GENDERED VOICES, FEMINIST VISIONS

CLASSIC AND CONTEMPORARY READINGS

SEVENTH EDITION

Susan M. Shaw

OREGON STATE UNIVERSITY

Janet Lee

OREGON STATE UNIVERSITY

NEW YORK   OXFORD

OXFORD UNIVERSITY PRESS

Oxford University Press is a department of the University of Oxford.
It furthers the University's objective of excellence in research,
scholarship, and education by publishing worldwide. Oxford is a
registered trade mark of Oxford University Press in the UK and
certain other countries.

Published in the United States of America by Oxford University
Press, 198 Madison Avenue, New York, NY 10016, United States
of America.

For titles covered by Section 112 of the US Higher Education
Opportunity Act, please visit www.oup.com/us/he for the latest
information about pricing and alternate formats.

Cataloging-in-Publication data is on file with the Library of Congress.

ISBN:9780190924874 (pbk)

Printing number: 9 8 7 6 5 4 3 2
Printed by LSC Communications, Inc.
Printed in the United States of America

Dedicated to all our WS 223 "Introduction to Women, Gender, and Sexuality Studies" students with thanks for all they have taught us.

CONTENTS

CHAPTER 5 **Media and Culture** *222*

CHAPTER 6 **Sex, Power, and Intimacy** *280*

CHAPTER **9**　　**Work Inside and Outside the Home**　*457*

Unpaid Labor in the Home　*458*

Paid Labor　*465*

CHAPTER **10**　　**Resisting Gender Violence**　*525*

Sexual Assault and Rape　*540*

Physical Abuse　*546*

Incest　*550*

PREFACE

We are thrilled to offer a new edition of *Gendered Voices, Feminist Visions: Classic and Contemporary Readings* with Oxford University Press at a time when our discipline is embarking on theoretical shifts, our academic programs are being both fully integrated and increasingly marginalized across the country, and threats to, and hopes for, social justice make the news daily. We know for sure the issues we deal with here are still very relevant! This book, formerly known as *Women's Voices, Feminist Visions*, has been revised—and renamed—to represent the shift from an essentialized notion of "woman" to a broader understanding of gender as socially constructed categories that shape our lives. It also better reflects the re-naming of academic programs nationwide from "Women's Studies" to "Women and Gender Studies" or just "Gender Studies." You will notice in chapter introductions that we straddle the realities of encouraging readers to question taken-for-granted normative categories of "women" and "men," applying the insights of postmodern and especially queer theoretical insights, and the recognition that these materially based normative categories represent distinct social groups whose members lead lives shaped and constrained by the realities of this very identity or group membership. We do not take these categories for granted, and we do recognize the realities of their existence.

We originally embarked on creating this book after finding that students were increasingly skipping assigned material in the introductory women's and gender studies course. They often found the readings to be mostly inaccessible, or, alternatively, they enjoyed reading the more testimonial first-person accounts included in some texts but were not grasping the theoretical frameworks necessary to make sense of these more experiential readings. We were tired of creating packets of readings, and students were tired of having to access alternative readings on top of purchasing a textbook. This book was crafted to include a balance of recent contemporary readings with historical and classic pieces as well as both testimonial and more theoretical essays that would speak to the diversity of human experience. Each chapter has an introduction that provides an overview of the topic and a framework for the readings that follow. Additionally, each chapter offers a variety of learning activities, activist profiles, ideas for activism, and other sidebars that can engage students with the material in various ways.

Although students of women's and gender studies today are in many ways like the students who have preceded them, they are also characterized by certain distinctions. Many of today's students come to our classes believing the goals of the women's and civil rights movements have already been accomplished, and, although most will say they believe in gender equity of some sort and some identify with feminism as a political theory or social movement, many still came of age benefiting from the gains made by feminist scholars and activists and taking for granted the social justice accomplishments of the last century. Moreover, as women's and gender studies has become institutionalized on college campuses and is fulfilling baccalaureate core requirements, more students are being exposed to this field than ever before. Many of these students "choose" women's and gender studies from a menu of options and may come to the discipline with varying levels of misunderstanding and resistance. Some of these students have been influenced by contemporary backlash efforts and by conservative religious ideologies that seek a return to traditional gender relations. All of these distinctions call for a new, relevant, and accessible introductory text.

In addition, another distinction of contemporary students compared to students in the past is their level of digital competency, which also means more traditional types of reading can be challenging. Students in women's and gender studies today are often the kind of visual learners who prefer reading from and interacting with a computer screen or a smart phone or watching video clips over reading traditional texts. We know from experience that a large percentage of students in introductory women's and gender studies classes read only a fragment of the required readings (especially dense theoretical texts that are often deemed "irrelevant" or "boring") and that our required readings end up as "fragmented texts." Our intention in this book is to address these challenges by presenting a student-friendly text that provides short, accessible readings that reflect the diversity of gender experiences and offer a balance of classic/contemporary and theoretical/experiential pieces. The goal is to start where students are rather than where we hope they might be, and to provide a text that enriches their thinking, encourages them to read, and relates to their everyday experiences. We have chosen accessible articles that we hope are readable. They are relatively short, to the point, and interesting in terms of both topics and writing styles. Although most articles are quite contemporary, we have also included earlier classic articles that are "must-reads." And although the articles we have chosen cover the breadth of issues and eras in women's and gender studies, we hope students will read them—and enjoy reading them—because of their relevance to their lives. Many pieces are written by young feminists, many are in testimonial format, and, on the whole, they avoid dense, academic theorizing. The cartoons, we hope, bring humor to this scholarship. Our hope is that these readings and the chapter introductions will invite students into productive dialogue with feminist ideas and encourage personal engagement in feminist work.

We also structure opportunities for students to reflect on their learning throughout the text, and, in this sense, the book is aimed at "teaching itself." It includes not only articles and introductions but also a number of features designed to engage students in active learning around the content. For example, we address students' tendencies to lose interest by creating a format that presents smaller, self-contained, more manageable pieces of knowledge that hold together through related fields and motifs that are woven throughout the larger text as boxes. This multiple positioning of various forms of scholarship creates independent but related pieces that enable students to read each unit in its entirety and make connections between the individual units and the larger text. We see this subtext as a way to address students' familiarity and comfort with contemporary design and multiple windows. By also presenting material in these familiar formats, we intend to create a student-friendly text that will stimulate their interest. We encourage them actually to read the text and then be actively engaged with the material.

Pedagogy is embedded within the text itself. In addition to the textual narrative, we include in each chapter learning activities, activism ideas that provide students with examples, and opportunities for the practical implementation of the content that help students explore chapter themes critically. Instructors will be able to utilize the various pedagogical procedures suggested in the text (and those in the accompanying instructor's manual found on the Ancillary Resource Center [ARC] at www.oup.com/us/shaw) to develop teaching plans for their class sessions. By embedding some pedagogy within the text, we hope to create a classroom tool that enables connections between content and teaching procedure and between assigned readings and classroom experience. Thus, students and instructors should experience the text as both a series of manageable units of information and a holistic exploration of the larger topics.

Like other women's and gender studies text-readers, this book covers a variety of issues that we know instructors address in the introductory course. We do not isolate race and racism and other issues of difference and power as separate topics, but thoroughly integrate them throughout the text into every issue addressed. We have also chosen not to present groups of chapters in parts or sections but to let the individual chapters stand alone. Pragmatically, this facilitates instructors being able to decide how they want to organize their own courses. At the same time, however, the chapters do build on each other. For example, after introducing students to women's and gender studies, Chapter 2 presents the systems of privilege and inequality that form the context for social justice education, and then Chapter 3 explores the social construction of gender, building on the previous chapter by introducing the plurality of sex/gender systems. The following chapters then examine how sex/gender systems are expressed and maintained in social institutions.

For this new edition, we have revised chapter framework essays to reflect the most up-to-date research and theory in the field. We've also included new readings that are contemporary and exciting. With each new edition, we strive to keep the textbook fresh and interesting for our students. We wish you all the best in your class and hope the book is a helpful addition to both teaching and learning.

NEW TO THIS EDITION

- **Fifty-eight new readings**, bringing in young feminist writers and contemporary topics such as disability and social justice, trans*masculinities, transgender issues, Cardi B, queer Muslim women, immigration policies, human trafficking, #SayHerName, sexual assault on campus, military femininities, white supremacist women, activism, and much more.

- **Revised chapter framework essays** to reflect the most up-to-date research and theory in the field.

- **A new feature in each chapter called "The Blog"**: posts written by Susan when she was blogging for the *Huffington Post* from 2015 to 2017. While most of these brief pieces were written in response to some current event, the feminist lens they offer remains timely, and the topics are still important for feminist conversations.

- **A new title**—*Gendered Voices, Feminist Visions*—to represent the shift from an essentialized notion of "woman" to a broader understanding of gender as socially constructed categories that shape our lives. This also reflects the renaming of academic programs nationwide from "Women's Studies" to "Women and Gender Studies" or just "Gender Studies."

ACKNOWLEDGMENTS

Writing a textbook is inevitably a community project, and without the assistance of a number of people this project would have been impossible. We would like to thank Karen Mills, administrator for the School of Language, Culture, and Society, and Leo Rianda, office assistant for Women, Gender, and Sexuality Studies, for their support; our graduate students and colleagues who wrote a number of sidebars for this edition; and students Lauren Grant and Nasim Basiri, who helped with fact-checking.

We also would like to acknowledge the work of the many reviewers who provided insights and suggestions for this edition:

Ozlem Altiok, University of North Texas
Josephine Beoku-Betts, Florida Atlantic University
Suzanne Bergeron, University of Michigan Dearborn
Adriane Brown, Augsburg College
Suzanne M. Edwards, Lehigh University
Kara Ellerby, University of Delaware
Julie Goodspeed-Chadwick, Indiana University-Purdue University Columbus
Tara Jabbaar-Gyambrah, Niagara University
Rachel Lewis, George Mason University
Hilary Malatino, East Tennessee State University
Amanda Roth, SUNY Geneseo
Robyn Ryle, Hanover College
Carissa Jean Sojka, Southern Oregon University
Beth Sutton-Ramspeck, Ohio State University
Martha Walker, Mary Baldwin University

Jan Wilson, University of Tulsa
One anonymous reviewer

Finally, we want to thank Sherith Pankratz and Grace Li at Oxford University Press, who have provided invaluable support and encouragement; Micheline Frederick, our production editor; and Mary Anne Shahidi, our amazing copyeditor. We'd also like to thank Serina Beauparlant, who initiated the first edition of the book with us when she was an editor at Mayfield Publishing.

ABOUT THE AUTHORS

Susan M. Shaw is professor of women, gender, and sexuality studies at Oregon State University. Her research interests are in feminist theology and women in religion. Professor Shaw teaches courses in global feminist theologies; feminist theologies in the United States feminism and the Bible; gender and sport; and gender, race, and pop culture. She is author of *Reflective Faith: A Theological Toolbox for Women* (Smyth & Helwys, 2014) and *God Speaks to Us, Too: Southern Baptist Women on Church, Home, and Society* (University Press of Kentucky, 2008), and co-author of *Intersectional Theology: An Introductory Guide* (Fortress Press, 2018) and *Girls Rock! Fifty Years of Women Making Music* (University Press of Kentucky, 2004). She is general editor of the four-volume *Women's Lives Around the World: A Global Encyclopedia* (ABC-CLIO, 2018). She is an avid racquetball player, reader of murder mysteries, hot tubber, and fan of Beavers women's basketball.

Janet Lee is professor of women, gender, and sexuality studies at Oregon State University, where she teaches a variety of courses on gender and feminism. Professor Lee's research interests include early-twentieth-century feminist and queer British histories and historical geographies of the relationships between space, modernity, and masculinities. She is author of *War Girls: The First Aid Nursing Yeomanry (FANY) in the First World War* (Manchester University Press, 2005) and *Comrades and Partners: The Shared Lives of Grace Hutchins and Anna Rochester* (Rowman and Littlefield, 2000); co-author of *Blood Stories: Menarche and the Politics of the Female Body in Contemporary U.S. Society* (Routledge, 1996); and co-editor with Susan Shaw of *Women Worldwide: Transnational Feminist Perspectives on Women* (McGraw-Hill, 2010). Her new book *Fallen Among Reformers: Miles Franklin, and the New Woman Writing from the Chicago Years* is forthcoming from Sydney University Press. She enjoys playing tennis and all things equestrian.

CHAPTER 1

WOMEN'S AND GENDER STUDIES

Perspectives and Practices

WHAT IS WOMEN'S AND GENDER STUDIES (WGS)?

WGS is an interdisciplinary academic field devoted to topics concerning women, gender, and feminism. It focuses on gender arrangements (the ways society creates, patterns, and rewards our understandings of femininity and masculinity) and examines the multiple ways these arrangements affect everyday life. In particular, WGS is concerned with gender as it intersects with multiple categories, such as race, ethnicity, social class, age, ability, religion, and sexuality. Exploring how we perform gender and how this interacts with other aspects of our identities, WGS focuses on the ways women and other feminized bodies experience discrimination and oppression. Simply put, WGS involves the study of gender as a central aspect of human existence.

The goal of WGS, however, is not only to provide an academic framework and broad-based community for inquiry about the impacts of gender practices on social, cultural, and political thought and behavior, but also to provide advocacy and work toward social change. This endeavor is framed by understandings of the social, economic, and political changes of the past half century that include a rapid increase in globalization and its impacts locally, including the deindustrialization of the global north, the blurring and dispersal of geopolitical boundaries and national identities, and the growth of new technologies that have not only transformed political and economic institutions, but supported mass consumerism. Such changes shape contemporary imperialism (economic, military, political, and/or cultural domination over nations or geopolitical formations) with implications for people in both local and global communities.

In this way, WGS seeks understanding of these issues and realities with the goal of social justice. In this endeavor it puts women and other marginalized peoples at the center of inquiry as subjects of study, informing knowledge through these lenses. This inclusion implies that traditional notions regarding men as "humans" and women as "others" must be challenged and transcended. Such a confusion of maleness with humanity, putting men at the center and relegating women to outsiders in society, is called androcentrism.

LEARNING ACTIVITY
WHY ARE WE READING THESE ESSAYS?

Margaret Stetz, University of Delaware

Imagine that you, not Susan Shaw and Janet Lee, have final responsibility for *Gendered Voices, Feminist Visions*. Shaw and Lee have finished arranging all the contents, which appear in their current order. Everything is ready to go to press, and at this point you cannot move anything around. Nonetheless, you have just received an urgent message from the publisher, who wants to include one additional essay in the book: Pandora L. Leong's "Living Outside the Box" from *Colonize This!* (2002). Your instructor will let you know how to access this article.

Now it is up to you to figure out where to place Leong's essay in the existing volume. Leong discusses a number of feminist issues, which means that the essay could go into any one of several different sections of the book. You will have to decide which is the most significant of the topics that Leong raises, as that will determine which chapter would be most appropriate for this inclusion.

But you will also have to choose where, within the chapter, to put the essay, and that, too, will be an important matter. If you place it at the start of a section, how might that affect readers' feelings about the essays that follow, especially the essay that comes right after it? If

you place it at the end of a section, how will its presence implicitly comment on the earlier essays in the section and perhaps color readers' reactions to the essay immediately preceding it? And if you sandwich it between two essays, midway through a section, how will that influence the way readers look at both the essay that comes before it and the one that comes after? You have a lot of power here, and you must think about how to exercise it.

Write a report to the publisher. In your report, you will need to do the following:

1. Identify the issue in Leong's "Living Outside the Box" that you think is most worth highlighting, and describe what she says about it.
2. Explain how you chose a place for "Living Outside the Box" in *Gendered Voices, Feminist Visions*, and make a case for your choice.
3. Discuss the possible implications of its placement, talking briefly about the essays that will surround it.

What do you think this activity suggests about the construction of an introductory women's and gender studies textbook? What kinds of decisions do you think Shaw and Lee had to make in developing *Gendered Voices, Feminist Visions*? If you were a co-author/co-editor, would you make similar or different decisions?

By making those who identify as women and other marginalized peoples the subjects of study, we assume that our opinions and thoughts about our own experiences are central in understanding human society generally. Adrienne Rich's classic essay from the late 1970s "Claiming an Education" articulates this demand for women as subjects of study. It also encourages you as a student to recognize your right to be taken seriously and invites you to understand the relationship between your personal biography and the wider forces in society that affect your life. As authors of this text, we also invite your participation in knowledge creation, hoping it will be personally enriching and vocationally useful.

HOW DID WGS ORIGINATE?

The original manifestation of WGS was the emergence of women's studies programs and departments in response to the absence, misrepresentation, and trivialization of women in the higher education curriculum, as well as the ways women were systematically excluded from many positions of power and authority as college faculty and administrators. This exclusion was especially true for women of color, who experienced intersecting obstacles based on both race and gender. In the late 1960s and early 1970s, students and faculty began demanding that the knowledge learned and shared in colleges around the country be more inclusive of women's issues. It was not unusual, for example, for entire courses in English or American literature to not include a single novel written by a woman, much less a woman of color. Literature was full of men's ideas about women—ideas that often continued to stereotype women and justify their subordination. History courses often taught only about men in wars and as leaders, and sociology courses addressed women primarily in the context of marriage and the family. Similarly, students and faculty asked to see more women in leadership positions on college campuses: entire departments often consisted exclusively of men with perhaps a small minority of (usually white) women in junior or part-time positions. Although there have been important changes on most college campuses as women's and multicultural issues are slowly integrated into the curriculum and advances are made in terms of leadership positions, unfortunately these problems still exist in higher education today. What kinds of people hold leadership positions on your campus?

It is important to note in terms of the history of WGS that making women subjects of study involved two strategies that together resulted in changes in the production of knowledge in higher education. First, it rebalanced the curriculum. Women as subjects of study were integrated into existing curricula through the development of new courses about women. This shifted the focus on men and men's lives in the traditional academic curriculum and gave some attention to women's lives and concerns by developing, for example, courses such as "Women and Art" and "Women in U.S. History" alongside "regular" courses that sometimes claimed to be inclusive but focused on (usually white) men. In addition, not only did traditional academic departments (such as sociology or English) offer these separate courses on women, but the development of women's studies programs and departments offered curricula on a variety of issues that focused specifically on (initially, mostly white) women's issues.

Second, the integration of women as subjects of study resulted in a transformation of traditional knowledge. People began questioning the nature of knowledge, how knowledge is produced, and the applications and consequences of knowledge in wider society. This means that claims to "truth" and objective "facts" were challenged by new knowledge integrating the perspectives of marginalized people. It recognized, for example, that a history of the American West written by migrating whites is necessarily incomplete and differs from a history written from the perspective of indigenous native people who had their land taken from them. Although the first strategy was an "add women and stir" approach, this second involved a serious challenge to traditional knowledge and its claims to truth. In this way, women's studies aimed not only to create programs of study where students might focus on women's issues and concerns, but also to integrate a perspective that would challenge previously unquestioned knowledge. This perspective questioned how such knowledge reflects women's lives and concerns, how it maintains patterns of male privilege and power, and how the consequences of such knowledge affect women and other marginalized people. This approach fostered heightened consciousness and advocacy about gendered violence and was also central in the development of other academic fields such as gay and lesbian and gender studies.

HISTORICAL MOMENT

THE FIRST WOMEN'S STUDIES DEPARTMENT

Following the activism of the 1960s, feminists in academia worked to begin establishing a place for the study of women. In 1970 women faculty at San Diego State University (SDSU) taught five upper-division women's studies classes on a voluntary overload basis. In the fall of that year, the SDSU senate approved a women's studies department, the first in the United States, and a curriculum of 11 courses. The school hired one full-time instructor for the program. Other instructors included students and faculty from several existing departments. Quickly, many other colleges and universities around the nation followed suit, establishing women's studies courses, programs, and departments. In 1977 academic and activist feminists formed the National Women's Studies Association (NWSA) to further the development of the discipline. NWSA held its first convention in 1979.

Women's studies has its origins in the women's movement of the 1960s and 1970s, known as the "second-wave" women's movement. The second wave refers to this twentieth-century period of social activism that addressed formal and informal inequalities associated, for example, with the workplace, family, sexuality, and reproductive freedom. The second-wave movement can be distinguished from "first-wave" mid-nineteenth-century women's rights and suffrage (voting) activity, which sought to overturn legal obstacles to women's participation in society, and more contemporary "third-wave" movements, discussed in more detail later. As an academic discipline, women's studies was influenced by the American studies and ethnic studies programs of the late 1960s. The demand to include women and other marginalized people as subjects of study in higher education was facilitated by broad societal movements in which organizations and individuals focused on such issues as work and employment, family and parenting, sexuality, reproductive rights, and violence. The objective was to improve women's status in society and therefore the conditions of women's lives. The U.S. women's movement emerged at a moment of widespread social turmoil as various social movements questioned traditional social and sexual values, racism, poverty and other inequities, and U.S. militarism. These social movements, including the women's movement and the civil rights movement, struggled for the rights of people of color, women, the poor, gays and lesbians, the aged and the young, and the disabled, and fought to transform society through laws and policies as well as changes in attitudes and consciousness.

Two aspects of the women's movement—commitment to personal change and to societal transformation—helped establish women's studies. In terms of the personal, the U.S. women's movement involved women asking questions about the cultural meanings of being a woman. Intellectual perspectives that became central to women's studies as a discipline were created from the everyday experiences of people both inside and outside the movement. Through consciousness-raising groups and other situations where some women were able to come together to talk about their lives, participants realized that they were not alone in their experiences. Problems they thought to be personal (like working outside the home all day and then coming home to work another full day's worth of domestic tasks involved in being a wife and mother) were actually part of a much bigger picture of masculine privilege and female subordination. Women began to make connections and coined the phrase "the personal is political" to explain how things taken as personal or idiosyncratic have broader social, political, and economic causes and consequences. In other words, situations that we are encouraged to view as personal are actually part of broader cultural patterns and arrangements. In addition, the idea that the personal is political encouraged people to live their politics—or understandings of the world and how it is organized—in their everyday lives: to practice what they preach, in other words. This concept is illustrated in the essay (originally presented as a leaflet) "No More Miss America," written in 1968 by members of an organization called the New York Radical Women. It accompanied a protest against the 1968 Miss America beauty pageant and was one of the first women's liberation protests covered widely by the national media. The 10 points in the leaflet present a feminist critique of the objectification of female "beauty" and its connection to sexism, racism, and consumerism. Is this critique still relevant today? Particularly interesting about the 1968 protest was the way the media produced the idea that women were "burning their bras." Even though no bra-burnings took place there, and there is no evidence that any ever took place, the notion has survived many decades and still exists as a fabricated, yet iconic, aspect of feminism. Why do you think this is the case?

By the 1970s questions were being raised about this generic notion of "woman" and the monolithic way "women's experiences" were being interpreted. In particular, critiques of the women's movement and women's studies centered on their lack of inclusivity around issues of race, class, sexual identity or orientation, and other differences. These critiques fostered, among other developments, a field of black women's studies that encouraged a focus on intersectionality that continues to transform the discipline. Intersectionality involves the ways all people's experiences of gender are created by the intersection, or coming together, of multiple identities like race, ethnicity, social class, and so forth. The need to provide more inclusive curricula involves the necessity of incorporating knowledge by and about people of color and those who do not identify with the binaries of gender (masculinity/femininity) or sexuality (heterosexuality/homosexuality) or who represent marginalized communities like immigrants, migrants, or people with disabilities. Although intersectionality is most easily understood as multifaceted identities, it also necessarily includes the organization of power in society and can be used as a tool of social justice. Kia M. Q. Hall addresses these intersections in the reading "A Transnational Black Feminist Framework," using the Black Lives Matter movement as an example of intersectionality and solidarity in activism. As readings in Chapter 2 also illustrate, intersectional analyses have shown how systems of power maintain patterns of privilege and discrimination.

The emergence of WGS within the last few decades represents not only the inclusion of intersectional analyses as mentioned earlier, but the movement away from a stable and fixed idea of "woman," as in "women's studies," toward a more inclusive focus on gender, as in "gender studies." The latter encourages the study of gender as socially constructed, historically and culturally variable, and subject to change through social and political action. Recognizing that "woman" and "man" are changeable and contested categories is central to the study of the ways gendered personhood is mapped onto physical bodies. In particular, gender studies provides knowledge and advocacy for understanding the ways bodies and gender expressions (as feminine or masculine) do not necessarily adhere to the typical female/male binary (implied in what is known as "trans" or gender fluid or gender nonbinary and discussed more in later chapters). However, while such a study emphasizes the ways social practices produce bodies that perform gender, it is important to note that gender performances are privileged and constrained by institutional structures that affect people who actually identify as "real" women and men. This means that even though gender studies may provide a more inclusive approach, there are social and political consequences of identifying as a woman, or living with a feminized body, that result in certain experiences and outcomes (for example, being more likely to live in poverty, or experience violence and sexual assault). The importance of understanding the experience of living as women in society, alongside the recognition of inclusivity and intersectionality, means that "women's studies" tends not to have been changed to "gender studies," but instead to have been transformed into "women's and gender studies." This move recognizes the historical development and contemporary reality of the field of women's studies as a site for social justice for those who live and identify as women in the world.

A key term for WGS writers and activists is "patriarchy," defined as a system where men and masculine bodies dominate because power and authority are in the hands of adult men. Discussions of patriarchy must recognize the intersectional nature of this concept whereby someone may be simultaneously privileged by gender but face limitations based on other identities. Men of color, for example, may benefit from patriarchy, but their expressions of masculine privilege are shaped by the politics of racism. It is important to remember that many men are supporters of women's rights and that many of the goals of the women's movement benefit men as well, although being a supporter of women's rights does not necessarily translate into men understanding how everyday privileges associated with masculinity maintain entitlements in a patriarchal society. It is one thing to feel indignant about inequality or compassion for marginalized people, and another to recognize that one's privilege is connected to the oppression of others. Connecting with the personal as political encourages men to potentially function as allies on a deeper, more authentic level. The concept of the personal as political has relevance for those with masculine privilege as understandings are made about the connections between social institutions that reward men and personal experiences of gendered entitlement.

In terms of societal change, the U.S. women's movement and other social movements have improved, and continue to improve, the lives of marginalized people through various forms of activism. The legal changes of the second wave include the passage of the Equal Pay Act of 1963 that sought equal pay for equal work, Title VII of the Civil Rights Act of 1964 that forbade workplace discrimination, and the creation of the Equal Employment Opportunity Commission (EEOC) in 1965 to enforce antidiscrimination laws (although

LEARNING ACTIVITY

WHAT'S IN A NAME?

What is the program that sponsors this introductory course at your institution called? Is it "Women's Studies," "Gender Studies," "Women's and Gender Studies," "Women, Gender, and Sexuality Studies," "Feminist Studies," or some other name? Have you ever stopped to think about the history and politics of the name of that unit?

In this chapter we have discussed how in its early years, women's studies tended to focus on women as an essential category and explored the ways women experienced discrimination based on sex or recovered the ways women had contributed to society. Soon a number of critiques and realizations challenged this understanding of the discipline, emphasizing that sex and gender are socially constructed ways of relating within systems of domination and subordination.

This realization that gave rise to "gender studies" as an interdisciplinary field examines the complex interactions of biology and society, sex and gender, with a specific emphasis on how gender is constituted across forms of difference.

Another contested area of study that related to but was not always central to women's studies and gender studies was sexuality. While many early second-wave feminists made important connections between women's oppression and the control of sexuality, others feared the intrusion of lesbian politics. As queer studies emerged, debates also arose about the place of gay men, transgender people, and queer-identified people in the women's studies and gender studies curricula.

Different colleges and universities have grappled with the controversies and developments in different ways. At Oregon State University, our program came into being in late 1972 as "Women Studies." Notice the absence of the apostrophe and "s." In the archives we have a number of memos back and forth between the founder of our program and university administrators about this. The founder argued (successfully) that women were the subject of study, not the owners of the discipline. Therefore, she contended, the program should be "Women Studies," not "Women's Studies." This name lasted for 40 years, even as the focus of our program shifted with changes in the discipline. From about 2008 to 2012 we added faculty members with expertise in multicultural, transnational, and queer feminisms, and so in 2013 we changed our name to "Women, Gender, and Sexuality Studies" to reflect growth both in the discipline and in our specific program. As our name change proposal moved through the approval process, we were asked several times why we wanted to keep the word "women." Our response was twofold: We did not want women to become invisible in our identity, and we wanted to acknowledge our history. So, as you can see, politics played a very important role in the naming of our program and shaping of our identity nearly 50 years ago and very recently.

What about your program? Research the history of your program's name, and find out why your institution made the decisions it did. Has the name changed over the years? Why or why not? Ask your professors how they think those choices have affected the courses and degrees the program offers. What difference do you think the name makes for you?

---

this enforcement did not occur until 1972). Rulings in 1978 and 1991 prohibited discrimination against pregnant women and provided women workers the right to damages for sex discrimination, respectively. The Family Medical Leave Act of 1993 provided 12 weeks of unpaid, job-protected leave for workers to care for children or ill relatives (although it is required only for businesses with more than 50 employees and for workers with at least a year's tenure in their job). Affirmative action as a legal mechanism to combat discrimination was first utilized in 1961 and was extended to women in 1967, although it is increasingly under attack. Similarly, although Supreme Court decisions such as *Roe v. Wade* legalized abortion and provided reproductive choices for women and the Freedom of Access to Clinic Entrances (FACE) Act of 1994 protected reproductive health care workers and patients accessing these services, such gains are currently under attack as well. In terms of legal changes directly aimed at higher education, Title IX of the Education

Amendments of 1972 supported equal education and forbade gender discrimination, including in sports, in schools. Since that time the Civil Rights Restoration Act of 1988 reversed a Supreme Court decision gutting Title IX, and more recent rulings (e.g., *Fitzgerald v. Barnstable School Committee*, 2009) established parents' right to sue for sex discrimination in schools under both Title IX and the Equal Protection Clause of the Fourteenth Amendment to the Constitution. Women's right to fight in combat positions and the overturning of the antigay military policy "Don't Ask, Don't Tell" in 2012 also reflect the activism of the women's and other civil rights movements, especially LGBTQ (lesbian, gay, bisexual, trans, queer) activism. These examples of civil rights legislation, often taken for granted today, are the result of organized resistance and a concerted effort to democratize the legal structure of U.S. society.

Legal changes in the United States have been accompanied by relatively significant increases in the numbers of women and people of color running for political office; taking positions of authority in government, business, education, science, and the arts; and becoming more visible and active in all societal institutions. These societal changes have strengthened the demand for alternative educational models: Not only is it the right thing to include women in college life, but it is illegal to prevent their participation. Alongside Jennifer Baumgardner and Amy Richards's classic essay "A Day Without Feminism," which encourages you to think about these second-wave gains, is Marge Piercy's plea to recognize the "heroines" who continuously strive every day in their families and communities to improve women's everyday lives. Her poem/reading "My Heroines" emphasizes that it is these people who write our future.

WHAT WERE THE ORIGINS OF WOMEN'S RIGHTS ACTIVISM IN THE UNITED STATES?

Although the original women's studies programs emerged out of the second wave of mid- to late-twentieth-century social activism, that activism itself was a part of an ongoing commitment to women's liberation that had its roots in late-eighteenth-century and nineteenth-century struggles for gender equity. Women had few legal, social, and economic rights in nineteenth-century U.S. society. They had no direct relationship to the law outside of their relationships as daughters or wives; in particular, married women lost property rights upon marriage. Women were also mostly barred from higher education until women's colleges started opening in the mid-nineteenth century. However, when socioeconomically privileged white women started to access higher education in the late nineteenth century, most women of color still faced obstacles that continued through the twentieth century and into the present. Despite this, African American women like Ida B. Wells, Mary Church Terrell, and Anna Julia Cooper (see "Activist Profile") offered strategies of resistance that provided an explicit analysis of patriarchy to address racial domination.

Most early women's rights activists (then it was referred to as "woman's" rights) in the United States had their first experience with social activism in the abolition movement, the struggle to free slaves. These activists included such figures as Elizabeth Cady Stanton, Lucretia Mott, Susan B. Anthony, Sojourner Truth, Sarah M. and Angelina Grimke, Henry

Blackwell, Frederick Douglass, and Harriet Tubman. Many abolitionists became aware of inequities elsewhere in society. Some realized that to improve women's status a separate social movement was required. In this way, for many abolitionists, their experiences with abolition inspired their desire to improve the conditions of all women's lives.

ACTIVIST PROFILE

ANNA JULIA COOPER

Anna Julia Cooper was born in North Carolina in 1858 to an enslaved woman and her white slave owner. By the latter part of the nineteenth century, she had become a profound voice for the rights and dignity of black women.

Even as a child, she protested the unequal treatment of women and girls, and when she attended Oberlin College, she refused to take the less rigorous course set out for women and insisted on enrolling in the men's course. By 1887, she had earned a master's degree in math, and she moved to Washington, DC, to work at the only all-black high school in the city. She became the school's principal in 1902.

Cooper saw education as the path to uplift and empower black women. She insisted on preparing students for college rather than for the trades, and she was successful in sending many students on to prestigious universities. She also founded the Colored Women's League of Washington and helped begin the first black women's chapter of the YWCA.

Her book *A Voice from the South* offered an early analysis of the intersections of gender and race. In it she wrote, "Only the BLACK WOMAN can say when and where I enter, in the quiet, undisputed dignity of my womanhood, without violence and without suing or special patronage, then and there the whole Negro race enters with me."

In 1924, Cooper became only the fourth black woman in the United States to earn a PhD. In 1930, she became president of Frelinghuysen University, a DC institution founded to provide access to education for local residents. She died in 1964 at the age of 105.

Learn more by visiting the website for the Anna Julia Cooper Project at www.cooperproject.org.

LEARNING ACTIVITY

THE NATIONAL WOMEN'S HALL OF FAME

How many significant American women can you name? Most students cannot name 20 women from American history. To learn more about some of the women who have made important contributions in the United States, visit the National Women's Hall of Fame at www.womenofthehall.org. What is the mission of the Hall of Fame? Select five inductees and read their biographies. Why do you think they were selected for the Hall of Fame? What do you think is the significance of having a National Women's Hall of Fame?

A Vindication of the Rights of Woman (1792), by English philosopher Mary Wollstone-craft, is seen as the first important expression of the demand for women's equality, al-though the beginning of the women's movement in the United States is usually dated to the Seneca Falls Convention of 1848. This convention was conceived as a response to the experience of Lucretia Mott and Elizabeth Cady Stanton, who, as delegates to the World Anti-Slavery Convention in London in 1840, were refused seating, made to sit behind a curtain, and not allowed to voice their opinions because they were women. Their experi-ence fueled the need for an independent women's movement in the United States and fa-cilitated the convention at Seneca Falls, New York, in July 1848. An important document, the "Declaration of Sentiments and Resolutions," came out of this convention. Authored primarily by Elizabeth Cady Stanton, it used the language of the U.S. Declaration of Inde-pendence and included a variety of demands to improve women's status in the family and in society. Woman's suffrage, the right of women to vote, was included. Other conven-tions were held across the country, and national organizations were formed to promote women's rights generally and suffrage in particular. These organizations included the Na-tional Woman Suffrage Association (NWSA) formed in 1869 and the National American Woman Suffrage Association (NAWSA) in 1890. NAWSA was formed from the merging of NWSA and the American Woman Suffrage Association and continues today as the League of Women Voters. It is important to understand that throughout all this history the rights of women of color were often subordinated and "women's rights" came to mean the lib-eration of white women. In some cases movement leaders conspired with racist forces to

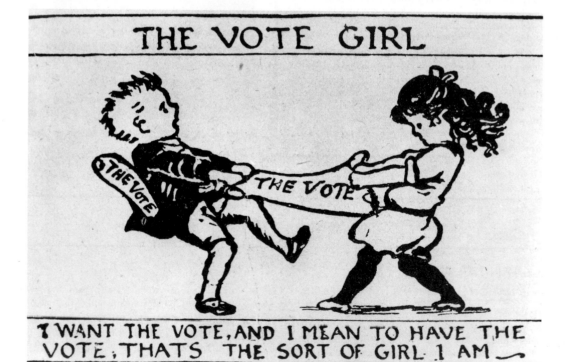

keep women of color subordinated, arguing, for example, for literacy requirements for voters that enhanced the status of economically privileged women and undermined the poor, ex-slaves, and many immigrants and migrants. Despite these serious problems, the first-wave women's movement fought for political personhood—a struggle that continues today. The "Anthony Amendment," a proposed women's suffrage amendment, was introduced into Congress in 1878; it took another 42 years for this proposal to be ratified as the Nineteenth Amendment in 1920, granting women the right to vote.

WHAT IS THE STATUS OF WGS ON COLLEGE CAMPUSES TODAY?

WGS has steadily become institutionalized, or established as a regular custom, on many college campuses. From a scattering of courses (often taught for free by committed faculty when colleges did not want to spend money on these courses) have come whole programs and departments with minors and majors of study and graduate degrees at both the master's and doctoral levels. Although most programs adopted the name "women's studies," some went with "gender studies" and others with "feminist studies," and over the years many have been renamed "women's and gender studies." These different names reflect different perspectives concerning knowledge about and for women. As the learning activity "What's in a Name?" asks, how is WGS institutionalized on your campus?

Professors of WGS might teach only in WGS, or they might do most of their work in another department like anthropology or history. This illustrates the multidisciplinary nature of our field: It can be taught from the point of view of many different disciplines. For the most part, however, WGS is interdisciplinary; that is, it combines knowledge and methodologies from across many academic disciplines. Knowledge integration has occurred at a more rapid rate in the humanities and social sciences than in the biological and physical sciences. This is primarily because those sciences are considered "objective" (free of values), with topics of study immune from consideration of issues of gender, race, and class. However, as scholars have pointed out, science is a cultural product and its methodologies are grounded in historical practices and cultural ideas. There are now courses on many campuses examining the history and current practices of science that integrate knowledge about science as a human (gendered and racialized) product.

A list of the goals or objectives of WGS might look like this:

- To understand the social construction of gender: the ways gendered personhood is mapped onto physical bodies.
- To examine the intersection of gender with other systems of inequality, including the effects of imperialism and globalization.
- To learn about the status of women and other marginalized peoples in society and ways to improve that status through individual and collective action for social change.
- To experience how institutions in society affect individual lives and to be able to think critically about the role of patterns of privilege and discrimination in our own lives.
- To develop critical thinking skills, improve writing and speaking skills, and empower self and others.

WHAT DOES WGS HAVE TO DO WITH FEMINISM?

WGS is generally associated with feminism as a paradigm for understanding self and society. Although there are many definitions of feminism and some disagreement concerning a specific definition, there is agreement on two core principles underlying any concept of feminism. First, feminism concerns equality and justice. Because feminism is a politics of equality and a social movement for social justice, it anticipates a future that guarantees human dignity and equality for all. A social movement can be defined as a sustained, collective campaign that arises as people with shared interests come together in support of a common goal. Second, feminism is inclusive and affirming of women across their differences; it celebrates women's achievements and struggles, and it works to provide a positive and affirming stance toward women and expressions of the feminine. As longtime feminist advocate and *Ms.* magazine cofounder Gloria Steinem explains in an interview with Rachel Graham Cody, feminism is about social, economic, and political equality. Steinem makes the case that reproductive freedom is the key to women's equality, emphasizing its role in explaining poverty, educational attainments, and health outcomes.

Feminism is a personal perspective as well as a political theory and social movement that has worked as a central force in advocating women's rights and making room for other liberatory possibilities. Put this way, feminism is hardly a radical notion. In the reading "Feminist Consciousness," Sara Ahmed points to the ways that people come to feminism and embrace its liberatory possibilities. In terms of transforming social inequality in a broad sense, however, it is important to note that feminism has worked alongside other social movements such as immigrant and migrant rights and indigenous peoples' movements that may or may not identify as feminist. And, while feminism is usually at the center of WGS and has embodied the discipline with advocacy for social justice and cultural plurality, the concept itself, and the often accompanying (although not always or necessarily present) "baggage" of its ideological location in the global north, can exclude those who do not identify as feminist from movements for the improvement of women's lives.

It is also important to understand that although this chapter addresses the origins of U.S. feminism, the movement for social justice takes different forms in societies around the world, and certainly feminism's multiple origins do not necessarily reside in the United States. In addition, transnational feminism, the movement for the social, political, and economic equality of women across national boundaries, is alive and well. Transnational feminism recognizes opportunities associated with the development of alliances and networks for the emancipation of marginalized peoples worldwide. It also educates about the problems of claiming a "universal sisterhood" that ignores differences between women and claims solidarity based on shared conditions, experiences, or concerns. Such claims often result in women in the global north or "First World" societies (those with political and economic privilege in the world order) making decisions for those in developing countries of the global south or "Third World" nations. Note how the terms "First World" and "Third World" imply a hierarchical ordering. The problematic nature of these terms is underscored by the phrase "Two-Thirds World" to emphasize that the global north has defined most of the world as coming in third.

In this way, feminism recognizes both the similarities and differences in women's status worldwide. This status in developing and nonindustrialized countries is often very low, especially in societies where strict religious doctrines govern gendered behaviors. Although women in various countries around the world often tend to be in subordinate positions, the form this subordination takes varies. As a result, certain issues, like the ability of women to maintain subsistence agriculture and feed their families—matters of personal survival—take priority over the various claims to autonomy that characterize women's issues in the global north or what is often termed "westernized" societies. What are considered feminist issues in the United States are not necessarily the most important concerns of women in other parts of the world. As already mentioned, it is important to understand this in order to avoid overgeneralizing about feminism's usefulness globally, even though the notion of global feminism or transnational feminism is real and useful for political alliances across national borders. It is also important to recognize that any claims for "Western" feminisms are necessarily interpreted internationally in the context of U.S. militarism, a history of colonialism, and international "development," as well as in regard to the power of U.S.-based corporations, consumerism, and popular culture. Nonetheless, transnational feminisms underscore the similarities women share across the world and seek strategies that take into account the interdependence of women globally. And, as communication technologies have advanced, the difficulties of organizing women in all parts of the world have decreased, despite issues of access for many people.

Some feminist peace and social justice movements have used the concept of the personal as political to make the case that diverse personal narratives shared within and across cultures encourage political awareness and have the potential to foster opportunities for communication and networking in an increasingly globalized world. Indeed, transnational feminist groups have worked against militarism, global capitalism, and racism, and for issues identified by local women in specific communities worldwide. Such actions were reflected in the United Nations (UN) Fourth World Conference on Women held in Beijing, China, in 1995 and the post-Beijing gatherings of the last decades. More than 30,000 women attended the Beijing conference, and 189 governments signed the "Platform for Action." This platform was a call for concrete action to include the human rights of women and girls as part of universal human rights, thus eradicating poverty of women, removing the obstacles to women's full participation in public life and decision making, eliminating all forms of violence against women, ensuring women's access to educational and health services, and promoting actions for women's economic autonomy.

Currently, much transnational feminist emphasis is on the passage of CEDAW (Convention on the Elimination of All Forms of Discrimination Against Women), adopted by the UN General Assembly in 1979 and already ratified by 186 countries (over 90 percent of UN countries). CEDAW prohibits all forms of discrimination against women by legally binding the countries that ratify it to incorporate equality of men and women into their legal systems. Measures include abolishing discriminatory laws and adopting new ones, establishing tribunals to ensure the protection of women, and eliminating acts of discrimination against women by persons, organizations, or enterprises. As of this writing, the United States is the only industrial society that has still not yet ratified the convention because of fear among some that it would give the UN power over U.S. legal statutes and institutions.

Various kinds of feminist thought (while embracing the two core concepts described earlier) differ in terms of their specific explanations for understanding the social organization of gender and their ideas for social change. An important distinction among U.S. feminisms is that between liberal and radical feminisms. Liberal feminists believe in the viability of the present system (meaning the system is okay) and work within this context for change in such public areas as education and employment. They attempt to remove obstacles to women's full participation in public life using strategies such as education, federal and state policies, and legal statutes.

Whereas liberal feminists want a piece of the pie, and have been critiqued as conservative reformists on account of this perspective, radical feminists (sometimes known as radical cultural feminists or difference feminists) want a whole new pie. Radical feminists recognize the oppression of women as a fundamental political oppression wherein women are categorized as inferior based on their gender. It is not enough to remove barriers to equality; rather, deeper, more transformational changes need to be made in societal institutions (like the government or media) as well as in people's heads. Patriarchy, radical feminists believe, shapes how women and men think about the world, their place in it, and their relationships with one another. Radical feminists assert that reformist solutions like those that liberal feminism would enact are problematic because they work to maintain rather than undermine the system. The "No More Miss America" manifesto by the radical feminist social organization New York Radical Women illustrates these points.

LEARNING ACTIVITY

GLOBAL FEMINISMS, TRANSNATIONAL ACTIVISM

Feminism is not simply a U.S. phenomenon. Indigenous feminisms have arisen all over the world to address the specific issues facing women in particular places. For example, in Botswana in the early 1990s a human rights attorney named Unity Dow challenged her country's Citizenship Act. That act, authorized in 1984, conferred citizenship on children born in Botswana only when the father was a citizen of Botswana. If the mother was a citizen of Botswana but the father was not, the children were not granted citizenship. Dow believed the law violated Botswana's constitution and challenged it in the high court. She won the case after four years of fighting. Another Botswanan woman, Musa Dube, a biblical critic and professor at the University of Botswana, uses her perspective as an African woman as a lens for interpreting the Bible. So, for example, when she reads the story of the hemorrhaging woman in Mark 5: 24–43 from an African postcolonial feminist perspective, she imagines the bleeding woman as Mama Africa, who is oppressed by sexism as well as colonialism and yet survives and participates in her own healing. Other feminists in

Botswana have worked diligently to support people living with HIV/AIDS and to stop the spread of the virus through the empowerment of women.

Choose one of the following nations and research feminisms in that country. What issues facing women do feminists confront? What forms does feminist activism take? How do these feminisms and forms of activism connect with feminist issues and activism in other countries? How do feminists work together across national borders to support one another's efforts?

- Australia
- Chile
- China
- Costa Rica
- Egypt
- Ghana
- India
- Lesotho
- Russia
- South Africa
- South Korea
- Turkey

Not surprisingly, although the focus of liberal feminism is on the public sphere, the focus of this radical approach is the private sphere of everyday individual consciousness and change. Radical feminist offshoots include lesbian feminism, which focuses on how compulsory heterosexuality (the cultural norm that assumes and requires heterosexuality) and heterosexual privilege (the rights and privileges of heterosexuality, such as legal marriage and being intimate in public) function to maintain power in society. Radical feminist thought also includes ecofeminism, a perspective that focuses on the association of women with nature and the environment and the simultaneous relationships among patriarchy, global economic expansion, and environmental degradation. Radical feminism tends to have a relatively fixed or biologically based idea of who is a "woman" and is often guilty of essentialism in treating all women as having common attributes and in minimizing differences among them.

Other feminist perspectives of "late modernity" (the latter part of the twentieth century) include Marxist feminism, a perspective that uses economic explanations from traditional Marxist theory to understand women's oppression. For Marxist feminists, the socioeconomic inequities of the class system are the major issues. This can be distinguished from socialist feminism, a perspective that integrates both Marxist and radical feminism. Socialist feminists use the insights of class analysis alongside radical feminist explanations of gender oppression. Contemporary socialist feminists seek to understand the workings of capitalist patriarchal institutions and often incorporate an environmental analysis that sees capitalism's push for private profits as the major cause of environmental degradation.

Many of these feminist approaches have been critiqued by the perspectives of women of color, who insist that theory be inclusive of all women's lives. Multiracial feminism or women of color feminism, for example, asserts that gender is constructed by a range of interlocking inequalities that work simultaneously to shape women's experience. This is the concept of intersections mentioned earlier. It brings together understandings drawn from the lived experiences of diverse women and influences all feminist writing today. Indeed, expressions of feminism grounded in the lives of women of color have included womanism, a social change perspective rooted in the lives of black women and other women of color that emphasizes that social change begins with self-change, and critiques the location of feminism in the ivory towers of academia. The name of this perspective was coined in 1983 by writer Alice Walker, who sought to distinguish this approach from that of white feminism. More recently, Latina/Chicana feminists have referred to themselves as Xicanistas to represent their indigenous roots and postcolonial histories.

Finally, some feminists have utilized a postmodern perspective that focuses on the relationship between knowledge and power. A postmodern approach questions the assumption that reality has an inherent order that is discernible through scientific inquiry, rejects binaries or dualistic thinking like male/female and heterosexual/homosexual, and attempts to destabilize such fixed identities. This approach recognizes changes in the organization of contemporary social life as a result, for example, of virtual technologies and increasing globalization and capitalist development. It also pays attention to how language constructs reality. Christine Garcia highlights the importance of language in disrupting hegemonic assumptions in the reading "In Defense of Latinx." Postmodernism emphasizes that humans actively construct or shape their lives in the context of various social systems, and often in the face of serious constraints. Queer theory is influenced by postmodernism and makes the case that gender and sexuality are socially produced and used as instruments of power. "Queer," once a derogatory term, is claimed back and celebrated in this approach that emphasizes fluid notions of power and identity and seeks to dismantle the binaries of gender and sexuality.

Many writers refer to a "third wave" of feminist activity influenced by postmodernism, queer theory, and multiracial feminism, that problematizes the universality and potential inclusivity of the term "woman." Third-wave feminism has its origins in the 1990s and reflects the thinking, writing, and activism of those who came of age taking for granted the gains of second-wave feminism, as well as the resistance or backlash to it. Third-wave perspectives are shaped by the material conditions created by globalization and techno-culture, and tend to focus on issues of sexuality and identity. Contemporary third-wave activity has been important in fueling feminist activism, especially through musical and art forms, such as "zines" (consciousness-raising magazines produced locally and often shared electronically), and through social networking and other virtual technologies.

Despite the advantages of using a "wave" metaphor to characterize the developments in feminism, the metaphor distracts attention from the continuity of feminist activity and runs the risk of setting up distinctions and potential intergenerational divisiveness between a more stodgy second-wave generation, devoid of sexuality and unwilling to share power, and a younger, self-absorbed generation obsessed with popular culture and uncritically

---

THANK A FEMINIST

Thank a feminist if you agree that . . .

- Women should have the right to vote.
- Women should have access to contraceptives.
- Women should have the right to work outside the home.
- Women should receive equal pay for equal work.
- Women should have the right to refuse sex, even with their husbands.
- Women should be able to receive a higher education.
- Women should have access to safe, legal abortion.
- Women should be able to participate in sports.
- Women should be able to hold political office.
- Women should be able to choose any career that interests them.
- Women should be free from sexual harassment in the workplace.
- Women should be able to enter into legal and financial transactions.
- Women should be able to study issues about women's lives and experiences.

One hundred years ago, none of these statements was possible for women in the United States. Only through the hard work and dedication of feminists in each decade of the twentieth century did these rights become available to women, and certainly access to each of these rights still continues to be shaped by race, social class, sexual identity, gender identity, ability, age, and other forms of difference.

Imagine a world without feminism. If you are a woman, you are not in college. You are not able to vote. You cannot play sports. Contraception is illegal. So is abortion. You're expected to marry and raise a family. If you must work, the only jobs available to you are in cleaning, clerical services, or teaching.

And you have no legal protection on the job if your boss pressures you for sex or makes lewd comments. Your husband can force you to have sex, and, if you were sexually abused as a child, most likely no one will believe you if you tell. If you are sexually attracted to women, you are considered mentally ill and may be subjected to an array of treatments for your illness.

Of course, much work remains to be done. Women across all their differences still do not have equality. Feminist work on issues of racial justice, gender identity, economic disparities, and other social justice issues is necessary to transform systems of oppression.

Still, today, young people who claim "I'm not a feminist, but . . ." benefit from the many gains made by feminists through the twentieth century. So the next time you see a woman go to class or vote or play basketball, thank a feminist!

IDEAS FOR ACTIVISM

TWO-MINUTE ACTIVIST

Many important legislative issues related to women come before elected officials regularly. You can make your voice to support women heard by contacting your senators and representatives. To become a two-minute activist ("one minute to read, one minute to act"), visit the website of the American Association of University Women (AAUW) at www.aauw.org. Click the "Take Action" button to find the Two-Minute Activist suggestions. There, you'll find links to information about the latest issues before Congress and to prewritten AAUW messages that you can personalize and send to your representatives. You can also sign up for Two-Minute Activist alerts.

sexualized. And, although contemporary feminism is accessible for many young women in the United States and is energizing in its focus on media, popular culture, sexuality, and so forth, it is critiqued as an "anything goes" movement. Some critics question its transformation of self rather than society, in part because of its potential ineffectiveness for collective action and structural change. In addition, they suggest it distorts the history of the second wave and fabricates a victim and/or anti-sex feminism that actually never existed. In this way, just as feminism encompasses diversity, so feminists do not all agree on what equality looks like or how to get there. As a social movement, feminism has always thrived on differences of ideology and practice. In "A Day Without Feminism," self-proclaimed third-wavers Jennifer Baumgardner and Amy Richards actively claim feminism as relevant to their lives and underscore the gains of second-wave feminist activism.

WHAT ARE THE MYTHS ASSOCIATED WITH FEMINISM?

A nationwide poll on feminism was published by the *Washington Post*–Kaiser Family Foundation in 2016. Sixty percent of women and 33 percent of men polled indicated they considered themselves to be either a feminist or a "strong feminist." Sixty-three percent of women aged 18–34 identified with these categories. Eighty-three percent of women aged 18–34 said feminism is empowering, and 45 percent have posted views about women's rights on social media. Only 16 percent of women younger than 35 viewed feminism as "outdated." Fifty-eight percent reported thinking that feminism is focused on the changes they want to see. An earlier poll from 2003 also found that when respondents were asked their opinion of the movement to strengthen women's rights, not the "women's rights movement," people's support was much higher. The misleading and negative connotations associated with the words "feminism" and "women's movement" play a central role in backlash, or organized resistance, to them and encompass what some call the "battered-word syndrome." The organized backlash to feminism also involves, for example, the ways certain groups who believe they would lose from a redistribution of power have worked hard to discredit and destroy the feminist movement and brand feminists in negative ways. This perspective is known as anti-feminism. Although such anti-feminist activity includes conservative groups and politicians, it also involves women who claim to be feminists yet are resistant to its core principles. These women, whose careers in part have been fueled by the gains brought about by the feminist movement, include such successful female academics as Christina Hoff Summers, Camille Paglia, Daphne Patai, Katie Roiphe, and Rene Denfield, and syndicated journalists like Mona Charen.

One result of this backlash has been the coining of the term "postfeminism" by those who recognize feminism as an important perspective but believe its time has passed and it is now obsolete. "We're already liberated" is the stance they take. The way this notion is accepted by public opinion is evidenced above by the number of people who believe the goals of the women's movement have already been met. Like other broad generalizations, there is some small truth to this: Things have improved for some women in some areas. Although generally it is accurate to say that women's status in the United States in the early decades of the twenty-first century is markedly improved, we still have a long way to go to reach full equality. In terms of the issues of poverty, violence, pornography, and health (to name just a few), things are worse for many women than they ever have been. There are still many areas in which women's status might be enhanced, and, for the majority of the world's women, life is very difficult indeed.

The idea that women have achieved equality is reinforced by the capitalist society in which we live. Surrounded by consumer products, we are encouraged to confuse liberation with the freedom to purchase products or to choose among a relatively narrow range of choices. Often personal style is mistaken for personal freedom as the body becomes a focus for fashion, hair, piercing, exercise, tattoos, and so forth. We are often encouraged to confuse such freedoms of expression with freedom in the sense of equality and social justice. Of course, popular culture and social media play a large part in this. We are encouraged to enjoy the freedoms that, in part, feminism has brought, often without recognition of this struggle or allegiance to maintaining such freedoms. Feminist writers explain that cultural changes exacerbated by virtual technologies often encourage young women to participate in their own objectification (being made into objects for male pleasure). They emphasize that these young women (who might consider themselves feminists) confuse their freedom to objectify themselves with authentic freedom.

LEARNING ACTIVITY

THE DINNER PARTY

In *Manifesta: Young Women, Feminism, and the Future*, Jennifer Baumgardner and Amy Richards tell the story of a dinner party they hosted, reminiscent of the consciousness-raising meetings of the 1970s during which women shared the stories and frustrations of their lives, most of which were directly related to sexism. The point of consciousness raising was to radicalize women, to help them develop the consciousness and motivation needed to make personal and political change in the world. One night many years ago, Jennifer and Amy brought together six of their friends around a dinner table to talk about current issues for women and directions needed for the contemporary women's movement. They found that the conversation wound its way around personal experiences and stories and their political implications and strategies. Their dinner party offered the beginnings of a revolution. They write, "Every time women get together around a table and speak honestly, they are embarking on an education that they aren't getting elsewhere in our patriarchal society. And that's the best reason for a dinner party a feminist could hope for."

Have a dinner party! Invite five or six of your friends over for dinner to discuss issues related to women, gender, and sexuality. What are the experiences of the people around the table in terms of sexuality, work, family, body image, media, and religion? What are the political implications of these experiences? What can be done to make the world better around these issues?

After your dinner party, write about what happened. What issues came up? What did various guests have to say about the issues? What strategies for change did the group identify? What plans for action did the group make? What did you learn from the experience?

Many people, groups, and institutions have attempted to discredit feminism (and therefore WGS) in other ways. Feminism has been subject to the following accusations: (1) Feminists are angry, whiny women who have an axe to grind, who have no sense of humor, and who exaggerate discrimination against women; (2) feminists hate men or want to be like men and selfishly want to create new systems of power over men; (3) all feminists are lesbians, women who choose romantic relationships with other women; (4) feminists reject motherhood, consider children a burden, and reject all things feminine; and (5) feminism is a white, middle-class movement that draws energy away from attempts to correct social and economic problems and discourages coalition building.

While several of these myths contain grains of truth, as a whole they can easily be shattered. First, although there are some feminists who respond, some would say rightly, to societal injustices with anger, most feminists work patiently with little resentment. Men as a social group demonstrate much more anger than women, feminists included. Even though male rage comes out in numerous acts of violence, wars, school shootings, and so on, men's anger is seen merely as a human response to circumstance. Note the androcentrism at work here. Because a few angry feminists get much more publicity than the majority of those working productively to change the status quo, a better question might be why women are not more angry, given the levels of injustice against women both in the United States and worldwide. Feminists do not exaggerate this injustice; injustice is a central organizing principle of contemporary society. We should also ask why women's anger provokes such a negative response. The cause of the relatively intense reaction to women's anger is grounded in a societal mandate against female anger that works to keep women from resisting their subordination—that is, it keeps them passive. Anger is seen as destructive and inappropriate, going against what we imagine to be feminine. As a result, organized expressions of anger are interpreted as hostile.

Second, it is often said that feminists hate men. It is accurate to say that in their affirmation of women and their desire to remove systems of inequality, feminists ask men to understand how gender privilege works in men's lives. Many men are more than willing to do this because the same social constructions of masculinity that privilege men also limit them. Because the demand for the examination of gender privilege is not synonymous with hating men, we might ask why these different concepts are so easily conflated. A more interesting question is why men are not accused more often of hating women, given the high levels of violence perpetrated by men against women. Certainly the world is full of misogyny—the hatred of, or contempt for, women—and every day we see examples of the ways misogyny influences, and sometimes destroys, the lives of women. The reality, of course, is that most feminists are in relationships of some kind (family, work, friends) with men, and some feminists are men. Some men eagerly call themselves pro-feminist because feminism is a perspective on life. The reading by Byron Hurt in Chapter 13, "Feminist Men," illustrates this practice. Nonetheless, the man-hating myth works to prevent many women who want to be in relationships with men from claiming feminism. They are encouraged to avoid a political stance that suggests antagonism toward men.

Feminists often respond to the declaration that they hate men with the observation that the statement illustrates a hypersensitivity about the possibility of exclusion and loss of power on the part of men. Only in a patriarchal society would the inclusion of women be interpreted as a potential threat or loss of men's power. It is a reflection of the fact that we live in a competitive patriarchal society when it is assumed that the feminist agenda is one that seeks to have power over men. Only in an androcentric society where men and their reality is center stage would it be assumed that an inclusion of one group must mean the exclusion of another. In other words, male domination encourages the idea that affirming women means hating men and interprets women's request for power sharing as a form of taking over. This projection of patriarchal mentality equates someone's gain with another's loss.

In response to the assertion that feminists want to be men, it is true to say that feminists might like to share some of the power granted to men in society. However, feminism is not about encouraging women to be like men; it's about valuing women for being women and respecting expressions of femininity no matter what body these expressions are mapped on. People opposed to feminism often confuse sameness with equality and say that women will never be equal to men because they are different (less physically strong, more emotional, etc.) or they say that equality is dangerous because women will start being like men. Feminism, of course, affirms and works to maintain difference; it merely asks that these differences be valued equally. That is the basis of social justice.

Third, feminists are accused of being lesbians in an effort to discredit feminism and prevent women both from joining the movement and from taking WGS classes. The term for this is "lesbian baiting." Feminism affirms women's choices to be and love whomever they choose. Although some lesbians are feminists, many lesbians are not feminists, and many feminists are heterosexual or have other sexual identities. Feminists do not interpret an association with lesbianism as an insult. Nonetheless, homophobia—the societal fear or hatred of lesbian, gay, bisexual, and queer people—functions to maintain this as an insult. There is considerable fear associated with being called a lesbian, and this declaration that all feminists are lesbians serves to keep women in line, apart from one another, and suspicious of feminism and WGS. Note that this myth is related to the earlier discussion on man hating because it is assumed that lesbians hate men too. Again, although lesbians love women, this does not necessitate a dislike of men.

Fourth, feminism does not reject motherhood but instead attempts to improve the conditions under which women mother. Contemporary legislation to improve working mothers' lives and provide safe and affordable health care, child care, and education for children (to name just a few examples) has come about because of the work of feminists. In terms of rejecting femininity, feminists have rejected some of the constraints associated with femininity such as corsets and hazardous beauty products and practices, but mostly they strive to reclaim femininity as a valuable construct that should be respected.

Fifth, feminism has been critiqued as a white, middle-class perspective that has no relevance to the lives of women of color. The corollary of this is that WGS is about only the lives of white, bourgeois women. This critique is important because, as discussed earlier, the history of the women's movement provides examples of both blatant and subtle racism, and white women have been the ones to hold most positions of power and authority in those movements. Similarly, working-class women have been underrepresented.

This is also reflected in the discipline of WGS as faculty and students have often been disproportionately white and economically privileged. Much work has been done to transform the women's movement into an inclusive social movement that has relevance for all people's lives. WGS departments and programs today are often among the most diverse units on college campuses, although most still have work to do. It is absolutely crucial that the study of women and other marginalized peoples as subjects both recognizes and celebrates diversity and works to transform all systems of oppression in society. Feminist scholar bell hooks claims back feminism as the movement to do just that. She emphasizes that any call to sisterhood must involve a commitment on the part of white women to examine white privilege and understand the interconnections among gender, race, and class domination.

Although the women's movement has had a profound impact on the lives of women in the United States and great strides have been made toward equality, real problems still remain. Women continue to face workplace discrimination and harassment, domestic violence, rape and abuse, education inequities, poverty, racism, and homophobia. WGS provides a forum for naming the problems women face, analyzing the root causes of these problems, envisioning a just and equitable world, and developing strategies for change. As you read the following articles, keep these questions in mind: What does the author identify as problems women face? What does the author suggest is the root of these problems? What strategies does the author suggest for bringing about change to improve the lives of women?

THE BLOG

WHY WE STILL NEED ETHNIC STUDIES AND WOMEN, GENDER & SEXUALITY STUDIES

Susan M. Shaw (2017)

Recently someone wrote a letter to the editor of our local paper criticizing our university's Ethnic Studies and Women, Gender, and Sexuality Studies programs for being divisive by their focus on "tiny subgroups" (African American, Latinx, Native American, Asian American, LGBTQ, women) rather than the larger human population.

In other words, this writer believes we don't need Ethnic Studies (ES) and Women, Gender, and Sexuality Studies (WGSS) because we should be teaching about our common humanity rather than our different identities, experiences, and cultures.

He could not be more wrong.

First of all, human beings do experience themselves as people who have gender, race, sexuality, and culture. And those differences lead to different experiences in the world. If we are to broaden and deepen our understanding of human experience, we have to examine it in all of its diversity and understand the difference difference makes. Ignoring social differences in human experience in academic study would make as much sense as ignoring differences in fish or stars or flowers. Commonalities don't negate differences.

Second, those "tiny subgroups" are actually the majority of the human population, and, yet, those subgroups are still mostly ignored or marginalized in much of the curriculum of higher education. Ethnic Studies and Women, Gender, and Sexuality Studies ensure that students have an opportunity to develop skills to understand how race, gender, sexuality, and other forms of difference work in the world.

Third, research shows that taking Ethnic Studies and Women, Gender, and Sexuality Studies classes is good for students and helps achieve the goals of higher education.

Many Ethnic Studies and Women, Gender, and Sexuality Studies students are members of the groups studied in these courses, and they are attracted to courses that focus on their communities, identities, and

(continued)

histories because they do not find their experiences and concerns centered in many other classes throughout the university. Research shows that ES and WGSS courses have positive impacts on these students. Taking these courses improves students' sense of empowerment and their sense of self-worth and enhances student engagement and academic achievement.

ES and WGSS courses also have positive impact on all students, especially heterosexual white men. White students who take Ethnic Studies courses experience reductions in prejudice and bias, and they become more democratic in their orientation. Students in ES and WGSS classes become more empathetic and more accepting of diversity.

Additionally, students who take ES and WGSS courses develop greater cognitive complexity and higher levels of thinking because of their exposure to diverse experiences and ideas.

And on campuses with strong attention to diversity, students across all groups report that they are more satisfied with their college experience than students who do not engage with diversity in college.

Finally, ES and WGSS faculty contribute essential scholarship to local and global communities. Here at Oregon State University my ES and WGSS colleagues are involved with research on motherhood, immigration, minority health, student success, and transnational adoption, to name a few topics. One just returned from supporting a medical team working with refugees in southern Iraq. Another works with Latinx communities in Oregon. One was nationally recognized [in 2016] for work on behalf of transgender people. Another was recently honored by our local community on MLK Day for his work with students and other people of color on campus and in the community.

Ethnic Studies and Women, Gender, and Sexuality Studies bring unique analytical lenses to academic study that help us understand how race, gender, sexuality, and other forms of difference shape individual and group experiences. They help us examine social institutions and the roles these institutions play in maintaining social inequality. And these academic disciplines also help us think about how people can work to bring about changes in the world that create more inclusive, equitable, and just workplaces, families, schools, churches, and other social organizations.

We still need Ethnic Studies and Women, Gender, and Sexuality Studies because race, gender, and sexuality are still important facets of human experience that give shape to the ways we are in the world. We need ES and WGSS because people from those "tiny subgroups" need an academic home to explore their concerns. We need ES and WGSS because all students benefit from exposure to diverse people and ideas. And we need ES and WGSS because the world still needs academics who can help us see things in a new way and develop skills to create a world that is life-affirming for us all.

1. CLAIMING AN EDUCATION
ADRIENNE RICH (1979)

For this convocation, I planned to separate my remarks into two parts: some thoughts about you, the women students here, and some thoughts about us who teach in a women's college. But ultimately, those two parts are indivisible. If university education means anything beyond the processing of human beings into expected roles, through credit hours, tests, and grades (and I believe that in a women's college especially it *might* mean much more), it implies an ethical and intellectual contract between teacher and student. This contract must remain intuitive, dynamic, unwritten; but we must turn to it again and again if learning is to be reclaimed from the depersonalizing and cheapening pressures of the present-day academic scene.

The first thing I want to say to you who are students is that you cannot afford to think of being here to *receive* an education; you will do much better to think of yourselves as being here to *claim* one. One of the dictionary definitions of the verb "to claim" is *to take as the rightful owner; to assert in the face of possible contradiction.* "To receive" is *to come into possession of; to act as receptacle or container for; to accept as authoritative or true.* The difference is that between

This talk was given at the Douglass College Convocation, September 6, 1977, and first printed in *The Common Woman*, a feminist literary magazine founded by Rutgers University women in New Brunswick, New Jersey.

acting and being acted upon, and for women it can literally mean the difference between life and death.

One of the devastating weaknesses of university learning, of the store of knowledge and opinion that has been handed down through academic training, has been its almost total erasure of women's experience and thought from the curriculum, and its exclusion of women as members of the academic community. Today, with increasing numbers of women students in nearly every branch of higher learning, we still see very few women in the upper levels of faculty and administration in most institutions. Douglass College itself is a women's college in a university administered overwhelmingly by men, who in turn are answerable to the state legislature, again composed predominantly of men. But the most significant fact for you is that what you learn here, the very texts you read, the lectures you hear, the way your studies are divided into categories and fragmented one from the other—all this reflects, to a very large degree, neither objective reality, nor an accurate picture of the past, nor a group of rigorously tested observations about human behavior. What you can learn here (and I mean not only at Douglass but any college in any university) is how men have perceived and organized their experience, their history, their ideas of social relationships, good and evil, sickness and health, etc. When you read or hear about "great issues," "major texts," "the mainstream of Western thought," you are hearing about what men, above all white men, in their male subjectivity, have decided is important.

Black and other minority peoples have for some time recognized that their racial and ethnic experience was not accounted for in the studies broadly labeled human; and that even the sciences can be racist. For many reasons, it has been more difficult for women to comprehend our exclusion, and to realize that even the sciences can be sexist. For one thing, it is only within the last hundred years that higher education has grudgingly been opened up to women at all, even to white, middle-class women. And many of us have found ourselves poring eagerly over books with titles like *The Descent of Man; Man and His Symbols; Irrational Man; The Phenomenon of Man; The Future of Man; Man and the Machine; From Man to Man; May Man Prevail?; Man, Science and Society;* or *One-Dimensional Man*—books pretending to describe a "human" reality that does not include over one-half the human species.

Less than a decade ago, with the rebirth of a feminist movement in this country, women students and teachers in a number of universities began to demand and set up women's studies courses—to *claim* a woman-directed education. And, despite the inevitable accusations of "unscholarly," "group therapy," "faddism," etc., despite backlash and budget cuts, women's studies are still growing, offering to more and more women a new intellectual grasp on their lives, new understanding of our history, a fresh vision of the human experience, and also a critical basis for evaluating what they hear and read in other courses, and in the society at large.

But my talk is not really about women's studies, much as I believe in their scholarly, scientific, and human necessity. While I think that any Douglass student has everything to gain by investigating and enrolling in women's studies courses, I want to suggest that there is a more essential experience that you owe yourselves, one which courses in women's studies can greatly enrich, but which finally depends on you, in all your interactions with yourself and your world. This is the experience of *taking responsibility toward your selves.* Our upbringing as women has so often told us that this should come second to our relationships and responsibilities to other people. We have been offered ethical models of the self-denying wife and mother; intellectual models of the brilliant but slapdash dilettante who never commits herself to anything the whole way, or the intelligent woman who denies her intelligence in order to seem more "feminine," or who sits in passive silence even when she disagrees inwardly with everything that is being said around her.

Responsibility to yourself means refusing to let others do your thinking, talking, and naming for you; it means learning to respect and use your own brains and instincts; hence, grappling with hard work. It means that you do not treat your body as a commodity with which to purchase superficial intimacy or economic security; for our bodies and minds are inseparable in this life, and when we allow our bodies to be treated as objects, our minds are in mortal danger. It means insisting that those to whom you give your friendship and love are able to respect your mind. It means being able to say, with Charlotte Bronte's *Jane Eyre*: "I have an inward treasure born with me, which can keep me alive if all the extraneous delights should be withheld or offered only at a price I cannot afford to give."

Responsibility to yourself means that you don't fall for shallow and easy solutions: predigested books and ideas, weekend encounters guaranteed to change your life, taking "gut" courses instead of ones you know will challenge you, bluffing at school and life instead of doing solid work, marrying early as an escape from real decisions, getting pregnant as an evasion of already existing problems. It means that you refuse to sell your talents and aspirations short, simply to avoid conflict and confrontation. And this, in turn, means resisting the forces in society which say that women should be nice, play safe, have low professional expectations, drown in love and forget about work, live through others, and stay in the places assigned to us. It means that we insist on a life of meaningful work, insist that work be as meaningful as love and friendship in our lives. It means, therefore, the courage to be "different"; not to be continuously available to others when we need time for ourselves and our work; to be able to demand of others—parents, friends, roommates, teachers, lovers, husbands, children—that they respect our sense of purpose and our integrity as persons. Women everywhere are finding the courage to do this, more and more, and we are finding that courage both in our study of women in the past who possessed it, and in each other as we look to other women for comradeship, community, and challenge. The difference between a life lived actively, and a life of passive drifting and dispersal of energies, is an immense difference. Once we begin to feel committed to our lives, responsible to ourselves, we can never again be satisfied with the old, passive way.

Now comes the second part of the contract. I believe that in a women's college you have the right to expect your faculty to take you seriously. The education of women has been a matter of debate for centuries, and old, negative attitudes about women's role,

women's ability to think and take leadership, are still rife both in and outside the university. Many male professors (and I don't mean only at Douglass) still feel that teaching in a women's college is a second-rate career. Many tend to eroticize their women students—to treat them as sexual objects—instead of demanding the best of their minds. (At Yale a legal suit [*Alexander v. Yale*] has been brought against the university by a group of women students demanding a stated policy against sexual advances toward female students by male professors.) Many teachers, both men and women, trained in the male-centered tradition, are still handing the ideas and texts of that tradition on to students without teaching them to criticize its antiwoman attitudes, its omission of women as part of the species. Too often, all of us fail to teach the most important thing, which is that clear thinking, active discussion, and excellent writing are all necessary for intellectual freedom, and that these require hard work. Sometimes, perhaps in discouragement with a culture which is both antiintellectual and antiwoman, we may resign ourselves to low expectations for our students before we have given them half a chance to become more thoughtful, expressive human beings. We need to take to heart the words of Elizabeth Barrett Browning, a poet, a thinking woman, and a feminist, who wrote in 1845 of her impatience with studies which cultivate a "passive recipiency" in the mind, and asserted that "women want to be made to *think actively*: their apprehension is quicker than that of men, but their defect lies for the most part in the logical faculty and in the higher mental activities." Note that she implies a defect which can be remedied by intellectual training—*not* an inborn lack of ability.

I have said that the contract on the student's part involves that you demand to be taken seriously so that you can also go on taking yourself seriously. This means seeking out criticism, recognizing that the most affirming thing anyone can do for you is demand that you push yourself further, show you the range of what you *can* do. It means rejecting attitudes of "take-it-easy," "why-be-so-serious," "why-worry-you'll-probably-get-married-anyway." It means assuming your share of responsibility for what happens in the classroom, because that affects the quality of your daily life here. It means that the student sees herself engaged *with* her teachers in an active, ongoing struggle for a real education. But for her to do this, her teachers must be committed to the belief that women's minds and experience are intrinsically valuable and indispensable to any civilization worthy [of] the name; that there is no more exhilarating and intellectually fertile place in the academic world today than a women's college—*if* both students and teachers in large enough numbers are trying to fulfill this contract. The contract is really a pledge of mutual seriousness about women, about language, ideas, methods, and values. It is our shared commitment toward a world in which the inborn potentialities of so many women's minds will no longer be wasted, raveled-away, paralyzed, or denied.

2. LIVING A FEMINIST LIFE

SARA AHMED (2017)

When did you begin to put the pieces together? Perhaps when you put the pieces back together you are putting yourself back together. We assemble something. Feminism is DIY: a form of self-assembly. No wonder feminist work is often about timing: sometimes we are too fragile to do this work; we cannot risk being shattered because we are not ready to put ourselves back together again. To get ready often means being prepared to be undone.

In time, with work, things begin to make more sense. You begin to recognize how violence is directed: that being recognized as a girl means being subjected to this pressure, this relentless assault on the senses; a body that comes to fear the touch of a world. Maybe you learn from that, from what that repetition does; you realize retrospectively how you came to take up less space. You might express feminist rage at how women are made responsible for the violence that is directed against them. Feminism helps you to make sense that something is wrong; to recognize a wrong is to realize that you are not in the wrong.

Becoming feminist: how we redescribe the world we are in. We begin to identify how what happens to me, happens to others. We begin to identify patterns and regularities. Begin to identify: this sounds too smooth. It is not an easy or straightforward process because we have to stay with the wrongs. And think about feeling: to direct your attention to the experience of being wronged can mean feeling wronged all over again.

We need to attend to the bumps; it is bumpy. You had already sensed something amiss. Maybe it was an uneasy feeling at first. As Alison Jaggar describes, "Only when we reflect on our initially puzzling irritability, revulsion, anger, or fear may we bring to consciousness our 'gut-level' awareness that we are in a situation of coercion, cruelty, injustice or danger" (1996, 181; see also Spelman 1989). A gut has its own intelligence. A feminist gut might sense something is amiss. You have to get closer to the feeling; but once you try to think about a feeling, how quickly it can recede. Maybe it begins as a background anxiety, like a humming noise that gradually gets louder over time so that it begins to fill your ear, canceling out other sounds. And then suddenly it seems (though perhaps it is not sudden) what you tried so hard not to notice is all you can hear. A sensation that begins at the back of your mind, an uneasy sense of something amiss, gradually comes forward, as things come up; then receding, as you try to get on with things; as you try to get on despite things. Maybe you do not even want to feel this way; feeling wrong is what brings a wrong home. Attending to the feeling might be too demanding: it might require you to give up on what otherwise seems to give you something; relationships, dreams; an idea of who it is that you are; an idea of who it is that you can be. You might even will yourself not to notice certain things because noticing them would change your relation to the world; it would change the world to which you exist in relation. We have to stay with the feelings that we might wish would go away; that become reminders of these things that happened that made you wary of being at all.

Perhaps there is just only so much you can take in. Perhaps you take in some things as a way of not taking in other things. As I have been putting a sponge to my own feminist past, I remembered another conversation. It was with a teacher of mine at university, Rosemary Moore, who taught the first feminist classes I took: Nineteenth-Century Women's Writing in 1988; Twentieth-Century Women's Writing in 1989. I hadn't thought about this conversation for a long time, though it is probably not true to say that I had forgotten it. I asked her whether my essay for the course had to refer to women or gender. Her answer was that it didn't but that it would be surprising if it didn't. Why did I ask her this question? I had come to university hoping to study philosophy. I was especially interested in what I called "scepticism," philosophies that proceeded by doubting what is as a way of questioning what's what. Sadly, philosophy at Adelaide University was pretty much straight analytical philosophy and scepticism was dismissed as self-refuting in the first lecture of Philosophy 101. To study the kind of work I was interested in, I ended up in the English literature department because there they taught what was referred to as "theory." And I chose the women's writing courses not because I was interested in feminist theory (even though I was passionate about feminism) but because I was interested in critical theory. I was interested in how we know things, in questions of truth, in perspective and perception, in experience and subjectivity. I wanted to ask how I know that what I see as green is what you see as green; those sorts of questions were my sort of questions.

Yes: I chose women's writing because I wanted to do critical theory. Our teacher was engaged with and by Lacanian psychoanalysis. If we began there, that wasn't what kept my attention; it was 1980s feminist literary theory and from there, feminist philosophy of science and feminist epistemology. I ended up writing my first feminist essay for that course. So why did it happen this way around: from critical theory to feminist theory, given that I thought of myself as a feminist and had been such an outspoken feminist

growing up? I think there was only so much feminism I could take in. I had thought that to be philosophical or to ask questions about the nature of reality was not to do feminism: that feminism was about something particular not general, relative not universal, that feminism was about questioning and challenging sexual violence, inequality, and injustice and not the nature of reality as such. I did not understand that feminism was a way of challenging the universal. I did not appreciate how questioning sexism is one of the most profound ways of disrupting what we take to be given and thus learning about how the given is given. Feminist theory taught me that the universal is what needs to be exploded. Feminist theory taught me that reality is usually just someone else's tired explanation. So if in my introduction to this book [*Living a Feminist Life*] I suggested that feminist theory is what gets you there, to the classroom, we might note how feminist theory can be what gets you out of there. By this I mean: I thought I wanted to be in the theory class; feminist theory taught me that that was not the class for me. Feminism is my theory class.

We learn also: how we recognize sexism or racism here can be a way of not recognizing it there. A location can be a reduction. Becoming feminist involves a process of recognizing that what you are up against cannot be located or reduced to an object or thing (which could then be discarded so we could start up again). The process of recognizing sexism was not smooth or automatic. I had multiple false starts because there was so much I resisted: I could take feminism in only bit by bit. Maybe there was only so much I could take in because it meant recognizing that I had been taken in. You can feel stupid for not having seen things more clearly before. You have to give up on a version of yourself as well as a version of events. And maybe we need to remember how hard it is to acknowledge that a world is not accommodating you because of the body you have. I didn't want feminism to be everywhere, as I didn't want to encounter these limits; I wanted there to be places to go where I could just leave my body behind.

If becoming feminist is not a smooth process, if we resist what we encounter because it is too much to take in, this is not to say when we do let go it is just difficult. When you begin to put the pieces together, it can feel magical: the wonder of the clicking moment, when things that had previously been obscured begin to make sense, when things fit into place. You blink and the world reappears: clarity can feel magical. For me reading feminist theory was a series of continuous clicks. And later, teaching women's studies was such a delight as you can participate in other people's clicking moments: what a sound it makes; how important it is that this sound is audible to others.

Finding feminism can be empowering as it is a way of reinhabiting the past. It is personal. There is no question: it is personal. The personal is structural. I learned that you can be hit by a structure; you can be bruised by a structure. An individual man who violates you is given permission: that is structure. His violence is justified as natural and inevitable: that is structure. A girl is made responsible for his violence: that is structure. A policeman who turns away because it is a domestic call: that is structure. A judge who talks about what she was wearing: that is structure. A structure is an arrangement, an order, a building; an assembly.

We need structure to give evidence of structure. To catalog instances of violence is to create a feminist catalog. I think one of the reasons I find the project *Everyday Sexism* so important and compelling is that it shows how the cataloging of instances of sexism is necessarily a collective project. The project involves the creation of a virtual space in which we can insert our own individual experiences of sexism, sexual violence, or sexual harassment so that we show what we know: that this or that incident is not isolated but part of a series of events: a series as a structure. These recent feminist strategies have revived key aspects of second-wave feminism; we are in the time of revival because of what is not over. Consciousness-raising was also about this: reaching a feminist account, as an account for oneself with and through others, connecting my experience with the experience of others. We need a deposit system to show the scale of sexism. When there is a place to go with these experiences—and feminism is about giving women places to go—the accounts tend to come out: a "drip, drip" becomes a flood. It is like a tap has been loosened, allowing what has been held back to flow. Feminism: the releasing of a pressure valve.

Feminism can allow you to reinhabit not only your own past but also your own body. You might over time, in becoming aware of how you have lessened your own space, give yourself permission to take up more space; to expand your own reach. It is not necessarily the case that we take up this permission simply by giving ourselves permission. It does take time, to reinhabit the body, to become less wary, to acquire confidence. Feminism involves a process of finding another way to live in your body. We might learn to let ourselves bump into things; not to withdraw in anticipation of violence. Of course I am describing a difficulty; I am describing how ways of resolving problems can enact the problems we are trying to resolve. We know we are not responsible for resolving the problem of violence; changing how we relate to the world does not change the world. And yet in refusing to withdraw, in refusing to lessen how much space we take up, in insisting on taking up space, we are not receiving the message that has been sent out. In order to put the pieces together, you cannot but get the message wrong, the message that makes a wrong a right. No wonder then, as I explore later, to become a feminist is to be perceived as in the wrong.

As we begin this process of putting ourselves back together we find much more than ourselves. Feminism, in giving you somewhere to go, allows you to revisit where you have been. We can become even more conscious of the world in this process of becoming conscious of injustices because we had been taught to overlook so much. A world can flood once we have let it in, once we have unlocked the door of our own resistance. Feminism too can become a flooding experience: one book read that leads to another, a trail that leads you to find feminism, more and more feminism, new words, concepts, arguments, models: patriarchy, phallocentrism, rape culture, the sex-gender system. In finding feminism, you are finding out about the many ways that feminists have tried to make sense, already, of the experiences you had, before you had them; experiences that left you feeling all alone are the experiences that lead you to others. We still have sorting to do: some of these ways of making sense make more sense to you than others. But I will always remember that feeling; a sense that there are others like you out there, that you are not on your own, that you were not on your own. Your own difficult history is written out in words that are sent out. I often think of reading feminist books as like making friends, realizing that others have been here before.

Even if you still feel pain, frustration, and rage, even if you feel these feelings more as you have given them more attention, they are directed in a different way. Knowledge is this achievement of direction. Your feelings are directed neither at some anonymous stranger who happened upon you (or not only), nor toward yourself for allowing something to happen (or not just), but toward a world that reproduces that violence by explaining it away.

3. NO MORE MISS AMERICA
NEW YORK RADICAL WOMEN (1968)

1. *The Degrading Mindless-Boob-Girlie Symbol.* The Pageant contestants epitomize the roles we are all forced to play as women. The parade down the runway blares the metaphor of the 4-H Club county fair, where the nervous animals are judged for teeth, fleece, etc., and where the best "Specimen" gets the blue ribbon. So are women in our society forced daily to compete for male approval, enslaved by ludicrous "beauty" standards we ourselves are conditioned to take seriously.

2. *Racism with Roses.* Since its inception in 1921, the Pageant has not had one Black finalist, and this has not been for a lack of test-case contestants. There has never been a Puerto Rican, Alaskan, Hawaiian, or Mexican-American winner. Nor has there ever been a *true* Miss America—an American Indian.

3. *Miss America as Military Death Mascot.* The highlight of her reign each year is a cheerleader-tour of American troops abroad—last year she went to Vietnam to pep-talk our husbands, fathers, sons and boyfriends into dying and killing with a better spirit. She personifies the "unstained patriotic American womanhood our boys are fighting for." The Living Bra and the Dead Soldier. We refuse to be used as Mascots for Murder.

4. *The Consumer Con-Game.* Miss America is a walking commercial for the Pageant's sponsors. Wind her up and she plugs your product on promotion tours and TV—all in an "honest, objective" endorsement. What a shill.

5. *Competition Rigged and Unrigged.* We deplore the encouragement of an American myth that oppresses men as well as women: the win-or-you're-worthless competitive disease. The "beauty contest" creates only one winner to be "used" and forty-nine losers who are "useless."

6. *The Woman as Pop Culture Obsolescent Theme.* Spindle, mutilate, and then discard tomorrow. What is so ignored as last year's Miss America? This only reflects the gospel of our Society, according to Saint Male: women must be young, juicy, malleable—hence age discrimination and the cult of youth. And we women are brainwashed into believing this ourselves!

7. *The Unbeatable Madonna-Whore Combination.* Miss America and Playboy's centerfold are sisters over the skin. To win approval, we must be both sexy and wholesome, delicate but able to cope, demure yet titillatingly bitchy. Deviation of any sort brings, we are told, disaster: "You won't get a man!!"

8. *The Irrelevant Crown on the Throne of Mediocrity.* Miss America represents what women are supposed to be: inoffensive, bland, apolitical. If you are tall, short, over or under what weight The Man prescribes you should be, forget it. Personality, articulateness, intelligence, and commitment—unwise. Conformity is the key to the crown—and, by extension, to success in our Society.

9. *Miss America as Dream Equivalent To—?* In this reputedly democratic society, where every little boy supposedly can grow up to be President, what can every little girl hope to grow to be? Miss America. That's where it's at. Real power to control our own lives is restricted to men, while women get patronizing pseudopower, an ermine clock and

a bunch of flowers; men are judged by their actions, women by appearance.

10. *Miss America as Big Sister Watching You.* The pageant exercises Thought Control, attempts to sear the Image onto our minds, to further make women oppressed and men oppressors; to enslave us all the more in high-heeled, low-status roles; to inculcate false values in young girls; women as beasts of buying; to seduce us to our selves before our own oppression.

4. A DAY WITHOUT FEMINISM

JENNIFER BAUMGARDNER AND AMY RICHARDS (2000)

We were both born in 1970, the baptismal moment of a decade that would change dramatically the lives of American women. The two of us grew up thousands of miles apart, in entirely different kinds of families, yet we both came of age with the awareness that certain rights had been won by the women's movement. We've never doubted how important feminism is to people's lives—men's and women's. Both of our mothers went to consciousness-raising-type groups. Amy's mother raised Amy on her own, and Jennifer's mother, questioning the politics of housework, staged laundry strikes.

With the dawn of not just a new century but a new millennium, people are looking back and taking stock of feminism. Do we need new strategies? Is feminism dead? Has society changed so much that the idea of a feminist movement is obsolete? For us, the only way to answer these questions is to imagine what our lives would have been if the women's movement had never happened and the conditions for women had remained as they were in the year of our births.

Imagine that for a day it's still 1970, and women have only the rights they had then. Sly and the Family Stone and Dionne Warwick are on the radio, the kitchen appliances are Harvest Gold, and the name of your Whirlpool gas stove is Mrs. America. What is it like to be female?

Babies born on this day are automatically given their father's name. If no father is listed, "illegitimate" is likely to be typed on the birth certificate. There are virtually no child-care centers, so all preschool children are in the hands of their mothers, a baby-sitter, or an expensive nursery school. In elementary school, girls can't play in Little League and almost all of the teachers are female. (The latter is still true.) In a few states, it may be against the law for a male to teach grades lower than the sixth, on the basis that it's unnatural, or that men can't be trusted with young children.

In junior high, girls probably take home ec; boys take shop or small-engine repair. Boys who want to learn how to cook or sew on a button are out of luck, as are girls who want to learn how to fix a car. *Seventeen* magazine doesn't run feminist-influenced current columns like "Sex + Body" and "Traumarama." Instead, the magazine encourages girls not to have sex; pleasure isn't part of its vocabulary. Judy Blume's books are just beginning to be published, and *Free to Be . . . You and Me* does not exist. No one reads much about masturbation as a natural activity; nor do they learn that sex is for anything other than procreation. Girls do read mystery stories about Nancy Drew, for whom there is no sex, only her blue roadster and having "luncheon." (The real mystery is how Nancy gets along without a purse and manages to meet only white people.) Boys read about the Hardy Boys, for whom there are no girls.

In high school, the principal is a man. Girls have physical-education class and play half-court basketball, but not soccer, track, or cross country; nor do they have any varsity sports teams. The only prestigious physical activity for girls is cheerleading, or being a drum majorette. Most girls don't take calculus or physics; they plan the dances and decorate the gym. Even when girls get better grades than their male counterparts, they are half as likely to qualify for a National Merit Scholarship because many of the test questions favor boys. Standardized tests refer to males and male experiences much more than to females and their experiences. If a girl "gets herself pregnant," she loses her membership in the National Honor Society (which is still true today) and is expelled.

Girls and young women might have sex while they're unmarried, but they may be ruining their chances of landing a guy full-time, and they're probably getting a bad reputation. If a pregnancy happens, an enterprising gal can get a legal abortion only if she lives in New York or is rich enough to fly there, or to Cuba, London, or Scandinavia. There's also the Chicago-based Jane Collective, an underground abortion-referral service, which can hook you up with an illegal or legal termination. (Any of these options are going to cost you. Illegal abortions average $300 to $500, sometimes as much as $2,000.) To prevent pregnancy, a sexually active woman might go to a doctor to be fitted for a diaphragm, or take the high-dose birth-control pill, but her doctor isn't likely to inform her of the possibility of deadly blood clots. Those who do take the Pill also may have to endure this contraceptive's crappy side effects: migraine headaches, severe weight gain, irregular bleeding, and hair loss (or gain), plus the possibility of an increased risk of breast cancer in the long run. It is unlikely that women or their male partners know much about the clitoris and its role in orgasm unless someone happens to fumble upon it. Instead, the myth that vaginal orgasms from penile penetration are the only "mature" (according to Freud) climaxes prevails.

Lesbians are rarely "out," except in certain bars owned by organized crime (the only businessmen who recognize this untapped market), and if lesbians don't know about the bars, they're less likely to know whether there are any other women like them. Radclyffe Hall's depressing early-twentieth-century novel *The Well of Loneliness* pretty much indicates their fate.

The Miss America Pageant is the biggest source of scholarship money for women. Women can't be students at Dartmouth, Columbia, Harvard, West Point, Boston College, or the Citadel, among other all-male institutions. Women's colleges are referred to as "girls' schools." There are no Take Back the Night marches to protest women's lack of safety after dark, but that's okay because college girls aren't allowed out much after dark anyway. Curfew is likely to be midnight on Saturday and 9 or 10 p.m. the rest of the week. Guys get to stay out as late as they want. Women tend

to major in teaching, home economics, English, or maybe a language—a good skill for translating someone else's words. The women's studies major does not exist, although you can take a women's studies course at six universities, including Cornell and San Diego State College. The absence of women's history, black history, Chicano studies, Asian-American history, queer studies, and Native American history from college curricula implies that they are not worth studying. A student is lucky if he or she learns that women were "given" the vote in 1920, just as Columbus "discovered" America in 1492. They might also learn that Sojourner Truth, Mary Church Terrell, and Fannie Lou Hamer were black abolitionists or civil-rights leaders, but not that they were feminists. There are practically no tenured female professors at any school, and campuses are not racially diverse. Women of color are either not there or they're lonely as hell. There is no nationally recognized Women's History Month or Black History Month. Only 14 percent of doctorates are awarded to women. Only 3.5 percent of MBAs are female.

Only 2 percent of everybody in the military is female, and these women are mostly nurses. There are no female generals in the U.S. Air Force, no female naval pilots, and no Marine brigadier generals. On the religious front, there are no female cantors or rabbis, Episcopal canons, or Catholic priests. (This is still true of Catholic priests.)

Only 44 percent of women are employed outside the home. And those women make, on average, fifty-two cents to the dollar earned by males. Want ads are segregated into "Help Wanted Male" and "Help Wanted Female." The female side is preponderantly for secretaries, domestic workers, and other low-wage service jobs, so if you're a female lawyer you must look under "Help Wanted Male." There are female doctors, but twenty states have only five female gynecologists or fewer. Women workers can be fired or demoted for being pregnant, especially if they are teachers, since the kids they teach aren't supposed to think that women have sex. If a boss demands sex, refers to his female employee exclusively as "Baby," or says he won't pay her unless she gives him a blow job, she has to either quit or succumb—no pun intended. Women can't be airline pilots. Flight attendants are "stewardesses"—waitresses in the sky—and necessarily female. Sex appeal is a job requirement, wearing makeup is a rule, and women are fired if they exceed the age or weight deemed sexy. Stewardesses can get married without getting canned, but this is a new development. (In 1968 the Equal Employment Opportunity Commission—EEOC—made it illegal to forcibly retire stewardesses for getting hitched.) Less than 2 percent of dentists are women; 100 percent of dental assistants are women. The "glass ceiling" that keeps women from moving naturally up the ranks, as well as the sticky floor that keeps them unnaturally down in low-wage work, has not been named, much less challenged.

When a woman gets married, she vows to love, honor, and obey her husband, though he gets off doing just the first two to uphold his end of the bargain. A married woman can't obtain credit without her husband's signature. She doesn't have her own credit rating, legal domicile, or even her own name unless she goes to court to get it back. If she gets a loan with her husband—and she has a job—she may have to sign a "baby letter" swearing that she won't have one and have to leave her job.

Women have been voting for up to fifty years, but their turnout rate is lower than that for men, and they tend to vote right along with their husbands, not with their own interests in mind. The divorce rate is about the same as it is in 2000, contrary to popular fiction's blaming the women's movement for divorce. However, divorce required that one person be at fault, therefore if you just want out of your marriage, you have to lie or blame your spouse. Property division and settlements, too, are based on fault. (And at a time when domestic violence isn't a term, much less a crime, women are legally encouraged to remain in abusive marriages.) If fathers ask for custody of the children, they get it in 60 to 80 percent of the cases. (This is still true.) If a husband or a lover hits his partner, she has no shelter to go to unless she happens to live near the one in northern California or the other in upper Michigan. If a woman is downsized from her role as a housewife (a.k.a. left by her husband), there is no word for being a displaced homemaker. As a divorcee, she may be regarded as a family disgrace or as easy sexual prey. After all, she had sex with one guy, so why not *all* guys?

If a woman is not a Mrs., she's a Miss. A woman without makeup and a hairdo is as suspect as a man with them. Without a male escort she may be refused service in a restaurant or a bar, and a woman alone is hard-pressed to find a landlord who will rent her an apartment. After all, she'll probably be leaving to get married soon, and, if she isn't, the landlord doesn't want to deal with a potential brothel.

Except among the very poor or in very rural areas, babies are born in hospitals. There are no certified midwives, and women are knocked out during birth. Most likely, they are also strapped down and lying down, made to have the baby against gravity for the doctor's convenience. If he has a schedule to keep, the likelihood of a cesarean is also very high. *Our Bodies, Ourselves* doesn't exist, nor does the women's health movement. Women aren't taught how to look at their cervixes, and their bodies are nothing to worry their pretty little heads about; however, they are supposed to worry about keeping their little heads pretty. If a woman goes under the knife to see if she has breast cancer, the surgeon won't wake her up to consult about her options before performing a Halsted mastectomy (a disfiguring radical procedure, in which the breast, the muscle wall, and the nodes under the arm, right down to the bone, are removed). She'll just wake up and find that the choice has been made for her.

Husbands are likely to die eight years earlier than their same-age wives due to the stress of having to support a family and repress an emotional life, and a lot earlier than that if women have followed the custom of marrying older, authoritative, paternal men. The stress of raising kids, managing a household, and being undervalued by society doesn't seem to kill off women at the same rate. Upon a man's death, his beloved gets a portion of his Social Security. Even if she has worked outside the home for her entire adult life, she is probably better off with that portion than with hers in its entirety, because she has earned less and is likely to have taken time out for such unproductive acts as having kids.

Has feminism changed our lives? Was it necessary? After thirty years of feminism, the world we inhabit barely resembles the world we were born into. And there's still a lot left to do.

5. A TRANSNATIONAL BLACK FEMINIST FRAMEWORK
KIA M. Q. HALL (2016)

INTRODUCTION

In many ways, today's Black Lives Matter (BLM) movement is breaking new ground in terms of Black freedom struggle in the United States. Digital technologies have propelled a bottom-up, grassroots movement: "New tools of technology—particularly social media and especially Twitter" have facilitated "a bottom-up insurgency led by ordinary people, and have displaced the top-down approach of old guard civil rights organizations"—a model that is no accident, but rather one that was adopted by design (Harris 2015, 37). The new movement has a broad and powerful base.

> Core activists of the Black Lives Matter movement have insisted on a group-centered model of leadership, rooted in ideas of participatory democracy. . . . Black Lives Matter organizers also operate on the principle that no one person or group of individuals should speak for or make decisions on behalf of the movement. They believe, as the legendary civil rights activist Ella Baker believed, that "strong people don't need strong leaders." (Harris 2015, 37)

Black Lives Matter cofounder Alicia Garza says the following about the importance of broad-based leadership: "We want to make sure there is the broadest participation possible in this new iteration of a black freedom movement. We can't afford to just follow one voice." She continues: "We have so many different experiences that are rich and complex. We need to bring all of those experiences to the table in order to achieve the solutions we desire" (Guynn 2015, 03B).

In addition to a different form of leadership, BLM is also correcting some important historical erasures in terms of how the "her-story" of Black freedom struggle is recorded:

> Although nascent, the emergent national (and arguably global movement) against anti-Black racial violence connects to a long tradition of African American activism. A troubling part of this tradition, however, is the regular erasure of Black women, queer

people, and trans* people from the historical record both as victims and as activists. Despite a robust field of scholarship that focuses on African American women as activists challenging anti-Black racism, dominant narratives about racial justice movements, both historically and contemporarily, often pivot around Black men's activism and, more specifically, Black heterosexual men's activism. (Lindsey 2015, 232–233)

Thus, the BLM movement embodies a thread of vindication, similar to that which Black feminist anthropologists have invoked in response to Black people's displacement and marginalization in the field of anthropology (McClaurin 2001a, 15). Certainly, the movement is marked by its openness to people of all genders and those who are gender nonconforming. "The hashtag that has become the movement's signature, #BlackLivesMatter, was itself coined by three black queer women, in response to George Zimmerman's acquittal in the killing of Trayvon Martin" (Pierre-Louis 2015). It has been noted that "BLM intentionally elevates both cis and trans women of color in its leadership and activism" (Cooper 2015, 31). Although women's leadership has been present all along, there is renewed visibility for unconventional women's leadership:

> Women are leading without suggesting they are the only leaders or that there is only one way to lead. ... It isn't a coincidence that a movement that brings together the talents of black women—many of them queer—for the purpose of liberation is considered leaderless, since black women have so often been rendered invisible. (Asoka 2015, 60)

More specifically, the presence of queer and lesbian women of color in leadership positions is not something new. As Gloria Anzaldúa (1987) wrote: "Colored homosexuals have more knowledge of other cultures; have always been at the forefront (although sometimes in the closet) of all liberation struggles in this country; have suffered more injustices and have survived them despite all odds" (85). In the BLM movement, the importance of women of color of all sexual orientations has been made explicit.

> Women across the generations are participating in this movement, but I think we've had a wonderful opportunity to see especially young, queer women play a central role. It's important to recognize that while they are organizing on behalf of victims of police brutality and cruelty broadly, they have to constantly remind the larger public that women are among those victims too. So, although these women are putting their bodies on the line for the movement, they also have to articulate that they are fighting for all lives, including their own. (Asoka 2015, 55)

Cofounder Alicia Garza consistently speaks to the importance of this radical inclusion:

> Speaking to issues of cooptation, heterosexism, homo-antagonism, sexism, patriarchy, and racism, Garza emphasizes the importance of a radical inclusivity and of a necessary acknowledgement of the tremendous work of Black women, trans˙ people, and queer people within contemporary racial justice movements. (Lindsey 2015, 232)

The group's actions reflect this radical commitment. For example, Black Lives Matter has organized nationwide rallies to bring attention to the murders of Black transgender women (Altman 2015, 121). Through words and deeds, BLM is highlighting lives of people who have been multiply marginalized, and engaging in radical inclusivity and visibility:

> When documentation and activism fail to encapsulate violence against trans˙ people, queer people, and women and girls, then we further marginalize and render invisible those surviving and living on the margins of marginalization. The push toward being more inclusive in our documentation and our activism surrounding anti-Black state violence opens up a dynamic space in which we can intentionally and collectively make visible and legible all victims of state and state-sanctioned violence. (Lindsey 2015, 237)

Thus, the BLM movement is both radically different and yet rooted in core values that are quite familiar to feminists, especially queer feminists of color.

This essay offers a theoretical framework, rooted in Black feminist and transnational feminist traditions, that provides a coherent feminist framing for this activist work. In particular, it speaks to the scholar-activist who might be inclined to explore the theoretical underpinnings of contemporary Black activism. What theoretical framing might the Black scholar-activist contribute to help analyze the feminist roots of the movement, contemporary activism, and potential futures? In response to this question, I offer a Transnational Black Feminist framework for engagement.

THEORIZING THE BLACK FREEDOM STRUGGLE

Some will wonder whether or not a movement such as Black Lives Matter needs theory. Should theory be left to the academics and freedom struggle be left to the activists? Of course, Black feminist scholar-activists have long argued the critical importance of embodied theoretical work. In 1994 bell hooks wrote the following:

> When our lived experience of theorizing is fundamentally linked to processes of self-recovery, of collective liberation, no gap exists between theory and practice. Indeed, what such experience makes more evident is the bond between the two—that ultimately reciprocal process wherein one enables the other. (61)

In developing a framework rooted in Black feminist traditions, I adopt Irma McClaurin's (2001b) conception of Black feminism as defined as follows:

> An embodied, positioned, ideological standpoint perspective that holds Black women's experiences of simultaneous and multiple oppressions as the epistemological and theoretical basis of a "pragmatic activism" directed at combating those social and personal, individual and structural, and local and global forces that pose harm to Black (in the widest geopolitical sense) women's well-being. (63)

In developing this embodied and practical theory, the voices of individuals on the margins of society are critical. In her book *Feminist Theory: From*

Margin to Center bell hooks (1984) wrote about growing up with this unique vantage point from the margins:

> Living as we did—on the edge—we developed a particular way of seeing reality. We looked both from the outside in and from the inside out. We focused our attention on the center as well as on the margin. We understood both. This mode of seeing reminded us of the existence of a whole universe, a main body made up of both margin and center. Our survival depended on an ongoing public awareness of the separation between margin and center and an ongoing private acknowledgement that we were a necessary, vital part of that whole. (ix)

Because of this nuanced view, people on the margins are well equipped for the project of developing transformative and visionary theory.

A critical question posed by bell hooks (1990) is: "How do we create an oppositional worldview, a consciousness, an identity, a standpoint that exists not only as that struggle which also opposes dehumanization but as the movement which enables creative, expansive self-actualization?" (15). A Transnational Black Feminist framework aims to chart a path forward while remaining rooted in feminist traditions. It points scholars, activists, and scholar-activists toward tools for advancing the freedom struggle, so that we may engage in the liberatory process that hooks (1990) described as follows:

> That process emerges as one comes to understand how structures of domination work in one's own life, as one develops critical thinking and critical consciousness, as one invents new, alternative habits of being, and resists from that marginal space of difference inwardly defined. (15)

Inspired by both Black feminist and transnational feminist traditions, the Transnational Black Feminist framework offers four guiding principles: intersectionality, scholar-activism, solidarity building, and attention to borders/boundaries. . . . Johnetta Cole (1993) wrote:

> When we think of oppression, we generally think in terms of the opportunities and life chances it robs its victims of; and rightly so, since this is the most

immediate and obvious sting. In the long run, however, the real horror of oppression is that it can rob people of their will to try, and make them take themselves out of the running of life. (111)

These principles are designed to bring together some of the critical feminist elements that have been crucial to movement building in the past, so that feminists of all walks of life can advance the current freedom movement.

TRANSNATIONAL BLACK FEMINIST GUIDING PRINCIPLES IN THE CONTEXT OF BLM

INTERSECTIONALITY

Legal scholar and Black feminist Kimberlé Crenshaw used the multidimensional experiences of Black women to demonstrate that a single-axis (e.g., race or gender) analysis is not only ineffective in capturing the experiences of Black women, but actually distorts their realities (Crenshaw 1998, 314). In place of a single-axis analysis, Crenshaw recommended an intersectional analysis that would analyze experiences at the intersection of multiple categories (e.g. race, class, and gender): "Because the intersectional experience is greater than the sum of racism and sexism, any analysis that does not take intersectionality into account cannot sufficiently address the particular manner in which Black women are subordinated" (1998, 315).

An intersectional approach is broadly applicable, and many observers have taken note of the intersectional analysis of the BLM movement. For example, Barbara Ransby (2015) has written that the "unapologetic intersectional analysis" of the BLM movement "reflect[s] the work of black women radicals and feminists such as Sojourner Truth, Angela Davis, Audre Lorde, Barbara Smith, bell hooks, Kimberlé Crenshaw, Beth Richie, Cathy Cohen, and Beverly Guy-Sheftal" (32). Black feminist sociologist Patricia Hill Collins could also be added to this list of influential feminists. Collins (2008) identified the importance of an intersectional approach as follows: "Intersectional paradigms remind us that oppression cannot be reduced to one fundamental type, and that oppressions work together in producing injustice" (21).

Intersectionality is critically important for understanding the diverse realities of Black lives:

> Because black bodies are still bound by racial apartheid, our humanist agenda is the same as an antiracist, anti-imperialist social justice agenda. It's not sufficient to recognize that "Black Lives Matter" . . . they also matter intersectionally—as female, queer, trans, poor, and disproportionately segregated. (Hutchinson 2015, 23)

Also, intersectionality has been critical to highlighting connections between diverse issues, such as mass incarceration and mass deportation within the movement (Asoka 2015, 59). As a concept developed in the academy, the utility of intersectionality in describing the Black experience only highlights the important relationship between scholarship—or academia—and activism.

SCHOLAR-ACTIVISM

Scholars (and students) have, and always have had, a critical role in activist movements. Black feminist anthropologist Irma McClaurin (2001b) argued that researchers are faced with the difficult task of "fashioning a research paradigm that decolonizes and transforms—in other words, one that seeks to alleviate conditions of oppression through scholarship and activism rather than support them" (57). Black feminist anthropologists and sociologists have pioneered Black feminist scholar-activism. Transnational feminists also are known for their activism, engaging states in international politics by reframing domestic issues in the context of international, transnational, or global issues (Tarrow 2005, 2–3). Keck and Sikkink (1998) have written about transnational advocacy networks:

> Transnational advocacy networks are proliferating, and their goal is to change behavior of states and international organizations. Simultaneously principled and strategic actors, they "frame" issues to make them comprehensible to target audiences, to attract attention and encourage action, and to "fit" with favorable institutional venues. (2–3)

BLM has engaged in the sort of activism that is typical of transnational feminists by reframing domestic violence issues in terms of international human rights.

> In framing racial discrimination in human rights terms, the Black Lives Matter movement is today picking up the baton of civil rights activists before them. The parents of Trayvon Martin and Jordan Davis have raised the issue of discriminatory policing with members of the UN Committee on the Elimination of All Forms of Racial Discrimination in Geneva. The parents of Mike Brown along with representatives of organizations in Ferguson and Chicago traveled to Geneva to share information about their cases with the UN Committee Against Torture in November 2014. (Harris 2015, 39)

The three women who launched the original Black Lives Matter hashtag in 2012—Alicia Garza, Opal Tometi, and Patrisse Cullors—are all professional organizers (Ransby 2015, 31). While they may or may not consider themselves feminist scholars, there is an important link between the reframing done by transnational feminist scholar-activists and the reframing being done in the context of BLM. It is important that scholars especially give theoretical and scholarly credit to this work, rooted in feminist concepts and advocating for Black freedom. Naming the scholarly significance of such political work is one way that scholars show their solidarity with this grassroots movement.

SOLIDARITY BUILDING

In distinguishing between solidarity and support, bell hooks has written:

> Solidarity is not the same as support. To experience solidarity, we must have a community of interests, shared beliefs and goals around which to unite, to build Sisterhood. Support can be occasional. It can be given and just as easily withdrawn. Solidarity requires sustained, ongoing commitment. (hooks 1984, 64)

Furthermore, "solidarity comes with an understanding of oppression and a commitment to act upon it with others and, when required, for others" (Matte 2010, ix). Such an understanding of oppression is facilitated by being positioned at the margins of society:

This sense of wholeness, impressed upon our consciousness by the structure of our daily lives, provided us an oppositional world view—a mode of seeing unknown to most of our oppressors, that sustained us, aided us in our struggle to transcend poverty and despair, strengthened our sense of self and our solidarity. (hooks 1984, ix)

It is important to recognize that solidarity does not presume sameness. Rather, it is in the context of bonds across diverse communities that Chandra Talpade Mohanty (2003) defined specific characteristics of solidarity.

I define solidarity in terms of mutuality, accountability, and the recognition of common interests as the basis for relationships among diverse communities. Rather than assuming an enforced commonality of oppression, the practice of solidarity foregrounds communities of people who have chosen to work and fight together. Diversity and difference are central values here—to be acknowledged and respected, not erased in the building of alliances. (7)

Toronto-based BLM activist Janaya Khan (2015) described the diverse nature of people uniting in solidarity as follows: "Black Lives Matter has become a transformative outlet for all black people from different historical, cultural, socioeconomic and political identities. It is a source of solidarity for the survivors of colonization, exploitation, capitalism and police brutality." In this way, BLM is bringing together different people in a solidarity that strengthens the movement. "Solidarity strengthens resistance struggle," hooks (1984) wrote. "There can be no mass-based feminist movement to end sexist oppression without a united front—women must take the initiative and demonstrate the power of solidarity" (44). Certainly, BLM seems to be approximating such a feminist mass movement:

Black Lives Matter is feminist in its interrogation of state power and its critique of structural inequality. It is also forcing a conversation about gender and racial politics that we need to have—women at the forefront of this movement are articulating that "black lives" does not only mean men's lives or cisgender lives or respectable lives or the lives that are legitimated by state power or privilege. (Asoka 2015, 57)

BLM is a radically inclusive feminist movement, challenging the idea that resistance and freedom struggle should be rooted in only one issue area. It is challenging boundaries and crossing borders.

ATTENTION TO BORDERS/BOUNDARIES

Too often, the legitimacy of state borders goes unquestioned by U.S. citizens. Gloria Anzaldúa, however, encouraged us to critically examine the borderlands that exist "wherever two or more cultures edge each other, where people of different races occupy the same territory, where under, lower, middle and upper classes touch, where the space between two individuals shrinks with intimacy" (Anzaldúa 1987, preface). Borders can be used to define spaces, as well as people:

Borders are set up to define the places that are safe and unsafe, to distinguish us from them. A border is a dividing line, a narrow strip along a steep edge. A borderland is a vague and undetermined place created by the emotional residue of an unnatural boundary. It is in a constant state of transition. The prohibited and forbidden are its residents. (Anzaldúa 1987, 3)

The United States is a state of many nations and nationalities, with borderlands throughout. The legacy of Jim Crow policies and forced racial segregation ensures that in many major cities, cultures continue to edge each other at the boundaries between neighborhoods, or across railroad tracks.

The Black freedom struggle is inextricably linked to the struggle of diverse groups within this country, as well as the struggle of marginalized people in other countries. Angela Y. Davis has long highlighted such connections:

The connections between the criminalization of young black people and the criminalization of immigrants are not random. In order to understand the structural connections that tie these two forms of criminalization together, we will have to consider the ways in which global capitalism has transformed the world. What we are witnessing at the close of the twentieth century is the growing power of a circuit of transnational corporations that belong to no particular nation-state, and that move across borders at will in perpetual search of maximizing profits. (Davis 2012, 44)

Our movements must keep pace with the corporations that direct our labor and the state forces that police our bodies. BLM is actively addressing such complexity: "What the Black Lives Matter protests have done, however, is not only put police reform on the policy agenda but demanded that American society reconsider how it values black lives" (Harris 2015, 34). BLM embodies a holistic approach to political engagement that challenges both boundaries that seek to contain issue areas of political engagement and borders that seek to contain the freedom movement geographically.

> As #BlackLivesMatter gained momentum, social media campaigns like #Palestine2Ferguson connected the violent erasure of Palestinian lives in Gaza to the mistreatment of black people in Ferguson and the U.S. at large. The mutual experiences of struggle and marginalization between African Americans and Palestinians created a real base of international solidarity, with Palestinians using Twitter to provide tips to Ferguson protesters on methods of neutralizing tear gas. (Khan 2015)

In spite of this global reach, BLM continues to be rooted in place-based transnationalisms that are "particularly relevant to movement-building transnational feminisms, and the particular political challenges of negotiating place-based difference in constructing transnational feminist and emancipatory geopolitics" (Conway 2008, 225).

Thus, the transnational movement continues to be rooted in local politics, even as "protests have emerged not just in Ferguson but in Washington, D.C., Oakland, Chicago, Bloomington, Minnesota, Los Angeles, New York, and internationally in London, Paris, and even Tokyo" (Pierre-Louis 2015). Local, bottom-up, and decentralized leadership ensures sensitivity to how transnational bonds are formed, so that power remains at the community base. Thus, there is the understanding that:

> Different modalities of transborder activism not only can have differential impacts on promoting desired policy changes, but also can have distinct political consequences for activist discourses and practices and for intramovement power relations on the home front. (Alvarez 2000, 32)

With control maintained at the popular base, these shifts in discourse and practice are more easily monitored.

REFERENCES

Altman, Alex. 2015. "Black Lives Matter: A New Civil Rights Movement Is Turning a Protest Cry into a Political Force." *TIME*, December 21, 116–125.

Alvarez, Sonia E. 2000. "Translating the Global Effects of Transnational Organizing on Local Feminist Discourses and Practices in Latin America." *Meridians: Feminism, Race Transnationalism* 1, no. 1: 29–67.

Anzaldúa, Gloria. 1987. *Borderlands/La Frontera: The New Mestiza*. San Francisco: Aunt Lute Books.

Asoka, Kaavya. 2015. "Women and Black Lives Matter: An Interview with Marcia Chatelain." *Dissent* (Summer): 54–61. https://www.dissentmagazine.org/article/women-black-lives-matter-interview-marcia-chatelain.

Cole, Johnetta B. 1993. *Conversations: Straight Talk with America's Sister President*. New York: Doubleday.

Collins, Patricia Hill. 2008. *Black Feminist Thought: Knowledge, Consciousness, and the Politics of Empowerment*. New York: Routledge.

Conway, Janet. 2008. "Geographies of Transnational Feminisms: The Politics of Place and Scale in the World March of Women." *Social Politics: International Studies in Gender, State and Society* 15, no. 2: 207–231.

Cooper, Brittney. 2015. "The Women of #Black Lives Matter." *Ms.*, Winter, 30–31.

Crenshaw, Kimberlé Williams. 1998. "Demarginalizing the Intersection of Race and Sex: A Black Feminist Critique of Antidiscrimination Doctrine, Feminist Theory, and Antiracist Politics." In *Feminism and Politics*, edited by Anne Phillips, 314–343. Oxford: Oxford University Press.

Davis, Angela Y. 2012. *The Meaning of Freedom: And Other Difficult Dialogues*. San Francisco: City Lights Books.

Guynn, Jessica. 2015. "3 Women, 3 Words, a New Movement." *USA Today*, March 5, 03B.

Harris, Fredrick C. 2015. "The Next Civil Rights Movement?" *Dissent* (Summer): 34–39. https://www.dissentmagazine.org/article/black-lives-matter-new-civil-rights-movement-fredrick-harris.

hooks, bell. 1984. *Feminist Theory: From Margin to Center*. Boston: South End Press.

———. 1990. *Yearning: Race, Gender, and Cultural Politics*. Boston: South End Press.

———. 1994. *Teaching to Transgress: Education as the Practice of Freedom*. New York: Routledge.

Hutchinson, Sikivu. 2015. "Do All Black Lives Matter? Feminism, Humanism & State Violence." *Humanist*, June 23. http://thehumanist.com/magazine/july-august-2015/features/do-all-black-lives-matter-feminism-humanism-and-state-violence.

Keck, Margaret E., and Kathryn Sikkink. 1998. *Activists Beyond Borders: Advocacy Networks in International Politics*. Ithaca, NY: Cornell University Press.

Khan, Janaya. 2015. "Black Lives Matter Has Become a Global Movement." *The Root*, August 7. http://www.theroot.com/articles/culture/2015/08/black_lives_matter_has_become_a_global_movement.html.

Lindsey, Treva B. 2015. "A 'Herstorical' Approach to Black Violability." *Feminist Studies* 41, no. 1: 232–237.

Matte, Diane. 2010. "Preface." In *Solidarities Beyond Borders: Transnationalizing Women's Movements*, edited by Pascale Dufour, Dominique Masson, and Dominique Caouette, vii–ix. Vancouver: UBC Press.

McClaurin, Irma. 2001a. "Introduction: Forging a Theory, Politics, Praxis, and Poetics of Black Feminist Anthropology." In *Black Feminist Anthropology: Theory, Politics, Praxis and Poetics*, edited by Irma McClaurin, 1–23. New Brunswick, NJ: Rutgers University Press.

———. 2001b. "Theorizing a Black Feminist Self in Anthropology: Toward an Autoethnographic Approach." In *Black Feminist Anthropology: Theory, Politics, Praxis and Poetics*, edited by Irma McClaurin, 49–76. New Brunswick, NJ: Rutgers University Press.

Mohanty, Chandra Talpade. 2003. *Feminism without Borders: Decolonizing Theory, Practicing Solidarity*. Durham, NC: Duke University Press.

Pierre-Louis, Kendra. 2015. "The Women behind Black Lives Matter." *In These Times*, January 22. http://inthesetimes.com/article/17551/the_women_behind_blacklivesmatter.

Ransby, Barbara. 2015. "The Class Politics of Black Lives Matter." *Dissent* (Fall): 31–34. https://www.dissentmagazine.org/article/class-politics-black-lives-matter.

Tarrow, Sidney. 2005. *The New Transnational Activism*. New York: Cambridge University Press.

6. IN DEFENSE OF LATINX
CHRISTINE GARCIA (2017)

"Latinx" is an intersectional identity term meant to be used by gender fluid and gender nonconforming people, LGBTQIA persons, cisgender men and women, and those taking a political stance that ethnicity and gender exist on a spectrum and are not dichotomous. The term was conceived around 2004 and popularized on social media outlets, experienced a waning in usage for a few years, and has since reemerged, most noticeably around 2014, on forums helmed by and dedicated to AfroLatinx and indigenous-centered Spanish speaking people (Gamio). The conceptualization of the "x" is rooted in the decolonization of the terms Latina/Latino on two levels: first, confronting and challenging the gender binary, and second, rejecting the silencing and erasure of AfroLatinx and indigenous languages by standard Spanish, the language of the colonizer of much of Latin America and the Southwestern United States. The term "Latinx" has since entered mainstream use, and, as an emergent term, it continues to be defined and contested.

The introduction of the "x" in lieu of the gendered endings was more of a gradual shift rather than a sudden debut. The evolution of the term began with the common gendered endings of "a" or "o" (Latina/feminine and Latino/masculine), which moved into a collapsing of the two onto the end of the word signifying inclusion of both genders (Latina/o) with one gendered ending placed first based on author discretion. Next was the short lived "Latin@," economical because it integrated both gendered endings into one symbol, but nonfunctional online due to the use of "@" for tagging purposes on social media. "Latine" has occasionally been proposed as an easy to pronounce gender neutral term such as "presidente," yet this erasure is counter to the semantic goal of acknowledgment and inclusion that the "x" represents.

It is within the argument of connotation that much of the battle over the "x" is located. The traditional use of the gender assumptive "a" or "o" was used innocuously for much of recent history with the gendered assignment all but accepted as unproblematic. Trouble arose as Latinas and Latinx of Afro and indigenous roots challenged the default to the masculine in mixed gender situations as well as the either/or identification based on Euro-Hispanic roots of the terms. Around two decades ago, woke users of the Spanish language in the United States began the collapsing of the endings in a move that signaled both inclusiveness and efficiency. Feminine and masculine were combined into one word, typically written with a slash separating gendered endings (i.e., Latina/o), which challenged the default to the masculine yet did not account for the myopic dichotomy of genders. The most raucous debates regarding the collapsed "a/o" gendered endings that occurred—prior to the shift to "x"—was whether the "a" or the "o" should appear first in the word. These debates over which gender ending would appear first were rhetorical in nature and situated in the connotative questions of preference and power. These challenges and changes to the gendered endings of "Latinx" reflect the evolution of U.S. Spanish speakers' initial acceptance of the masculine as default and eventual resistance against essentialization and erasure. The "x" adaptation contains within it the movement towards intersectionality and the acknowledgement that ethnicity and gender are interlocked identity constructs, which is a direct linguistic manifestation of what is happening socioculturally in our academic institutions and in our communities and families.

The move away from the usage of "a/o" to "x" marks an amelioration of "Latina/o" and its variants through the dismissal of the gender binary in a move that marks gender and ethnicity inclusion. Not all Latinx identify with Euro-Hispanic roots and not all Latinx identify as either female or male, and the "x" accounts for these important identity markers. This semantic shift is indicative of a larger sociocultural shift, one in which Spanish language users in the United States, many, but not all of whom are multilingual, are becoming more sensitive to the denotative power of words; specifically, users recognize that concretizing words with gender markers often creates false implications and incorrect representations of referents. While imperfect and not applicable to all Spanish-speaking peoples, the evolution of the term "Latina/o" into "Latinx" is the most functional contemporary label for many of us. The imperfectness of the term, especially this hotly debated shift to "x," is but one step in the continual decolonization of the Spanish language. Whether Latinx is a temporary buzzword, as some detractors claim, or the springboard for further acts of linguistic decolonization, the term is proof positive that language is alive, evolving, and is a tool and a reflection of our humanness. And, for those still struggling to find the right articulation of the term, it is pronounced / la"ti:nɛks/ or "Lah-teen-ecks."

WORKS CITED

Gamio, Arlene. *Latinx: A Brief Guidebook*. Princeton LGBTQ Center. 2016. Accessed 02 July 2017. https://www.academia.edu/29657615/Latinx_A_Brief_Guidebook.

7. MY HEROINES

MARGE PIERCY (2010)

When I think of women heroes,
it's not Joan of Arc or Molly Pitcher
but mothers who quietly say
to their daughters, *you can*.
Who stand behind attempts
to open doors long bolted shut
to teams or clubs or professions.

I think of women who dress
'respectably' and march and march
and march again, for the ability
to choose, for peace, for rights
their own or others. Who form
phone banks, who stuff envelopes
who do the invisible political work.

They do not get their faces on
magazine covers. They don't get fan
mail or receive awards. But without
them, no woman or liberal man

would ever be elected, no law
would be passed or changed. We
would be stuck in sexist mud.

It's the receptionist in the clinic,
the escorts to frightened women,
the volunteers at no kill shelters,
women sorting bottles at the dump,
women holding signs in the rain,
women who take calls of the abused,
of rape victims, night after night.

It's the woman at her computer
or desk when the family's asleep
writing letters, organizing friends.
Big change turns on small pushes.
Heroes and heroines climb into
history books, but it's such women
who actually write our future.

CHAPTER 2

SYSTEMS OF PRIVILEGE AND INEQUALITY

"Women" are as different as we/they are alike. Although sharing some conditions, including having primary responsibility for children and being victims of male violence, individual lives are always marked by difference. This is a result of the varying conditions and material practices of women's existence in global communities and the societies in which these communities are embedded. We inhabit different cultures whose norms or cultural expectations prescribe different ways of acting as women and men and impose different sanctions if these norms are broken. It is therefore important to recognize difference and, as already discussed in Chapter 1, avoid using "woman" as a universal or homogeneous category that assumes sameness. Many of the readings in this chapter are essays illustrating how power in society works, how differences are ranked or valued differently, and how privilege and discrimination operate. Although several may seem "dated" because they were written during the critique of second-wave feminism in the 1980s, they are used intentionally here as examples of classic scholarship in WGS. They make suggestions for change in both personal and social lives. They emphasize that what it means to identify as a "woman" is a complex interaction of multiple identities.

In the United States our differences are illustrated by the material conditions of our lives; the values, cultures, behavioral practices, and legal structures of the communities in which we live; and even the geographic region of the country we inhabit. In particular, we inhabit different identities in terms of race and ethnicity, religion, age, looks, sexual identity, socioeconomic status, and ability. For people in the United States these identities are also situated within a global context that positions the United States within the world order. In particular, this means understanding colonialism and imperialism: the practices that subordinate one society to another and exercise power through military domination, economic policies, and/or the imposition of certain forms of knowledge. As discussed in Chapter 1, just as it is important to question the homogenizing notions of sameness in terms of the category "woman" across societies, it is also important to understand that these universalizing tendencies work against our understanding of women in the United

States as well. Often we tend to think of women in comparison to a mythical norm: a white, middle-class, cisgender, heterosexual, abled, thin, young adult, which is normalized or taken for granted such that we often forget that whites are racialized and men are gendered. Asking the question "Different from what?" reveals how difference gets constructed against what people think of as "normal." "Normality" tends to reflect the identities of those in power. This is especially apparent in the issue of disability: It is impossible for someone to be "disabled" or "impaired" without reference to a constructed idea of "normal." As many disability scholars emphasize, any notion of "normal" is an artifact or by-product produced by the discipline that measures it. In other words, this normality is created and has no physical reality apart from the practice that constructs the idea of normality in the first place. Poet Jim Ferris explores meanings of disability in the reading "Poems with Disabilities." In the reading "Disability and Social Justice," Teodor Mladenov also argues that attentiveness to disabilities in social transformation will benefit not only people with disabilities, but all marginalized people.

In this way, it is important to recognize that the meanings associated with differences are socially constructed. These social constructions would not be problematic were they

"I have two mommies. I know where the apostrophe goes."

not created against the notion of the mythical norm. Being a lesbian or identifying as "queer" would not be a "difference" that invoked cultural resistance if it were not for compulsory heterosexuality, the notion that everyone should be heterosexual and have relationships with the opposite sex. Implicit here, of course, is also the idea that sexuality must be categorized into the binaries of heterosexuality and homosexuality in the first place.

In this chapter we focus on differences among women and explore the ways systems of privilege and inequality are created out of these differences. Such systems, however, are shaped by broader forces of imperialism at home and abroad. As already mentioned, imperialism refers to the economic, political, and cultural domination over nations or communities. Early forms of imperialism (such as the U.S. conquest of Hawaii) subjugated indigenous populations and extracted resources. Contemporary imperialism continues to do this, but also destroys indigenous forms of production by usurping and privatizing land and forcing economies into market or capitalist production. Often this involves military occupation or the strategic military use of colonized land. Also included is cultural imperialism, the destruction of indigenous languages, and the imposition of certain forms of knowledge: a particularly insidious problem with the rapid growth of digital and other technologies. In this way, although imperialism often involves colonialism (the building and maintenance of colonies in one region by people from another region), it must be understood in terms of broader economic, military, and cultural practices of domination. These forces of imperialism provide the global context for our discussion of systems of inequality and privilege in the United States. It is also important to consider the privileges afforded citizens of the global north as a result of this global structuring. Privileges include the availability of cheap goods produced elsewhere (often under problematic conditions) and the ability to remain "innocent" of the consequences of U.S. economic and military policies abroad.

In addition, however, we must consider the notion of internal colonialism (sometimes called settler colonialism) that has colonized indigenous people in North America. Colonizing processes include the following: imposition of the dominant group's culture and language, denial of citizenship rights, relegation to subordinate labor markets, and entrance into a host country by force. We can recognize the history of U.S. racism in this brief discussion of internal colonialism. Examples include the importation of black slaves forced to leave their African homelands, the removal from indigenous lands of native people who are forced into reservations, and the construction of "illegal" to describe immigrants and migrants who lost their land in Mexico through military conquest and yet are needed by the economic system to participate in menial and often dangerous work.

DIFFERENCE, HIERARCHY, AND SYSTEMS OF PRIVILEGE AND INEQUALITY

Simply put, society recognizes people's differences and assigns group membership accordingly; at the same time, society also ranks the differences and institutionalizes them into the fabric of society. "Institutionalized" means officially placed into a structured system or set of practices. In other words, "institutionalized" means to make something part of a structured and well-established system. For example, there may be feelings and attitudes that women do not belong in certain disciplines or positions in higher education, but these beliefs and practices that disparage women become institutionalized when standardized tests (such as SATs, GREs, and intelligence tests) contain language and gendered content that is less accessible for girls and more familiar to boys, thus facilitating lower scores for girls and women that provide the "evidence" or justification for these beliefs. This would be an example of institutionalized sexism. The concept of institutionalization in this context also implies that meanings associated with difference exist beyond the intentions of individual people. This distinction between the "micro" (focusing on the level of individuals) and "macro" (focusing on the large-scale, societal level) is important. Your experience of reading this chapter as a class assignment, for example, centers on the individual micro level, but it is embedded in, and part of, a more macro, systematically organized set of practices associated with education as an institution. Whether you actually read or study this on the micro level is independent of the fact that education as an institution functions in certain ways. In other words, studying course readings is institutionalized into education (whether you actually study your readings or not).

Even though differences associated with various identities intersect, they are also ranked. Masculine is placed above feminine, thin above fat, cisgender above transgender, economically privileged above poor, and so forth. These rankings of groups and their members create a hierarchy in which some ways of being, like being able-bodied or heterosexual, are valued more than others, like having a disability or being gay or lesbian. Some have advantages in accessing resources, whereas others are disadvantaged by unequal access to economic opportunities; some are unable to exercise the rights of citizenship, and others have clearer access to rights to life and happiness. For example, U.S. rights of citizenship should include equal participation in the political process to ensure that laws reflect the will of the people with the knowledge that the government exists to serve the people, and to serve all equally. Although civil rights legislation removed many of the barriers set up to prevent nonwhites from voting, intimidation (such as discarding votes for various reasons and requiring different ID for certain voters) and gerrymandering (drawing voting district lines in a way that neutralizes the power of nonwhite voters) still occur.

LEARNING ACTIVITY

UNPACK YOUR KNAPSACK

In her famous essays on white and male privilege, professor Peggy McIntosh lists a number of ways she experiences privilege as a white person. For example, in her 46 instances of white privilege, Macintosh notes, "I am never asked to speak for all the people of my racial group"; "I can talk with my mouth full and not have people put this down to my color"; "If a traffic cop pulls me over or if the IRS audits my tax return, I can be sure I haven't been singled out because of my race"; and "I can do well in a challenging situation without being called a credit to my race." In the reading "Cisgender Privilege," Evin Taylor lists the ways privilege is experienced by those whose gender

assignment and gender identity pretty well align. Choose from the following various nontarget statuses and make lists of the ways you experience the following categories of privilege:

White
Middle or upper class
Male
Young
Heterosexual
Able-bodied
Cisgender
Native born in the United States
Christian
Thin

LEARNING ACTIVITY
TEST FOR HIDDEN BIAS

The Implicit Association Test, developed by researchers at Harvard University, tests for unconscious bias. Even though most of us believe we view everyone equally, we still may hold stereotypes and biases of which we are unaware. These tests can determine if perhaps you hold hidden biases concerning race, sexual identity, age, gender, or body image. To take one or more of these tests, go to Project Implicit's website at www.implicit .harvard.edu/implicit. After you finish the tests, take a few minutes to jot down a few things you learned about yourself. Were there any surprises? Do you hold hidden biases? How do you feel about your test results? Now that you know about your hidden biases, what can you do?

LEARNING ACTIVITY
FIVE FACES OF OPPRESSION

Iris Young identifies the following characteristics of systems of oppression. Think about a group of people—American Indian women or queer Chicanas or trans women, for example. How might these categories apply to them? Why, according to Young's categories, would young, heterosexual white men not qualify as an oppressed group?

1. EXPLOITATION
   - A steady process of the transfer of the results of the labor of one social group to benefit another.
   - Social relations produced and reproduced through a systematic process in which the energies of the subordinate group are continuously expended to maintain and augment the power, status, and wealth of the dominant group.

2. MARGINALIZATION
   - The expulsion of entire groups of people from useful participation in social life that potentially subjects them to severe material deprivation and possible extermination.
   - Even those with material resources experience feeling useless, bored, and lacking in self-respect.

3. POWERLESSNESS
   - The powerless lack authority; they are those over whom power is exercised without their exercising it; they are situated so that they must take orders and rarely have the right to give them.
   - The powerless have little or no work autonomy, exercise little creativity or judgment in their work, and do not command respect.
   - A lack of "respectability"—respect is not automatically given.

4. CULTURAL IMPERIALISM
   - The universalization of a dominant group's experience and culture—its establishment as the norm.
   - These norms render the experiences and cultures of subordinate groups invisible and create stereotypes about these groups, marking them as Others.

5. VIOLENCE
   - Members of subordinate groups live with the threat of violence based on their status as group members.
   - To a great extent, this violence is legitimated because it is tolerated.

Source: Iris Young, "Five Faces of Oppression," in *Readings for Diversity and Social Justice* (2nd ed.), ed. Maurianne Adams et al. (New York: Routledge, 2010), pp. 35–45.

The hierarchical ranking of difference is constructed through social processes such that patterns of difference become systems of privilege and inequality. Inequality for some and privilege for others is the consequence of these processes. Privilege can be defined as advantages people have by virtue of their status or position in society. This can be distinguished from earned privilege that results, for example, from earning a degree or fulfilling responsibilities. In her oft-referenced essay "White Privilege and Male Privilege," Peggy McIntosh writes that white privilege is the "invisible package of unearned assets" that white people can count on cashing in every day. And, as McIntosh explains, it is easier to grant that others are disadvantaged than to admit being privileged. Men might be supportive of women's rights but balk at the suggestion that their personal behavior is in need of modification. Whites might be horrified by stories of racial injustice but still not realize that taken-for-granted white privilege is part of the problem. This is similar to the discussion in Chapter 1 where being supportive of women's rights does not necessarily translate into an understanding of how the entitlements of masculine privilege work. Gina Crosley-Corcoran's reading "Explaining White Privilege to a Broke White Person" notes the ways intersections shape white privilege and points out that some of McIntosh's assumptions are rooted in class privileges that not all white people share.

Systems of oppression can be understood as systems that discriminate and privilege based on perceived or real differences among people. Systems that facilitate privilege and inequality, subordination and domination, include sexism based upon gender: something you will be reading a lot about in this book. However, although sexism is understood and lived as discrimination against women, it is also important to understand that gender conformity itself entails privilege. What this means is that people who are recognized as fitting into the gender binary of "female" and "male" receive collective advantages. Cisgender people are those whose gender identity or expression matches their assigned gender by societal standards. Those who change or cross these gender binaries are transgender individuals who do not enjoy the privileges that cisgender individuals do. This is the topic of Evin Taylor's short piece titled "Cisgender Privilege," an essay originally published in the anthology *Gender Outlaws* by Kate Bornstein and S. Bear Bergman. The essay invokes Peggy McIntosh's invisible knapsack to explore the question of cisgender privilege. The author encourages readers to adapt the questionnaire to suit their own gender positioning and to come up with questions that can be added to the list.

Systems of inequality and privilege also include racism based upon racial/ethnic group membership (African American, Asian American, Latinx, Native American—note this also includes anti-Semitism, or discrimination against Jews, as well as discrimination against Muslims and Arab Americans); classism associated with socioeconomic status; ageism relating to age; looksism and sizeism, concerning looks and body size; and ableism, about physical and mental ability. Also included is heterosexism, which concerns sexual identity or orientation. As already mentioned, systems function by discriminating and privileging based on perceived or real differences among people. Given this, sexism discriminates and privileges on the basis of gender, resulting in gender stratification; racism discriminates and privileges on the basis of racial and ethnic differences; and so forth for classism, heterosexism, ageism, looksism, and ableism. Homophobia, the fear and dislike of those who do not identify as heterosexual or "straight," functions to support heterosexism as well as sexism. The latter occurs, for example, through misogyny directed at gay men and as a threat to encourage women to give up the love of other women to gain male approval. It is important to understand that homophobia is an example of prejudice, and, although it plays a part in the maintenance of heterosexism, it is not equivalent to it as a structured system of power. A similarly functioning concept is transphobia, the fear and dislike of transgender individuals.

As introduced in the discussion of intersectionality in Chapter 1, all people are in multiple places vis-à-vis these systems. A person might not have access to race and gender privilege because she is African American and a woman; she might have access to heterosexual privilege because she is straight, cisgender privilege because her gender identity matches her gender assignment, and class privilege because she lives in a family that is financially secure. All of these privileged and disadvantaged identities then intersect and shape one another within systems of power to create a unique social position and experiences for our hypothetical person. This is the intersection or confluence, the flowing together of various identities within binary and hierarchical structures of power. As Patricia Hill Collins explains in "Toward a New Vision," it is not as useful to think of these various identities as being stacked or arranged in a cumulative manner. Lives are not experienced as "Here I'm a woman, here I'm able-bodied, here I'm poor," as if all of our various statuses are all stacked up; we experience ourselves as ordinary people who struggle daily with the inequities in our lives and who usually take the privileges for granted. Various identities concerning these systems of equality and privilege are usually thoroughly blended and potentially shifting depending on subjective orientation and cultural context. This means that cultural forces of race and class, and others such as age and ability, all shape gender expression. It is important to emphasize that people experience race, class, gender, and sexual identities differently depending on their social location in various structures of inequality and privilege. This means that people of the same race or same age, for example, will experience race or age differently depending on their location in gendered structures (whether they are women or men) or class structures (such as working class, professional class, or unemployed), as well as structures associated with sexual identity (whether they identify as heterosexual, bisexual, lesbian, gay, or queer), and so on. This is also Audre Lorde's point in the reading "There Is No Hierarchy of Oppression." She writes about these intersections and advocates solidarity among multiple intersecting identities.

"Intersectionality" is the topic and title of the essay by Vivian M. May. She describes the approach as incorporating an intersecting matrix that allows an understanding of simultaneous privilege and oppression. Among her vision of future possibilities for this approach is a focus on lived experience and a shift toward this more complex subjectivity as central to both theory construction and liberatory strategies.

LEARNING ACTIVITY

QUEER DISRUPTIONS

"Queer" is one of those tricky words that has a particular historical meaning (its denotation) and specific cultural meanings (its connotations) that can be either positive or negative. Originally, "queer" just meant "odd," but in the early twentieth century it was applied to gays in a derogatory way. In the 1980s people who in many ways were part of nonheteronormative categories began to reclaim the word to mean "sexually dissident" and to reflect a growing activism that challenged fixed sexual categories and heteronormativity. In academic circles, queer theory became a method of analysis that disrupted fixed meanings and exposed underlying contradictions and structures of power, particularly as they pertained to the regulation of sexual behavior and the oppression of people who do not conform to societal expectations around sexuality. Beyond the goals of acceptance and equal treatment pursued by gay and lesbian rights activists, queer theory seeks to destabilize cultural ideas and norms that are used to oppress nonconforming people.

(continued)

Let's look at an example: queer theology. Queer theology seeks to deconstruct and disrupt normative theologies, especially heteronormative theologies. It is a transgressive theology. So a simple question queer theology asks of sacred texts is about the reader's assumption that the characters in the text are heterosexual. Queer theology also questions cultural norms about sexuality and sexual identity drawing on characters from the biblical texts. This opens up space to understand, for example, the relationship of David and Jonathan from the Hebrew Bible or Jesus and the apostle John from the Christian testament in ways that do not force contemporary understandings of sexuality on the text. How might we understand these as queer relationships, as relationships that contest heteronormative standards? This is not to say that we are arguing that these characters had sex with one another. Rather, we are asking how these relationships reflect a larger continuum of intimate behaviors than traditional masculinity (in these cases) might allow. Queer theology asks how we might understand divinity from queer perspectives or how we might use "coming out" as a metaphor in Christianity to understand Jesus as the incarnation of God's love or how we might through the character of the Virgin Mary understand the sexual oppression/denial of women in the contemporary world.

Queering Your Discipline

Identify an important text (a book, a story, a movie, a song, a painting) in your own discipline. Think about how you might do a queer reading of this text:

- How might you challenge the heteronormative assumptions of the text?
- What are the underlying norms of power and domination in the text?
- How does the text (and its typical reading) regulate sexual behavior?
- How might the text be read to disrupt essential notions of gender and sexuality?

CHALLENGING YOUR ASSUMPTIONS

Read the following sentences and identify the assumptions inherent in each regarding age, ability, appearance, ethnicity, gender, race, religion, sexual identity, and socioeconomic power or status.

Identify the "norm" (a standard of conduct that should or must be followed; a typical or usual way of being or behaving, usually said of a certain group) and discuss how the assumptions reflect this norm.

Discuss how these assumptions operate in your cultural situation. How are you affected by cultural assumptions about the "norm"?

Our founding fathers carved this great state out of the wilderness.

Mrs. Imoto looks remarkably good for her age.

Fashion tights are available in black, suntan, and flesh color.

Someday I intend to visit the third world.

We need more manpower.

Our facilities all provide handicapped access.

A real man would never act that way.

The network is down again. We'd better get Kevin in here to do his voodoo on it.

Our boys were having a rough time of it, and the black regiment was too.

How Neanderthal man existed for so long is a mystery. He must have had the ability to adapt to his environment.

I see she forgot to sign her time sheet. She's acting a little blonde today.

Mitochondrial DNA testing should help us determine when our race split off from the lower creatures.

Confined to a wheelchair, Mr. Garcia still manages to live a productive life.

Pat really went on the warpath when the budget figures came out.

I won't be associated with you and your pagan behaviors!

The Academy now admits women and other minorities.

We have a beautiful daycare center where women can leave their children while they work.

See if you can Jew him down to $50.

Personally, I don't think it's right that the foreign students come in here before term and buy up all the insignia bags. Our kids don't get a chance at them.

I completely forgot where I put my car keys. I must be having a senior moment.

Win a fabulous lovers' weekend in Hawaii! Prizes include a day at the spa for her and a relaxing game of golf for him.

That is not a very Christian attitude.

We welcome all guests, their wives, and their children.

May I speak to Mr. or Mrs. Williams?

Source: Janet Lockhart and Susan Shaw, *Writing for Change: Raising Awareness of Issues of Difference, Power, and Discrimination*, www.teachingtolerance.org.

Systems of inequality interconnect and work together to enforce inequality and privilege, each mostly supporting the other. The intersections of racism and classism, for example, are demonstrated by the fact that according to 2017 U.S. Census data, almost 20 percent of Latinx, 23 percent of African Americans, and 25 percent of Native Americans compared to 9 percent of white Americans are living in poverty. Social class always intersects with other identities but is particularly intertwined with race. While about half of all poor people are white, wealthy people are disproportionately white. The reading "What Determines How Americans Perceive Their Social Class?" by Robert Bird and Frank Newport explores how Americans' perceptions of their own social class often reflect notions of the American myth of a society with few class distinctions, despite growing gaps of inequality. Similarly, although ageism or age discrimination is very much connected to classism, it is also intertwined with sexism as well as with looksism. Women learn to "age pass"; that is, we do not want to be mistaken for 40 when we are in our 30s, or mistaken for 70 when only 60. This is part of the pursuit of youth and beauty that encourages women to participate as agents of ageism as we fulfill the expectations of gender. Ellie Mamber rejects such ideas in the poem "Don't Laugh, It's Serious, She Says." She refers to the "double standard of aging" whereby society interprets women's aging differently than men's (remembering too that "women" and "men" imply intersections of various identities with age and other identities and not just gender). Mamber observes the cultural acceptance of men being able to romantically pursue much younger women but refuses to let this affect her sense of self.

IDEAS FOR ACTIVISM

- Find out how your university ensures access for people with disabilities. If some structures on your campus are inaccessible, advocate with your administration to create accessibility.
- Plan a celebration of black women during Black History Month.
- Find out what programs your university offers to recruit and retain students and faculty of color. If programs are not in place, advocate with your administration to develop such programs.
- Find out if your university's antidiscrimination policy includes sexual and gender identities as protected

classifications, and find out if your university provides benefits for domestic partners. If not, advocate with your administration to include sexual and gender identities in its policy and/or to provide domestic partner benefits.
- Research your university's policy for student names. Does your university use names from only legal documents such as a birth certificate? Or does your school use students' chosen names? Advocate for policies and processes that allow students to indicate and use chosen names in employment, transportation, and other spaces such as public accommodations.

Awareness of intersecting inequalities and advocacy for social justice was inspired by civil rights, feminist, and other social movements of the late twentieth century. In particular, intersectionality theory was shaped by the theoretical writings of women of color who, as described in Chapter 1, decried the lack of inclusivity and racism of the white women's movement. Intersectionality was applied to disability studies, for example, as a result of the work of the disability rights movement that worked to ensure the passage of the Americans with Disabilities Act in 1990, which protected people with disabilities from discrimination in employment, transportation, and public accommodations. Like other intersectionality theorists, disability scholars like Rosemarie Garland-Thompson emphasize that integrating understandings of ableism is not an additive endeavor but a "conceptual shift that strengthens our understanding of how these multiple oppressions intertwine, redefine, and mutually constitute each other." In the reading "Disability and Social Justice," Teodor Mladenov argues that societies are only just when people have a say in policies that affect them and when societies provide equitable support for all people, including people with disabilities.

DISCOURSE, POWER, AND KNOWLEDGE

A focus on difference, hierarchy, and systems of inequality and privilege implies the study of power. In this chapter we have presented this discussion of power as something individuals or groups have—or do not have. It is important, however, to recognize that power does not necessarily operate in a binary or top-down fashion. Rather, power can be dispersed and multidimensional, and can function in all aspects of our everyday lives. Postmodern scholar Riki Wilchins calls this "small power exercised in hundreds of everyday transactions."[1] And, instead of imagining power as something individuals acquire, share, or demand, we can imagine a concept of power as diffused and embedded in "discourse." This notion is central to Evin Taylor's discussion of the ways cisgender privilege involves a "cultural currency" or power enjoyed by people who possess desired characteristics such as "normal" gender expressions.

---

1   Riki Wilchins, "Changing the Subject," in *Gender Queer: Voices From Beyond the Sexual Binary*, ed. Joan Nestle, Clare Howell, and Riki Wilchins (Los Angeles: Alyson Books, 2002), p. 51.

Discourse is the process of creating knowledge or a culturally constructed representation of reality. It involves language and other categories of meaning that work with social, material practices to produce "regimes of truth." These regimes of truth tell us what is "appropriate" in any given context. This involves the taken-for-granted rules about what people can say, who it is possible to be, and what it is possible to do (or not say or not do). In this way, discourse provides a range of being ("subjectivity") that we recognize as identity. This is what is meant by identities being produced through discourse. In other words, power produces discourses of difference, normality, and truth that shape bodies and identities. Moving beyond the notion of hierarchies, postmodern theorists focus on the diffuse and microlevel powers that produce multiple "truths" about gender, desire, and bodies.

Importantly, each community or society has its regimes of truth connected to power that inform what counts as knowledge. Imagine, for example, the different knowledge accepted among people in your family or different groups of friends; your academic classes; or your church, mosque, or synagogue, if you attend one. Regimes of truth are shaped by general truths/discourses such as science, or religion, for example; other levels of discourse, such as patriotism, are framed by these broader, general discourses. There are also discursive fields such as law that provide meaning and organize social institutions and processes. Scholars who focus on discourse are interested in understanding the ways some discourses have created meaning systems that have gained the status of "truth" and shape how we define and organize our social world (such as science) when other discourses are marginalized. These marginalized discourses offer a site for challenge and resistance. In this way it is interesting to consider how some discourses maintain their authority, how some "voices" get heard when others are silenced, and who benefits and how. These are all questions addressing issues of power/empowerment/disempowerment associated with knowledge, power, and discourse. We know this is a more complicated notion of power, but it is one you will encounter as you take more classes in the humanities and the social sciences.

Language, or the symbolic means by which we communicate, is a key aspect of regimes of truth as just described. Language is an incredibly sophisticated process of symbols that we learn at an early age and mostly take for granted unless we are confronted with trying to communicate in a language not our own. Because language allows us not only to name the objects of our experience but also to typify them (experience them as similar to something of a similar type), it creates as well as reflects our reality. It shapes as well as expresses thought. And because language helps us sort and anticipate our experiences, it has a primary influence on our lives. Language influences how its speakers focus their attention, remember events and people, and think about the world. This shapes how we understand space, time, and even justice. English, for example, tends to assign an agent to an action regardless of the agent's intent. In Japanese or Spanish, however, intent matters and requires different verb forms. Language maintains sexism and racism, for instance, by shaping our understandings and limiting options for self-definition. In this way, it is important to consider how language shapes our reality and helps structure the everyday realities of our lives. When you grow up knowing 20 different words synonymous with "slut" and fewer, more positive words for men who have multiple sexual partners, for example, you learn something powerful about gender and sexuality.

These categories of meaning or regimes of truth discussed earlier involve ideas and values (such as stereotypes and jokes) or sets of beliefs (sometimes called ideologies) that provide rationales for injustice. Hill Collins calls this the "symbolic dimension" of systems of domination and subordination. For example, media often reinforce negative stereotypes about women such as dumb blondes, passive Asian Americans, or pushy African Americans. Another example of gendered messages comes from the institution of religion. This institution is especially powerful because it implies the notion of divine sanction. Traditional religious texts tell stories (of, for instance, Eve's behavior that led to the banishment from the Garden of Eden or the chaste role of the Virgin Mary) that convey important messages about moral thought and behavior as well as women's place in society. These messages tend to be strongly gendered and often support different behaviors for women and men. A central code of some religious teaching is that women should be subordinate to men in their spiritual and everyday lives.

An example of discourse supported by institutional power is the bootstrap myth concerning economic success. The bootstrap myth and other dominant economic ideologies are propagated by economic systems that paint economic success as a result of hard work and ambition. People, if properly motivated and willing to work hard, can pull themselves up by their bootstraps. Given this set of ideas, those individuals who are not able to provide for their families must have deficiencies. Perhaps they were unmotivated, did not work hard enough, or were not smart enough. Such ideas encourage blaming the poor for their poverty rather than understanding the wider societal forces that shape people's existence and maintain classism. Notwithstanding the fact that of course hard work and ambition may facilitate some measure of success in the short term, they do not guarantee such success, nor do they tend to transform the bigger picture of structural inequalities. Notice that a particular truth claim need not be supported unanimously for it to influence society. Many people would disagree vehemently with the bootstrap myth; yet, this is still a key part of the ideology of capitalist countries. In this way, institutions construct and are constructed by truth claims that provide authority about how people should be and live.

Discourses that result in marginalization involve prejudices. Prejudice means, literally, to prejudge and involves making premature judgments without adequate information or with inaccurate information. Often prejudice is adopted when there is no other basis for understanding. For example, many white people have little contact with people of color, and many young people do not interact on an everyday basis with old people. As a result, there is a lack of accurate information to destabilize oppressive regimes of truth, and stereotypes or images from movies or other media are used instead. This kind of ignorance and misinformation breeds prejudice. Prejudices are internalized (assimilated, integrated, or incorporated into our thoughts and behavior) by all of us, and, as already mentioned in the discussion of homophobia and transphobia, they play a part in maintaining systems of inequality and privilege. However, because humans have active agency and will, prejudices can be resisted. Generally we can say that individuals negotiate these ideologies, accepting, resisting, and/or modifying them. If we are members of the target group, the group against whom the prejudice is aimed, we can succumb to low self-esteem, self-loathing, and shame. Sadly, this can mean individuals are encouraged to believe they are not worthy of social justice and therefore are less likely to seek equality. Although members of target groups may accept oppressive regimes of truth, members of nontarget groups, groups (often part of the mythical norm) against whom the prejudice is not aimed, also internalize these messages as well as messages about their own privilege. This can encourage or justify hostility.

Internalizing oppression means that we self-police as a result of discourses that "discipline" bodies and encourage self-surveillance. In addition, however, we also police one another, encouraging compliance with institutions that may oppress. When individuals direct the resentment and anger they have about their situation toward those who are of equal or lesser status, this process is called horizontal hostility. As a strategy, it is similar to the military tactic of "divide and conquer" in which groups are encouraged to fight with one another in order to avoid alliances that might collaboratively overpower an enemy. Women might do this when they compete with each other over appearance or put other women down with verbal and/or nonverbal behavior.

INSTITUTIONS

Postmodern notions of power described earlier transcend the practices of who acquires what and how by seeing power as an everyday embodied phenomenon. This discursive notion of power as being everywhere replaces the notion of institutions set apart from the systems of meanings they create. Some postmodern scholars, including Michel Foucault, still prioritize themes of institutionalized power, and it is to these that we now turn.

Institutions are social organizations that involve established patterns of behavior organized around particular purposes. They function through social norms (cultural expectations), which as explained earlier are institutionalized and patterned into organizations and sometimes established as rules and/or laws. Major institutions in our society include the family, marriage, the economy, government and criminal justice systems, religion, education, science, health and medicine, mass media, the military, and sports. Usually patterns of rules and practices implicit in major societal institutions have a historical component and reflect political, military, legal, and socioeconomic decisions made over decades and centuries. Although institutions are intended to meet the needs of society generally, or people in particular, they meet some people's needs better than others. These social organizations are central in creating systems of inequality and privilege because they pattern and structure differences in relatively organized ways. Institutions are important channels for the perpetuation of what Hill Collins calls "structures of domination and subordination." Institutions encourage the channeling of various systems of gendered inequality to all aspects of women's lives. In terms of the patterning of resources and practices, institutions function to support systems of inequality and privilege. First, institutions assign various roles to women and men and are also places of employment where people perform gendered work. K–12 educational institutions, for example, employ a considerable number of women. However, as the prestige of the teaching position increases, the number of white males in these positions increases, and salaries become higher. Additionally, it is very difficult for openly lesbian teachers to find employment in some schools, and some states have attempted to pass laws preventing lesbians and gay men from teaching in state-funded educational establishments.

Second, to return to a more resource-based notion of power where power is imagined as something people acquire, own, or share, institutions distribute resources and extend privileges differentially to different groups. Sports are a good example of this. As an institution, athletics has traditionally been male dominated. Men's sports are more highly valued than women's sports and are a major focus of sports entertainment. Compared to men's professional sports, women's are grossly underrepresented. Despite Title IX of the Educational Amendments of 1972, which barred discrimination in education, many colleges still are not in compliance and spend considerably more money on men's sports than on women's. Female athletes on some campuses complain that men receive better practice times in shared gymnasiums and more up-to-date equipment. And, within women's sports, some are more "white" than others. Examples that immediately come to mind

GENDER AND STEM

Kryn Freehling-Burton

After the passage of Title IX in 1972, increasing numbers of girls and women gained access to courses that prepared them to achieve dreams of higher education, graduate school, and careers in the sciences and engineering. However, problems with the institutions of science remain, including the association of STEM with masculinity, heterosexuality, and whiteness. Recent studies show that when asked to draw a scientist, 34 percent of children draw a woman, up from 1 percent in 1970, and when girls draw scientists today, more than half draw women (Miller et al. 2018). But women are still less likely to go into certain fields like neurosurgery or nuclear engineering, are less likely to advance to the upper levels in any field, and are more likely to opt out of careers in STEM for a variety of reasons. And the numbers of women in computer science have been declining. These numbers are even starker for women of color. A full 100 percent of women of color in STEM fields report experiencing gender bias, and 77 percent report having to prove themselves over and over again as experts in their field (Williams, Phillips, and Hall 2014). Across all STEM disciplines, women earn only 35 percent of bachelor's degrees; only in the life sciences is this percentage over 50 percent. For women of color only a paltry 11 percent earn bachelor's degrees in STEM fields (National Center for Education Statistics 2016). Women are still more likely to study and practice in STEM areas connected to health and receive lower salaries across fields and positions. For instance, only 18 percent of computer science program graduates in the United States are women, and only 26 percent of jobs in computer science and mathematics are held by women. Responsibilities for child-rearing and domestic labor in the home continue to fall disproportionately on women, and the maternal wall bias at work affects not only women with children, but also women without.

Explore the websites of your university's STEM majors. How are women and other underrepresented students and faculty represented? What kinds of programs are available to help women, students and faculty of color, and first-generation students succeed in STEM education?

Explore the website of one of the following organizations: the American Association of University Women, the National Science Foundation's Advance program, Chick Tech, or Black Girls Code. How does the organization work to increase the numbers of girls and women in STEM? What kinds of programs or activities might be successful at your college?

Watch the 2017 film *Hidden Figures*, starring Taraji P. Henson, Octavia Spencer, and Janelle Monáe. How is this film an important step in the recovery of the stories of black women in mathematics and computer science? Why does it matter that a black woman, Margot Lee Shetterly, wrote the book on which it is based?

References

Miller, D., Nolla, K. M., Eagly, A. H., and Uttal, D. H. (2018). "The Development of Children's Gender-Science Stereotypes: A Meta-analysis of 5 Decades of U.S. Draw-a-Scientist Studies." *Child Development*, 89:6, 1–13.

National Center for Education Statistics (2016). "Table 318.45: Number and Percentage Distribution of Science, Technology, Engineering, and Mathematics (STEM) Degrees/Certificates Conferred by Postsecondary Institutions, by Race/Ethnicity, Level of Degree/Certificate, and Sex of Student: 2008-09 Through 2014–15." *Digest of Education Statistics: 2016 Tables and Figures.* https://nces.ed.gov/programs/digest/d16/tables/dt16_318.45.asp

Williams, J. C., Phillips, K. W., and Hall, E. V. (2014). *Double Jeopardy? Gender Bias Against Women of Color in Science.* Work Life Law, UC Hastings College of the Law. Retrieved from www.worklifelaw.org/publications/Double-Jeopardy-Report_v6_full_web-sm-2.pdf

are gymnastics, ice skating, equestrian sports, tennis, golf, and to some extent soccer (all relatively expensive pursuits). Most women's sports—outside of basketball and track—are dominated by white women. In this way, sports and athletics are an example of an institution where resources are inequitably distributed.

Another blatant example of inequitable distribution concerns the economic system. Other than inherited wealth, the major way our economic system distributes resources is in remuneration for the work that we do. Women tend to work in jobs that are heavily occupied by women; examples include clerical work, service and retail sales, and professional occupations such as teaching and nursing. These jobs are undervalued in our society, contributing to the fact that generally a woman's average salary for all occupations tends to be less than a man's average salary. Some women work under deplorable conditions at minimum wage levels; some work with hazardous chemicals or have to breathe secondhand smoke throughout their workday. Older women and women of color own a tiny percentage of the wealth in this society—another example of the inequitable distribution of resources by an intersection or confluence of multiple identities.

Third, major institutions in society are interconnected and work to support and maintain one another. Often this means that personnel are shared among major institutions; more likely it means that these institutions mutually support one another in terms of the ways they fulfill (or deny) the needs of people in society. For example, close ties to economic institutions include the military (through the military-industrial complex), the government (corporate leaders often have official positions in government and rely on legislative loopholes and taxation systems to maintain corporate profits), health and medicine (which have important ties to pharmaceutical companies), the media (whose content is controlled in part by advertising), and sports (through corporate sponsorship).

In closing, we have emphasized that systems of inequality and privilege are maintained through institutionalized power and various regimes of truth. However, it is also

---

HISTORICAL MOMENT
WOMEN OF COLOR FEMINISM

Acutely aware of the intersections of gender, race, sexual identity, and social class were women of color who daily experienced the material realities of the confluence of oppressions. From the beginning of the women's movement, women of color participated actively, although their specific concerns were often overlooked by some of the middle-class white women in the movement. In the early 1970s, women of color spoke out about their experiences of racism, sexism, and heterosexism. Barbara Smith co-founded the Combahee River Collective, a black feminist group that confronted racism and homophobia in the women's, gay, and black movements. The Collective took its name from a river in South Carolina where Harriet Tubman led a military action that freed hundreds of slaves.

In the late 1970s, Smith joined forces with Cherríe Moraga to found Kitchen Table/Women of Color Press when Moraga and Gloria Anzaldúa could not find a publisher for *This Bridge Called My Back: Writings by Radical Women of Color*. Kitchen Table/Women of Color Press was the first independent press to publish exclusively works by feminists of color. *This Bridge Called My Back* won an American Book Award from the Columbus Foundation.

In 1983 poet and novelist Alice Walker coined the term "womanism" to describe black feminism in contrast to "feminism," which has generally been associated with white women. Walker situates womanists in a long line of black women who have struggled for social change and liberation. Womanists are, in her words, "outrageous, audacious, courageous, and willful, responsible, in charge, serious." They love black women's culture, black women's beauty, and themselves.

MENTAL HEALTH AND SYSTEMS OF OPPRESSION

Lzz Johnk

The scholarship of intersectional feminists tells us that aspects of identity, embodiment, and positionality are overlapping and imbricated, such that disability, race, gender, and so on cannot be understood separately from one another. However, modern Eurowestern psychology and psychiatry focus on a largely decontextualized individual whom they claim to treat without regard to race, gender, sexuality, and so on. These scientific systems hold diagnostic and pathologizing power over a supposedly neutral individual.

Mad studies scholars refer to these systems as "the psy sciences," or the psy industrial complex, indicating the way psy power is intrinsically connected with neoliberal, racist, misogynist, and other forms of power. These systems pursue social control of individuals through pathologization, psychiatric incarceration, forced treatment, and other forms of what transnational feminist disability studies scholar Eunjung Kim calls "curative violence" (2017). Such normalized "treatment" and other forms of discrimination against people with mental disability (e.g., psychiatric disability, neurodivergence, madness, and mental illness) are examples of sanism.

Sanism is a form of structural oppression comprised of beliefs and practices that are predicated upon the presumed existence of a "sound mind," leading to harm of all kinds being directed at those determined to be of "unsound mind." Sanism intersects with other forms of systemic oppression (racism, classism, sexism, queermisia, xenomisia, etc.) in ways that compound harm for those in multiply marginalized positionalities.[1] Moreover, ideals of "able-mindedness"—the notion that some minds are more "sound," "able," or "rational" than others—are co-constructed with white supremacy, heteropatriarchy, and colonialism. This means that the violence of sanism falls disproportionately across race, class, gender, sexuality, nationality, and so on, such that certain groups of people (e.g., women of color, indigenous people, queer people, immigrants) are much more likely to be perceived, diagnosed, and treated as "mentally ill," "feeble-minded," or "insane" within the context of white supremacist colonialism. For instance, during U.S. chattel slavery, black slaves who attempted to run away from enslavement were thought to be "mentally ill" by Eurowestern settlers such as Samuel Cartwright, who created the diagnosis of "drapetomania" to describe the "unfit" behavior of runaway slaves.

The historical trajectory of sanism stretches across space-time. Psychiatric survivor Colin King (2016), who identifies as an African man living in the United Kingdom, asserts that black men who emigrate from African and Caribbean nations to Eurowestern nations experience sanism in conjunction with anti-black racism, xenomisia, and gendered colonial white supremacist beliefs about black men as innately violent and irrational. Thus, black African men are viewed as "mentally disordered" within converging systems of colonial white supremacy (e.g., psychiatry, public health, and immigration services). Stories such as King's reveal that psy systems are premised on white supremacist colonialism and pathologize individual body-minds with the intent to control racialized and gendered "Others." Systems wielding psy power against mad, disabled, and neurodivergent body-minds are frequently targeting them with eugenicist intent (e.g., incarceration, sterilization), especially the body-minds of queer, indigenous, immigrant, and/or people of color.

Read More:

> https://theicarusproject.net/
> https://thebodyisnotanapology.com/

Dig deeper: 1. Perpetrators of mass shootings are often labeled "mentally ill" by authorities. How does this serve sanism and intersecting systems of gender and race? 2. How does the prison system serve the purposes of sanism? 3. Identify recent incidents of the use of psy power against members of non-dominant groups.

References

Kim, E. (2017). *Curative Violence: Rehabilitating Disability, Gender, and Sexuality in Modern Korea.* Durham, NC: Duke University Press.

King, C. (2016). "Whiteness in Psychiatry: The Madness of European Misdiagnosis." In J. Russo and A. Sweeney, *Searching for a Rose Garden: Challenging Psychiatry, Fostering Mad Studies* (pp. 69–76). Monmouth, UK: PCCS Books Ltd.

---

[1] Among mad, crip, and neurodivergent communities, there is a growing practice of replacing the suffix "phobia" (which is a form of neurodivergent experience) with "misia" (meaning "hate") to avoid replicating sanism/ableism in our language.

---

important to recognize the ways hate crimes (also known as bias-motivated crimes) are central to these power relations. Hate crimes reflect the ways power produces regimes of truth, difference, and normalcy that regulate people's lives. As already explained, we are expected to police ourselves and indulge in self-surveillance, often to keep ourselves in narrow boxes of "appropriate" behavior. However, in addition, disciplinary acts to regulate others who are perceived as not conforming (for example, not dressing like a woman is "supposed" to dress, or not acting like a man is supposed to act, or a person of color not showing the appropriate amount of deference expected by whites who hold racist views about people of color) result in hate crimes. And for some, the very act of living and being in a certain body is enough to cause anger and resentment. This kind of foundational bigotry is often at the heart of hate crimes.

Hate crimes include the threat of coercion and violence as well as the actual practice of them, and their motives are hate and bigotry. Evidence shows that perpetrators of hate crimes are most likely to be heterosexual white males. For example, there has been a substantial increase in hate crimes in the past few years, especially against people of color and lesbian,

ACTIVIST PROFILE

FANNIE LOU HAMER

She began life in Mississippi in 1917 as the granddaughter of slaves and the daughter of sharecroppers, but Fannie Lou Hamer was to become one of the most important leaders of the U.S. civil rights movement. Although Hamer became a sharecropper herself, by 1962 she'd had enough of the second-class life of the segregated South. She joined 17 other African Americans taking a bus to the county seat to register to vote. On the way home, they were stopped by police and arrested. After Hamer returned home, she was visited by the plantation owner, who told her that if she insisted on voting, she would have to get off his land, which she did that same day.

The next year, when Hamer joined other civil rights workers in challenging the "whites only" policy at a bus terminal diner, she was arrested and jailed. The police ordered two other African American prisoners to beat her with a metal-spiked club. Hamer was blinded in one eye from the beating and suffered permanent kidney damage.

In 1964 Hamer helped organize the Mississippi Freedom Democratic Party (MFDP) to challenge the all-white Mississippi delegation to the Democratic National Convention. Hamer spoke to the credentials committee of the convention, and although her live testimony was preempted by a presidential press conference, it was aired by national networks in its entirety later that evening. The MFDP and the credentials committee reached a compromise, giving voting and speaking rights to two MFDP delegates and seating the others as honored guests. Hamer responded, "We didn't come all this way for two seats when all of us is tired." In 1968 the Mississippi Democratic Party did seat an integrated delegation.

Throughout her life, Hamer continued to work for justice, supporting Head Start for black schools and jobs for poor African Americans, opposing the Vietnam War, and helping to convene the National Women's Political Caucus in the 1970s.

Hamer died in 1977 and was buried in Mississippi. Her tombstone reads, "I am sick and tired of being sick and tired."

gay, queer, and trans people, although improved reporting systems are also increasing awareness of this social problem and providing hate-crime statistics. Hate groups include the Ku Klux Klan, racist skinheads, the Christian Identity movement, neo-Confederates, and neo-Nazis (including Aryan Nations). Since the election of Donald Trump as president, white nationalist groups have felt empowered to engage in much more public displays of hate. In 2017, white nationalists organized a "Unite the Right" rally in Charlottesville, Virginia, that led to the death of a counter-protester and dozens of injuries to other people. One of the best sources for understanding hate crimes is the Southern Poverty Law Center (www.splcenter.org). It is important to emphasize that gender as a category is omitted from most hate-crime statutes despite the fact that women, transgender, and queer/gay men suffer from crimes of misogyny. People are often hurt and/or killed because they are perceived as women, or are expressing feminine behavior. In the case of transgender individuals, this reflects the ways regimes of truth discipline bodies that do not perform in expected ways. The United Nations now recognizes crimes against women, although in 2018 the Trump administration announced it would no longer consider domestic violence against women in other countries as a basis for an asylum request. Hate crimes against women just because they are women, as well as hate crimes against, for example, lesbians or women of color, often involve sexual terrorism, the threat of rape and sexual assault that controls a woman's life whether or not she is actually physically or sexually violated.

In concluding this chapter, we underscore the need for social change and transformation to improve the conditions of women's lives. Almost all of the readings focus on this need. Patricia Hill Collins, for example, writes about awareness and education, the need to build empathy for one another, and the need to work to form coalitions for structural change around common causes. Evin Taylor tells us to recognize our privilege and work on internalized prejudices and privileges. Ellie Mamber suggests identifying and acknowledging sources of inequality and specifically the ways we are taught contempt for aging women.

All authors, and especially the late Audre Lorde, hope for alliances across our differences. The message in all of these articles is the need to recognize difference, to understand how the meanings associated with intersecting differences and the material conditions of everyday lives get translated into privilege and inequality, and to celebrate difference through coalitions for social justice and other expressions of personal and social concern.

LEARNING ACTIVITY

COMBATING HATE

Many web pages provide valuable information about hate, hate crimes, and hate groups in the United States. Go to the Southern Poverty Law Center's homepage at www.splcenter.org, and click on "Hate Map." Then enter your state to discover which hate groups operate where you live. Click on "Intelligence Files" to learn more about these hate groups. You may also want to visit the following websites as well: www.adl.org, www.campuspride.org/stop-the-hate, www.hatewatch.org, www.hrc.org, and www.wiesenthal.com. Using information from these sites, make a list of ways you can help stop hate.

LEARNING ACTIVITY

TRANSGENDER EXPERIENCES AROUND THE WORLD

Go to YouTube and find videos made by transgender people in the following countries:

- Brazil
- India
- Kenya
- New Zealand
- Ukraine
- United States

What common experiences do these people have? How have they experienced being transgender differently?

What difficulties and forms of oppression do they face? What do they celebrate about their lives? How do their lives and experiences offer challenges to fixed notions of gender identity?

The United Nations adopted the Universal Declaration of Human Rights in 1948. In 2012 the UN Secretary-General called for an end to discrimination based on gender identity. Take a look at the UN declaration (http://www.un.org/en/universal-declaration-human-rights/), and identify cultural and social changes that would be needed to bring about equity for transgender people.

CHALLENGING THE PSEUDOGENERIC "MAN"

Examine the following phrases that use male nouns as "generic." Describe the mental image created for you by each phrase. Do you see yourself and people like you in the images?

Next, choose a term representing a group of people of a specific age, religion, class, or ethnicity, and substitute that term for the male noun (example: "mankind" becomes "childkind"). Does use of the new, specific term sound incongruous or unusual? Why?

Describe the mental images created by using the substitute terms. Do you see yourself and people like you In the images?

Finally, suggest a gender-inclusive term for each (example: for "mankind," "humanity" or "people").

> For the benefit of all mankind
> "All men are created equal"

May the best man win
Prehistoric man
Man the pumps!
The first manned mission to Mars
Chairman of the Board
We need more manpower
Not fit for man or beast
The relationship between men and machines
Man's best friend
"To boldly go where no man has gone before"
Man of the Year
"Peace on Earth, goodwill toward men"
The founding fathers
"Crown thy good with brotherhood"
"Friends, Romans, countrymen; lend me your ears"

Source: Janet Lockhart and Susan M. Shaw, *Writing for Change: Raising Awareness of Difference, Power, and Discrimination*, www.teachingtolerance.org.

THE BLOG

IS PATRIARCHY THE RELIGION OF THE PLANET?

Susan M. Shaw (2015)

Decades ago, feminist philosopher Mary Daly claimed that patriarchy is the prevailing religion of the planet. As I watch the headlines, I think she may be right.

Patriarchy is a system of domination of men over women. It's racialized. It's shaped by economic resources and political access. It benefits some people more than others and in different ways across genders. But at its core it is a system that worships power—whether it be physical, political, social, or economic—and devalues women and anything associated with them.

Let's take the Pope's recent visit as an example. While the media were heralding his commitments to the poor and his kinder approach to those the church has often condemned (and these are commendable changes), let's not forget that poverty is gendered, with women significantly more likely to be poor than men.

(continued)

We cannot end poverty without ending the oppression of women, and yet the Pope offered no gender analysis of the problems of poverty. Additionally, while the Pope may have ended the inquisition against American nuns, the Church still forbids the ordination of women to the priesthood. Catholic women are still not allowed control of their own reproductive lives. The Pope even made a saint of a man who was a key figure in the colonization of the indigenous peoples of the West. And the Pope chose to meet with and encourage Kim Davis, the Kentucky county clerk who has refused to follow the law and issue marriage licenses to lesbian and gay couples because of her religious convictions.

Of course, the Catholic Church is not the only one that excludes women from leadership—Mormons, Seventh Day Adventists, Southern Baptists, all likewise believe that only a man can represent God in a religious leadership capacity. Very, very few Muslim women have ever led prayers in a Mosque. Some ultra-Orthodox Jewish men harass Jewish women who want to pray at the Western Wall and have spit on Jewish girls whose dress does not conform to their strict standards.

Despite laws banning the practices—and a great deal of local activism and resistance—some Hindu women are subject to dowries that amount to extortion payments to take women off of families' hands; instead of burning on funeral pyres, some widows are now victims of so-called suicides, found hanging or poisoned or burned inside their homes. We know that ISIS kidnaps and rapes women—with a ready religious justification built from their misreadings of the Qur'an and some Islamic scholars, while Boko Haram kidnaps and rapes girls in Nigeria.

Even the Dalai Lama, who claims to be a feminist, recently said that, while he believed a female Dalai Lama would be possible, she would have to be attractive or she would be of no use.

But as the religion of the planet, patriarchy is not simply a matter of religion. The worship of power and its parallel devaluing of women are pervasive, which was Mary Daly's point.

A recent report by the World Bank found that laws around the world impede women's progress. Ninety percent of the 173 countries surveyed had at least one law on the books that discriminated against women. Delegates at the UN's 1995 Beijing conference on women set a target of 30 percent participation by women in national legislatures by 2015. Only 44 of 190 countries have met that goal. In the United States, women are 23 percent of the House and 24 percent of the Senate. No woman has ever led the United Nations, or the United States, for that matter.

Other distressing headlines have included Donald Trump's comments about women, including an insult about Carly Fiorina's appearance. Conservatives are attacking Planned Parenthood (again), despite the fact that Planned Parenthood receives no federal funding for abortions. In fact, most of Planned Parenthood's funding comes from Medicaid reimbursements for the wide variety of necessary health services the organization provides, particularly to low-income women. The recently released documentary, *The Hunting Ground*, documents the epidemic of sexual assault on college campuses—which mirrors the epidemic of sexual assault elsewhere in the United States. Leaders told U.S. soldiers in Afghanistan to ignore the abuse of boys by Afghan allies. Amnesty International wants to decriminalize pimping, which is not the same as decriminalizing the selling of sex by sex workers themselves. We know of at least 27 transgender women of color who have been murdered in the United States in 2017. And making black women's lives (and deaths) visible in Black Lives Matter has been difficult.

On and on we could go. Watching the nightly news is generally watching a parade of misogyny. I don't deny that progress happens for women. But often our need to talk about progress is a way of avoiding talking about the ongoing problems of sexism, racism, and other interlocking forms of oppression. Progress is never even, and people benefit differently from progress, usually in ways related to their status in the system. So, for example, affirmative action programs have actually benefited white women more than women and men of color. So-called progress may also mask the ways that discrimination simply changes. For example, while race-based housing discrimination is illegal, apartments may suddenly be no longer available when a person of color shows up; people of color also have a more difficult time securing home loans and are often saddled with higher interest rates for those loans than whites. If those people happen to be gay, in many states, they can simply be denied housing on the basis of sexual identity.

So, yes, I do think patriarchy is the prevailing religion of the planet—or to make it more complex, nuanced, and intersectional, as feminist bell hooks does, white, capitalist heteropatriarchy is the prevailing religion of the planet.

And that's why, as Nigerian author Chimamanda Adichie argues, we should all be feminists. Then she answers the question, why feminist? She writes:

> "Why not just say you are a believer in human rights or something like that?" Because that would be dishonest. Feminism is, of course, part of human rights in general—but to choose to use the vague expression *human rights* is to deny the specific and particular problem of gender. (*We Should All Be Feminists* [New York: Anchor, 2014], 41)

The world has a problem of gender of religious proportions. We need a reformation, perhaps a revolution, to tear down the altars to male power and rebuild a global sanctuary of inclusion, equity, justice, peace, and love.

8. TOWARD A NEW VISION
Race, Class, and Gender as Categories of Analysis and Connection
PATRICIA HILL COLLINS (1993)

The true focus of revolutionary change is never merely the oppressive situations which we seek to escape, but that piece of the oppressor which is planted deep within each of us.
—*Audre Lorde*, Sister Outsider, *123*

Audre Lorde's statement raises a troublesome issue for scholars and activists working for social change. While many of us have little difficulty assessing our own victimization within some major system of oppression, whether it be by race, social class, religion, sexual orientation, ethnicity, age or gender, we typically fail to see how our thoughts and actions uphold someone else's subordination. Thus, White feminists routinely point with confidence to their oppression as women but resist seeing how much their White skin privileges them. African Americans who possess eloquent analyses of racism often persist in viewing poor White women as symbols of white power. The radical left fares little better. "If only people of color and women could see their true class interests," they argue, "class solidarity would eliminate racism and sexism." In essence, each group identifies the type of oppression with which it feels most comfortable as being fundamental and classifies all other types as being of lesser importance.

Oppression is full of such contradictions. Errors in political judgment that we make concerning how we teach our courses, what we tell our children, and which organizations are worthy of our time, talents and financial support flow smoothly from errors in theoretical analysis about the nature of oppression and activism. Once we realize that there are few pure victims or oppressors, and that each one of us derives varying amounts of penalty and privilege from the multiple systems of oppression that frame our lives, then we will be in a position to see the need for new ways of thought and action.

[This discussion] addresses this need for new patterns of thought and action. I focus on two basic questions. First, how can we reconceptualize race, class and gender as categories of analysis? Second, how can we transcend the barriers created by our experiences with race, class and gender oppression in order to build the types of coalitions essential for social exchange? To address these question[s] I contend that we must acquire both new theories of how race, class and gender have shaped the experiences not just of women of color, but of all groups. Moreover, we must see the connections between these categories of analysis and the personal issues in our everyday lives, particularly our scholarship, our teaching and our relationships with our colleagues and students. As Audre Lorde points out, change starts with self, and relationships that we have with those around us must always be the primary site for social change.

HOW CAN WE RECONCEPTUALIZE RACE, CLASS, AND GENDER AS CATEGORIES OF ANALYSIS?

To me, we must shift our discourse away from additive analyses of oppression (Spelman 1982; Collins 1989) Such approaches are typically based on two key premises. First, they depend on either/or, dichotomous thinking. Persons, things and ideas are conceptualized in terms of their opposites. For example, Black/White, man/woman, thought/feeling, and fact/opinion are defined in oppositional terms. Thought and feeling are not seen as two different and interconnected ways of approaching truth that can coexist in scholarship and teaching. Instead, feeling is defined as antithetical to reason, as its opposite. In spite of the fact that we all have "both/and" identities (I am both a college professor and a mother—I don't stop being a mother when I drop my child off at school, or forget everything I learned while scrubbing the toilet), we persist in trying to classify each other in either/or categories. I live each day as an African-American woman—a race/gender specific experience. And I am not alone. Everyone has a race/gender/class specific identity. Either/or, dichotomous thinking is especially troublesome when applied to theories of oppression because every individual must be classified as being either oppressed or not oppressed. The both/and position of simultaneously being oppressed and oppressor becomes conceptually impossible.

A second premise of additive analyses of oppression is that these dichotomous differences must be ranked. One side of the dichotomy is typically labeled dominant and the other subordinate. Thus, Whites rule Blacks, men are deemed superior to women, and reason is seen as being preferable to emotion. Applying this premise to discussions of oppression leads to the assumption that oppression can be quantified, and that some groups are oppressed more than others. I am frequently asked, "Which has been most oppressive to you, your status as a Black person or your status as a woman?" What I am really being asked to do is divide myself into little boxes and rank my various statuses. If I experience oppression as a both/and phenomenon, why should I analyze it any differently?

Additive analyses of oppression rest squarely on the twin pillars of either/or thinking and the necessity to quantify and rank all relationships in order to know where one stands. Such approaches typically see African-American women as being more oppressed than everyone else because the majority of Black women experience the negative effects of race, class and gender oppression simultaneously. In essence, if you add together separate oppressions, you are left with a grand oppression greater than the sum of its parts.

I am not denying that specific groups experience oppression more harshly than others—lynching is certainly objectively worse than being held up as a sex object. But we must be careful not to confuse this issue of the saliency of one type of oppression in people's lives with a theoretical stance positing the interlocking nature of oppression. Race, class and gender may all structure a situation but may not be equally visible and/or important in people's self-definitions. In certain contexts, such as the antebellum American South and contemporary South America, racial oppression is more visibly salient, while in other contexts, such as Haiti, El Salvador and Nicaragua, social class

oppression may be more apparent. For middle class White women, gender may assume experiential primacy unavailable to poor Hispanic women struggling with the ongoing issues of low-paid jobs and the frustrations of the welfare bureaucracy. This recognition that one category may have salience over another for a given time and place does not minimize the theoretical importance of assuming that race, class and gender as categories of analysis structure all relationships.

In order to move toward new visions of what oppression is, I think that we need to ask new questions. How are relationships of domination and subordination structured and maintained in the American political economy? How do race, class and gender function as parallel and interlocking systems that shape this basic relationship of domination and subordination? Questions such as these promise to move us away from futile theoretical struggles concerned with ranking oppressions and towards analyses that assume race, class and gender are all present in any given setting, even if one appears more visible and salient than the others. Our task becomes redefined as one of reconceptualizing oppression by uncovering the connections among race, class and gender as categories of analysis.

1. THE INSTITUTIONAL DIMENSION OF OPPRESSION

Sandra Harding's contention that gender oppression is structured along three main dimensions—the institutional, the symbolic, and the individual—offers a useful model for a more comprehensive analysis encompassing race, class and gender oppression (Harding 1986). Systemic relationships of domination and subordination structured through social institutions such as schools, businesses, hospitals, the workplace, and government agencies represent the institutional dimension of oppression. Racism, sexism and elitism all have concrete institutional locations. Even though the workings of the institutional dimension of oppression are often obscured with ideologies claiming equality of opportunity, in actuality, race, class and gender place Asian-American women, Native American men, White men, African-American women, and other groups in distinct institutional niches with varying degrees of penalty and privilege.

Even though I realize that many ... would not share this assumption, let us assume that the institutions of American society discriminate, whether by design or by accident. While many of us are familiar with how race, gender and class operate separately to structure inequality, I want to focus on how these three systems interlock in structuring the institutional dimension of oppression. To get at the interlocking nature of race, class and gender, I want you to think about the ante-bellum plantation as a guiding metaphor for a variety of American social institutions. Even though slavery is typically analyzed as a racist institution, and occasionally as a class institution, I suggest that slavery was a race, class, gender specific institution. Removing any one piece from our analysis diminishes our understanding of the true nature of relations of domination and subordination under slavery.

. . .

A brief analysis of key American social institutions most controlled by elite White men should convince us of the interlocking nature of race, class and gender in structuring the institutional dimension of oppression. For example, if you are from an American college or university, is your campus a modern plantation? Who controls your university's political economy? Are elite White men overrepresented among the upper administrators and trustees controlling your university's finances and policies? Are elite White men being joined by growing numbers of elite White women helpmates? What kinds of people are in your classrooms grooming the next generation who will occupy these and other decision-making positions? Who are the support staff that produce the mass mailings, order the supplies, fix the leaky pipes? Do African-Americans, Hispanics or other people of color form the majority of the invisible workers who feed you, wash your dishes, and clean up your offices and libraries after everyone else has gone home?

If your college is anything like mine, you know the answers to these questions. You may be affiliated with an institution that has Hispanic women as vice-presidents for finance, or substantial numbers of Black men among the faculty. If so, you are fortunate. Much more typical are colleges where a modified version of the plantation as a metaphor for the institutional dimension of oppression survives.

2. THE SYMBOLIC DIMENSION OF OPPRESSION

Widespread, societally-sanctioned ideologies used to justify relations of domination and subordination comprise the symbolic dimension of oppression. Central to this process is the use of stereotypical or controlling images of diverse race, class and gender groups. In order to assess the power of this dimension of oppression, I want you to make a list, either on paper or in your head, of "masculine" and "feminine" characteristics. If your list is anything like that compiled by most people, it reflects some variation of the following:

Masculine	**Feminine**
aggressive	passive
leader	follower
rational	emotional
strong	weak
intellectual	physical

Not only does this list reflect either/or, dichotomous thinking and the need to rank both sides of the dichotomy, but ask yourself exactly which men and women you had in mind when compiling these characteristics. This list applies almost exclusively to middle class White men and women. The allegedly "masculine" qualities that you probably listed are only acceptable when exhibited by elite White men, or when used by Black and Hispanic men against each other or against women of color. Aggressive Black and Hispanic men are seen as dangerous, not powerful, and are often penalized when they exhibit any of the allegedly "masculine" characteristics. Working-class and poor White men fare slightly better and are also denied the allegedly "masculine" symbols of leadership, intellectual competence and human rationality. Women of color and working class and poor White women are also not represented on this list, for they have never had the luxury of being "ladies." What appear to be universal categories representing all men and women instead are unmasked as being applicable to only a small group. It is important to see how the symbolic images applied to different race, class and gender groups interact in maintaining systems of domination and subordination. If I were to ask you to repeat the same assignment, only this time, by making separate lists for Black men, Black women, Hispanic women and Hispanic men, I suspect that your gender symbolism would be quite different. In comparing all of the lists, you might begin to see the interdependence of symbols applied to all groups. For example, the elevated images of White womanhood need devalued images of Black womanhood in order to maintain credibility.

Assuming that everyone is affected differently by the same interlocking set of symbolic images allows us to move forward toward new analyses. Women of color and White women have different relationships to White male authority, and this difference explains the distinct gender symbolism applied to both groups. Black women encounter controlling images such as the mammy, the matriarch, the mule and the whore, that encourage others to reject us as fully human people. Ironically, the negative nature of these images simultaneously encourages us to reject them. In contrast, White women are offered seductive images, those that promise to reward them for supporting the status quo. And yet seductive images can be equally controlling. Consider, for example, the views of Nancy White, a 73-year-old Black woman, concerning images of rejection and seduction:

> My mother used to say that the black woman is the white man's mule and the white woman is his dog. Now, she said that to say this: we do the heavy work and get beat whether we do it well or not. But the white woman is closer to the master and he pats them on the head and lets them sleep in the house, but he ain't gon' treat neither one like he was dealing with a person. (Gwaltney 1980, 148)

Both sets of images stimulate particular political stances. By broadening the analysis beyond the confines of race, we can see the varying levels of rejection and seduction available to each of us due to our race, class and gender identity. Each of us lives with an allotted portion of institutional privilege and penalty, and with varying levels of rejection and seduction inherent in the symbolic images applied to us. This is the context in which we make our choices. Taken together, the institutional and symbolic dimensions of oppression create a structural backdrop against which all of us live our lives.

3. THE INDIVIDUAL DIMENSION OF OPPRESSION

Whether we benefit or not, we all live within institutions that reproduce race, class and gender oppression. Even if we never have any contact with members of other race, class and gender groups, we all encounter images of these groups and are exposed to the symbolic meanings attached to those images. On this dimension of oppression, our individual biographies vary tremendously. As a result of our institutional and symbolic statuses, all of our choices become political acts.

Each of us must come to terms with the multiple ways in which race, class and gender as categories of analysis frame our individual biographies. I have lived my entire life as an African-American woman from a working-class family, and this basic fact has had a profound impact on my personal biography. Imagine how different your life might be if you had been born Black, or White, or poor, or of a different race/class/gender group than the one with which you are most familiar. The institutional treatment you would have received and the symbolic meanings attached to your very existence might differ dramatically from what you now consider to be natural, normal and part of everyday life. You might be the same, but your personal biography might have been quite different.

I believe that each of us carries around the cumulative effect of our lives within multiple structures of oppression. If you want to see how much you have been affected by this whole thing, I ask you one simple question—who are your close friends? Who are the people with whom you can share your hopes, dreams, vulnerabilities, fears and victories? Do they look like you? If they are all the same, circumstance may be the cause. For the first seven years of my life I saw only low-income Black people. My friends from those years reflected the composition of my community. But now that I am an adult, can the defense of circumstance explain the patterns of people that I trust as my friends and colleagues? When given other alternatives, if my friends and colleagues reflect the homogeneity of one race, class and gender group, then these categories of analysis have indeed become barriers to connection.

I am not suggesting that people are doomed to follow the paths laid out for them by race, class and gender as categories of analysis. While these three structures certainly frame my opportunity structure, I as an individual always have the choice of accepting things as they are, or trying to change them. As Nikki Giovanni points out, "we've got to live in the real world. If we don't like the world we're living in, change it. And if we can't change it, we change ourselves. We can do something" (Tate 1983, 68). While a piece of the oppressor may be planted deep within each of us, we each have the choice of accepting that piece or challenging it as part of the "true focus of revolutionary change."

HOW CAN WE TRANSCEND THE BARRIERS CREATED BY OUR EXPERIENCES WITH RACE, CLASS, AND GENDER OPPRESSION IN ORDER TO BUILD THE TYPES OF COALITIONS ESSENTIAL FOR SOCIAL CHANGE?

Reconceptualizing oppression and seeing the barriers created by race, class and gender as interlocking categories of analysis is a vital first step. But we must transcend these barriers by moving toward race, class and gender as categories of connection, by building relationships and coalitions that will bring about social change. What are some of the issues involved in doing this?

1. DIFFERENCES IN POWER AND PRIVILEGE

First, we must recognize that our differing experiences with oppression create problems in the relationships among us. Each of us lives within a system that vests us with varying levels of power and privilege. These differences in power, whether structured along axes of race, class, gender, age or sexual orientation, frame our relationships. African-American writer June Jordan describes her discomfort on a Caribbean vacation with Olive, the Black woman who cleaned her room:

> . . . even though both "Olive" and "I" live inside a conflict neither one of us created, and even though

both of us therefore hurt inside that conflict, I may be one of the monsters she needs to eliminate from her universe and, in a sense, she may be one of the monsters in mine. (1985, 47)

Differences in power constrain our ability to connect with one another even when we think we are engaged in dialogue across differences. . . .

In extreme cases, members of privileged groups can erase the very presence of the less privileged. When I first moved to Cincinnati, my family and I went on a picnic at a local park. Picnicking next to us was a family of White Appalachians. When I went to push my daughter on the swings, several of the children came over. They had missing, yellowed and broken teeth, they wore old clothing and their poverty was evident. I was shocked. Growing up in a large eastern city, I had never seen such awful poverty among Whites. The segregated neighborhoods in which I grew up made White poverty all but invisible. More importantly, the privileges attached to my newly acquired social class position allowed me to ignore and minimize the poverty among Whites that I did encounter. My reactions to those children made me realize how confining phrases such as "well, at least they're not Black," had become for me. In learning to grant human subjectivity to the Black victims of poverty, I had simultaneously learned to demand White victims of poverty. By applying categories of race to the objective conditions confronting me, I was quantifying and ranking oppressions and missing the very real suffering which, in fact, is the real issue.

One common pattern of relationships across differences in power is one that I label "voyeurism." From the perspective of the privileged, the lives of people of color, of the poor, and of women are interesting for their entertainment value. The privileged become voyeurs, passive onlookers who do not relate to the less powerful, but who are interested in seeing how the "different" live. Over the years, I have heard numerous African-American students complain about professors who never call on them except when a so-called Black issue is being discussed. The students' interest in discussing race or qualifications for doing so appear unimportant to the professor's efforts to use Black students' experiences as stories to make the material come alive for the White student audience. Asking Black students to perform on cue and provide a Black experience for their White classmates can be seen as voyeurism at its worst.

Members of subordinate groups do not willingly participate in such exchanges but often do so because members of dominant groups control the institutional and symbolic apparatuses of oppression. Racial/ethnic groups, women, and the poor have never had the luxury of being voyeurs of the lives of the privileged. Our ability to survive in hostile settings has hinged on our ability to learn intricate details about the behavior and worldview of the powerful and adjust our behavior accordingly. I need only point to the difference in perception of those men and women in abusive relationships. Where men can view their girlfriends and wives as sex objects, helpmates and a collection of stereotyped categories of voyeurism—women must be attuned to every nuance of their partners' behavior. Are women "naturally" better in relating to people with more power than themselves, or have circumstances mandated that men and women develop different skills? . . .

Coming from a tradition where most relationships across difference are squarely rooted in relations of domination and subordination, we have much less experience relating to people as different but equal. The classroom is potentially one powerful and safe space where dialogues among individuals of unequal power relationships can occur. . . .

2. COALITIONS AROUND COMMON CAUSES

A second issue in building relationships and coalitions essential for social change concerns knowing the real reasons for coalition. Just what brings people together? One powerful catalyst fostering group solidarity is the presence of a common enemy. African-American, Hispanic, Asian-American, and women's studies all share the common intellectual heritage of challenging what passes for certified knowledge in the academy. But politically expedient relationships and coalitions like these are fragile because, as June Jordan points out:

> It occurs to me that much organizational grief could be avoided if people understood that partnership in misery does not necessarily provide for partnership for change: When we get the monsters off our backs

all of us may want to run in very different directions. (1985, 47)

Sharing a common cause assists individuals and groups in maintaining relationships that transcend their differences. Building effective coalitions involves struggling to hear one another and developing empathy for each other's points of view. The coalitions that I have been involved in that lasted and that worked have been those where commitment to a specific issue mandated collaboration as the best strategy for addressing the issue at hand.

. . .

None of us alone has a comprehensive vision of how race, class and gender operate as categories of analysis or how they might be used as categories of connection. Our personal biographies offer us partial views. Few of us can manage to study race, class and gender simultaneously. Instead, we each know more about some dimensions of this larger story and less about others. . . . Just as the members of the school had special skills to offer to the task of building the school, we have areas of specialization and expertise, whether scholarly, theoretical, pedagogical or within areas of race, class or gender. We do not all have to do the same thing in the same way. Instead, we must support each other's efforts, realizing that they are all part of the larger enterprise of bringing about social change.

3. BUILDING EMPATHY

A third issue involved in building the types of relationships and coalitions essential for social change concerns the issue of individual accountability. Race, class and gender oppression form the structural backdrop against which we frame our relationship—these are the forces that encourage us to substitute voyeurism . . . for fully human relationships. But while we may not have created this situation, we are each responsible for making individual, personal choices concerning which elements of race, class and gender oppression we will accept and which we will work to change.

One essential component of this accountability involves developing empathy for the experiences of individuals and groups different than ourselves. Empathy begins with taking an interest in the facts of other people['s] lives, both as individuals and as groups. If you care about me, you should want to know not only the details of my personal biography but a sense of how race, class and gender as categories of analysis created the institutional and symbolic backdrop for my personal biography. How can you hope to assess my character without knowing the details of the circumstances I face?

Moreover, by taking a theoretical stance that we have all been affected by race, class and gender as categories of analysis that have structured our treatment, we open up possibilities for using those same constructs as categories of connection in building empathy. For example, I have a good White woman friend with whom I share common interests and beliefs. But we know that our racial differences have provided us with different experiences. So we talk about them. We do not assume that because I am Black, race has only affected me and not her or that because I am a Black woman, race neutralizes the effect of gender in my life while accenting it in hers. We take those same categories of analysis that have created cleavages in our lives, in this case, categories of race and gender, and use them as categories of connection in building empathy for each other's experiences.

Finding common causes and building empathy is difficult, no matter which side of privilege we inhabit. Building empathy from the dominant side of privilege is difficult, simply because individuals from privileged backgrounds are not encouraged to do so. For example, in order for those of you who are White to develop empathy for the experiences of people of color, you must grapple with how your white skin has privileged you. This is difficult to do, because it not only entails the intellectual process of seeing how whiteness is elevated in institutions and symbols, but it also involves the often painful process of seeing how your whiteness has shaped your personal biography. Intellectual stances against the institutional and symbolic dimensions of racism are generally easier to maintain than sustained self-reflection about how racism has shaped all of our individual biographies. Were and are your fathers, uncles, and grandfathers really more capable than mine, or can their accomplishments be explained in part by the racism members of my family experienced? Did your mothers stand silently by and watch all this happen?

More importantly, how have they passed on the benefits of their whiteness to you?

These are difficult questions, and I have tremendous respect for my colleagues and students who are trying to answer them. Since there is no compelling reason to examine the source and meaning of one's own privilege, I know that those who do so have freely chosen this stance. They are making conscious efforts to root out the piece of the oppressor planted within them. To me, they are entitled to the support of people of color in their efforts. Men who declare themselves feminists, members of the middle class who ally themselves with antipoverty struggles, heterosexuals who support gays and lesbians, are all trying to grow, and their efforts place them far ahead of the majority who never think of engaging in such important struggles.

Building empathy from the subordinate side of privilege is also difficult, but for different reasons. Members of subordinate groups are understandably reluctant to abandon a basic mistrust of members of powerful groups because this basic mistrust has traditionally been central to their survival. As a Black woman, it would be foolish for me to assume that White women, or Black men, or White men or any other group with a history of exploiting African-American women have my best interests at heart. These groups enjoy varying amounts of privilege over me and therefore I must carefully watch them and be prepared for a relation of domination and subordination.

Like the privileged, members of subordinate groups must also work toward replacing judgments by category with new ways of thinking and acting. Refusing to do so stifles prospects for effective coalition and social change. Let me use another example from my own experiences. When I was an undergraduate, I had little time or patience for the theorizing of the privileged. My initial years at a private, elite institution were difficult, not because the course work was challenging (it was, but that wasn't what distracted me) or because I had to work while my classmates lived on family allowances (I was used to work). The adjustment was difficult because I was surrounded by so many people who took their privilege for granted. Most of them felt entitled to their wealth. That astounded me.

I remember one incident of watching a White woman down the hall in my dormitory try to pick out which sweater to wear. The sweaters were piled up on her bed in all the colors of the rainbow, sweater after sweater. She asked my advice in a way that let me know that choosing a sweater was one of the most important decisions she had to make on a daily basis. Standing knee-deep in her sweaters, I realized how different our lives were. She did not have to worry about maintaining a solid academic average so that she could receive financial aid. Because she was in the majority, she was not treated as a representative of her race. She did not have to consider how her classroom comments or basic existence on campus contributed to the treatment her group would receive. Her allowance protected her from having to work, so she was free to spend her time studying, partying, or in her case, worrying about which sweater to wear. The degree of inequality in our lives and her unquestioned sense of entitlement concerning that inequality offended me. For a while, I categorized all affluent White women as being superficial, arrogant, overly concerned with material possessions, and part of my problem. But had I continued to classify people in this way, I would have missed out on making some very good friends whose discomfort with their inherited or acquired social class privileges pushed them to examine their position.

Since I opened with the words of Audre Lorde, it seems appropriate to close with another of her ideas. . . .

Each of us is called upon to take a stand. So in these days ahead, as we examine ourselves and each other, our works, our fears, our differences, our sisterhood and survivals, I urge you to tackle what is most difficult for us all, self-scrutiny of our complacencies, the idea that since each of us believes she is on the side of right, she need not examine her position. (1985)

I urge you to examine your position.

REFERENCES

Collins, Patricia Hill. 1989. "The Social Construction of Black Feminist Thought." *Signs.* Summer 1989.

Gwaltney, John Langston. 1980. *Drylongso: A Self-Portrait of Black America.* New York: Vintage.

Harding, Sandra. 1986. *The Science Question in Feminism.* Ithaca, NY: Cornell University Press.

Jordan, June. 1985. *On Call: Political Essays.* Boston: South End Press.

Lorde, Audre. 1984. *Sister Outsider.* Trumansberg, NY: The Crossing Press.

———. 1985. "Sisterhood and Survival." Keynote address, conference on the Black Woman Writer and the Diaspora, Michigan State University.

Spelman, Elizabeth. 1982. "Theories of Race and Gender: The Erasure of Black Women." *Quest* 5: 36–32.

Tate, Claudia, ed. 1983. *Black Women Writers at Work.* New York: Continuum.

9. INTERSECTIONALITY

VIVIAN M. MAY (2012)

The struggle to comprehend and implement intersectionality is epistemologically and politically significant for Women's and Gender studies (WGS), and suggests a problem of understanding that must be accounted for. As Susan Babbitt describes it, unpacking a problem of understanding entails first examining how "dominant expectations"—about rationality, subjectivity, narrative style, or form—tend to "rule out the meaningfulness of important struggles" and impede their ability to be understood (2001, 298).

Some discourses "are not able to be heard" (300); they seem unimaginable because of power asymmetries and injustices (308). Moreover, this implausibility is rarely questioned. Often, "people think they have understood . . . when they have not in fact understood what most needs to be understood" (303), so that, any difficulty in understanding (i.e., that there is something important that is still not yet understood from a normative stance) and the fundamental differences in world view are thereby put to the side. The alternative way of seeing becomes characterized merely as different or illogical: its meaning is flattened. I would argue that intersectionality's recursiveness signifies the degree to which its practices go against the grain of prevailing conceptualizations of personhood, rationality, and liberation politics, even in WGS.

PROBLEMS OF UNDERSTANDING AND NOMINAL USE

To better illustrate how elusive this shift in thinking can be, and because I am interested in well-intended applications of intersectionality that fall short, I first turn to a text that is widely taught in Women's and Gender Studies: Marilyn Frye's essay, "Oppression"—regularly included across the WGS curriculum because Frye's delineation of systemic "double-binds" (1983, 2) is useful. . . . Yet despite Frye's important contributions to examining oppression, and notwithstanding her intent to focus on how gender is interwoven with race, class, and sexuality, she slips away from developing the multifaceted analyses she sets out to undertake.

For example, Frye concludes her essay with a gender-universal analysis of patriarchy that posits the divide between men and women as primary, since, she argues, "men" are never denigrated or oppressed "as men." Frye explains, "whatever assaults and harassments [a man] is subject to, being male is not what selects him for victimization; . . . men are not oppressed as men" (1983, 16). To be taken up, Frye's analysis requires a form of "pop-bead" logic (Spelman 1988, 136, 186), wherein the gender "bead" of masculinity can be pulled apart from race, sexuality, social class, and other factors. Masculinity seems, therefore, not to be impacted by or intersected with disability, race, sexuality, or citizenship status, in an inextricable, dynamic way.

This atomization of multiplicity is also evident in that Frye is confident, in analyzing the politics of anger or of the smile, that "it is [her] being a woman that reduces the power of [her] anger to a proof of [her] insanity" (1983, 16). Perhaps Frye can presume it is her "being a woman" alone that is causal because she is white, able-bodied, and middle class—since

people who are marked as "different" by means of race, disability, and social class, for instance, are also often stereotyped as more irrationally "angry" than are members of privileged groups. Some women are perceived as "angrier" (or as inappropriately angry) in comparison to other women; likewise, some women are expected to show docility or compliance via smiles or silences to other women because of intertwined factors of (and asymmetries of power related to) race, class, sexuality, and ability.

Additionally, Frye's analysis of how women's dependency (4, 7–10) is derogated (while structurally reinforced) obscures how different forms of gendered dependency are differently derogated because gender is not isolatable from other facets of identity. Some forms of dependence (heteronormative, middle class) are more idealized (e.g., women's dependence on men who are their fathers or husbands for protection and care), whereas others are stigmatized as deviant and in need of remediation (e.g., poor women's dependency on the state via welfare). Both types of institutionalized dependency can be understood as oppressive, but differently so; one carries social stigma, the other social approval (even if, as feminist scholars, we may think it should not). Throughout her analysis of the workings of oppression, Frye includes reference to (and seeks to acknowledge) differences among women (of race, class, and sexuality), yet reverts to statements about women as a general group and to analyses of gender processes as not only homogenized but also isolatable from other factors and processes.

. . .

A SNAPSHOT OF INTERSECTIONALITY

Rather than assume "everyone understands intersectionality," I want to pause to summarize some of its central insights. Intersectionality calls for analytic methods, modes of political action, and ways of thinking about persons, rights, and liberation informed by multiplicity. It is both metaphorical and material, in that it seeks to capture something not adequately named about the nature of lived experience and about systems of oppression.

Intersectionality adds nuance to understanding different sites of feminism(s) and the multiple dimensions of lived experience, it lends insight into the interrelationships among struggle[s] for liberation, and . . . it shifts what "counts" as a feminist issue and what is included as gendered experience. Intersectionality offers a vision of future possibilities that can be more fully realized once a shift toward the multiple takes place. Its critical practices include:

- *Considering lived experience as a criterion of meaning:* Intersectionality focuses on how lived experience can be drawn upon to expose the partiality of normative modes of knowing (often deemed neutral) and to help marginalized groups articulate and develop alternative analyses and modes of oppositional consciousness, both individually and collectively.[1]
- *Reconceptualizing marginality and focusing on the politics of location:* Intersectionality considers marginalization in terms of social structure and lived experience and redefines "marginality as a potential source of strength," not merely "tragedy" (Collins 1998, 128). Lugones and Price insist that the marginalized, "create a sense of ourselves as historical subjects, not exhausted by intermeshed oppressions" (2003, 331). While hooks characterizes the margins as a "site of radical possibility, a space of resistance" (1990, 149), Lugones describes marginality as a site of the "resistant oppressed" wherein "you have ways of living in disruption of domination" (2006, 78, 79). Methodologically, attending to the politics of location entails accounting for the contexts of knowledge production (Bowleg 2008, 318; Jordan-Zachery 2007, 259) and thinking about the relevance of the knower to the known-factors usually considered outside the realm of knowledge "proper."[2]
- *Employing "both/and" thinking and centering multiracial feminist theorizing:* Moving away from "dichotomized" thought (Lugones 1990, 80) and "monolithic" analyses of identity, culture, and theory (Christian 1990, 341), intersectionality theorizes from a position of "simultaneity" (Nash 2008, 2; V. Smith 1998, xv).[3] Bridging the

theoretical and empirical (McCall 2005, 1780), and using "double vision " (Lugones 2006, 79), intersectionality "refers to both a normative theoretical argument and an approach to conducting empirical research that emphasizes the interaction of categories" (Hancock 2007, 63). While it is not merely the descriptive for which intersectionality was developed, it is often reduced to this.[4] As Shields explains: "Most behavioral science research that focuses on intersectionality . . . employs [it] as a perspective on research rather than as a theory that drives the research question. . . . [Intersectionality's] emergent properties and processes escape attention" (2008, 304).

- *Shifting toward an understanding of complex subjectivity:* Alongside an epistemological shift toward simultaneity and both/and reasoning is a shift toward subjectivity that accounts for "compoundedness" (Crenshaw 2000, 217); critiques of unitary knowledge and the unitary subject are linked (McCall 2005, 1776). Rather than approach multiple facets of identity as "noninteractive" and "independent" (Harnois 2005, 810), an intersectional approach focuses on indivisibility, a "complex ontology" (Phoenix and Pattynama 2006, 187) conceptualized as woven (Alarcón 1990, 366), kneaded (Anzaldúa 1990e, 380), and shifting (Valentine 2007, 15). This approach "denies any *one* perspective as the only answer, but instead posits a shifting tactical and strategic subjectivity that has the capacity to re-center depending upon the forms of oppression to be confronted" (Sandoval 2000, 67).
- *Analyzing systems of oppression as operating in a "matrix":* Connected to complex subjectivity are analyses of domination that account for relationships among forms of oppression. As Pauli Murray aptly put it, "The lesson of history that all human rights are indivisible and that the failure to adhere to this principle jeopardizes the rights of all is particularly applicable" (1995, 197). The Combahee River Collective insists on "the development of an integrated analysis and practice based upon the fact that the major systems of oppression are interlocking" (1983, 261).[5] A "single axis" approach "distorts" and "theoretically erases" differences

within and between groups (Crenshaw 2000, 209–17); multiple systems of power must therefore be addressed simultaneously.

- *Conceiving of solidarity or coalition without relying on homogeneity:* Rather than sameness as a foundation for alliance, Lorde attests, "You do not have to be me in order for us to fight alongside each other" (1984, 142).[6] Intersectionality pursues "'solidarity' through different political formations and . . . alternative theories of the subject of consciousness" (Alarcón 1990, 364). Mohanty advocates thinking about feminist solidarity in terms of mutuality, accountability, and the recognition of common interests as the basis for relationships among diverse communities. Rather than assuming an enforced commonality of oppression, the practice of solidarity foregrounds communities of people who have chosen to work and fight together. . . . [It] is always an achievement, the result of active struggle (2003, 78). This requires acknowledging that marginalization does not mean "we" should "naturally" be able to work together. Lugones urges us to "craft coalitional gestures" both communicatively and politically, since there is no guarantee of "transparency" between us, even margin to margin (2006, 80, 83).
- *Challenging false universals and highlighting omissions built into the social order and intellectual practices:* Intersectionality exposes how the experiences of some are often universalized to represent the experiences, needs, and claims of all group members. Rather than conceptualize group identity via a common denominator framework that subsumes within-group differences, creates rigid distinctions between groups, and leads to distorted analyses of discrimination, intersectionality explores the politics of the unimaginable, the invisible, and the silenced. Intersectionality understands exclusions and gaps as meaningful and examines the theoretical and political impact of such absences.[7]
- *Exploring the implications of simultaneous privilege and oppression:* In addition to focusing on the "relational nature of dominance and subordination" (Zinn and Dill 1996, 327)[8] and breaking open false universals, intersectionality focuses on how

personhood can be structured on internalized hierarchies or "arrogant perception" (Lugones 1990); thus "one may also 'become a woman' in opposition to other women" not just in opposition to "men" (Alarcón 1990, 360).[9] Normative ideas about identity categories as homogenous "limit[s] inquiry to the experiences of otherwise-privileged members of the group," and "marginalizes those who are multiply burdened and obscures claims that cannot be understood as resulting from discrete sources of discrimination" (Crenshaw 2000, 209). Intersectionality seeks to shift the logics of how we understand domination, subordination, personhood, and rights.

- *Identifying how a liberatory strategy may depend on hierarchy or reify privilege to operate:* Intersectionality offers tools for seeing how we often uphold the very forms of oppression that we seek to dismantle.[10] For instance, Crenshaw identifies how the court's normative view of race and sex discrimination means that the very legal frameworks meant to address inequality require a certain degree of privilege to function (2000, 213). She lays bare the court's "refusal to acknowledge compound discrimination" (214) and highlights the problem Lugones characterizes as a collusion with divide and conquer thinking (2006, 76).

We must ask some difficult questions. Do nods to intersectionality in WGS provide a "conceptual warrant" to avoid, if not suppress, multiplicity? Has intersectionality's critical lexicon, forged in struggle, been co-opted and flattened rather than engaged with as an epistemological and political lens? We must address the common notion that "everyone" already "does" intersectionality; even if one agrees, for the sake of argument, that "we" all "do" intersectional work, the question remains, how? Does intersectionality shape research, pedagogy, or curriculum structure from the start, or is it tacked on or tokenized? How does intersectionality translate into methodology, be it qualitative, quantitative, literary, or philosophical? Is it reduced to a descriptive tool or conceptualized as impossible? Do its key insights slip away, even in well-intended applications? Statements about intersectionality's having "arrived" beg the question Collins raises when she wonders whether it is being adopted primarily as the latest "overarching" terminology to explain both the matrices of identity and of systems of oppression, but in a way that obscures complexities. She writes: "If we are not careful, the term 'intersectionality' runs the . . . risk of trying to explain everything yet ending up saying nothing" (2008, 72).

NOTES

1. See Anzaldúa 1999; Christian 1990; Collins 1990; Crenshaw 2000; Combahee 1983; Guy-Sheftall 1995.
2. See Anzaldúa 1999; Zinn and Dill 1996, 328; Lugones 2006, 76–78; Sandoval 2000, 86.
3. See Anzaldúa 1990a, 145 and 1990b, 378; Henderson 1989, 117; Phoenix and Pattynama 2006, 187; Sandoval 2000, 88.
4. See Bowleg 2008, 316–18; Hancock 2007, 66; Harnois 2005, 813; Jordan-Zachery 2007, 261.
5. See Beale 1970, 92–93; Collins 2008, 72 and 2004, 95–96; Jordan-Zachery 2007, 259; King 1988; Lemons 2001, 87; Lorde 1984, 140; B. Smith 1983, xxxii–xxviii; Zinn and Dill 1996, 237.
6. See Alarcón 1990, 366; Lemons 2001, 87; B. Smith 1983, xliii.
7. See Alarcón 1990, 356; Bowleg 2008, 312; Crenshaw 2000, 223; A. Davis 1984; DuCille 2001, 254; Henderson 1989, 117; Jordan Zachery 2007, 254; Ringrose 2007, 267; Sandoval 2000, 75–76.
8. See Anzaldúa 1990c, xix; and Minh-ha 1990, 375.
9. See Crenshaw 2000, 209–13; Lorde 1984, 67, 132; Lemons 2001, 86–87; Neal 1995.
10. See Alarcón 1990; Anzaldúa 1990c and 1990d; McCall 2005; Murray 1995; Nnaemeka 2003.

REFERENCES

Alarcón, Norma. 1990. "The Theoretical Subject(s) of This Bridge Called My Back and Anglo American Feminism." In *Making Face, Making Soul* Haciendo Caras: *Creative and Critical Perspectives by Feminists of Color*, edited by Gloria E. Anzaldúa, 356–69. San Francisco: Aunt Lute Books.

Anzaldúa, Gloria. 1990a. "*En rapport*, In Opposition: Cobrando cuentas a las nuestras." In *Making Face, Making Soul* Haciendo Caras: *Creative and Critical Perspectives by Feminists of Color*, edited by Gloria E. Anzaldúa, 143–48. San Francisco: Aunt Lute Books.

Anzaldúa, Gloria. 1990b. "*Hanblando cara a cara/* Speaking Face to Face." In *Making Face, Making Soul* Haciendo Caras: *Creative and Critical Perspectives by Feminists of Color*, edited by Gloria E. Anzaldúa, 46–54. San Francisco: Aunt Lute Books.

Anzaldúa, Gloria. 1990c. "*Haciendo caras, una entrada.*" In *Making Face, Making Soul* Haciendo Caras: *Creative and Critical Perspectives by Feminists of Color*, edited by Gloria E. Anzaldúa, xv–xxviii. San Francisco: Aunt Lute Books.

Anzaldúa, Gloria. 1990d. "*La conciencia de la mestiza:* Towards a New Consciousness." In *Making Face, Making Soul* Haciendo Caras: *Creative and Critical Perspectives by Feminists of Color*, edited by Gloria E. Anzaldúa, 377–89. San Francisco: Aunt Lute Books.

Anzaldúa, Gloria. 1990e. "Bridge, Drawbridge, Sandbar, Island: Lesbians of Color Hacienda Alianzas." In *Bridges of Power*, edited by L. Albrecht and R. Brewer, 316–31. Philadelphia: New Society.

Anzaldúa, Gloria. 1999. *Borderlands*/La frontera: *The New Mestiza*. San Francisco: Aunt Lute Books. First published 1987.

Babbitt, Susan E. 2001. "Objectivity and the Role of Bias." In *Engendering Rationalities*, edited by Nancy Tuana and Sandra Morgen, 297–314. Albany: SUNY Press.

Bailey, Alison. 1998. "Privilege: Expanding on Marilyn Frye's 'Oppression'." *Journal of Social Philosophy* 29 (3): 104–19.

Beale 1970. "Double Jeopardy: To Be Black and Female." In *The Black Woman*, edited by Toni Cade, 90–100. New York: Mentor.

Bowleg, Lisa. 2008. "When Black + Lesbian + Woman ≠ Black Lesbian Woman: The Methodological Challenges of Qualitative and Quantitative Intersectionality Research." *Sex Roles* 59 (5–6): 312–25.

Carbado, Devon W. 1999. *Black Men on Race, Gender, and Sexuality.* New York: New York University Press.

Christian, Barbara. 1990. "The Race for Theory." In *Making Face, Making Soul* Haciendo Caras: *Creative and Critical Perspectives by Feminists of Color,* edited by Gloria E. Anzaldúa, 335–45. San Francisco: Aunt Lute Books.

———. 1998. *Fighting Words: Black Women and the Search for Justice.* Minneapolis: University of Minnesota.

———. 2004. *Black Sexual Politics: African Americans, Gender, and the New Racism.* New York: Routledge.

———. 2008. "Reply to Commentaries: Blacks Sexual Politics Revisited." *Studies in Gender and Sexuality* 9: 68–85.Collins, Patricia Hill, *Black Feminist Thought: Knowledge, Consciousness, and the Politics of Empowerment.* Boston: Unwin Hyman, 1990.

Collins, Patricia Hill. 1998. *Fighting Words: Black Women and the Search for Justice.* Minneapolis: University of Minnesota Press.

———. 2008. *Black Feminist Thought: Knowledge, Consciousness and the Politics of Empowerment.* New York: Routledge.

Combahee River Collective. 1983. "The Combahee River Collective Statement." In *Home Girls: A Black Feminist Anthology,* edited by Barbara Smith, 272–82. New York: Kitchen Table Press. First Published 1977

Cooper, Anna Julia. 1988. *A Voice from the South by a Black Woman of the South.* New York: Oxford University Press. First Published 1892.

———. 1925. *L'Attitude de la France à l'égard de l'esclavage pendant la Révolution.* Paris: impr. de la cour d'appel, L. Maretheux.

Crenshaw, Kimberlé. 2000. "Demarginalizing the Intersection of Race and Sex: A Black Feminist Critique of Antidiscrimination Doctrine, Feminist Theory, and Antiracist Politics." In *The Black Feminist Reader,* edited by Joy James and T. Denean Sharpley-Whiting, 208–38. Maiden: Blackwell.

Davis, Angela Y. 1984. *Women, Race and Class.* New York: Vintage.

Davis, Kathy. 2008. "Intersectionality as Buzzword: A Sociology of Science Perspective on What Makes a Feminist Theory Successful." *Feminist Theory* 9 (1): 67-85.

DuCille, Anne. 2001. "The Occult of True Black Womanhood: Critical Demeanor and Black Feminist Studies." In *Feminism & "Race,"* edited by Kum-Kum Bhavnani, 233–60. New York: Oxford University Press.

Frye, Marilyn. 1983. "Oppression." In *The Politics of Reality: Essays in Feminist Theory,* 1–16. Trumansburg: Crossing Press.

Giddings Paula J. 2006. "Editor's Introduction." *Meridians* 7 (1): v–vii.

———. 1995b. "The Evolution of Feminist Consciousness Among African American Women." In *Words of Fire,* 1–22. New York: New Press.

Guy-Sheftall, Beverly. *Words of Fire: An Anthology of African-American Feminist Thought.* New York: The New Press, 1995.

Hancock, Ange-Marie. 2007. "When Multiplication Doesn't Equal Quick Addition: Examining Intersectionality as a Research Paradigm." *Perspectives Politics* 5 (1): 63–79.

Harnois, Catherine. 2005. "Different Paths to Different Feminisms? Bridging Multiracial Feminist Theory and Quantitative Sociological Gender Research." *Gender & Society* 19 (6): 309–28.

Henderson, Mae Gwendolyn. 1989. "Speaking in Tongues: Dialogism and the Black Woman Writer's Literary Tradition." In *Changing Our Own Words: Essays on Criticism, Theory, and Writing by Black Women,* edited by Cheryl A. Wall, 16–37. New Brunswick, NJ: Rutgers University Press.

Holloway, Karla F. C. 2006. "'Cruel Enough to Stop the Blood': Global Feminisms and the U.S. Body Politic, Or: 'They Done Taken My Blues and Gone'." *Meridians: Feminism, Race, Transnationalism* 7 (1): 1–18.

hooks, bell. 1990. *Yearning: Race, Gender, and Cultural Politics.* Boston: South End Press.

Jordan-Zachery, Julia. 2007. "Am I a Black Woman or a Woman Who Is Black? A Few Thoughts on the Meaning of Intersectionality." *Politics & Gender* 3 (2): 254–63.

King, Deborah K. 1988. "Multiple Jeopardy, Multiple Consciousness: The Context of a Black Feminist Ideology." *Signs: Journal of Women in Culture and Society* 14 (1): 42–72.

Lemons, Gary L. 2001. "'When and Where [We] Enter': In Search of a Feminist Forefather— Reclaiming the Womanist Legacy of W.E.B. DuBois." In *Traps: African American Men on Gender and Sexuality*, edited by Rudolph P. Byrd and Beverly Guy-Sheftall, 71–89. Bloomington: Indiana University Press.

Lorde, Audre. 1984. *Sister Outsider: Essays and Speeches by Audre Lorde*. Berkeley: The Crossing Press.

Lugones, Maria. 1990. "Playfulness, 'World' Traveling and Loving Perception." In *Making Face, Making Soul* Haciendo Caras: *Creative and Critical Perspectives by Feminists of Color*, edited by Gloria E. Anzaldúa, 390–402. San Francisco: Aunt Lute Books.

———. 2006. "On Complex Communication." *Hypatia* 21 (3): 75–85.

Lugones, María, and Joshua Price. 2003. "The Inseparability of Race, Class, and Gender." *Latino Studies Journal* 1 (2): 329–32.

Lugones, María, and Elizabeth Spelman. 2005. "Have We Got a Theory for You!: Feminist Theory, Cultural Imperialism and the Demand For 'The Woman's Voice'." In *Feminist Theory: A Reader*, edited by Wendy Kolmar and Frances Bartkowski. New York: McGraw Hill.

Maparyan, Layli. 2012. *The Womanist Idea*. New York: Routledge.

McCall, Leslie. 2005. "The Complexity of Intersectionality." *Signs: Journal of Women in Culture and Society* 30 (3): 1771–1800.

Min-ha, Trinh T. 1990. "Not You/Like You: Post-Colonial Women and the Interlocking Questions of Identity and Difference." In *Making Face, Making Soul* Haciendo Caras: *Creative and Critical Perspectives by Feminists of Color*, edited by Gloria E. Anzaldúa, 371–75. San Francisco: Aunt Lute Books.

Mohanty, Chandra Talpade. 2003. *Feminism without Borders: Decolonizing Theory, Practicing Solidarity*. Durham, NC: Duke University Press.

Murray, Pauli. 1995. "The Liberation of Black Women." In *Words of Fire: An Anthology of African-American Feminist Thought*, edited by Beverly Guy-Sheftall, 186–97. New York: New Press.

Nash, Jennifer. 2008. "Re-Thinking Intersectionality." *Feminist Review* 89 (1) 1–15.

Neal, Mark Anthony. 1995. *New Black Man*. New York: Routledge.

Nnaemeka, Obioma. 2003. "Nego-Feminism: Theorizing, Practicing, and Pruning Africa's Way." *Signs: Journal of Women in Culture and Society* 29 (2): 357–85.

Phoenix, Ann, and Pamela Pattynama. 2006. "Intersectionality." *European Journal of Women's Studies* 13 (3): 187–92.

Ringrose, Jessica. 2007. *Am I That Name?: Feminism and the Category "Women" in History*. New York: MacMillan.

Sandoval, Chela. 2000. *Methodology of the Oppressed*. Minneapolis: University of Minnesota Press.

Shields, Stephanie. 2008. "Gender: An Intersectionality Perspective." *Sex Roles* 59 (5–6): 301–11.

Smith, Barbara, ed. 1983. *Home Girls: A Black Feminist Anthology*. New York: Kitchen Table, Women of Color Press.

Smith, Valerie. 1998. *Not Just Race, Not Just Gender: Black Feminist Readings*. New York: Routledge.

Spelman, Elizabeth V. 1988. *Inessential Woman: Problems of Exclusion in Feminist Thought*. Boston: Beacon.

Valentine, Gill. 2007. "Theorizing and Researching Intersectionality: A Challenge for Feminist Geography." *The Professional Geographer* 59 (1): 10–21.

Zinn, Maxine Baca, and Bonnie Thornton Dill. 1996. "Theorizing Difference from Multiracial Feminism." *Feminist Studies* 22 (2): 321–33.

10. THERE IS NO HIERARCHY OF OPPRESSION

AUDRE LORDE (1983)

I was born Black, and a woman. I am trying to become the strongest person I can become to live the life I have been given and to help effect change toward a livable future for this earth and for my children. As a Black, lesbian, feminist, socialist, poet, mother of two, including one boy, and a member of an interracial couple, I usually find myself part of some group in which the majority defines me as deviant, difficult, inferior, or just plain "wrong."

From my membership in all of these groups I have learned that oppression and the intolerance of difference come in all shapes and sizes and colors and sexualities; and that among those of us who share the goals of liberation and a workable future for our children, there can be no hierarchies of oppression. I have learned that sexism (a belief in the inherent superiority of one sex over all others and thereby its right to dominance) and heterosexism (a belief in the inherent superiority of one pattern of loving over all others and thereby its right to dominance) both arise from the same source as racism—a belief in the inherent superiority of one race over all others and thereby its right to dominance.

"Oh," says a voice from the Black community, "but being Black is NORMAL!" Well, I and many Black people of my age can remember grimly the days when it didn't used to be!

I simply do not believe that one aspect of myself can possibly profit from the oppression of any other part of my identity. I know that my people cannot possibly profit from the oppression of any other group which seeks the right to peaceful existence. Rather, we diminish ourselves by denying to others what we have shed blood to obtain for our children. And those children need to learn that they do not have to become like each other in order to work together for a future they will all share.

The increasing attacks upon lesbians and gay men are only an introduction to the increasing attacks upon all Black people, for wherever oppression manifests itself in this country, Black people are potential victims. And it is a standard of rightwing cynicism to encourage members of oppressed groups to act against each other, and so long as we are divided because of our particular identities we cannot join together in effective political action.

Within the lesbian community I am Black, and within the Black community I am a lesbian. Any attack against Black people is a lesbian and gay issue, because I and thousands of other Black women are part of the lesbian community. Any attack against lesbians and gays is a Black issue, because thousands of lesbians and gay men are Black. There is no hierarchy of oppression.

It is not accidental that the Family Protection Act,[1] which is virulently antiwoman and antiblack, is also antigay. As a black person, I know who my enemies are, and when the Ku Klux Klan goes to court in Detroit to try and force the board of education to remove books the Klan believes "hint at homosexuality," then I know I cannot afford the luxury of fighting one form of oppression only. I cannot afford to believe that freedom from intolerance is the right of only one particular group. And I cannot afford to choose between the fronts upon which I must battle these forces of discrimination, wherever they appear to destroy me. And when they appear to destroy me, it will not be long before they appear to destroy you.

NOTE

1. A 1981 congressional bill repealing federal laws that promoted equal rights for women, including coeducational school-related activities and protection for battered wives, and providing tax incentives for married mothers to stay at home.

11. EXPLAINING WHITE PRIVILEGE TO A BROKE WHITE PERSON

GINA CROSLEY-CORCORAN (2014)

Years ago some feminist on the Internet told me I was "privileged."

"THE F&CK!?!?" I said.

I came from the kind of poor that people don't want to believe still exists in this country. Have you ever spent a frigid northern-Illinois winter without heat or running water? I have. At 12 years old were you making ramen noodles in a coffee maker with water you fetched from a public bathroom? I was. Have you ever lived in a camper year-round and used a random relative's apartment as your mailing address? We did. Did you attend so many different elementary schools that you can only remember a quarter of their names? Welcome to my childhood.

So when that feminist told me I had "white privilege," I told her that my white skin didn't do crap to prevent me from experiencing poverty. Then, like any good, educated feminist would, she directed me to Peggy McIntosh's now-famous 1988 piece "White Privilege: Unpacking the Invisible Knapsack."

After one reads McIntosh's powerful essay, it's impossible to deny that being born with white skin in America affords people certain unearned privileges in life that people of other skin colors simply are not afforded. For example:

> "I can turn on the television or open to the front page of the paper and see people of my race widely represented."
>
> "When I am told about our national heritage or about 'civilization,' I am shown that people of my color made it what it is."
>
> "If a traffic cop pulls me over or if the IRS audits my tax return, I can be sure I haven't been singled out because of my race."
>
> "I can if I wish arrange to be in the company of people of my race most of the time."

If you read through the rest of the list, you can see how white people and people of color experience the world in very different ways. But listen: This is not said to make white people feel guilty about their privilege. It's not your fault that you were born with white skin and experience these privileges. But whether you realize it or not, you *do* benefit from it, and it *is* your fault if you don't maintain awareness of that fact.

I do understand that McIntosh's essay may rub some people the wrong way. There are several points on the list that I felt spoke more to the author's status as a middle-class person than to her status as a white person. For example:

> "If I should need to move, I can be pretty sure of renting or purchasing housing in an area, which I can afford and in which I would want to live."
>
> "I can be pretty sure that my neighbors in such a location will be neutral or pleasant to me."
>
> "I can go shopping alone most of the time, pretty well assured that I will not be followed or harassed."
>
> "If I want to, I can be pretty sure of finding a publisher for this piece on white privilege."

And there are so many more points in the essay where the word "class" could be substituted for the word "race," which would ultimately paint a very different picture. That is why I had such a hard time identifying with this essay for so long. When I first wrote about white privilege years ago, I demanded to know why this white woman felt that my experiences were the same as hers when, no, my family most certainly could not rent housing "in an area which we could afford and want to live," and no, I couldn't go shopping without fear in our low-income neighborhoods.

The idea that any ol' white person can find a publisher for a piece is most certainly a symptom of class privilege. Having come from a family of people who didn't even graduate from high school, who knew not a single academic or intellectual person, it would never occur to me to assume that I could be published. It is absolutely a freak anomaly that I'm in graduate school, considering that not one person on either side of my family has a college degree. And it took me until my 30s to ever believe that someone from my stock could achieve such a thing. Poverty colors nearly everything about your perspective on opportunities for advancement in life. Middle-class, educated people assume that anyone can achieve their goals if they work hard enough. Folks steeped in poverty rarely see a life past working at the gas station, making the rent on their trailer, and self-medicating with cigarettes and prescription drugs until they die of a heart attack. (I've just described one whole side of my family and the life I assumed I'd be living before I lucked out of it.)

I, maybe more than most people, can completely understand why broke white folks get pissed when the word "privilege" is thrown around. As a child I was constantly discriminated against because of my poverty, and those wounds still run very deep. But luckily my college education introduced me to a more nuanced concept of privilege: the term "intersectionality." The concept of intersectionality recognizes that people can be privileged in some ways and definitely not privileged in others. There are many different types of privilege, not just skin-color privilege, that impact the way people can move through the world or are discriminated against. These are all things you are born into, not things you earned, that afford you opportunities that others may not have. For example:

Citizenship: Simply being born in this country affords you certain privileges that non-citizens will never access.

Class: Being born into a financially stable family can help guarantee your health, happiness, safety, education, intelligence, and future opportunities.

Sexual orientation: If you were born straight, every state in this country affords you privileges that non-straight folks have to fight the Supreme Court for.

Sex: If you were born male, you can assume that you can walk through a parking garage without worrying that you'll be raped and then have to deal with a defense attorney blaming it on what you were wearing.

Ability: If you were born able-bodied, you probably don't have to plan your life around handicap access, braille, or other special needs.

Gender identity: If you were born cisgender (that is, your gender identity matches the sex you were assigned at birth), you don't have to worry that using the restroom or locker room will invoke public outrage.

As you can see, belonging to one or more category of privilege, especially being a straight, white, middle-class, able-bodied male, can be like winning a lottery you didn't even know you were playing. But this is not to imply that any form of privilege is exactly the same as another, or that people lacking in one area of privilege understand what it's like to be lacking in other areas. Race discrimination is not equal to sex discrimination and so forth.

And listen: Recognizing privilege doesn't mean suffering guilt or shame for your lot in life. Nobody's saying that straight, white, middle-class, able-bodied males are all a bunch of assholes who don't work hard for what they have. Recognizing privilege simply means being aware that some people have to work much harder just to experience the things you take for granted (if they ever can experience them at all).

I know now that I *am* privileged in many ways. I am privileged as a natural born white citizen. I am privileged as a cisgender woman. I am privileged as an able-bodied person. I am privileged that my first language is also our national language, and that I was born with an intellect and ambition that pulled me out of the poverty that I was otherwise destined for. I was privileged to be able to marry my way "up" by partnering with a privileged, middle-class, educated male who fully expected me to earn a college degree.

There are a million ways I experience privilege, and some that I certainly don't. But thankfully, intersectionality allows us to examine these varying dimensions and degrees of discrimination while raising awareness of the results of multiple systems of oppression at work.

Tell me: Are you a white person who's felt uncomfortable with the term "white privilege"? Does a more nuanced approach help you see your own privilege more clearly?

12. WHAT DETERMINES HOW AMERICANS PERCEIVE THEIR SOCIAL CLASS?

ROBERT BIRD AND FRANK NEWPORT (2017)

The term "social class" is commonly used in American culture today but is not well-defined or well-understood. Most of us have a sense of a hierarchy in society, from low to high, based on income, wealth, power, culture, behavior, heritage and prestige. The word "class" appended after terms such as "working," "ruling," "lower" and "upper" is a shorthand way to describe these hierarchical steps, but with generally vague conceptions of what those terms mean.

A focus on *objective* social class entails a direct determination of a person's social class based on socioeconomic variables—mainly income, wealth, education and occupation. A second approach to social class, the one that occupies us here, deals with how people put themselves into categories. This is *subjective* social class—an approach that has its difficulties but helps explain class from the perspective of the people. This is important since the way people define a situation has real consequences on its outcome.

Gallup has, for a number of years, asked Americans to place themselves—without any guidance— into five social classes: upper, upper-middle, middle, working and lower. These five class labels are representative of the general approach used in popular language and by researchers. Gallup's last analysis showed that 3% of Americans identified themselves as upper class, 15% as upper-middle class, 43% as middle class, 30% as working class and 8% as lower class—with noted changes in these self-categorizations over time.

What goes into determining the class into which Americans put themselves? We can't measure all possible variables theoretically related to class self-placement, including, in particular, family heritage and background, prestige of residential area, behavior relating to clothes, cars, houses, manners, spouses and family context. But, we can look at the statistical relationship between social class placement and a list of socioeconomic and demographic variables included in an aggregation of three Gallup surveys conducted in the fall of 2016. This analysis controls for all other variables, allowing us to pinpoint the independent impact of each variable on social class identification.

As we would expect, income is a powerful determinant of the social class into which people place themselves, as is, to a lesser degree, education. Age makes a difference, even controlling for income and education, as does region, race, whether a person is working, and one's urban, suburban, or rural residence.

Americans' political party identification, ideology, marital status and gender make no difference in how they define themselves, once the other variables are controlled for.

The accompanying graph displays the relationship between income and subjective social class. The statistical model we discussed above is based on the complex analysis of the totality of all of the variables at once; the data represented in the table are the simple display of social class identification at each income level.

- At the lowest level of yearly household income included in this study (under $20,000 a year), people are equally likely to identify as "lower," "working" and "middle."

- Identification as lower class drops rapidly as income increases, while identification as working and middle class increase. Among Americans with incomes between $30,000 and $40,000, for example, well below the median income for the U.S., less than 10% identify as lower class. Working class is modestly more prevalent than middle class.

- We see a change at around $40,000; people at that level become more likely to say they are middle class and less likely to say they are working class.

- Working class identification shrinks significantly at the $75,000–$99,000 yearly income level. Middle class still dominates, but upper-middle class becomes somewhat more predominant.

- $150,000 is the income level at which upper-middle class becomes the most dominant social class identification—with almost all of those who don't choose upper-middle class settling on middle class.

- Finally, a third of Americans making $250,000 a year and more, the highest broad group we

Social class identification by household income

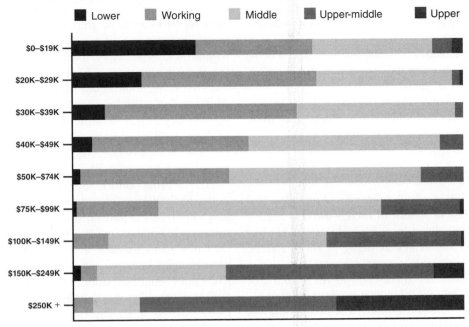

Gallup, Sep 14–18, Oct 5–9, Dec 7–11, 2016

represent in the graph, identify as upper class, with most of the rest as upper-middle. There are few people in our survey who say they make $500,000 a year or more, and of this small group—not represented in the chart because of small sample sizes—only about half say they are upper class. Most of the rest identify as upper-middle class.

The biggest impact of **education** on subjective social class comes at the college graduate level, at which point working-class identification drops significantly, with a concomitant rise in identification as upper-middle class. Middle-class identification is surprisingly constant across all levels of education. Less than half identify as working class at any educational level.

Social class identification by education level

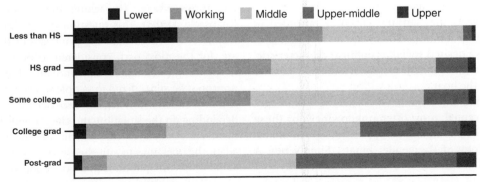

Gallup, Sep 14–18, Oct 5–9, Dec 7–11, 2016

The biggest impact of **age** comes among those who are 65 and older, who are more likely to identify with a higher social class compared with younger people.

There is an impact of **race**. Everything else being equal, whites are more likely than nonwhites to identify with a higher social class.

People living in **rural areas** are less likely to identify in a higher social class compared with those living in urban and suburban areas.

FINAL THOUGHTS

While in many minds there may be a lower class and an upper class in American society today, relatively few Americans at any income or education level like to think of themselves as being in those classes. Americans with very low socioeconomic status are just as likely to see themselves in the working or middle class as in the lower class, while Americans with very high socioeconomic status view themselves in the upper-middle class rather than the upper class.

The data support, to some degree, the popular conception of a dividing point at the college graduate level between those who are working class and those who are not. Still, less than 40% of Americans without a college degree identify as working class. For those with a high school degree or some college education, middle class edges out working class, while for those with less than high school education, the majority identify as either middle or lower class. In short, Americans' resonance with the label "working class" is not as substantial as might have been expected, even for those without college degrees.

The fact that political identity doesn't affect subjective social class is important, given the extraordinary importance of partisanship on so much else that shows up in our data. In other words, for people with the same socioeconomic and demographic characteristics, being a Democrat doesn't make one more likely than being a Republican to identify as working class. Nor does being a Republican make one more likely than being a Democrat to identify as upper-middle or upper class.

13. CISGENDER PRIVILEGE

EVIN TAYLOR (2010)

The latin prefix "cis," loosely translated, means "on this side," while the prefix "trans" is generally understood to mean "change, crossing, or beyond" Cisgender people are those whose gender identity, role, or expression is considered to match their assigned gender by societal standards. Transgender people are individuals who change, cross, or live beyond gender.

Privilege is the "cultural currency" afforded to a person or group of persons who are recognized as possessing a desired social or political characteristic. Privilege is the stability society affords us when we don't rock the boat.

Gendered privilege is the collective advantages that are accepted, most often unknowingly, by those who are not positioned in opposition to the dominant ideology of the gender binary. Simply put: A person who is able to live in a life and/or body that

is easily recognized as being either man/male or woman/female generally needs to spend less energy to be understood by others. The energy one need not expend to explain their gender identity and/or expression to others is gendered privilege.

The following questionnaire was inspired by Peggy McIntosh's article "Unpacking the Invisible White Knapsack" (1988). This questionnaire is intended to inspire some insight into the privileges of those who are, for the most part, considered to be performing normative gender. It is certainly not an exhaustive list, nor can it be generalized to people in every social position. Gendered privilege is experienced differently depending on the situation and the individual people involved. Readers of this article are encouraged to adapt the questions to suit their own positioning and to come up with questions that can be added to the list.

1. Can you be guaranteed to find a public bathroom that is safe and equipped for you to use?
2. Can you be sure to find a picture of someone whose gender expression resembles yours somewhere on a magazine rack?
3. Can you be reasonably sure whether to check the M or F box on a form?
4. Can you be reasonably sure that your choice of checked box on such forms will not subject you to legal prosecution of fraud or misrepresentation of identity?
5. Are you able to assume that your genitals conform relatively closely to portrayals of "normal" bodies?
6. Can you expect to find a doctor willing to provide you with urgent medical care?
7. Are you able to make a decision to be a parent without being told that you are confused about your gender?
8. Can you be confident that your health care providers will not ask to see your genitals when treating you for a sore throat?
9. Can you be confident that your health care providers will provide treatment for your health concerns without assuming that you chose to be ill?
10. Can you obtain a passport and travel without government employees asking explicit questions regarding your genitals?
11. Do people often act as if they are doing you a favor by using the appropriate pronouns for your gender?
12. Can you undress in a public changing room without risk of being assaulted or reported?
13. Are you able to discuss your childhood without disguising your gender?
14. Can you provide government identification without risking ridicule for your name or legal sex status?
15. Do you need to prove your gender before others will refer to you with your chosen name and pronouns?
16. Can you wear a socially acceptable bathing suit?
17. Does the government require proof of the state of your genitals in order to change information on your personal identification?
18. Are incidental parts of your identity defined as a mental illness?
19. Can you reasonably expect to be sexual with your consenting partner of choice without being told you have a mental illness?
20. Do other people consider your lifestyle a mental illness?
21. How many mental illnesses can be put into total remission through medical surgeries?
22. Can you expect that your gender identity will not be used against you when applying for employment?
23. Do your sexual preferences cause people to assume that your gender identity is mistaken?
24. Can you expect to be reasonably eligible to adopt children if you should choose to?
25. Do people assume that they know everything about you because they saw an investigative news episode about plastic surgery?
26. On most days, can you expect to interact with someone of a gender similar to your own?
27. Can you expect to find a landlord willing to rent to someone of your gender?
28. Do teachings about your national and cultural history acknowledge the existence of people of your gender identity?
29. Can you be sure that your children will not be harassed at school because of your gender?
30. Can you be sure that school teachers will not try to convince your children that their understanding of their family members' bodies is incorrect?
31. Are you able to use your voice and speak in public without risk of being ridiculed?
32. Can you discuss feminism with others without the appearance of your genitals being called into question?
33. Can you freely use checks, credit cards, or government-issued ID in a grocery store without being accused of using stolen finances?
34. Can you wait at a bus stop at noon without passers-by assuming that you are working in the survival sex trade?
35. If you are asked for proof-of-age in order to purchase tobacco or alcohol, can you be reasonably sure that the cashier is trying to prove your age, not your gender?

36. Can you be reasonably sure that, when dating someone new, they will be interested in getting to know your personality over and above your medical history?

37. Can you smile at a young child without their parents scorning or explaining you to the child?

38. Can you be sure that your gender identity doesn't automatically label you as an outsider, an anomaly, abnormal, or something to be feared?

39. Can you argue for gender equality without your right or motivation to do so being questioned?

40. Does the state of your genitals cause you to fear violence if they are discovered?

41. Are your height, weight, muscle mass, or hair follicles used as "proof" that your gender identity is mistaken?

42. Are your height, weight, muscle mass, or hair follicles consistently pointed out as being incongruent with your gender?

43. Are your basic healthcare needs minimized by others who contrast them in priority with lifesaving surgeries?

44. Can you find a religious community that will not exclude you based upon your genital or hormonal structures?

45. If you are having a difficult time making new friends, can you generally be sure that it is not because of your gender identity?

46. Can you choose whether or not to think of your gender as a political or social construct?

47. When you tell people your name, do they ask you what your "real" name is?

48. Can you consider social, political, or professional advancements without having to consider whether or not your gender identity will be called into question as being appropriate for advancement?

49. Do people assume that they have a right to hear, and therefore ask, about your intimate medical history or future?

50. Can you find gendered privilege in other places?

14. DON'T LAUGH, IT'S SERIOUS, SHE SAYS

ELLIE MAMBER (1985)

At 55, I'm trying to meet men.
But though I look my best
(beautiful say some
of my friends) & am spirited
& very interesting (you can
tell this, can't you?)
most men look at me with blank eyes,
no part of them flickering.
At parties they talk around me
as though I weren't there,
choose less attractive
partners to dance or talk with.
Such a puzzle! I try
so hard not to let them know
that I am smarter, more
talented, classier & more

interesting than they. Nicer, too.
I cover this so well
with a friendly smile
& a cheerful word
that they could never tell
I want them to pursue me
so I can reject them.
Bug off, you bastards,
balding middle-aged men with paunches
hanging around women 20 years
younger, who the hell
do you think you are?
You'd better hurry up
and adore me or
it will be too late.

15. DISABILITY AND SOCIAL JUSTICE

TEODOR MLADENOV (2016)

Disability has consistently been marginalised by critical theorists and social activists alike. Most thinkers and campaigners concerned with social justice have perceived their work as unrelated to what has routinely been regarded as a specialist domain of research and campaigning. This point about the side-lining of disability has previously been made by disability scholars—for example, Davis (2002, 147) lamented the widespread assumption that disability does not constitute 'a serious category of oppression', contrasting the progressives' indignation with racism and sexism to their indifference towards ableism. Let me provide two recent examples of such disregard of disability taken from the domains of critical theory and activism.

In a radical critique of contemporary capitalism, Jonathan Crary (2014) characterises our technologically interconnected world by the injunction to perform that incorporates people into homogeneous space and time of uninterrupted and constantly accelerating production and consumption. Crary regards sleep as the last frontier before the total submission of humans to the profit-making imperatives of the globalised techno-capital. He conceptualises sleep as a vulnerability that defies the instrumental calculus of the 24/7 world of contemporary capitalism: "Sleep is the only remaining barrier, the only enduring 'natural condition' that capitalism cannot eliminate" (Crary 2014, 74). I find it remarkable that Crary does not see disability in similar terms, considering disability's resistance to instrumentalisation that, although far from 'natural', has nevertheless been repeatedly highlighted by disability scholars (for example, Hartblay 2014; Mitchell and Snyder 2010; Mladenov 2015a). The only place in the book that includes a discussion of disability is Crary's brief recourse to autism. Yet autism is used by Crary as way to condemn television that, according to a quoted study (2014, 86; original emphasis), "might have a catastrophic *physical* impact on the developing human being— . . . it could produce extreme, permanent impairments in the acquisition of language and

in the capacity for social interaction." In this account, autism is a pathology created by techno-capitalism rather than an impediment to its total instrumentalisation of life, as sleep is argued to be.

My second example concerns the side-lining of disability in contemporary social activism. The case in question is the Leap Manifesto,[1] a campaigning tool promoting social and environmental justice in Canada. It was written in 2015 by Canadian activists and has been supported by Naomi Klein and other well-known public figures (Klein 2016). The document weaves together measures intended to rectify injustices suffered by the planet, indigenous peoples, women, workers, migrants and refugees. Accordingly, it insightfully highlights the intersections between the issues of climate change, economic inequality, racism, sexism, economic exploitation, globalisation and migration. Yet despite this impressive intersectionality, the Leap Manifesto does not mention disability or injustices of ableism.

In this article I will explore the importance of disability for accounts concerned with social justice, be they critical-theoretical as the one provided by Crary (2014), or practical-activist as the one advanced in the Leap Manifesto (Klein 2016). To this end, I will focus on what I consider to be the most powerful critical-theoretical conceptualisation of social justice produced in recent decades—that of Nancy Fraser. In the mid-1990s, Fraser (1995) developed an account of social justice intended to bring together in a synthesis the two main left-wing strands of twentieth-century thinking and acting on justice—the socialist strand that had focused on issues of economic redistribution, and the postsocialist strand that had focused on issues of cultural recognition. This account was later expanded to accommodate issues of political representation (Fraser 2005), thus creating a comprehensive theory and a versatile instrument for critique of present-day injustices.

Fraser has meticulously explored injustices of gender, class, race and sexuality, but has so far hardly ever mentioned disability. In the early 2000s,

Michael Bérubé (2003) highlighted this omission of Fraser's and insisted on the importance of "mak[ing] disability central to our theories of egalitarian social justice." Taking this suggestion as my point of departure, I will argue that the mechanisms which produce and maintain injustices along other axes of difference such as class or gender cannot be completely understood nor fully dismantled without taking disability into account. First, I will briefly present Fraser's theory of social justice. Then, I will explore the significance of disability for the formulation and advancement of some prominent transformative strategies for social change aimed at economic redistribution, cultural recognition and political representation. The conclusion will emphasise the interrelations between these three spheres of action.

FRASER'S THEORY OF SOCIAL JUSTICE

Fraser's theory of social justice (Fraser 1995, 1996, 2000, 2005, 2007, 2013; Fraser and Honneth 2003) has been summarised by disability scholars on several occasions (Danermark and Gellerstedt 2004; Dodd 2016; Hugemark and Roman 2007; Mladenov 2016). These reviews have been devised in view of applying Fraser's framework to disability, whereas the summary provided here is tailored to the purpose of looking at social justice from the perspective of disability. With this intention in mind, the first thing to note is that for Fraser (1996) social justice means 'parity of participation' and that this normative standard has been central for disability campaigning and thought at least since the 1970s (UPIAS 1976). From the perspective of parity of participation, a society is just only when it enables all of its adult members to interact with each other as peers, and this necessarily includes disabled people.

According to Fraser's (1996) initial formulation, parity of participation requires economic redistribution and cultural recognition. Later, Fraser (2005, 2007) added political representation to her originally two-dimensional framework in order to take into account the impact of transnational structures and processes on social justice. Fraser expanded the familiar scope of the terms 'redistribution', 'recognition' and

'representation'. In her theory, redistribution is not reduced to "the sort of end-state reallocations that are associated with the liberal welfare state. Rather, it also encompasses the sort of deep-structural economic changes that have historically been associated with socialism" (Fraser and Honneth 2003, 95–96, n. 8). Accordingly, a strategy of redistribution could be either affirmative or transformative—it could promote surface reallocations of economic outputs without touching the underlying structures that generate economic inequality, or it could attempt deep-level economic restructuring. Fraser's understanding of recognition is similarly broader than usual—in her usage, the term is "not limited to the sort of valorization of group differences that is associated with mainstream multiculturalism. Rather, it also encompasses the sort of deep restructuring of the symbolic order that is associated with deconstruction" (Fraser and Honneth 2003, 96, n. 9). Accordingly, a strategy of recognition could seek to affirm, on the surface level, previously devalued differences or commonalities that transcend differences; or, alternatively, could attempt to transform culture in-depth by deconstructing the underlying frameworks that produce differences in the first place.

As far as representation is concerned, for Fraser (2005, 2007) this term encompasses both ordinary-political democratic processes such as political association within national civil society or voting in national elections, and meta-political processes that determine who is entitled to participate in ordinary-political processes. Fraser (2005, 12) points out that strategies of political representation which limit democratisation to the bounded polity of the nation-state reproduce the seventeenth-century principle that "the territorial state is the appropriate unit within which to pose and resolve disputes about justice". In the context of contemporary globalisation, such strategies are bound to remain affirmative. In contrast, transformative strategies of political representation seek to democratise decision-making on a transnational basis, recognising that the principle of the nation-state is "out of synch with the structural causes of many injustices in a globalizing world, which are not territorial in character" (2005, 12). Such injustices include global division of labour, global inequalities in access to communicative power and global biopolitics of climate, weaponry, cure and biotechnology that take lives and injure bodies (2005, 13).

Fraser's distinction between redistribution, recognition and representation forms the backbone of the discussion that follows. Because of institutional differentiation that accompanied the development of capitalism (Fraser 2000), the three dimension[s] of justice have become relatively autonomous—therefore, they require different but equally important strategies for overcoming associated injustices. Indeed, Fraser (2005, 10–11, n. 9) has acknowledged that, for tactical reasons, struggles for justice are sometimes justified in emphasising one of the dimensions at the expense of the other two. However, in general, "struggles against maldistribution and misrecognition cannot succeed unless they are joined with struggles against misrepresentation—and vice-versa"; therefore, "efforts to overcome injustice cannot, except in rare cases, address themselves to one such dimension [of justice] alone" (2005, 11).

. . .

Besides the distinction between redistribution, recognition and representation, the following analysis also relies on Fraser's (1995) distinction between affirmative and transformative strategies for overcoming injustice. Affirmative strategies correct the outcomes of social arrangements while transformative remedies correct social arrangements themselves (1995, 82). Therefore, affirmative strategies are less likely to produce substantial change because they leave the underlying structures intact; they can even enhance injustice. Transformative strategies are more promising because they reach deeper and change structures and frames, although they may be harder to implement because they are removed from the immediate concerns of the oppressed (Fraser 1995, 90; Fraser and Honneth 2003, 77–78). In the following three sections, I will explore the significance of disability for three prominent transformative strategies for achieving parity of participation—decommodification of labour in the dimension of redistribution, deconstruction of self-sufficiency in the dimension of recognition, and transnationalisation of democracy in the dimension of representation.

DISABILITY AND ECONOMIC REDISTRIBUTION

On the level of economy, capitalism generates maldistribution through commodification of labour. This is not the only way in which capitalism impairs distributive justice, but it is nevertheless a key one. Capitalism commodifies labour by putting pressure on people to work for a wage (Marx 1978). The stronger the pressure to sell one's labour, the less room one has to negotiate conditions of employment and the more unequal society becomes. Therefore, a transformative strategy of redistribution would seek to decommodify labour (Esping-Andersen 1990; see also Mladenov 2015b)—for example, through the introduction of a basic income:

> According to proponents, if the level of the grants were set high enough, Basic Income would alter the balance of power between capital and labor, creating a more favorable terrain on which to pursue further change. The long-term result could be to undermine the commodification of labor power. (Fraser and Honneth 2003, 78)

But in order to be truly transformative, a strategy of redistribution that aims to decommodify labour needs to improve the access to disability support. The structural reasons for this could be clarified by drawing a political-economic comparison between gender and disability.

In their analyses of capitalism, feminist thinkers have emphasised the centrality of gender for this political-economic system. Capitalism requires gender division of labour for its smooth functioning—both a division between paid and unpaid (caregiving and homemaking) labour and a gender division within paid labour (Fraser 1995, 78). The coding of an activity as 'feminine' legitimates its exploitative incorporation in the system of capital accumulation—keeping overfeminised activities such as caregiving, homemaking and certain kinds of service provision unpaid or underpaid is an essential tool for value appropriation: "Women who care are thought to be exercising their natural proclivities to nurture and this invidious assumption translates into low wages" (Watson et al. 2004, 338). Disability is equally important for capitalism, as Marxist and neo-Marxist thinkers within disability studies have argued (Finkelstein 1980; Oliver and Barnes 2012; Russell 2001, 2002; Stone 1984). For example, according to Abberley (1987, 17), "a theory of disability as oppression will attempt to flesh out the claim that historically specific categories of 'disabled people' were constituted as a product of the development of capitalism, and its concern with the compulsion to work." The category of disability is a major instrument used by the capitalist state to regulate the supply of labour in the interests of capital accumulation. So if gender (in addition to class and race) is key for division of labour, disability is key for commodification of labour.

In her book *The Disabled State*, Deborah Stone (1984) has shown that tightening of eligibility criteria which allow a person to be officially recognised as 'disabled' makes access to need-based distribution harder, thus putting additional pressure on workers to accept unfavourable conditions of employment within the system of work-based distribution. Notably, this regulation of eligibility concerns all workers and non-workers in capitalism (rather than only disabled ones), which allows Stone to argue that:

> The very notion of disability is fundamental to the architecture of the welfare state; it is something like a keystone that allows the other supporting structures of the welfare system and, in some sense, the economy at large to remain in place. (1984, 12)

The more difficult the access to the disability category (and therefore—to the need-based system of distribution), the more pressure there will be on both actual and potential workers to sell their labour for a wage irrespective of the conditions of employment:

> Enlarging the active reserve army of labour [by decreasing disability support and pushing more people into employment] is 'good' for business because it disciplines labour. Having more people desperate for work keeps competition for jobs high and workers' wages down, thereby protecting the corporate profit margins and class privilege, which are sacred to the interests of capital. (Russell 2002, 125)

In contrast to the tightening of eligibility, the liberalisation of eligibility criteria makes it possible for some unemployed or underemployed people to be reclassified as disabled people, which could potentially reduce the pressure of commodification. However, liberalisation of eligibility is not enough for effective decommodification because meagre, conditional or stigmatised benefits deter people from seeking exemption from work-based distribution by way of the disability category (Russell 2001, 93). The point about stigma suggests that the economic mechanisms of commodification are intertwined with the cultural mechanisms of ableism (explored in the next section)—nevertheless, the two have autonomous causal force. Therefore, economic mechanisms need to be addressed in systemic rather than communicative terms (e.g. in terms of creation and appropriation of value rather than construction of meaning) and require a distinctive strategy of redistribution that could correspond to but does not coincide with the strategy of recognition (see Vehmas and Watson 2014, 647). What does such a strategy look like?

The foregoing analysis suggests that a transformative strategy of redistribution which seeks to decommodify labour should necessarily take disability into account. Labour could be effectively decommodified only when: the access to disability support is improved by liberalising disability assessment; the access to disability support is decoupled from means-testing, prior contributions and workfare conditionality; and disability support is expanded to ensure proper standard of living for those who rely on it. An actual benefit approximating this ideal type was the Disability Living Allowance (DLA) in the United Kingdom (Roulstone and Prideaux 2012, 162). The DLA was designed to cover the additional costs of living with impairment in present-day society and, according to Morris (2011, 4), was "the only aspect of the benefit system [in the United Kingdom] which [was] implicitly based on creating a 'level playing field' for disabled people". Notably, the DLA was non-means tested, non-contributory and free from workfare conditionality. As such, it was based on "a mixture of welfare and rights thinking" rather than "simple compensation" (Roulstone and Prideaux 2012, 53).

A transformative strategy of redistribution that seeks to decommodify labour would thus advocate for public provision of disability support based on principles approximating those incorporated in the United Kingdom's DLA. Since 2013, the DLA for people of working age has been gradually replaced by the more restrictive Personal Independence Payment (Roulstone 2015). This transformation has been part of a wider programme of austerity (Dodd 2016; Mladenov 2014). Disabled people in the United Kingdom have been amongst the 'disproportionally affected' (Taylor-Robinson, Whitehead, and Barr 2014) by the cuts to public services systematically implemented since 2010. The impact of these cuts on disability policy in the United Kingdom has been described as 'systematic retrogression' by disability organisations (Inclusion London 2015) and a 'great leap backwards' by policy analysis (Taylor-Robinson, Whitehead, and Barr 2014). . . .

DISABILITY AND CULTURAL RECOGNITION

On the level of culture, capitalism generates misrecognition by promoting self-sufficiency.[2] Although self-sufficiency is not the only term that confers cultural value within capitalism, it is certainly a key one. The paradigmatic subject of capitalism is the rational utility maximiser who is free from social and natural restraints or external interferences. In the era of neoliberal capitalism, this subject is sleepless, tireless, hyper-able, flexible and mobile, continuously enhancing one's capacity to produce and consume (Crary 2014):

> A subject of (market) choice and a consumer of services, this individual is obligated to enhance her quality of life through her own decisions. In this new "care of self," everyone is an expert on herself, responsible for managing her own human capital to maximal effect. (Fraser 2003, 168)

This overvaluation of self-sufficiency has a negative recognitive impact on those involved in caring relationships such as women and disabled people (Hughes et al. 2005); it forces the latter "to embolden the ability side of the dis/ability complex in order to survive, hopefully thrive, but definitely make do and mend" (Goodley, Lawthom, and

Runswick-Cole 2014, 981). Therefore, a transformative strategy of recognition would seek to deconstruct self-sufficiency—for example, by exposing self-sufficiency as rooted in relations of interdependence. This point could be clarified by juxtaposing critiques of self-sufficiency focused on gender with those concerned with disability.

Utilising the perspective of gender, Fraser and Gordon (1994) point out that in pre-industrial societies dependence was a nearly universal and therefore normalised condition that did not entail moral-psychological stigma. Pre-industrial women were dependent but so were most pre-industrial men, which precluded feminisation of dependence. On this basis, Fraser and Gordon (1994) argue that, in the pre-industrial phase of historical development, to be economically, socio-legally and politically dependent did not entail stigma. But what about dependence on assistance, be it physical, emotional or cognitive? Histories of disability suggest that premodern societies in Europe stigmatised disabled people for their appearance or behaviour but not for their reliance on external support: "There is significant evidence that people with disabilities used networks of support in their communities to survive in times that were harsh for nearly everyone" (Braddock and Parish 2001, 21). In other words, similarly to economic dependence, dependence on support was widespread and was therefore equally normalised in premodern Europe. Consequently, at least until the onset of modernity in the fifteenth and sixteenth centuries, it was uncommon to construct disabled people as deviant due to their perceived dependence (Finkelstein 1980; Oliver and Barnes 2012)—in this regard, disabled people were not only like women, but also like most of the men.

With the advance of industrial capitalism in the eighteenth and nineteenth centuries, self-sufficiency gradually became the norm and dependence —a deviation. The (hitherto strong) association between wage labour and dependence was weakened and, eventually, effaced: "Radical workingmen, who had earlier rejected wage labor as 'wage slavery,' claimed a new form of manly independence within it" (Fraser and Gordon 1994, 315–316). This shift allowed male workers to (falsely) perceive themselves and be perceived as self-sufficient, but the corollary was the feminisation, marginalisation and, eventually, stigmatisation of dependence (in all its forms, but now excluding wage labour). The demise of welfarism and the rise of neoliberalism in the post-industrial age further devalued dependence. The pressure to engage in wage labour extended towards women, as well as towards disabled people. Two-earner families became the norm, public campaigns stigmatised 'dependency culture', receipt of benefits became conditional on labour market participation and eligibility criteria were tightened. "In this context, the worker tends to become the universal social subject: everyone is expected to 'work' and to be 'self-supporting.' Any adult not perceived as a worker shoulders a heavier burden of self-justification" (1994, 324). This analysis suggests that the cultural norm of self-sufficiency is intrinsically related to the economic mechanism of commodification of labour explored in the previous section. However, it would be a mistake to reduce self-sufficiency to a superstructural manifestation of underlying economic forces—as a cultural norm, self-sufficiency is relatively autonomous and should be analysed and challenged in its own right. With the development of capitalism, self-sufficiency has become deeply embedded in public and private discourses that, on their behalf, have become sufficiently differentiated from the economic order of society to merit separate analysis (Fraser 2000, 118).

Fraser and Gordon's (1994) 'genealogy of dependency' exposes the stigmatisation of dependence as a historically contingent cultural construct, highlights the disparaged experience of women as traditional caregivers, and on this basis valorises interdependence. Their analysis thus engages in a transformative politics of recognition that deconstructs self-sufficiency. This approach is highly relevant to disability because the experience of disabled people as care-receivers has been similarly disparaged by the capitalist overvaluation of self-sufficiency. Until relatively recently, both caregivers and care-receivers were completely excluded from wage labour and with this also excluded from the opportunity to acquire the status of self-sufficient individuals, however fake this status has been in the case of wage labourers. In consequence, both female caregivers and disabled

care-receivers have maintained strong experiential and cultural links with interdependence—links that have been broken in the case of allegedly self-sufficient (male, able-bodied) wage labourers, and links that could provide the excluded with a common ground for deconstructing self-sufficiency. . . .

Seen from the perspective of disability, the feminist valorisation of interdependence informed by the experiences of caregivers risks an ableist slippage without taking into account the position of care-receivers. Activists and thinkers within disability studies have been suspicious of the term 'care' because of its historical association with paternalism, benevolence and charity: "For many disabled people the concept 'care' is both patronising and oppressive" (Oliver and Barnes 2012, 66; see also Watson et al. 2004, 335). Sharing these concerns, in my own work I have abstained, as much as possible, from talking about 'care' and instead have used terms connoting contract such as 'support' or 'assistance' (Mladenov 2015a). The discourse of contract is favoured by the Independent Living advocates because it challenges paternalism (Watson et al. 2004, 336–338), but it also tends to cover up relations of interdependence (Mladenov 2012). Feminist ethics of care, as opposed to capitalist work ethic, is a more promising way to illuminate and valorise interdependence (Watson et al. 2004). That said, the perspective of the caregiver endorsed by feminists needs to be complemented by the perspective of the recipient of care highlighted by disability scholars—otherwise, the citizenship of the former could overpower the citizenship of the latter. A reconciliatory fusion of perspectives is proposed by Hughes et al.:

> the parties involved in the caring relationship are perpetually invalidated because the value of care is measured against the autonomous adult male who neither requires nor delivers care. To be a carer or cared for—male or female, disabled or non-disabled in either role—is to be found wanting, to be other in relation to the masculine subject of modernity, to be reduced to 'the other of the same'. Those who give and receive care are marginalized, 'used and wasted' bodies, existing, by and large, on the margins of what counts as the truly human community. (2005, 265)

A transformative strategy of recognition that de-constructs self-sufficiency "think[s] past or beyond a world in which women and disabled people are constituted as the 'negative of the positive,' as inferior or defective men" (Hughes et al. 2005, 269). Thus it reconciles the interests of caregivers, the overwhelming majority of whom are women, with the interests of care-receivers, a great number of whom are disabled people. Critical disability studies emphasises that all humans rely on infrastructures and relations of support (Mladenov 2015a). We are just temporarily able-bodied, but even when able-bodied we are still interdependent—it is just that in such periods, the infrastructures of support and care that we depend on remain invisible or unrecognised, receding in the background of familiarity or hidden in the realm of the 'private'. Finkelstein's seminal phenomenology of 'hand washing' clearly illuminates this point:

> The fact that an able-bodied person requires a wash-basin, tap, plumbing and so on, as well as an army of people to plan, build and maintain the water works so that he or she can wash indicates that *dependency is not unique to disabled people.* (1980, 25; original emphasis)

The disability studies perspective complements the insights of feminists into care by suggesting that self-sufficiency could be effectively deconstructed only when: the interdependence illuminated by disabled people's lives and experiences is universalised and normalised; and the self-sufficiency experienced by able-bodied people is unmasked as underpinned by infrastructures of support and caring relationships. This task requires confronting mainstream cultural patterns that overvalue self-sufficiency and devalue interdependence. . . .

DISABILITY AND POLITICAL REPRESENTATION

On the level of political participation, misrepresentation is generated by keeping democracy national in a capitalist system that is transnational. This is not the only mechanism for undermining democratic justice under capitalism, but it is a key one and its salience has increased with globalisation. Restricting the opportunities for democratic participation to the citizens of the nation-state makes it impossible for many of those affected by the economic and cultural injustices generated by transnational capital to make claims for redistribution and recognition. This disjunction between national framing of political membership and transnational socio-economic structures, although far from being new, has become especially pronounced since the onset of globalisation in the late twentieth century. The ensuing political injustice has been termed 'misframing' by Fraser (2005, 8; original emphasis): "Here the injustice arises when the community's boundaries are drawn in such a way as to wrongly exclude some people from the chance to participate *at all* in its authorized contests over justice." In order to redress the injustice of misframing, a transformative strategy of representation would seek to transnationalise democracy—for example, by reconstituting the public sphere along transnational lines (Fraser 2007). My argument is that disability has a central role to play in such efforts.

This argument is supported by research in the emerging field of transnational disability studies (for example, McRuer 2010; Meekosha 2011; Sherry 2007). Building on this expanding body of work, Soldatic (2013) and Soldatic and Grech (2014) have suggested that the production of impairment—which they conceptualise as the bodily component of disability—makes visible the structural violence of colonialism and globalisation, the otherwise "invisible debts of the global North that are owed to the South" (Soldatic 2013, 749). In this account, produced impairment is a material trace left by the capitalist world-system on subaltern people's bodies. As such, it becomes a ground for challenging, in a uniquely powerful way, the national misframing of political contestation and decision-making in view of its negative implications:

> for the free movement of disabled people across borders, whether this is forced migration such as disabled refugees and asylum seekers, for disabled citizens who are seeking to make claims against a nation state to which they are not a citizen, or for disabled citizens residing within the South who wish to make claims against transnational institutions such as the World Bank, WTO, and the IMF for the devastating impacts

of their economic and social restructuring programs on local livelihoods, communities and environments. (Soldatic and Grech 2014, n.p.)

For disability studies and activism, the significance of embracing a transnational perspective is potentially as far-reaching as was the significance of embracing the social model of disability in the 1980s and the 1990s (Oliver 1996). The social model challenged the individual or medical model on the basis of a paradigmatic shift from methodological individualism to methodological holism. Similarly, what could be identified in the work of transnational disability scholars as an emerging transnational model of disability challenges the national framing of disability issues by promoting a paradigmatic shift away from 'methodological nationalism' (Beck 2006, 24). Such a shift is pivotal when it comes to exploring disability in the Global South, because disability here "is firmly linked to northern imperialism, centuries of colonisation and globalisation" (Meekosha 2011, 671). Considering that the overwhelming majority of disabled people reside in the Global South, it follows that only a transnational model of disability could effectively address the issues faced by most of the disabled people in the world.

The importance of transnationalisation for disability studies seems undeniable, but what could disability add to the transnational perspective? In the approach proposed by Soldatic (2013) and Soldatic and Grech (2014), the bodily component of disability is historicised, contextualised and foregrounded to underpin transnationalisation of democracy. Here, produced impairments provide a unique and powerful justification for including non-citizens in the public sphere according to the 'all-affected principle'. This principle holds that "what turns a collection of people into fellow members of a public is not shared citizenship, but their co-imbrication in a common set of structures and/or institutions that affect their lives" (Fraser 2007, 22). In brief, produced impairments illuminate transnational 'affectedness' like no other personal characteristic and in this sense are central to a transformative strategy of political representation that seeks to transnationalise democracy.

Let me provide an example. The collapse of the Rana Plaza building in 2013 in Dhaka, Bangladesh, killed more than 1100 garment factory workers and injured over 2000 (Human Rights Watch 2015). These people—mostly women from rural areas—produced clothes for prominent international fashion brands. They lost their lives or were injured as a result of an accident precipitated by unsafe and grossly exploitative working conditions. Their injuries illuminated the ways in which workers in Bangladesh are negatively affected by the profit-seeking activities of the international garment industry:

> Some of this [abuse of workers] can also be blamed on the branded retailers who place bulk orders and say 'Scale up production lines because it is a big order, and improve your margins'. Even 2–3 cents can make the difference, but these companies don't want to factor in [labor rights and safety] compliance into costing. (Bangladeshi garment factory owner as quoted in Human Rights Watch 2015, 9)

The public recognition that garment factory workers in Dhaka were (bodily) affected by global structures of capital accumulation justified demands for redistribution on a transnational scale. In the aftermath of the collapse of the Rana Plaza building, a global fund was set up to secure financial support for the victims[3] and international retailers were publicly admonished to contribute (Human Rights Watch 2015, 66–67). In 2015, the General Secretary of the British Trade Union Congress wrote in an open letter to the Chairmen of the Benetton Group: 'Benetton was one of the companies with a relationship with at least one of the factories housed in the Rana Plaza building. As such *your company has a responsibility for ensuring those families affected receive the compensation they need*' (TUC 2015, n.p.; emphasis added).

The produced impairments of the workers in Dhaka illuminated transnational affectedness, shaped transnational public opinion and justified demands for transnational redistribution (albeit an affirmative rather than a transformative one). It may be argued that the motivation of international companies to compensate affected workers boils down to fears of falling profits due to reputational damage. However, such an explanation does not justify a reduction of "the political" to "the economic" because it still admits that economic pressure on international retailers has mounted as a result of political pressure underpinned by transnationalisation of democracy.

. . .

CONCLUSION

Let me recap the arguments so far presented. According to Fraser, social justice means parity of participation. Parity of participation requires strategies of economic redistribution, cultural recognition and political representation. Such strategies are either affirmative or transformative, but only the latter achieve real change. Capitalism could be transformed economically by decommodifying labour, culturally by deconstructing self-sufficiency, and politically by transnationalising democracy. Yet to be really transformative, decommodification of labour needs to enhance disability support and deconstruction of self-sufficiency—to valorise interdependence illuminated by disabled people's lives by emphasising its universality and highlighting the ways in which interdependence underpins self-sufficiency. On its behalf, transnationalisation of democracy needs to make recourse to produced impairments in order to reveal affectedness, but this strategy bears the risk of devaluing non-conforming bodies and experiences and should be approached with caution.

The redistributive enhancement of disability support interacts with the recognitive valorisation of disability-illuminated interdependence in a mutually reinforcing way. Improving the access to disability support and increasing the entitlements associated with it strengthen the understanding of disability-illuminated interdependence as universal and natural. On its behalf, universalising and naturalising disability-illuminated interdependence legitimises the expansion of disability support. This interrelationship is key when addressing the austerity agenda because the latter brings about material deprivation and cultural devaluation in similarly mutually reinforcing loops (Dodd 2016, 154; Mladenov 2014).

Using the perspective of gender, Fraser (2013, 133–135) has argued that social justice could be achieved by transforming public policy and attitudes according to a 'universal caregiver' model. This model promotes the caregiving of men, thus providing the conditions for men to become more like women

have traditionally been. The disability perspective espoused by this article suggests that social justice requires complementing 'universal caregiving' with the principle of 'universal care-receiving'. The latter would normalise and facilitate care-receiving, thus emphasising the (routinely disavowed) common ground of interdependence that underpins the lives of disabled and non-disabled people alike. An integrated 'universal caregiver/care-receiver' model could pave the way to 'think[ing] past or beyond a world in which women and disabled people are constituted as ... inferior or defective men' (Hughes et al. 2005, 269). The practical measures that promote 'universal caregiving'—for example, shorter working week, publicly supported care work (Fraser 2013, 134)—are commensurate with the practical measures promoting 'universal care-receiving'—for example, liberalised access to disability support, elimination of means-testing and workfare conditionality, adequate benefit levels. Both advance decommodification of labour and both presuppose deconstruction of self-sufficiency.

The transnationalisation of democracy 'on the grounds of produced impairment emerging from the South' (Soldatic and Grech 2014, n.p.) provides subaltern people with the opportunity to have a say in the governance of global economic and cultural affairs. On this basis, it becomes possible to advance claims for redistribution and recognition along the lines of 'universal caregiving/care-receiving'. However, the risk of devaluing non-conforming bodies should be taken into consideration when using impairment to shed light on global injustices. In other words, illumination of transnational affectedness or, to use a sharper term, colonial violence should not overshadow the violence of ableism. A potential way out of this dilemma is Abberley's (1987, 9) 'attitude of ambivalence towards impairment' that allows one to perceive impairment simultaneously as something bad and something good: "Impairment must be identified as a bad thing, insofar as it is an undesirable consequence of a distorted social development, as the same time as it is held to be a positive attribute of the individual who is impaired." Abberley links his 'attitude of ambivalence' to a distinction between prevention of the social production of impairments and treatment of impairments that have already been produced—from the perspective of the former, impairment is bad; whereas the perspective of the latter calls for a positive attitude towards impairment. Note also that for Abberley (1987, 11), the overwhelming majority of impairments are produced by conditions of work, consumption or maldistribution under capitalism, and therefore are socially (or, to be more precise, politico-economically) produced.

My final point is that the three disability-informed strategies for social transformation promoted in this article, when pursued together, bear the potential to improve parity of participation not only for disabled people, but for everyone else as well. Conversely, disregarding disability risks enhancing injustice for all.

NOTES

1. https://leapmanifesto.org/en/the-leap-manifesto/ (accessed October 6, 2016).
2. Within the liberal framework that ideologically underpins capitalism, 'self-sufficiency' is synonymous with 'independence'. However, within disability thought and activism, the Independent Living movement has shifted the meaning of 'independence' from liberal-individualist self-sufficiency to a particular type of interdependence (Mladenov 2012). In order to avoid confusion with the revised 'independence' of the Independent Living advocates that has a strong (albeit sometimes implied rather than explicitly stated) emphasis on interdependence, in this text I use the term 'self-sufficiency' instead of independence.
3. http://www.ranaplaza-arrangement.org/ (accessed October 6, 2016).

REFERENCES

Abberley, P. 1987. "The Concept of Oppression and the Development of a Social Theory of Disability." *Disability, Handicap & Society* 2 (1): 5–19.

Beck, U. 2006. *The Cosmopolitan Vision*. Cambridge: Polity Press.

Bérubé, M. 2003. "Citizenship and Disability." *Dissent Magazine*, Spring 2003. https://www .dissentmagazine.org/article/citizenship-and-disability.

Braddock, D., and S. Parish. 2001. "An Institutional History of Disability." In *Handbook of Disability Studies*, edited by G. Albrecht, K. Seelman, and M. Bury, 11–68. London: Sage.

Crary, J. 2014. *24/7: Late Capitalism and the Ends of Sleep*. London: Verso.

Danermark, B., and L. C. Gellerstedt. 2004. "Social Justice: Redistribution and Recognition—A Non-Reductionist Perspective on Disability." *Disability & Society* 19 (4): 339–353.

Davis, L. J. 2002. *Bending over Backwards: Disability, Dismodernism, and Other Difficult Positions*. New York: New York University Press.

Dodd, S. 2016. "Orientating Disability Studies to Disablist Austerity: Applying Fraser's Insights." *Disability & Society* 31 (2): 149–165.

Esping-Andersen, G. 1990. *The Three Worlds of Welfare Capitalism*. Cambridge: Polity Press.

Finkelstein, V. 1980. *Attitudes and Disabled People: Issues for Discussion*. New York: World Rehabilitation Fund.

Fraser, N. 1995. "From Redistribution to Recognition? Dilemmas of Justice in a 'Post-Socialist' Age." *New Left Review* 212 (July/August 1995): 68–93.

Fraser, N. 1996. "Social Justice in the Age of Identity Politics: Redistribution, Recognition and Participation." *The Tanner Lectures on Human Values*, Stanford University, April 30—June 2. http:// tannerlectures.utah.edu/_documents/a-to-z/f/ Fraser98.pdf.

———. 2000. "Rethinking Recognition." *New Left Review* 3, May–June 2000: 107–120.

———. 2003. "From Discipline to Flexibilization? Rereading Foucault in the Shadow of Globalization." *Constellations* 10 (2): 160–171.

———. 2005. "Reframing Justice in a Globalizing World." *New Left Review* 36: 1–19.

———. 2007. "Transnationalizing the Public Sphere: On the Legitimacy and Efficacy of Public Opinion in a Post-Westphalian World." *Theory, Culture & Society* 24 (4): 7–30.

———. 2013. *Fortunes of Feminism: From State-Managed Capitalism to Neoliberal Crisis*. London: Verso.

Fraser, N., and L. Gordon. 1994. "A Genealogy of Dependency: Tracing a Keyword of the U.S. Welfare State." *Signs* 19 (2): 309–336.

Fraser, N., and A. Honneth. 2003. *Redistribution or Recognition? A Political-Philosophical Exchange.* London: Verso.

Goodley, D., R. Lawthom, and K. Runswick-Cole. 2014. "Dis/Ability and Austerity: Beyond Work and Slow Death." *Disability & Society* 29 (6): 980–984.

Hartblay, C. 2014. "A Genealogy of (Post-)Soviet Dependency: Disabling Productivity." *Disability Studies Quarterly* 34 (1): n.p.

Hugemark, A., and C. Roman. 2007. "Diversity and Divisions in the Swedish Disability Movement: Disability, Gender, and Social Justice." *Scandinavian Journal of Disability Research* 9 (1): 26–45.

Hughes, B., L. McKie, D. Hopkins, and N. Watson. 2005. "Love's Labours Lost? Feminism, the Disabled People's Movement and an Ethic of Care." *Sociology* 39 (2): 259–275.

Human Rights Watch. 2015. *"Whoever Raises Their Head Suffers the Most." Workers' Rights in Bangladesh's Garment Factories.* New York: Human Rights Watch.

Inclusion London. 2015. "Evidence of Breaches of Disabled People's Rights under the UN Convention on the Rights of Persons with Disabilities." "Information Paper," report published online. London: Inclusion London. https://www.inclusionlondon.org.uk/campaigns-and-policy/facts-and-information/equality-and-human-rights/evidence-of-breaches-of-disabled-peoples-rights-under-the-un-convention-on-the-rights-of-persons-with-disabilities/.

Klein, N. 2016. "Let's Make This a Real 'Leap' Year, and Go Fossil Fuel-Free." *The Guardian.* Accessed 4 February 2016. http://www.theguardian.com/commentisfree/2016/feb/04/leap-year-fossil-fuel-leap-maifesto-naomi-klein

Marx, K. 1978. ([1849 and 1891]). "Wage Labour and Capital." In *The Marx-Engels Reader,* edited by R. C. Tucker, 203–217. New York: W. W. Norton & Company.

McRuer, R. 2010. "Disability Nationalism in Crip Times." *Journal of Literary & Cultural Disability Studies* 4 (2): 163–178.

Meekosha, H. 2011. "Decolonising Disability: Thinking and Acting Globally." *Disability & Society* 26 (6): 667–682.

Mitchell, D. T., and S. L. Snyder. 2010. "Disability as Multitude: Re-Working Non-Productive Labor Power." *Journal of Literary & Cultural Disability Studies* 4 (2): 179–194.

Mladenov, T. 2012. "Personal Assistance for Disabled People and the Understanding of Human Being." *Critical Social Policy* 32 (2): 242–261.

Mladenov, T. 2014. "Disability and Austerity." *Cost of Living.* Accessed August 1 2014. http://www.cost-ofliving.net/disability-and-austerity/

Mladenov, T. 2015a. *Critical Theory and Disability: A Phenomenological Approach.* New York: Bloomsbury.

Mladenov, T. 2015b. "From State Socialist to Neoliberal Productivism: Disability Policy and Invalidation of Disabled People in the Postsocialist Region." *Critical Sociology.* Advance online publication. doi: 10.1177/0896920515595843.

Mladenov, T. 2016. "Postsocialist Disability Matrix." *Scandinavian Journal of Disability Research.* Advance online publication. doi:10.1080/15017419.2016.1202860.

Morris, J. 2011. "'Rethinking Disability Policy,' a Joseph Rowntree Foundation Report." London: Joseph Rowntree Foundation. https://www.jrf.org.uk/report/rethinking-disability-policy.

Oliver, M. 1996. *Understanding Disability: From Theory to Practice.* London: Macmillan.

Oliver, M., and C. Barnes. 2012. *The New Politics of Disablement.* Basingstoke: Palgrave Macmillan.

Roulstone, A. 2015. "Personal Independence Payments, Welfare Reform and the Shrinking Disability Category." *Disability & Society* 30 (5): 673–688.

Roulstone, A., and S. Prideaux. 2012. *Understanding Disability Policy.* Bristol: The Policy Press.

Russell, M. 2001. "Disablement, Oppression, and the Political Economy." *Journal of Disability Policy Studies* 12 (2): 87–95.

———. 2002. "What Disability Civil Rights Cannot Do: Employment and Political Economy." *Disability & Society* 17 (2): 117–135.

Sherry, M. 2007. "(Post)Colonising Disability." *Wagadu—A Journal of Transnational Women's and Gender Studies* 4 Summer: 10–22.

Soldatic, K. 2013. "The Transnational Sphere of Justice: Disability Praxis and the Politics of Impairment." *Disability & Society* 28 (6): 744–755.

Soldatic, K., and S. Grech 2014. "Transnationalising Disability Studies: Rights, Justice and Impairment." *Disability Studies Quarterly* 34 (2): n.p.

Stone, D. 1984. *The Disabled State*. London: Macmillan.

Taylor-Robinson, D., M. Whitehead, and B. Barr. 2014. "Great Leap Backwards: The UK's Austerity Programme Has Disproportionately Affected Children and People with Disabilities." *BMJ* 349: g7350.

TUC. 2015. "TUC Urges Benetton to Compensate Rana Plaza Victims." Letter by Frances O'Grady published online at https://www.tuc.org.uk/international-issues/globalisation/international-development/global-economic-justice-campaigns/tuc-rana-plaza-compensation.

UPIAS. 1976. *Fundamental Principles of Disability*. London: Union of the Physically Impaired Against Segregation. http://www.leeds.ac.uk/disability-studies/archiveuk/UPIAS/fundamental%principles.pdf.

Vehmas, S., and N. Watson. 2014. "Moral Wrongs, Disadvantages, and Disability: A Critique of Critical Disability Studies." *Disability & Society* 29 (4): 638–650.

Watson, N., L. McKie, B. Hughes, D. Hopkins, and S. Gregory. 2004. "(Inter)Dependence, Needs and Care: The Potential for Disability and Feminist Theorists to Develop an Emancipatory Model." *Sociology* 38 (2): 331–350.

16. POEMS WITH DISABILITIES

JIM FERRIS (2000)

I'm sorry—this space is reserved
for poems with disabilities. I know
it's one of the best spaces in the book,
but the Poems with Disabilities Act
requires us to make all reasonable
accommodations for poems that aren't
normal. There is a nice space just
a few pages over—in fact (don't
tell anyone) I think it's better
than this one, I myself prefer it.
Actually I don't see any of those
poems right now myself, but you never
    know
when one might show up, so we have to
    keep
this space open. You can't always tell
just from looking at them either. Sometimes
they'll look just like a regular poem

when they roll in . . . you're reading along
and suddenly everything
changes, the world tilts
a little, angle of vision
jumps, your entrails aren't
where you left them. You
remember your aunt died
of cancer at just your age
and maybe yesterday's twinge means
something after all. Your sloppy,
fragile heart beats
a little faster
and then you know.
You just know:
the poem
is right
where it
belongs.

CHAPTER 3

LEARNING GENDER

Our typical in-class exercise while teaching a unit on the social construction of gender is to ask how many students identified as "tomboys" when they were growing up. A sea of hands usually results as many remember resisting traditional notions of femininity. When students are asked whether they identified as "sissies," usually the whole group laughs as one lone student sheepishly raises a hand and remarks about always being a sissy. Why is it so easy to say you were a tomboy and so difficult to admit to being a sissy? This has a lot to do with the meanings associated with masculinity and femininity and the ways these are ranked in society. In this chapter we focus specifically on gender and sexism, keeping in mind two important points: first, how gender is constructed through intersection with other differences such as race, ethnicity, and class, and second, how sexism as a system of oppression is related to other systems of inequality and privilege.

GENDER, CULTURE, AND BIOLOGY

In Chapter 1 we explained gender as the way society creates, patterns, and rewards our understandings of femininity and masculinity, or the process by which certain behaviors and performances are ascribed to "women" and "men." Society constructs and interprets perceived differences among humans and gives us "feminine" and "masculine" people. These words are intentionally placed in quotation marks to emphasize that notions of femininity and masculinity are fluid and socially constructed—created by social processes that reflect the various workings of power in society. Therefore gender is culturally and historically changeable. There is nothing essential, intrinsic, or static about femininity or masculinity; rather, they are social categories that might mean different things in different societies and in different historical periods. The reading "Trans*forming College Masculinities" by T. J. Jourian recognizes ways trans*masculine students are constructing gender and challenging hegemonic masculinities.

It is important to emphasize that gender is embedded in culture and various forms of knowledge are associated with any given community. What it might mean to be "feminine" or "masculine" may differ from culture to culture. This implies that people growing up in different societies in different parts of the world at different historical moments perform different gender expressions. As the boxed insert later in this chapter called "Rites of Passage" suggests, gender performances vary around the world.

In addition, contemporary life in the twenty-first century, which involves global systems of production, consumption, and communication, means that patterns of gender in the United States are exported worldwide and are increasingly linked to patterns of global economic restructuring. This encourages us to consider the ways the social and economic dynamics of globalization (including economic and political expansion, militarism and colonial conquest and settlement, disruption/appropriation of indigenous peoples and resources, and the exportation of ideas through media and world markets, etc.) have shaped global gender arrangements and transformed gender relations. Whatever our global location, it is important to consider the ways we interact with globalized cultures and particularly the ways in which products of world media feature in our lives and shape our ideas about femininity and masculinity.

Femininities and masculinities are performed by bodies in a series of repetitive acts that we usually take for granted and tend to see as "natural." As we "do" gender, these practices (such as walking, speaking, or sitting in a certain way) are always shaped by discourses or regimes of truth that give these actions meaning. However, it is important not to reduce this "performativity" associated with gender to a voluntary act or understand it as something over which we have perfect control. In this sense it is not merely a theatrical performance. Rather, performativity is constrained by social norms. What this means is that gender is not only what we "do"; it is a process by which we "are" or "become."

In addition, the relationship between biology and culture is more complicated than the assertion that sex is a biological fact and gender is the societal interpretation of that fact. First, there is greater gender diversity in nature than once thought. Many species are not just female or male, but can be both female and male at the same time, or be one or the other at different times. As will be discussed later, this ambiguity relates to humans too. Some children are born without distinct sex characteristics and are assigned a sex at birth. Anne Fausto-Sterling's classic reading "The Five Sexes, Revisited" critiques the traditional binaries we call female and male. Second, while biology may imply some basic physiological "facts," culture gives meaning to these in such a way that we must question whether biology can exist except within the society that gives it meaning in the first place. This implies that sex, in terms of raw male or female, is already gendered by the culture within which these physiological facts of biology exist. In other words, although many people make a distinction between biological sex (female/male) and learned gender (feminine/masculine), it is really impossible to speak of a fixed biological sex category outside of the sense that a culture makes of that category.

We know this is a complicated idea, but basically it is saying that we must no longer understand biological femaleness and maleness as the fixed foundation upon which gender is imposed. The body is given meaning by preexisting beliefs about gender, including those of medical and scientific authorities. Science is a human (and necessarily gendered) product. This is what it means to say that "sex," as in "male/female," has actually been gender all along.

An example that highlights how biology is connected to culture concerns the processes by which ambiguous sex characteristics in children are handled. When "intersex" children (those with reproductive or sexual anatomies that do not seem to fit the typical binary definitions of "female" or "male") are born, families and health professionals often make an immediate sex determination. Hormone therapy and surgeries may follow to make such a child fit normative constructed binary categories, and gender is taught in accordance with this decision. In other words, physicians and others use gendered norms to construct the sexed bodies of ambiguously sexed infants. This is an example of the way a breakdown in taken-for-granted tight connections between natural biology and learned gender is interpreted as a medical and social emergency. As already mentioned, Anne Fausto-Sterling's reading "The Five Sexes, Revisited" questions this tidy organization of human sex into the two categories female and male, emphasizing that sex is not as easy as genetics and genitalia and arguing for theories that allow for human variation.

Another illustration of the variable relationships between gender, biology, and culture is exemplified by indigenous "Two Spirit" status, whereby people with multiple or integrated genders held/hold places of honor in native communities. The Navajo, for instance, have believed that to maintain harmony, there must be a balanced interrelationship between the feminine and the masculine within the individual, in families, in the culture, and in the natural world. Two Spirit reveals how these beliefs are expressed in a broad range of gender diversity that is accepted as normative within certain communities. The reading "Native American Men-Women, Lesbians, Two-Spirits" by Sabine Lang examines female gender variability within native cultures.

A focus on gender assignment, identity, and expression involves three ways to understand the forces shaping gender and how we experience and express gender as individuals. Gender assignment is usually given to us at birth and determined by our physical body type to be male or female. This assignment, decided by doctors and parents, is the first classification an individual receives. Corresponding gender performances (behavior, dress, activities that one may participate in, etc.) are usually enforced based on the individual's gender assignment at birth. Gender identity concerns how one feels internally about one's own gender. This is a gendered sense of self that comes from within and may or may not match one's assigned gender at birth. The ways we present ourselves to the world are our expression of gender. Our gender expression is how we perform and express gender to those around us. In this way, gender is a pervasive theme in our world, shaping social life and informing attitudes, behavior, and an individual's sense of self. Basically, it is one of the foundational ways that societies are organized.

Gender is always experienced, however, in intersection with other identities. As emphasized in Chapter 2, a person's sense of self is multifaceted and shaped by multiple (and sometimes conflicting) social patterns and practices. In other words, experiences of gender differ by race, class, age, and other factors. For example, due to historical and cultural reasons, many African American women have not internalized the association of femininity with passivity and dependency characteristic of white femininities.

The pervasiveness of gender is a focus of Judith Lorber's article "The Social Construction of Gender." She explains gender as a process that involves multiple patterns of interaction created and re-created constantly in human interaction. Lorber also makes the important point that because gender is so central in shaping our lives, much of what is gendered we do not even recognize; it's made normal and ordinary and occurs on a subconscious level. In other words, the differences between "femininity" (passive, dependent, intuitive, emotional) and "masculinity" (strong, independent, in control, out of touch emotionally) are made to seem natural and inevitable despite the fact that gender is a social script that individuals learn. Cordelia Fine also addresses this "naturalizing" of gender in her book *The Delusions of Gender*, which focuses on research in gendered brain chemistry. She disputes the belief that gendered traits are "hardwired" into the brain and critiques the "biology is destiny" argument that claims innate psychological differences between the minds of women and men.

In reality, gender is a practice in which all people engage; it is something we perform over and over in our daily lives. As already mentioned, gender is something we "do" rather than "have." Through a process of gender acquisition, we practice the performative aspects of gender and learn the "appropriate" thinking and behaviors associated with our gender assignments. Sometimes there are harsh responses to children who do not follow these patterns, especially, as mentioned earlier, to boys who embrace "girly" things such as nail polish or pink clothes. As an aside, it is interesting to note that the association of color options with gender is a relatively recent phenomenon. Traditionally, pink had been associated with males as a diminutive of the reds favored in men's clothing. It was not until the 1940s that manufacturers dictated specific color options for boys and girls.

Our gender expression is not always the same as our gender identity and may or may not match our assigned gender at birth. As discussed in Chapter 2, transgender people,

---

LEARNING ACTIVITY

MORE GENDERS

Across history, many cultures have recognized more than two genders. For example, in Albania, the *burrnesha* are "sworn virgins." These people are born with typical female bodies, but they take a vow of chastity and, in exchange, can live as men. Until very recently, women's roles in Albania were severely limited. Becoming burrnesha allowed women to escape their restraints and gain freedom and power. By taking the oath of virginity, burrnesha became patriarchs of their families. They wear men's clothing, carry weapons, own property, and move about society freely. As women have gained status in recent years, the tradition of burrnesha has diminished, leaving only a small number of them in Albania. In Samoa, *fa'afafine* are people born with typical male bodies raised as girls by their families. Historically, parents chose to raise a child as a fa'afafine when the family had many boys in it and few or no girls. In recent years, parents may have recognized more traditionally feminine behaviors in a young boy and acknowledged

him as fa'afafine. Other boys may choose to become fa'afafine and then may begin to adopt more traditionally feminine behaviors, dressing as women and learning the traditional duties of Samoan women. The Bugis in Indonesia recognize five genders: male and female; *Calabi*, people born with typical male bodies who express typically feminine behaviors and gender roles; *Calalai*, people born with typical female bodies who express typically male behaviors and gender roles; and *Bissu*, people who embody aspects of all genders. In the indigenous Zapotec culture in Oaxaca in Mexico, *muxes* are a third gender, people born in typically male bodies who identify as women or mixed gender.

What do these additional genders suggest about our dominant notion of only two genders? Why is the dominant culture so invested in maintaining the illusion of only two genders? How does the dominance of the ideology of only two genders intersect with the history and legacy of colonialism? What are the implications for liberation of all people in the recognition of many genders?

in the words of Evin Taylor, are individuals "who change, cross, or live beyond gender." Transgender individuals who claim a gender identity or expression different from the one assigned at their birth by their family and community resist the social construction of gender in two distinct binary categories, masculinity and femininity, and subvert these taken-for-granted categories that in most cultures are set in opposition to each other. Genderqueer and gender nonconforming people push at the boundaries of gender and help reveal its constructed nature by refusing to identify in any distinct category. In comparison to transgender, cisgender identity is one where gender identity and expression match the gender assignment given at birth. Cisgender individuals can be said to experience conformity between gender assignment, identity, and expression.

GENDERED VOCABULARY

LZZ JOHNK

The language of gender, sex, and sexuality is highly context-dependent and constantly shifts over time. Even the distinction between "sex" (the "biological") and "gender" (the "social") as we understand and deploy it today is relatively recent, dating from the 1940s. Words that were once commonly accepted within in-groups might be considered inappropriate or derogatory today (e.g., the increasing use of "transgender" and the decreasing use of "transsexual"); words that were once derogatory might now be claimed as terms of pride and collective identification (e.g., "queer"). Words used by people who identify with a given term (e.g., "queer") frequently should not be used by people outside of the communities for whom a term carries negative historical weight. Therefore, we should discuss gendered vocabulary with a heightened consciousness around the ways words and their meanings shift in different spaces and times.

The temptation to define particular identities connected to gender, sex, and sexuality is great, especially when many cis-hetero people feel the need to clarify "who is what." However, many definitions are generated on an individual level and thus reflect only that individual's understanding of a given identity or gendered term—and very often that individual is also a member of a dominant group (e.g., white/Eurowestern, Christian, able-body-minded, middle-class, educated, citizen-status). Moreover, the tendency of "gender glossaries" to utilize "umbrella terms" often results in the reiteration of a colonial worldview. For instance, "genderqueer" is an umbrella term often used by white Eurowestern people (including genderqueers) to describe *all* "third gender," nonbinary, and other genders that fall outside of "the gender binary," but doing so recenters and reinforces the hegemonic power of colonial binary gender (man/woman; male/female). Many Two-Spirit and queer indigenous/people of color, such as b. binaohan, are opposed to the use of and disidentify with Eurowestern umbrella terms (e.g., "nonbinary") (binaohan 2014).

Taking a cue from gender/queer communities, an increasingly common practice within women, gender, sexuality, and queer studies spaces is including one's pronouns during introductions. Though some transgender and genderqueer people have expressed concerns that this practice leads to "outing" in certain cases, such practice highlights the ways that normative cissexist assumptions tend to map colonial binary cisgender pronouns and identities onto everyone, frequently resulting in the erasure of anyone not recognizable to that binary. Pronouns are one aspect of everyday gendered language that is taken for granted, often at the expense of multiply marginalized embodiments and positionalities. Asking for a person's pronouns may be growing more common, but we should continue to exercise sensitivity to the contexts in which we are asking about pronouns, as it is sometimes unsafe for transgender and genderqueer people to assert their pronouns.

When it comes to respecting someone's sex, gender, and/or sexuality, a few simple guidelines can help: Never make assumptions and, if contextually appropriate, respectfully ask the person, keeping in mind that they are not obligated to educate you.

Read More:

> http://www.transstudent.org/definitions/
> https://srlp.org/resources/trans-101/

References

binaohan, b. (2014). *decolonizing trans/gender 101*. Toronto: biyuti publishing.

OED Online. (2018, March). *gender, n*. Retrieved from Oxford English Dictionary: http://www.oed.com/view/Entry/77468?

Although the term "transgender" illustrates the ways a person's gender identity might not match the gender assignment given at birth based on physical or genetic sex characteristics, it is often used interchangeably with the term "transsexual" (and simply labeled trans). Transsexual is an older term, however, still used by some people who have transitioned genders with hormone therapy and surgery. Transgender is an umbrella term that encompasses gender identities that do not fit within the binary categories of male and female assigned at birth. While many transgender people do take hormones and have surgeries to align their bodies with their gender identities, many do not. Some people transition fully from the gender assigned at birth (male-to-female, or MtF, or transwoman; or female-to-male, or FtM, or transman), while others identify as genderqueer, gender nonbinary, gender nonconforming, gender fluid, or any of another number of gender identity descriptors. Not all gender nonconforming people identify as trans, and not all trans people identify as gender nonconforming. The most important thing is to acknowledge that each of us has the right to name our gender identity and be recognized as that identity. The best way to do this is simply to ask people how they would like to be referenced. Gender pronouns are a significant way to support gender identity. Always use people's chosen names and pronouns. Using the pronoun "they" as singular has become an increasingly popular way to recognize the variety of people's gender identities.

As a category, transgender also overlaps with cross-dressing, the practice of wearing the clothes of a sex different from that to which a person was assigned in childhood. Cross-dressing is a form of gender expression that is most typically done by heterosexual men and is not done for entertainment. Drag performances that involve makeup and clothing worn on special occasions for theatrical or comedic purposes are not necessarily transgender behavior, although within the genre of drag there are drag performers who also identify as transgender. In most although not all cases, drag queens are men doing female impersonation, and drag kings are women doing male impersonation.

As a concept, transgender is different from androgyny, although in practice, one performance of a transgender identity might be androgyny. Androgyny can be defined as a lack of gender differentiation or a balanced mixture of recognizable feminine and masculine traits. It is an example of transgender behavior because it attempts to break down the binary categories of femininity and masculinity. It is interesting to note that contemporary ideas about androgyny tend to privilege the "andro" (masculine) more than the "gyny" (feminine), with the presentation of androgyny looking a lot more like masculinity than femininity. The trappings of femininity seem to be the first things that are shed when a body is constructed as androgynous. This is related to androcentrism and the ways masculinity more closely approximates our understanding of (nongendered) "human."

It is also interesting to consider the ways the Internet and other virtual technologies have facilitated transgender identities through a disruption of the expected relationship between self and body ("feminine" identity/"female" body). These technologies remove physical, bodily cues and potentially allow "gender swapping," or the creation of identities that attempt to avoid the binaries of "femininity" and "masculinity." This supports the postmodern view of gender as performative and identity as multiple and fluid.

Transgender does not imply any specific form of sexual identity: Transgender people may identify as heterosexual, gay, lesbian, bisexual, queer, or asexual. It is important not to confuse gender and sexuality here. Transgender identities are about gender performance and might involve any sexual identity. It can be confusing, however, because on many campuses there are LGBTQ (lesbian/gay/bisexual/trans/queer) alliances or centers where resources for transgender students are incorporated into a coalition about sexual rights. In addition, transgender theory has been heavily influenced by queer theory and its insistence on fluid identities (discussed in Chapter 1). Both trans and queer theory emphasize that "woman" and "man" are changeable, evolving, and contested categories that must not be seen as fixed, static, normalized, and taken for granted. Both are interested in the ways diverse notions of personhood are mapped onto the physical body.

Another potential confusion that encourages the merging of gender and sexuality is the term "genderqueer," which combines alternative gender identities and sexualities, although you might see it used to imply someone who is transgender without concern for sexual identity. Generally, "genderqueer" describes a person who is a nonconformist in challenging existing constructions and identities. You might also see it used to describe a social movement resisting the traditional categories of gender. In other words, although genderqueer focuses on the integration of gender and sexual identities and therefore is a useful concept in terms of individual empowerment, social commentary, and political change, again, it is important to understand that, conceptually, these identities (gender and sexuality) are distinct from each other even though they are lived simultaneously. Gender performances are associated with meanings about femininity and masculinity (discussed in this chapter), whereas sexuality concerns sexual desire, feelings, and practices (discussed more fully in Chapter 6). A person could potentially combine any combination of gendered performances with sexual identities.

We actively learn the skills and practices of gender, accepting, rejecting, and negotiating them until most of us become very accomplished in our various performances. For example, throwing a ball is a learned act and one that anybody can perform. However, because girls are less likely to be taught this skill, even today, the way they do throw is often the object of derision. Throwing "like a boy" is learned, then performed again and again until it becomes a skill valued in organized sports. Men are not necessarily better athletes than women; rather, sports as an institution has developed to reflect the particular athletic competencies of men, even though upper-body strength is only one aspect of athleticism. For example, if long-distance swimming or balance beam (activities where women generally outperform men) were popular national sports, then we might think differently about the athletic capabilities of women and men. Sporting activities where upper-body strength is a plus and where women perform less well than men are most valued in the United States.

LEARNING ACTIVITY

SPEAKING OF WOMEN AND MEN AND GENDER

Think about the adjectives we typically use to describe women and men, and list these words in the following columns. A couple of examples are provided to get you started. What do you notice about the words we use to describe women and men? How does our language reinforce stereotypical notions about women and men?

WOMEN	MEN
Passive	Active
Nurturing	Strong

Think about the words we use to designate women and men, and list these names in the following columns. Also, try to find parallel names for women and men. Think about the profanities we use as well. Again, a couple of examples are provided. What do you notice about the terms we use to name women and men? What is the significance of the words for which you could not identify parallels? How do you think language plays a role in shaping the ways we think about and "do" gender?

WOMEN	MEN
Slut	Stud
Chick	

What words does the dominant culture use to describe transgender, genderqueer, gender nonbinary, and gender nonconforming people? How can transgender, genderqueer, gender nonbinary, and gender nonconforming thinking and experiences disrupt essentialist language about gender?

In addition to sports, there are many other major U.S. institutions that support gendered practices. You need only go to a toy store and cruise the very different girls' and boys' aisles to witness the social construction of gender in contemporary U.S. society. What does it mean to get a child-size ironing board instead of a toy gun, and what kinds of behaviors and future roles do these toys help create and justify? Increasingly, and at earlier ages, children are preoccupied with video and cell phone games and computerized activities that also teach lessons about gender.

HISTORICAL MOMENT
GENDER TESTING IN THE OLYMPICS

Rebecca Lambert

The International Olympic Committee (IOC) instituted gender testing in the 1960s. These tests were administered to women athletes who were accused of being men. Initially conducted as visual exams of athletes' naked bodies, the IOC moved to testing chromosomes (XX for female and XY for male). These tests typically reproduce binaries around ideas of femininity and masculinity and reinforce the idea that biology determines gender.

In 1967 Polish sprinter Ewa Klobukowska failed the sex test and was banned from competition. Later, doctors found that she had a condition that, once identified, would have allowed her to compete.

In 1985 Spanish hurdler Maria Patino expected to compete in the World University Games in Kobe, Japan. Patino had lived her entire life as a woman, and her body type and sex characteristics were typically female. Unfortunately for Patino, however, her sex test revealed that she did not have two X chromosomes. She was barred from the competition. A few months later, she competed in Spain and won her event. Following her win, however, she was kicked off the Spanish national team, stripped of her titles, and banned from all future competition. Her fight to be reinstated by the International Amateur Athletics Federation took two years.

South African runner Caster Semenya was subjected to gender testing in 2009 after she won the women's 800-meter race and questions arose around her gender and appearance. Based on the results, she was withdrawn from subsequent competitions. After a year of psychological, gynecological, and endocrine tests, her eligibility to compete was reinstated.

While our society generally operates under the assumption that people are either female or male, variations from this typical biological pattern are common. Some forms of intersexuality may occur in as many as 1 in 100 births. Generally, 1 in 400 female athletes will fail the sex identification test. For many years, women athletes engaged in activism to stop the sex test. The test was suspended for the 2000 Olympics, although the Olympic Committee reserved the right to reinstate the test at any point in the future.

Recently, the International Association of Athletics Federations (IAAF), which governs the sport of track and field, announced that in November, new rules will go into effect that will again target female athletes with naturally higher levels of testosterone. These rules stipulate that female athletes with elevated testosterone levels will have to take certain measures to lower testosterone in order to compete. These measures range from hormone therapy to changing the distance they run to pulling out of the competition altogether.

These tests have been conducted only on female athletes, often focusing on women of color. Why do you suppose this is true? What role do race and gender play in this practice? How does the existence of people who do not fit neatly into one or the other of the biological categories of female and male disrupt the notion of fixed sexes and fixed genders?

References

Longman, Jeré. (April 25, 2018). "Track's New Gender Rules Could Exclude Some Female Athletes." Retrieved from https://www.nytimes.com/2018/04/25/sports/caster-semenya.html

Schaffer, Amanda. (July 25, 2012). "Gender Games: The Olympics Has a New Way to Test Whether Athletes Are Men or Women. Is It Fair?" Retrieved from http://www.slate.com/articles/health_and_science/fivering_circus/2012/07/olympics_sex_test_the_international_olympic_committee_has_a_way_to_test_whether_athletes_are_men_or_women_is_it_fair_.html

Sengupta, Anuradha. (August 15, 2016). "Sex Testing for Female Olympic Athletes Is a Thing of the Past (at Least for Now)." Retrieved from www.womensmediacenter.com/news-features/sex-testing-for-female-olympic-athletes-is-a-thing-of-the-past-at-least-for

This discussion of gender identities and practices does not imply that all men in contemporary North American society are ambitious and independent and all women domestic and emotional. Far from it! However, this discussion clarifies the social norms or shared values associated with the two kinds of human beings our society has created. Regimes of truth about gender and other identities provide the standards or parameters through which thoughts and behaviors are molded.

MASCULINITY

In mainstream contemporary U.S. society, the "regimes of truth" associated with masculinity are constructed from the classical traits of intelligence, courage, and honesty, with the addition of two other key dimensions. One of these dimensions revolves around potent sexuality and an affinity for violence: the machismo element. Machismo involves breaking rules, sexual potency contextualized in the blending of sex and violence, and contempt for women and femininity (misogyny). To be a man is to not be a woman. Weakness, softness, and vulnerability are to be avoided at all costs. Boys are often socialized into contemporary masculinity through shaming practices that ridicule expressions of femininity. As Michael Kimmel explained in a 2013 HuffPost "Let's Talk" feature, boys are relentlessly policing each other, "pressured to conform to a narrow definition of masculinity by the constant spectre of being called a fag or gay." Kimmel's solution to the academic disengagement of boys (as evidenced by the fact that girls do better in school) is "to empower boys' resilience in the face of this gender policing." He emphasizes that there are actually more differences among boys than between boys and girls, emphasizing that the stereotype of the rough-and-tumble, boys-will-be-boys type of boy flattens the differences among boys and crushes those who do not conform to the stereotype.

It is no coincidence that the symbol of male ♂ represents Mars, the Roman god of war. A second dimension of masculinity is the provider role, composed of ambition, confidence, competence, and strength. Early research by Deborah David and Robert Brannon characterized four dictates of masculinity that encompass these key dimensions: (1) "no sissy stuff," the rejection of femininity; (2) the "big wheel," ambition and the pursuit of success, fame, and wealth; (3) the "sturdy oak," confidence, competence, stoicism, and toughness; and (4) "give 'em hell," the machismo element.[1] Although these scripts dictate masculinity in a broad sense, there are societal demands that construct masculinity differently for different kinds of men. Of course, masculinity is also experienced through intersections with other identities. Middle-class masculinities, for example, put emphasis on the big-wheel dimension; the dictates of white masculinity often involve the sturdy oak; and men of color often become associated with the machismo element (with the exception of Asian American men, who are sometimes feminized, when they are not being portrayed as karate warriors).

The last decades have seen changes in the social construction of contemporary masculinity. Although the machismo element is still acted out by countless teenage boys and men, it is also avoided by many men who genuinely do not want to be constrained by its demands. Often these men have realized that moving away from machismo does not necessarily imply a loss of power. In fact, it seems contemporary women may prefer men who are a little more sensitive and vulnerable. In part, these changes have come about as a result of the focus on gender provided by the women's movement and the work of such organizations as the National Organization of Men Against Sexism (NOMAS). As feminist

---

1   Deborah S. David and Robert Brannon, eds., *The Forty-Nine Percent Majority: The Male Sex Role* (Reading, MA: Addison-Wesley, 1976), 13–35.

writer and activist Gloria Steinem once said, gender is a prison for both women and men. The difference, she explained, is that for men it's a prison with wall-to-wall carpeting and someone to bring you coffee. Understanding the limitations associated with masculine social scripts has encouraged some men to transform these scripts into more productive ways of living. Many pro-feminist men and men's organizations have been at the forefront of this work.

RITES OF PASSAGE

In almost every culture, adolescents participate in some rite of passage to mark entry into adulthood. Quite often, these rites reinforce gender distinctions. Most rites of passage share four basic elements: (1) separation from society, (2) preparation or instruction from an elder, (3) transition, and (4) welcoming back into society with acknowledgment of changed status.* Notice in the following examples how gender is reinforced through rites of passage:

- Among the Okrika of Africa, girls participate in the Iria, a rite that begins in the "fatting rooms" where the girls are fed rich foods to cause the body to "come out." The girls learn traditional songs from the elderly women, and these songs are used to free the girls from their romantic attachments to water spirits so they can become marriageable and receive mortal suitors. On the final day of their initiation, the water spirits are expected to try to seize the girls, but the Osokolo (a male) strikes the girls with sticks and drives them back to the village, ensuring their safety and future fertility.*
- The Tukuna of the Amazon initiate girls into womanhood at the onset of menstruation through the Festa das Mocas Novas. For several weeks, the girl lives in seclusion in a chamber in her family's home. The Tukuna believe that during this time, the girl

is in the underworld and in increasing danger from demons, the Noo. Near the end of the initiation period, the girl is painted with black genipapo dye for two days to protect her from the Noo, while guests arrive, some wearing masks to become incarnations of the Noo. On the third day, she leaves the chamber to dance with her family until dawn. The shaman gives her a firebrand to throw at the Noo to break the Noo's power and allow her to enter into womanhood.*

- In Ohafia in Nigeria, a father provides his son with a bow and arrows around age seven or eight. The boy practices shooting at targets until he develops the skill to kill a small bird. When this task is accomplished, the boy ties the dead bird to the end of his bow and marches through his village singing that his peers who have not yet killed their first bird are cowards. His father then dresses him in finery and takes him to visit, often for the first time, his maternal family. His new social role distinguishes him from the "cowards" and marks his entrance into manhood.

What are some rites of passage in the United States? How do these rites reinforce gender? How might rites of passage be developed that acknowledge entrance into adulthood without reinforcing gender distinctions?

*Cassandra Halle Delaney, "Rites of Passage in Adolescence," *Adolescence* 30 (1995): 891–987.

LEARNING ACTIVITY
PERFORMING GENDER IN THE MOVIES

Many movies offer gender-bending performances. Choose one or more of the following movies to watch. During the movie, record your observations about how the various characters learn and perform gender. Also note the ways race intersects with gender in these performances. How is sexual identity expressed in the

performance of gender? Are these performances of gender disruptive of gender norms? Or are they problematic in their reinforcement of the gender binary and gender stereotypes?

- *The Adventures of Priscilla, Queen of the Desert*
- *Albert Nobbs*
- *The Associate*

(continued)

- *Big Momma's House*
- *The Birdcage*
- *Boys Don't Cry*
- *Connie and Carla*
- *The Danish Girl*
- *Kiss of the Spiderwoman*
- *M. Butterfly*
- *Ma Vie en Rose*
- *Mrs. Doubtfire*
- *Mulan*
- *Nutty Professor*
- *Nutty Professor II: The Klumps*

- *Orlando*
- *Shakespeare in Love*
- *Sorority Boys*
- *Switch*
- *To Wong Foo, Thanks for Everything! Julie Newmar*
- *Tomboy*
- *Tootsie*
- *Transamerica*
- *Victor/Victoria*
- *White Chicks*
- *Yentl*

Some men have responded to the limitations of masculinity and the advances of women brought about by feminism by focusing on themselves as victims, as demonstrated by the mytho-poetic men's movement, which encourages men to bond and reclaim their power. While this may empower individual men, private solutions to social problems do little to transform patriarchal social structures. Other men more overtly express their desire to take back the power they believe they have lost as a result of changes in contemporary notions of femininity and the gains of the women's movement. These include the Promise Keepers, a group of Christian-affiliated men who want to return men to their rightful place in the family and community through a strong reassertion of traditional gender roles. They believe that men are to rule and women are to serve within the traditional family system. The reading "The Connection Between White Men, Aggrievement, and Mass Shootings" by Arvind Dilawar demonstrates how gendered and racialized expectations intersect in white masculinity to produce mass violence.

ACTIVIST PROFILE

QWO-LI DRISKILL

Qwo-Li Driskill is a queer Two-Spirit noncitizen Cherokee poet, performer, and activist and our colleague at Oregon State University, where they are an associate professor of queer studies in the Women, Gender, and Sexuality Studies program. Raised in Colorado, they earned a BA from the University of Northern Colorado; an MA from Antioch University, Seattle; and a PhD from Michigan State University.

Qwo-Li explains, "My activism is committed to radical social transformation and intersectional politics. It is deeply rooted in and informed by Native decolonization movements, Queer/Trans/GLBT communities of color, feminisms, poor/working-class politics, and (dis)ability movements. My work as a poet, performer, scholar, and educator (both inside and outside of the university) is entwined with struggles for social justice and healing."

Their first book of poetry, *Walking with Ghosts: Poems* (2005), confronts the forced removal of the Cherokee from their native lands, as well as the ongoing attacks on the LGBTQ community. As reviewer Janice Gould commented, "Qwo-Li Driskill's poetry, part lament and part manifesto, is haunted by ghost dancers. It is a record of those we've lost to the irrational hatred and fear of racism and homophobia. The voice within these poems chants, croons, sasses, and sings, for this is poetry meant to be spoken into being. In the tradition of other queer, socially-conscious poets, like Chrystos, Pat Parker, and Audre Lorde, the question of whether justice exists for all—especially for the poorest and most despised among us—burns at the center of this fine first collection." The book was named Book of the Month by *Sable: The LitMag for New Writing* and was nominated for the Griffin Poetry Prize. More of Qwo-Li's poems have appeared in a variety of journals and anthologies. They also published co-edited volumes including *Scars Tell Stories: A Queer and Trans (Dis)ability Zine* (2007) and *Queer Indigenous Studies: Critical Interventions in Theory, Politics, and Literature* (2011), a collection of essays that critique the intersections of colonialism and heteropatriarchy. They are the author of *Asegi Stories: Cherokee Queer and Two-Spirit Memory* (2016).

FOR MARSHA P. (PAY IT NO MIND!) JOHNSON

by Qwo-Li Driskill

> found floating in the Hudson River shortly after NYC Pride, 1992 "You are the one whose spirit is present in the dappled stars."
>
> —Joy Harjo, from "For Anna Mae Pictou Aquash . . ."

Each act of war
    is whispered from Queen to Queen
    held like a lost child
then released into the water below.
    Names float into rivers
    gentle blooms of African Violets.
I will be the one that dangles
    from the side but
    does not let go.
The police insisted you leapt
    into the Hudson
    driftwood body
    in sequin lace
    rhinestone beads
    that pull us to the bottom,
    No serious investigation—just
    another
    dead Queen.
I am the one who sings Billie Holiday
    as a prayer song to you, Marsha P.
We all choke on splintered bones,
    dismembered screams,
    the knowledge that each
    death is our own.
I pour libations of dove's blood,
    leave offerings of yam and corn
    to call back all of our lost spirits.

Marsha P, your face glitters with
    Ashanti gold
    as you sashay across the moonscape
    in a ruby chariot ablaze.
    Sister, you drag
    us behind you.
We are gathered on the bridge between
    survival and despair.
    I will be the one wearing gardenias
    in my hair,
    thinking about
    how we all go back to water.
    Thinking about
    the night
    you did not jump.
I will make voodoo dolls
    of the police and other thugs,
    walk to the edge,
    watch the river rise to meet them.
I will be the one
    with the rattlesnake that binds
    my left arm and
    in my right hand I will carry
    a wooden hatchet to
    cut away at the
    silence of your murder.
Each of us go on,
    pretend to pay it no mind,
    bite down hard on the steel of
    despair.
We will be the ones that gnaw off our own
    legs rather than let them win.
We will be the ones mourning
    the death of yet another Queen.
Girl, I will put your photo
    on my ancestral altar
    to remember all of us
    who never jumped.
Miss Johnson, your meanings
    sparkle like stars dappled
    across the piers of the
    Hudson River.
Gathered on the bridge
    we resist the water.

(Published in *Lodestar Quarterly*, Fall 2004)

FEMININITY

Adjectives associated with traditional notions of femininity in contemporary mainstream North American society include soft, passive, domestic, nurturing, emotional, dependent, sensitive, delicate, intuitive, fastidious, needy, fearful, and so forth. These are the qualities that have kept women in positions of subordination and encouraged them to do the

GENDER ON THE WEB

JANET LOCKHART

As with many other phenomena, the ways people are portrayed on the Internet can either reinforce stereotypical ideas about gender or challenge them. Stereotypical/idealized views of women as passive, emotional, supportive, and secondary; and men as active, intelligent, aggressive, and primary are propagated in advertising, entertainment—and news. Of course, many women do embody some of the stereotypical traits described (as many men embody some of the opposite), but the overwhelming depiction of this narrow range ignores the enormous variety of traits, interests, skills, and abilities women have: In short, it limits them.

In groups or individually, do the following:

Examine a mainstream website (choose a major provider or have your instructor assign one) and start with a simple tally: *How many* women are pictured or mentioned in text, compared to how many men; how many transgender or gender nonbinary people are found in news articles, entertainment, advertisements, and so on? How many women are shown or mentioned on the opening screen, home page, or "above the fold"? Then go further: What *types* of women are shown or mentioned: What is their race, size, appearance, sexual identity, socioeconomic status, religion, and so on? What types of women are not shown? Are there any women of color, women with disabilities, transwomen, bisexual women, women with large bodies, Muslim women, and so on? Why do you think this is?

Finally, *how* are the women depicted? Are they central or secondary to the story? Are they shown posing or actively doing something? Are they named, or are they described in terms of their relationship to a man (girlfriend or "GF," wife, ex-wife, Mrs. Smith, etc.)? Are they shown for traditional reasons such as getting married or wearing high fashion? Or are they shown doing their jobs skillfully, making a discovery, giving their opinion on something, or taking a political action? Are any women shown doing physically arduous tasks, leading groups of people, engaging in scientific work, and the like?

What do you think are the reasons for the limited variety of women's depictions online? How do the depictions of females and males influence (overtly or subtly) the way you think about the people shown? What are some ways these depictions could be expanded?

Dig Deeper

Find an activist news agency, feminist organization's website, or blog and do the same kind of analysis as just outlined. Were there any surprises? What patterns did you see? Did this exercise give you anything to think about? Will you do anything differently as a result of this exercise? How will you use your web surfing time?

Variation: Do some in-depth research and identify how women and men are present in owning, developing, controlling, and profiting from online content.

---

domestic and emotional work of society. Again, it is no surprise that the symbol of female ♀ represents Venus, the goddess of love. "Doing gender" in terms of femininity involves speaking, walking, looking, and acting in certain ways: in feminine ways. The performative quality involved in being a drag queen (someone who is acting out normative femininity) highlights and reveals the taken-for-granted (at least by cisgender women) affectations of femininity. Yet femininity, like masculinity, varies across cultures and intersects with other identities. As already discussed, African American women may not identify with some aspects of femininity more readily associated with white femininity, such as passivity. Asian American women, on the other hand, often have to deal with societal stereotypes that construct femininity very much in terms of passivity and dependence: the "exotic gardenia" or "oriental chick" described in Nellie Wong's poem "When I Was Growing Up."

A key aspect of femininity is its bifurcation or channeling into two opposite aspects. These aspects involve the chaste, domestic, caring mother or madonna and the sexy, seducing, fun-loving playmate or whore (sometimes known in popular mythology as women

LEARNING ACTIVITY
WALK LIKE A MAN, SIT LIKE A LADY

One of the ways we perform gender is by the way we use our bodies. Very early on, children learn to act their gender in the ways they sit, walk, and talk.

Try this observation research:

- Observe a group of schoolchildren playing. Make notes about what you observe concerning children's gendered behaviors, particularly how they use their bodies in their play and communication.

- Find a place where you can watch people—any age— sitting or walking. A public park or mall may offer an excellent vantage point. Record your observations about the gendered ways people walk and sit.

Also try this experiment: Ask a friend who identifies with another gender to participate in an experiment with you. Take turns teaching each other to sit and to walk like the other gender. After practicing your newfound gender behaviors, write down your reflections about the experience.

you marry and women with whom you have sex). These polar opposites cause tension as women navigate the implications of these aspects of femininity in their everyday lives. A woman may discover that neither sexual activity nor sexual inactivity is quite right. If she is too sexually active, she will be censured for being too loose, the whore; if she refrains from sexual activity, she might similarly be censured for being a prude or frigid. Notice there are many slang words for both kinds of women: those who have too much sex and those who do not have enough. This is the double bind: You're damned if you do and potentially damned if you don't. These contradictions and mixed messages serve to keep women in line.

Unlike contemporary masculinity, which is exhibiting very small steps into the realms of the feminine, femininity has boldly moved into areas that were traditionally off-limits. Today's ideal woman (perhaps from a woman's point of view) is definitely more androgynous than the ideal woman of the past. The contemporary ideal woman might be someone who is smart, competent, and independent; beautiful, thin, athletic, and sexy; yet also loving, sensitive, competent domestically, and emotionally healthy. Note how this

image has integrated characteristics of traditional masculinity with feminine qualities at the same time that it has retained much of the feminine social script. The contemporary ideal woman is strong, assertive, active, and independent rather than passive, delicate, and dependent. The assumption is that she is out in the public world rather than confined to the home. She has not completely shed her domestic, nurturing, and caring dimension, however, or her intuitive, emotional, and sensitive aspects. These attributes are important in her success as a loving and capable partner to a man, as indeed are her physical attributes concerning looks and body size.

To be a modern woman today (we might even say a "liberated woman") is to be able to do everything: to be a superwoman. It is important to ask who is benefiting from this new social script. Women work in the public world (often in jobs that pay less, thus helping employers and the economic system) and yet still are expected to do the domestic and emotional work of home and family as well as stay fit and "beautiful." In many ways, contemporary femininity tends to serve both the capitalist economic system and individual men better than the traditional, dependent, domestic model.

GENDER FLUIDITY

Masculinity and femininity are socially constructed categories that have little to do with biology and much to do with social hierarchies. While many people are comfortable performing in cisgender ways, a number of people do not fit either category of femininity or masculinity and may label themselves gender fluid, gender nonconforming, gender nonbinary, genderqueer, or any of a number of terms that reflect more complicated ways of experiencing and expressing gender. Because of the dominance of the gender binary, however, societal norms and enforcements often discourage gender nonconformity and reinforce conformity with assigned gender. People who do not conform to the expected binaries may express themselves as a combination of traditional masculine and feminine characteristics, or they may move along a continuum, some days expressing themselves as more masculine, some days as more feminine. These expressions blur binary gender lines and disrupt hegemonic femininity and masculinity. In fact, a recent poll found that half of millennials believe gender is a spectrum, and a GLAAD survey found that 12 percent of millennials identify as transgender or gender nonconforming. In practice, this has meant that more babies are being given names not associated with one gender or another; parents are dressing their children in both pink and blue; people are taking on once-gendered roles in ways that have nothing to do with gender. And, not surprisingly, corporations are paying attention, eager to capitalize on the growing awareness of gender fluidity and nonconformity. The fashion industry is starting to create clothes that aren't gendered, as are the cosmetic and fragrance industries. Many brands are starting to focus on personality attributes and passions rather than gender in developing and marketing products. Of course, none of this means that discrimination and violence against people who do not conform to traditional gender roles are no longer problems. The rejection of the gender binary is often met with bullying, insults, discrimination, rejection, and violence. At least 25 transgender or gender nonconforming people were killed in 2017, 84 percent of whom were people of color and 80 percent of whom were transwomen. Being harassed at work is a nearly universal experience for trans and gender nonconforming people, another survey found. Three-quarters of trans and gender nonconforming students feel unsafe at school, and nearly 60 percent have been denied use of the bathroom that most closely corresponds with their gender identity. So even as some acceptance increases and corporations work to turn a profit from gender nonconformity, the realities of marginalization and discrimination remain, demonstrating the power of systems of gender to police, enforce, and punish non-adherence to the gender binary.

GENDER RANKING

Gender encompasses not only the socially constructed, intersecting differences prescribed for different kinds of human beings but also the values associated with these differences. Recall the sissy/tomboy exercise at the beginning of this chapter. Those traits assigned as feminine are less valued than those considered masculine, illustrating why men tend to have more problems emulating femininity and trans people moving into femininity are viewed with somewhat more hostility than those transitioning toward masculine identities. It is okay to emulate the masculine and act like a boy, but it may not be okay to emulate the feminine. This is gender ranking (the valuing of one gender over another). "When genders are ranked," writes Judith Lorber in "The Social Construction of Gender," the "devalued genders have less power, prestige, and economic rewards than the valued genders." Just as white is valued above brown or black, young (though not too young) above old, and heterosexual above homosexual, masculinity tends to be ranked higher than femininity. To be masculine is to have privileges vis-à-vis gender systems; to be feminine means to identify with members of a target group. As already discussed, the social system here that discriminates and privileges on the basis of gender is sexism, although any one person experiencing entitlements or obstacles associated with sexism may also experience entitlements and/or obstacles associated with other intersecting differences or identities. Sexism works by viewing the differences between women and men as important for determining access to social, economic, and political resources. As defined in Chapter 2, sexism is the system that discriminates and privileges on the basis of gender and that results in gender stratification. Given the ranking of gender in our society, sexism works to privilege men and limit women. In other words, men receive entitlements and privilege in a society that ranks masculinity over femininity even while they may be limited by virtue of other intersecting identities such as race or social class.

This discussion, however, must be nuanced by an understanding that masculine privilege tends to be granted first and foremost to cisgender masculinity. Transgender individuals often face transphobia as well as hate crimes as a result of their gender expressions. It can be especially difficult for male-bodied individuals to identify as girls since their gender performances are ranked as a result of both breaking gender norms and identification with a target group. This encourages us to pay attention to the varied forms of regulation and violence associated with gender ambiguity and transgender identification. Gender expressions that do not adhere to traditional female/male binaries are often subject to discipline in a society that expects and enforces "opposite" genders.

Although women are limited by sexism as a system of power that privileges men over women, the social category "woman," as you will recall from Chapter 2, is hardly homogeneous and constantly in flux. Location in different systems of inequality and privilege shapes women's lives in different ways; they are not affected by gender in the same ways. Other systems based on class, race, sexual identity, and so forth interact with gender to produce different experiences for individual women. This means that the effects of gender and understandings of both femininity and masculinity are mediated by other systems of power. This is another way that ranking occurs. Forms of gender-based oppression and exploitation depend in part on other social characteristics in people's lives, and gender practices often enforce other types of inequalities. This reflects the confluence that occurs as gender categories are informed/constructed through social relations of power associated with other identities and accompanying systems of inequality and privilege (such as racial identities and racism, sexual identities and heterosexism, and so forth). These identities cannot be separated, and certainly they are lived and performed through a tangle of multiple (and often shifting) identities. In this way, ranking occurs both across gender categories (masculinity is valued over femininity) and within gender categories (economically privileged women are represented differently than poor women and receive economic and social entitlements, abled women live different lives than disabled women, and so forth).

Examples of this latter type of gender ranking also include the ways African American women may be characterized as promiscuous or matriarchal and African American men are described as hyperathletic and sexually potent. Jewish women are painted as materialistic and overbearing, whereas Jewish men are supposedly very ambitious, thrifty, good at business, yet still tied to their mothers' apron strings. Latinas and Chicanas are stereotyped as sexy and fun loving, and, likewise, Latinos and Chicanos are seen as oversexed, romantic, and passionate. Native American women are portrayed as silent and overworked or exotic and romantic, whereas Native American men are stereotyped as aloof mystics, close to nature, or else as "savages" and drunks. Asian Americans generally are portrayed as smart and good at science and math, with Asian American women further typed as exotic, passive, and delicate. Such stereotypes are part of regimes of truth that keep power systems intact. Remember that you will always find examples of people who may fit a certain stereotype to some extent; but stereotypes are used to shape meaning about, and often denigrate, a whole category of humans without respect to accurate information about them.

Finally, other examples of this gender ranking include the ways certain women (the poor and women of color) were historically regarded as carrying out appropriate womanhood when they fulfilled the domestic labor needs of strangers. Upper-class femininity meant that there were certain jobs these privileged women could not perform. This demonstrates the interaction of gender with class and race systems. Old women endure a certain brand of femininity that tends to be devoid of the playmate role and is heavy on the mother aspect. Sexually active old women are violating the norms of femininity set up for them: This shows the influence of ageism in shaping gender norms. Other stereotypes that reveal the interaction of gender with societal systems of privilege and inequality include disabled women's supposedly relatively low sexual appetite or lesbians' lack of femininity (they are presumed to want to be like men at the same time they are said to hate them).

All of these problematic constructions are created against the norm of whiteness and work to maintain the privileges of the mythical norm. This concept is illustrated in Nellie Wong's poem. She longed to be white, something she saw as synonymous with being a desirable woman. Note there are ethnic and regional stereotypes for white women (such as the dizzy blonde, Southern belle, sexually liberated Scandinavian, or hot-tempered Irish), even though whites are encouraged not to see white as a racial category. Whiteness is just as racialized as any other racial group. The fact that being white can be claimed as the mythical norm strips whiteness from the historical and political roots of its construction as a racial category. As discussed in Chapter 2, this ability for nontarget groups to remain relatively invisible is a key to maintaining their dominance in society.

IDEAS FOR ACTIVISM

- Be a gender traitor for a day. Act/dress in ways that are not generally considered to be appropriate for your gender.
- Develop and perform on campus a street theater piece about gender performance.

- Plan, create, publish, and distribute a zine challenging traditional gender roles.
- Examine how masculinity is valued above femininity on your campus. Write a letter about your findings to your campus newspaper.

THE BLOG

ACADEMIA'S WAR ON MEN—THAT ISN'T

Susan M. Shaw with Bradley Boovy (2017)

The University of Wisconsin has launched a war on men. At least, that's what Republican state senator Steve Nass says. According to Nass, the university's undergraduate program on masculinity is an assault on men that is part of higher education's "politically correct agenda."

Apparently, Nass has no clue what a men and masculinities program is, nor the benefits such a program provides both men and women.

The academic study of gender has its roots in the second wave of the women's movement, with the first women's studies courses offered in the early 1970s. These initial courses brought women's contributions in history, literature, art, theology, and other disciplines to the fore and for the first time centered gender as a significant topic for study.

Because gender generally and women specifically had essentially been omitted from academic study until this point, women's studies began as a way to claim a place for women in the curriculum and to make women's issues central. The accepted premise was that men's lives and experiences were well represented in the rest of the curriculum, and so the study of women was a necessary additive.

Quickly, early feminist scholars realized that simply adding women to existing course content or offering courses about women was not enough. Rather, gender needed to become a primary lens for analysis because of the inextricable link between gender and power, in this case, as represented in the academic disciplines.

Inevitably, asking questions about gender led to asking questions not only about women and femininity but also about men and masculinity, and so the field of masculinity studies arose in the 1990s, not as a competitor to women's studies but as its complement.

Masculinity studies ask questions of how we understand what a "real man" is, how notions of men and masculinity are also shaped by race, social class, sexuality, and other forms of difference, and how ideas about masculinity affect men and women.

(continued)

At our institution, we teach a course on men and masculinities that is grounded in the important contributions that feminist scholars have made to our understanding of gender. The course attracts many young men who are interested in asking questions about what role masculinity plays in maintaining structural inequality, how ideas of what is masculine and what is feminine have changed over time and vary from one culture to another, and how masculinity is represented in media and the arts. Most importantly, students ask critical questions about how masculine ideals affect society and people's lives in terms of everyone's access to power and resources.

As an example of the kinds of thinking we encourage our students to engage in today, take the report that Oxfam published that revealed that eight men own the same wealth as 3.8 billion people. Students who have taken courses on masculinity and gender in society are equipped to understand that it is no accident that the world's wealthiest people are men. (It's also no accident that of these eight men, most are white, speak English, and live in the United States.) We train our students to take a hard look at such inequalities, ask critical questions about history and unequal distribution of power and resources, and—we hope—go out and change the social systems that perpetuate such inequality. Honestly, isn't *that* what Mr. Nass is really worried about?

Of course, the Right has reacted (a bit hysterically) to this field of study: It's part of "the Left's feminization of male culture in America," "propaganda" to reduce "young men to brainwashed nancy-boys," "a men's auxiliary of women's studies," and part of a "plan to subvert Christian and traditional values and replace them with diversity and multicultural mush."

Just days after Nass unleashed his invective against the University of Wisconsin's masculinity studies program, Fox News contributor Todd Starnes targeted two other universities (one of them Oregon State University) for supporting programming that encourages critical thinking about men and masculinities from multiple scholarly perspectives. Starnes's attempt at satire relies on a grab bag of conservative rhetoric about men and women that does nothing to help any of us understand and respond to the challenges we face as a country and in our communities.

Such absurd fearmongering is made possible by dominant Western ideals of what men "should be." Expressions like "Man up!" and "Boys don't cry" perpetuate patterns of belief and social behavior that have a negative impact not only on the lives of women and other marginalized groups but also on men themselves. The evidence from fields like psychology, public health, history, and law is overwhelming and continues to grow. Young men on college campuses, for example, are more likely to engage in high-risk behavior such as alcohol and drug abuse (Miller 2008; Swartout and White 2010). More troubling still is that suicide rates among young college-aged (as well as working-class) men are consistently very high for a variety of reasons (see, for example, Pitman et al. 2012).

Failure to pay close attention to masculinity—in ways that are informed by critical scholarly approaches from fields like women studies, queer studies, and critical race theory—is to fail society as a whole and young men in particular. Outside of universities, community organizations such as domestic violence centers, churches, and peer-support groups also provide men with the opportunity to learn about and understand male privilege as they work to create change in the world.

If anyone is "waging a war on men," it's not academics, scholars, teachers, or community organizers who work to help men understand that they don't need to buy into the misogynistic, homophobic, and racist rhetoric of "traditional values." It is people in positions of power who legitimize violent and destructive expressions of masculinity, in part by rehashing the same tired language of "war" and "attack" that the Right has used at least since the 1980s to incite aggressive responses to social issues that require the kind of critical thinking and dialog that students in courses on masculinity and gender practice.

References

Miller, K. (2008). "Wired: Energy Drinks, Jock Identity, Masculine Norms, and Risk Taking." *Journal of American College Health*, 56(5), 481–490.

Pitman, A., Krysinska, K., Osborn, D., and King, M. (2012). "Suicide in Young Men." *Lancet*, 379(9834), 2283–2392.

Swartout, K., and White, J. (2010). "The Relationship Between Drug Use and Sexual Aggression in Men Across Time." *Journal of Interpersonal Violence*, 25(9), 1716–1735.

17. THE FIVE SEXES, REVISITED*

ANNE FAUSTO-STERLING (2000)

As Cheryl Chase stepped to the front of the packed meeting room in the Sheraton Boston Hotel, nervous coughs made the tension audible. Chase, an activist for intersexual rights, had been invited to address the May 2000 meeting of the Lawson Wilkins Pediatric Endocrine Society (LWPES), the largest organization in the United States for specialists in children's hormones. Her talk would be the grand finale to a four-hour symposium on the treatment of genital ambiguity in newborns, infants born with a mixture of both male and female anatomy, or genitals that appear to differ from their chromosomal sex. The topic was hardly a novel one to the assembled physicians.

Yet Chase's appearance before the group was remarkable. Three and a half years earlier, the American Academy of Pediatrics had refused her request for a chance to present the patients' viewpoint on the treatment of genital ambiguity, dismissing Chase and her supporters as "zealots." About two dozen intersex people had responded by throwing up a picket line. The Intersex Society of North America (ISNA) even issued a press release: "Hermaphrodites Target Kiddie Docs."

It had done my 1960s street-activist heart good. In the short run, I said to Chase at the time, the picketing would make people angry. But eventually, I assured her, the doors then closed would open. Now, as Chase began to address the physicians at their own convention, that prediction was coming true. Her talk, titled "Sexual Ambiguity: The Patient-Centered Approach," was a measured critique of the near-universal practice of performing immediate, "corrective" surgery on thousands of infants born each year with ambiguous genitalia. Chase herself lives with the consequences of such surgery. Yet her audience, the very endocrinologists and surgeons Chase was accusing of reacting with "surgery and shame," received her with respect. Even more remarkably, many of the speakers who preceded her at the session had already spoken of the need to scrap current practices in favor of treatments more centered on psychological counseling.

What led to such a dramatic reversal of fortune? Certainly, Chase's talk at the LWPES symposium was a vindication of her persistence in seeking attention for her cause. But her invitation to speak was also a watershed in the evolving discussion about how to treat children with ambiguous genitalia. And that discussion, in turn, is the tip of a biocultural iceberg—the gender iceberg—that continues to rock both medicine and our culture at large.

Chase made her first national appearance in 1993, in [*The Sciences*], announcing the formation of ISNA in a letter responding to an essay I had written for [*The Sciences*], titled "The Five Sexes" [March/April 1993]. In that article I argued that the two-sex system embedded in our society is not adequate to encompass the full spectrum of human sexuality. In its place, I suggested a five-sex system. In addition to males and females, I included "herms" (named after true hermaphrodites, people born with both a testis and an ovary); "merms" (male pseudohermaphrodites, who are born with testes and some aspect of female genitalia); and "ferms" (female pseudohermaphrodites, who have ovaries combined with some aspect of male genitalia).

I had intended to be provocative, but I had also written with tongue firmly in cheek. So I was surprised by the extent of the controversy the article unleashed. Right-wing Christians were outraged, and connected my idea of five sexes with the United Nations–sponsored Fourth World Conference on Women, held in Beijing in September 1995. At the same time, the article delighted others who felt constrained by the current sex and gender system.

Clearly, I had struck a nerve. The fact that so many people could get riled up by my proposal to revamp our sex and gender system suggested that change—as well as resistance to it—might be in the offing.

---

*   This article uses the term "transgendered," which was the term primarily used in 2000 when the essay was written. "Transgendered" is no longer used. Instead, the appropriate term in contemporary discussion is "transgender."

Indeed, a lot has changed since 1993, and I like to think that my article was an important stimulus. As if from nowhere, intersexuals are materializing before our very eyes. Like Chase, many have become political organizers, who lobby physicians and politicians to change current treatment practices. But more generally, though perhaps no less provocatively, the boundaries separating masculine and feminine seem harder than ever to define.

Some find the changes under way deeply disturbing. Others find them liberating.

Who is an intersexual—and how many intersexuals are there? The concept of intersexuality is rooted in the very ideas of male and female. In the idealized, Platonic, biological world, human beings are divided into two kinds: a perfectly dimorphic species. Males have an X and a Y chromosome, testes, a penis and all of the appropriate internal plumbing for delivering urine and semen to the outside world. They also have well-known secondary sexual characteristics, including a muscular build and facial hair. Women have two X chromosomes, ovaries, all of the internal plumbing to transport urine and ova to the outside world, a system to support pregnancy and fetal development, as well as a variety of recognizable secondary sexual characteristics.

That idealized story papers over many obvious caveats: some women have facial hair, some men have none; some women speak with deep voices, some men veritably squeak. Less well known is the fact that, on close inspection, absolute dimorphism disintegrates even at the level of basic biology. Chromosomes, hormones, the internal sex structures, the gonads and the external genitalia all vary more than most people realize. Those born outside of the Platonic dimorphic mold are called intersexuals.

In "The Five Sexes" I reported an estimate by a psychologist expert in the treatment of intersexuals, suggesting that some 4 percent of all live births are intersexual. Then, together with a group of Brown University undergraduates, I set out to conduct the first systematic assessment of the available data on intersexual birthrates. We scoured the medical literature for estimates of the frequency of various categories of intersexuality, from additional chromosomes to mixed gonads, hormones and genitalia. For some

conditions we could find only anecdotal evidence; for most, however, numbers exist. On the basis of that evidence, we calculated that for every 1,000 children born, seventeen are intersexual in some form. That number—1.7 percent—is a ballpark estimate, not a precise count, though we believe it is more accurate than the 4 percent I reported.

Our figure represents all chromosomal, anatomical and hormonal exceptions to the dimorphic ideal; the number of intersexuals who might, potentially, be subject to surgery as infants is smaller—probably between one in 1,000 and one in 2,000 live births. Furthermore, because some populations possess the relevant genes at high frequency, the intersexual birthrate is not uniform throughout the world.

Consider, for instance, the gene for congenital adrenal hyperplasia (CAH). When the CAH gene is inherited from both parents, it leads to a baby with masculinized external genitalia who possesses two X chromosomes and the internal reproductive organs of a potentially fertile woman. The frequency of the gene varies widely around the world: in New Zealand it occurs in only forty-three children per million; among the Yupik Eskimo of southwestern Alaska, its frequency is 3,500 per million.

Intersexuality has always been to some extent a matter of definition. And in the past century physicians have been the ones who defined children as intersexual—and provided the remedies. When only the chromosomes are unusual, but the external genitalia and gonads clearly indicate either a male or a female, physicians do not advocate intervention. Indeed, it is not clear what kind of intervention could be advocated in such cases. But the story is quite different when infants are born with mixed genitalia, or with external genitals that seem at odds with the baby's gonads. Most clinics now specializing in the treatment of intersex babies rely on case-management principles developed in the 1950s by the psychologist John Money and the psychiatrists Joan G. Hampson and John L. Hampson, all of Johns Hopkins University in Baltimore, Maryland. Money believed that gender identity is completely malleable for about eighteen months after birth. Thus, he argued, when a treatment team is presented with an infant who has ambiguous genitalia, the team could make a gender assignment solely on the basis of what made the best surgical sense. The physicians could then simply encourage the parents to raise the child according to the surgically assigned gender. Following that course, most physicians maintained, would eliminate psychological distress for both the patient and the parents. Indeed, treatment teams were never to use such words as "intersex" or "hermaphrodite"; instead, they were to tell parents that nature intended the baby to be the boy or the girl that the physicians had determined it was. Through surgery, the physicians were merely completing nature's intention.

Although Money and the Hampsons published detailed case studies of intersex children who they said had adjusted well to their gender assignments, Money thought one case in particular proved his theory. It was a dramatic example, inasmuch as it did not involve intersexuality at all: one of a pair of identical twin boys lost his penis as a result of a circumcision accident. Money recommended that "John" (as he came to be known in a later case study) be surgically turned into "Joan" and raised as a girl. In time, Joan grew to love wearing dresses and having her hair done. Money proudly proclaimed the sex reassignment a success.

But as recently chronicled by John Colapinto, in his book *As Nature Made Him,* Joan—now known to be an adult male named David Reimer eventually rejected his female assignment. Even without a functioning penis and testes (which had been removed as part of the reassignment) John/Joan sought masculinizing medication, and married a woman with children (whom he adopted).

Since the full conclusion to the John/Joan story came to light, other individuals who were reassigned as males or females shortly after birth but who later rejected their early assignments have come forward. So, too, have cases in which the reassignment has worked—at least into the subject's mid-twenties. But even then the aftermath of the surgery can be problematic. Genital surgery often leaves scars that reduce sexual sensitivity. Chase herself had a complete clitoridectomy, a procedure that is less frequently performed on intersexuals today. But the newer surgeries, which reduce the size of the clitoral shaft, still greatly reduce sensitivity.

The revelation of cases of failed reassignments and the emergence of intersex activism have led an increasing number of pediatric endocrinologists, urologists and psychologists to reexamine the wisdom of early genital surgery. For example, in a talk that preceded Chase's at the LWPES meeting, the medical ethicist Laurence B. McCullough of the Center for Medical Ethics and Health Policy at Baylor College of Medicine in Houston, Texas, introduced an ethical framework for the treatment of children with ambiguous genitalia. Because sex phenotype (the manifestation of genetically and embryologically determined sexual characteristics) and gender presentation (the sex role projected by the individual in society) are highly variable, McCullough argues, the various forms of intersexuality should be defined as normal. All of them fall within the statistically expected variability of sex and gender. Furthermore, though certain disease states may accompany some forms of intersexuality, and may require medical intervention, intersexual conditions are not themselves diseases.

McCullough also contends that in the process of assigning gender, physicians should minimize what he calls irreversible assignments: taking steps such as the surgical removal or modification of gonads or genitalia that the patient may one day want to have reversed. Finally, McCullough urges physicians to abandon their practice of treating the birth of a child with genital ambiguity as a medical or social emergency. Instead, they should take the time to perform a thorough medical workup and should disclose everything to the parents, including the uncertainties about the final outcome. The treatment mantra, in other words, should be therapy, not surgery.

I believe a new treatment protocol for intersex infants, similar to the one outlined by McCullough, is close at hand. Treatment should combine some basic medical and ethical principles with a practical but less drastic approach to the birth of a mixed-sex child. As a first step, surgery on infants should be performed only to save the child's life or to substantially improve the child's physical well-being. Physicians may assign a sex—male or female—to an intersex infant on the basis of the probability that the child's particular condition will lead to the formation of a particular gender identity. At the same time, though, practitioners ought to be humble enough to recognize that as the child grows, he or she may reject the assignment—and they should be wise enough to listen to what the child has to say. Most important, parents should have access to the full range of information and options available to them.

Sex assignments made shortly after birth are only the beginning of a long journey. Consider, for instance, the life of Max Beck: Born intersexual, Max was surgically assigned as a female and consistently raised as such. Had her medical team followed her into her early twenties, they would have deemed her assignment a success because she was married to a man. (It should be noted that success in gender assignment has traditionally been defined as living in that gender as a heterosexual.) Within a few years, however, Beck had come out as a butch lesbian; now in her mid-thirties, Beck has become a man and married his lesbian partner, who (through the miracles of modern reproductive technology) recently gave birth to a girl.

Transsexuals, people who have an emotional gender at odds with their physical sex, once described themselves in terms of dimorphic absolutes—males trapped in female bodies, or vice versa. As such, they sought psychological relief through surgery. Although many still do, some so-called transgendered people today are content to inhabit a more ambiguous zone. A male-to-female transsexual, for instance, may come out as a lesbian. Jane, born a physiological male, is now in her late thirties and living with her wife, whom she married when her name was still John. Jane takes hormones to feminize herself, but they have not yet interfered with her ability to engage in intercourse as a man. In her mind Jane has a lesbian relationship with her wife, though she views their intimate moments as a cross between lesbian and heterosexual sex.

It might seem natural to regard intersexuals and transgendered people as living midway between the poles of male and female. But male and female, masculine and feminine, cannot be parsed as some kind of continuum. Rather, sex and gender are best conceptualized as points in a multidimensional space. For some time, experts on gender development have

distinguished between sex at the genetic level and at the cellular level (sex-specific gene expression, X and Y chromosomes); at the hormonal level (in the fetus, during childhood and after puberty); and at the anatomical level (genitals and secondary sexual characteristics). Gender identity presumably emerges from all of those corporeal aspects via some poorly understood interaction with environment and experience. What has become increasingly clear is that one can find levels of masculinity and femininity in almost every possible permutation. A chromosomal, hormonal and genital male (or female) may emerge with a female (or male) gender identity. Or a chromosomal female with male fetal hormones and masculinized genitalia but with female pubertal hormones—may develop a female gender identity.

The medical and scientific communities have yet to adopt a language that is capable of describing such diversity. In her book *Hermaphrodites and the Medical Invention of Sex*, the historian and medical ethicist Alice Domurat Dreger of Michigan State University in East Lansing documents the emergence of current medical systems for classifying gender ambiguity. The current usage remains rooted in the Victorian approach to sex. The logical structure of the commonly used terms "true hermaphrodite," "male pseudohermaphrodite" and "female pseudohermaphrodite" indicates that only the so-called true hermaphrodite is a genuine mix of male and female. The others, no matter how confusing their body parts, are really hidden males or females. Because true hermaphrodites are rare—possibly only one in 100,000—such a classification system supports the idea that human beings are an absolutely dimorphic species.

At the dawn of the twenty-first century, when the variability of gender seems so visible, such a position is hard to maintain. And here, too, the old medical consensus has begun to crumble. Last fall the pediatric urologist Ian A. Aaronson of the Medical University of South Carolina in Charleston organized the North American Task Force on Intersexuality (NATFI) to review the clinical responses to genital ambiguity in infants. Key medical associations, such as the American Academy of Pediatrics, have endorsed NATFI. Specialists in surgery, endocrinology, psychology, ethics, psychiatry, genetics and public health, as well as intersex patient-advocate groups, have joined its ranks.

One of the goals of NATFI is to establish a new sex nomenclature. One proposal under consideration replaces the current system with emotionally neutral terminology that emphasizes developmental processes rather than preconceived gender categories. For example, Type I intersexes develop out of anomalous virilizing influences; Type II result from some interruption of virilization; and in Type III intersexes the gonads themselves may not have developed in the expected fashion.

What is clear is that since 1993, modern society has moved beyond five sexes to a recognition that gender variation is normal and, for some people, an arena for playful exploration. Discussing my "five sexes" proposal in her book *Lessons from the Intersexed*, the psychologist Suzanne J. Kessler of the State University of New York at Purchase drives this point home with great effect:

> The limitation with Fausto-Sterling's proposal is that . . . [it] still gives genitals . . . primary signifying status and ignores the fact that in the everyday world gender attributions are made without access to genital inspection. . . . What has primacy in everyday life is the gender that is performed, regardless of the flesh's configuration under the clothes.

I now agree with Kessler's assessment. It would be better for intersexuals and their supporters to turn everyone's focus away from genitals. Instead, as she suggests, one should acknowledge that people come in an even wider assortment of sexual identities and characteristics than mere genitals can distinguish. Some women may have "large clitorises or fused labia," whereas some men may have "small penises or misshapen scrota," as Kessler puts it, "phenotypes with no particular clinical or identity meaning."

As clearheaded as Kessler's program is—and despite the progress made in the 1990s—our society is still far from that ideal. The intersexual or trans-gendered person who projects a social gender—what Kessler calls "cultural genitals"—that conflicts with his or her physical genitals still may die for the transgression. Hence legal protection for people whose cultural and physical genitals do not match is needed during the current transition to a more gender-diverse world. One easy step would be to eliminate the category of "gender" from official documents, such as driver's licenses and passports. Surely attributes both more visible (such as height, build and eye color) and less visible (fingerprints and genetic profiles) would be more expedient.

A more far-ranging agenda is presented in the International Bill of Gender Rights, adopted in 1995 at the fourth annual International Conference on Transgender Law and Employment Policy in Houston, Texas. It lists ten "gender rights," including the right to define one's own gender, the right to change one's physical gender if one so chooses and the right to marry whomever one wishes. The legal bases for such rights are being hammered out in the courts as I write and, most recently, through the establishment, in the state of Vermont, of legal same-sex domestic partnerships.

No one could have foreseen such changes in 1993. And the idea that I played some role, however small, in reducing the pressure—from the medical community as well as from society at large—to flatten the diversity of human sexes into two diametrically opposed camps gives me pleasure.

Sometimes people suggest to me, with not a little horror, that I am arguing for a pastel world in which androgyny reigns and men and women are boringly the same. In my vision, however, strong colors coexist with pastels. There are and will continue to be highly masculine people out there; it's just that some of them are women. And some of the most feminine people I know happen to be men.

18. THE SOCIAL CONSTRUCTION OF GENDER

JUDITH LORBER (1994)

Talking about gender for most people is the equivalent of fish talking about water. Gender is so much the routine ground of everyday activities that questioning its taken-for-granted assumptions and presuppositions is like thinking about whether the sun will come up.[1] Gender is so pervasive that in our society we assume it is bred into our genes. Most people find it hard to believe that gender is constantly created and re-created out of human interaction, out of social life, and is the texture and order of that social life. Yet gender, like culture, is a human production that depends on everyone constantly "doing gender" (West and Zimmerman 1987).

And everyone "does gender" without thinking about it. Today, on the subway, I saw a well-dressed man with a year-old child in a stroller. Yesterday, on a bus, I saw a man with a tiny baby in a carrier on his chest. Seeing men taking care of small children in public is increasingly common—at least in New York City. But both men were quite obviously stared at—and smiled at, approvingly. Everyone was doing gender—the men who were changing the role of fathers and the other passengers, who were applauding them silently. But there was more gendering going on that probably fewer people noticed. The baby was wearing a white crocheted cap and white clothes. You couldn't tell if it was a boy or a girl. The child in the stroller was wearing a dark blue T-shirt and dark print pants. As they started to leave the train, the father put a Yankee baseball cap on the child's head. Ah, a boy, I thought. Then I noticed the gleam of tiny earrings in the child's ears, and as they got off, I saw the little flowered sneakers and lace-trimmed socks. Not a boy after all. Gender done.

. . .

For the individual, gender construction starts with assignment to a sex category on the basis of what the genitalia look like at birth.[2] Then babies are dressed or adorned in a way that displays the category because parents don't want to be constantly asked whether their baby is a girl or a boy. A sex category becomes a gender status through naming, dress, and the use of other gender markers. Once a child's gender is evident, others treat those in one gender differently from those in the other, and the children respond to the different treatment by feeling different and behaving differently. As soon as they can talk, they start to refer to themselves as members of their gender. Sex doesn't come into play again until puberty, but by that time, sexual feelings and desires and practices have been shaped by gendered norms and expectations. Adolescent boys and girls approach and avoid each other in an elaborately scripted and gendered mating dance. Parenting is gendered, with different expectations for mothers and fathers, and people of different genders work at different kinds of jobs. The work adults do as mothers and fathers and as low-level workers and high-level bosses, shapes women's and men's life experiences, and these experiences produce different feelings, consciousness, relationships, skills—ways of being that we call feminine or masculine.[3] All of these processes constitute the social construction of gender.

. . .

To explain why gendering is done from birth, constantly and by everyone, we have to look not only at the way individuals experience gender but at gender as a social institution. As a social institution, gender is one of the major ways that human beings organize their lives. Human society depends on a predictable division of labor, a designated allocation of scarce goods, assigned responsibility for children and others who cannot care for themselves, common values and their systematic transmission to new members, legitimate leadership, music, art, stories, games, and other symbolic productions. One way of choosing people for the different tasks of society is on the basis of their talents, motivations, and competence—their demonstrated achievements. The other way is on the basis of gender, race, ethnicity—ascribed membership in a category of people. Although societies vary in the extent to which they use one or the other of these ways of allocating people to work and to carry out other responsibilities, every society uses gender and age grades. Every society classifies people as "girl and boy children," "girls and boys ready to be married," and "fully adult women and men," constructs similarities among them and differences between them, and assigns them to different roles and responsibilities. Personality characteristics, feelings, motivations, and ambitions flow from these different life experiences so that the members of these different groups become different kinds of people. The process of gendering and its outcome are legitimated by religion, law, science, and the society's entire set of values.

GENDER AS PROCESS, STRATIFICATION, AND STRUCTURE

As a social institution, gender is a process of creating distinguishable social statuses for the assignment of rights and responsibilities. As part of a stratification system that ranks these statuses unequally, gender is a major building block in the social structures built on these unequal statuses.

As a process, gender creates the social differences that define "woman" and "man." In social interaction throughout their lives, individuals learn what is expected, see what is expected, act and react in expected ways, and thus simultaneously construct and maintain the gender order. . . .

Gendered patterns of interaction acquire additional layers of gendered sexuality, parenting, and work behaviors in childhood, adolescence, and adulthood. Gendered norms and expectations are enforced through informal sanctions of gender-inappropriate behavior by peers and by formal punishment or threat of punishment by those in authority should behavior deviate too far from socially imposed standards for women and men.

. . .

As part of a *stratification* system, gender ranks men above women of the same race and class. Women and men could be different but equal. In practice, the process of creating difference depends to a great extent on differential evaluation. . . . The dominant categories are the hegemonic ideals, taken so for granted as the way things should be that white is not ordinarily thought of as a race, middle class as a class, or men as a gender. The characteristics of these categories define the Other as that which lacks the valuable qualities the dominants exhibit.

In a gender-stratified society, what men do is usually valued more highly than what women do because men do it, even when their activities are very similar or the same. In different regions of southern India, for example, harvesting rice is men's work, shared work, or women's work: "Wherever a task is done by women it is considered easy, and where it is done by [men] it is considered difficult" (Mencher 1988, 104). A gathering and hunting society's survival usually depends on the nuts, grubs, and small animals brought in by the women's foraging trips, but when the men's hunt is successful, it is the occasion for a celebration. Conversely, because they are the superior group, white men do not have to do the "dirty work," such as housework; the most inferior group does it, usually poor women of color (Palmer 1989).

. . .

When gender is a major component of structured inequality, the devalued genders have less power, prestige, and economic rewards than the valued genders. In countries that discourage gender discrimination, many major roles are still gendered; women still do most of the domestic labor and child rearing, even while doing full-time paid work; women and men are segregated on the job and each does work considered "appropriate"; women's work is usually paid less than men's work. Men dominate the positions of authority and leadership in government, the military, and the law; cultural productions, religions, and sports reflect men's interests.

In societies that create the greatest gender difference, such as Saudi Arabia, women are kept out of sight behind walls or veils, have no civil rights, and often create a cultural and emotional world of their own (Bernard 1981). But even in societies with less rigid gender boundaries, women and men spend much of their time with people of their own gender because of the way work and family are organized. This spatial separation of women and men reinforces gendered differences, identity, and ways of thinking and behaving (Coser 1986).

Gender inequality—the devaluation of "women" and the social domination of "men"—has social functions and social history. It is not the result of sex, procreation, physiology, anatomy, hormones, or genetic predispositions. It is produced and maintained by identifiable social processes and built into the general social structure and individual identities deliberately and purposefully. The social order as we know it in Western societies is organized around racial, ethnic, class, and gender inequality. I contend, therefore, that the continuing purpose of gender as a modern social institution is to construct women as a group to be the subordinates of men as a group.

THE PARADOX OF HUMAN NATURE

To say that sex, sexuality, and gender are all socially constructed is not to minimize their social power. These categorical imperatives govern our lives in the most profound and pervasive ways, through the social experiences and social practices of what Dorothy Smith calls the "everyday/everynight world" (1990, 31–57). The paradox of human nature is that it is always a manifestation of cultural meanings, social relationships, and power politics; "not biology, but culture, becomes destiny" (J. Butler 1990, 8). Gendered people emerge not from physiology or sexual orientations but from the exigencies of the social order, mostly, from the need for a reliable division of the work of food production and the social (not physical) reproduction of new members. The moral imperatives of religion and cultural representations guard the boundary lines among genders and ensure that what is demanded, what is permitted, and what is tabooed for the people in each gender is well known and followed by most (C. Davies 1982). Political power, control of scarce resources, and, if necessary, violence uphold the gendered social order in the face of resistance and rebellion. Most people, however, voluntarily go along with their society's prescriptions for those of their gender status, because the norms and expectations get built into their sense of worth and identity as [the way we] think, the way we see and hear and speak, the way we fantasy, and the way we feel.

There is no core or bedrock in human nature below these endlessly looping processes of the social production of sex and gender, self and other, identity and psyche, each of which is a "complex cultural construction" (J. Butler 1990, 36). *For humans, the social is the natural. . . .*

NOTES

1. Gender is, in Erving Goffman's words, an aspect of *Felicity's Condition*: "any arrangement which leads us to judge an individual's . . . acts not to be a manifestation of strangeness. Behind Felicity's Condition is our sense of what it is to be sane" (1983, 27). Also see Bem 1993; Frye 1983, 17–40; Goffman 1977.
2. In cases of ambiguity in countries with modern medicine, surgery is usually performed to make the genitalia more clearly male or female.
3. See J. Butler 1990 for an analysis of how doing gender is gender identity.

REFERENCES

Bem, Sandra Lipsitz. 1993. *The Lenses of Gender: Transforming the Debate on Sexual Inequality.* New Haven: Yale University Press.

Bernard, Jessie. 1981. *The Female World.* New York: Free Press.

Butler, Judith. 1990. *Gender Trouble: Feminism and the Subversion of Identity.* New York and London: Routledge.

Coser, Rose Laub. 1986. "Cognitive structure and the use of social space." *Sociological Forum* 1:1–26.

Davies, Christie. 1982. "Sexual taboos and social boundaries." *American Journal of Sociology* 87: 1032–63.

Dwyer, Daisy, and Judith Bruce (eds.). 1988. *A Home Divided: Women and Income in the Third World.* Palo Alto, Calif.: Stanford University Press.

Frye, Marilyn. 1983. *The Politics of Reality: Essays in Feminist Theory.* Trumansburg, N.Y.: Crossing Press.

Goffman, Erving. 1977. "The arrangement between the sexes." *Theory and Society* 4:301–33.

Mencher, Joan. 1988. "Women's work and poverty: Women's contribution to household maintenance in South India." In Dwyer and Bruce 1988.

Palmer, Phyllis. 1989. *Domesticity and Dirt: Housewives and Domestic Servants in the United States, 1920–1945.* Philadelphia: Temple University Press.

Smith, Dorothy. 1990. *The Conceptual Practices of Power: A Feminist Sociology of Knowledge.* Toronto: University of Toronto Press.

West, Candace, and Don Zimmerman. 1987. "Doing gender." *Gender & Society* 1: 125–51.

19. NATIVE AMERICAN MEN-WOMEN, LESBIANS, TWO-SPIRITS

SABINE LANG (2016)

INTRODUCTION

Ever since the beginning of European colonization of the Americas, there have been reports of male-bodied individuals in indigenous cultures taking up the work tasks of women, often also entering into relationships with men. To a lesser extent, chroniclers (and, from the early twentieth century onward, ethnographers) also documented cases in Native North America—the subcontinent with which the present contribution is concerned—where female-bodied persons adopted a masculine role and entered into sexual relationships or marriages with women. While they were accepted and sometimes even revered by their respective indigenous societies, the status and role particularly of the "feminine males" was usually met with disdain by the colonizers, to the extent that the Spaniards—the first Europeans (after the Vikings' brief sojourn in Newfoundland several centuries earlier) to set foot on American soil—attempted to physically exterminate the supposed "sodomites," committing what has been termed gendercide on them both in Middle America and California (cf. Miranda 2010; see also Lang 1998: 323–325; Trexler 1995). In the works of early Spanish chroniclers on the Native cultures they encountered, "sodomy," which in sixteenth-century Spanish law came directly after heresy and crimes against the king, is often mentioned in connection with idolatry and cannibalism (cf. Guerra 1971: 221), and the presence of that triad of "godless acts" served as a legitimization for conquest, colonization, and forced conversion to Christianity.

In the centuries that followed, Native people who were considered "deviant" in terms of gender and/or sexuality continued to be targeted by missionaries, Indian agents, boarding school teachers, and other representatives of the dominant non-Native society, who used violence and ridicule to make such people conform to European norms. In 1879, for example, the only surviving Hidatsa *miati* (male in a woman's role) was forcibly stripped of her/his female attire by the local government agent, who also dressed her/him in men's clothes and cut off her/his braids (Bowers 1965: 315). The sources indicate that in the second half of the nineteenth century at the latest, the massive impact of colonization and forced acculturation resulted in a decline of the special roles and statuses held by "women-men" (males in a feminine role) and "men-women" (females in a masculine role) in indigenous North American cultures (cf. Lang 1998: 115–127; Williams 1986a: Part II).

This development was exacerbated by the fact that people in many Native communities began to adopt the negative attitude held by Europeans on "homosexuality." Today, the overall impression is that while indigenous ways are generally cherished, preserved, and in many cases revived in Native American communities, the traditions of gender diversity are quite obviously something most people do not wish to see revitalized. Homophobia was rampant both on the reservations and in urban Native contexts when I did my fieldwork in the early 1990s, and more recent studies, such as Gilley's (2006) book, Denetdale's (2009) article on the Diné Marriage Act prohibiting same-sex marriages in the Navajo Nation, and contributions in the edited volumes by Justice, Rifkin, and Schneider (2010) and Driskill, Finley, Gilley, and Morgensen (2011a) convey the impression that not much has since changed in that respect. Gilley observed that the two-spirited/gay Native men he talked to "see the respect once given gender diversity as a part of the historic traditional values that Indian people now venerate. In contrast, many non-gay Indians see same-sex relationships and gender difference as something that did not exist historically and should not be recognized as associated with contemporary Native peoples" (2006: 61).

. . .

In the most recent academic approaches to the two-spirit, many of whose proponents have Native roots, the term and concept undergoes still another change. "Two-spirit" becomes a key concept, a liberating icon in a larger political project: a radical vision of decolonizing not only indigenous communities but also the settler states/societies they live in, including the academy and research.[1] As is stated by Driskill et al. in their introduction to *Queer Indigenous Studies*, this project is about designing "practices and futures—both inside and outside the academy—that can both remember and create radical, decolonial LGBTQ2 [the '2' denotes two-spirit people, S.L.] Indigenous communities. (. . .) The book invites looking to Indigenous genders and sexualities—both 'traditional' and contemporary—for their potential to disrupt colonial projects and to rebalance Indigenous communities. Beginning to articulate and practice specific LGBTQ2 Indigenous critiques is a way of continuing radical movements and scholarship that work for collective decolonial futures" (2011b: 18). The unifying power of two-spirit as a collective, inclusive LGBTQ Native identity, as well as its potential in developing an indigenist approach to sexuality and gender, are also emphasized by authors who discuss two-spirit issues from the perspective of social work and health (e.g., Walters, Evans-Campbell, Simoni, Ronquillo, and Bhuyan 2006).

. . .

MEN-WOMEN AND WOMEN-MEN: SOME GENERAL REMARKS

> Greater honor was paid to her than to the Great chief, for she occupied the 1st place in all the Councils, and, when she walked about, was always preceded by four young men, who sang and danced the Calumet to her. She was dressed as an Amazon; she painted her face and Wore her Hair like the men. (Gravier 1959 [1700]: 147–148; orthography as in the original)

The account by the French Jesuit Missionary Jacques Gravier, from which the above quote is taken, is arguably the first description of a Native American female-bodied person in a masculine role. Being a member of the Houma tribe in what today is Louisiana, the "femme chef" (woman chief) had so distinguished herself in war that she was awarded the highest honors. She participated in the council meetings of

the men and, like members of the nobility, was laid to rest in the temple of the Houma (Gravier 1959: 147). This "woman chief" exemplifies one among several categories of female-bodied people who assumed a status resembling that of men in indigenous North American cultures. Among the Houma and other tribes across the Subcontinent, it was not unusual for women to go to war. In rare individual cases remembered for generations, they would perform such extraordinary feats as warriors that they were assigned a quasi-male status in their respective society (cf. Lang 1998: 303–308; . . .). Far more common and much less spectacular, however, were institutionalized statuses, usually based on occupational preferences, within gender systems that acknowledged gender variability or gender diversity, that is, "cultural expressions of multiple genders (i.e., more than two) and the opportunity for individuals to change gender roles and identities over the course of their lifetimes" (Jacobs and Cromwell 1992: 63–64). Such special statuses for people who were neither women nor men but genders of their own existed in a considerable number of pre-reservation and early reservation Native American tribal societies both for male and female individuals who chose to live—completely or partially—in the culturally defined role of the "other sex." Due to the massive impact of colonization, missionary work, and forced acculturation, these traditions of gender diversity, which often included same-sex relationships for reasons to be discussed below, have now largely disappeared in indigenous North American communities, to the extent that people will even deny their former existence (cf. Jacobs 1997: 25).

The first to give accounts of indigenous North American males in a woman's role and females in a man's role were travelers, traders, and missionaries, followed by representatives of the then budding discipline of U.S. anthropology from the early twentieth century onward. In anthropological literature, the traditions of what is now referred to as gender variability in Native North America were formerly subsumed under the term "berdache." However, that word has fallen into disuse due to its original Arab/French meaning of male prostitute or "kept boys" (Angelino and Shedd 1955; Williams 1986a: 9–10), which has come to be viewed as inappropriate not only by contemporary LGBTQ Native Americans, but also by Native and non-native anthropologists (cf. Jacobs, Thomas, and Lang 1997a). In addition, the term becomes downright absurd when applied to females in a man's role. In academic literature, it has been largely replaced by the term "two-spirit" from the mid-1990s onward as a result of two conferences on "The 'North American Berdache' Revisited," whose participants included Native gay and lesbian activists as well as non-Native anthropologists (Jacobs, Thomas, and Lang 1997a). In addition, the term has gained almost universal currency in LGBTQ Native American contexts and activism.

Like "berdache," however, "two-spirit," which originated at an intertribal gathering of LGBT Native Americans/First Nations people in the late 1980s, encompasses an entire host of identities and sexualities across history, ranging from the pre-reservation and early reservation systems of multiple genders to contemporary LGBTQ indigenous people. While the inclusiveness of the term has great advantages when it comes to uniting LGBTQ Native Americans/ First Nations in supra-tribal political and HIV/AIDS organizing, I nevertheless prefer to use the terms woman-man (male in a woman's role) and man-woman (female in a man's role) to refer to people past and present who were, and are, neither women nor men.[2] As I learned in conversations with contemporary women-men and men-women who were raised on their people's reservation to fulfill their special role, this is very much in line with how they view themselves, as has already been alluded to above. While they will agree to be subsumed under the label of "two-spirit" in intertribal contexts (e.g., at meetings of LGBTQ indigenous people from all over the United States and Canada), they will usually make a clear distinction between themselves and LGBTQ2 Native Americans/members of First Nations. They do neither identify as gay, lesbian, bisexual, or queer, nor as transgender, but will refer to themselves by the term appropriate for their specific gender status in their respective culture, such as *nádleeh* (Navajo), *tainna wa'ippe* (Shoshone), *dubads* (Paiute), and so on.

. . .

While gender diversity at least traditionally was a widespread trait of indigenous North American cultures, its individual expressions varied. Women-men and men-women would sometimes adopt the role of the "other" sex completely, sometimes only partially (cf. Lang 1998: 59–90, 261–267). As a rule, however, and regardless of the degree to which they mixed or did not mix gender role components, they were classified as neither men nor women, but as genders of their own within systems of three or four genders, as becomes apparent from the words used [to] refer [to] them. These differ from the terms for man and woman, and often indicate that men-women and women-men are viewed as combining the masculine and the feminine (cf. Roscoe 1988; Lang 1998: 248–251, 263–265). The Shoshone, for example, call both men-women and women-men *tainna wa'ippe*, "man-woman" (Michael Owlfeather, personal communication). Among the Diné (Navajo), there likewise exists a common term for both, *nádleeh* ("someone who is in a constant process of change," Wesley Thomas, personal communication).[3] The Sduk-al-bixw (Quinault) word for men-women is "man acting" (Olson 1936: 99), and the Akimel O'odham (Pima) call women-men *wik'ovat*, "like a girl" (Hill 1938: 339).

As I have argued elsewhere (Lang 2011), the gender statuses of women-men and men-women can be characterized as being "hermaphroditic," that is, a mixture of the masculine and feminine, and this dual nature—rather than a complete transition from the masculine to the feminine gender role or vice versa—was also emphasized particularly by traditionally raised women-men I talked to. Their ambiguity reflects general patterns found in Native American world views which appreciate and emphasize transformation, ambiguity, and change. For example, humans can transform into animals and vice versa, or beings can be both humans and animals at the same time. Individuals combining the masculine and the feminine are therefore just another aspect of the transformations and ambiguities that are a central feature of indigenous North American systems of thought. Within world views that recognize that the act of creation did not necessarily establish everything in binary categories, human beings who are ambiguous in terms of their sexual features, or display a discrepancy between their physical sex and their occupational preferences, are accepted as part of the natural order of things. In other words, they are not what in Western culture is termed "deviant." In some cases they are even welcomed as people who have been blessed, or touched, by the supernatural (cf. Lang 2011).

MEN-WOMEN IN TRIBAL SOCIETIES

When the systems of multiple genders were still intact in Native American cultures, the classification of a person as a woman-man or man-woman was usually based on her/his occupational preferences, which often became manifest as early as in childhood. A gendered division of labor, which assigned specific work tasks to either the feminine or the masculine sphere, existed in all tribal societies on the Subcontinent, and while there was some flexibility in gender roles, activities within that division of labor were decisive in defining an individual's gender. Prospective men-women usually showed a profound interest in masculine occupations in childhood. As became apparent from conversations I had with contemporary women-men and men-women, this is still the case today. . . . "Men pretenders" among the Ingalik (autonym: Deg Xit'an) in Alaska, for example, refused to learn women's skills when they were children, so their fathers would take them under their wings and teach them men's work. They joined the boys and men in the *kashim* (men's house), and are said to have concealed their female physical characteristics during the sweat bath. As adults they assumed the complete social role of a man but only rarely married women (Osgood 1958: 262–263). Female-bodied *nádleeh* also began to behave like boys in childhood (Hill 1935: 273). Young Cocopa *warrhameh* played with the boys, made arrows and bows for themselves, and went hunting for rabbits and birds (Gifford 1933: 294).

In some cultures, girls' entrance into the role and status of men-women was not due to their personal inclinations; parents would decide to raise daughters as sons in the interest of the respective community. This was the case in the Arctic and Subarctic, where the diet was largely composed of meat obtained by the men by hunting, and vegetable food gathered by

women played a less important role. If there were not enough boys in a community or family, some fathers would teach their daughters hunting skills and raise them to fulfill a hunter's role. Among some Inuit groups, for example, such girls learned to hunt seals from a kayak, acquired a quasi-masculine status, and wore men's garb (Mirsky 1937: 84; Kjellström 1973: 180). . . .

From time to time, parents among the Canadian Anishinaabe (Ojibwa) whose only child was a girl decided to raise her as a boy, and sometimes fathers would choose their favorite daughter to fulfill such a man-woman role. Such girls were treated like boys in every respect and, like boys, were sent on a vision quest to summon a guardian spirit, or supernatural helper (Landes 1937: 119, 121). Masculine occupations of men-women in Native American cultures included hunting, fishing, trapping, trade, and participation in warfare. Sometimes they practiced specialized occupations in their tribal societies. In some California groups such as the Achomawi, Klamath, and Tolowa, as well as among the Mohave living in the Mojave Desert, they were traditionally curers or "shamans" (Lang 1998: 286). This might or might not be related to their gender status. In some indigenous North American cultures, curers were predominantly men, and men-women chose that specialization as part of their masculine role. In others, there is no predominance of either women or men in healing, and men-women probably became healers if they were gifted for it but were not expected to pursue that profession if they did not possess that gift (cf. Lang 1998: 286–289). Among some tribes, men-women and women-men were believed to possess special powers due to their specific nature. Mohave *hwame* were said to be particularly powerful "shamans" (Devereux 1937: 516), and according to Michael Owlfeather (personal communication) Shoshone *tainna wa'ippe* of either sex are born with the gift of being medicine people. In some cases their dual nature predestines them to be mediators between the human and supernatural worlds, and women-men in particular were sometimes popular as matchmakers and mediators between women and men (Grinnell 1962, II: 39; Hill 1935: 275; Mead 1932: 189, Fn. 2).

. . .

INDIGENOUS DEFINITIONS OF HOMOSEXUALITY AND HETEROSEXUALITY

Both women-men and men-women often entered into sexual or even marital relationships with members of the same sex. Hence, their roles have long been interpreted as institutionalized homosexuality in anthropological writings. This "homosexuality" was usually considered innate, and sometimes classified according to Western psychiatric concepts of perversion and deviance,[4] even though some authors early on pointed to the fact that definitions of "deviance" vary widely between cultures: behavior considered deviant in one culture may be part of social norms in another (cf. Benedict 1934: 60; Mead 1961: 1454). In addition, this interpretation of gender variability as a way to culturally integrate, or accommodate, "homosexual" people ignores the fact that by no means all men-women and women-men entered into same-sex relationships. The sources, as well as conversations I had with people who are familiar with their tribe's traditions of gender variability, reveal that women-men had sex, or partner relationships, with women in a number of tribes, and men-women had relationships with men (Lang 1998: 189–195, 190–291). In some tribes women-men and men-women were, and still are, apparently free to have relationships with both women and men. With regard to Shoshone *tainna wa'ippe*, for example, Michael Owlfeather (personal communication) commented: "Some of those [male-bodied] two-spirited people were married people. They dressed in feminine clothes, they dressed in women's things, but they were married. Some of them even had children." The same is true of female-bodied *tainna wa'ippe*.

. . .

What, then, is the implication of cultural systems of more than two genders for possible concepts of heterosexuality and homosexuality in indigenous North American cultures? Given the presence of multiple genders, sexual relationships between a woman-man and a man or a man-woman with a woman are "homosexual" on the level of physical sex, but not on the level of gender. If a man-woman has sex with either a man or a woman, he/she is having sex with someone whose gender differs from his/her own; the same is true for sexual relationships between women-men and either women or men. Regardless of whether they are of the same sex or not—the partners in such relationships are never of the same gender. Within such systems of multiple genders, Native classifications of sexual partner choice are based on the gender rather than the physical sex of those involved in a relationship.

In most cases, little is known about the details of these classifications, but thanks to the work of Wesley Thomas (Diné) and information generously shared by Michael Owlfeather (Shoshone/Métis) in personal conversations it is possible to compare Diné and Shoshone concepts of appropriate and non-appropriate sexual relationships. Among the Diné (Navajo), there traditionally existed four genders—women, men, women-men, and men-women. As has been mentioned above, the latter two genders were called *nádleeh*. The same term is, by the way, also applied to intersex people; the latter's supernatural prototypes feature in the Diné Origin Story, and the human *nádleeh* (whether physically ambiguous or not) are viewed as the worldly likenesses of these mythical hermaphrodite beings. Within the Diné classification, the equivalent to a homosexual relationship is a sexual relationship between people of the same gender (two women, two men, two female-bodied *nádleeh*, two male-bodied *nádleeh*), or of closely related genders (woman and male-bodied *nádleeh*, man and female-bodied *nádleeh*).

Among the Shoshone, *tainne-wa'ippe* of both sexes are viewed as acting on a vision that demands them to adopt the occupations, ways of behavior, and garb of the "other sex." However, their gender status does not limit their partner choice. In contrast to *nádleeh*, they are free to have relationships with both men and women. The same is true for women-men and men-women in some other Native cultures, as has been pointed out above; we can thus assume that the Shoshone classification of sexual relationships is representative of other indigenous North American cultures as well. The only type of relationship that was at least traditionally forbidden—not only among the Shoshone and Diné, but universally in Native American cultures—was between two women-men and two men-women. Where multiple genders continue to exist, women-men, for example, are still believed to be connected by a bond of kinship, sometimes referring to each other as "sisters." Hence, a sexual relationship between them is considered incestuous (Michael Owlfeather, personal communication; Thomas 1997 and personal communication; Williams 1986b: 93–94).

. . .

A distinction between themselves and gay/lesbian Native Americans is also made by contemporary women-men and men-women. This distinction is based on varying criteria. Among the Shoshone, a "gay" Native person as opposed to a *tainna wa'ippe* is defined as lacking the spiritual component that is so essential to the *tainna wa'ippe*'s role and status:

> One person told me, "Well, those old-time 'berdaches,' they were nothing but drag queens, weren't they?" And I said, "No, they weren't," because they didn't dress in women's clothes just because of personal preference. It was because of the manifestation of Spirit. They *had* to do it. You know, (. . .) they had to act on this vision in order to be a complete person. (Michael Owlfeather, personal communication; emphasis his)

Among the Diné, the distinction between *nádleeh* and gay/lesbian is based on the fact that the *nádleeh* role and status is based on occupational preferences while "gay" is viewed as being based on sexual preference. According to Wesley Thomas (personal communication), "a true *nádleeh* or traditional *nádleeh* is somebody who is one hundred percent—[he pauses to think:] a woman, who was born as a man but is a woman in Navajo society, not in their sexual preferences or sexual persuasion, but as an occupational [preference]."

TWO-SPIRIT PEOPLE

The old-time statuses and roles of women-men and men-women have disappeared on many reservations and in urban Native communities. When I talked to members of the first generation of Native LGBT activists in the early 1990s, they told me that the last "true" *winkte, tainna wa'ippe,* and so on, had lived on the reservations in the 1930s and 1940s. When one

of my friends grew up as a male-bodied *nádleeh* on the Navajo Reservation in the 1950s, there was no role model around. However, her/his grandmother, who had been born in the early 1920s, recognized her/his special nature. She remembered the *nádleeh*, their rootedness in Diné religion and philosophy, and raised her grandchild to fulfill that special role. The same was true for other people I met; they, too, had been raised by grandparents who still remembered and appreciated the traditions of gender diversity in their respective cultures.

On the other hand, there were a growing number of Native lesbians, gays, and bisexuals, the large majority of them urban, who sought to gain acceptance by their Native communities, began to make their voices heard, and researched into the history of same-sex relationships in their indigenous cultures. From the mid-1970s onward, and largely unnoticed by non-Native anthropologists and historians who began to explore "old-time" gender systems, Native American gay and lesbian writers and activists made their voices heard as well, addressing their concerns and experiences, including the impact of colonialism on gay/lesbian and "straight" indigenous North Americans alike. These authors include Maurice Kenny (Mohawk), Paula Gunn Allen (Laguna Pueblo), Beth Brant (Mohawk), Chrystos (Menominee), Vickie Sears (Cherokee), Joy Harjo (Muskogee), Janice Gould (Concow), and many others. Native lesbians were represented, for example, in the women of color anthology *This Bridge Called My Back* (Moraga and Anzaldúa 1983), Beth Brant's *A Gathering of Spirit: A Collection of Writing and Art by North American Indian Women* (1984), and the first anthology composed (with the exception of one contribution by the non-Native historian Will Roscoe) of writings by Native gays and lesbians, *Living the Spirit: A Gay American Indian Anthology* (1988), edited by Gay American Indians and Will Roscoe. Today, analyses of poetry and prose written by Native LGBT, including the first generation but also more recent authors, are at the focus of literary studies in the context of queer indigenous studies (e.g., Rifkin 2012; Scudeler 2011; Tatonetti 2011, 2014; . . .).

At the same time, the first Native gay and lesbian organization, Gay American Indians (GAI), was founded in San Francisco in 1975. What was to become the two-spirit identity had been originally emerging in such urban settings as well as in "pan-tribal" contexts such as the annual Two-Spirit Gatherings, not on the reservations. The concept and term of two-spirit are the result of urban gay and lesbian Native Americans' search for and rediscovery of the cultural roots of homosexual behavior in indigenous North American cultures. Initially, these activists did research into the written historical and anthropological sources, as the traditions of gender diversity were often forgotten or repressed in their communities. While anthropological approaches to multiple genders in Native American cultures are now criticized for ignoring indigenous knowledge and the concerns of contemporary LGBTQ2 indigenous North Americans (cf. Driskill et al. 2011a, b), the emergent two-spirit identity initially reflected, ironically, the very way non-Native researchers interpreted the roles and statuses of men-women and women-men: as ways to culturally integrate "homosexual"/LGBT individuals who, in addition, often held revered and highly respected statuses in their respective communities.

While "two-spirit" has come to be widely used in LGBTQ indigenous contexts and organizations, it needs to be mentioned that not all LGBTQ Native Americans/First Nations people identify as two-spirit. The gay poet, teacher, and social worker Gregory Scofield (Cree/Métis), for example, stated: "First of all, in relation to the ideology of Two-Spirited theory, I always back away from that three-hundred fold. I mean I don't consider myself Two-Spirited. (. . .) Not that I'm disparaging of it. It's just that I think it's very multi-layered insofar as the politicization of the word and how it's come about and its interpretation and its reinvention and the reinterpretation of things" (McKegney 2014: 218; cf. also Gilley 2006: 90–95, 113–121).

A key feature of the concept, and identity, of "two-spirit" is that unlike for many "white" gays and lesbians, people's (homo)sexuality is not a prime marker of their identity even though sexuality and desire are, of course, important in their lives. Their primary identity is as Native Americans and/or members of a specific ethnic group, as was stressed again and again by people I talked to. Erna Pahe (Navajo),

for example, commented with regard to GAI: "One of our major emphases is that we are Indian first, we're Navajo, we're Pima, we're Apaches. And we do not divide our group and say that we're gay, and making us different. We're all Indians, and that's the way we portray our feelings, and that's the priority in terms of our organization." This was echoed by Randy Burns (Paiute), who told me: "I used to say I was gay first and I was Indian second, and then I, of course, through peer pressure got convinced that, 'No, you're Indian! Remember who you are!' And, you know, 'When you're born into this world, you're born Native, you're not born queer.'" Another recurrent aspect of being two-spirit is spirituality; the very term/concept of "two-*spirit*" expresses a connection of contemporary Native American LGBTQ to indigenous spirituality in the broadest sense. As has been observed by Lüder Tietz with regard to Canada, "For some *two-spirited people*, the word *spirit* seems to be at the core of the use of the term 'Two-Spirited.' (. . .) The concept of 'two-spirited' can be seen as the attempt to transcendentally substantiate a modern lesbian/gay identity that is specifically First Nations" (Tietz 1996: 207, emphasis his, translation mine).

This priority in identity needs to be seen in the context of two-spirit people's life experiences and concerns, which have much more in common with those of "straight" Native Americans than with those of white lesbians and gays, or even other LGBTQ people of color (cf. Driskill 2010: 78, 80). With heterosexual Native Americans, they share the experience and impact of five hundred years of colonization, cultural genocide, and forced acculturation. Just like other Native Americans, middle-aged two-spirits raised on reservations still vividly remember the physical and emotional violence they suffered in boarding schools run under the motto of "Kill the Indian, save the Man," which was given out in 1879 by Richard E. Pratt, the founder of Carlisle Indian School. Given these shared experiences of ongoing historical trauma, which have left a deep, lasting impact on heterosexual and LGBTQ Native Americans alike, and the Native-oriented priority in their identity, most two-spirit people do not wish to set themselves apart from their Native communities. Many of them feel that they are innately imbued with special spiritual and/or practical gifts that they would like to use for the benefit of their ethnic group and/or the Native American community at large.

This desire to be an integral part of Native communities implies that two-spirit people are not prone to separatism on the grounds of their sexual orientation. For example, they do not strive for any type of new religious community shared exclusively by two-spirit people; for them, Native religions are not a matter to be eclectically trifled with. If they engage in religious practices of their respective ethnic group, they attach importance to doing so in the customary and appropriate manner of their people. An example of this is a women-only Sun Dance founded by a Lakota woman in the mid-1980s (cf. Lang 2013; see also below). Though specifically addressing Native lesbian women, the focus is not on "lesbianism" but on the proper performance of a sacred ceremony. It is also important to note that the Women's Sun Dance was not created out of some lesbian or feminist separatist whim. Its founder would have preferred to continue to participate in the Sun Dances held on her tribe's reservation, but found herself unable to do so because of the homophobia experienced by herself and her partner. While some elements of the ceremony have been modified due to its all-female attendance, others are not supposed to be changed lest the supernatural powers be offended.

TWO-SPIRIT WOMEN/NATIVE LESBIANS

This primary identity as Native Americans influences the way two-spirit women see themselves, and the way they relate to Native gays in particular and their communities in general. For example, the concept of lesbian separatism seemed to hold little appeal for most Native lesbians/two-spirit women I talked to. While they acknowledge that some of their experiences, identities, and goals differ from those of male two-spirits, there is an emphasis on solidarity due to shared experiences of colonization, racism, and social marginalization. In addition, a very common concept in North American indigenous cultures is that the feminine and masculine qualities are complementary, and that it is advisable to combine them in both worldly and spiritual matters for efficiency. Similar observations were made by Walters et al. (2006), and summed up by one of their Native lesbian respondents:

> A lot of times in the White community, lesbians will say, you know, "I just don't like men." Actually, I think that identifying as two-spirit, I have more of an alliance with Native men (. . .) because they're Native men and they have experienced a lot of similar racist attitudes as well as homophobic attitudes on the reservation that I have. Um, we seem to bond together better, the male and the female sides sort of complement one another. I have difficulty explaining it to White lesbians who would say, "Well, why would you want gay men at an event?" Because Native gay men are not gay men, they're my two-spirit brothers. (132)

Another feature of both two-spirit women and men is that they do not wish to set themselves apart from their Native communities on the grounds of their sexuality, as has already been pointed out above. There are specific roles they assume, or wish to assume, for the benefit of these communities; these roles are culturally attributed to two-spirit people in general, so it makes no sense to treat women and men separately in the present context.

One of the specific gifts attributed to two-spirit people is caretaking. The caretaker role was already associated with the traditional women-men and men-women, and continues to be stressed both by contemporary two-spirit people and their communities (Evans-Campbell, Fredriksen-Goldsen, Walters, and Stately 2007; Jacobs, Thomas, and Lang 1997; Lang 1998). Michael Owlfeather told me: "We have always been the caretakers, we have always been the cultural keepers," and went on to elaborate on other culturally ascribed roles of two-spirits/men-women/women-men: "We are the ones that people go to when they want to know how to do things right, be it funerals, be it giveaways, be it a way of dressing, a style of beadwork, a song. We are the people that keep those things. We always have been, and we always will be." The role and contribution of two-spirit people as caregivers for the elderly and children, and positive reactions to these activities by families and Native communities, have been stressed by the respondents in Evans-Campbell et al. (2007). The authors conclude:

> Caregiving is perceived as an important and integral role of two-spirit people, and it is clear that many two-spirit people already engage in caregiving or expect to provide care for others at some point during their lifetime. (. . .) Based on culturally proscribed roles, two-spirit people may be asked to care for the elderly, relatives, or children. In some communities, they may be asked to care for the community as a whole as they take on specific social or ceremonial responsibilities. (88)

This role was also emphasized by people I talked to. A Nez Percé woman pointed out in a conversation that elders will pass on their knowledge to the two-spirit people who take care of them, and who thus become keepers of their tribe's traditions. Being caretakers of children in particular was an important aspect of the role of women-men and men-woman. In Native American communities, it is not unusual for children to be raised by people other than their parents. Navajo *nádleeh* of both sexes are traditionally expected to adopt and raise children (Wesley Thomas, personal communication). George (pseudonym), a Colville *wenatcha* (woman-man) I talked to, had raised no less than twenty-six children from her/his extended family, and Michael Owlfeather raised three of his nieces because their parents had alcohol abuse problems and could not properly take care of the girls.

Another recurrent aspect in the lives of Native lesbians/two-spirit women is motherhood. Many of those I met had become pregnant "the natural way," as one of them said with a wink, that is, the children were not conceived by artificial insemination but by intercourse with men. Quite a few of the Native lesbians I talked to had started out having sexual relationships with men, or had had such relationships at some time in their lives. Within their Native American cultural frames of reference they would stress motherhood as an essential aspect of womanhood, regardless of whether a woman identifies as lesbian or straight. George told me that the female-bodied *wenatcha* of his tribe usually give birth to and raise children, explaining that this is just part of their nature, which requires a balance of the feminine and the masculine rather than switching completely from one to the other. Erna Pahe (Navajo), who was married twice and has two children, stressed the importance of children to Diné women:

> There is a special role that women play, too, as the bearers of the next generation. There is a very distinct position that women play within our tribe, so even though *nádleeh* [used by Erna in the meaning of "lesbian," S.L.] women exist, it's of a different level. They're *mothers*. I mean, like myself, I am a mother. The first thing is you're a child. And you become the young woman. And then you become a mother, so whether you're *nádleeh* or not, the first, before anything else, is you are a mother. And then you become a grandmother. (. . .) So when you speak about *nádleeh* women, the thing is that they're mothers first. (Erna Pahe, personal communication; emphasis hers)

Other two-spirit women, rather than subscribing to rigid European categories of "gay," "lesbian," or "straight," will rather self-label as bisexual due to their recognition of the fact that sexual preferences may change in the course of an individual's lifetime. In other cases, they will use the term "lesbian" in a sense that includes the possibility of having sexual relationships with both women and men; in still others, they will use "lesbian" synonymous with "man-woman," referring to contemporary manly women on the reservations including their relationships that are by no means exclusively homosexual.

The role of two-spirit women as parents, and the Native definition of "lesbian" as not excluding sexual relationships with men, was also emphasized by Michael Owlfeather in one of our conversations. Among the Shoshone, there were manly women of his grandmother's generation who would have male husbands and female lovers: "My grandmother was a two-spirited person herself, and it's known among the lesbian people here. (. . .) [Women like her] took pride in doing anything a man could do, and doing it better, you know? But these women also had children, got married. But they had their 'women friends' and were always respected for that and everything else. It was nothing overt, they didn't hold it out to the community, but everybody knew what was going on."

Most Native lesbians/two-spirit women I talked to were acutely aware of the triple discrimination they are exposed to as women, lesbians, and Native Americans. Recent studies address the impact of historical trauma, discrimination, and other stressors on the health and wellness of Native American lesbian, gay, bisexual, transgender, and two-spirit men and women (see, e.g., Burks, Robbins, and Durtschi 2010; Walters et al. 2006; Walters 2010). The health status of LGBTQ2 Native Americans/First Nations people reflects, in many ways, that of the indigenous population of the United States and Canada in general. Issues related to physical and mental health include a high prevalence of chronic illnesses and premature mortality related to these, disproportionately high levels of poverty and socioeconomic deprivation, exposure to racism, and the persistent impact of colonization.

Given the discrimination and racism they encounter even within the "white" lesbian subculture, some lesbians of Native American or mixed descent have come to prefer partners who share the same, or at least a related, ethnic background. One of the reasons for this is doubtlessly the fact that, no matter how sensitive the white partner of a Native woman may be as far as matters of racism are concerned, racism often seems to become an issue in a relationship between a Native American and a white woman. White lesbians may also have a yearning for Native spirituality and a romanticized image of their Native partners, which is likewise annoying to the latter (cf. Chrystos' poem "I am not your princess," 1988: 66–67). Native lesbians may feel that they do not want to cope with these issues in their relationships anymore, having to deal with them already in all spheres of their lives. They may reach the conclusion that it will further their personal growth if they are in a relationship with a woman where no strength and energy is consumed by suffering from and educating their partner on racism and related issues.

In some cases, Native lesbians/two-spirit women have become so disenchanted with the culture and values of the colonizers that they have established small communities restricted to Native women or women of color. And in spite of the fact that many two-spirit women emphasize and appreciate

cooperation with Native gays in projects and organizations, they feel that their specific experiences and needs sometimes require women-only gatherings. One example is the Women's Sun Dance founded by a Lakota woman in the mid-1980s (Lang 2013). While white women and non-Native women of color are welcome to attend as long as they behave respectfully toward the ceremony and its participants, only Native women may pledge to actually be Sun Dancers. The Women's Sun Dance has meanwhile become integrated into a larger project called Kunsi Keya Tamakoce (the Lakota term for "Grandmother Turtle Land") located in a remote rural mountain area. Its mission is very clearly outlined in terms of indigenous knowledge, a decided stance against heteronormativity and racism, and a focus on ecology. According to its homepage, it "preserves indigenous religious heritage and fights against racism, sexism, classism, homophobia, ageism and ecological violence experienced in tribal populations and the world at large" (http://www.kunsikeya.org/about.html). . . .

SOME CONCLUDING THOUGHTS

From the above discussion, it becomes apparent that Native traditions of gender variability lent themselves for diverse interpretations, and these interpretations, in turn, served diverse purposes. The Spaniards invoked particularly women-men and their "sodomite" practices in attempts to justify colonization and forced conversion to the Christian faith. Several centuries later, two-spirit people became exactly the reverse in recent academic indigenist approaches, which credit LGBTQ2 indigenous people with what might be termed the "queer" potential needed to create a decolonial future in settler states. Up to the 1970s and from a psychological perspective, women-men and men-women viewed as examples of the cultural integration of innately "homosexual" individuals in tribal societies. In the 1970s, a new look at their roles and statuses opened researchers' eyes to the non-universality of Western concepts of sexual relationships and gender. Research refocused away from sexual behavior towards transcultural studies of gender constructions. And from the 1980s onward particularly the roles of women-men became elevated by some non-Native scholars to some universal supreme spiritual status held by people who were not heterosexual. While Native two-spirit/lesbian women significantly contribute to the field of interdisciplinary queer indigenous studies, and while contemporary LGBT Native activists and writers have made their voices and concerns heard from the 1970s onward, earlier non-Native historical and anthropological research tended to focus on women-men in pre-reservation and early reservation times; there was, and still is, a shortage of research on men-women.

All these non-Native and Native perspectives have in common that they largely relegate the traditions of gender variability to the past. But men-women and women-men do still exist. They keep their tribes' traditions alive and pass on their knowledge to two-spirit and other Native people largely outside urban academic and political activist contexts.

NOTES

1. With regard to its research agenda and desiderata, this approach is situated within a larger current of efforts toward decolonization in the academy and beyond as outlined, for example, in the pioneering book *Decolonizing Methodologies* by Linda Tuhiwai Smith (2012 [1999]). On decolonization strategies in research with/on contemporary two-spirit people see, for example, Walters and Simoni (2009).

2. This differs from the way these terms are used in other anthropological writings (e.g., Roscoe 1991; Fulton and Anderson 1992), where "man-woman" usually refers to male-bodied persons in a woman's role. However, in Native American cultures more importance is attached to an individual's gender status than to his/her physical sex. Hence, it seems logical to follow Bleibtreu-Ehrenberg (1984), who titled her monograph on male gender diversity in various cultures *Der Weibmann* ("The Woman-Man"), and to put the gender to which the chosen gender role belongs first and the physical sex second.

3. Michael Owlfeather (Shoshone/Métis) and Prof. Wesley Thomas (Diné) are experts in the traditions of gender diversity in their respective cultures. On the *nádleeh*, see also Hill (1935); Thomas (1997); Epple (1997). In Shoshoni, *tainkwa* or *tainna* means "man," and *wa'ippe* "woman" (Miller 1972: 136, 172).

4. For a discussion of anthropological interpretations of gender diversity, see, for example, Lang (1998: 17–56).

REFERENCES

Angelino, H., and C. L. Shedd. 1955. A note on berdache. *American Anthropologist* 57(1): 121–126.

Benedict, R. F. 1934. Anthropology and the abnormal. *Journal of General Psychology* 10: 59–82.

Bleibtreu-Ehrenberg, G. 1984. *Der Weibmann: Kultischer Geschlechtswechsel im Schamanismus.* Frankfurt am Main: Fischer.

Bowers, A. 1965. Hidatsa social and ceremonial organization. *Bureau of American Ethnology, Bulletin* 194. Washington, DC: Smithsonian Institution Press.

Brant, B. (ed.). 1984. *A gathering of spirit.* Ithaca, NY: Firebrand Books.

Burks, D. J., R. Robbins, and J. P. Durtschi. 2011. American Indian gay, bisexual and two-spirit men: A rapid assessment of HIV/AIDS risk factors, barriers to prevention and culturally-sensitive intervention. *Culture, Health and Sexuality: An International Journal for Research, Intervention and Care* 13(3): 283–298.

Chrystos. 1988. *Not vanishing.* Vancouver: Press Gang Publishers.

Denetdale, J. N. 2009. Securing Navajo national boundaries: War, patriotism, tradition, and the Diné Marriage Act of 2005. *Wicazo Sa Review* 24(2): 131–148.

Devereux, G. 1937. Homosexuality among the Mohave Indians. *Human Biology* 9: 498–527.

Driskill, Q.-L. 2010. Doubleweaving two-spirit critiques: Building alliances between native and queer studies. *GLQ: A Journal of Lesbian and Gay Studies* 16(1–2): 69–92.

Driskill, Q.-L., C. Finley, B. J. Gilley, and S. L. Morgensen (eds.). 2011a. *Queer indigenous studies: Critical interventions in theory, politics, and literature.* Tucson: University of Arizona Press.

———. 2011b. Introduction. In Q.-L. Driskill, C. Finley, B. J. Gilley, and S. L. Morgensen (eds.), *Queer indigenous studies: Critical interventions in theory, politics, and literature.* Tucson: University of Arizona Press, pp. 1–28.

Epple, C. 1997. A Navajo worldview and *nádleehí:* Implications for western categories. In S.-E. Jacobs, W. Thomas, and S. Lang (eds.), *Two-spirit people: Native American gender identity, sexuality, and spirituality.* Urbana and Chicago: University of Illinois Press, pp. 174–191.

Evans-Campbell, T., K. I. Fredriksen-Goldsen, K. L. Walters, and A. Stately. 2007. Caregiving experiences among American Indian two-spirit men and women: Contemporary and historical roles. *Journal of Gay and Lesbian Social Services* 18(3/4): 75–92.

Fulton R., and S. W. Anderson. 1992. The Amerindian "man-woman": Gender liminality and cultural continuity. *Current Anthropology* 33(5): 603–609.

Gifford, E. W. 1933. The Cocopa. *University of California Publications in American Archaeology and Ethnology* 31(5): 257–333.

Gilley, B. J. 2006. *Becoming two-spirit: Gay identity and social acceptance in Indian country.* Lincoln and London: University of Nebraska Press.

Gravier, J. 1959. Relation ou Journal du voyage du Père Gravier de la Compagnie de Jesus en 1700. In R. G. Thwaites (ed.), *The Jesuit relations and allied documents,* vol. 65. New York: Pageant Book Company, pp. 100–179. [Reprint.]

Grinnell, G. B. 1962. *The Cheyenne Indians.* 2 vols. New York: Cooper Square.

Guerra, F. 1971. *The pre-Columbian mind.* New York: Seminar Press.

Herdt, G. (ed.). 1994. *Third sex, third gender: Beyond sexual dimorphism in culture and history.* New York: Zone Books.

Hill, W. W. 1938. Note on the Pima berdache. *American Anthropologist* 40: 338–340.

———. 1935. The status of the hermaphrodite and transvestite in Navaho culture. *American Anthropologist* 37: 273–279.

Jacobs, S.-E. 1997. Is the "North American berdache" merely a phantom in the imagination of western social scientists? In S.-E. Jacobs, W. Thomas, and S. Lang (eds.), *Two-spirit people: Native American gender identity, sexuality, and spirituality.* Urbana and Chicago: University of Illinois Press, pp. 21–44.

———. 1968. Berdache: A brief review of the literature. *Colorado Anthropologist* 1: 25–40.

Jacobs, S.-E., W. Thomas, and S. Lang (eds.). 1997a. *Two-spirit people: Native American gender identity, sexuality, and spirituality.* Urbana and Chicago: University of Illinois Press.

———. 1997b. Introduction. In S.-E. Jacobs, W. Thomas, and S. Lang (eds.), *Two-spirit people: Native American gender identity, sexuality, and spirituality.* Urbana and Chicago: University of Illinois Press, pp. 1–19.

Jacobs, S.-E., and J. Cromwell. 1992. Visions and revisions of reality: Reflections on sex, sexuality, gender, and gender variance. *Journal of Homosexuality* 23(4): 43–69.

Justice, D. H., M. Rifkin, and B. Schneider (eds.). 2010. Sexuality, nationality, indigeneity. *GLQ: Special issue, A Journal of Lesbian and Gay Studies* 16(1–2).

Kjellström, R. 1973. Eskimo marriage: An account of traditional Eskimo courtship and marriage. Stockholm: Nordiska museets handlingar 80.

Landes, R. 1937. The Ojibwa of Canada. In M. Mead (ed.), *Cooperation and competition among primitive people.* New York: McGraw-Hill, pp. 87–126.

Lang, S. 2013. Re-gendering sacred space: An all-women's sun dance. In A. Blätter and S. Lang (eds.), "Contemporary Native American studies." Special issue, *Ethnoscripts* 15(1): 124–139.

———. 2011. Transformations of gender in Native American cultures. In R. Potter-Deimel and K. Kolinská (eds.), "Transformation, translation, transgression: Indigenous American cultures in contact and context." Special issue, *Litteraria Pragensia* 21(4): 70–81.

———. 1998. *Men as women, women as men: Changing gender in Native American cultures.* Austin: University of Texas Press.

McKegney, S. 2014. *Masculindians: Conversations about indigenous manhood.* East Lansing: Michigan State University Press.

Mead, M. 1961. Cultural determinants of sexual behavior. In E. C. Young (ed.), *Sex and internal secretions.* Baltimore: Williams and Wilkins, pp. 1433–1479.

———. 1932. *The changing culture of an Indian tribe.* New York: Columbia University Press.

Miller, W. R. 1972. *Newe natekwinappeh: Shoshoni stories and dictionary.* Salt Lake City: University of Utah Press.

Miranda, D. A. 2010. Extermination of the joyas: Gendercide in Spanish California. *GLQ: A Journal of Lesbian and Gay Studies* 16(1–2): 253–284.

Mirsky, J. 1937. The Eskimo of Greenland. In M. Mead (ed.), *Cooperation and competition among primitive people.* New York: McGraw-Hill, pp. 51–86.

Moraga, C., and G. Anzaldúa (eds.). 1983. *This bridge called my back: Writings by radical women of color.* New York: Kitchen Table Women of Color Press.

Olson, R. L. 1936. The Quinault Indians. *University of Washington Publications in Anthropology* 6(1): 1–194.

Osgood, C. 1958. Ingalik social culture. *Yale University Publications in Anthropology* 53: 1–289.

Rifkin, M. 2012. *The erotics of sovereignty: Queer native writing in the era of self-determination.* Minneapolis and London: University of Minnesota Press.

Roscoe, W. 1991. *The Zuni man-woman.* Albuquerque: University of New Mexico Press.

———. 1988. North American tribes with berdache and alternative gender roles. In Gay American Indians and W. Roscoe (eds.), *Living the spirit: A gay American Indian anthology.* New York: St. Martin's Press, pp. 217–222.

Scudeler, J. 2011. Gifts of Maskihkîy: Gregory Scofield's Cree-Métis stories of self-acceptance. In Q.-L. Driskill, C. Finley, B. J. Gilley, and S. L. Morgensen (eds.), *Queer indigenous studies: Critical interventions in theory, politics, and literature.* Tucson: University of Arizona Press, pp. 190–210.

Tatonetti, L. 2014. *The queerness of Native American literature.* Minneapolis: University of Minnesota Press.

———. 2011. Indigenous fantasies and sovereign erotics: Outland Cherokees write two-spirit nations. In Q.-L. Driskill, C. Finley, B. J. Gilley, and S. L. Morgensen (eds.), *Queer indigenous studies: Critical interventions in theory, politics, and literature.* Tucson: University of Arizona Press, pp. 155–171.

Thomas, W. 1997. Navajo cultural constructions of gender and sexuality. In S.-E. Jacobs, W. Thomas, and S. Lang (eds.), *Two-spirit people: Native American gender identity, sexuality, and spirituality.* Urbana and Chicago: University of Illinois Press, pp. 156–173.

Tietz, L. 1996. *Moderne Rückbezüge auf Geschlechtsrollen indianischer Kulturen.* Unpublished Master's thesis. University of Hamburg, Germany, Institut für Ethnologie.

Trexler, R. C. 1995. *Sex and conquest: Gendered violence, political order, and the European conquest of the Americas.* Ithaca, NY: Cornell University Press.

Tuhiwai Smith, L. 2012. *Decolonizing methodologies: Research and indigenous peoples* (second edition). New York: Zed Books.

Walters, K. L. 2010. Critical issues and LGBT-two spirit populations: Highlights from the HONOR project study. IOM Presentation, March 2010. http://www.iom.edu/~/media/Files/Activity%20 Files/SelectPops/LGBTHealthIssues/Walters%20 presentationl.pdf.

Walters, K. L., and J. M. Simoni. 2009. Decolonizing strategies for mentoring American Indians and Alaska Natives in HIV and mental health research. *American Journal of Public Health* 99(1): S71–S76.

Walters, K. L., T. Evans-Campbell, J. M. Simoni, T. Ronquillo, and R. Bhuyan. 2006. "My spirit in my heart": Identity experiences and challenges among American Indian two-spirit women. *Journal of Lesbian Studies* 10(1/2): 125–149.

Williams, W. L. 1986a. *The spirit and the flesh: Sexual diversity in American Indian culture.* Boston: Beacon Press.

———. 1986b. Persistence and change in the berdache traditions among contemporary Lakota Indians. In E. Blackwood (ed.), *The many faces of homosexuality: Anthropological approaches to homosexual behavior.* New York and London: Harrington Park Press, pp. 191–200.

20. THE CONNECTION BETWEEN WHITE MEN, AGGRIEVEMENT, AND MASS SHOOTINGS

ARVIND DILAWAR (2018)

[In 2018], two seemingly unrelated bits of news came to light. The first was that Nikolas Cruz had etched Nazi swastikas into the ammunition magazines he used in the school shooting that claimed 17 lives in Parkland, Florida. The second was that the United States' white jail population doubled from 1990 to 2013, according to analysis conducted by the Vera Institute of Justice, a research non-profit that studies the criminal justice system.

The thread that connects these two stories is aggrievement, and it offers a unique insight into the cause of mass shootings—at least 57 percent of which are committed by white men, according to data from *Mother Jones*. The perpetuation of these crimes is deeply entangled with both the actual and perceived downward mobility of white men, as well as their mistaken attribution of that decline to African Americans, feminists, immigrants, and other "boogeymen" of social justice movements.

Michael Kimmel, a professor of sociology and gender studies at Stony Brook University, examined "aggrieved entitlement" in his 2013 book *Angry White Men*. He defines aggrieved entitlement as a deal between white men and the nation, which they feel the nation has reneged on.

"These white men made a bargain with American society, which is, if I do all of these things that you've asked me to do—be solid, responsible, tax-paying, hardworking citizens—then I should expect to get these rewards," Kimmel tells me. Those rewards include societal markers such as home ownership and wages high enough to support a family on a single income.

But those supposed promises have not been fulfilled. According to data from the Census Bureau, homeownership rates for non-Hispanic whites has been falling since at least 2004, while the number of white dual-income families has grown by almost 34 percent since 1980—a reflection of economic necessity as much as feminist independence.

An artificially adopted sense of victimhood is a common theme, says Mike King, an assistant professor of criminal justice at Bridgewater State University who has written extensively on the subject of white identity politics. King says that, in the pursuit of reclaiming the ostensible ability to play the part of the marginalized, aggrieved white men fail to see that the very people they're angry with are suffering from the same failures and consequences of a broken system.

"Real problems that face working people of all races—de-unionization, drug addiction, suicide, mass incarceration, family disintegration, foreclosure or loss of home equity, underemployment or delayed retirement, increasing costs of health care and education, the mounting impacts of environmental crisis, and a lack of real political power—these problems are not addressed by aggrieved whiteness," King says.

"It's not immigrants who are responsible for climate change, it's not LGBT people who outsourced their jobs, it's not feminist women who issued those predatory loans," Kimmel adds. "They're rightfully angry, but they're delivering their mail to the wrong address."

The fallout from these broken promises manifests instead in a host of other ways. Middle-aged white men are the fastest-growing segment of the population committing suicide. But that rage and despair can also be turned outward—such as with the rise in economic property crimes, like burglary, larceny, and theft, being perpetrated by white men.

Often, this anger is directed at fellow victims rather than the true perpetrators. Whereas the school shooters of yesterday were committing "suicide by mass murder"—that is, murdering as many people as possible before being gunned down by the police or killing themselves—a newer breed of school shooters is operating more along the lines of Anders Breivik, the neo-Nazi who killed 77 people in a joint bombing and mass shooting in Norway. Breivik's behavior—one that didn't end in his own suicide—is echoed in the actions of Dylann Roof, the white supremacist who killed nine African Americans in Charleston, South Carolina, in 2015, and Cruz, who had expressed hatred for African Americans, Hispanic people, and homosexuals prior to his shooting at Marjory Stoneman Douglas High School.

"These guys don't want to die, they want to see the fruits of their labor," Kimmel says. "They want to ignite a civil war that they want to watch. They want to be hailed as heroes for starting things."

The victims of aggrieved whiteness, then, are the victims of white supremacy, whether they be African-American churchgoers in Charleston, or the mostly white students in Parkland. When all of the forces of progress—from Black Lives Matter activists to Women's Marchers to Dreamers—are supposedly conspiring against you, everyone is the enemy.

21. WHEN I WAS GROWING UP

NELLIE WONG (1981)

I know now that once I longed to be white.
How? you ask.
Let me tell you the ways.
    when I was growing up, people told me
    I was dark and I believed my own darkness
    in the mirror, in my soul, my own narrow vision
       when I was growing up, my sisters
       with fair skin got praised
       for their beauty, and in the dark
       I fell further, crushed between high walls
    when I was growing up, I read magazines
    and saw movies, blonde movie stars, white skin,
    sensuous lips and to be elevated, to become
    a woman, a desirable woman, I began to wear
    imaginary pale skin
       when I was growing up, I was proud
       of my English, my grammar, my spelling
       fitting into the group of small children
       smart Chinese children, fitting in,
       belonging, getting in line
when I was growing up and went to high school,
I discovered the rich white girls, a few yellow girls,
their imported cotton dresses, their cashmere
    sweaters,
their curly hair and I thought that I too should have
what these lucky girls had
       when I was growing up, I hungered
       for American food, American styles,
       coded: white and even to me, a child
       born of Chinese parents, being Chinese
       was feeling foreign, was limiting,
       was unAmerican

when I was growing up and a white man wanted
to take me out, I thought I was special,
an exotic gardenia, anxious to fit
the stereotype of an oriental chick
    when I was growing up, I felt ashamed
    of some yellow men, their small bones,
    their frail bodies, their spitting
    on the streets, their coughing,
       their lying in sunless rooms,
       shooting themselves in the arms
when I was growing up, people would ask
if I were Filipino, Polynesian, Portuguese.
They named all colors except white, the shell
of my soul, but not my dark, rough skin
       when I was growing up, I felt
       dirty. I thought that god
       made white people clean
       and no matter how much I bathed,
       I could not change, I could not shed
       my skin in the gray water
    when I was growing up, I swore
    I would run away to purple mountains,
       houses by the sea with nothing over
       my head, with space to breathe,
       uncongested with yellow people in an area
       called Chinatown, in an area I later
         learned
       was a ghetto, one of many hearts
       of Asian America
I know now that once I longed to be white.
How many more ways? you ask.
Haven't I told you enough?

22. TRANS*FORMING COLLEGE MASCULINITIES

T. J. JOURIAN (2017)

Men and masculinities studies in higher education are gaining prominence within the literature, illuminating how cisgender men understand and grapple with masculinity/ies on college campuses. The study of men and masculinities broadly emerged in the 1970s and 1980s as a profeminist response to the men's rights movement, itself a conservative backlash to the gains made by women in society up to that point (Brod, 1987; Clatterbaugh, 1990). As an interdisciplinary study "of men *as men*" (Shapiro, 1981, p. 122), the investigation of men and masculinities is a relatively new endeavor, with the focus on college men's identities and developmental needs barely a couple of decades old (Capraro, 2004). Within higher education as well, scholars have argued there is a need to study college men's experiences from a gendered perspective. Despite much of the foundational literature used in the field being based on men's lives and development (Patton, Renn, Guido, & Quaye, 2016), gender as a construct or process was not purposefully examined, thus this literature is also relatively new (Davis & Laker, 2004; Edwards & Jones, 2009; Harris & Barone, 2011). However, there is a significant gap in this emerging literature as the discussion of masculinities is solely restricted to men's experiences, all of whom are assumed to be or are cis men, and the constructs of "men," "male," and "masculinities" are used interchangeably (Marine, 2013). In addition to masculine-identified women (Person, 1999), these studies fail to include the experiences and understandings of trans* students.

Similarly emergent, literature on trans* students is incredibly limited in scope and quantity, most of it being derived from broader lesbian, gay, bisexual, trans* and queer (LGBTQ) studies, sometimes regardless of whether trans* students were a part of the study (Renn, 2010). This practice uncritically conflates sexual orientation with gender identity, and thus assumes concerns and experiences associated with one are reflective of the other (Marine, 2011; Pusch, 2003; Renn & Reason, 2013). Furthermore,

trans* students' understandings of masculinity/ies, femininity/ies, or variations thereof are not explored, and trans* students are treated as a monolithic entity in the literature, without attention to the diversity among the population or in intersection with identities other than gender. One noteworthy exception is Catalano's (2015) work exploring how trans* men's experiences in higher education shape their understanding of their gender identities.

This study fills gaps in both men and masculinities studies in higher education, as well as in trans* college student literature. The study is significant in that it asks us to consider masculinities from a divergent perspective, offering us much in the pursuit of meaning and potential interventions. By centering trans*masculine students' understandings of masculinities with particular attention to trans*masculine students with multiple marginalized identities, this study advances an intersectional and transformative investigation of masculinities and understanding of trans*masculine students. Thus, this study's findings could point to liberatory potentials for everyone, including cis men and women, and trans* people. Additionally, a trans*-centered study provides opportunity for trans* students to reflect and amplify their self-awareness, as well as validate trans* lives, perspectives, and resilience. Such validation is important if we are to improve trans* students' sense of belonging, involvement, persistence, and academic success on campus, and may provide invaluable insight into how we may dismantle the gender binary and undo the oppression that trans* students face on hostile campuses (e.g. Beemyn, 2003; Bilodeau, 2009; Rankin, Blumenfeld, Weber, & Frazer, 2010). Finally, the study also begins to build a bridge between masculinity studies and trans* studies in higher education, an interaction that is missing despite the glaring commonality of gender in the two strands.

This study illuminates how masculinities are understood, defined, and conceptualized on college campuses from the perspective of those who figuratively and/or literally move across genders. Thus, the study poses the following questions:

- How, if at all, do trans*masculine students conceptualize a masculine identity?
- How, if at all, do their salient intersecting identities inform this conceptualization?

CONCEPTUAL FRAMEWORK

The conceptual framework informing the literature review and the study situates hegemonic masculinity (Connell, 2005) and genderism (Bilodeau, 2009) as part of the social and institutional context in which trans*masculine students understand themselves and the world around them. Hegemonic masculinity is 'the pattern of practice . . . that allowed men's dominance over women to continue' (Connell & Messerschmidt, 2005, p. 832), as well as over subordinated masculinities that do not meet patriarchal standards (Connell, 2005). Hegemonic masculinity is invisible, ubiquitous, and maintained and reconstructed by all genders simply by continuing to perform gender-scripted behaviors and practices. Genderism—also referred to as cissexism or cisgenderism—is a cultural and systemic ideology that regulates gender as an essentialized binary based on sex assignment at birth (Bilodeau, 2009). It pathologizes and denigrates nonconforming gender identities through binary sorting and privileging of conforming identities, punishing nonconformity, and isolating gender nonconforming people and identities.

The contexts of hegemonic masculinity and genderism are examined and challenged through the lenses of intersectionality (Crenshaw, 1991), disidentification (Muñoz, 1999), critical trans politics (Spade, 2011), and theory as liberatory practice (hooks, 1994). Intersectionality (Crenshaw, 1991) is an analytical tool that seeks to name and deconstruct the interlocked nature of systems of oppression. Rooted in Black feminist thought, intersectionality was conceptualized and advanced by Black women who experienced marginality in both the civil rights and the women's liberation movements through the collusion of racism, sexism, and classism (Combahee River

Collective, 1981; Springer, 2002). The theory has since evolved and [been] repurposed to include additional systems of oppression, such as heterosexism, ableism, and genderism (Abes, Jones, & McEwen, 2007; Andersen & Collins, 2013; Renn, 2010). Building off intersectionality and women of color feminism, queer of color analysis and critique offer disidentification (Muñoz, 1999). Disidentification is the disruption of normative narratives of belonging that situate individuals as either aligning with and conforming to dominant ideologies and ways of being ('identification' or good) or in active opposition ('counter-identification' or bad). Thus, to disidentify is an agentic political act of resistance that creates new truths rather than either adopting the dominant reality or opposing it entirely.

Outlining disidentification as a political survival tool that is especially useful for queer (including trans*) people with multiple marginalized identities, comes to focus when examined from a critical trans politics (Spade, 2011) lens. Critical trans politics challenges mainstream assumptions that institutional structures are neutral, and positions administrative systems such as higher education institutions as constantly reproducing dominant meanings and boundaries of gender. These lenses collectively push for the examination and critique of the (re)production of intersecting systems of power and the pursuit of transformative theory that aims to enact practice for liberation (hooks, 1994). 'Theory is not inherently healing, liberatory, or revolutionary' (hooks, 1994, p. 61), thus we must intentionally ask it to do so and create theory that shifts our daily lives. It is not enough to ask whether masculinities can include trans*masculine representations, but rather how trans* realities and conceptions might transform masculinities, how we think about them, value them, and enact them. . . .

LITERATURE REVIEW

. . .

The increased visibility of lesbian, gay, bisexual, trans*, and queer (LGBTQ) students on college campuses has led to the expansion of related literature in higher education publications, particularly examining identity development, surveying campus climate, and sharing personal narratives (Renn, 2010). However, much of that work either does not include trans* students or uncritically aggregates them with the whole LGBTQ population, assuming trans* students' needs and experiences to be similar to those of lesbian, gay, and bisexual (LGB) students and making little to no distinctions between sexual orientation and gender identity (Marine, 2011; Pusch, 2003; Renn & Reason, 2013). This practice is not useful, particularly when LGB/LGBTQ campus organizations and centers, often sources of LGBTQ study participants, have not always been supportive or inclusive (Beemyn, 2003; Bilodeau, 2009), with the 'T' in the acronym being 'more symbolic than substantive' (Beemyn, 2003, p. 34). Some would even characterize these spaces to be trans* exclusionary, with trans* people's contributions to LGBTQ advocacy and activism often overlooked, co-opted, or marginalized (Marine, 2011; Spade, 2011).

Studies on the experiences of trans* college students provide a dismal outlook (e.g. deVries, 2012; Effrig, Bieschke, & Locke, 2011; McKinney, 2005; Morgan & Stevens, 2008, 2012; Rankin, 2004; Rankin et al., 2010), illuminating the hardships and the many areas that need to be addressed to alleviate those hardships, but also making it hard to envision how trans* students can succeed in the collegiate environment. Although there is still a need to unearth hostile campus climates with the intention of transforming them, there is also a need to foreground the ways that trans* students' resiliency, support networks, and leadership aid in their persistence and contributions to campus and society (Nicolazzo, 2016). As some quantitative studies relied on small sample sizes (e.g., Dugan, Kusel, & Simounet, 2012; Effrig et al., 2011; Rankin, 2004), there is a need for additional studies to aid in comparative insight, as well as larger studies to allow for nuanced perspective on trans* subpopulations. The monolithic and aggregated narrative thus far has been overwhelmingly drawn from the voices of white trans*masculine students at large public institutions, with few studies including trans* students of color, trans*feminine and gender nonconforming students, and students at single-sex and community colleges. There is also an over-reliance on policy recommendations, with little if any discussion on systemic/cultural change

to transform postsecondary environments (Bilodeau, 2009; Spade, 2011).

. . .

Although there are only a few non-pathologizing models of identity development for trans* students (Beemyn & Rankin, 2011; Bilodeau, 2005, 2009; Catalano, 2015), these studies aid in 'the dismantling of dual gender systems, promoting greater freedom from rigid gender roles' (Bilodeau & Renn, 2005, p. 32). These benefit trans* individuals, normalizing their existence, validating their perspectives, and providing necessary insight for campus support. Additionally, the relaxing of the gender binary and restrictive identity manifestations benefits all students (Bilodeau, 2009), and thus ought to inform and motivate studies examining the gender identity development processes of all students.

METHODOLOGY

This study utilizes post-intentional and queer approaches to phenomenology (Ahmed, 2006; Vagle, 2014). Although traditional phenomenology concerns itself with essentializing a concept, the post-intentional approach opens up phenomenology to 'multiplicity, difference, and partiality' (Vagle, 2014, p. 114), making it a 'dialogic philosophy' (p. 114). It seeks out what a phenomenon might become rather than what it is by hearing multiple, complex, and variant voices rather than seeking out a singular common voice. Queer phenomenology concerns itself with orientation and the revelations of how queerness disrupts and disorients accepted paths and directions dictated by social relations (Ahmed, 2006). It positions phenomenology to be political and transformative by making disorientation a necessary experience in order to understand how we are orientated. Queer phenomenology acknowledges that certain orientations are scripted and organized, while being interested in the deviations from those scripts. Similar to this study, queer phenomenology has been used to theorize and understand different embodiments and orientations, such as athletic embodiments and identity (Allen-Collinson, 2009, 2011), the governance of embodiment and disability (Titchkosky, 2011), and the interlocking orientations of queers and migrants to politics (Chávez, 2013).

To maximize the potentials of these phenomenological approaches to resist the construction of a homogeneous trans*masculinity (singular), this study employed maximum variation sampling to seek out diverse and divergent perspectives (Merriam, 2009).

My in-group access to trans*masculine communities and spaces allowed for the purposeful selection of individuals that span regional, institutional, racial, and other identity-related representations, as demonstrated in Table 1.

TABLE 1   STUDY PARTICIPANTS

Pseudonym (pronouns)	Race	Sexuality	Disability	SES	Class*	Inst type and region
RJ (they/them/theirs)	Borica/Latinx	Pansexual	Disabled	Working class/ poor	G	Private, South
James (he/him/his)	white, Black, Native American, Asian	Queer	—	Middle class	UG	Public, Northeast
Demian (they/them/theirs)	white	Queer	Dissociative Depressedish	Upper-middle class	UG	Private, West
Jack (he/him/his)	white	Queer	Disabled	<$10,000/year	G	Private, South
Coffee Bean (they/them /theirs)	Latin@-NicaMexiGreek	Queer	PTSD	Working class	UG	Public, Northeast
Charles (he/him/his and they/them/theirs)	Japanese, Hawaiian, Chinese, Portuguese, and Irish	Queer— attracted to femininity	—	Raised middle(ish) working class	UG	Public, West
Blake (they/them/theirs)	white	Queer	Arthritis and anxiety	Upper class	G	Public, Northeast
Jay (he/him/his)	Black	Queer	Yes?	Working class	G	Public, Midwest
Daniel (he/him/his)	white	Queer	—	Middle class	UG	Private, Midwest
Earl (he/him/his)	African American	Queer	—	Poor	G	Public, West
Kyle (he/him/his)	Black Cherokee	Queer	—	Working poor	UG	Public, South
Seth (he/him and they/ze)	Latino	Pansexual	Occasional anxiety	Lower middle class	UG	Private, West
Bastian (he/him/his)	Lakota Jew	Heteroflexible, sapioromantic, demisexual, Two Spirit	Several mental and chronic health conditions	Raised upper-middle, currently poor	G	Public, Midwest
Mohammad (they/them and he/him)	Middle Eastern	| <3 femmes	—	Lower middle class	UG	Public, West
Eli (he/him/his)	white	Asexual	—	Middle class	UG	Private, South
Peter (he/him/his)	white	Bisexual	—	Upper-middle class	UG	Private, South
Stephen (he/him/his)	white	Queer	—	Working/lower middle class	CE	Private, Northeast
Gabriel (he/him/his)	white	Attracted to women	—	Upper class	UG	Private, West
Jones (he/him/his, they /them/theirs)	Korean–American	Queer	—	Low middle	G	Public, South

Note: Participants' own articulations of identities used.

*UG = undergraduate; G = graduate; CE = continuing education.

Participant criterion included (i) individuals assigned female at birth, (ii) who at the time of the study attended an institution of higher education, and (iii) whose gender identity and/or expression is self-described as trans*masculine in some way. . . .

Data collection occurred through semi-structured individual and two-person interviews. Both the Patton and Spradley models (as cited in Madison, 2012) were used to construct the interview questions. The Patton model was useful in constructing questions regarding opinions, feelings, physiological senses, and sources of knowledge (e.g. 'what words do you use to describe your masculinity, and where do these terms come from?'), while the Spradley model primarily guided the construction of descriptive questions to elicit stories and examples (e.g. 'can you share a story about an instance when you remember feeling masculine?').

A total of 19 individuals were interviewed, in person or via phone or Skype as preferred by participants, and interviews lasted anywhere from 40 min to 2 h. These 19 individuals were selected out of a pool of 57 respondents who filled out an online demographic form to indicate interest, aiding in the selection of a diverse participant pool. The interviews were recorded and transcribed. Data analysis occurred using post-intentional phenomenology's whole-part-whole method (Vagle, 2014). This allowed for a whole picture context-taking, followed by a deep dive into individual transcripts, and situating parts and quotes from those transcripts into the whole context. Informed by post-intentional phenomenology's inclination toward multiplicity and variance (Vagle, 2014), coding was deemed as insufficient and reductive. Thus, analysis was driven by a motivation to 'avoid [creating] a coherent and interesting narrative . . . bound by themes and patterns' (Jackson & Mazzei, 2012, p. viii). By utilizing theory, including the literature reviewed and the conceptual framework described, to think with and through data, a 'dense and multi-layered treatment of data' was achieved.

Study trustworthiness and authenticity were established through a variety of measures. These included using multiple data collection methods (single and dual interviews), multiple data sources, and twice piloting the interview protocol. Member checking, community feedback forums, and the use of auditors aided in the study's transferability, credibility, dependability, and neutrality. Member checking involved summarizing and restating participants' comments to them, sending their individual transcripts to them, and sharing the findings with them to provide multiple opportunities to clarify any inaccuracies or misunderstandings. A few participants added notes and further explanations in their transcripts and these were also included in the data analysis. Presentations of initial findings at two conferences (Gender Odyssey, August 2015 in Seattle; Translating Identity Conference, October 2015 in Vermont) served as community feedback forums to solicit reactions and input from other trans*masculine individuals to increase validity of the findings. Two auditors were recruited for their lived and scholarly content expertise to conduct verification that procedures were followed through and findings could be substantiated. This was done through regular meetings with each auditor individually, where steps and evolving analysis would be discussed. It was in part through these discussions, locating the data within queer orientations (Ahmed, 2006) and disidentifications (Muñoz, 1999), that the insufficiency of coding data revealed itself, thus allowing for pathways to emerge in the findings. Trustworthiness and authenticity were further strengthened by engaging in reflexivity throughout the research process, providing rich descriptive data, and using maximum variation sampling to elevate marginalized voices.

I must also acknowledge my own positionality in this process. As a trans*masculine person of color who entered the field of higher education emboldened by experiences in student activism, I am partial to scholarship that seeks to name and destabilize systems of oppression and taken-for-granted constructs. Current conceptions of gender in particular, but always in relation to and fused with other social statuses, do not account for conceptions and experiences like my own and those of other trans* people, including within higher education. The exclusion of our multifaceted realities shapes the oppressive landscape of these institutions and has an impact on the matriculation, persistence, success, and well-being of trans* people within and beyond its bounds. This study is motivated by a desire to reimagine that landscape by unveiling its current state and recognizing its severe limitations. My involvement in different queer and trans* communities gave me access to a variety of networks. I minimized my personal bias by asking probing questions, especially when I thought I might know what a participant meant by making a particular statement. Additionally, I utilized a reflexion journal to bracket my own thoughts, experiences, and reactions to the participants' narratives, so as not to analyze the data in relation to my personal journey.

FINDINGS

This study sought to answer how, if at all, do trans*masculine college students understand, define, and adopt a masculine identity, as well as how that identity is informed by their various and salient intersecting identities. The presentation of the findings in the form of a threshold and pathways disputes notions of a singular trans*masculinity that trans*masculine college students arrive at or even aspire to realize. I utilize pathways as metaphor to describe the limitless paths or possibilities of (trans*) masculinities that the study's participants took on, pathways that exist within the contexts of hegemony and dominance, not independent of them. This metaphor is illustrated in Figure 1, with an image of trans*masculine pathways that exist within the aforementioned contexts, which are invisible and ubiquitous. This manuscript will present a description of the threshold and the many ways it presented itself in participants' worldview. This will be followed by an overview of the pathways, and minimal explorations of individual pathways and some subpathways.

THE THRESHOLD OF DOMINANT MASCULINITIES OR DOMINANCE IN MASCULINITIES

It is through the contexts of hegemony and dominance that trans*masculine college students first experience the threshold of dominant masculinities or dominance in masculinities (including as reflected in themselves), represented by the dark gray area in Figure 1. This threshold functions as an entry point

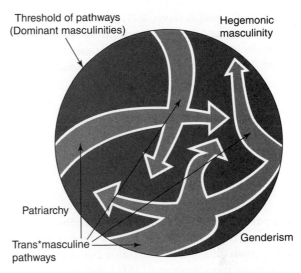

FIGURE 1 Trans*masculine threshold and pathways.

that all trans*masculine students talked about negotiating. Dominant or hegemonic representations of masculinity were the first things on participants' minds, demonstrating how omni-present and unavoidable they are (Connell, 2005), particularly as trans*masculine individuals begin considering how to define and construct their own masculinities. As the negotiation with this entry point occurred, students variously resisted, leveraged, or even internalized dominance. Within the threshold students talked about identifying how dominance showed up in themselves and others around them, how dominant masculinities were institutionalized at their campuses, and how non-dominant college masculinities showed up as pleasant and surprising exceptions in a few individuals. These various exceptional acts of affirmation and non-dominant performances often catalyzed the exposure of dominant masculinities as not the only masculine paths that participants could take, but rather positioned dominant masculinities as a threshold of excess that served 'as a site for transformation' (Jackson & Mazzei, 2012, p. 7).

UN/LEARNING FROM FATHERS

Not unlike cisgender college men, fathers came up as one of the most prevalent conveyors of dominant and hegemonic masculinities beyond an institutional context (Kimmel & Davis, 2011). Many talked about questioning and critically examining their fathers' masculinities, rather than uncritically adopting them. Talking about their father, Blake said,

> I so much don't want to become my father and don't want to emulate that same kind of masculinity. To me he's very emotionally closed off and the only emotion is anger or like being upset. It's interesting because . . ., I see a lot of him in myself and I think that's part of why I've been so intentional in self-reflection about the type of masculinity I want to embody.

Others had similar resistive responses to being compared to their fathers. Daniel described his father's and paternal grandfather's masculinity as a lazy masculinity and exclaimed how I don't ever want to be those guys and I think that happens to a lot of us [trans*masculine people]. We get these bad examples of masculinity and we're like I don't want to do that. Seth similarly described their father as very emotionally weak. He is easy to anger at times and he doesn't know how to navigate his emotions. It's something I associate with masculinity, a really big negative aspect of it. This was in contrast to associating femininity with being emotionally strong, like his mother's, which Seth talked about admiringly and more like themselves than their father's masculine and weak emotionality. Daniel's and Seth's articulations of emotions and how they are associated with femininity (strong capacities) and masculinity (weak capacities), stand in contrast to the guy code (Kimmel, 2008), which associates emotionality with weakness and femininity.

Earl spoke to noticing and learning the dictates of the guy code, ". . . growing up as far as something's wrong, just be like 'whatever, it's fine' or like my feelings are hurt and not really talking about that." This meant that what ailed him was not addressed and he was left carrying the hurt around. He attributed these learned behaviors to masculinity's focus on doing and action ("if something was going on or something was wrong you just handle your business") rather than taking the time to reflect or emote ("You didn't stop and talk about how you feel or if you're tired or sick or whatever"), which has an adverse impact on health and well-being (Courtenay, 2010).

Although, most talked about their fathers' masculinities as embodying dominance, lack of emotionality, and being toxic or unhealthy, some participants' fathers did model more positive or desirable representations of masculinity in their behaviors and expressions. Incidentally, the three students who shared having these positive examples were all students of color (Jay, Charles, and Mohammed). These counter-narratives stand in opposition to racist attributions of danger, threat, violence, and hyper-masculinity to men of color with which masculine students of color contend (Dancy, 2011; Harper, 1996; Lee, 2004). Charles talked about his stepfather's expressions of masculinity as being non-normative and in contrast to other participants' fathers who were described as closed off emotionally.

> I think of my stepdad, who while is very masculine, he has feminine traits. He's very emotional, he cries all the time and he's such an emotional man that sometimes I think he's embarrassed because of it. If anything I so admire that because I'm like, this is also masculinity.

DOMINANCE WITHIN

Not all participants necessarily saw themselves always resisting traditional and dominant masculinities. James in particular often talked about willingly and consciously adopting traits and expectations associated with masculinity. For example, James gravitated toward the image of the husband who brings home the bacon kind of things, that masculinity is being the bread winner. Being able to support your family even if it's not [your passion]. He saw his father's ability to financially support the family vs. his mother who was a stay-at-home parent during his childhood, as a model he wished to follow, including physiologically. Since he considered his father to have a lot of power and status at his job and is seen as the man, James took "a lot of social cues from him. Like how to walk into a room and how to present as a powerful male . . . So I mimic some of these habits, good and bad."

James reflected how some of his behaviors, expressions, and attitudes around gender help compensate for what he believed he lacked, specifically in terms of physical characteristics he wanted that would clearly mark him as a man. He reflected on a time he watched himself on a video recording and how,

> everything about my outer person screams girl so I think I overcompensate to try and mask that. I dominate conversations, I try and answer every question in class, I work out a ton, I push myself to excel academically, professionally, I try to come off as a stud, I try to see how many girls I can get to like me. Kinda fucked, but it's about changing what I can.

Others also reflected on how they internalized dominance or would notice dominance being imposed on them through gendered expectations changing the more masculine they presented or identified. Even as they developed their own internal definitions of masculinity, they needed to contend with the external pressures of hegemonic masculinity (Edwards & Jones, 2009). Mohammad talked about these shifting expectations being a central reason in wanting to participate in the study, to intentionally take time to think about what masculinity means to him, to empower himself to challenge or resist some of these imposed expectations. Even as awareness of one's masculine privilege rises to the surface, some students talked about not knowing how to respond without asserting masculine dominance. Bastian talked about an undergraduate class when another man in the class was,

> talking about sexism and whether women that are wearing skimpy clothes are like asking for it . . . I really wanted to deck him. I kind of wish that I had, but then again that would just be a different [negative] representation of masculinity right there if I had.

INSTITUTIONALIZED MASCULINITY, DOMINANCE, AND LEADERSHIP

Participants had specific conceptualizations and experiences of dominant masculinities as they showed up on their campuses as embodied among their peers and other individuals, but often as reflections of the institutions themselves and institutional discourse. Jack named the pervasiveness of masculinity at his institution, and how it played out within the Deaf community on campus, as related to power.

> Even in the Deaf community, who (*sic*) is an oppressed minority, in this Deaf community you have a system of power . . . Men have much more power than women because of the patriarchy obviously . . . That is actually a huge issue at [my institution]; domestic violence and sexual assault on campus is like out of control.

RJ spoke to institutional masculine culture and rape culture when they said, "Currently, like, this is horrible to say but the culture of [my institution], masculinity equals rape. It's bad shit; it's fucked up to say . . . There is a culture of, 'Who gives a shit,' or 'She was asking for it.'" The institutionalized framing of rape and sexual assault as only a women's issue and men 'as the definite enemy,' as well as the embeddedness of the gender binary in this framing, left Kyle feeling conflicted about his role and positionality as a man of transgender experience, who wanted "to engage in these conversations . . . [but] not knowing how to balance the amount of space I take up." He also spoke to his knowledge of what it "feels like to be seen and treated as a woman, [but] find it hard to find space for me to be able to have these conversations and not feel invalidated by them." Gabriel also talked about recognizing how rape culture impacts interpersonal interactions and women's perceptions of him and his masculinity, despite his own self-concept.

> I do have to be conscious of my masculinity I think because sometimes I'm like I know I'm a trans* guy, I know what I'm *not* going to do but then I'm like, wait, unfortunately a lot of women on college campuses are afraid of sexual assaults and things like that and I have to remember . . . so if I see someone who's drunk I'll be like, "hey are you okay" or something like that, but then I have to be conscious of things people might assume [about what] my intentions are.

The connection between institutionalized masculine and rape cultures was just one way in which participants understood how their institution portrayed a dominant and privileged masculinity. Trans*masculine students of color in particular talked about the whiteness of institutional masculinity. Earl very directly stated that "when I think of masculinity with regards to my school I think of white guys." Jay was similarly direct as he stated, "It's like people [in higher education] don't have expectations of you as a Black man." As a returning student, who had already experienced a lack of belonging during his first tenure as an undergraduate student, he was severely disengaged from the institution.

> I don't live on campus, I don't fuck with campus, I don't have anything to do with campus. I just go in, get my classes and go back to the south side with the other Black people and I'm good, you know what I'm saying?

Institutionalized masculinity, in its racist and misogynistic form, was often paralleled with Greek life on campus. At Coffee Bean's institution, these elements, along with class, all coalesced into dude-bro masculinity. For them,

> a dude-bro is a Whitefraternity dude, upper class, of course. And that upper class is deeply tied to their whiteness. I think of someone who is in Fiji [Phi Gamma Delta] and Sammy [Sigma Alpha Mu]. I think of someone who is obnoxious, someone who is entitled. And that's Whitemasculinity, right, because for me, especially coming to [my institution], it was hard for me to disentangle whiteness from upper class-ness.

Others also discussed how institutionalized masculinity presented itself in campus leadership. For example, Mohammed described administrators and campus police as being patriarchal and policing on people, mirroring Ayman and Korabik's 2010) contention that leadership is considered masculine. Thus, hegemonic masculinity was pervasive on college campuses at both the interpersonal and institutional cultural level. In contrast, Seth, who attended a traditionally women's institution, talked about the centering of femininity as an experience he appreciated, describing his campus as a feminist institution. For him, this meant that masculinity was,

> just not something that [the institution] prioritizes. I think because society does place such a high value on masculinity, that being a woman on this college is a point of pride and says, "Hey, femininity is like the cultural, subcultural standard in this area, and not masculinity." I guess personally, being a trans* man at [this campus], I feel like I'm both intimidated and

inspired, because of having all these strong female figures. . . . It doesn't really take away from my experience of being a trans* man aside from I don't really run into a lot of guys, and ones I can look up to. It enhances my appreciation for strong female figures.

So for students like Seth, Eli, and Peter, who all attended traditionally women's colleges, the decentering of masculinity as the cultural . . . standard at traditionally women's colleges allowed them to be in environments where dominant and hegemonic masculinity was not the institutionalized norm. They experienced diverse genders on campus, including masculinities, being affirmed rather than discarded. These institutions counteracted the overvaluing of masculinity and undervaluing of femininity that they saw throughout society, and thus were spaces where they could also exist. Their experiences at these specific institutions and with trans*-affirming staff and faculty differs from what researchers have uncovered at other women's colleges (Hart & Lester, 2011; Marine, 2009).

NON-DOMINANT COLLEGE MASCULINITIES

Despite the institutionalization of masculinity at most students' campuses, there were individuals on those campuses that consciously or unconsciously resisted dominant social scripts. This meant, some participants experienced validations from other non-script following masculine people on campus and found examples of non-dominant masculinities they related to or saw as models. These were often staff and faculty, often—but not always—queer and trans*, and participants discussed them as exceptions or alternatives to the embeddedness of dominance in institutional masculinity. Daniel referred to two queer staff as mentors in queer masculinity. As someone who predominantly dated other men, there was "Landon (a pseudonym), who like seeing him marry some other man but still sort of owning his masculinity, but doing it in a real gentle way." Whereas Mike (a pseudonym), who "really strongly identifies as queer and masculine, but also is in a hetero-romantic relationship," has become significant in Daniel's life now that he finds himself in a relationship with a woman and has the ability to discuss how to negotiate his masculinity in that realm with Mike. Thus, for Daniel it was significant to know both Mike and Landon and see the varying ways they embodied gentle, queer masculinities, regardless of the gender makeup of their relationships.

Coffee Bean met their trans* father figure, Ryan (a pseudonym), when they visited the institution before matriculating. Ryan was the director of the campus LGBTQ resource center at the time, and it was his openness with his trans* identity that captured Coffee Bean's attention.

> He was so open about yeah, when I transitioned and a couple of years passed, blah, blah, blah, and I'm just like you transitioned?! Que?! The scandalousness, like what do you mean? And he was just like yeah, whatever. I've got my partner. And I was just like oh my god you have a partner? Oh my god. You can have a life and be trans? Like, get the fuck out. And the fact that he talked about, I love my job, I was just like, damn, and you've got a job where you can be like out and you're happy, and your family is cool with it . . . like, all of these things that I thought were insurmountable. And he's someone who was just chilling, living their life like yeah, whatever, fuck it. I know Ryan now and it's not like he's totally fucking perfect but the fact that those things are accessible, they're real and they can happen to someone like me, wow, you're someone like me, damn! Like it was, and I'm starting to tear up, that was so life changing, it really was.

Meeting and getting to know trans*masculine staff in their full humanity, their struggles and their resilience, even when their gender identities and presentations did not completely align with theirs, was an entry point to imagining multiple possibilities of trans*masculinities for students like Coffee Bean. This wasn't limited to meeting other trans*masculine people on campus, as was the case for Seth and their understanding of masculinity/ies and trans*ness.

> My chemistry professor, she is a trans*woman. She tells me that she isn't the most feminine individual. She can kind of be like a tomboy or whatever. It's kind of helped me realize that as a trans* person I don't really have to adhere to anything.

Cisgender peers also could play a positive role, when they themselves acknowledged and pointed out that masculinities did not look one particular way. When Jones talked about masculinity with some of his friends, they pointed out that,

> there's this guy and that guy in our class and they're not super masculine. So they're trying to explain to me that there's different ways of being a dude. So it comforts me to know that there are, just like there are so many types of women, there are different types of men. So that gives me the freedom to be myself and however sensitive I am it's okay.

SUMMARY

Participants in the study described dominant masculinities as the first and most present masculinities in their lives. They often learned about them from their fathers, who were action-oriented, concerned with careers and financial stability, and unable or unwilling to be emotionally vulnerable. At times they found themselves struggling or not wanting to resist dominant narratives of masculine expression and identity. At an institutional level, hegemonic and toxic masculinity was pervasive, often associated with rape culture, Greek Life, athletics, and whiteness. Many found encouragement and alternatives in exceptional models of positive and non-oppressive masculinities around them. This included staff, faculty, alumni, and peers, across genders and sexualities. These models meant that dominant masculinity, the threshold where trans*masculine college students began to conceptualize what being masculine means, was not the only option and they could negotiate different pathways for themselves.

PATHWAYS

Through negotiations and interactions with the threshold of dominant masculinities, including individual representations of non-dominance, various pathways emerged. Thus, the threshold functions as an entry point for trans*masculine college students into deviated possibilities of masculinity pathways. The pathways represent the various (trans*)masculinities that the study's participants took on to (re) define their gendered identities. These (re)definitions were informed by their intersecting and salient identities and realities. These pathways are understood to exist within—and not independent of—the contexts of dominance, hegemony, genderism, and patriarchy (as well as racism, classism, and other systems of oppression, as represented by the white/invisible area in Figure 1). The pathways do not remove trans*masculine people or trans*masculinities from these contexts, but rather offer alternative, i.e. dis-identified (Muñoz, 1999), possibilities within them. Some of these pathways may start from a similar point, but diverge, while others get closer to each other, and others find themselves in a similar space at a particular point in time only. The pathways are represented by the light gray arrows in Figure 1 and are listed in Table 2.

The order in which the pathways are listed do not suggest an order by which trans*masculine college students explore said pathways or that the pathways are mutually exclusive. Thus, to read this presentation as a trans*masculine developmental model whereby trans*masculine college students start with

dominance and arrive at authenticity with a number of ordered steps in between would be an inaccurate reading. A linear understanding would fail to witness how many of these pathways and sub-pathways emerge and re-emerge at different times and can occur concurrently, rarely if ever being completely resolved. Rather the order demonstrates how individuals' definitions of masculinity/ies become increasingly complex and authentic as they (re)visit pathways. Further, the separate naming of the pathways and sub-pathways ought not to suggest that they are mutually exclusive. Meaning their separate presentations does not suggest for example that there is an inauthenticity inherent in reoriented (trans*) masculine embodiments, or that authentic (trans*) masculinities are not informed by race. In fact, the majority if not all the pathways and sub-pathways are variously intersectional. For example, Kyle, who participated in BBP's Leadership Retreat, talked about,

> connecting back to indigenous roots and the different tribes that existed that actually understood that masculinity and femininity are fluid, [that] they flow into each other rather than just being binary or either side of the spectrum . . . I think that if it wasn't for Brown Bois I would probably still have that anxiety, that pressure, to be rigid, to be cold, to try to be hard and all that other stuff. I guess getting connected back to the ancestry that says this never existed before colonialization. This wasn't a part of our culture. We don't even understand what that means . . . is what kind of transformed my view of what masculinity means to me and what it can mean in another context.

Kyle's reflection of the impact of his BBP experience intersects at the sub-pathways of (trans*)masculinities of color and non-binary (trans*)masculinities, as they begin to flow into Kyle's authentic (trans*) masculine pathway. Traversing multiple pathways and sub-pathways simultaneously is analogous to taking multiple classes in a semester, allowing learnings from one to inform approaches in another, and with subsequent semesters becoming more and more integrated and complex in one's tackling of assignments and learning.

Additionally, the pathways are intentionally named as *(trans*)masculine* rather than as either

TABLE 2   PATHWAYS AND SUB-PATHWAYS

Pathways	Sub-pathways
Racialized (trans*)masculinities	
	(Trans*)masculinities of color
	Black (trans*)masculinities
	white (trans*)masculinities
Reoriented (trans*)masculine embodiments	
	Fashioned (trans*)masculinities
	Sexua-romanticized (trans*) masculinities
	(Dis)abled (trans*)masculinities
	Non-binary (trans*)masculinities
Authentic (trans*)masculinities	
	Intentional (trans*)masculinities
	Gentle (trans*)masculinities

*trans*masculine* or *masculine*. To remove *trans** entirely from the names of the pathways is to dismiss the role that the students' trans*ness has played in shaping and informing their gendered conceptions and experiences. However, to tether *trans** and *masculine* together without parenthetical disruption might allow for two suggestions to be made: (a) that these pathways are only possibilities for trans*masculine individuals and irrelevant for other masculine people, and (b) that for these students trans*ness and masculinities are always integrated and fused, and thus they cannot be trans* and not masculine or vice versa.

RACIALIZED TRANS*MASCULINITIES

Race and racism played an underlying role across all pathways, as well as the threshold as mentioned earlier. Race also interacted with masculinity/ies in a manner that informed how individuals read others and how they believed they were perceived by others. This is exemplified by Blake, a white non-binary transmasculine person, who said, "I think I fall into the same pattern of reading Black men as more dangerous than white men. Although I also think I do read white men as dangerous but not as dangerous perhaps."

(Trans*)masculinities of color

Trans*masculine students of color experienced whiteness, white supremacy, and racism as impediments to their desire to embody or witness representations of masculinities that were both positive and culturally affirming. Specifically, trans*masculine students of color brought up colonialism, respectability politics, and being seen as threats as racialized beings as mediators in their experience of masculinities within and outside of their racial and cultural communities. Bastian talked about how "the Two Spirit community is still being influenced by some colonialist ideas regarding gender." As an example, he talked about how "the ones that were born and assigned male at birth tend to speak over the trans members and the women," and how he believed Western values have polluted Lakota masculinity to mean that wives should submit. His testimony is an articulation of colonialism's influence in disrupting traditional

Indigenous masculine roles that existed as complimentary rather than as superior to or in conflict with feminine roles (Innes & Anderson, 2015).

Black (trans*)masculinities

For Black-identified participants in the study, their experiences and masculinities were often additionally shaped by anti-Blackness. The ways Black-identified participants in the study discussed anti-Blackness and the significance of specifically Black spaces and history on their lives and gender conceptions necessitated examining their stories in a distinctive manner within the (trans*)masculinities of color subpathway.

Kyle, Earl, and Jay's experiences of anti-Blackness was particularly salient for them within queer and trans* spaces as others began to progressively perceive them as Black men. Jay felt his masculinity stripped of its queerness and trans*ness by others' interpretations of Black masculinity as inherently heterosexual and cisgender. He believed others assumed him to be cishet, experiencing the ways that queerness is often underwritten by whiteness. As he transitioned, Jay tracked the microaggressions he experienced and felt disoriented, remarking how he did not know where he stood. "I'm automatically an aggressor, I'm automatically someone causing a problem, I'm automatically a troublemaker, I'm automatically a suspect." To mitigate these perceptions, Earl talked about modifying his masculine performance to "try not to be the angry Black guy." The feeling of exhaustion was palpable as he described the ways he silenced and shrank himself to not "take up a lot of space in class." As he struggled to find space for his Blackness to exist in queer spaces, Kyle found "solace [in] other Black guys who are kind of like me and creating our own kind of pocket community that is very much Black pride . . . but also has this inclusive kind of masculinity."

White (trans*)masculinities

Although race was a fairly consistent part of the interviews with trans*masculine students of color, it did not come up as particularly salient for most of the white trans*masculine students that participated in the study, with many not mentioning race at all, either on a personal level or conceptually. For some, their experiences of marginality as trans* people acted as an entry point into reflecting on their privileged identities, including race, but this was not the case for all. The four participants who spoke to being white, having white privilege, and seeking to understand the role of whiteness in their lives were Daniel, Blake, Stephen, and Eli. Stephen for example talked about what it meant to have a plethora of white (trans*)masculine images and people around him.

> I'm white so I honestly think that I've been presented with images of masculinity, of what my masculinity could look like . . . I mean white men are in everything so your ideas about what it means to be, for the most part I think that masculine standards are based on what traditional white men, [say] masculinity is.

REORIENTED (TRANS*)MASCULINE EMBODIMENTS

Many of the participants in the study talked about deconstructing and reconstructing (their) masculinities, constantly (re-)negotiating their identities as they learned and unlearned scripts they were exposed to or were trying on. This also involved reorienting and disidentifying with stereotypically masculine constructs (Ahmed, 2006; Muñoz, 1999). For example, Mohammad described himself as a competitive person and stated,

> I think in that sense masculinity, just like striving towards the goal, finishing college . . . striving towards being successful and in my terms successful means helping others. I think that masculinity in a lot of ways helped me with that. Society's ideas of masculinity has helped me with that . . . I want to be a teacher. I really enjoy teaching. And I think it's one of the best things you can do to help the revolution, whatever you think that is. Because you're really teaching the next generation and education is really important.

Thus Mohammad is simultaneously taking advantage of hegemonic masculine expectations of competition and success, while redefining what success means—one that involves helping others and the revolution rather than just himself, something he had learned growing up among Arab people. His aspirations to joining a feminized and care-based profession such as teaching furthered that redefinition. This practice in disidentification was in line with how he defined

being masculine, "like embodying this masculine performance, it's kind of like, this is who I am. I'm a trans* guy, and kind of like, 'Fuck you and what you think of masculinity.'"

Having the agency, desire, and ability to redefine identity for self and others was often tied to social position and how gender intersected and was influenced by identities such as class, (dis)ability status, religion, and sexuality. These intersections and influences are variably explored in the sub-pathways of fashion, sexuality and romance, (dis)ability, and non-binary masculinities. RJ spoke often about the intersection of class, fashion, and their masculine embodiment. Unable to access transition, RJ found power and redefinition by "always wear[ing] jewelry" such as "earrings and stuff and some other [masculine of center (MOC) people] are not too comfortable doing that. I don't see [MOC] folks with earrings."

It was almost impossible for many participants to talk about gender and masculinity without discussing sexuality and relationships. Participants talked about their masculinity in terms of roles (imposed, desired, and their closeness to power) in romantic and sexual relationships, their sexual identities (assumed, imposed, and fluidness), and ways they and others saw themselves as sexual beings. Daniel talked about navigating his first serious relationship with a woman, as someone who identifies as queer and had "pretty exclusively been interested in other male-identified people." Daniel spoke to being intentional about roles and how certain practices might be read by others, as a way to be intentional about interrogating how his masculine privilege might present itself.

> I think about how I show up in space with her . . . I think about what does it look like if I put my arm around [her] in public when we're with friends? What does it look like in public at all? And what does it look like for a person that's been romantically submissive to ask a woman out as a man?

Masculine embodiment was a salient pathway for participants with disabilities. Trans*masculine students with various (dis)abilities talked about how their disabilities and experiences with ableism intersected with masculinities. In most of these conversations there was a sense of conflict between disability and masculinity with the former having a diminishing effect on the latter, as tied to physicality and self-sufficiency, with few talking about reclaiming their simultaneously masculine and (dis)abled bodies. Blake attributed struggling to build muscle and thus embodying a more masculine physique to having arthritis. Thinking about how arthritis had shaped their body thus far made them think about their body in "the future and kind of wondering what is going to happen and not being sure."

What it means to embody a masculine body or identity was also a space of negotiation and resistance for students who explored and pushed for nonbinary ways of being and understanding themselves and their masculinities and/or manhoods. Contending with binaries in both cis and trans* contexts, in campus environments and non-campus environments made non-binary students feel silenced, unsafe, othered, and bore an emotional toll on them. Some found online communities to be spaces where they could exist more authentically and avoid contending with feelings of not being man/masculine/trans* enough (Catalano, 2015). Genderism had influenced the narratives of trans*ness that Peter was exposed to, dictating that trans* men were masculine, that his androgyny conflicted with trans* manhood and thus he surmised that he could not be a trans* man. Through Tumblr, a microblogging platform, Peter began to learn that there is no such thing as someone who's the perfect paragon of masculinity, who has every single trait that is associated with masculinity.

AUTHENTIC (TRANS*)MASCULINITIES

Participants' experiences and reflections drew them to desiring masculinities that felt authentic to them, without performing restrictive, prescriptive, and harmful scripts just to be recognized as masculine and/or as men. Authenticity had varying meanings to different students, but many talked about crafting their masculinities with intentionality and imbuing them with gentleness. Intentionality was tied to taking up physical space, voice, and language. As an example, Charles mentioned how amongst his friends he used to say things like,

oh my god you're being such a bitch, right, and talking to my friends that way. It's clearly banter-y and that's just our way of speaking, but I realize now when I say the word bitch in public to anyone, joking or not, my male presence makes it different and I have to be really mindful of my presence and how I say things because I don't want to be *that* guy.

The balancing of gentleness and intentionality in many of the students' authentic (trans*)masculinities often meant not resisting early female socialization. Earl saw being "raised and socialized as female" as an asset, and that "it's okay to use what you learn and experience from being raised and conditioned as female to let that influence what masculinity is or how it looks to you or presents through you." Always thinking about their gender through a racialized lens, Coffee Bean was,

not interested in denying the fact that I was socialized as a woman of color . . . That's real and that shapes me and that's who I was and that will always be a little part of who I am and I think that also informed some of my reason for joining [my Latina sorority].

Having resisted trying "to fit into this really restrictive feminine role," Jones was not interested in replacing that with a restrictive masculine one, preferring to give himself "the freedom to move the way I've always wanted to move, just the freedom to be." RJ believed that "[vulnerability] should be at [masculinity's] center." RJ's demand stood in disidentified opposition to hegemonic ideas that masculine people "can't really show emotion all the time." Part of gentleness and vulnerability involved self-preservation. In describing their masculinity succinctly, RJ stated "my trans*masculinity is . . . self-care and survival." For Kyle this meant "not forget[ting] about myself in these larger movements, while also supporting [and advocating for] other people as well."

CONCLUSION

Trans*masculine college students notice and conceptualize masculinity in particularly nuanced ways with their perspectives informed by their varied lived experiences as trans* individuals. The pathways upon which trans*masculine college students construct and reconstruct (trans*)masculinities are racialized, reoriented, and seek authenticity in intentional and gentle ways. A diverse participant pool unveiled a slew of disidentified and reoriented (trans*) masculine pathways that demonstrated their abilities to shift the conversation on and practice of masculinities. When we are surrounded by endless examples of toxic and hegemonic masculinity unleashing itself unapologetically and with little if any accountability (Chemaly, 2015; Devega, 2015; Tourjee, 2015), trans*masculine students are creating and offering life-saving alternatives, resisting genderism and hegemonic masculinity simultaneously, demanding and exemplifying liberatory masculinities (hooks, 1994).

REFERENCES

Abes, E. S., Jones, S. R., & McEwen, M. K. (2007). Reconceptualizing the model of multiple dimensions of identity: The role of meaning-making capacity in the construction of multiple identities. *Journal of College Student Development, 48*(1), 1–22.

Ahmed, S. (2006). *Queer phenomenology: Orientations, objects, others*. Durham, NC: Duke University Press.

Allen-Collinson, J. (2009). Sporting embodiment: Sports studies and the (continuing) promise of phenomenology. *Qualitative Research in Sport and Exercise, 1*, 279–296. doi:10.1080/19398440903192340

Allen-Collinson, J. (2011). Feminist phenomenology and the woman in the running body. *Sports, Ethics and Philosophy, 5*, 297–313. doi:10.1080/17511321 .2011.602584

Andersen, M. L., & Collins, P. H. (2013). Systems of power and inequality. In M. L. Andersen & P. H. Collins (Eds.), *Race, class, & gender: An anthology* (8th ed., pp. 61–90). Belmont, CA: Thomson Wadsworth.

Ayman, R., & Korabik, K. (2010). Leadership: Why gender and culture matter. *American Psychologist, 65*, 157–170.

Beemyn, B. (2003). Serving the needs of transgender college students. *Journal of Gay & Lesbian Issues in Education, 1*, 33–49.

Beemyn, G., & Rankin, S. (2011). *The lives of transgender people*. New York, NY: Columbia University Press.

Bilodeau, B. (2005). Beyond the gender binary: A case study of two transgender students at Midwestern research university. *Journal of Gay & Lesbian Issues in Education, 3*, 29–44.

Bilodeau, B. (2009). *Genderism: Transgender students, binary systems and higher education*. Saarbrücken: Verlag Dr. Müller.

Bilodeau, B., & Renn, K. A. (2005). Analysis of LGBT identity development models and implications for practice. In R. L. Sanlo (Ed.), *Sexual orientation and gender identity: New directions for student services* (Vol. 111, pp. 25–40). San Francisco, CA: Jossey-Bass.

Brod, H. (1987). The new men's studies: From feminist theory to gender scholarship. *Hypatia, 2*, 179–196.

Capraro, R. L. (2004). Men's studies as a foundation for student development work with college men. In G. E. Kellom (Ed.), *New directions for student services 107: Developing effective programs and services for college men* (pp. 23–34). San Francisco: Jossey-Bass.

Catalano, D. C. J. (2015). "Trans enough?" The pressures trans men negotiated in higher education. *TSQ: Transgender Studies Quarterly, 2*, 411–430. doi:10.1215/23289252-2926399

Chávez, K. R. (2013). *Queer migration politics: Activist rhetoric and coalitional possibilities*. Champaign: University of Illinois Press.

Chemaly, S. (2015, October 5). Mass killings in the US: Masculinity, masculinity, masculinity. *Huffington Post: Crime*. Retrieved from http://www.huffingtonpost.com/ soraya-chemaly/mass-killings-in-the-us-w_b_8234322 .html

Clatterbaugh, K. (1990). *Contemporary perspectives on masculinity: Men, women, and politics in modern society*. Boulder, CO: Westview Press.

Combahee River Collective. (1981). The Combahee River Collective statement. In C. Moraga & G. Anzaldúa (Eds.), *This bridge called my back: Writings by radical women of color* (pp. 210–218). Watertown, MA: Persephone Press.

Connell, R. W. (2005). *Masculinities* (2nd ed.). Berkeley: University of California Press.

Connell, R. W., & Messerschmidt, J. W. (2005). Hegemonic masculinity: Rethinking the concept. *Gender and Society, 19*, 829–859.

Courtenay, W. H. (2010). Constructions of masculinity and their influence on men's well-being: A theory of gender and health. In S. R. Harper & F. Harris, III (Eds.), *College men and masculinities: Theory, research, and implications for practice* (pp. 307–336). Indianapolis, IN: Wiley.

Crenshaw, K. (1991). Mapping the margins: Intersectionality, identity politics, and violence against women of color. *Stanford Law Review, 43,* 1241–1299.

Dancy, T. E., II (2011). Colleges in the making of manhood and masculinity: Gendered perspectives on African American males. *Gender and Education, 23,* 477–495.

Davis, T., & Laker, J. (2004). Connecting men to academic and student affairs programs and services. In G. E. Kellom (Ed.), *New directions for student services 107: Developing effective programs and services for college men* (pp. 47–57). San Francisco, CA: Jossey-Bass.

Devega, C. (2015, July 7). The plague of angry White men: How racism, gun culture & toxic masculinity are poisoning America. *Salon.* Retrieved from http://www.salon.com/2015/07/07/the_plague_of_angry_white_men_how_racism_gun_culture_toxic_masculinity_are_poisoning_america_in_tandem

deVries, K. M. (2012). Intersectional identities and conceptions of the self: The experience of transgender people. *Symbolic Interaction, 35,* 49–67.

Dugan, J. P., Kusel, M. L., & Simounet, D. M. (2012). Transgender college students: An exploratory study of perceptions, engagement, and educational outcomes. *Journal of College Student Development, 53,* 719–736.

Edwards, K. E., & Jones, S. R. (2009). "Putting my man face on": A grounded theory of college men's gender identity development. *Journal of College Student Development, 50,* 210–228.

Effrig, J. C., Bieschke, K. J., & Locke, B. D. (2011). Examining victimization and psychological distress in transgender college students. *Journal of College Counseling, 14,* 143–157.

Harper, P. B. (1996). *Are we not men? Masculine anxiety and the problem of African–American identity.* New York, NY: Oxford University Press.

Harris, F., III, & Barone, R. P. (2011). The situation of men, and situating men in higher education: A conversation about crisis, myth, and reality about college students who are men. In J. A. Laker & T. Davis (Eds.), *Masculinities in higher education: Theoretical and practical considerations* (pp. 50–62). New York, NY: Routledge.

Hart, J., & Lester, J. (2011). Starring students: Gender performance at a women's college. *NASPA Journal about Women in Higher Education, 42,* 192–217.

hooks, b. (1994). *Teaching to transgress: Education as the practice of freedom.* New York, NY: Routledge.

Innes, R. A., & Anderson, K. (2015). *Indigenous men and masculinities: Legacies, identities, regeneration.* Winnipeg: University of Manitoba Press.

Jackson, A. Y., & Mazzei, L. A. (2012). *Thinking with theory in qualitative research: Viewing data across multiple perspectives.* New York, NY: Routledge.

Kimmel, M. S. (2008). *Guyland: The perilous world where boys become men.* New York, NY: HarperCollins.

Kimmel, M. S., & Davis, T. (2011). Mapping guyland in college. In J. A. Laker & T. Davis (Eds.), *Masculinities in higher education: Theoretical and practical considerations* (pp. 3–15). New York, NY: Routledge.

Lee, S. J. (2004). Up against whiteness: Students of color in our schools. *Anthropology & Education Quarterly, 35,* 121–125.

Marine, S. B. (2009). Navigating discourses of discomfort: Women's college student affairs administrators and transgender students. *Dissertation Abstracts International, 70*(2), UMI 3349517.

Marine, S. B. (2011). Stonewall's legacy: Bisexual, gay, lesbian, and transgender students in higher education. *ASHE Higher Education Report, 37*(4). San Francisco: Jossey-Bass.

Marine, S. B. (2013). Book review [Review of the book *Masculinities in higher education: Theoretical and practical considerations,* by J. A. Laker & T. Davis (Eds.)]. *NASPA Journal about Women in Higher Education, 6,* 131–134.

Marine, S. B., & Nicolazzo, Z. (2014). Names that matter: Exploring the tensions of campus LGBTQ centers and trans* inclusion. *Journal of Diversity in Higher Education, 7,* 265–281.

McKinney, J. S. (2005). On the margins: A study of experiences of transgender college students. *Journal of Gay and Lesbian Issues in Education, 3,* 63–76.

Merriam, S. B. (2009). *Qualitative research: A guide to design and implementation.* San Francisco, CA: Jossey-Bass.

Morgan, S. W., & Stevens, P. E. (2008). Transgender identity development as represented by a group of female-to-male transgendered adults. *Issues in Mental Health Nursing, 29,* 585–599.

Morgan, S. W., & Stevens, P. E. (2012). Transgender identity development as represented by a group of transgendered adults. *Issues in Mental Health Nursing, 33,* 301–308.

Muñoz, J. E. (1999). *Disidentifications: Queers of color and the performance of politics.* Minneapolis: University of Minnesota Press.

Nicolazzo, Z. (2016). *Trans* in college: Transgender students' strategies for navigating campus life and the institutional politics of inclusion.* Sterling, VA: Stylus Publishing.

Patton, L. D., Renn, K. A., Guido, F. M., & Quaye, S. J. (2016). *Student development in college: Theory, research, and practice* (3rd ed.). San Francisco, CA: Jossey-Bass.

Person, E. S. (1999). Some mysteries of gender: Rethinking masculine identification in heterosexual women. In *Sexual Century: Selected Papers on Sex and Gender* (pp. 296–315). New Haven, CT: Yale University Press.

Pusch, R. S. (2003). The bathroom and beyond: Transgendered college students' perspectives of transition. *Dissertation Abstracts International, 64*(2), 456. UMI 3081653.

Rankin, S. (2004). Campus climate for lesbian, gay, bisexual, & transgender people. *The Diversity Factor, 12*(1), 1–3.

Rankin, S., Blumenfeld, W. J., Weber, G. N., & Frazer, S. (2010). *State of higher education for LGBT people.* Charlotte, NC: Campus Pride.

Renn, K. A. (2010). LGBT and queer research in higher education: The state and status of the field. *Educational Researcher, 39,* 132–141.

Renn, K. A., & Reason, R. D. (2013). *College students in the United States: Characteristics, experiences, and outcomes.* San Francisco, CA: Jossey-Bass.

Shapiro, J. (1981). Anthropology and the study of gender. In E. Langland & W. Gove (Eds.), *A feminist perspective in the academy: The difference it makes* (pp. 110–129). Chicago, IL: University of Chicago Press.

Spade, D. (2011). *Normal life: Administrative violence, critical trans politics, and the limits of law.* Brooklyn, NY: South End Press.

Springer, K. (2002). Third wave black feminism? *Signs, 27,* 1059–1082.

Titchkosky, T. (2011). *The question of access: Disability, space, and meaning.* Toronto: University of Toronto Press.

Tourjee, D. (2015, December 16). Why do men kill trans women? Gender theorist Judith Butler explains. *Broadly.* Retrieved from https://broadly .vice.com/en_us/article/why-do-men-kill-trans-women-gender-theorist-judith-butler-explains

Vagle, M. D. (2014). *Crafting phenomenological research.* Walnut Creek, CA: Left Coast Press.

CHAPTER 4

INSCRIBING GENDER ON THE BODY

Human bodies illustrate the most obvious expressions of gender. Indeed, this inscription of gender onto bodies is the key to gender identities as we recognize bodies as "masculine" or "feminine." Bodies that are not easily and immediately recognizable as fitting within this binary often cause anxiety and consternation when we cannot place them neatly into either masculine/male or feminine/female boxes. This binary aspect of bodies as "either this or that" is so thoroughly taken for granted that we rarely question it. If you have ever attended a drag show or parade where bodies act outside of gender expectations, you might have noted these exaggerated gender performances. They are especially instructional because drag performances accentuate traditional gendered bodies through the clothes people wear and the ways they walk and talk. They help illustrate how gender is normalized and usually experienced as "natural." When gender is performed in these ways, it can be entertaining, in part because it emphasizes this "taken-for-grantedness" of most individuals' experiences of gender. As emphasized in the previous chapter, there is nothing "natural" about gender at all. Instead, it is constructed and repeated over and over again every minute of the day. However, as also explained in Chapter 3, "performativity" must not be reduced to a voluntary act or something that is totally willful. Rather, performativity is constrained by social norms.

Actions performed by our bodies provide a sense of agency (the "me" that separates me from "you") and are shaped by social forces that give them meaning. Gender performances are not only what we "do"; they are also who we "are" or "become." This implies that we are what we do, and what we do is shaped by cultural ideas, social practices, and structured institutions that give those everyday actions meaning. In addition, remember that all bodies are racialized. "White" is a racialized concept too. The mythical norm serves to assume race is just about people of color, but white is a diverse category also constructed through history, culture, and politics. In terms of bodies, however, the stereotype of the hypersexualized black male body, for example, has been used to control communities of color, just as the expectation that certain bodies are "naturally" good at sports or science and so forth has functioned to reinscribe racialized discourses on human bodies. As already mentioned, there are also discourses or regimes of truth about the aging body that regulate behaviors, just as there are many discourses in contemporary societies about ability and disability that provide meaning about the body. As discussed in Chapter 2, these include the very notions of disability or differently abled as bodily "impairment" that implies a lack or pathology rather than a different set of attributes. "Impaired" has meaning only against something that is defined as "normal." In this way, bodies, and the ways bodies are interpreted, are contextualized in cultural meanings informed by our ideas about gender and other identities. Many of these cultural ideas, for example, come from contemporary media, the focus of the next chapter. Indeed, bodies are foundational for many issues discussed in this book: sexuality, reproductive justice, health, and violence, to name just a few.

In this chapter we focus on this social construction of the body and go on to explore "beauty": one of the most powerful discourses associated with gendered bodies that regulates our lives, affecting what we do and how we think. Everyone knows what a beautiful person, and especially a beautiful woman, looks like, even though this notion is constantly in flux and varies across time and culture. We close the chapter with a discussion of eating disorders and methods for negotiating "beauty" ideals.

LEARNING ACTIVITY

CONSIDERING BODY SIZE, SHAPE, AND MOVEMENT

Take a tour examining the public facilities of your campus, which may include:

> Drinking fountains
> Bleachers
> Sinks and stalls in public restrooms
> Curbs, ramps, and railings
> Chairs and tables
> Turnstiles
> Elevators and escalators
> Stairs and staircases
> Vending machines
> Doors and doorways
> Fire alarm boxes

Answer the following questions:

> What assumptions about the size and shape of the users (height, weight, proportionate length of arms and legs, width of hips and shoulders, hand preference, mobility, etc.) are incorporated into the designs?
> How do these design assumptions affect the ability of you and people you know to use the facilities satisfactorily?
> How would they affect you if you were significantly:
> Wider or narrower than you are?
> Shorter or taller?
> Heavier or lighter?

Rounder or more angular?
More or less mobile/ambulatory?

Identify any access or usage barriers to people with physical disabilities. Answer the following questions:

> Are classrooms accessible to people who can't walk up or down stairs? Are emergency exit routes usable by people with limited mobility?
> Are amplification devices or sign language interpreters available for people with hearing impairments?
> Are fire alarms low enough to be reached by people who are seated in wheelchairs or who are below average height?

Identify one assumption incorporated into the design of one of the facilities (drinking fountain, conference room, lab, etc.). Gather formal or informal data about the number of people on campus that might not be able to use the facility satisfactorily based on the design assumption. Suggest one or two ways to make the facility more useful for all people.

Choose one of the access or usage barriers you have identified and suggest a way to remove the barrier. Research the cost involved. Identify one or two ways of funding the access strategy you have suggested.

Source: Janet Lockhart and Susan M. Shaw, *Writing for Change: Raising Awareness of Difference, Power, and Discrimination*, www.teachingtolerance.org.

THE SOCIAL CONSTRUCTION OF THE BODY

A social constructivist approach to understanding the body recognizes attributes as arising out of cultures in which the body is given meaning. For example, in some communities large-bodied women are considered more beautiful than slim women, illustrating that there is no fixed idea of "beauty." Contrary to this is the concept of biological determinism, where a person's biology or genetic makeup, rather than culture or society, determines destiny. This approach sees people in terms of their reproductive and biological bodies and allows men to avoid the constraints of biological determinism through a construction of the male body as less grounded in, and able to transcend, nature (as evident in mythology, art, and philosophy). This association of women with the body, earth, nature, and the domestic is almost universal and represents one of the most basic ways that bodies are gendered. Males, because of historical and mythological associations with the spirit and sky, have been associated with culture and the mind rather than the body, and with abstract reason rather than with earthly mundane matters.

In addition, many societies have incorporated not only a distinction between nature and culture, but often a domination of culture and mind over nature and body. In particular, imperialist notions of "progress" have involved the taming and conquering of nature in favor of "civilization." As a result, the female/nature side of this dichotomy is valued less and often denigrated and/or controlled.

A prime example of this association and denigration of women with the body is the way menstruation has often been seen as smelly, taboo, and distasteful. Menstruation has often been regarded negatively and described with a multitude of derogatory euphemisms like "the curse" and "on the rag," and girls are still taught to conceal menstrual practices from others (and men in particular). As Gloria Steinem suggests in the classic essay "If Men Could Menstruate," the experience would be something entirely different if men menstruated. Advertisements abound in magazines and on television about tampons, pads, douches, feminine hygiene sprays, and yeast infection medicines that give the message that women's bodies are constantly in need of hygienic attention. Notice we tend not to get ads for jock itch during prime-time television like we do ads for feminine "ailments." In this way, there is a strange, very public aspect to feminine bodily processes at the same time that they are coded as very private. This is an example of the discourses or regimes of truth that shape bodies in contemporary culture.

In this way, although the body is an incredibly sophisticated jumble of physiological events, our understanding of it cannot exist outside of the society that gives it meaning. Take, for example, the ways we recognize "the heart," not just as a physiological organ, but also as symbolic of cultural meaning: in this case, love and care. "Head" is sometimes opposed to "heart." In this way, even though bodies are biophysical entities, what our bodies mean and how they are experienced is intimately connected to the meanings and practices of the society in which we reside. And, while meanings about the body are always contextualized in local communities, ideas about bodies are transported around the globe, and their commercialization supports imperialism and global capitalism alongside sexism and misogyny.

The favoring of certain looks (including size, shape, and color, as well as certain clothes or fashion) associated with the global north is an example of how imperialism and globalization frame meanings about the body, as well as shape bodies in a more literal sense. As we emphasize in this chapter and others in the book, this is about power and control over women through practices associated with the body. An example is female genital cutting (FGC), practiced in some parts of North Africa and the Middle East, as well as other regions, that ensures a girl's marriageability. The cutting varies from ritually "nicking" the clitoris to full infibulation in which external genitalia are removed and the labia stitched together. Advocates against FGC argue that its health consequences are detrimental and decry the inability of girls to give consent. It is important for feminists of the global north to understand the cultural and economic contexts in which FGC occurs. In addition, we must recognize the surgical modifications of genitalia that occur in the global north, such as labia remodeling and vaginoplasty (discussed later in this chapter), as well as the surgical assignment of "sex" that may occur with intersex children.

Bodies are thus cultural artifacts; culture becomes embodied and is literally inscribed or represented through the body. Gender and other identity performances are scripted, for example, by the ways more women (and particularly white women) want to shrink their bodies compared to men, who are more likely to want bigger bodies, especially in terms of height and muscle mass. The fact that many more women than men would willingly want to be characterized as "petite" is an example of gender norms associated with the body. Indeed, scholars suggest that women's decisions for cosmetic surgery reflect their desire to attain normative standards of "beauty," whereas men are more likely to want cosmetic changes in order to be more competitive in the marketplace. Again, remember that these discussions of "men" and "women" assume intersection with other identities. They also assume a symmetry between identification as a man or woman and a masculine or feminine body, respectively. Transgender individuals identify with identities that may not match the bodily assignment given at birth, or they may portray an androgynous mixture in the same body. Trans bodies illustrate the ways bodies may subvert taken-for-granted social norms and practices.

Trans bodies also act as a site for power struggles against dominant norms as trans people decide how to embody their genders. In "Understanding Transgender and Medically Assisted Gender Transition," Jamie Lindemann Nelson explores the ways issues of gender and power play out in the medical community's role in assisting in gender transition for people who desire medical intervention.

An essential aspect of the gendering of bodies is objectification (seeing the body as an object and separate from its context) as supported by media and entertainment industries as well as by fashion. Both female- and male-identified bodies are objectified, although the context for objectification of female-identified bodies is different. This means that the turning of women into objects is contextualized in what Andrea Smith calls a racist heteropatriarchy. In other words, there is broad institutional support for the objectification of multifaceted femininities in our culture. This does not mean that men cannot be objectified, but rather that the contexts for, and thus the consequences of, such objectification are different. Kimberly Springer writes, "Know that our bodies are our own—our bodies do not belong to the church, the state, our parents, our lovers, our husbands, and certainly not Black Entertainment Television (BET)."

TRANS BODIES ARE NOT "WRONG" BODIES

Andrés López

"Born in the 'Wrong' Body"

I'm told I was born in the "wrong" body,
because somehow the physicality of my
spirit
tells you more about me than the soul
within it.
I look in the mirror wanting to see myself
and all I find are borders raised upon my
person (Anzaldúa 2012).
Borders mapped onto my body,
and the "wrongness" of a body that
betrays me.
A body that does not really tell you anything about me.
And yet, you go on believing that my
"wrong" body
Is the source of all my problems.
That because you think I'm in the
"wrong" body
I will automatically want to change it.
My body is not "wrong"
My body is more complex than that.
My body is the physical manifestation of
my being,
It is the conglomeration of the changes
that occur within me
It is the vessel that holds my history,
my thoughts, and my spirit together.
My body is NOT "wrong"!
Even if you choose to believe it is.

When I was first starting to come out as trans, I kept getting questions directed at me that focused on my body. "When are you having *the* surgery?" "When are you starting hormones?" "When will you get a penis?" were some of the ones I heard over and over again. While at the time I couldn't quite put my finger on why these sorts of questions made me uncomfortable, I very quickly realized that the reasons folks around me kept misgendering me or using the wrong pronouns and name for me was because of how my body looked. It was the way that other people saw my body that made them gender me.

This form of gendering bodies is not something that is new, or that has just emerged as more and more trans people start to share our stories. Making gender seem like it is somehow biological or natural is something that started off in the late eighteenth century when scientists were starting to categorize bodies in order to find the root causes of differences between people of different races (Stryker 2017). This particular story of how bodies can tell you something about a person's gender has been taken on by trans folks ourselves as a way to gain access to services, rights, and resources. You can see this whenever you read, watch, or hear about a trans narrative that focuses on being "born in the 'wrong' body." Now, some trans folks actually feel like this is their experience of being trans, others like myself feel like this notion of a "wrong" body gets put on us by societal pressures, and others still have different types of relationships with their bodies.

There really are no "right" or "wrong" bodies—just ideas of what bodies that get labeled as female or male should look like, and this gets more complicated when race, ability, class, and other systems of power are included. Most of us learn these ideas at a very young age and are told by parents, teachers, peers, media, and a lot of other sources how to make sure other people can see our bodies the way they should; that is as matching what our genitals got labeled as. But in reality bodies come in a variety of shapes, anatomies, and sizes that we might see as more masculine or feminine or somewhere in between. Some of us like these categories, some of us don't really care much for them, and many more of us want to get away from these expectations of what bodies should look like to match gender because it winds up putting us all into boxes we might or might not feel speak to our own experiences.

Have you ever been questioned about your body's gender? What it looks like? How it doesn't fit ideals of femininity or masculinity? How did that make you feel?

Who gets erased when we only think of trans bodies within a binary gender structure?

References

Anzaldúa, G. (2012). *Borderlands/La Frontera: The New Mestiza*, 4th ed. San Francisco: Aunt Lute Books.
Stryker, S. (2017). *Transgender History*, 2nd ed. New York: Seal Press.

In this way, the assertion "Our bodies are our own" reminds us that alongside objectification is the opportunity for the body to serve as a site of identity and self-expression. When Muslim women, for example, choose to wear the hijab or headscarf, they are responding to personal desires that may include identity and self-reliance, piety, and safety.

When transwomen don feminine attire, they are presenting themselves to the world as women: This is their identity and their sense of agency. This concept of agency is discussed by Minh-Ha T. Pham. She claims the politically conscious understanding of fashion as a source of empowerment, and also cites feminist fashion blogs as ways to celebrate non-normatively raced, gendered, sexed, and sized bodies.

As our lives become more complex and we have less power over the way we live them, we are encouraged to focus more on the body as something we can control and as something we can use to express our identity. As a result, the body becomes something to be fashioned and controlled; at the same time, this control over body—and the ability to shape, clothe, and express it—becomes synonymous with personal freedom. We might question

ACTIVIST PROFILE

MAGGIE KUHN

Most people are getting ready to retire at 65. Maggie Kuhn began the most important work of her life at that age. In 1970 Kuhn was forced to retire from her career with the Presbyterian Church. In August of that year, she convened a group of five friends, all of whom were retiring, to talk about the problems faced by retirees— loss of income, loss of social role, pension rights, age discrimination. Finding new freedom and strength in their voices, they also concerned themselves with other social issues, such as the Vietnam War.

The group gathered in Philadelphia with college students opposed to the war at the Consultation of Older and Younger Adults for Social Change. A year later, more than 100 people joined the Consultation. As this new group began to meet, a New York television producer nicknamed the group the Gray Panthers, and the name stuck.

In 1972 Kuhn was asked at the last minute to fill in for someone unable to speak during the 181st General Assembly of the United Presbyterian Church. Her stirring speech launched the Gray Panthers into national prominence, and calls began to flood the organization's headquarters. Increased media attention came as the Gray Panthers became activists. They co-sponsored the Black House Conference on Aging to call attention to the lack of African Americans at the first White House Conference on Aging, and they performed street theater at the American Medical Association's 1974 conference, calling for health care as a human right. At the core of Panther activities was the belief that older people should seize control of their lives and actively campaign for causes in which they believe.

The Gray Panthers have been instrumental in bringing about nursing home reform, ending forced retirement provisions, and combating fraud against the

elderly in healthcare. Kuhn, who was active with the Panthers until her death at age 89, offered this advice to other activists: "Leave safety behind. Put your body on the line. Stand before the people you fear and speak your mind—even if your voice shakes. When you least expect it, someone may actually listen to what you have to say. Well-aimed slingshots can topple giants."

whether the ability to change and adorn the body in new ways is really "freedom," as is political or economic freedom. Indeed, scholars discussing backlash (organized resistance) have emphasized that the contemporary preoccupation with the body illustrates the ways society encourages us (members of marginalized groups in particular) to focus on the body and its management as a "distraction" from real economic and political concerns. In the reading "'I Click and Post and Breathe, Waiting for Others to See What I See," Minh-Ha T. Pham offers an analysis of the complex ways the #feministselfie campaign both displayed "network vanity" and offered alternative notions of beauty and selfhood, particularly by minoritized people.

Tattoos and piercing among young women are examples of a trend toward self-expression in the context of mass-market consumerism. Having a tattoo or multiple tattoos— traditionally a masculine or an outlaw, rebellious act—is a form of self-expression for many. Similarly, multiple piercing of many body parts, including erogenous and sexually charged

---

BODY ART

Across practically all times and cultures, humans have practiced various forms of body modification for such differing reasons as warding off or invoking spirits, attracting sexual partners, indicating social or marital status, identifying with a particular age or gender group, and marking a rite of passage. People all over the world have pierced, painted, tattooed, reshaped, and adorned their bodies, turning the body itself into an artistic canvas.

The earliest records of tattoos were found in Egypt around the time of the building of the pyramids. Later, the practice was adopted in Crete, Greece, Persia, Arabia, and China. The English word tattoo comes from the Polynesian *tatau*, a practice observed by James Cook when he visited Tahiti on his first voyage around the world. In the Marquesas, Cook noted that the men had their entire bodies tattooed, but women tattooed only their hands, lips, shoulders, ankles, and the area behind the ears.

Today, many of the Maori men of New Zealand are returning to the practice of wearing the elaborate tattoos of their ancestors. In Morocco, henna designs on the hands and feet are an integral part of significant celebrations, such as weddings and religious holidays. In Ethiopia, Hamar men earn raised scars made by cutting with a razor and then rubbing ash into the wounds for killing a dangerous animal or enemy. Surma girls have their earlobes stretched by clay plates and paint their faces during courtship season.

As you may have noted, body art is a gendered practice. Tattooing, piercing, painting, and reshaping the body also serve the purpose of marking gender. What are common body modification practices in the United States? How do these practices express and reinforce gender? How do they challenge gender?

Sources: Monica Desai, "Body Art: A History," *Student BMJ* 10 (2002): 196–197; Michael Lemonick et al., "Body Art," *Time South Pacific* (December 13, 1999), 66–68; Pravina Shukla, "The Human Canvas," *Natural History* 108 (1999): 80.

LEARNING ACTIVITY

ON THE RAG

Collect a wide variety of women's magazines such as *Cosmopolitan*, *Glamour*, *Vogue*, *Elle*, and so on. Identify advertisements for "feminine hygiene products"— such as tampons, pads, douches, feminine hygiene sprays, and yeast infection medicines. What do the visual images in the ads suggest? What do the words tell readers? What messages do these advertisements send about bodies with vaginas? Now collect a variety of men's magazines such as *GQ*, *Maxim*, *Men's Journal*, and so on. Identify advertisements for "masculine hygiene products." What do you find? What do these differences imply about various bodies? How does this implication reinforce structures of gender subordination?

areas of the body, can be seen as a form of rebellion against the constraints of gender and sexuality. This expression is certainly less rebellious from society's point of view than activities for real social and political justice, especially when trends involve the purchase of products and services that support the capitalist economy. Indeed, both tattooing and piercing can also be interpreted as reactionary trends and as examples of the many ways women are encouraged to mutilate and change parts of their bodies. Note that these "rebellious" behaviors have now been appropriated as relatively ordinary fashion practices. You can buy nose and belly-button rings, for example, that clip on without ever having to pierce anything, just as you can buy temporary tattoos. In fact, the self-consciousness involved in the parody of the real thing is now a form of self-expression all its own. This issue of body image and its consequences for women's lives is a central issue for contemporary feminism, mobilizing many young people.

THE "BEAUTY" IDEAL

In contemporary U.S. society we are surrounded by images of "beautiful," thin (although fit, sculpted, and large-breasted), young, abled, smiling women. Most of these bodies are white, and when women of color are depicted, they tend to show models with more typically white features or hair. Obviously, real women come in all shapes and sizes. Our diversity is part of our beauty! Nonetheless, these images set standards for appearance and "beauty" that are internalized—standards that affect how we feel about our own bodies. Such internalization is mediated though multifaceted identities arising out of diverse community memberships. Although different communities have different standards and expectations associated with how bodies should look, the permanence of some standard means that most of us grow up disliking our bodies or some parts of them. Many of us are especially troubled by parts of our bodies perceived as larger than societal ideals or, in the case of breasts and perhaps bottoms, we might be troubled because these parts are not big enough.

As men are increasingly tapped as a market for beauty and body management products, they are also increasingly confronted with idealized images. Anxiety over the presence of back hair or baldness is a case in point, as is the anxiety among some men that they are not muscled enough. Penis size, of course, while a source of amusement in popular culture, is a sensitive issue that is supported by extensive industries catering to penis enlargements as advertised on TV and in your email inbox. In addition, the metrosexual market is one marketing niche for men's consumption. 'Metrosexual' is derived from "metropolitan" and "heterosexual" and alludes to men who are meticulous about grooming and have disposable income to spend on clothes and other products. Again, all these standards of how bodies should look are mediated through communities that interpret for people who identify as men what a masculine body should look like. However, because women's worth is more tied to bodily appearances than men's worth, portrayals of female "beauty" are more significant in women's lives. This is called the double standard associated with "beauty" or normative bodily standards. What this means is that despite the increasing focus on male bodies in society and popular culture, women are particularly vulnerable to the cultural preoccupation with, and the measuring of their worth against, the body. Physical appearance is more important in terms of the way women are perceived and treated. This is especially true in terms of the aging body; there is a much stronger mandate for women than for men to keep their bodies looking young. In U.S. society, men's beer bellies, for example, provoke less aversion than women's tummy fat (either by traditional cultural definitions or by individuals themselves). Again, while we attempt to trouble these binary categories of "women" and "men" with a discussion of gender and the ways gender is inscribed onto bodies, the reality that most people in the world identify as women and as men, and experience the consequences of that identification in terms of privilege and limitations or discriminations, means that these categories are experienced as relatively fixed.

In this section we discuss four points associated with the "beauty" ideal: (1) the changeable, fluid notion of beauty; (2) the ways beauty ideals illustrate power in society; (3) the ways beauty standards are enforced in complex ways; and (4) the relationship between contemporary beauty standards and consumerism and the growth of global capitalist expansion. First, contemporary images of female beauty are changeable. What is considered beautiful in one society is different from standards in others: Practices in one society might ostracize you—or might certainly prevent you getting a date—in another. Some societies encourage the insertion of objects into earlobes or jawline or other mechanics to increase neck length or head shape. Others consider large women especially attractive and see their fat as evidence of prosperity; again, in most contemporary societies of the global north, thin is closer to standards of ideal beauty, although there are differences within specific communities within the United States. In other words, what is considered beautiful is culturally produced and changes across different cultures. In addition, as already discussed, standards of body appearance are exported along with fashion and other makeup products. A poignant example of this is the trend in limb-lengthening surgeries where bones are broken and then stretched. In some cultures the painful and expensive procedure is seen as an investment in the future, especially for men. Minimum heights, for example, are often quoted in personal and job advertisements in China, and to join the foreign service men are required to be at least 5'7" tall. Although this controversial operation was banned in China in 2006, surgeries are still performed in many countries, including the United States. Such procedures reinscribe certain ideals of beauty and body standards.

What is considered "beautiful" also varies across historical periods. Most adult women can clearly see these changes in feminine "beauty" even within their own lifetimes. Fashion trends are particularly implicated in these practices. Minh-Ha Pham explains that fashion industries shape how we're perceived by others, especially in terms of gender, class, race, and sexual identity across different time periods. "That most ordinary and intimate of acts, getting dressed, has very real political and economic consequences," writes Pham in *Ms.*

For example, a focus on standards of "Western" female beauty over time reveals that in the nineteenth century white, privileged women were encouraged to adopt a delicate, thin, and fragile appearance and wear bone-crushing (literally) corsets that not only gave them the hourglass figure but also cramped and ruptured vital organs. Such practices made women faint and appear frail, delicate, dependent, and passive—responses to notions of middle-class femininity. Victorian furniture styles accommodated this ideal with special swooning chairs. Standards for weight and body shape changed again in the early twenti-eth century when a sleek, boyish look was adopted by the flappers of the 1920s. Women bound their breasts to hide their curves. Although more curvaceous and slightly heavier bodies were encouraged through the next decades, body maintenance came to dominate many women's lives. Fueled by the fashion industry, the 1960s gave us a return to a more emaciated, long-legged look, but with very short skirts and long hair. At the beginning of this new century, we see a more eclectic look and a focus on health and fitness, but norms associated with ideal female beauty still construct the thin, large-breasted and full bottomed, white (tanned, but not too brown) body as the most beautiful. Note this cur-vaceous yet slender body type is quite rare and represents a very small minority. Most large-breasted women also have larger hips and waists for instance. Nonetheless this body

HISTORICAL MOMENT
THE DISABILITY RIGHTS MOVEMENT

Much like the other civil rights movements of the late twentieth century, the disability rights movement sought to provide equal access and equal opportunity for people living with disabilities. This movement had its roots in earlier actions directed toward improving the lives of people with disabilities. In 1817, the American School of the Deaf in Hartford, Connecticut, opened as the first educational institution to use sign language. The New England Asylum for the Blind opened in 1829, and Braille was introduced in 1832. In 1911, the U.S. gov-ernment approved compensation for disabled workers and in 1946 passed the Hill-Burton Act that provided assistance for rehabilitation. Social Security disability insurance was created in 1950.

Unfortunately, the progression of disability rights was not smooth. In the 1880s, eugenics, a pseudosci-ence with the goal of "improving" the genetic composi-tion of humanity, discouraged reproduction by people considered "undesirable," including people with dis-abilities (as well as people of color, immigrants, and the poor). Many disabled people underwent forced steril-ization as a result, and in 1927 the U.S. Supreme Court upheld the constitutionality of forced sterilization. By the 1970s, tens of thousands of people with disabilities had been sterilized without their consent.

Throughout the twentieth century, disability rights advocates continued to organize. The Blinded Veter-ans Association, the Cerebral Palsy Society of New York City (which became the United Cerebral Palsy Associations), the National Mental Health Foundation, Paralyzed Veterans of America, the National Wheelchair Basketball Association, Little People of America, the National Association of the Physically Handicapped, and the American Council of the Blind are just a few of the organizations founded in the 1940s through 1960s. In 1963 President John F. Kennedy called for the dein-stitutionalization of the mentally ill and increased com-munity services for them.

More radical disability rights groups formed in the 1970s and pushed for greater legislation and accom-modation. In 1972, the first independent living center opened and sparked the independent living movement. In 1973, Congress passed the Rehabilitation Act that for the first time addressed discrimination against people with disabilities, and the litigation coming from the act gave rise to concepts such as "reasonable modification," "reasonable accommodation," and "undue burden." In 1990, the most comprehensive legislation about disabili-ties became law—the Americans with Disabilities Act. The act mandates accessibility and reasonable accom-modations in government and public areas.

While such legislation has improved conditions for people with disabilities, disability rights activists con-tinue to advocate for access and change. Cultural groups such as the National Theater of the Deaf and sports events such as the Paralympics provide opportunities for people with disabilities to participate in social activities, and these events also function as consciousness-raisers about disabilities. Universal access to buildings contin-ues to be an issue, even on college campuses, as many old buildings do not provide easy access for people in wheelchairs or people with visual impairment who need Braille signage. Individuals with mental disabilities still face stigma, and, as the population ages, the need for greater attention to disabilities in the elderly grows.

The successes of the disability rights movement are many, but, as in other civil rights movements, work re-mains to be done. For more information, visit the website of the National Disability Rights Network at ndrn.org.

type is still the standard of beauty to which most women aspire, reflected in the increasing numbers of cosmetic surgeries involving augmentation among fashion models, celebrities, and the general population.

A second point concerning beauty ideals is that such ideals reflect various relations of power in society. Culture is constructed in complex ways, and groups with more power and influence tend to set the trends, create the options, and enforce the standards. As Susie Orbach explains in the reading *"Fat Is Still a Feminist Issue,"* about 40 years since she published her groundbreaking work, sizeism has remained a consistent problem, even as the ways sizeism is expressed in society have changed. Nonetheless, the adverse impacts, especially on girls and women, remain. As explained in Chapter 2, these deleterious outcomes as a result of weight bias have a significant impact on health, quality of life, and socioeconomic outcomes.

In U.S. culture, beauty standards are very much connected to the production and consumption of various products, and the beauty product and fashion industries are multibillion-dollar enterprises. As the reading excerpted from Joan Jacobs Brumberg's *The Body Project* explains, garment industries in the United States helped sexualize women's breasts through their development of the bra. Corporate powers, advertising, and the fashion, cosmetics, and entertainment industries all help create standards for us and reinforce gender relations. Even the "natural look" is sold to us as something to be tried on, when obviously the real natural look is devoid of marketing illusions in the first place. Most of these industries are controlled by white males or by other individuals who have accepted what many scholars call ruling-class politics. The main point is that most of us get offered beauty and fashion options constructed by other people. Although we have choices and can reject them, lots of resources are involved in encouraging us to adopt the standards created by various industries.

In this way, beauty ideals reflect white, abled, and middle-class standards. Such standards of beauty can humiliate fat or nonwhite women as well as the poor, the aged, and the disabled. These norms help enforce racism, classism, ableism, ageism, and fat oppression, as well as sexism generally. Many communities, however, have alternative notions of feminine beauty and actively resist such normalizing standards of Anglo culture. Research suggests Latinas and African American women are less likely to rely on others' approval, less likely to idealize (white, thin) cultural norms about "beauty," and less likely to experience body dissatisfaction than white women. Other sources of discrimination, however, might overshadow those attributable to body size. Still, this "resilience" to traditional beauty norms seems to occur as women of color experience a decreased self-relevance associated with these norms. In other words, Latinas and African American women are less likely to indulge in social comparisons with typical (white, thin) media images precisely because they do not see themselves in such images. However, when they do indulge in comparisons, they are just as susceptible as white women to body dissatisfaction.

Physically challenged individuals are also claiming the right to redefine beauty and the body. Aimee Mullins, a spokeswoman for high-tech prosthetics and an activist for disability rights, illustrates this goal. Although she was born without fibular bones and both her legs were amputated when she was an infant, she learned to use prosthetics and competed as a champion sprinter in college. She explains that a prosthetic limb "doesn't represent the need to replace loss anymore. It can stand as a symbol that wearers have the power to create whatever it is that they want to create in that space. So people once considered disabled can now become the architects of their own identities and indeed continue to change those identities by designing their bodies from a place of empowerment."[1] It is also important to point out that Mullins is a fashion model and actress and very closely fits the normative standard of feminine beauty in the global north. These characteristics do not detract from her important message, but they are important features in terms of understanding how her message is received.

The third point concerning beauty practices is that standards are enforced in complex ways. Of course, "enforcement" does not mean, as feminist scholar Sandra Bartky has said, that someone marches you off to electrolysis at gunpoint. Instead, we adopt various standards and integrate them as "choices" we make for ourselves. Self-objectification, seeing ourselves through others' eyes, impairs women's body image. At the same time that young girls are sexualized and objectified by contemporary media, they also learn that their body is a project that must be altered before they can attract others. It is estimated that the average woman is exposed to hundreds of advertisements a day, in part as a result of the Internet and especially advertising on social networking sites. At the same time that girls and women "police" themselves, they also learn to regulate one another in a general sense. The surveillance of women by other women around body issues (such as imposing standards and sanctions like negative talk, withdrawing friendship, or exclusion from a group or party) is an example of horizontal hostility (see Chapter 2). The reading "Asian American Women's Body Image Experiences" by Jennifer L. Brady and others explores how race intersects with gender to facilitate body dissatisfaction among Asian American women. Norms (cultural expectations) of female beauty are produced by all forms of contemporary media and by a wide array of products. For example, Victoria's Secret, a lingerie company, sells more than underwear. Models are displayed in soft-porn poses, and the company's advertisements shape ideas about gender, sexuality, and the body. Other companies have emphasized body acceptance, paralleling a surge in the acceptance of "plus size" models. It is interesting to note that these models, although called "plus size," more closely mirror average U.S. women's bodies than do traditional fashion models.

Beauty norms are internalized, and we receive various positive and negative responses for complying with or resisting them. This is especially true when it comes to hair, which plays significant roles in women's intimate relationships. It is interesting to think about these everyday behaviors that maintain the body: the seemingly trivial routines, rules, and practices. Some scholars call these disciplinary body practices. They are "practices" because they involve taken-for-granted, routinized behaviors such as shaving legs, applying makeup, or curling/straightening/coloring hair; they are "disciplinary" because they involve social control in the sense that we spend time, money, and effort, and imbue meaning in these practices that regulate our lives. Again, disciplinary beauty practices are connected to the production and consumption of various products. Of particular concern

---

1   Aimee Mullins, "Prosthetic Power," TED 2009, https://www.utne.com/science-and-technology/prosthetic-power-aimee-mullins-disability

is the connection between practices associated with weight control and smoking. A recent study from the National Institutes of Health reported that weight concerns and a "drive for thinness" among both black and white girls at ages 11 to 12 years were the most important factors leading to subsequent daily smoking.

You can probably think of many disciplinary beauty practices in which you or your friends take part. Men's practices tend to be simpler and involve a narrower range of (usually less expensive) products. Alongside fashion and various forms of cosmetics and body sculpting, women are more likely to get facelifts, eye tucks, rhinoplasties (nose reshaping), collagen injections to plump up lips, Botox injections, liposuction, tummy tucks, stomach bands and stapling, and, of course, breast augmentation (implants) as well as breast reductions. The American Society of Plastic Surgeons reports twice as many women electing to have breast augmentation than a decade ago, even though the U.S. FDA (Food and Drug Administration) has been concerned about the safety of both silicone-gel-filled and saline-filled breast implants and banned the widespread use of silicone-gel-filled implants some years ago. Known risks involve leakage and rupture, loss of sensation in the nipples, permanent scarring, problems with breastfeeding, potential interference with mammography that may delay cancer diagnoses, and fibrositis, or pain and stiffness of muscles, ligaments, and tendons.

Breast implants require ongoing maintenance and often need periodic operations to replace or remove the devices. In 2006 the FDA again approved the marketing of silicone-gel-filled implants by two companies for breast reconstruction in women of all ages and breast augmentation in women aged 22 years and older. The companies are required to conduct postapproval studies of potential health risks.

Another increasingly popular surgery is vaginal cosmetic surgery, which includes labiaplasty (a procedure to change the shape and size of the labia minora [inner lips of the vagina] and/or labia majora [outer lips], although most often it involves making the labia minora smaller), vaginoplasty (creating, reshaping, or tightening the vagina; the latter procedure is often called "vaginal rejuvenation"), and clitoral unhooding (exposing the clitoris in an attempt to increase sexual stimulation). There is no agreement, for example, on what is the "normal" size for labia and no reliable studies on the impact of labia size on sexual functioning and sexual pleasure. The most recent data from the American Society for Aesthetic Plastic Surgery reports a 64 percent increase in vaginal cosmetic surgeries from 2,142 performed in 2011 to 3,521 in 2012). Although these surgeries are sometimes performed for medical reasons, their increase is related to what has been called "aesthetic" motivations. It is important to understand that the aesthetics of the pelvic area is related to norms about gender, the body, and sexuality, and especially norms created by media and contemporary pornography.

A 2018 report from the American Society of Plastic Surgeons notes nearly 1.8 million plastic surgeries were performed in 2017, with breast augmentation the number one procedure, closely followed by liposuction. In particular, the number of African American women electing cosmetic surgery has increased (with the most favored procedures being rhinoplasty, liposuction, and breast reduction), reflecting the imposition of white standards of beauty as well as increases in disposable income and acceptance of cosmetic surgery among some groups in the African American community. More than 15 million "cosmetic minimally invasive procedures" were also performed, with Botox injections leading the way with over 7 million procedures. Women account for 90 percent of all individuals undergoing procedures, although rates of men electing cosmetic procedures have increased by more than 100 percent since the late 1990s. In order to understand all these trends, it is necessary to recognize the crucial role of the media. Celebrities, for example, often set trends that "ordinary" people try and emulate. It is known that Jennifer Lopez, for instance, had three cosmetic surgery procedures when she was just 15 years old that included liposuction, breast implants, and buttock fillers.

The enormous popularity of "reality" television shows like *Fit to Fat to Fit* and *I Used to Be Fat*, plus the increased number of websites encouraging young girls to change the way they look, has fueled these changes. These shows take people (especially women) out of communities, isolate them, and then transform their bodies through surgery, cosmetics, and other technologies of body management, before reintroducing them into their communities as radically transformed people (implying that their lives will now be better, more successful, happier, etc.). Such shows encourage people to pass for a younger age and to consider cosmetic surgery (especially breast implants and argumentation) as something women of all ages should seek and want. Though they are often entertaining and seductive in their voyeuristic appeal, it is important to recognize the role they play in the social construction of "beauty," the advertising of products and body management technologies, and the social relations of power in society. In considering these practices—from following fashion and buying clothes, accessories, and makeup to breast enhancement and all the practices in between—we need to keep in mind how much they cost, how they channel women's energies away from other (perhaps more productive) pursuits, and how they may affect the health and well-being of people and the planet.

These technologies of the body have global impact and appeal. Desire to script the body in accordance with cultural notions of attractiveness is worldwide. As discussed earlier, standards of "beauty" that vary across cultures are maintained by diverse practices that are both traditional to specific cultures as well as shaped by global media. Developments in

---

MY 600-POUND LIFE

My 600-Pound Life is a popular reality TV show that follows an individual who weighs at least 600 pounds for a year while that person prepares for and undergoes weight loss surgery (either gastric bypass or a sleeve to reduce both stomach size and the amount of food a person can eat at a time). Watch a few episodes of this show with a critical feminist eye. What do you see?

1. How does gender play out in the show? What about intersections with disability, race, and social class?
2. How are the people seeking weight loss surgery depicted? How are they situated in relation to the power of the medical community? The power of the director and camera? The power of the viewer?
3. How are we as viewers implicated in the judgments on large people offered by the show?
4. How does the show pursue individual rather than structural solutions?
5. How much agency does the show grant to the people seeking weight loss surgery?
6. What role does sexual violence play in the show? Does the show address sexual violence in its solutions?
7. What does the show suggest about the control of bodies? By individuals? By families? By medicine? By the state? By corporations? By viewers?
8. How does the show reinforce hegemonic notions of ideal bodies? How does it contribute to sizeism, sexism, ableism, and classism?
9. Could a show like this ever be disruptive or resistant to dominant views of bodies, size, disabilities, and sexuality?

Iran illustrate such practices: This country now has the world's highest number of rhinoplasties per capita (as well as a problematic number of botched surgeries).

The body and the various practices associated with maintaining the female body are probably the most salient aspects of what we understand as femininity, and they are crucial in social expressions of sexuality. Note how many bodily practices of contemporary femininity encourage women to stay small, not take up space, and stay young. Maturity in the form of body hair is unacceptable; we are encouraged to keep our bodies sleek, soft, and hairless—traits that some scholars identify with youth and powerlessness. The trend to shave and remove pubic hair so that the genitalia appear prepubertal is an example of this. Such hair removal, mimicking the display of female genitalia in pornography, may send the message that the mature female body is "gross" or should be altered. It also sexualizes children's bodies.

The fourth and final point regarding the "beauty" ideal is that while beauty standards and practices shape our bodies and lives, they are a huge aspect of consumerism and global capitalism that support imperialist cultural practices worldwide. Although enormous profits accrue to the fashion, cosmetics, beauty, and entertainment industries yearly, they sell not only products, but also ideas and values and transform communities. The underlying message for all of us, however, is that we are not good enough the way we are but need certain products to improve our looks and relationships. This does not help the development of positive self-esteem. We are bombarded with messages to buy products to fix these kinds of "flaws." As will be discussed in Chapter 5, advertising messages teach unattainable and unrealistic notions of body perfection that leave us thinking we are never quite good enough. Images present flawless young bodies that give the illusion of absolute perfection. In reality these images tend to be airbrushed and computer enhanced or

---

EXPANDING ON BODY IMAGE

Jennifer Venable

1. What comes to mind when you think about an "ideal" body? Using a blank silhouette of a person, add details to the image to represent the specific attributes of a culturally attractive person.

   - What do they look like?
   - What is their gender? Does their gender fall into the gender binary?
   - What is the color of their skin?
   - What does their hair look like?
   - How old are they?
   - Are they able-bodied?
   - What is the shape of their body?

   What social pressures reinforce these bodily expectations? How do these body standards represent social norms in terms of race, class, ability, and gender? How are messages about these social norms circulated?

2. Contemplate how an "ideal" body represents what (and who) is culturally attractive in the United States today. Reimagine a more inclusive vision of body image and beauty. How would you draw your ideal person differently to represent a more positive body image? How might your renewed body image promote acceptance and celebration of diverse bodies and their changes over time? Decorate a new silhouette to represent an expansion of acceptance of varying bodies as beautiful and culturally acceptable. How does your person:

   - Challenge beauty standards?
   - Subvert societal expectations that limit our individual expressions?
   - Represent the uniqueness of individuality?
   - Celebrate bodies that represent various ages, shapes, colors, and movements?

Source: Loosely adapted from © One Circle Foundation, Body Image Program (Revised 2009).

THE COMMODIFICATION OF BEAUTY

Liddy Detar

The social construction of female beauty has resulted in a multimillion-dollar cosmetic surgery industry that shapes, tucks, pinches, lightens, and cuts away women's bodies, "sculpting" them with knives, lasers, and needles into ideal shapes and forms. Even as notions of beauty have changed over time, this industry continues to find a market in the insecurities and social norms that construct our relationships to our bodies. The industry capitalizes on dominant social constructions of gender, gender normativity, and heteronormative sexual scripts. It reproduces and perpetuates Western ideals and cultural values, capitalizing on internalized racisms and other forms of self-loathing and promising to lighten skin, lift eyelids, and otherwise "erase" features that mark difference. It has even succeeded in a postfeminist era in packaging its violent interventions on the body in feminist frameworks, selling "new bodies" for personal happiness and empowerment. Media plays a powerful role in how beauty is defined in American culture, and this extends to create global standards of beauty. In the early 2000s, television shows such as *The Swan*, *Extreme Makeover*, and *Nip/Tuck* popularized the notion of creating a new self through surgery. Even as the ad and media industries have increasingly begun to incorporate a greater range of body types, identities, ethnicities, abilities, and races, our media continues to construct the conventions of beauty against which all female-presenting bodies are measured—and then made to conform.

TRY THIS: Look at the commodification of beauty in magazines, commercials, ads, and even music videos. Include in your search all kinds of bodies along the gender spectrum, both conforming and deviant. Which bodies are represented, and which are not? What dominant stories of gender, sexuality, beauty, race, ability, class, and ethnicity do these bodies and ads tell? How are the constructions of these narratives of identity related to what products they are supposed to sell? Try to find ads that conform to normative social constructions of beauty and gender, as well as those that challenge and resist these norms. Try selecting a single company and review its media campaigns over time. How have they changed? How are the conventions of beauty and gender norms maintained through the marketing of products? How is resistance articulated and "marketed" as well?

---

completely computer generated. These digital representations integrate all of the "positive" features associated with contemporary North American "beauty" in one image. Such images of perfect bodies are fabricated by a male-dominated culture and are reinforced by multibillion-dollar industries organized around corporate profit making.

One of these industries concerns weight loss. Millions of dollars are spent every year by people who seek to cram their bodies into smaller-size clothing. Of course, many individuals want to shrink their bodies out of a concern for better health and mobility, and the weight and exercise industries help them attain these goals. But we often do not recognize that you can be both fit and fat. We fail to acknowledge the ways we have been taught to both despise fat and participate in consumerism out of a desire to more closely fit certain cultural standards. Again, there is a double standard here whereby fat women have a harder time than fat men in our culture. This is not to say that fat men have an easy time; certainly, as already mentioned, prejudice against large-size people of all genders is one of the last bulwarks of oppression in U.S. society. Many people have no qualms about blatantly expressing their dislike and disgust for fat people even when they might keep sexist or racist attitudes hidden. However, fat women have an especially difficult time because of the interaction between sexism and fat phobia. In this way the beauty ideal supports the weight loss industry and encourages looksism and fat oppression.

At the very same time that we are bombarded with messages about being thin, the food industry in the United States (the third largest industry nationally) has considerable clout. Never before have North Americans (and, increasingly, people in developing countries)

HOW COMFORTABLE ARE YOU IN YOUR OWN BODY?

Beauty ideals and social pressures to look a certain way have adverse impacts on our feeling about our bodies. At least 80 percent of women are unhappy with their bodies, and research shows that unhappiness begins in childhood. Men too feel pressure to conform to certain kinds of bodies, and trans folks also struggle with body image. An important form of feminist resistance is learning to be comfortable in and happy with our own bodies. While consumerist culture would have us always feeling ill at ease with the way we look to encourage us to buy products to change our appearance, we can resist by paying attention to our feelings about our bodies and working to reject the culture's messages about body size, shape, abilities, and image.

Place yourself in front of a mirror. Now look at yourself and try not to evaluate or criticize how you look. It's hard, isn't it?

Besides judging yourself in front of a mirror, what other practices do you do that may contribute to discomfort in your own body?

Do you compare the way you look to the ways others look? Do you seek sexual partners to make you feel attractive? Are you preoccupied with what you eat, counting calories or grams of fat? Do you eat less when you're with other people?

Certainly there are individual things you can do to feel better about your body. There's a whole-body positivity movement that focuses on helping people improve their body images.

And while the work of having a better body image is important, it doesn't address the actual structural problems that create the social context that reproduces body dissatisfaction. Corporations that want to sell you products so you can achieve a beauty ideal, media that reinforce a narrow range of ideal bodies, pharmaceutical companies and medical practitioners that pathologize bodies—all of these and other institutions conspire to maintain a system of sizeism that is also marked by gender, race, class, ability, age, and sexual identity. Perhaps the best thing we can do to feel better about our bodies is to challenge the system that makes us uncomfortable in our own bodies to begin with.

Brainstorm ways you can challenge institutions that reinforce the system of sizeism.

been bombarded with advertising for cheap and often toxic (high in sugar, fat, salt, or preservatives) food to such a degree. Many of these agricultural products are subsidized by the U.S. government. In addition, children watch more than 10,000 food ads per year on television, 90 percent of which are for four types of "food": sugarcoated cereals, soft drinks, fast food, and candy. A study from the United Kingdom found that the more overweight a child was, the more she or he would eat when exposed to advertisements following a television show. Obese children increased food intake by 134 percent and normal-weight children by 84 percent. Chocolate was the food source of choice. The need for healthy nutrition is underscored by a study at Brigham and Women's Hospital in which researchers found that although as many as one in four children under the age of 14 years diet, these behaviors not only were ineffective but often tended to lead ultimately to weight gain.

EATING DISORDERS

Today, models weigh about 23 percent less than the average woman, and this fact alone sends many women into despair as they compare themselves against these mostly unattainable images. It is distressing that people often experience their bodies as sources of anxiety rather than joy and celebration. Such images encourage body loathing and can precipitate eating disorders and other unhealthy disordered thinking. In the reading "Race, Online Space and the Feminine," Nicole Danielle Schott notes the ways pro–eating disorder, or "thinspiration," websites encourage young black women to reject fuller bodies and embrace dominant racialized and gendered notions of attractiveness through detrimental practices of dieting, purging, using laxatives, and other forms of control.

Contemporary eating disorders are compulsive disorders that include a variety of behaviors. Among these are anorexia nervosa (self-starvation), bulimia nervosa (binge eating with self-induced vomiting and/or laxative use), compulsive eating (uncontrolled eating or binge eating), and muscle dysmorphia (fear of being inadequately muscled). Alongside these diagnostic categories are general eating-disordered behaviors that may include occasional binge eating and fasting and overly compulsive food habits such as eating only certain foods, not being able to eat in public, and general problems associated with compulsive dieting and/or compulsive overexercising (sometimes called anorexia athletica, although at this time this is not recognized as a formal diagnosis). The latter catchall category of generalized disordered eating/exercising seems to be widespread among North American women.

These disorders are culturally mediated in that they are related to environmental conditions associated with the politics of gender and sexuality. It appears that the number of eating-disordered women in any given community is proportional to the number of individuals who are dieting to control weight. Dieting seems to trigger the onset of an eating disorder in vulnerable individuals. According to a British study, teenage girls who dieted even "modestly" were five times more likely to become anorexic or bulimic than those who did not diet. Those on strict diets were 18 times more likely to develop an eating disorder. The extent of this problem is illustrated by a 2015 study that found that 80 percent of girls have dieted by age 10, one quarter by age 7. About 50 percent of all elementary school girls (ages 6 to 12) are concerned about their weight or about becoming too fat. These fears and concerns are foundational in understanding eating disorders.

Anorexics become very thin and weak by refusing to maintain a healthy body weight, have intense fears of gaining weight, and tend to strive for perfection. Bulimics also display intense body dissatisfaction. They eat large amounts of food in a short time (binge) and then purge by making themselves vomit or taking laxatives, diuretics, and/or amphetamines, or overexercising. Bulimics are more likely to be of normal weight than anorexics, although they both share emotions and thoughts associated with self-punishment, or feelings of being overwhelmed because they feel fat, or feelings of frustration and/or anger with other factors in their lives. Compulsive eating (which may involve bingeing) is understood as an addiction to food and often involves using food as comfort and includes eating to fill a void in life, hide emotions, or cope with problems. Compulsive eaters often have low self-esteem and feel shame about their weight. Individuals with muscle dysmorphia believe that their physiques are too small and unmuscular rather than too large. They participate in maladaptive exercise and dietary practices, and many use performance-enhancing substances. Although early studies focused on male bodybuilders, recent scholarship suggests that such symptoms can appear in the general population and that women are increasingly demonstrating this disorder. Similarly, while boys and men tend to use steroids more than women to increase athletic performance, new scholarship has shown that girls and women are also using steroids. Steroid use among women is more likely to be used to improve body image and muscle tone and control weight than for purely athletic reasons.

Eating disorders (with the exception of muscle dysmorphia) affect women primarily; the ratio of women to men among anorexia nervosa and bulimia sufferers is 10:1, and the figure is 3:1 for binge eating. In North America, these disorders primarily affect young (aged 15 to 25 years) women. Current statistics suggest that about 1 percent of female adolescents have anorexia, 4 percent have bulimia (with about half of the former also developing bulimic patterns), and approximately 3.5 percent experience binge eating in any six-month period. Accurate numbers associated with generalized eating problems are unknown, although it is assumed that the number of women who indulge in disordered eating patterns of some kind is quite substantial. Recent research also suggests that transgender youth may be even more susceptible to eating disorders than cisgender youth.

While these disorders occur in all populations in the United States, white women and those with higher socioeconomic status are somewhat more likely to suffer from these problems. Women of color are not immune from body dissatisfaction and potential eating disorders. This is corroborated by new data showing the prevalence of eating disorders as similar among white women and women of color, with the exception that anorexia nervosa is more common among white women. However, it is also important to understand reporting bias whereby reports tend to reflect the ways "incidence" is tied to resource availability for treatment in various communities. We do not know the incidence of unacknowledged or untreated eating disorders that occur in communities where treatment resources are scarce or unavailable. Finally, while eating disorders are associated with the developed global north and usually not manifested in countries with food scarcity, Asian countries have recently experienced a surge in the incidence of eating disorders as a result of increased development, especially urbanization. There are often serious physical and emotional complications with these disorders, and up to 20 percent of people with serious eating disorders die from the disorder, usually of complications associated with heart problems and chemical imbalances, as well as suicide. With treatment, mortality rates fall to 2–3 percent, about 60 percent recover and maintain healthy weight and social relationships, 20 percent make only partial recoveries and remain compulsively focused on food and weight, and approximately 20 percent do not improve. The latter often live lives controlled by weight—and body—management issues, and they often experience depression, hopelessness, and loneliness. Chronic obesity that may follow compulsive eating also has important consequences for health and illness.

Many students who live in dorms and sororities report a high incidence of eating disorders; perhaps you have struggled with an eating disorder yourself or have had a close friend or sister similarly diagnosed. If the huge number of women who have various issues with food—always on a diet, overly concerned with weight issues, compulsive about what they do or do not eat—are also included in the figures on eating disorders, then the number of women with these problems increases exponentially. Indeed, although teenage boys are actually more likely to be overweight than girls, they are less likely to diet. A study published in the *American Journal of Health Promotion* found that 21 percent of the teenage girls in the study were overweight, 55 percent said they were dieters, and 35 percent were consistent dieters. Although more teenage boys in the study were overweight, only a quarter said they were dieters and only 12 percent were consistent dieters. Because food and

---

IDEAS FOR ACTIVISM

- Organize an eating disorders awareness event. Provide information about eating disorders and resources for help. Invite a therapist who specializes in treating eating disorders to speak. Create awareness posters to hang around your campus.
- Organize a letter-writing campaign to protest the representation of such a small range of women's shapes and sizes in a particular women's magazine.
- Organize a speak-out about beauty ideals.
- Organize a tattoo and piercing panel to discuss the politics of tattooing and piercing. Have a tattoo and piercing fashion show, and discuss the meaning of the various tattoos/piercings.

---

bodies are central preoccupations in so many women's lives, we might ask, Why women and why food?

First, women have long been associated with food and domestic pursuits; food preparation and focus on food are a socially accepted part of female cultural training. Given that women have been relegated to the private sphere of the home more than the public world, food consumption is easily accessible and unquestioned. Second, food is something that nourishes and gives pleasure. In our culture, food has been associated with comfort and celebration, and it is easy to see how eating can be a way of dealing with the anxieties and unhappiness of life. Put these two together, and we get food as the object of compulsion; when we add the third factor, the "beauty" ideal, with all the anxieties associated with closely monitoring the size and shape of women's bodies, the result can be eating disorders.

Scholars also emphasize that eating disorders reflect the ways women desire self-control in the context of limited power and autonomy. In other words, young women turn to controlling their bodies and attempt to sculpt them to perfection because they are denied power and control in other areas of their lives. Central in understanding eating disorders, however, is the pressure in our society for women to measure up to cultural standards of beauty and attractiveness, what is often called the "culture of thinness." These standards, discussed throughout this chapter, infringe on all of our lives whether we choose to comply with them or to resist them. Messages abound telling women that they are not good enough or beautiful enough, encouraging us to constantly change ourselves, often through the use of various products and practices. The result is that girls learn early on that they must aspire to some often-unattainable standard of physical perfection. Such bombardment distracts girls and women from other issues, "disciplining" them to focus energy on the body, affecting their self-esteem, and constantly assaulting the psyche as the body ages. In this way, eating disorders can be read as cultural statements about gender.

NEGOTIATING "BEAUTY" IDEALS

Although many women strive to attain the "beauty" ideal on an ongoing, daily basis, some actively resist such cultural norms. These women are choosing to not participate in the beauty rituals, to not support the industries that produce both images and products, and to create other definitions of beauty. Some women are actively appropriating these standards by highlighting and/or exaggerating the very norms and standards themselves. They are carving out their own notions of beauty through their use of fashion and cosmetics. For them, empowerment involves playing with existing cultural standards. Most women comply with some standards associated with the beauty ideal and resist others. We find a place that suits us, criticizing some standards and practices and conforming to others, usually learning to live with the various contradictions that this implies and hopefully appreciating the bodies we have.

A question that might be raised in response to ideas about resisting beauty ideals and practices is, What's wrong with being beautiful? Feminists answer that it is not beauty that is a problem but, rather, the way that beauty has been constructed by the dominant culture. This construction excludes many "beautiful" women and helps maintain particular (and very restricted) notions of femininity. Another common question is, Can you wear makeup and enjoy the adornments associated with femininity and still call yourself a feminist? Most feminists (especially those who identify as third-wave) answer with a resounding yes. In fact, you can reclaim these trappings and go ultra-femme in celebration of your femininity and your right to self-expression. What is important from a feminist perspective is that these practices are conscious. In other words, when women take part in various reproductions of femininity, it is important to understand the bigger picture and be aware of the ways "beauty" ideals work to limit and objectify women, encourage competitiveness (Is she better looking than me? Who is the cutest woman here? How do I measure up?), and ultimately lower women's self-worth. Understand also how many beauty products are tested on animals, how the packaging of cosmetics and other beauty products encourages the use of resources that end up polluting the environment, and how many fashion items are made by child and/or sweatshop labor and then exported overseas as examples of cultural imperialism. The point is for us to make conscious and informed choices about our relationships to the "beauty" ideal and to respect, love, and take care of our bodies.

THE BLOG
WHAT IS IT ABOUT BATHROOMS?

Susan M. Shaw (2016)

In 2015 the citizens of Houston voted on an equal rights ordinance that among other things would have given protections to transgender people. Opponents were worried about bathrooms. They printed up signs that said: "NO Men in Women's Bathrooms." They worried that predatory men would use the ordinance as a way to enter public bathrooms and assault girls and women.

This reminds me of the campaign against the ERA. I remember as a child in a conservative church being warned that if the ERA passed, women would have to use the same restrooms as men. And so we needed to oppose the ERA to protect the sanctity of women's bathrooms.

What is it about civil rights that gets some people so worked up about bathrooms?

Of course, we know bathrooms are important. In Beverly Cleary's children's book *Ramona the Pest*, on the first day of kindergarten the teacher reads the class the story of Mike Mulligan and his steam shovel that had to dig the basement for the town hall in a single day. At the end of the story, Ramona's hand goes up so she can ask her burning question: "How did Mike Mulligan go to the bathroom when he was digging the basement of the town hall?" Miss Binney tells the class she doesn't know and that it's not important. But the class is not convinced. They know the bathroom is important. After all, the first thing Miss Binney had shown them was the bathroom.

(continued)

Bathrooms are important. We all need them, and perhaps that is part of the reason bathrooms become central in conservative Christian challenges to civil rights around issues of gender. Bathrooms level the playing field. As my mother used to say, "Everybody has to go."

That fact, however, does not ameliorate the deep discomfort many people feel about sex, bodies, and bodily functions. After all, in many traditions the body is equated with sin and worldliness—and mostly women. The body therefore needs to be controlled, and clear gender roles need to be kept in place to maintain order (read patriarchy). The body is also a site of vulnerability, especially when it is not controlled. For girls and women in particular, the sense of vulnerability to sexualized violence is particularly heightened in a culture in which abuse, sexual assault, and rape are commonplace.

Some conservative Christians of Houston used this sense of vulnerability to mask the misogyny and homophobia that are the roots of their opposition to the equal rights ordinance. Men are not suddenly going to claim to be women so they can lurk in bathrooms and attack girls and women. The truth of the matter is that bathrooms are much more dangerous for transgender and gender non-conforming people right now than they ever will be for girls and women because of a civil rights ordinance. And, in fact, the most dangerous place for a woman in the United States is not a public bathroom but her own home. As we know, most violence against women and girls does not come from strangers but from family and friends.

By focusing arguments on some supposed danger to girls and women, opponents of the ordinance claimed a high moral ground on gender, but the truth is the opposite. This is the same misogyny that asserts that women need protection, and it's the same misogyny that targets transgender people for violating the gender norms that uphold patriarchy. Were this not about more than bathrooms, perhaps the citizens of Houston might have suggested the very simple solution of building more single-user bathrooms or gender inclusive bathrooms alongside the women's and men's bathrooms rather than policing who goes into which bathroom.

Especially distressing is the willingness of some conservative Christians intentionally to use fear, misinformation, bigotry, and misunderstanding of what transgender means to perpetuate stereotypes and to try to block equal protections for all citizens. This fear-mongering and misinforming seems a far cry from the truth-telling Christians claim for themselves.

While transgender and gender non-conforming people may bring up discomforts about bodies and vulnerabilities for some cis-gender people, we should not allow discomforts to lead us to dehumanize and marginalize others. Bathrooms, while incredibly important to all of us, should not be battlegrounds for human rights. After all, everybody has to go.

23. BREAST BUDS AND THE "TRAINING" BRA
JOAN JACOBS BRUMBERG (1997)

In every generation, small swellings around the nipples have announced the arrival of puberty. This development, known clinically as "breast buds," occurs before menarche and almost always provokes wonder and self-scrutiny. "I began to examine myself carefully, to search my armpits for hairs and my breasts for signs of swelling," wrote Kate Simon about coming of age in the Bronx at the time of World War I. Although Simon was "horrified" by the rapidity with which her chest developed, many girls, both in literature and real life, long for this important mark of maturity. In Jamaica Kincaid's fictional memoir of growing up in Antigua, *Annie John*, the main character, regarded her breasts as "treasured shrubs, needing only the proper combination of water and sunlight to make them flourish." In order to get their breasts to grow, Annie and her best friend, Gwen, lay in a pasture exposing their small bosoms to the moonlight.

Breasts are particularly important to girls in cultures or time periods that give powerful meaning or visual significance to that part of the body. Throughout history, different body parts have been eroticized in art, literature, photography, and film. In some eras, the ankle or upper arm was the ultimate statement of female sexuality. But breasts were the particular preoccupation of Americans in the years after World War II, when voluptuous stars, such as Jayne Mansfield, Jane Russell, and Marilyn Monroe, were popular box-office attractions. The mammary fixation of the 1950s extended beyond movie stars and shaped the experience of adolescents of both genders. In that era, boys seemed to prefer girls who were "busty," and American girls began to worry about breast size as well as about weight. This elaboration of the ideal of beauty raised expectations about what adolescent girls should look like. It also required them to put even more energy and resources into their body projects, beginning at an earlier age.

The story of how this happened is intertwined with the history of the bra, an undergarment that came into its own, as separate from the corset, in the early twentieth century. In 1900, a girl of twelve or thirteen typically wore a one-piece "waist" or camisole that had no cups or darts in front. As her breasts developed, she moved into different styles of the same garment, but these had more construction, such as stitching, tucks, and bones, that would accentuate the smallness of her waist and shape the bosom. In those days, before the arrival of the brassiere, there were no "cups." The bosom was worn low; there was absolutely no interest in uplift, and not a hint of cleavage.

The French word *brassière*, which actually means an infant's undergarment or harness, was used in *Vogue* as early as 1907. In the United States, the first boneless bra to leave the midriff bare was developed in 1913 by Mary Phelps Jacobs, a New York City debutante. Under the name Caresse Crosby, Jacobs marketed a bra made of two French lace handkerchiefs suspended from the shoulders. Many young women in the 1920s, such as Yvonne Blue, bought their first bras in order to achieve the kind of slim, boyish figure that the characteristic chemise (or flapper) dress required. The first bras were designed simply to flatten, but they were superseded by others intended to shape and control the breasts. Our current cup sizes (A, B, C, and D), as well as the idea of circular stitching to enhance the roundness of the breast, emerged in the 1930s.

Adult women, not adolescents, were the first market for bras. Sexually maturing girls simply moved into adult-size bras when they were ready—and if their parents had the money. Many women and girls in the early twentieth century still made their own underwear at home, and some read the advertisements for bras with real longing. When she began to develop

breasts in the 1930s, Malvis Helmi, a midwestern farm girl, remembered feeling embarrassed whenever she wore an old summer dimity that pulled and gaped across her expanding chest. As a result, she spoke to her mother, considered the brassieres in the Sears, Roebuck catalog, and decided to purchase two for twenty-five cents. However, when her hardworking father saw the order form, he vetoed the idea and declared, "Our kind of people can't afford to spend money on such nonsense." Although her mother made her a make-shift bra, Malvis vowed that someday she would have store-bought brassieres. . . .

The transition from homemade to mass-produced bras was critical in how adolescent girls thought about their breasts. In general, mass-produced clothing fostered autonomy in girls because it took matters of style and taste outside the dominion of the mother, who had traditionally made and supervised a girl's wardrobe. But in the case of brassieres, buying probably had another effect. So long as clothing was made at home, the dimensions of the garment could be adjusted to the particular body intended to wear it. But with store-bought clothes, the body had to fit instantaneously into standard sizes that were constructed from a pattern representing a norm. When clothing failed to fit the body, particularly a part as intimate as the breasts, young women were apt to perceive that there was something wrong with their bodies. In this way, mass-produced bras in standard cup sizes probably increased, rather than diminished, adolescent self-consciousness about the breasts.

Until the 1950s, the budding breasts of American girls received no special attention from either bra manufacturers, doctors, or parents. Girls generally wore undershirts until they were sufficiently developed to fill an adult-size bra. Mothers and daughters traditionally handled this transformation in private, at home. But in the gyms and locker rooms of postwar junior high schools, girls began to look around to see who did and did not wear a bra. Many of these girls had begun menstruating and developing earlier than their mothers had, and this visual information was very powerful. In some circles, the ability to wear and fill a bra was central to an adolescent girl's status and sense of self. "I have a figure problem," a fourteen-year-old wrote to *Seventeen* in 1952: "All of my friends are tall and shapely while my figure still remains up-and-down. Can you advise me?"

In an era distinguished by its worship of full-breasted women, interest in adolescent breasts came from all quarters: girls who wanted bras at an earlier age than ever before; mothers who believed that they should help a daughter acquire a "good" figure; doctors who valued maternity over all other female roles; and merchandisers who saw profits in convincing girls and their parents that adolescent breasts needed to be tended in special ways. All of this interest coalesced in the 1950s to make the brassiere as critical as the sanitary napkin in making a girl's transition into adulthood both modern and successful.

The old idea that brassieres were frivolous or unnecessary for young girls was replaced by a national discussion about their medical and psychological benefits. "My daughter who is well developed but not yet twelve wants to wear a bra," wrote a mother in Massachusetts to *Today's Health* in 1951. "I want her to wear an undervest instead because I think it is better not to have anything binding. What do you think about a preadolescent girl wearing a bra?" That same year a reader from Wilmington, Delaware, asked *Seventeen*: "Should a girl of fourteen wear a bra? There are some older women who insist we don't need them." The editor's answer was an unequivocal endorsement of early bras: "Just as soon as your breasts begin to show signs of development, you should start wearing a bra." By the early 1950s, "training" or "beginner" bras were available in AAA and AA sizes for girls whose chests were essentially flat but who wanted a bra nonetheless. Along with acne creams, advertisements for these brassieres were standard fare in magazines for girls.

Physicians provided a medical rationale for purchasing bras early. In 1952, in an article in *Parents' Magazine*, physician Frank H. Crowell endorsed bras for young girls and spelled out a theory and program of teenage breast management. "Unlike other organs such as the stomach and intestines which have ligaments that act as guywires or slings to hold them in place," Crowell claimed, the breast was simply "a growth developed from the skin and held up only by the skin." An adolescent girl needed a bra in order to prevent sagging breasts, stretched blood vessels,

and poor circulation, all of which would create problems in nursing her future children. In addition, a "dropped" breast was "not so attractive," Crowell said, so it was important to get adolescents into bras early, before their breasts began to sag. The "training" that a training bra was supposed to accomplish was the first step toward motherhood and a sexually alluring figure, as it was defined in the 1950s.

…

Breasts were actually only one part of a larger body project encouraged by the foundation garment industry in postwar America. In this era, both physicians and entrepreneurs promoted a general philosophy of "junior figure control." Companies such as Warners, Maidenform, Formfit, Belle Mode, and Perfect Form (as well as popular magazines like *Good Housekeeping*) all encouraged the idea that young women needed both lightweight girdles and bras to "start the figure off to a beautiful future."

The concept of "support" was aided and abetted by new materials—such as nylon netting and two-way stretch fabrics—developed during the war but applied afterward to women's underwear. By the early 1950s, a reenergized corset and brassiere industry was poised for extraordinary profits. If "junior figure control" became the ideal among the nation's mothers and daughters, it would open up sales of bras and girdles to the largest generation of adolescents in American history, the so-called baby boomers. Once again, as in the case of menstruation and acne, the bodies of adolescent girls had the potential to deliver considerable profit.

There was virtually no resistance to the idea that American girls should wear bras and girdles in adolescence. Regardless of whether a girl was thin or heavy, "junior figure control" was in order, and that phrase became a pervasive sales mantra. "Even slim youthful figures will require foundation assistance," advised *Women's Wear Daily* in 1957. In both *Seventeen* and *Compact*, the two most popular magazines for the age group, high school girls were urged to purchase special foundation garments such as "Bobbie" bras and girdles by Formfit and "Adagio" by Maidenform that were "teen-proportioned" and designed, allegedly, with the help of adolescent consultants. The bras were available in pastel colors in a variety of special sizes, starting with AAA, and they were decorated with lace and ribbon to make them especially feminine. In addition to holding up stockings, girdles were intended to flatten the tummy and also provide light, but firm, control for hips and buttocks. The advertisements for "Bobbie," in particular, suggested good things about girls who controlled their flesh in this way; they were pretty, had lots of friends, and drank Coca-Cola. As adults, they would have good figures and happy futures because they had chosen correct underwear in their youth.

By the mid-1950s, department stores and specialty shops had developed aggressive educational programs designed to spread the gospel of "junior figure control." In order to make young women "foundation conscious," Shillito's, a leading Cincinnati department store, tried to persuade girls and their mothers of the importance of having a professional fitting of the first bra. Through local newspaper advertisements, and also programs in home economics classes, Shillito's buyer, Edith Blincoe, promoted the idea that the purchase of bras and girdles required special expertise, which only department stores could provide. (*Seventeen* echoed her idea and advised a "trained fitter" for girls who wanted a "prettier" bosom and a "smoother" figure.) Blincoe acknowledged that teenage girls were already "100% bra conscious," and she hoped to develop the same level of attention to panty girdles . . .

In home economics classes, and also at the local women's club, thousands of American girls saw informational films such as *Figure Forum* and *Facts About Your Figure*, made by the Warner Brassiere Company in the 1950s. Films like these stressed the need for appropriate foundation garments in youth and provided girls with scientific principles for selecting them. They also taught young women how to bend over and lean into their bras, a maneuver that most of us learned early and still do automatically. Most middle-class girls and their mothers embraced the code of "junior figure control" and spent time and money in pursuit of the correct garments. . . .

In the postwar world, the budding adolescent body was big business. Trade publications, such as *Women's Wear Daily*, gave special attention to sales strategies and trends in marketing to girls. In their reports from Cincinnati, Atlanta, and Houston, one thing was clear: wherever American girls purchased bras, they wanted to be treated as grownups, even if they wore only a AAA or AA cup. In Atlanta, at the Redwood Corset and Lingerie Shop, owner Sally Blye and her staff spoke persuasively to young customers about the importance of "uplift" in order "not to break muscle tissue." And at Houston's popular Teen Age Shop, specially trained salesgirls allowed young customers to look through the brassieres on their own, and then encouraged them to try on items in the dressing room without their mothers. Although many girls were shy at first, by the age of fourteen and fifteen most had lost their initial self-consciousness. "They take the merchandise and go right in [to the dressing room]," Blincoe said about her teenage clientele. Girls who could not be reached by store or school programs could send away to the Belle Mode Brassiere Company for free booklets about "junior figure control" with titles such as "The Modern Miss-Misfit or Miss Fit" and "How to Be Perfectly Charming." In the effort to help girls focus on their figures, Formfit, maker of the popular "Bobbies," offered a free purse-size booklet on calorie counting.

Given all this attention, it's not surprising that bras and breasts were a source of concern in adolescents' diaries written in the 1950s. Sandra Rubin got her first bra in 1951, when she was a twelve-year-old in Cleveland, but she did not try it on in a department store. Instead, her mother bought her a "braziere" while she was away on a trip and sent it home. "It's very fancy," Sandra wrote. "I almost died! I ran right upstairs to put it on." When she moved to New York City that September and entered Roosevelt Junior High School, Sandra got involved with a clique of seven girls who called themselves the "7Bs." Their name was not about their homeroom; it was about the cup size they wanted to be. . . .

Breasts, not weight, were the primary point of comparison among high school girls in the 1950s. Although Sandra Rubin called herself a "fat hog" after eating too much candy, her diary reportage was principally about the bosoms, rather than the waistlines, she saw at school. Those who had ample bosoms seemed to travel through the hallways in a veritable state of grace, at least from the perspective of girls who considered themselves flat-chested. "Busty" girls made desirable friends because they seemed sophisticated, and they attracted boys. In December 1959, when she planned a Friday-night pajama party, thirteen-year-old Ruth Teischman made a courageous move by inviting the "gorgeous" Roslyn, a girl whom she wrote about frequently but usually only worshiped from afar. After a night of giggling and eating with her junior high school friends, Ruth revealed in her diary the source of Roslyn's power and beauty: "Roslyn is very big. (Bust of course.) I am very flat. I wish I would get bigger fast." Many girls in the 1950s perused the ads, usually in the back of women's magazines, for exercise programs and creams guaranteed to make their breasts grow, allegedly in short order.

The lament of the flat-chested girl—"I must, I must, I must develop my bust"—was on many private hit parades in the 1950s. There was a special intensity about breasts because of the attitudes of doctors, mothers, and advertisers, all of whom considered breast development critical to adult female identity and success. Although "junior figure control" increased pressure on the entire body, and many girls wore waist cinches as well as girdles, it was anxiety about breasts, more than any other body part, that characterized adolescent experience in these years. As a result, thousands, if not millions, of girls in early adolescence jumped the gun and bought "training bras" at the first sight of breast buds, or they bought padded bras to disguise their perceived inadequacy. In the 1950s, the bra was validated as a rite of passage: regardless of whether a girl was voluptuous or flat, she was likely to purchase her first bra at an earlier age than had her mother. This precocity was due, in part, to biology, but it was also a result of entrepreneurial interests aided and abetted by medical concern. By the 1950s, American society was so consumer-oriented that there were hardly any families, even among the poor, who would expect to make bras for their daughters the way earlier generations had made their own sanitary napkins.

Training bras were a boon to the foundation garment industry, but they also meant that girls' bodies were sexualized earlier. In contemporary America, girls of nine or ten are shepherded from undershirts into little underwear sets that come with tops that are protobrassieres. Although this may seem innocuous and natural, it is not the same as little girls "dressing up" in their mother's clothing. In our culture, traditional distinctions between adult clothing and juvenile clothing have narrowed considerably, so that mature women dress "down," in the garments of kids, just as often as little girls dress "up." While the age homogeneity of the contemporary wardrobe helps adult women feel less matronly, dressing little girls in adult clothing can have an insidious side effect. Because a bra shapes the breasts in accordance with fashion, it acts very much like an interpreter, translating functional anatomy into a sexual or erotic vocabulary. When we dress little girls in brassieres or bikinis, we imply adult behaviors and, unwittingly, we mark them as sexual objects. The training bras of the 1950s loom large in the history of adolescent girls because they foreshadowed the ways in which the nation's entrepreneurs would accommodate, and also encourage, precocious sexuality.

24. IF MEN COULD MENSTRUATE

GLORIA STEINEM (1978)

A white minority of the world has spent centuries conning us into thinking that a white skin makes people superior—even though the only thing it really does is make them more subject to ultraviolet rays and to wrinkles. Male human beings have built whole cultures around the idea that penis-envy is "natural" to women—though having such an unprotected organ might be said to make men vulnerable, and the power to give birth makes womb-envy at least as logical.

In short, the characteristics of the powerful, whatever they may be, are thought to be better than the characteristics of the powerless—and logic has nothing to do with it.

What would happen, for instance, if suddenly, magically, men could menstruate and women could not?

The answer is clear—menstruation would become an enviable, boast-worthy, masculine event:

Men would brag about how long and how much.

Boys would mark the onset of menses, the longed-for proof of manhood, with religious ritual and stag parties.

Congress would fund a National Institute of Dysmenorrhea to help stamp out monthly discomforts.

Sanitary supplies would be federally funded and free. (Of course, some men would still pay for the prestige of commercial brands such as John Wayne Tampons, Muhammad Ali's Rope-a-dope Pads, Joe Namath Jock Shields—"For Those Light Bachelor Days," and Robert "Baretta" Blake Maxi-Pads.)

Military men, right-wing politicians, and religious fundamentalists would cite menstruation ("*menstruation*") as proof that only men could serve in the Army ("you have to give blood to take blood"), occupy political office ("can women be aggressive without that steadfast cycle governed by the planet Mars?"), be priests and ministers ("how could a woman give her blood for our sins?"), or rabbis ("without the monthly loss of impurities, women remain unclean").

Male radicals, left-wing politicians, and mystics, however, would insist that women are equal, just different; and that any woman could enter their ranks if only she were willing to self-inflict a major wound every month ("you *must* give blood for the revolution"), recognize the preeminence of menstrual issues, or subordinate her selfness to all men in their Cycle of Enlightenment.

Street guys would brag ("I'm a three-pad man") or answer praise from a buddy ("Man, you lookin' *good!*") by giving fives and saying, "Yeah, man, I'm on the rag!"

TV shows would treat the subject at length. ("Happy Days": Richie and Potsie try to convince Fonzie that he is still "The Fonz," though he has missed two periods in a row.) So would newspapers. (SHARK SCARE THREATENS MENSTRUATING MEN. JUDGE CITES MONTHLY STRESS IN PARDONING RAPIST.) And movies. (Newman and Redford in "Blood Brothers"!)

Men would convince women that intercourse was *more* pleasurable at "that time of the month." Lesbians would be said to fear blood and therefore life itself—though probably only because they needed a good menstruating man.

Of course, male intellectuals would offer the most moral and logical arguments. How could a woman master any discipline that demanded a sense of time, space, mathematics, or measurement, for instance, without that in-built gift for measuring the cycles of the moon and planets—and thus for measuring anything at all? In the rarefied fields of philosophy and religion, could women compensate for missing the rhythm of the universe? Or for their lack of symbolic death-and-resurrection every month?

Liberal males in every field would try to be kind: the fact that "these people" have no gift for measuring life or connecting to the universe, the liberals would explain, should be punishment enough.

And how would women be trained to react? One can imagine traditional women agreeing to all these arguments with a staunch and smiling masochism. ("The ERA would force housewives to wound themselves every month": Phyllis Schlafly. "Your husband's blood is as sacred as that of Jesus—and so sexy, too!": Marabel Morgan.) Reformers and Queen Bees would try to imitate men, and *pretend* to have a monthly cycle. All feminists would explain endlessly that men, too, needed to be liberated from the false idea of Martian aggressiveness, just as women needed to escape the bonds of menses-envy. Radical feminists would add that the oppression of the nonmenstrual was the pattern for all other oppressions. ("Vampires were our first freedom fighters!") Cultural feminists would develop a bloodless imagery in art and literature. Socialist feminists would insist that only under capitalism would men be able to monopolize menstrual blood. . . . In fact, if men could menstruate, the power justifications could probably go on forever.

If we let them.

25. RACE, ONLINE SPACE AND THE FEMININE
NICOLE DANIELLE SCHOTT (2016)

INTRODUCTION

There are online forums, such as social networking websites, where individuals refer to themselves or their eating disorders as 'pro-ana' and 'pro-mia' (pro-anorexia/pro-bulimia). A major component of the pro-eating disorder culture (pro-ana/mia) is what is referred to as 'thinspiration' or 'thinspo', which consists of images, slogans and videos aimed at inspiring the pursuit of extreme thinness. Through the application of a spatial analysis, I contend that pro-eating disorder environments are spaces where women are attempting to de-mark their bodies through hard work, will-power and mastery over their desires. Women on these websites promote and seek to control the mind over the urges of the body, as a display of perfection and ardent work ethic. The large majority of images displayed on thinspiration videos are of white women. More recently, there is a specific kind of thinspiration, labeled online as 'black girl thinspiration' that seeks to inspire black women to reject fuller-figured body shapes as beautiful and responsible. Women, out of survival, are participating in the racialized project of ridding excess fat that marks the body as out-of-control and savage-like. The women on these sites who are seeking to achieve a white elite citizenship status are, paradoxically, further racialized through the medicalization of pro-ana/mia as a mental illness that is marked by irrationality and a loss of control. I present a spatial analysis that allows for an attunement to intersectionality, which recognizes how forms of oppression (sizism, racism, sexism, ableism, etc.) are interconnected. This analysis disrupts the white hegemony of the thin ideal by unmapping how modern capitalism, sexism, and racism operate in unison to produce women who starve, purge, abuse laxatives and hate their bodies, while highlighting the tremendous violence embedded in these practices. In order to achieve this disruption I draw on critical race and feminist postmodern scholarship.

. . .

EATING DISORDERS AND RACE

In much of the scholarly literature, the two most well-known eating disorders, anorexia nervosa (AN) and bulimia nervosa (BN), are described as mental illnesses that primarily afflict white, middle to upper class women (Root, 1990; Rucker and Cash, 1992; Taylor et al., 2013; Wildes et al., 2001). Root (1990: 525) states that "in fact, anorexia nervosa, coined the 'Golden Girls Disease,' specifically refers to a pursuit of a White, Western European ideal of beauty run amuck." Empirical studies that compare the rates of AN and BN in black versus white women consistently have found that black women suffer from considerably lower rates of eating disorders (Powell and Kahn, 1995; Rucker and Cash, 1992; Taylor et al., 2013; Wildes et al., 2001). Scholars have found that the lower rates of eating disorders among black women are associated with black women having a more positive self-body image, experiencing less internalization of hegemonic standards of white beauty and its conflation with success, experiencing less pressure to be thin and being less fat-phobic (Powell and Kahn, 1995; Root, 1990; Rucker and Cash, 1992). However, Taylor et al. (2013: 290) found that black women had "equal to or higher rates of binge eating disorder (BED) than Whites." All of these findings have been challenged by scholars who have argued that these claims are tainted with race and class bias (Bordo, 2013; Riley, 2002).

In a meta-analytic review of the literature, Roberts et al. (2006) comment on the great body of literature that finds that black women have higher body image satisfaction compared to white women. Many researchers now question the common belief and academic findings that suggest blacks and whites significantly differ regarding body image satisfaction (Dolan et al., 1990; Shaw et al., 2004; Wilfley et al., 1996). However, Bordo (2013: 268) notes that "many people *do* still believe that just because a woman is black, she has greater cultural permission to be large" (emphasis in original). Further, a footnote provided by Roberts et al. (2006) notes that most previous studies uncritically assumed that white women and black women represent homogeneous groups instead of considering heterogeneity among ethnic groups. The insight into the heterogeneity of black and white women suggests yet another flaw in the eating disorder and race literature that could dismantle some of the findings that black women suffer from lower rates of eating disorders. For example, Sirena Riley (2002: 358–359 as referenced by Bordo, 2013: 268) states that "just because women of color aren't expressing their body dissatisfaction the same way as heterosexual, middle-class white women, it doesn't mean that everything is hunky-dory and we should just move on." It is likely that many of the academic investigations of eating disorders have been problematic because they did not consider ethnic variations.

Historically, black women have been characterized as either asexual or hypersexual. For example, black women have been imagined as the asexual 'plump, maternal Mammy' who cooks fried chicken and only cares for white people (Bordo, 2013: 267), or as the hyper-sexual, large-bodied 'Hottentot Venus' with a voluptuous buttocks (Fuller, 2011). Further, Bordo (2013) explains how class and race are conflated with beliefs that poor women, and therefore women of color, cannot get eating disorders. A study by Girls Incorporated (2007: 4) reports that "it is a myth that eating disorders are restricted to middle and upper-class White young women." The study found that non-white women experience eating disorders, and noted that young Latina women in particular were found to be striving for thinness. Franko et al. (2007: 165) specifically found that:

> The frequency of binge-eating, restrictive eating, vomiting, and amenorrhea did not differ significantly across ethnic groups. However, significant between-group differences were found with respect to modes of purging. Binge correlates (e.g. eating until uncomfortably full) were significantly more frequent among Caucasian than African American participants ($p < .001$). Binge eating was the best predictor of distress among Caucasians, African Americans, and Latinos, whereas vomiting was the best predictor of

distress among Asians. Asian participants who used laxatives were significantly less likely to receive a recommendation for further evaluation than non-Asian participants.

Further, Franko et al. (2007) found that out of all of the ethnic groups examined, Native American women reported the highest use of obsessive exercise, multiple methods of purging and laxative use for weight loss. These findings lay in stark contrast with studies that suggest only privileged white women experience eating and body image disturbances and challenge the belief that if black women experience an eating disorder it is most likely to be a binge-eating disorder.

It has been argued that the common psychological themes across disordered eating, "the pursuit of identity, power, specialness, validation, self-esteem, and respect" (Root, 1990: 526), are experiences that are shared by women in general, people of color and all other oppressed persons. Therefore, it would make sense that black women would not be immune to eating disorders. Root (1990: 526) suggests that it is very possible that "the limitations of current theory and discussion of who is vulnerable to developing an eating disorder reflects racial/ethnic stereotyping, Western Euro-centrism, and the lack of experience of mainstream researchers in working with a diversity of people." It is clear that the academic space for eating disorder and race research is racialized and this racialization has material consequences for our understandings and responses to women experiencing disordered eating. Having this understanding in mind helps us enter into the world of thinspiration and 'black girl thinspiration' from a position that has challenged the 'common knowledge' about eating disorders and race.

. . .

ETHNOGRAPHIC FINDINGS

. . .

As of January 2016, typing 'black girl thinspiration' into YouTube's search engine results in 4570 results, compared to 30,300 video results for the search terms 'thinspiration' (type in 'black girl thinspo playlists' to find a playlist containing 178 videos). The YouTube video 'thinpo: black girls luv ana too' (Coco_CHANEL, 2008) was posted on 15 September 2008, and as of January 2016 the video has received 13,367 views, 85 likes, 12 dislikes and 83 comments. After several slides of different thin black women played to music, the final slide reads: 'because not all black girls want to be big bootied hoes'. Black girl thinspiration contains the exact same types of slogans and quotes as 'non-designated' thinspiration, such as quotes that highlight will-power, strength, self-control (mastery over bodily urges) and perfection (examples will be provided throughout my analyses).

The six verbatim comments presented below in order of appearance have all been taken from the YouTube video titled 'thinspo: black girls luv ana too' (Coco_CHANEL, 2008). The six selected comments represent repetitive themes I have found throughout my ethnographic immersion on many other black girl thinspiration YouTube video comment sections, as well as on other black girl thinspiration websites (all relative times below are as of January 2016):

1) "most black women don't have anorexia disorder, they have an overeating disorder" (Posted 2 years ago, black woman in profile picture).

2) ". . . it's hard to be inspired when there's so many thin white chicks and black girls are known for being curvacious. i want to be thin and perfect, not fat and big bootied and large . . ." (Posted 4 years ago, default profile picture).

3) ". . . I mean this with no disrespect but the reason there aren't a lot of black women who have anorexia is because most black MEN don't think thin/skinny is sexy . . ." (Posted 5 years ago, default profile picture).

4) "Thanks for posting! Finally, there is a black ana video!" (Posted 5 years ago, default profile picture).

5) ". . . I hate the 'black people want to be fat, or ur supposed to have a fat ass cuz ur black! etc' remarks . . ." (Posted 6 years ago, default profile picture).

6) ". . . only my white friends understand but i get kind of discouraged sometimes looking at regular thinspo be there's no one who looks like me. thanks for putting this up!" (Posted 6 years ago, black woman in profile picture).

These six excerpts represent some of the major themes found in comments across many videos and websites: 1) belief that black women do not get eating disorders that involve a restriction of food, but instead get eating disorders that involve binge-eating; 2) many black women do want to be thin and reject full body figures as desirable; 3) black women shape their bodies in accordance to what men 'want' (same theme is prevalent on all thinspiration); 4) an appreciation for having thinspiration made for black women; 5) annoyance about how there is a common perception that black women are supposed to be large bodied; and 6) 'regular' thinspiration does not represent black women. It is important to mention that many of the comments found under these videos express that they are against black girl thinspiration, just like there are many who 'fight' for the censorship of pro-ana/mia thinspiration in general. One example is: "woooow. the equating of thinness with perfection (whatever that is) is really startling to me. if you aren't thin than something is wrong w/you? if you have a 'booty' or 'rumpshaker' than you're automatically 'disgusting'? or a 'beastly bitch'? just. . . . wow . . ." (Posted 5 years ago, default profile picture). Other anti-thinspiration comments are much more aggressive and demeaning than this example.

PART 1: HOW DO WE KNOW THINSPIRATION IS ABOUT WHITENESS?

At first glance, it may appear that women travel through thinspiration spaces because they are simply striving to achieve beauty or because they have an eating disorder. However, I am contending that the pursuit of thinness is actually a journey in which these women are trying to achieve the status and privilege granted to whiteness (Cartesian subjecthood). The cartography of the pro-ana/mia landscape has been mapped with the neoliberal architecture of hard work, self-control and body-surveillance (so-called 'white' characteristics). Women are trying to distinguish themselves as thin, and therefore in control of their body, as opposed to the racialized 'other' who gives into bodily desires. Pro-ana/mia's thinspiration is a space that women enter in an attempt to gain Cartesian subjecthood that allows them access to elite social spaces and movement up the ladder of neoliberal defined success.

As Mohanram (1999) has argued, the racialized 'other' is seen as animal-like and as part of the flora and fauna of the landscape. I am arguing that the geographies of the woman's body are seen as an irrational and wild space that needs to be tamed. Weight loss is often described as a 'battle', and within thinspiration I have found that the body has been described as a 'battleground'—like colonial logic positions nature/land as something man had to conquer (Kirby, 1998), woman has been positioned as needing to conquer her chaotic body. Women are not given human status as they are inherently marked by disorder and unruliness, and therefore they are deemed to be closer to nature. Particularly, women menstruate every month, making them 'more body' than mind, which prevents women from entering the citizenship of humanity. Razack (2002: 11) states that "the new citizen subject was a figure who, through self-control and self-discipline, achieved mastery over his own body." There are countless examples of thinspiration pictures available that exemplify messages of self-control, self-discipline, and mastery over the body and desire, such as the thinspiration images with the slogans: "If you want to be thin you have to have control" (0WannaBeThin0, 2009) and "You've come too far to take orders from a cookie" (Shamaya Mikel, 2013). Thinspiration is an online space that women venture into in order to achieve mastery over their bodies through self-control and self-discipline.

On these websites, thinspiration quotes and slogans conflate skinny with 'perfection', 'beauty', 'choice', 'hard work', 'strength', 'control', 'self-worth' and 'will-power', which have all been constructed as 'white'. Thinspiration mantra on YouTube tells you: 'Mind over matter, and you won't get FATTER' (Coco_CHANEL, 2009). Women are quite literally trying to rid themselves of excess fat, to become less body and more mind. Heather Sykes (2011: 54) explains that "in Cartesian logic, then, not only is fat feminine, but it is also racialized." Women of all ethnicities are trying to distinguish themselves as thin as opposed to the beastial 'other' who gives in to desire

and is marked by fat. As the black girl thinspiration video expressed: "not all black girls want to be fat ass beastly bitches, with big 'booties' and 'rumpshakers'" (Coco_CHANEL, 2008). It is also important to note the racialized conflation of hyper-sexuality and big black female bodies that is demonstrated in the many comments that express that the commenters do not want to be 'big bootied hoes'.

. . .

PART 2: CAN BLACK WOMEN WHITEN THEMSELVES THROUGH EXTREME DIETING?

> The category of the 'black body' can come into being only when the body is perceived as being out of place, either from its natural environment or its national boundaries. (Mohanram, 1999: xii)

Black women have been excluded from mapping their bodies into whiteness, as those who identify as black women online have commented on thinspiration YouTube Videos: "thanks for this video! i typed in thinspiration and all i got were videos of white girls i was like . . . hmm . . . never gonna look like that. Thank you for this!!" (AngelAmyAnna, 2009). King (2010: 45), who discusses abject female bodies in relation to One Strike evictions, has argued that the "production of social space that excludes black female bodies is predicated on legacies of racism and colonial dispossession." In response to black women's lack of inclusion in regards to thinspiration, black women have produced their own 'black girl thinspiration' spaces online in order to not only join the pursuit for the status and privilege of whiteness, but as an act of social and material survival. The inclusion of black women on thinspiration is perceived as unnatural because they are not considered the glamorous beauty ideal that women should be striving to achieve: "The black woman had not failed to be aware of America's standard of beauty nor the fact that she was not included in it; television and motion pictures had made this information very available to her" (Wallace, 1979: 157–158, as cited by Patton, 2006: 26). Since Wallace's observation in 1979, we have seen an emergence of black women in hit television shows (i.e. *Scandal* and *Suits*) and movies where they are portrayed as beautiful. However, it is my casual observation that these mainstream actors in North America are presented as beautiful and desirable if they are thin, light-skinned, have straightened hair and more Eurocentric features. A recent notable exception is actress Lupita Nyong'o who, although very thin, has dark skin (to listen to Lupita discuss black beauty and desires to become lighter see: https://www.youtube.com/watch?v=ZPCkfARH2eE). Patton (2006: 26) has argued that "Black beauty and Black inferiority are inextricably bound," and black women strive for white beauty in order to become mobile, *not* because they want to be white—this fits with my observation of how black women have moved into popular entertainment.

. . .

Only some bodies are granted mobility and access to civilized femininities, while others are immobile, restricted from moving into civilized spaces. Mohanram (1999: 4) contends that "whiteness has the ability to move . . . [and] the ability to move results in the unmarking of the body. In contrast, blackness is signified through a marking and is always static and immobilizing." I am contending that thinness has the same mobility features of whiteness; thinness has the ability to move, which unmarks the body, whereas 'fatness' is signified through a marking and is always static and immobilizing for women. The immobilizing marker of 'fat' that excludes and marginalizes has severe material consequences (van Amsterdam, 2013). If this demobilizing feature of thinness is accurate, it begs the question: can black women increase their mobility by shedding some pounds?

It has been argued that "thinness, associated with higher social class (power, resource, and opportunity) in North America, is often a woman's ticket to upward mobility (Shultz, 1979)" (as reference by Root, 1990: 526). The research suggests that, indeed, thinner women are more successful, including thin black women (Patton, 2006). More specifically, Patton (2006) has found that black women who are thin, straighten their hair and are lighter skinned have better employment opportunities and higher social mobility. Mohanram (1999: 82) states that "women with weak passports are normally confined within their borders." Therefore, it seems that thinness for all women can increase mobility; black women who are successful dieters can obtain a social passport that allows them to move beyond their confined social borders.

Sherene Razack (2002: 6) has contended that "racial hierarchies come into existence through patriarchy and capitalism, each system of domination mutually constituting the other," and I am adding that the pursuit of thinness/whiteness is intrinsically tied to this perpetual social ordering. The marketing of insecurity and inferiority (i.e. 'too fat', 'too dark') within a neoliberal 'self-improvement' culture results in big bucks because women are sold the notion that we need to improve ourselves by gaining mastery over our bodies by purchasing consumer goods, such as weight loss, fitness, and cosmetic products. This insidious structuring of society allows for a population of people, women, who have easy access to food, yet are essentially starving themselves while paying (money, time, energy) into the system that oppresses them. Black women have even more 'body work' to do than white women in order to demark their bodies, which means it costs them even more resources.

There is a rather blatant hierarchical racial division of beauty, and thinness seems to be a strategy to bridge the gap. Thinness, improved social status, becomes a woman's 'social passport', allowing her movement into respectability and elite spaces. Not adhering to these Euro-American beauty standards has resulted in job loss, the inability to move into elite social spaces and various other forms of violence (Bordo, 2013; Patton, 2006; van Amsterdam, 2013). For example, black girl thinspiration YouTube videos demonstrate that even black girl thinspo is saturated with Eurocentric ideal features: thin, straight hair, and light skin. It is important to note that I am not arguing that black women can unmark their body of color through thinness. Oprah Winfrey is not able to completely unmark her black body through material success, but just as Oprah's money increases her mobility, thinness increases other women's ability to move in and through civilized spaces.

PART 3: CAN ANY WOMAN RETURN FROM THE THIN PURSUIT UNSCATHED?

Dieting appears to be a rite of passage into adulthood for females in a culture . . . Dieting also appears to be a strategy women rather than men use to increase self-esteem, obtain privileges, increase credibility in the workforce . . . In essence, dieting is a strategy many women attempt to obtain power and acceptance. Although this strategy appears to be superficial, mythology, fairy tales, television, movies, and advertising lead women to believe that thinness is beauty, success, power, and acceptance, and therefore, dieting is a viable strategy. (Root, 1990: 526)

. . .

Pro-ana/mia women's racial journeys into personhood involve the simultaneous movement through, and mastering of, two spaces: the landscape of her body and the landscape of online thinspiration territory. Both of these spaces are understood as degenerate, irrational and 'sick' places for individuals striving for extreme thinness. Alternatively, I suggest that the female body is the main space that needs unmapping, and it is online thinspiration that is used as a map by the contemporary body-mapping woman. Thinspiration acts as a map of how the ideal feminine body should be landscaped, and provides the tools to prune her unruly garden into a lush showcase that maintains hegemonic masculinities. The journey through the landscape of the female body and thinspiration online space "materially and symbolically secures h[er] dominance" (Razack, 2002: 13) over "other" women who cannot control their appetites.

I would like to adapt Razack's concept, referring to my adaption as the 'racial journey into personhood trap'. Mohanram (1999) argues that women are unable to mature, like black people are unable to unmark themselves, because 'animals' cannot move into consciousness. The trap is built into the thinspiration online environments with the mirages of neoliberal self-determination because even if you are a successful dieter you are likely to be labeled as being mentally ill for being found in these 'dangerous and disgusting' places. The label of an eating disorder evicts women from rationality, self-control and civility. Very few succeed in achieving the balance between controlling one's appetite and being marked as mentally ill, making the thin and healthy feminine status extremely elite:

Because of this exclusionary standard of beauty, not all Euro American women emulate the stereotypical White woman; only a few women are privileged to be in this 'beautiful club'. Those Euro American women who deviate from this standard of whiteness are displaced like ethnic minority women for their departure from 'pure' White womanhood. (Patton, 2006: 119)

Sherene Razack (2010) explains how Palestinian women are evicted from femininity through the physicality of the wall at Al-Jeeb that they are forced to climb to get to school or work. Both men and women are evicted from personhood and labeled as criminals through scaling this wall, which maintains the understanding that Palestinians are pre-modern and animal-like. Razack (2010: 97) states that "the lessons for the body are clear: Palestinians do not simply walk or ride to work or school but instead scramble, crawl and climb." I contend that the lessons for the feminine body are clear: 'pure' white women must starve, purge, exercise and use laxatives in order to reach the thin ideal. Both Palestinian women and women pursuing thinness are participating in the broader neoliberal social order: civilized and responsible people go to work or school, and they control their body size. However, the physical barriers that marked bodies must overcome in order to reach the civilized side of humanity make the journey a trap. Women must cross many barriers in order to journey into personhood, but that very journey inscribes lessons onto the body, marks the body as animal-like and degenerate. The white male body is able to move into degenerate spaces and return to civilized space unscathed. Most women are unable to return to civilized space because during the journey they are evicted from personhood, from social spaces, and from online spaces through censorship efforts.

Pro-ana/mia thinspiration space is a paradox: is it white space marked by neoliberal discourse (hard work, will-power, self-determination and self-control) or is it degenerate space marked by mental illness (irrationality, disgust, danger and lack of control)? . . .

As women deprive their brains of food they slip into blackness and reinforce the domination of their bodies by men, legitimizing violence. Women are quite literally evicted from social space through the dieting journeys where they seek to shrink their bodies in order to be desirable for men, as this thinspiring quote found online exemplifies: 'feel small for him'. Women are engaged in body modification that will ensure that they are inferior, by taking up less physical and social space than men do. This violent process of shrinking one's body was also discussed in Kawash's (1998: 330) article about the homeless body: "without a proper place, the homeless body is obliged to become small, to minimize its surface, its extension." Kawash (1998) explains how the homeless body experiences 'placelessness' because it belongs nowhere. Women's bodies also experience 'placelessness'; they belong nowhere, and if they try to journey into personhood the spaces they must trek through are filled with landmines that will bring them right back to savagery. Women can attempt the dieting rite of passage in hopes that it will bring them to personhood, but most of their bodily landscapes will be blown up by violent messages that they are inferior along the way.

CONCLUDING REMARKS

Throughout this paper, I have contended that women's bodies, thinspiration online space and social space are places that are "saturated with relations of domination which are relevant to the construction of [feminine] identity" (Mohanram, 1999: xv). In order to contextualize my spatial analyses, I detailed how the academic literature on eating disorders is racialized. Next, I introduced 'black girl thinspiration' to the scholarly conversation on race, space and citizenship. The first analytic section of the paper argued that online pro-ana/mia thinspiration is all about whiteness and moving away from blackness. The second part of this paper suggested that black women can increase their mobility by obtaining a social passport that only thin women can obtain. The access that the social passport provides is material: thinner women experience less prejudice, get better jobs and are seen as responsible human beings. The third section of the paper suggests that most women are unable to return from the journey into extreme dieting unscathed because traps along the way evict them from personhood, femininity, online space and other social spaces. The multiple evictions that women experience throughout their dieting rite of passage, unfortunately, may be worth the

risk because having a 'fat' body also has violent consequences. The machinery of the status quo is hard to overcome because patriarchal, racist, and neoliberal capitalist structures have been built in such a way that women, and racialized persons, cannot truly win: they can never fully unmark their bodies.

REFERENCES

0WannaBeThin0 (2009) Thinspo Pro Ana quotes [video online]. Available (consulted 5 May 2016) at: https://www.youtube.com/watch?v=M8Uzi8FFVOk

AngelAmyAnna (2009) *Black Girl Thinspiration* [video online]. Available (consulted 5 May 2016) at: https://www.youtube.com/watch?v=EmNClbpAp18

Bordo S (2013) Not just "a white girl's thing": The changing face of food and body image problems. In: Counihan C and Van Esterik P (eds) *Food and Culture: A Reader*, 3rd edn. New York, NY: Routledge, 265–275.

Coco_CHANEL (2008) *Thinspo: Black Grls Luv Ana Too* [video online]. Available (consulted 5 May 2016) at: https://www.youtube.com/watch?v=9fA0E2-Jzy0

Coco_CHANEL (2009) *Thinspo: Mind over Matter* [video online]. Available (consulted 5 May 2016) at: https://www.youtube.com/watch?v=X-B0VKyqZFs

Dolan B, Lacey JH and Evans C (1990) Eating behaviour and attitudes to weight and shape in British women from three ethnic groups. *British Journal of Psychiatry* 157: 523–528. Available (consulted 4 May 2016) at: http://bjp.rcpsych.org/content/157/4/523.full-text.pdf+html

Franko DL, Becker AE, Thomas JJ, et al. (2007) Cross-ethnic differences in eating disorder symptoms and related distress. *International Journal of Eating Disorders* 40(2): 156–164. Available (consulted 4 May 2016) at: http://onlinelibrary.wiley.com.libproxy.wlu.ca/doi/10.1002/eat.20341/epdf

Fuller J (2011) The "black sex goddess" in the living room. *Feminist Media Studies* 11(3): 265–281. Available (consulted 4 May 2016) at: http://journals1.scholarsportal.info.libproxy.wlu.ca/pdf/14680777/v11i0003/265_tsgitlr.xml

Girls Incorporated (2007) *Girls and their bodies: striving for good health and a positive body image.* Available (consulted 4 May 2016) at: http://

www.girlsinc-monroe.org/styles/girlsinc/defiles/Girls_and_Their_Bodies.pdf

Kawash S (1998) The homeless body. *Public Culture* 10(2): 319–339. Available (consulted 4 May 2016) at: http://publicculture.dukejournals.org.libproxy.wlu.ca/content/10/2/319.full.pdf

King TL (2010) One Strike evictions, state space and the production of abject black female bodies. *Critical Sociology* 36(1): 45–64. Available (consulted 4 May 2016) at: http://crs.sagepub.com.libproxy.wlu.ca/content/36/1/45.full.pdf+html

Kirby K (1998) Re: mapping subjectivity: Cartographic vision and the limits of politics. In: Duncan N (ed.) *Body Space*. New York, NY: Routledge, 45–55.

Mikel S (2013) *Motivational Quotes (Thinspo)* [video online]. Available (consulted 5 May 2016) at: https://www.youtube.com/watch?v=P421OFxfkyE

Mohanram R (1999) *Black Body, Women, Colonialism, and Space*. Minneapolis, MN: University of Minnesota Press.

Patton TO (2006) Hey girl, am I more than my hair? African American women and their struggles with beauty, body image, and hair. *NWSA Journal* 18(2): 24–51. Available (consulted 4 May 2016) at: http://www.jstor.org.libproxy.wlu.ca/stable/4317206

Powell AD and Kahn AS (1995) Racial differences in women's desires to be thin. *International Journal of Eating Disorders* 17(2): 191–195.

Razack S (1998) Race, space and prostitution. The making of the bourgeois subject. *Canadian Journal of Women and the Law* 10(2): 338–376. Available (consulted 4 May 2016) at: http://heinonline.org.myaccess.library.utoronto.ca/HOL/Page?handle=hein.journals/cajwol10&collection=journals&id=359

Razack S (2002) When place becomes race. In: Razack S (ed.) *Race, Space and the Law: Unmapping a White Settler Society*. Toronto: Between the Lines, 1–20.

Razack S (2010) A hole in the wall, a rose at a checkpoint: The spatiality of colonial encounters in occupied Palestine. *Journal of Critical Race Inquiry* 1(1): 90–108. Available (consulted 4 May 2016) at: http://ojs.library.queensu.ca/index.php/CRI/article/view/3551/3559

Riley S (2002) The black beauty myth. In: Hernandez D and Rehman B (eds) *Colonize This!* Emeryville, CA: Seal Press, pp. 357–369.

Roberts A, Cash TF, Feingold A, et al. (2006) Are black-white differences in females' body dissatisfaction decreasing? A meta-analytic review. *Journal of Consulting and Clinical Psychology* 74(6): 1121–1131. Available (consulted 5 May 2016) at: http://journals2.scholarsportal.info.libproxy.wlu.ca/pdf/0022006x/v74i0006/1121_abdifbddamr.xml

Root M (1990) Disordered eating in women of colour. *Sex Roles* 22(7): 525–536. Available (consulted 5 May 2016) at: http://link.springer.com.libproxy.wlu.ca/article/10.1007/BF00288168

Rucker C and Cash T (1992) Body images, body-size perceptions, and eating behaviors among African-American and white college women. *International Journal of Eating Disorders* 12: 231–299. Available (consulted 5 May 2016) at: http://onlinelibrary.wiley.com.libproxy.wlu.ca/doi/10.1002/1098–108X(199211)12:3%3C291::AID-EAT2260120309%3E3.0.CO;2-A/epdf

Shaw H, Ramirez L, Trost A, et al. (2004) Body image and eating disturbances across ethnic groups: More similarities than differences. *Psychology of Addictive Behaviors* 18: 12–18. Available (consulted 5 May 2015) at: http://journals2.scholarsportal.info.libproxy.wlu.ca/pdf/0893164x/v18i0001/12_biaedaegm-std.xml

Sykes H (2011) *Queer Bodies: Sexualities, Genders & Fatness in Physical Education*. New York, NY: Peter Lang.

Taylor JY, Caldwell CH, Baser RE, et al. (2013) Classification and correlates of eating disorders among blacks: Findings from the national survey of American life. *Journal of Health Care for the Poor and Underserved* 24(1): 289–310. Available (consulted 5 May 2016) at: https://muse.jhu.edu.libproxy.wlu.ca/article/496952/pdf

Van Amsterdam N (2013) Big fat inequalities, thin privilege: An intersectional perspective on "body size." *European Journal of Women's Studies* 20(2): 155–169. Available (consulted 5 May 2016) at: http://ejw.sagepub.com.libproxy.wlu.ca/content/20/2/155.full.pdf+html

Wildes J, Emery R and Simons A (2001) The roles of ethnicity and culture in the development of eating disturbance and body dissatisfaction: A meta-analytic review. *Clinical Psychology Review*

21: 521–551. Available (consulted 5 May 2016) at: http://journals2.scholarsportal.info.libproxy.wlu .ca/pdf/02727358/v21i0004/521_troeacabdamr .xml

Wilfley D, Schreiber G, Pike K, et al. (1996) Eating disturbance and body image: A comparison of a community sample of adult black and white women. *International Journal of Eating Disorders* 20: 377–387. Available (consulted 5 May 2016) at: http://online library.wiley.com.libproxy.wlu.ca/doi/10.1002/ (SICI)1098–108X(199612)20:4%3C377::AID-EAT5%3E3.0.CO;2-K/epdf

26. "I CLICK AND POST AND BREATHE, WAITING FOR OTHERS TO SEE WHAT I SEE"

MINH-HA T. PHAM (2015)

To hear some commentators and critics tell it, vanity is the scourge of our times. The advent of participatory media—Facebook, YouTube, blogs, and so on—is blamed for unleashing a cyberpsychological surge of pent up exhibitionist desires. In the book that helped to define this technocultural affliction called *The Narcissism Epidemic* Jean Twenge and W. Keith Campbell describe the problem as a: "'Look at me!' mentality" (2010: 4). The Internet, they argue, "serves as a giant narcissism multiplier" that, among other things, has normalized "provocative and self-promoting public dress" (2010: 271). Fashion journalist Suzy Menkes echoes Twenge and Campbell in a scathing op-ed piece titled "The Circus of Fashion" published in *New York Times Magazine* in February 2013. For Menkes, the "look-at-me mentality" has turned the sanctified institution of fashion journalism into a circus. In contrast to the old guard of fashion journalists or "black crows," social media "peacocks" are more interested in promoting themselves than reporting about fashion. (The peacock is a popular symbol of vanity in Western art.) Menkes, like so many other critics of Internet narcissism, lays much of the blame on bloggers. She calls out personal style bloggers like "Susie Bubble" (Susanna Lau) and "BryanBoy" (Bryan Grey Yambao) by name, excoriating them for their "look-at-me" fashion sense. "Look at me wearing the dress! Look at these shoes I have found! Look at me loving this outfit in 15 different images!" (Menkes 2013). Beneath the self-aggrandizing self-absorption, Menkes suggests, lies a desperate need for external validation. Bloggers are not only "ready and willing" to objectify themselves, she writes, they are "gagging for attention."

Yet another highly gendered iteration of the desperately vain social media user appeared in the Gawker Media feminist website *Jezebel* in November 2013. Commenting on the broader selfie phenomenon of which fashion bloggers are key figures, Erin Gloria Ryan concludes that selfies are "a high tech reflection of the fucked up way society teaches women that their most important quality is their physical attractiveness" (2013). For Ryan, selfies technologize sexism by extending and making more efficient well-established ideologies and practices of objectifying women. With the selfie, women are encouraged to become a collaborating partner in their own objectification and their own devaluation as individuals whose significance is reduced to their physical appearance. As with Twenge and Campbell who describe vanity in terms of an epidemic, and Menkes who suggests bloggers' vanity betray[s] a certain desperation, Ryan also casts a psychopathological shade on vanity when she posits that selfies are illustrative of a widespread cultural and gendered dysmorphia: "they're a reflection of the warped way we teach girls to see themselves as decorative" (2013).

These commentaries on vanity in the digital age from three very different sources are representative of the prevailing view of post-Internet vanity or what is derisively termed "digital narcissism." As these examples illustrate, vanity is generally interpreted in very narrow terms as practices and desires that are organized around an unhealthy focus on and promotion of the self. But, in fact, vanity is a many and contradictory thing. As Claire Tanner, JaneMaree Maher, and Suzanne Fraser (authors of *Vanity: 21st Century Selves*) point out, "vanity can be natural or unnatural [when applied to men or women], a sign of agency or a sign of victimhood [when interpreted as self-confidence or self-absorption]" (2013: 8). Likewise, its effects can be liberating or oppressive. In their book, the authors introduce what they see as "an emergent notion of twenty-first century vanity . . . in which self regard is intertwined with relationality and responsiveness to others" (2013: 153). They give the examples of writing personal profiles on online dating sites and personal blogging, pointing out that these practices of online self-promotion serve social needs. Efforts to promote one's personality, image, and life to gain attention are "created in the hope of *enhancing connection* with others" (2013: 157; emphasis in original). As such, "relational vanity" is, in their words, a model of "good vanity" (2013: 18).

Others including James R. Baker and Susan M. Moore and Andrew L. Mendelson and Zizi Papacharissi have suggested much the same thing in their research. In their article in *Cyberpsychology and Behavior*, Baker and Moore posit, "it seems reasonable that blogs might help increase feelings of being part of a group" (2008: 748). Likewise, Mendelson and Papacharissi's analysis of Facebook photo galleries concludes, "while narcissistic behavior may be structured around the self, it is not motivated by selfish desire, but by a desire to better connect the self to society" (2011: 270).

In this article, I provide a discussion of a new formation of vanity that I call "networked vanity" that is similar to but also diverges significantly from "relational vanity." In the above revised conceptualizations of vanity, relational vanity is still understood as serving individual and individualistic goals. The practices of online self-regard and self-promotion attributed to relational vanity remain steadfastly self-serving. They are still aimed at producing individual benefits (e.g. a personal sense of belonging). While relational vanity is suggestive of the creative, collaborative, and communicative potential of vanity that is the primary

concern of this article, it does not adequately capture the ways new participatory media and its capacity for self-presentation and self-promotion are being used for purposes beyond self-interest. Today, individual and public acts of vanity (particularly those that centrally involve sartorial and corporeal displays of physical attractiveness) are being incorporated into social activist movements.

In what follows, I discuss [one example] of networked vanity. The . . . #feministselfie hashtag campaign . . . emerged on Twitter in November 2013 in which women (and to a lesser extent, men) silently but powerfully declared their self (or rather "selfie") love using the popular microblogging platform. The #feministselfie hashtag campaign wonderfully demonstrates the importance of self-reflexivity in social activism. Feminist selfie tweets and photo tweets are not simply digital forms of self-regarding. They are a decentralized mode of political action based on a key tenet of women of color feminism that political movements be informed by and grounded in embodied experiences and situated knowledges. In this way, we can understand the #feministselfie hashtag campaign as an extension of a longer tradition of critiquing mainstream liberal white feminism's universalist foundations.

. . .

[This] and other instances of networked vanity make clear that subjectivity has become a primary representational object of visual media. The networked subject is now caught in the regime of ubiquitous visibility constituted by mass distributed technologies and technical platforms. Yet the networked subject-as-object has unprecedented control of the frames of vision within which they are seen. Participatory media allows the networked subject-as-represented object a hand in shaping and controlling their representation. They make choices about when to take a selfie or fashion blog style outfit photo; where to position the head, face, and body in relation to the camera; which blog platform, HTML tags, and hashtags to use; how to caption, crop, and otherwise edit the image; and when to share it online or whether to share it at all.

Participatory media has moved us into a new visual paradigm where the relations of power between the object of looking and the looking subject are significantly more dynamic. Traditionally, the represented object has been consigned to a position of subordination. The terms and conditions of their representation are imposed from above. User-generated media provide new, if limited, means by which those being looked at are both an object and agent of representation. In participating in the representational process, individuals who are the objects of the gaze are also co-creators of the interpretative conditions through which media images of their bodies and selves are seen (see also Rocamora 2011 on personal fashion blogs).

It is precisely this shift in the visual relations of participatory media that make practices of networked vanity potentially so powerful for minoritized groups who have historically bore the greater burden of the dominating gaze—whether it is the surveillant gaze of the state or the voyeuristic gaze of film, television, and photographic camera. The projects of networked vanity discussed here will demonstrate that the larger work of transforming institutionalized structures of visuality can sometimes begin with the self(ie).

A HISTORY OF NETWORKED VANITY

Networked vanity is particular to the age of social media but it is also coextensive with a wider multiracial history of vanity. The #feministselfie tweets and photo tweets . . . are part of a longer tradition of the politics of vanity. Indeed, fashion has long served as a powerful medium in the struggle for social visibility and social recognition for racially, economically, and sexually marginalized people. Public displays of showy dress and spectacular adornment were radical assertions of agency that functioned to restore the dignity of one's body and image through sartorial and corporeal pleasure. Writing about Black style under slavery, scholars such as Stephanie M. H. Camp (2002), Elisa F. Glick (2003), Patricia K. Hunt (1996), and most notably Monica L. Miller have illuminated the ways dandyism and other modes of fancy dress that were generally viewed as an excessive and indeed dangerous amount of self-admiration

were actually political acts that recuperate[d] laboring Black bodies through leisure activities of fashion parading, cakewalking, and conspicuous consumption. As well as an expression of self-worth against the physical, social, and emotional assault of slavery capitalism, fashion also produced political effects. As Miller explains, "wearing clothing beyond their station or of the other gender [facilitated slaves'] efforts to appear free and be mobile" (2009). Black dandyism instrumentalized "the negotiation between slavery and freedom." In other words, what was disparaged as gratuitous vanity was actually a political tactic based in a "fake it till you make it" belief that personal transformation [is] part and parcel of social transformation.

Asian Americans and Mexican Americans share a similar but not identical history and politics of vanity. Key to the production of alternative racial and gender identities for Filipino male laborers in California in the 1930s and 1940s is the McIntosh suit, an expensive suit with "padded shoulders and wide lapels worn by some of Hollywood's most famous men like William Powell" (España-Maram 2006: 123). By retailoring the suit, literally and figuratively, to fit their bodies Filipino men resignified this sartorial sign of white masculinity. Linda España-Maram explains, "Dressing up in the latest style was always important to Filipinos, in part because a snazzy ensemble transformed brown bodies from overworked, exploited laborers to symbols of sensuality, style, and pleasure" (2006: 138). The love and attention Filipino working men gave to their bodies which were socially and economically devalued was puzzling if not objectionable to others in the larger culture. But for these Filipino men public displays of vanity in taxi dancehalls and other commercialized sites of popular culture were at once pleasurable and political activities that unsettled dominant racial meanings, social relationships, and identity categories.

Around the same time as the McIntosh suit, the zoot suit became a key site of anti-racist struggle especially for Mexican but also Japanese and Filipino American men. First worn by African Americans and popularized by jazz legends such as Duke Ellington, Cab Calloway, and Dizzy Gillespie, the zoot suit's distinctive baggy pants, extra-long jacket, and wide lapels flouted wartime calls for rationing and moderation. Disaffected Mexican American youth or so-called pachucos' adoption of the zoot suit signaled their rejection of the nation-state's authority specifically with respect to its formal and informal anti-Mexican policies. On the bodies of Mexican American women, the zoot suit also defied gender expectations, queering white American and Mexican American ideas of femininity. In her study *The Woman in the Zoot Suit*, Catherine S. Ramirez notes, "both *la pachuca* and the lesbian are queer in that they signify excess: both exceed the limits of the heteropatriarchal family" (Ramirez 2009: 133). The zoot suit's exaggerated style, its excess material, and its fashioning of excessive identities that disregard racial, gender, and class boundaries of propriety and normativity drew both public attention and public ire. Recurring racial attacks on pachucos and pachucas sometimes as young as twelve and thirteen years old by mostly white servicemen were tacitly and openly supported by middle-class white America. One article published in the *Los Angeles Times* in 1943[1] even praised the attacks as a moral lesson pachucos and pachucas sorely deserved.

Vanity as both a personal feeling and a cultural political tactic is the lynchpin of all these fashion histories and many others. [See also Nan Enstad's fabulous study of white working women's use of flamboyant fashion—what the middle class viewed as a "vulgar vanity"—to construct a political identity as workers but also as women who deserved better treatment from their male supervisors (Enstad 1999: 69).] Ostentatious dress, by the choice of garment and/or by the very choice to dress beyond the prescribed limits of racial, gender, and class norms, has always been a cultural, political, and affective practice rooted in specific social realities. The tendency to dismiss practices of sartorial display and extravagance as mere vanity risks ignoring the lived experience of minoritized people for whom the right to be seen on their own terms and the right to take pleasure in their bodies and self-images has never been a given.

Participatory media technologies and techniques increase the capacity and reach of sartorial and corporeal self-presentations. What African American

dandies, Chicano zoot suiters, and McIntosh-clad Filipino dancehall patrons managed to achieve locally, . . . the #feministselfie women have been able to do on a greater scale using new technologies of self-promotion and self-broadcasting. In critically considering the #feministselfie hashtag campaign . . . , what emerges is a crucial insight about the importance of the politics of self-composure that is at the heart of networked vanity.

#FEMINISTSELFIE

As I have already mentioned, in November 2013, *Jezebel* published an article under a headline that declared, "Selfies Aren't Empowering: They're a Cry for Help." As the headline suggests, the journalist of the feminist Gawker Media website offers a quasi-psychosocial diagnosis of the selfie phenomenon. Briefly stated, the article castigates women who take selfie photographs for falling prey to systemic sexism. Its message and Ryan's condescending tone ignited a firestorm of protest. One of the first critical tweets against the article came from journalist Mikki Kendall who achieved recent notoriety for initiating the #SolidarityIsForWhiteWomen Twitter hashtag campaign. In the spirit of the earlier hashtag campaign, Kendall's selfie tweet took white feminists to task for failing to consider racial inequalities in feminist online media discourses and representations. Kendall's tweet pointedly asks, "can we talk about what #selfies mean to people who never get a chance to see themselves in mainstream media?" (see Figure 1).

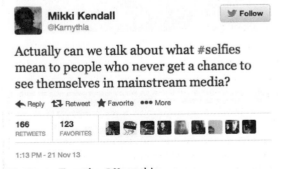

FIGURE 1   Tweet by @Karnythia.

Responding to Kendall's provocation, tweets with the #feministselfie hashtag—frequently accompanied by a selfie photo tweet—began trending online. The tweets fell into three major categories of response. The first category involve tweets that directly called out Ryan for her dismissive and as many saw it, her racial and gender normative, attitude (see Figures 2–4).

The second category of tweets emphasized the racial biases and omissions in mainstream feminist media outlets like *Jezebel* (see Figures 5–7).

The third category of #feministselfie tweets were those in which individuals simply but defiantly reveled in the pleasure of their own image (see Figures 8 and 9).

The #feministselfie hashtag campaign and the media coverage it attracted from websites as diverse

as *Colorlines* (a news site that covers issues of race and politics) and *Bustle* (a women's entertainment and lifestyle website), as well as from the circuitry of shared links on Facebook, Tumblr, and Instagram

A. Lynn
@anerdyfeminist   Follow   ⌄

Bc of fabulous fat gals posting selfies on Tumblr, I feel happier in my own skin. Thank goodness they don't listen to Jez
#feministselfie

11:37 AM - 21 Nov 2013

4 Likes

FIGURE 4   Tweet by @anerdyfeminist.

dulce de leche @bad_dominicana   21 Nov
selfies are the only place I see women like me. unlike whites, I dont have entire industries made in my image. #feministselfie
Details

FIGURE 5   Tweet by @bad_dominicana.

Elle
@FireinFreetown   Follow   ⌄

Need a White woman to come teach me about feminism. This is my cry for help #feministselfie

FIGURE 2   Tweet by @FireinFreetown.

Mary @OHTheMaryD · Nov 21
I'll be damned if an able-bodied, cis, White woman is gonna make me feel bad for taking a damn selfie. HELL NO!! #FeministSelfie
Collapse
                         ← Reply ⇄ Retweeted ★ Favorite ••• More
RETWEETS   FAVORITES
8   12
1:49 PM - 21 Nov 2013 · Details

FIGURE 3   Tweet by @OHTheMaryD.

dulce de leche @bad_dominicana   21 Nov
taking time out of my day to admire myself in the midst of constant antiblack misogynist degradation. #feministselfie
pic.twitter.com/7mgZOfU8dg
    Reply Retweet Favorite   Flag media

FIGURE 6   Tweet by @bad_dominicana.

standing in the soft light of a world that sees me as hard. #feministselfie

11:01 AM - 21 Nov 2013

7 Retweets 36 Likes

FIGURE 7   Tweet by @so_treu.

whatever Erin Gloria Ryan I look fab #feministselfie pic.twitter.com/rdrsmDOxCu

Reply   Retweet   Favorite   ••• More

FIGURE 8   Tweet by @ixolotl.

affirmed that at stake in these selfies was the struggle over the value and right of self-composure. A blogger named Maurice Tracy posted a powerful meditation on the reasons why he takes selfies. Although the blog post was published several months before the hashtag campaign, it is a salient articulation of the campaign's broader message. On his blog, *Blaqueer*, Tracy writes:

> I take my selfies because I am that guy who, unless he takes the picture or suggests it, doesn't get his picture taken . . . I live in a world where either body privilege or race privilege is always against me. So I point my camera at my face . . . and I click; I upload it to instagram [sic], and I hold my breath because the world is cruel and I am what some would call ugly, but I don't see it . . . I click and post and breathe, waiting for others to see what I see: beautiful dark skin, Afrika's son, a dream un-deferred, pretty eyes, and nice lips, and a nose that fits my face; I want them, you, to see that I am human. (Tracy 2013)

FIGURE 9   Tweet by @ChiefElk.

The #feministselfie campaign and images exemplify the potential of user-generated media to allow minoritized individuals the means to self-create and self-name identities that challenge dominant ways of seeing and knowing beauty and person-hood. As a do-it-yourself technique of visibility, the selfie and related methods of networked vanity can direct our attention to bodies and experiences that are invisible in traditional sites of fashion and beauty imagery or, when they are visible at all, are only visible as the inferior Other in the beautiful/ugly binary.

When Tracy writes, "I click and post and breathe, waiting for others to see what I see: beautiful dark skin, Afrika's son . . . I want them, you, to see that I am human," he makes important links between networked vanity and dominant Western aesthetic discourses epitomized by Kant's essay, "On National Characteristics So Far as They Depend upon the Distinct Feeling of the Beautiful and the Sublime" (2003 [1961]). This discursive tradition, as Sarah Nuttall explains, "present[s] the African continent as the metaphor *par excellence* for physical ugliness and moral decay" (Nuttall 2006: 9).

The #feministselfie participants' use of social media technologies and practices is an exercise in networked vanity that is both centered on the self but with the understanding that the self is situated within larger transmedia, transhistorical, and transnational systems of seeing and knowing race, gender, beauty, and personhood. The #feministselfie tweets and photo tweets challenge the political history of aesthetic visibility and the racist and colonial projects they empower by demanding that we see minoritized people on their own terms and in their own vision.

As well as fashioning alternative public visibilities—alternative ways of seeing beauty and personhood—the #feministselfie tweets effectively reappropriate public space for radical feminist critique. By uploading #feministselfies onto Twitter and sharing them on Facebook and Instagram, for example, participants seize valuable space for their body and image in what are today the most dynamic environments of public culture. According to a 2013 Pew Internet report, 73 percent of adult Internet users (age 18 and older) worldwide use social media networks

(Duggan and Smith 2014). The top three are Facebook, Twitter, and Instagram. The numbers of active users these sites have are staggering. Respectively, they have 1.19 billion, 241 million, and 150 million monthly active users (with a significant amount of overlap between them). Twitter and Instagram are, in some ways, niche sites that have "particular appeal to younger adults [ages 18–29], urban dwellers, and non-whites" (Duggan and Smith 2014). All of this is to say that popular social media sites constitute an enormous part of digital public culture and public interactivity today.

#Feministselfie participants are doing more than inserting themselves into popular public spaces. They transform these digital public spaces by changing the narratives and images that define them as sites of subjectification and objectification. What is on display in actual #feministselfie tweets—not the images of people taking selfies that typically accompany media stories about them but actual #feministselfies—is a minority perspective. Unlike representations of people taking selfies in which we see individuals admiring themselves in front of a (visible) camera, actual #feministselfies make visible the self-perspective of the user not the "selfie scene" (as viewed from the critic's perspective). What is on display in actual #feministselfies are alternative ways of seeing beauty and personhood shaped by the styles of embodiment, lived experiences, and creative efforts of minoritized people.

When networked vanity is discounted as merely narcissism and showing off, not only is the perspective of the networked subject-as-object elided for the perspective of the critic, the particular relationship between public appearance and public space for minoritized women is ignored. As many of the #feministselfie participants point out, critiques of digital narcissism by Ryan and other would-be white feminist allies rest on the presumptuousness of white feminists to assume they are in a position to dictate standards of personal and public behavior to all women. The cultural political value of participatory media technologies and techniques is that they enable people whose images are invisible or are distorted in traditional media to capture and direct attention to non-normative bodies and identity presentations that remain generally invisible in traditional media outlets—even those that are attentive to feminist concerns.

NOTE

1. "Zoot Suiters Learn Lesson in Fights with Servicemen: Gangs Stay Off Streets after Dark." *Los Angeles Times* June 7: 1943, A1: 1.

REFERENCES

Baker, James R. and Susan M. Moore 2008. "Blogging as a Social Tool: A Psychological Examination of the Effects of Blogging." *Cyberpsychology and Behavior* 11(6): 747–9.

Camp, Stephanie M. H. 2002. "The Pleasures of Resistance: Enslaved Women and Body Politics in the Plantation South, 1830–1861." *The Journal of Southern History* 68(3): 533–72.

Duggan, Maeve and Aaron Smith. 2014. "Social Media Update 2013." Pew Research Center, January. http://pewinternet.org/~/media//Files/Reports/2013/Social%20Networking%202013_PDF.pdf (accessed March 20, 2014).

Enstad, Nan. 1999. *Ladies of Labor, Girls of Adventure: Working Women, Popular Culture, and Labor Politics at the Turn of the Twentieth Century*. New York: Columbia University Press.

España-Maram, Linda. 2006. *Creating Masculinity in Los Angeles's Little Manila: Working-Class Filipinos and Popular Culture, 1920s–1950s*. New York: Columbia University Press.

Glick, Elisa F. 2003. "Harlem's Queer Dandy: African-American Modernism and the Artifice of Blackness." *MFS: Modern Fiction Studies* 49(3): 414–42.

Hunt, Patricia K. 1996. "The Struggle to Achieve Individual Expression through Clothing and Adornment: African American Women under and after Slavery." In P. Morton (ed.) *Discovering the Women in Slavery: Emancipating Perspectives on the American Past*, pp. 227–40. Athens, GA: University of Georgia Press.

Kant, Immanuel. 2003 [1961]. "Of National Characteristics, So Far as They Depend upon the Distinct Feeling of the Beautiful and the Sublime." *Observations on the Feeling of the Beautiful and the Sublime*. Trans. John T. Goldthwait. Berkeley, CA: University of California Press.

Mendelson, A. L. and Z. Papacharissi. 2011. "Look at Us: Collective Narcissism in College Student Facebook Photo Galleries." In Z. Papacharissi (ed.) *A Networked Self: Identity, Community, and Culture on Social Network Sites*, pp. 251–73. New York and London: Routledge.

Menkes, Suzy. 2013. "The Circus of Fashion." *New York Times Magazine* February 17: 91–4.

Miller, Monica L. 2009. *Rorotoko* October 16. http://rorotoko.com/interview/20091016_miller_monica_on_slaves_fashion_black_dandyism_styling_black_ident/?page=2 (accessed March 17, 2014).

Nuttall, Sarah. 2006. *Beautiful/Ugly: African and Diaspora Aesthetics*. Durham, NC: Duke University Press.

Ramirez, Catherine S. 2009. *The Woman in the Zoot Suit: Gender, Nationalism, and the Cultural Politics of Memory*. Durham, NC: Duke University Press.

Rocomora, Agnès. 2011. "Personal Fashion Blogs: Screens and Mirrors in Digital Self-portraits." *Fashion Theory* 15(1): 407–24.

Ryan, Erin Gloria. 2013. "Selfies Aren't Empowering: They're a Cry for Help." *Jezebel* November 21. http://jezebel.com/selfies-arent-empowering-theyre-a-cry-for-help-1468965365 (accessed March 25, 2014).

Tanner, Claire, JaneMaree Maher and Suzanne Fraser. 2013. *Vanity: 21st Century Selves*. New York: Palgrave Macmillan.

Tracy, Maurice. 2013. "The Fat Boi Diaries: Why Selfies?" *Blaqueer* March 16. https://blaqueer.wordpress.com/2013/03/16/the-fat-boi-diaries-why-selfies/ (accessed March 25, 2014).

Twenge, Jean and W. Keith Campbell. 2010. *The Narcissism Epidemic: Living in the Age of Entitlement*. New York: Simon & Schuster.

27. ASIAN AMERICAN WOMEN'S BODY IMAGE EXPERIENCES

JENNIFER L. BRADY, AYLIN KAYA, DEREK IWAMOTO, ATHENA PARK, LAUREN FOX, AND MARCUS MOORHEAD (2017)

Body dissatisfaction, or the negative evaluation of one's physical body (Stice & Shaw, 2002), is a serious public health concern that intensifies risk for a number of other negative health outcomes, including depression (Johnson & Wardle, 2005), low self-esteem (Koff, Benavage, & Wong, 2001), and substance abuse (Wilson, 2000). Despite the well-documented harmfulness of body dissatisfaction for all women, most models of body dissatisfaction have been tested with White women or draw on comparisons between White women and women of color (Bordo, 2009). This is highly problematic because it obscures the complexity of women's experiences by positioning White women as the "norm," which in turn underemphasizes racially salient features and distinct experiences for marginalized groups (Cummins & Lehman, 2007). Although some research in the past decade has challenged the cultural-boundedness of body dissatisfaction (Cummins, Simmons, & Zane, 2005; Lau, Lum, Chronister, & Forrest, 2006), Asian American women are underrepresented. The current study sought to extend the research literature by qualitatively exploring the experiences of oppression at the intersections of gender and race, and the forms of resilience that influence body image among Asian American women.

BODY DISSATISFACTION AMONG ASIAN AMERICAN WOMEN

Research investigating the prevalence of body dissatisfaction among Asian American women has yielded contradictory findings. Some studies suggest that White, Asian, Hispanic, and Black women experience similar levels of body dissatisfaction (Cachelin, Veisel, Barzegarnazari, & Striegel-Moore, 2000; Grabe & Hyde, 2006) and that Asian American women, compared to White and Hispanic American women, are more likely to be dissatisfied

with specific body parts, including breast size (Forbes & Frederick, 2008) and eye appearance (Frederick, Kelly, Latner, Sandhu, & Tsong, 2016). Other studies suggest Asian American women actually have thinner body ideals than White women (Barnett, Keel, & Conoscenti, 2001), yet other studies purport that Asian American women experience less body dissatisfaction than White women (Nouri, Hill, & Orrell-Valente, 2011). On the whole, these findings suggest that Asian American women experience somewhat similar or elevated levels of dissatisfaction compared to other racial groups, suggesting the need for greater understanding of cultural factors that predispose risk (Cheng, 2014; Smart, Tsong, Mejia, Hayashino, & Braaten, 2011; Tsong & Smart, 2015).

CULTURAL AND RACIAL INFLUENCES OF BODY DISSATISFACTION

One prominent cultural factor that has been studied in relation to body dissatisfaction among Asian American women is ethnic identity. Some studies suggest that ethnic identity can be a direct or interactive protective factor against eating concerns by facilitating a positive sense of self and identity and discouraging adoption of Western beauty ideals (Rakhkovskaya & Warren, 2014). Yet, other research suggests ethnic identity intensifies the relation between pressure for thinness and body preoccupation (Phan & Tylka, 2006) and is positively associated with a drive for thinness (Sabik, Cole, & Ward, 2010) and disordered eating (Tsai, Curbow, & Heinberg, 2003). It is possible that women with stronger ethnic identification may compare their bodies to other Asian peers, who are often physically petite (Smart & Tsong, 2014; Tsai et al., 2003). Feeling overweight compared to other Asian women, coupled with cultural expectations to be dainty, slim, and feminine

(Wardle, Haase, & Steptoe, 2006), may contribute to even stricter standards of thinness and may facilitate unhealthy attempts to lose weight. Given that other studies have found no direct association between ethnic identity and eating disorders (Cheng, 2014; Iyer & Haslam, 2003), it is essential to clarify the nature of these relations.

Acculturation is another salient predictor of body dissatisfaction among Asian American women. There is some consensus that acculturation can result in a double-bind for Asian American women, where adherence to either U.S. or traditional cultural values can confer risk for body image concerns. Some researchers suggest assimilation can intensify body surveillance and awareness of racialized features that may be considered non-normative or unattractive (Cummins & Lehman, 2007). Other research suggests that the retention of traditional cultural beauty norms within more patriarchal societies can increase pressures to appear thin, modest, and attractive (Smart & Tsong, 2014). Although some studies found no evidence supporting these relations among diverse ethnic groups (Reddy & Crowther, 2007), others found that stronger adherence to Asian values, and in turn lower acculturation, was more predictive of greater overall body dissatisfaction (Lau et al., 2006). Adding to the complexity, Tsong and Smart (2015) found that body dissatisfaction might be related to cultural conflict, or biculturative stress, suggesting that Westernization or traditional cultural beliefs alone may not confer risk. The collective research on ethnic identity, acculturation, and body dissatisfaction among Asian American women has provided equivocal findings. Investigating other meaningful contextual factors, including racism, could potentially yield a more comprehensive and nuanced understanding of risk factors for this group.

Asian American women have a unique racialized experience that may contribute to higher body dissatisfaction. They are often exoticized, depicted as hypersexual and submissive sexual objects, and are targets of race-related-teasing that marginalizes and denigrates race-related features (e.g., eye size, skin tone). Research suggests that frequency and exposure to race-related or ethnic teasing intensified body shape concern and maladaptive eating attitudes (Cummins & Lehman, 2007; Iyer & Haslam, 2003; Reddy & Crowther, 2007). In addition, perceived discrimination has been associated with greater endorsement of media beauty ideals and body dissatisfaction (Cheng, 2014). Given the abundance of research documenting the deleterious effects of racial discrimination on Asian Americans' mental health (Lee & Ahn, 2011), it is essential to better understand how various oppressive experiences may relate to body dissatisfaction among this marginalized group. We reasoned that an intersectional theoretical lens would assist in understanding how body dissatisfaction among Asian American women is embedded within interlocking systems of oppression (e.g., gender, race, and class).

INTERSECTIONALITY: A RECOMMENDED THEORETICAL APPROACH

Intersectionality approaches, particularly within feminist perspectives, have been praised for their ability to provide new answers to long-standing questions in psychology (Else-Quest & Hyde, 2016). Intersectionality attends to the meaning and experiences embedded within multiple categories of identity, difference, and inequality and recognizes that such social categories are inextricably interconnected or intertwined (Cole, 2009; Shields, 2008; Warner, 2008). An intersectional perspective emphasizes both the shared experiences and differences among group members and the fluidity of the social categories, with some identities emerging more prominently in certain contexts than others (Cole, 2009). It also emphasizes dimensions of power and oppression and how these forces are embedded within, or perpetuated by, membership in multiple social categories (Else-Quest & Hyde, 2016; Shields, 2008). Within the body image literature, most researchers of Asian American women's body image experiences neglect to investigate how race and gender intersect and inform one another, such that the experience of one identity (e.g., gender) is shaped by the contextual experiences created by the other (e.g., race). We sought to understand women's occupation of multiple social categories and the salience of these categories in different social contexts in influencing how women perceive their bodies and how they perceive that their bodies are externally evaluated. Given gender and race are highly visible social identities, others are likely to categorize and stereotype Asian American women based on their membership in these groups (Lott & Saxon, 2002). It is thus critical to understand the compounded effects of racism and sexism to better understand within-group variability in body image experiences among Asian American women. A qualitative approach offers an ideal way to explore women's distinct experiences and racially salient body image beliefs that are often not captured in present body image measures.

PRESENT STUDY

Using an intersectional framework, we sought to qualitatively explore the body image experiences of undergraduate U.S.-born Asian American women. Evidence suggests that college-aged women experience disproportionately higher rates of body image discontent (Britton, Martz, Bazzini, Curtin, & Lea-Shomb, 2006) and that U.S.-born Asian American women may exhibit heightened levels of body image concern due to biculturative stress (Tsong & Smart, 2015). Asian American women may experience distinct racial discrimination (i.e., "yellow fever" or the fetishization of Asian women's bodies) and must contend with criticism and pressure from multiple cultures with potentially incongruent values (Smart et al., 2011). Women born in the United States may also experience greater family conflict, particularly in navigating differences in acculturation and cultural expectations in their families (Castillo, Zahn, & Cano, 2012). As current literature lacks an inclusive model to understand the etiology of body dissatisfaction for Asian American women, we sought to develop a new model through grounded theory methodology (Strauss & Corbin, 1998). This study explored the following research questions through semi-structured interviews: (a) How do Asian American women perceive their bodies? (b) How are Asian American women's body image beliefs influenced by their gender and race? and (c) How do Asian American women manage their body image beliefs in contexts of power, inequality, and privilege?

METHOD

PARTICIPANTS

Twenty women who identified as Asian or Asian American from a large Mid-Atlantic university were invited to participate using criterion-based sampling to identify information-rich cases (Patton, 2002). Any participant who met the following inclusion criteria at the time of the interview was invited to participate: (a) self-identified as an Asian or Asian American woman, (b) currently a full-time student, (c) aged 17–25 years, and (d) born in the U.S. Participants ranged in age from 18 to 22 years (mean age = 19.35) and represented a variety of ethnicities: Chinese ($n = 6$), Korean ($n = 3$), Indian ($n = 2$), Bengali ($n = 1$), Vietnamese ($n = 1$), and Pakistani ($n = 1$). Six women reported mixed racial and ethnic backgrounds and were included because they self-identified as Asian American (see Table 1 for more detailed information). . . .

. . . The semi-structured interview questions were constructed using a feminist lens (White et al., 2001) to engage the participants in a shared and collaborative dialogue about their body image experiences, cultural beauty norms, and body image comparison processes. The interviewers encouraged flexibility and spontaneity in responses; the researchers allowed the participants to select their own wording so their subjective body image experiences could naturally emerge. The questions were continuously readjusted to reflect relevant and meaningful topics for each woman (Glaser & Strauss, 1967). . . .

GROUNDED THEORY ANALYSIS

Grounded theory offers a process for exploring the subjective experiences of participants to facilitate the generation of a new theory or framework (Charmaz, 2006; Glaser & Strauss, 1967). An inductive constructivist approach assumes previous theories tested with other women of color and White women may not apply. Grounded theory acknowledges women as the true experts of their experiences (Charmaz, 2006) and allows for the coexistence of multiple realities and an understanding of how power dynamics interact in various social and historical arenas.

Data analysis was conducted with the grounded theory methods outlined by Glaser and Strauss (1967).

TABLE 1 PARTICIPANT DEMOGRAPHIC INFORMATION

Pseudonym	Ethnicity	Generational Status	Age	BIR	Liked Features	Disliked Features
Chloe	½ Chinese ½ Laotian	2.5	19	6.5	Eyes, hair	Stomach, weight
Jenny	½ Korean ½ White	2.5	18	7	Hair, height, leanness	Stomach, acne
Shabani	Indian	2.0	21	6.5	Hips	Stomach, weight
Lin	Chinese	2.0	20	6	Eyes, eyebrows, hair	Stomach, weight, lack muscles
Yun	Chinese	2.0	18	6	Hair, having curves	Stomach, eyebrows, eyes
Nancy	Chinese	2.0	20	7.5	Eyes, smaller frame	Calves, legs, shortness
Connie	Chinese	2.0	20	6	Lips, face, hands, curves	Stomach, fatness in legs, nose
Esther	Korean	2.0	18	7	Stomach, skinny	Face shape, weight, eye color
Sana	Pakistani	2.0	19	8.5	Hair, weight	Breast size, lack of curves
Chrissie	½ Singaporean ½ Taiwanese	2.0	19	4	Hair	Thighs, weight, acne
Jamie	Korean	2.0	20	6.5	Lips	Skin, shortness
Jacqueline	Vietnamese	2.0	21	3.5	Legs, height, flawless skin	Stomach, body hair, breast size
Grace	Korean	2.0	19	4.5	Calves, smiley eyes	Stomach, short torso, breast size, height
Adeline	Chinese	2.0	20	6.5	High-cheek bones	Stomach, height, eye-size, weight, acne
Min	½ Chinese ½ Burmese	2.0	20	8	Eyes, curves	Nose, acne, height
Sunita	½ Indian ½ White	2.5	18	7.5	Legs, all parts	Feet, flat butt, body hair, lack of muscles
Indra	Indian	2.0	22	8.5	Waist, skinny, light skin tone	Love handles, breasts
Arpana	Bengali	2.0	19	2	Lips, skin tone, face shape, body proportions	Weight, body hair, acne, height, feet
Elaine	Chinese	2.0	18	5.5	Eyes, legs	Small breasts, lack of curves, eyes
Fatima	¼ White ¼ African American ½ Pakistani	3.0	18	7.5	Eyes, feet	Back, small butt, acne

Note. BIR = body image rating. BIR was a self-identified score out of 10, with 1 representing *strong dissatisfaction* and 10 representing *strong satisfaction*. Generational status: 2.0 = both parents foreign-born, 2.5 = one U.S.-born parent and one foreign-born parent, 3.0 = both parents U.S.-born.

In the first step of the analysis, all members of the research team individually read each interview transcript and thoughtfully recorded interpretative notes that influenced their understanding of the data. Two smaller coding teams, composed of two researchers and the first author, subsequently met biweekly to investigate the complexities and nuances of participant experiences. These smaller coding meetings encouraged more active participation among all members and improved decision-making quality.

. . .

RESULTS

Five major categories emerged that informed body image: (a) navigating cultural beauty norms, (b) experiences of sexism and racism, (c) parental influences, (d) peer influences, and (e) identity management processes. Each category is composed of multiple properties. The following sections describe how Asian American women conceptualize body image, the categories that appear to influence body image, the consequences of these categories on women's appearance evaluation, and women's sources of resiliency and coping strategies.

CORE CONCEPT: BODY IMAGE

All women described feelings (e.g., dissatisfaction), attitudes (e.g., beliefs about attractiveness), and behaviors (e.g., exercise, make-up routines) related to their body image. Many participants defined body image as both self-perceptions and evaluations from others, particularly family members, romantic partners, and peers, about their appearance, body shape, or specific features. Women commonly described their thoughts and feelings about their bodies based upon racialized features and stereotypes perpetuated by others (e.g., mono-lids, Asians as "doll-like") and the media. Overall, Asian American women described their body image experiences in terms of (a) body structure, (b) facial features, and (c) skin complexion or tone.

Body Structure

All women discussed some degree of self-consciousness, dissatisfaction, or self-criticism surrounding their body weight, shape, and size. Many women commented on their desire for a flatter, thinner stomach; longer and leaner limbs; larger breasts; or slender overall physique. Most women ($n = 14$) expressed specific discontent with their weight and fat distribution throughout their body, with many women feeling overweight due to comparisons with slimmer Asian peers. Shabani noted:

> I am kind of self-conscious of my lankiness, or the overall fat distribution of my body. I feel like it's kind of weird sometimes. There are just certain little things that I pick up on that I'm sure no one else really notices . . . I am, like, jealous of people that are completely comfortable in their own skin and in their bodies.

A few women ($n = 5$) expressed satisfaction and appreciation for their body structure yet many times this self-acceptance was placed in a context of adherence to idealized cultural beauty norms. Nancy and Indra shared their privileged role of having a skinny frame, Jacqueline discussed the benefits of being taller than her relatives, and Yun discussed possessing more desirable curves than her other Asian peers.

Facial Features

Many women ($n = 13$) discussed a range of feelings and beliefs about visible facial features, including eye color, shape, or size; nose bridges; and eyebrows. Women disclosed discontent with their "button nose" (Fatima), self-consciousness about their lack of eyebrows (Yun), and desire for dark hair to emphasize paleness (Connie). Most women juxtaposed these features against White features, which were often perceived as more desirable, privileged, or sought after. A few women described how racialized features symbolize racial hierarchies and oppression and how they feel uniquely objectified. Min stated:

> I think some ideals are kind of the same in the way that, like, I think Asian women have a lot of problems with how they think about their eyes, because people object them. So Asian women always want to make their eyes bigger and their noses smaller.

Many women discussed the desirability of eye shape, size, or color ($n = 10$) and perceived bigger eyes (Esther) that were double-lidded (Adeline) and light-colored (Fatima) as more attractive.

Skin Complexion or Tone

Many women ($n = 13$) commented on their desire for a smooth, acne-free complexion and their difficulty navigating disparate cultural beauty norms of attractive skin color. Many of these women reported struggling to manage breakouts and felt more insecure when family members or peers pointed out these imperfections. Jenny stated, "I feel like I put myself down a little, just because I see flaws when I look in the mirror and, oh, I have scabs here and I have a pimple here." These women described flawless, youthful, wrinkle-free skin as a desirable Eastern beauty norm that was often associated with social class (e.g., financial resources to buy beauty products). Many women discussed possessing darker or tanner skin color than their other Asian peers and how this is remarkably different from Eastern beauty norms that emphasize fair skin. While women often described a slew of products and practices they could use to obtain lighter skin, many ($n = 9$) reported feeling satisfied with achieving a tanner complexion in part as a way to assimilate to Western cultural beauty norms, as noted by Arpana:

> I think it's different. A lot of my friends want to tan, they think it's cool to tan and like when I go home my mom is like, have you been wearing sunscreen? Like here's a hat, here's sunglasses, wear all of that.

In sum, women's beliefs about their body structure, facial features, and skin complexion were influenced by their exposure to distinct contextual and interpersonal stressors.

CATEGORY I: NAVIGATING CULTURAL BEAUTY NORMS

All participants devoted significant time to exploring cultural messages that dictated standards of attractiveness. Women discussed navigating (a) cultural differences in defining attraction ($n = 11$), (b) White beauty ideals ($n = 8$), and (c) biological limitations in attaining Eurocentric features ($n = 12$). Collectively, women were exposed to various cultural beauty norms that influenced their likes and dislikes about their bodies yet often these expectations of attractiveness prized Eurocentric features and devalued Asian features.

Cultural Differences in Defining Attraction

All women discussed their roles in actively negotiating and navigating multiple, and at times conflicting, standards of beauty. Almost all women described a shared understanding of desirable Eastern beauty norms; however, South Asian women described curvy hips and minimal body hair as attractive features. These standards of beauty were often part-focused (e.g., fair skin, porcelain features, petite physique, and black thick hair) and more narrowly defined compared to Western beauty norms, which were perceived as more accepting of multiple images of beauty. Five women described the sociopolitical and historical context that shaped this narrow conceptualization of attraction by stating that appealing features were a way of demonstrating social class and status, rather than mirroring Western beauty ideals (e.g., fair skin). Min disclosed:

> Certain things are kind of seen as Asian women trying to look more Western. I think there definitely is sort of an ideal, especially that the pale skin, maybe, but I think people misconstrue that a little bit because a lot of that is also from where you are born in China and how you grew up. So women of mobility wouldn't have to go outside and they wouldn't have to work in the fields. So they, like, they generally had a lot more paler skin, which, like, also could have been a European influence but like a lot of it is just your rank.

> . . .

Despite feeling restricted to fit a certain ideal, women often positioned their own disliked or unattractive features in relation to the absence of perceived desirable features in Asian countries. Many women expressed wishing for "better skin like those Korean stars" (Adeline), "jet black hair" like the ideal Chinese woman (Min), deep-set eyes (Yun), smaller feet (Nancy), and less body hair compared to other South Asian women (Arpana). This is illustrated in Connie's comment about desire for a petite body frame:

> I guess, since my family background and my culture emphasizes on kind of a petite body frame, that kind of resulted in my dissatisfaction of my neck

down, sort of, just because it's like, oh, I naturally have—not a wider body frame but like my shoulders are bigger than average. I have more muscle or more flesh in my arms and legs, and a little bit on my stomach than average. So I guess there's dissatisfaction from that.

In contrast to their perceived dislikes about their body, women's self-prescribed likes about their body shape and features were often juxtaposed with declarations of their distinctness, uniqueness, or deviation from how Asian women typically look. Jacqueline shared "I kind of like my legs, because I don't know, in Vietnam we're all small. 'Cause Asians are small in general. But then whenever I go to family parties, I'm always like taller than half the people there." Chloe described:

> I feel like that also isn't as much of a problem for me because there are lots of Asian women that have, like, mono-lids and their eyes are like smaller than mine are, so I feel like that never really was an issue for me that much growing up.

Women also described liking features that are highly valued across geographic contexts, such as slenderness, thinness, lighter skin tone, and longer limbs.

White Beauty Ideals

Women's body image narratives were often contextualized within multiple hierarchies of beauty, with Whiteness recognized as the most revered representation of beauty. Eurocentric features, while not explicitly idealized, were often sought after and preferred in a heteronormative context as a way to appear attractive and sexy to men. Women received messages that Eurocentric features are normalized and desirable, which often instilled feelings of inadequacy, self-doubt, and body criticism. For instance, Jenny recounted:

> In particular my last boyfriend, he was very, very White. His ex-girlfriend was this pretty blond girl with curly long blond hair . . . So it was just like comparing myself being like, okay, well this is the type of person he dates and I'm not like that, so what's going to happen? Just like kind of self-doubt. I think it used to really bother me just because I'd be like why, why

am I not this way, why do I not look a certain way, why am I built this way?

. . .

These women were often sensitively attuned to external cues in their environments that dictated expectations of attractiveness with some noting that their consumption of American media induced more negative feelings about their body. Many women ($n = 16$) described the unattainable and unrealistic media images that generally lacked representation of women of color (Blake Lively, Cara Delevingne, Kim Kardashian, and Emma Watson). Yet it was only when women internalized Eurocentric beauty standards that they experienced heightened awareness of their perceived appearance-related deficits. Elaine shared:

> I think I definitely compare myself more to American pop culture. So when you watch, like, movies or listen to songs and stuff, a lot of the women are very curvaceous and it's like beautiful and they have the perfect hourglass figure. So for me, because I don't have that, it's hard for me to be at an 8 [out of 10] on the scale. Maybe if I had compared myself to more Asian women maybe I would like myself a little bit better, or I mean like my body a little bit more.

Biological Limitations in Attaining Eurocentric Features

Most women expressed difficulty in adhering to Western beauty norms because of biological differences in genetic make-up. They expressed discontent in their ability to achieve Western standards of attractiveness, particularly curvaceous butts, lighter eyes, double eyelids, and larger breasts. Some women shared that they perceived their bodies as substandard, while they also felt powerless because Eurocentric features are biologically impossible to attain. Jamie stated,

> In around middle school, I understood that I would probably not measure up to the curvy body type, because of just, you know, my basic body structure. So I guess in that way I saw it as a kind of unattainable kind of thing, where like I know that's the image that

a lot of people want, but I just don't think that I can achieve that.

Even though women could recognize their own biological limitations, several women normalized and justified cosmetic practices necessary to achieve Eurocentric features, including plastic surgery to acquire double eyelids or to enhance breast size. Women described this as a common cultural practice in many East-Asian countries, particularly in Korea, as a way to achieve "perfection." For some women, plastic surgery represented a way to reclaim power over their bodies by acquiring sought-after features (e.g., eyebrow tattoos); yet for other women, plastic surgery was too severe and they preferred smaller behavioral changes (e.g., wearing make-up) to change their appearance.

. . .

CATEGORY 2: EXPERIENCES OF SEXISM AND RACISM

Many women shared experiences of sexism and racism that undermined their individuality and increased self-consciousness and self-objectification. This was composed of (a) expectations to be hyper-feminine ($n = 13$), (b) sexual objectification experiences ($n = 9$), and (c) microaggressions and race-related teasing ($n = 11$). These reported occurrences demonstrate the unique disadvantages Asian American women encounter relative to women of other racial groups.

Expectations to be Hyper-Feminine

Many women reported a distinct awareness of societal feminine expectations to be nurturing, submissive, obedient, and quiet. The intersection of racism and sexism resulted in unique challenges for Asian American women who described messages to be hyper-feminine in traditional cultural contexts (e.g., subservient to men) that seemed devaluing, degrading, and constraining. This is illustrated by Jamie:

> I still feel like there is just that awful stigma that Asian American women are supposed to be, you know, like really gentle and docile and submissive and, I don't know, to speak really frankly, that really bothers me.

Women discussed endorsing hyper-feminine expectations as a way to appease men. Sana shared that a good "prospect for marriage" is a woman who is pure, innocent, shy, and acquiescent and that Pakistani women can compensate for deficits in appearance by excelling in domestic roles. Furthermore, Chloe articulated the pressure she feels to "do whatever the male says" and shared feeling restricted to perform her femininity in a way that is attractive to men. Hyper-femininity also seemed to be communicated through body language and body image features, particularly in striving to be delicate and dainty.

Sexual Objectification Experiences

Many women shared instances in which they navigated limiting and racialized expectations of appearance that objectified their bodies in ways that are different from women of other racial groups. These experiences overvalued women's bodies, either by reducing women to inanimate objects or to a series of parts, and devalued their personhood and uniqueness. Women described messages that an attractive Asian woman is "doll-like" (Jenny) or child-like, with porcelain-like features (Chrissie), including doe-eyed, smooth complexion, and skinny physique, that can resemble cartoons (Grace). A few women discussed being exoticized for their racialized features and "presented to everyone else" (Connie) to be evaluated and critiqued based upon race. As a result of feeling on display, Connie engaged in a variety of impression management strategies to craft an image of perfection, by wearing her hair and make-up just right or dressing a certain way.

Some women reported adhering to cultural expectations to dress modestly as a way to shield themselves from unwelcome attention on their bodies. A few women ($n = 7$) discussed the importance of covering one's body to avoid unwanted attention, body evaluations, and sexual advances from men. Shabani, for example, described wanting to hide her body:

> I am mostly comfortable with my body it's just, I think, it's just being exposed and the idea of having people look at me like observers. Like, I just feel like that in general, not even just with my body, but in

anything that I do, like I don't like having too much attention on me. And that's a part of the reason that I don't feel completely comfortable necessarily being like exposed . . . Yeah I'd prefer kind of hiding under my layers and stuff, maybe. Because I'm more aware of people looking at me, I guess, when I am wearing less clothing.

. . .

Women's hyper-vigilance about their appearance and increased body monitoring as a result of their sexual objectification experiences, when coupled with cultural expectations of modesty, seemed to result in downplaying body image features they liked.

Microaggressions and Race-Related Teasing

In addition to exotification and sexual objectification of Asian women's bodies, many women described exposure to race-related teasing and stereotyping about their Asian identity. A few women discussed hurtful instances of being typecast by peers and authority figures as "good at math" (Jenny) or pigeonholed as a housewife who knows "how to do chores really well" (Chrissie). Moreover, even though all women were born in the United States, they were objectified as perpetual foreigners and felt pressured to defend their nationality. Other women discussed heightened feelings of vulnerability and awareness of their race and appearance when peers would tease them about their accent, their "caramel" skin color (Arpana), or make comments about their "chinky" eyes (Esther). Most women reported feeling exposed, increasingly self-conscious, and critiqued differently because of their outward appearance as an "Asian woman." Esther explained:

> I wanted to rush next semester, but it's weird because a majority of sorority girls are White and all that stuff, so it's just going to be weird rushing because everyone is going to be the same. I will probably stand out, which is uncomfortable . . . I guess we grow up learning to conform with everyone else and kind of blend in with everyone, but being in that kind of environment where you're the only Asian, or one of the few Asians, it makes you stand out and feel self-conscious, like there's a spotlight on you.

Exposure to racial microaggressions seemed to increase women's body surveillance and appearance

preoccupation. In sum, receiving messages to be hyper-feminine, and experiencing racism, sexual objectification, and race-related teasing, presented distinct challenges for Asian American women and appeared to contribute to their body dissatisfaction.

CATEGORY 3: PARENTAL INFLUENCES

All women explored how meaningful close relationships with others shaped their beliefs about attraction, the salience of appearance, and attitudes toward body image features. Women most often described the roles of their parents, particularly their mothers, in influencing their body image. Women discussed encounters with (a) family members who "point out flaws" ($n = 13$) and (b) family conflict ($n = 6$), both of which seemed to increase body dissatisfaction.

Point Out Flaws

Many women described instances of receiving unsolicited feedback and criticism from family members about their body shape or features, most of which concerned body weight or acne. Women reported receiving conflicting feedback, such as being told to gain weight after previously being told to lose weight. These instances appeared to intensify body dissatisfaction because women believed they could never fulfill their parents' expectations of attractiveness. Although parents' teasing and vocalized disapproval about disliked features were perceived as hurtful and intrusive by many women, a few women were quick to defend these experiences by rationalizing them as a normal cultural practice. For example, Chrissie reflected on the customary nature of these exchanges:

> Well, for example, there's fat-shaming in the U.S., where everybody is saying that it's not okay and you're supposed to embrace how you look, but then, I feel like in Asian cultures, it's perfectly acceptable for someone to go up to you and be like, "You're too fat, you need to lose weight."

A few women perceived these unsolicited comments as a gesture of affection within their family, particularly when family members encouraged them to eat more. Shabani noted plumpness was associated with health in her Indian community and could signify social class and ability to afford resources. Some women, including Lin, minimized and made light of these experiences as a protective mechanism to maintain appearances and preserve respect for their family, stating: "I don't want to make my mom kind of look bad, but she did tell me that I was fat a lot . . . not a lot, just like, sometimes, just in passing." Yet other women noted feeling resentful, aggravated, embarrassed, self-critical, and dissatisfied with certain features because of the recurring body criticism. Some women shared feelings of helplessness and powerlessness in their family dynamics to prevent further instances of body criticism. . . .

These women noted that family members often rationalize pointing out flaws by framing them as a "joke" (Chloe) or "poking fun" (Elaine) to make them less upsetting. Other women, including Chrissie, voiced their resentment and questioned the futility of offering negative feedback, particularly when the perceived appearance deficits are something they cannot control. . . .

Family Conflict

Unsolicited comments from family members seemed to intersect with the quality of the family relationships. Women who reported more instances of tension, intergenerational family conflict (e.g., discrepancies and disagreements over adherence to family values, practices, expectations), and lack of affection in their families appeared more negatively affected by instances of family criticism. . . . Conversely, women who reported feeling accepted and supported in their family relationships were less likely to internalize instances of teasing as a reflection of their self-worth. These women, like Nancy, tended to deemphasize the value of appearance and recognized the importance of appreciating other desirable parts of the self, such as health, intelligence, and personality:

> I think it's just 'cause, like, I get a lot of love from my family because we have a close relationship. So it's like, I think from that, I feel good about myself . . . And so it's sort of, like, this feeling that even if your body changes they'll still accept you for who you are, like it doesn't matter what you look like on the outside 'cause they know what you are on the inside.

CATEGORY 4: PEER INFLUENCES

Women also described the roles of peers in influencing their body image. Women described the normalization of women, commenting on each other's bodies and instances where feedback is (a) "supposed to be a compliment" ($n = 9$) but instead casts doubt and fuels insecurity. Feedback from women motivated upward body image comparisons ($n = 19$) and seemed to increase self-objectification of disliked body parts. Unlike feedback from same-sex peers, women believed men evaluate their attractiveness ($n = 14$).

It's Supposed to Be a Compliment

All women shared detailed accounts of receiving feedback about their appearance from same-sex peers. A few women discussed the confusing dynamics of receiving compliments from other women; these women were often skeptical of these compliments, which may be due to modesty but also reflective of the self-deprecating context in which it is given, as noted by Nancy:

> I don't really know how to respond to it. Because it's like, this is how I was born. This is what I look like, I can't change anything about it. And it's, I guess it's meant as a compliment, but it's, I dunno, I mean I don't go around saying like, "Oh you're normal size."

. . . Furthermore, a few women, including Elaine, described the difficulty of accepting compliments about features (e.g., small breast size) they were not comfortable with or wanted to change. Some women described feeling infantilized by being called "cute" rather than "hot" (Jenny, Grace) and self-critical when comments from women occurred in a context where they are already vulnerable and exposed (e.g., undressing). During these moments, women shared feeling hyper-vigilant about their body image and perceived appearance-deficits and engaged in more negative self-talk about their bodies. Unlike feedback from family members, feedback from female friends was more often disputed, rather than accepted at face value.

Upward Body Image Comparisons

Same-sex peer feedback often motivated further body image comparisons between women that intensified self-consciousness and accentuated disliked body image features. Even though a majority of women identified the self-destructive risks of body image comparisons, almost all women reported engaging in some form of comparisons. Shabani described it as a "cycle of self-consciousness" where the subsequent anxiety and self-criticism from body image comparisons often motivated further appearance checking and comparisons to other women.

Nearly all women, including Esther, reported instances of upward body image comparisons, whereby they evaluated their own bodies in reference to a woman who seemed more desirable, attractive, or confident than themselves:

> I went to [School name] a few weeks ago to visit one of my friends, and she's the ideal woman, like she's blonde, she has blue eyes, and she's skinny but she also has curves. So being around her made me self-conscious, 'cause she basically had everything . . . I felt really self-conscious about my body. And usually I'm not, like when I'm by myself, but when I compare myself to other people like her, it's like wow, I'm not like her?

These comparisons seemed to increase body dissatisfaction but also a degree of envy, awe, and appreciation for others' beauty. A few women ($n = 3$) reported actively engaging in healthier body image comparisons that were less self-deprecating in nature and less likely to be personalized to their own appearance. Lin illustrates this phenomenon:

> Mostly I think, "Oh wow, she's really pretty. I wish I was this pretty." But also like, I'm glad for her that she's pretty and I hope she's happy with herself. I used to be a lot more jealous. But like, I said, as I've become more okay with my own body I've become less prone to feelings like that.

Most women ($n = 11$) reported comparing their bodies to other Asian women due to "genetic factors" that make it seem like it "would be a waste of time for [them] to try to compare [themselves] to other people" (Chrissie). Yet sometimes comparisons to other Asian women would heighten awareness of body image concerns, particularly in feeling fatter (Jacqueline) or curvier (Lin) than other Asian female peers. . . .

Men Evaluate Your Attractiveness

Many women expressed ambivalence about feedback from male peers and expressed that their feelings were contingent on the context in which it is received. In more sexualized domains (e.g., bars), heterosexual women such as Adeline reported wanting to impress men and wishing for compliments or approval about their appearance:

> I think that with men, I definitely try to check up on my appearance more because I want to be attractive to them, I guess. I definitely would want to look better to them versus if I'm just going to hang out with some girlfriends, it's not really a big deal. I can look like a bum. I feel like I can be more natural around females versus males because I feel like males have a certain expectation of what you're supposed to look like, and I don't feel like defying that.

Yet simultaneously, these women reported feeling more evaluated, uncomfortable, and exposed in these contexts because the feedback sexually objectified their bodies thereby making it appear more threatening. The inherent power differentials between men and women made it difficult for women to believe that they could negotiate, challenge, or dispute the feedback. Unlike feedback from women, feedback from male peers, while acceptable in desexualized contexts (e.g., dorm room with friends), was more unwelcome in sexualized domains. While women engaged in strategies to monitor and manage their body image beliefs, a majority of women appeared to feel "constantly under scrutiny" (Chrissie) from both male and female peers.

CATEGORY 5: IDENTITY MANAGEMENT PROCESSES

Many women described their process of identity management, which often either enhanced or hindered their ability to navigate restrictive beauty ideals, multiple minority stressors, and interpersonal difficulties. We identified two subgroups of women with distinct identity management processes: (a) the integrated identity appreciation group ($n = 5$), which included women with a sense of positive regard about their identities as Asian American women and an ability to integrate multiple identity statuses into a unified self-image, and (b) the disintegrated identity depreciation group ($n = 5$), which included women with a negative regard about their identity(s) and difficulty integrating multiple identity statuses into a unified self-image.

Integrated Identity Appreciation

Some women ($n = 5$) possessed a heightened sense of self-appreciation, self-respect, and critical consciousness that served as a protective buffer against minority stressors (e.g., experiences of racism, sexism). Regardless of their multiple marginalized identities (e.g., race, gender, and sexual orientation), their unwavering self-compassion and acceptance promoted a sense of individuality and self-efficacy to navigate experiences that could increase body dissatisfaction, such as family body criticism. These women often discussed the racial socialization processes in their family, whereby their parents would explain racial inequalities, express pride in their heritage, and explore tactics (e.g., code-switching) for coping with stereotypes. Many of these women were also surrounded by feminist female family members who imbued the importance of self-confidence and authenticity, while deemphasizing the salience of physical appearance and comparisons to peers. The messages learned from family members and feminist role models were often internalized by women and used to challenge restrictive beauty standards and increase body acceptance. These women expressed resourcefulness and agency in crafting a personal definition of what it means to be an Asian American woman. Sunita described her understanding that her identity as an Indian woman can be fluid and crafted in ways that promote belonging without negating other aspects of who she is. She shared "feeling comfortable" with her appearance and uninterested in putting effort into her appearance simply to appease men. Similarly, Jenny and Fatima described their journeys of integrating multiple racial backgrounds into a cohesive identity, which might permit greater flexibility in ascribing to multiple cultural beauty norms because of their racially ambiguous features. Fatima's sense of pride in her identities as a multiracial, bisexual woman and her confidence helped her sustain a positive body image and restrain from making comparisons:

> I don't really think I find myself looking at beauty norms because, I mean, those people who you see, like those people are very rare. Like not everyone is going to look like that. So you can't expect to look like that. So then, what's the point of comparing yourself to them?

. . .

Disintegrated Identity Depreciation

Unlike women with integrated identities and a sense of self-appreciation, other women ($n = 5$) expressed less self-acceptance and more difficulty functioning in multiple cultural contexts without compromising their racial or gender identity. In comparison, they did not possess the same resiliency in coping with their multiple, marginalized identities and this in turn may be reflected in more negative body image beliefs. These women often described feeling like a "third culture kid" and felt a lack of belonging in both their host culture and the U.S. culture. For example, Jacqueline shared that traditional gender role expectations of Vietnamese women "clash" with American culture and that the normalization in Vietnam to "cover up flaws" was contributing to her desire for plastic surgery. Some women also immersed themselves more fully in Western culture by dating White men or by socializing primarily with White peers. At times, this resulted in their idealization of White features and heightened self-criticism.

These women often described being "on-guard" (Chrissie) and hyper-vigilant about their outward appearance. They also experienced difficulty fully embracing their Asian identity or described a fragmented sense of self, whereby one or more identities were concealed or depreciated. Chloe shared worrying that others think she is "ugly" and believed that it would be "easier if she were White" because she would "fit in." Arpana was diagnosed with Polycystic Ovarian Syndrome, which resulted in hair loss, weight gain, and acne. She described disconnecting from her Bengali community at school, the lack of openness in her family, exposure to race-related teasing, and a pressure to be the "perfect daughter." Her experience with multiple minority-status stressors across locations of gender, race, and disability appeared to heighten self-denigration and self-objectification:

> I had, like, hair loss and like a lot of hair is something that is seen as something you should value [in Bengali culture]. Just having, like being constantly reminded, that I have to make sure I'm tweezing my eye brows, especially because my hair grows faster, like body hair, so like keeping on top of that can be exhausting. And just, like, seeing my other friends that don't have that issue at all. Acne as well, like that sucks.

Experiences of oppression, coupled with negative evaluations of their social identities and feelings of exclusion and isolation, seemed to make it harder for women to develop a sense of self-validation and body acceptance.

COPING AND RESILIENCY

All women reported a range of coping strategies to increase body satisfaction, confidence, and self-worth. Some women expressed an appreciation for their body ($n = 12$), which encompassed admiration and appreciation for diverse beauty representations, valuing the functionality of the body (i.e., what the body can do), and valuing health over appearance. Through recognizing that multiple body shapes and sizes can be attractive, women were able to challenge unrealistic beauty ideals and restrain from making comparisons as with Chloe:

> I guess because, like, I have a lot of friends on the internet and, like, they are all different shapes and sizes and it just kind of makes you more aware how normal it is to not have a completely flat stomach or a thigh gap or something.

Women also described a sense of body acceptance ($n = 15$) or a genuine acceptance and respect for all aspects of their bodies. Women described creating an individualized appearance, rather than attempting to strictly replicate Western or Asian standards of beauty, and embracing their bodies in spite of flaws, as stated by Indra, "you don't always have to work and be prettier or have a better body image, sometimes you just need to work on feeling more comfortable with yourself."

Some women discussed restructuring cognitions about their appearance ($n = 12$), most of which entailed reframing self-defeating, distorted ideas about their bodies. Some women discounted negative feedback from family members about their weight, focused on positive or liked aspects of their bodies when feeling self-conscious, or sought additional perspectives about their appearance from peers. Jamie described consciously challenging negative thoughts about her appearance that arose from family criticism:

> I kind of wanted to be stronger than that, and so, I didn't want to give in to what other people thought. I wanted to you know, build myself up on the inside so that it wouldn't matter to me as much. I feel like that was more important to me than to be what they wanted me to be.

. . .

Moreover, women discussed the value of finding positive role models ($n = 7$) who are empowering, supportive, and strengths-focused. These role models were often female peers who deemphasized the importance of appearance and offered encouraging feedback, as reported by Sunita:

> I always surrounded myself by people who I really liked. So all of my friends are really supportive. And it's not like that friend group whose like, aw man, I gained like three pounds. Like I can't eat this and this. The people I surround myself with have the same kind of viewpoints in terms of body image. I never really felt pressured to change what I do to fit a better body image.

. . .

DISCUSSION

. . . We found that Asian American women's body image narratives were contextualized within numerous systems of oppression, including racism, sexism, restrictive gender expectations, and cultural definitions of beauty. Women described their difficulties navigating cultural differences in defining attraction, race-related teasing, and sexual objectification, family body criticism, appearance-related comparisons, and identity management. These experiences influenced women's positive and negative beliefs about their body structure, facial features, and skin complexion or tone, which in turn prompted appearance-related consequences, such as body surveillance or body dissatisfaction. Although most women disclosed experiences in which they felt exposed, objectified, and exoticized, all women developed numerous coping strategies and resiliencies. Women described appreciating and accepting their bodies, restructuring self-defeating thoughts, seeking empowering role models, and investing more effort into their appearance. These coping strategies acted as a buffer against experiences of oppression by promoting positive body image beliefs and appeared to directly influence positive appearance-related consequences, such as feeling confident.

The experiences of oppression at the intersections of gender and race may contribute to unique sources of strain that distinctly influence body image beliefs for Asian American women. Given that only a few quantitative studies (see Cheng, 2014) examine how race-related factors (e.g., racism, race-related teasing) correspond with body image dissatisfaction among Asian American women, this study contributes to the literature by exploring the roles of both racism and sexism in shaping body image beliefs. . . .

BODY IMAGE BELIEFS

Consistent with prior conceptualizations of body image (Cash, Morrow, Hrabosky, & Perry, 2004), women described the multifaceted nature of their body images that were constructed and managed based on evaluations from self, important others (e.g., parents, romantic partners, and peers), and society (e.g., media). Previous research (Bearman, Martinez, & Stice, 2006) indicates that a desire for thinness and weight loss represent the most salient body image concerns for women. However, Asian American women in our study suggested that specific racialized features (e.g., eye shape) also influenced how they perceived their bodies. Our findings are supported by quantitative studies (Forbes & Frederick, 2008; Frederick et al., 2016) that suggest Asian American women experience dissatisfaction with racialized physical characteristics (e.g., face

shape, eye size, and skin tone) that may predispose risk for eating disorder symptoms. Racialized features appear to play an important role in appearance evaluation for Asian American women.

CAUSAL CONDITIONS AND CONSEQUENCES

Women frequently described the role of cultural beauty standards in perpetuating hierarchies of beauty and unattainable beauty ideals. Although women in our study, across ethnicities, described a normalized pressure to be thin, they received unique racialized messages that Asian women in particular are expected to be thin. Other studies also suggest that Asian American women are subject to an even stricter standard of thinness (Smart & Tsong, 2014; Wardle et al., 2006) than other women. The women in our study experienced unique conflict in being considered "fatter" than other Asian women while striving to obtain idealized Western curvaceous features. It is possible that these women experienced heightened levels of biculturative stress, or difficulty integrating and balancing multiple salient cultural identities, which increased risk for body image dissatisfaction (Tsong & Smart, 2015).

Women, across ethnic backgrounds, also shared unique experiences of racialized sexual objectification (i.e., being perceived as doll-like or exotic) that appeared to increase body surveillance and self-consciousness. A majority of women described experiencing racial microaggressions that were associated with a loss of individuality and increased self-objectification. It is possible that women who experience race-related teasing and racial microaggressions may feel more pressure to assimilate to Western standards of attractiveness to avoid being singled out. The biological limitations of achieving Western beauty norms may leave some women vulnerable to body dissatisfaction. These results support findings from quantitative studies that found that perceived discrimination and race-related teasing were associated with more body dissatisfaction and greater endorsement of media ideals (Cheng, 2014; Iyer & Haslam, 2003; Reddy & Crowther, 2007).

Family body criticism, particularly weight-related teasing, was a recurring theme that also appeared to heighten body dissatisfaction. Although many comments were unwanted, a few women described family body criticism as a normal cultural practice and a display of affection. It is possible that due to cultural styles of communication and a desire to respect elders (Smart et al., 2011), women did not dispute or contest this feedback. While these findings coincide with other studies (Smart & Tsong, 2014), this study extends the literature by describing how family body criticism intersects with the quality of family dynamics. That is, women who reported expectations of perfectionism in their families, and who reported more intergenerational family conflict, seemed more likely to internalize instances of family body criticism and felt worse about their bodies. This is partly supported by Frederick, Kelly, Latner, Sandhu, and Tsong's (2016) results that expectations of perfectionism in the family were associated with heightened self-criticism and preoccupation with appearance.

Aside from body criticisms, women recounted instances of receiving compliments, from mostly female Asian peers, about their thinness, daintiness, and small breast size. During these instances, women described feeling exposed and vulnerable, which fueled body image comparisons to Asian peers who were often viewed as more physically desirable and petite. This upward social comparison feedback loop, wherein feedback motivates further appearance checking and comparisons which provoke further feedback, seemed to intensify body dissatisfaction. Smart and Tsong (2014) also found that body dissatisfaction increased when women compared themselves to ethnically similar peers. While comparisons to those with "superior" appearance has been linked to body dissatisfaction (Myers, Ridolfi, Crowther, & Ciesla, 2012), the race of the comparison target group is an underexplored area of research that may influence appearance evaluation.

Small subgroups of women also described their experiences of identity management and how they either intensified or buffered against contextual conditions that predisposed them for risk of negative body image. To our knowledge, no other study has explored how management of multiple marginalized identities may relate to body image. . . . In our sample, Asian American women managed structural inequalities associated with marginalized identities by either forming a holistic identity (e.g., integrated

identity appreciation) or silencing aspects of the self and by compartmentalizing identities (e.g., disintegrated identity depreciation). Women with integrated identity appreciation described a positive regard about their multiple identities and self-appreciation for their uniqueness and individuality. Compared to other women, they seemed to use more coping strategies, such as discounting negative feedback and restraining from making comparisons. These women also discussed more supportive family relationships, which seemed to facilitate more acceptance of their bodies and less emphasis on appearance as a determinant of one's worth. In contrast, women with disintegrated identity depreciation reported feeling less affirmed in their identities and were subsequently more self-critical and preoccupied with their appearance. They discussed more family conflict and the difficulty of navigating minority stressors independently, particularly when their parents did not model how to cope with race-related distress. Previous literature has suggested that protective and proactive socialization messages transmitted in the family, such as promoting cultural pride, can promote resilience in overcoming race-related stressors (Hughes et al., 2006). The unique stressors of these women across identities of gender, race, and disability, coupled with limited protective racial socialization messages, might have played a role in their body dissatisfaction.
. . .

CONCLUSIONS

Our study provides an inclusive, comprehensive model for understanding Asian American women's body image experiences. We sought to understand how Asian American women conceptualize body image, the sociocultural factors that influence body image, the consequences of these factors on appearance evaluation, and sources of coping and resiliency for managing these experiences through an intersectional lens. This study advances the current literature by underscoring how structures of inequality, such as hierarchies of beauty and power differentials between men and women, and interpersonal contexts (e.g., media, family, and peers), influence Asian American women's body image. By understanding Asian American women's body image as socially constructed, fluid, and embedded in systems of power, clinicians and researchers can more deeply understand how experiences of exclusion and marginalization can heighten risk for body dissatisfaction. Our study suggests that understanding the intersectional effects of racism and sexism is integral to understanding Asian American women's body dissatisfaction.

REFERENCES

Barnett, H. L., Keel, P. K., & Conoscenti, L. M. (2001). Body type preferences in Asian and Caucasian college students. *Sex Roles, 45*, 867–878. doi:10.1023/A:1015600705749

Bearman, S. K., Martinez, E., & Stice, E. (2006). The skinny on body dissatisfaction: A longitudinal study of adolescent girls. *Journal of Youth and Adolescence, 35*, 217–229. doi:10.1007/s10964-005-9010-9

Bordo, S. (2009). Not just "a White girl's thing": The changing face of food and body image problems. In M. Burns & H. Mason (Eds.), *Critical feminist perspectives on eating disorders* (pp. 46–59). New York, NY: Routledge.

Britton, L., Martz, D., Bazzini, D., Curtin, L., & LeaShomb, A. (2006). Fat talk and self-presentation of body image: Is there a social norm for women to self-degrade? *Body Image, 3*, 247–254. doi:10.1016/j.bodyim.2006.05.006

Cachelin, F. M., Veisel, C., Barzegarnazari, E., & Striegel-Moore, R. H. (2000). Disordered eating, acculturation, and treatment-seeking in a community sample of Hispanic, Asian, Black, and White Women. *Psychology of Women Quarterly, 24*, 244–253. doi:10.1111/j.1471-6402.2000.tb00206.x

Cash, T. F., Morrow, J. A., Hrabosky, J. I., & Perry, A. A. (2004). How has body image changed? A cross-sectional investigation of college women and men from 1983–2001. *Journal of Consulting and Clinical Psychology, 72*, 1081–1089. doi:10.1037/0022-006X.72.6.1081

Castillo, L. G., Zahn, M. P., & Cano, M. A. (2012). Predictors of familial acculturative stress in Asian American college students. *Journal of College Counseling, 15*, 52–64. doi:10.1002/j.2161-1882.2012.00005.x

Charmaz, K. (2006). *Constructing grounded theory: A practical guide through qualitative analysis*. London, England: Sage.

Cheng, H. (2014). Disordered eating among Asian/Asian American women: Racial and cultural factors as correlates. *The Counseling Psychologist, 42*, 821–851. doi:10.1177/0011000014535472

Cole, E. R. (2009). Intersectionality and research in psychology. *American Psychologist, 64*, 170–180. doi:10.1037/a0014564

Cummins, L. H., & Lehman, J. (2007). Eating disorders and body image concerns in Asian American women: Assessment and treatment from a multicultural and feminist perspective. *Eating Disorders, 15*, 217–230. doi:10.1080/10640260701323474

Cummins, L. H., Simmons, A. M., & Zane, N. S. (2005). Eating disorders in Asian populations: A critique of current approaches to the study of culture, ethnicity, and eating disorders. *American Journal of Orthopsychiatry, 75*, 553–574. doi:10.1037/0002-9432.75.4.553

Else-Quest, N. M., & Hyde, J. S. (2016). Intersectionality in quantitative psychological research: I. Theoretical and epistemological issues. *Psychology of Women Quarterly, 40*, 155–170. doi:10.1177/0361684316629797

Forbes, G. B., & Frederick, D. A. (2008). The UCLA Body Project II: Breast and body dissatisfaction among African, Asian, European, and Hispanic American college women. *Sex Roles, 58*, 449–457. doi:10.1007/s11199-007-9362-6

Frederick, D. A., Kelly, M. C., Latner, J. D., Sandhu, G., & Tsong, Y. (2016). Body image and face image in Asian American and White women: Examining associations with surveillance, construal of self, perfectionism, and sociocultural pressures. *Body Image, 16*, 113–125. doi:10.1016/j.bodyim.2015.12.002

Glaser, B. G., & Strauss, A. L. (1967). *The discovery of grounded theory*. New York, NY: Adline.

Grabe, S., & Hyde, J. S. (2006). Ethnicity and body dissatisfaction among women in the United States: A meta-analysis. *Psychological Bulletin, 132*, 622–640. doi:10.1037/0033-2909.132.4.622

Hughes, D., Rodriguez, J., Smith, E. P., Johnson, D. J., Stevenson, H. C., & Spicer, P. (2006). Parents' ethnic racial socialization practices: A review of research and directions for future study. *Developmental Psychology, 42*, 747–770. doi:10.1037/0012-1649.42.5.747

Iyer, D. S., & Haslam, N. (2003). Body image and eating disturbance among south Asian-American women: The role of racial teasing. *International Journal of Eating Disorders, 34,* 142–147. doi:10.1002/eat.10170

Johnson, F., & Wardle, J. (2005). Dietary restraint, body dissatisfaction, and psychological distress: A prospective analysis. *Journal of Abnormal Psychology, 114,* 119–125. doi:10.1037/0021-843X.114.1.119

Koff, E., Benavage, A., & Wong, B. (2001). Body-image attitudes and psychological functioning in Euro-American and Asian-American college women. *Psychological Reports, 88,* 917–928. doi:10.2466/pr0.2001.88.3.917

Lau, A. S. M., Lum, S. K., Chronister, K. M., & Forrest, L. (2006). Asian American college women's body image: A pilot study. *Cultural Diversity and Ethnic Minority Psychology, 12,* 259–274. doi:10.1037/1099-9809.12.2.259

Lee, D. L., & Ahn, S. (2011). Racial discrimination and Asian mental health: A meta-analysis. *The Counseling Psychologist, 39,* 463–489. doi:10.1177/0011000010381791

Lott, B., & Saxon, S. (2002). The influence of ethnicity, social class, and context on judgments about U.S. women. *Journal of Social Psychology, 142,* 281–299. doi:10.1080/00224540209603913

Myers, Taryn A., Ridolfi, Danielle R., Crowther, Janis H., & Ciesla, Jeffery A. (2012). The impact of appearance-focused social comparisons on body image disturbance in the naturalistic environment: The roles of thin-ideal internalization and feminist beliefs. *Body Image, 9*(3), 342–351.

Nouri, M., Hill, L. G., & Orrell-Valente, J. K. (2011). Media exposure, internalization of the thin ideal and body dissatisfaction: Comparing Asian American and European American college females. *Body Image, 8,* 366–372. doi:10.1016/j.bodyim.2011.05.008

Patton, M. Q. (2002). *Qualitative research and evaluation methods* (3rd ed.). Thousand Oaks, CA: Sage.

Phan, T., & Tylka, T. L. (2006). Exploring a model and moderators of disordered eating with Asian American college women. *Journal of Counseling Psychology, 53,* 36–47. doi:10.1037/0022-0167.53.1.36

Rakhkovskaya, L. M., & Warren, C. S. (2014). Ethnic identity, thin-ideal internalization, and eating pathology in ethnically diverse college women. *Body Image, 11,* 438–445. doi:10.1016/j.bodyim.2014.07.003

Reddy, S. D., & Crowther, J. H. (2007). Teasing, acculturation, and cultural conflict: Psychosocial correlates of body image and eating attitudes among South Asian women. *Cultural Diversity and Ethnic Minority Psychology, 13,* 45–53. doi:10.1037/1099-9809.13.1.45

Sabik, N. J., Cole, E. R., & Ward, L. M. (2010). Are all minority women equally buffered from negative body image? Intra-ethnic moderators of the buffering hypothesis. *Psychology of Women Quarterly, 34,* 139–151. doi:10.1111/j.1471-6402.2010.01557.x

Shields, S. A. (2008). Gender: An intersectionality perspective. *Sex Roles, 59,* 301–311. doi:10.1007/s11199-008-9501-8

Smart, R. H., & Tsong, Y. (2014). Weight, body dissatisfaction, and disordered eating: Asian American women's perspectives. *Asian American Journal of Psychology, 5,* 344–352. doi:10.1037/a0035599

Smart, R., Tsong, Y., Mejia, O. L., Hayashino, D., & Braaten, M. E. T. (2011). Therapists' experiences treating Asian American women with eating disorders. *Professional Psychology: Research and Practice, 42,* 308–315. doi:10.1037/a0024179

Stice, E., & Shaw, H. E. (2002). Role of body dissatisfaction in the onset and maintenance of eating pathology: A synthesis of research findings. *Journal of Psychosomatic Research, 53,* 985–993. doi:10.1016/S0022-3999(02)00488-9

Strauss, A. L., & Corbin, J. (1998). *Basics of qualitative research: Techniques and procedures for developing grounded theory* (2nd ed.). London, England: Sage.

Tsai, G., Curbow, B., & Heinberg, L. (2003). Sociocultural and developmental influences on body dissatisfaction and disordered eating attitudes and behaviors of Asian American women. *The Journal of Nervous and Mental Disease, 191,* 309–318. doi:10.1097/01.NMD.0000066153.64331.10

Tsong, Y., & Smart, R. (2015). The role of cultural beliefs in disordered eating among Asian-American women. *Asian American Journal of Psychology, 6,* 342–349. doi:10.1037/aap0000029

Wardle, J., Haase, A. M., & Steptoe, A. (2006). Body image and weight control in young adults: International comparisons in university students from 22 countries. *International Journal of Obesity, 30,* 644–651. doi:10.1038/sj.ijo.0803050

Warner, L. R. (2008). A best practices guide to intersectional approaches in psychological research. *Sex Roles, 59,* 454–463. doi:10.1007/s11199-008-9504-5

White, J. W., Russo, N. F., & Travis, C. B. (2001). Feminism and the decade of behavior. *Psychology of Women Quarterly, 25,* 267–279. doi:10.1111/1471-6402.00028

Wilson, T. G. (2000). Eating disorders and addiction. *Drugs and Society, 15,* 87–101. doi:10.1300/J023v15n01_05

28. *FAT IS STILL A FEMINIST ISSUE*

SUSIE ORBACH (2018)

When I sat down to write *Fat Is A Feminist Issue* 40 years ago I never dreamed, or feared, it would still be in print today. I naively hoped my book would change the world. By analysing and suggesting solutions to body and eating problems, I imagined they would disappear. But in truth, of course, when I was writing about girls' and women's body and eating problems, I was writing about inequality, too. And inequality is stubborn. It didn't look it in 1978, at the height of what we now call second wave feminism. Everything was up for being rethought—families, bodies, education, science, medicine, class, racism, money, sex.

When feminism first appeared, I hadn't much understood it. At school, we were encouraged to compete with boys for Oxbridge places while soaking in knowledge which would, when the time came for marriage, delight and please our husbands. It seemed ever so dull. Then, suddenly the Sixties spoke to women about their own experience. There was a spectacular protest at the Miss America beauty contest in New Jersey in 1968. There, a woman's body was marked up as a cow ready for butchering, while a "freedom" trash can was ready for women to dump in bras and hair rollers, and pots and pans. It was the first hint that the way we personally felt about (and suffered) beauty, bodies and caring was a social issue. It looked like the world was changing. And when I published *Fat Is A Feminist Issue*, the message was taken to a wide audience through women's magazines such as *Woman's Own*, aimed mainly at working-class mothers.

Fat Is A Feminist Issue talked about our lived experience: how preoccupied we could become with eating, not eating and avoiding fat. Emotionally schooled to see our value as both sexual beings for others and midwives to their desires, we found ourselves often depleted and empty, and caught up in a kind of compulsive giving. Eating became our source of soothing. We stopped our mouths with food, and I proposed we could learn to exchange food—when we weren't hungry—for words.

So far so good. Many of us started challenging the homogeneity of what constituted beauty. We stopped worrying and dared to live from our bodies. But we never saw the backlash coming, or the ingenious forms it would take, from the now rather innocent ("Because you're worth it") to the downright nefarious practices of industries that were growing rich on the making of body insecurity. And that was way before social media and the beauty bloggers with their, yes, millions of followers, would begin to reap money as daily beauty labour got instituted in a way that before then perhaps only a Hollywood makeup artist would recognise. Beauty work became relentless and, with it, the ubiquity of judgment and failure. Judgments and failures which, once internalised, destabilised girls' relationship to their bodies and—as if that wasn't enough—created an insecurity that hurt their minds.

The story of the past 40 years is grim. It's a story of malice, of greed and of mendacity. Not content with destabilising the eating of many western women and exporting body hatred all over the world as a sign of modernity, the combined forces of what investigative health reporter Alicia Mundy so aptly termed "Obesity Inc" set about to create new so-called disease entities; these would medicalise and pathologise people's relationship to food and bodies so successfully that vast industries would grow up to treat problems that these industries had themselves instigated. In January we learned that one in three women in the UK won't go for their smear tests. Why? Is it because they don't know about them? No, they are invited by their doctors by text, email and letter. Why then? Because they feel so bad about their bodies.

This should alarm us. And yet sadly it doesn't, because we know how ubiquitous bad body feeling is. It is constantly stoked by visual images which invade us, by pronouncements disguised as health directives, by blandishments to do, be, brand, mark ourselves in ways that reward not the human body as a place we dwell in but as an object to enhance the profits of the beauty, fashion, diet, cosmetic surgery, food and exercise industries, no matter one's age.

So what has changed? Go back 20 years. The porn industry is being mainstreamed. Fashion magazines are normalising pornographic images of girls. Preteen girls with legs spread wide apart are looking to camera with a combination of allure, innocence and nonchalance. The girls who read them start going for Brazilian waxes. They don't learn about labias and clitorises in school, they learn about how to put on a condom. Their genitals are not to be in view for themselves. And when they are in view, they are presented as inadequate and available for labiaplasty.

If we go back four years, we see the development of cosmetic surgery apps, games marketed to little girls in which they prepare for the surgery they will have when they are old enough. Already at six they will have been targeted with make-up and fashion and bras. Hourly vigilance is yet to come but the notion of a body ready and available for reconstruction is firmly planted. Indeed, many a girl will already have seen baby pictures of herself that have been digitally altered, so that the idea of "perfecting" and "fixing" becomes part of just what is. It is as normalised as the troubled eating she can expect in her journey through life.

By the time they become preteens, girls have been living on their smartphones. That is where life happens and the saturation of the screen with images and likes, with its constant entreaty to be approved

of, should give us pause. Beauty labour has become part of girls' and women's lives and now that feminism is back on the agenda we can say, once again, part of our oppression. But, of course, it isn't experienced like that. It is felt as the expression of personal agency, with the promise that looking good is doing good. But I know from the young women I work with that the search for likes is rather more troubling than that. It is an often desperate search for approval, for safety, for body acceptance—a frequently elusive quest.

If that young woman comes to parenting, frantic body preoccupation may have so invaded and insinuated itself into her that she will have schemes for managing food and managing appearance. Midwives and health professionals tell me they have noticed a dramatic change. Today pre- and postpartum mums can show considerable anxiety about their body self, so much so that the rhythm of early bonding is interrupted by rules and regulations, rather than the getting to know of one's own body's capacities and the wishes of the baby. For many, the parenting websites with their contradictory and commercially led "advice," from recommendations for tummy tucks after your C-section to making a bespoke spreadsheet to track your feeding schedule, have turned postpartum into a straitjacket in which getting into pre-pregnancy jeans is the goal. And the anxiety the mothering person might well feel will be inadvertently transmitted to their baby, who will journey through life frightened of food and confused about their body self. A further tragedy.

This is then exacerbated by a rapacious food industry—from the diet promoters to the so-called clean eating movement to the manufacturers of non-food foods. The sole aim of the latter is to produce replicas masquerading as potato chips or cheese for children's lunchboxes but whose chemical composition strives to stimulate their bliss point: the umami, sweet, crispy feel that means taste buds are stimulated rather than hunger addressed. Appetite, desire, is being undermined by the smells and tastes which beckon all day and yet often don't deliver the nourishment we crave.

When you grow up absorbing the idea that food is quasi-dangerous, it is hard to know how to handle it.

There are no end of experts selling their wares whose books and products end up generating enormous profits, and Weight Watchers' newest push into the teen market has been criticised for potentially leading to teenagers becoming fixated on dieting. So, too, with other food and diet fads. The desperation that exists to be at peace and dwell in our bodies clashes with the knowledge that such schemas promote or reinforce confusion about appetite and desire. They don't deliver peace. They deliver confusion. They deliver hurt.

Another huge industry is the world fashion market, worth $2.4tn. The UK market alone is worth £26bn a year, with a £1,000 spend per inhabitant. I love clothes but how have we been persuaded to buy that much? The penetration of visual culture says how we look is so essential to our existence that we must spend, spend, spend. And that spend doesn't include the cost of the clean-up from the fashion industry, the toxins in the water and the sweatshop conditions here and in China and Bangladesh. If the industry continues at its current rate, it will be using a staggering 26% of the carbon budget in 2050. I mention these statistics because it is sometimes possible to feel that when we are talking of bodies we aren't engaging in serious economic and social issues, but we are. We are talking of large industries and excessive hours spent in persuading us to labour over transforming while attempting to live from our bodies.

It's hard to get the figures that big pharma makes from products aimed at our bodily transformations.

They guard them. But we do know that when they launch a diet drug, they spend a fortune marketing and defending it even when it doesn't work or causes medical damage. I could go on. There is the cosmetic industry, the cosmetic surgery industry, the doll market, the role of internet beauty bloggers who have followers in their millions and of course the horror for youngsters of living online and being continually scrutinised. But I want us to think for a moment about #MeToo and Time's Up, where we can see a line, not such a wiggly line, from pervasive bad body feeling to the compromising positions women have been put into in all the spaces where they work and love. If we weren't continually assaulted by the merchants of body hatred, we would not be as vulnerable to the assaults. I'm not saying they wouldn't happen; misogyny ensures that. But the shame, the hiding, the confusions that beset us would diminish and we would be stronger in our fightback and our fight to control our own bodies.

The body has become a political project. From rape as a weapon of war to the internal belief that we must be constantly wary about our appetites, to limiting ourselves individually and collectively because so much of our energy is misemployed, we have to act together to find ways through these minefields. The energy from #MeToo, with its reinvigoration of feminism, can help us say enough is enough. There's just too much anguish, too much sorrow. We need more rage, more refusal and more love.

29. UNDERSTANDING TRANSGENDER AND MEDICALLY ASSISTED GENDER TRANSITION
JAMIE LINDEMANN NELSON (2016)

INTRODUCTION

It's an interesting time to be alive if your sense of yourself is out of alignment with parts of your body that traditionally have been taken to determine your gender. "Transgender" has in recent years become a (generally) viable, commodious, diverse social identity, one that has achieved some semblance of legal parity with other fundamental parts of people's identities. We can see people like ourselves in positions of responsibility in government, industry, academia, health care, in the police and military, and the arts. We see more realistic depictions of transgender lives in the media, conveyed without scorn.

Yet if scorn is no longer routine in the media, it is still painfully, and for some of us, fatally present in day-to-day interactions; if laws at the national level and in some states and localities are moving us toward recognition as full and equal citizens, there are many people who still fear and disdain us. We've become targets for politicians seeking to ban access to public accommodations in an effort to curry favor with the fearful by blocking further social uptake of how we make sense of ourselves and of gender [1].

This is not to say that transgender people are the only group who has sought to revise what gender means—or who have experienced backlashes for these efforts. Reimagining what gender is, and what it means in our own and other's lives, has been an increasingly important feature of social life throughout the last century. Women in particular have challenged limitations on their lives that traditionally had been seen as part and parcel of the "natural facts" of gender. Feminist thinkers and activists have done substantial work in responding to these challenges and in articulating the values and concepts—for example, that the agency of women must be fully respected, that their physical integrity must be honored, that the importance of their needs and desires are not lessened by their biology—that they embody. The upshot for both women and men has been slow but steady movement toward the possibility of living in ways that are more equitable, less hemmed in by rigid gender roles, and more reflective of these values.

MEDICINE AND WHAT GENDER MEANS

Medicine has played both progressive and regressive roles in this general process and has had a distinctive involvement in the lives of transgender people that extends at least back into the early decades of the twentieth century. Medical engagement gained momentum as the century wore on and academic centers and specialty societies dedicated to transgender-specific care began to appear. Authoritative standards of care governing access to endocrinological and surgical responses to "gender identity disorder" were first promulgated in 1979, and have been in continual evolution since [2]. However, while medicine was

trying to help some people liberate themselves from the alienating experiences and expectations attached to their birth-assigned gender, it also tried to isolate the challenge such efforts posed to ordinary understandings of gender. That is, if your gender identity did not match your anatomy, you were understood to have a mental illness resistant to psychiatric intervention, but amenable to physical intervention. Surgery, for example, was often depicted in a *faute de mieux* fashion—as facilitating not a real "change of sex" but merely a harm-reducing simulacrum that preserved a familiar and safe gender binary. That is, society could rest easy with medicine pathologizing gender "deviance" and proposing a clinical strategy for explaining and containing it: nobody's genitals were going under the knife unless they had the right kind of illness, and besides, nothing that happened in an operating room on any single patient could really challenge gender's "fundamental truths"—e.g., that there are two and only two, that everyone has one or the other, and which one you are is determined by some deep and immutable fact.

Very little of this has any direct connection to medical knowledge or practice: a person could be, for instance, a highly skilled surgeon, endocrinologist, or psychiatrist without believing that transpeople suffer from a disease or a disorder, or that gender is fundamentally bivalent and unalterable. The "fundamental truths" are much more matters of ideology than science, and feminists and transgender people themselves have been busy replacing them with conceptions better equipped to consider adequately the complexities of gender.

Medicine no longer needs to make transgender unthreatening by portraying it as a disease whose therapies must preserve the gender binary. Yet giving up a disease model may seem to leave medicine in a quandary. The kinds of psychiatrically mediated gatekeeping to medical help required by various iterations of the World Professional Association for Transgender Health standards of care—for example, a mental health assessment and a referral from a mental health practitioner for gender-affirming interventions—make most sense if transgender is a sort of illness. If transgender is not an illness, it might be wondered, what business has medicine with it at all? Perhaps surgical and hormonal interventions should be seen as merely a sort of extreme cosmetic intervention—involving the destruction of healthy organs and the removal of reproductive abilities—legitimated solely by consumers' (informed) choice. Yet seeing transgender interventions in this way seems hardly more likely to reflect most transgender people's experience of themselves than would the mental illness story. Achieving a recognizable gender identity that reflects one's sense of self is not merely one choice among others aiming at more social or professional success. A habitable gender identity is not important because it is chosen; it is chosen because it is important. Understanding transgender interventions as elective cosmetic surgery could also threaten the insurance coverage that does exist for transgender-directed medical interventions and make any expansion of that coverage less likely, as it would not be seen as medically necessary.

Yet if neither "medically indicated" pathology nor elective cosmetic surgery are good ways of understanding what is going on in medically assisted gender transitioning, how can it be best understood? Here, some prominent strands in feminist thinking about gender can be helpful.

The relationship between transgender and important currents of thought within feminism is complex; over the years, feminists and feminisms have served as allies as well as critics of transgender people. Feminists agree, however, on the enormous social importance of how people are gendered and, in particular, about how damaging practices associated with gender typically are for women and girls. Disagreements among feminists concerning transgender often pivot on whether transgender and, particularly, medically assisted forms of gender crossing, reinforce or erode damaging features of gender [3].

In my view, transgender can do either, and it has done both; it has both challenged and reinforced norms and practices associated with gender that have hampered people's lives. Part of the way forward is to tap the potential of *transgender* to make of *gender* a more humane set of social relations, as well as subjective experiences. A big question for medicine is how to understand and respond to transgender in ways that will promote these conceptual, social, and cultural goals.

GENDER, AUTHORITY, AND ANALOGIES

Gender Differences Are not Simply Natural "Givens"

There is a lingering temptation to think that gender differences are straightforwardly natural facts and that social organizations have to accommodate those facts in one way or another. Some have even thought that transgender must abet this temptation: something presocial *must* be happening to explain why transpeople so strongly resist assimilation to the gender socialization to which most so readily succumb.

Yet, as many feminists and other theorists have argued, this temptation too readily accepts the idea that "natural facts" can be clearly and distinctly separated from the social contexts in which they occur [4]. What those facts mean to us, how they are taken up into our lives, reflect and reinforce the ways in which respect, authority, and access to goods are distributed in human societies; they cannot by themselves justify those distributions.

What might accepting a broadly feminist—which is at least to say a highly social and critically inclined—account of the nature of gender mean for clinicians involved with transgender patients? Feminism would provide reason to resist the notion that there is something artificial, not natural, and therefore second-best in the ways transgender people live out their gender identities. This realization might help clinicians recall that how we express our genders is important to many of us, not just to transgender people. Most people engage in practices—how they walk, talk, or wear clothing, for example—designed to make their gender identities plain to others; virtually all of us are addressed by gender-distinctive standards of behavior and of aspiration, not all of which seem unwelcome. In this sense, gender's subjective and social dimensions are not so different for trans- and nontranspeople. What the existence of transpeople can do is to testify that gender-related expectations can be assessed, resisted, and reworked, as well as affirmed.

Transpeople, then, face a certain set of problems as they live out their lives in ways that simultaneously challenge and converge with what tends to be important for most people. Medicine has resources to help some of them better resolve those problems and achieve goals—personal peace, social acceptance—that are in many respects quite commonplace. Understanding transgender also might relieve some of the social anxieties that may have prompted clinicians to continue to insist on psychiatric endorsement of transpeople's self-understanding [5]. Furthermore, it might well improve the experience of transgender people in all their dealings with health care—dealings that go far beyond what occurs in a gender identity clinic. Perhaps most importantly of all, it might speed the spread through social life of supportive and welcoming attitudes to transgender people. There is reason to believe that such attitudes can go a long way toward causing the rate of trans suicide, particularly among trans youth, to plummet [6].

The Authority of Women over Their Bodies and Their Lives Must be Honored

This is a key tenet of feminism, but why should we think it has special relevance for transgender people? There are, after all, transmen as well as transwomen, and transpeople who seek to live insofar as possible beyond the gender binary, resisting identification as either women or men. But in general, medicine's engagement with gender crossing involves people who have either been socially configured as women, or who understand themselves to be women, despite their anatomy. Like everyone else, these people have a presumptive authority over the fundamental terms of how they are understood by others. Yet, as is the case with many forms of authority, women face particular resistance to its recognition. This resistance can hamper gender identity expression for transmen and transwomen both. If medicine is to align itself with defensible values as it aids gender crossing, it needs to do so in a way that fully endorses both the worthiness of women's choices and the choiceworthiness of women's lives. Psychiatric assessment as a required hurdle to gender-affirming hormone therapy or surgery tends to undermine that endorsement. Counseling—including peer counseling—should be readily available and can be an important part of achieving fully informed consent, but psychotherapy

should not be mandatory for access to hormone treatment or surgical procedures.

Being a woman, or a man, or a nonbinary person are worthy ways of living, not pathological impulses; those who seek medical assistance to help them live so are not on that basis alone ill or confused, and there is every reason to avoid giving the impression that they are. It then might seem that the feminist perspectives discussed here support an elective cosmetic surgery model.

But feminism, in its insistence that women's experiences need to be acknowledged as central features of human experience, might remind us that we are not limited to merely two options in thinking about the relationship between medicine and transgender.

Birth Giving as a Model

Motherhood is a social role that many people deeply want to occupy. Moreover, many of them want to achieve that role in a way that crucially involves their bodies. Medical assistance in the project is often welcome and sometimes needed to avert poor, or even tragic, outcomes. Yet it is not strictly necessary for becoming a mother. There are analogies here with transgender: while many transgender people see medical interventions as essential for social acceptance and personal integrity, others do not. Many different transition strategies are used by transpeople. Consider further how giving birth to a child can transform one's life. The process is arduous and not without dangers; the outcomes may well bring as much heartbreak as joy. Yet women aren't required to undergo any form of screening or therapy as a condition of getting medical help with pregnancy and delivery.

Pregnancy is not a disease. Nor is the decision to begin or add to a family likely to be of only instrumental significance; often, it emerges from a person's sense of what matters deeply to her. Here too, analogies with gender crossing seem clear. As medical assistance with pregnancy and with birth giving are altogether appropriate, and insurable, it would seem that policies withholding insurance coverage for medical assistance with transgender would need to be able to cite significant disanalogies between the two to escape the charge that refusal of coverage is arbitrary.

There have always been ideologies of gender expressed in medicine's dealings with transgender people—messages sent and received in ways that do not require them to be explicitly endorsed by any particular caregiver. It seems to me, however, that now medicine should openly ally itself with ways of making sense of gender that affirm the value of transgender people's experiences and choices, in preference to conveying a hodgepodge of confused attitudes that may disrespect transgender people and slow the bend of history's arc toward justice [7].

NOTES

1. Human Rights Campaign. Anti-transgender legislation spreads nationwide. http://hrc-assets.s3-website-us-east-1.amazonaws.com//files/assets/resources/HRC-Anti-Trans-Issue-Brief-FINAL-REV2.pdf. Published February 2016. Accessed March 20, 2016.

2. Meyerowitz JJ. *How Sex Changed: A History of Transsexuality in the United States.* Cambridge, MA: Harvard University Press; 2002.

3. Stryker S. Transgender feminism: queering the woman question. In: S Gillis, G Howie, R Munford, eds. *Third Wave Feminism: A Critical Exploration.* 2nd ed. New York, NY: Palgrave Macmillian; 2007.

4. Kessler SJ, McKenna W. *Gender: An Ethnomethodological Approach.* Chicago, IL: University of Chicago Press; 1978.

5. Nelson J. Medicine and making sense of queer lives. *Hastings Cent Rep.* 2014:44(suppl 4):S12–S16.

6. Bauer GR, Scheim AI, Pyne J, Travers R, Hammond R. Intervenable factors associated with suicide risk in transgender persons: a respondent driven sampling study in Ontario, Canada. *BMC Public Health.* 2015;15:525. https://bmcpublichealth.biomedcentral.com/articles/10.1186/s12889-015-1867-2. Accessed September 29, 2016.

7. The phrase "the arc [of the moral universe] . . . bends toward justice" is from Parker T. *Ten Sermons of Religion.* Boston, MA: Crosby, Nichols; 1853: 84-85.

CHAPTER 5

MEDIA AND CULTURE

Although literature and the arts remain important cultural forms, popular culture, television, movies, music, print media, and the Internet also play a significant role in reflecting, reinforcing, and sometimes subverting the dominant systems and ideologies that help shape gender. Popular culture is very seductive; it reflects and creates societal needs, desires, anxieties, and hopes through consumption and participation. Popular culture also provides stories and narratives that shape our lives and identities. It gives us pleasure at the end of a long day and enables us to take our minds off work or other anxieties. In this regard, some scholars have suggested that popular culture regulates society by "soothing the masses," meaning that energy and opposition to the status quo are redirected in pursuit of the latest in athletic shoes or electronic gadgets.

Of course, popular culture creates huge multibillion-dollar industries that themselves regulate society by providing markets for consumption and consolidating power and status among certain groups and individuals. Media conglomerates have merged technologies and fortunes, consolidating resources and forming powerful corporations that control the flow of information to the public. Over the last few decades globalization (those forces integrating communities and economies into a global marketplace) has created global media with powerful mass media corporations that both dominate domestic markets and influence national governments. Ninety percent of what is on television is owned by six companies—GE (which owns Comcast, NBC, and Universal Pictures), News-Corp, Disney, Viacom, Time Warner, and CBS. The world's largest media company is Alphabet, formerly known as Google, followed closely by Facebook.

At the same time, corporations such as Disney spark resistance as women of color and LGBTQ individuals, for example, respond to their absence and misrepresentation in contemporary media. The FAAN (Fostering Activism and Alternatives Now!) Project is a media literacy and media activism project formed by young women of color in Philadelphia. They seek to critique and create media, with the goal of social change. Another organization is the Queer Women of Color Media Arts Project that creates, exhibits, and distributes new films that reflect the lives of queer women of color and address vital social justice issues that concern them. Blogs and zines, discussed shortly, and various online communities also provide feminist media activism, including cyberactivism, that seeks to empower and change society.

As emphasized in Chapter 4, popular culture plays a huge role in setting standards of beauty and encouraging certain bodily disciplinary practices. Popular culture is culture for many people; the various forms pop culture takes help shape identity and guide people's understandings of themselves and one another. This chapter addresses such issues by focusing on the Internet and cell/mobile phone technology and their relationship to television, movies, the music industry, and print media. In this discussion we emphasize issues of power and access, gender stereotyping, and obstacles to active participation in contemporary media that include both technological (obtaining the hardware) and social aspects (knowledge of and relationship to cultural norms about technology and who should use it, as well as literacy skills). The final section of this chapter addresses literature and the arts.

DIGITAL TECHNOLOGIES

The Internet is a global system of interconnected private, public, academic, business, and governmental computer networks that serve billions of users worldwide. These are linked by electronic, wireless, and optical networking technologies and carry a wide range of information resources and services, such as the World Wide Web and infrastructure to support email. The Internet is central in enabling and accelerating interactions through Internet forums, instant messaging, and especially social networking and the use of personalized services tailored to users. Most traditional communications media, including music, film, and television, have been reshaped or redefined by the Internet, as have newspapers and other print media, by blogging and web feed features, for example, often accessed through mobile wireless technologies. Of course the pornography and gambling industries have also taken advantage of the Internet and provide a significant source of advertising revenue for other websites. Although many governments have attempted to restrict both industries' use of the Internet, in general, this has failed to stop their widespread popularity.

As of this writing (and of all the chapters in this book, this is the one where knowledge most quickly goes out of date), more than half of the world's approximately 7.6 billion people have used the services of the Internet. Despite this scope, accessibility (to the Internet and other media) is one focus of this chapter, as is the relationship of new technologies to imperialism and global capitalist development. New media both support traditional imperialist practices as well as provide opportunities for subversion and resistance through online communities organized to improve the lives of marginalized people. Indeed, over the last couple of decades there have been several global policy directives like the World Summits on Information Society (WSIS) by, for example, the United Nations, the World Bank, and various nongovernmental organizations to improve women's access to information and communication technologies generally.

In terms of expansion of global capitalist development, online shopping opportunities are now challenging and in many cases surpassing traditional consumer behaviors, with staggering profits for major corporations. In 2018, Amazon founder Jeff Bezos became the richest person in modern history, with $150 billion in wealth. Much of this commerce

MAKING THE NEWS: A GUIDE TO GETTING THE MEDIA'S ATTENTION

1. *Have a clear message.* Decide what you are calling for and keep repeating it clearly and concisely. Don't dilute strong arguments by going off on tangents or harping on trivialities. Relate your cause to everyday concerns. For example, if you're campaigning for ethical investment, point out that it is financially viable and has a positive effect on the world. If you speak calmly and appeal to common understandings, radical ideas can appear not only sensible but even obvious.

2. *Make media a priority.* Effective campaigning means making media engagement a priority. I have often seen activists organize an event and then think about promoting it to the media. Put media at the center of your planning from the beginning.

3. *Offer news.* Something is news only if it is new. Discussions of opinions are not news—but you can make them news. When the University of London Union campaigned on fair trade, they couldn't make headlines simply by repeating its benefits. But by conducting a survey that showed that London students were among Britain's most enthusiastic fair trade buyers, they made a good news story. Don't forget to be imaginative!

4. *Watch your timing.* If you are aiming for a weekly paper that goes to print on Tuesday afternoon, don't hold an event on Tuesday evening. Be where journalists are, both literally and metaphorically. It's difficult to get journalists to come to a protest outside a company's offices, but if you demonstrate outside the company's big annual meeting, business correspondents will already be there. Contact them in advance and there's a good chance they'll come over to speak with you.

5. *Talk to journalists.* It sounds obvious, but it is often overlooked. Issue a news release when you act or respond to events, but don't rely on the release alone. Get on the phone with the journalists who have received it. Be concise and brace yourself for disappointments—most of them will not be interested. But chances are you will find someone who wants to know more eventually.

6. *Build contacts.* Go back to journalists every time you have a story, especially those who seemed interested earlier. If you're concise and reliable, and give them good stories, they will soon be phoning you for comments. When this happens, make sure that someone is available. A good relationship with a few journalists is worth a thousand press releases.

7. *Choose the right media.* Who are you trying to influence? If you're aiming to shift local public opinion, the local press is, of course, vital. When the UK student group People and Planet launched its Green Education Declaration, it targeted specialist education media. The news was read by fewer people than if it had been in mainstream media, but that audience included the decision makers whom the initiative was targeting.

8. *Keep it human.* A single death is a tragedy; a million deaths is a statistic. For example, Disarm UCL is a group of students campaigning for an end to their university's arms investments. They discovered that a University College London graduate named Richard Wilson had written a book about his sister's death as a result of the arms trade. By involving Wilson in their campaign, they made the story more human and made it harder for their opponents to dismiss them as inexperienced and unrealistic.

9. *Make it visual.* A good image can make or break your chances of coverage. Photo stunts should be original and meaningful but not too complicated. A great example is students who dressed in military jackets and mortarboards to illustrate military influence on universities. With photos of protests, be careful about the background. I'm amazed how often people protest outside a shop or company without ensuring that the company's name is visible in shots of the demonstration. Specialist media will often use photos provided by campaigners, so it's worth finding someone who's good with a camera.

10. *Keep going.* Media liaison is hard work, especially when you are new to it. But don't give up! The more you do, the more contacts you will acquire and the more coverage you will get. Keep your press releases and your phone calls regular. It will all be worth it when you see the coverage making a difference to your campaign.

Source: Symon Hill, *Utne*, March–April 2009. Reprinted from Red Pepper.

relies on the cheap labor of millions, especially women, worldwide. Data mining allows companies to improve sales and profitability by creating customer profiles that contain information about demographics and online behaviors. Cloud computing merges business with social networking concepts by developing interactive communities that connect individuals based on shared business needs or experiences. Many provide specialized networking tools and applications that can be accessed via their websites, such as business directory and reviewing services. However, the Internet also provides market opportunities for artisans and craftspeople (through websites such as Etsy).

It is also important to note the environmental consequences of the marketing of these technologies worldwide—especially in terms of "e-waste" and its relationship to global climate change. Consequences of electronic production and use include the following: (1) raw material extraction of nonrenewable natural resources, including coltan, a rare metal that is found mostly in the Democratic Republic of Congo, where its mining is currently helping finance a war; (2) material manufacturing that involves greater use of fossil fuels than other traditional manufacturing; (3) computer and accessory manufacturing, packaging, and transport that involve extensive use of plastics and styrofoam; (4) energy use to deal with the explosion of e-data generated, transmitted, and stored; and (5) despite recycling efforts, problems associated with the rapid obsolescence of electronic products containing toxic metals that end up in landfills and pollute the earth and its water sources. A concern is that large amounts of e-waste are sent to China, India, and Africa, where many unprotected workers are exposed to hazardous materials such as mercury and lead in the process of burning electronics in search of copper and aluminum to resell.

An important feature of the Internet is that it allows greater flexibility in working hours and location, especially with the spread of unmetered high-speed connections and tools such as virtual private networks, Skype, Zoom, and videoconferencing. The relatively low cost and nearly instantaneous sharing of ideas, knowledge, and skills have increased opportunities for collaborative work nationally and transnationally. Such collaboration occurs in a wide variety of areas, including scientific research, software development, conference planning, political activism, and creative writing. Publishing a web page or a blog or building a website involves little initial cost, and many cost-free services are available. However, "cyberslacking" has been identified as a drain on business and other organizational resources. Employees who use a computer at work spend one to three hours per workday surfing the web.

The term Web 2.0 is commonly associated with web applications that facilitate interactive information sharing, user-centered design, and collaboration. Web 2.0 sites provide opportunities for users to collaborate and interact as initiators of user-generated content in virtual communities. This can be compared to websites where users consume online content created for them. Web 2.0 innovations include applications such as mashups, which use or combine data from several sources to create new services, and folksonomies, or collaborative tagging or indexing, which allow users to collectively classify and find information. Most familiar applications include blogs, wikis, video-sharing sites, hosted services, and social networking sites. Facebook, for example, the most popular social network service and website, has 2.32 billion monthly active users as well as 65 million pages, and 6 percent of digital time is spent on Facebook. Similarly Twitter and Tumblr offer social networking and microblogging with millions of users. LinkedIn is a business-oriented site offering opportunities for professional networking with 467 million active users, Yelp is a business directory service and review site with social networking features, and

Flickr provides image and video hosting, creating an online community that allows users to embed images in blogs and social media. WhatsApp is one of the fastest-growing applications and is now the top messenger app in 128 countries. These technologies rely not only on expensive hardware, but also, ultimately, on literacy, a key issue worldwide as women are less likely than men to be able to access education, and thus are more likely to be illiterate.

Increasingly, people access the Internet through mobile devices such as cell phones and tablets. Two-thirds of the world's 7.6 billion people now have a cell phone, 2 billion of which are smartphones. Currently about 95 percent of U.S. adults have a cell phone, and two-thirds of them access the Internet through a smartphone. There are very few significant differences in terms of cell and smartphone usage by gender or ethnicity. The greatest uptick in cell phone usage in recent years has been among older adults: Now, nearly three-quarters of 50–64-year-old Americans have a cell phone, and 42 percent older than 65 use one (an increase of 12 percent over 2015). Of U.S. adults using smartphones, 97 percent use them for text messaging, 92 percent make voice or video calls, 75 percent access news and social networking sites, 60 percent take and upload photos, and 41 percent listen to music or podcasts and play games. About 50 percent watch videos on their smartphones.

Seventy-five percent of teenagers own cell phones; 72 percent of those use the phone to send text messages, and 54 percent text daily. Eleven percent send more than 200 texts per day! At least one in three have texted while driving. Girls send and receive significantly more text messages than boys. Around a quarter of teens use their phones for going online and accessing social media sites. Four percent have texted a nude or semi-nude photo of themselves (sexted), and 15 percent have received a nude or semi-nude photo of someone else. Teenagers and young adults represent the leading edge of mobile connectivity, and the patterns of their technology use signal future changes in the adult population. It is interesting, and frightening, to note that more people on earth have access to mobile or

cell phones than toilets. A recent study estimated that out of the world's 7.6 billion people, 6 billion have access to mobile phones. Far fewer—only 4.5 billion people—have access to working toilets. Of the 2.5 billion who don't have proper sanitation, more than 1 billion defecate in the open. In one second on the Internet, there are 54,907 Google searches, 7,252 tweets, 125,406 YouTube video views, and 2,501,018 emails sent. Certainly these technologies are changing the ways we interact with each other and how we anticipate friendship and community. Ninety percent of American adults carry a cell phone with them most of the time, and most always keep their phone on. Americans spend an average of six hours a day on their phone; college students spend 8–10 hours. People in the United States check their social media accounts on average 17 times a day.

Is unlimited access to information and communication always beneficial? Is the opportunity to have hundreds of friends on social networking sites helping us build community? The answers to such questions are complex, and the case can be made that these devices are providing more knowledge at our fingertips, yet knowledge that is unfiltered as well as voluminous and therefore more easily forgettable. Social networking sites provide opportunities for us to keep in touch with a broad range of people in important ways, yet the case can be made that these are "faux friendships" without the interpersonal intimacies of "real" face-to-face friendship. What are your thoughts on this? Sherry Turkle, founder and director of the MIT Initiative on Technology and Self and someone at the forefront of technological innovation, recently gave her opinion on the future of social life in this rapidly changing time. We are "networked and we are together," she said. "But so lessened are our expectations of each other that we feel utterly alone. And there is the risk that we come to see others as objects to be accessed—and only for the parts we find useful, comforting, or amusing." Scholars and clinicians have underscored her reservations with identification of various forms of Internet addiction disorder whereby excessive computer use interferes with daily life in relatively serious ways. Although Internet users are more efficient at finding information and have developed strong visual acuity and eye-hand coordination, these practices appear to interfere with deeper-level thought related to creativity. And, although cell phones are usually considered devices that connect people, a study at the University of Maryland found that cell phone use for both women and men reduced empathic and prosocial behavior (measured via willingness to aid a charity). Researchers suggested that cell phone use evokes perceptions of connectivity to others, thereby fulfilling the basic human need to belong and reducing the desire to indulge in prosocial behavior. The ultimate risk of heavy technology use is that it not only fragments our life through multiple, diverse, and often superficial stimulation, but it also diminishes our empathy by limiting how much we really engage (offline) with one another. More significantly, how are digital technologies changing our brains? What does it mean for someone who has spent, since birth, large portions of the day in front of screens, interrupted constantly, and encouraged to juggle various streams of information? Some scientists say without hesitation that juggling multiple sources of information and responding to ongoing communication are changing how we think and behave. It appears that the technology is actually rewiring the brain as neural networks continue to develop through life. Scientists say our ability to focus is undermined by bursts of information that stimulate (through a dopamine surge) the primitive impulse to respond to immediate opportunities and threats. This is why people experience digital technologies as addictive and feel bored or anxious when they are not "connected" to their devices. Along with this surge comes stress hormones that also have powerful effects on the body. Educators explain that children have reduced attention span, difficulties focusing, and increased problems with obesity as a direct consequence of the ways we structure life around digital devices.

Originally the web was imagined as a utopian space where gender, race, class, and sexuality would be neutral forces or where alternative subjectivities could be performed. Although this potential still remains, virtual realities tend to reinforce current social standards about gender and other identities. This occurs in two ways. First, traditional standards are scripted through gendered and racialized content supported by advertising, entertainment, and pornography. This "content" is saturated with traditional ideas about gender, which comes through downloading music and videos, watching television shows, and reading narratives about other people's lives and activities on social networking sites.

Many advertisements that accompany websites and a significant percentage of Internet traffic are pornography related. About 15 percent of internet traffic is pornography. Globally, porn brings in about $97 billion, with between $10 and $12 billion of that coming from the United States. In 2017, Pornhub averaged 81 million visitors per day (28.5 billion visitors for the year), 50,000 searches per minute, and 800 per second. About a quarter of American men admit to consuming porn; only 8 percent of American women say they watch. In addition, pornography is often credited as the fuel behind technological innovation and adoption. For example, pornography companies were attempting to perfect video streaming long before mainstream media in order to offer live sex performances that could be streamed directly to consumers. Live chat rooms between pornography consumers and performers also innovated much of the technology used today in other arenas. Finally, of course, it is important to mention the levels of violence in online entertainment. Of particular concern are violent video games marketed to adolescent boys and the relationship between these activities and teen violence. This concern has precipitated hearings in the U.S. House of Representatives to discuss the regulation of certain games that depict the death, maiming, and harassment of people and animals. Violent video games tend to glorify violence and desensitize individuals to suffering, and may legitimize and trivialize violence and hate crimes against marginalized groups.

Second, despite the fact that Internet technologies provide new opportunities and help people connect across wide geographical expanses, these technologies are not available to everyone. Social class limits access to all information and communication technologies, irrespective of gender. The speed with which technology evolves or becomes obsolete (the "technology turnover" that pushes new gadget accessories through the marketplace at astonishing speeds) exacerbates these issues of equity associated with Internet technologies. There are few gender differences in Internet access in the United States, although in terms of usage women are more likely to use it for communication (email, blogs, and fan following) and participation on social networking sites. Men are more likely to use the Internet for recreation. Women participate in more streaming content, whereas men download more. Men also have a higher use of Internet pornography and violent gaming, as just discussed. In this way, although in the global north a majority of women have access to the Internet, it is still a contested site where girls and women may experience marginalization, discrimination, abuse, and/or disempowerment. Online predation of girls and young women is an increasingly important problem as computers are installed in children's bedrooms and phones with Internet capabilities are owned by younger and younger individuals, making the Internet a central feature of teen and preteen life. It is estimated that one in five children is approached by an Internet predator, mostly through social networking sites.

Although a global perspective on women's access to the Internet reveals similar gendered usage, there are important gender and class differences associated with access. Where resources are scarce, the gap widens between those with resources, access, and skills and those without. This means that because women as a group are limited by poverty and lack of education, they are less likely to be able to access digital technologies. In addition, cultural differences also come into play as some communities encourage women's access to the Internet and some do not. In this way, women's access to media is limited by socioeconomic factors as well as literacy and numeracy skills and "user" characteristics such as time constraints associated with family obligations.

Finally, at the same time that the Internet reinscribes power issues on multiple levels, as already mentioned, it provides opportunities for subversion and resistance. Its relevance as a political tool facilitating various forms of cyberactivism is now well known. For example, recent U.S. presidential campaigns have been notable for their success in organizing voters and soliciting donations through the Internet as well as for the involvement of cyberterrorism influencing the electoral process. Russia's alleged meddling in democratic elections in the United States and Europe is a case in point. Digital technologies are also increasingly employed in resistance against standing regimes outside the United States, as in the case of the 2012 Arab Spring uprisings. In particular, social networking sites such as Facebook and Twitter have helped citizens organize protests, communicate grievances, and share information. China's attempts to censor and filter material on the Internet also reflect the growing civic potential of online communities and cyberactivism generally. Indeed, this activism is responding to the explosion of mass media globally that have grown with the expansion of markets on local, national, and global scales. Media corporations have grown stronger in their reach of audiences and in their ability to shape production and distribution processes worldwide.

The content and organization of the web also provide opportunities to dispute and create new knowledge. Many women have fought to make a place for themselves in the technological world, developing their own activist websites, blogs, and computer games.

Blogs allow opportunities for citizen journalism that enables people to critique and provide social commentary on their lives or the world around them. Blogging has also changed the face of publishing. Although bloggers are not usually formally trained and may not have professional credentials, they have been able to publish their opinions or beliefs about any number of subjects, appearing in school projects, on activism websites, and on political web pages, often with accompanying video. Similarly, wikis are knowledge databanks in which any user can add, edit, and create definitions for common words,

LEARNING ACTIVITY

GENDER AND SOCIAL MEDIA

Jeana Moody

For younger generations, online lives take up a significant amount of time and emotional energy. For many young people, social media in particular have provided opportunities for activism. The #MeToo movement offers a powerful example of how online activism can support resistance to sexist behavior.

#MeToo took hold in 2017 thanks to Alyssa Milano, but the hashtag was actually created in 2006 by activist and senior director of Girls for Gender Equity in Brooklyn Tarana Burke. The 2017 campaign shone a light on the prevalence of sexual harassment in workplaces and called for more structural and formal support of victims. #MeToo led many women, trans people, and some men from all over the United States and other countries to share their stories in solidarity and to contextualize how sexual harassment plays out in daily life. The Time's Up movement was born from #MeToo and focused on the imbalance of power within the workplace, informing people of their rights, providing resources, and educating people on what they can do to help.

Social media have been able to amplify women's voices and experiences and expose white male privilege. While social media are used for feminist actions, not all online interactions are positive. Often social media's anonymity and lack of accountability allow discriminatory and harmful online behaviors. We may not often think of social media as a gendered space, but of course social media are created and used by people who are gendered, and cultural expectations of gender are enacted in digital space. Let's consider the different ways social media are used to create community and amplify voice but yet also have the power to create echo chambers within communities gathered in support of oppression.

Activity 1: Take a look at some of the people you follow online:

> In what ways are they using their platform?
> In what ways do they perform gender?
> Do they use their platforms for activism or for selling products or for some other purpose?
> Who else follows these people? And how do they react to their online presence?

Activity 2: Go to a website that allows anonymous commentary (on videos or postings):

> How are commenters performing gender?
> Do they use the platform for activism? If so, how?
> Is their behavior sexist, racist, or otherwise derogatory? How do others respond to discriminatory postings?
> Or is their behavior resistant and liberatory?

Activity 3: Take a look at the communities you participate in online:

> For what purposes are these communities using their social media platforms?
> Is the community welcoming?
> How is gender performed in these spaces?
> Do these communities engage in nonsexist and nonracist behavior?
> How might your online communities be more effectively activist?

LEARNING ACTIVITY

ANALYZING SOCIAL MEDIA

1. Follow a celebrity on Twitter for a few days. Then complete a gender analysis of the person's tweets: What issues are important to this celebrity? Who is the audience for the tweets? What is this person trying to accomplish with these tweets? How does this celebrity perform gender in these tweets? Does this person address gender issues in tweets? Do the tweets reinforce or challenge gender norms? Do you think tweeting can be an effective form of feminist activism?

2. Search for YouTube videos on a topic related to feminism. Watch a selection of these videos and analyze them: Who is the intended audience? How does the video frame feminist issues? What is the goal of the video? How does the video make its argument? How would you assess the video's contribution to feminist dialogue? Can YouTube videos be an effective form of feminist activism?

3. Identify three feminist bloggers and read a selection of their blogs on feminist issues. Who is their audience? How do they construct their arguments to reach this audience? What kinds of comments get posted in response to their blogs? How effective do you think these blogs are as a form of feminist activism?

concepts, histories, or biographies. It is important to note that although wikis can be good sources of common information, they are not always accurate and should not be confused with academic databases! These sites reflect a democratic construction of knowledge to which individuals can contribute (the website Wikipedia is one example). Emma Turley and Jenny Fisher's reading "Tweeting Back While Shouting Back" examines possibilities for digital spaces as platforms for feminist activism.

SLACKTIVISM

Janet Lockhart

Showing Up, or Showing Off?

"Slacktivism" is the tug between wanting to help a cause and wanting to stay comfortable at home. Or maybe it's the desire to look good, to come across as a concerned citizen, without giving any of your time, property, or money.

Originally, the word had a positive connotation. "Slacktivism" was used for a small, individual act that really could make a difference, like planting a tree. Coined in 1995 (Clark, 2009), it was a term for the young adults of that generation, a combination of "slacker" and "activism," meant to show that not all young people were lazy and indifferent.

Now the connotation is almost always negative—and can refer to people of any generation. It still means a small action, but one that is, or essentially is, meaningless. Slacktivists are often "preaching to the choir," taking a stand on an issue or cause—but only in front of their friends, family, or others who already share their beliefs. Slacktivists may be active only on social media, retweeting, forwarding links, and "liking" others' posts without ever moving away from their computer.

Slacktivism can happen offline as well, and includes things like displaying a bumper sticker or wearing a T-shirt supporting a cause without taking any other action. Wikipedia calls these actions "virtue signaling" (2018)—essentially, showing off, making yourself look good, without really doing anything.

It's not that there is anything wrong with signing a petition or sharing a link to a website that may interest others. Making others aware of an issue can be a first step—but, by itself, is not enough. Make sure you raise the awareness of others in *addition* to taking effective action, not *instead* of acting.

Active, or "Slacktive"?

So, what is the difference between "slacktivism" and true activism? The answer: *Activism has the potential to create real change.* It's not necessarily the *size* of the action, but how *effective* it is: Will the online petition be delivered to someone with decision-making power, such as your senator or representative in Congress? Did the cost of your bumper sticker go directly to the cause it publicizes? Ask yourself, What will *happen*, or what will *change*? What *real action* will be taken?

Rate each activity from **1** (indirect or no effect) to **5** (direct, immediate effect). If you rated an activity 1, 2, or 3, what action could you take to make it more effective?

"Liking" your friend's Facebook post about LGBTQ rights	1	2	3	4	5
Donating money to a GoFundMe account	1	2	3	4	5
Emailing the local newspaper opinion column	1	2	3	4	5
Buying fair trade coffee	1	2	3	4	5
An action you took this week: _____	1	2	3	4	5

What power do *you* have for change? *How will you use it?*

References

Clark, F. (2009). Slacktivist. *Patheos* [blog], June 11. http://www.patheos.com/blogs/slacktivist/2009/06/11/etymology/

Wikipedia (2018) Slacktivism. Retrieved from https://en.wikipedia.org/wiki/Slacktivism

TELEVISION

Television is one of the most influential forms of media because it is so pervasive and its presence is taken for granted in most households in the United States. Television impacts family life because it encourages passive interaction, often replacing alternative family interaction. In addition, television is a visual medium that broadcasts multiple images on a continual basis in digitized, high-density formats. The ways people watch television, however, are changing as viewers increasingly record shows rather than watch them in real time, watch parts of shows in other formats (for example, YouTube), and view television shows through computers and other mobile devices. However, although television viewing habits are increasingly diverse and fragmented, still these images come to be seen as representing the real world and influence people's understanding of others and the world around them. This is especially significant for children because it is estimated that most children, on average, watch far more television than is good for them. Of course, the range and quality of television shows vary, and a case can be made for the benefits of educational television. Unfortunately, educational programming is only a small percentage of television viewing.

The explosion of cable and satellite availability and subscription services such as Netflix, Amazon Prime, and Hulu has resulted in an unlimited number of television channels and viewing options. Such choice, however, has not meant greater access to a wide range of alternative images of gender. Reality shows—and makeover shows, in particular—reinforce dominant notions of gender and standards of beauty, as do entertainment shows such as *American Idol, America's Got Talent,* and *The Voice.* In addition, a host of shows such as *Teen Mom* and *Pregnant and Dating* provide sometimes contradictory messages about the challenges and benefits of unplanned pregnancies (although recent research suggests these shows may increase contraceptive usage). Shows incorporating shame and humiliation can be said to "discipline" an audience even while they present other people's misfortune as entertainment. Ultimately these programs are engaged in the selling of products.

Advertising sponsors control the content of most commercial television. During male sporting events, for example, the commercials—for beer, cars, electronic products, Internet commerce, and other products—target a male audience. During daytime soap operas or evening family sitcoms, on the other hand, the commercials are aimed at women and focus on beauty and household products. As a result, commercial sponsors have enormous influence over the content of television programming. If they want to sell a certain product, they are unlikely to air the commercial during a feature that could be interpreted as criticizing such products or consumerism generally. In this way, commercial sponsors shape television content. Some corporations have recently tried to capitalize on their public embrace of so-called girl power and feminism. Judith Taylor, Josée Johnston, and Krista Whitehead's reading "A Corporation in Feminist Clothing?" examines Dove's "Real Beauty" campaign to see if corporate advertising can really help bring about feminist transformation.

Television messages about gender are often very traditional, even when they are attempting to capitalize on new trends. The popular show *Modern Family* is a case in point. Although it depicts a secure, loving gay couple, for example, it reinscribes many stereotypes about gay men. Similarly, while it also presents a very likeable Latina struggling to cope with life in the United States, it supports stereotypes of the ditzy Latin woman in most episodes. In fact, the assumed differences between the genders very often drive the plot of television programming. The format of shows is also gendered. For example, daytime soap operas focus on relationships and family and employ rather fragmented narratives with plots weaving around without closure or resolution, enabling women to tune in and out as they go about multiple tasks. Daytime soaps are only part of the story. Shows with drama and overt sexuality, such as the long-running *Scandal*, target an evening audience, as do crime and thriller shows such as *How to Get Away with Murder* and *NCIS*. In these shows, women can be competent and successful, but they're also attractive and sexy. The popularity of the historical drama *Downton Abbey* represented not only the interest in romance and intrigue, fashion and stately homes, but a nostalgia for the past. Cable networks such as Showtime and AMC feature dramatic series such as *Homeland* that garner popular acclaim and then become profitable as boxed-set DVDs. *Homeland* features a strong woman lead who struggles with bipolar disorder and often makes bad choices that get other characters killed. Similarly, popular series like *Game of Thrones* offer sexualized violence and misogynous male characters alongside some dynamic female characters. Even *Broadchurch*, a show with high hopes from a feminist perspective, provided fodder for debate about contradictory messages about gender. Scholars have pointed out that these shows reconcile women to male-dominated interpersonal relationships and help enforce gendered social relations. Others argue that these shows enable women viewers to actively critique blatant male-dominated situations in ways that help them reflect on their own lives.

A similar analysis can be made of evening family sitcoms. Shows such as *Modern Family* and *The Good Wife* are funny and entertaining because they are relatively predictable. The family or work group (as in *Veep*) is made up of characters with distinct personalities and recognizable habits; each week this "family" is thrown into some kind of crisis, and the plot of the show is to resolve that crisis back to the situation as usual. Sometimes it involves a group of roommates or neighbors, as in the classics *Friends*, *Seinfeld*, *The Big Bang Theory*, or *New Girl*. For the most part, the messages are typical in terms of gender, race, class, and other differences, and they often involve humor that denigrates certain groups of people and ultimately maintains the status quo. As already mentioned, reality television is especially influential. The appeal of "reality" shows such as *The Bachelor*, *Survivor*, *The Biggest Loser*, *Hell's Kitchen*, and *Real Housewives* relies on creative casting, scripting, and editing to make the shows seem spontaneous, incorporating character traits and personalities that viewers love to hate and adore. These shows also rely on a cult of the celebrity, rampant in popular culture. HGTV has also made home improvement and house-hunting shows a staple of entertainment, but the network has challenged some barriers, frequently showing gay or lesbian couples purchasing or renovating a home. And its renovation show *Rehab Addict* features self-taught renovator Nicole Curtis, who is as comfortable driving a backhoe as picking out wallpaper. Still most of the shows reflect stereotypical gender roles, with women designing and men swinging hammers and operating power tools.

The Ellen DeGeneres Show and gay-themed decorating and personal styling shows may have helped normalize gay life for the broader society even while they often relied on traditional stereotypes. While still a relative rarity, in recent years more LGBTQ characters have found a spot on TV shows, even occasionally in a central role. *The Fall*'s Stella Gibson is bisexual, as is *Orange Is the New Black*'s Piper Chapman. The groundbreaking *Will and Grace*, which first premiered in the late 1990s and featured a gay man, Will Truman, made a comeback in 2017. In other shows, for example, Connor Walsh is a gay man in a relatively stable relationship in *How to Get Away with Murder*, Sophia Burset is a transwoman prisoner in *Orange Is the New Black*, Harry Doyle is a gay former MI6 agent now working with the FBI in *Quantico*, and Tammy Gregorio is a lesbian agent on *NCIS: New Orleans*. In 2018, the CW network premiered the first transgender superhero, Nia Nal, on *Supergirl*.

Increasingly, we are seeing shows and advertisements that resist traditional representations, or at least present them with a new twist. Empowering roles for women are actually more likely to appear in television than in the movies because the former expects a female audience, whereas the latter relies on young male viewers. In addition, changes in society's views of gender and other differences have made sponsors realize that they have a new marketing niche. The BBC's *Killing Eve* offers two strong women as primary characters, the protagonist and the villain, although both women are much more complicated than that. The show also features an Asian American woman as lead, and Sandra Oh became the first Asian woman nominated for an Emmy for leading actress. While she didn't win the Emmy, she did win a Golden Globe for her portrayal of MI5 officer Eve Polastri. *Killing Eve* is part of a new wave of limited-series shows that tell a story over fewer episodes (often six to eight) and may or may not last longer than one season (such as *Big Little Lies*). These shorter series seem to offer an opportunity for more shows centered on strong women. In particular, subscription services like Netflix, Hulu, and Amazon Prime have presented shows like *The Handmaid's Tale*, *The Fall*, and *The Marvelous Mrs. Maisel*. An

---

LEARNING ACTIVITY
QUEER OF COLOR IN MEDIA

Queer people, especially queer people of color, haven't often had great positive visibility in media, although, as mentioned at the start of the chapter, this has improved somewhat in recent years. *Moonlight* (2016) focused on issues of identity, gender, race, and sexuality as it followed a young gay black man growing up in Miami. The film won that year's Academy Award for Best Picture. Transwoman of color Laverne Cox became well known for her work in *Orange Is the New Black* and remains one of the few transgender people of color in TV and film, although Mya Taylor was honored with an Independent Spirit Award for her work in *Tangerine*, making her the first transgender actor to win one of the awards.

Check out the Queer Women of Color Media Wire at www.qwoc.org. QWOC is a media advocacy organization that creates space for art, books, music, film, and other media created by queer women of color.

Who are some of the queer women of color you learn about on the site?

Watch one of the shows featured on the site's TV page. What do you notice? How does the show address issues of gender identity, sexuality, and race?

Read some of the entries on the blog page. What issues are important for queer women of color in media? What barriers do they face? How are they resisting and succeeding?

Recent controversies have arisen around cisgender actors playing transgender roles (see for example Chloë Sevigny in Hit & Miss). Do some research about the controversy. Why is this practice problematic? Why do you think it has been pervasive? What is Hollywood doing (or not) to address the problem? How might this practice specifically disadvantage trans people of color actors?

especially prevalent British genre focuses on women police officers, detectives, or investigators who are often themselves a mess but are superb at solving crimes. Examples are *Marcella* and *Happy Valley*. Subscription service to international shows has also made available many Scandinavian detective noir shows with strong female leads, such as *The Bridge* and *The Killing*. Media expert Susan Douglas writes about the proliferation of empowered female characters. Douglas makes the case for these representations as fantasies of power that are especially seductive for girls and young women in that they provide the illusion and postfeminist message that "all has been won." She explains that such "enlightened sexism" embeds feminism into its representations and insists that because women are now equal to men, it is okay—and merely entertainment—to present the old, tired stereotypes under new glitter. Often, unfortunately, these new representations involve the same old package tied up in new ways; typically they involve women and men resisting some of the old norms while keeping most intact.

For example, although women are starting to be shown as competent, strong, athletic, and in control of their lives rather than ditzy housewives or sex symbols, they still are very physically attractive and are often highly sexualized. Crime dramas such as *Law & Order: SVU* and *Criminal Minds* also demonstrate how strong women must also be put in their place. Often the women leads are placed in peril, particularly sexual peril, or must choose between their jobs and their families or personal lives. These shows provide strong, intelligent women as primary characters, but at the same time these women fulfill the stereotypical standards of beauty. They can track down criminals using forensic science and look gorgeous while doing it. Unfortunately, most of the victims are female, too. Despite some empowered characters in shows like *Criminal Minds*, the focus on sexy female corpses ultimately associates women, queer cultures, and sexual subcultures with traditional and shallow stereotypes, negativity, and death.

Finally, news programs play an important role in shaping public opinion. Fox News, for example, is known for its support of conservative political opinion. Media scholars are particularly interested in the relationship between political ideologies and news media and especially the role of organizations like Fox News in supporting a conservative Republican agenda. One of the most influential pundits shaping popular opinion is Sean Hannity, whose net worth is estimated to be around $80 million and who is a close advisor to Donald Trump. Satire news shows such as *The Daily Show with Trevor Noah* and *The Late Show with Stephen Colbert* provide alternative, more liberal takes on domestic and international news.

MOVIES

In her groundbreaking work on cinema, feminist film theorist Laura Mulvey identifies the "male gaze" as a primary motif for understanding gender in filmmaking. Mulvey argues that movies are essentially made through and for the male gaze and fulfill a voyeuristic desire for men to look at women as objects. Viewers are encouraged to "see" the movie through the eyes of the male protagonist who carries the plot forward. In other words, the focus is on the production of meaning in a film (including television and digital media), how it imagines a viewing subject, and the ways the mechanisms of cinematic production shape the representation of women and marginalized others, reinforcing intersecting systems of inequality and privilege. Mulvey makes the point that traditional feminine subjects in film are bearers of meaning, not meaning making. Meaning making in Hollywood tends to incorporate heteronormative (centering of heterosexuality) themes that reinforce gender ranking through such genres as gangster films, action films, and westerns that celebrate heterosexual masculine power (with exceptions, of course, such as *Brokeback Mountain*). In other words, these films portray heterosexuality as the dominant theme representing masculinities.

Some feminist scholars have suggested the possibility for "subversive gazing" by viewers who refuse to gaze the way filmmakers expect and by making different kinds of movies. A key aspect of this criticism is recognizing the way identities are constructed and performed (in everyday life as well as in the movies) rather than essentialist and intrinsic to people. Coming from a black feminist perspective, bell hooks writes about the "oppositional gaze," encouraging women of color in film to reject stereotypical representations in film and actively critique them. In addition, film theorists are increasingly taking global or transnational perspectives, responding to critiques of Eurocentrism or the centering of a white, European, as well as straight and economically privileged perspective that has traditionally excluded disparate approaches across class, racial, and ethnic groups throughout the world. Bollywood, for example, a Hindi-language film industry in India, demonstrates the popularity of non-"Western" consciousness. Feminist film theorists such as Claire Johnson, hooks, and Mulvey emphasize that alternative (to traditional Hollywood) films can function as "counter cinema" by integrating alternative cinematic forms and images and by putting women and other marginalized people in charge of directing and producing films. Finally, the integration of lesbian/gay/queer politics in film attempts to destabilize traditional Hollywood themes. For example, the Queer Film Society, a consortium of LGBT film critics, historians, artists, and scholars, focuses on the production and celebration of queer images in world cinema. One of their mottos is "We're here, we're queer, we're watching movies."

Probably the best genre of film in which to observe gender is the romantic comedy or romantic drama. Romantic comedies have become the de facto film produced for female audiences that shape notions of multifaceted femininities. Their heteronormative formula reinforces myths about romantic love and marriage as the most important keys to women's happiness. This popular and seductive genre sometimes contains glimpses challenging heteropatriarchy (such as the blockbuster film *He's Just Not That Into You*). These films are packed with subtle and not-so-subtle notions of gender. For example, the now-classic movie *Pretty Woman* is a contemporary retelling of the Cinderella story, in which a young woman waits for her Prince Charming to rescue her from her undesirable situation. In this case, the prostitute-with-a-heart-of-gold is swept away in a white limousine by the older rich man who procured her services and then fell in love with her. Some films like *Enchanted* are trying to challenge the idea that all women need to be saved by a handsome prince. The *Shrek* series of movies satirizes traditional fairy tale elements, with the princess choosing to become an ogre and exhibiting her own sense of self and agency. Yet even these films that seem to challenge masculinist assumptions still often reproduce patriarchal understandings. So while Fiona in *Shrek* forsakes traditional femininity, she still embraces the roles of wife and mother as the ultimate goals for women.

Other genres of film are also revealing in terms of norms about gender. Slasher films and horror movies are often spectacular in terms of their victimization of women. The killers in these movies, such as Norman Bates in the classic *Psycho* (a spin-off television show in 2013, *Bates Motel*, capitalized on this plot and revealed his ambiguous childhood psyche),

---

INDEPENDENT FEMINIST FILMS

Janet Lockhart

Increasing Visibility on the Big Screen

Mainstream, big-studio films usually show stories reflecting the cultural "norm." The characters as well as the action mirror the filmmakers' assumptions, values, and ideas about who is important to include and what is important to show. Since making a film takes power—influence, money, access to skilled people and specialized equipment—it is not surprising that most films are made by the people in control of those resources: mostly men, mostly white. Their worldview mostly leaves out or only peripherally includes women, people of color, those with disabilities, LGBTQ people, and people of religions other than Christianity. The action in the stories reflects the filmmakers' ideas about what constitutes a good story: often heroes, engaged in conflict, competition, action, and/or violence.

Anyone, including feminists, who wants to tell a *different* story faces challenges. Independent films are one attempt to overcome biases and bring a greater diversity of characters and stories to the screen. Award-winning filmmaker Sofia Coppola (*Lost in Translation, The Beguiled*) has had opportunities to direct big-budget films but prefers to continue making independent films: "I love making small, low-budget films where I'm really allowed to do it the way I want," she says (Mottram, 2017).

Other self-identified feminist filmmakers have recently appeared in mainstream theaters: Patti Jenkins directed *Wonder Woman* (2017), and Ava DuVernay directed *A Wrinkle in Time* (2018), both of which included central female characters (one white and one African American). These films have received mixed responses about whether they are "feminist," based partly on the ways in which the female characters do and don't behave in accordance with the expected norm. As for mainstream acceptance (reflected in reviews and box office earnings), responses have also been mixed—based on the same norm.

Another attempt to change the face of mainstream filmmaking is the USC Annenberg Inclusion Initiative. This group uses research, advocacy, and action to promote diversity in entertainment media. Visit its website at https://annenberg.usc.edu/research/aii and explore its initiatives. Scroll down and read its "Inclusion Rider" (Kotagal et al. 2018). What does it ask filmmakers to do? What might be the importance of having a diversity of people working on films behind the scenes as well as on screen?

Look Further

Ask yourself these questions: What constitutes a "feminist" film? Is any story centered around a woman a feminist story? Can a woman-directed film be feminist if the main character is male? Can a film directed by a man be feminist? Are the stories told by feminist filmmakers significantly different from those told by mainstream filmmakers? If so, how?

Then, visit "12 Feminist Indies Every Film Lover Must See" (www.indiewire.com/2015/10/12-feminist-indies-every-film-lover-must-see-56249/). View one or more of these films and report on your impressions: Does the film conform to your idea of good storytelling? Does it challenge any of your assumptions or expectations? How does the depiction of women's lives conform to your definition of "feminist"? How does it differ?

References

Kotagal, K., Smith, S., Cox DiGiovanni, F., and Fischman, L. (2018). "Inclusion Rider." https://annenberg.usc.edu/research/aii

Mottram, J. (2017). "Sofia Coppola: My Feminist Retelling of 'The Beguiled' May 'Flip' the Male Fantasy—But It's No Castration Wish." *Independent*, July 12 https://www.independent.co.uk/arts-entertainment/films/features/sofia-coppola-feminist-retelling-of-the-beguiled-flip-male-fantasy-castration-nicole-kidman-kirsten-a7837711.html are often sexually disturbed and hound and kill women who arouse them. This is also the subtext of other old films such as *The Texas Chainsaw Massacre* movies and *Prom Night*.

Often it is sexually active couples who are killed, either after sex or in anticipation of it. Another standard plot line in horror movies is the crazed and demanding mother driving her offspring to psychosis. The "final girl" trope is also a staple of slasher films. She is the last girl left alive, the one who confronts the killer and presumably lives to tell the story. She's seen in classic films such as *Halloween, Friday the 13th, Scream, A Nightmare on Elm Street*, and *Hatchet*. Although both women and men claim to be entertained by these films, it is important to talk about the messages they portray about men, women, and the normalization of violence.

Pornography is an extreme example of the male gaze and the normalization of violence against women (discussed in Chapter 10). With its print media counterpart, pornography extends the sexualization and objectification of women's bodies for entertainment. In pornographic representations, women are often reduced to body parts and are shown deriving pleasure from being violated and dominated. Additionally, racism intersects with sexism in pornography when women of color are portrayed as the "exotic other" and are fetishized and portrayed in especially demeaning and animalistic ways. Although many feminists, ourselves included, oppose pornography, others, especially those described as "sex radicals," feel that pornography can be a form of sexual self-expression for women. They argue that women who participate in the production of pornography are taking control of their own sexuality and are profiting from control of their own bodies.

Advertisers have targeted young girls with stripper- and porn-inspired merchandise that creates a very narrow definition of what constitutes sexiness for women. Such pressures encourage young women to identify with this objectification and sexualization and confuse it with notions of self-empowerment. As already discussed, young people often follow blogs that feature gossip and photos about their favorite movie and music celebrities. Although this "cult of the celebrity" is not something new in popular culture, the growth of the Internet has facilitated public fascination with famous people and encourages young people to seek their few minutes of fame. It has been suggested that this celebration of fame not only shapes young people's ideas about self and body with unrealistic expectations, but has also facilitated the growth and interest in reality television. Ella Fegitz and Daniela Pirani's reading "The Sexual Politics of Veggies" explores how vegan and vegetarian diets have become hip and sexy because of celebrity endorsements, such as Beyoncé's.

Some of the more pervasive and lasting gender images in U.S. culture derive from Walt Disney feature films. As mentioned, Disney Corporation is one of the world's largest media conglomerates. A key source of its profits comes from tie-in products: Disney heroines live not only on the big screen, but also as dolls in little girls' rooms, on their sheets and curtains, and on their lunchboxes and clothes. On the whole, Disney characters reflect white, middle-class, heteropatriarchal, and imperialist norms. More recent representations in Disney movies have attempted to be more inclusive, but they still rely largely on these traditional norms. For example, new Disney heroines are empowered to make choices for themselves, but they still tend to be represented in sexualized ways with Anglo features.

As women have made societal gains, Hollywood filmmaking has changed and become more inclusive of new norms about gender and other forms of social difference. Indeed, as Susan Douglas explains, film media contain multiple images of female empowerment and gay-friendly narratives. Douglas asks why these images of female empowerment are not aligned with the realities of most women's lives and makes the case for a seductive appropriation of feminism for corporate gain. These empowered characters are more likely to be white and economically privileged at the same time that narratives about them tend to rely on heterosexual romance. Notice also the dearth of people of color or LGBTQ characters in leading roles in most films. Bringing a critical eye to the movies we watch helps us notice how films play a role in maintaining privilege and moves us from being passive recipients of the movies' message to active viewers who can offer informed analysis.

The dominance of Marvel's superhero series at the box office offers a glimpse into the pervasiveness of gender bias and stereotypes in the movies. Most Marvel superheroes are men—Spider-Man, Captain America, Iron Man, Thor, the Incredible Hulk. The Black Widow is highly feminized and sexualized and is underrepresented in the action compared with the male superheroes. Agent Peggy Carter, despite having her own successful superhero career, is defined primarily by her relationship to Steve Rogers, aka Captain America. Of course, these characters are also white. Only in 2019 did Captain Marvel present a woman superhero who was not defined by her relationship to a man. In 2018 *Black Panther* was one of the biggest hits of the year. It offered a plethora of strong black characters, including black women who fight, spy, go on missions, and do tech. This was in contrast to DC Comics' *Wonder Woman* While a powerful (white) woman is the central character, the film often focuses on her appearance and, of course, her relationship with a man. In *Justice League*, she becomes the one woman among all the male superheroes.

CONTEMPORARY MUSIC AND MUSIC VIDEOS

Popular music genres such as rock, grunge, punk, metal, techno, and hip-hop are contemporary cultural forms targeted at youth. Often this music offers resistance to traditional cultural forms and conveys a lot of teenage angst attractive to young people who are figuring out who they are in relation to their parents and other authority figures. In this way, such music serves as contemporary resistance and can work to mobilize people politically. Certainly music functions to help youth shape notions of identity. The various musical forms offer different kinds of identities from which people can pick and choose to sculpt their own sense of self. In this way, music has played, and continues to play, a key role in the consolidation of youth cultures in society. There is a huge music industry in the United States, and it works in tandem with television, film, video, radio, and, of course, advertising. The Internet and personalized music devices and software like the iPod and iTunes allow people to download music and create their own personalized collections rather than purchasing complete CDs. Similarly, personalized radio like Spotify, Pandora, and Slacker allows individuals to indicate and provide feedback on a song or artist they like, and the service responds by playing selections that are musically similar. These technologies have changed industries and listening practices.

Just as rock music was an essential part of mobilizing the youth of the 1960s to rebel against traditional norms, oppose the war, and work for civil rights, hip-hop music and culture have been influential in recent decades as critiques of racial cultural politics. Originating in African American urban street culture of the late 1970s, rap was influenced by rhythm and blues and rock and quickly spread beyond its roots into television, fashion, film, and, in particular, music videos. At the same time that the rap music industry has been able to raise the issues of racism, poverty, and social violence in the context of its endorsement of black nationalism, it has also perpetuated misogyny and violence in its orientation and lyrics. There are women performers in hip-hop and new female rappers are receiving much more attention, but their status in the industry is far below that of male performers. Women's success in hip-hop is illustrated by the success of such artists as Queen Latifah, Lil' Kim, Nicki Minaj, and Missy Elliot. Elliott in particular is known not only as a writer and performer but also as a producer of other artists' music. In the reading "Cardi B: Love & Hip Hop's Unlikely Feminist Hero," Sherri Williams examines how Cardi B has used her platform as a reality TV star to promote feminism. These women continue in the footsteps of blues and soul artists such as Billie Holiday, Aretha Franklin, and Etta James.

About 30 years after the advent of rock music, the combination of music with visual images gave rise to the music video genre, which gained immense popularity in the 1980s with the prominence of MTV, a music video station that has now branched into specialized programming. Music videos serve as both entertainment and advertisement. While viewers enjoy the product of the music video itself, the video also serves as a commercial for the recording that can be purchased with an easy click. Most music videos are fairly predictable in the ways they sexualize women, sometimes in violent ways. As in movies, women are generally present in music videos to be looked at. In fact, music videos featuring male musicians are aired in greater numbers than those featuring female musicians.

Nonetheless, we could also argue that the music video industry has allowed women performers to find their voice (literally) and to script music videos from their perspective. This opportunity gave women audience recognition and industry backing. Music videos also helped produce a feminine voice with the potential to disrupt traditional gendered perspectives. At its peak in the mid-1980s, MTV helped such women as Tina Turner, Cyndi Lauper, and Madonna find success. Madonna is especially interesting because she was cast simultaneously as both a feminist nightmare perpetuating gendered stereotypes about sexualized women and an important role model for women who want to be active agents in their lives. Lady Gaga (Stefani Germanotta) is similarly positioned as an icon who simultaneously supports and resists female sexualization. Both Madonna and Lady Gaga have been regarded as returning the male gaze by staring right back at the patriarchy. Similarly, Beyoncé, for example, has declared her feminism with empowering songs like "Single Ladies (Put a Ring on It)" and Destiny's Child's classic "Independent Women." Other artists like Christina Aguilera and Pink are also celebrated for being both sexual and assertively feminist in much the same way.

Performing rock music has generally been seen as a male activity, despite the presence of women rockers from the genre's beginnings in the 1950s. The male-dominated record industry has tended to exclude women rockers and tried to force women musicians into stereotypical roles as singers and sex objects. But the advent of new, accessible technologies has allowed women greater control of their own music. Now, instead of needing a recording contract with one of the big labels, an aspiring rocker can write, record, produce, and distribute her own music. For years, independent artists sold most of their music out of the back of a van, but now the Internet has made global distribution possible for just about every musician—without a large budget, agent, manager, or record label. New technologies both inside and outside the music industry have provided more ways for women to express themselves. Opportunities for self-promotion on YouTube and various social networking sites have encouraged a new generation of women musicians. Musicians can share their music and promote themselves for free with minimal effort. This allows them to break out of expected norms and potentially avoid industry stereotyping. Online communities such as Girlschool or Soundgirls and Women in Music also support and help launch new artists.

IDEAS FOR ACTIVISM

- Write letters to encourage networks to air television shows that depict the broad diversity of women and LGBTQ people.
- Write letters to sponsors to complain about programs that degrade or stereotype women and LGBTQ people.
- Form a reading group to study novels by women and LGBTQ authors.

- Create your own zine about a feminist issue that's important to you.
- Sponsor a media awareness event on campus to encourage other students to be aware of media portrayals of women and LGBTQ people. Use social media to promote awareness of women's and LGBTQ issues.
- Create a YouTube video to promote your women's and gender studies program.

Other strategies for independence include "indie" artists and bands whose music is produced within networks of independent record labels and underground music venues that emerged in the United States and elsewhere in the 1980s and 1990s. Indie is also seen as a distinct genre of rock music with a specific artistic aesthetic that includes many female artists. Singer-songwriters such as Ani DiFranco, the Indigo Girls, Tracy Chapman, and Tori Amos were important in providing feminist music as were the "riot grrl" feminist punk artists and bands of the 1980s. Many of these artists continue to serve as role models for young women seeking to gain a more independent place in contemporary music.

PRINT MEDIA

No discussion of popular culture is complete without a discussion of print media, even while most of its content is also available online. These mass media forms include magazines, newspapers, comic books, and other periodicals that are usually simultaneously available online. Like other media, they are a mix of entertainment, education, and advertising. Fashion magazines are heavy on advertising, whereas comic books tend to be geared toward entertainment and rely more on product sales of the comic books themselves. Newspapers fall somewhere in between.

Women's magazines are an especially fruitful subject of study for examining how gender works in contemporary U.S. society. As discussed in Chapter 4, women's magazines are a central part of the multibillion-dollar industries that produce cosmetics and fashion and help shape the social construction of "beauty." Alongside these advertising campaigns are bodily standards against which women are encouraged to measure themselves. Because almost no one measures up to these artificially created and often computer-generated standards, the message is to buy these products and your life will improve.

Generally, women's magazines can be divided into three distinct types. First are the fashion magazines that focus on beauty, attracting and satisfying men, self-improvement, and (occasionally) work and politics. Examples are *Vogue* (emphasizing fashion and makeup), *Cosmopolitan* (emphasizing sexuality and relationships with men), and *Self* (emphasizing self-improvement and employment), although the latter two are also heavy on beauty and fashion and the former is also preoccupied with sex. Most of these magazines have a white audience in mind; *Ebony* is one similar kind of magazine aimed at African American women. Note that there are also a number of junior magazines in this genre, such as *Seventeen*, aimed at teenage women. However, although its title suggests the magazine might be oriented toward 17-year-olds, it is mostly read by younger teenagers and even preadolescent girls. Given the focus of teen magazines on dating, fashion, and makeup, the effects of such copy and advertisements on young girls are significant.

A second genre of women's magazines includes those oriented toward the family, cooking, household maintenance and decoration, and keeping the man you already have. Examples include *Good Housekeeping*, *Redbook*, and *Better Homes and Gardens*. These magazines (especially those like *Good Housekeeping*) also include articles and advertising on fashion and cosmetics, although the representations of these products are different. Instead of the seductive model dressed in a shiny, revealing garment (as is usually featured on the cover of *Cosmo* or *Glamour*), *Redbook*, for example, usually features a less glamorous woman

LEARNING ACTIVITY

LOOKING GOOD, FEELING SEXY, GETTING A MAN

Locate a number of women's magazines, such as *Cosmopolitan*, *Vogue*, *Elle*, *Glamour*, *Redbook*, and *Woman's* *Day*. Read through the magazines and fill in the chart listing the number of articles you find about each topic. What do you observe from your analysis? What messages about gender are these magazines presenting?

Magazine Title	Makeup	Clothes	Hair	Sex/Dating	Dieting	Food/Recipes	Home Decoration	Work	Politics

WOMEN'S VOICES IN THE PUBLISHING INDUSTRY

Nancy Staton Barbour

Feminist consciousness-raising efforts in the late 1960s and early 1970s increased women's awareness that their personal experiences needed articulation in wider sociopolitical contexts. Like their first-wave sisters before them, second-wave feminists worked to spread their critical knowledge to greater numbers of women by distributing newsletters, pamphlets, and zines. The now famous book *Our Bodies, Ourselves* (1973), by the Boston Women's Health Book Collective, began as a 35-cent feminist pamphlet that aimed to demystify women's reproductive health and sexuality. But the women's movement faced resistance from mainstream publishers.

High-circulation magazines for "ladies" rejected feminist articles that addressed issues of real concern to women. Instead, they often published "puff" pieces—articles that appear to be informative but are really advertisements designed to sell a product. Feminists understood that these publications, although marketed directly to women, were controlled and edited almost entirely by men. In 1970, over 100 feminists descended upon the offices of *Ladies' Home Journal* and staged an 11-hour sit-in. They demanded that the magazine hire women to fill all editorial and advertising positions, that it hire a proportionate number of women of color at all levels, and that it cease publishing advertisements that were degrading to women. The editor did not immediately capitulate, but the August 1970 issue included an eight-page insert, "The New Feminism," written by protesters. In 1973, *LHJ* hired a woman as editor-in-chief.

Today, a handful of conglomerates control over 80 percent of the U.S. trade book market. Feminist publishers once relied on independent women's and lesbian bookstores as their major retailers, but many of these stores were driven out of business by chain and online booksellers. The feminist presses that have survived into the twenty-first century continue to promote the work of women writers, including women of color and queer and trans-identified women. Visit these feminist publishers' websites, join their mailing lists, read their books, and spread the word. You can also apply for an internship to learn more about feminist nonprofit publishing.

CALYX Press: An independent, nonprofit publisher of fine art and literature by women. *CALYX Journal* was the first in the United States to publish color reproductions of Frida Kahlo's art. CALYX has published work by Julia Alvárez, Barbara Kingsolver, Cherríe Moraga, Haunani-Kay Trask, Gail Tremblay, and Nellie Wong. *Into the Forest* by Jean Hegland (1996) was adapted as a 2015 film starring Ellen Page and Evan Rachel Wood. www.calyxpress.org

The Feminist Press: An educational publisher of classic and new writing from around the world that aims to advance women's rights and amplify feminist perspectives. It has published books by Ama Ata Aidoo, Justin Vivian Bond, Barbara Ehrenreich, and Paule Marshall, as well as reprinted work by Zora Neale Hurston and Charlotte Perkins Gilman. www.feministpress.org

Aunt Lute Books: A nonprofit multicultural women's press highlighting the perspectives of women from a broad range of communities. Aunt Lute has published many well-known feminist and lesbian authors, including Paula Gunn Allen, Gloria Anzaldúa, Judy Grahn, LeAnne Howe, Melanie Kaye/Kantrowitz, Audre Lorde, and Alice Walker. www.auntlute.com

(although one who is still very normatively beautiful) in more conservative clothes, surrounded by other graphics or captions featuring various desserts, crafts, and so forth. The focus is off sex and onto the home.

A third genre of women's magazines is the issue periodical that focuses on some issue or hobby that appeals to many women. *Parents* magazine is an example of an issue periodical aimed at women (although not exclusively). *Ms.* magazine is one aimed at feminists, as are *Bitch* and *Bust*. Examples of hobby-type periodicals include craft magazines on needlework or crochet and fitness magazines. There are many specialized issue periodicals aimed at men (such as hunting and fishing and outdoor activities periodicals, computer and other electronic-focused magazines, car and motorcycle magazines, and various sports periodicals). The best known of the latter is *Sports Illustrated*, famous also for its "swimsuit edition," which always produces record sales in its sexualization of female athletes' bodies. That there are more issue periodicals for men reflects the fact that this group is assumed to work and have specialized interests, and women are assumed to be preoccupied with looking good, working on relationships, and keeping a beautiful home.

Again, as in music, technology has also provided a way for women to express their voices through publishing. Zines are quick, cheap, cut-and-paste publications that have sprung up in both print and online formats in recent years. These publications, which range in quality, often provide a forum for alternative views on a wide variety of subjects, especially pop culture. As Alison Piepmeier notes, zines provide an opportunity for young feminists to resist ideas in mainstream publications that sustain women's subordination. Piepmeier explores the ways zines have allowed girls and young women to both critique and embrace girlishness and femininity. She suggests zine authors focus on the pleasures of girlhood even while they critique racist, heteropatriarchal social structures.

LITERATURE AND THE ARTS

In the reading "Thinking About Shakespeare's Sister," Virginia Woolf responds to the question "Why has there been no female Shakespeare?" Similarly, in the early 1970s, Linda Nochlin wrote a feminist critique of art history that sought to answer the question "Why have there been no great women artists?" Woolf and Nochlin reached very similar conclusions. According to Nochlin, the reason there had been no great women artists was not that no woman had been capable of producing great art but that the social conditions of women's lives had prevented such artistic endeavors.

Woolf wrote her essay in the late 1920s, but still today many critics and professors of literature raise the same questions about women's abilities to create great literature. Rarely, for example, does a seventeenth- or eighteenth-century British literature course give more than a passing nod to women authors of the period. Quite often, literature majors graduate having read perhaps only Woolf, George Eliot, Jane Austen, and Emily Dickinson. The usual justification is that women simply have not written the great literature that men have or that to include women would mean leaving out the truly important works of the literary canon (those written by white men).

In her essay, Woolf argues that it would have been impossible due to social constraints for a woman to write the works of Shakespeare in the age of Shakespeare. Although women did write, even in the time of Shakespeare, their works were often neglected by the arbiters of the literary canon because they fell outside the narrowly constructed definitions of great literature. For example, women's novels often dealt with the subjects of women's lives—family, home, love—subjects not deemed lofty enough for the canon of literature. Additionally, women often did not follow accepted forms, writing in fragments rather than unified texts. As the canon was defined according to white male norms, women's writing and much of the writing of both women and men of color were omitted. Jane Austen is still a popular novelist despite having written her books two centuries ago. Her current popularity is based in part on the dramatization of her work in a series of blockbuster movies as well as the fact that Austen was both a romantic and a feminist. The still-relevant romantic plots in Austen's novels provide a foundation for her strong critique of sexism and classism. We include in this chapter Emily Dickinson's short poem "The Wife," with its lament about the wife who "rose to his requirement, dropped / The playthings of her life / to take the honorable work / Of woman and of wife." Writing in the mid-nineteenth century, Dickinson was very aware, as women still are today, of the duties and expectations of women as they become wives.

Yet, toward the end of the twentieth century, more women began to publish novels and poetry, and these have been slowly introduced into the canon. These works have dealt with the realities of women's lives and have received wide acclaim. For example, writers such as Toni Morrison (who received the Nobel Prize in Literature), Alice Walker, and Maya Angelou have written about the dilemmas and triumphs faced by black women in a white, male-dominated culture. Annie Dillard won a Pulitzer Prize at the age of 29 for her nature essays about a year spent living by Tinker Creek. Feminist playwrights such as Wendy Wasserstein, Suzan Lori-Parks, Lynn Nottage, Migdalia Cruz, and Eve Ensler; performance artists such as Lily Tomlin and Lori Anderson; and feminist comedians such as Suzanne Westenhoffer, Tracey Ullman, Wanda Sykes, Hannah Gadsby, and Margaret Cho have also been very influential in providing new scripts for women's lives. Audre Lorde talks about the importance of literature in "Poetry Is Not a Luxury." She describes poetry as an opportunity to bring forth dreams, longings, and all that we dare make real. She implores us to speak and write the truths of our lives.

Just as female writers have been ignored, misrepresented, and trivialized, so too female artists and musicians have faced similar struggles. Women's art has often been labeled "craft" rather than art. This is because women, who were often barred from entering the artistic establishment, tended to create works of art that were useful and were excluded from the category of art. Often, female artists, like their sisters who were writing novels and poetry, used a male pen name and disguised their identity in order to have their work published or shown. With the influence of the women's movement, women's art is being reclaimed and introduced into the art history curriculum, although it is often taught in the context of "women's art." This emphasizes the ways the academy remains androcentric, with the contributions of "others" in separate courses. Female artists such as Frida Kahlo, Georgia O'Keeffe, and Judy Chicago have revitalized the art world by creating women-centered art and feminist critiques of masculine art forms. Similarly, graphic artists such as Barbara Kruger and mixed-media artists such as Jennifer Linton have incorporated feminist critiques of consumerism and desire. Photographers such as Cindy Sherman and Lorna Simpson have also raised important questions about the representation of women and other marginalized people in media and society. Joyce Wieland has famously created quilted art pieces using a traditionally feminine art form, and Kiki Smith has sculpted feminist imagery focusing on bodily secretions such as blood and sweat. Finally, the Guerrilla Girls, an anonymous feminist group wearing gorilla masks, use the names of dead female artists to highlight the ways women and people of color are disproportionately excluded from the art world through posters, postcards, and public appearances.

The works of female composers and musicians (such as Fanny Mendelssohn Hensel and Clara Schumann) have also been ignored as barriers to female achievement in this arena prevented recognition of their talents. Women of color faced almost insurmountable obstacles by virtue of both race and gender discrimination as well as the effects of class. It was mostly economically privileged women who were able to devote themselves to music. In 1893 Margaret Ruthven Lang was the first female composer in the United States to compose a piece performed by a major American symphony orchestra. Contemporary women composers still face challenges despite achievements by such women as Kaija Saariaho,

---

ACTIVIST PROFILE

MAXINE HONG KINGSTON

As a young girl, Maxine Hong Kingston could not find herself among the images in the books she read. The public library in her hometown of Stockton, California, had no stories of Chinese Americans and very few that featured girls. For Kingston, this meant a significant need and open space for the telling of her stories.

Kingston was born in Stockton in 1940 to Chinese immigrant parents. Her mother was trained as a midwife in China, and her father was a scholar and teacher. Arriving in the United States, Tom Hong could not find work and eventually ended up working in a gambling business. Maxine was named after a successful blonde gambler who frequented her father's establishment.

Growing up in a Chinese American community, Kingston heard the stories of her culture that would later influence her own storytelling. By earning 11 scholarships, she was able to attend the University of California at Berkeley, where she earned a BA in literature. She married in 1962, and she and her new husband moved to Hawaii, where they both taught for the next 10 years.

In 1976 Kingston published her first book, *The Woman Warrior: Memoirs of a Girlhood Among Ghosts*. This story of a young Chinese American girl who finds her own voice won the National Book Critics Circle Award. Kingston's portrayal of her own struggle with silence was met with a great deal of criticism from many Chinese men, who attacked Kingston's exploration of critical gender and race issues among Chinese Americans.

Kingston followed *Woman Warrior* with *China Men* in 1980, which also won the National Book Critics Circle Award. This book explored the lives of the men in Kingston's family who came to the United States, celebrating their achievements and documenting the prejudices and exploitation they faced. Her 1989 novel, *Tripmaster Monkey: His Fake Book*, continued her explorations of racism and oppression of Chinese Americans. Although some critics have accused Kingston of selling out because her stories have not reflected traditional notions of Chinese culture, she has maintained her right to tell her story in her own words with her own voice.

The Fifth Book of Peace, published in 2003, uses her personal tragedy of losing her house, possessions, and an unfinished novel in the Oakland–Berkeley fire of 1991 as a metaphor for war. She asks repeatedly the questions "Why war? Why not peace?" In 2006, she edited *Veterans of War, Veterans of Peace*, a collection of essays written by survivors of war who participated in her healing workshops. She published another memoir, *I Love a Broad Margin to My Life*, in 2012.

Cynthia Wong, Yu-Hiu Chang, and Paola Prestini. Similarly, very few women have been given the opportunity to conduct orchestras until recently, with the debut of contemporary female conductors such as Marin Alsop, Susanna Mälkki, Emmanuelle Haïm, Julia Jones, Anu Tali, Odaline de la Martinez, and Xian Zhang. Nadia Boulanger was the first woman to conduct a symphony orchestra in the early twentieth century and was known as one of the best music teachers of her time. Women were limited in music by the gendered nature of certain musical instruments that rendered them inappropriate. In fact, through the nineteenth century, only certain instruments such as the keyboard and harp were considered appropriate for women to play, and, even today, women are still directed away from some instruments and toward others. Despite these obstacles, they continue to produce literature and art and to redefine the canon. As in other male-dominated arenas, however, women have had to struggle to create a place for themselves. This place is everchanging, providing women with opportunities for fame, empowerment, self-validation, and respect.

HISTORICAL MOMENT

THE NEA FOUR

Chartered by the U.S. Congress in 1965, the National Endowment for the Arts (NEA) provides funding for artists to develop their work. In 1990 Congress passed legislation that forced the NEA to consider "standards of decency" in awarding grants. Four performance artists—Karen Finley, Holly Hughes, John Fleck, and Tim Miller—had been selected to receive NEA grants, but following charges by conservatives, particularly Senator Jesse Helms (R–North Carolina), that the artists' works were obscene, the NEA denied their grants. All but Finley are gay, and Finley herself is an outspoken feminist.

Finley's work deals with raw themes of women's lives. She gained notoriety for a performance in which she smeared her nude body with chocolate to represent the abuse of women. Latching onto this image, conservatives referred to Finley as "the chocolate-smeared woman." Her work is shocking, but she uses the shocking images to explore women's horrific experiences of misogyny, and she uses her body in her performances in ways that reflect how society uses her body against her will.

Hughes's work explores lesbian sexuality, and, in revoking her NEA grant, then–NEA chairman John Frohnmeyer specifically referenced Hughes's lesbianism as one of the reasons she had lost her grant. Some of her performances have included *Well of Horniness*, *Lady Dick*, and *Dress Suits to Hire*.

Following the revocation of their grants, the four sued the U.S. government, and in 1992 a lower court ruled in favor of the plaintiffs, reinstating the grants. The government appealed in 1994 and lost again. Then, in a surprise move, the Clinton administration appealed the decision to the U.S. Supreme Court. In 1998 the Supreme Court overturned the lower court's rulings and held that the "standards of decency" clause is constitutional. Since the ruling, the budget and staff of the NEA have been slashed, and artists like Finley and Hughes must seek funding from other sources to continue their performances.

If you're interested in finding out more about feminism and censorship, visit the website of Feminists for Free Expression at https://ffeusa.livejournal.com.

THE BLOG

LOVE AND WOMEN'S BASKETBALL

Susan M. Shaw (2017)

My love affair with basketball began when I was 10 years old and started playing on my elementary school team. Of course, that was a couple of years before Title IX, and so our coaches were well-meaning but untrained moms, and we played half-court ball, since a lot of people believed girls couldn't and shouldn't run up and down the entire court.

(continued)

Fast-forward 45 years. My beloved Oregon State Beavers are headed to the NCAA tournament as a number two seed. They ended the regular season ranked sixth in the country, the highest ranking ever for our team. As I watch them play, I see what's been so great about the impact of the Women's Movement, and I see the work we still have to do to achieve true equity between women and men—and not just in basketball.

In the mid-1970s my best friend played basketball for the University of South Carolina (today one of the number one seeds in the tournament) for one season before she blew out her knee. She's 5'10". She was a tall player back then. Today, our point guard is 6'1".

Because of Title IX, girls now start playing basketball with real coaches. They have trainers. They go to basketball camps. They grow strong and fast in ways we could not have imagined in the 1970s. In fact, Bernice Sandler, one of the driving forces behind Title IX, once told me that those early feminists had no idea the impact Title IX would have on women's sports. We just hoped for a few more games at field day, she told me.

The advances on the court have been paralleled by advances in the classroom. Our 6'6" center who holds the Pac 12 career record for blocks is a rocket scientist (seriously) with a stellar grade point average.

Fans are wild about this team. We are Beaver Believers. We cheer them on with such passion that I truly believe that in a couple of close games the home crowd willed them to the win. Community members, students, women and men, girls and boys come to these games. I took my nine-year-old goddaughter to a game a few weeks ago, and I was thrilled to see her watching women being strong and competitive and hearing a crowd cheer for women. So many Beavers fans made the trek north that when we played in the Pac 12 tournament in Seattle, organizers announced that this year's tournament had set an attendance record. Meanwhile, the University of South Carolina has led the way nationally with an average attendance of around 15,000 fans at each game.

One could almost think the dream of equality has been reached. Almost. The distance we still have to go, however, shows up now and again in subtle ways in what we value and how we behave.

I'm grateful that all of our sports teams are Beavers. We have no "Lady" Beavs. I was always a little puzzled at a previous institution where our women's basketball team was the "Lady Lancers." While most college teams have gotten rid of the "Lady" designation, high schools have "Lady Knights," "Lady Rebels," "Lady Warriors," and even "Lady Friars." Not long ago, the University of Tennessee rebranded all of its teams as simply "Volunteers," except for the women's basketball team, which remains the "Lady Vols" in honor of what Pat Summit

did there (and I believe Pat Summit did more to advance women's basketball nationally than anyone). Still, 2016, and women athletes are "Ladies."

This season and last, OSU led the Pac 12 conference in attendance for women's basketball. We usually have between 4,000 and 5,000 fans at home games. I believe our best-attended game this year was around 7,000. But no matter how good our women's team has been the past two years, attendance at our men's games is better (and I love our men's basketball team too—nothing against them), even though they have not had the successes the women have.

People often suggest the men's game is just more exciting. But women's basketball and men's basketball are really two different games, and we should ask why we define dunking as more exciting than actually shooting the ball. In other words, we've made the facet of the game that most women can't do the defining skill that makes the game exciting. But for those of us who love women's basketball, we know just how exciting pinpoint accuracy in shooting the three can be.

We also know the thrill of watching a group play as a team. This year very few of our players were recognized for individual achievements; we had very, very few Pac 12 players of the week. We won as a team.

Media coverage of women's and men's basketball is different too. From our local paper and local TV stations to *the New York Times*, I've noticed the greater coverage given to men's basketball. An article this week in our local paper highlighted the dilemma for OSU students who can't travel to the men's first-round NCAA game in Oklahoma because this is finals week here. The article ended by saying that students could go to the women's game on Friday because it's in Corvallis. I guess the women's game is the consolation prize.

Second-class status continues into professional women's basketball as well. No matter what UConn's Breanna Stewart has accomplished as one of the greatest players ever, she'll never make as much money as the top players in the men's game. Her team will never draw the same crowds, and she'll have to play in the summer because that's the WNBA season.

Nonetheless, Friday afternoon when the Beavers take the court I'll be there in my orange and black, cheering proudly, yelling at the officials, and clapping along with the fight song. I'll think about how far we've come and how far we still have to go. I'll fume that we didn't sell out the coliseum, and I'll form the letters with my arms as we chant, "Ohhhhhh—Esssssss—Uuuuuuu! Oregon State, fight, fight, fight!" And I'll spend March Madness marveling at powerful, capable women, the fruit of Title IX, and the challenge for a more equitable future.

30. THINKING ABOUT SHAKESPEARE'S SISTER

VIRGINIA WOOLF (1929)

. . . [I]t is a perennial puzzle why no woman wrote a word of extraordinary literature when every other man, it seemed, was capable of song or sonnet. What were the conditions in which women lived, I asked myself; for fiction, imaginative work that is, is not dropped like a pebble upon the ground, as science may be; fiction is like a spider's web, attached ever so lightly perhaps, but still attached to life at all four corners. Often the attachment is scarcely perceptible; Shakespeare's plays, for instance, seem to hang there complete by themselves. But when the web is pulled askew, hooked up at the edge, torn in the middle, one remembers that these webs are not spun in midair by incorporeal creatures, but are the work of suffering human beings, and are attached to grossly material things, like health and money and the houses we live in.

I went therefore, to the shelf where the stories stand and took down one of the latest, Professor Trevelyan's *History of England*. Once more I looked up Women, found "position of," and turned to the pages indicated. "Wifebeating," I read "was a recognized right of man, and was practiced without shame by high as well as low. . . . Similarly," this historian goes on, "the daughter who refused to marry the gentleman of her parents' choice was liable to be locked up, beaten and flung about the room, without any shock being inflicted on public opinion. Marriage was not an affair of personal affection, but of family avarice, particularly in the 'chivalrous' upper classes. . . . Betrothal often took place while one or both of the parties was in the cradle, and marriage when they were scarcely out of the nurses' charge." That was about 1470, soon after Chaucer's time. The next reference to the position of women is some two hundred years later, in the time of the Stuarts. "It was still the exception for women of the upper and middle class to choose their own husbands, and when the husband had been assigned, he was lord and master, so far at least as law and custom could make him. Yet even so," Professor Trevelyan concludes, "neither Shakespeare's women nor those of authentic seventeenth-century memoirs, like the Verneys and the Hutchinsons, seem wanting in personality and

character." Certainly, if we consider it, Cleopatra must have had a way with her; Lady Macbeth, one would suppose, had a will of her own; Rosalind, one might conclude, was an attractive girl. Professor Trevelyan is speaking no more than the truth when he remarks that Shakespeare's women do not seem wanting in personality and character. Not being a historian, one might go even further and say that women have burnt like beacons in all the works of all the poets from the beginning of time—Clytemnestra, Antigone, Cleopatra, Lady Macbeth, Phèdre, Cressida, Rosalind, Desdemona, the Duchess of Malfi, among the dramatists; then among the prose writers: Millamant, Clarissa, Becky Sharp, Anna Karenina, Emma Bovary, Madame de Guermantes—the names flock to mind, nor do they recall women "lacking in personality and character." Indeed, if woman had no existence save in fiction written by men, one would imagine her a person of the utmost importance, very various; heroic and mean; splendid and sordid; infinitely beautiful and hideous in the extreme; as great as a man, some think even greater. But this is woman in fiction. In fact, as Professor Trevelyan points out, she was locked up, beaten and flung about the room.

A very queer, composite being thus emerges. Imaginatively she is of the highest importance; practically she is completely insignificant. She pervades poetry from cover to cover; she is all but absent from history. She dominates the lives of kings and conquerors in fiction; in fact she was the slave of any boy whose parents forced a ring upon her finger. Some of the most inspired words, some of the most profound thoughts in literature fall from her lips; in real life she could hardly read, could scarcely spell, and was the property of her husband.

. . .

Be that as it may, I could not help thinking, as I looked at the works of Shakespeare on the shelf . . . it would have been impossible, completely and entirely, for any woman to have written the plays of Shakespeare in the age of Shakespeare. Let me imagine, since facts are so hard to come by, what would have happened had Shakespeare had a wonderfully gifted sister, called Judith, let us say. Shakespeare himself went, very probably—his mother was an heiress—to the grammar school, where he may have learnt Latin—Ovid, Virgil and Horace—and the elements of grammar and logic. He was, it is well known, a wild boy who poached rabbits, perhaps shot a deer, and had, rather sooner than he should have done, to marry a woman in the neighbourhood, who bore him a child rather quicker than was right. That escapade sent him to seek his fortune in London. He had, it seemed, a taste for the theatre; he began by holding horses at the stage door. Very soon he got work in the theatre, became a successful actor, and lived at the hub of the universe, meeting everybody, knowing everybody, practising his art on the boards, exercising his wits in the streets, and even getting access to the palace of the queen. Meanwhile his extraordinarily gifted sister, let us suppose, remained at home. She was as adventurous, as imaginative, as agog to see the world as he was. But she was not sent to school. She had no chance of learning grammar and logic, let alone of reading Horace and Virgil. She picked up a book now and then, one of her brother's perhaps, and read a few pages. But then her parents came in and told her to mend the stockings or mind the stew and not moon about with books and papers. They would have spoken sharply but kindly, for they were substantial people who knew the conditions of life for a woman and loved their daughter—indeed, more likely than not she was the apple of her father's eye. Perhaps she scribbled some pages up in an apple loft on the sly, but was careful to hide them or set fire to them. Soon, however, before she was out of her teens, she was to be betrothed to the son of a neighbouring wool-stapler.

She cried out that marriage was hateful to her, and for that she was severely beaten by her father. Then he ceased to scold her. He begged her instead not to hurt him, not to shame him in this matter of her marriage. He would give her a chain of beads or a fine petticoat, he said; and there were tears in his eyes. How could she disobey him? How could she break his heart? The force of her own gift alone drove her to it. She made up a small parcel of her belongings, let herself down by a rope one summer's night and took the road to London. She was not seventeen.

The birds that sang in the hedge were not more musical than she was. She had the quickest fancy, a gift like her brother's, for the tune of words. Like him, she had a taste for the theatre. She stood at the stage door; she wanted to act, she said. Men laughed in her face. The manager—a fat, loose-lipped man—guffawed. He bellowed something about poodles dancing and women acting—no woman, he said, could possibly be an actress. He hinted—you can imagine what. She could get no training in her craft. Could she even seek her dinner in a tavern or roam the streets at midnight? Yet her genius was for fiction and lusted to feed abundantly upon the lives of men and women and the study of their ways. At last—for she was very young, oddly like Shakespeare the poet in her face, with the same grey eyes and rounded brows—at last Nick Greene the actor-manager took pity on her; she found herself with child by that gentleman and so—who shall measure the heat and violence of the poet's heart when caught and tangled in a woman's body?—killed herself one winter's night and lies buried at some cross-roads where the omnibuses now stop outside the Elephant and Castle.

That, more or less, is how the story would run, I think, if a woman in Shakespeare's day had had Shakespeare's genius. . . .

This may be true or it may be false—who can say?—but what is true in it, so it seemed to me, reviewing the story of Shakespeare's sister as I had made it, is that any woman born with a great gift in the sixteenth century would certainly have gone crazed, shot herself, or ended her days in some lonely cottage outside the village, half witch, half wizard, feared and mocked at. For it needs little skill in psychology to be sure that a highly gifted girl who had tried to use her gift for poetry would have been so thwarted and hindered by other people, so tortured and pulled asunder by her own contrary instincts, that she must have lost her health and sanity to a certainty. No girl could have walked to London and stood at a stage door and forced her way into the presence of actor-managers without doing herself a violence and suffering an anguish which may have been irrational—for chastity may be a fetish invented by certain societies for unknown reasons—but were none the less inevitable. . . .

But for women, I thought, looking at the empty shelves, these difficulties were infinitely more formidable. In the first place, to have a room of her own, let alone a quiet room or a sound-proof room, was out of the question, unless her parents were exceptionally rich or very noble, even up to the beginning of the nineteenth century. Since her pin money, which depended on the good will of her father, was only enough to keep her clothed, she was debarred from such alleviations as came even to Keats or Tennyson or Carlyle, all poor men, from a walking tour, a little journey to France, from the separate lodging which, even if it were miserable enough, sheltered them from the claims and tyrannies of their families. Such material difficulties were formidable; but much worse were the immaterial. The indifference of the world which Keats and Flaubert and other men of genius have found so hard to bear was in her case not indifference but hostility. The world did not say to her as it said to them, Write if you choose; it makes no difference to me. The world said with a guffaw, Write? What's the good of your writing? . . .

31. THE WIFE

EMILY DICKINSON (C. 1860)

She rose to his requirement, dropped
The playthings of her life
To take the honorable work
Of woman and of wife.

If aught she missed in her new day
Of amplitude, or awe,

Or first prospective, or the gold
In using wore away.

It lay unmentioned, as the sea
Develops pearl and weed,
But only to himself is known
The fathoms they abide.

32. POETRY IS NOT A LUXURY

AUDRE LORDE (1902)

The quality of light by which we scrutinize our lives has direct bearing upon the product which we live, and upon the changes which we hope to bring about through those lives. It is within this light that we form those ideas by which we pursue our magic and make it realized. This is poetry as illumination, for it is through poetry that we give name to those ideas which are—until the poem—nameless and formless, about to be birthed, but already felt. That distillation of experience from which true poetry springs births thought as dream births concept, as feeling births idea, as knowledge births (precedes) understanding.

As we learn to bear the intimacy of scrutiny and to flourish within it, as we learn to use the products of that scrutiny for power within our living, those fears which rule our lives and form our silences begin to lose their control over us.

For each of us as women, there is a dark place within, where hidden and growing our true spirit rises, "beautiful/and tough as chestnut/stanchions against (y)our nightmare of weakness/"[1] and of impotence.

These places of possibility within ourselves are dark because they are ancient and hidden; they have survived and grown strong through that darkness. Within these deep places, each one of us holds an incredible reserve of creativity and power, of unexamined and unrecorded emotion and feeling. The woman's place of power within each of us is neither white nor surface; it is dark, it is ancient, and it is deep.

When we view living in the european mode only as a problem to be solved, we rely solely upon our ideas to make us free, for these were what the white fathers told us were precious.

But as we come more into touch with our own ancient, noneuropean consciousness of living as a situation to be experienced and interacted with, we learn more and more to cherish our feelings, and to respect those hidden sources of our power from where true knowledge and, therefore, lasting action comes.

At this point in time, I believe that women carry within ourselves the possibility for fusion of these two approaches so necessary for survival, and we come closest to this combination in our poetry. I speak here of poetry as a revelatory distillation of experience, not the sterile word play that, too often, the white fathers distorted the word *poetry* to mean—in order to cover a desperate wish for imagination without insight.

For women, then, poetry is not a luxury. It is a vital necessity of our existence. It forms the quality of the light within which we predicate our hopes and dreams toward survival and change, first made into language, then into idea, then into more tangible action. Poetry is the way we help give name to the nameless so it can be thought. The farthest horizons of our hopes and fears are cobbled by our poems, carved from the rock experiences of our daily lives.

As they become known to and accepted by us, our feelings and the honest exploration of them become sanctuaries and spawning grounds for the most radical and daring of ideas. They become a safe-house for that difference so necessary to change and the conceptualization of any meaningful action. Right now, I could name at least ten ideas I would have found intolerable or incomprehensible and frightening, except as they came after dreams and poems. This is not idle fantasy, but a disciplined attention to the true meaning of "it feels right to me." We can train ourselves to respect our feelings and to transpose them into a language so they can be shared. And where that language does not yet exist, it is our poetry which helps to fashion it. Poetry is not only dream and vision; it is the skeleton architecture of our lives. It lays the foundations for a future of change, a bridge across our fears of what has never been before.

Possibility is neither forever nor instant. It is not easy to sustain belief in its efficacy. We can sometimes work long and hard to establish one beachhead of real resistance to the deaths we are expected to live,

only to have that beachhead assaulted or threatened by those canards we have been socialized to fear, or by the withdrawal of those approvals that we have been warned to seek for safety. Women see ourselves diminished or softened by the falsely benign accusations of childishness, of nonuniversality, of changeability, of sensuality. And who asks the question: Am I altering your aura, your ideas, your dreams, or am I merely moving you to temporary and reactive action? And even though the latter is no mean task, it is one that must be seen within the context of a need for true alteration of the very foundations of our lives.

The white fathers told us: I think, therefore I am. The Black mother within each of us—the poet—whispers in our dreams: I feel, therefore I can be free. Poetry coins the language to express and charter this revolutionary demand, the implementation of that freedom.

However, experience has taught us that action in the now is also necessary, always. Our children cannot dream unless they live, they cannot live unless they are nourished, and who else will feed them the real food without which their dreams will be no different from ours? "If you want us to change the world someday, we at least have to live long enough to grow up!" shouts the child.

Sometimes we drug ourselves with dreams of new ideas. The head will save us. The brain alone will set us free. But there are no new ideas still waiting in the wings to save us as women, as human. There are only old and forgotten ones, new combinations, extrapolations and recognitions from within ourselves—along with the renewed courage to try them out. And we must constantly encourage ourselves and each other to attempt the heretical actions that our dreams imply, and so many of our old ideas disparage. In the forefront of our move toward change, there is only poetry to hint at possibility made real. Our poems formulate the implications of ourselves, what we feel within and dare make real (or bring action into accordance with), our fears, our hopes, our most cherished terrors.

For within living structures defined by profit, by linear power, by institutional dehumanization, our feelings were not meant to survive. Kept around as unavoidable adjuncts or pleasant pastimes, feelings were expected to kneel to thought as women were expected to kneel to men. But women have survived. As poets. And there are no new pains. We have felt them all already. We have hidden that fact in the same place where we have hidden our power. They surface in our dreams, and it is our dreams that point the way to freedom. Those dreams are made realizable through our poems that give us the strength and courage to see, to feel, to speak, and to dare.

If what we need to dream, to move our spirits most deeply and directly toward and through promise, is discounted as a luxury, then we give up the core—the fountain—of our power, our womanness; we give up the future of our worlds.

For there are no new ideas. There are only new ways of making them felt—of examining what those ideas feel like being lived on Sunday morning at 7 A.M., after brunch, during wild love, making war, giving birth, mourning our dead—while we suffer the old longings, battle the old warnings and fears of being silent and impotent and alone, while we taste new possibilities and strengths.

NOTE

1. From "Black Mother Woman," first published in *From a Land Where Other People Live* (Broadside Press, Detroit, 1973), and collected in *Chosen Poems: Old and New* (W. W. Norton and Company, New York, 1982), p. 53.

33. TWEETING BACK WHILE SHOUTING BACK

EMMA TURLEY AND JENNY FISHER (2018)

'Shouting back' or responding using a hashtag in digital spaces is a way of exposing the prejudice faced by people on a daily basis, while sharing and reacting to it, and provoking responses; social networking sites (SNSs) provide a visible platform for feminists to address experiences relating to sexism and misogyny. Guillard (2016, p. 1) argues that digital spaces are central to defining 'a fourth wave of feminist practice' and allow for global engagement, yet the use of digital media can be tokenistic (Kristofferson, White, & Peloza, 2014) and use of the Internet is insufficient to demarcate a new wave of practice. As feminist academics (Braun, 2011) writing from the United Kingdom, who have engaged with social media for a number of years, we seek to explore some of the issues related to social media-based feminist campaigns and examine the process of 'shouting back' against hegemony, misogyny and sexism. Digital spaces are a powerful influence on social movements (Earl & Kimport, 2011), and we consider some of the ways in which social media has contributed to the feminist movement. We will first briefly reflect on why social media and SNSs are useful to feminists, before discussing the impact of two social media based feminist campaigns and the implications of this for the feminist movement. Following Kitzinger (2000), we consider the feminist movement to be a social movement to challenge the patriarchal and societal systems that serve to oppress women, to advocate for social justice and issues that affect women around the world. Further, we use the terms feminist groups and feminist individuals in recognition that there is both collective action and individual protest.

Since 2010, there has been a global digital explosion of feminists using SNSs and blogs to raise consciousness and expand awareness about a myriad of issues related to patriarchy, sexism, misogyny, gendered violence and inequality (Baer, 2016). Baer (2016, p. 30) argues that due to neoliberalism, with its emphasis on the individual and the shift from public to private politics, feminist social media campaigns are political actions that are reframing feminism and "deploy the precarious female body to make visible contradictions of contemporary social reality." Taking advantage of digital platforms can facilitate the broadening of feminist space(s), thus enabling a wider reach and more open engagement with and promotion of feminism and feminist ideas (Crossley, 2015). Further, for Schuster (2013), social media can connect people beyond their locality, and involve those who may not be able to connect face to face. National, transnational and global academic literature is increasingly focused on the connections between feminism and social media, and much of the literature is transdisciplinary (see for example, Baer, 2016; Gillard, 2016; Hutton, Griffin, Lyons, Niland, & McCreanor, 2016; Manago, 2013).

We note here that digital spaces are not a utopia for feminist campaigning. Women are frequently attacked online (to the extent of rape or death threats) or 'trolled' for airing their views and experiences relating to inequality and sexism. As Boynton (2012, p. 539) stated, "[t]he mobilizing power social media creates also enables mobbing, bullying and harassment" for feminists. Social media can expand the means to proliferate misogynistic and sexist narratives, and shame women and maintain power inequalities in the offline world. Digital spaces have potential to exclude people for their gender, ethnicity, social class and other structural inequalities (Hutton et al., 2016), and their levels of digital literacy or disabilities.

Further, the digital stage is crowded and so various feminist organisations (and individuals) compete for publicity, recognition and resources (Fotopoulou, 2016). Digital labour (often unpaid) is essential for establishing and maintaining an online presence. In addition, the use of social media by feminists takes place alongside offline action, and as Baer (2016, p. 22) argues, "[t]he interface between online and offline spaces appears to be crucial for establishing modes of feminist protest." Social media can be further used for reach and scope through celebrity endorsement such as actor Emma Watson's #heforshe, which encourages men to become feminists and strive for equality. These enable rapid dissemination of feminist information and news, that is then often picked up and covered by the mainstream media because of celebrity involvement. The use of a hashtag makes the campaigns accessible to a larger audience, immediate and easy to track, and using social media can be less intimidating than actually confronting a misogynist in the real, offline world (Eagle, 2015), as well as encouraging a collective sense of support and empathy.

Turning to 'shouting back' social media campaigns, that have challenged hegemony, misogyny and inequalities, there are a number of examples of hashtags. Acknowledging that spaces here are limited for a wide consideration of hashtags, we selected two that we are familiar with, and have made an impact beyond feminist circles and in the offline world: #everydaysexism and #AskThicke. We chose #everydaysexism as this is part of an online active feminist campaign by British feminist writer, Laura Bates, that aims to collate examples of everyday experiences of sexism in one space. #AskThicke is an example of a hashtag that has been appropriated by feminists to raise awareness about a particular issue. Both campaigns have been widely cited in the mainstream U.K. press including the *Guardian*, the *Independent*, the *Telegraph* and the *Daily Mail* newspapers, and discussed on television shows ranging from political programmes to talk shows. This illustrates that these campaigns have had a broader influence through reaching a mainstream, not actively feminist, audience.

Founded by Laura Bates in 2012 in the U.K., in reaction to the explicit and implicit sexism she encountered [and] frequently heard about from other women, the global Everyday Sexism Project's #everydaysexism and linked Twitter account, has acted as a platform for feminists to share lived experiences of harassment, misogyny and sexism in public and private spheres, raise consciousness and challenge dominant hegemonic discourses. The website's Twitter account uses two main hashtags, #everydaysexism and #shoutingback, aims to document macro and micro examples to expose implicit patriarchal culture and the unequal treatment of women and the collection of women's stories includes over 85,000 examples. Indeed, as a result of the accessibility of Twitter hashtags, interaction with the project has been wide ranging and covered significantly by the mainstream press in the U.K, and by television programmes, including the BBC news. The project has been documented in a book *Everyday Sexism* cited by Feminist Press as essential reading for young people.

Laura Bates writes weekly for the *Guardian* and has recently covered the ways in which the media portrays female politicians and sportswomen.

Turning to #AskThicke, a controversial number one hit song "Blurred Lines" written by Robin Thicke and Pharrell Williams, was called out as a "rape anthem" and banned from some university campuses. This provided feminists with an opportunity to raise awareness of rape culture. In 2014, the VH1 music channel used the #AskThicke hashtag on Twitter, originally intended as an online Q&A session for fans to interact with Robin Thicke. The hashtag was quickly appropriated by feminists to challenge Thicke about his misogynistic lyrics and music video, and to speak out against the prevalence of rape culture more broadly. Two examples of tweets are:

@kittyknits: #AskThicke It might seem like some of the questions on this hashtag are cruel and abusive but Robin, I know you want it

@MariaJPrice: #AskThicke Did you really write a rape anthem as a love song for your wife and are you still wondering why she left you?

For Thicke and his record label, Star Trak Recordings, the social media engagement mobilised by feminists was a public relations disaster, as the story was picked up by the media in both the U.K. and the United States (The *Telegraph*, 2014; *Time*, 2014) and highlighted the issue of rape culture more widely. Discussion of the #AskThicke hashtag was unconfined to online spaces; the media produced articles mentioning misogyny and sexism as a central feature, referring to Thicke as "the poster boy for misogyny" (*Independent*, 2014: online), and "creepy and manipulative" (*Time*, 2014: online), and sexism within the music industry and more widely in society was given prominent coverage. In the U.K., some students' associations successfully lobbied for the song to be banned at a number of universities, including Leeds University and the University of Edinburgh. Other prominent men within the music industry have recently been accused of sexual harassment and assault. Heathcliff Berru, founder of a music public relations company, has been accused by seven women of a range of sexual offences, and the American singer Kesha has filed a lawsuit against her manager for sexual assault and rape. Once again,

Twitter was used by the singers to document and share their experiences, and also by supporters to show solidarity with the women, using the hashtag #FreeKesha. The media reported on these allegations (*New York Times*, 2016; The *Guardian*, 2016) opening up debate regarding sexual harassment at work and more broadly.

Here, we have considered the use of two hashtags on Twitter relating to feminist campaigns. We are aware that there are limitations in the use of hashtags and indeed social media. However, digital media has radical potential for shouting back and highlighting sexism, equality misogyny and rape culture, along with generating a space for discussions of other everyday issues. We recognise that social media is not the only modality of feminism and the importance and value of offline feminist movements should not be overlooked.

REFERENCES

Baer, H. (2016). Redoing feminism: Digital activism, body politics and neoliberalism. *Feminist Media Studies*, 16, 17–34.

Bates, L. (2012). Everydaysexism.com. Retrieved from http://everydaysexism.com/.

Boynton, P. (2012). Getting the press we deserve: Opportunities and challenges for innovative media practice. *Feminism & Psychology*, 22(4), 536–540.

Braun, V. (2011). Petting a snake? Reflections on feminist critique, media engagement and "making a difference." *Feminism & Psychology*, 22(4), 528–535.

Crossley, A. (2015). Facebook Feminism: Social Media, Blogs, and New Technologies of Contemporary U.S. Feminism. *Mobilization: An International Quarterly*, 20, 253–268.

Eagle, R. B. (2015). Loitering, lingering, hashtagging: Women reclaiming public space via #BoardtheBus, #StopStreetHarassment, and the #Everydaysexism Project. *Feminist Media Studies*, 15, 349–353.

Earl, J., & Kimport, K. (2011). *Digitally enabled social change: Activism in the Internet age*. Cambridge, MA: MIT Press.

Fotopoulou, A. (2016). Digital and networked by default? Women's organisations and the social imaginary of networked feminism. *New Media and Society, 18*(6), 989–1005.

Guillard, J. (2016). Is feminism trending? Pedagogical approaches to countering (Sl)activism. *Gender and Education, 28*(5), 609–626.

Hutton, F., Griffin, C., Lyons, A., Niland, P., & McCreanor, T. (2016). "Tragic girls" and "crack whores": Alcohol, femininity and Facebook. *Feminism & Psychology, 26*(1), 73–93.

Independent. (2014) Robin Thicke trolled after #Ask-Thicke Twitter publicity stunt goes horribly wrong. Retrieved from www.independent.co.uk/news/people/robin-thicke-mercilessly-trolled-after-askthicke-publicity-stunt-goes-horribly-wrong-9575740.html

Kitzinger, C. (2000). Doing feminist conversation analysis. *Feminism & Psychology, 10*(2), 163–193.

Kristofferson, K., White, K., & Peloza, J. (2014). The nature of slacktivism: How the social observability of an initial act of token support impacts subsequent prosocial action. *Journal of Consumer Research, 40*, 1149–1166.

Manago, A. M. (2013). Negotiating a sexy masculinity on social networking sites. *Feminism & Psychology, 23*(4), 478–497.

Schuster, J. (2013). Invisible feminists? Social media and young women's political participation. *Political Science, 65*, 8–24.

The *Guardian.* (2016). Kesha: Leading the fight against sexism at the music industry's core. Retrieved from www.theguardian.com/music/2016/feb/27/kesha-profile-court-case-dr-luke-sony

The *New York Times.* (2016). Retrieved from www.nytimes.com/2016/02/24/arts/music/kesha-dr-luke.html?mcubz=0

The *Telegraph.* (2014). Robin Thicke's Twitter disaster: The best of #AskThicke. *The Telegraph.* Retrieved from www.telegraph.co.uk/culture/music/music-news/10937764/Robin-Thickes-Twitter-disaster-the-best-of-AskThicke.html

Time. (2014). Robin Thicke's #AskThicke Hashtag Completely Backfired. *Time.* Retrieved from: http://time.com/2945115/askthicke-robin-thicke-twitter-hashtag-disaster/

34. THE SEXUAL POLITICS OF VEGGIES

ELLA FEGITZ AND DANIELA PIRANI (2017)

INTRODUCTION

Choosing to adopt a vegetarian or vegan diet can be motivated by several concerns: animal welfare and treatment, the environment, health issues, as well as unequal power relations and capitalism. Some strands of the feminist movement have conceptualized veg*an diets as ethical choices that resist patriarchal, capitalist, white culture. However, in the past 10 years we have witnessed a noteworthy shift in mainstream media representations of veg*an diets: vegetables have become sexy. PETA's advertisement campaigns are among several recent examples, including *Sexy Vegan Cookbook* by L. Brian Patton (2012), and, most importantly for this paper, the pop singer Beyoncé's endorsement of a vegan diet. While traditionally vegetables have been associated with femininity, sexual abstention, and frigidity, in the examples above this association has been challenged: vegetarian and vegan diets have become associated with eroticized images of women and sexual prowess.[1]

This article explores this shift by focusing on the media spectacle of Beyoncé's connection with the "22 days diet," often referred to as "The Beyoncé Diet" in popular media (such as in the articles by Michele Persad [2015], Kate Winick [2015], Laura Mitchell [2015], and Emma Firth [2015]) due to the pop-star's endorsement. The diet, created by Paul Borges, Beyoncé's personal trainer, involves adopting a vegan diet for at least 22 days, stressing the health benefits and weight loss that it can bring. Focusing our analysis on Beyoncé originates from her centrality in debates about post-feminist culture, the "media spectacle" (Douglas Kellner 2003) that was created around her weight-loss attributed to a vegan diet, and her enormous popularity.

Through the analysis of the discursive production of Beyoncé's endorsement of a vegan diet, we argue that the availability of a discourse of "vegetables as sexy" in popular culture resides in its connection with post-feminism. The term "post-feminism" has been used by Angela McRobbie (2004, 2009) and Rosalind Gill (2007b, 2008) to indicate the way mainstream culture has employed some of the vocabulary and concerns of the feminist movement, but has twisted them in such a way as to support an individual ethic of success, rather than political engagement against gender and other inequalities. Although the connection between veganism and sexuality has already been claimed by vegansexual culture, post-feminist culture articulates it differently: rather than an ethical choice, veganism is made available as a commodified diet.

In our analysis, we detect three main dimensions that connect in the discursive production of Beyoncé's uptake of a vegan diet: empowerment in terms of consumer choice; full agency and responsibilization; and the investment in a sexy body while at the same time imposing strict self-surveillance, management, and discipline. Through an exploration of these elements, we argue that what has been conceptualized as an ethical and political choice by eco-feminism throughout the years, as well as other eco-friendly and anti-capitalist movements, becomes depoliticized and deradicalized, becoming part of an individualistic project of the self. Hence, we claim that alongside "commodity feminism" (Robert Goldman, Deborah Heath, and Sharon L. Smith 1991) we are witnessing "commodity veg'ism," fully enmeshed with post-feminist culture.[2] We use the term veg'ism to indicate the fluid definitions of vegan and vegetarian diets, in which the avoidance of animal meat and products relies more on individual choice than on compliance with an actual regime. Veg'ism does not negate the existence of other simultaneously occurring practices that foreground vegan and vegetarian diets as ethical and political choices, but its study casts light on how food cultures are appropriated within post-feminism.

THE GENDERED PANTRY: FOOD GENDER AND SEXUALITY

Food tastes and choices are not subjective: they follow social scripts and discourses too (for relevant debates see, among others, Jukka Gronow [1997]). In his foundational work, Pierre Bourdieu (1984) has shown that how we display taste in food is similar to one's taste in art, sport, and fashion, and is closely connected to the habitus. Through this concept, Bourdieu argues that we are prompted to align our personal taste with that of the class we belong to, reproducing social disparities. However, taste in food is not only related to class: through the food we choose, prepare, and share, we reproduce a wide range of social boundaries, such as gender, ethnicity, religion, and sexuality.

Scholarship on the relationship between food and gender claims that food practices are interlaced with gendered ones (Carol Counihan 1998; Eileen Fischer 2000), both at the symbolic level and through everyday practices. On a symbolic level, masculinity is strongly linked to red meat, understood also as a symbol of virility and sexual prowess. Femininity instead is bound to sweetness, when conceptualized as sinful and irrational, or to vegetables, when conceived as asexual and pure. More often, though, it is the practices around food that contribute to establishing the "correct" roles and behaviours attributed to each gender. Indeed, "through the everyday practice of food consumption, gender performances take place" (Bethan Irvine 2015, 40), from the level of representation (for example in media and advertising) to the mundane level of everyday meal planning, provisioning and eating. These two elements, however, are often connected because the consumption of "gendered foods" bestows meaning onto the one who consumes them.

Meat creates the strongest polarity of gendered food. Even if it does not hold an exclusive connection with masculinity (see, for example, the work on coffee by Eminegül Karababa and Guliz Ger [2011] and Julie Kjendal Reitz [2007]), it is certainly the most powerful one. However, the specificity of the meat product is important: chicken or fish do not have the same connection with macho masculinity

(Paul Rozin, M. Julia Hormes, S. Myles Faith, and Brian Wansink 2012). Red meat, instead, evokes a traditional notion of manhood that is tightly bound with sexual drive and domination (J. Carol Adams 1990; Erika Cudworth 2008; Irvine 2015; Annie Potts and Jovien Parry 2010; Jeffrey Sobal 2005)—eating red meat means to eat like a man (C. Wesley Buerkle 2009; A. Mark Newcombe, B. Mary McCarthy, M. James Cronin, and N. Sinead McCarthy 2012).

Along with sweetness, vegetables are symbolically associated with femininity, especially when considered in antithesis with red meat (Newcombe et al. 2012). Furthermore, because female sexuality has been historically connected with a lack of sexual desire and pleasure, vegetables are the epitome of the asexual, where the term is used to describe lack of sexual desires and sex drive (F. Anthony Bogaert 2012).

. . .

THE POLITICS OF VEG*ANISM

The feminine virtue of vegetables has been appropriated as a political statement. Formalized from the early 1980s, vegetarian eco-feminism incorporated the work previously done not only by feminists, but also by activists who operated in the countercultural movement. It must be mentioned, however, that vegetarian eco-feminism is a distinct strand within the broad eco-feminist movement, and does not represent the whole of eco-feminism (Greta Gaard 2002). Unlike "masculine" culture, eco-feminist vegetarianism has engaged in a vision of compassion towards nature, animals being included in the moral community as well as humans, in an effort to condemn a consumer culture founded on patriarchal and capitalist values (Adams 1990; J. Carol Adams 2003; Josephine Donovan 1990; Sheri Lucas 2005). Ethical vegetarianism does not end with food, since it affects other areas of living, from clothing to cosmetics.

Meat eating also engages with a broader conversation of the deployment of natural resources that the capitalist economy perpetrates. Indeed, a proper sense of social and environmental justice has animated the eco-feminist debate (Greta Gaard 2010), where critical reflections on feminism stand within the context of environmental concern. The

association between culture and masculinity versus nature and femininity supports the patriarchal and capitalist understanding that Mother Nature has to be bent to masculine domination (Elizabeth Dodson Gray 1981). That is why, as a belief system, it cannot be reduced only to a diet, but reflects an ethical way of inhabiting the world (Joanne Stepaniak 2000).

Carol Adams (1990) most famously framed vegetarianism as in opposition to the patriarchal system, and stated that eating meat corresponded to the reproduction of politics of oppression, not only towards animals but also towards women. Thus, eco-feminism argues that there is an important connection between the domination of women and the domination of nature (Adams 1990, 127), and the same structure of oppression defines women and animals as subordinated subjects. This argument resonates more recently with those of Potts and Perry (2010), who explain that consuming products such as meat, eggs, milk, and honey, all of which come from female animals, involves supporting the reproduction of patriarchal power over women through violence and abuse. In this theoretical framework, the vegetarian choice refuses to reproduce this logic of domination using the body (and its feeding) as a site of protest.

The gendered relation between culture and nature is not only one of domination, but also one of heterosexual consumption (Dodson Gray 1981). Eco-feminists argue that by rejecting meat, women can refuse to perform the logic of becoming flesh, to be sexually consumed by men and to be "ontologized as sexual beings" (Adams 1990, 137). In eco-feminism, the domination over nature is the sexual domination over the feminine, and one cannot be overcome without the other (Andrée Collard and Joyce Contrucci 1989; Mary Daly 1978; Irene Diamond and F. Gloria Orenstein 1990; Martin Kheel 1991). Hence, the eco-feminist vegetarian/vegan lifestyle is paired with the feminist refusal to become objectified to men's consumption, and to be considered as mere sexual objects within a patriarchal system.

Similarly, some black vegans articulate veganism as a way to decolonize the black body. Aph-Ko (2015) explains how black people have been oppressed also via their identification with animals. Hence, by rejecting the discourse that animals are inferior to humans and thus can be exploited, black people stop supporting the same oppression they have endured. Furthermore, Amie "Breeze" Harper (2009) highlights how popular race-neutral veganism is oblivious to racial issues, as it concentrates on animal rights and health claims. According to her, a race-informed perspective adds to the debate on how race and class intersect in reproducing health disparities among the black community, with veganism being employed to heal the manifestations of white supremacist culture upon the black body (Queen Afua 1999).

Vegan and vegetarian diets also have a longstanding presence in the Lesbian, Gay, Bisexual, Trans and Queer (LGBTQ) community. For example, the Michigan Womyn's Music Festival has served vegetarian food since its beginning in 1976. In a study of the festival, Laurie J. Kendall (2008) reports that "becoming vegetarian is part of claiming a lesbian identity, which many conceptualise as both a spiritual and political act" (81). The queer vegan manifesto (Rasmus R. Simonsen 2012) also attends to "veganism as marker of identity" (54), claiming that deviating from eating meat means deviating from the heteronormative reproduction of gender identity.

However, recently, vegan/vegetarian diets have made a shift: vegetables have become sexy (A. Sherrie Inness 2006) and directly associated with sexual properties. This is not entirely new, as shown by the vegansexual movement. What is new, however, is the extent to which vegetable-based diets are represented, and seen as, sexy in mainstream media. A striking example is the promotional campaign by PETA, which has rearticulated the relationship between gender and food, in particular the one between masculinity and vegetarianism/veganism. These campaigns have made vegetables sexy, and aphrodisiacs, often through hypersexualized images of women and questionable sexual innuendos. In fact, PETA has a history of adopting hypersexualized women and celebrities as main subjects for its advertising posters. The gaze implied is often male; at times clearly so, as in the slogan: "Fight impotence. Go vegetarian" written across the image of a pin-up girl holding an "unerect" hotdog. According to PETA's heteronormative campaigns, male omnivores are to be reassured that removing meat from their diets will not affect their masculinity and virility, while women will benefit from their enhanced sexual performances.

While PETA's communication has been heavily criticized for its open sexism, Beyoncé's link with the "22 days diet" is different because she openly labels herself as a feminist. She is not the only celebrity openly endorsing a vegan lifestyle: actress Gwyneth Paltrow is the editor of Goop, a successful blog on lifestyle and wellness. Her second book *It's All Good: Delicious, Easy Recipes That Will Make You Look Good and Feel Great* (Gwyneth Paltrow, Julia Turshen, and Ditte Isager 2013), written with chef Julia Turshen, is just a step away from being entirely vegan. Hence, there is a clear shift between the eco- and black-vegan feminist movements, which refuse meat along with the white, patriarchal, and capitalist system, and a celebrity culture that makes a business out of a veg*an diet, while conveying a message of female emancipation. The move towards sensual commodified veg*an feminism is possible only through a new vision of the body and the self as offered by post-feminism, the cultural trend that frames our analysis of Beyoncé's participation in the 22 days diet.

BEYONCÉ AS POST-FEMINIST CELEBRITY

Angela McRobbie's (2004, 2008, 2009) and Rosalind Gill's (2007a, 2007b, 2008) theories about post-feminism have been useful for understanding how media culture participates in a new gender regime in which women's freedom, empowerment, and achievements are celebrated, while at the same time they are subjected to old and new forms of discrimination and control. While Gill (2007a, 2007b, 2008) describes post-feminism in terms of a "sensibility" made of several recurring themes, tropes and constructions, McRobbie (2004, 2009) thinks of it in terms of a "double entanglement" in which feminism is taken into account, only to be repudiated as passé, outdated, and even backwards. Both authors see a close connection between post-feminism and neo-liberalism, arguing that the emergence of post-feminist subjectivities is related to the process of neo-liberalization that characterizes many Western countries.[3]

However, more recently there has been a resurgence of feminism and particular forms of feminist politics in mainstream media culture, with many female and male celebrities and personalities claiming the term feminist for themselves. . . . Beyoncé is one of the celebrities who claimed the term "feminist" in 2014, famously incorporating the word into her MTV Video Awards performance by writing it in blazing capital letters on a giant screen, while performing the song ***Flawless (Beyoncé 2014). The song itself contains several lines of the speech by Chimamanda Ngozi Adichie as part of the TED talk titled "We should all be feminists" (2013).

For Beyoncé and other celebrities to claim the term "feminist," and for them to speak of gender inequality and feminist issues, might seem to contradict theories of post-feminism such as McRobbie's and Gill's, and instead signify a new "wave" of feminism. Indeed, a number of scholars, including Catharine Lumby (2011), Imelda Whelehan (2010), Hanna Retallack, Jessica Ringrose, and Emilie Lawrence (2016), have questioned whether the term "post-feminism" is still useful, or if it should at least be problematized. However, as we aim to illustrate through our analysis, we agree with Rosalind Gill (2016) that "a postfeminist sensibility informs even those media productions that ostensibly celebrate the new feminism" (610).

More specifically, Beyoncé's engagement with feminist themes and issues has been debated on mainstream and online media, as well as in academic circles. The singer Annie Lennox has famously described Beyoncé's feminism as "Lite" and "tokenistic," suggesting that hypersexual performances dilute the message (Chris Azzopardi 2014), yet for many others Beyoncé's feminism is a cause for celebration and joy (Eliana Dockterman 2013; Quinn Keaney 2014). At this juncture, we stress that the aim of this article is not to express a judgment on whether Beyoncé is a feminist. Instead, our objective is to contribute to the literature on the intersection of gender, race, class, and sexuality, in Beyoncé's music, commercial enterprises, performances, media representations, and self-representations.

Critiques of Beyoncé have described her as lacking an intersectional approach, through neglecting the history of slavery, exploitation, and devaluation of black bodies in the USA, in particular that of black female bodies (Lucy R. Short 2015; Nathalie Weidhase 2015). According to Weidhase (2015), Short (2015), Shirley Anne Tate (2015) and Daphne A. Brooks (2008), Beyoncé speaks of and to the positions of black women in the US culture, challenging white supremacist culture's dehumanization and devaluation of black femininity, and fear/eroticization of black female sexuality. Ultimately, they argue, Beyoncé succeeds in reclaiming her agency and subjecthood from a white cultural system that denies it.

Other scholars have rejected this interpretation, with bell hooks famously calling Beyoncé a "terrorist" in a panel discussion at the New School called *Are You Still a Slave? Liberating the Black Female Body* (The New School 2014). hooks criticizes Beyoncé for reproducing white culture's construction of female black bodies as sexual objects. She makes a similar point in relation to *Lemonade*, claiming that, while she commends the diverse representation of the female body, and the will to challenge its devaluation and dehumanization in mainstream culture, it nonetheless reproduces stereotypical representations of black women as victims or enraged. Celeste Manoucheka (2015) agrees with hooks, and states: "Knowles is indeed represented as the centre of admiration, but she is in that position partially because she plays the roles carved out for black women in this capitalist consumer culture" (151).

However, we argue that neither position fully grasps the complexity of Beyoncé's relation to femininity and feminism. Fabio Parasecoli (2007), Aisha Durham (2012), and Farah Jasmine Griffin (2011) produced more nuanced readings of the Beyoncé phenomenon, stressing, on the one hand, the deep connection of her work with a personal and collective racial past, while, on the other, pointing out the ambivalences and contradictions within her songs, videos, and performances. Hence, we suggest it is possible for multiple and nuanced readings of her work and persona to coexist—she can be an inspirational figure for young (black) women, challenging white heteropatriarchal culture's exclusion and devaluation of black female bodies, while at the same time reproducing normative discourses about female beauty, sexual availability, and heterosexuality.

. . .

Building on both McRobbie (2009) and Chatman's (2015) arguments, we agree that Beyoncé represents the ideal post-feminist subject. However, this is not because she already held the appropriate cultural and economic capital, but because she portrays the possibility for every woman, and black women especially, to be as successful as her, despite their social and economic position. What Beyoncé tells her fans is that with hard work, motivation, and commitment, they can overcome poverty, gender, class, sexuality, and dis/ability constraints. In this way female success is defined in individualistic terms, stressing competition, ambition, meritocracy, and self-reliance, at the expense of collectivity and political mobilization.

Furthermore, Beyoncé is an industry in her own right, and the 22 days diet is a side investment of her enterprise. Indeed, not only has Beyoncé actively endorsed a vegan diet, but she herself has invested in the business, partnering up with Marco Borges in an enterprise that delivers vegan meals door to door. With each meal costing between $9.24 and $14.85 (three meals a day for 22 days coming to a total just under $630), the diet plan is in fact accessible only to the middle-classes, making "healthy eating" an exclusive and exclusionary practice. While Beyoncé can campaign for and afford healthy and vegan diets, many people have to rely on a much smaller budget to feed themselves (and often their household too). Thus, veg*an diets become a way through which economic and cultural capital are manifested, reproducing class divisions while at the same time providing income for the rich (i.e., Beyoncé).

. . .

Beyoncé's iconic role in post-feminism becomes even more significant when contrasting the aspirational Beyoncé to what American society perceives to be the abject black female body. Indeed, while in the British context the figure of the working class, single mother is particularly charged, the USA has had a similar attitude toward the "welfare queen," the abject maternal figure introduced by the Reagan administration (Patricia Hill Collins 1990). Cultural representations of this dreaded figure have often centered on the black, poor, welfare-dependent, single mother, who is also often depicted as fat. These representations work to complement Beyoncé's ethics of empowerment, such that, taken together, they produce a dichotomization of "bad" and "good" femininity. The competitive, ambitious, entrepreneurial Beyoncé, fully integrated in upper middle-class tastes and lifestyles, who has built for herself a normative heterosexual nuclear family, comes to represent the ideal post-feminist subject, having made the right choices with respect to marriage, motherhood, career, and, most importantly for this article, dietary choices and health concerns.

VEG*ISM AS A POST-FEMINIST DIETARY PRACTICE

Beyoncé's association with the 22-days diet confirms the central place that the discursive production of Beyoncé has in post-feminist culture. The appropriation of a vegan diet is mobilized as part of a post-feminist ethics that promotes an individualistic form of emancipation, which sustains existent patterns of discrimination and inequality, consumerism and neoliberalism. In this context, the endorsement of veganism is radically different from the ethical and political stance of eco-feminism or black veganism, becoming commodified as just another lifestyle choice. This commodification of veganism is articulated through three main interlinking issues: the understanding of empowerment in terms of participation in consumer culture[4]; a stress on autonomous choice and agency, in life and in consumption, that leads to the responsibilization of the individual about the choices they make; and the focus on having a sexy body, which subsumes new techniques of self-management, -control, and -discipline.

Yvonne Tasker and Diane Negra (2007) argue that besides incorporating and negotiating feminist goals, post-feminism also works to commodify feminism through the articulation of women as empowered consumers. The term "empowerment" is an important trope of post-feminism, with women being sold make up, sex toys, and even pole dancing classes as manifestations of their empowerment. For Beyoncé, the uptake and promotion of a vegan diet is connected with the ambiguous notion of empowerment as well. In the preface to the book by Marco

Borges (2015) called *The 22 day revolution*, Beyoncé galvanizes the audience: "you deserve to give your self the best life you can. Empowerment starts within you and your decisions. You can control the quality of your life with the food you eat" (par. 6). In such a way, the vegan diet becomes one of the many lifestyle choices that consumer culture makes available, and one that has in itself the promise of "empowerment."

Indeed, Beyoncé's uptake and promotion of a vegan diet highlights what Elspeth Probyn (1993) has called "choicechoisie," by which she means the bourgeois, neo-liberal logic of shaping personal identity through the exercise of consumer choice, but also the way in which individuals are made responsible for the choices they make, assuming a position of blame if these reveal themselves not to be the correct choices (Gill 2008). Within the same preface, Beyoncé claims "I decided I wanted to take a more pro-active role in my health, and knowing all the amazing benefits [of the vegan diet], I knew this was the one" (par. 3). This statement stresses the post-feminist responsibilization of the individual for making the correct life choices and seeking self-improvement (McRobbie 2009)—in this case, the correct consumer choices in regards to fitness and health. Furthermore, the narrative produced by Beyoncé is one that stresses the full autonomy and agency of the subject. Beyoncé appears as an individual completely free from external constraints of gender, wealth, and class in the choices available to her, and this is assumed to be the case for those toward whom the promotional video and preface are directed.

While Beyoncé herself does not directly address "sexiness" in her uptake and promotion of the 22 days diet, the central focus that her sexy, curvy body has had in the discursive production of her persona inevitably brings the two together. Beyoncé has made her body one of the most significant aspects of her career. She is well known for taking pride in her "nonhegemonic" body: curvy but well maintained, with a specific focus on the "big" booty. This is further strengthened by the media frenzy created around the news that Beyoncé's spectacular weight loss was due to her uptake of a vegan diet. Indeed, not only was this news a staged "scoop," but the aftermath involved many publications making the connection between the vegan diet

and her return to a "bootylicious" body.[5] In such a way, vegetables become sexy, challenging traditional (and sexist) associations between meat as male and sexual, and women as vegetable and asexual.

This "nonhegemonic" body is the assemblage of elements from ideal Western (white) beauty standards, such as blonde hair and fair skin, and from popular culture signifiers of black culture—a voluptuous butt. As Manoucheka (2015) reports, Beyoncé is often presented as a hybrid whose ethnicity can be flexible and is able to appeal to multiple audiences: she is often described as beautiful by European standards, yet her buttocks remain a spectacle and a marker of her blackness. Furthermore, one can argue that Beyoncé has contributed to changing beauty standards for women, or at least expanding them, although in a very circumscribed direction.[6]

Yet, Beyoncé's sexy and curvaceous body is not as "natural" as it appears to be. While the aforementioned song ***Flawless** is also a hymn to accepting your body as it is, suggesting that any form and shape of body is flawless in itself, Beyoncé's body is a result of intense work and discipline, the vegan diet becoming part of this lifestyle. In her preface to Marco Borges's book (2015), and the promo video for his website (*22 Days Nutrition* 2015), she acknowledges that her body has been the result of extreme dieting habits and exercise routines. The choice of a vegan diet results from her need to lose weight quickly, but healthily. Thus, the uptake of a vegan diet becomes completely detached from ethical and political concerns, but is simply one of the many possible "diets" one can employ not only to lose weight quickly and keep it off, but also to experience "increased energy, better sleep, weight loss, improved digestion, clarity, and an incredibly positive feeling" (Beyoncé 2015, par. 4).

Furthermore, the uptake of a vegan diet is closely attached to motherhood, both in Beyoncé's own narratives and in media representations. In the preface, she claims

> [a]fter having my daughter, I made a conscious effort to regain control of my health and my body [. . .] [s]o I turned to no one other than my good friend and fitness and nutrition confidant, Marc Borges. I've worked with him for years to keep me on-track, motivated and ahead of the health game (par. 2).

Similarly, the media frenzy was centered on how the vegan diet had allowed Beyoncé to lose the "pregnancy weight" so effectively, showing off her newly fit and toned body at the Met Gala four months after having given birth to her child.

As McRobbie (2013) argues, the post-feminist focus on women's bodies in the media extends to motherhood, such that women are required to maintain their (hetero)sexual desirability throughout, as well as after, pregnancy, and achieve "affluent, middle-class maternity," which is visually translated via "a spectacularly slim body, a well groomed and manicured appearance, with an equally attractive baby and husband" (131). Indeed, the "yummy mummy," the mother who has not lost her sexiness despite motherhood, has become commonplace in media representations and in society at large (Jo Littler 2013). However, as the example of Beyoncé shows, this praised status is achieved through intense self-management and self-monitoring, which includes a change in food habits.

Hence, Beyoncé's uptake and promotion of a vegan diet reconfigures the relationship between food and gender, making vegetables sexy. Through the vegan diet, Beyoncé can be sensual but not carnal: she is in charge of her body and of her desires, to the point where failing to control what enters one's body resembles a failure to perform an appropriate femininity The post-feminist endorsement of veganism borrows this rhetoric of control from vegetarian feminisms, where vegan and vegetarian rules are used to resist capitalist consumption, patriarchal power, and white supremacy, but this appropriation only works to promote consumerism, an individualistic ethic, and a sexy body, rather than challenging unequal power relations.

The result is that veg'n diets stop being ethical, they become "commodity veg'anism." Food morality, what is good and bad to eat, loses its political ground and does not go further than the ingredients' nutritional profile, leading to a wider ecological indifference. Moreover, this means that post-feminist veg'ism is not a way of living, but simply another lifestyle to be chosen among the many, which can be as easily picked up as discarded. As a result, you do not need to *be* vegan or vegetarian, but you can buy veg'an meals or prepare veg'an recipes to participate in the commodified veg'an trend. This participation is confined in time and variety (22 days, 185 recipes) and in the field of action (one's own kitchen). . . .

CONCLUSION

By incorporating vegetable-based diets in the profile of self-owned, sexually liberated women, post-feminist practices have integrated and redefined the symbolic gendered associations between vegetables and women. Historically closer to purity and asexuality, vegetables have now become sexy and linked to a voluptuous femininity. This reconfigures a feminist critique of cultural associations of food and gender, relegating it to the sphere of the personal, such that the selection of a vegetable-based diet becomes fully integral to the post-feminist trend. Hence, post-feminism extends to the field of food, such that alongside "commodity feminism" (Goldman, Heath, and Smith 1991), we are witnessing a "commodity veg'ism," fully enmeshed with postfeminist culture.

Through the analysis of Beyoncé's involvement with the "22 days diet," we have uncovered how commodity veg'ism supports a post-feminist understanding of empowerment in terms of participation in consumer culture; a stress on autonomous choice and agency, in life and in consumption, and full responsibilization of the individual; and the focus on having a sexy body, which subsumes new techniques of self-management, -control, and -discipline. Through these interlacing aspects, we have argued that commodity veg'ism does not challenge the status quo, but instead promotes a post-feminist ethic that emphasizes individualism, consumer choice, and empowerment.

While eco-feminists sustain their resistance to a patriarchal economy of exploitation through this diet, post-feminists fully align their vegetarian choices with the capitalist marketplace. It should be acknowledged that the endorsement of feminism and veg'ism by a public black figure such as Beyoncé has the potential to open up these discourses to people who might have previously felt excluded and/or alienated from them. However, ultimately, the post-feminist endorsement of veg'ism becomes a business opportunity, with celebrities such as Beyoncé capitalizing and aggrandizing their wealth through a dietary practice that eco-feminism has employed for political and ethical reasons.

Conclusively, this paper highlights how food choices cannot be reduced to a private matter, because consumption practices and access to the marketplace are always interlaced with power discourses (Roberta Sassatelli 2007). The incorporation of veg*ism into post-feminist culture has reinforced a configuration of gender and class, reproducing systems of inequalities and putting them on people's tables.

NOTES

1. We acknowledge that separating politics from the body and subjectivity is impossible. Indeed, the choice of a vegan or vegetarian diet is not only and not always motivated by political factors; personal experiences equally contribute. Despite this, in this article we would like to focus specifically on the eco-feminist discourses that make this choice an ethical and political one.

2. Others who have dealt with the commodification of veganism, but in different contexts, are L. Gary Francione (2012), and Kim Socha and Sarajane Blum (2013).

3. Until recently, the literature on post-feminism has been based mostly in Europe and the USA. However, in the past few years a number of scholars have engaged in exporting and modifying these theories to analyze non-Western countries (see, for example, Simidele Dosekun [2015]).

4. Consumer culture is defined as a society in which consumption works as privileged means for meaning sharing and creation (B. Douglas Holt 2002; Don Slater 1997), such that "cultural reproduction is largely understood to be carried through the exercise of free personal choice in the private sphere of everyday life" (Slater 1997, 8).

5. *Bootylicious* is the name of a song by Destiny's Child, former band of Beyoncé that popularized the term. Since then, it has been employed by Beyoncé herself to describe a voluptuous body, characterized by a prominent backside.

6. Durham (2012) references a newspaper article that indicates a significant increase in buttocks

augmentation, with patients openly requesting Beyoncé- or Jennifer Lopez-style bottoms.

REFERENCES

22 Days Nutrition. 2015. Accessed October 15, 2015. https://www.22daysnutrition.com

Adams, J. Carol. 1990. *The Sexual Politics of Meat: A Feminist-Vegetarian Critical Theory.* New York: Continuum.

Adams, J. Carol. 2003. *The Pornography of Meat.* New York: Continuum.

Adichie, N. Chimamanda. 2013. "We Should All Be Feminists." *TEDx*, April 29. Accessed June 11, 2016. https://tedxtalks.ted.com/video/We-should-all-be-feminists-Chim

Afua, Queen. 1999. *Sacred Woman: A Guide to Healing the Feminine Body, Mind, and Spirit.* New York: One World.

Aph-Ko [Black Vegans Rock]. 2015. "Aphro-Ism: What Does Animal Oppression Have to Do with Our Anti-Racist Movements?" You Tube. Accessed October 23, 2016. https://www.youtube.com/watch?v=rLG_nanqdAl

Azzopardi, Chris. 2014. "Q&a: Annie Lennox on Her Legacy, Why Beyonce Is 'Feminist Lite.'" *Pride Source: From the Publishers of between the Lines*, September 25. Accessed October 26. https://www.pridesource.com/article.html?article=68228

Beyoncé. 2014. ***Flawless.* Music Single. USA: Parkwood/Columbia.

Beyoncé. 2015. "Foreword." In *The 22-Day Revolution: The Plant-Based Program That Will Transform Your Body, Reset Your Habits, and Change Your Life*, written by Marco Borges [e-book]. New York: Penguin Books. Available through: the British Library database. Accessed May 3, 2016. https://explore.bl.uk/primo_library/libweb/action/search.do?dscnt=1&tab=local_tab&dstmp=1459841530105&vl(freeText0)=22-day%20revolution&fn=search&vid=BLVU1&mode=Basic&fromLogin=true

Bogaert, F. Anthony. 2012. *Understanding Asexuality.* Lanham: Rowman & Littlefield Publishers.

Borges, Marco. 2015. *The 22-Day Revolution: The Plant-Based Program That Will Transform Your Body, Reset Your Habits, and Change Your Life.* New York: Penguin Books.

Bourdieu, Pierre. 1984. *Distinction: A Social Critique of the Judgement of Taste.* Cambridge, MA: Harvard University Press.

Brooks, Daphne A. 2008. "'All That You Can't Leave Behind': Black Female Soul Singing and the Politics of Surrogation in the Age of Catastrophe." *Meridians* 8 (1): 180–204.

Buerkle, C. Wesley. 2009. "Metrosexuality Can Stuff It: Beef Consumption as (Heteromasculine) Fortification." *Text and Performance Quarterly* 29 (1): 77–93.

Chatman, Dayna. 2015. "Pregnancy, Then It's 'Back to Business.'" *Feminist Media Studies* 15 (6): 926–941.

Collard, Andrée, and Joyce Contrucci. 1989. *Rape of the Wild: Man's Violence against Animals and the Earth.* Bloomington: Indiana University Press.

Collins, Patricia. 1990. *Black Feminist Thought: Knowledge, Consciousness and the Politics of Empowerment.* London: HarperCollins.

Counihan, Carol. 1998. *Food and Gender: Identity and Power.* Oxon: Routledge.

Cudworth, Erika. 2008. "Most Farmers Prefer Blondes: The Dynamic of Anthroparchy in Animals' Becoming Meat." *Journal for Critical Animal Studies* 6 (1): 32–45.

Daly, Mary. 1978. *Gyn/Ecology: The Metaethics of Radical Feminism.* Boston, MA: Beacon Press.

Diamond, Irene, and F. Gloria Orenstein. 1990. *Reweaving the World: The Emergence of Eco-Feminism.* San Francisco: Sierra Club Books.

Dockterman, Eliana. 2013. "Flawless: 5 Lessons in Modern Feminism from Beyonce." *Time*, December 17. Accessed October 26, 2016. https://time.com/1851/flawless-5-lessons-in-modern-feminism-from-beyonce/

Dodson Gray, Elizabeth. 1981. *Green Paradise Lost.* Wellesley: Roundtable Press.

Donovan, Josephine. 1990. "Animal Rights and Feminist Theory." *Signs* 15 (2): 350–375.

Dosekun, Simidele. 2015. "For Western Girls Only?" *Feminist Media Studies* 15 (6): 960–975.

Durham, Aisha. 2012. "Check on It." *Feminist Media Studies* 12 (1): 35–49.

Firth, Emma. 2015. Beyoncé's Vegan Diet: 3 Recipes You Need to Try from the Star's Nutritionist. *Marie Claire*, June 9. Accessed October 14, 2015. https://www.marieclaire.co.uk/blogs/549263/beyonc-3-comforting-vegan-recipes-you-need-to-try-from-the-star-s-nutritionist.html

Fischer, Eileen. 2000. "Consuming Contemporaneous Discourses: A Postmodern Analysis of Food Advertisements Targeted toward Women." In *Advances in Consumer Research*, edited by Stephen J. Hoch and Robert J. Meyer, 288–294. 2000 Provo, Association for Consumer Research.

Francione, L. Gary. 2012. "Animal Welfare, Happy Meat and Veganism as the Moral Baseline." In *The Philosophy of Food*, edited by David M. Kaplan, 169–189. Berkeley: University of California Press.

Gaard, Greta. 2002. "Vegetarian Eco-Feminism: A Review Essay." *Frontiers: A Journal of Women Studies* 23 (3): 117–146.

Gaard, Greta. 2010. "New Directions for Eco-Feminism: Toward a More Feminist Ecocriticism." *Interdisciplinary Studies in Literature and Environment* 17 (4): 643–665.

Gill, Rosalind. 2007a. *Gender and the Media.* Cambridge: Polity Press.

Gill, Rosalind. 2007b. "Post-Feminist Media Culture: Elements of a Sensibility." *European Journal of Cultural Studies* 10 (2): 147–166.

Gill, Rosalind. 2008. "Empowerment/Sexism: Figuring Female Sexual Agency in Contemporary Advertising." *Feminism Psychology* 18(1): 35–60.

Gill, Rosalind. 2016. "Post-Postfeminism?: New Feminist Visibilities in Postfeminist times." *Feminist Media Studies* 16 (4): 610–30.

Goldman, Robert, Deborah Heath, and L. Sharon Smith. 1991. "Commodity Feminism." *Critical Studies in Mass Communication* 8 (3): 333–351.

Griffin, Farah Jasmine. 2011. "At Last . . .?: Michelle Obama, Beyoncé, Race & History." *Daedalus* 140 (1): 131–41.

Gronow, Jukka. 1997. *The Sociology of Taste.* London: Routledge.

Harper, A. Breeze. 2009. *Sistah Vegan: Black Female Vegans Speak on Food, Identity, Health, and Society.* New York: Lantern Books.

Holt, B. Douglas. 2002. "Why Do Brands Cause Trouble? A Dialectical Theory of Consumer Culture and Branding." *Journal of Consumer Research* 29 (1): 70–90.

Inness, A. Sherrie. 2006. *Secret Ingredients: Race, Gender, and Class at the Dinner Table*. New York: Palgrave Macmillan.

Irvine, Bethan. 2015. *Vegetarian Masculinities: How Discourses of Normative Masculinities Are Challenged and (Re)Produced through Food Consumption*. Birmingham, AL: University of Birmingham.

Karababa, Eminegül, and Guliz Ger. 2011. "Early Modern Ottoman Coffeehouse Culture and the Formation of the Consumer Subject." *The Journal of Consumer Research* 37 (5): 737–760.

Keaney, Quinn. 2014. "Beyonce Schools Everyone on Body Image and Feminism in Her Latest Surprise Video." *MTV News*, December 12. Accessed October 26. https://www.mtv.com/news/2024545/beyonce-yours-mine-video-feminism/

Kellner, Douglas. 2003. *Media Spectacle*. New York: Routledge.

Kendall, Laurie J. 2008. *The Michigan Womyn's Music Festival: An Amazon Matrix of Meaning*. Baltimore, MD: Spiral Womyn's Press.

Kheel, Martin. 1991. "Eco-Feminism and Deep Ecology: Reflections on Identity and Difference." *Trumpeter* 8 (2): 62–72.

Littler, Jo. 2013. "The Rise of the 'Yummy Mummy': Popular Conservatism and the Neoliberal Maternal in Contemporary British Culture." *Communication, Culture and Critique* 6 (2): 227–243.

Lucas, Sheri. 2005. "A Defense of the Feminist-Vegetarian Connection." *Hypatia* 20 (1): 150–177.

Lumby, Catharine. 2011. "Past the Post in Feminist Media Studies." *Feminist Media Studies* 11 (1): 95–100.

Manoucheka, Celeste. 2015. "Ch.8: Black Women and U.S. Pop Culture in the Post-Identity Era: The Case of Beyoncé Knowles." In *Transatlantic Feminisms: Women and Gender Studies in Africa and the Diaspora*, edited by Cheryl R. Rodriguez, Dzodzi Tsikata, and Akosua Adomako Amopofo, 137–158. London/Lanham, Maryland: Lexington Books.

McRobbie, Angela. 2004. "Post-Feminism and Popular Culture." *Feminist Media Studies* 4 (3): 255–264.

McRobbie, Angela. 2008. "Pornographic Permutations." *The Communication Review* 11 (3): 225–236.

McRobbie, Angela. 2009. *The Aftermath of Feminism: Gender, Culture and Social Change*. London: Sage.

McRobbie, Angela. 2013. "Feminism, the Family and New 'Mediated' Maternalism." *New Formations* 80–81: 119–138.

Mitchell, Laura. 2015. Fit for a Queen Bee: Copy Beyoncé's Vegan Diet Plan from £6.31. *Daily Star*, June 11. Accessed June 12, 2016. https://www.dailystar.co.uk/diet-fitness/447494/Beyonce-vegan-diet-Instagram-swimming-costume-pictures-diet-plan

Newcombe, A. Mark, B. Mary McCarthy, M. James Cronin, and N. Sinead McCarthy. 2012. "'Eat like a Man.' A Social Constructionist Analysis of the Role of Food in Men's Lives." *Appetite* 59 (2): 391–398.

Paltrow, Gwyneth, Julia Turshen, and Ditte Isager. 2013. *It's All Good: Delicious, Easy Recipes That Will Make You Look Good and Feel Great*. New York: Grand Central Life & Style.

Parasecoli, Fabio. 2007. "Bootylicious: Food and the Female Body in Contemporary Black Pop Culture." *Women's Studies Quarterly* 35 (1/2): 110–125.

Patton, L. Brian. 2012. *The Sexy Vegan Cookbook: Extraordinary Food from an Ordinary Dude*. Novato: New World Library.

Persad, Michele. 2015. "I Tried the 22-Day Beyoncé Vegan Diet . . . and I'm Starving." *Huffington Post*, August 4. Accessed 11 June, 2016. https://www.huffingtonpost.com/2015/04/08/beyonce-vegan-diet-_n_7025122.html

Potts, Annie, and Jovian Parry. 2010. "Vegan Sexuality: Challenging Heteronormative Masculinity through Meat-Free Sex." *Feminism & Psychology* 20 (1): 53–72.

Probyn, Elspeth. 1993. "Choosing Choice: Images of Sexuality and 'Choiceoisie' in Popular Culture." In *Negotiating at the Margins: The Gendered Discourses of Power and Resistance*, edited by Sue Fisher and Kathy Davis, 278–294. New Brunswick, NJ: Rutgers University Press.

Reitz, Julie Kjendal. 2007. "Espresso: A Shot of Masculinity." *Food, Culture & Society: An International Journal of Multidisciplinary Research* 10 (1): 7–21.

Retallack, Hanna, Jessica Ringrose, and Emilie Lawrence. 2016. "Ch.6: 'Fuck Your Body Image': Teen Girls' Twitter and Instagram Feminism in and around School." In *Learning Bodies: The Body in Youth and Childhood Studies*, edited by J. Coffey, S. Budgeon, and H. Cahill, 85–103. London: Springer.

Rozin, Paul, M. Julia Hormes, S. Myles Faith, and Brian Wansink. 2012. "Is Meat Male? A Quantitative Multimethod Framework to Establish Metaphoric Relationships." *Journal of Consumer Research* 39 (3): 629–643.

Sassatelli, Roberta. 2007. *Consumer Culture History, Theory and Politics*. Los Angeles, CA: Sage.

Short, Lucy R. 2015. Still Haunted: Tending to the Ghosts of Marriage and Motherhood in White Feminist Critiques of Beyoncé Knowles-Carter and Michelle Obama. *Tapestries: Interwoven Voices of Local and Global Identities* 4(1): p. n.a.

Simonsen, Rasmus R. 2012. "A Queer Vegan Manifesto." *Journal for Critical Animal Studies* 10 (3): 51–81.

Slater, Don. 1997. *Consumer Culture and Modernity*. Cambridge: Blackwell Publishers.

Sobal, Jeffrey. 2005. "Men, Meat, and Marriage: Models of Masculinity." *Food and Foodways* 13 (1/2): 135–158.

Socha, Kim, and Sarahjane Blum. 2013. *Confronting Animal Exploitation: Grassroots Essays on Liberation and Veganism*. Jefferson, North Carolina: McFarland & Company.

Stepaniak, Joanne. 2000. *Being Vegan: Living with Conscience, Conviction, and Compassion*. Los Angeles, CA: Lowell House.

Tasker, Yvonne, and Diane Negra. 2007. *Interrogating Post-Feminism: Gender and the Politics of Popular Culture*. London: Duke University Press.

Tate, Shirley Anne. 2015. *Black Women's Bodies and the Nation: Race, Gender and Culture*. New York: Palgrave Macmillan.

The New School. 2014. "Are You Still a Slave?" *Livestream*. Accessed October 26, 2016. https://livestream.com/TheNewSchool/Slave

Weidhase, Nathalie. 2015. "'Beyoncé Feminism' and the Contestation of the Black Feminist Body." *Celebrity Studies* 6 (1): 128–131.

Whelehan, Imelda. 2010. "Remaking Feminism: Or Why Is Postfeminism So Boring?" *Nordic Journal of English Studies* 9 (3): 155–172.

Winick, Kate. 2015. "I Tried the Beyoncé Diet: And It Changed My Foodie Life." *Elle*. Accessed October 26, 2016, https://www.elle.com/beauty/health-fitness/how-to/a27210/i-tried-the-beyonce-diet/ElleMarch

35. CARDI B
Love & Hip Hop's *Unlikely Feminist Hero*
SHERRI WILLIAMS (2017)

In just a short time, Belcalis Almanzar has emerged as a feminist hero who is vocal about women's rights and supporting women's choices. But she is not often celebrated. She is often overlooked, dismissed and disregarded. She is an Afro Latina who is a former stripper, Instagram model turned reality television star who transformed into one of the most talked about rappers. Almanzar, known by her stage name Cardi B, has become one of the most popular reality stars in recent years.

In a time when one of the most controversial of words, feminism, turns people off Cardi B adopts that label and ideology with pride. She often talks about feminism and takes a feminist position on the show that made her a star, *Love & Hip Hop*, and on her social media channels. But she has found herself as the target of classist and perhaps even racist critiques because her brand of feminism has not met the standards of those in more formal feminist spaces. In November 2016 she defended and explained the feminism that she embodies in a video statement to her millions of Instagram followers:

> If you believe in equal rights for women, that makes you a feminist. I don't understand how you bitches feel like being a feminist is a woman that have a

education, that have a degree. That is not being a feminist. You discouraging a certain type of woman, that certainly doesn't make you one. Some bitches wanna act like "oh you have to read a book about feminists." That's only a definition for a simple word. The problem is that being a feminist is something so great and y'all don't want me to be great but too bad. Because at the end of the day I'm going to encourage any type of woman. You don't have to be a woman like me to encourage and support you and tell you "yes bitch, keep on going." And that's why you mad you little dusty ass bitch.

Cardi B is not perfect and neither is feminism. But it is through her position in pop culture as a reality television star on VH1's heavily watched franchise that she introduced feminism and feminist practices to people who have been closed off to them. With her 10.1 million Instagram followers, 3.1 million Facebook followers and 1 million Twitter followers, Cardi B has access to a massive audience that is influenced by her. But it is my hope that Cardi B will influence feminists inside the academy to not be so rigid in their definition(s) of feminism.

In her contemporary feminist classic *When Chickenheads Come Home to Roost: A Hip Hop Feminist Breaks It Down* Joan Morgan wrote, "I needed a feminism brave enough to fuck with the grays. And this was not my foremothers' feminism" (Joan Morgan 1999, 59). Morgan is advocating for a comprehensive form of feminism that has enough courage to address issues that do not have clear cut and easy solutions, a feminism that is intersectional and fights for the liberation of all. In her Instagram video Cardi B is calling on feminists to have a broader, more inclusive form of feminism that does not just restrict it to women with advanced degrees who have read the canons of feminist scholarship and literature. Like Morgan, nearly 20 years later Cardi B is advocating for feminism that can work through complicated and complex identities and scenarios. Essentially what Cardi B is doing is what hip-hop feminist scholar Gwendolyn Pough (2004) calls "bringing wreck" to classist and even racist notions of what is perceived as legitimate feminism. By bringing wreck, resisting traditional ways and seeing things and reclaiming and recreating spaces (Pough 2004), Cardi B is demanding a space

in feminism and carving out room for herself. Hip-hop feminists resist compliance to restrictive and exclusive forms of feminism (Aisha Durham, Brittney C. Cooper, and Susana M. Morris 2013). Cardi B does the same. Hip-hop feminists demand that we confront differences and conflicts because not to do so would restrict feminism to a purely scholarly project that stays within the halls of academia and does not move outside to be a sustainable force for social justice and political change (Durham, Cooper, and Morris 2013). Cardi B also resists the notion that feminism is only saved for women formally educated in university halls.

Pop culture and media are where many women artists are expressing their feminism and how they are introducing it to their fans. Beyonce's feminism was criticized, rebuffed, and castigated for not being feminist enough. Chimamanda Ngozi Adichie, the feminist writer whose TED Talk *We Should All Be Feminists* is featured on Beyonce's 2013 *Flawless* song, said she appreciates Beyonce taking a stand on social issues but "her type of feminism is not mine, as it is the kind that gives quite a lot of space to the necessity of men" (Aimee Kiene 2016). For others Beyonce's feminism was too capitalist or hypersexual or simply not robust enough. After the release of Beyonce's 2016 *Lemonade* album, pioneering feminist writer and scholar bell hooks wrote that Beyonce's was "fantasy feminism" and that "her construction of feminism cannot be trusted. Her vision of feminism does not call for an end to patriarchal domination" (bell hooks 2016). But we have seen Beyonce's feminism evolve, grow and contribute to the creation of intersectional and transformative art that has done everything from explain black women's joy and pain to call for resistance to the white supremacy embedded in this nation's institutions. Beyonce's generalized girl power anthems *Run the World Girls* and *Flawless* progressed to songs with stronger calls for liberation with the songs *Freedom* and *Formation*.

What if feminists allow Cardi B's feminism to evolve? Black feminists are already using social media as a tool to fight against the sexual violence that women of color experience (Sherri Williams 2015). Imagine enlisting Cardi B in feminist movements and utilizing her massive social media reach to convey messages about gender equality. What if feminists incorporated Cardi B into their digital activism and exposed her millions of followers to messages of gender justice? Cardi B's visibility is important in popular culture because she challenges traditional ideas about women, especially women of color. Cardi B was an exotic dancer before she became a social media sensation and reality television star. Most media representations of exotic dancers are shrouded in shame. In fact, the media strongly reinforce the shame of women. Media are one layer in the shame web, a complex set of rigid, gendered and contradictory social expectations that serve to regulate and shame women (Brene Brown 2006). Media help to reinforce those unattainable ideals that leave women feeling cornered and ashamed (Brown 2006). Cardi B is a multimedia entertainer with a prominent presence on reality television, social media and in hip hop. On those multiple platforms Cardi B shreds the same web by being authentic and true to herself, her past, and all of her identities. In media interviews and on *Love & Hip Hop* Cardi B owns and discusses her past employment in strip clubs without shame. In her massively popular summer 2017 hit song *Bodak Yellow* she says: "Look, I don't dance now/I make money moves/Say I don't gotta dance/I make money move." Cardi B's very presence is an act of resistance to oppressive and restrictive ideologies. She does feminist work through pop culture but it is not validated because her path to feminism is not traditional and, most importantly, she is a sex-positive woman of color from a working class background who challenges some of the traditional views that even feminists possess.

Cardi B came to the nation's attention . . . when she debuted on *Love & Hip Hop* in December 2015. On the show she challenged patriarchal relationships and ideas about women's ability to succeed in fields dominated by men, including hip hop. On the show we see several rappers work toward stardom and success but we actually see Cardi B achieve it. Pop culture often challenges traditional gender norms. But this reality television show and its breakout star do not receive the same credit because it is through a format, hip-hop reality television, that some perceive as without value because it is so raw—and perhaps because it is so black. We often see white women entertainers from Madonna to Katy Perry and Taylor Swift lauded for their mainstream versions of girl power and feminism which we know are not perfect but the same has not happened with Cardi B. She recently announced that she will not return to *Love & Hip Hop* because she is too busy pursuing her rising music and acting careers. Will feminists and others take her seriously now that she is no longer on reality television? That remains to be seen. But we also should not have to wait for people to ascend to what may be perceived to [be] more legitimate social spaces before we pay attention to them and value what they say. If we give so-called low-brow popular culture such as reality television and social media the same consideration that we do more widely accepted genres in pop culture we might find the value in the representations and the feminist work that is happening across all forms of media.

REFERENCES

Brown, Brene. 2006. "Shame Resilience Theory: A Grounded Theory Study on Women and Shame." *Families in Society* 87 (1): 43–52.

Durham, Aisha, Brittney C. Cooper, and Susana M. Morris. 2013. "The Stage Hip-Hop Feminism Built: A New Directions Essay." *Signs: Journal of Women in Culture and Society* 38 (3): 721–737.

hooks, bell. 2016, May 9. "Moving beyond the Pain." https://www.bellhooksinstitute.com/blog/2016/5/9/moving-beyond-pain.

Kiene, Aimee. 2016, October 7. *Ngozi Adichie: Beyoncé's Feminism Isn't My Feminism.* deVolkskrant. https://www.volkskrant.nl/boeken/ngozi-adichie-beyonce-s-feminismisn-t-my-feminisma4390684/.

Morgan, Joan. 1999. *When Chickenheads Come Home to Roost: A Hip Hop Feminist Breaks It Down.* New York: Simon & Schuster.

Pough, Gwendolyn. 2004. *Check It While I Wreck It: Black Womanhood, Hip-Hop Culture and the Public Sphere.* Boston, MA: Northeastern University Press.

Williams, Sherri. 2015. "Digital Defense: Black Feminists Resist Violence with Hashtag Activism." *Feminist Media Studies* 15 (2): 341–344. doi:10.1080/14680777.2015.1008744.

36. A CORPORATION IN FEMINIST CLOTHING?

JUDITH TAYLOR, JOSÉE JOHNSTON, AND KRISTA WHITEHEAD (2016)

INTRODUCTION

CAPITALIST REBELLION THROUGH CONSUMPTION

Capitalist enterprise has been subjected to numerous critiques from disgruntled citizens and activists. While free market ideals retain a canonical presence in contemporary culture (McKinnon, 2013), progressive social ideas have been readily incorporated into capitalist marketing and promotional campaigns (Barkay, 2013; Frank, 1997; Heath and Potter, 2004), and even into business school pedagogy (Cabrera and Williams, 2012). The phenomenon of "commodifying dissent" is not unusual, but has been argued to constitute a key feature of contemporary capitalist culture (e.g. Boltanski and Chiapello, 2007; Frank and Weiland, 1997; Gordon, 1995; Newfield, 1995; Vogel, 2005). Whole Foods Market trades on images of ethical consumption, Nike sells women's empowerment via lycra shorts, and the Dove Real Beauty Campaign sell products by critiquing dominant media-constructions of beauty and promoting body acceptance. Scholars have analyzed various aspects of this trend and its implications (e.g. Cabrera and Williams, 2012; Johnston, 2008; Johnston and Taylor, 2008; Messner, 2002), but less studied is how individuals think and feel when they see their politics appropriated by corporations. In other words, critiques of corporate cooptation have focused primarily on the production, rather than the reception of these messages.

This research gap is significant since it is not clear to what extent social movement adherents support or disapprove of the corporate appropriation of their ideals. Do people appreciate seeing their grass-roots views amplified on a large scale, or do they see these corporate incarnations as crass, manipulative, and politically harmful? Do those committed to social change resent that personal ideals are being peddled to sell products, or do they think that corporations can play a positive role in the dissemination of social movement ideals? The answers to these questions can help clarify how corporate appropriation of movement ideals affects movement adherents' political

consciousness. In this article, we focus on Unilever Corporation's use of feminism to sell Dove brand products, and draw from focus groups with young, feminist-identified women to analyze their understandings of this campaign.

Previous research on the Dove Campaign for Real Beauty (Johnston and Taylor, 2008) identified the phenomenon of *feminist consumerism*, a corporate strategy that employs feminist themes of empowerment to market products to women. The Dove initiative—a multi-million dollar, global advertising campaign with innumerable print ads and billboards, and viral videos—has been exceptionally successful. In this study, we focus on:

1. whether the Dove campaign is seen as compatible with their vision of feminism, and
2. whether these women see corporations as potential vehicles for achieving feminist change.

. . .

Drawing on the experiences of the women's movement, feminist theorists have shed light on the dynamic of capitalist critique, cooptation, and resistance. While the commodification of feminist ideals has been a topic of critical importance (e.g. McRobbie, 2009; Messner, 2002), it is also important to investigate how lifestyles and consumption can serve as meaningful channels for women's activism (Micheletti, 2003: 17). This is especially the case given women's historical oppression (and resistance) within the private realm of home, family, and social reproduction (Bezanson and Luxton, 2006; Laslett and Brenner, 1989; Wilson, 2003). A key insight of both feminist and new social movement theory is that political inequalities are not abstract entities, but are intimately constituted through personal relationships, corporeal practices, and affect. A focus on internalized feelings of inferiority should not necessarily be dismissed as apolitical or narcissistic. Individually scaled changes can challenge broader power relationships if they connect personal problems with political institutions (see Taylor, 1996). Feminist scholars have productively drawn from Foucault's insights on power relationships, emphasizing how "a society's imposition of discipline upon bodies depends on those bodies learning *to regulate themselves*" (Hartley, 2001: 63). As such, resisting the corporeal regulation of dominant beauty ideology, and questioning the negative emotions linked to deviant physical forms (e.g. fatness, aging) may be a way to resist dominant power relationships, even if such resistance does not offer a full-scale rejection of capitalism. These tendencies have been contentious, and third wave feminism in particular has been criticized as myopically focused on a politics of the self (Faludi, 2010; Gilmore, 2005; Heath and Potter, 2005; for defenses, see Harris, 2008; Orr, 1997; Redfern and Aune, 2010; Reger, 2012).

One particularly sympathetic and sophisticated critique comes from British sociologist Angela McRobbie (2009). Looking at current popular culture, McRobbie identifies a 'post-feminist' backlash where feminist ideas are undermined at the same time as women are sold ideas of empowerment, choice and individualism—ideas that take particular hold in a neoliberal consumer culture. Because feminist ideals are thought to have been 'taken into account', serious contemporary concerns about gender inequality and exploitation can be minimized, or even forgotten. In McRobbie's (2009: 12) words: "post-feminism positively draws on and invokes feminism as that which can be taken into account, to suggest that equality is achieved, in order to install a whole repertoire of new meanings which emphasize that it is no longer needed, it is a spent force." In a post-feminist context, it is possible for women to see themselves (and be seen as) empowered agentic beings when they *choose* to buy painful and expensive high-heel shoes (e.g. *Sex and the City*), spend tremendous effort radically transforming their appearance (e.g. reality shows featuring cosmetic surgery make-overs), or publicly show off their breasts (e.g. *Girls Gone Wild*). . . .

. . . Beauty ideology is embedded in political economic systems of capital accumulation, but it is also deeply and literally embodied in the feelings and material practices of women's lived experience (e.g. Weitz, 2004; Wolf, 1990). Analysis of feminist resistance and incorporation in the Dove Campaign for Real Beauty (Johnston and Taylor, 2008) suggests that while feminist analyses must remain critical of corporate interests and the political-economy of the beauty industries, it must also take seriously transformative potential occurring at the scale of personal ideas, practices, and emotions. This research also highlighted the importance of identifying change at the level of individual thoughts, feelings, and actions. This is especially significant with regard to beauty ideology, in which capitalist exploitation intersects with race and gender inequality in daily practices, ideals, and self-esteem (Banet-Weiser, 1999, 2012; Banner, 1983; Gimlin, 2002; Jeffreys, 2005). At the same time, since the Dove campaign specifically targets women's insecurities about their physical form, it is clear that individual resistance to dominant beauty ideologies can be channelled back into new beauty products (with a subversive feel), rather than challenging the dominant nature of beauty ideology and the accompanying commodities.

. . .

We conducted six focus groups, stopping when the data became saturated and little new discussion emerged (Morgan, 1996). Each group consisted of a pre-existing network of close friends or members of a community-based organization who identified as feminist or were concerned with women's empowerment. Rather than parachute into an unknown group as an 'official outside expert' we first facilitated a discussion with a group of friends who were familiar with one of the authors. We used a snowball-sampling technique with this first group, asking members to suggest people outside their racial-ethnic group and occupation if possible, to obtain a theoretically broader sample. Groups included 5–15 participants, for a total of 40 participants in the study. Four of the groups consisted of women in their 20s working in professions such as teaching, the arts, social work, human resources, and media. Two groups consisted of adolescents and teens in school and community centre girls' clubs. . . . [W]e sought participants under the age of 30, reasoning that participants from this demographic grew up in a post-consciousness-raising era and therefore would not likely have focused on social questions and issues in a group setting as older cohorts might have. . . . [W]e only used pre-existing groups of friends, increasing the likelihood they would continue the political dialogue after the completion of the focus group.[1]

. . .

FINDINGS

This section outlines answers to two central questions asked in the focus group discussions:

1. Is the Dove Campaign for Real Beauty 'feminist?' and
2. Should corporations engage in the cause of feminism?

The discussions generated by these questions helped participants gain a deeper understanding of the scope of feminism as a movement and set of ideas, the multiple axes of their identities that informed their personal responses to the campaign, and the structure, work, and purpose of corporations. Before addressing these questions, we describe the general tone of focus group conversations, the evolving nature of the conversations, and how participants moved from surface impressions to more critical discussion.

Discussions usually began with participants' recounting their initial observations or feelings upon first seeing the Dove campaign. Many were very good at recalling and describing the first thing they felt when they saw a Dove billboard or subway advertisement. A minority of participants were straightforwardly positive, such as Julie (FG4), who said, "Phew, it was a breath of fresh air. Something new, more realistic, that represented like, how people actually are." A few participants reacted immediately with suspicions about corporate cooptation of feminist ideals, which rejected the conflation of opposites between corporate marketing and feminist ideals:

ANNIE (FG1): The first time I saw it I was livid. It's a gimmick. It creates the notion that we don't have to worry about this stuff anymore because Dove is taking care of it. It made me nervous.

MELINDA (FG1): I saw the white underwear and I was so worried. My reaction to anything that is remotely trying to use feminism is great caution.

More commonly, participants were initially happy to see less stereotypical images of women in mainstream media, and to see their politics amplified on such a large scale. However, these initially positive impressions generally gave way to concerns about the larger meaning of the campaign, and the disingenuous or rhetorical use of feminist concerns. In other words, one-dimensional support for the campaign may have characterized their initial thoughts, but further reflection and dialogue led to a more critical appraisal of the conflation between corporate and feminist objectives. For example:

MINDY (FG2): I was torn, I was like, okay, this is a step in the right direction, but they didn't give you a lot of information so I was kind of like, hmm, I'm not sure if I like this or not.

ANIKA (FG3): At first I thought it was great, you know, celebrating women, but then I felt there was something really forced about it, something artificial.

SADIA (FG6): I think it's good that they're trying to advertise diferent sizes, but really, *that* is not real beauty either.

Because most participants had mixed opinions, focus group discussions often involved identifying the different registers through which a response was possible: as a woman, a consumer, and a feminist. Opinions wove through understandings of one's own physical appearances, feelings about the business of advertising, personal consumption habits, and overall understandings of feminist politics and feminist change. Typical of participants' contributions, Maya gave varying responses to the campaign in the space of a 15-minute discussion. She initially complimented the campaign's potential positive impact on women's self-esteem and self-image, and talked about her own emotional response to its images, using examples related to her own physical appearance, and self-image. However, Maya later tempered her initial reaction by saying, "There is nothing radical about saying bigger women can be clean too." This later comment signals Maya's cognizance of the Dove campaign's primary goal—selling products—and her critical assessment of its limited transformative agenda.

. . .

QUESTION I. IS THE DOVE CAMPAIGN FOR REAL BEAUTY FEMINIST?

Focus group participants found this question challenging. Many commented that there are many different kinds of feminism so they were hesitant to say definitively whether or not the Dove Campaign was *truly* feminist. Half of the groups began by discussing two challenges: *first*, feminists are an unwieldy group with little consensus among them; and *second*, movements cannot control what happens to the ideas they produce. Participants identified a challenge inherent to the popularization of feminism, appreciating its wider reach but worrying about the watering down of ideas.

MINDY (FG1): Part of the problem is that feminism is so disjointed and not united. Some will see [the campaign] as good and others won't.

MYERA (FG1): It's also awkward because you want feminism to take off, when you create a movement you want it to take off, and then it becomes more accessible and then you're angry about it. I don't know how to feel about that.

Despite the challenge of defining feminism in a way all adherents would subscribe to, most participants found the Dove Campaign for Real Beauty to be a kind of faux feminism, or inauthentic engagement with feminist ideas. This judgment required them to articulate the campaign's insufficiencies: that unlike feminism, the campaign is not transgressive, nor does it encourage women to see beyond the confines of their own appearance and self-interest. Rather than accepting the conflation of 'feminism' with 'corporation,' our participants actively resisted this conflation and used discussion to clarify the points of distinction.

1A. Feminism Promotes Transgression

Participants in all focus groups argued that feminism should 'shake things up,' shock people out of complacency, and transgress accepted norms. . . . Feminism should push boundaries, forcing people to think about the taken-for-granted aspects of their lives and thought processes. Most participants found Dove's central message—that women should prioritize

being beautiful—incompatible with this objective. The campaign does not challenge the imperative of what we call 'compulsory beauty'—the ideology that beauty is not only a priority for women, but is a necessary component of a woman's self-worth and social value. Our participants, however, *did* challenge this idea, and said if the campaign asked women to let go of the beauty imperative, it would be more transformative. Others noted that while the campaign may have been intended to subvert dominant notions of beauty, it actually reinforced the significance of being 'beautiful' in mainstream society. One participant said that the campaign "reiterates the surface level focus of our culture" (Ella FG2).

. . .

. . . Five of the six groups contended that there was nothing terribly feminist or norm-busting about using women dancing in their underwear to sell products—a comment which reveals these young women's critical consciousness of post-feminist norms (Gill, 2003). Several women pointed out images of women hugging and posing for the camera with seeming delight, asking rhetorically whether they were celebrating the fact that thanks to Dove, they could delight in their own objectification. These focus group participants clearly rejected the conflation of "feminism" with Dove's corporate interests.

Some participants went further, suggesting what a truly transgressive campaign might look like if it applied the aesthetics of their feminist politics, and moved beyond Dove's images of women deriving pleasure from fitting in to dominant beauty ideals.

MELISSA (FG2): [Dove] is not pushing the envelope, it's not making you uncomfortable. As a feminist, there's a lot of other things that I could give them that I know they would not do. You know, like have someone with their chest bound, or maybe someone who is really large and happy with her body. [Dove is] still pretty palatable to the mainstream audience, and it silences all of these people who still don't fit. Maybe there should be two women in their underwear making out.

For Melissa, a feminist advertisement would be aimed at questioning the aspiration to be thin and conventionally pretty, would acknowledge the very real battles women have with their bodies such as chronic pain or disliking having breasts, and would contest the imperative to be found attractive by men. In other words, "compulsory beauty" could be challenged by a campaign that didn't glamorize or domesticate gender conformity.

The politics of size was a central feature in focus group discussions; so were other axes of inclusion such as religion, race and ethnicity. One group of teens, some of whom were black, Latina, and Muslim, criticized Dove's implicit colorism and limited presentation of diversity:

JOY (FG5): They look more real because they are in different shapes and colours.

ULI (FG5): Most of the models are light skinned people, not really dark-skinned.

CAM (FG5): There is a wider range of skin colours, but not types of religion. No magazine that I have ever seen has a girl with a hijab on.

JOY (FG5): Hair sells products. That's why they can't show girls in hijab.

ULI (FG5): Our hair isn't there either, nothing puffy or nappy.

These participants acknowledged that the campaign made some effort to represent diversity, but that it did not significantly upset hegemonic understandings of compulsory beauty. Their impression was that women of colour were lighter-skinned, and appeared to have had their features 'computerized' to look more European (Lani FG5). They also noted the absence of images that might challenge Western notions of beauty, like unstraightened black hair, or images that challenge the expectation that women should display their beauty for others, such as the hijab. Many non-white participants noted that Dove's version of diversity did not challenge hegemonic beauty norms based on white ideals, nor did it address the racism that underpins myriad beauty practices and expectations. These participants distinguished a corporate cosmetic approach from a feminist approach; the latter would challenge beauty norms, include women across the colour spectrum, enable women to resist using skin lighteners, affirm diversity in skin tone, and honor the range of embodied existence.

. . .

1B. Feminism Moves beyond the Self

The Dove Campaign for Real Beauty focuses on improving the self-esteem of girls and women by affirming their beauty. Rather than reject beauty, it positions beauty as a democratic good, fundamental to the self-esteem and self-worth of women everywhere (Johnston and Taylor, 2008). Many of its advertisements involve young girls who are unhappy with their appearance, and Dove developed a think tank about women's self-esteem and curricula for use in schools and community-based organizations (see Banet-Weiser, 2012).

Participants considered this pairing of beauty and self-esteem, and concluded that a feminist approach to self-esteem should aim to decouple appearance and feelings of self-worth, rejecting the idea of compulsory female beauty. Many argued that self-esteem is inherently apolitical, and that feminist causes should be oriented away from an isolated self, and toward a broader sense of social justice. Even if Dove's campaign broadened the social definition of beauty, thereby improving women's self-esteem, they argued that without a broader political analysis of gender inequality, such a shift would not significantly change the balance of power in society. In other words, some participants felt that resistance to conformist notions of beauty was insufficient to bring about political or economic change.

TARA (FG2): It kind of bugs me, reminds me of when we were in grade seven or eight and we had self-esteem talks, and I just don't feel like it's critical of anything else, self-esteem is such an easy thing to focus on, it's not very political.

MINDY (FG2): It's pretty palatable to a mainstream audience. They might make fun of it, they might not love it, but it's not like whoa, this is different.

TARA (FG2): I guess it could be very empowering for women, which is fine. But that doesn't make a difference, not enough.

For these participants, a campaign focused on self-esteem misses the larger goal of feminism, to effect change within the self as well as *beyond the self*. Consciousness-raising, they argued, should be the starting but not the ending point. In contrast to analyses that critique third-wave feminists as myopically focused on the self (e.g. Heath and Potter, 2005), our participants suggested that women could begin with social awareness about the injustices or insecurities of their lives, but optimally make larger connections between their own marginality and larger structural problems. Taya (FG3) compared Dove with another company, The Body Shop, whose campaigns focus on free-trade, fair labour, and environmental sustainability:

> You have this company [Dove] advocating positive self-image, it's a personal concept, whereas The Body Shop is preaching huge social issues. Dove is saying feel good about you, and the Body Shop is saying look at the Earth, the people around the world, look at these huge global issues.

Taya's comment reflects how participants did not immediately criticize Dove simply because it was a corporation engaging with feminist ideals; they used a different company to highlight what they perceived as Dove's comparative superficiality. These women found Dove's focus on the self encouraged preoccupation with the achievement of social affirmation and self-acceptance to the exclusion of broader social objectives.

. . .

ANNIE (FG3): Dove is saying 'Celebrate you,' and that seems to me kind of backward. If you are a conscious person who cares about the world and what happens as a result of your choices then you would be in the long run, more secure, you know, you'll have higher self-esteem and you'll be happier. The other way just seems sort of more myopic—focus on you and you and you.

For Annie and most participants in her group, feminism was about larger problems like social inequality and global warming, rather than democratizing access to beauty. They felt that self-esteem is accrued not through feeling beautiful, but through awareness of, and conscientious behaviour in relation to larger social issues. Believing that feminism is about 'moving past yourself' leads these women to critique Dove's focus on the self as myopic. For these participants, looking outside oneself is not simply a way to generate social change; it is also a recipe for happiness and personal growth.

. . .

QUESTION 2. SHOULD CORPORATIONS DO FEMINISM?

Focus group discussions about whether and how corporations should be involved in social change initiatives were more contentious than discussions about the Dove campaign's feminist status. Debates about the role of corporations in society were often unresolved, and participants were left to think about these issues after they left the focus groups. Each group produced a series of questions about the purview of corporations that led them to reflect critically on their own responsibilities as feminists, consumers and citizens. Even with the dissenting views, we observed a significant degree of critical consciousness about the extent to which corporate and feminist interests could be conflated. However, we also heard pessimistic accounts of how a ubiquitous world of corporate capitalism made such a conjoining inevitable.

Questions were wide-ranging and related to the mission of corporations, how social change occurs in practice, whether feminists should strive to be ethical consumers, what it means to hate corporations and love consumption, and whether it is legitimate to criticize corporate activism if one is not engaging in activist causes. Participants also struggled with the enormity and constancy of capitalism. Cynicism about capitalism appeared to temper their initial criticisms of the Dove campaign, as most participants found it difficult or impossible to imagine non-market possibilities for social change. Failing a new economic and social order, the overwhelming majority of participants agreed that the Dove campaign, with its flaws and contradictions, is 'better than nothing'—possibly justifying Marcuse's (1964) pessimism about imagining alternatives to capitalism.

2A. Anti-Capitalist Feminism

While participants found it difficult to imagine alternatives to capitalism, many agreed that feminism should at least *resist* capitalism. These participants argued that when a corporation engages in feminist politics, it dilutes feminists' criticisms of capitalism and their ability to envision non-commodified alternatives. They saw feminism as a daily practice reminding them that the central goal of a corporation (and its marketing) is to generate insecurities that drive consumption.

PAULINE (FG1): Every time you see advertising, people are trying to make money. Is it a bunch of guys sitting around in suits [thinking] oh, how are we going to get 40-year-old women to buy our products?

SUE (FG1): You're coming at it as a feminist, they are selling it to you as a feminist campaign, but the campaign is steeped in capitalism. It doesn't make sense, how can you mix those two?

. . . Women in all groups commented that even if some people who work in corporations sincerely care about forwarding feminist ideals, they care most about selling products, and that the profit motive will ultimately trump other ideals. Shale (FG2) said, "Is it a corporation's job to be political? . . . do I want Dove Corporation to show me politics? I want a more grassroots analysis." For women like Shale, corporate advocacy is inevitably influenced by the profit-motive, and usurps grassroots actors and ideas. While the groups did not develop a grand vision of post-capitalist life, there was still normative space to imagine grassroots ideals as important alternatives to capitalist commodification and corporate solutions.

Others women objected to the commodification of feminism—the idea that feminist beliefs should be expressed through buying a product. Several found it insidious how Dove paired products with realms of life that had little to do with purchasing products, such as self-help therapy or the arts. For example, Dove sponsored a feminist photography exhibit at one of Toronto's largest shopping malls, and gave free product samples to viewers as they exited the show. Other participants did not like the implication that one must purchase (corporate) products to support grassroots initiatives. Tanya (FG4) observed, "It's like turning feminism into something you can buy, I don't know if I like that. It's an idea or a way of life, I don't know if you can buy that. I'm a feminist because I bought this hand cream? It's the lazy way out." . . .

2B. Accomplishing Feminist Change in a Capitalist Context

There was general agreement in focus groups that Dove's parent company, Unilever, would profit from the campaign, but that aesthetic norms and women's insecurities about their physical appearances would not be radically changed. In Taya's words (FG6), "[i]n terms of making a difference in society, it's not going to happen. They're gonna make a bit of money off it and then when everybody realizes it's bull then it's time for a new idea." Scepticism about the efficacy of the Dove campaign raised the question of how feminist change might actually occur. At this point participants tempered their corporate critiques, and asked practical questions: how am I personally enacting feminism in the world? Should feminists partner with power holders to affect society? Don't we want corporations to support movements? Isn't it useful for us as consumers to know which companies support our politics so we can buy from them? These questions reflected a mixed critical consciousness and conflicted emotions about personal contributions to feminist social change.

Teenaged participants tended to be self-critical about the extent to which they were promoting feminist social change, seeing themselves as not doing enough. Older participants expressed guilt about their complex relationship to capitalism, and debated whether it was hypocritical to criticize corporations and still enjoy consumer culture. Women in their 20s were also conflicted about the role of the corporation in the landscape of social change: some felt corporations should spearhead initiatives, others felt they should stay out of the realm of ideas and simply donate money to non-profit organizations.

ANNA (FG1): There are people whose job it is—and who genuinely want—to find good places for money to go. Would we really want to prevent a corporation from donating?

MENA (FG1): Do we need to be partners with the bad guys in order to create change?

ANNA (FG1): You know—we like to spend money. We like clothing, we like a certain standard of living. We also need to learn how to work from within the corporation.

MENA (FG1): But to what degree will feminism be compromised? Are corporations going to start shaping social justice movements?

In addition to imagining feminists who might work within or cooperate with corporations, in these pragmatic discussions participants evaluated their own complicity with capitalism as a way of life, and debated whether feminism is discrete from capitalism and should be protected from its influences. Others made useful comparisons with other industries to debate the role of corporations promulgating feminist ideals and social change:

SHEILA (FG2): Change has to come from inside the [beauty] industry.
ASTRID: (FG2): I totally disagree. I don't think change happens from inside an industry. It hasn't happened with food. Consumer demands led to changes. And with the beauty industry, it's got to be women who say I am not going to wear stilettos or makeup. It is dollars and cents that drive industry to change.

The idea of 'dollars and cents' driving social change was not unusual in our discussions. Most participants were ambivalent about feminism partnering with corporations, but interestingly, still generally supported some notion of ethical consumerism involving political expression through targeted consumption choices. Heather (FG1) said, "I am still going to buy shampoo and soap, why not buy it from someplace that at least purports to have some good values?" Most participants, regardless of how pointedly they criticized Dove, found corporate engagement with movement ideals 'better than nothing'—a sentiment which sometimes reflected an underlying sense of powerlessness.

. . .

Those who begrudgingly agreed with the sentiment the Dove campaign was 'better than nothing' were incredulous that corporations harm people through their business practices, but then participate in philanthropy, seemingly 'paying dues' for the social and environmental havoc they cause. Maya (FG1) said, "Where is the line? Where do they stop being a corporation and start helping people?" . . .

The inherent struggle in many of these conversations was related to the inevitability of capitalism, the depth of capitalist entrenchment in every aspect of life, and a sense of powerlessness when it came to imagining alternatives. Some participants accepted this reality and promoted the idea of pragmatically working within these logics, while others held fast to the desire to preserve distinctions between their own feminist ideals and corporate marketing. While Jenine (FG4) insisted that "you have to attach [social issues] to a company or a product" to get people to pay attention, Wanda (FG6) protested, "I just don't see why there has to be a product that is being sold for these [feminist] messages to be up there." . . .

CONCLUSION

One important conclusion from our focus group research is that young women positively predisposed to feminism exhibit notable critical capacities and political consciousness, even in a culture marked by post-feminist individualism (McRobbie, 2009). The sophisticated feminist consciousness we observed leads us to believe that one factor that keeps social movements alive in times of quiescence is not just organizations, but intellectual work. While social movement organizations preserve networks, goals, and collective identity (Taylor, 1989), our results suggest that critical consciousness can be active and vibrant in periods of movement abeyance, as supporters maintain the ability to think critically and generate analyses that sustain and justify political identities. Our focus groups clearly demonstrate how young women were skilled at unpacking power relations, using everyday observations to elaborate their critiques and identifying the contradictions and trespasses that oppose their visions for the future.

The critical analyses of young feminists also refute understandings of third wave feminists as unduly and narcissistically attuned to lifestyle and popular culture, to the exclusion of concerns about material inequality and structural obstacles (Faludi, 2010; Heath and Potter, 2005). While our sample is neither exhaustive nor representative of the general population, our findings suggest that young women who respond positively to feminism are *inclined* to make political sense of personal obstacles, even if this is likely not true among the general populace (e.g. Eliasoph, 1998). . . .

In terms of feminism's relationship to political agency and corporate capitalism, our participants agreed the Dove Campaign for Real Beauty was not feminist because it preached conformity rather than transgression, and encouraged women to focus on their self-esteem to the neglect of the world around them. The majority argued that corporations should not 'do the work' of feminism, reasoning that feminism is intrinsically anti-capitalist, and that political expression through consumption is not a legitimate strategy for progressive movements. While not all groups were in agreement, most spent the session collectively disentangling feminist goals from corporate behaviour—although participants (even those who did not support the Dove campaign) were open to the idea that targeted shopping practices could achieve social benefits. . . . Participants left the sessions simultaneously aware of capitalism's effects—and its durability.

. . . In all focus groups, the majority of participants did not appreciate a corporation amplifying the ideals of the feminist movement, and they challenged the 'feminist' status of the ideals used in the Dove campaign. Participants discussed how feminist ideals were rendered politically ineffectual by their use in the Dove campaign, and the importance of separating feminist and corporate interests, and maintaining this boundary. Most participants rejected the idea that profit motive and social change engine could be effectively combined, but they were also pragmatic—they evaluated corporations' forays into social change comparatively, and found some corporate projects more egregious than others.

Participants discredited the Dove campaign's apparent goal to democratize beauty, by suggesting that genuine feminism (rather than feminist consumerism) rejects compulsory beauty and inspires empowerment by other means. Women talked about how the promise of beauty paired with products is not feminist, but involves the most basic consumer logic of commodification. Participants openly explored the numerous contradictory feelings the campaign inspired in them—for example, gratitude for seeing more women of colour represented on billboards, but

irritation at the saturation of the cultural landscape with advertising. While most participants were pessimistic about the possibilities of decentering consumerism as a dominant social value and economic model, they still envisioned spaces of resistance, and doing so is constitutive of their political identities. Through dialogue, women honed their critiques and developed new understandings of feminism as a politics that goes beyond self-care, transgresses accepted norms, and is anti-capitalist. . . .

NOTE

1. One methodological limitation to note is that our use of pre-existing networks limited participants' opportunities to share their ideas outside their circle.

REFERENCES

Banet-Weiser S (1999) *The Most Beautiful Girl in the World: Beauty Pageants and National Identity.* Berkeley, CA: University of California Press.

Banet-Weiser S (2012) "Free self-esteem tools"? Brand culture, gender, and the Dove Real Beauty Campaign. In: Banet-Weiser S and Mukherjee R (eds) *Commodity Activism.* New York, NY: New York University Press, 39–56.

Banner LW (1983) *American Beauty.* Chicago, IL: University of Chicago Press.

Barkay T (2013) When business and community meet: a case study of Coca-Cola. *Critical Sociology* 39(2): 277–293.

Bezanson K and Luxton M (eds) (2006) *Social Reproduction: Feminist Political Economy Challenges Neo-Liberalism.* Montreal: McGill Queens University Press.

Boltanski L and Chiapello E (2007) *The New Spirit of Capitalism.* Brooklyn, NY: Verso Press.

Cabrera SA and Williams C (2012) Consuming for the social good: marketing, consumer citizenship, and the possibilities of ethical consumption. *Critical Sociology.* Published online before print. DOI: 10.1177/0896920512458599.

Eliasoph N (1998) *Avoiding Politics: How Americans Produce Apathy in Everyday Life.* Cambridge: Cambridge University Press.

Faludi S (2010) American Electra: feminism's ritual matricide. *Harper's Magazine* October: 29–42.

Frank T (1997) *The Conquest of Cool: Business Culture, Counterculture, and the Rise of Hip Consumerism.* Chicago, IL: University of Chicago Press.

Frank T and Weiland M (eds) (1997) *Commodify Your Dissent: Salvos from the Baffler.* New York, NY: Norton and Company.

Gill R (2003) From sexual objectification to sexual subjectification: The resexualisation of women's bodies in the media. *Feminist Media Studies* 3(1): 100–105.

Gilmore S (2005) Rethinking the liberal/radical divide: the National Organization for Women in Memphis, Columbus, and San Francisco, 1971–1982. PhD dissertation, Ohio State University, Columbus OH, USA.

Gimlin D (2002) *Body Work: Beauty and Self-Image in American Culture.* Berkeley, CA: University of California Press.

Gordon A (1995) The work of corporate culture: diversity management. *Social Text* 44: 3–30.

Harris A (ed.) (2008) *New Wave Culture: Feminism, Subcultures, Activism.* London: Routledge.

Hartley C (2001) Letting ourselves go: making room for the fat body in feminist scholarship. In: Braziel JE and LeBesco K (eds) *Bodies Out of Bounds: Fatness and Transgression.* Berkeley: University of California Press, 60–73.

Heath J and Potter A (2004) *The Rebel Sell. Why the Culture Can't Be Jammed.* Toronto: Harper Collins.

Heath J and Potter A (2005) Feminism for sale. *This Magazine* 38(6): 20.

Jeffreys S (2005) *Beauty and Misogyny: Harmful Cultural Practices in the West.* New York, NY: Routledge.

Johnston J (2008) The citizen-consumer hybrid: ideological tensions and the case of Whole Foods Market. *Theory and Society* 37(3): 229–270.

Johnston J and Taylor J (2008) Feminist consumerism and fat activists: a comparative study of grassroots activism and the Dove "Real Beauty" campaign. *Signs: A Journal of Women in Culture and Society* 33(4): 941–966.

Laslett B and Brenner J (1989) Gender and social reproduction: historical perspectives. *Annual Review of Sociology* 15: 381–404.

McKinnon A (2013) Ideology and the market metaphor in rational choice theory of religion: a rhetorical critique of "religious economies." *Critical Sociology* 39(4): 529–543.

McRobbie A (2009) *The Aftermath of Feminism: Gender, Culture and Social Change.* Los Angeles, CA: Sage.

Marcuse H (1964) *One-Dimensional Man.* Boston, MA: Beacon Press.

Messner M (2002) *Taking the Field: Women, Men, and Sports.* Minneapolis, MN: University of Minnesota Press.

Micheletti M (2003) *Political Virtue and Shopping: Individuals, Consumerism and Collective Action.* New York, NY: Palgrave MacMillan.

Morgan DL (1996) Focus groups. *Annual Review of Sociology* 22: 129–152.

Newfield C (1995) Corporate pleasures for a corporate planet. *Social Text* 44(3): 1–44.

Orr C (1997) Charting the current of the Third Wave. *Hypatia* 12(3): 29–45.

Redfern C and Aune K (2010) *Reclaiming the F Word.* New York, NY: Zed.

Reger J (2012) *Everywhere and Nowhere: The State of U.S. Contemporary Feminist Communities.* Cambridge: Cambridge University Press.

Taylor V (1989) Social movement continuity: the women's movement in abeyance. *American Sociological Review* 54(5): 761–775.

Taylor V (1996) *Rock-a-by Baby: Feminism, Self-Help, and Post-Partum Depression.* New York, NY: Routledge.

Turkle, S (2011). "Alone Together: Why We Expect More from Technology and Less from Each Other," p.154, Basic Books

Vogel D (2005) *The Market for Virtue: The Potential and Limits of Corporate Social Responsibility.* Arlington, VA: Brookings Institute Press.

Weitz R (2004) *Rapunzel's Daughters: What Women's Hair Tells Us about Women's Lives.* New York, NY: Farrar, Straus and Giroux.

Wilson E (2003) *Bohemians: The Glamorous Outcast.* London: Tauris Park.

Wolf N (1990) *The Beauty Myth.* Toronto: Random House.

CHAPTER 6

SEX, POWER, AND INTIMACY

Sexuality is one topic of great interest to many. It entertains and intrigues and can be a source of both personal happiness and frustration. It is also an aspect of our lives that is highly regulated as communities shape and control sexual desires and behaviors. Scholars emphasize that this control has emerged as a principal means of governing contemporary societies through regulation, which includes laws and social policies condoning certain relationships and sexual expressions. Regulation also involves "regimes of truth" discussed in earlier chapters, where power is more dispersed and individuals shape normative behaviors in themselves and others. A central aspect of such contemporary discourses on sexuality is the fundamental assumption that all adults should experience sexual desire. Asexual individuals who do not experience desire, and have no inclination to do so, radically challenge the prevailing normative culture.

The flip side of this focus on the regulatory regimes of sexuality is that sex when freely chosen and practiced has the potential to be a liberating force. To enjoy and be in control of one's sexuality and to be able to seek a mutually fulfilling sexual relationship can be a very empowering experience. Feminists tend to value this notion of an empowered sexuality but may disagree about the definition of, and the path to, such empowerment, especially among adolescents. Certainly media literacy education and proficient sexuality education are central in this endeavor. Sexual empowerment is a central theme of this chapter. We not only discuss the social construction of sexuality and provide key terms, but also focus on two themes: first, the politics of sexuality, and second, intimacy, romance, and interpersonal communication. In these sections we emphasize the shifts and fluidity in gender and sexual identities.

THE SOCIAL CONSTRUCTION OF SEXUALITY

Human sexuality involves erotic attractions, identity, and practices, and it is constructed by and through societal sexual scripts. In this sense, we perform sexuality just as we perform gender and other identities. Sexual scripts are guidelines for how we are supposed to feel and act as sexual persons. They are shaped by the communities and societies in which we participate and therefore are socially constructed (they emerge from communities and societies). The focus on these scripts is meant to emphasize the ways they create our understanding of "normal."

People are thus not "naturally" anything; individuals' sexual desires and identities change over the course of their lives, and "normal" is a historically specific, constructed concept emerging out of human communities. In this way social scripts are socially produced and part of the discourses and broader regimes of truth that reflect social norms and practices; in other words, they provide frameworks and guidelines for sexual feelings and behaviors in particular communities at a particular time. Foundational in these scripts is the oppositional binary of heterosexuality and homosexuality that constructs normative sexuality and shapes sexual feelings and expression. By opposing heterosexuality to homosexuality and setting it up as unquestioningly normative, heterosexuality gains its credibility. This is the meaning of heteronormativity: the centering and normalizing of heterosexuality.

Sometimes there is embarrassment, shame, and confusion associated with sexual scripts, and they may easily become fraught with potential misunderstandings. As Jessica Valenti explains in "The Cult of Virginity," an excerpt from her book *The Purity Myth*, the contemporary focus on virginity as an indicator of female moral worth (the "good girl") is both problematic and confusing in an era when girls and young women are increasingly sexualized and yet simultaneously faced with abstinence movements aiming to control sexual activity. Surveys show that more than half of participating teens in "virginity pledges" become sexually active anyway, and the numbers who take precautions against pregnancy and STIs (sexually transmitted infections) are significantly lower among nonpledgers.

Sexual scripts, contextualized in specific communities and nations, shape how individuals come to develop a sense of their own sexual lives. We learn these subjective understandings by assimilating, rejecting, and ultimately negotiating the sexual scripts available to us. These subjective understandings are called sexual self-schemas. They can be defined as ideas and beliefs about sexual aspects of the self that are established from past and present experiences and that act to guide sexual feelings and behavior. What is desirable or acceptable to one person may be unacceptable or even disgusting to another. The reading "The Future of Fat Sex" by Francis Ray White argues that contemporary culture has constructed "fat sex" as a type of "failure" in dominant sexual scripts.

Sexual identity is one aspect of sexual self-schemas that can be defined as a person's attraction to, or preference for, certain people. It is an individual's romantic and/or sexual (also called erotic) identity and behavior. Note that sexual identity does not necessarily require sexual experience or behavior. Heterosexuality is a sexual identity of romantic and/or sexual attachments between people of the "opposite sex" (popularly termed "straight"). Homosexuality is a sexual identity of romantic and/or sexual attachments between people of the "same sex." Note also how these terms rely on polarized binaries and on assumptions that individuals are cisgender (remember this concept from Chapter 3). Because the term "homosexual" is stigmatized and because it seems to overemphasize sexual behaviors, many communities have preferred the term gay. Gay and homosexual are terms inclusive of women, although they are used mainly to describe men. The term lesbian means the romantic and/or sexual attachment and identification between women specifically. You might also hear the terms dyke, butch, and femme. Dyke is synonymous with lesbian, although it connotes a masculine or mannish lesbian. Like queer, dyke is a word that is used against lesbians as an insult and has been appropriated or reclaimed by lesbians with pride. This means that if you are not a member of the lesbian, gay, or queer communities, you should use these terms with care. Butch and femme are roles adopted by some lesbians, especially in the past. Butch means acting as the masculine partner, and femme means acting in a feminine role. Although today many lesbians avoid these role types because there is little incentive to mimic traditional heterosexual relationships, others enjoy these identities and appropriate them to suit themselves.

Bisexuality implies a sexual identification with both women and men. There are derogatory social connotations of bisexuality as hypersexualized. Of course, to be bisexual does not imply this at all; it just means the choice of lover can be either a woman or a man. Nonetheless, these connotations reflect the fact that there are many stigmas associated with bisexuality from both the straight and the lesbian and gay communities. Although these identities are experienced and enjoyed by individuals, and therefore pragmatic for our understanding of sexuality, such definitions rely on fixed notions of "woman" or "man." In response, the term "polysexual," defined as the attraction to multiple genders and sexual identities, is used intentionally to disrupt the binary implied in the foregoing definitions. In other words, polysexual people are attracted to individuals from the full range of sexual identities. Importantly, the gendering of "people" is broader than the "woman" and "man" used earlier. Polysexuals are attracted to diverse sexual identities performed by a broad array of gender identities. In particular, this term critiques the heterosexual/homosexual binary implicit in the term "bisexuality." Individuals who identify as polysexual may be attracted to transgender, Two-Spirit, or those who identify as "genderqueer." They may also, however, still be attracted to cisgender people of all sexual identities. Polysexuality as a sexual identity is different from polyamory. Polyamory does not imply that a person is attracted to a diversity of sexual identities: Instead, it is defined as the practice, desire, or acceptance of having more than one intimate relationship at a time with the knowledge and consent of everyone involved. Often abbreviated as "poly," it is often described as consensual, ethical, and responsible non-monogamy. The practice emphasizes ethics, honesty, and transparency.

As already discussed, the word queer, traditionally meaning out of the ordinary or unusual, and historically an insult when used in the context of sexualities (most often as a derogatory term for effeminate and/or gay boys and men), has in recent times taken on new meaning and been reclaimed as a source of self-empowerment by those who reject the categories of straight, gay, lesbian, and bisexual, and who seek to live alternative identities that are more fluid and less rigidly assigned to binary boxes in terms of both gender and sexuality. "Queer" critiques the confined aspect of these boxes themselves, even if they are nontraditional boxes like LGBT (lesbian, gay, bisexual, trans). As a result, it is important to recognize that queer is not a synonym for LGBT identities. Instead it is a critique of

UNDERSTANDING TRANS SEXUALITIES: DIVING INTO THE BINARY

Andrés López

Just like trans people's bodies can come in all sorts of shapes, anatomies, and sizes, trans people experience their sexualities in a multitude of ways. Often, when we first come out to those closest to us, there's an assumption that our gender identities have something to do with our sexual orientation—meaning that others place expectations of who we might be sexually attracted to on us based on our gender identities and presentations. However, trans folks experience sexuality on a spectrum. We feel attracted to people who are masculine, as well as to feminine-presenting folks. We can feel attraction toward both. We feel attracted to people who have no gender. We also might not feel any sexual attractions toward anyone at all.

To make sense of this we need to dive into the gender binary. Here is a helpful model from YES Institute's "Gender Continuum" course (2010).

BINARY GENDER MODEL

Body	Gender	Orientation
Female	Feminine	Male
Male	Masculine	Female
Assigned	Assumed	Expected

Notice how there is a clear one-directional line that moves from Body to Gender to Orientation. When we're in the binary, anyone born is assigned a category based on the appearance of their genitals. This assignment creates assumptions about this person's gender. Subsequently there's an expectation that this person will be attracted to those who have the opposite assignment and assumed gender. There's an unnamed expectation that *all people* fit into this model neatly all of the time. Do you fit into this model all of the time?

It's okay if you do fit into this model. The problem is not that people fit into this model or that there are folks who don't. The problem is that this is expected of everyone all of the time! The problem is that through these assumptions about our genders there are expectations as to how and who we should feel attracted to. In reality, there are behaviors that we do that get labeled as feminine and masculine. And these behaviors, presentations, and bodies don't really tell us anything about who people feel attracted to.

What happens to people who cross any of these clearly defined lines? It is when people cross these imaginary binary lines that others perpetuate violence. Because most of us are taught that everyone's experiences of their body, gender, and orientation are the same, there are people who feel threatened or afraid when they encounter others who do not fit into their conceptions of "reality." This is why instances of violence against trans people, and trans women of color in particular, are so high. Folks assume that because the genitalia of someone they're attracted to (body) looks a particular way, they will be labeled as "gay." In reality, body parts don't tell us anything about anyone.

How does the gender binary affect your own sexuality? What might be some ways to counter the assumptions we've been taught about gender and sexuality?

To learn more, check out the YES Institute at https://yesinstitute.org/resource/gender-resource-guide/.

Reference

YES Institute. (2010). "Gender Continuum" (Course Power-Point). Miami, FL.

"all things oppressively normal," including nontraditional categories like lesbian and gay. Nowadays this distinction is often lost, and "queer" tends to be used as another alternative identity for lesbian and gay, thus creating a new fixed category—even though, of course, this gesture toward re-creating yet another box has important functions in terms of building solidarity and pursuing collective action for social justice.

Finally, asexuality, as already mentioned, involves a person who does not experience desire and attraction to others. Asexuality has been pathologized and medicalized and is often seen as a "deviance" or a "deficit." In fact, asexuality may be regarded as a "queer" orientation in its resistance to contemporary normative standards that expect adults to want to experience sexual desire. Note that asexuality is not about people who experience a decrease in sex drive and are distressed by it. Asexual people are those who do not experience sexual desire and are not distressed by this "lack."

Again, as emphasized in Chapter 3 and mentioned earlier in this chapter, it is important to understand both the ways gender (the focus of Chapter 3) and sexuality (the focus of this chapter) are simultaneously distinct and intertwined. We know this can be confusing, but try to remember that gender is about femininity and masculinity, and sexual identity is about sexual desire and behaviors. It is possible to have multiple combinations of gendered individuals identifying with varying sexual scripts, although heterosexuality relies on cisgender performances to maintain its stability.

Finally, the term "coming" out refers to someone adopting a gay, lesbian, bisexual, or queer identity. Coming out is understood as a psychological process that tends to involve two aspects: first, recognizing and identifying this to oneself, and second, declaring oneself in a "public" (broadly defined) way. In terms of this second aspect, individuals usually come out to affirming members in their own community before they (if ever) face a general public. Some never come out to families or coworkers for fear of rejection, reprisals, and retaliation. For some, coming out means becoming part of an identifiable political community; for others, it means functioning for the most part as something of an outsider in a straight world. "In the closet" means not being out at all. In the closet can imply that people understand themselves to be lesbian, gay, or queer but are not out to others. It can also imply that people are in denial about their sexuality and are not comfortable claiming nonheterosexual identities.

Given homophobia and the potential for bullying in many communities, it is easy to see how individuals are encouraged to police themselves and each other. It is important to emphasize that homophobia (fear or hatred of homosexuals, gays, lesbians, bisexuals, and/or those identifying as queer) can be especially hurtful to young people. Indeed, gay, lesbian, bisexual, and queer youth are especially at risk for suicide, resulting in a relatively higher rate of suicides among these teens. Data show a higher rate of attempted suicides among girls and a higher rate of suicide deaths among boys. Suicidal behavior can be understood, in part, by examining risk factors—the conditions or experiences that increase the likelihood of suicide. Overall, risk factors are greater and more severe for trans, lesbian, gay, bisexual, and queer youth, especially in situations where there is bullying and stigma. They experience higher rates of depression and substance abuse: factors associated with increased risk of suicide. They also are more likely than teens overall to lack family and community support. It is transphobia, homophobia, and institutionalized heterosexism that lead these youth to kill themselves.

A focus on sexual scripts highlights the ways these discourses vary across cultures and through time and always concern issues of power (such as which groups get the authority to define "appropriate" sexual activity and the means to regulate it). Compulsory heterosexuality, the expectation that everyone should be heterosexual, is a central component of the regulation of sexual scripts worldwide. Also implicit in this script is the notion of heteronormativity, already discussed, which means the assumption of heterosexuality as the norm or normative behavior in any given setting that also regulates at the level of social policy. For example, historically in the United States, anti-miscegenation laws prevented people from different races from engaging in sexual relationships, and the "Don't Ask, Don't Tell" law, now repealed, once prevented gays and lesbians from openly serving

DISRUPTING NARRATIVES ABOUT QUEER AND TRANS* FOLKS AROUND THE WORLD

Sasha A. Khan

Often within Western Europe and North America, people imagine that the rest of the world is lagging behind or failing to make progress on LGBT rights. This narrative, called "Western sexual exceptionalism," creates a false binary between "the West" (progressive, free, equal, civilized) and the rest of the world (backward, repressive, patriarchal, barbaric). It is accomplished through the flattening and obscuring of power relations.

Brainstorm examples of Western sexual exceptionalism. You might have encountered these narratives in popular culture, the news, or daily conversations. For example, an episode of the TV show *Scandal* depicted a gay man from a fictional Muslim-majority Middle Eastern country seeking political asylum in the United States because he would rather die than return home, where the show assumes that he will be killed. This is an oft-repeated and unquestioned narrative in Western media. Then, consider the following questions. What are the assumptions underlying Western sexual exceptionalism? How do these narratives homogenize queer and trans* communities in "the West" and elsewhere? How are the categories queer and trans* coded in terms of race, gender, sexuality, nationality, and class? Who is rendered legible and who is rendered illegible? How do these distinctions feed ongoing power dynamics including heteropatriarchy, ableism, white supremacy, colonialism, and imperialism? How might you disrupt narratives of Western sexual exceptionalism that you encounter in your daily life? Why, if at all, is this important?

In the midst of narratives of Western sexual exceptionalism, education can be a powerful tool. Conduct a web search to learn more about queer and trans* activism taking place around the world. Some useful starting points for your research might include the following: the Sylvia Rivera Law Project in the United States, the Society of Transsexual Women of the Philippines, Fem Alliance Uganda, Equal Ground in Sri Lanka, and Mosaic in Lebanon.

in the military. Cisgender scripts shape sexual norms, as the recent National Transgender Discrimination Survey[1] attests. This survey highlights systemic anti-transgender bias and structural violence as endless challenges for transgender people. Finally, current marriage laws in many states also provide examples of the institutionalization of sexual scripts endorsing compulsory heterosexuality as social policy, just as marriage equality laws have now institutionalized marriage equality, commonly known as "same-sex marriage." In June, 2015, marriage equality was established in all 50 states as a result of the U.S. Supreme Court ruling, which held that "same-sex" couples had the rights and responsibilities to marry on the same terms and conditions as "opposite-sex" couples, as guaranteed by the Equal Protection Clause of the Fourteenth Amendment to the U.S. Constitution.

In this age of globalization, women's bodies and sexuality are increasingly the site of intense conflict as control of female sexuality carries symbolic value in many societies, both in the United States and worldwide. The reading by Carl Collison, "Queer Muslim Women Are Making Salaam with Who They Are," addresses the disjuncture between Muslim women's sexuality and/or gender nonconformity and their religious affiliations. The article points out that these obstacles are social rather than spiritual and quotes religious scholars encouraging queer Muslims to create their own interpretations of the relationships between sexuality and spirituality. A key point of this reading is that imperialism and globalization have played significant roles in shaping sexual politics worldwide, in part through colonialism that functioned to organize sexual power by constructing the sexual norms and morality of indigenous societies as "exotic" and/or "uncivilized." Indeed, in terms of the colonization of the Americas, the depiction of colonized peoples as

---

1   National Center for Transgender Equality (2015) https://www.transequality.org/sites/default/files/docs/USTS-Full-Report-FINAL.PDF

LEARNING ACTIVITY

QUEER CINEMA

The depictions of LGBTQ people in movies tell us a lot about how a culture frames non-dominant sexual relationships. The following movies were made in very different cultures and time periods.

1. Watch several of these movies and think about what they tell us about how the culture and time period understood various sexual identities and sexual relationships. How have depictions of LGBTQ people in film changed or not over time?
2. Do some research on the web to learn about the people who produced and directed these films. Did these filmmakers have a political agenda?
3. Read reviews of the films. How were the films received?
4. How do you think the movement from lesbian and gay identity and politics to queer theory may affect how we analyze these films?

Movies:

- *Rope* (USA, 1948)
- *Un Chant d'Amour* (France, 1950)
- *The Children's Hour* (USA, 1961)
- *Victim* (UK, 1961)
- *In a Year with Thirteen Moons* (Germany, 1978)
- *Making Love* (USA, 1982)
- *Personal Best* (USA, 1982)
- *The Hunger* (USA, 1983)
- *My Beautiful Laundrette* (UK, 1985)
- *The Color Purple* (USA, 1985)
- *The Kiss of the Spider Woman* (USA, 1985)
- *Desert Hearts* (USA, 1985)
- *I've Heard the Mermaids Singing* (Canada, 1987)
- *Torch Song Trilogy* (USA, 1988)

- *Paris Is Burning* (USA, 1990)
- *Longtime Companion* (USA, 1989)
- *My Own Private Idaho* (USA, 1991)
- *The Crying Game* (USA, 1992)
- *Philadelphia* (USA, 1993)
- *The Sum of Us* (Australia, 1994)
- *When Night Is Falling* (Canada, 1995)
- *The Incredibly True Adventures of Two Girls in Love* (USA, 1995)
- *Fire* (India, 1996)
- *The Watermelon Woman* (USA, 1996)
- *Happy Together* (Hong Kong, 1997)
- *All About My Mother* (Spain, 1999)
- *Before Night Falls* (USA, 2000)
- *Hedwig and the Angry Inch* (USA, 2001)
- *Tropical Malady* (Thailand, 2004)
- *The Blossoming of Maximo Oliveros* (Philippines, 2005)
- *Brokeback Mountain* (USA, 2005)
- *Milk* (USA, 2008)
- *A Single Man* (USA, 2009)
- *The Kids Are All Right* (USA, 2010)
- *Albert Nobbs* (UK/Ireland 2011)
- *Blue Is the Warmest Color* (France, 2013)
- *The Imitation Game* (UK, 2014)
- *Pride* (UK, 2014)
- *Carol* (USA/UK, 2015)
- *The Danish Girl* (USA, 2015)
- *Moonlight* (USA, 2016)
- *Battle of the Sexes* (USA, 2017)
- *Professor Marston and the Wonder Women* (USA, 2017)
- *Boy Erased* (USA, 2018)
- *Bohemian Rhapsody* (USA/UK, 2018)

---

sexually perverse and/or sinful was fundamental to colonial projects. Colonialism tends to reorganize sexual relationships among indigenous communities and devalue those that are not organized around heteropatriarchy. In response to colonial rule, many nationalist movements in the Caribbean, Asia, and Africa after World War II protested and secured formal political independence. Unfortunately, these gains did not necessarily ensure greater sexual autonomy for women, who were often seen as the "mothers of the nation" and vital to maintaining the purity and sanctity of the nation. In addition, because women are often associated with national culture, controlling women's sexual behaviors under the guise of morality has become a question of national concern. Efforts to control women's sexual lives by religiously inspired fundamentalist social groups such as the Taliban of Afghanistan or the Religious Right in the United States are cases in point. Such forces have often criminalized LGBTQ issues in many regions of the world.

The economic, social, and cultural aspects of globalization also shape sexual identities by constraining people's sexual expressions and practices and normalizing particular sexual identities, delegitimizing and sometimes destroying local culture, and making sex into a commodity that can be bought and sold. These processes involve new media and the rapid circulation of cultural representations of sexuality worldwide, including pornography. Commodification and consumerism include increased demand for women's sexual labor, with growth in sex tourism and the global sex industry generally. However, globalization also provides opportunities for resistance and the possibilities of new sexual identities.

Certainly analyses of sexuality focusing on the United States must be contextualized in a global perspective and the struggle for sexual justice must be understood within a

---

RAINBOW HISTORY

1. At what New York bar did the modern gay liberation movement begin?

   a. Studio 54
   b. Stonewall
   c. Club 57
   d. Scandals

2. What were homosexuals required to wear to identify them in concentration camps during World War II?

   a. A yellow star
   b. A lavender H
   c. A pink star
   d. A pink triangle

3. What Greek letter symbolizes queer activism?

   a. Lambda
   b. Alpha
   c. Delta
   d. Sigma

4. What is the name of the religious organization that supports queer Catholics?

   a. Spirit
   b. Celebration
   c. Dignity
   d. Affirmation

5. What is the country's largest political organization working specifically for queer rights?

   a. Human Rights Campaign
   b. ACT-UP
   c. NOW
   d. Christian Coalition

6. In what year did the U.S. Congress vote to repeal "Don't Ask, Don't Tell," the military policy that prohibited gay and lesbian service members from being open about their sexual identity?

   a. 1968
   b. 1993
   c. 2001
   d. 2010

7. What show made television history by having the first gay lead character?

   a. *Soap*
   b. *Roseanne*
   c. *Ellen*
   d. *All in the Family*

8. Who was the first openly gay man elected in California (to the San Francisco Board of Supervisors in 1977)?

   a. Harvey Milk
   b. Barney Frank
   c. Allen Ginsberg
   d. Elton John

9. What was the first openly black lesbian novel published in the United States (1974)?

   a. Alice Walker's *The Color Purple*
   b. Ann Allen Shockley's *Loving Her*
   c. Gloria Naylor's *The Women of Brewster Place*
   d. Ntozake Shange's *Sassafrass, Cypress, and Indigo*

10. In 2004, which state became the first to legalize gay marriage?

    a. Iowa
    b. California
    c. Vermont
    d. Massachusetts

Answers: 1. b, 2. d, 3. a, 4. c, 5. a, 6. d, 7. c, 8. a, 9. b, 10. d

broader struggle for social justice. All liberation struggles that do not challenge heteronormativity cannot challenge imperialism and white supremacy. This relationship between settler colonialism that subjugates native peoples in the United States and around the world is also noted in Janice Gould's essay "Lesbian Landscape." In this article about first love, Gould discusses her coming of age as a lesbian who is also tribally affiliated. She writes about the difficulties of being accepted as a lesbian by her family and society.

As Gould's essay suggests, sexual scripts vary across intersecting differences such as gender, race, class, age, ability, and so forth. This means that although gender is a significant dimension of sexual scripts, it must be understood as intersecting with other identities. Like fat individuals, those with physical disabilities, for example, are often faced with stigma that asexualizes them and refuses to represent them as sexual beings. Kimberly Springer also discusses intersections in her essay on the racialized constructions of heterosexuality for black women ("Queering Black Female Heterosexuality"). Gendered and racialized double standards of sexual conduct have condoned certain activities for men as opposed to women and for white women as opposed to black women and white men compared to black men. She suggests that the history of segregation and lynching, and of caricaturing black women as asexual mammies and promiscuous "jezebels," is reproduced today as the "black woman-as-whore image in a new mass-media age." These examples emphasize how sexual scripts are heavily informed by multifaceted notions of gender.

As discussed in Chapter 3, feminine sexual scripts have often involved a double bind: To want sex is to risk being labeled promiscuous and to not want sex means potentially being labeled frigid and a prude. For many women, sexuality is shrouded in shame and fear, and, rather than seeing themselves as subjects in their own erotic lives, women may understand themselves as objects, seen through the eyes of others. Valenti makes this point in "The Cult of Virginity" when she writes about the "ethics of passivity" that defines subjects by what they do not do. This can be compared to an ethics of autonomy or self-actualization involving the ability to initiate and enjoy being the center of one's erotic experience. Springer also advocates such autonomy and suggests black heterosexual women adopt the language of queer rights and make the case for enjoying sex "on our own terms." She advocates straight black women's refusal to acquiesce to sexist and racist representations. In addition, the relentless youth-oriented culture of contemporary U.S. society also sees "older" ("older than whom?" you may ask—note how this term encourages a mythical norm associated with young adulthood) people as less sexual, or interprets their sexuality as humorous or out of place. Many of these scripts are learned from the media and enacted in peer groups. Indeed, the increasing sexualization of young girls in the media normalizes demands for younger sexual partners, teaches girls that to be acceptable they must be sexual, and can rob children of their childhoods.

THE POLITICS OF SEXUALITY

The term "politics" used here implies issues associated with the distribution of power in sexual relationships. There are politics in sexual relationships because they occur in the context of a society that assigns power based on gender and other systems of inequality and privilege. Interconnections of these systems are reflected in the concept of heteropatriarchy:

the dominance associated with a gender binary system that presumes heterosexuality as a social norm. As mentioned earlier, this presumption is also called heteronormativity. Many of the readings in this section make the case that heteropatriarchy is a logic that normalizes social hierarchies. This highlights the role of binary systems (such as straight versus gay or lesbian) in maintaining hierarchies and advocates a breaking down of these polarized categories in order to transform society.

When people get together romantically, what results is more than the mingling of idiosyncratic individuals. The politics of this relationship implies that people bring the baggage of their gendered lives into relationships. We negotiate gender and intersecting identities associated with systems of inequality and privilege that inform sexual scripts and shape our lives through internalized self-schemas. Although much of this is so familiar that it is thoroughly normalized and seen as completely "natural," the experiences of differently gendered lives implies power, just as the intersection or confluence of all identities involves power on multiple levels.

As many feminists have pointed out, heterosexuality is based on cisgender performances and organized in such a way that men's power in society gets carried into relationships and can encourage women's subservience, sexually and emotionally. Practically, this might mean that a woman sees herself through the eyes of men, or a particular man, and strives to live up to his image of who she should be. It might mean that a woman feels that men, or again, a particular man, owns or has the right to control her body or sexuality, or that she should be the one to ease the emotional transitions of the household or tend to a man's daily needs—preparing his meals, cleaning his home, washing his clothes, raising his children—while still working outside the home. Even though a woman might choose this life and enjoy the role she has, feminists would argue that this is still an example of male domination in the private sphere where individual men benefit. They have their emotional and domestic needs filled by women and are left free to work or play at what they want. Of course, their part of the bargain for these services is the expectation (whether it is fulfilled or not) that men should provide for women economically. This is an arrangement many women choose rationally.

We know that heterosexual relationships are a source of support and strength for many women; it is not heterosexuality that is faulted here but the context in which heterosexual coupling takes place. When heterosexual intimacies are grounded in unequal power relationships, it becomes more and more difficult for women and men to love in healthy ways. The politics of sexuality also come into play in lesbian/gay, bisexual, and queer relationships. Some, for example, may enter relationships with the baggage of gender expectations to work out and often internalized homophobia as well. These relationships also have fewer clear models for successful partnering. An example of this is the "Are we on a date?" syndrome that occurs as individuals attempt to deal with the boundaries between being platonic friends and being romantically interested in each other. These relationships also occur in the context of heteronormativity and compulsory heterosexuality. For example, various institutions support and encourage heterosexual coupling and dating. Schools offer heteronormative dances and proms, the entertainment industry generally assumes heterosexual dating, with of course, some celebrity exceptions, and there is a public

ACTIVIST PROFILE

EMMA GOLDMAN

According to J. Edgar Hoover, she was one of the most dangerous women in America in the early twentieth century. Emma Goldman came to the United States from Russia as a teenager in 1885, but for a Jewish immigrant, America was not the land of opportunity she had envisioned. Rather, she found herself in slums and sweatshops, eking out a living. Goldman had witnessed the slaughter of idealistic political anarchists in Russia, and in 1886 she saw the hangings of four Haymarket anarchists who had opposed Chicago's power elite. As a result of these experiences, Goldman was drawn to anarchism and became a revolutionary.

Goldman moved to New York, where she met anarchist Johann Most, who advocated the overthrow of capitalism. Most encouraged Goldman's public speaking, although she eventually began to distance herself from him, recognizing the need to work for practical and specific improvements such as higher wages and shorter working hours. In 1893 she was arrested and imprisoned for encouraging a crowd of unemployed men to take bread if they were starving.

In New York, Goldman also worked as a practical nurse in New York's ghettos, where she witnessed the effects of lack of birth control and no access to abortion. She began a campaign to address this problem, and her views eventually influenced Margaret Sanger and Sanger's work to make contraception accessible. Goldman was even arrested for distributing birth control literature.

Goldman was particularly concerned about sexual politics within anarchism. She recognized that a political solution alone would not rectify the unequal relations between the sexes. Rather, she called for a transformation of values, particularly for women—by asserting themselves as persons and not sex commodities, by refusing to give the right over their bodies to anyone, and by refusing to have children unless they wanted them.

Her involvement in no-conscription leagues and rallies against World War I led to her imprisonment and subsequent deportation to Russia. There she witnessed the Russian Revolution and then saw the corruption of the Bolsheviks as they amassed power. Her experience led her to reassess her earlier approval of violence as a means to social justice. Instead, she argued that violence begets counterrevolution.

Goldman remained active in Europe and continued to exercise influence in the United States. In 1922 *Nation* magazine named her one of the 12 greatest living women. In 1934 she was allowed to lecture in the United States, and in 1936 she went to Spain to participate in the Spanish Revolution. Goldman died in 1940 and was buried in Chicago near the Haymarket martyrs.

holiday (Valentine's Day) that celebrates it. Even though gays and lesbians are thoroughly visible in popular media (although sometimes, as in the case of the depiction of women showing sexual interest in other women, for the titillation of heterosexual men), these are

LEARNING ACTIVITY

REALITY TV

Tune into some reality TV shows. As you watch, record observations about gendered behaviors, roles, and interactions. If all anyone knew about gender and heterosexual relationships was what she or he saw on reality TV, what would this person believe? How does race shape perception of these reality TV actors? Social class? Sexual identity?

Work with one or two other people in your class to devise an episode of a feminist reality TV show. What would the premise be? Into what situation would you place participants? What would the rules be? Would you have a winner? What would you call your show? Is feminist reality TV possible? Would anyone watch?

LEARNING ACTIVITY

HETERONORMATIVITY: IT'S EVERYWHERE

Heterosexism is maintained by the illusion that heterosexuality is the norm.

This illusion is partly kept in place by the visibility of heterosexuality and the invisibility of other forms of sexuality. To begin to think about the pervasiveness of heterosexuality, grab a clipboard, pen, and paper and keep a tally.

- Go to a card store and peruse the cards in the "love" and "anniversary" sections. How many depict heterosexual couples? How many depict queer couples? What options are there for customers who wish to buy a card for a queer partner?

- Look at the advertisements in one of your favorite magazines. How many pictures of heterosexual couples do you find? How many pictures of same-sex couples? If a photo is of a person alone, do you automatically assume the person is heterosexual? Or is that assumption so deep-seated that you don't even think about it at all?
- Watch the commercials during your favorite hour of television. How many images of heterosexual couples do you see? Of queer couples?
- Go to the mall or a park and people-watch for an hour. How many heterosexual couples holding hands do you see? How many queer couples?

overshadowed by the barrage of public displays of heterosexual intimacy in social media, on the Internet, on billboards, on magazine covers, in television shows, in the movies, and so forth.

One of the most vivid examples of the politics of sexuality is that of consent associated with sexual relations and its role in sexual assault, especially on college campuses. "The Complexities of Sexual Consent Among College Students" by Charlene L. Muehlenhard, Terry P. Humphreys, Kristen N. Jozkowski, and Zoë D. Peterson addresses the recent upsurge in attention to sexual consent policies on college campuses, problematizes conceptions of consent, and discusses student risk as examples of the politics of sexuality.

Despite changes in favor of marriage equality, nonheterosexual individuals and couples often encounter obstacles when adopting children and gaining custody of and raising their biological children (products of previous heterosexual relationships, planned hetero-sexual encounters with the goal of conception, or artificial insemination). This is because these sexual identities are still often constructed by society as an immoral and abnor-mal "choice" that could have negative consequences for children. It has generally been assumed by the dominant culture that children of homosexual parents will grow up to be homosexual, although all the evidence shows that this is indeed not the case. Despite research that suggests that lesbians, gay men, and those who identify as queer make fine parents, there are still relatively strong social imperatives against nonheterosexual child-rearing in some communities. See the reading in Chapter 8, "The Kids Are OK," written by Ken Knight and colleagues, for more discussion. A related prejudice is the notion that gays, lesbians, bisexuals, and queer-identified people abuse or recruit children. These negative and misinformed stereotypes reinforce homophobia and help maintain heterosexism. Re-search shows absolutely overwhelmingly that it is heterosexual males who are the major predators of children. Nonetheless, because of these societal stigmas these nontraditional parents may encounter obstacles concerning voluntary parenting, and are often not wel-come in occupations involving children.

In this way, sexual self-schemas develop in a social context and are framed by the vari-ous workings of power in society. This section has emphasized how politics—the workings of power—influence and shape every aspect of sexual relationships. On the macro (soci-etal) level, these politics are often represented in the forms of public debates about sexual-ity (like marriage equality, reproductive rights, sex education, and interpersonal violence) that are also experienced on the individual level. This micro- (individual) level analysis is the topic of the next section of this chapter.

INTIMACIES

"Courtship" is an old-fashioned word, but it means that period when individuals are at-tracted to each other, develop intimacy, enjoy each other's company, and identify as a ro-mantic couple. In contemporary U.S. society this period usually involves dating, although what "dating" means changes across time and place and is heavily influenced by popular culture and the technologies of the time. Cell phones and online dating sites, for example, have influenced communication in relationships, altering notions of public and private conversations, and encouraging the accessibility of individuals to each other. An essential aspect of courtship and dating is the development of romantic love: a mainstay of our culture and one of the most important mythologies of our time. Romantic love is about a couple coming together, sharing the excitement of an erotic relationship, and feeling united with the other in such a way that the object of their love is unique and irreplaceable. The clichés of love abound: Love is blind, love is painful, love means never having to say you're sorry, love conquers all, and so forth. "Gate C22," a poem by Ellen Bass, counters the idea that love happens only for young, "beautiful" people, and shows how expressions of love move us as humans.

Romantic love is a cultural phenomenon and not necessarily a basis for marriage. While of course romantic love and sexual attraction have been present in marriage and other domestic relationships through time, their value as prerequisites for most contemporary marriages in societies of the global north is a relatively modern notion. Indeed, there is a tight relationship between romantic love as an ideology and consumer culture as an industrial development. Prior to the twentieth century, dating as we know it did not exist. As dating developed after the turn of the twentieth century, it quickly became associated with consuming products and going places. The emerging movie industry glamorized romance and associated it with luxury products; the automobile industry provided those who could afford it with the allure of travel, getaways, and private intimacy; and dance halls allowed close contact between people in public. Romance became a commodity that could be purchased, and it made great promises. People were (and still are) encouraged to purchase certain products with the promise of romantic love. The fashion and makeup industries began revolving around the prospect of romantic love, and the norms associated with feminine beauty became tied to glamorous, romantic images. Romantic love came to be seen as a special feminine domain; both cisgender and transwomen are encouraged to spend enormous emotional energy, time, and money in the pursuit and maintenance of romantic love.

Romantic love is fun; it can be the spice of life and perhaps one of the most entertaining features of life. In particular, it often contrasts starkly with our working lives because romance is associated with leisure, entertainment, and escape. At the same time, however, romantic love and its pursuit have become the means by which many, and women in particular, are encouraged to form relationships. It has also provided justification for tolerating inequities in interpersonal relationships, both straight and lesbian/gay/queer. Many scholars suggest that romance is one of the key ways that sexism is maintained in society.

When it comes to sexuality, romantic love plays a large part in feminine sexual scripts. Research suggests that women as a social group still seem to be more likely than men to make sense of sexual encounters in terms of the amount of intimacy experienced so that love becomes a rationale for sex. If I am in love, they might reason, sex is okay. Men as a social group are more easily able to accept sex for its own sake, with no emotional strings necessarily attached. In this way, sexual scripts for men have been described as more instrumental (sex for its own sake), whereas for women they tend to be more expressive (sex involving emotional attachments). There is also evidence to suggest that women are moving in the direction of sex as an end in itself without the normative constraints of an emotional relationship, in part as a result of a "hookup" culture associated with social media. By and large, however, women as a group are still more likely than men to engage in sex as an act of love. These assertions assess women and men as statistical social groups, and there are always exceptions to these generalizations. In addition, of course, these

LEARNING ACTIVITY

IT'S IN THE CARDS

Go to a local card shop and browse through the cards in the "love" or "romance" sections. What are their messages about heterosexual relationships? How do cards targeted toward women differ from cards targeted toward men?

Now get creative. Design a feminist romance greeting card. How does it differ from the ones you saw at the card shop? How do you think the recipient will feel about this card? Now, if you're really brave, send it to the one you love.

gender categories deserve scrutiny, even though our society—and social research—tends to be organized around them. The point we make throughout the book is that although we recognize the problematics of essentialized gender categories, society is rooted in these binary systems and people do identify with them. Individuals perform real and tangible everyday practices based on gender expectations associated with these identities, and they are treated accordingly—often in discriminatory ways—because they identify, for example, as "women." As we explained in earlier chapters, this is a reality of gender categories.

In heterosexual relationships, sexual scripts tend to encourage men to be sexual initiators and sexually more dominant. Although this is not always the case, women who do initiate sex often run the risk of being labeled with terms that are synonymous with "slut." Having one person in the relationship more sexually assertive and the other more passive is different from sadomasochistic sexual practices (S&M) in which one person takes a domineering role and the other becomes dominated. People of diverse sexual identities may enjoy sadomasochistic practices. Although usually consensual, S&M can also be coercive, in which case it functions as a form of violence.

VIRTUAL SEX

Janet Lockhart

"Hooking Up" in Cyberspace

Cybersex is not the first simulated sexual experience—people went to "peep shows" and had phone sex before the Internet appeared—but the wide availability of computers and smart phones means that access to virtual sex is also widely available. There are many ways to do it: You can "sext" (sex + text), send and receive photos or videos, chat (in real time or asynchronously), video chat, or create an avatar in an online simulation. You can know the person you are having virtual sex with, or it can be anonymous. In short, it is easy to find, do, and do again.

Virtual sex can be a way to explore. For someone inexperienced, it can be an opportunity to experiment a little. For people who want to try something different from the accepted norm, it can be exciting and fun, a safe outlet for behavior they wouldn't try in the real world.

But is it safe? Although it's true that you can't get a disease from cybersex, there are still risks. For those who want to keep their virtual sex activity anonymous, social embarrassment can be a real concern. And, since people can present themselves however they want online, in-person meetings can lead to disappointment or worse.

There are differing views about whether virtual sex is acceptable outside of a committed relationship. Some people believe that virtual sex is cheating on one's real-life partner, arguing that the sexual feelings it creates are real. Others argue that since it is simulated physically, or they are unlikely to meet the other person in the real world, virtual sex doesn't "count."

Finally, some wonder if virtual sex is addictive. Like many other electronic phenomena, it gives an immediate pleasure "hit." Like other electronic phenomena, people can spend a lot more time doing it than they realize. And when the pleasure hit wears off, users can end up feeling let down, isolated, and lonely.

Ask yourself some questions. If you have engaged in virtual sex, did you consider it real sex? Did you feel a connection, and if so, what was it like for you? For you, was it healthy or unhealthy? Would you do it again?

If you have not engaged in virtual sex, would you try it, and if so, under what conditions? For you, do you think it would be healthy or unhealthy? Do you think virtual sex can potentially lead to a fulfilling real-world relationship? Why do you think so many people try it?

Ask Around

Take an anonymous poll of students on your campus: How many have engaged in virtual sex? What did they get out of it? How many of them considered it to be cheating on one's partner? How many found it fulfilling or pleasurable? How many were disappointed or regretted doing it? How many are still doing it, or would do it again?

Did you notice any patterns? Were there differences in the ways people of various genders experienced and thought about virtual sex? Were there differences in students' experiences based on ethnicity or socioeconomic status? Religion? Age? Sexual identity? Ability?

Emotional intimacy can be defined as sharing aspects of the self with others with the goal of mutual understanding. Intimacy can sometimes be a source of conflict in heterosexual relationships because those who identify as women tend to be more skilled at intimacy than men. Traditionally, they have been socialized to be emotional and emotionally expressive, and those who identify as men have been socialized to put their energy into shaping culture and society and to be more reserved about interpersonal emotional issues. As explained in Chapter 3, these behaviors illustrate gendered sexual performances that we call "feminine" or "masculine" and which intersect with social learning associated with other identities. Although girls and women are more likely to be socialized to perform femininity, and boys and men masculinity (whatever that might mean in a given community), anyone can act in feminine ways and/or masculine ways in intimate relationships. We all know of boys or men who demonstrate more feminine traits and are more skilled at expressing emotions than some women even though this might not be the norm. Gender is a learned performance that shapes the experiences of sexual intimacy in any given setting.

Some scholars have suggested that women are inherently better at connecting with others and that this skill is rooted in early childhood psychosexual development that reflects the fact that girls have a continuous relationship and identification with a maternal figure, unlike boys, who have to break from the mother to identify with the masculine. Others have focused on the social context of childhood skill acquisition. They suggest that the interpersonal skills girls learn at an early age are a result of social learning. Certainly these skills are useful for women in terms of intimacy generally, and in terms of their role as keepers of heterosexual relationships in particular. For example, girls are more likely to play games that involve communication: talking and listening, as well as taking the role of the other through imaginary role-playing games. Boys, on the other hand, are more likely to play rule-bound games where the "rights" and "wrongs" of the game are predetermined rather than negotiated. As a result, girls learn to notice and are trained to be perceptive. They learn to be sensitive of others' feelings and become more willing to do emotional work. Boys are often raised to repress and deny their inner thoughts and ignore their fears. As discussed in Chapter 3, boys are often taught that feelings are feminine or are for sissies. Girls become more comfortable with intimacy, and boys learn to shy away from it because intimacy is often seen as synonymous with weakness. Boys may learn to camouflage feelings under a veneer of calm and rationality because fears are not manly. Importantly, as boys grow up they learn to rely on women to take care of their emotional needs, and girls learn that this request is part of being a woman.

Because emotional intimacy is about self-disclosure and revealing oneself to others, when people are intimate with each other, they open themselves to vulnerability. In the process of becoming intimate, people share feelings and information about themselves, and then their partners (if they want to maintain and develop intimacy) respond by sharing too. In turn, they give away little pieces of themselves, and, in return, mutual trust, understanding, and friendship develop. Given the baggage of gender, however, what can happen is that one person does more of the giving away, and the other reveals less; one opens up to being vulnerable, and the other maintains personal power. That one person also takes on the role of helping the other share, drawing them out, translating ordinary messages for their hidden emotional meanings, and investing greater amounts of energy into interpersonal communication. This person doing the emotional work has taken the role prescribed by femininity and the other the role that masculinity endorses. The important point here is that intimacy is about power. People who take on these masculine scripts tend to be less able to open themselves up because of anxiety associated with being vulnerable and potentially losing personal power. Again, anyone can take on masculine or feminine sexual scripts.

Central in understanding masculine sexual scripts and issues around emotional intimacy is the mandate against homosexuality. Because boys and men may play rough and work closely together—touching each other physically in sports and other masculine pursuits—there are lots of opportunities for homoeroticism (arousal of sexual feelings through contact with people of the same sex). In response to this, strong norms against homosexuality (examples of "regimes of truth") regulate masculine behavior. These norms are fed by homophobia and enforced by such institutions as education, sports, media, family, and the military. In the United States these norms tend to discourage men from showing affection with each other and thus discourage intimacy between men. They also encourage male bonding in which women may function as objects in order for men to assert sexual potency as "real" heterosexuals. Examples of this include objectifying women as entertainment for various kinds of stag parties, women as pinups in places where men live and/or work together, and, in the extreme, gang rape. Homophobia serves to keep women apart too, of course. In particular, women are encouraged to give up the love of other women in order to gain the approval of men. However, compared with men, women in the United States tend to have more opportunities for intimacies between friends. This is also demonstrated in language about friendships: Women friends call each other "girlfriend" with no sexual innuendo, while men tend not to call their platonic male friends "boyfriend."

A key aspect of intimacy, and thus sexuality, is interpersonal communication. Again, the ways we communicate in relationships have a lot to do with gender, as well as membership in other communities with specific norms about social interaction, including verbal language spoken and nonverbal language expressed. Feminine and masculine speech varies in the following ways: First, in terms of speech patterns, feminine speech is more polite and less profane and uses more standard forms. More fillers like "um," hedges like "sort of" and "I guess," and intensifiers like "really" and "very" are used. In addition, feminine speech involves tag questions on statements like "It's hot today, isn't it?" and often turns an imperative into a question: "Would you mind opening the door?" rather than "Open the door." All of these forms of speaking are less authoritative. Note again that although women in U.S. society are more likely to use feminine speech and men to use masculine speech, anyone can learn these speech patterns, and they also vary by membership in other identities and communities. Indeed, people are often trained in masculine speech to function effectively in authority positions or careers in which an assertive communication style is necessary or most productive.

Second, feminine speech tends to use different intonations with a higher pitch that is recognized as less credible and assertive than a lower pitch. This speech has more emotional affect and is more likely to end with a raised pitch that sounds like a question and gives a hesitant quality to speaking. There is evidence that many young women today use this "upspeak" in their speech mannerisms, along with what is known as "vocal fry": a low tone that produces a creaky or breathy sound.

Third, feminine speech differs from masculine speech in that the latter involves more direct interruptions of other speakers. Listening to individuals talking, we find that although men and women interrupt at about the same rate in same-sex conversations (women interrupting women, and men interrupting men), in mixed groups men interrupt other speakers more than women do, and men are more likely to change the subject in the process, whereas women tend to interrupt to add to the story with their own experiences and thoughts. Although there are cultural differences around interruptions, it is clear that who interrupts and who gets interrupted is about power.

Fourth, feminine speech patterns involve more confirmation and reinforcement, such as "Yes, go on" or "I hear you" or "Uh-huh." Examples of nonverbal confirmation of the speaker might include leaning forward, making eye contact, and nodding, although these behaviors may vary (as does all social interaction) across communities.

Finally, feminine speech and masculine speech fulfill different functions. Feminine speech tends to work toward maintaining relationships, developing rapport, avoiding conflict, and maintaining cooperation. Masculine speech, on the other hand, is more likely to be oriented toward attracting and maintaining an audience, asserting power and dominance, and giving information. Given these gendered differences in communication, it is easy to see how problems might arise in interpersonal interaction generally and in sexual relationships in particular, and how these issues are related to the give and take of interpersonal power.

In this way, sexual intimacy is as much about sexual scripts taught and regulated by society as it is about physiology. Sexuality is wound up with our understandings of gender as well as other intersecting identities that shape our sense of ourselves as sexual persons. These social constructs encourage us to feel desire and enjoy certain sexual practices and relationships, and they guide the meanings we associate with our experiences.

IDEAS FOR ACTIVISM

- Work with various social justice groups on your campus to develop, publish, and distribute a "Check Up on Your Relationship" brochure. This brochure should contain a checklist of signs for emotional/physical/sexual abuse and resources to get help.
- Organize and present a forum on healthy dating practices.
- Organize a clothes drive for your local domestic violence shelter.
- Research LGBTQ rights, such as protection against discrimination in employment or housing, domestic partner benefits, or hate crimes legislation in your city or state. If you find that gay, lesbian, bisexual, transgender, or queer people in your area do not enjoy full civil rights, write your government officials to encourage them to enact those policies.
- Organize a National Coming Out Day celebration on your campus.
- Organize an event on your campus in recognition of World AIDS Day, which is December 1.
- Connect with a national organization that supports women's and LGBTQ rights, such as Gay and Lesbian Advocates and Defenders (GLAD), the Family Equality Council, the National Center for Transgender Equality, or the National Organization for Women.

THE BLOG

BACHELORETTE PARTIES, DRAG, AND THE APPROPRIATION OF QUEER SPACE

Susan M. Shaw (2017)

My partner and I took my sister to Darcelle XV Showplace Saturday night for her birthday. Darcelle XV hosts the longest continuously running drag show on the West Coast, and its iconic founder and star at 86 is the oldest performing drag queen in the world.

I first went to Darcelle's about 25 years ago, just as I was coming out myself and as LGBTQ people in Oregon were fighting off discriminatory ballot measures. Darcelle's was a safe space, a rite of passage, and a haven for queer culture and queer people. Sure, a couple of bridal parties were there celebrating, and a few straight couples came to enjoy the show. Mostly, though, the crowd of around 100 or so was gay men, lesbians, a few drag queens, maybe a drag king or two. Despite the presence of a handful of straight people, we were decidedly in queer space.

Saturday night was a completely different experience. While in line to enter, I noticed pretty quickly that almost everyone else waiting was either a (heterosexual) bride-to-be or a bridesmaid. I felt strangely out of place. I wondered why all of these straight women saw this as a space that was theirs to inhabit, especially for that most heteronormative of rituals, the bachelorette party. I asked the door manager what he thought of this appropriation of queer culture. "They're here for the dog and pony show," he responded. "That's what we are to them. It's just a show."

It is a show, but it's so much more than a show. While men performing as women has a long history all the way back to ancient societies and through Elizabethan England, contemporary drag is associated primarily with gay men (though some women also perform as drag kings). In the twentieth century, drag became one way for gay men to claim self-expression for diverse sexualities and to challenge restrictive gender norms at a time when homosexuality was outlawed and wearing the clothes of another gender could lead to arrest and imprisonment. Drag conferred a kind of liberation, but it also often came at a high cost.

While queer folks had long resisted bigotry and discrimination, a pivotal moment came in 1969 at the Stonewall Bar in New York City when the drag queens and butch lesbians fought back. The Stonewall riots marked a visible beginning for the gay liberation movement and the subsequent struggle for LGBTQ rights that continues in the present.

When Walter Cole, who would become Darcelle, bought the old Demas Tavern in Portland in 1967, he hired a lesbian bartender, and with her came a clientele of lesbians and gay men who found a home at the bar in a time when homosexuality was illegal and considered a mental disorder. Darcelle became a fixture in Portland and an activist and fundraiser for LGBTQ causes. Darcelle and her club reached out to straight Portland, building allies and strengthening LGBTQ rights in the city.

I don't imagine any of those brides or members of their entourages have a clue about this history. Apparently, Darcelle's has become *the* place for bachelorette parties, a stamping of heterosexual privilege over the invisibility of LGBTQ struggle in queer space. When we entered, my partner turned to me and asked, "Do you think it's ok to act like we're together?" After all, it's one thing to pay to watch drag queens perform. It's entirely another to see real live lesbians holding hands right in front of you at your bachelorette party. I felt defiant. "Of course we're going to act like we're together," I said. "They will not take that from us in our own space."

A couple of the bridesmaids in the audience looked terribly uncomfortable. They didn't laugh or clap with the music. They ducked their heads and averted their eyes. Even Darcelle noticed. She walked out to one of these women and commented, "You look scared sh*tless." She did. I think she was.

Once the show started, I noticed something else new to me since I was last at the show 25 years ago. These young women had handfuls of one-dollar bills that they gleefully tucked into the performers' cleavage. I realized that Darcelle's also gave them a space where they could indulge in some homoerotic fantasy with no risk of the actual costs of lesbian or queer identity. They could safely engage in the fantasy of stuffing bills in a performer's bra with none of the risk or stigma of actual same-sex sexuality since they knew these were "really men." They could exert the capitalist power of heteropatriarchy by pretending drag queens were other women without risking the lesbian label or imagining how they might feel if strangers wanted to shove dollar bills in their cleavage. For a moment, they possessed the sexualized power of straight men in a strip bar.

I also noticed that a lot of these heterosexual women felt free to hang all over each other. Our hard-fought struggles for lesbian visibility made this possible. We have managed to dilute some of the stigma of same-sex love and attraction, and so now heterosexuals can use our space to engage in physicality with one another without fear of being labeled "lesbian." In fact, right by the stage two women were so physically engaged with one another that I thought, "Oh, perhaps we do have a queer couple getting married" (since we did at last win that right just two years ago today). I took comfort in that belief until Darcelle recognized all the brides-to-be (there were 14 of them). Darcelle asked the young woman where she was getting married, and she replied, "In a Catholic church." So much for my fantasy of a lesbian bachelorette party at Darcelle's.

I also noticed how racialized this phenomenon was. I don't think there was a person of color in the bar other than one performer and one person working sound. These young straight women were white. Every single one of them. So the consumption of queer culture and queer space was their right not only as straight women but also as white women. For some reason, young, straight white women feel absolutely free to invade queer space, and, because of their privilege as young, straight, and white, they never even have to think about the fact that they might be invading someone else's space, that their overwhelmingly white and heterosexual presence might create unsafe space for queer people, especially queers of color. They can just be out for a good time without ever questioning what their presence in queer space might mean for queer people. That is the very definition of privilege.

When we left, the line for the next show extended down the block. More bachelorette parties. More young, straight, white women. As we crossed the street toward our car, two young queer women walking down 3rd hailed us. "How are you tonight? What have you been doing?" We locked eyes in recognition of our shared queerness. "We're great. We celebrated a birthday at Darcelle's." "That's great. Have a good night." They continued down the street. I felt at home again. Maybe now that we can walk down the street out and proud a little more easily than we could 25 years ago, we don't need the safe spaces of Darcelle's quite as much. Maybe that's why so few queer folk were there. Or maybe it's like the dance club we lost as more and more straight people started to come, and eventually we felt unsafe in our own club. Maybe we don't feel like we belong at Darcelle's anymore because we only see queer on the stage as spectacle and not in the audience as full human beings.

Maybe the straightening of Darcelle's is progress. It didn't feel like it. It felt like loss. So on this day we celebrate the Supreme Court's decision for marriage equality, we also realize the work that remains to be done. We aren't equal yet, and white and heterosexual privilege still marginalize us, even in our own spaces. But Darcelle is still cracking queer jokes and wearing the mantle of queerness, and, after 50 years, her showplace still stands as queer space, even when invaded by straight white bridal parties. So the struggle goes on. But we're still here, and we're still queer.

37. THE CULT OF VIRGINITY

JESSICA VALENTI (2009)

In the moments after I first had sex, my then-boyfriend—lying down next to me over his lint-covered blanket—grabbed a pen from his nightstand and drew a heart on the wall molding above his bed with our initials and the date inside. The only way you could see it was by lying flat on the bed with your head smashed up against the wall. Crooked necks aside, it was a sweet gesture, one that I'd forgotten about until I started writing this book.

The date seemed so important to us at the time, even though the event itself was hardly awe-inspiring. There was the expected fumbling, a joke about his fish-printed boxers, and ensuing condom difficulties. At one point, his best friend even called to see how things were going. I suppose romance and discretion are lost on sixteen-year-olds from Brooklyn. Yet we celebrated our "anniversary" every year until we broke up, when Josh left for college two years before me and met a girl with a lip ring.

I've often wondered what that date marks—the day I became a woman? Considering I still bought underwear in cutesy three-packs, and that I certainly hadn't mastered the art of speaking my mind, I've gotta go with no. Societal standards would have me believe that it was the day I became morally sullied, but I fail to see how anything that lasts less than five minutes can have such an indelible ethical impact so it's not that, either.

Really, the only meaning it had (besides a little bit of pain and a lot of postcoital embarrassment) was the meaning that Josh and I ascribed to it. Or so I thought. I hadn't counted on the meaning my peers, my parents, and society would imbue it with on my behalf.

From that date on—in the small, incestuous world of high school friendships, nothing is a secret for long—I was a "sexually active teen," a term often used in tandem with phrases like "at risk," or alongside warnings about drug and alcohol use, regardless of how uncontroversial the sex itself may have been. Through the rest of high school, whenever I had a date, my peers assumed that I had had sex because my sexuality had been defined by that one moment when my virginity was lost. It meant that I was no longer discriminating, no longer "good." The perceived change in my social value wasn't lost on my parents, either; before I graduated high school, my mother found an empty condom wrapper in my bag and remarked that if I kept having sex, no one would want to marry me.

I realize that my experience isn't necessarily representative of most women's—everyone has their own story—but there are common themes in so many young women's sexual journeys. Sometimes it's shame. Sometimes it's violence. Sometimes it's pleasure. And sometimes it's simply nothing to write home about.

The idea that virginity (or loss thereof) can profoundly affect women's lives is certainly nothing new. But what virginity is, what it was, and how it's being used now to punish women and roll back their rights is at the core of the purity myth. Because today, in a world where porn culture and reenergized abstinence movements collide, the moral panic myth about young women's supposed promiscuity is diverting attention from the real problem—that women are still being judged (sometimes to death) on something that doesn't really exist: virginity.

THE VIRGINITY MYSTERY

Before Hanne Blank wrote her book *Virgin: The Untouched History*, she had a bit of a problem. Blank was answering teens' questions on Scarleteen[1]—a sex education website she founded with writer Heather Corinna so that young people could access information about sex online, other than porn and Net Nanny—when she discovered that she kept hitting a roadblock when it came to the topic of virginity.

"One of the questions that kept coming up was 'I did such-and-such. Am I still a virgin?'" Blank told me in an interview. "They desperately wanted an authoritative answer."

But she just didn't have one. So Blank decided to spend some time in Harvard's medical school library to find a definitive answer for her young web browsers.

"I spent about a week looking through everything I could—medical dictionaries, encyclopedias, anatomies—trying to find some sort of diagnostic standard for virginity," Blank said.

The problem was, there was no standard. Either a book wouldn't mention virginity at all or it would provide a definition that wasn't medical, but subjective.

"Then it dawned on me—I'm in arguably one of the best medical libraries in the world, scouring their stacks, and I'm not finding anything close to a medical definition for virginity. And I thought, *That's really weird. That's just flat-out strange.*"

Blank said she found it odd mostly because everyone, including doctors, talks about virginity as if they know what it is—but no one ever bothers to mention the truth: "People have been talking authoritatively about virginity for thousands of years, yet we don't even have a working medical definition for it!"

Blank now refers to virginity as "the state of having not had partnered sex." But if virginity is simply the first time someone has sex, then what is sex? If it's just heterosexual intercourse, then we'd have to come to the fairly ridiculous conclusion that all lesbians and gay men are virgins, and that different kinds of intimacy, like oral sex, mean nothing. And even using the straight-intercourse model of sex as a gauge, we'd have to get into the down-and-dirty conversation of what constitutes penetration.

Since I've become convinced that virginity is a sham being perpetrated against women, I decided to turn to other people to see how they "count" sex. Most say it's penetration. Some say it's oral sex. My closest friend, Kate, a lesbian, has the best answer to date (a rule I've followed since she shared it with me): It isn't sex unless you've had an orgasm. That's a pleasure-based, non-heteronormative way of marking intimacy if I've ever heard one. Of course, this way of defining sex isn't likely to be very popular among the straight-male sect, given that some would probably end up not counting for many of their partners.

But any way you cut it, virginity is just too subjective to pretend we can define it.

Laura Carpenter, a professor at Vanderbilt University and the author of *Virginity Lost: An Intimate Portrait of First Sexual Experiences*, told me that [when] she wrote her book, she was loath to even use the word "virginity," lest she propagate the notion that there's one concrete definition for it.[2]

"What is this thing, this social phenomenon? I think the emphasis put on virginity, particularly for women, causes a lot more harm than good," said Carpenter.[3]

This has much to do with the fact that "virgin" is almost always synonymous with "woman." Virgin sacrifices, popping cherries, white dresses, supposed vaginal tightness, you name it. Outside of the occasional reference to the male virgin in the form of a goofy movie about horny teenage boys, virginity is pretty much all about women. Even the dictionary definitions of "virgin" cite an "unmarried girl or woman" or a "religious woman, esp. a saint."[4] No such definition exists for men or boys.

It's this inextricable relationship between sexual purity and women—how we're either virgins or not virgins—that makes the very concept of virginity so dangerous and so necessary to do away with.

Admittedly, it would be hard to dismiss virginity as we know it altogether, considering the meaning it has in so many people's—especially women's—lives. When I suggest that virginity is a lie told to women, I don't aim to discount or make light of how important the current social idea of virginity is for people. Culture, religion, and social beliefs influence the role that virginity and sexuality play in women's lives—sometimes very positively. So, to be clear, when I argue for an end to the idea of virginity, it's because I believe sexual intimacy should be honored and respected, but that it shouldn't be revered at the expense of women's well-being, or seen as such an integral part of female identity that we end up defining ourselves by our sexuality.

I also can't discount that no matter what personal meaning each woman gives virginity, it's people who have social and political influence who ultimately get to decide what virginity means—at least, as it affects women on a large scale.

VIRGINITY: COMMODITY, MORALITY, OR FARCE?

It's hard to know when people started caring about virginity, but we do know that men, or male-led institutions, have always been the ones that get to define and assign value to virginity.

Blank posits that a long-standing historical interest in virginity is about establishing paternity (if a man marries a virgin, he can be reasonably sure the child she bears is his) and about using women's sexuality as a commodity. Either way, the notion has always been deeply entrenched in patriarchy and male ownership.

> Raising daughters of quality became another model of production, as valuable as breeding healthy sheep, weaving sturdy cloth, or bringing in a good harvest. . . . The gesture is now generally symbolic in the first world, but we nonetheless still observe the custom of the father "giving" his daughter in marriage. Up until the last century or so, however, when laws were liberalized to allow women to stand as full citizens in their own right, this represented a literal transfer of property from a father's household to a husband's.[5]

That's why women who had sex were (and still are, at times) referred to as "damaged goods" because they were literally just that: something to be owned, traded, bought, and sold.

But long gone are the days when women were property . . . or so we'd like to think. It's not just wedding traditions or outdated laws that name women's virginity as a commodity; women's virginity, our sexuality, is still assigned a value by a movement with more power and influence in American society than we'd probably like to admit.

I like to call this movement the virginity movement. And it is a movement, indeed—with conservatives and evangelical Christians at the helm, and our government, school systems, and social institutions taking orders. Composed of antifeminist think tanks like the Independent Women's Forum and Concerned Women for America; abstinence-only "educators" and organizations; religious leaders; and legislators with regressive social values, the virginity movement is much more than just the same old sexism; it's a targeted and well-funded backlash that is rolling back women's rights using revamped and modernized definitions of purity, morality, and sexuality. Its goals are mired in old-school gender roles, and the tool it's using is young women's sexuality. (What better way to get people to pay attention to your cause than to frame it in terms of teenage girls' having, or not having, sex? It's salacious!)

And, like it or not, the members of the virginity movement are the people who are defining virginity—and, to a large extent, sexuality—in America. Now, instead of women's virginity being explicitly bought and sold with dowries and business deals, it's being defined as little more than a stand-in for actual morality.

It's genius, really. Shame women into being chaste and tell them that all they have to do to be "good" is not have sex. (Of course, chastity and purity, as defined by the virginity movement, are not just about abstaining sexually so much as they're about upholding a specific, passive model of womanhood.)

For women especially, virginity has become the easy answer—the morality quick fix. You can be vapid, stupid, and unethical, but so long as you've never had sex, you're a "good" (i.e., "moral") girl and therefore worthy of praise.

Present-day American society—whether through pop culture, religion, or institutions—conflates sexuality and morality constantly. Idolizing virginity as a stand-in for women's morality means that nothing else matters—not what we accomplish, not what we think, not what we care about and work for. Just if/how/whom we have sex with. That's all.

Just look at the women we venerate for not having sex: pageant queens who run on abstinence platforms, pop singers who share their virginal status, and religious women who "save themselves" for marriage. It's an interesting state of affairs when women have to simply do, well, nothing in order to be considered ethical role models. As Feministing .com commenter electron-Blue noted in response to the 2008 *New York Times Magazine* article, "Students of Virginity," on abstinence clubs at Ivy League colleges, "There were a WHOLE LOTTA us not having sex at Harvard . . . but none of us thought that that was special enough to start a club about it, for pete's sake."[6]

But for plenty of women across the country, it *is* special. Staying "pure" and "innocent" is touted as the greatest thing we can do. However, equating this inaction with morality not only is problematic because it continues to tie women's ethics to our bodies, but also is downright insulting because it suggests that women can't be moral actors. Instead, we're defined by what we don't do—our ethics are the ethics of passivity. (This model of ethics fits in perfectly with how the virginity movement defines the ideal woman.)

. . .

But it's not only abstinence education or conservative propaganda that are perpetuating this message; you need look no further than pop culture for stark examples of how young people—especially young women—are taught to use virginity as an easy ethical road map.

A 2007 episode of the MTV documentary series *True Life* featured celibate youth.[7] Among the teens choosing to abstain because of disease concerns and religious commitments was nineteen-year-old Kristin from Nashville, Tennessee. Kristin had cheated on her past boyfriends, and told the camera she'd decided to remain celibate until she feels she can be faithful to her current boyfriend. Clearly, Kristin's problem isn't sex—it's trust. But instead of dealing with the actual issues behind her relationship woes, this young woman was able to circumvent any real self-analysis by simply claiming to be abstinent. So long as she's chaste, she's good.

Or consider singer and reality television celebrity Jessica Simpson, who has made her career largely by playing on the sexy-virgin stereotype. Simpson, the daughter of a Baptist youth minister, started her singing career by touring Christian youth festivals and True Love Waits events. Even when she went mainstream, she publicly declared her virginity—stating that her father had given her a promise ring when she was twelve years old—and spoke of her intention to wait to have sex until marriage. Meanwhile, not surprisingly, Simpson was being marketed as a major sex symbol—all blond hair, breasts, and giggles. Especially giggles. Simpson's character (and I use the word "character" because it's hard to know what was actually her and not a finely honed image) was sold as the archetypal dumb blond. Thoughtless moments on *Newlyweds*, the MTV show that followed her short-lived marriage to singer Nick Lachey, became nationally known sound bites, such as Simpson's wondering aloud whether tuna was chicken or fish, since the can read "Chicken of the Sea."

Despite Simpson's public persona as an airhead (as recently as 2008, she was featured in a Macy's commercial as not understanding how to flick on a light switch), women are supposed to want to be her, not only because she's beautiful by conventional standards, but also because she adheres to the social structures that tell women that they exist purely for men: as a virgin, as a sex symbol, or, in Simpson's case, as both. It doesn't matter that Simpson reveals few of her actual thoughts or moral beliefs; it's enough that she's "pure," even if that purity means she's a bit of a dolt.

For those women who can't keep up the front as well as someone like Simpson, they suffer heaps of judgment—especially when they fall off the pedestal they're posed upon so perfectly. American pop culture, especially, has an interesting new trend of venerating and fetishizing "pure" young women—whether they're celebrities, beauty queens, or just everyday young woman—simply to bask in their eventual fall.

And no one embodies the "perfect" young American like beauty queens. They're pretty, overwhelmingly white, thin, and eager to please. And, of course, pageant queens are supposed to be pure as pure can be. In fact, until 1999, the Miss America pageant had a "purity rule" that barred divorced women and those who had obtained abortions from entering the contest—lest they sully the competition, I suppose.[8]

So in 2006, when two of those "perfect" girls made the news for being in scandalous photos on the Internet, supposed promiscuity, or a combination thereof, Americans were transfixed.

First, twenty-year-old Miss USA Tara Conner was nearly stripped of her title after reports surfaced that she frequented nightclubs, drank, and dated. Hardly unusual behavior for a young woman, regardless of how many tiaras she may have.

The *New York Daily News* could barely contain its slut-shaming glee when it reported on the story: "'She really is a small-town girl. She just went wild when she came to the city,' one nightlife veteran said. 'Tara just couldn't handle herself. They were sneaking those [nightclub] guys in and out of the apartment'. . . Conner still brought boyfriends home. . . . Soon she broke up with her hometown fiancé and started dating around in the Manhattan nightclub world. . . ."[9]

Instead of having her crown taken away, however, Conner was publicly "forgiven" by Miss USA co-owner Donald Trump, who appeared at a press conference to publicly declare he was giving the young woman a second chance.[10] In case you had any doubts about whether this controversy was all tied up with male ownership and approval, consider the fact that Trump later reportedly considered giving his permission for Conner to pose for *Playboy* magazine. He played the role of dad, pimp, and owner, all rolled into one.[11]

Mere days later, Miss Nevada USA, twenty-two-year-old Katie Rees, was dethroned after pictures of her exposing one of her breasts and mooning the camera were uncovered.[12] When you're on a pedestal, you have a long way to fall.

. . .

Shaming young women for being sexual is nothing new, but it's curious to observe how the expectation of purity gets played out through the women who are supposed to epitomize the feminine ideal: the "desirable" virgin. After all, we rarely see women who aren't conventionally beautiful idolized for their abstinence. And no matter how "good" you are otherwise—even if you're an all-American beauty queen—if you're not virginal, you're shamed.

The desirable virgin is sexy but not sexual. She's young, white, and skinny. She's a cheerleader, a baby sitter; she's accessible and eager to please (remember those ethics of passivity!). She's never a woman of color. She's never a low-income girl or a fat girl. She's never disabled. "Virgin" is a designation for those who meet a certain standard of what women, especially younger women, are supposed to look like. As for how these young women are supposed to act? A blank slate is best.

NOTES

1. www.scarleteen.com.

2. Laura M. Carpenter. *Virginity Lost: An Intimate Portrait of First Sexual Experiences* (New York: New York University Press, November 2005).

3. Laura M. Carpenter. Interview with the author, March 2008.

4. Dictionary.com definition of "virgin," http://dictionary.reference.com.

5. Hanne Blank. *Virgin: The Untouched History* (New York: Bloomsbury USA, 2007), 29.

6. Feministing.com. "Ivy Hymens: Why glorifying virginity is bad for women," March 31, 2008, www.feministing.com/archives/008913.html.

7. MTV. "True Life: I'm Celibate," July 2007, www.mtv.com/videos.

8. Denise Felder. "Miss America 'Purity Rule' Change Halted," September 14, 1999, www.ktvu.com/ entertainment.

9. *New York Daily News.* "Miss USA Tara Conner Sex & Cocaine Shame," December 17, 2006, www.feministing.com/archives/006220.html.

10. Mark Coulton. "Trump deals disgraced Miss USA a new hand," *The Age*, December 21, 2006, www.theage.com.au.news.

11. Page Six. "Duck and Cover," *New York Post*, January 4, 2007, www.nypost.com/seven/01042007/gossip/pagesix/duck_and_cover_pagesix_.htm.

12. Fox News. "Miss Nevada Katie Rees Fired Over Raunchy Photos," December 22, 2006, www.foxnews.com.

38. GATE C22

ELLEN BASS (2007)

At gate C22 in the Portland airport
a man in a broad-band leather hat kissed
a woman arriving from Orange County.
They kissed and kissed and kissed. Long after
the other passengers clicked the handles of their
    carry-ons
and wheeled briskly toward short-term parking,
the couple stood there, arms wrapped around
    each other
like he'd just staggered off the boat at Ellis Island,
like she'd been released at last from ICU, snapped
out of a coma, survived bone cancer, made it down
from Annapurna in only the clothes she was
    wearing.
Neither of them was young. His beard was gray.
She carried a few extra pounds you could imagine
her saying she had to lose. But they kissed lavish
kisses like the ocean in the early morning,
the way it gathers and swells, sucking
each rock under, swallowing it
again and again. We were all watching—
passengers waiting for the delayed flight
to San Jose, the stewardesses, the pilots,

the aproned woman icing Cinnabons, the man
    selling
sunglasses. We couldn't look away. We could
taste the kisses crushed in our mouths.
But the best part was his face. When he drew back
and looked at her, his smile soft with wonder,
    almost
as though he were a mother still open from giving
    birth,
as your mother must have looked at you, no
    matter
what happened after—if she beat you or left you
    or
you're lonely now—you once lay there, the varnix
not yet wiped off, and someone gazed at you
as if you were the first sunrise seen from the
    Earth.
The whole wing of the airport hushed,
all of us trying to slip into that woman's middle-
    aged body,
her plaid Bermuda shorts, sleeveless blouse,
    glasses,
little gold hoop earrings, tilting our heads up.

39. THE COMPLEXITIES OF SEXUAL CONSENT AMONG COLLEGE STUDENTS

CHARLENE L. MUEHLENHARD, TERRY P. HUMPHREYS, KRISTEN N. JOZKOWSKI, AND ZOË D. PETERSON (2016)

- Pop star Lady Gaga and Governor Andrew Cuomo coauthored an essay, published in *Billboard* magazine, urging support for a bill requiring all New York colleges and universities to address sexual assault by adopting affirmative consent policies (Gaga & Cuomo, 2015).
- In a highly publicized protest, Columbia University student Emma Sulkowicz carried a mattress around campus for months until May 2015, when she and the student she accused of raping her both graduated (Bazelon, 2015). In response, the accused student, Paul Nungesser, sued Columbia University for sex discrimination under Title IX for allowing Sulkowicz to receive course credit for her protest (Kutner, 2015).
- Jameis Winston—Florida State University (FSU) star quarterback, Heisman Trophy winner, and number-one National Football League (NFL) draft pick—is being sued by Erica Kinsman for sexual battery and assault while both were students at FSU (Axon, 2015; Hanzus, 2015).
- *Rolling Stone* published an article about a gang rape at a University of Virginia fraternity house, but later apologized and retracted the article when it became clear that the incident could not have happened the way the article described it (Coronel, Coll, & Kravitz, 2015).
- At Saint Mary's University in Halifax, student orientation leaders led a chant during frosh week celebrating underage, nonconsensual sex and posted it on Instagram: "SMU boys we like them YOUNG! Y is for your sister. O is for oh so tight. U is for underage. N is for no consent. G is for grab that ass" (National Post Staff, 2013).

These stories, taken from recent headlines, make clear that sexual assault among university students is a hotbed of controversy. In the United States and Canada, universities are under pressure to investigate and address students' complaints of sexual assault. Often the complaining student and the accused student both acknowledge that sexual contact occurred; the issue of contention—the issue that university investigators need to decide—is whether this sexual contact was consensual. Many sexual assault educational and awareness campaigns stress the importance of getting sexual consent before having sex, without clarifying what counts as consent. What is meant by sex being consensual or nonconsensual?

In this article, we review the literature on sexual consent as it relates to sexual assault. We begin by discussing how the term *sexual assault* and related terms are typically defined. Next, we discuss issues specifically related to sexual assault and sexual consent at colleges and universities in the United States and Canada: the reasons behind the increased media and political attention paid to sexual assault among college students, the prevalence of sexual assault among college students, and aspects of college life associated with risk of sexual assault. We then discuss issues related to conceptualizing sexual consent, including factors that complicate sexual consent and controversial questions about standards of sexual consent. Against this background, we review research on how college students and other young people convey and infer sexual consent. Integrating these conceptual issues and research findings, we discuss implications for consent policies, and we present five principles that could be useful for thinking about consent. Finally, we discuss some of the limitations of existing research and suggest directions for future research.

Some topics related to sexual consent are beyond our scope. We cannot answer nonempirical questions such as "What *is* consent?" or "What *should* count as consent?" We can, however, answer questions about how young people typically express consent and what behaviors they interpret as signaling consent.

Because we are focusing on college students, we do not address questions related to the inability to consent because of youth (Oudekerk, Guarnera, & Reppucci, 2014), developmental disabilities (Kennedy, 2003), or dementia (Tarzia, Fetherstonhaugh, & Bauer, 2012). We do, however, address the inability to consent due to alcohol and drug intoxication, which is common among students.

DEFINITIONS OF SEXUAL ASSAULT AND RELATED TERMS

There are no universally accepted definitions of the terms *sexual assault, rape,* or *sexual battery.* Legal definitions vary across jurisdictions (Eileraas, 2011; Palmer, 2011); researchers' operational definitions vary across studies (Muehlenhard, Powch, Phelps, & Giusti, 1992). Generally, these terms refer to sexual acts that are obtained by force or threat of force or without the victim's consent. *Rape* is typically defined more narrowly than these other terms; it typically includes sexual penetration (vaginal, and in some jurisdictions also anal or oral penetration) that is obtained by force or threat of force or when the victim is incapacitated (Cantor et al., 2015). In many jurisdictions, *sexual battery* includes sexual touching obtained in these ways, and *sexual assault* includes sexual penetration or sexual touching obtained in these ways (Cantor et al., 2015). In 1983 Canadian law "was amended to replace the offences of rape and indecent assault with a three-tier structure of sexual assault" (Sinha, 2013, p. 29). In the United States, these crimes and their definitions vary from state to state (Eileraas, 2011; Palmer, 2011).

In the present article, we use the term *sexual assault* to refer to sexual penetration or sexual touching done without the victim's consent. What constitutes consent, however, is a contentious issue.

. . .

PREVALENCE: HOW COMMON IS SEXUAL ASSAULT AMONG COLLEGE STUDENTS?

If sexual assault is defined as sexual penetration or sexual touching obtained by physical force, threats of force, or incapacitation, studies suggest that roughly 20% of female university students in the United States and Canada experience attempted or completed sexual assault (for a review, see Muehlenhard, Peterson, Humphreys, & Jozkowski, 2015). This one-in-five prevalence rate is not uniform across all campuses, however; a recent study of students at 27 institutions of higher education across the United States (N = 150,072), undertaken by the Association of American Universities, found that prevalence rates across campuses varied from 13% to 30% (Cantor et al., 2015, p. 16).

A student's risk of sexual assault is affected by numerous factors. Women (American College Health Association, 2013; Brener, McMahon, Warren, & Douglas, 1999; Cantor et al., 2015; Krebs, Lindquist, Warner, Fisher, & Martin, 2007) and transgender students (Cantor et al., 2015) are at greater risk than are men (e.g., in the Association of American Universities [AAU] study, the percentages of senior undergraduates who reported having experienced nonconsensual penetration involving physical force or incapacitation since enrolling in college were 13.5% for women; 2.9% for men; and 15.2% for transgender, genderqueer, gender-nonconforming, and questioning students; Cantor et al., 2015, p. 67, Table 3-11). First-year students are at greatest risk; this risk declines in subsequent years, with seniors and graduate students at the lowest risk (Cantor et al., 2015; Cranney, 2015; Krebs, Lindquist, Warner, Fisher, & Martin, 2009). Much—probably most—of the sexual assault that occurs among college students involves alcohol or drugs—usually alcohol (Cantor et al., 2015; Krebs et al., 2009; Testa & Livingston, 2009). In some cases, alcohol impairs victims' ability to recognize risky situations or to resist effectively (Testa & Livingston, 2009). In other cases, it is the victim's level of intoxication that makes the act nonconsensual; according to laws in the United States and Canada, sex with someone who is incapacitated because of alcohol or drugs qualifies as rape or sexual assault (Eileraas, 2011).

The risk of sexual assault does not begin in college. For girls and women, the greatest risk of rape occurs during adolescence and young adulthood. Many college women have a history of sexual assault before entering college (Black et al., 2011; Tjaden &

Thoennes, 2006). Young women who are not college students are also at risk (Sinozich & Langton, 2014). However, research on sexual *consent* in noncollege populations is rather limited, and there are particular characteristics of college life that may complicate sexual consent; these issues are reviewed in the section that follows.

The percentage of men who report having sexually assaulted a woman is far smaller than the percentage of women who report having been sexually assaulted by a man. Likely explanations are that some men sexually assault numerous women, some sexually aggressive men intentionally underreport their aggressive behavior because of social desirability or legal concerns, and some sexually aggressive men do not consider their behavior to be coercive (Kolivas & Gross, 2007; Lisak & Miller, 2002; Strang, Peterson, Hill, & Heiman, 2013).

CHARACTERISTICS OF COLLEGE LIFE THAT INCREASE WOMEN'S RISK OF SEXUAL ASSAULT AND COMPLICATE CONSENT

Many aspects of college life make college students, especially women in their first year of college, vulnerable to sexual assault (Cranney, 2015; Krebs et al., 2009). Many college students are living away from their parents for the first time. This newfound freedom, in conjunction with a social script of college as a "time to experiment" (Kuperberg & Padgett, 2015, p. 518), encourages students to "try on" new personalities and behaviors. From a developmental perspective this is perfectly natural, but when these circumstances are combined with limited knowledge about sex, gendered sexual expectations, male-controlled party culture, and heavy alcohol consumption, many young women are at heightened risk of sexual assault.

COLLEGE STUDENTS' LIMITED KNOWLEDGE ABOUT SEX

Many students enter college with limited knowledge about sex. Instead of comprehensive sex education, many U.S. high school students have been exposed exclusively to abstinence-only programs, many of which treat gender stereotypes as factual representations and disseminate inaccurate information about contraception and condoms (Kantor, Santelli, Teitler, & Balmer, 2008). These programs do not provide space for students to consider their own criteria for engaging in sex; they do not address topics such as how to give, ask for, or infer sexual consent; the only message is "Don't."

Popular culture exposes students to messages suggesting that sexual communication, negotiation, and equality are unnecessary or impossible in the face of strong passion (Reinholtz, Muehlenhard, Phelps, & Satterfield, 1995). Without accurate information to counter these messages, many students are poorly prepared for the many new situations they face when entering college.

COLLEGE STUDENTS' GENDERED SEXUAL EXPECTATIONS

Young women and men are exposed to different cultural messages about sexuality. In schools, girls typically get messages of risk, disease, and immorality, consistent with traditional gender ideologies of feminine passivity (Fine, 1988; Grose, Grabe, & Kohfeldt, 2014). In popular culture, they get mixed messages: Look "'hot' but not 'slutty'" (Armstrong, Hamilton, & Sweeney, 2006, p. 488); be popular, not prudish; be seductive and responsive but not too sexually available (Wiederman, 2005).

In contrast, boys and young men face pressure to be sexually active. Culturally prescribed sexual scripts portray men as always interested in and ready for sexual activity. According to these scripts, men's sexual performance is evidence of their masculinity; if they do not show strong sexual interest, their masculinity might be questioned (Pascoe, 2005; Sweeney, 2014; Wiederman, 2005). Thus, many men and women enter college with different "sexual agendas" (Armstrong et al., 2006, p. 483).

The sexual double standard (Muehlenhard, Sakaluk, & Esterline, 2015) also complicates women's and men's sexual choices. Many young women want to have fun, to fit in, and to be popular; however, women who engage in sex freely or who "flaunt" their sexuality are sometime labeled "sluts" or "whores" (Armstrong et al., 2006; Sweeney, 2014). In contrast, men gain social status by having numerous sexual partners, gaining labels such as "player" or "stud" (DeSantis, 2007; Sweeney, 2014). Women might feel pressured to refuse sex—even sex that they desire— to avoid negative social repercussions (Hamilton & Armstrong, 2009). If a woman refuses a man's sexual advances, he might assume she is refusing for appearance's sake (Muehlenhard, 2011; Osman, 2007; Osman & Davis, 1999), or he might assume that she will eventually give in, and he might feel justified continuing his advances (Jozkowski & Hunt, 2014). Men might pursue sex—even sex that they do not desire—to appear more masculine (Pascoe, 2005; Sweeney, 2014; Wiederman, 2005).

COLLEGE STUDENTS AND PARTY CULTURE

Socializing among college students often involves partying and heavy drinking (Armstrong et al., 2006). Because many residence halls have strict policies forbidding alcohol, students often drink at off-campus residences or fraternities (Armstrong et al., 2006; Wechsler, Lee, Nelson, & Kuo, 2002). Students end up consuming alcohol provided by others, in locations controlled by others, in sexualized environments (Armstrong et al., 2006). Women are expected to be "nice" to the men who host the parties; part of being "nice" may be tolerating some unwanted sexual contact, even when it makes women feel uncomfortable, because they believe that they owe it to the men (Armstrong et al., 2006). Many young women drink to the point of incapacitation; even for women who are not incapacitated, many aspects of this party culture—an environment controlled by men, social expectations to be sexy and to defer to men, alcohol, and "a disproportionate targeting of newly arrived women" (Cranney, 2015, p. 11)—combine to pressure young women into sex.

Armstrong et al. (2006) described party culture in the U.S. fraternity system: "Fraternities control every aspect of parties at their houses: themes, music, transportation, admission, access to alcohol, and movement of guests. Party themes usually require women to wear scant, sexy clothing and place women in subordinate positions to men," such as "'Pimps and Hos,' 'Victoria's Secret,' and 'Playboy Mansion'" (p. 489). Some fraternities provide women

with transportation from dormitories to these parties—but not with transportation back to the dorms. Women "cede control of turf, transportation, and liquor" and are "expected to be grateful for men's hospitality" (p. 491).

Not all sexual assaults occur at parties. Sometimes similar dynamics occur during a hookup or date. Some sexually aggressive men look for opportunities at bars, seeking out women who seem intoxicated and vulnerable to coercion (Graham et al., 2014). Cranney (2015) found that college women were most likely to be sexually victimized at parties and while "hanging out" (i.e., spending time with a man in an unstructured social situation; p. 6).

COLLEGE STUDENTS AND ALCOHOL

Many college students drink heavily, especially in the context of parties and bars (McCauley, Ruggiero, Resnick, Conoscenti, & Kilpatrick, 2009; Wechsler et al., 2002). Many students enter college having little experience with alcohol and how it affects them. New students are typically too young to buy alcohol legally; nevertheless, most underage students drink (e.g., Wechsler et al., 2002, found that almost two-thirds of the underage students studied reported having consumed alcohol in the past month). Many underage women are given alcohol by older male students, resulting in a situation where intoxicated young women feel beholden to older, more experienced men (Armstrong et al., 2006). Underage students drink alcohol less often than their older peers, but when they do drink, they are more likely to binge drink (defined as consuming at least four [for women] or five [for men] alcoholic drinks in a row; Wechsler et al., 2002).

Numerous studies of college students and the general population have found that most sexual assaults involve alcohol consumption by the victim, the perpetrator, or both (Abbey, 2002; Abbey, McAuslan, & Ross, 1998; Cantor et al., 2015; Harrington & Leitenberg, 1994; Mohler-Kuo, Dowdall, Koss, & Wechsler, 2004; Tjaden & Thoennes, 2006). Alcohol consumption linked to sexual assaults is usually voluntary, rather than forcefully or covertly administered by a perpetrator (Krebs et al., 2009; Lawyer, Resnick, Bakanic, Burkett, & Kilpatrick, 2010; McCauley et al., 2009).

Alcohol alters the dynamics of sexual consent in several ways. Individuals who are consuming alcohol are perceived as being more sexually interested and available than those who are not consuming alcohol (for reviews, see Farris, Treat, Viken, & McFall, 2008; Lindgren, Parkhill, George, & Hendershot, 2008). Men with strong alcohol expectancies—that is, men who believe "in alcohol's disinhibitory and aphrodisiac powers" (George, Cue, Lopez, Crowe, & Norris, 1995, p. 166)—are especially likely to perceive alcohol-drinking female targets as higher in sexual arousal and intent (Abbey, Buck, Zawacki, & Saenz, 2003; George et al., 1995). This is important because men's ratings of a woman's sexual arousal are positively related to their ratings of how appropriate it is for a man to repeatedly pressure her to have sex, despite her verbal refusals and physical resistance (Abbey et al., 2003).

. . .

Furthermore, intoxicated men perceive more sexual intent in women than do sober men, attending more to women's cues of sexual interest and less to their cues of uncertainty or disinterest (Abbey, Zawacki, & Buck, 2005; Farris, Treat, & Viken, 2010). These findings could be examples of alcohol myopia, "a state of shortsightedness in which superficially understood, immediate aspects of experience have a disproportionate influence on behavior and emotion" (Steele & Josephs, 1990, p. 923). The most salient and immediate cues might be noticed, but more subtle cues and long-term consequences are likely to be missed.

Likewise, intoxication can inhibit women's attention to cues of sexual risk (Davis, Stoner, Norris, George, & Masters, 2009; Fromme, D'Amico, & Katz, 1999; Stoner et al., 2008). Compared with sober women, intoxicated women showed less awareness of, and less discomfort with, sexual assault risk cues in hypothetical dating scenarios, especially more ambiguous risk cues. Even at fairly low doses, alcohol can decrease women's ability to detect signs that the situation is becoming risky.

In summary, alcohol use among college students increases the risk of sexual assault in numerous ways. The sexual assault of individuals who are intoxicated to the point of incapacitation is prevalent among college students (Cantor et al., 2015). Even if they are not incapacitated, intoxicated women are likely to be perceived as more sexually permissive and available, and they may be less aware of risk cues and early warning signs of sexual aggression. Intoxicated men are likely to focus on women's positive cues rather than negative cues and on short-term goals rather than long-term consequences. This, in combination with young people's limited knowledge about sex, gendered sexual expectations, and participation in party culture, can create a "perfect storm" of risk factors.

. . .

What Counts as Giving Consent?

Under an affirmative consent standard, individuals trying to initiate sexual activity need to get the other person's consent before proceeding—but what is necessary to infer that the other person has consented?

Some affirmative consent standards require verbal consent. Probably the best known of these policies is Antioch College's Sexual Offense Prevention Policy, which, in the 1990s, received attention and ridicule from news media around the world (including being mocked on the comedy sketch show *Saturday Night Live*). This policy states, "All sexual interactions at Antioch College must be consensual. Consent means verbally asking and verbally giving or denying consent for all levels of sexual behavior" (Antioch College, 2014–2015, p. 42). In contrast, other affirmative consent policies, such as those mandated for California universities and in Canada's Criminal Code, do not require that consent be given verbally.

When affirmative consent policies allow for consent to be communicated nonverbally, which nonverbal behaviors should count as consent? There are numerous behaviors that some people interpret as indicative of sexual consent: dressing in revealing clothing, drinking alcohol, going home with someone, flirting, and so on. If nonverbal behaviors can count as expressions of affirmative consent, the affirmative consent standard becomes less distinguishable from the traditional sexual script.

. . .

Are There Circumstances in Which Even an Explicit "Yes" Should Not Be Interpreted as Consent?

Usually saying yes is interpreted as indicative of consent. This is not always the case, however. As an extreme example, if someone says yes while being threatened at gunpoint, few people would interpret this as indicative of consent. What about other, less extreme, situations?

VERBAL PRESSURE AND COERCION. Affirmative consent policies require that for consent to be valid it must be given willingly or voluntarily (e.g., California Senate Bill SB-967, 2014; Antioch College, 2014–2015). This suggests that consent is not valid if it occurs in the context of threats, pressure, or other types of coercion. Numerous authors have discussed this principle as important for sexual consent (e.g., Beres, 2007; Muehlenhard, 1995–1996; Pineau, 1989; Tuerkheimer, 2013; West, 2008). In several major surveys of the prevalence of sexual assault and sexual coercion, using threats to obtain sexual activity is classified as sexual coercion (Black et al., 2011; Cantor et al., 2015). There is no consensus, however, about "how much duress is required to render consent only apparent rather than real" (West, 2008, p. 41). Furthermore, the duress caused by a threat could vary depending on the nature of the threat and the individuals and circumstances involved.

Consider, for example, the National Intimate Partner and Sexual Violence Survey (NISVS; Black et al., 2011) sponsored by the Centers for Disease Control and Prevention (CDC). This survey includes "threatening to end your relationship" as a type of pressure associated with sexual coercion (Black et al., 2011, pp. 17, 106; to clarify, in the NISVS, sex after this type of pressure is not considered rape; it is considered sexual coercion, a broader category). Other studies have also included threatening to end the relationship as a verbally coercive technique for obtaining sex (e.g., Kanin, 1967; Koss et al., 2007; Koss et al., 1987; Livingston, Buddie, Testa, & VanZile-Tamsen, 2004; Struckman-Johnson, Struckman-Johnson, & Anderson, 2003; Zurbriggen, 2000). Opinions vary about whether and when this should be considered coercive. For many people, it depends on the circumstances. For example, if someone threatens divorce unless their spouse has sex with them whenever they

demand it, many people would regard this as coercive. In contrast, if someone informs their dating partner that they want a relationship that includes sex, so if the partner is not ready for a sexual relationship, they will seek a partner who also wants a sexual relationship, this probably seems less coercive. Other factors could include the timing and tone of the statement and the individual's circumstances: "Threats to leave a relationship are more serious if they would result in the partner's being destitute or being unable to be with his or her children" (Zurbriggen, 2000, p. 577).

Similar questions could be asked about other verbally coercive behaviors. For example, "wearing you down by repeatedly asking for sex, or showing they were unhappy" is another type of coercion included in the NISVS (Black et al., 2011, pp. 17, 106). Other studies have also included repeated requests for sex and continual verbal pressure as coercive techniques for obtaining sex (Koss et al., 2007; Koss et al., 1987; Livingston et al., 2004; Struckman-Johnson et al., 2003). Under an affirmative consent standard, if someone says yes after the initiator repeatedly asks for sex, would this be considered coercive and thus render consent invalid? What counts as "repeatedly" asking? What circumstances might influence such judgments?

. . .

RESEARCH ON SEXUAL CONSENT

In this section, we review empirical research on how college students communicate sexual consent to their partner, how they infer their partner's sexual consent, and what they think about sexual consent. Most studies asked specifically about heterosexual encounters or used samples unscreened for sexual orientation, in which most participants identified as heterosexual; a few studies, however, focused specifically on same-sex sexual encounters. . . .

RESEARCH ON COMMUNICATING SEXUAL CONSENT TO A PARTNER

. . .

. . . Across studies, students reported typically communicating consent by using nonverbal behaviors or by not resisting their partners' advances; verbal consent was reported least frequently (Beres et al., 2004; Hall, 1998; Hickman & Muehlenhard, 1999; Jozkowski, 2013; Jozkowski, Sanders, et al., 2014; Jozkowski & Wiersma, 2015; McLeod, 2015). Verbal consent was more likely to be used for PVI [penile-vaginal intercourse] than for other behaviors, and it was more likely to be used by same-sex couples than by heterosexual couples. Regardless of sexual orientation, however, participants reported expressing consent nonverbally more frequently than verbally.

In contrast, most participants reported that they would refuse sex verbally (Jozkowski, Peterson, et al., 2014; Kitzinger & Frith, 1999; O'Byrne et al., 2006; O'Byrne et al., 2008). Many young women, however, reported that refusing could be difficult, and many reported softening their refusals to avoid sounding rude or arrogant. Kitzinger and Frith (1999) argued that such softening techniques are culturally normative ways of refusing requests, so even indirect or softened refusals should be readily understood as refusals.

. . .

RESEARCH ON INTERPRETING A PARTNER'S SEXUAL CONSENT SIGNALS

Researchers have also explored how people make inferences about a prospective partner's consent. . . .

Students interpreted direct verbal expressions of consent as highly indicative of consent (Hickman & Muehlenhard, 1999). However, such direct verbal expressions were not the norm. Verbal consent was generally regarded as unnecessary because, participants thought, it is easy to tell if a prospective partner is interested (Beres, 2010; Jozkowski & Hunt, 2013). Both men and women reported that women usually communicate consent nonverbally (Burkett & Hamilton, 2012; Burrow et al., 1998; Byers, 1980).

Expressing nonconsent, however, was a different situation. Both men and women reported that women usually communicate nonconsent verbally (Burrow et al., 1998; Byers, 1980). Many said that for men to understand that women are not consenting, women need to be clear; unless women's refusals are clear and direct, miscommunication is likely (Burkett & Hamilton, 2012; O'Byrne et al., 2006; O'Byrne et al., 2008; Starfelt et al., 2015).

These ideas—that verbal consent is unnecessary because it is obvious, but miscommunication is likely—seem contradictory. However, both are consistent with the traditional sexual script; men's sexual advances are assumed to be consensual as long as the woman does not resist; if she does not consent, it is her responsibility to communicate this, and if sexual assault occurs, she might be blamed for not communicating clearly enough.

Not everyone, however, described women's refusals as hard to interpret or as resistance to be overcome. For example, the young men in Beres's (2010) study reported several cues—some straightforward and some more subtle—signaling women's nonconsent. In addition, almost all of them endorsed a higher standard than mere lack of resistance; they looked for signals that their partner was enjoying the encounter. We return to the idea of gender-based miscommunication later in this article.

In many of the studies reviewed here, researchers focused on *men's* interpretations of *women's* consent and nonconsent signals. This made sense because many of these studies were done to investigate the idea that sexual assaults often result from men's misunderstandings of women['s] cues. Beres (2007), however, noted that in much of the sexual consent literature in psychology, sociology, and the law, the focus is on women's sexual consent. In much of this literature, men's sexual consent is assumed, consistent with the "'male sexual drive' discourse, in which men are viewed as always desiring sex and always in pursuit of sex. Through this discourse, men's consent is assumed" (p. 97). This assumption is, of course, untrue and can be harmful to women and men.

RESEARCH ON ATTITUDES AND BELIEFS ABOUT CONSENT

Researchers have used a variety of methods to assess young people's attitudes and beliefs about sexual consent, including focus groups, hypothetical vignettes, and attitudes scales. These studies provide an understanding of norms and expectations.

. . .

. . . Women's and men's attitudes and beliefs about sexual consent reflected substantial agreement (Humphreys, 2004; Humphreys & Herold,

2007; Jozkowski, Peterson, et al., 2014). Women were somewhat more likely than men to endorse explicitly communicating—rather than assuming or inferring—consent, but in general both women and men agreed that consent was important. The majority of women and men agreed that an Antioch College type of verbal consent policy might be a good way to encourage communication between partners but thought that it was unrealistic.

Almost all participants could provide a definition of consent, when asked to do so. Their context-free definitions of consent seem to be influenced by legal definitions and/or affirmative consent policies, reflecting the idea that consent is mutual agreement made while unimpaired by alcohol or drugs. In real-life situations, however, their expressions of consent did not match their abstract definitions (Beres, 2014; Jozkowski, Peterson, et al., 2014). In fact, some of them said that consent no longer applied to their relationships because they did not explicitly request sex from each other (Beres, 2014, p. 383). If the word *consent* has taken on legal connotations, it might be advisable to use other terms, such as *agree*, in questionnaires.

. . .

CONSENT AND GENDER: GENDER SIMILARITIES AND GENDER DIFFERENCES

The consent literature shows gender similarities and gender differences. In some areas (e.g., how individuals interpret various consent cues; how they would show consent if their partner initiated), gender differences are small. In other areas (e.g., how likely individuals are to be pressured sexually or to experience nonconsensual sex), gender differences are large.

Gender-Based Miscommunication: Do Women and Men Understand Each Other's Consent and Refusal Cues?

A large body of literature has demonstrated that, on average, men perceive female targets as displaying more sexual interest and intent than women perceive (for a review, see Farris et al., 2008). Thus, men might misperceive women as expressing sexual interest or willingness when the women intended to express friendliness or politeness. As noted, some circumstances (e.g., men's intoxication; men's expectancies

that alcohol increases sexual arousal and decreases inhibitions) are likely to intensify the problem (Abbey et al., 2003; Farris et al., 2008, George et al., 1995; Lindgren et al., 2008).

Some students expressed the idea that miscommunication can result in sexual assault (Burkett & Hamilton, 2012; O'Byrne et al., 2008). Is this plausible? Do men really misunderstand whether women are consenting? If so, can such misunderstandings actually lead to sexual assault?

. . .

Most cases of sexual assault . . . are likely not attributable to miscommunication. In most cases of sexual assault, the man knows that the woman has not consented but nevertheless chooses to continue. He could have numerous reasons for continuing. Perhaps he recognizes that she is currently unwilling but thinks that she will eventually get aroused and will actually enjoy it—a theme conveyed in pornography and even in mainstream movies and television programs (Warshaw, 1994). Perhaps he does not care how she feels about it or—given that many abusive relationships involve sexual as well as physical and psychological violence (Sabina & Straus, 2008)—perhaps his intention is to hurt and humiliate her.

When Gender Differences Are Important

Women and men often behave similarly when they are in similar situations or roles. Often, however, women and men are in different situations or roles. There are many gender-related differences related to sexuality. The traditional sexual script dictates very different roles for women and men (Wiederman, 2005). Women face a double standard in which they are evaluated more negatively than men for engaging in sexual behavior (Muehlenhard, Sakaluk, et al., 2015). A system in which heterosexual encounters can enhance men's status as "players" but stigmatize women as "sluts" (Sweeney, 2014) is not a level playing field. Women, especially women who are new to campus, are disproportionately targeted for sexual victimization (Cranney, 2015). Women are much more likely than men to be sexually assaulted while in college (American College Health Association, 2013; Brener et al., 1999; Cantor et al., 2015; Krebs et al., 2007).

Although this system generally disadvantages women, it can also have negative consequences for some men. Often, women's sexual consent is treated as an open question, but men's consent is assumed (Beres, 2007). Kanga (2015) found that less than 10% of the women and men in her sample thought that men should assume women's sexual consent, but 15% of the women and 33% of the men thought that it would be fine for women to assume men's sexual consent. In their recommendations for preventing sexual assault among college students, Krebs et al. (2007) recommended "informing men that they are ultimately responsible for determining (1) whether or not a women [sic] has consented to sexual contact, and (2) whether or not a women [sic] is capable of providing consent" (pp. xix, 6-5). They did not, however, make a parallel recommendation in which women are responsible for determining whether a man has consented or is capable of providing consent.

Of course, men do not always consent to sex. Some men are sexually assaulted (for a review, see Peterson, Voller, Polusny, & Murdoch, 2011). Some men agree to unwanted sex because they feel awkward or uncomfortable refusing sex (O'Sullivan & Allgeier, 1998). Some men report engaging in unwanted sexual activity to enhance or maintain their social status (Muehlenhard & Cook, 1988). Vannier and O'Sullivan (2011) noted that men are more likely than women to initiate their own unwanted sexual activity, reflecting external pressure to conform to cultural standards of masculinity.

. . .

CONCLUSION

Consent can be conceptualized in numerous ways: as a feeling or decision, as an explicit agreement, or as behavior indicative of willingness; as something that can be assumed or as something that must be given explicitly; and as a discrete event or as an ongoing, continuous process. All this is further complicated by numerous factors: Individuals are often ambivalent or uncertain about what they want or are willing to do. Gendered expectations and sexual double standards create unequal environments for women and men. Many college students engage in partying and heavy drinking. Even

expressions of agreement can be questioned under certain conditions (e.g., if the individual was intoxicated or was being pressured or threatened); determining whether these conditions exist often involves judgment calls (e.g., how intoxicated is too intoxicated to consent, or what types of pressure or threats are serious enough to preclude meaningful consent).

All this presents challenges to university officials who are trying to create policies that will reduce sexual assault but that are realistic and flexible enough to accommodate consensual sex between willing students. Research can provide data that might inform these policies, feedback about how these policies are working, and ideas for programming aimed at encouraging communication about sexual consent and preventing sexual assault.

REFERENCES

Abbey, A. (2002). Alcohol-related sexual assault: A common problem among college students. *Journal of Studies on Alcohol, 14*(Suppl. 14), 118–128. doi:10.15288/jsas.2002.s14.118

Abbey, A., Buck, P. O., Zawacki, T., & Saenz, C. (2003). Alcohol's effects on perceptions of a potential date rape. *Journal of Studies on Alcohol, 64,* 669–677. doi:10.15288/jsa.2003.64.669

Abbey, A., McAuslan, P., & Ross, T. L. (1998). Sexual assault perpetration by college men: The role of alcohol, misperception of sexual intent, and sexual beliefs and experiences. *Journal of Social and Clinical Psychology, 17,* 167–195. doi:10.1521/jscp.1998.17.2.167

Abbey, A., Zawacki, T., & Buck, P. O. (2005). The effects of past sexual assault perpetration and alcohol consumption on men's reactions to mixed signals. *Journal of Social and Clinical Psychology, 25,* 129–155. doi:10.1521/jscp.24.2.129.62273

American College Health Association. (2013). *American College Health Association–National College Health Assessment II: Canadian reference group data report, spring 2013.* Hanover, MD: American College Health Association. Retrieved from http://www.cacuss.ca/_Library/documents/NCHA-II_WEB_SPRING_2013_CANADIAN_REFERENCE_GROUP_DATA_REPORT.pdf

Antioch College. (2014–2015). *Student handbook 2014–2015*. Yellow Springs, OH: Author. Retrieved from http://www.antiochcollege.org/sites/default/files/pdf/student-handbook.pdf

Armstrong, E. A., Hamilton, L., & Sweeney, B. (2006). Sexual assault on campus: A multilevel, integrative approach to party rape. *Social Problems, 53*, 483–499. doi:10.1525/sp.2006.53.4.483

Axon, R. (2015, April 16). Accuser sues Jameis Winston over alleged rape in 2012. *USA Today*. Retrieved from http://www.usatoday.com/story/sports/ncaaf/2015/04/16/erica-kinsman-civil-lawsuit-jameis-winston-rape-florida-state/25896871/

Bazelon, E. (2015, May 29). Have we learned anything from the Columbia rape case? *New York Times*. Retrieved from http://www.nytimes.com/2015/05/29/magazine/have-we-learned-anything-from-the-columbia-rape-case.html?_r=0

Beres, M. A. (2007). "Spontaneous" sexual consent: An analysis of sexual consent literature. *Feminism and Psychology, 17*, 93–108. doi:10.1177/0959353507072914

Beres, M. A. (2010). Sexual miscommunication? Untangling assumptions about sexual communication between casual sex partners. *Culture, Health, and Sexuality, 12*, 1–14. doi:10.1080/13691050903075226

Beres, M. A. (2014). Rethinking the concept of consent for anti-sexual violence activism and education. *Feminism and Psychology, 24*, 373–389. doi:10.1177/0959353514539652

Beres, M. A., Herold, E., & Maitland, S. B. (2004). Sexual consent behaviors in same-sex relationships. *Archives of Sexual Behavior, 33*, 475–486. doi:10.1023/B:ASEB.0000037428.41757.10

Black, M. C., Basile, K. C., Breiding, M. J., Smith, S. G., Walters, M. L., Merrick, M. T., . . . Stevens, M. R. (2011). *The National Intimate Partner and Sexual Violence Survey (NISVS): 2010 summary report*. Atlanta, GA: Centers for Disease Control and Prevention. Retrieved from http://www.cdc.gov/ViolencePrevention/pdf/NISVS_Report2010-a.pdf

Brener, N. D., McMahon, P. M., Warren, C. W., & Douglas, K. A. (1999). Forced sexual intercourse and associated health-risk behaviors among female college students in the United States. *Journal of Consulting and Clinical Psychology, 67*, 252–259. doi:10.1037/0022-006X.67.2.252

Burkett, M., & Hamilton, K. (2012). Postfeminist sexual agency: Young women's negotiations of sexual consent. *Sexualities, 15*, 815–833. doi:10.1177/1363460712454076

Burrow, J. J., Hannon, R., & Hall, D. (1998). College students' perceptions of women's verbal and nonverbal consent for sexual intercourse. *Electronic Journal of Human Sexuality, 1*. Retrieved from http://www.ejhs.org/volume1/burrow/burrow.htm

Byers, E. S. (1980). Female communication of consent and nonconsent to sexual intercourse. *Journal of the New Brunswick Psychological Association, 5*, 12–18.

California Senate Bill SB-967. (2014). Student safety: Sexual assault. Section 1. (a) (1). Retrieved from http://leginfo.legislature.ca.gov/faces/billNavClient.xhtml?bill_id=201320140SB967

Cantor, D., Fisher, B., Chibnall, S., Townsend, R., Lee, H., Bruce, C., & Thomas, G. (2015). *Report on the AAU Campus Climate Survey on Sexual Assault and Sexual Misconduct*. Washington, DC: Association of American Universities. Retrieved from http://www.aau.edu/uploadedFiles/AAU_Publications/AAU_Reports/Sexual_Assault_Campus_Survey/Report%20on%20the%20AAU%20Campus%20Climate%20Survey%20on%20Sexual%20Assault%20and%20Sexual%20Misconduct.pdf

Coronel, S., Coll, S., & Kravitz, D. (2015, April 5). *Rolling Stone* and UVA: The Columbia University Graduate School of Journalism report: An anatomy of a journalistic failure. *Rolling Stone*. Retrieved from http://www.rollingstone.com/culture/features/a-rape-on-campus-what-went-wrong-20150405

Cranney, S. (2015). The relationship between sexual victimization and year in school in U.S. colleges: Investigating the parameters of the "red zone." *Journal of Interpersonal Violence, 30*, 3133–3145. doi:10.1177/0886260514554425

Davis, K. C., Stoner, S. A., Norris, J., George, W. H., & Masters, N. T. (2009). Women's awareness of and discomfort with sexual assault cues: Effects of alcohol consumption and relationship type. *Violence Against Women, 15,* 1106–1125. doi:10.1177/1077801209340759

DeSantis, A. (2007). *Inside Greek-U: Fraternities, sororities, and the pursuit of power; pleasure, and prestige.* Lexington: University Press of Kentucky.

Eileraas, K. (2011). Legal definitions of rape. In M. Z. Stange, C. K. Oyster, & J. E. Sloan (Eds.), *Encyclopedia of women in today's world* (pp. 1205–1209). Thousand Oaks, CA: Sage.

Farris, C., Treat, T. A., & Viken, R. J. (2010). Alcohol alters men's perceptual and decisional processing of women's sexual interest. *Journal of Abnormal Psychology, 119,* 427–432. doi:10.1037/a0019343

Farris, C., Treat, T. A., Viken, R. J., & McFall, R. M. (2008). Sexual coercion and the misperception of sexual intent. *Clinical Psychology Review, 28,* 48–66. doi:10.1016/j.cpr.2007.03.002

Fine, M. (1988). Sexuality, schooling, and adolescent females: The missing discourse of desire. *Harvard Educational Review, 58,* 29–53. doi:10.17763/haer.58.1.u0468k1v2n2n8242

Fromme, K., D'Amico, E. J., & Katz, E. C. (1999). Intoxicated sexual risk taking: An expectancy or cognitive impairment explanation? *Journal of Studies on Alcohol, 60,* 54–63. doi:10.15288/jsa.1999.60.54

Gaga, L., & Cuomo, A. (2015, June 8). Lady Gaga, Gov. Cuomo pen essay urging passage of "Enough Is Enough" bill: Exclusive. *Billboard.* Retrieved from http://www.billboard.com/articles/news/6590572/lady-gaga-andrew-cuomo-enough-is-enough-legislation

George, W. H., Cue, K. L., Lopez, P. A., Crowe, L. C., & Norris, J. (1995). Self-reported alcohol expectancies and postdrinking sexual inferences about women. *Journal of Applied Social Psychology, 25,* 164–186. doi:10.1111/j.1559-1816.1995.tb01589.x

Graham, K., Bernards, S., Osgood, D. W., Abbey, A., Parks, M., Flynn, A., & Wells, S. (2014). "Blurred lines?" Sexual aggression and barroom culture. *Alcoholism: Clinical and Experimental Research, 38,* 1416–1424. doi:10.1111/acer.12356

Grose, R. G., Grabe, S., & Kohfeldt, D. (2014). Sexual educational, gender ideology, and youth sexual empowerment. *Journal of Sex Research, 51,* 742–753. doi:10.1080/00224499.2013.809511

Hall, D. S. (1998). Consent for sexual behavior in a college student population. *Electronic Journal of Human Sexuality, 1.* Retrieved from http://www.ejhs.org/volume1/consent1.htm

Hamilton, L., & Armstrong, E. A. (2009). Gendered sexuality in young adulthood: Double binds and flawed options. *Gender and Society, 23,* 589–616. doi:10.1177/0891243209345829

Hanzus, D. (2015, May 1). Jameis Winston signs rookie contract with Buccaneers. *Around the NFL.* Retrieved from www.nfl.com/news/story/0ap3000000489828/article/jameis-winston-signs-rookie-contract-with-buccaneers

Harrington, N. T., & Leitenberg, H. (1994). Relationship between alcohol consumption and victim behaviors immediately preceding sexual aggression by an acquaintance. *Violence and Victims, 9,* 315–324.

Hickman, S. E., & Muehlenhard, C. L. (1999). "By the semi-mystical appearance of a condom": How young women and men communicate sexual consent in heterosexual situations. *Journal of Sex Research, 36,* 258–272. doi:10.1080/00224499909551996

Humphreys, T. (2004). Understanding sexual consent: An empirical investigation of the normative script for young heterosexual adults. In M. Cowling & P. Reynolds (Eds.), *Making sense of sexual consent* (pp. 209–225). Burlington, VT: Ashgate.

Humphreys, T., & Herold, E. (2007). Should universities and colleges mandate sexual behavior? Student perceptions of Antioch College's consent policy. *Journal of Psychology and Human Sexuality, 15,* 305–315. doi:10.1007/s11199-007-9264-7

Jozkowski, K. N. (2013). The influence of consent on college students' perceptions of the quality of sexual intercourse at last event. *International Journal of Sexual Health, 25,* 260–272. doi:10.1080/19317611.2013.799626

Jozkowski, K. N., & Hunt, M. (2013, November). *Beyond the "bedroom": When does consent to sex begin?* Paper presented at the Annual Meeting of the Society for the Scientific Study of Sexuality, San Diego, CA.

Jozkowski, K. N., & Hunt, M. (2014, November). *"Who wants a quitter? . . . So you just keep trying":*

How college students' perceptions of sexual consent privilege men. Paper presented at the Annual Meeting of the Society for the Scientific Study of Sexuality, Omaha, NE.

Jozkowski, K. N., & Peterson, Z. D. (2013). College students and sexual consent: Unique insights. *Journal of Sex Research, 50,* 517–523. doi:10.1080/00224499.2012.700739

Jozkowski, K. N., Peterson, Z. D., Sanders, S. A., Dennis, B., & Reece, M. (2014). Gender differences in heterosexual college students' conceptualizations and indicators of sexual consent: Implications for contemporary sexual assault prevention education. *Journal of Sex Research, 51,* 904–916. doi:10.1080/00224499.2013.792326

Jozkowski, K. N., Sanders, S., Peterson, Z. D., Dennis, B., & Reece, M. (2014). Consenting to sexual activity: The development and psychometric assessment of dual measures of consent. *Archives of Sexual Behavior, 43,* 437–450. doi:10.1007/s10508-013-0225-7

Jozkowski, K. N., & Wiersma, J. D. (2015). Does drinking alcohol prior to sexual activity influence college students' consent? *International Journal of Sexual Health, 27,* 156–174. doi:10.1080/19317611.2014.951505

Kanga, M. R. (2015). *College students' perceptions of sexual consent* (Unpublished doctoral dissertation). University of Kansas, Lawrence, KS.

Kanin, E. J. (1967). An examination of sexual aggression as a response to sexual frustration. *Journal of Marriage and Family, 29,* 428–433. doi:10.2307/349577

Kantor, L. M., Santelli, J. S., Teitler, J., & Balmer, R. (2008). Abstinence-only policies and programs: An overview. *Sexuality Research and Social Policy, 5,* 6–17. doi:10.1525/srsp.2008.5.3.6

Kennedy, C. H. (2003). Legal and psychological implications in the assessment of sexual consent in the cognitively impaired population. *Assessment, 10,* 352–358. doi:10.1177/1073191103258592

Kitzinger, C., & Frith, H. (1999). Just say no? The use of conversation analysis in developing a feminist perspective on sexual refusal. *Discourse and Society, 10,* 293–316. doi:10.1177/0957926599010003002

Kolivas, E. D., & Gross, A. M. (2007). Assessing sexual aggression: Addressing the gap between rape victimization and perpetration prevalence rates *Aggression and Violent Behavior, 12,* 315–328. doi:10.1016/j.avb.2006.10.002

Koss, M. P., Abbey, A., Campbell, R., Cook, S., Norris, J., Testa, M., . . . White, J. (2007). Revising the SES: A collaborative process to improve assessment of sexual aggression and victimization. *Psychology of Women Quarterly, 31,* 357–370. doi:10.1111/j.1471-6402.2007.00385.x

Koss, M. P., Gidycz, C. J., & Wisniewski, N. (1987). The scope of rape: Incidence and prevalence of sexual aggression and victimization in a national sample of higher education students. *Journal of Consulting and Clinical Psychology, 55,* 162–170. doi:10.1037/0022-006X.55.2.162

Krebs, C. P., Lindquist, C. H., Warner, T. D., Fisher, B. S., & Martin, S. L. (2007). *The Campus Sexual Assault (CSA) Study.* Washington, DC: National Institute of Justice. Retrieved from https://www.ncjrs.gov/pdffiles1/nij/grants/221153.pdf

Krebs, C. P., Lindquist, C. H., Warner, T. D., Fisher, B. S., & Martin, S. L. (2009). College women's experiences with physically forced, alcohol- or other drug-enabled, and drug-facilitated sexual assault before and since entering college. *Journal of American College Health, 57,* 639–647. doi:10.3200/JACH.57.6.639-649

Kuperberg, A., & Padgett, J. E. (2015). Dating and hooking up in college: Meeting contexts, sex, and variation by gender, partner's gender, and class standing. *Journal of Sex Research, 52,* 517–531. doi:10.1080/00224499.2014.901284

Kutner, M. (2015, April 28). The anti-mattress protest: Paul Nungesser's lawsuit against Columbia University. *Newsweek.* Retrieved from http://www.newsweek.com/anti-mattress-protest-paul-nungessers-lawsuit-against-columbia-university-326319

Lawyer, S., Resnick, H., Bakanic, V., Burkett, T., & Kilpatrick, D. (2010). Forcible, drug-facilitated, and incapacitated rape and sexual assault among undergraduate women. *Journal of American College Health, 58,* 453–460. doi:10.1080/07448480903540515

Lindgren, K. P., Parkhill, M. R., George, W. H., & Hendershot, C. S. (2008). Gender differences in perceptions of sexual intent: A qualitative review and integration. *Psychology of Women Quarterly, 32,* 423–439. doi:10.1111/j.1471-6402.2008.00456.x

Lisak, D., & Miller, P. M. (2002). Repeat rape and multiple offending among undetected rapists. *Violence and Victims, 17,* 73–84. doi:10.1891/vivi.17.1.73.33638

Livingston, J. A., Buddie, A. M., Testa, M., & VanZile-Tamsen, C. (2004). The role of sexual precedence in verbal sexual coercion. *Psychology of Women Quarterly, 28,* 287–297. doi:10.1111/j.1471-6402.2004.00146.x

McCauley, J. L., Ruggiero, K. J., Resnick, H. S., Conoscenti, L. M., & Kilpatrick, D. G. (2009). Forcible, drug-facilitated, and incapacitated rape in relation to substance use problems: Results from a national sample of college women. *Addictive Behaviors, 34,* 458–462. doi:10.1016/j.addbeh.2008.12.004

McLeod, L. (2015). *Towards a culture of consent: Sexual consent styles and contemporary social interventions* (Unpublished thesis). James Cook University, Cairns, Australia.

Mohler-Kuo, M., Dowdall, G. W., Koss, M. P., & Wechsler, H. (2004). Correlates of rape while intoxicated in a national sample of college women. *Journal of Studies on Alcohol, 65,* 37–45. doi:10.15288/jsa.2004.65.37

Muehlenhard, C. L. (1995–1996). The complexities of sexual consent. *SIECUS Report, 24*(2), 4–7. Retrieved from http://www.siecus.org/_data/global/images/SIECUS%20Report%202/24-2.pdf

Muehlenhard, C. L. (2011). Examining stereotypes about token resistance to sex. *Psychology of Women Quarterly, 35,* 676–683. doi:10.1177/0361684311426689

Muehlenhard, C. L., & Cook, S. W. (1988). Men's self-reports of unwanted sexual activity. *Journal of Sex Research, 24,* 58–72. doi:10.1080/00224498809551398

Muehlenhard, C. L., Peterson, Z. D., Humphreys, T. P., & Jozkowski, K. N. (2015). *Evaluating the one-in-five statistic: The prevalence of sexual assault among college students.* Manuscript submitted for publication.

Muehlenhard, C. L., Powch, I. G., Phelps, J. L., & Giusti, L. M. (1992). Definitions of rape: Scientific and political implications. *Journal of Social Issues, 48*(1), 23–44. doi:10.1111/j.1540-4560.1992.tb01155.x

Muehlenhard, C. L., Sakaluk, J. K., & Esterline, K. M. (2015). Double standard. In P. Whelehan & A. Bolin (Eds.), *International encyclopedia of human sexuality* (Vol. 1, pp. 309–311). Chichester, UK: Wiley-Blackwell.

National Post Staff. (2013, September 5). Saint Mary's University under fire for frosh-week chant championing non-consensual sex with under-age girls. *National Post.* Retrieved from http://news.nationalpost.com/news/canada/halifax-university-under-fire-for-frosh-week-chant-championing-non-consensual-sex-with-underage-girls

O'Byrne, R., Hansen, S., & Rapley, M. (2008). If a girl doesn't say "no" . . . : Young men, rape, and claims of "insufficient knowledge." *Journal of Community and Applied Social Psychology, 18,* 168–193. doi:10.1002/casp.922

O'Byrne, R., Rapley, M., & Hansen, S. (2006). "You couldn't say 'no,' could you?" Young men's understandings of sexual refusal. *Feminism and Psychology, 16,* 133–154. doi:10.1177/0959-353506062970

O'Sullivan, L. F., & Allgeier, E. R. (1998). Feigning sexual desire: Consenting to unwanted sexual activity in heterosexual dating relationships. *Journal of Sex Research, 35,* 234–243. doi:10.1080/00224499809551938

Osman, S. L. (2007). Predicting perceptions of sexual harassment based on type of resistance and belief in token resistance. *Journal of Sex Research, 44,* 340–346. doi:10.1080/00224490701586714

Osman, S. L., & Davis, C. M. (1999). Belief in token resistance and type of resistance as predictors of men's perceptions of date rape. *Journal of Sex Education and Therapy, 24,* 189–196. doi:10.1080/01614576.1999.11074300

Oudekerk, B. A., Guarnera, L. A., & Reppucci, N. D. (2014). Older opposite-sex romantic partners, sexual risk, and victimization in adolescence. *Child Abuse and Neglect, 38,* 1238–1248. doi:10.1016/j.chiabu.2014.03.009

Palmer, B. (2011, February 17). What's the difference between "rape" and "sexual assault"? *Slate.* Retrieved from http://www.slate.com/articles/news_and_politics/explainer/2011/02/whats_the_difference_between_rape_and_sexual_assault.html

Pascoe, C. J. (2005). "Dude, you're a fag": Adolescent masculinity and the fag discourse. *Sexualities, 8,* 329–346. doi:10.1177/1363460705053337

Peterson, Z. D., Voller, E. K., Polusny, M. A., & Murdoch, M. (2011). Prevalence and consequences of adult sexual assault of men: Review of empirical findings and state of the literature. *Clinical Psychology Review, 31,* 1–24. doi:10.1016/j.cpr.2010.08.006

Pineau, L. (1989). Date rape: A feminist analysis. *Law and Philosophy, 8,* 217–243. doi:10.1007/BF00160012

Reinholtz, R. K., Muehlenhard, C. L., Phelps, J. L., & Satterfield, A. T. (1995). Sexual discourse and sexual intercourse: How the way we communicate affects the way we think about sexual coercion. In P. J. Kalbfleisch & M. J. Cody (Eds.), *Gender, power, and communication in human relationships* (pp. 141–162). Hillsdale, NJ: Erlbaum.

Sabina, C., & Straus, M. A. (2008). Polyvictimization by dating partners and mental health among U.S. college students. *Violence and Victims, 23,* 667–682. doi:10.1891/0886-6708.23.6.667

Sinha, M. (2013). *Measuring violence against women: Statistical trends. Canadian Centre for Justice Statistics Profile Series* (No. 85-002-X). Retrieved from http://www.statcan.gc.ca/pub/85-002-x/2013001/article/11766-eng.pdf

Sinozich, S., & Langton, L. (2014, December). Victimization among college-age females, 1995–2013, U.S. Department of Justice, Bureau of Justice Statistics, NCJ 248471. Retrieved from http://www.bjs.gov/content/pub/pdf/rsavcaf9513.pdf

Starfelt, L. C., Young, R., Palk, G., & White, K. M. (2015). A qualitative exploration of young Australian adults' understandings of and explanations for alcohol-involved rape. *Psychiatry, Psychology and Law, 22,* 337–354. doi:10.1080/13218719.2014.945639

Steele, C. M., & Josephs, R. A. (1990). Alcohol myopia: Its prized and dangerous effects. *American Psychologist, 45,* 921–933. doi:10.1037/0003-066X.45.8.921

Stoner, S. A., Norris, J., George, W. H., Morrison, D. M., Zawacki, T., Davis, K. C., & Hessler, D. M. (2008). Women's condom use assertiveness and sexual risk-taking: Effects of alcohol intoxication and adult victimization. *Addictive Behaviors, 33,* 1167–1176. doi:10.1016/j.addbeh.2008.04.017

Strang, E., Peterson, Z. D., Hill, Y., & Heiman, J. R. (2013). Discrepant responding across self-report measures of men's coercive and aggressive sexual strategies. *Journal of Sex Research, 50,* 458–469. doi:10.1080/00224499.2011.646393

Struckman-Johnson, C., Struckman-Johnson, D., & Anderson, P. B. (2003). Tactics of sexual coercion: When men and women won't take no for an answer. *Journal of Sex Research, 40,* 76–86. doi:10.1080/00224490309552168

Sweeney, B. N. (2014). Sorting women sexually: Masculine status, sexual performance, and the sexual stigmatization of women. *Symbolic Interaction, 37,* 369–390. doi:10.1002/SYMB.113

Tarzia, L., Fetherstonhaugh, D., & Bauer, M. (2012). Dementia, sexuality, and consent in residential aged care facilities. *Journal of Medical Ethics, 38,* 609–613. doi:10.1136/medethics-2011-100453

Testa, M., & Livingston, J. A. (2009). Alcohol consumption and women's vulnerability to sexual victimization: Can reducing women's drinking prevent rape? *Substance Use and Misuse, 44,* 1349–1376. doi:10.1080/10826080902961468

Tjaden, P., & Thoennes, N. (2006). *Extent, nature, and consequences of rape victimization: Findings from the National Violence Against Women Survey.* Washington, DC: U.S. Department of Justice.

Tuerkheimer, D. (2013). Sex without consent. *Yale Law Journal Online.* Retrieved from http://www.yalelawjournal.org/forum/sex-without-consent

Vannier, S. A., & O'Sullivan, L. F. (2011). Communicating interest in sex: Verbal and nonverbal initiation of sexual activity in young adults' romantic dating relationships. *Archives of Sexual Behavior, 40,* 961–969. doi:10.1007/s10508-010-9663-7

Warshaw, R. (1994). *I never called it rape* (2nd ed.). New York, NY: Harper & Row.

Wechsler, H., Lee, J. E., Nelson, T. F., & Kuo, M. (2002). Underage college students' drinking behavior, access to alcohol, and the influence of deterrence policies. *Journal of American College Health, 50,* 223–236. doi:10.1080/07448480209595714

West, R. (2008). Sex, law, and consent. In A. Wertheimer & W. Miller (Eds.), *The ethics of consent: Theory and practice.* Retrieved from http://scholarship.law.georgetown.edu/cgi/viewcontent.cgi?article=1073&context=fwps_papers.

Wiederman, M. W. (2005). The gendered nature of sexual scripts. *Family Journal, 13,* 496–502. doi:10.1177=1066480705278729

Zurbriggen, E. L. (2000). Social motives and cognitive power–sex associations: Predictors of aggressive sexual behavior. *Journal of Personality and Social Psychology, 78,* 559–581. doi:10.1037/0022-3514.78.3.559

40. QUEER MUSLIM WOMEN ARE MAKING SALAAM WITH WHO THEY ARE

CARL COLLISON (2017)

"The day I left for Mecca, I told myself and God that if, by the time I came back to Cape Town, I still feel this way towards women—still attracted to them—then so be it. I would make peace with it. But it won't stop me from being a Muslim, because I am a Muslim first."

So says Fatima Ahmed of the pilgrimage she undertook to Mecca many years ago.

"In the six weeks I was there, I stood on Mount Arafat asking God for forgiveness; I cried, asking Allah to take this feeling away from me. When I did tawaf [the spiritual walk around the Kaaba, Islam's most sacred site], there wasn't a minute I didn't ask Allah—beg him, in fact—to take this feeling away from me."

Still a practising Muslim and together with her partner for the past 13 years, Ahmed, who did not want to have her real name used, says: "I have been living a double life for 20 years now."

For many queer Muslim women, the disjuncture between their sexuality or gender-nonconformity and the prescripts of their religion sees them having to do this.

A devout Muslim, Layla Adams* (who chose to use a pseudonym) decided to devote her life to spreading the teachings of Islam. After completing her religious studies qualification, Adams became an alimah (a woman with a formal qualification in Islamic education). "It's basically the equivalent of being a nun in Christianity," she says with pride.

But she did not experience the reverence usually afforded this high position. "Because I am a religious teacher, a Muslim person who might know I am gay would not take advice from me. Their thinking is along the lines of: 'Hell is waiting for you, so why would I want to ask you anything?' or 'You're living in sin already, so what good could come out of your mouth?'"

Adams says: "Initially, when I discovered my attraction to women, I prayed that God would take it away from me.

"Sometimes it still haunts me, because all your life you have been indoctrinated that being gay is a sin. It weighed on me. It affected every aspect of my life. I questioned my faith. I was scared because, if you're gay, you're going to go to jahannam [hell]. At one stage of my life, I asked God: 'If me being gay displeases you, please take it away.'"

Although in a relationship now for the past 10 years, Adams says: "I can't be affectionate or loving with my partner in public. Only my very close friends know—and those who do know keep it to themselves."

Muhsin Hendricks is South Africa's first openly gay imam and the founder of The Inner Circle, the Cape Town–based organisation focused on helping queer Muslims to reconcile with their Islamic identity, sexual orientation and gender identity.

"The main problem Muslim women face is patriarchy, which is inexpungible from Islam. Orthodox Islam has always taught that women should be in the back row when they pray and their roles confined to the home.

"With queer women, they already feel marginalised because of that, and then still opening themselves up to more abuse by openly stating that they are lesbian. It's a double discrimination for them.

"Whereas with gay men, they still have the privilege of being men. So it's easier for them. Many lesbians feel uncomfortable even in gay men's spaces because, even then, it is still very patriarchal."

In the hopes of creating a safe space for queer Muslim women—albeit a virtual one—queer rights activist Midi Achmat has created a Facebook page, Unveiling the Hijab.

Although no longer a practising Muslim, Achmat—who has had no contact with her family for nearly 30 years after being rejected because of her sexual orientation—conducted research into the difficulties queer Muslim women face in coming out as part of her honours degree thesis.

"What I found was that people are going through exceptionally difficult times. Many are married in heterosexual relationships but have lesbian relationships on the side."

After being approached by the University of the Western Cape to continue her research into the subject, Achmat refused.

"I didn't do it because, after interviewing so many people and hearing the things they went through and were going through, I was too depressed. It was heartbreaking.

"With one of the people I interviewed, for example, rumours of her being gay had got to her mother. Her mother then approached her, asking if she wants to be a man. She told me how she then got undressed in front of her mother, looked her straight in the eye, and asked: 'Who am I? Did you not give birth to me?'

"She wanted her mother to see her as what she was—her child. Her story really broke me, because, even after that, her family still completely rejected her.

"Another subject, a trans woman, spoke of how she was serving women at a tea party and it was discovered that she was a trans woman.

"The women started mocking her but, when a well-known sheik came in and saw what they were doing, he asked them to stop, asking them: 'Wie het haar ru in haar geblaas?' [Who blew her soul into her?] God has blown her soul into her—the same God that has blown your soul into you. So why are you making fun of God's creation?'

"This was very surprising because our religious leaders tend to endorse homophobia, transphobia and queerphobia."

Having queer Muslim patients, clinical psychologist Soraya Nair has seen first-hand the effect religion-sanctioned queerphobia can have.

"Any person or religious doctrine that discriminates on any basis, including gender and sexual identity, presents a significant risk to the sense of self-worth of those discriminated against."

Nair says being a woman and identifying as queer is core to one's sense of self. "So any messaging that rejects either is devaluing of the self. Given that our psychological wellbeing is primarily dependent on a healthy sense of self, it stands to reason that those subjected to messages that say 'you do not have value' or 'you are an aberration' are at risk of psychological as well as physical illness.

"However, in families that have been both accepting and embracing of the sexual identity of their daughters, we see much more resilience in those daughters."

Following Hendricks's appearance in the 2007 documentary *A Jihad for Love*, which looked into the challenges faced by gay Muslims, the Muslim Judicial Council (MJC) issued a fatwa declaring Hendricks "out of the fold of Islam and the work I do as propaganda."

A decade later, however, Hendricks believes there are changes afoot.

"In 2007, we hardly had any imams supporting our work. We never had the Forum for Religious Leaders, which has now grown from five imams to 20 internationally."

Ludovic-Mohammed Zahed is an imam, author and founder of Europe's first inclusive mosque, who has recently finished work on the soon-to-be-released documentary *Islam and Homosexuality*.

In his research paper, titled Feminist and Gay-Friendly Islamic Theologians, Zahed notes: "For 20 years, remarkable changes have taken place in the field of theology and interpretations of Islam."

The paper added: "Homosexuals and transsexuals also find themselves in this reformist current that grows in the United States, Canada, South Africa, Indonesia and Europe since the 2000s."

Following the Orlando massacre—in which 49 lesbian, gay, bisexual, transsexual and intersex people were gunned down—the imam of the Claremont

Main Road mosque in Cape Town, Rashied Omar, delivered an Eid sermon in which he stated: "Homophobia is not exclusive to any religious or ethnic group. There are homophobic Jews, homophobic Christians, homophobic Hindus, homophobic Muslims, homophobic atheists, homophobic whites and homophobic blacks. So, this is not a Muslim problem, but it would be disingenuous to claim it is not also a Muslim problem.

"Our radical equality before God prohibits us from thinking of another human being as lesser merely because they are different. Moreover, from this Qur'anic perspective, protecting the dignity of all people should be the primary objective of human rights and social justice advocacy."

Zahed says: "The patriarchal and discriminatory attitudes faced by queer Muslim women has nothing to do with Islam as a spirituality but rather with Islam as a civilisation, going through tremendous crises over the last century. My advice would be to read and create your own interpretation of the relationship between spirituality and sexuality."

Creating their own interpretations is something younger queer Muslim women appear to be doing.

"I have no problem reconciling my spirituality and my sexuality," says Mishka Wazar (19), a practising Muslim who identifies as pansexual.

She says. "I went to an extremely homophobic school, so always got into shit for calling people out about their homophobia and queerphobia.

"Many don't come out because it can be a very dangerous thing to do. It is an extremely patriarchal space to inhabit, with gender roles very clearly defined, especially for women of colour.

"Stepping out of those gender roles can be very dangerous. There is the actual physical threat of violence, so many just don't think it is worth it to come out. For me, I'm really not worried what people think of me. I'm worried about whether they have the power structure to hurt me."

Imaan Latif is a practising Muslim, queer rights activist and conceptual artist.

"It has been quite a journey of realising what my religion is and how much of an impact it has had on my life; the depths of the indoctrination of my upbringing and cultural lens.

"I live a carefree, liberalist, spiritualist lifestyle. Choosing to study Arabic and Islamic politics and economics has led me to my own personal reconciliation of being a Muslimah [a Muslim woman]. My intention every day is to embody the dimensions of Islam and to perform each and every salaah [prayer], no matter where I am and what I am doing.

"Initially, it was like choosing between the right life and the wrong one. But I came to the understanding that it is compatible to be all things, although there are conflicts between traditionalism and modernisation.

"It doesn't make any sense to compare your sexuality to your religion and ask if those can exist together. Do who you pray to and who you fuck really matter to one another?"

Years after having undertaken her pilgrimage to the holy city, and despite continuing to live a double life, Ahmed might finally be at a similar place of self-acceptance.

"I don't care what anybody says. They have no right to judge me. This journey that I am on is between God and me. I will be answerable for it—nobody else."

41. LESBIAN LANDSCAPE

JANICE M. GOULD (2016)

I met my first girlfriend, Lia, on a Girl Scout "Burro Trip" into the Sierra Nevada. It was 1965; I was sixteen, she was twenty-four. The girls who signed up for this trip were a rowdy bunch, most of whom were not yet interested in boys, either because they were incipient lesbians, as I was, or tomboys. Or maybe they were simply shy. We enjoyed hanging out with other girls, hiking, sailing, swimming, folk-dancing, and camping, activities that were more fun and adventurous than having to primp for some boy and then keep him from pawing and insulting us. Some girls had parents who were life-long members of the

Sierra Club, so their knowledge of trails and maps and backpacking had long been a part of their lives, and we young women wanted to know what they knew.

The beauty of a Burro Trip, of course, is that sturdy animals carry the foodstuff in rectangular containers, with rolled sleeping bags and duffle bags piled up over these, and the whole thing covered by a tarp, secured by rope or twine over and under the burro. We wore daypacks and learned to lead the burros and to load them carefully and securely so that none lost their baggage. In the evenings, we camped at sites where the burros could graze. We took the John Muir Trail from Dana Meadows, went south past Lake Ediza and the Minarets, down to Fish Creek, over the pass to Big McGee Lake, and then hiked east at McGee Creek, down the steep slopes of the Sierra Nevada, out to the Owens Valley, a total distance of perhaps forty miles in seven days of hiking.

Many of us outfitted ourselves at the Army-Navy surplus store with striped, long-sleeved jerseys from the French navy, and blue wool turtlenecks. Most of us wore cut-off jeans, although one of our friends looked really cute in a pair of lederhosen with suspenders. I also had a dark khaki Boy Scouts of America shirt that was very nice. But as for our hiking boots, these had to be gray Pivettas with Vibram soles, bought at the Ski Hut on University Avenue in Berkeley. My Pivettas replaced some old crepe sole work boots that had belonged to my best friend Darcy's youngest brother. The following year, my new Trailwise backpack with a contour frame replaced a straight aluminum pack frame to which—on Sierra Club trips—I would lash a sleeping bag, a thin piece of Insulite, a duffel bag of clothes, and two Number Ten size tins of food for hikes that Darcy (I always called her by her last name, Hutchins) and I took— usually the only two teenagers in a small party of Sierra Clubbers.

Lia was a college student at the University of Oregon and already married. In fact, her husband, a lanky, quiet, sunburned guy, was on the Burro Trip to take care of the animals. I didn't really talk with her much till two or three nights before the trip ended. I remember we were at Fish Creek on a "lay over day" (a day camping rather than moving), and Hutchins and

I had wandered up the creek a ways to do our laundry and wash our hair. That afternoon, I noticed Lia taking photographs. I had my camera with me, too, so I hopped from rock to rock, and joined her across the creek. I asked if I could see her camera because I wanted to compare them. Secretly, I also wanted to take her picture, so it gave me an opportunity. I showed her how my camera focused and the setting I would use for just the kind of bright conditions we were experiencing—and, so doing, I snapped her photo. It made her laugh, though. She had been peering down at our cameras and suddenly looked up. I caught her that way, in a bemused, upward gaze. She was wearing a blue hooded sweatshirt, and her long brown hair was rolled at the back of her neck, held in place by a leather and wood hairclip. She did not seem like a woman who smiled a lot, so I felt good that I could make her laugh. In fact, I think I made her laugh as well when I told her that I could keep thunderstorms away. She wanted to know how I could do that. I forked my index and middle finger into a V, pointed them at the sky, and said, "Zot!" It worked, too.

That afternoon she took a picture of me, as well, smiling at her in my blue wool sweater, my hair clean and shaggy, a bandana around my neck. I thought of that time often, after that trip was over and she had gone home to Oregon. I remembered the warmth of that meadow, my clean clothes drying on the willows, the sound of the creek, the open sky, the granite mountains that rose up out of that little valley. It was a pretty place. On some level I knew I had charmed a woman, and that a flirtation had gone on; but this was not something I could articulate to my best friend Hutchins, let alone to myself. In the months and years that passed, I would return in my mind to that grassy stretch near the creek and to other mountain places. These were refuges from both the loneliness I felt and the intense shame and fear of not being "normal."

That August, before eleventh grade started, I received a package from Lia. It contained a small eight-by-eight reel of folksongs. One of the things we had bonded over was the fact that I had memorized many songs and could accompany myself on guitar. I had learned just about everything Joan Baez sang, and had even learned her guitar arrangements. Lia sent me songs by singers I had never heard of. There were funny lyrics—"Seven Beers with the Wrong Woman," for example, sung by Janet Stuart, and Stuart's version of "Frankie and Johnny." And there were love songs, like "Brandy, Leave Me Alone," by Gale Garnett, and Richard Dyer-Bennett's version of the Byron poem, "So We'll Go No More A-Roving." I learned a lot of those songs, and still sing them to this day. After that reel came, I received cards and long letters over the months, with whole poems scripted out in red ink on narrow-lined paper, poems by Edna St. Vincent Millay and Jacques Prévert and Khalil Gibran. And I wrote long letters back, not in cursive, but printing, much as she did. She introduced me to authors I had never read, Miguel de Unamuno and Federico García Lorca, Antoine de St.-Exupéry's *Wind, Sand, and Stars*, Fyodor Dostoevsky, Erich Fromm, Eugène Ionesco, and Jean-Paul Sartre.

Although she was majoring in French and Spanish, she herself was half Italian and, like me, had grown up in Berkeley. She was a good artist; it may have been her minor while at university. She sent me prints she had made, one of a meadowlark curled in a nest, another the silhouette of a girl sitting on a hill beneath tall trees. I treasured everything she sent me and kept all her letters in the yellow boot box that had held my Pivettas. I kept taking pictures and had an unspoken interest in becoming a photographer.

Lia and I met in the mid-1960s. The Free Speech Movement would soon be underway, sending shock waves through the city of Berkeley and across the nation, transforming not only how people talked, but what they talked about. At that time, the issue of race, for example, was spoken of only in black and white terms. As an urban, middle class, mixed-blood California Indian, my being Native American (Concow in the anglicized version of our tribal name[1]) was seldom considered by my friends. While it might have been a factor for me in how I was treated out in the world, this was not something my friends or their families were particularly aware of. In addition, when I was "raced" by someone, I was usually mistaken for being Asian—sometimes Japanese, sometimes Chinese. In the San Francisco Bay Area, prejudice against Asians still persisted, a legacy of the anti-Asian laws passed in the nineteenth-century, and of the Second World War and the battles against the Japanese military. My being Indian—and a California Indian at that—had no reality to most people, since Indians, it was believed by many, had long since vanished. If I were "something," I must be Asian. Of course, in my family, we talked about racial prejudice against Indians. It was a reality my mother, my older sister, and I experienced, most pronouncedly from our father's mother, but Mom's marrying a white man (an immigrant from Great Britain) and landing among the bourgeoisie in Berkeley no doubt offered my mother, my older sister, and me some security from the out and out racism that other Indians experienced.

The year Lia and I met, or some time the following year, she divorced her husband. I knew little about their relationship, only that they had been in Mexico together, but by the time of the burro trip, they seemed estranged from each other. I don't think they had been married long, not more than a couple of years. That she had been to Mexico, had studied there, intrigued me, but I was too shy to ask her much about it. We saw one another again, the following March—it must have been spring break—when the trees were in full flower for one sunny week, and the iris and poppies, narcissus and freesias were opening in Berkeley gardens. We hiked to one of her favorite places in Strawberry Canyon, above the eastern edge of the University of California. We sat beneath the redwoods, talking. Probably my parents met Lia during that week, so when she invited me to visit her in Oregon in the summer, they had no objection. They seemed to think it was a good idea that I had an older friend who shared so many of my interests.

That June I took the train to Oregon—a journey of several hours. I boarded in Oakland early in the morning, around 6 a.m., and arrived in Eugene that evening, as it was growing dark. I remember Lia, waiting, slim in her seersucker summer dress. It had pale green stripes, and her leather sandals were the kind people in Berkeley bought at the leather goods shop on Shattuck Avenue. Her long hair was pulled back. Probably she was smoking a cigarette. She was driving her friend Sylvie's blue VW bug that had a sunroof that could be opened.

The day's warmth in the Willamette Valley was starting to give way. We drove some miles west of town to the little farmhouse she rented, a typical Oregon clapboard house painted white, with a blue spruce growing in front. I loved that place immediately—small, rural, cozy—at the end of a narrow dirt and gravel track called McMorrot Lane. There were hills behind the farmhouse covered with Douglas fir and hemlocks. I could feel their presence, the vast quiet of nighttime trees, for it was nearly dark by the time we arrived. Walking along the gravel drive, I smelled wild oats and tarweed, scents I always associate with Oregon. The stars were beginning to brighten in the eastern sky. We came through the backdoor into the mud-room, which doubled as a darkroom, for she had an enlarger set up on a table and all the equipment for developing and printing photographs. She would teach me how to develop my pictures, and we did that together as the days progressed.

I stayed with her from some time in June until after the Fourth of July. I was by myself a good deal while my friend took classes, so after she showed me how to frail on a five-string banjo, I practiced that instrument, played Clementi on the upright piano, and read. Lia's roommate, Sylvie, was not around, but her books were still in the bedroom that was hers, so I borrowed book after book, and lay on the sofa to read. On days off, Lia and I took drives on her Honda motor scooter, went shopping for groceries, and cooked together. She taught me to make a beef stew *al suga* (in tomato-basil sauce) and *gnocchi* (potato dumplings), chow mein, and what she called "Raisin Baddies" because they were so good. On rainy days, I sat at the table and looked out the window, smelled rain on the wet earth, on the meadow, listened to rain falling on the farmhouse roof. On Sunday, we sat in bed together working the crossword puzzle that was printed in the Eugene *Register-Guard*. I would sometimes make up words to fit the spaces, and when she discovered one of these creations, she would scold me laughingly. "Grnocks" became a favorite seven letter word for "an expression of surprise."

We traveled. Up to Silver Falls, out to the wild McKenzie River, down to Diamond Lake, over to the Oregon coast, where we spent a foggy night and found, next morning, large slug-like sea creatures beached up on the shore. Usually we took the VW bug on our excursions, but sometimes Sylvie needed it, so then we drove in an old two-tone, black and brown 1955 Studebaker, the "coche," that Lia's father had given her. One time we packed up our sleeping bags and food and headed out past the Cascades into central Oregon, out along the John Day River. We got to a campsite late at night. The next day we found a logging road and followed it south and west, through clear-cut forests, devastated tracts of land, raising a huge cloud of pale brown dust behind us. That night we pitched a tent and, after dinner, sat by an open fire for a long time, not talking, just watching the flames. I took pine needles and broke them into little pieces, and with those pieces I spelled out on the earth the words *TE QUIERO*. I was afraid to say aloud, "I love you," but I had learned some Spanish from Lia, and I had delved into her Spanish–English dictionary to translate a song I had learned that began, *"Eres alta, delgada, como tu madre, morena y salada"* (You are tall and slender like your mother, dark and salty). How did she answer me that night? Perhaps she said I love you, too.

My time with Lia came to an end and I returned home. Ocean fogs poured over the Berkeley Hills, pulled in from the sea as the heat of the valley began to lift in the afternoon. I spent time in the open space near my home—property owned by the University of California—watching fog drift through the Golden Gate and over the San Francisco bay. I was not prepared to return to high school. I had taken another Girl Scout pack trip in early August, again following the John Muir Trail south, this time exiting the mountains to the west, down Mono Creek to where it emptied into Lake Edison, a manmade lake dug into the rich red soil of the mountains. My mother, Lia, and another mother, Mrs. Bjork, drove to meet our group. Driving home, Lia and I held hands under a blanket in the backseat of my mom's big Ford.

I must have met Lia's father and mother that August, before she returned to college in Eugene. She had grown up on Spruce Street, just off Cedar, near our church, All Souls' Episcopal, and across from the church of the Christian Scientists. Their house, probably built in the 1930s, was pale green and had a long driveway and a garage at the back. The lot was deep, and the entire backyard was taken up with a garden. Her parents grew flowers and vegetables: zinnias, roses, tomatoes, zucchini. I remember having dinner at their house. Her father gave me wine, and when I cautiously tasted it, he laughed and told me that my face looked flushed. At that, I'm sure I turned even redder. The next day, Lia and I hiked on the trail above Strawberry Canyon, held hands and kissed beneath the redwood trees. Then she was gone.

Twelfth grade began strangely. The school placed me in a class for students who, by virtue of test scores or other measures, could not read well. I was terrified. I knew my grades were low, but I didn't think so low as to warrant being tracked into a "slow reader" track. I wondered if it had to do with my being Native American. Every student in that class was a kid of color, which was how Berkeley High kept us segregated back then. Our first assignment was to list all the books we had read that summer. I included all the books I had read at Lia's, plus some others I had picked up at home. When the instructor saw my list, he called me to his desk and told me the administration had made some kind of mistake. He sent me to another classroom, what would today be the equivalent of an Advanced Placement (AP) class, but which was called in those days a "college prep" course.

I was miserable in the AP class, even though the books we were to read were exciting: *Lazarillo de Tormes, Candide, Wuthering Heights, The Great Gatsby.* I was shy and seldom spoke up in class. I felt intimidated by the other students, who seemed competitive, wanting to impress one another and the teacher, Miss Kalfas, with smart talk and jokes. Miss Kalfas, a young, pretty Greek, loaned me books from her own collection when she saw me eyeing them—*The Last Temptation of Christ* by Kazantzakis and Cavafy's *Collected Poems.* I had never read anything like "Body, remember not only how much you were loved/ not only the beds you lay on/ but also those desires that glowed openly/ in eyes that looked at you . . ." and "We were lovers for a month./ Then he went away to work, I think in Smyrna,/ and we never met again." I didn't know how to think about such lines for I had never read gay poetry and didn't know such work could exist.

It depressed me that Cavafy lived so secretly and in such despair, and I thought I could feel what he meant when he wrote, "With no consideration, no pity, no shame,/ they have built walls around me, thick and high./ And now I sit here feeling hopeless." I lived very much in my own mind and heart, telling no one of my desires and dreams. Little by little, I turned solitary, did not speak in class, declined to go out with my friends. Hutchins had a boyfriend by this time and was spending time with him. I was more hurt than jealous about this, because Hutchins and I had been close for a long time, pals who shared adventures, who enjoyed camping and hiking, or sitting by a river, talking. Now I talked to no one. Overwhelmed by a sense of anomie and dislocation, silenced because I knew no one else who shared a reality anything like mine, my studies and grades slipped more and more. I hated my bright classmates, who spoke of applying at Harvard, MIT, Stanford, and "Cal," feeling confident that they would be accepted. I barely knew what a Grade Point Average (GPA) was, or how to find it on the grade report that was delivered to my home every six weeks; I didn't know what a good score on the Scholastic Aptitude Test (SAT) or ACT was supposed to be.

My affair with Lia, a relationship that was really very chaste, if passionate, went on for almost four years. Over time it became too risky for Lia to love me because I was so badgered by my mother, who suspected I was a lesbian, but could not bring herself to ask me. Instead, Mom mocked my love for my friend, made snide remarks about the way I walked and sat, told me that *real* women cannot love other women, *real* women want a man, and so on. She was merely informing me about these facts of life for my own good. Finally one day she got into my stash of letters from Lia. There she found evidence of a physical relationship, and when I came home from school repeated in a voice laden with sarcasm words Lia had written to me—how good it felt to be held by me, how sweet it was to be kissed. "It disgusts me," my mother told me, "what you and Lia do together." I was both mortified and angry, but I also felt ashamed that the intimacies of Lia's and my relationship had been found out. I could say nothing. That my mother violated my privacy was in no way equal to the deeper transgression of my willfully and knowingly violating a "law of nature."

But it was in nature that I felt most alive and most real, most myself. In daydreams, I hiked trails in the high Sierra, sat by clear lakes, watched clouds move overhead, lay on a granite slab near a fast running creek or icy mountain tarn. Other times I remembered sailing on Tomales Bay with Hutchins in her family's Pelican, a gaff-rigged craft that was wonderful to sail in a full breeze. I imagined the sun on my face, the feel of wind tugging the sails, the sound of the hull slapping its way through choppy water. I could almost smell salt and anise and eucalyptus, could imagine lying on the warm sand at Heart's Desire Beach, listening to the screech of seagulls, to water lapping against the shore. I believed I could somehow have this fantasy life with Lia, who accepted me just as I was, who seemed to love me. I wasn't certain I was a lesbian, never having met anyone else like me. And I wasn't even certain I was a woman, though I bled every month—because I knew that my inner life and desires did not align with what *real* women felt or did, according to society. I knew I was not male, but whatever I felt and experienced, it was presumably more like what a man was supposed to feel. This was, of course, confusing. So I decided that I was neither female nor male, but some odd, deviant creature who would always have to hide and suppress its inner life, inner feelings. I decided, therefore, that I would not feel anything anymore, and I trained myself to shut down, to freeze my feelings. But such a decision is very hard to implement, and I was only partially successful. Besides, it was very hard for me to convince myself that loving someone—yes, a woman—was a bad thing, or a crime.

I decided to run to Lia. It was 1966, the Fall of my senior year in high school. I didn't care whether I finished school or not, since I was already flunking out. I got up early one morning, placing my small suitcase on the front porch, where it wouldn't be detected. As usual, only my dad was up. He was reading the *San Francisco Chronicle*, sipping coffee, spreading marmalade on his toast. After a quick breakfast, I told Dad "bye" and went out to wait for the city bus that would take me downtown. From there, I would transfer to another bus that would take me to the Oakland Greyhound depot. At the bus terminal, I bought a ticket for Eugene. My suitcase had just gotten loaded onto the Greyhound, and I was standing in line, waiting to board, when I saw my father walk into the depot. He came over to me.

"Let's go home," he said.

"No, Dad," I told him. "I don't want to. Mom hates me."

"I know," he answered. I seldom hugged my father, but I did that morning. I had never had a real talk with my father. This was as close as I would ever come to learning what he thought until, years later, after Mom had passed away, he confessed to me that he was going through sex reassignment surgery to become a woman.[2]

I went with him to his car and he drove me home. We didn't say anything. I was afraid to face my mom, who would be angry and upset with me for wanting to run away.

I was expected to graduate from Berkeley High that June of 1967. At the beginning of my last semester I went to my school counselor—something I had never done before—and asked him to assign me to a lower track. I felt that I might be able to improve my grades if I didn't have to work so hard for them. I hated being the stupid one in the "college prep" class, the one who failed exams, the "dumb Indian." Things at home were not good. There was constant turmoil: daily arguments, people yelling, screaming, crying. My older sister was running around with cowboys, going to bars, smoking. My mother disapproved, but at the same time loved the young men who hung around our house. She eventually invited my sister's boyfriend to live with us. She treated him like a son, did his laundry, ironed his shirts, bought him new Levis and boots. Even if I had been studious, our home conditions were so disruptive I would have had a hard time concentrating. But my tumultuous inner life kept me wary, unsettled, unfocused.

Despite mediocre grades, my ACT scores were respectable enough that I was accepted to a private college in Oregon, about an hour's drive from Eugene. I intended to major in music—I had played oboe for the past five years, studying with some fine musicians in the Bay Area. I had no car, so if Lia and I were to see one another, she would have to drive to where I was. One weekend in early November 1967, we arranged for her to pick me up, and Lia brought me to her place for a weekend. I'm not sure what we did, but the cheerfulness and lightness of our time together was gone. I was angry with Lia, but not able to understand why. Perhaps she was distant with me. Finally she told me that we couldn't see each other again, that she couldn't watch me suffer, that she was afraid my mother was driving me crazy, driving me to commit suicide. She didn't want to be accused, blamed, made to be responsible. Her decision devastated me. But it also made me aware of my own evasive and dishonest behavior, the ways I had to hide my feelings, lie about my thoughts, or pretend things I didn't feel. I had lost much of my playfulness; in fact, I was deeply depressed and unhappy, and had been for months.

I remember it was rainy and cold, already dark when I got back to my dorm room. It may have been around that time that I simply stopped going to classes. Soon after that the Dean of Women asked me to come talk with her. The Dean probed gently, perhaps wanting to know more about who I was, what I thought and felt. At first I hesitated then, even though I knew it was risky, finally confessed that I had just broken up with a woman I loved. I suppose I wanted this older woman to care about me enough not to judge me. Instead, the Dean lectured me, told me it was bizarre that I should have such strong feelings for this woman. I felt sick at heart, and when she suggested I see a therapist and said the college would pay for the first appointment, I decided to go. I somehow managed to get through the therapy session without discussing my feelings about Lia; I stuttered out other reasons for being miserable. The guy prescribed some pills for me. I took one, threw the rest down the toilet. I knew about electro-shock therapy, and was aware that if I were deemed "crazy," I might be a candidate for this kind of treatment. This depressed me even further.

I never went back to classes, and in December my dad drove to Oregon and packed up the car with my belongings and we headed back to Berkeley. I was bereft, of course, but could tell no one how I felt or why I felt as I did.

What's puzzling is that, while my mother may have distrusted Lia, who she felt may have "corrupted"

me, she sort of respected my friend too. She admired that Lia was a gifted artist, a hard worker, intelligent, and that she had what my mom called "independence of thought." That spring Lia wrote to inform me that she was joining the Peace Corps. She went overseas to Uganda. When she returned, a year or so later, she brought my mother strange, bright fabrics. My mother had sometimes found things for Lia, as well—one time a woven *rebozo* from Mexico, which Lia wore stylishly, like Frida Kahlo—another time a green wool plaid that she made into a skirt for Lia.

Later, after I had moved away from home, I went through a period of cutting myself, slicing my forearms, then a long period of heavy drinking to get drunk. Finally I tried to commit suicide, but couldn't go through with it. I was working on a ranch, again in Oregon, in the Columbia River gorge, a beautiful place with distant views of mountains, the timbered slopes of the Cascades, and wheat fields far to the east. I had had other girlfriends by then, but these relationships remained more or less clandestine; the word lesbian was almost never said aloud in reference to these romances. One lover had informed me that she could not bring me home because their parents hated Indians; another had made herself crazy by taking LSD almost daily.

What had drawn me back to that state? I loved that land, even though I could barely support myself when I lived there. I loved rain, deep rivers, damp forests, the wild beaches along the Pacific coast. Over the years, I disconnected from Lia. We stopped communicating, stopped seeing one another. I came home to Berkeley, and little by little, began to find language for my lesbianism, began to find ways to talk about being Indian. Eventually my mother changed her views as discourse about being Gay became more prevalent through the 1970s, and especially after Mom met a young Gay man named Robert Hillsborough, who became a friend. Mom was working as a seamstress for a new outdoor retail store called Mountain Traders. My mother had an interest in designing clothes, and Robert, who worked as a gardener for the city of San Francisco, had an interest in becoming a tailor. They bonded over this work.

Mom and Robert seemed to get along well; perhaps he found she was someone he could talk to about his dreams. He would sometimes come to our house for supper. Then one morning the news reported that Robert had been murdered, the result of a "gay-bashing" that took place outside a nightclub in the Mission District in San Francisco. It was 1977. Although it was a horrifying reminder of the danger of being "out" in a world that still hated and derided Gay people, I think this sad incident helped my mother to understand that Gays and Lesbians had a right to live openly and freely, without fear. In time, she decided to accept her "two-spirit" daughter and stopped insisting that I "pass" for straight. We forgave one another for the pain we had caused each other. Instead of having to remain a stranger to my family, I was somehow brought home, brought in, returned. It took many years.

As for Lia, in time I learned that she married an older man and seemed content in her life. Perhaps twenty years ago we reconnected. At Christmas she sends me one of her holiday newsletters, which includes descriptions of her many adventures in the outdoors: raft trips in Idaho, or winter camping in the Harney Basin in Southeastern Oregon, vast and open landscapes I remember from taking family road trips north. Sometimes, traveling through the sagebrush country in northern New Mexico, or southern

Colorado where I now live, I look northwest across a great landscape of mountains, and I imagine the extensive salt flats that were once an inland sea; the dry, lava plateau of the Snake River plain; the Great Basin lands full of juniper and sage, antelope, deer, migrating birds, stands of cottonwoods among the hills, the wide Columbia River and the Cascades. Inscribed in my mind is a map of those western lands that comprise my history and formed the bones, blood, and flesh of my traveling ancestors who settled in mountains, along rivers, in meadows. My spirit feels as wide as the blue sky arching overhead, and as mobile as the clouds pushed by strong winds. I am grateful that I met my first love in mountains, that she nurtured poetry and music in me, that she let me love her, and that she was—and remains—my friend.

NOTES

1. Concow is one variant among many. Other designations and spellings include Northwestern Maidu, Konkau, Konkow, and Koyangk'auwi.
2. I have told my father's story elsewhere: "My Father, Cynthia Conroy," *GLQ: A Journal of Lesbian and Gay Studies* 16(1–2), 2010, pp. 93–103.

42. THE FUTURE OF FAT SEX
FRANCIS RAY WHITE (2016)

Obesity can sink your sex life. (*USA Today*, 2010)

Tough love: obese women have less satisfying sex lives than cancer survivors. (*Daily Mail*, 2011)

Obese have worse sexual health despite less sex. (Kelland, 2010)

Infertility crisis looms in the west as obesity levels soar. (Curtis, 2007)

If these stories are to be believed, being fat is chronically bad for your sex life. How much you're getting (if any), how satisfying it is and how likely it is to lead to conception on the one hand, or infection on

the other, can all now be predicted from your body mass index (BMI). Even the UK government agrees. In one of its recent Change4Life public health advertisements (Department of Health, 2011), a brightly coloured Claymation figure called Alfie laments the slide from a slim 'Jack the lad' to 'Jack the rather porky middle-aged bloke'. A literal spare tyre (complete with tread-marks) has grown around Alfie's middle and moving about has become a struggle. 'It's harder getting up the stairs,' Alfie says, 'or up to anything else for that matter.' Anything else being sex. We see Alfie in a bedroom, a rose clenched between the teeth enthusiastically lunging towards a female figure, also sporting the telltale spare tyre. At the moment of contact their tyres repel, bouncing the figures to opposite sides of the room. Fat sex is rendered an impossibility, fat people marked as fucking failures.

The idea that 'obesity can sink your sex life', as *USA Today* so succinctly puts it, or that putting on weight will impair one's ability to have 'sex', positions fat people negatively in relation to a hegemonic model of sexual 'success' which assumes certain (hetero) normative standards of sexual desire, function and reproductivity which originate largely in medical discourses (Tiefer, 2004: 9–12). It is no coincidence then that recent media interest in the 'failing' sex lives of fat people also draws on medical and scientific research which is then disseminated in media news reports and drawn on in public health campaigns such as Change4Life. It is this medical research which will form the focus of this article. By far the greatest attention in the medical literature on obesity has been on attempts to establish clear links between obesity and various co-morbidities (cancer, type II diabetes, cardiovascular disease), the result of which has been the increasing pathologization of fat people and an intensification of stigmatization in the search for 'cures' to the problem of obesity (see Gard and Wright, 2005 and Saguy, 2013 for developed critiques of the medicalization of obesity). It is within this context that research into the supposed effects of raised BMI on sexual behaviour, sexual functioning and human reproduction/fertility has become a significant and persistent sub-field of obesity science. However, little attention has been paid thus far to this research in critical studies of the obesity 'epidemic' or in fat studies.

The aim of this article is to analyze how fat sex is constructed in a small sample of articles from medical journals, in order to examine how it is produced as a kind of 'failure'. It will attempt to explore the discourses that make this production possible, including those of the obesity 'epidemic' and the medicalization of both fatness and sexual function. Rather than simply attempting to disavow the association of fat sex with failure, the later discussion will draw on antisocial queer theory, and in particular the work of Lee Edelman (2004) and Judith Jack Halberstam (2011) in order to rethink the meaning of fat sex within "reproductive futurism" (the future-oriented, heteronormative social order). Antisocial queer theory provides a particularly rich and apt frame in which to do this and not only allows for a reconceptualization of fat sex as queer, but also offers new avenues for resistance and subversion that may be meaningful to ongoing fat political projects.

THE CONSTRUCTION OF FAILURE

The analysis was conducted using a sample of 25 articles from medical journals published in the past decade (2004–2014). The journals were all peer-reviewed publications from the UK or USA specializing in publishing clinical research in the medical subfields of obesity, reproduction, obstetrics, gynaecology, diabetes, vascular disease, impotence, urology, behavioural science and family and sex therapy. Articles were selected for the sample that reported on or reviewed research on the connection between obesity and sexual relationships, sexual function, sexual behaviour, or reproduction. Because of the large amount of research in the latter area, articles on reproduction have been limited to those concerned with fertility, conception and pregnancy. To attempt to engage with the immense discourse on, for example, parenting while obese and childhood obesity is beyond the scope of this article, though these issues have been analyzed to great effect elsewhere in the fat studies literature (see for example, Boero, 2009; McNaughten, 2011).

. . .

Following selection, the articles were categorized into two central themes. The first comprised research on sexual behaviour, sexual (dys)function and sexual quality of life (n = 15). Of these articles only three explicitly refuted the association between weight and lesser sexual function. The second category covered the multiple issues around reproduction (n = 10). Within each of the categories the individual articles cover a wide range of issues. Those in the sexual behaviour, (dys)function and sexual quality of life group explore the possible correlations between overweight and obesity and perceived sexual attractiveness, rates and frequency of sexual relationships/activity (particularly (hetero)sexual intercourse), sexual desire, arousal, performance and satisfaction and a range of more medicalized sexual 'disorders' such as erectile dysfunction, female sexual dysfunction, vaginismus and dyspareunia (see Bajos et al., 2010; Brody, 2004; Esposito et al., 2008; Kolotkin et al., 2006; Larsen et al., 2008; Østbye et al., 2011).

The research reported in these studies is inconclusive and subject to numerous methodological and interpretive limitations. However, often despite the evidence of their own data, the authors of many of these studies still succeed in discursively producing fat people's sex lives as failure. Østbye et al.'s (2011) study of 'sexual functioning in obese adults' is one such example. Like many studies, it begins with the hypothesis that, 'increasing BMI would be associated with decreased sexual functioning' (2011: 226), and sets out to investigate it using a 'Sexual Functioning Questionnaire' (SFQ) originally developed for cancer survivors. The results show varying, though not particularly striking, degrees of difference in the sexual functioning of obese participants, and Østbye reports that, "although we hypothesized that higher BMIs would be associated with reduced sexual functioning, there was little decrease in SFQ with increasing BMI, especially after adjustment for covariates" (2011: 232).

However, further down the same page these findings appear to be contradicted when Østbye claims that "our findings *support* a growing body of research that indicates that obesity is associated with reduced sexual functioning or sexual quality of life for men and women" (2011: 232, emphasis added). Hence, despite a disproved hypothesis and some rather underwhelming findings further tempered by a range of mitigating factors, Østbye produces fat sex as failed. This is subsequently reinforced through the novel comparison between the sexual functioning of the obese study participants and that of a group of cancer survivors—the comparison that made the headline of the *Daily Mail*'s coverage of this research (2011). No rationale is given for why this comparison might be a meaningful one, but it has the discursive effect of further associating fatness with disease and malfunction and reinforces the legitimacy/necessity of medical intervention into fat people's sex lives.

The selective reporting of findings in both the articles themselves and media coverage of them is common to several of the other studies analyzed. Bajos et al.'s (2010) study of the sexual behaviour of 12,000 men and women in France, for example, was widely reported in the news media as having found that obese people have 'less sex' (Cheng, 2010; *Daily Mail*, 2010; *Daily Telegraph*, 2010; Kelland, 2010; *USA Today*, 2010). What the study itself reports is less clear-cut. It found that single obese women were less likely to report a sexual partner in the past year, but were "as likely as normal weight women to be living with a sexual partner" (Bajos et al., 2010: 3). Obese men were less likely to report having more than one sexual partner in the past year, but the rates of having at least one, or living with a sexual partner were not significantly different from men with a 'normal' BMI (2010: 3).

Of course, findings like these do not make good headlines; however it is notable that in Bajos' article the findings that associate irregular sexual behaviour or functioning with overweight or obesity are highlighted whilst discussion of other correlations visible in the data is absent. For example, the various tables of data reproduced in the article show that men in the underweight category are the least likely to have had sex in the previous month, experience premature ejaculation and lack of sexual desire three times more frequently than obese men, and reported the lowest rates of sexual satisfaction of all groups (Bajos et al., 2010: 4–5). Despite their apparent significance, these findings are not discussed in the report nor the media coverage of it, thus presenting obesity as the only weight-related factor relevant to sexual behaviour and function.

Given the work done in the articles on sexual behaviour and (dys)function to produce the idea that fat people's sex lives are pretty much nonexistent, it is something of a paradox that there is simultaneously such a wide literature on obesity and reproduction, suggesting that at least some fat people do manage to successfully enter into (hetero)sexual relationships. However, the focus of the articles dealing with reproduction construct a new sphere of fat sexual failure as they attempt to posit obesity as a cause of subfertility, increased time to conception, anovulation, reduced sperm quality and quantity, reduced egg and uterine quality (fat women have 'inhospitable' uteruses—see Luke et al., 2011; Mahmood, 2009; Rittenberg et al., 2011) and a whole host of pregnancy and childbirth-related problems such as: gestational diabetes, pre-eclampsia, thromboembolic disease, miscarriage, neonatal mortality, premature birth, caesarean, postpartum haemorrhage, difficulties using ultrasound, increased in-patient admission, neural tube defects, larger or small neonates and maternal death (Mahmood, 2009; Metwally et al., 2007; Ramsey et al., 2006).

As with the articles on sexual behaviour and (dys)function, the studies of obesity and reproduction are subject to varying degrees of conclusiveness. Although there seems to be some certainty that high(er) BMI does have a negative effect on reproductive success for both men and women, the reasons why this might be remain largely unknown, and the articles invariably include a call for further research to be conducted. The other major similarity between the two categories of article is their endorsement of weight loss as *the* solution to the entire range of sex-related problems 'caused' by obesity. Weight loss is advocated in all of the articles analyzed on reproduction, despite a professed lack of evidence that it will have a beneficial effect.

. . .

Weight loss is also advocated in 12 of the 15 articles in the sexual behaviour and (dys)function category. Esposito et al., for example, expound at length on the possible benefits of physical exercise and a Mediterranean diet for improving sexual function in women (2008: 363), despite having earlier stated that "evidence linking FSD [female sexual dysfunction] to obesity is very scanty" (2008: 361). Perhaps it is the unswerving belief the articles display in the curative power of weight loss that most strongly constructs fat sex as failure. The 'solvable' problem is not sexual dysfunction, or infertility per se, but fatness, and in recommending it be removed from the equation the articles make clear their prescription for successful sex: don't be fat.

. . .

CRITIQUING FAILURE

From a critical fat studies perspective the sample articles present a highly problematic account of the relationship between fatness and sex. The following

discussion will elaborate a possible critique of the assumptions and knowledges underpinning the discursive production of fat sex as failure. To begin, it seems almost too obvious to note that the sample articles approach obesity from within a medical framework. However, it is this that fundamentally shapes why the articles are produced at all, as well as how they contextualize the problems and solutions they identify. All but three of the articles in the sample contain an explicit reference to population-wide increases in obesity or the obesity 'epidemic'. These references function to rationalize the research being conducted/discussed and operate to preclude the need for any further explanation of the value or necessity of that research.

. . .

Implicit in fat studies critiques . . . is an understanding of the obesity epidemic as a kind of moral panic that operates to intensify social control and the stigmatization of fat people (see Campos et al., 2006; Gard and Wright, 2005). The endorsement of weight loss in the articles can be seen as part of this process wherein responsibility (or more often blame) for sexual function or fertility is placed on the individual. What makes the continued recommendation of weight loss in the sample articles even more problematic is the absence of any [of] the counter-literature that presents evidence of the failure of most weight-loss attempts long term and questions its benefits to health (see for example Aphramor, 2005). Similarly, Hanne Blank's ground-breaking fat-positive sex guide *Big Big Love* (2011) raises issues around weight loss and sex that are completely neglected in the sample articles. Blank argues that "dieting is likely to be bad for your sex life" (2011: 47) because of the stress and anxiety it causes and the physical effects of under-nutrition which are documented to lower libido. This is aside from the general observation that, "dieters can become obsessive, tedious, and boring" (2011: 49)—presumably something that would be problematic for both the dieter and their (potential) sexual partner(s).

Blank's assertions not only challenge the medical opinion that weight loss will improve sexual functioning, but also highlight some methodological questions about the studies reported on in the articles. Some of the studies explicitly recruit their participants through hospital-based weight-loss programmes

(Kadioglu et al., 2010; Kolotkin et al., 2008; Østbye et al., 2011) but do not discuss the impact of this on their findings. The majority do not report on the dieting status of their participants at all, with the exception of one study which compared the sexual quality of life of two groups engaged in medically supervised weight loss with a group of non-treatment seeking obese control subjects (Kolotkin et al., 2006). Results showed the control group experienced less 'impairment' in sexual quality of life, though the reasons for this are not discussed. This is typical of the sample articles' tendency not to consider social factors in relation to sexual behaviour, as Aphramor and Blank imply. Hence, a separate study by Kolotkin that did find weight loss improved the sex lives of a sample population, did not explain *why* this happened given that at the end of the study, participants' BMIs were still in the 'obese' range, and some had regained some of their original weight (2008: 490).

The same neglect of social factors cannot be said of Jeannine Gailey's (2012) study of fat women's sexual and dating experiences. Gailey interviewed 36 women who had had some involvement in the US size acceptance movement and found their sexual confidence and satisfaction improved as a result. This is credited to changes in how the women viewed their bodies—a shift from 'shame' to 'pride' (2012: 122—123). Gailey argues: "women who accept their bodies, or are beginning to, not only experience freedom from the pressure to diet or change their bodies, but also the freedom to be sexual" (2012: 124). However, perhaps what is most striking about Gailey's study are the accounts given by the women of disrespectful or abusive relationships, sexual ridicule, fetishization, dehumanization, lack of self-worth and absence of sexual agency that characterized their sex lives prior to any involvement in size acceptance politics. These are aspects of fat sex related to stigmatization and fatphobia. From a fat studies perspective this is crucial to understanding fat people's sex lives, yet it is only considered in a minority of the sample articles and even then in rather limited ways (Bajos et al., 2010; Chen and Brown, 2005; Halpern et al., 2005; Swami and Tovée, 2009).

. . .

. . . The discussion thus far has attended only to questions around weight while the larger problem

with medical research may be not its inconclusive results or inadequate methodologies, but rather the models of sexual 'function' and 'normality' it operates with. Historically, medically defined sexual function/dysfunction has been understood in terms of Masters and Johnson's human sexual response cycle, a framework feminist sexologist Leonore Tiefer considers to be mechanistic and biologically reductionist as well as overly focused on genital functioning (or not) during/for sexual intercourse (Tiefer, 2004). Tiefer argues that "full genital performance during heterosexual intercourse is the essence of sexual functioning, which excludes and demotes nongenital possibilities for pleasure and expression" (2004: 55). Moreover, although Tiefer does not "doubt that many (most? all?) human bodies can produce genital vasocongestion and orgasm," there is little to justify the claim that "absence of these features constitutes a 'disorder'" (Tiefer, 2004: 190). Yet, this is how disorder is constituted, despite the absence of any acknowledgement of the interpersonal and social factors affecting sexual behaviour and activity or a widely agreed standard for measuring 'function' or 'dysfunction' (Tiefer, 2004: 192).[1]

This is the model of sexual (dys)function reflected in the medical articles analyzed. 'Sexual behaviour', when it is quantified at all, equates to heterosexual intercourse (Bajos et al., 2010; Brody, 2004; Kaneshiro, 2008). Nowhere is this more apparent than in Brody's study of the correlation between slimness and greater frequency of intercourse (2004). Brody states unequivocally that "there are many differences between penile-vaginal intercourse and other sexual activities, with only the former being associated with indices of better physical and psychological health" (2004: 252). Further, despite not actually surveying any people whose BMI would put them in the obese category, Brody is able to claim by the end of the analysis that "this study provides yet another example of an index of better health (slimness) being positively and specifically associated with frequency of penile-vaginal intercourse" (2004: 259). The disturbing hetero-superiority of this argument hardly needs further comment here. Suffice to say that by establishing such a narrow parameter for (fat) sexual success, Brody manages to produce a wide range of potential failures.

QUEER FAILURE

. . .

Even fat heterosexual sex is queered in the medical articles, effected ironically via the erasure of homosexual sexuality from the studies. The majority of studies simply fail to mention the existence of non-heterosexuals. One gathered data on the sexual orientation of participants, but deemed the sample too small to be significant (Bajos et al., 2010: 6) and another merely 'assumed' the majority of its participants would be heterosexual (Chen and Brown, 2005). Elsewhere there is an entire(ly heterosexual) sub-field dedicated to studying the links between marriage and weight (Sobal and Hanson, 2011). As previously discussed, all of the articles in the sample operate within a particular biologically rooted, genitally centred model of sexual function which defines heterosexual intercourse *as* sex. The effect of erasing non-heterosexual sex serves to further establish this as *the* standard of sexuality so that not only homosexual but also non-normative heterosexual practices are ranked beneath it. This also explains why in the rare instances that sexual activity that is not penis-in-vagina sex is mentioned, fat people are reported as doing it more often. Brody (2004) claims a higher BMI is linked with more frequent masturbation. Bajos reports that fat people are more likely to have seen a pornographic film in the past 12 months, met their partner online, have an also-obese partner or to have engaged in 'risky' sexual behaviour (2010: 4–6). In each case these differences are reported as evidence of disorder and of fat people's failure to live up to a mythical model of sexual success.

Fat people's divergence from the heterosexual gold standard also manifests in the medical discourse via the construction of fat gender as less than fully binary. The articles on fertility frequently reiterate the idea that obesity alters 'natural' gender through references to the 'elevated oestrogen levels' (Kay and Barratt, 2009: 238) and 'decreased levels of testosterone' (Shayeb and Bhattacharya, 2009: 7) in overweight and obese men and to 'ovarian androgen secretion' (Ramsey et al., 2006: 1159) or 'hyperandrogenism' (Metwally et al., 2007: 516) in women. While these references are to gendered characteristics

operating at the hormonal level, they strongly insinuate fat men and women's failure to produce the sexual dimorphism required for successful (reproductive) heterosexuality. One article goes even further. In a scenario reminiscent of Emily Martin's classic feminist restaging of 'the sperm and the egg' as a patriarchal fertilization narrative (1991), Binder (2012) constructs what might be read as the story of the 'fat sperm and the egg'.

In a study investigating the 'functional effect of male obesity on sperm quality' (Binder et al., 2012: 2), mice were fed a high fat diet said to "emulate a Western-style fast food diet" (2012: 2) before their sperm was used to fertilize an egg. Results showed that "male obesity negatively affects sperm function, reducing its ability to generate a competent embryo capable of developing into a viable offspring" (2012: 2). The image conjured here of the incompetent, incapable and generally ineffectual fat sperm is not only suspiciously reminiscent of the worst stereotypes of obese people as lazy and stupid, but emphasizes how far from the model of virile hegemonic masculinity fat men are. To further compound these associations, when Binder's research was reported in the media it was under the title "men need to be 'match fit' to conceive" (*Daily Telegraph*, 2012)—the sporting metaphor here reinforcing fat men's distance from heteronormative gender.

This is not the only example of the way, as Gailey notes, "weight is connected to the heteronormative system of meaning and value that constitutes what it means to be feminine or masculine" (2012: 116; see also Graves and Kwan, 2012). It is also connected to the shape of gender difference within heterosexual couples where the female partner is expected to be smaller than the male (Blank, 2011: 15). Moreover, the physicality of fatness can work to prevent the achievement of certain kinds of symbolically heterosexual body configurations. . . .

The sheer volume of medical literature on obesity and its role, or not, in fertility, conception and pregnancy perhaps speaks to the perceived threat(s) fat sex poses to the possibility of a future, namely in the form of an 'infertility crisis' (Curtis, 2007). The literature on fertility is, somewhat ironically, littered with references to death. Not only are there invariably references to the health consequences associated with obesity, most often conjuring the spectre of (mass) death as obesity rates rise throughout the population over time, but sex and death are inextricably linked in discussions of maternal, foetal and neonatal death. While this is nihilistic enough, the prospect of a more apocalyptic social death is also raised via warnings that when fat people do reproduce, their offspring will be susceptible to more disease, obesity, infertility and early mortality. As Mahmood puts it, "maternal death is just the tip of the iceberg" (2009: 19). Luke elaborates the lurid long-term scenario in more detail:

> The excess reproductive morbidity associated with obesity may increase with longer duration, making the current trends among children and young adults particularly critical in terms of their future reproductive potential . . . Recent findings from the Study of Women's Health Across the Nation indicate that adolescent obesity is associated with a 3-fold increased risk of lifetime nulliparity and a 4-fold increased risk of lifetime nulligravidity. (Luke et al., 2011: 245–246)

Not only are fat people reproductive failures in the present, but any offspring they do bring forth will only hasten the degenerative downfall of the human race. The only thing fat people succeed in doing in this scenario, is breeding a next generation of even bigger failures.

. . .

CONCLUSION: THE FUTURE OF FAT SEX

The future for fat sex imagined in the medicalized discourses of the obesity 'epidemic' is a depressingly bleak one. Not only is fat sex not happening often enough in the 'right' kinds of ways with the 'right' kinds of outcomes, but it is only going to get worse as more people get fatter. At heart, fatness and sex are incompatible, leaving would-be fat lovers like Alfie from the Change4Life video with only two possible choices: lose weight or die a swift, sexless death.

In this context it is valuable to articulate a thorough understanding of how fat sex is being pathologized, how it is being 'artifactually' (Guthman, 2013) produced as a public health concern and how this in turn intensifies both the surveillance and stigmatization of fat people. It is crucial that fat people construct

their own knowledge of fat sex (e.g. Blank, 2011). However, if this work is done and it succeeds only in producing a new model of sexual success (and hence a new class of fucking failures) it is unclear that the future would be any different from the present.

While I have argued in this article for the usefulness of antisocial queer theory and its call to 'embrace negativity', translating this into action is less straightforward. It can appear churlish, if not irresponsible, to 'celebrate failure' if that entails tolerating sexual frustration, bad or abusive sex, body shame or the inability to conceive a child, if that is what one desires. If this were all that antisocial queer politics could offer its value would certainly be questionable. Happily, it has the potential to offer more. The point is not to accept failure, but to reimagine it, to "recognize failure as a way of refusing to acquiesce to dominant logics of power and discipline and as a form of critique" (Halberstam, 2011: 88). It does not mean accepting things the way they are, but forging alternatives that do not reproduce the measures of 'success' or 'failure' that characterize the past and present of fat sex.

NOTE

1. See also Adolfsson et al., 2004; Kadioglu et al., 2010; Kolotkin et al., 2006; Larsen et al., 2008; Østbye et al., 2011 for the range of scales used to measure elusive sexual 'satisfaction'.

REFERENCES

Adolfsson B, et al. (2004) Are sexual dissatisfaction and sexual abuse associated with obesity? A population-based study. *Obesity Research* 12(10): 1702–1709.

Aphramor L (2005) Is a weight-centred health framework salutogenic? Some thoughts on unhinging certain dietary ideologies. *Social Theory & Health* 3: 315–340.

Bajos N et al. (2010) Sexuality and obesity, a gender perspective: Results from French national random probability survey of sexual behaviours. *BMJ* 340. Available at: http://www.bmj.com/content/340/bmj.c2573 (accessed 29 June 2013).

Binder NK, et al. (2012) Paternal diet-induced obesity retards early mouse embryo development, mitochondrial activity and pregnancy health. *PLoS ONE* 7(12): e52304 1–10.

Blank H (2011) *Big Big Love: A Sex and Relationships Guide for People of Size (and Those Who Love Them)*. New York, NY: Celestial Arts.

Boero N (2009) Fat kids, working moms, and the "epidemic of obesity": Race, class, and mother blame. In: Rothblum E and Solovay S (eds) *The Fat Studies Reader*. New York, NY: New York University Press, pp. 113–119.

Brody S (2004) Slimness is associated with greater intercourse and lesser masturbation frequency. *Journal of Sex and Marital Therapy* 30(4): 251–261.

Campos P, et al. (2006) The epidemiology of overweight and obesity: Public health crisis or moral panic? *International Journal of Epidemiology* 35(1): 55–60.

Chen E and Brown M (2005) Obesity stigma in sexual relationships. *Obesity Research* 13(8): 1393–1397.

Cheng M (2010) Being obese raises the risk of sexual problems. Available at http://www.guardian.co.uk/world/feedarticle/9129139 (accessed 29 June 2013).

Curtis P (2007) Infertility crisis looms in the west as obesity levels soar. Available at: http://www.guardian.co.uk/society/2007/aug/24/health.healthandwellbeing (accessed 29 June 2013).

Daily Mail (2011) Tough love: obese women have less satisfying sex lives than cancer survivors. Available at: http://www.dailymail.co.uk/news/article-1383593/Obese-people-satisfying-sex-lives-researchers-find.html (accessed 29 June 2013).

Daily Telegraph (2010) Obese women have less sex but more accidental pregnancies. Available at: http://www.telegraph.co.uk/news/7829743/Obese-women-have-less-sex-but-more-accidental-pregnancies.html?fb (accessed 29 June 2013).

Daily Telegraph (2012) Overweight men warned they need to become "match fit" if they want to be fathers. Available at: http://www.telegraph.co.uk/health/healthnews/9503465/Overweight-men-warned-they-need-to-become-match fit if they want to be fathers.html?fb (accessed 29 June 2013).

Department of Health (2011) Alfie. *Change4Life*. Available at: http://www.nhs.uk/video/Pages/change-for-life-alfie.aspx?searchtype=Tag&searchterm=About+the+NHS&offset=49& (accessed 29 June 2013).

Edelman L (2004) *No Future: Queer Theory and the Death Drive*. Durham, NC: Duke University Press.

Esposito K, et al. (2008) Obesity and sexual dysfunction, male and female. *International Journal of Impotence Research* 20: 358–365.

Gailey JA (2012) Fat shame to fat pride: Fat women's sexual and dating experiences. *Fat Studies: An Interdisciplinary Journal of Body Weight and Society* 1(1): 114–127.

Gard M and Wright J (2005) *The Obesity Epidemic: Science Morality and Ideology*. London: Routledge.

Graves JL and Kwan S (2012) Is there really "More to Love"? Gender, body and relationship scripts in romance-based reality television. *Fat Studies: An Interdisciplinary Journal of Body Weight and Society* 1(1): 47–60.

Guthman J (2013) Fatuous measures: The artifactual construction of the obesity epidemic. *Critical Public Health* 23(3): 263–273.

Halberstam J (2011) *The Queer Art of Failure*. Durham, NC: Duke University Press.

Halpern C, et al. (2005) Body mass index, dieting romance, and sexual activity in adolescent girls: Relationships over time. *Journal of Research on Adolescence* 15(4): 535–559.

Kadioglu P, et al. (2010) Obesity might not be a risk factor for female sexual dysfunction. *British Journal of Urology International (BJUI)* 106: 1357–1361.

Kaneshiro B (2008) Body mass index and sexual behavior. *Obstetrics and Gynecology* 112(3): 586–592.

Kay V and Barratt CLR (2009) Male obesity: Impact on fertility. *British Journal of Diabetes and Vascular Disease* 9(5): 237–241.

Kelland K (2010) Obese have worse sexual health despite less sex. Available at: http://www.reuters.com/article/2010/06/15/us-obesity-sex-idUSTRE65E6LC20100615 (accessed 29 June 2013).

Kolotkin R, et al. (2006) Obesity and sexual quality of life. *Obesity* 14(3): 472–479.

Kolotkin R, et al. (2008) Improvements in sexual quality of life after moderate weight loss. *International Journal of Impotence Research* 20: 487–492.

Larsen SH, et al. (2008) Sexual function and obesity. *International Journal of Obesity* 31: 1189–1198.

Luke B, et al. (2011) Female obesity adversely affects assisted reproductive technology (ART) pregnancy and live birth rates. *Human Reproduction* 26(1): 245–252.

Mahmood TA (2009) Review: Obesity and pregnancy: An obstetrician's view. *British Journal of Diabetes and Vascular Disease* 9(1): 19–22.

Martin E (1991) The egg and the sperm: How science has constructed a romance based on stereotypical male-female roles. *Signs* 16(3): 485–501.

McNaughten D (2011) From the womb to the tomb: Obesity and maternal responsibility. *Critical Public Health* 21(2): 179–190.

Metwally M, et al. (2007) The impact of obesity on female reproductive function. *Obesity Reviews* 8: 515–523.

National Center for Transgender Equality (2015) https://www.transequality.org/sites/default/files/docs/USTS-Full-Report-FINAL.PDF

Østbye T, et al. (2011) Sexual functioning in obese adults enrolling in a weight loss study. *Journal of Sex and Marital Therapy* 37(3): 224–235.

Ramsey J, et al. (2006) ABC of obesity: Obesity and reproduction. *BMJ* 333: 1159–1162.

Rittenberg V, et al. (2011) Influence of BMI on risk of miscarriage after single blastocyst transfer. *Human Reproduction* 26(10): 2642–2650.

Saguy A (2013) *What's Wrong With Fat?* Oxford: Oxford University Press.

Shayeb AG and Bhattacharya S (2009) Review: Male obesity and reproductive potential. *British Journal of Diabetes and Vascular Disease* 9(1): 7–12.

Sobal J and Hanson KL (2011) Marital status, marital history, body weight, and obesity. *Marriage and Family Review* 47(7): 474–504.

Swami V and Tovée MJ (2009) Big beautiful women: The body size preferences of male fat admirers. *Journal of Sex Research* 46(1): 89–96.

Tiefer L (2004) *Sex Is Not a Natural Act and Other Essays.* Boulder, CO: Westview Press.

USA Today (2010) Obesity can sink your sex life. Available at: http://usatoday30.usatoday.com/news/health/weightloss/2010-06-16-obese-sex_N.htm (accessed 29 June 2013).

43. QUEERING BLACK FEMALE HETEROSEXUALITY

KIMBERLY SPRINGER (2008)

How can black women say yes to sex when our religious institutions, public policy, home lives, media, musical forms, schools, and parents discuss black women's sexuality only as a set of negative consequences? When mentioned at all, the words I recall most associated with black female sexuality were edicts against being "too fast." "Oooh, that girl know she fas'!" my aunty would tut as the neighborhood "bad girl" swished on by. Just looking too long at a boy could provoke the reprimand "Girl, stop being so fas'." Notably, it was only us girls who were in danger of being labeled "fast." Women in church, passing through the hairdressers, and riding by in cars with known playas were simply dismissed. They were already gone; "respectable" women uttered "jezebel" in their wake. The culture that's embedded in these subtle and not-so-subtle passing judgments tries to take away my right to say yes to sex by making me feel like if I do, I'm giving in to centuries of stereotypes of the sexually lascivious black woman.

Public assumptions about black female sexuality mirror the contradiction we deal with daily: hypersexual or asexual. We use silence as a strategy to combat negative talk. Perhaps if we do not speak about black women and sex, the whole issue will go away? After all, for centuries black women tried to escape sexual scrutiny by passing unnoticed through white America as nurturing mammies. It's the nasty jezebels who give black people a bad name, and it's Mammy's duty to keep those fast women in check. The mammy and jezebel caricatures were forged in the complex and perverse race relations of the post–Civil War South.

. . .

After slavery, though black women were no longer needed to supply offspring for sale, persistent racial and economic segregation required the jezebel image. Perpetuating the myth of black women as hypersexual served to set white women on a pedestal and excuse white men's rape of black women. If black women were always ready and willing sexual partners, it was impossible to have sex with them against their will. . . .

Black female sexuality in pop culture has not moved very far from these stereotypes. What better place to see this continued history of the asexual mammy than in the films of Queen Latifah? Whether she's *Bringin' Down the House* or having a *Last Holiday*, she's the queen of teaching white people how to be more human at the expense of her own sexuality, save the improbably chaste and deferred romance with a hottie like LL Cool J.

. . .

As sociologist Patricia Hill Collins points out in her book *Black Sexual Politics*, the more things change, the more they remain the same. Collins describes the continuous link between the mammy and a contemporary image of the "black lady." Stereotypes about black women's sexuality have met with resistance, particularly among middle-class blacks in the nineteenth century who advocated racial uplift and self-determination. Proving that blacks could be good citizens required silence about sexuality and sexual pleasure. Between respectability and silence, black women found little space to determine who they were as sexual beings. Black women might never be "true ladies" capable of withdrawing from the workplace and into the home and motherhood. The realities of racism and sexism in terms of wages and employment meant that black families needed two incomes long before white Americans needed or wanted double paychecks. Still, though most black women had to work, they could endeavor to be respectable and asexual. Respectable black women were professionals, good mothers, dutiful daughters, and loyal wives. Each role depended on their being traditionally married and in a nuclear family. Most certainly, one was not a loose woman.

Just as nineteenth-century black leaders advocated respectability, modern-day public policies that belittle black women as "welfare queens," "hoochie mamas," and "black bitches" work to control and define the parameters of black women's sexuality. If black women's sexuality—particularly poor and working-class black women's sexuality—is routinely described as the root of social ills, then once again black women are left with little room to maneuver if they want respect

in America's classrooms, boardrooms, and religious sanctuaries. Collins claims that the ideal of the "black lady" is what black women have to achieve if they want to avoid undesirable labels like "bitchy," "promiscuous," and "overly fertile."

The nonsexual black lady has become a staple in television and film. She wears judicial robes (Judges Mablean Ephriam and Lynn Toler of *Divorce Court*), litigates with stern looks (district attorney Renee Radick in *Ally McBeal*), is a supermom who seems to rarely go to the office (Claire Huxtable on *The Cosby Show*), delegates homicides (Lieutenant Anita Van Buren in *Law and Order*), and ministers to a predominantly white, middle-class female audience (Oprah Winfrey).

. . .

Today in black communities, women's communities, the hiphop community, and popular culture, the main way of viewing black female sexuality is as victimized or deviant. No one could have anticipated the proliferation of the black woman-as-whore image in a new mass-media age that is increasingly the product of black decision makers. Fans and detractors these days uncritically call women who perform in music videos "hoes," "ho's," or "hoez." No matter how it's spelled, the intent is still the same: to malign black women who use their bodies in sexual ways. An equal-opportunity sexist might claim, "Video hoes aren't only black—there are Asian hoes, white hoes, Latin hoes, all kinds of hoes!" How very exciting and magnanimous—an age of racial equality when little girls of any race can be called hoes.

They wear very little clothing (it might be generous to call a thong "clothing"). The camera shots are either from above (for the best view of silicone breasts) or zoomed in (for a close-up on butts). And the butts! They jiggle! They quake! They make the beat go *boom*, papi!

. . .

Jezebel has become a video ho, video honey, or video vixen—depending on your consumer relationship to the women who participate in making music videos.

There are also female rappers willing to play the jezebel role to get ahead in the game. As Collins and others observe, they have added another stereotype to the mix: the Sapphire. Sapphire is loud and bitchy.

She is abusive to black men and authority figures, especially her employer. Embodied in raunchy rappers like Lil' Kim, Trina, and Foxy Brown, this combination Jezebel/Sapphire is hot and always ready for sex . . . but she just might rip your dick off in the process. Is this empowerment?

Listening to people debate black women's sexualized participation in rap music videos, but seeing asexual black women only on film and television, what's a girl to do? Young black girls and teenagers are aspiring to be well-paid pole dancers. Black women, such as Melanie in the CW's sitcom *The Game*, think that the only way to attract and keep their man is to adopt a position of "stripper chic," which means clinging comically to a newly installed pole in the living room. Black female heterosexuality seems to move deeper and deeper into unhealthy territory that is less about personal satisfaction and more about *men's satisfaction*.

This acquiescence is akin to a nationwide black don't ask/don't tell policy. In her documentary film *Silence: In Search of Black Female Sexuality in America* (2004), director Mya B asks young black women how they learned about sex. They all give a similar, familiar answer: not in my parents' house.

. . .

There is, of course, an intergenerational aspect to silence around discussions of sexuality that cuts across race and ethnicity. Puritanical views on sexuality are not confined by race. In the case of the black community, however, our silence is further enforced by traumatic intersections of race, sexuality, and often violence. In other words, there are nuances to silence that will take more than merely urging openness in dialogue between mothers and daughters to address. Ending this silence around sexuality needs to be more than telling girls how not to get pregnant or catch STDs. Speaking about black women's sexuality today should be as much about pleasure as it is about resistance to denigration.

This "damned if you do, damned if you don't" approach to black women's sexuality is a *crisis situation*. It might not have Beyoncé ringin' the alarm, but until black women find a way to talk openly and honestly about our private sexual practices, the terms of black female sexuality will always be determined

by everyone but black women. The women in the videos are merely the emissaries delivering a skewed message.

Also of urgent concern is black women's acceptance of negative representations of our sexuality. Is the disavowal that we are not like the video hoes on our screens any better than silence? Is even accepting the term "video ho" resignation that the insult is here to stay? Postmodern sexuality theorist Michel Foucault wrote about how people will serve as their own surveillance by policing their own thoughts and actions. Our silence about our sexuality becomes the border that we must not cross if we too want to assume the role of the black lady. Racism, sexism, classism, and heterosexism are the sentinels on that border, but there is very little for these guardians to do when we keep ourselves within the designated zone with our own silence or condemnation of other women. There are women, increasingly young women, who believe that if they do not behave in sexually promiscuous ways, they will be exempt from public scorn. Unfortunately, that is not the case. Just as we can all take a bit of pride in Oprah's achievements, we also are all implicated in the mockery and contempt heaped upon Janet Jackson. Clearly, the strategies we've used since the end of slavery have not worked. What have we been doing? Being silent in an effort to resist the normalization of deviant representations of black female sexuality is a failed tactic.

. . .

In 1982 at Barnard College, a controversial conference, 'Towards a Politics of Sexuality," exposed the tensions and anxieties inherent in wrestling with sexuality. Coming out of the conference was a key book, *Pleasure and Danger: Exploring Female Sexuality*, edited by Carol Vance. Vance asks questions in her introduction that remain, for me, unanswered: "Can women be sexual actors? Can we act on our own behalf? Or are we purely victims?" When applied to women of color, these questions become even more pressing, given that our sexuality is what is used as the dark specter to keep white women in line. Can black women be sexual actors in a drama of our own construction? Will black women act on our own behalf . . . even if doing so includes fantasies that incorporate racist or sexist scenarios? Or are black women destined to always be victims of a racial and sexual history that overwhelms hope for transformation and liberation?

. . .

We need new visions and new ways of talking about black female sexuality.

Historically, white women parlayed their experiences working with blacks for the abolition of slavery into the drive for women's voting rights. In the early 1970s, many social-change groups adopted the language of the Black Power movement. Why? Because the notion of power was potent and, dare I say, *virile* language. The notion of pride and refusing to be ashamed had a confrontational edge to it that Chicanos, women's libbers, Asians, American Indians, and gays recognized as a new direction: Rather than ask for integration into a corrupt system, why not demand the resources to build a new world according to one's own agenda?

In developing that vision, gays, lesbians, bisexuals, and transgender (LGBT) activists not only declared a form of gay pride, but also later would even co-opt the language of civil rights. We see it today in demands for same-sex marriage as a right. And while LGBT uses of civil rights language might rub some African Americans the wrong way, I would say it is time for blacks—specifically, black women—to take something back. Isn't it time for heterosexual black women to adopt the language of queerness to free us from Mammy's apron strings? Wouldn't the idea of coming out of the closet as enjoying sex on our own terms make Jezebel stop in her tracks to think about getting *herself* off, rather than being focused on getting her man off? It is time to queer black female *heterosexuality.* As it stands, black women acquiesce to certain representations as if taking crumbs from the table of sexual oppression. Our butts are in vogue, we're nastier than white women in the bedroom, we're wilder than Asian women—all stereotypes derived in a male fantasy land of "jungle" porn and no-strings-attached personal ads. A queer black female heterosexuality isn't about being a freak in the bedroom; it's about being a sexual person whose wants and needs are self-defined.

. . .

Queerness, then, is not an identity, but a position or stance. We can use "queer" as a verb instead of a noun. Queer is not someone or something to be treated. Queer is something that we can *do.* The black woman is the original Other, the figure against which white women's sexuality is defined. Aren't we already queer? To queer black female sexuality means to do what would be contrary, eccentric, strange, or unexpected. To be silent is, yes, unexpected in a world whose stereotype is of black women as loud and hypersexual. However, silence merely stifles *us.* Silence does not change the status quo.

Queering black female sexuality would mean straight black women need to:

1. Come out as black women who enjoy sex and find it pleasurable.
2. Protest the stereotypes of black female sexuality that do not reflect our experience.
3. Allow all black women—across class, sexual orientation, and physical ability—to express what we enjoy.
4. Know the difference between making love and fucking—and be willing to express our desires for both despite what the news, music videos, social mores, or any other source says we should want.
5. Know what it is to play with sexuality. What turns us on? Is it something taboo? Does our playfulness come from within?
6. Know that our bodies are our own—our bodies do not belong to the church, the state, our parents, our lovers, our husbands, and certainly not Black Entertainment Television (BET).

Queering black female heterosexuality goes beyond language. Black communities go 'round and 'round about the use of "nigger" with one another. Is it a revolutionary act of reclaiming an oppressive word? Or does it make us merely minstrels performing in the white man's show? Older and younger feminists debate the merits of embracing the labels of "bitch" and "dyke" as a bid for taking the malice out of the words. There are some black women who say, "Yes, I am a black bitch" or, "Yes, I am a ho." These claims do little to shift attitudes. If nothing else, we merely give our enemies artillery to continue to shoot us down or plaster our asses across cars in rap videos. How does the saying go? You act like a trick, you get played like a trick. Claiming queerness is linguistic, but ultimately about action that does not reinforce the stereotypes.

I am not suggesting a form of political lesbianism, which was a popular stance for some feminists who struggled against male domination in the 1970s. In addition to adopting a political position, queering black female sexuality means listening to transformative things that have already been said about black sexuality. Black lesbians and gay men have something to tell straight black women about sexuality if we care to listen. Poets such as Audre Lorde, writer/activists such as Keith Boykin, and cultural theorists such as Cathy Cohen and Dwight McBride offer insights about African American sexuality that move beyond boundaries of sexual orientation and that we would do well to heed. Cohen, for example, challenges queer politics for lacking an intersectional analysis. That is, queer theory largely ignores questions of race and class when those categories in particular are the straw men against which marginalization is defined, constructed, and maintained.

Queer theory isn't just for queers anymore, but calling on the wisdom of my black, gay sisters and brothers runs the risk of reducing them solely to their sexuality. Thus, the challenge for me in bringing an intersectional perspective to queering black female heterosexuality is to remain mindful of my own heterosexual privilege and the pitfalls of appropriating queerness as identity and not as a political position.

What I must also claim and declare are all the freaky tendencies that I consider sexy and sexual. Sexual encounters mined from Craigslist's Casual Encounters, where I both defy and play with stereotypes about black women's sexuality. Speaking frankly about sex with friends—gay, straight, bisexual, trans, male, and female. Enjoying the music and words of black women, such as Jill Scott, who are unabashed about their sexual desire and the complexity of defining nontraditional relationships—monogamous and otherwise. All of these sexual interventions/adventures in daily existence play against my own conditioning to be a respectable, middle-class young lady destined to become an asexual black lady. That biology is *not* my destiny.

There is no guarantee that straight black women adopting queerness will change how the dominant culture perceives black female sexuality. I do not think black women embracing our sexuality and being vocal about that will change how politicians attempt to use our sexuality as a scapegoat for society's ills, as they did with the "welfare queen" in the 1980s and 1990s. However, I do believe that queering black female sexuality, if enough of us participate in the project, will move us collectively toward a more enlightened way of being sexual beings unconstrained by racialized sexism. Instead of trying to enact a developmental approach (we were asexual mammies or hot-to-trot jezebels, but now we are ladies), claiming queerness will give us the latitude we need to explore who we want to be on a continuum. It is a choice that both black women as a group and black women as individuals must make.

. . .

It may not seem like much, but overcoming centuries of historical silence will create different perceptions about black women and sex that will reshape our culture, society, and public policies. In calling for heterosexual black women to queer their sexuality, I am expressing the fierce belief that . . . we can dramatically change how black female sexuality is viewed in America. More important, though, I believe we can change how black girls and women *live* and *experience* their sexuality: on their own terms and free from a past of exploitation. Historians often refer to the "long shadow" that slavery has cast over African Americans. While it is important to acknowledge the reverberations of this human atrocity in black family structure, economic disadvantage, and especially black sexuality, it is just as critical that we push along a dialogue that reinvents black sex in ways that do not merely reinstate the sexual exploitation that was inflicted and that some of us now freely adopt.

Can black women achieve a truly liberated black female sexuality? Yes. If we continue to say no to negative imagery—but that alone has not been effective. In addition, we must create and maintain black female sexuality queerly. Only then can we say, and only then will society hear, both yes and no freely and on our own terms.

CHAPTER 7

HEALTH AND REPRODUCTIVE JUSTICE

HEALTH AND WELLNESS

Health is a central issue in all our lives. Ask parents what they wish for their newborns and they speak first about hoping the baby is healthy; quiz people about their hopes for the New Year and they speak about staying healthy; listen to politicians debate their positions before an election and health care is almost always a key issue. In contemporary U.S. society, good health is generally understood as a requirement for happy and productive living. To make sense of the complexities of our relationships to health care systems, we discuss five themes: equity, androcentrism, medicalization, stereotyping, and corporate responsibility. After this discussion we address reproductive justice and focus specifically on contraceptive technologies and abortion debates in the United States.

First, in terms of equity, despite the 2010 passage of President Obama's Patient Protection and Affordable Care Act (PPACA), commonly called the Affordable Care Act, or simply Obamacare, medical institutions in the United States continue to provide different levels of service based on health insurance status and the general ability to pay. This issue of equity affects all aspects of health care, including access to fertility, contraceptive, and abortion facilities. Poor families are less healthy than those who are better off, whether the benchmark is mortality, the prevalence of acute or chronic diseases, or mental health. This is the issue of equity. Some people have better health care than others because of a two-tiered system that has different outcomes for those who can pay or who have health insurance and those who cannot afford to pay and do not have health insurance through their jobs or are not covered by welfare programs. This is a special problem as health care costs continue to rise. Some states are providing less coverage for low-income people, a problem because the United States, unlike most industrialized societies in the global north, does not yet have a nationalized health care system.

As of this writing, the Affordable Care Act, together with the Health Care Education Reconciliation Act, represents the most significant government expansion and regulatory overhaul of the health care system in the United States since the passage of Medicare and

Medicaid in 1965. It was aimed at increasing health insurance coverage and reducing the overall costs of health care. It provided a number of mechanisms, including individual mandates, subsidies, and tax credits, to employers and individuals in order to increase the coverage rate.

In particular, the Affordable Care Act stated that, with a few exceptions, an individual cannot "be excluded from participation in, be denied the benefits of, or be subjected to discrimination under any health program or activity, any part of which is receiving federal financial assistance." This meant that public or private entities receiving federal funds (private insurance companies often receive federal funds) cannot discriminate on the basis of gender, national origin, ethnicity, age, or disability. "Gender rating"—charging, for example, women more than men for health insurance—is disallowed for individual and employer plans with more than 100 employees. It was estimated that women with individual health insurance plans had been paying up to 48 percent higher premiums. The legislation also required insurers to provide maternity coverage (about three-quarters of plans had not included this) and that companies with more than 50 employees provide breastfeeding mothers with breaks and room to express milk. In addition, midwives and birth centers were covered by the Affordable Care Act. Other key aspects of this health care reform important for women's health included promises for preventive care provisions, mental health coverage, increased coverage for Medicaid and SCHIP (State Children's Health Insurance Program), and increased access for individuals to group rates. In addition, young people could stay on parents' health insurance policies until age 26, Medicare patients got better coverage, coverage denials for preexisting conditions and lifetime caps on coverage were eliminated, and employers were prohibited from giving lesser plans to lower-paid workers.

Despite these gains, extreme opposition to President Obama's health care reform efforts resulted in the absence of a public option and limits on abortion coverage. Still, these changes in health care attempted to ensure that everyone in the United States had some kind of health insurance coverage. This legislation was especially important for women because growth in health costs over the last decade had a disproportionate effect on them due to women's lower incomes, higher rates of chronic health problems, and greater need for reproductive health services. As discussed earlier, discriminatory practices charging women higher rates than men and refusing to cover essential service associated with reproductive health have had important consequences for women's health and well-being.

Although the U.S. Supreme Court upheld the constitutionality of this law in 2012, President Donald Trump and House Republicans waged a concerted effort to repeal the act—unsuccessfully as of this writing. What they have done is strip the law of the individual mandate tax penalty for individuals who do not carry health insurance, decrease the advertising budget associated with open enrollment by 90 percent, cut the open enrollment period from three months to six weeks a year, and reduce funds for personal enrollment assistance by 41 percent. Efforts are also under way to support increased Medicaid work requirements.

Health insurance coverage is a critical factor for health outcomes. Among the 98 million women aged 19 to 64 years residing in the United States, most had some form of coverage in 2016. However, gaps in private sector and publicly funded programs left a little over 1 in 10 women uninsured. Overall, the rate of uninsured Americans rose from 12.7 percent in 2016 to 15.5 percent in 2018. In those states that chose not to participate in Medicaid expansion, the rate increased from 16 percent to almost 21 percent over the same years. Uninsured women are more likely to have inadequate access to care, get a lower standard of care in the health system, and have poorer health outcomes. They are more likely to postpone care—including often delaying or skipping important preventive care such as mammograms and Pap tests—and to forgo filling prescriptions than their insured counterparts. One study found that insurance, or the lack of it, proved to be the most powerful predictor of rates of women's late-stage cancer. In addition, uninsured children are at greater risk of experiencing health problems such as obesity, heart disease, and asthma that will continue to affect them as (potentially uninsured) adults, resulting in increased costs for public health care services. Such adverse effects of health care inequity carry long-term implications for families and society.

Another issue of equity in health access and outcome is that women are more likely to be employed in part-time work or full-time work without health insurance benefits and, compared to men, are more likely to be covered as a "dependent" by another adult's employer-based insurance. As a result, women are more vulnerable to losing their insurance coverage if they divorce or become widowed, if a spouse or partner loses a job, or if a spouse or partner's employer drops family coverage or increases premium and out-of-pocket costs. In addition, of course, employment has not necessarily ensured access to health insurance, as more than two-thirds of uninsured women live in families in which they or a partner are working full time. As discussed, these obstacles cause low-income women (who are disproportionately women of color) to postpone care and delay preventive procedures.

Health club memberships and healthy foods are outside the reach of many low-income people, who also are more likely to live in neighborhoods that provide unhealthy environments with unsafe water because of the presence of hazardous waste associated with industrial production and the dumping of toxic chemicals in neighborhoods with little economic and political power. Environmental racism has fostered an environmental justice movement. Low-income women are more susceptible to chronic conditions as well as acute problems that might have been avoided had preventive care been available. These problems are unethical, cost the state millions of dollars annually, and are not fiscally responsible ways to provide health care services. People of color are especially at risk for not having health care coverage and for receiving substandard care when they enter the system. They have higher maternal and infant mortality rates and higher rates of HIV infection, and their reproductive health is threatened by limited access to basic reproductive health care, including family planning services and abortion care. Services such as these can be understood as human rights, emphasizing the importance of such rights for social justice.

Professional health-related organizations (such as the American Medical Association [AMA]), health maintenance organizations (HMOs), insurance companies, pharmaceutical companies, and corporations representing other medical products and practices have enormous influence over health politics. In addition, health is not just about medical services. Health conditions, including incidence and mortality rates, are related to such socioeconomic factors as poverty, poor nutrition, interpersonal violence, substandard housing, and lack of education. Many of the social issues that affect women on a daily basis and that contribute to their increased tobacco use, chemical addictions, stress, and poor nutrition lead to increased rates of disease—heart disease, cancer, chronic obstructive pulmonary disease, diabetes, and obesity, to name just a few. Health problems are compounded by the aging of the population, such that by the year 2030, women (who are likely to have fewer economic resources than men) will represent approximately 81 percent of those older than 85 years. In addition, the consequences of catastrophic weather conditions in this era of climate change also differentially impact the health and safety of many families around the globe.

Globally, women's health access is one of the most important issues determining justice and equity for women. As already discussed in previous chapters, "globalization" refers to the processes by which regional economies, societies, and cultures have become integrated through an interconnected global network of communication, transportation, and trade. Several of the readings in this chapter specifically make this claim about the importance of health for facilitating equity and social justice. In the reading "On Being Transnational and Transgender" Don Operario and Tooru Nemoto, for example, write about the health needs of transgender people and the challenges they face in transnational perspective, making the case for the human rights of transgender individuals as legitimate public health issues. They emphasize the importance of moving beyond individual-level concerns (even though these are crucially important) to a focus on the structural and legal transnational issues that affect health outcomes. These issues are fraught with violence as discrimination against nontraditional forms of gender identities shapes such health outcomes. Operario and Nemoto suggest the need to contextualize transgender health needs within human rights frameworks. Jallicia Jolly makes this point in terms of reproductive justice in the article "On Forbidden Wombs and Transnational Reproductive Justice," as does Sarah Combellick-Bidney in "Reproductive Rights as Human Rights: Stories from Advocates in Brazil, India, and South Africa," both discussed later in the chapter.

The HIV/AIDS global pandemic and its consequences for marginalized people worldwide is also an important illustration of issues of gender and racial/ethnic equity in transnational context. Worldwide the number of HIV-related deaths has been cut nearly in half since the height of the epidemic, but HIV is still a leading cause of death of women of reproductive age in low- and middle-income countries, particularly in sub-Saharan Africa. Sarah Combellick-Bidney addresses nonconsensual sterilization "in the shadow" of the HIV/AIDS crisis in South Africa in "Reproductive Rights as Human Rights." The author highlights the stigma associated with the disease and its role in non-consensual sterilization practices.

By the end of 2016, according to the most recent data published by the U.S. Centers for Disease Control and Prevention, about 1.1 million people in the United States were living with HIV, with almost a quarter of these identifying as women. In addition, women accounted for almost one-fifth of the new HIV infections in 2016, with approximately 87 percent of these cases infected by heterosexual contact. See the box "Women and HIV in the United States" for more information. However, not all women are equally at risk for

WOMEN AND HIV IN THE UNITED STATES

Meghan Fitzgerald

Of the one million people living with HIV in the United States, more than 24 percent are women (Kaiser Family Foundation [KFF], 2018). Women accounted for 19 percent of new HIV infections in 2016 (Centers for Disease Control and Prevention [CDC], 2018). Women living with HIV tend to be clustered in major urban areas. In 2009, half of all women with an HIV diagnosis were living in just 10 large metropolitan areas of the United States (KFF, 2018).

The most common mode of HIV transmission among women is heterosexual contact, accounting for 87 percent of diagnoses. The second most common mode is injection drug use, which increases the potential for risky behavior (CDC, 2018). In cities with high HIV rates, 72 percent of women who injected drugs reported having had sex without a condom in the previous year (Office on Women's Health [OWH], 2018). Women with a history of being sexually abused are also at greater risk for HIV infection due to increased likelihood of risky behavior such as having multiple sex partners, having sex without a condom, or exchanging sex for drugs (CDC, 2018; OWH, 2018).

There are several physiological factors that make women more vulnerable to contracting HIV during sex. Generally, receptive sex carries greater risk than insertive sex, putting women at higher risk during vaginal or anal sex than their partners (CDC, 2018). Additionally, women with untreated sexually transmitted infections are at increased risk of contracting HIV, and women with HIV are at increased risk of contracting various other adverse conditions (KFF, 2018; CDC, 2018; OWH, 2018).

Among women affected by HIV, disparities exist in subgroups of the population that experience discrimination and oppression in the United States. According to the CDC, 59 percent of women living with HIV in 2015 were African American, 19 percent were Latina, and 17 percent were white (2018). In 2010, the rate of new HIV infections for African American women was 20 times greater than the rate for white women (KFF, 2018). Another group with disproportionately high risk for HIV is transgender women, especially transgender women of color (Sevelius, Keatley, and Gutierrez-Mock, 2011). HIV prevalence estimates among this group range from 22 percent to 68 percent across five major U.S. cities (Garafalo et al., 2006; Xavier et al., 2005; Risser et al., 2005; Clements-Nolle et al., 2001; Elifson et al., 1993). Barriers to HIV testing and treatment include lack of knowledge, transgender-friendly testing sites, and transgender-specific prevention programs; further, there are unique cultural challenges in adherence to treatment, such as stigma in health care and potential adverse reactions between antiretroviral medication and hormone therapy (Sevelius, Keatley, and Gutierrez-Monk, 2011).

Despite declining rates of infection, many challenges remain for women at risk for or living with HIV. Barriers to accessing services and knowledge include sexual violence, poverty, cultural inequities, and societal gender norms (White House, 2012; Health Resources and Services Administration [HRSA], 2012; Denning and DiNenno, 2010). Only 70 percent of women diagnosed with HIV have been linked to care (KFF, 2018). However, resources for women with HIV in the United States are increasing through developments in policy like the Affordable Care Act and federal programs like Medicaid and the Ryan White Program, designed to increase access to care (KFF, 2018).

a.

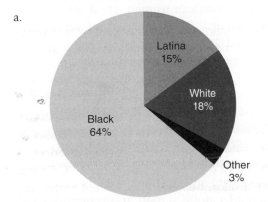

b.

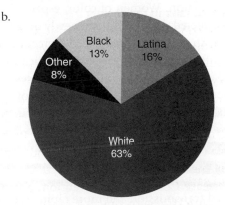

FIGURE 1 (a) New HIV Infections Among Women and Girls and (b) U.S. Female Population, by Race/Ethnicity, 2010 Note: Data are estimates among those ages 13 and older and do not include U.S. dependent areas. Source: Kaiser Family Foundation (2018).

(continued)

Discussion Question

• Given the inequitable burden of HIV on African American and transgender women in the United States, and what we know of the factors that increase risk of contracting HIV, how do you think such disparities come to exist? How might discrimination play a role for a woman with HIV in getting tested and/or accessing treatment? What structural changes should be made to decrease vulnerability to HIV infection and ensure greater access to resources and support for HIV-positive people?

References

Centers for Disease Control and Prevention [CDC]. (2018). "Fact Sheet: HIV Among Women." https://www.cdc.gov/hiv/group/gender/women/index.html

Clements-Nolle, K., Marx, R., Guzman, R., and Katz, M. (2001). "HIV Prevalence, Risk Behaviors, Health Care Use, and Mental Health Status of Transgender Persons: Implications for Public Health Intervention." *American Journal of Public Health*, 91, 915–921.

Denning, P., and DiNenno, E. (2010, August). "Communities in Crisis: Is There a Generalized HIV Epidemic in Impoverished Urban Areas of the United States?" [Poster]. Atlanta, GA: Centers for Disease Control and Prevention, National Center for HIV Viral Hepatitis STD and TB Prevention.

Elifson, K., Boles, J., Posey, E., Sweat, M., Darrow, W., and Elsea, W. (1993). "Male Transvestite Prostitutes and HIV Risk." *American Journal of Public Health*, 83, 260–262.

Garafalo, R., Deleon, J., Osmer, E., Doll, M., and Harper, G. (2006). "Overlooked, Misunderstood, and At-Risk: Exploring the Lives and HIV Risk of Ethnic Minority Male-to-Female Transgender Youth." *Journal of Adolescent Health*, 38, 230–236.

Health Resources and Services Administration [HRSA], U.S. Department for Health and Human Services. (2012, September). CAREAction Newsletter: Ryan White HIV/AIDS Program Providers Address HIV/AIDS Among African-American Women.

Kaiser Family Foundation [KFF]. (2018). "Women and HIV/AIDS in the U.S." https://www.kff.org/hivaids/fact-sheet/women-and-hivaids-in-the-united-states/

Office on Women's Health [OWH]. (2018). "Women and HIV." U.S. Department of Health and Human Services. https://www.womenshealth.gov/hiv-and-aids/women-and-hiv

Risser, J., Shelton, A., McCurdy, S., Atkinson, J., Padgett, P., Useche, B., et al. (2005). "Sex, Drugs, Violence, and HIV Status Among Male-to-Female Transgender Persons in Houston, Texas." *International Journal of Transgenderism*, 8, 67–74.

Sevelius, K., Keatley, J., and Gutierrez-Mock, L. (2011, March). "HIV/AIDS Programming in the United States: Considerations Affecting Transgender Women and Girls." *Women's Health Issues*, 21(6S), S278–S282.

Xavier, J., Bobbin, M., Singer, B., and Budd, E. (2005). "A Needs Assessment of Transgender People of Color Living in Washington DC." *International Journal of Transgenderism*, 8, 31–47.

White House. (2012, March). "Presidential Memorandum Establishing a Working Group on the Intersection of HIV/AIDS, Violence Against Women and Girls, and Gender-Related Health Disparities." https://obamawhitehouse.archives.gov/the-press-office/2012/03/30/presidential-memorandum-establishing-working-group-intersection-hivaids-

HIV infection. Women of color, especially African American women, are disproportionately affected. Indeed, among newly diagnosed cases in 2016, over 60 percent were African American, 19 percent white, 16 percent Latina, and 5 percent "other." Even though new HIV infections among African American women have decreased consistently since 2010, compared with members of other races and ethnicities they continue to account for a higher proportion of cases at all stages of HIV from new infections to deaths. Both African American women and men are at higher risk because of higher rates of poverty and less access to HIV prevention education and affordable health care. These socioeconomic issues directly and indirectly increase the risk for HIV infection and affect the health of people living with, and at risk for, HIV. Late diagnosis of HIV infection, in particular, results in lack of early medical care and facilitates transmission to others. High prevalence means increased transmission and more rapid acceleration of a problem than in communities with low prevalence. Also, the fact that African Americans tend to have sexual relations with partners of the same race/ethnicity means the smaller population encourages an increased risk of HIV infection. In other words, the higher prevalence of HIV infection in African

American and Latino/a communities and the fact that people tend to have sexual relationships with partners of the same race/ethnicity mean that women from these communities face a greater risk of HIV infection with each new sexual encounter. However, today medical treatment can lower levels of the virus in the body (viral suppression) such that it is no longer detectable. HIV patients who are virally suppressed in this way can stay healthy and have effectively no risk of sexually transmitting HIV to HIV-negative partners.

HIV risk factors for women, both in the United States and globally, include lack of power in relationships (as reflected by sexual violence against women; their lack of input into decisions such as whether a male partner wears a condom, visits a prostitute, or has multiple sexual partners, etc.), inadequate health care and HIV prevention education, lack of education about the body and sexuality, and the biological vulnerability of women during sexual intercourse that provides more sources of entry for the virus. The riskiest behavior for getting HIV is unprotected (without a condom) receptive anal sex. Scholars suggest that many students in the United States are at risk for HIV infection when they have multiple sex partners, use condoms inconsistently, and combine alcohol and/or other drugs with their sexual experiences. Although students tend to be knowledgeable about HIV, this does not always lead to condom use.

Although there has been increased funding for HIV/AIDS prevention, treatment, and care in Africa and the Caribbean, a U.S. "global gag rule" (temporarily lifted by President Obama in 2009, but reinstated and expanded 15 times by President Trump) on the U.S. Agency for International Development (USAID) population-control program has restricted foreign nongovernmental organizations (NGOs) from receiving USAID family-planning funds if they provided certain services. These services include providing legal abortion services, lobbying their own governments for abortion law reform, or even providing accurate medical counseling or referrals regarding abortion. However, the gag rule coincided with another U.S. policy that blocked contributions to the United Nations Population Fund. This fund supported programs in some 150 countries to improve poor women's reproductive health, reduce infant mortality, address sex trafficking, and prevent the spread of HIV/AIDS. Such policies undermine funding for other related health issues (as well as health and infant screening, nutritional programs, and health education) and encourage narrow, often religious, and abstinence-based approaches to HIV/AIDS prevention that exclude condom use. Officially known as the "Mexico City Policy," the global gag rule is an indirect method of targeting reproductive justice worldwide. As of this writing, the global gag rule applies to all U.S. global health assistance (a total of about $9 billion), including that related to international family planning and reproductive health. For the first time, however, funding for maternal and child health, nutrition, malaria, tuberculosis, and infectious and tropical diseases has been jeopardized, and providers must choose between offering comprehensive health care or receiving critical U.S. funding. Importantly, roughly two-thirds of the funding affected by the expanded global gag rule is for HIV/AIDS programs around the world, under the President's Emergency Plan for AIDS Relief (PEPFAR). PEPFAR, created in 2003 by the George W. Bush administration, has received broad bipartisan support and has been successful in reaching more than 13 million men, women, and children with lifesaving antiretroviral treatment.

The second theme of this chapter is androcentrism, or male centeredness (see Chapter 1). The male body is constructed as normative, and medical research has tended to focus on men (mostly white men), overgeneralizing the results of this research to others. Baseline data for heart monitors, for example, were based on middle-aged white men, causing serious complications for patients who did not fit this description. Until recently, women often were not included in clinical trials to determine the safety and effectiveness of drugs and other medical devices because it was thought that women's hormonal cycling or other factors peculiar to being female might constitute variables that could skew trial results. It was declared that excluding women protected them, because a woman might be pregnant or the drug might prevent future fertility. Drug companies did not want to get sued. Recently it has become increasingly clear that research from male-only trials may not apply equally to women or may not provide data on important effects of drugs on women. Originally, researchers believed most sex differences in terms of reactions to drugs were most likely a result of differences in hormones, height, and/or weight. Scientists now know that these differences are more complex. Differences in the livers of men and women may explain why most women seem to metabolize drugs differently than men, for example. There may also be sex differences in pain tolerance and the ways individuals respond to pain medications. Today the National Science Foundation (NSF) and National Institutes of Health (NIH) have implemented regulations to ensure that funded research is free of gender discrimination and other kinds of bias, although the application of medical research to clinical practice moves slowly, and assumptions about gender evolve slowly too. These assumptions about gender in health assessments are aptly illustrated in Kate Horowitz's essay "Performance of a Lifetime: On Invisible Illness, Gender, and Disbelief." Horowitz writes about her own diagnosis and the years spent battling a medical establishment keen to shape interpretations of her illness through the lens of gender expectations and performances.

More money is spent on diseases that are more likely to afflict men. Related to this is the notion of "anatomy as destiny" (an example of biological determinism, already discussed in other chapters) whereby female physiology, and especially reproductive anatomy, is seen as central in understanding women's behavior. These trends have a long history. Social norms about femininity, for instance, have guided medical and scientific ideas about women's health, and female reproductive organs have long been perceived as sources of some kind of special emotional as well as physical health. "Female hysteria," for example, was a once-common nineteenth-century medical diagnosis of women in the United States and Europe that was "treated" by various practices that included hysterectomy (surgical removal of the uterus). Women thought to be suffering from it exhibited a wide array of symptoms, including nervousness, sexual desire or lack of desire, anxiety, and irritability. Basically women who transgressed cultural notions of femininity and had a tendency to cause trouble were suspected of suffering from the condition.

Third, medicalization is the process whereby normal functions of the body come to be seen as indicative of disease. This affects women in two ways. One, because some women have more episodic changes in their bodies as a result of childbearing (for example, menstruation, pregnancy, childbirth, lactation, and menopause), they are more at risk for medical personnel interpreting these natural processes as problematic. Note how this tends to reinforce the argument that biology is destiny. Two, medicalization supports business and medical technologies. It tends to work against preventive medicine and encourages the use of sophisticated medical technologies to "fix" problems after they occur. Medical services tend to be dominated by drug treatments and surgery, and controlled by pharmaceutical companies, HMOs, and such professional organizations as the American Medical Association.

MEDICAL MODEL OF DISABILITY

Abigail C. Mulcahy

Start Here

Draw a body. It doesn't have to be yours. It doesn't have to be good—this isn't an exercise in artistry. Just draw a body. Be respectful. Label all parts however it makes the most sense to you.

Now, draw a body with a disability. The same rules apply—it doesn't have to be your body, it doesn't have to be an artistic masterpiece, but please be respectful. Again, label all the parts in whatever way makes the most sense to you.

Looking at your first drawing:

- What did you draw?
- Was it humanoid? (There was no requirement that you draw a human.)
- Did it have two arms? Two legs?
- Was it symmetrical?

Looking at your second drawing:

- How is this body different from your first drawing?
- Does it have a clear visible disability?
- Is it in a wheelchair? Walking with a cane?
- Is it in profile? Is it looking at you?

The Medical Model

The medical community pathologizes the concept of disability; that is, the disabled body is read as inherently abnormal and/or unhealthy. Under this model, mental disability is almost always separated from physical disability. Moreover, disabilities are ranked and measured, with some disabilities considered more significant (and therefore more deserving of certain types of treatment or accommodation) than others (Goering, 2002).

Feminist Perspectives on Disability

Feminist disability scholar activists like Margaret Price and Alison Kafer, as individuals with disabilities and/or in conversation with other people living with disabilities, critique the medical model of disability. Price refuses to play by the mind/body binary in the medical model, aligning the mental and physical in the concept of the "bodymind" (2015). Kafer, in her book *Feminist Queer Crip* (2013), makes a point of referring to people not living with a disability as "temporarily able bodied" (pointing to the fact that all of us—outside of an untimely end—are headed for old age and disability) as an attempt to engage as many people as possible in the fight for accessibility. But out of context, language like "temporarily able bodied" can be read as oversimplification (bordering on threat) that distracts from issues like genetic testing and selective abortion (Kafer, 2013).

Toward a Better Model

Take another look at your drawings. Considering your first drawing:

- Does it look like you? Like someone(s) you know?
- Is it what you would consider a normative or default body?

Now, looking at your second drawing:

- Does it look like you? Like someone you know?
- Did you depict both mental and physical disability? How?
- Is this what you would consider an abnormal or deviant body?

A better model of disability is neither the default body nor the deviant body. Rather, it is a defiant body, one that rejects the mind/body binary of the medical model while also engaging with issues of accessibility without veiled threats or indulgent appeals. The defiant body is one that, where possible, leverages its privilege in the interest of those who cannot.

How can you represent a defiant body? How can you become one?

References

Goering, S. (2002). "Beyond the Medical Model? Disability, Formal Justice, and the Exception for the 'Profoundly Impaired.'" *Kennedy Institute of Ethics Journal*, 12(4), 373–388. https://muse.jhu.edu/article/37518/pdf.

Kafer, A. (2013). *Feminist, Queer, Crip*. Bloomington: Indiana University Press.

Price, M. (2015). "The Bodymind Problem and the Possibilities of Pain." *Hypatia*, 30(1), 268–284.

Fourth, stereotyping, including the practices of gender and ethnic profiling, encompasses how notions about gender, race/ethnicity, and other identities inform everyday understanding of health care occupations and influence how medical practitioners treat their patients. For example, patients still often assume that white-coated white male orderlies are doctors and call women doctors "nurse." In this way, certain gendered individuals not only interact differently with the health care system, but are treated differently, often to the detriment of health outcomes.

Such differential treatment may occur as a result of provider bias, which concerns the ways stereotypes about people influence how providers and clinicians interpret identical behaviors and clinical findings. Research in provider bias suggests several key interrelated factors. First, providers' conscious beliefs may be inconsistent with their automatic, unconscious reactions to those in certain identity groups. Second, when providers make complex judgments quickly, with insufficient and imperfect information or little time to gather information, they may "fill in the gaps" with beliefs associated with patients' social categories. Third, providers tend to be more likely to rely on stereotypes for "out-group members" or people who do not act or look like them; and finally, providers may unconsciously favor those they feel to be similar to themselves, regardless of their conscious beliefs and politics.

For example, transgender patients often suffer gender bias and transphobic responses at the hands of the medical establishment. Operario and Nemoto make this point in their reading on the challenges faced by transgender people when accessing health systems and liken it to a form of structural violence, a concept also discussed in Chapter 10. Homophobia and transphobia prevent LGBTQ individuals from receiving fully informed care, which affects their options and access. In addition, in terms of gender and ethnic profiling, one study found that blacks, Latinx, and women generally waited longer for care. Whites waited an average of 24 minutes, blacks 31 minutes, and Latinx 33 minutes.

Research suggests that physicians generally are more likely to consider emotional factors when diagnosing women's problems, and they are more likely to assume that the cause of illness is psychosomatic when the patient presents as female, prescribing more anxiety-mediating and mood-altering medication for women than for men. Indeed, about 1 in 10 people in the United States older than age 12 takes antidepressant medication. This includes approximately 6 percent of men and more than 15 percent of women, with white women having the highest rate. It is also interesting to note that the rate of antidepressant use in the United States has increased nearly 400 percent in the last 25 years, and, according to the Centers for Disease Control and Prevention, antidepressants are the most frequently used medication by persons aged 18 to 44 years. The reading by Aisha Wagner, "Doctors Need to Talk Openly About Race—Our Patients Depend on It," articulates the need for physicians to understand how attitudes about race affect medical care, as well as how discrimination and oppression shape health care systems. Wagner also emphasizes the ways that training of physicians falls short and makes the case for medical education to address these issues.

Finally, a focus on health must discuss the issue of corporate responsibility and the role of the state in guiding and establishing that responsibility. This relates to how national and transnational corporations with strong profit motives affect our lives in terms of environmental degradation and toxic exposure, food additives, and problematic medical practices, and the ways decisions at national and international levels affect these practices. Examples include concern with greenhouse gases and global climate change, use of pesticides and herbicides, genetically modified food and corporate control of bioresources, and growth hormones in beef and dairy food products. All of these issues are related to the corporatization of life and the global economy, the stresses of life in postindustrial societies, and ultimately the quality of life on the planet.

There is increasing interest in exploring the role of stress in our lives, as well as the connections between mind and body in terms of illness. Scientists have long known about these connections and have emphasized that it is less stress itself (over work, relationships, trauma, etc.) that affects the immune system, and more how individuals interpret or make meaning of that stress. It seems that stresses we control evoke different responses from those we cannot control, with feelings of helplessness being worse than the stressor itself. What this means is that stress as a result of structural violence such as poverty or living in high-crime areas is deadly and has consequences for health outcomes. Robert Horton's reading, "Racism—The Pathology We Choose to Ignore," emphasizes that health is about power and politics. The author addresses microaggressions in health care systems associated with racism, heterosexism, and other systems of inequality experienced by LGBTQ individuals who are also racial/ethnic minorities. This reading, which emphasizes that health professionals have an important part to play in addressing these dangers through their work and values, starts out with this important quote: "Social oppression in its many forms takes a toll on the health of individuals." Although stress affects everyone, there is differential impact based on marginalized identities that shape people's everyday lives, including where they live, the kind of work they perform, the food they can afford to eat, and so forth. Again, these stresses and the discriminations associated with being a target group member are examples of what scholars call structural violence. Horton's point is that structural violence must be addressed by those working within health professions.

As mentioned earlier, marginalized peoples' differential exposure to environmental problems has fostered an environmental justice movement to resist these inequities that occur as a result of lack of economic, social, and political power. In particular, environmental racism reflects the fact that people of color in the United States are disproportionately exposed to toxic environments due to the dumping of chemical and other waste on Native American lands and in urban areas where more people of color live. Environmental waste tends not to be located in areas populated by people of high socioeconomic status or where property values are high. The dumping of radioactive waste at Yucca Mountain, Nevada, despite the impact of this on the Western Shoshone tribe that considers the mountain sacred, is a case in point, as is the way the Dakota Access Pipeline traversed the sacred lands of the Standing Rock Indian Reservation. People in developing countries who work in factories and sweatshops within the global economy (especially young women, who are often hired because they are cheap, dispensable, and easily controlled workers) are particularly at risk for occupational disease.

Breast cancer is one important health issue closely tied to environmental problems and therefore to corporate responsibility. According to a 2013–2018 National Cancer Institute fact sheet, 1 in 8 women will be diagnosed with breast cancer over a lifetime (compared to 1 in 20 in 1960). The relative increase in women's life expectancy does not fully explain this increase in breast cancer incidence. Except for skin cancer, breast cancer is the most common form of cancer in women and the number-two cause of cancer death (lung and bronchial cancer causes the most deaths), except in the case of Latinas, for whom breast cancer is the number-one cause of cancer death. Although over a quarter of a million new cases of invasive breast cancer are diagnosed yearly, there has been a decrease in death rates from breast cancer since 1989, especially among women under 50 years old. These decreases are understood as a result of treatment advancements, earlier detection through screening, and increased awareness. However, even though African American women are not more susceptible to breast cancer, African American women aged 35 to 44 years are more than twice as likely to die from it than women generally. This is because they tend to have more advanced tumors as a result of poorer screening and reduced access to health care services.

Breast cancer research works to find a "cure," despite the fact that a focus on environmental contributors could work effectively to prevent breast cancer. The pink ribbon campaign for the cure, while a formidable support for breast cancer research and the empowerment of survivors, inadequately addresses environmental links to breast cancer. This is especially important because less than 10 percent of breast cancer cases have a genetic cause. About half of all breast cancer cases cannot be explained by known risk factors, encouraging scientists to suspect toxic chemicals in the environment playing a role. In particular, researchers have hypothesized that environmental estrogens play a role in the increasing incidence of breast cancer, testicular cancer, and other problems of the human reproductive system.

Environmental estrogens (also known as xenoestrogens) mimic the effects of human estrogen or affect its level in the body indirectly by disrupting the ways human estrogen is produced or used. Although some are naturally occurring (for example, phytoestrogens in plants such as soybeans), the greatest concern is synthetic estrogens that are not easily broken down and can be stored in the body's fat cells. Almost 40 years ago, researchers showed that organochlorines, a family of compounds including the pesticide DDT and the industrial chemicals known as polychlorinated biphenyls (PCBs), could mimic human estrogen and induce mammary tumors in laboratory animals. Organochlorines are organic compounds containing chlorine bonded to carbon. Virtually unknown in nature, they are primarily products or by-products of the chemical industry. Their largest single use is in the manufacture of polyvinyl chloride (PVC) plastics, but they are also used in bleaching, disinfection, dry cleaning, fire prevention, refrigeration, and such pesticides as DDT and atrazine. Although PCBs and DDT were banned years ago, they are still with us because they persist in the environment. An EPA (Environmental Protection Agency) report on dioxin, another highly toxic organochlorine, reports that North Americans have far higher levels of dioxin in their systems than was previously thought, raising new questions about the chemical's relationship to breast cancer and other health problems. It is also known that the plastic chemical BPA (Bisphenol A) (present in cash register receipts, the lining of canned goods, and sporting equipment and medical supplies) is carcinogenic (cancer-promoting) and can cause lowered male sperm count.

Focusing on environmental issues necessarily involves addressing the effects of U.S. corporations and businesses on environmental quality. Even if exposure to toxic chemicals in the environment has been shown to be associated with only 10 to 20 percent of breast cancer cases (a very conservative estimate, because, as already mentioned, about half of all breast cancer cases cannot be explained by known risk factors), policy enforced by the U.S. government to control individual and corporate use of toxic chemicals could prevent between 9,000 and 36,000 women and men from contracting the disease every year. In this way, the "cure" is much more within reach than is acknowledged. See the sidebar "Breast Science" for links to help you explore the complex causes of breast cancer in the United States.

BREAST SCIENCE

Janet Lockhart

Female Breasts: Under the Male Gaze

Enter the phrase "breast science" in your favorite search engine, and alongside articles about breast cancer, your results will include titles such as "New Theory on Why Men Love Breasts" (Wolchover and Pappas, 2016) and "Men's Favourite Boob Type Revealed by Scientists Who Analysed Every Shape and Size" (Murphy, 2017). At first glance, the erotic and the medical approaches to female breasts may seem like polar opposites. But these results shed light on the concept of the "male gaze": the unspoken assumption that women—or, in this case, women's breasts—are there for men to look at, touch, evaluate, alter, and control.

As you will read in this chapter, modern medicine has been primarily the purview of males. As such, cultural stereotypes, biases, and assumptions about females have been incorporated into all aspects of the field. For example, assumptions have been made that male-centered research questions and findings simply transfer over to females—even in the case of breast cancer. Service delivery—even by women, to women—has largely been overseen, controlled, and regulated by men. And differences between men and women have been problematized, with women's regular physiological functions being treated as disorders (look up the origins of the word "hysterical" for one example).

In terms of breast health, the effects of this male-oriented viewpoint (androcentrism) have included the treatment of women's breasts as parts that pose a problem, puzzle, or challenge to the provider. Treatment is often impersonal and detached, with more emphasis on the skill of the provider "fixing" the problem than on the patient herself. There can be a focus on illness rather than health, passivity rather than proactivity. Even under the most compassionate and state-of-the-art conditions, the way women's breasts are handled—during mammograms, biopsies, surgeries, and chemo- and radiation therapies—can be invasive and traumatic.

Women are not simply passive participants in health care, however. They validate each other's experiences in support groups, work to establish government funding for research on women's health issues, and collaborate with researchers to make sure their perspectives as survivors and caregivers are included (see, for example, the UCSF "Breast Science Advocacy Core," 2018).

Further Reflection

Alter the male gaze in breast health care by challenging assumptions, building bridges, and seeing differences as just that—differences. Identify one aspect of female breast science in which you want to make a woman-centered change and envision how this could happen. Would you work to prevent release of carcinogens into the environment? Educate women about breast self-examination for early detection? Advocate to ensure that women and minorities are included in research and drug trials? Improve three-dimensional body imaging techniques? Encourage more collaboration between patients and medical providers? *What would a feminist breast science look like?*

References

Murphy, M. (2017, April 7). "Which Breast Is Best? Men's Favourite Boob Type Revealed by Scientists Who Analysed Every Shape and Size." Retrieved from https://www.thesun.co.uk/tech/2497834/mens-preferred-boob-type-revealed-according-to-scientists-who-analysed-every-shape-and-size/

UCSF, Helen Diller Family Comprehensive Cancer Center. (2018). "Breast Science Advocacy Core." Retrieved from http://cancer.ucsf.edu/research/programs/breast/breast-science-advocacy-core

Wolchover, N., and Pappas, S. (2016, March 17). "New Theory on Why Men Love Breasts." Retrieved from https://www.livescience.com/23500-why-men-love-breasts.html

These environmental toxins are also affecting men's health, of course, and not only because men are also diagnosed with breast cancer. In particular, as well as other cancer risks, environmental estrogens as well as pesticides, parabens, and chemical compounds like phthalates and bisphenol are linked to the decrease in testosterone levels among men today (other causes include increased weight and decreased smoking since nicotine is an aromatase inhibitor). A 2017 international study analyzed data from nearly 43,000 men in industrialized countries around the world and also found that sperm counts have dropped by more than half over the past four decades.

REPRODUCTIVE JUSTICE

Reproductive justice involves access to safe and affordable birthing and parenting options; reliable, safe, and affordable birth control technologies; freedom from forced sterilization; and the availability of abortion. However, in demanding these freedoms, reproductive justice moves beyond "rights" and matters of individual choice by addressing the multiple forces of domination faced by women of color and other marginalized people, which shape these demands and their outcome. In the reading "On Forbidden Wombs and Transnational Reproductive Justice," Jallicia Jolly makes this point by underscoring the efforts of reproductive justice to understand how racialized, classed, and gendered state-sanctioned violence interact to shape marginalized bodies as sites for political conflicts over law, welfare, and health. Quoting the reproductive justice advocate Loretta Ross, Jolly writes that reproductive justice addresses "the impact of interlocking systems of dominations on the quality of life of women of color, which offers a comprehensive way to address the multifaceted forces that constrain women's reproductive futures and their capacity to live healthy lives."

Worldwide, over 215 million women have an "unmet need" for reproductive health, meaning they want to either space or limit births but do not have access or lack consistent access to reliable methods of birth control that fit their personal needs. Women with unmet needs make up approximately 82 percent of the estimated 75 million unintended pregnancies that occur each year. The remaining 18 percent are due to inconsistent method use or method failure. Providing all women with basic family planning services is first and foremost a matter of basic human rights and bodily integrity. However, despite the importance of reproductive justice in the United States and worldwide, it is increasingly under attack. As the reading "Reproductive Rights as Human Rights" by Sarah Combellick-Bidney emphasizes, resisting population control while simultaneously claiming the right to freedom from domination and bodily self-determination is at the heart of reproductive struggles. Although in sharing narratives of human rights advocates in South Africa, India, and Brazil Combellick-Bidney uses a reproductive rights approach rather than one of reproductive justice, she articulates the necessity of access to contraception and abortion as well as the right to have children. She also recognizes the complex systems of discrimination and oppression that shape women's reproductive lives in these regions. In the sections that follow, we elaborate on these issues through a focus on the politics of sterilization, contraceptive technologies, and abortion.

STERILIZATION PRACTICES

Female sterilization options include tubal ligation, a surgical procedure in which the fallopian tubes are blocked ("having the tubes tied"), and hysterectomy, in which the uterus is removed. A less invasive alternative to tubal ligation is implantation of a device called Essure that blocks the fallopian tubes. Flexible coils are inserted through the vagina and cervix and into the fallopian tubes: the tubes that carry the eggs from the ovaries to the uterus. As tissue builds up, it creates a barrier that keeps sperm from reaching the eggs, thus preventing conception. Although hysterectomy is usually performed for medical reasons not associated with a desire for sterilization, this procedure results in sterilization. Vasectomy is permanent birth control for men, or male sterilization. It is effective and safe and does not limit male sexual pleasure. Countless women freely choose sterilization as a form of permanent birth control, and it is a useful method of family planning for many. "Freely choose," however, assumes a range of options not available to some women. In other words, "freely choose" is difficult in a racist, class-based, and sexist society that does not provide all people with the same options from which to choose. This is a key component of what is meant by reproductive justice.

As a result, women on welfare are more likely to be sterilized than women who are not, and women of color and women in nonindustrialized countries are disproportionately more likely to receive this procedure rather than being offered more expensive contraceptive options. Lingering here is the racist and classist idea that certain groups have more right to reproduce than others: a belief and social practice called eugenics, which assumes

---

HISTORICAL MOMENT

THE WOMEN'S HEALTH MOVEMENT

From the beginnings of the medical industry, women often suffered from the humiliation and degradation of medical practitioners who treated women as hysterical and as hypochondriacs, who medicalized normal female body functions, and who prevented women from controlling their own health. In 1969, as the women's movement heightened consciousness about other issues, women also began to examine the ways they had been treated and the ways women's biology and health had been largely unexplored. In the spring of that year, several women participated in a workshop on "women and their bodies" at a Boston conference. As they vented their anger at the medical establishment, they also began to make plans to take action. Although most had no medical training, they spent the summer studying all facets of women's health and the health care system. Then they began giving courses on women's bodies wherever they could find an audience. These women, who became known as the Boston Women's Health Collective, eventually published their notes and lectures as a book called *Our Bodies, Ourselves.*

Their efforts resulted in a national women's health movement. In March 1971, 800 women gathered for the first women's health conference in New York.

Women patients began to question doctors' authority and to bring patient advocates to their appointments to take notes on their treatment by medical professionals. Feminists questioned established medical practices such as the gendered diagnosis and treatment of depression, the recommendation for radical mastectomies whenever breast cancer was found, and the high incidence of cesarean deliveries and hysterectomies.

Although the original members of the women's health movement tended to be well-educated, middle-class white women, the movement quickly expanded to work with poor women and women of color to address the inequities caused by the intersections of gender with race and social class. Together, these women worked on reproductive rights, recognizing that for many poor women and women of color, the right to abortion was not as paramount as the right to be free from forced sterilization. Their work shaped the agenda of the National Women's Health Network, founded in 1975 and dedicated to advancing the health of women of all races and social classes.

some groups have more right to reproduce than others. Policies providing support for sterilization that make it free or very accessible obviously no longer require or force women to be sterilized. Rather, policies like these make the option attractive at a time when other options are limited.

One of the unfortunate legacies of reproductive history is that some women have been sterilized against their will, usually articulated as "against their full, informed consent." In the 1970s it was learned that many poor women—especially women of color, and Native American women in particular, as well as women who were mentally disabled or incarcerated—had undergone forced sterilization. Situations varied, but often they included women not giving consent at all, not knowing what was happening, believing they were having a different procedure, being strongly pressured to consent, or being unable to read or to understand the options told to them. The latter was especially true for women who did not speak or read English. Of course forced sterilization is now against the law, although problems remain. One consequence of forced sterilization for women of color in the United States was suspicion of birth control technologies as another potential tool of genocide. For example, when the contraceptive pill became available in the 1960s, some women of color remembered this history of forced sterilization and resisted its marketing, fearing the pill was another way to limit the nonwhite population. This was especially significant since the pill had been originally tested on women in Puerto Rico.

PARENTING OPTIONS AND CONTRACEPTIVE TECHNOLOGIES

In considering reproductive choice, it is important to think about the motivations for having children as well as the motivations for limiting fertility. Most people, women and men, assume they will have children at some point in their lives, and, for some, reproduction and parenting are less of a choice than something that people just do. Although in many nonindustrial societies children can be economic assets, in contemporary U.S. society, for the most part, children consume much more than they produce. Some women do see children as insurance in their old age, but generally today we have children for emotional reasons such as personal and marital fulfillment, and for social reasons such as carrying on the family name and fulfilling religious mandates. This freedom to have children as well as control conception is at the heart of another key issue: assisted reproductive technologies (ART) for infertile individuals who want children. These technologies include fertility medication; in vitro fertilization, in which eggs are retrieved from ovarian follicles, fertilized outside the body, and implanted in the uterus; and surrogacy. In response to current debates about whether these technologies are ultimately good or bad, we make the case that they are neither inherently liberating nor entirely oppressive. Rather, the consequences of these technologies can be understood only by considering how they are actually taken up within specific communities. What is clear, however, is that differential access to these technologies is increasingly an issue of reproductive justice.

Childbirth is an experience that has been shared by millions the world over. Women have historically helped other women at this time, strengthening family and kinship bonds and the ties of friendship. As the medical profession gained power and status and developed various technologies (forceps, for example), women's traditional authority associated with birthing was eclipsed by an increasing medicalization of birthing. Childbirth became seen as an irregular episode that requires medical procedures, often including invasive forms of "treatment." As these trends gained social power, women who could afford it started going to hospitals to birth their children instead of being attended at home by relatives, friends, or midwives. Unfortunately, in those early days, hospitals were relatively dangerous places where sanitation was questionable and women in childbirth were attended by doctors who knew far less about birthing than did midwives. As the twentieth century progressed and birthing in hospitals became routine, women gave birth lying down in the pelvic exam position with their feet in stirrups, sometimes with their arms strapped down; they were given drugs and episiotomies (an incision from the vagina toward the anus to prevent tearing) and were routinely shaved in the pubic area. By the late twentieth century, thanks to a strong consumer movement, women were giving birth under more humane conditions. Birthing centers now predominate in most hospitals, and doctors no longer perform and administer the routine procedures and drugs they used to. Nonetheless, a large number of pregnant women (especially women of color) do not receive any health care at all, and a larger number still receive inadequate health care, with some resorting to emergency rooms to deliver babies and having their first contact with the medical establishment at this time. As you can imagine, this scenario results in increased complications and potential unhealthy babies, and costs society much more than if routine health screening and preventive health care had been available.

Why might women want to control their fertility? The first and obvious answer concerns health. Over a woman's reproductive life, she could potentially birth many children and be in a constant state of pregnancy and lactation. Such a regimen compromises maximum health. Second, birthing large numbers of children might be seen as irresponsible in the context of world population and a planet with finite resources. Third, birthing is expensive and the raising of children even more expensive. Fourth, given that women have primary responsibility for child care and that in the global north and many other regions the organization of mothering tends to isolate women in their homes, it is important to consider the emotional effects of constant child-rearing. And, finally, if women had unlimited children, the constant caretaking of these children would preempt women's ability to be involved in other productive work outside the home. This "indirect cost" concept involves the loss or limitation of financial autonomy, work-related or professional identity, and creative and ego development. Overall, women are having children later in life and, as discussed in Chapter 8, are more likely than in the past to be raising them alone or in diverse family situations. In addition, about 1 in 10 babies is born to a teenage mother, although these rates have been falling since 1991 with the exception of a two-year increase between 2005 and 2007 (which coincided with increased funding for abstinence-only sex education programs). Half of young women who have babies in their teens do not earn a high school diploma by age 22. A third of their children will go on to become teen parents and are also more likely to do poorly in school and drop out. Teens of color are especially susceptible to early pregnancy as a result of poverty and the interlocking systems of domination that shape their everyday lives.

Unwanted births to solo mothers, especially among teenagers, may result from lack of knowledge and support about reproduction and contraception in the context of an increasing sexually active population, poverty and lack of opportunities for education and employment, failure of family and school systems to keep young people in school, the increased use of alcohol and other drugs, and increasing restrictions on access to abortion services. Some girls see motherhood as a rite of passage into adulthood, as a way to escape families of origin, or as a way to connect with another human being whom they may believe will love them unconditionally. Because the largest increase in solo births has been among women aged 25 years and older, these changes also reflect changing norms about raising a child "out of wedlock," either alone or in a heterosexual, gay/lesbian, or queer cohabiting (living together) arrangement, and the fact that many are wary of marriage, feel it is no longer a relevant institution, and/or choose and have the resources to maintain families outside of legal marriage. Media and television shows such as *Teen Mom* also help shape the cultural context for these changing norms.

Birth control technologies have been around for a long time. Many preindustrial societies used suppositories coated in various substances that blocked the cervix or functioned as spermicides; the condom was used originally to prevent the spread of syphilis, although it was discovered that it functioned as a contraceptive; and the concept of the intrauterine device was first used by Bedouins who hoped to prevent camels from conceiving during long treks across the desert by inserting small pebbles into the uterus. Nineteenth-century couples in the United States used "coitus interruptus" (withdrawal before ejaculation), the rhythm method (sexual intercourse only during nonfertile times), condoms, and abstinence. Although technologies of one kind or another have been around for generations, the issue for women has been the control of, and access to, these technologies. Patriarchal societies have long understood that to control women's lives, it is necessary to control women's reproductive options. In this way, information about, access to, and denial of birth control technologies are central aspects of women's role and status in society.

In 1873 the Comstock Act made it illegal to send "obscene, lewd, and/or lascivious" materials through the mail, including contraceptive devices and information. In addition to banning contraceptives and "quack" medicines, this act also banned the distribution of information on abortion. The state and federal restrictions became known as the Comstock Laws. Women understood that the denial of contraception kept them in the domestic sphere and, more importantly, exposed them to repetitive and often dangerous pregnancies. In response, a social movement emerged that was organized around reproductive choice. Called "voluntary motherhood," this movement not only involved giving women access to birth control, but also worked to facilitate reproduction and parenting under more safe, humane, and dignified conditions. Many of its followers sought to control male sexual behaviors and advocated a social purity politics that saw male "vice" (prostitution, sexually transmitted infections, and sexual abuse) as the problem. Margaret Sanger was a leader of this movement and in 1931 wrote *My Fight for Birth Control* about her decision to become involved in the struggle for reproductive choice.

One unfortunate aspect, however, was the early birth control movement's affiliation with an emerging eugenics movement that argued only the "fit" should be encouraged to

ACTIVIST PROFILE

SISTERLOVE

The beginnings of SisterLove can be traced to a small group of women in Atlanta who organized to educate women about HIV/AIDS, self-help, and safer sex.

Founded in 1989, SisterLove "is on a mission to eradicate the adverse impact of HIV/AIDS and other reproductive health challenges upon women and their families through education, prevention, support and human rights advocacy in the United States and around the world" (http://sisterlove.org/about-us/). A part of the reproductive justice movement that centers on the reproductive health needs of women of color, Sister-Love focuses on HIV prevention and outreach to women of color in Atlanta.

The organization's "Healthy Love" workshop provides prevention strategies. The facilitators take their programs into communities and offer them in spaces where participants feel safe and comfortable. Sister-Love's website explains, "The workshop encourages participants to be confident in approaching their own sexuality and to demand safe behaviors from themselves and their partners. It also provides the opportunity for women to explore, discuss and dispel the barriers to practicing safer sex. The HLW respects the cultural traditions of African-American women who, throughout time, have gathered to support one another in times of crisis and growth" (http://sisterlove.org/our-work/health-education-prevention/). Another outreach program focuses on HIV prevention education with women attending historically black colleges and universities.

SisterLove also offers a "Bridge Leadership" program that connects the group to a variety of other reproductive justice organizations, including SisterSong, and supports collaborative projects. The organization also has a capacity-building project in South Africa to enhance the capacity and leadership capabilities of NGOs and community-based organizations working with women and youth to prevent HIV.

As staff member Omisegun Pennick reminds us: "Indeed, 30 years into the epidemic we still have to drive the conversation around the absolute inclusion of women, especially women of color, in the movement to eradicate HIV/AIDS throughout the globe. We have to actively engage researchers in remembering to include women of color when talking about Pre-Exposure Prophylaxis (PreP) and other clinical treatments. We must support the critical work of campaigns such as the 30 for 30 to ensure that a minimum of 30% of the national resources for HIV/AIDS are given to organizations that directly serve women. We have to rally at the local, regional, and national level to ensure that policies and plans such as the National AIDS Strategy directly include women" (http://sisterloveinc.blogspot.com/).

reproduce. Birth control was therefore necessary to prevent the "unfit" from engaging in unlimited reproduction. The "unfit" included poor and immigrant populations, the "feeble-minded," and criminals. Using a rationale grounded in eugenics, birth control proponents were able to argue their case while receiving the support of those in power in society. Nonetheless, although contraceptive availability varied from state to state, it was not until a Supreme Court decision (*Griswold v. Connecticut*) in 1965 that married couples were allowed legal rights to birth control. The Court's ruling said that the prohibition of contraceptive use by married people was unconstitutional in that it violated the constitutional right to privacy. This legal right was extended to single/solo people in 1972 and to minors in 1977.

Today there are a variety of contraceptive methods available. Their accessibility is limited by the availability of information about them, by cost, and by health care providers' sponsorship. As you read about these technologies, consider the following questions: Whose body is being affected? Who gets to deal with the side effects? Who is paying for these methods? Who will pay if these methods fail? Who will be hurt if these side effects become more serious? These questions are framed by racialized gender relations and the context of the U.S. economy and its health organizations.

Alongside permanent methods of birth control mentioned earlier (tubal ligation and vasectomy) are other forms. These include the intrauterine device (IUD), a small, *t*-shaped device made of flexible plastic that is inserted into the uterus and prevents the implantation of a fertilized egg. IUDs are available only by prescription, must be inserted by a clinician, and are a popular form of reversible birth control. IUDs are divided into two types: copper IUDs, such as ParaGard, which provide protection from pregnancy for up to 12 years; and hormonal IUDs, such as Mirena, Kyleena, Liletta, and Skyla, which use the hormone progestin and provide protection for 3 to 5 years depending on the device. IUDs with hormones claim to reduce menstrual cramping and flow, but they may increase the risk of pelvic inflammatory disease among women with multiple sexual partners and do not protect against HIV/AIDS and other sexually transmitted infections.

Hormone regulation is another birth control method. The combined oral contraceptive pill (COCP), often referred to as the birth control pill or colloquially as "the pill," contains a combination of two hormones: progestin and estrogen. It became widely available in the United States in the 1960s and quickly became the most popular means of contraception despite such side effects as nausea, weight gain, breast tenderness, and headaches. Combination pills usually work by preventing a woman's ovaries from releasing eggs (ovulation). They also thicken the cervical mucus, which keeps sperm from joining with an egg. Extended-cycle pills are COCPs designed to reduce or eliminate menstrual bleeding. They usually produce a period every three months. The progestin-only or "mini pill" contains no estrogen and has fewer side effects than the regular pill; it works by thickening cervical mucus and/or preventing ovulation. Taking the pill daily maintains the level of hormone that is needed to prevent pregnancy, and it is important that this pill be taken at exactly the same time every day.

Contraception options also include implants such as Norplant, a contraceptive device inserted under the skin of the upper arm that releases a small amount of the hormone progestin for up to five years. As a result of lawsuits associated with unanticipated side effects, the maker of Norplant no longer markets this device in the United States, although it is available worldwide. Depo-Provera, which also uses progestin, is a contraceptive injection that provides protection for three months. It inhibits the secretion of hormones that stimulate the ovaries and prevents ovulation. It also thickens cervical mucus to prevent the entrance of sperm into the uterus. It has been used safely, although risks include loss of bone density and side effects generally associated with the pill—such as weight gain; irregular, heavy, or no bleeding; headaches; depression; and mood changes. In addition, it may take up to a year after discontinuing use of Depo-Provera before a woman is fertile again. Alongside implants and injections are contraceptive patches, such as Ortho Evra, placed on the arm, buttocks, or abdomen, which release hormones.

Vaginal rings are also relatively popular contraceptives in the United States. One device marketed under the name NuvaRing was approved in 2001. It is a flexible, transparent ring about 2 inches in diameter that women insert vaginally once a month. The ring releases a continuous dose of estrogen and progestin. The ring remains in the vagina for 21 days and is then removed and discarded, and a new ring inserted. None of these hormone methods protect against HIV/AIDS and other sexually transmitted infections.

Next are the barrier methods. The diaphragm, cervical cap, and shield are barrier devices that are inserted into the vagina before sexual intercourse, fit over the cervix, and prevent sperm from entering the uterus. These methods work in conjunction with spermicidal jelly, which is placed along the rim of the device, or spermicidal foam, which is inserted into the vagina with a small plunger. Unlike supplies for the other methods, spermicides are available at any drugstore, but the diaphragm or cervical cap must be obtained from a physician or clinic. Also available at drugstores are vaginal sponges that are coated with spermicide, inserted into the vagina, and work to block the cervix and absorb sperm. All these barrier methods work best when used in conjunction with a condom and are much less effective when used alone. The male condom is a rolled-up latex rubber tube that is unrolled on the penis. The female condom is a floppy polyurethane tube with an inner ring at the closed end that fits over the cervix and an outer ring at the open end that hangs outside the vagina. Condoms block sperm from entering the vagina and, when used properly in conjunction with other barrier methods, are highly effective in preventing pregnancy. Another very important aspect of condoms is that they are the only form of contraception that offers protection against sexually transmitted infections (STIs) generally and HIV/AIDS in particular. All health care providers emphasize that individuals not in a mutually monogamous sexual relationship should always use condoms in conjunction with other methods.

Finally, levonorgestrel emergency contraception (EC), commonly known as the "morning-after pill," is currently available under trade names that include Plan B, My Way, and Next Choice B. Used after unprotected heterosexual intercourse, EC is most effective if taken within 12 hours, although it offers protection for three days with some protection for up to five days. EC provides a high dose of the same hormones that are in birth control pills to prevent ovulation and fertilization. Morning-after pills are available for purchase over the counter and without a prescription or ID at drugstores and pharmacies, irrespective of a person's age or gender; however, sometimes the morning-after pill is locked up or kept behind the counter. Plan B usually costs about $40 to $50, but other brands tend to be cheaper. A new EC, EllaOne (ulipristal acetate), is also available. Note that EC is different from the drug Mifeprex (the U.S. trade name for mifepristone), also known as RU-486 and discussed in the following section, that works by terminating an early pregnancy and is known as a "medical abortion." Emergency contraception does not terminate a pregnancy but prevents one from occurring. It is important to understand the ways these two medications serve two different purposes and work completely differently. As mentioned, RU-486 results in a termination of a pregnancy and is used only after pregnancy is established (and no more than 49 days since a woman's last menstrual period). On the other hand, EC is used to prevent pregnancy. It will not harm an existing pregnancy and does not cause an abortion.

ABORTION

Although induced abortion—the removal of the fertilized ovum or fetus from the uterus—is only one aspect of reproductive justice, it has dominated discussion of this topic. This is unfortunate because reproductive rights are about much more than abortion. Nonetheless, this is one topic that generates unease and often heated discussion. Pro-choice advocates believe that abortion is women's choice, women should not be forced to have children against their will, a fertilized ovum should not have all the legal and moral rights of personhood, and all children should be wanted children. Pro-choice advocates tend to believe in a woman's right to have an abortion even though they might not make that decision for themselves. Pro-life advocates believe that human personhood begins at conception and a fertilized ovum or fetus has the right to full moral and legal rights of personhood. They believe the sanctity of human life outweighs the rights of mothers. Some pro-life advocates see abortion as murder and doctors and other health care workers who assist in providing abortion services as accomplices to a crime.

According to a 2018 Gallup poll, and 46 years after the Supreme Court issued its opinion in *Roe v. Wade* that legalized abortion, 70 percent of people in the United States believe abortion should be legal in all or some circumstances. However, in a follow-up question probing what "some circumstances" means, the majority of respondents said it should be legal in a "few" rather than "most" circumstances. The result is that 43 percent say abortion should be legal in all (29 percent) or most (14 percent) circumstances, while 53 percent say it should be legal in only a few (35 percent) or no circumstances (18 percent). Twenty-six percent of men and 31 percent of women say that abortion should be legal in all circumstances. This figure jumps from 31 percent of women generally to 42 percent for college-educated women. Eighteen percent of both women and men say abortion should be totally illegal.

A 2017 Pew Research Center study also reported different attitudes on abortion by race and ethnicity. The majority of black respondents (62 percent) believe abortion should be legal in all or most circumstances, compared to 58 percent of whites, while attitudes among Latinx are split, with 50 percent advocating for the legality of abortion and 49 percent the illegality in all or most circumstances. About 65 percent of young adults under 30 years also believe abortion should be legal in all or most circumstances. In addition, differences exist across religious affiliations, with 70 percent of white evangelical Protestants believing that abortion should be illegal in all or most circumstances. In comparison, approximately 65 percent of white mainline Protestants, slightly over 50 percent of Catholics, and 80 percent of those religiously unaffiliated believe that abortion should be legal in all or most circumstances. Finally, not surprisingly, there are distinct differences in attitudes toward abortion based on political party affiliation. The Pew report indicated that two-thirds of Republicans felt abortion should be illegal and three-quarters of Democrats that it should be legal, both in all or most circumstances.

All of this suggests that there is a distinct divide in opinion and that most people do not favor an outright ban, but want limits on abortions. These data show that relatively few Americans are positioned at either extreme of the spectrum of beliefs: abortion should be legal in all circumstances or illegal in all circumstances. Despite this "middle ground" position, the public debate on abortion tends to be highly polarized.

As of this writing, the ideological makeup of the Supreme Court has shifted along with the Trump presidency and the controversial addition of Judge Brett Kavanaugh, who is known for his anti-choice position, and there is discussion about whether *Roe v. Wade* will eventually be overturned, giving rights to the states to decide abortion policy. Most scholars suggest the current "chipping away" of abortion access, discussed shortly, will

REPRODUCTIVE JUSTICE AND ABORTION: LET'S THINK TRANSNATIONALLY!

Maria Cristina Lenzi Miori

Data

According to the World Health Organization (WHO, 2017), approximately 56 million induced abortions took place annually between the years 2010 and 2014. In each of those years, around 25 million of the abortions were performed in circumstances considered unsafe by WHO, which categorizes unsafe abortion into "less safe" or "least safe." "Less safe" means that these procedures were performed either by trained professionals who were using unsafe methods or by untrained people who had access to safe abortion-inducing drugs, and "least safe" denotes abortions induced by untrained persons using unsafe methods.

As the following infographic shows, the regions where most unsafe abortions occur are Asia, Africa, and Latin America.

Laws

Abortion laws around the world vary drastically, and each country's restrictions play a major role regarding access to both safe providers and safe abortion methods. The data show that in countries that regulate and legalize abortion, 9 out of 10 procedures are categorized as safe, contrasting with the alarming 1 out of 4 safe procedures in countries with restricted policies (Sedgh et al., 2016; WHO, 2017).

The next image shows the World's Abortion Laws map. This is an interactive map that allows you to explore the laws of specific countries around the world, describing the level of restriction of each place (http://worldabortionlaws.com/map/).

Accessibility, Prevention, and Protection

Unsafe abortion is an issue that affects a vast part of the world population and can cause a series of lasting health complications or even death (Sedgh et. al., 2016). To change the current scenario and prevent unsafe abortions, it is crucial to first guarantee worldwide

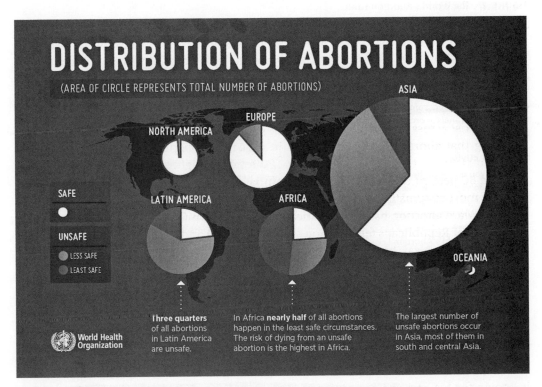

FIGURE 1 Distribution of Abortions
Source: World Health Organization (2019)

(continued)

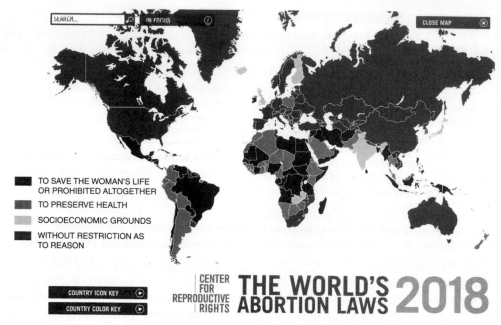

FIGURE 2 The World's Abortion Laws
Source: Center for Reproductive Rights (2018)

accessibility to both comprehensive sex education and multiple contraceptive methods and family planning counseling (WHO, 2003). Besides prevention, it is important to hold each country accountable for providing accessible, legal, and safe abortion methods done by trained professionals in order to avoid risks and promote public health.

Learning Activity

1. Were you aware of the global aspects of abortion? What do you think is the importance and/or benefits of looking at abortion issues through transnational lenses? Why is it important to consider abortion a human right?

2. Visit the "World's Abortion Laws" map at http://worldabortionlaws.com/ and compare it to the infographic "Distribution of Abortions." Can you identify any relevant correlations between the map and the infographic?

3. Choose two countries with abortion law systems that are unfamiliar to you and discuss them. Consider the laws, geographical locations, socioeconomic aspects, and historical context in which they are immersed.

References

Center for Reproductive Rights. (2018). "The World's Abortion Laws" (Map). Retrieved from http://worldabortionlaws.com/map/

Sedgh, G., et al. (2016). "Abortion Incidence Between 1990 and 2014: Global, Regional, and Subregional Levels and Trends." *Lancet*, 388(10041), 258–267.

World Health Organization. (2003). *Safe Abortion: Technical and Policy Guidance for Health Systems.* Geneva: World Health Organization.

World Health Organization. (2017, September 28). "Worldwide, an Estimated 25 Million Unsafe Abortions Occur Each Year" (News Release). Retrieved from http://www.who.int/en/news-room/detail/28-09-2017-worldwide-an-estimated-25-million-unsafe-abortions-occur-each-year

World Health Organization. (2019). "Distribution of Abortions" (Infographic). Retrieved from http://www.who.int/reproductivehealth/publications/unsafe_abortion/infographic-distribution-abortions.jpg

continue. Indeed, the number of U.S. abortion-providing facilities has declined dramatically. Over 90 percent of all U.S. counties lack a clinic, and about 40 percent of women of reproductive age live in those counties. Whatever the future holds, however, abortion is a divisive topic, with 48 percent of those polled identifying as pro-choice and 48 percent as pro-life, with the rest undecided. Note that this is a different question than whether abortion should be legal or not. The 2018 Gallup poll mentioned earlier reported women being somewhat more pro-choice than men, with 50 percent of women describing themselves as pro-choice and 44 percent as pro-life, whereas 46 percent of men reported themselves as pro-choice and 46 percent as pro-life.

In addition, a majority of adults aged 18 to 49 identify as pro-choice whereas older adults as a group are more likely to be pro-life. Others more oriented to the pro-choice position include those with a college education, high-income earners, those who live in the eastern part of the United States, and city dwellers. On the other end of the spectrum, religiously affiliated individuals, low-income individuals, adults with no college education, and those who live in the southern part of the United States are more likely to join Republicans and conservatives as the least pro-choice.

There are several issues associated with feminist pro-choice politics. These include, for example, the moral responsibilities associated with requiring the birth of unwanted children, because the forces attempting to deny women safe and legal abortions are the very same ones that call for reductions in the social, medical, educational, and economic support of poor children. Does "pro-life" include being "for life" of these children once they are born? "Pro-life" politicians often tend to vote against increased spending for services that benefit women and families. Second, there are the moral responsibilities involved in requiring women to be mothers against their will. If you do grant full personhood rights to a fertilized ovum or fetus, then at what point do these rights take priority over the rights of another fully established person, the mother? What of fathers' rights? Third, studies have shown that between two-thirds and three-quarters of all women accessing abortions would have an illegal abortion if abortions were banned. Illegal abortions have high mortality rates; issues do not go away just by making them illegal. In the years since *Roe v. Wade*, the Supreme Court ruling legalizing abortion in the United States, thousands of women's lives have been saved by access to legal abortion. It is estimated that before 1973, 1.2 million U.S. women resorted to illegal abortions each year, and that botched

LEARNING ACTIVITY

FRAMING THE DEBATE

The words we choose to talk about issues matter, and the frames we create for understanding reproductive justice shape the conversation. Following are some of the ways anti-choice activists frame the debate. Search on the web, newspapers, TV, or social media to find examples of these frames. How do you think these frames shape the debate? How do advocates of reproductive justice frame the debate? What differences do these frames make?

"Abortion as murder"   "Fetal personhood"
"Partial-birth abortion"   "Abortion as holocaust/
                              genocide"

"Rape exemptions"   "Abortion as harm to
                            women"
"Sexual morality"   "Abstinence-only until
                            marriage"
"The right to conscience"

Source: These frames are identified in Political Research Associates, *Defending Reproductive Justice: An Activist Resource Kit* (Somerville, MA: Political Research Associates, 2013). Retrieved from http://www.politicalresearch.org/wp-content/uploads/ downloads/2013/04/Defending-Reproductive-Justice-ARK-Final.pdf

illegal abortions caused as many as 5,000 annual deaths. Finally, although most feminists consider themselves pro-choice, there are exceptions, most notably the Feminists for Life of America organization. Their motto is "Women Deserve Better than Abortion," and they advocate opposition to all forms of violence, characterizing abortion as violence against women as well as against the fetus.

According to the Guttmacher Institute, rates of abortion in the United States are at a historic low. However, nearly half (45 percent) of U.S. pregnancies are unintended and about 4 in 10 of these are terminated by abortion. Of all pregnancies (wanted and unwanted, but excluding miscarriages), about 2 in 10 end in abortion. By age 45, at least half of all American women will have experienced an unintended pregnancy and about one-third will have had an abortion. Almost 9 in 10 abortions occur in the first 12 weeks of pregnancy (the first trimester) and 62 percent of all abortions take place in the first 9 weeks. Less than 2 percent occur at 21 weeks or later. Women who have abortions come from all racial, ethnic, socio-economic, and religious backgrounds, and their motivations vary. Among women obtaining abortions, approximately half are younger than 25 years and 12 percent are teenagers. The abortion rate is highest among women who are 20 to 24 years old.

The Guttmacher Institute also reports that white women account for 39 percent of abortion procedures, blacks 28 percent, Latinas 25 percent, and those of other races and ethnicities 9 percent. Religious affiliation varies: 17 percent are mainline Protestant, 13 percent evangelical Protestant, 24 percent Catholic, 8 percent "other" religions, and 38 percent no religious affiliation. In addition, 46 percent of those accessing abortion procedures have never married and are not cohabitating, although nearly half were living with a male partner in the month they became pregnant, including 14 percent who were married and 31 percent who were cohabiting. Slightly over half were using a contraceptive method during the time they became pregnant, and 59 percent of abortions are obtained by women who have at least one child. Finally, 75 percent of those accessing an abortion are poor or low-income with annual incomes below the federal poverty level.

In the United States, abortion was not limited by law or even opposed by the church until the nineteenth century. In 1800 there were no states with antiabortion laws and abortion was a relatively common occurrence through the use of pills, powders, and mechanical devices. Generally, abortion was allowed before "quickening," understood as that time when the fetus's movements could be felt by the mother (usually between three and four months). Between 1821 and 1840, 10 states enacted laws that included provisions on abortion, although in 5 these applied only to abortions after quickening. Between 1840 and 1860 the numbers of abortions increased such that some scholars estimate one abortion for every five or six live births. According to James Mohr's *Abortion in America*, abortion became more popular among married women and those of the middle and upper classes. This alarmed physicians in the rapidly growing medical profession. Mohr explains that physicians' concerns centered on ethical issues such as lower birth rates among the white middle classes, scientific reasons to question the importance of quickening, the dangers of abortion for women, and the desire of physicians to rid themselves of some competitors such as midwives and others who helped provide abortions. He suggests that physicians were the major force in the enactment of laws against abortion in the nineteenth century, working through the American Medical Association to campaign state legislatures to further restrict abortion. Between 1860 and 1880 more than 40 laws restricted abortion and remained largely intact for a century. Abortion became less visible, and the Comstock Laws prevented the sharing of information about them. Abortions continued to be performed, but they were called something else, and in some states they were performed to save a mother's health and life. Not surprisingly, illegal abortions were rampant and often unsafe. By 1860 the Catholic Church officially had ruled against abortion even though, as already explained, religious objections were not at the root of antiabortion legislation. By the mid-twentieth century, resistance to abortion laws had increased such that in 1959 the American Law Institute proposed revisions that were later adopted by a number of states. It is important to understand that the Supreme Court decisions of the 1970s were not a modern "weakening" of moral standards, but a return to what many Americans believed and practiced in the past.

In 1969 Planned Parenthood supported the repeal of antiabortion laws. Then in 1970 Hawaii and New York repealed their abortion legislation, but a 1972 referendum in Michigan to do so was defeated. Change came in 1973 when the U.S. Supreme Court ruled in *Roe v. Wade* that a Texas antiabortion statute was unconstitutional and overturned all states' bans on abortion. The ruling used the *Griswold v. Connecticut* decision to argue that the right to privacy encompassed a woman's decision of whether or not to terminate a pregnancy. It did not, however, attempt to decide the religious or philosophical issue about when life begins. The Court did agree that, under the law, a fetus is not treated as a legal person with civil rights. The ruling went on to divide pregnancy into three equal stages, or trimesters, and explained the differential interventions that the state could make during these different periods. The *Roe v. Wade* ruling held that the U.S. Constitution protects a woman's decision to terminate her pregnancy and allowed first-trimester abortions on demand. It declared that only after the fetus is viable, capable of sustained survival outside the woman's body with or without artificial aid, may the states control abortion. Abortions necessary to preserve the life or health of the mother must be allowed, however, even after fetal viability. Prior to viability, states can regulate abortion, but only if the regulation does not impose a "substantial obstacle" in the path of women.

There has been a general chipping away of women's rights to abortion since that ruling. Subsequent legislative and legal challenges have made abortion access more difficult and dangerous. Activities limiting legal rights to abortion currently include the following: heartbeat bans that attempt to outlaw abortion as soon as a heartbeat is detected, which is often at the embryonic stage; laws restricting poor and young women's access; debates over refusal clauses, such as whether pharmacists may choose not to dispense medication if such practices offend their religious or political beliefs; bans on rarely occurring late-term abortion methods that protect women's health; violent tactics that intimidate doctors and patients; and pregnancy crisis centers that mislead women by purporting to offer full services but work by misleading and dissuading women from accessing an abortion.

One of the first restrictions on abortion rights was the Hyde Amendment, sponsored by Henry Hyde, a Republican senator from Illinois. It was an amendment to the 1977 Health, Education, and Welfare Appropriations Act and gave states the right to prohibit the use of

Medicaid funds for abortion, thus limiting abortion to those women who could afford to pay and restricting abortion for poor women. Note that this was accompanied by Supreme Court rulings (*Beal v. Doe*, 1977) that said that states could refuse to use Medicaid funds to pay for abortions and that Congress could forbid states from using federal funds (including Medicaid) to pay for abortion services (*Harris v. McRae*, 1980). The latter ruling also allowed states to deny funds even for medically necessary abortions.

Second, the 1989 *Webster v. Reproductive Health Services*, sponsored by Missouri state attorney William Webster, upheld a state's right to prevent public facilities or public employees from assisting with abortions, to prevent counseling concerning abortion if public funds were involved, and to allow parental notification rights. The latter restrict abortion for young women because parental involvement laws require young women who seek abortion care to tell their parents or get their permission, regardless of their family circumstances.

Third, *Planned Parenthood v. Casey*, although upholding *Roe v. Wade* in 1992, also upheld the state's right to restrict abortion in various ways: parental notification, mandatory counseling and waiting periods, and limitations on public spending for abortion services. Refusal clauses and counseling bans limit women's access to honest information and medical care, making it virtually impossible for some women to access abortion services altogether. Refusal clauses permit a broad range of individuals and/or institutions—hospitals, hospital employees, health care providers, pharmacists, employers, and insurers—to refuse to provide, pay for, counsel, or even give referrals for medical treatment that they personally oppose. Counseling bans, also known as "gag rules," prohibit health care providers—including individuals, under certain circumstances—from counseling or referring women for abortion care, preventing doctors from treating their patients responsibly and severely limiting women's ability to make informed decisions. In 2013 there were 21 states with laws prohibiting some or all state organizations that receive state funds from providing counseling or referring women for abortion services. There have also been state rulings that require pregnant women to be offered ultrasound images of her fetus before she can have an abortion (even in the case of pregnancy due to rape or incest) and that shield physicians from lawsuits if they choose not to tell a pregnant patient that her fetus has a birth defect for fear she might opt for abortion. Other bills in Mississippi and Virginia have been debated that require women to have ultrasounds before abortions can be performed.

LEARNING ACTIVITY
DEBATING REPRODUCTIVE RIGHTS

Select one of the following topics to research from various perspectives. Be sure to represent perspectives that both support and oppose the topic, and be sure to examine various feminist analyses of the topic. Present your findings to your classmates. You may want to present your findings in the form of a debate, a Q&A session, or a pros/cons list.

TOPICS

1. The morning-after pill
2. The right to have children (particularly for lesbians, women with disabilities, single women, and older women)
3. Assisted reproductive technologies
4. Abstinence-only education
5. Distributing condoms in public schools
6. Selective reduction (abortion of one or more fetuses when pregnancy results in multiple fetuses)

Congress has also imposed restrictions on abortion care for women who depend on the government for their health care needs, including women serving in the military. With very rare exceptions, almost all women who obtain health care through federal programs are subject to additional restrictions on their right to choose. Unlike women who can use their own funds or private health insurance to pay for abortion care, women insured by federal health plans often lack the means to pay for an abortion. These include low-income women who receive health care through Medicaid, federal employees and military personnel and their dependents, and women in federal prisons.

Webster v. Reproductive Health Services and *Planned Parenthood v. Casey* both gave states the right to impose parental involvement laws. Attempts to mandate parental involvement, while often seemingly reasonable, unfortunately may endanger vulnerable teenagers. Some young women feel they cannot involve their parents because they come from homes where physical violence or emotional abuse is prevalent, because their pregnancies are the result of incest, or because they fear parental anger and disappointment. Mandatory parental involvement laws (regarding both notice and consent: "notice" requires notification of intent to terminate a pregnancy; "consent" requires the permission of one or both biological parents) do not solve the problem of troubled family communication; they only exacerbate a potentially dangerous situation. In other words, although in a perfect world it would be positive for parents to provide guidance at this time, we do not live in a perfect world and instead of protecting young women, these laws have been shown to have serious consequences such as illegal and self-induced abortion, family violence, and suicide. Most states'

IDEAS FOR ACTIVISM

TEN THINGS YOU CAN DO TO PROTECT CHOICE

1. Volunteer for a pro-choice organization. Pro-choice organizations need volunteers. There are dozens of organizations working in various ways to help women get the services they need.
2. Write a letter to a local clinic or abortion provider thanking them for putting themselves on the line for women. Doctors and clinic workers hear vociferously from those opposed to abortion. Hearing a few words of thanks goes a long way.
3. Monitor your local paper for articles about abortion. Write a letter to the editor thanking them for accurate coverage or correcting them if coverage is biased.
4. Find out how your elected representatives have voted on abortion. Call and ask for their voting records, not just on bills relating to the legality of abortion, but also on related issues such as funding for poor women, restrictions meant to impede a woman's access to services (such as waiting periods and informed consent), and contraceptives funding

and/or insurance coverage. Whether or not you agree with the votes of your elected officials, write and let them know that this is an issue on which you make voting decisions. Antichoice activists don't hesitate to do this; you should do it too.

5. Talk to your children now about abortion. Explain why you believe it's a decision only a woman can make for herself.
6. If you have had an abortion, legal or illegal, consider discussing it with people in your life. More than 40 percent of American women will have at least one abortion sometime during their life. More openness about the subject might lead to less judgment, more understanding, and fewer attempts to make it illegal.
7. Volunteer for a candidate whom you know to be pro-choice.
8. Be an escort at a clinic that provides abortions.
9. Vote!
10. Hold a house meeting to discuss choice with your friends.

Source: Adapted from www.choice.org.

laws make it harder for teens to make a responsible and safe decision in a difficult situation. For example, 23 states currently require parental consent, 15 require parental notice, and 11 have parental notice and/or consent laws but permit other adults to stand in for a parent.

The fourth "chipping away" of *Roe v. Wade* occurred in 2003 when the U.S. Congress passed the Federal Abortion Ban and President George W. Bush signed it into law. The ban outlaws certain second-trimester abortions that leading medical and health organizations, doctors, medical school professors, and other experts have repeatedly declared under oath as necessary to protect women's health. These are performed when the life or health of the mother is at risk or when the baby is too malformed (for example, in severe cases of hydrocephalus in which the baby cannot live outside the uterus and a normal delivery would kill the mother). In 2007 the U.S. Supreme Court upheld this first ever federal ban on an abortion procedure. Surprisingly, and reversing three decades of legal rulings, the federal ban does not allow an exception when women's health is in danger. The Court's decision gives the go-ahead to the states to restrict abortion services (discussed shortly) and paves the way for new legislation to enact additional bans on abortion, including those that doctors say are safe and medically necessary. Following this federal ban on abortion have been other restrictions at the state level. A case in point as of this writing is a Tennessee state bill that passed the state house and bans abortions after a fetal heartbeat is detected. It would become the most restrictive state abortion policy in the nation, despite the fact that a similar law adopted in Iowa was recently ruled unconstitutional. More than half of all states have informed consent laws that require doctors to counsel patients before the procedure and/or reflect for a period of time (usually 24 hours, although some states mandate up to three days) before being allowed to access a legal abortion. These states also require abortion clinics to carry written informed consent brochures containing information about fetal development stages and risks associated with abortion, and its alternatives.

In addition, state restrictions also include those on rare, late-term abortions. In 2010, for example, Nebraska passed the country's most restrictive abortion law that barred abortions after 20 weeks. In 2011, Alabama, Idaho, Indiana, Kansas, and Oklahoma followed suit; and in 2012, Arizona, Georgia, and Louisiana passed curbs of their own. If laws provide exceptions for the life or health of the woman, they may be considered constitutional under *Roe v. Wade*. Many scholars, however, have emphasized that the movement to limit rare, late-term abortions is a "straw man" argument in which a perceived opponent is misrepresented in order to create the illusion of having refuted the argument by replacing it with a superficially similar, yet unequivalent, position (the "straw man"). The misrepresentation is the notion that late-term abortions occur frequently and willingly rather than rarely and usually as a result of a medical emergency. Such tactics have been used throughout history in polemical debates, particularly in cases of highly charged, emotional issues. With the exception of laws in Arizona, Idaho, and Georgia, many of these cases have not been challenged as unconstitutional (Idaho's law was found to be unconstitutional as of this writing). This is in part because they do not really have a serious effect: As already discussed, less than 2 percent of abortions occur after 20 weeks. Still, their real effect is twofold: misrepresentation and the energizing of a movement to limit women's reproductive freedom, and the hope among anti-choice activists to force these laws to be considered by the U.S. Supreme Court with the goal of overturning women's right to a legal abortion.

As of this writing, the latter may occur as states move to pass earlier bans. For example, in 2013 Arkansas passed a ban on all abortions after 12 weeks (despite the veto of its governor), and North Dakota proceeded to pass the most restrictive law banning all abortions after 6 weeks. While the Arkansas law still does not affect many procedures, the North Dakota law, although seemingly unconstitutional, basically bans all abortions in the state. Again, the goal is to put abortion back in front of the Supreme Court, get *Roe v. Wade* overturned, and return abortion policymaking power to the states. Currently four states—Louisiana, Mississippi, North Dakota, and South Dakota—have "trigger laws" imposing near-total criminal bans on abortion if *Roe v. Wade* is overturned. A trigger law in this context means that the state has a law that says its policy is to ban abortion at a delayed date. Ten other states have pre-*Roe* antiabortion legislation on the books, although it is not clear how these laws might be reactivated. An additional seven states have expressed "intent to limit abortion to the maximum extent permitted" in the absence of the federal mandate.. As of this writing, a legal challenge has delayed implementation. In addition, the U.S. Supreme Court in 2018 allowed an Arkansas ban on RU-486, the abortion pill, to stand.

The fifth "chipping away" of abortion rights occurred in April 2004 when President George W. Bush signed the Unborn Victims of Violence Act into law, giving the zygote, embryo, or fetus the same legal rights as a person and preparing the groundwork for further restrictions on abortion access. Also known as the Laci Peterson Law, in reference to the murder of a woman and her unborn child, this law creates the notion of double homicide in the case of the murder of a pregnant woman, although the law has jurisdiction only for homicides committed on federal property. This law is somewhat controversial for women's rights supporters. Though written to support survivors of violence by establishing that a fetus of any gestational age has equal personhood with a woman, it jeopardizes women's rights to safe and legal abortions.

Sixth, versions of the Child Interstate Abortion Notification Act were again introduced to Congress in 2017, but the act is not yet law. It seeks to make it a crime to take a minor woman (under 18 years of age) residing in a state with parental notification and/or consent laws across state lines to access an abortion. It also seeks to create a national requirement for parental notification for underage women wanting to terminate a pregnancy and requires a 24-hour waiting period for a minor's abortion. Doctors and others could be prosecuted under the legislation. Supporters of the bill declare it necessary to protect young women because an adult predator could impregnate a girl and then force her to have an abortion to hide the crime. Opponents say the bill is too far reaching, explaining that it sets up more roadblocks for women who have the right to safe and legal abortion, and could further isolate young women by making it a crime for a family member or other caring adult to provide assistance. Major medical and public health organizations, including the American Medical Association and the American Academy of Pediatrics, oppose such efforts to prevent young women from receiving confidential health services.

Finally, restrictions on abortion occur as a result of new requirements for clinics that provide a certain number of surgical abortions per year and that publicly advertise outpatient abortion services. These clinics must meet the licensing requirements of usually more extensive freestanding outpatient surgical facilities: a hardship for small facilities whose only surgery is abortion. Other restrictions on abortion access associated with abortion facilities include violence and harassment of medical personnel who provide legal abortion services. These violent tactics intimidate medical personnel and patients seeking reproductive health care. In May 2009, for example, Dr. George Tiller was murdered inside his church in Wichita, Kansas. He was killed because he was a doctor who provided abortion services. Such medical personnel providing legal services face ongoing threats of murder, violence, and intimidation. They continue to face harassment, bombings and arson, death threats, kidnapping, assault, and stalking. Patients visiting clinics may also be targeted, as antiabortion extremists often use such tactics to block patients' access to medical care.

One piece of legislation, however, was passed in 1994 to safeguard women's right to access their legal rights. After the public outcry associated with the public harassment, wounding, and death of abortion services providers, and the vandalism and bombing of various clinics, the Supreme Court in *Madsen et al. v. Women's Health Center, Inc.* ruled to allow a buffer zone around clinics to give patients and employees access and to control noise around the premises. The same year, the Freedom of Access to Clinic Entrances (FACE) Act made it a federal crime to block access, harass, or incite violence in the context of abortion services. FACE provides federal protection against unlawful tactics used by abortion opponents. It provides civil remedies and criminal penalties for a range of violent, obstructive, or threatening conduct directed at reproductive health providers or patients. Courts repeatedly have upheld the law as constitutional, and scholars describe FACE as a significant factor in reducing clinic violence. In addition, 16 states and the District of Columbia have laws that protect health care facilities, providers, and/or patients from blockades, harassment, and/or other violence. Finally, seven states have passed Freedom of Choice Acts that codify a woman's right to choose, making the protections of *Roe v. Wade* part of state law. These states include California, Connecticut, Hawaii, Maine, Maryland, Nevada, and Washington. The latter three states passed this through ballot initiatives.

In closing this chapter, it is important to emphasize that only 12 percent of ob-gyn medical residency programs offer routine training in abortion procedures. There has also been a significant increase in crisis pregnancy centers (CPCs) that claim to offer comprehensive services but are actually focused on reducing abortions. Currently, it is estimated there are between 2,300 and 4,000 CPCs in the United States. Many of these are unregulated and unlicensed and may not be required to follow privacy protection laws required of physicians and comprehensive health clinics. They have been well documented as operating in close proximity to health clinics, mimicking the style or names of clinics that offer abortion services, and functioning to actively dissuade women from seeking an abortion. They use deceptive tactics to mislead women about pregnancy-related issues, making false claims, such as the claim that abortion causes breast cancer or mental illness or can lead to sterility. Many CPCs receive state and federal funding, and a recent study found that 87 percent of CPCs that receive federal funding provide false and unscientific information about abortion.

THE BLOG

WHEN BELIEF BECOMES MORE IMPORTANT THAN PEOPLE

Susan M. Shaw (2015)

[A conservative evangelical college] has decided to stop offering health insurance plans to students rather than comply with federal requirements under the Affordable Care Act. The school is suing the Department of Health and Human Services claiming that the requirement to notify the federal government about the college's religious beliefs about contraceptive coverage violates the school's freedom of religion. This notification would require the college's insurance provider to offer coverage for contraception directly to students and would thereby, according to college officials, implicate the college in providing contraceptive coverage.

[The college] opposes certain forms of contraception that leaders there consider to be abortifacients, primarily IUDs and morning-after pills or emergency contraception. The American Medical Association, National Institutes of Health, and the American Congress of Obstetricians and Gynecologists reject the notion that IUDs and emergency contraception cause abortions. Pregnancy, as defined by these medical professionals, begins once a fertilized embryo has implanted in the uterus. Before that, a fertilized egg is not considered a viable pregnancy. Morning-after pills, then, do not end a pregnancy (they prevent fertilization or implantation) but rather prevent pregnancy.

Leaders at [the college], however, argue that life begins the moment an egg is fertilized, and therefore preventing implantation of a fertilized egg is an abortion. Note that this is a theological belief, not a medical fact.

My goal here, however, is not to engage in a theological debate about when life begins. My concern is that the leaders at [the college] find a theological proposition to be more important than the actual students within their care. [The college]'s vice president of student development acknowledged that students had been hurt by the college's decision to end insurance coverage rather than notify DHHS of the college's religious objections and trigger direct coverage by their insurance carrier.

Given the timing of the announcements, students have only a short time to find new coverage before the old coverage ends. The school did say it would set up a fund to help financially strapped students pay for the increased cost in coverage.

Nonetheless, the college has made a profound choice—belief over people. While claiming a position that values life, the college has made choices that value the potential life of a possible fertilized egg over the actual lives of students who may well require insurance coverage in the present to avoid or treat life-threatening and health-compromising conditions. So in the name of fidelity to a theological belief, the college has prioritized potential human beings over actual ones.

I'm not saying theological beliefs are unimportant, but I am disturbed that in the name of Christianity, a college would put its principles over its people. People of faith disagree about abortion. [The college] is free to believe as it chooses about the issue. But when "right belief" becomes more important than right practice, we should give pause to see if the belief really is right or if the principle is worth harming the very people entrusted to our care. Let me paraphrase the Apostle Paul: If you say you have principles, but you do not care for the people right in front of you, what good are those principles?

44. ON FORBIDDEN WOMBS AND TRANSNATIONAL REPRODUCTIVE JUSTICE[1]

JALLICIA JOLLY (2016)

INTRODUCTION: WHAT IS REPRODUCTIVE JUSTICE?

In recognizing the interrelated forces of domination faced by women of color, reproductive justice moves beyond matters of individual choice and privacy central to white feminist agendas and the pro-choice movement to address the race- and class-based reproductive politics that impede the ability of multiply marginalized women to govern themselves (Asian Communities for Reproductive Justice 2005; Ross 2006a, 2006b). It recognizes the need to appropriately address the configurations of state power that link our contemporary penal state to our judicial, welfare, and health-care systems in ways that subject poor and queer women of color to inhumane and lethal laws, policies, and practice (Roberts 1997; Dalley 2002; Chieko 2006). Such an agenda acknowledges that abuses of power affect intimate aspects of all women's lives, especially those who are socially, politically, and economically marginalized and whose bodies remain crucial sites for political battles over health, welfare, and law and order. This approach shows us that, like access to contraceptives and critical health services, police brutality and the rights to life, to give life, to not give life, and to parent are human rights issues that must intersect with our agendas for racial justice and gender equality.

In the wake of unconscionable tragedies caused by racialized, gendered, state-sanctioned violence, we must strategize productively and organize effectively. A reproductive justice approach addresses the constellation of dominating forces that have deprived women of color of the economic, social, and political resources to live, birth, parent, and sustain their families. More than ever before, our lives, families, communities, and futures depend on our ability to address entrenched inequities that impede our ability not only to survive, but to thrive.

REPRODUCTIVE JUSTICE?

Heightened rates of racialized, gendered, and classed violence and its embodiment in the psychological, physical, and social worlds of multiply marginalized women of color demands that we seek interventions that are multidimensional. As noted by Patricia Hill Collins (1986), intersectionality is a "holistic approach that treats the interaction among multiple systems as the object of study" (20). Reproductive justice centers this approach to address the impact of interlocking systems of dominations on the quality of life of women of color, which offers a comprehensive way to address the multifaceted forces that constrain women's reproductive futures and their capacity to live healthy lives (Ross 2006b). Its emphasis on intersectionality offers an expansive framework for both interrogating and intervening in the ways that marginalization and relational privilege shape the

intellectual, emotional, and material lives of individuals and/or communities. This crucial deviation from the "add and stir" diversity approach that combines identity categories without critically considering their concrete impacts helps us strategically unpack the ways that identity markers such as race, gender, class, sexuality, and (dis)ability coalesce in our daily lives, structuring the possibilities for life and death as they shape who the deserving and non-deserving members of society are. Thus, a reproductive justice agenda understands that the right to a healthy life and the conditions necessary for living and parenting requires that we also address the varied components that shape our well-being, such as the right to quality education, housing, health services, clean drinking water, and safe and toxin-free environments.

REPRODUCTIVE JUSTICE IN THE CONTEXT OF U.S. STATE-SANCTIONED VIOLENCE

Understanding the significance of reproductive justice today requires an exploration of the United States government's restrictions of the rights of women of color to determine their own reproductive futures. The growing eugenics movement in the early twentieth century helped popularize the idea that socially undesirable characteristics were hereditary and could be eliminated by destroying the reproductive capacity of those with "undesirable traits" (Solinger 2005). The widespread acceptance of the eugenic theory that deviant behavior was biologically determined coupled with social anxieties regarding the reproduction of the poor, immigrants, and people of color coincided with the dominant racist ideologies of the time (Gordon 2002). These ideas also supported the widespread claim that social problems are caused by reproduction and can be cured by population control, thereby providing the context in which marginalized populations such as women of color and queer women were deemed unfit to parent (Levi et al. 2010). The legacies of eugenics lingers in the involuntary mass sterilization of working-class women of Mexican origin in California through family planning initiatives of the War on Poverty and of

Indigenous women as part of a "genocidal strategy of decimation," as well as in punitive judicial responses that rendered Black mothers "unfit to parent" (Stern 2005a, 2005b; Flavin 2009).

In centering the rights of women to control their own fertility and access the resources to create the circumstances for healthy living conditions, reproductive justice addresses the tensions that have historically evolved amidst calls against sterilization and for access to birth control. Recognizing the need for more expansive reproductive health agendas, Frances Beal, coordinator of the Black Women's Liberation Committee of the Student Non-Violent Coordinating Committee (SNCC) stated in 1970:

> We are not saying that black women should not practice birth control. Black women have the right and the responsibility to determine when it is [in] the interest of the struggle to have children or not to have them, and this right must not be relinquished to anyone. It is also her right and responsibility to determine when it is in her own best interests to have children, how many she will have and how far apart. The lack of the availability of safe birth control methods, the forced sterilization practices, and the inability to obtain legal abortions are all symptoms of a decadent society that jeopardizes the health of black women (and thereby the entire black race) in its attempt to control the very life processes of human beings. (quoted in Silliman et al. 2004)

Beale's appeal to more comprehensive approaches to reproductive health is applicable to marginalized women of color whose intersecting identity categories make them vulnerable to a host of coercive laws and policies. Reproductive justice reconciles the conflicts in claims for access to birth control with involuntary sterilization by relying on the legacies and techniques used by women of color to strategically negotiate spaces infused with competing interests, desires, and needs.

The evolving faces of state-sanctioned abuse invite further discussions about strategies to address the fatal impacts of state violence on the lives of women of color. The recent murders of Black women and their continuous subjection to calculated, violent assaults on their humanity have shed light on a critical truth: Black women's bodies are used as a terrain to work out contested notions about sexuality, motherhood, and womanhood (Hammonds 1997; Agard 2014). Beyond just showing that the systems of law enforcement, health care, and welfare as currently practiced are broken, these acts of terror reveal the dynamic dehumanization reserved for women of color. It is a violence that runs deep, starting from the womb. It jeopardizes their right to live, give birth, parent, and sustain life. It springs from a history of violent neglect that has helped continue their abuse in jail cells, courtrooms, and hospitals. At their core, the callous assaults on the lives of women of color detail the importance of embracing a reproductive justice framework in our fight against attacks on our humanity (Lindsey 2015).

A reproductive justice framework further highlights the daily violations of the rights of women of color to safe conditions critical to living healthy lives. In November of 2014, Ann Arbor police executed Aura Rosser after they were called to address a domestic dispute between Rosser and her boyfriend. On July 13, 2015, Sandra Bland was viciously assaulted by a Waller County sheriff in Texas for failing to signal before changing lanes. She was later found dead in her jail cell. The expression of their humanity, as well as their rage, remained a site of deadly contention. Together, these egregious attacks reveal a harsh reality: the exposed Black female body yields the immorality of Black womanhood and the criminality of Black motherhood in U.S. society. The dominance of stereotypical images of Black female sexuality as "untamed" and "dangerous" continue to shape Black womanhood as an incurable immorality and Black reproduction as degeneracy, creating the context for fatal exertions of authority (Roberts 1997).

The beliefs that Black women are the source of social ills are inextricably linked to ideas of women of color and queer women as groups afflicted with pathological tendencies (Gordon 2002; Jordan-Zachery 2009). These ideas don't just help create fertile ground for the aggressive enforcement of coercive laws and policies. The reliance of U.S. social policies on cultural images and symbols of non-white womanhood and non-heteronormative sexualities as dishonorable and immoral also help dictate responses to social and economic inequity in ways that invoke class and racial biases in value-laden discourses (Jordan-Zachery 2009). Such depictions frame women of color as unentitled and unpitiable and, thus, undeserving of the freedom to move and thrive without being subjected to coercive force.

The ongoing terror reigned against women of color is evident not only in cases of forced sterilization and police brutality, but also in recent attempts to reduce access to quality and affordable health care (Kerby 2012; Hiltzik 2015). The increasing attempts of the federal government to reduce funding of public health centers coupled with inadequate health care in under-resourced communities create more barriers for many marginalized women, whose inability to pay for health-care services remains a major stumbling block to safe and healthy reproduction.

Conservative legislators have continued to impose restrictions on access to life-saving treatment and services for members of federally funded programs like Medicaid. These barriers include provisions that exclude low-income Black and Latina women who do not meet categorical eligibility criteria such as disability and having dependents. This presents a "catch-22" for many women who do not qualify for Medicaid until they are sick and disabled, although early access to preventative care and treatment could potentially stave off disability and prevent illness (Andrews 2013; Henry J. Kaiser Family Foundation 2013). Alongside the vulnerability of women of color to coercive federal health policies, they also suffer at the hands of judicial attempts at welfare reform (Alexander 2011; Roberts 2009). For instance, decisions that restrict Black women's ability to procreate, parent, and legally care for their children reveal invasive rationales that underpin judicial discretion in setting probation conditions (Ross 2004; Levi et al. 2010). Court-ordered birth control and no-procreation orders represent bold assaults along economic lines and erroneously link social ills with the fertility of Black women (Corneal 2003; Levi et al. 2010).

The current functioning of the child welfare and criminal justice systems work to systematically deny Black women the right to parent. In New Jersey, Black mothers are more likely than white and Latino parents to lose custody of their children as a result of drug use or having a half-empty pantry—stipulations that legally cannot justify the placement of children into foster care. Although Black children make up only 14% of the child population in the state, they make up 41% of those entering foster care (Gonzalez 2015). The vulnerability of Black mothers to state supervision in parental decisions is strengthened by the "fifteen out of twenty-two-month" unfitness ground of the 1997 Adoption and Safe Families Act, which authorizes the termination of parental rights. The conscious decision of social workers, lawyers, and judges to remove Black children from Black mothers imposes an "ideal parent" standard, which systematically demonizes Black motherhood as it criminalizes maternal incarceration (Corneal 2003; Roberts 2009).

The Adoption and Safe Families Act precludes the possibility of children retaining a legal relationship with their mothers while also limiting understandings and expressions of parenting. The varied manifestations of structural inequality and systematic violence have required that Black families create networks and kinships that provide a host of parental responsibilities—emotional support, psychosocial care, and other intangible qualities—that can be fulfilled while parents are physically separated from their children.

Punitive legislative measures by federal and state governments to restrict women's reproductive and parenting capacities create distinctive vulnerabilities for all women, especially low-income women of color, many of whom lack the economic resources, social recognition, and political capital needed to resist such pervasive reproductive regulations. The murderous enactment of these laws and policies sends a clear message: poor women of color are disposable and fundamentally ungrievable. The violent inconsideration of their lives demands that activists embrace a reproductive justice framework. As noted by reproductive justice activist Loretta Ross, reproductive justice is "the complete physical, mental, spiritual, political, social, and economic well-being of women and girls, based on the full achievement and protection of women's human rights" (Ross 2006b, 14). It emphasizes the need for women of color to access the resources and services needed to control their reproductive capacity amidst the brute force of law enforcers, the state-sanctioned criminalization of their pregnancies, the forced removal of their children, the destruction of the welfare system, and the insensitivity of the foster care system.

A reproductive justice approach acknowledges that in the current state of recognition and belonging, multiply marginalized women are systematically denied certain social and human rights associated with reproduction. It addresses the systemic variations in the ways that the rights of citizenship—the right to bear children, access to education, quality health care, and equal protection under the law—are filtered, conferred, and withheld from women according to their race, class, sexuality, and nationality.

REPRODUCTIVE JUSTICE IN A TRANSNATIONAL CONTEXT

The emphasis of reproductive justice on the right of multiply marginalized women to determine their reproductive futures engages with the possibilities of solidarity across borders of race, class, sexuality, culture, and nationality. This approach requires a consideration of women's agency within a broader system of relational power and privilege that shapes transnational commodified markets in bodies, babies, and reproductive labor (Alexander and Mohanty 2010; Fixmer-Oraiz 2013). Eliminating interlocking systems of domination not only invites an interrogation of social and economic injustice, but also requires that we address the connections between racialized misogyny and increasing anti-Black state-sanctioned violence globally.

Centering transnational reproductive justice requires a thorough understanding of the unique ways that "misogynoir" constrains marginalized women's ability to negotiate the risks, barriers, and opportunities associated with their reproductive capacity. Misogynoir, a term coined by Moya Bailey to refer to the intersectionality of racism, misogyny, and anti-Blackness, further reveals the trauma of mothering while Black and living in an anti-Black, anti-queer, heteropatriarchal world (Bailey 2013). Agendas, collectives, syllabi, and various forms of political mobilization that interrogate the systematic denigration and dehumanizing objectification of Black women shed light on the reoccurring psychological, emotional, and physical trauma that Black women face as they strategically address the chronic dehumanization of Black female life globally. They reveal a striking reality: Black motherhood is the direct antithesis to the ideals of the twenty-first century militarized, carceral world. Its proliferation of Black life in uteri and beyond places it in a dangerously ambiguous relation to white power structures, particularly their historical investment in the dynamic dispossession of Black people through calculated exploitation, structural violence, and lethal abuse.

Few works and political agendas have explored the transnational dimensions of reproductive justice and its significance in addressing the processes and practices that both authorize and mask various inequities that constrain the reproductive futures of multiply marginalized women of color. A transnational approach to reproductive justice offers an analytical lens that centers relational power and vulnerability as it invests in the possibility of a shared consciousness in our efforts to address the terror and suffering faced by multiply marginalized women. In prioritizing transnational and transdisciplinary approaches to addressing the disenfranchisement of women of color, it also offers frameworks to craft and expand interventions aimed at maintaining the conditions necessary for safe and healthy lives and living conditions globally. This includes various initiatives such as policy, advocacy, research, and education strategies that support living wages, affordable and supported housing, high quality public health and medical care, accessible sexual and reproductive health services, and clean living environments.

In connecting the framework of reproductive justice to pressing concerns and needs, collectives have implemented strategies that target environmental toxins, sexual autonomy, parenting, and access to health care among immigrant groups. For instance, Alaska Community Action on Toxics addresses policies that link environmental contaminants and the major reproductive justice concerns of Indigenous villages, such as premature births, stillbirths, and birth defects (Alaska Community Action on Toxics 2016).

This culturally-based policy advocacy is mirrored in the efforts of California Latinas for Reproductive Justice, which uses policy, community education, and communication strategies to educate and mobilize Latina women at local and state levels on issues related to the reproductive and sexual health of low-income, undocumented, adolescent, lesbian, bisexual, queer, and transgender women (California Latinas for Reproductive Justice 2016).

In Latin America and the Caribbean, community groups such as Women's Link Worldwide and Eve for Life have mobilized resources to allow marginalized women to make informed reproductive decisions. Women's Link Worldwide has provided emergency contraceptives to poor and rural women living in Columbia who are disproportionately affected by the growing outbreak of the Zika virus, a mosquito-borne disease associated with adverse pregnancy outcomes (Barragan 2016). Eve for Life has revolutionized HIV care through their directed and prolonged provision of quality psychosocial care to HIV-positive young mothers in Jamaica. Embodying a guided mentorship and education approach that centers holistic HIV/AIDS care, Eve for Life trains young mothers in gender-based violence and intimate partner violence awareness, sexual and reproductive health rights and education, STI and HIV/AIDS prevention, group facilitation, and peer communication to allow them to develop the skills to educate themselves and their peers (Eve for Life 2016).

At their core, these initiatives illuminate the local, national, and transnational forces that work to impede the ability of women of color to determine their reproductive futures. Yet they also illuminate the possibilities inherent in expansive agendas that address the unique needs, desires, and interests of multiply marginalized women of color. In our move toward our collective liberation, transnational reproductive justice allows us to envision more strategic, meaningful, and sustainable strategies critical to the survival of women of color.

NOTE

1. The exclusions of trans people and men are limitations of this article. While I primarily emphasize the experiences of women throughout the piece, I consider reproductive justice an expansive framework fighting for the rights of all people (of all genders) to live, birth or not birth, parent, and sustain their families. Though it is heavily grounded in the needs/rights of women of color, it is not limited to women of color. As the needs and rights of trans women, trans men, and non-binary people remain critical to our efforts to address overlapping and unique assaults on the quality of Black lives, I encourage future works to productively engage with these areas.

WORKS CITED

Agard, Veronica. 2014. "Black Women's Lives Matter Too: The Forgotten Victims of Police Killings." *The Grio*, December 14. http://thegrio.com/2014/12/14/black-women-lives-matter.

Alaska Community Action on Toxics. 2016. "What We Do." Accessed October 20. http://www.akaction.org/tackling_toxics/.

Alexander, Amanda. 2011. "Criminalizing Reproduction: The Rise of Judicial Welfare Reform." Seminar paper, Yale Law School.

Alexander, Jacqui, and Chandra Mohanty. 2010. "Cartographies of Knowledge and Power: Transnational Feminism and Radical Praxis." In *Critical Transnational Feminist Praxis*, edited by Amanda Lock Swarr and Richa Nagar, 23–45. New York: State University of New York.

Andrews, Michelle. 2013. "A Costly Catch-22 in States Forgoing Medicaid Expansion." *New England Public Radio*, March 5. http://www.npr.org/sections/health-shots/2013/03/04/173455000/a-costly-catch-22-in-states-forgoing-medicaid-expansion.

Asian Communities for Reproductive Justice. 2005. *A New Vision for Advancing Our Movement for Reproductive Health, Reproductive Rights and Reproductive Justice*. Atlanta: SisterSong Women of Color Reproductive Health Collective. http://strongfamiliesmovement.org/assets/docs/ACRJ-A-New-Vision.pdf.

Bailey, Moya. 2013. "New Terms of Resistance: A Response to Zenzele Isoke." *Souls: A Critical Journal of Black Politics, Culture, and Society* 14, no. 14: 341–343.

Barragan, Yesenia. 2016. "Zika and Reproductive Justice in Latin America." *teleSUR*, February 25, 2016. http://www.telesurtv.net/english/opinion/Zika-and-Reproductive-Justice-in-Latin-America-20160225-0019.html.

California Latinas for Reproductive Justice. 2016. "What We Do." Accessed October 20. http://www.californialatinas.org/about-us/what-we-do/.

Centers for Disease Control and Prevention. 2016a. "Health of Black or African American Non-Hispanic Population." Last modified October 6. http://www.cdc.gov/nchs/fastats/black-health.htm.

———. 2016b. "HIV among Women." http://www.cdc.gov/hiv/pdf/group/gender/women/cdc-hiv-women.pdf.

Chieko, Clarke. 2006. "Maternal Justice Restored: Redressing the Ramifications of Mandatory Sentencing Minimums on Women and Their Children. *Howard Law Journal* 50: 263–64.

Chrisler, Joan. 2012. *Reproductive Justice: A Global Concern*. Santa Barbara, CA: Praeger.

Collins, Patricia Hill. 1986. "Learning from the Outsider Within: The Sociological Significance of Black Feminist Thought." *Social Problems* 30, no. 6: 14–32.

Corneal, Devon A. 2003. "Limiting the Right to Procreate: *State v. Oakley* and the Need for Strict Scrutiny of Probation Conditions." *Seton Hall Law Review* 33, no. 2: 447–478.

Dalley, Lanette P. 2002. "Policy Implications Relating to Inmate Mothers and Their Children: Will the Past Be Prologue?" *The Prison Journal* 82, no. 2: 234–68. doi:10.1177/003288550208200205.

Eve for Life. 2016. "About Us." Accessed October 20. http://www.eveforlife.org/about-us.

Fixmer-Oraiz, Natalie. 2013. "Speaking of Solidarity: Transnational Gestational Surrogacy and the Rhetorics of Reproductive (In)Justice, Frontiers." *A Journal of Women Studies* 34, no. 1: 126–163.

Flavin, Jeanne. 2009. *Our Bodies, Our Crimes: The Policing of Women's Reproduction in America*. New York: New York University Press.

Gonzalez, Sarah. 2015. "Black Mothers Judged Unfit at Higher Rate Than White Mothers in NY." *New York Public Radio*, May 26. http://www.wnyc.org /story/black-parents-nj-lose-custody-their-kids-more-anyone-else.

Gordon, Linda. 2002. *The Moral Property of Women: A History of Birth Control Politics in America*. Chicago: University of Illinois Press.

Hammonds, Evelynn. 1997. "Toward a Genealogy of Black Female Sexuality: The Problematic of Silence." In *Feminist Genealogies, Colonial Legacies, Democratic Futures*, edited by Alexander, M. Jacqui and Chandra Talpade Mohanty, 170–182. New York: Routledge.

Henry J. Kaiser Family Foundation, The. 2013. "Women of Color More Likely to Be Uninsured or Covered by Medicaid, 2012." November 12. http://kff.org/womens-health-policy/slide/women-of-color-more-likely-to-be-uninsured-or-covered-by-medicaid-2012.

Hiltzik, Michael. 2015. "The Cost of Defunding Planned Parenthood: Less Healthcare for 650,000 Women." *Los Angeles Times*, September 22. http://www.latimes.com/business/hiltzik/la-fi-mh-cost-of-defunding-planned-parenthood-20150922-column.html.

Jordan-Zachery, Julia Sheron. 2009. *Black Women, Cultural Images and Social Policy*. New York: Routledge.

Kerby, Sophia. 2012. "The State of Women of Color in the United States." *Center for American Progress*, July 17. https://www.americanprogress.org/issues/race/report/2012/07/17/11923/the-state-of-women-of-color-in-the-united-states.

Levi, Robin, Nerissa Kinakemakorn, Azadeh Zohrabi, Elizaveta Afanasieff, and Nicole Edwards-Masuda. 2010. "Creating the 'Bad Mother': How the U.S. Approach to Pregnancy in Prisons Violates the Right to Be a Mother." *UCLA Women's Law Journal* 18, no. 1: 1–77.

Lindsey, Treva. 2015. "Race in the U.S. History." *Aljazeera*, September 5. http://www.aljazeera.com/indepth/features/2015/09/race-herstory-150904052450065.html.

Roberts, Dorothy. 1997. *Killing the Black Body: Race, Reproduction, and the Meaning of Liberty*. New York: Vintage.

Roberts, Dorothy E. 2009. "Race, Gender, and Genetic Technologies: A New Reproductive Dystopia?" *Signs* 34, no. 4: 783–804.

Ross, Catherine. 2004. "The Tyranny of Time: Vulnerable Children, Bad Mothers, and Statutory Deadlines in Parental Termination Proceedings." *Virginia Journal of Social Policy and Law* 176: 1–67.

Ross, Loretta. 2006a. "The Color of Choice: White Supremacy and Reproductive Justice." In *Color of Violence: The INCITE! Anthology,* edited by INCITE! Women of Color Against Violence, 53–65. Cambridge, MA: South End Press.

———. 2006b. "Understanding Reproductive Justice: Transforming the Pro-Choice Movement." *Off Our Backs: The Feminist Newsjournal* 36: 14–20.

Silliman, Jael, Marlene Gerber Fried, Loretta Ross, and Elena Gutierrez. 2004. *Undivided Rights: Women of Color Organizing for Reproductive Justice.* Cambridge, MA: South End Press.

Solinger, Rickie. 2005. *Pregnancy and Power: A Short History of Reproductive Politics in America.* New York: New York University Press.

Stern, Alexandra Minna. 2005a. *Eugenic Nation: Faults and Frontiers of Better Breeding in Modern America.* Berkeley: University of California Press.

———. 2005b. "Sterilized in the Name of Public Health: Race, Immigration, and Reproductive Control in Modern California." *American Journal of Public Health* 95, no. 7: 1128–1138.

45. REPRODUCTIVE RIGHTS AS HUMAN RIGHTS

SARAH COMBELLICK-BIDNEY (2017)

REPRODUCTIVE RIGHTS AS HUMAN RIGHTS: AN UNFOLDING STORY

> I'm seeing the human rights field as so much more diverse, there's just so many more people who are in the fray.—Raksha

Reproductive rights are human rights. To this day, this claim meets with disagreement in groups convened to promote human rights, where human rights are a *raison d'être*. Where there is no consensus that reproductive rights should be included among basic rights for all human beings, the notion that reproductive rights are human rights is an unfolding story made from countless small examples and narratives: specific and deliberate work to link the two concepts in the realm of universal rights. This is the work of reproductive rights advocates who traverse human rights circles, and it can be systematically and comparatively studied.

A frequent counterargument to the claim that reproductive rights are human rights is cultural relativity: that the degree to which rights language applies to issues of human reproduction depends largely on one's culture.[1] It is notable that while there are those who hail from many different cultural backgrounds who might not support reproductive rights as human rights for one reason or another, the cultural relativity argument necessarily focuses on cultures which did not become globally dominant through colonialism and globalisation, that is, cultures of the Global South. This is not to say that consensus has been reached in the Global North—it has not, and reproductive rights are under constant threat in much of the US and Europe. But it is overwhelmingly non-Western cultures which are frequently essentialised in human rights discourse.[2] It is for this reason that I chose to talk with reproductive rights workers in the Global South, eventually settling on cases from Brazil, India and South Africa. While their perspectives and stories are absolutely unique and cannot be generalised, each voice has distinct value for the conversation about reproductive rights happening around the world.

Human rights frames resonate across borders and oceans, with or without reference to specific treaties, wherever mistreatment and abuse occur. However, "Human rights messages are intrinsically hard to deliver and hard to hear. A government engaged in repression does not want to hear messages about human rights."[3] It is even more difficult to craft an effective human rights message that engages reproductive health and freedom, which despite their centrality to human well-being, may at first glance appear to be marginal sites of controversy and debate.

. . .

In this dynamic moment in human rights history, international treaties are only one part of the nuanced dynamics of this high-stakes discourse. In fact, Julie Hollar says the over-reliance on human rights treaties as proxies for human rights action leads scholars to

> miss crucial aspects of how human rights struggles play out because they make two problematic assumptions about human rights. First, that they are fixed, desired outcomes rather than contested fields; and, second, that they can be measured fruitfully at the state level using the available datasets.[4]

Instead, this study focuses on the micro- and meta-levels of human rights work, tracing the processes of constructing and connecting reproductive rights-focused human rights claims across communities. "Scholars have been slow to recognise either the rationality or the significance of activist networks," say Keck and Sikkink, because "these networks fall outside of our established categories."[5] Researchers often ignore this undercurrent of activity simply because it may be less formalised and visible than the official actions of governments.

. . .

METHODS AND METHODOLOGICAL TENSIONS

The 'Global South' is a term that describes the majority of the world; it is a construct that cannot be elucidated in any meaningful way with interviews with a few select individuals in far flung parts of the globe. While I necessarily use the term frequently as a descriptor to distinguish this piece from projects that focus on the US and Europe, I try to do so in ways that deconstruct the term rather than reify it in any way. My interpretive methods are predicated on a critical understanding of the historical processes that led to the creation of a concept of 'Global South': colonial discourses followed by globalised ones that

reinforced hierarchies even as they purported to analyse them, and made some places seem more central to academic inquiry than others. It would thus be an irony if this piece were understood as an attempt to describe reproductive rights in the Global South. Rather, it is a picture of how some individuals navigate this concept and context in their lives— embodied very differently for each person—and what stories they encounter and use in the process.

The initial curiosity that spawned this project fuelled two years of interviews, correspondences and archival research on reproductive rights in various parts of the world. The first phase of research focused on the US and it was only in the second phase that I expanded to regions across the Global South.[6] This article focuses on the second phase, on the most detailed cases that emerged from Brazil, India and South Africa, examining how advocates use local discourses of gender, sexuality, race, ethnicity and class to construct reproductive rights and other human rights as intersectional and interdependent. The interviews gathered here are regarded as reflections only of the individuals who gave them and not representative of anyone other than the speaker. They contribute to the field in that they are a product of the unique intersection of place, time and identity from which they develop their practice. Local issues, which each practitioner knows well, are understood and articulated differently by different speakers even if they are in the same organisation.

. . .

PROFILES OF PARTICIPANTS

The study yielded a diverse group of respondents from ages 29–72, with widely varying racial and ethnic backgrounds. The most extensive interviews (an hour or longer via Skype, or with multiple exchanges of follow-up correspondence) were with participants in Brazil, India, South Africa and Lebanon; and included a medically trained abortion advocate in India, a teen health delegate in Brazil and a reproductive rights attorney in South Africa. Most were women, but there were two men and three persons who did not indicate their gender identity. At least two identified as being of an ethnic minority in the region where they work. Those who consented to more extended interviews obviously had occasion to disclose more about their backgrounds, and I include the information where appropriate to contextualise their responses. From these longer interviews, I was able to find more supplementary information about the current context of reproductive rights in the first three countries, hence the choice of cases. Though Lebanon would have been a helpful addition as a less 'hegemonic' power in the Global South, I decided late in the process to focus on the other three due to my greater access to information about the legal-policy framework in those areas.

. . .

SOUTH AFRICA: ADDRESSING NONCONSENSUAL STERILISATION IN THE SHADOW OF THE HIV/AIDS CRISIS

Jelka was the first legal advocate I interviewed and the only attorney. Her work demonstrates how litigation can complement other tactics in the battle for reproductive rights. But on a deeper level, Jelka has a compelling perspective that stories are already used in the forging of national laws and that they might be used to achieve broader protection for reproductive rights as part of South Africa's comprehensive commitment to human rights.

South Africa's approach to the HIV crisis has improved dramatically in the last decade, but gender inequity and HIV stigma interact to put HIV positive women at high risk of violence and coercion. Particularly alarming for human rights advocates is the imposition of nonconsensual sterilisation procedures on HIV positive women. These compounding effects of the HIV crisis are not unpredictable, given that South Africa has high rates of gendered violence and had an egregiously delayed response to the HIV/AIDS epidemic under the Mbeki presidency. Subsequent administrations struggled to catch up by dramatically increasing the budget for addressing the crisis. The country has an 18% rate of HIV infection to Brazil's 1%, which had a rate similar to South Africa's in the 1990s.[7]

There is no explicit protection of reproductive rights with relation to HIV/AIDS under international law, and states generally do a poor job of protecting the reproductive autonomy of individuals living with HIV.[8] But the mid-2000s brought HIV into the international human rights discourse, to the point that 89% of countries explicitly mention human rights in their national HIV/AIDS strategies.[9] South Africa is one of these countries, with a comprehensive human rights plan for addressing HIV and tangible gains in treatment and prevention. The latest UNAIDS report showed decreased infection rates among young people.[10] Even more notably, South Africa's treatment to prevent mother to child HIV transmission is the best in sub-Saharan Africa, with almost 90% coverage across the country.[11]

Jelka is an attorney at a reproductive rights organisation. Her daily work focuses on strategic litigation of human rights cases. She described her academic background as 'all human rights'. Today, much of her work involves gathering and sharing stories of women who have had nonconsensual sterilisations. It is not a headline issue in South Africa, but common enough to constitute a pattern of human rights violations. Even in a country with a strong history of human rights discourse—from the African National Congress' (ANC) successful campaign against the Apartheid system to the human rights imperative of the HIV crisis—sterilisation is not a recognisable human rights issue. Jelka makes her case by learning as much as possible about the experiences of women who have experienced these procedures nonconsensually in different parts of South Africa and sharing it in the language of human rights law. In short, she must identify key incidents that will build the pattern, and translate these local stories into legal language.

Jelka's law degree allows her to act as a bridge between local communities and the legal system. She says it is her work in legal advocacy that made her commitments 'a lived reality as opposed to something theoretical in books'. She is currently representing two women who were sterilised without their consent. Her hope is that these cases will bring to light a systemic problem across the country, and add impetus to include nonconsensual sterilisation in the definition of torture prohibited in South Africa. She takes cases which 'will end up making an impact for women beyond the individual we represent in court', to improve health services for women in marginalised communities across South Africa.

South African laws since 1996 uphold rights to abortion and other reproductive health care services. The legislation passed in 1996

> repeals the restrictive and inaccessible provisions of the Abortion and Sterilization Act, 1975, and promotes reproductive rights and extends freedom of choice by affording every woman the right to choose whether to have an early, safe, and legal termination of pregnancy according to her beliefs.[12]

The law is also notable for its notion of reproductive freedom, which recognises "that both women and men[13] have the right to be informed of and to have access to safe, effective, affordable, and acceptable methods of fertility regulation of their choice."[14] The definitions were updated in 2008 for accuracy and applicability, for example, to add registered nurses as reproductive health care providers.

The reality in South Africa is murkier than the laws might indicate, and, with progressive laws still unenforced, reproductive rights advocates are seeking to improve access through human rights legislation. Human rights discourse has historically privileged demands of autonomy over demands of access,[15] but Jelka and many other reproductive rights advocates want to include health care access along with decisional autonomy as a human right. The stories of clients who experienced nonconsensual procedures make it difficult to gloss over issues of access. The gap between rich and poor is visible in the divergent outcomes for mothers who seek reproductive health care in various parts of the country:

> In South Africa we have a very startling Gini coefficient, which means that we have very deep-rooted inequality in our society. So you see one portion of the population being able to access any kind of services right up to very expensive kinds of fertility treatment, whereas the majority of the population are living in abject poverty and are unable to even go to the local clinic and give birth without the threat of death. (Jelka)

Maternal mortality from preventable complications also correlates with poverty. South Africa has robust programmes in testing, counselling and treatment of HIV. But even with these programmes, the number of mothers who died from AIDS after giving birth rose 5% from 2004 to 2007. Medical experts consider these deaths to be 'clearly avoidable' given South Africa's access to antiretroviral therapy.[16] Jelka concurs, "We have a very high maternal and infant mortality rate in South Africa. Even [the Millennium Development Goals] don't reflect accurately what's really going on. So it really is very scary." While medical advancements have helped HIV patients live longer and have full lives, women are still dying of the disease in disproportionately high numbers.

Jelka chooses to work on nonconsensual sterilisation because it is one of the routes by which women can lose access to body autonomy, i.e. when stigma and stereotypes get in the way of a routine hospital visit. She uses her clients' stories to indicate a pattern of human rights abuses, ultimately aiming to include protection against nonconsensual sterilisation in human rights legislation. The first story she told was a more clear-cut case in which "the client didn't even speak any of the languages the nurses or doctors addressed her in, so there really was no informed consent." But for the second client, "the line was a little more blurry. She did speak the language and also signed the form, but the nurse failed to explain to her exactly what a sterilisation entails." She thought they were giving her an IUD. Since she was not given information about the procedure being offered to her, there could be no informed consent. "Both of these clients were sterilised after undergoing a C-section, after the baby was delivered, and both—we believe—on the basis of their HIV positive status. The events seem to point in that direction."

Though her clients had somewhat different experiences in the facilities where the sterilisations were performed, it is significant that both were HIV positive. Feminist research finds that gender dynamics shape the emerging picture of the HIV/AIDS crisis in many ways, including gendered patterns in ability to implement safe sex practices, transmission rates, stigma and access to treatment.[17] It is not a coincidence that both of these women were HIV positive, as discrimination against and persecution of women living with HIV persists despite the national government's assiduous efforts to uphold the rights of those living with the condition. Jelka sees the anti-sterilisation movement as one that is just beginning, in contrast to the HIV movement that has been gaining ground for decades. She says, "The HIV/AIDS movement has done quite well, but other movements are still very young." Her work gives her an opportunity to expand the movement and coordinate efforts with other advocacy groups working against nonconsensual sterilisation and other violations of reproductive rights in South Africa. Jelka believes most South Africans have not yet grasped the scope of the issue. "They still don't think it's a systemic problem. They think it might be a couple of rogue practitioners. But that can't be the case, since we are seeing it happen all over in all the provinces." She works with other groups to organise advocacy efforts, and hopes that they can systematically document the abuses to show how they form a pattern.

. . .

INDIA: SECURING ABORTION AMID OUTCRY OVER SEX-SELECTIVE ABORTIONS

> These issues raise questions about what a wanted pregnancy is and what an unwanted pregnancy is, in this complex fabric within which women are forced to make their decisions.—Abhaya

India's laws against abortion derived from British colonial law and persisted until 1964, when a high maternal mortality rate led to a process of liberalisation and decriminalisation of abortion. Reformers used the term "medical termination of pregnancy (MTP)" to evade opposition from religious groups, and in 1971 the MTP Act legalised abortion in all of India except the states of Jammu and Kashmir. The Indian Parliament then amended the law in 2002–2003 to allow more practitioners and health facilities to perform abortions.[18] Abortion is now legal in India, but there are still restrictions and inconsistencies. For example, the law still requires an opinion from one registered medical practitioner for abortions to take place up to 12 weeks into a pregnancy and concurring opinions from two practitioners for procedures from 12 to 20 weeks; requires abortion providers to

be licensed doctors (which are often scarce in rural areas); uses the term 'married women' that could be construed to deny the procedure to those who are unmarried or require a husband's consent; requires women to report contraceptive use after abortions (MTP regulations, form 2); and holds private facilities to a potentially higher standard of safety than public ones by providing an approval process for the former but not the latter.

In India, many abortions are sex-selective—that is, patients request ultrasounds to determine the biological sex of the fetus, and more frequently opt for an abortion if the fetus is designated female to avoid the greater economic burden of raising a girl to adulthood. As sex selection is difficult to detect, debates about the practice often bring up proposals for more restrictive abortion laws. I spoke with two reproductive rights advocates in different parts of India who have different views on this issue: one, Abhaya, who works primarily in the area of abortion access; and another, Raksha, who works on a wide range of issues including female infanticide, HIV/AIDS, and sex worker rights. The former works more directly with women seeking abortions and creates media to educate the public about issues related to reproductive rights, while the latter works on a more administrative level to write grants for her organisation. But both used stories to highlight changes in the way they approach their work, and emphasised how the debate over sex-selection abortion affects human rights work in India.

Abhaya is a medically trained reproductive health advocate who makes videos and accessible educational media about reproductive issues in India. She also works directly with women seeking abortions. When we spoke, she began by telling the story of one of the first women who came to her seeking an abortion. The woman had sought treatment for infertility and had subsequently adopted two children but then got accidentally pregnant with twins. She wanted an abortion because she could afford to raise only two children and wanted to focus all her energies on parenting the two adopted ones. She was afraid that if her husband found out about the pregnancy he would prefer to parent biological children and force her to send their adopted children back to the orphanage. Abhaya said the woman's situation "revealed to me that this is not black and white. This is the same woman who is a mother, who was an infertility patient, and who now needs an abortion." She did not fit the stereotype of a woman in need, but she required Abhaya's assistance to obtain an abortion.[19]

The woman's story also raised Abhaya's awareness of gender oppression in India. Abhaya says, "This is quite a patriarchal country, to be honest, and in spite of the recent economic development, I cannot say that it has done anything in particular for women." One year before we spoke, a gang rape and fatal assault on a bus in India made international headlines. On a less visible front, dowry-related violent crimes against women in India are not diminishing, despite predictions that globalisation would end the tradition of dowries altogether.[20] While the subcontinent continues to boast economic growth every year, gender violence is not going away.

Although the gang rape incident was heavily sensationalised, it provided opportunities for conversations about reproductive rights and human rights in India and beyond. The victim was a middle-class woman, and therefore did not carry as much of the stigma associated with rape as lower-caste women. Reproductive rights advocates use the story as an opening to dismantle stereotypes that continue to stigmatise and silence survivors of sexual assault or rape.

Destigmatisation is a necessary first step to discussing reproductive health care, and the language of rights is a way to move from stigma to empowerment. Some of the stories Abhaya tells are from her own experience as a reproductive rights advocate. She has learned to be gradual but open when discussing her work. Here she spells out some of the ways she begins conversations about abortion and how she introduces the concept of rights:

> If someone asks me randomly what I do, if I think they are going to be receptive, I say I work for safe abortion. When I say receptive, I don't want them to be 100% open to it; I just don't want them to jump at me. And people usually say, yes, I have heard that is necessary. And it's almost always women who respond like this. They might say, well, I wouldn't need it, but someone else might. And then I like to explain

a little bit more, and say it's not just us and them, it's for all of us. Because abortion is just one part of a whole spectrum of reproductive health and rights. If I don't know whether they are going to be receptive, I start the other way around. I say I work for reproductive health and rights.

This quotation also illustrates the process of human rights theory-building that is implicit in advocates' work. Abhaya's narration of encounters with strangers lays out a clear position in favour of "rights" language. In the following section on Brazil, one source raised abortion as a public health issue. But Abhaya prefers to emphasise rights over public health framing. "I want to look at everything through a very feminist lens. Because abortion could become just about the health issue. To me, it's a woman's right." She is emphasising reproductive rights to guard against the downplaying of abortion access in the context of the debate on sex-selective abortion. She is wary of depoliticising abortion, and when it seems to be framed as a health issue, she redirects the conversation back to rights.

For sex-selective abortion, this is an especially sensitive conversation. Says Abhaya, "The moment someone says 'sex ratio' ... the focus turns to abortion." Restrictions on abortion are a common proposal for reducing sex selection, but Abhaya is strongly against this. Not only does it not solve the problem of sex selection—those abortions would only be done in less safe conditions—but it raises the prospect of increased female infanticide. "I would wish that there was no sex selection, but at the same time, I don't think abortion is the problem. If you say no abortion, that just means you are saying no to safe abortion."

She traces some of the acrimonious tone of the sex selection debate back to the Global North, and specifically the negative portrayals of abortion in the US. "Recently," she says, "a lot of these anti-sex-selection campaigns have started using those fetal images that you see in a lot of anti-choice movements in the US." She says there are some anti-abortion efforts on the part of religious groups in India, and they do not limit their scope to abortion. They also oppose access to contraception and promote narrow views of reproduction. In conversations on sex selection, she is careful not to let the anti-abortion movement define human rights in terms of the rights of the fetus but rather emphasises the rights of already existing individuals to determine their reproductive lives. She must simultaneously explain gender issues and human rights. . . .

BRAZIL: CALLING FOR SEXUAL AND REPRODUCTIVE RIGHTS IN THE FACE OF RESTRICTIVE NATIONAL POLICIES

Rubens works with youth on issues of sexual health and sees his work in the context of a broad human rights platform for Brazil that will include protections for sexual freedom as well as other fundamental reproductive rights. He has a highly nuanced and critical perspective on reproductive rights language, having taken part in conversations about these topics in academic as well as non-profit spaces, internationally as well as locally. He spoke of his experience as a man in a relatively woman-centred field and as a youth worker in a part of the world where rhetoric does not match reality for youth, especially those who are lesbian, gay, bisexual, transgender or queer (LGBTQ).

Brazil is a technologically advanced, economically active industrialised country, but it has been resistant to change the abortion policy from the Penal Code of 1940, which made abortion a crime except in very narrow circumstances of rape and to preserve the life of the pregnant person.[21] Dilma Rousseff's administration passed an amendment in 2013 to guarantee a treatment protocol for rape survivors that could lead to further decriminalisation, but abortion is still effectively illegal in Brazil in the vast majority of cases. Sterilisation and fertility regulation procedures common in most industrialised countries are also difficult to access legally in Brazil, due to the pronatalist stance of the government. In contrast, HIV policies have been more proactive than in other states in the Global South; government responded to demands for human rights protections after democratisation by making HIV education, prevention and treatment free and universally available in Brazil since the early 1990s.[22]

But pressure on the government to change its restrictive reproductive policies has not yielded much change. The most notable shift was the 1988 Constitution which recognised the importance of 'educational and scientific resources' to help persons access their 'right to family planning', but these words have not yet translated into real gains for reproductive rights in Brazil.[23] Each year, many Brazilians seek illegal abortions, often facing unsafe and insecure conditions where complications are likely. Deaths sometimes result, or infections that can cause infertility. Yury Puello Orozco, the director of Catholics for the Right to Choose, says,

> The majority of women who are at risk from abortions are black, poor, uneducated, and live in the marginal neighborhoods. We estimate that one in five Brazilian women have had an insecure abortion. So we see this as an issue of public health.[24]

Brazilian non-governmental organisations work constantly to support citizens to access their rights, even in the restrictive national climate that seems so slow to change. Brazil is the site of feminist health projects to empower sex workers to take charge of their sexual and reproductive health.[25] It is common for advocates in these areas to be conversant in both the progressive international discourse of human rights, and the national discourse on reproductive health, which is necessarily much more muted. When speaking with colleagues outside Brazil, advocates are often impatient with their government and eager to connect with allies who can strengthen the transnational movements that can help to bring countries up to speed across Latin America.

I spoke with Rubens in the midst of the 2013 protests in Brazil. He was in favour of the protests, with their progressive and even radical agenda of social change including sexual freedom and access to health care. He pushes for these very changes in his professional life. He says,

> I work politically on various levels to advocate for the needs of young people—young women, young men, LGBT communities, young people living with disabilities, living with HIV, depending on the context—and discuss how to influence and shape programs to serve their needs.

He shares their stories with other advocates at international conferences, and "then I go back to my country and try to get the government to implement what we discussed at the international level."

The protests were a topic of great interest for Rubens, and he wove them into the stories he shared. The protests began when the government announced bus fare hikes, and eventually escalated into widespread demonstrations across the country. Targets included the government's massive construction projects for the 2014 FIFA World Cup, which protesters decried as a misuse of funds. They demanded the money be redirected towards social services, along with other sweeping political and economic changes, some of which they achieved. By June, President Dilma Rousseff and the National Chamber reversed or voted down most of the specific measures opposed by the protesters, including the bus fare hikes and a so-called 'gay cure' bill, and increased funds for education and health care.[26]

On 1 August 2013, Dilma Rousseff and Brazilian Minister for Women Eleonora Menicucci announced a new law to permit abortion in cases where a pregnancy resulted from violence, where the definition of violence included nonconsensual sex. This was a major step in a country which alternates between headlines of women leaders calling for full legalisation of abortion and Catholic protests against the few abortion laws on the books. Reports indicate that churchgoing is declining and many Catholics are changing their stance on abortion.[27] The new pope, hailing from Latin America, has not signalled change on the issue of abortion, but slightly more liberal papal messages on LGBTQ issues indicate that the Catholic world is by no means of one mind on issues of reproductive and sexual rights.

Brazil's lack of movement on abortion is an unacceptable anachronism for Rubens, who says, "everyone knows someone who has had an abortion." The stigma affects even activists. "We don't talk about it." Rubens feels incredibly frustrated with the situation, which he says has dire consequences for young people. When he was young, his friends knew of his activist work and would talk to him to try to get access to contraception or abortion. These experiences instilled in him a strong drive to change policies that restrict access to health services and force young people to go through personal connections.

"Reproductive justice has been present in my life from an early age," he says.

While Rubens enjoys a sense of forward motion at the international gatherings, there is catch-up work to be done at home. Talking to communities on the ground in Brazil, he notices an abrupt shift in receptivity when he moves from a general human rights stance to specific issues: "When you're talking about human rights, it's more like a very common concept, and nobody will go against it. But when you are talking about families, that's a very tricky one, because a lot of people will go against it." His task is to show that the rights of families *are* human rights, and this linkage must be made repeatedly and from various angles depending on the audience.

Having a long history in advocacy work (he began his first human rights campaign as a teenager), Rubens is well positioned to make his case. But he is lighter-skinned and male, while many of the people for whom he advocates do not benefit from the privileges he enjoys. He is in the, sometimes uncomfortable, position of seeking a graduate education, advancing his knowledge of transnational feminism, and advocating for the rights of marginalised young people in his own country. In particular, his gender can be a barrier, in some contexts:

> It's very interesting how I can be blocked—because I'm a man—to, for example, identifying myself as a feminist. Or to even work supporting families. This whole area, it's a very tricky area because they would say, "oh, but we don't want a man taking over again," and . . . how hard it is because I understand that at some point in the history, it was very crucial for women to work together, just women. Because they needed that space to identify as a group and to get a chance to work for their rights. But now, in 2013, I do think that we should try to look at ways that we can grow this movement . . . like, this movement needs to be transcended by other partners, not only women.

His entry into feminist spaces is careful, but insistent. He does not refute that women may have reasons not to want to work with a man in his position. But he persists in making space for his work. He is comfortable with young people and works with diverse communities, construing feminism in a broad way to include voices that have historically been silenced in Brazil. The young people he works with will face issues he himself has never faced, including HIV discrimination, gender violence, and barriers to accessing reproductive health care.

Given the interconnected social issues that affect his work, Rubens says the concept of intersectionality is 'crucial' to his current projects. He encountered the notion of intersectional identities first in his activist work, and later in academia, where he continues to advocate for reproductive rights through his writing. "With everything you write, you are positioning yourself." The university does not always recognise the knowledge he gathered in activist work or on the streets working with youth. He feels a tension in academic environments between lived experience and scholarly research, and finds that his decades of experience in human rights activism are not always respected in classrooms and graduate committees. Even in conferences, where there is an opportunity to learn from each other, he feels that activists can be edged out of the conversation by academic experts. In particular, he is frustrated with the lacklustre response to his proposals to change the frame of youth work from family planning to reproductive and sexual rights. . . . Family planning continues to be a focus of grants and conferences, and he sees this as evidence that the conversation has not yet evolved to place women at the centre. The concept of family planning constructs women's reproductive lives normatively, and praises having fewer children and fitting the profile of a straight, monogamous, married woman in a stable, long-term relationship. It marginalises individuals' sexual rights, as well, and focuses mainly on sex as it relates to reproduction. Programmes seek to change women's behaviour and to reduce birth rates, but not to empower women as agents of change. "They do speak of empowerment, but only in terms of using contraception, waiting to marry, or having fewer children. But if a woman wants to marry and have ten children, because it's her right too, then no." Rubens echoes the voices of advocacy groups such as SisterSong which define reproductive justice in terms of human rights rather than public health or population.

. . .

CONCLUDING THOUGHTS ON THE (RE)INTEGRATION OF REPRODUCTIVE RIGHTS AS HUMAN RIGHTS

These unique context-specific cases offer many examples of a narrative focus in advocating for reproductive rights as human rights. Stories serve to do many things at once, connecting human experiences from widely varying locations in the Global South to a wider discourse that often marginalises or essentialises them. They are unique local stories, but as tends to be the case with human rights work, they are also critical interventions in the global debate on which rights count as universal rights and how they might be protected as such.

To promote a concept of human rights inclusive of reproductive rights means engaging in many acts of translation across differences. It means assembling and presenting stories that bridge divides between local and global publics who may have divergent understandings of human rights, to acknowledge these differences and find points of entry from one discourse into another. Reproductive rights advocates in the Global South are using stories about reproductive rights to make transnational human rights networks more accessible to local people, as human rights workers do around the world, and also to explain complex local situations to outsiders in the human rights community who often stereotype or essentialise them. As Abhaya noted, the woman seeking an abortion in India is not necessarily who you portray her to be. Stories reduce the stigma that so often surrounds reproductive and sexual health issues; make differences in access easier for listeners to grasp; and connect reproductive rights to other substantive rights that may be more familiar in a given social context.

At the start of this project, I anticipated that reproductive rights, like human rights more generally, take time to become real and accessible through complex and sometimes nonlinear political processes, as transnational activist networks construct pathways in and among available institutions to articulate and construct them over time.[28] But it is only through interviews with advocates operating in vastly different contexts that the specific routes came to light by which the connection can be made that reproductive rights are human rights for any given case. Whether carefully introducing critical gender frameworks into discussions of sex-selective abortion in India, or relentlessly documenting cases of nonconsensual sterilisation in South Africa, reproductive rights advocates are using local stories to prompt broader conceptions of human rights.

Another point that comes through in the interviews is that reproductive rights advocates are making a way for human rights to have a more real and grounded connection to the human body. Much of the confusion and prevarication around reproductive human rights stems from the stigma around sexuality and the body. Destigmatisation tends to be a feature of reproductive rights work in a way that it may not be in other human rights advocacy. The stigma of reproductive issues continues to be a barrier to addressing gender violence, for example, as a human rights issue. It is therefore a core part of reproductive rights advocacy to address and dismantle stigma that disproportionately affects women and other marginalised groups seeking access to their rights. . . . Even with case studies and comparisons that allow for some degree of nuance, generalisations can creep in. But it would be a mistake to construe the human rights frameworks of the advocates in this study as wholly unified. Through these interventions in disparate regions of the Global South, there are significant divergences in how advocates conceptualise human rights work. For example, while some emphasise the role of laws to facilitate access, others rail against the hyper-regulation of women's bodies. Advocates engage these dialogues, often comparing their approach to campaigns and movements in other regions. . . .

An equally important element of reproductive rights work is fluency in the language of intersectionality, i.e. the intersecting oppressions that create inequities in access to human rights. Advocates use stories to go outside of their own experiences and engage the complexity of the social fabric in which they work. They do not use universal terms or emphasise commonalities among human beings as much as differences in the ways diversely situated individuals are treated. While the South African attorney uses broad categories like "women," she also imagines the dynamics of discrimination that affect some women more than others:

> I don't have evidence for this, but sometimes I have this vision of a male doctor saying, well, you're HIV positive, and you're obviously wanton and engage in risky behaviors because you got HIV in the first place, and we really don't want you to have any more kids because you're just going to die, and leave us with these orphans who will be a burden on the state. So this idea that women are the ones who are weak, women are the ones who get sick, and are a burden on the state because of their HIV status. So it's interesting how the state and the health care system that is meant to protect people hijacks a woman's autonomy over her body and over her reproductive health. (Jelka)

However fundamental reproductive rights may be to the well-being of a person, the claim that they are as basic as any other human right is not an unopposed truth. Reproductive human rights work can require a level of courage and nonconformity which can invite unprecedented opposition, but also serendipitous alliances. . . .

The ongoing political project of linking reproductive and human rights involves transnational human rights movements, governments, and nongovernmental organisations in local communities around the world, at a time when not all issues are given equal weight in human rights circles. Adjusting heavily bureaucratised definitions of human rights to incorporate reproductive rights is a daunting task, especially when audiences differ in their familiarity with formal concepts or local situations. Issues in the Global South often get short shrift in global human rights debates, and are often presented as problems endemic to certain cultures because of a perceived failure to accept modern ideas. This creates a challenging context for doing human rights work, and one in which advocates relate to a multitude of audiences at the same time. Advocates in the Global South are using stories of individuals as vehicles for translating issues across diverse publics; to destigmatise reproductive issues, challenge stereotypes that might be getting in the way of understanding individual cases, and reintegrate sexual and reproductive life into the concept of human rights. It is through stories that advocates invite audiences in their local community and around the world to grapple with the realities of reproductive oppression and work towards a more inclusive definition of human rights.

NOTES

1. J. Murdoch, "Human Rights," *Human Rights* 15, no. 1 (2003): 989–1018. doi:10.1016/ S0140-6736(11)61458-X; Jack Donnelly, "Cultural Relativism and Universal Human Rights," *Human Rights Quarterly* 6, no. 4 (1984): 400–19. doi:10.2307/762182; and Abdullahi Ahmed An-Na'im, "Human Rights in Cross-Cultural Perspectives: A Quest for Consensus," *Human Rights Quarterly* 14 (1992): 467. doi:10.2307/762319.

2. Susan Moller Okin, "Feminism, Women's Human Rights, and Cultural Differences," *Hypatia* 13, no. 2 (1998): 32–52. doi:10.1111/j.1527-2001.1998 .tb01224.x; and Heiner Bielefeldt, "'Western' versus 'Islamic' Human Rights Conceptions?: A Critique of Cultural Essentialism in the Discussion on Human Rights," *Political Theory* 28, no. 1 (2000): 90–121. doi:10.1177/0090591700028001005.

3. Kathryn Sikkink, *Mixed Signals: U.S. Human Rights Policy and Latin America* (Ithaca, NY: Cornell University Press, 2004), 216.

4. Julie Hollar, "Human Rights Instruments and Impacts," *Comparative Politics* 46, no. 1 (2013): 104.

5. Margaret E. Keck and Kathryn Sikkink, *Activists Beyond Borders: Advocacy Networks in International Politics* (Ithaca, NY: Cornell University Press, 1998), 2.

6. I sent recruitment materials in English and Spanish to reproductive rights organisations across Latin America, and English materials to organisations in the Middle East, Africa, South and Southeast Asia, and the Pacific Islands. For those requesting interviews, I conducted Skype interviews ranging from 45 minutes to two hours, and then conducted archival research and correspondence as necessary.

7. Paul Gready, "Introduction—'Responsibility to the Story'" *Journal of Human Rights Practice* 2, no. 2 (2010): 177–90.

8. Lance Gable, "Reproductive Health as a Human Right," *Case Western Reserve Law Review* (2010): 956–57.

9. Julie Hollar, "Human Rights Instruments and Impacts," *Comparative Politics* 46, no. 1 (2013): 103–20.

10. UNAIDS, http://www.unaids.org/sites/default/ files/media_asset/UNAIDS_Gap_report_en.pdf

11. Sonia Corrêa, "Holding Ground: The Challenges for Sexual and Reproductive Rights and Health: In Dialogue with Sonia Corrêa," *Development* 48, no. 4 (2005): 11–15.

12. Choice on Termination of Pregnancy Act, 1996, preamble.

13. Gendered language is not ideal when it comes to conversations about reproductive health care, because it essentialises gender as biological sex and marginalises the reproductive health care needs of transgender, intersex and gender nonconforming individuals. Much of the legislation on reproductive rights refers to women only, so while less overtly gendered language would be more inclusive, the mention of men in the South African law is of interest.

14. Choice on Termination of Pregnancy Act, 1996, preamble.

15. Keck and Sikkink, *Activists Beyond Borders*.

16. Ibid.

17. Niamh Reilly, "Cosmopolitan Feminism and Human Rights," *Hypatia* 22 (2007): 180–98.

18. Amy Nunn, "The impacts of AIDS movements on the policy responses to HIV/AIDS in Brazil and South Africa: A comparative analysis," *Global Public Health* 7, no. 10 (2012): 1031–1044.

19. Abortion is legal in India up to 20 weeks into a pregnancy, but some doctors use the stigma of abortion to coerce patients to pay them an extra fee, claiming that the doctors themselves are taking a risk by providing the abortion. This illegal practice puts safe abortions out of the range of affordability for many low-income women in India, especially if they do not know their rights.

20. Sofia Gruskin, Laura Ferguson, and Jeffrey O'Malley, "Ensuring Sexual and Reproductive Health for People Living with HIV: An Overview of Key Human Rights, Policy and Health Systems

Issues," *Reproductive Health Matters* 15, no. 29 (2007): 4–26.

21. Keck and Sikkink, *Activists Beyond Borders.*

22. UNAIDS, http://www.unaids.org/sites/default/files/media_asset/UNAIDS_Gap_report_en.pdf

23. Gable, "Reproductive Health."

24. Keck and Sikkink, *Activists Beyond Borders.*

25. Anna Bredstrom, "Intersectionality: A Challenge for Feminist HIV/AIDS Research?" *European*

Journal of Women's Studies 13, no. 3 (2006): 229–43. doi:10.1177/1350506806065754.

26. Ibid.

27. Ibid.

28. Varun Gauri and Evan S. Lieberman, "Boundary Institutions and HIV/AIDS Policy in Brazil and South Africa," *Studies in Comparative International Development* 41, no. 3 (2006): 47. doi:10.1007/BF02686236.

46. DOCTORS NEED TO TALK OPENLY ABOUT RACE— OUR PATIENTS DEPEND ON IT

AISHA WAGNER (2018)

Once again, Black History Month has ended and led us directly into Women's History Month. Despite these back-to-back opportunities, we are still not talking enough about the ways our society is failing these populations, especially women of color.

I confess that I've been a part of the problem—keeping my head down and mouth shut as I made my way through training. But this year is different for me—it's the first year I am in practice as a "full-fledged" physician, the first year where a president is injecting hate and fear into my heart and the hearts of my patients and community. It is also my first year as a pregnant Black woman in a country filled with health disparities, where pregnancy-related deaths are three times more likely in Black women than in White women.

My practice is one place where I strive to address these health disparities—this racism—by incorporating social justice principles and awareness of unintentional biases. This does not come easily; I have been trained—and even raised—to ignore or excuse these differences. However, as I grow as a provider and as a person, my deep concern with our medical education, and its lack of teaching around racism and reproductive justice, grows. In medicine, we talk about the distrust of people of color toward the medical community, but we do not talk about why. We struggle to explore why these differences in health equity exist—thinking 'there must be a scientific explanation,' not accepting that all of this dark history,

as reproductive justice activist Loretta Ross put it, "is in our bones."

In elementary school for Black History Month, my predominately white classmates and I completed reports about Harriet Tubman and Dr. Martin Luther King Jr., but the teaching of Black history stopped there. In college, the few Black people on campus would make an effort to bring attention to our past and present, but it fell on deaf ears. In medical school, not only did we not pay special attention to Black History Month, we didn't pay attention to Black history at all. There was no mention of reproductive justice, which—as defined by reproductive justice collective SisterSong—is a grassroots movement that places the focus on the reproductive health and rights of "people of color, low-income and uninsured women, Indigenous women, immigrant women, women with disabilities and people whose sexual expression [is] not respected."

We did not learn that Dr. James Marion Sims, the "father of modern gynecology," perfected his procedures on un-anaesthetized black slaves. We do not learn that in Puerto Rico in the 1950s the US performed its first large-scale human birth control pill trial on women without adequate consent. We were not taught that in 1990 when Norplant (an implantable birth control) was initially released, it was marketed exclusively to low-income women and teens as a way to "reduce poverty." Or that within two days of the FDA approval, an editorial in the *Philadelphia*

Inquirer suggested that Norplant should be used as a "tool in the fight against black poverty." Within a few years, legislators throughout the U.S. had proposed multiple bills to make Norplant a requirement for welfare recipients and parolees.

Instead, in medical school we were taught to emphasize long active reversible contraceptives (LARCs) such as IUDs and implants for women deemed to be "at risk" for pregnancy—women of color, young women, and poor women.

Today we further control the reproductive rights of underserved women with the Hyde Amendment, which forbids federal money to go toward abortion services, though Medicaid will cover cost of sterilization with few legal barriers.

Thankfully, the movement to incorporate social justice and reproductive justice frameworks into medicine has begun and, for the first time, conversations with my patients have seamlessly transformed into conversations about race and immigration. The day after the election—when the fear and confusion was palpable on the streets—I sat in a small exam room with a patient. She said to me "You're beautiful." I smiled back at her smooth brown face and she continued, "Girl, you know we have to lift each other up." And I said, "Thank you, we do. Now more than ever."

In the East Bay clinic where I now work, a middle-aged Black man smiled as he told me about his past distrust of doctors and how he talked to his white friends in dialysis about how contrasting their medical care has been. Last week, a young Black woman came in crying. She was pregnant, having been denied a tubal ligation by providers in the past because she was, in their eyes, "too young" to make that decision. She had an appointment at Planned Parenthood for an abortion. I held back tears as she thanked me for being so understanding and supportive. I left the visit furious that she had been treated any other way.

There is so much more to tell, so much more to say. It is time to have these conversations and talk openly in the medical community about race and racism. As providers, we have the privilege and the power to work with our communities to effect change. This is not Black history, this is history, and we can no longer ignore it—our relationships with our patients depend on this movement forward—no matter your skin color, your history, or your geographic location.

In a few short months, my life will be forever changed as I welcome my first child. But in all of the excitement and anticipation remains the dread of one day needing to teach them what their schooling won't. I will teach them Black history and women's history: the history of injustice, imbalance of power, of the slow steady march to regaining what was taken away through the work of social and reproductive justice. And I will teach them of the courage, strength, beauty, love and vibrancy of women of color. Our history must be redefined for not just my future child, but for all of her future peers.

47. ON BEING TRANSNATIONAL AND TRANSGENDER
DON OPERARIO AND TOORU NEMOTO (2017)

There has been a notable increase in attention to the lives and health needs of transgender people.[1,2] The growing burden of HIV among transgender communities during the 1990s brought visibility to this population, spurring two decades of research on individual-level health behaviors, mental health, substance use, and sex work as drivers of transgender women's HIV risk.[3] The Institute of Medicine called for a broader research agenda on transgender-specific health needs in 2011—the same year that the National Transgender Discrimination Survey highlighted systematic antitransgender bias and structural violence as enduring challenges for transgender people.[4] The human rights of transgender people have more recently been garnering attention as a legitimate public health issue, demonstrated by the study by Cheney et al. ["Living Outside the Gender Box in Mexico: Testimony of Transgender Mexican Asylum Seekers,

AJPH 107, no. 10 (October 1, 2017): 1646–1652], on transgender women from Mexico seeking asylum in the United States. This work demonstrates how the arc of research on transgender health has evolved from initially focusing on individual-level behaviors to considering transnational and legal issues that affect health outcomes.

The study analyzed asylum declarations filed through a legal service organization in California by transgender women immigrating from Mexico. Although Mexico has instituted national policies that acknowledge the rights of sexual minority populations, such as the legalization of same-sex marriage, there remains resistance to progress among religious institutions and local communities that acknowledge only heterosexual lifestyles and that discriminate against nontraditional forms of gender identity and expression. According to their document analysis, systemic community violence was a key impetus for transgender women's immigration from Mexico.

Forms of violence included childhood insults by family members, intimidation in school settings, and more extreme acts of physical victimization, sexual assault, and murder of transgender adults. Transgender women reported a lack of support from police and the legal system in Mexico; some officers were perpetrators of transgender violence. The authors noted limitations of their research, including a non-representative sample of transgender women from Mexico who had access and comfort using legal services in the United States, which might not be the case for many transgender immigrants.

Violence and other human rights violations among transgender people are not geographically unique. Findings reported in the National Transgender Discrimination Survey revealed the "banality" of violence in transgender communities in the United States,[4] and our research findings have documented the prevalence and health correlates of antitransgender violence in the United States[5] and throughout the Global South.[3] For example, research with transgender women in Thailand (known locally as *kathoey*) reported violence inflicted by family members (generally fathers and brothers) while participants were questioning their gender and expressing nonnormative gender traits.[6] In Malaysia, transgender women (known locally as *mak nyah*) are frequently exposed to physical violence and harassment from police and religious authorities, and the systematic employment discrimination of *mak nyah* can lead to survival sex and an elevated risk of trauma, exposure to violence, HIV, sexually transmitted infections, and substance abuse.[7]

Many transgender women immigrants and asylum seekers bring a history of violence and trauma with them as they resettle in the United States. Consequently, they may avoid institutions that require disclosure of their gender history, such as health care and legal support agencies, to protect themselves against the antitransgender stigma that has been well documented in the United States. Unhealthy trajectories may continue in the United States for transgender immigrants because of the intersection of antitransgender bias, anti-immigrant bias, and racism and because of health systems that traditionally have a myopic view on individual-level determinants of health.

We urge public health researchers and providers to contextualize the health needs of transgender immigrants within a transnational and human rights backdrop. Individual-focused health interventions, guided by individual-level theories and frameworks, may have limited success without recognition of the structural and life course challenges that transgender immigrants experienced before, during, and after their migration to the United States. Future study must address transgender immigrants' and asylum seekers' access to and utilization of health and social service[s] in the United States in relation to their cumulative exposure to antitransgender discrimination, violence, and trauma. Transnational public health and policy efforts are necessary to advance the human rights of transgender people globally and must promote basic safety, freedom of expression, freedom from violence, and access to legal protections as foundations for public health for transgender people.

REFERENCES

1. Stall R, Matthews DD, Friedman MR, et al. The continuing development of health disparities on

lesbian, gay, bisexual, and transgender individuals. *Am J Public Health.* 2016;106(5):787 789.

2. Meyer IH. The elusive promise of LGBT equality. *Am J Public Health.* 2016;106(8):1356–1358.

3. Poteat T, Wirtz AL, Radix A, et al. HIV risk and preventive interventions in transgender women sex workers. *Lancet.* 2015;385(9964):274–286.

4. Grant JM, Mottet L, Tanis JE, Harrison J, Herman J, Keisling M. *Injustice at Every Turn: A Report of the National Transgender Discrimination Survey.* Washington, DC: National Center for Transgender Equality; 2011.

5. Nemoto T, Bödeker B, Iwamoto M. Social support, exposure to violence and transphobia, and correlates of depression among male-to-female transgender women with a history of sex work. *Am J Public Health.* 2011;101(10):1980–1988.

6. Nemoto T, Cruz T, Iwamoto M, et al. Examining the sociocultural context of HIV-related risk behaviors among kathoey (male-to-female transgender women) sex workers in Bangkok, Thailand. *J Assoc Nurses AIDS Care.* 2016;27(2):153–165.

7. Nemoto T, Iwamoto M, Perngpam U, Areesantichai C, Teh Y. Access to health care in relation to discrimination due to gender identity and sexual orientation among transgender women and men who have sex with men (MSM) in Thailand and Malaysia. Paper presented at the International Conference on Sexuality; July, 2017; Bangkok, Thailand.

48. RACISM—THE PATHOLOGY WE CHOOSE TO IGNORE

RICHARD HORTON (2017)

London (July 7, 2005; 52 dead). Woolwich (May 22, 2013; one dead). Westminster (March 22, 2017; five dead). Manchester (May 22, 2017; 23 dead). London Bridge (June 3, 2017; eight dead). Finsbury Park (June 19, 2017; one dead). Grenfell Tower (June 14, 2017; 79+ dead). These tragedies are connected. Hate is a health issue. Racism is a health issue. Xenophobia is a health issue. And terror is a health issue too. Our societies are struggling to find solutions to these threats—threats that are causing deaths with increased frequency. Deaths directly from premeditated violence. Deaths indirectly by a structurally racist society that creates unsafe, isolated, and abandoned ethnic enclaves. Health professionals, together with medical and public health scientists, have an important part to play in addressing these dangers through their work and values—peace, equity, solidarity, diversity, community, and social justice. Health is about power and politics. Now is an important moment to recommit ourselves professionally and politically—across the entire spectrum of medicine and public health—to defeat the insidious social pathologies of hate, racism, xenophobia, and terror.

Medicine and public health have so far failed to meet these growing challenges. Preoccupied as they are with the conventional causes and determinants of disease, broader political influences shaping health have been neglected, even ignored. The motives of social and political reform that once animated medicine and public health have been lost, forgotten, or deliberately erased. For example, during recent decades, public health practitioners have been co-opted by government into guiding service provision in increasingly bankrupt health systems. They have become the actuaries of efficiency, the accountants of decline. They have traded their critical perspective for collusion with a state whose coercive policies have abjured all notions of the right to health. In return, public health leaders have accepted government patronage. Having sacrificed moral authority, they capitulated to government emoluments. Meanwhile, the science of public health has shrouded itself within the worm-eaten veneer of a medical model of disease that has long failed to meet the objectives of equity and justice. Epidemiology is indeed the basic science of health. But the scaffold of knowledge that epidemiology provides is just that—a skeleton on which must be draped garments of truth about the lives people live today. Those lives seem as distant from the concerns of medicine and public health as they can possibly be.

We live in racist societies where hate and xenophobia flourish and where politicians demonise migrant communities. Remember Theresa May's 2013 "Go Home or Face Arrest" campaign? The acts of terror seen across Europe are the result of a complex assemblage of factors. But those factors certainly include the rhetoric and practice of racism. Hate, racism, xenophobia, and terror all lead to poor health, diminished wellbeing, and limited access to health care. The terrorist attacks in Britain, together with the inferno at Grenfell, are linked through the collapse of microcivilisations. Communities from which terrorists emerge are prey to incitement because of a collapse of hope regarding schools, jobs, homes, safety, welfare, and health. Those living in Grenfell Tower were a diverse mix of Moroccans, Eritreans, and more, conveniently packaged and parked with few protections by a council that revelled in its exclusive status. Hate, racism, xenophobia, and terror will be hard to defeat. But medicine and public health can play a part. First, they must find their voice and join the public discussion. Second, they must put at the centre of their concern those who are most vulnerable in our societies, and use a political as well as a biomedical lens to interpret and understand their predicaments. Third, they must examine the accumulating body of evidence about community-specific, multisector, equity-oriented interventions that can make inroads into racism. Inequality does not hurt us equally. There can be neither health nor health equity while racism is tolerated and, in today's aggressive anti-immigration culture, even encouraged. If our society is to achieve better health, we have to work out a better way to live together, we have to embrace the full humanity of our neighbourhoods, and we have to, as Jeff Chang put it in his recent chronicle of racial injustice in America (*We Gon' Be Alright*, 2016), learn to look again, and never stop looking.

49. PERFORMANCE OF A LIFETIME
On Invisible Illness, Gender, and Disbelief
KATE HOROWITZ (2017)

Dr. Moran tapped his heavy silver pen against a sheaf of test results. "Well," he said, "I've found the problem."

I had arrived enervated in his office a few weeks ago, drifting through the door in a fog of weakness and fatigue. Headaches hammered me all day. I was 23 years old and my bones ached. I couldn't feel my feet. My guts felt oily and torqued. Once a month or so, I would slip into a hot, dizzy spell that made the floor slant and my eyes blur. None of this was new.

I was there because he had a reputation as a diagnostic virtuoso. I had heard that he once traced one man's seizures back to a rare South American parasite. They said no ailment was too obscure to escape his scope. I would put my name on his lengthy waiting list.

He was as thorough as they said. He wired me up like a dead auto battery, switched on the current, and measured each muscle twitch. He stuck syringes into strategic locations on my scalp. He timed me as I clumsily pushed plastic pegs into a puzzle board.

Now it had arrived: the moment my strange, bumbling body would start making sense. Dr. Moran's eyes flicked toward mine, and then returned to his pages of data.

"It's called conversion disorder," he said, enunciating every syllable. "At some point in your childhood you likely experienced a traumatic event. Rather than processing that trauma, you're unconsciously converting that trauma into physical sensations—performing illness, so to speak."

I couldn't think of a single thing to say.

"I'm going to write you a referral to a psychiatrist," he continued, still looking down. "He'll be able to help you sort this out."

The skies opened up as I wrote out a check for the receptionist. I ran to my car and landed hard in the driver's seat, wiping rainwater from my eyes. I dialed my mother with wet, shaking hands.

"Lovey, what is it? What's wrong?"

"What happened to me?"

"What? What are you talking about?"

"When I was a kid. Dr. Moran says my sickness has something to do with trauma, that something awful must have happened, that I'm repressing it."

My mother was quiet.

"Mommy, what happened?" My voice rose and broke. I swallowed the slick saliva pooling in my throat. "What happened to me?"

"Nothing happened, honey. Nothing happened to you that you don't remember."

"Mom?"

"Nothing. I swear."

***

Dr. Moran was not the first physician to tell me my illness was psychological, nor would he be the last.

Experts in every imaginable specialty labeled me a malingerer, hypochondriac, hysteric, drama queen. I was diagnosed with an eating disorder and an anxiety disorder. I was prescribed Xanax and threatened with institutionalization. An emergency room doctor sent me home with "women just have pain sometimes." An allergist told me I was breaking into hives because I wanted attention. "You must like feeling special," he said.

I wish he was right. I wish this was about me, that this story was mine alone. I wish I couldn't name a dozen friends who have been through the same thing, or recite a litany of horrific statistics: A man in pain waits an average of 49 minutes for treatment in the emergency room, compared to the average woman's wait of 65 minutes. Women's symptoms are more likely to be downplayed, disbelieved, or dismissed. Men in pain are generally given painkillers; women, sedatives.

Women are also far more likely than men to be diagnosed with conversion disorder, which was rebranded as "functional neurological disorder" by the American Psychiatric Association in 2013. The term "conversion disorder" was itself a rebranding. For nearly 2,000 years, it was simply called hysteria.

My doctors made it clear that there were two kinds of illness: those they could identify, and those that didn't exist. My symptoms were simply shadow puppets cast by a mind that couldn't control itself. I was confused. They were certain.

They were wrong.

***

The person who finally got it right was not even my doctor. Dr. Renault was a cardiologist specializing in chronic fatigue. I was a graduate student in science writing interviewing him for a summer project. He asked me why I had chosen him.

It had been six years since I had seen Dr. Moran. I was still so weak. So tired.

"I'm sick," I said flatly. "I'm sick, and I don't know why."

"Ah." He gestured toward two chairs around a broad conference table.

Eventually I ran out of questions. When I looked up from my notebook, he was observing me with an expression I didn't understand. "I bet you're hypermobile," he murmured, almost to himself.

Gently, he explained what he saw. My fingertips bent backward like plastic straws as I gripped my pen. I supported my neck with one hand as if to keep my heavy head from dropping onto the table. The whites of my eyes, on closer examination, were pale blue.

"May I?" he asked, reaching for my arm and extending it outward. "Look at your elbow." I did. It looked fine to me. He pointed at the hyperextended joint. "It's not supposed to do that." In a five-minute cursory examination, knowing almost nothing about me, he had spotted a body's worth of signs and symptoms that scores of specialists had overlooked.

Dr. Renault gave me nearly an hour of his time, slowly explaining his suspicions. He recommended a good doctor in my city who would know what to do. That night he e-mailed me a packet of papers on the illnesses he was pretty sure I had.

Hypermobile Ehlers-Danlos syndrome (hEDS) is a genetic disorder that corrodes connective tissue. Postural orthostatic tachycardia syndrome (POTS) affects the autonomic nervous system, which is responsible for breathing, digestion, and pumping blood to the extremities and brain. Mast cell activation syndrome (MCAS) causes overblown allergic reactions to things like sunlight, exercise, food, and medications.

Three acronyms explained every symptom I'd ever experienced—the pain, the exhaustion, the nausea, the dizziness, fainting spells, headaches, even the hives—and some things I hadn't realized were symptoms. The bruises perpetually spattering my legs. My laughable clumsiness. My translucent, fragile skin. Trouble focusing in school and at work. The difficulty absorbing nutrients that led to the weight loss, which had looked, in a teenage girl, a lot like an eating disorder. My racing heart.

With a diagnosis, my experience suddenly had a name. With diagnosis came the possibility of treatment and information with which I could reframe and reclaim my life.

There are no cures for these diseases, and I will likely never be well. But I have medication for the pain now and braces for my knees, shoulders, and wrists. I have supplements and exercises to help me sleep and make me strong. I've learned what warrants a trip to the emergency room and what will likely pass. I've accepted that, for now, I need a job I can do from home. I've attended conferences and met other women with my conditions. I've held their bruised hands and looked into their tired, understanding eyes.

***

Although I waited 29 years for answers, I was lucky. Eventually I got them. If I hadn't had the economic privilege to go to graduate school, I never would have met Dr. Renault. I would either still be searching, or I would have given up.

In all my years of research and doctors appointments, I had never heard of any of these illnesses. One might think, as I did, that they must be incredibly rare.

They are not rare. But they are rarely diagnosed.

Symptoms such as pain, exhaustion, and weakness are invisible to the dubious eye and the CT scanner. There's little room for a patient's subjective experience in a medical system organized around quantifiable results.

All three illnesses are deceptively multi-systemic. Symptoms rotate through the body, sending sufferers from specialist to specialist in vain. The gastroenterologist you see for abdominal pain will not ask about your easily torn skin. A rheumatologist will not ask about your difficulty finding words.

Then there's the scientific neglect. POTS, hEDS, and MCAS are not taught in medical school, and there has been very little research into their causes or treatments.

It's probably not a coincidence that all three disproportionately affect women.

My illnesses are the result of molecular abnormalities brewed up in my body before I was even born. They're indisputably real. I didn't imagine them or bring them on myself.

The average EDS diagnosis takes 10 years. But most women will never be diagnosed at all. They'll be referred to psychiatrists, or left to their pain, or sent home with prescriptions for Xanax.

People with POTS and hEDS are more likely to experience depression and anxiety. Researchers don't know why. It could be neurological. It could be pain-related. It could, they say, be the consequence of being accused, over and over, of playacting.

***

My sleep this morning was unsettled by a familiar dream.

It started out promising, with a flyer on a telephone pole announcing auditions. A local theater was staging a play about invisible illness. I clambered onto the dusty black stage and read for the lead role, the sick woman. The scene flowed naturally. I felt good about my chances.

Then the director called and explained that he'd given the part to someone else.

He sounded like he was standing somewhere windy.

"We appreciated your approach," he shouted, "but you just weren't that convincing."

CHAPTER 8

FAMILY SYSTEMS, FAMILY LIVES

The title of this chapter reflects the reality of the family as both a major societal institution and a place where individuals experience intimate relationships. Using the definition of institution as established patterns of social behavior organized around particular purposes, the family is constituted through general patterns of behavior that emerge because of the specific needs and desires of human beings and because of societal conditions. At the institutional level, the family maintains patterns of privilege and inequity and is intimately connected to other institutions in society such as the economy, the political system, religion, and education, which together produce social discourses or "regimes of truth" that create meaning associated with family and its relationship to these institutions. At the level of experience, the family fulfills basic human needs and provides most of us with our first experiences of love and relationship as well as power and conflict. Families are complex entities, as the poem "My Grandmother Washes Her Feet in the Sink of the Bathroom at Sears" by Mohja Kahf illustrates. This poem demonstrates relationships among families, religion, and culture, emphasizing how young family members often serve as a bridge or translator between traditional cultures within families and contemporary institutions and practices.

Scholarship on the family has demonstrated that family forms are historically and culturally constructed in global contexts and that family is a place for the reproduction of power relations both nationally and transnationally. Families worldwide are increasingly shaped not only by social structures within each society, but also by uniquely global forces, including worldwide demographic shifts, transnational employment across national and political borders, regional and international violence, and worldwide culture systems. In this way, families are primary social units that maintain other institutions and reinforce existing patterns of domination. At the same time, however, family networks provide support systems that can reduce the indignities and/or challenge the inequities produced by various systems of inequality in society.

DEFINITIONS OF FAMILY

Families are part of what social scientists call kinship systems, or patterns of relationships that define family forms. In most societies worldwide, people live together on the basis of kinship ties and responsibilities for raising children. Such ties involve rules about who has sexual access to whom, what labor should be done and by whom, and how power should be distributed. In virtually all societies, there is a publicly announced contract and/or ritual that makes sexual and economic ties legitimate. Kinship systems vary widely around the world and determine matters such as family descent or claims to common ancestry (for example, through the line of the father [patrilineal], mother [matrilineal], both parents [bilateral], or either parent [unilateral]) and distribution of wealth.

Kinship rules also govern norms about the meanings of marriage or romantic partnerships and the numbers of partners allowed. Monogamy is a form of relationship in which an individual has only one partner, or in terms of marriage, only one spouse, or only one partner or spouse at any one time (known as serial monogamy). This can be compared to non-monogamy, meaning multiple partners or spouses. There are overlapping and non-mutually exclusive definitions of monogamy that include marital monogamy (marriage of two people), social monogamy (two partners living together in a sexual and cooperative economic relationship), and sexual monogamy (two partners remaining sexually exclusive with each other and having no outside sex partners). Non-monogamy includes both polygamy (multiple partners or spouses) and polyamory (discussed in Chapter 6 and meaning the practice, desire, or acceptance of having more than one intimate relationship at a time with the knowledge and consent of everyone involved). In terms of marriage, within polygamy is cenogamy (group marriage), polygyny (multiple wives), and the least common form of polygamy, polyandry (multiple husbands). In this way, families are central organizing principles among humans around the world and, as a result, the status and role of individuals in families are not only dependent on their access to power in society generally, but also related to the status of families within a society, and especially their access to economic resources.

In the United States, there is no "normal" family, although this still tends to be constructed as the nuclear family of the middle-class, white, married, heterosexual couple with children even though this is no longer the most frequently occurring contemporary family formation. "Nuclear family" implies a couple residing together with their dependent children, and it can be distinguished from an extended family, in which a group of related kin, in addition to parents and children, live together in the same household. U.S. Census Bureau data show that traditional nuclear families have dropped to about a quarter of all households and multiple family forms are now the rule rather than the exception—even though more than two-thirds of all children live with two parents, broadly defined. Frequently occurring family forms in the United States today include single/solo-parent families; blended families; families headed by lesbian, gay, and/or queer domestic partners; and families including other cohabiting couples with children. These changes have occurred, in part, because there has been a significant drop in the number of legally married heterosexual couples in the last few decades, with more women never marrying, delaying marriage, cohabiting in heterosexual and gay/lesbian and queer relationships, and raising families alone.

In addition, there has been an increase in multigenerational families over the last decades (now about 16 percent of all families) that reflect economic forces, especially the job losses and home foreclosures of recent years, and the rise in numbers of immigrants, who, like their European counterparts from earlier centuries, are far more likely than native-born North Americans to live in multigenerational family households.

In 2018 barely half of all U.S. adults were married (compared to almost three-quarters of all adults in the 1960s) and 40 to 50 percent of all marriages ended in divorce. The median age of first marriage is 28 years for men and 26 years for women, up from 23 and 21 years, respectively, in 1980. African American women marry at lower rates than whites (even though most eventually do marry). Educated women are more likely to marry, and although they often marry at a later age, they are less likely to divorce, and, especially at ages 35 and 40, college-educated women of all races are significantly more likely to be married than any other group.

The share of U.S. children living with an unmarried parent has doubled since 1968, increasing from 13 percent to about a third of all children in 2017. That trend is accompanied by a drop in the numbers of children living with two married parents, from 85 percent in 1968 to 65 percent in 2017. Most children in unmarried parent households are living with a solo mother, but a growing share are living with cohabiting parents. Overall, about one in five children (21 percent) are living with a solo mother, up from 12 percent in 1968. Seven percent of children are now living with cohabiting parents, about twice the number in 1997, when the U.S. Census Bureau first started asking this question. Numbers

GLOBAL FAMILIES FACTS AND STATS

The definition of "family" has been argued within academia, religious groups, governments, and even families themselves. How researchers define family directly impacts statistical outcomes and presents a challenge to comparative analysis of family structure, stability, roles, and trends over time. How do *you* define family?

Three multi-year studies, the *United Nations Demographic Yearbook* and *Population and Vital Statistics Report* (United Nations Statistics Division, 2016), MLK Global's "1968 and Today: Stats to Shock" (2017), and the Social Trends Institute and the Institute for Family Studies' *World Family Map* (Wilcox and DeRose, 2017), have followed trends in world family structure and stability.

Using these resources, compare the original study findings to the most recent findings, and create your own family map that answers the following questions:

1. Is marriage trending up or down? How does this trend impact family stability, individual roles within the family, and child development?
2. How has the definition of family changed over the last decade? How has this impacted the health and well-being of children? Of women? Of the LGBTQ population?
3. What is the impact of location on family trends and stability?
4. What are other factors that impact family trends and stability? How has the level of impact by these factors changed over time?
5. Based on your findings, where do you see families trending in the next decade, and what new factors might impact those trends?

Resources

MLK Global. (2017). "1968 and Today: Stats to Shock." https://mlkglobal.org/2017/11/23/1968-and-today-stats-to-shock/

United Nations Statistics Division. (2016). *United Nations Demographic Yearbook* and *Population and Vital Statistics Report 2016*. https://unstats.un.org/unsd/demographic-social/products/dyb/index.cshtml

Wilcox, W. B., and DeRose, L. (2017). *The World Family Map 2017: Mapping Family Change and Child Well-Being Outcomes*. http://www.socialtrendsinstitute.org/publications/family/the-world-family-map-2017-mapping-family-change-and-child-well-being-outcomes

of children living with a solo father have also increased to 4 percent from 1 percent in 1968. It is important in interpreting these figures to know that although children are classified based on the parent with whom they live most of the time, those splitting their time equally between households are classified based on the household they were in at the time the data were collected.

The numbers of children living with an unmarried parent vary by race and ethnicity. Over half of all black children live with an unmarried parent, and most live with a solo mother. Similarly, about a third of Latinx children live with an unmarried parent, as do a quarter of white children. The share of Asian American children living with unmarried parents is markedly lower at 13 percent. In addition, currently about two million children are raised by lesbian, gay, or queer-identified parents. About one-third of lesbian and one-fifth of gay male households include children.

One of the most distinct characteristics of families today reflects the fact that solo women who get pregnant are much more likely to live alone or in a cohabiting relationship. In the 1970s about 30 percent of women chose to marry before their child was born compared to only 5 percent who chose to marry and one-fifth to begin cohabiting in 2017. Patterns of cohabitation and marriage also vary according to social class, with better-off pregnant women more likely to move into marriage and more disadvantaged pregnant women remaining solo or cohabiting.

This diversity of family forms actually more closely parallels U.S. families of the nineteenth century rather than the recent past. In the premodern era before industrialization, households were made up of various kin and unrelated adults and children, reflecting the ways an agricultural way of life meant that households contained many people—not just kin, but others who came to help work the land or maintain the household. These social, economic, and demographic facts underscore the myth of the nuclear family in the United States, either currently or in the distant past. In other words, traditional "regimes of truth" about the normative family hide the reality of the wide diversity of family life in the United States.

Although today women are as likely to have children as they ever were, three facts stand out. First, the average family size has decreased. Second, women in industrialized societies are having children later in life than they did in earlier times. Both of these trends are related to changes in health care technologies that have raised health care standards and encouraged parenting at later ages, the availability of birth control and abortion, and the increase in women's education and participation in paid labor with subsequent postponement of marriage and child-rearing. Third, as already mentioned, there has been a significant increase in the number of children born to solo and cohabiting women outside of marriage, especially among nonwhite populations since the 1970s. Because the largest increase in unmarried births has been among women aged 25 years and older, these changes also reflect changing norms discussed in Chapter 7 about raising a child "out of wedlock," either alone or in a heterosexual, gay/lesbian, or queer cohabiting arrangement, and the fact that many are wary of marriage, feel it is no longer a relevant institution, and/or choose—and have the resources—to maintain families outside of legal marriage.

LEARNING ACTIVITY

WHAT MAKES A FAMILY?

Conduct an informal survey of the people on your dorm floor or in an organization to which you belong about the structure of their family of origin. Whom do they consider to be in their family? What relation do these people have to them?

Did all of these people live in the same house? Who had primary responsibility for caring for them as children? Who was primarily responsible for the financial well-being of the family? For the emotional well-being of the family? Was the family closely connected to extended family? If so, which extended family members and in what ways?

Compare your findings with those of your classmates. What do your findings lead you to surmise about what makes a family? How closely do the families of your interviewees resemble the dominant notion of the nuclear family—a husband and wife (in their first marriage) and their two or three children? What do you think is the impact of our stereotype of the nuclear family on social policy? How do you think this stereotype affects real families dealing with the real problems of everyday family life?

MYTHS AND FACTS ABOUT LESBIAN FAMILIES

Myth 1: Lesbians don't have lasting relationships.

Fact: Many lesbians are in long-term partnerships. In fact, around 10 percent of lesbian and gay people in the United States are in same-sex marriages. Unfortunately, social supports and civil rights are not accorded to lesbian partnerships as they are to heterosexual marriages. While lesbian and gay people won the right to marriage with the Supreme Court's 2015 decision, more than half of U.S. states still do not provide employment, housing, and public accommodation protections for queer people. Additionally, the Right has continued to fight equality by using religious liberty arguments to suggest that bakers, florists, photographers, and venues don't have to provide services for lesbian and gay weddings if the business owners have a sincere religious conviction against marriage equality.

Myth 2: Lesbians don't have children.

Fact: Millions of American children are being raised by lesbian or gay parents. Many lesbians have children from previous heterosexual relationships before they came out. Others have children through artificial insemination, and others adopt children. Unfortunately, because the courts may believe stereotypes about lesbians, lesbian mothers still sometimes lose custody of their children in a divorce, despite research indicating the fitness of lesbian mothers. While gay men and lesbians can adopt in all 50 states, some religious adoption agencies are seeking to deny gay and lesbian couples using a religious liberty argument.

Myth 3: Children of lesbian parents develop psychological disorders.

Fact: Research indicates that there is no difference in the development or frequency of pathologies between children of heterosexual parents and children of homosexual parents. In fact, study after study suggests that children in lesbian families are more similar to, rather than different from, children in heterosexual families. Studies of separation-individuation, behavior problems, self-concept, locus of control, moral judgment, and intelligence have revealed no major differences between children of lesbian mothers and children of heterosexual mothers.

Myth 4: Children of lesbian parents become gay themselves.

Fact: Research indicates no difference between children raised in lesbian families and children raised in heterosexual families with respect to gender identity, gender role behavior, and sexual orientation. Studies suggest that children in lesbian families develop along the same lines as children in heterosexual families; they are as likely to be happy with their gender, exhibit gender role behaviors, and be heterosexual as children of heterosexual mothers.

In conclusion, U.S. Census data also show a dramatic increase in the last few years among cohabiting couples. Demographers believe the increase involves individuals delaying marriage because of the cost, avoiding marriage altogether, or moving in together without a long-term plan because of short-term financial pressures. At the same time, the increase in the number of women not marrying, and the age of those who do, reflects the improved status of women where they have relative control over their reproductive and economic lives. Such data illustrate the complex role of economic factors in marriage trends.

FAMILY DIVERSITY

The diversity of families includes solo parents; extended and multigenerational families; lesbian, gay, and queer families with and without children; people (married or not and with or without children) living in community with other adults; grandparents raising grandchildren or nieces and nephews; and so forth. These families represent all social classes, sexualities, and racial and ethnic groups, and one in five children in the United States speaks a language other than English in their homes. Globally, family structure is affected by the consequences of the global economy as well as by militarism and colonial expansion. Examples include the effects on family life as a result of immigration patterns associated with exportation and consolidation of global capital and the consequences for women in families as a result of their labor in industries such as textiles or electronic components worldwide.

Diversity among U.S. families was strengthened in June 2015, when marriage equality was established in all 50 states as a result of the U.S. Supreme Court ruling that held that "same-sex" couples had the rights and responsibilities to marry on the same terms and conditions as "opposite-sex" couples, as guaranteed by the Equal Protection Clause of the Fourteenth Amendment. Indeed, more than 50 percent of the U.S. population endorses marriage equality at this point. It is estimated that a greater number of people in the United States currently supports marriage equality than believe in evolution as a scientific principle. Gay, lesbian, and queer rights activists made the case that the values of these couples are indistinguishable from those of their straight neighbors. They are no less loyal to their partners, they value and participate in family life, and they are just as committed to their neighborhoods and communities. They also pay the same taxes. As such, the case was made for their rights as citizens to the rights that all straight people have: the right to legal marriage. Nonetheless, the ongoing political debate concerning "family values" illustrates how supporters of the status quo (or existing power relations) in society have made the term "family values" synonymous with traditional definitions of the family and its role in society. This includes seeing women defined in terms of their domestic and reproductive roles, men as the rightful sources of power and authority, and married heterosexual families as the only legitimate form of family. Many people are offended by this narrow construction of family and its association with a repressive political agenda, and reject such values as their family values. Determining what kinds of families get to be counted as "real" and determining whose "family values" are used as standards for judging others are heated topics of debate in the United States, despite the achievements of marriage equality advocates.

It is also important to note, however, that not all lesbian/gay/queer committed couples advocate marriage for themselves or necessarily endorse the legal recognition of gay marriage as a primary goal of the lesbian/gay/queer movements. They recognize the right to equal domestic partnerships and the basic economic benefits that come with that, but understand marriage as a key feature of a heterosexist culture that underpins the very discrimination they experience as nonheterosexual people. In other words, they resist legal marriage because of its role in maintaining the heteropatriarchy that justifies homophobia. They ask, Why mimic practices associated with an institution central to supporting heterosexism (the discrimination against nonheterosexual people)? In addition, the critique has been made that people in more affluent developed countries often focus on "gay marriage" to the detriment of addressing other issues such as violence, discrimination, and social exclusion. The term "homonationalism" is often used to describe the ways LGBTQ issues get positioned as the great "civilizational gifts" the United States has to offer less developed countries.

The notion of family—with all its connotations of love, security, connectedness, and nurturing—is a prime target for nostalgia in the twenty-first century. This is especially pertinent as economic forces transform the ways families function and we yearn for a return to the "traditional" family, with its unconditional love and acceptance, to escape from the complexities and harsh realities of society. Although many families do provide this respite, dominant ideologies about the family have idealized and sometimes glorified the family, and women's roles in the family, in ways that hide underlying conflict and violence. In addition, these ideologies present a false dichotomy between public (society) and private (family) spheres. Poor and nonwhite families have rarely enjoyed the security and privacy assumed in this split between family and society and instead experience the effects of interlocking systems of domination and the configurations of state power that link penal systems to the judicial, welfare, and health care systems in ways that subject marginalized families to oppressive laws, policies, and practices. This is the topic of the next section: the connections between the family and other social institutions.

INSTITUTIONAL CONNECTIONS

The family interacts with other institutions in society and provides various experiences for family members. For example, economic forces shape women's family roles and help construct the balance between work and family responsibilities. As discussed in Chapter 9, women perform more than two-thirds of household labor—labor that is constructed as family work and often not seen as work. In addition, the family work that women do in the home is used to justify the kinds of work women are expected to perform in the labor force. It is no coincidence that women are congregated in a small number of occupations known for their caretaking, educating, and servicing responsibilities. In addition, the boundaries between women's paid work and home life are more fluid than men's. This is structured into the very kinds of jobs women tend to perform, as well as the expectations associated with hiring women. These assumptions can be used against women very easily as they attempt to advance in careers. At the same time, the more rigid boundaries between work and home for male-dominated jobs mean that men have a more difficult time negotiating parenting responsibilities when they want to be more actively involved in their children's lives.

The economic system impacts families in many ways; in turn, families support and impact economic systems. Women care for and maintain male workers as well as socialize future generations of workers, thus supporting economic institutions that rely on workers to be fed, serviced, and able to fulfill certain work roles. Although in contemporary U.S. society some families are still productive units in that they produce goods directly for family consumption or for exchange on the market, most families are consumptive units in that they participate in the market economy through goods purchased for family consumption. As a result, advertisers target women as family shoppers. The family is a consumptive unit that provides the context for advertising, media, and other forms of entertainment. In these ways, family systems are intimately connected to economic forces in society. Some scholars and activists are making the case for a return to the family as a productive, ecologically mindful unit that consumes local goods and supports local businesses.

The impact of shifting economies and changing technologies on families varies considerably by gender, class, sexuality, and race, such that a family's placement in the larger political economy directly influences diverse patterns of family organization. The ways

---

THE FEMINIZATION OF POVERTY

Jennifer Venable

Recent scholarship indicates that a clear connection exists between gender and poverty. In particular, statistics from the European Parliament show that globally, women earn little more than 50 percent of what men earn on average (Debusscher, 2015, 8). The "feminization of poverty" is the process by which the poverty population is increasingly comprised of women regardless of race and age (Starrels, Bould, and Nicholas, 1994, 590). Poverty is multifaceted, and a number of causes contribute to the poverty of women:

1. The gendered division of labor in which women are delegated domestic responsibilities (Research and Library Services Division, 2006). Sixty-six percent of caregivers (of children, elderly, and disabled individuals in one's family) are women (National Center on Caregiving at Family Caregiver Alliance, 2003). Because care work is often unpaid labor, women's opportunities within the workforce are drastically reduced.
2. Single motherhood and lack of child care. Approximately 20 percent of women's unemployment is directly connected to lack of child care (Starrels et al., 1994, 592–593). This impacts children in particular because women customarily receive custody of their children over men. Yet, many divorced mothers receive little to no child support (Starrels et al., 1994, 592–593).
3. While women make up a little under half the workforce, they continue to earn less than men in nearly all occupational sectors (Milli, Huang, Hartman, and Hayes, 2017, 1). According to the U.S. Census

Bureau's Current Population Survey Annual Social and Economic Supplement, 2014–2016, 50 percent of households rely on women as the sole breadwinners or as earners who contribute 40 percent to the household. Consequently, women's earnings are essential to the economic stability of their families (Milli et al., 2017, 1).

To learn about poverty in your state, go to https://talkpoverty.org/poverty/.

References

Debusscher, P. (2015). *Evaluation of the Beijing Platform for Action +20 and the Opportunities for Achieving Gender Equality and the Empowerment of Women in the Post-2015 Development Agenda*. Brussels: European Parliament. Retrieved from http://www.europarl.europa.eu/RegData/etudes/STUD/2015/519191/IPOL_STU(2015)519191_EN.pdf

Milli, J., Huang, Y., Hartman, H., and Hayes, J. (2017). "The Impact of Equal Pay on Poverty and the Economy." *Institute for Women's Policy Research*. Retrieved from http://www.iwpr.org/publications/impact-equal-pay-poverty-economy/

National Center on Caregiving at Family Caregiver Alliance. (2003, May). *Women and Caregiving: Facts and Figures*. Retrieved from https://www.caregiver.org/women-and-caregiving-facts-and-figures

Research and Library Services Division, Legislative Council Secretariat. (2006, February 23). *Fact Sheet: Causes of Women's Poverty*. Retrieved from http://www.legco.gov.hk/yr05-06/english/sec/library/0506fs07e.pdf

Starrels, M. E., Bould, S., and Nicholas, L. J. (1994). "The Feminization of Poverty in the United States: Gender, Race, Ethnicity, and Family Factors." *Journal of Family Issues*, 15(4), 590–607.

economic systems affect family organization and life are demonstrated by the fact that African American children are twice as likely to enter U.S. foster care systems because of the conditions of poverty in their lives. In addition, solo-female-headed families are approximately five times more likely than married-couple-headed families to live in poverty (28 percent to 5 percent, respectively). Economic factors impact single-headed families such that households headed by women have about half the income and less than a third of the wealth (assets) of other U.S. households and are about three times as likely to be at or below the poverty level. Most recent census data show that the poverty rate for single mothers is twice as high as the rate for single fathers. As already mentioned, almost half of children living in single-headed households live in poverty. Race impacts this economic situation such that households headed by women of color are the most likely to experience poverty. It is well known that the most effective antipoverty program for families is one that includes educational opportunities, a living wage with benefits, and quality child care. In this way, families are shaped by their relationship to systems of inequality in society.

This means, for example, that working-class women's lack of flexible work scheduling affects how families are able to meet their needs, as does the lower pay of working-class family members, making them less able to afford quality day care. Similarly, higher unemployment among men of color as compared to white men impacts families. Jobs with different incomes and levels of authority and seniority affect access to such family-friendly benefits as flextime, on-site child care, and company-sponsored tax breaks for child care. For example, although unpaid parenting leave is a legal right of all U.S. employees, many companies provide better family benefits for their higher-level and better-paid employees than they do for their lower-level employees.

Around the world 169 countries guarantee paid maternity leave, with 98 of these providing 14 or more weeks. The United States provides no paid parenting leave, although the Family Medical Leave Act (FMLA) establishes the rights of workers in certain occupations to take unpaid leave, continue to receive benefits and job protection, and use their own accumulated "sick leave" to maintain their salary for a certain number of days annually. However, almost half of employed private sector women workers lack a single paid sick day that they could use in a medical or family emergency. Institutional support in the form of family-friendly policies is thus a necessity for healthy families and effective parenting.

Economic factors are especially influential for determining incidence and age of marriage. Worldwide poverty often increases the incidence of marriage, especially among young women. It is the lack of opportunities, extreme poverty, and the importance placed on female virginity that encourages girls to be married as children. And, even though countries may set a minimum marriageable age, such as 16 years, traditional marriages of girls of younger ages are widespread in sub-Saharan Africa as well as many regions of South Asia. Goods received as the bride price of a daughter—including, for example, livestock, cash, or other valuables—are often essential for sustaining the rest of the family. Unfortunately, child brides are subject to interpersonal violence and health problems such as obstetric fistula. Organizations such as Human Rights Watch advocate for the end of these practices, as does Girls Not Brides, a global partnership of almost 200 nongovernmental organizations committed to addressing child marriage.

The family experience is also affected by the state and its legal and political systems. Prison systems, for example, shape experiences of family for incarcerated women, who are disproportionately mothers and women of color. Other examples of relationships between families and state systems include the ways governments closely regulate families and provide certain benefits to legally married couples. Couples need a license from the state to marry, and the government says they may file a joint tax return, for instance. Benefits accrue to certain family members and not to people who, even though they might see themselves as family, are not recognized as such by the state. And, although an advanced industrial society, the United States has no national funding of day care centers. This affects the social organization of the family and the experience of parenting. Federal and state policies also impact the family, of course, through legal statutes that regulate marriage and divorce legislation, reproductive choice, and violence in families.

A key example of interactions between family and state policies is immigration policy, especially that of undocumented immigrants. As of this writing, the Trump administration is embroiled in controversial policies that were signature issues during his presidential campaign when he characterized certain immigrants as criminals—although research repeatedly finds that such immigrants have lower crime and incarceration rates than those who are born in the United States. President Trump has imposed a "zero tolerance" immigration policy, requiring the arrest of all illegal immigrants at the border, which has resulted in the separation of children from their parents—a policy that provoked intense resistance as inhumane and a human rights violation. In the meantime, he has promised to build a wall on the Mexico–U.S. border. The reading "Beyond the Wall," by Ashley McKinless, examines the plight of Central American immigrants and refugees, with a focus on Guatemala, where 60 percent of the population live in poverty.

President Trump has also imposed a travel ban prohibiting entry into the United States for people from seven Muslim-majority countries, although in response to legal challenges, the plan was revised twice. The third version was upheld by the U.S. Supreme Court in 2018 in a 5–4 ruling. The president also attempted to end the Deferred Action for Childhood Arrivals program (DACA), but a legal injunction as of this writing has allowed the policy to continue. Leila Schochet's reading "Immigration Policies Are Harming Children" addresses DACA and focuses on ways harsh immigration policies "create toxic stress for young children by breaking families apart, instilling fear in the immigrant community, and preventing families from accessing programs that meet children's most basic needs."

Indeed, the family has connections to all societal institutions, and these connections help shape the kind and quality of experiences that we have as family members. Religion and the family are closely tied as social institutions. Religious socialization of children occurs in the family through religious and moral teachings, and religious institutions often shape societal understandings of families as well as provide rituals (such as baptisms, weddings, and funerals) that help symbolize family and kin relations. As the reading "The Reciprocal Relationship Between Religious Beliefs and Acceptance of One's Gay or Lesbian Family Member" suggests, such an acceptance process involves a complex relationship between family members' attitudes toward LGBTQ issues and their general proclivity toward acceptance. This reading about familial reactions to the coming out of a family member is authored by Katherine Zeininger, Mellisa Holtzman, and Rachel Kraus.

Educational institutions also rely on the family as a foundation for the socialization, care, and maintenance of children. Health systems rely on parents (and women in particular) to nurse and care for sick and elderly family members, as well as provide adequate nutrition and cleanliness to prevent disease. Military institutions need the family as a foundation for ideologies of combat and for socialization and support of military personnel. Sports and athletics are tied to the family through gender socialization, the purchase of certain equipment and opportunities, and the consumption and viewing of professional sports in the home. Although we might like to think of the family as an "oasis" apart from society, nothing could be further from the truth.

POWER AND FAMILY RELATIONSHIPS

At the direct level of experience, the family is the social unit in which most people are raised, learn systems of belief, experience love and perhaps abuse and neglect, and generally grow to be a part of social communities. It is in the family that most of us internalize messages about ourselves, about others, and about our place in the world. Some learn that love comes with an abuse of power as large people hit little people, all in the name of love. Some also learn that love means getting our own way without responsibility—a lesson that may detract from the hopes of a civil society where individuals care about one another and the communities of which they are a part. Others learn that love is about trust, care, compassion, and responsibility.

Family is where many of us first experience gender because societal understandings of the differences between girls and boys are transferred through early teachings by family members, facilitating the binaries we associate with gender performances. Parents bring home baby girls and boys, dress them in gender-"appropriate" colors, give them different toys, and decorate their bedrooms in different ways that tend to facilitate and enforce cisgender behaviors. As Chapter 3 emphasizes, the family is a primary institution for teaching about gender. In addition, experiences of gender are very much shaped by the gender composition of family members. A girl growing up in a family of brothers and a boy growing up with only women and girls have different experiences of gender.

Central in any discussion of family is a focus on power. Power in families can be understood as access to resources (tangible or intangible) that allows certain family members to define the reality of others, have their needs met, and access more resources. In most U.S. families today, power is distributed according to age and gender. Older family members (although not always the aged, who often lose power in late life) tend to have more power than children and young people, who are often defined as "dependents." Men (both cisgender and transmen, although the status of the latter may of course vary, and "men" is always understood through other identity categories) tend to have more power in families if this is measured in terms of resource management and allocation and decision-making authority. Women often have "power" if this is defined as day-to-day decisions about the running of the household and how certain household chores get done. Sociologists tend to

ACTIVIST PROFILE
HANNAH SOLOMON

Hannah Greenbaum Solomon believed that "woman's sphere is the whole wide world" and her first responsibility was to her family. Solomon worked tirelessly in turn-of-the-century Chicago for social reform. Laboring alongside Jane Addams at Hull House, Solomon worked to improve child welfare. She reformed the Illinois Industrial School for Girls, established penny lunch stations in the public schools, and led efforts for slum clearance, low-cost housing, child labor laws, mothers' pensions, and public health measures.

In 1876 Solomon became the first Jewish member of the Chicago Woman's Club, where she developed a sense of women's ability to work together for social good. In 1893 she organized the Jewish Women's Congress at the Chicago World's Fair, which led to her founding the National Council of Jewish Women (NCJW) to enhance social welfare and justice. Solomon saw her commitment to justice as a part of her responsibility as a Jew, a woman, and an American.

Under Solomon's leadership, the NCJW sponsored programs for the blind, formed the Port and Dock Department to assist immigrant women in finding housing and jobs, established a permanent immigrant aid station on Ellis Island, supported Margaret Sanger's National Birth Control League, raised relief dollars during World War I, and participated in the presidential effort to create jobs during the Depression.

Solomon's legacy has continued in the NCJW since her death in 1942. Following World War II, the NCJW provided assistance to Holocaust survivors in Europe and Israel. During the McCarthy era, the NCJW organized the Freedom Campaign to protect civil liberties. Additionally, the organization helped develop Meals on Wheels, built the Hebrew University High School in Jerusalem, helped establish the Court Appointed

Advocate Project (CASA) to protect the rights of children in court cases, and launched a national campaign to try to ensure that children were not harmed by changes in welfare law.

Currently, the National Council of Jewish Women has 90,000 members and continues the work of Hannah Solomon by bringing her vision of justice to bear in the world.

---

emphasize that this latter sort of power is vulnerable to changes in broader family dynamics and subject to decisions by economic providers or heads of household.

The United States has among the highest marriage and the highest divorce rates of any industrialized country. Although a large number of people get divorced, this does not seem to indicate disillusionment with marriage because large numbers of people also remarry. Marriage traditionally has been based on gender relations that prescribe authority of husbands over wives and that entail certain norms and expectations that are sanctioned by the state. Still today, the traditional marriage contract assumes the husband will be the head of household with the responsibility to provide a family wage and the wife will take primary responsibility for the home and the raising of children and integrate her personal identity with that of her husband. As in "Mrs. John Smith" and "Dr. and Mrs. John Smith," Mrs. Smith easily can become someone who loses her identity to a husband. The declaration of "man and wife" in the traditional marriage ceremony illustrates how men continue to be men under this contract and women become wives.

Today these norms are increasingly being challenged by contemporary couples who have moved from this traditional contract to one whereby women are expected to contribute financially and men are expected to fulfill family roles. Despite these modifications, husbands still tend to hold more power in families and wives do the majority of physical and emotional family work. The rituals of marriage ceremonies illustrate these normative gender relations: the father "giving away" his daughter, representing the passage of the woman from one man's house to another; the wearing of white to symbolize purity and virginity; the engagement ring representing a woman already spoken for; and the throwing of rice to symbolize fertility and the woman's obligation to bear and raise children. Finally, as already mentioned, the traditions of naming are illustrative of power in families. Despite contemporary changes in attitudes and gender performances, approximately 8 out of 10 women in heterosexual marriages still take the name of their husband, and among those who keep their name, most give their children their husband's name and not their own. An additional 1 in 10 choose a third option, such as hyphenating or continuing to use a birth name professionally. However, if the number of married women taking a husband's name today is approximately 78 percent, in the 1970s it was 86 percent: not a dramatic decrease.

Writing in 1910, socialist anarchist Emma Goldman saw marriage as an economic transaction that binds women into subservience to men (through love and personal and sexual services) and society (through unpaid housework). In the reading "Marriage and Love," she advocates "free love" that is unconstrained by marriage and relations with the state. Goldman believed love found in marriages occurred in spite of the institution of marriage and not because of it. Also, as Goldman notes, it is especially in the family that many girls and women experience gender oppression. It is in close relationship with men, such as in heterosexual marriage and as daughters in patriarchal families, that women often experience gender domination and feel the consequences of masculine power and privilege.

Sexism in interpersonal relationships among family members reduces female autonomy and lowers women's and girls' self-esteem. Consequences of masculine privilege in families can mean that men dominate women in relationships in subtle or not-so-subtle ways, expecting or taking for granted personal and sexual services, making and/or vetoing important family decisions, controlling money and expenditures, and so forth. In addition, power in family and marital relationships may lead to psychological, sexual, and/or physical abuse against women and children. Often the double standard of sexual conduct allows sons more freedom and autonomy compared to daughters. Also, daughters are very often expected to perform more household duties than brothers, duties that may include cleaning up after their brothers or father. Studies have shown that boys spend about a third less time doing chores than their sisters and are more likely than girls to get paid

LEARNING ACTIVITY

DIVORCE LAW: WHO BENEFITS IN MY STATE?

Research your state's divorce laws. How is property divided in a divorce? How is custody determined? How are alimony and child support determined? How do these laws affect women and children in actuality in your state?

What are the poverty rates for divorced women and their children in your state? How many parents do not pay child support as ordered by the court? How does your state deal with nonpaying parents? What can you do to challenge the legal system in your state to be more responsive to women's and children's needs following divorce?

IDEAS FOR ACTIVISM

- Become a court-appointed special advocate (CASA) for children.
- Offer to babysit for free for a single parent one evening a month.
- Find out your university's family leave policies and child care support for faculty/staff.

- Organize a campus campaign to improve these if needed.
- Become a Big Brother or Big Sister. To learn more, visit www.bbbs.org.
- Organize an educational activity on your campus around alternative family models.

or receive an allowance for doing the work. Mirroring the housework data for adults (see Chapter 9), chores—such as dishwashing and cooking, often regarded as routine and performed for free—are more likely to be done by girls than boys. This sets up gender inequities in the family, impacts the amount of free time girls can enjoy, and sets a precedent for adult behavior.

In particular, the balance of power in domestic partnerships depends in part on how couples of all kinds negotiate paid labor and family work in their relationships. These partnerships can be structured according to different models that promote various ways that couples live and work together. Models include "head-complement," "junior partner/ senior partner," and "equal partners"—relationships that each have different ways of negotiating paid work and family work, and, as a result, provide different balances of power within these relationships.

The "head-complement" model reflects the traditional marriage contract, as discussed previously, whereby the head has the responsibility to provide a family wage and the complement takes primary responsibility for the home and the raising of children. In addition, complements see their role as complementing the head's role by being supportive and encouraging in both emotional and material ways. The balance of power in this family system is definitely tilted in the direction of the "head" of the head-complement couple. Power for the complement is to a large extent based on the goodwill of the head as well as the resources (educational and financial in particular) that the complement brings into the relationship. This model has been embraced and articulated as a theological concept, "complementarianism," by Christian conservatives, as noted in Chapter 12. Although the

HISTORICAL MOMENT
THE FEMININE MYSTIQUE

In 1963 Betty Friedan, a housewife and former labor activist, published the results of a series of interviews she had conducted with women who had been educated at Smith College. Despite their picture-perfect lives, these women reported extreme despair and unhappiness and, unaware that others shared this experience, blamed themselves. To deal with this "problem that has no name," these women turned to a variety of strategies, ranging from using tranquilizers to having affairs to volunteering with church, school, and charitable organizations.

What had happened to these educated women? Following World War II, when women had found a prominent role in the workforce, a national myth emerged that the place for (middle-class, white) women was in the home. To conform to this ideal, women sublimated their dreams and desires and fell in line with "the feminine mystique."

When Friedan's book *The Feminine Mystique* appeared in 1963, it spoke loudly to the unspoken misery of millions of American housewives. In its first year, it sold three million copies. Unfortunately, during the era immediately following the repressive, anti-Communist McCarthy years, Friedan feared that were she to push the envelope in her book to include an analysis of race and social class, her work would be discredited. So, rather than choosing to address the more complex problems of working-class women and women of color and likely be dismissed, she chose to be heard and addressed the safer topic of middle-class housewives.

Despite its shortcomings, *The Feminine Mystique* found a readership that needed to know that they were not alone in believing that something was seriously wrong with their lives. Friedan suggested that the something wrong was a conspiracy of social institutions and culture that limited the lives of women. She challenged women to find meaningful and purposeful ways of living, particularly through careers.

Friedan encouraged women to move out into the workforce and to examine the social and economic, as well as psychological, forces at work in limiting women's lives. Although she did not go so far as to question the need for men to move into equitable work in the home, she did bring to national attention the problem of women's circumscribed existence and offered a call for women to begin to examine the limitations imposed on them.

Source: Ruth Rosen, *The World Split Open: How the Modern Women's Movement Changed America* (New York: Viking, 2000).

complement does tend to have control over the day-to-day running of the household, this power may disappear with divorce or other internal family disruption.

As already mentioned, the percentage of married-couple households with children younger than 18 has declined to about a fifth of all households. Less than 5 percent of stay-at-home parents in the United States are fathers, although this number has tripled in the last decade. However, there is also a trend in educated women choosing to give up their careers and live the head-complement lifestyle. This does not contradict the longitudinal trend of an increasing number of women with children entering the workplace since 1950; rather, it points to the slight decrease in this trend in the last five years specifically among affluent couples. These choices reflect the difficulties in juggling the demands of work and home and the fact that these families can afford for wives not to work outside the home.

The "junior partner/senior partner" model is one in which the traditional marriage contract has been modified. Both members of the couple work outside the home, although junior partners consider their work to be secondary to senior partners' jobs. They also take primary responsibility for the home and child care. This means that junior partners have taken on some of the provider role while still maintaining responsibility for the domestic role. In practice this might mean that if the senior partner is transferred or relocated because of work, the junior partner experiences a disruption in work or career to follow. When children are sent home from school sick, junior partners are the ones contacted. They might enter and leave the labor force based on the needs of the children and family. This model, the most frequently occurring structure for marriage or domestic partnerships today in the United States, encourages the double day of work as junior partners in particular tend to work long hours inside and outside the home. In the traditional family it is wives or those fulfilling that role in domestic partnerships, who tend to fulfill these junior partner roles.

In terms of power, there is a more equitable sharing in this junior partner/senior partner model than in the head-complement model because the junior partner is bringing resources into the family and has control over the day-to-day running of the household. Note that in both models described here, the head or senior partner loses out to a greater or lesser degree on the joys associated with household work—especially the raising of children. Junior partners tend to fare better after divorce than the "complements" of the head-complement model. But junior partners do have the emotional stress and physical burdens of working two jobs. These stresses and burdens are affected by how much the senior partner "helps out" in the home.

The "equal partners" model is one in which the traditional marriage contract is completely disrupted. Neither partner is more likely to perform provider or domestic roles. In practice this might mean both jobs or careers are valued equally such that one does not take priority over the other and domestic responsibilities are shared equally. Alternatively, it might mean an intentional sharing of responsibilities such that one partner agrees to be the economic provider for a period of time and the other agrees to take on domestic responsibilities, although neither is valued more than the other, and this is negotiated rather than implied. In this model financial power is shared, and the burdens and joys of domestic work and child care are also shared. Although this arrangement gives women the most power in marriage or domestic partnerships, not surprisingly it is a relatively infrequent arrangement, at least among contemporary cisgender heterosexual couples (there is little data on trans/queer couples). This is because, first, most men in these domestic relationships are socialized to expect the privileges associated with having women service their everyday needs or raise their children, and most women in these relationships expect to a greater or lesser degree to take on these responsibilities. Second, masculine-oriented and male-dominated jobs are more likely to involve a separation of home and work, and it is more difficult for these workers to integrate these aspects of their lives. Third, these occupations ensure higher pay on average, and although it might be relatively easy to value feminine-oriented, female-dominated paid work equally in theory, it is difficult to do so in practice if one job brings in a much higher salary than the other. For example, imagine an equal partner relationship between a dentist and a dental hygienist, which involves relatively gender-segregated occupations with distinct salary differences. Although a couple may value each other's work equally, it might be difficult for a family to make decisions concerning relocation and so forth in favor of the one partner who works as the dental hygienist and makes a small percentage of the partner's salary as a dentist.

It is important to emphasize that despite these various arrangements and the differential balance of power in marriage or domestic partnerships, the family is where many individuals feel most empowered. Many women in particular find the responsibilities of maintaining a household or the challenges of child-rearing fulfilling and come to see the family as a source of their competency and happiness. Sometimes this involves living in traditional family forms, and sometimes it means devising new ways of living in families. In this way the family is a positive source of connection, community, and/or productive labor. These diverse experiences associated with family life suggest how family relationships are a complex tangle of compliance with and resistance against various forms of inequities. Parenting, in particular, is one experience that often brings individuals great joy and shapes their experiences of family relations at the very same time that in patriarchal societies it may function as a form of behavioral constraint, especially for those who identify as women. The reading "Where Are the Mothers?" by Katherine Goldstein focuses on journalism as a profession and addresses the ways it has responded to efforts that create more diversity and gender balance in newsrooms. It points out that mothers in particular are often ignored in these efforts and suggests a series of strategies to make the newsroom a more family-friendly environment. This issue of mothering is the topic to which we now turn.

MOTHERING

Both cis-and transwomen are mothers and virtually anyone can perform the role of mother whether they actually identify as a mother or not. Indeed, our understanding of motherhood is conflated with notions of innate, biologically programmed behavior and expectations of unconditional love and nurturance. In other words, even though the meanings associated with motherhood vary historically and culturally, women are expected to want to be mothers, and they are expected to take primary responsibility for the nurturing of children. Unlike the assumptions associated with "to father," "to mother" implies nurturing, comforting, and caretaking. You might mother a kitten or a friend without the assumption of having given birth to them. To have fathered a kitten implies paternity: You are its parent; you did not cuddle and take care of it. Similarly, to father a friend makes no sense in this context.

In contemporary U.S. society, there is a cultural construction of "normal motherhood" that is class and race based, and sees motherhood as a practice that implies devotion to, and sacrifice for, children. Despite these imperatives, mothering roles include three types of child care: activities to meet children's basic physical needs; work that attends to children's emotional, cognitive, and recreational needs; and activities for maintaining children's general well-being. In traditional families, mothers tend to be involved with children more than fathers in all these ways—except with their recreational activities. This is especially true for fathers with male children, illustrating how gender informs parenting behaviors. In addition, as global societies have developed and the expectations associated with the role of motherhood have been framed by patterns of consumption in postindustrial societies of the global north, middle-class motherhood has been modified to include the detailed management of children's lives, including social, recreational, and educational opportunities, alongside the management of mothers' own careers in many cases. This scenario may cause stress for both mothers and children.

This primary association between women and the nurturing aspects of mothering has brought joys and opportunities for empowerment as well as problems and hardships. It has justified the enormous amount of work done in the home and encouraged girls to set their sights on babies rather than on other forms of productive work, or, more likely today, on both babies and jobs, without enough conversation about the sharing of responsibilities or an understanding of the often exhausting consequences of attempting to juggle the needs of families and careers. It has justified the types of labor that women have traditionally done in the labor force as well as women's lower pay; it has kept women out of specific positions, such as in the military, where they might be involved in taking life rather than giving life; and it has encouraged all kinds of explanations for why men are, and should be, in control in society. For example, one study asked volunteers to evaluate a pool of equally qualified job applicants and found that mothers were consistently viewed as less competent and less committed, and they were held to higher performance and punctuality standards than other female or male candidates. Mothers were 79 percent less likely to be hired and, if hired, would be offered a starting salary $11,000 lower than nonmothers. Fathers, by contrast, were offered the highest salaries of all. In addition, the nonmothers were more than twice as likely as equally qualified mothers to be called back for interviews.[1]

The close relationship between traditional notions of "womanhood" and mothering has caused pain for women who are not able to have children as well as for those who have intentionally chosen to not have any. Mothering a disabled child brings its own challenges and joys: Ableism and the normatively abled notion of childhood construct institutional responses that affect the experience of mothering.

In this way, contemporary constructions of mothering, like the family, tend to be created around a mythical norm that reflects a white, abled, middle-class, heterosexual, and young adult cisgender experience. But, of course, mothers come in all types, abilities, and sexual identities, and reflect the wide diversity of those who identify as women in the United States. Their understandings of their roles and their position within systems of inequality and privilege are such that mothering is a diverse experience. This is because society has varied expectations of mothers depending on class, culture, and other differences—at the same time that these differences create diverse attitudes toward the experience of mothering. For example, although society often expects poor mothers to work outside the home rather than accept welfare, middle-class mothers might be made to feel guilty for "abandoning" their babies to day care centers. Because of class, ethnicity, and/or religious orientation, some mothers experience more ambivalence than others when it comes to combining work and family roles. Further, there are thousands of mothers in the United States who attempt to parent while they are incarcerated and experience stigma on an ongoing basis. The 2018 estimate is two million U.S. children with one or more parents in prison.

---

1 Shelley J. Correll, Stephen Benard, and In Paik. "Getting a Job: Is There a Motherhood Penalty?" *American Journal of Sociology* 112, no. 5 (2007): 1297–1339.

Interracial or LGBTQ couples or people who adopt a child of another race are often accused of not taking into account the best interests of their children. Of course, it is society that has these problems and the families are doing their best to cope. This illustrates the narrow understandings of motherhood as well as the stereotypes associated with being a mother. As emphasized in the reading "The Kids Are OK," by Ken W. Knight and others, although there is misinformation about the health and well-being of children raised in LGBTQ families, the consensus of all research is that they do as well emotionally, socially, and educationally as children raised by heterosexual parents, despite the discrimination that their families often endure.

In this way, North American families are increasingly diverse forms of social organization that are intricately connected to other institutions in society. The family is a basic social unit around which much of society is built; it is fundamental to the processes of meeting individual and social needs. The centrality of the family in U.S. society encourages us to think about the way the family reproduces and resists gender relations and what it means to each of us in our everyday lives.

THE BLOG

INSIDE OCHO TIJAX: MEET THE WOMEN IN GUATEMALA OFFERING SUPPORT IN THE FACE OF HORROR

Susan M. Shaw (2017)

Five friends were watching the horror on the news from their homes on March 8. A shelter was going up in flames with girls inside. Stephany Arreaga picked up the phone and called her mom. "Are you seeing this?" she asked. "What can we do?"

"Let's go down there," Mayra Jimenez suggested. And so, Arreaga and Jimenez gathered their friends—Maria del Carmen Peña, Hane Herrera, and Kimy De León—and went to help.

Until this moment, these women weren't really activists: They were a graphic designer, a journalist, a sociologist, a dentist, and a photographer making the nearly hour-long drive to Hogar Seguro Virgen de la Asunción, just outside Guatemala City.

By the time they arrived, emergency workers were bringing out survivors and bodies.

The women started to help by meeting the families as they arrived and going with them to the hospital or to the morgue. "I knew, at that moment, that people were suffering and that I could be useful, somehow, for those families," Jimenez told *Ms.* "But in relation to the girls, it was a tremendous feeling of pain and love; it was wanting to be with them in their final moments, even knowing that they were dying one by one."

By the time it was all over, 41 girls were dead, and 15 were severely burned.

The girls were in the shelter because they had been reported missing at some point—running away from abuse, kidnapped, trafficked. They were not criminals. They were there to be protected as the government sorted out a safe space for them to go. But at the shelter, they were mistreated. They were physically and sexually abused, medicated against their will, forced to undergo abortions, and fed spoiled food. Some were even trafficked again.

Things weren't much better at the boys' shelter. The children tried to escape, but the national police were waiting. Rather than help these vulnerable children, Guatemala's president Jimmy Morales and other government officials abdicated responsibility and turned them over to the police. The boys were locked in an auditorium; the girls in a small 22'-by-23' room with a few mattresses but no blankets.

When the girls begged to be allowed to go to the bathroom, the police refused. They built a makeshift bathroom using the mattresses that had been left on the floor to create some small place of privacy. Quickly, however, the area overflowed, and the stench became unbearable. Again, the girls begged to be released. They refused the food the police brought because they suspected their food at the shelter had been drugged to make them compliant for abuse and trafficking.

Finally, with no other apparent options, officials think some of the girls moved a mattress near a window and set it on fire, believing the police would respond to the smoke and let them out. Instead, the police kept them locked in the room as it burned.

As the five friends accompanied the families of the victims through the medical and legal processes, they quickly realized that the Guatemalan government was taking little responsibility for assisting the survivors or the families or seeking justice by identifying and prosecuting perpetrators—and that they needed a longer-term strategy to address the atrocities of the fire and its aftermath.

They founded Ocho Tijax, an organization to accompany families, support survivors, and seek justice—a "collective of love that is born in the midst of pain."

"Love is the purest emotion, and the one that has sustained me for more than six months working alongside these families and girls," Arreaga said. "At the moment of the tragedy, my first instinct was that of providing protection, as a woman and a mother. Offering my solidarity from afar, to the families and the survivors, was not going to be enough. There was so much need and zero government support. This is still the case today."

Ocho Tijax currently coordinates with lawyers from the Human Rights Law Firm to provide legal aid for four survivors and their families, as well as for the families of eight victims of the fire. They provide counseling for the families of these 12 girls and facilitate counseling and physical and emotional healing therapy for the four survivors in coordination with "Camino de Sol" and a psychologist from the Human Rights Law Firm. They also create media campaigns to dignify the memory and lives of the 56 victims with the assistance of Prensa Comunitaria.

As the cases move through Guatemala's legal system, they offer support and accompaniment during the hearings and trials of the Hogar Seguro case, provide financial aid to cover transportation and other costs for the families, facilitate testimonies to serve as evidence for the public prosecutor's office, and help the survivors and family members understand and navigate the complexities of the legal case and their search for justice. "These women are true heroes," Rob Mercatante, co-director of the Human Rights Defenders Project in Guatemala, an organization that provides support for human rights activists, said of Ocho Tijax. "When they became aware of the fire, instead of posting about it on social media, they went to the scene of the tragedy. They were present with the grieving families during moments of unimaginable loss and suffering. They provided loving support—to these complete strangers—in the hospitals, the morgues, and the funeral parlors. But it didn't end there. These courageous women continue to stand in solidarity with the young girls who survived the massacre and the families of those who didn't make it out alive."

One of the survivors, Cynthia, was only 14 years old at the time of the fire. Over 60 percent of her body was burned. She was in a coma for months, and she had to undergo multiple surgeries to address the physical damage from the fire. Now, she hopes for the quinceañera celebration many Latin American girls experience to mark their coming of age—and since her family can't afford the traditional party, the women of Ocho Tijax are raising funds for her celebration.

Ocho Tijax is still devoted to the legal battles ahead. "Their next challenge is to bring to justice those government officials responsible for this horrific crime," Mercatante said. "This is a very dangerous endeavor, as seeking truth and justice in Guatemala is a high-risk activity . . . especially when those implicated are high-ranking government officials, including the president of the country."

Mercatante, however, has faith. "The women of Ocho Tijax," he declared, "are the very definition of selfless courage."

50. MARRIAGE AND LOVE
EMMA GOLDMAN (1910)

The popular notion about marriage and love is that they are synonymous, that they spring from the same motives, and cover the same human needs. Like most popular notions this also rests not on actual facts, but on superstition.

Marriage and love have nothing in common; they are as far apart as the poles; are, in fact, antagonistic to each other. No doubt some marriages have been the result of love. Not, however, because love could assert itself only in marriage; much rather is it because few people can completely outgrow a convention. There are today large numbers of men and women to whom marriage is naught but a farce, but who submit to it for the sake of public opinion. At any rate, while it is true that some marriages are based on love, and while it is equally true that in some cases love continues in married life, I maintain that it does so regardless of marriage, and not because of it.

On the other hand, it is utterly false that love results from marriage. On rare occasions one does hear of a miraculous case of a married couple falling in love after marriage, but on close examination it will be found that it is a mere adjustment to the inevitable. Certainly the growing-used to each other is far away from the spontaneity, the intensity, and beauty of love, without which the intimacy of marriage must prove degrading to both the woman and the man.

Marriage is primarily an economic arrangement, an insurance pact. It differs from the ordinary life insurance agreement only in that it is more binding, more exacting. Its returns are insignificantly small compared with the investments. In taking out an insurance policy one pays for it in dollars and cents, always at liberty to discontinue payments. If, however, woman's premium is a husband, she pays for it with her name, her privacy, her self-respect, her very life, "until death doth part." Moreover, the marriage insurance condemns her to life-long dependency, to parasitism, to complete uselessness, individual as well as social. Man, too, pays his toll, but as his sphere is wider, marriage does not limit him as much as woman. He feels his chains more in an economic sense.

Thus Dante's motto over Inferno applies with equal force to marriage. "Ye who enter here leave all hope behind."

...

From infancy, almost, the average girl is told that marriage is her ultimate goal; therefore her training and education must be directed towards that end. Like the mute beast fattened for slaughter, she is prepared for that. Yet, strange to say, she is allowed to know much less about her function as wife and mother than the ordinary artisan of his trade. It is indecent and filthy for a respectable girl to know anything of the marital relation. Oh, for the inconsistency of respectability, that needs the marriage vow to turn something which is filthy into the purest and most sacred arrangement that none dare question or criticize. Yet that is exactly the attitude of the average upholder of marriage. The prospective wife and mother is kept in complete ignorance of her only asset in the competitive field—sex. Thus she enters into life-long relations with a man only to find herself shocked, repelled, outraged beyond measure by

the most natural and healthy instinct, sex. It is safe to say that a large percentage of the unhappiness, misery, distress, and physical suffering of matrimony is due to the criminal ignorance in sex matters that is being extolled as a great virtue. Nor is it at all an exaggeration when I say that more than one home has been broken up because of this deplorable fact.

If, however, woman is free and big enough to learn the mystery of sex without the sanction of State or Church, she will stand condemned as utterly unfit to become the wife of a "good" man, his goodness consisting of an empty brain and plenty of money. Can there be anything more outrageous than the idea that a healthy, grown woman, full of life and passion, must deny nature's demand, must subdue her most intense craving, undermine her health and break her spirit, must stunt her vision, abstain from the depth and glory of sex experience until a "good" man comes along to take her unto himself as a wife? That is precisely what marriage means. How can such an arrangement end except in failure? This is one, though not the least important, factor of marriage, which differentiates it from love.

Ours is a practical age. The time when Romeo and Juliet risked the wrath of their fathers for love, when Gretchen exposed herself to the gossip of her neighbors for love, is no more. If, on rare occasions, young people allow themselves the luxury of romance, they are taken in care by the elders, drilled and pounded until they become "sensible."

The moral lesson instilled in the girl is not whether the man has aroused her love, but rather it is, "How much?" The important and only God of practical American life: Can the man make a living? Can he support a wife? That is the only thing that justifies marriage. Gradually this saturates every thought of the girl; her dreams are not of moonlight and kisses, of laughter and tears; she dreams of shopping tours and bargain counters. This soul poverty and sordidness are the elements inherent in the marriage institution. The State and the Church approve of no other ideal, simply because it is the one that necessitates the State and Church control of men and women.

Doubtless there are people who continue to consider love above dollars and cents. Particularly is this true of that class whom economic necessity has forced to become self-supporting. The tremendous change in woman's position, wrought by that mighty factor, is indeed phenomenal when we reflect that it is but a short time since she has entered the industrial arena. Six million women wage workers; six million women, who have the equal right with men to be exploited, to be robbed, to go on strike; aye, to starve even. Anything more, my lord? Yes, six million wage workers in every walk of life, from the highest brain work to the mines and railroad tracks; yes, even detectives and policemen. Surely the emancipation is complete.

Yet with all that, but a very small number of the vast army of women wage workers look upon work as a permanent issue, in the same light as does man. No matter how decrepit the latter, he has been taught to be independent, self-supporting. Oh, I know that no one is really independent in our economic treadmill; still, the poorest specimen of a man hates to be a parasite; to be known as such, at any rate.

The woman considers her position as worker transitory, to be thrown aside for the first bidder. That is why it is infinitely harder to organize women than men. "Why should I join a union? I am going to get married, to have a home." Has she not been taught from infancy to look upon that as her ultimate calling? She learns soon enough that the home, though not so large a prison as the factory, has more solid doors and bars. It has a keeper so faithful that naught can escape him. The most tragic part, however, is that the home no longer frees her from wage slavery; it only increases her task.

According to the latest statistics submitted before a Committee "on labor and wages, and congestion of population," ten percent of the wage workers in New York City alone are married, yet they must continue to work at the most poorly paid labor in the world. Add to this horrible aspect the drudgery of housework, and what remains of the protection and glory of the home? As a matter of fact, even the middle-class girl in marriage can not speak of her home, since it is the man who creates her sphere. It is not important whether the husband is a brute or a darling. What I wish to prove is that marriage guarantees woman a home only by the grace of her husband. There she moves about in his home, year after year, until her aspect of life and human affairs becomes as flat, narrow, and drab as her surroundings. Small wonder if she becomes a nag, petty, quarrelsome, gossipy, unbearable, thus driving the man from the house. She could not go, if she wanted to; there is no place to go. Besides, a short period of married life, of complete surrender of all faculties, absolutely incapacitates the average woman for the outside world. She becomes reckless in appearance, clumsy in her movements, dependent in her decisions, cowardly in her judgment, a weight and a bore, which most men grow to hate and despise. . . .

The institution of marriage makes a parasite of woman, an absolute dependent. It incapacitates her for life's struggle, annihilates her social consciousness, paralyzes her imagination, and then imposes its gracious protection, which is in reality a snare, a travesty on human character.

51. WHERE ARE THE MOTHERS?

KATHERINE GOLDSTEIN (2017)

"We're having a bit of a baby boom," says Lauren Williams, executive editor of Vox.com and the mother of an 18-month-old. When the news startup began in 2014, there wasn't a single parent working at the site. But as the website has grown, so have employees' families. Now, around 15 percent of the 90-person staff have children.

Margaret Wheeler Johnson, who has a 2-year-old and an infant, was the first person to have a baby while working at Bustle.com, a startup women's site. She's now managing editor of Romper.com, owned by the same company, a site for millennial moms that is also experiencing a surge in new children among staff.

"We're all in that early- to mid-30s life shift," is how Kate Sheppard, with a 20-month-old son, describes the leaders of HuffPost's Washington, D.C. bureau. Three quarters of the senior staff have children under 2.

"Any company that wants to employ millennials needs to address this," says Laura Wides-Muñoz, mother of a 7- and an 8-year-old and vice president of special projects and editorial strategy at Fusion. She's seen a wave of new parents enter her workplace. In contrast to even 10 years ago, she's noticed these staffers have often been more upfront about their parenting realities and more vocal about their desire for better policies. "I think it's a positive development," she says.

In the conversation about how to create more diversity and gender balance in newsrooms, one group has been routinely ignored: mothers. What are newsrooms doing to retain women who have or plan to have children, to make sure more women stay in the talent pipeline?

While legacy news organizations have had some working mothers and (sometimes less than ideal) family leave policies for many decades, for a certain set of younger digital news organizations, this is all unfolding in real time. What happens when the people who took blogging mainstream in the mid-2000s, and who now hold demanding jobs in national news, start to have babies? A recent Pew study puts the median age for a first child among highly educated women at 30, and one million millennial women (born between 1981 and 1997) are becoming mothers each year in America.

A 2015 University of Kansas study found female journalists were at higher risk of burnout and more plan to leave the industry than their male counterparts, citing a feeling of less support from their organizations. Their dissatisfaction with the field was, in part, attributed to women's desires to balance work with family responsibilities.

How both legacy organizations, hungry for journalists with 21st-century skills, and startups with nascent HR policies handle this may determine how diverse news leadership and coverage is for decades to come. What follows is a four-point plan for helping women—and men—with young families better manage work and parenthood.

When I found out I was pregnant with my first child, I had been working for six months as a leader at a fast-paced news website. I was to be the first person on this digital team to be a parent. I'd spent my 20s deftly climbing the career ladder in digital journalism, reaching senior management positions at a young age. I had a loving and supportive husband, who was happy to go down a less intense career path while I was the breadwinner. I presumed after our son was born I would take 12 weeks of maternity leave and keep charging ahead in journalism.

My son, Asher, was born in July of 2015. There were the joyous moments—the discovery that listening to Stevie Wonder at full blast seemed to make Asher stop crying, and his love of making eye contact and cuddling. What wasn't typical was, when my son was 6 weeks old, we took him for a follow-up appointment to a specialist because of a potential issue originally identified on a prenatal sonogram. My husband, Travis, and I were in the middle of laughing at a joke when the doctor with well-coiffed hair and a TV anchor smile came in with a somber look on his face.

We were shocked to learn that our son had a number of serious problems with his kidneys and would need surgery as soon as possible. What followed was a multi-week saga involving surgery, two hospitalizations, endless blood tests, and a spinal tap in the longest day of my life at the pediatric ER. I remember walking out of the hospital in a dress covered in a mixture of my son's blood and urine. My eyes were glazed, but the clearest thought in my mind was, "I will never be the same person after this."

I'm so grateful my son has recovered from those early ordeals, but as I prepared to go back to work, thoughts about his need for a second surgery loomed. Warnings about monitoring him for infections were sternly passed on by doctors, along with the directive that continuing to nurse him was "the best thing I could do for him." Despite the traumas of Asher's early life, I was back at my desk when my 12 weeks of maternity leave were up.

Many mothers find the early weeks and months of being back at work difficult. In the only developed country in the world with no requirement for paid maternity leave, the average length of maternity leave, when taken, was 10.3 weeks in 2006–2008, according to a federal study. A 2014 Careerbuilder.com survey found that 11 percent of working mothers took a maternity leave of two weeks or less. There's some hope this could change in the near future—in the 2018 budget, President Trump included a proposal for six weeks of paid leave for all new mothers, fathers, and adoptive parents—but the current reality is far from ideal. And while my son's health crises weren't typical, there is not a parent on the planet who hasn't dealt with some kind of acute stress, whether it's a sleepless baby, colic, or the inability to find reliable and affordable childcare.

Although I was the first person within my digital news team to have a child, I started to notice something on social media that made me realize I wasn't alone. More and more journalist colleagues from past jobs, acquaintances, and women I'd met at conferences over the years were starting to post pregnancy announcements, followed by that newborn photo with the blue and white hospital blanket. As I saw their sleeping infant photos or their anguished first-day-back-at-work posts I wondered: How do they manage the demands of this industry?

And, if all, most, or even many of the new mothers leave this business, who's going to be left?

Increasingly, journalists are asking questions about how their own newsrooms and the industry at large can do better at creating policies that specifically support parents. Rebecca Ruiz asked journalists to report on the family-friendliness of their newsrooms for the Poynter Institute, and Melody Kramer, also for Poynter, has surveyed newsrooms' family leave policies. Both efforts are important first steps in starting conversations and getting data on these issues. Additionally, journalists are bringing their unions into the conversation about better family leave policies and employer support for childcare needs. *The Wall Street Journal*'s editorial staff wrote a letter in March demanding more newsroom diversity, gender pay equity, and specific protections for the careers of parents. William Lewis, the CEO of Dow Jones, the parent company of *The Wall Street Journal*, recently released a statement about this, promising to address gender equality and other diversity issues at the paper, but did not mention mothers or parents specifically.

To research this article, I interviewed nearly 20 mothers at a wide variety of news organizations. I picked women who work in senior leadership or management positions: women who work in digital mediums and will have the most capacity to direct news coverage and story topics for years to come. I chose women who are fully immersed in newsroom environments and culture—editors, managers, strategists, assigners, and idea generators. I chose this group to get better insights into how newsrooms operate and what official and unofficial policies are in place to support them. In focusing specifically on how to retain mothers in the news industry, I hope to promote solutions for tackling the pernicious gender gap in journalism. Most women spoke to me on the record, but some asked for their names to not be used when discussing sensitive workplace situations that could upset current or former employers.

While the women I spoke with earned more than many working mothers, they also frequently lived in expensive metropolitan areas, like New York or Washington, D.C. with some of the highest housing and childcare costs in the nation. While financial resources undoubtedly relieve many kinds of parenting stress, education and salary doesn't seamlessly translate to an easier experience for working mothers. A Pew study found that 65 percent of parents with college degrees found it tough to balance family and job responsibilities, compared to 49 percent of non-graduates. According to the same study, mothers are more likely to find it difficult than fathers, and women still do a majority of household and childcare tasks, even when both parents work full time.

As detailed in the 2014 Nieman Reports feature "Where Are the Women?" there is a crisis in American journalism where fewer women are leading newspapers than ever before, and the number of women in supervisory roles at papers has remained flat since the 1980s, around 37 percent. The Women's Media Center 2017 report found "Men still dominate media across all platforms—television, newspapers, online and wires—with change coming only incrementally. Women are not equal partners in telling the story, nor are they equal partners in sourcing and interpreting what and who is important in the story."

Today, women make up about two-thirds of graduates in journalism programs, but little progress has been made overall in terms of byline representation and gender parity in leadership at legacy news organizations. Some of the lack of gender balance must be attributed to a failure to retain mothers. Aminda Marqués Gonzalez, executive editor of the *Miami Herald*, observed in the 2014 Nieman Reports article, "Of the women in my peer group who had kids, I'm the only one who stayed in the newsroom or came back after some time away. Most of them quit."

Digital news organizations and people working at the forefront of new forms of storytelling—in video, multimedia, data visualization, social media, and audience development—have the opportunity to break traditional newsroom hierarchies. Many digital news operations are relatively flat; it's not uncommon for talented journalists to reach management positions while still in their 20s. In its 2016 report, the American Society of News Editors found 50 percent of online news employees were women, compared to 38 percent of daily newspaper employees.

If all, most, or even many of the new mothers leave this business, who's going to be left?

The gender makeup of news organizations has an outsize influence on society at large, in how newsrooms cover all topics, from sports to public health to national politics. The 2017 Women's Media Center report found that more than half of stories about reproductive rights were written by men at major outlets like the Associated Press and *The New York Times*. Women were quoted, on an issue that is central to their lives, only 33 percent of the time. On the hot button topic of campus rape, the same study found that men wrote a majority of the stories, and more often focused on the crime's impact on the alleged perpetrator rather than the alleged victim. Editors often draw on their own experiences in deciding which stories to pursue and that is as true with mothers as anyone else. Julia Turner, editor in chief of *Slate*, pursued an editorial partnership to cover the science and policy around education. She says, "My interest in advocating for us to do that work was informed by my own experience navigating early childhood education for my own kids and becoming much more aware of the vast disparity of

opportunity available to kids with different kinds of resources."

Turner sees it as a clear-cut case that newsrooms must have a diversity of perspectives in order to thrive.

"Journalism is an incredibly competitive landscape," Turner says. "If you create a workplace where [women] see that if they make the fairly common life choice [to have kids] they will no longer have opportunities to do amazing work or to be promoted to take on leadership roles, then you're shooting yourself in the foot. We need that brainpower, talent, and those ideas."

Certainly, it's not just birth mothers who need better support in the workplace. Fathers and non-birth parents, people caring for aging parents, and even those without family responsibilities can also benefit greatly from progressive family policies and supportive work cultures. But the reality is that the news industry and society at large don't have the same systemic problem retaining and promoting talented men after they have children. The U.S. Bureau of Labor Statistics found that 93 percent of fathers with children under 18 are participating in the workforce, compared to 71 percent of mothers. Fathers are also more likely than mothers to be granted requests for childcare-related flexibility and to be seen more favorably than women by their employers after asking.

The Affordable Care Act mandates insurance companies to provide breast pumps for free to new moms, and because of the lack of mandated paid family leave, many mothers who choose to breast-feed attempt to pump a majority of their infants' food not long after birth. The logistics and time commitment related to this can be strenuous. Pumping sessions can last anywhere from 15 minutes to an hour and must be done on a regular schedule, so figuring out how to fit pumping into a busy day of meetings, commuting, or breaking news is no small feat. (One woman I interviewed on the phone managed to pump milk, eat her lunch, and answer urgent emails while we spoke.) Producing breast milk can for some women be physically demanding, and many of the mothers I spoke to gave up on breastfeeding sooner than they'd initially planned. Ruiz's survey for Poynter found that nearly a third of respondents said their employer was unsupportive of breastfeeding.

But the challenges around being a working mother in news don't stop when you throw away your breast pump.

The reality of the job can mean long hours, high levels of unpredictability, and working for companies that are often strapped for resources and demand a lot from their employees. This can often come to a head when dealing with the relentless pace of the 24-hour news cycle, which has only accelerated after the 2016 election. Jill Abramson, former executive editor of *The New York Times*, who has two grown children, saw supporting female journalists and parents as a priority when she was at the helm. "There's no way I would have managed to keep my career going if I was starting out now," she says.

Elizabeth Bruenig, assistant editor for the Outlook section at *The Washington Post* and mother of a 1-year-old, describes how the current intensity, if it keeps up, will influence her life: "It will definitely strongly impact my future childbearing because it is tough to imagine having another kid in this kind of [news] environment."

While an understanding boss helps create a good work environment for all employees, especially mothers, it's hardly a retention strategy. Women who are met with a lack of understanding about family realities and have been refused flexibility often leave the industry. Anne Hawke was a producer on NPR's "Morning Edition" when it was announced that every three months, producers would be required to rotate their shifts to nights, evenings, or weekends. As the single mother of an 18-month-old, this was untenable. Her requests for flexibility or a job change were not accommodated. When the company announced buyouts the next month, she leaped at the chance. "It was very bittersweet because I really wanted to stay," she says. "I loved the place and thought I'd spend my whole career there, but I had to find the exit door." She now works in communications for a nonprofit.

Asked to comment on Hawke's story, NPR released a statement that pointed out the demands of 24/7 breaking news and defended the rotating shift schedule as a good solution so tough shifts are shouldered more fairly by the whole "Morning Edition" staff. The statement says, "NPR is committed to retaining talented staff before and after they have

children: we offer maternity/paternity leave, rollover vacations and sick days, and a leave-sharing program." It also mentions that NPR offers a number of other employee well-being initiatives, including assistance with childcare.

If you want to see your newsroom better support working mothers, a highly instructive story is how a group of women at *The New York Times* demanded—and got—a better family leave policy.

The *Times* has a formal organization called the Women's Network, which provides networking and mentorship opportunities and arranges discussions and speakers. About two years ago, five senior women who were involved in the Women's Network, all in their 30s and beginning to start families, felt the group should start focusing on policy changes around family leave. "We did this because we felt like, as new mothers, there was no one looking out for us," says Erin Grau, who is vice president of operations and has two young children.

At the time, the family leave policy was 11.1 weeks paid for birth mothers with vaginal deliveries, and 6 weeks for a non-birth parent. The group didn't feel it was adequate, given the company's aggressive growth goals, stated interest in gender diversity and retaining top talent, and the fact that the *Times* now competes with tech companies, not just other newspapers, for sought-after employees. The women decided to focus on the business case for why the company needed to think differently about family leave. "We worked on it with the same rigor and structure we bring to [our regular jobs]," says Grau. "We became the most educated people on the issue in any room."

The women, four of five of whom had given birth in the last 6 months, prepared a memo and presentation for President and CEO Mark Thompson and members of the *Times* executive committee. They had found an ally on the executive committee, now chief operating officer Meredith Kopit Levien, who advised them, supported their efforts, and helped broker the high-level meeting. The group was armed with arguments and data from a compelling source: articles touting the economic benefits of paid family leave that had appeared in *The New York Times*, such as the money-saving success of California's paid family leave policy, the fact that mothers who take leave are more likely to be working a year later, and turnover of female employees is often significantly reduced when leave benefits are increased. At Google, for example, the attrition rate of female employees decreased by 50 percent when the firm increased maternity leave from three to five months and from partial to full pay. Grau and colleagues also included research and estimates on how much their proposals would cost.

The threat was implicit, Grau recalls. "Basically, we were saying, if you don't want to lose any of us, or all us, you should change these policies."

Thompson was persuaded by their case, and told them so at the meeting. "We believe family leave policies that work well for employees make good business sense for the company. The Women's Network presented us with a cogent, well-researched case and we quickly changed our parental leave policy as a result," says Thompson. Maternity leave was extended to 16–18 weeks paid (for vaginal versus cesarean-section births); partners, birth fathers, and adoptive parents get 10 weeks paid leave. Employees are eligible the day they are hired. The policy went into effect in March of 2016.

Jeremy Bowers, a senior editor who works in interactive news at the *Times*, last year took his 10 weeks paternity leave after the birth of his second child and treasured his experience. He had wanted to take the full 10 weeks, but worried that taking that much time could be seen as selfish. A female colleague made a comment that changed his perspective.

"She said, 'I really wish men would take their leave because of the examples it sets. If 100 percent of women take the leave, and only 50 percent of men do, it makes a male employee appear more valuable and less of a liability.' When she said that, my perspective changed. I started to see that family leave wasn't just a personal decision, but something that we should embrace collectively." Ultimately, Bowers ended up taking four weeks when his child was born and six after the election, a decision, he notes, that was his choice, not one the *Times* urged him to make.

There's evidence that taking paternity leave is actually contagious. An *American Economic Review* study found that when a man's co-workers took paternity leave, it increased the chance that he would take it by 11 percentage points—and that if his brother took it, by 15 points.

Bowers is now such a big fan of the *Times*'s policy, he mentions it in all the job descriptions he posts for his team and brings it up with candidates in interviews. He believes the new, more generous policy helps the *Times* stand out with top talent and assists with his recruiting efforts.

Grau's advice to others wanting to advocate for policy changes is, "Don't wait for someone else, or HR, to do the work for you." She believes part of the network's success was having a concrete, well-researched proposal that bosses could just say yes to. Creating allies at the top, and "safety in numbers" through an organized group, rather than just one individual who could be seen as complaining, is also a smart strategic move.

As a next step, Grau and others in the Women's Network are advocating for an official flextime policy and an on-boarding and preparation handbook for those who are going on leave. It doesn't exist at the company, so they are writing it themselves. The one part of their initial proposal that wasn't approved involved creating pools of money to hire freelancers to backfill for people on leave. This was the most expensive aspect of their ask, so they are continuing to look for new ways to advocate for it.

Another important part of the success of the women's efforts is that everyone at the *New York Times* is eligible, from copy editors to vice presidents. I've spoken with several men and women who have negotiated better family leave for themselves than was officially offered by their companies. While understandable, this practice reinforces the idea of family leave as a "perk" and flexibility as something granted to "valuable" employees. It also leaves too much up to an individual manager's discretion and doesn't push companies to make fair and smart policies that benefit everyone.

Throughout my interviews, recurring themes highlighted what some organizations were doing well to help retain mothers as well as areas that must be improved if companies are serious about keeping talented women in the workforce. Here are four recommendations all companies should consider to create news organizations that support the growing millennial workforce and diversity in family responsibilities. All of these recommendations are given in the context of the realities of the news business in the United States. While some recommendations are informed by successful, progressive policies in other industries, some of these suggestions cost nothing to implement.

GIVE PAID MATERNITY LEAVE

There is no "industry standard" for maternity leave in news organizations. With no mandated paid leave in the United States, companies are free to set widely varying policies. Only 14 percent of U.S. workers even have access to paid leave.

As a culture, we too often frame parental leave as a "perk" rather than an essential component of healthy families and productive companies. But paid leave reduces the infant mortality rate, leads to less postpartum depression, and improves the chance women will return to work. Women who receive paid leave are more likely to subsequently work more hours and earn more money than their counterparts who don't.

According to the Center for American Progress, an independent public policy think tank, replacing a skilled worker costs about 20 percent of the employee's salary. The more senior the position, the higher the cost, with executive replacement costs ballooning up to 213 percent of the original salary. Many news organizations have recently been more focused on buyouts and layoffs than retention strategies, but to ignore gender diversity and younger employees with valuable 21st-century skills in an effort to cut costs further puts an organization's long-term viability in peril.

Many of the women I spoke with worked in large cities at organizations with 50 or more employees and are therefore subject to the Family Medical Leave Act, which guarantees 12 weeks of unpaid job projection after one year of employment. Virtually all the women I spoke with were able to get 12 weeks of mostly paid leave, often combining a paid policy with vacation days and short-term disability payments that covered part of their salary. In Melody Kramer's survey about family leave in newsrooms, she found cases of women who were only paid if they had sick time accrued or women who were required to ask colleagues to "donate" their sick days to cover a

maternity leave. Several newsrooms surveyed had no formal parental leave policies in place.

A start for all news organizations would be to offer a blanket 12 weeks of gender-neutral paid leave, without forcing employees to use vacation and sick time to reach that number. Additionally, companies should follow the *Times*'s lead and make the policy effective on the first day of employment. This might help companies attract talented men and women who are planning or expecting children.

GIVE FATHERS AND NON-BIRTH PARTNERS PAID FAMILY LEAVE

The first person to kick off the baby boom at *Vox* was one of the co-founders, Matt Yglesias. He took a four-week paternity leave and even wrote about what he learned from the experience. At the time, Vox.com was still very small, and everyone usually stayed quite late at the office. It was immediately noticeable that Yglesias began coming in much earlier in the morning, leaving at 5 p.m. and then logging on later.

"We didn't have a real template in place [for being a working parent]," Yglesias says. "Ideally, I wanted to set a tone. I'm aware that websites, particularly new ones, often operate on an unsustainable, exploitative culture. They are creating a work environment that's maybe an OK place for young people to get their start, but doesn't really work as an adult job for people who want to have families. We want Vox.com to be a place where people can work for a long time, so that means thinking seriously about the needs of people in their 30s and 40s and beyond."

"It was really helpful for all the women who got pregnant after he had a child," Lauren Williams says of Yglesias's example. "He pioneered a sense of work-life balance for parents. No one else really had to fight for understanding or anything like that. A [new kind of culture] became established. It was a big deal, and I think it would have been hard for someone who wasn't a co-founder to start that precedent."

Newsroom leaders should encourage men to take their full parental leave, and make public what they are doing. Over the last 20 years, the number of men taking parental leave has increased by nearly

400 percent—something that's not just beneficial for fathers and their children, but for women, too, who see improvements in everything from their health to their earnings and career advancement.

Most importantly, perhaps, greater access to paternity or gender-neutral leave policies helps increase gender equity, both at home and in the workplace, in part by lessening hiring and promotion bias against women.

Paternity leave has been shown to have a long-term impact on how involved men are in childcare duties and household work. A recent study from the National Partnership for Women and Families found that fathers who take two or more weeks of leave after the birth of a child are more involved in the child's care nine months after birth. A more equitable division of childcare and chores would undoubtedly increase women's participation in the workforce, considering more than 60 percent of women cited family responsibilities as a reason they weren't working in a 2014 Kaiser Family Foundation/*New York Times*/CBS survey, compared to only 37 percent of men.

CREATE OFFICIAL WORK-FROM-HOME AND FLEX POLICIES

S. Mitra Kalita is the vice president of programming for CNN Digital and has two daughters who are 12 and 5. She found out she was pregnant with her first child while working as a general assignment reporter at *The Washington Post*. Her own mother had been a stay-at-home mom for most of her childhood, and she had imagined she might become one, too, especially while she had young children. She decided to take a six-month maternity leave when her first daughter was born, some of which was unpaid.

As the six months of leave came to a close, she met with a senior editor who was also a working mother and expressed her trepidation about coming back to work. She told her she was considering leaving the job to stay at home. The woman offered her a deal to come back part-time. Kalita was thrilled with the arrangement, and eventually returned to full-time work.

When her second daughter was born, continuing to breastfeed after maternity leave was extremely important to her. She was upfront with her boss at Quartz about her desire to work from home on certain days so she could nurse her baby. Her male boss, the son of a lactation consultant, was supportive of her commitment to breastfeeding and the logistics she needed to make it work.

It's hard to imagine that Kalita would have advanced as far as she has in her career if her requests for flexibility were refused and if, as a result, she decided to take off several years when her children were young. In accommodating her, her bosses saw—and expressed—the value of her as an employee.

But, again, relying on good bosses is not enough. Flexible work options should become part of stated company policies, rather than leaving them up to an individual's negotiation skills. Pamela Stone, author of the book *Opting Out?: Why Women Really Quit Careers and Head Home*, found that when women were offered flexibility, it was often offered as a "privately-brokered special favor," making her vulnerable if the boss left the company or changed his or her mind.

Flexible work policies can take many forms, including compressed work weeks, partial work from home days, and full or part-time telecommuting. Many news organizations use chat software like Slack to communicate about work assignments, and ubiquitous video software allows for teleconferencing. And these policies are not just sought after by parents. A 2014 survey found that 43 percent of workers would choose flexibility over a pay raise, something that should be noted by cash-strapped newsrooms. And flexibility has become the norm at many professional services firms. PricewaterhouseCoopers, Deloitte, and Ernst & Young LLP, among others, are well represented on the Working Mother's 100 Best Companies list, and collectively these firms top the list in the use of flextime.

Studies have shown that when flexible policies are thought out and well-adopted, they can improve productivity and reduce stress. Codifying flexibility can also help attract and retain millennial talent, with people in their childbearing years more likely to prioritize paid parental leave policies and flexible telecommuting in evaluating potential jobs. A study conducted by Stanford University found that when an employer allowed workers to opt-in to a work-from-home arrangement, employees were happier, more productive, and less likely to quit.

"We really need to think much bigger in terms of redesigning and redefining excellent work because right now we think excellent work means you have to work all the time and be physically present in an office," says Brigid Schulte, a veteran journalist, author, and director of the Better Life Lab at New America, which focuses on gender roles and family policy, in and out the workplace. "Newsrooms need to start understanding that that's actually not the way to do the best work. It leads to burnout. It leads to inefficient work. It leads to fewer innovative, creative, and breakthrough ideas, and it punishes people who have caregiver responsibilities, who tend to be women and mothers, but also are increasingly men."

Going from being totally disconnected from work to being back in the office full time can be great for some, but others crave a different on-ramp and have specific, short-term flexibility needs immediately after maternity leave.

One woman I spoke with was put off by having to commit to her exact leave schedule before her baby was born. She saved two weeks for when her daughter was a bit older, and she felt like everyone just treated it as her going on vacation, with work requests coming in throughout that period. Others I spoke with didn't feel there was much leeway to adjust their initial plans once maternity leave began.

Some women I spoke with were able to negotiate a four-day-a-week schedule, additional work from home options, or leaving earlier in the afternoons at the beginning of their time back to ease the transition. One woman I spoke with wished she could have started smaller projects earlier, at the end of her leave, to give her a window back into work life.

Fusion's Wides-Muñoz, who at the time worked at the Associated Press, arranged to work from home on Wednesdays while her nanny cared for her child in order to give her a break from commuting and pumping. This one day a week of flexibility made a world of difference to her, and she thinks could for others as well. "It was the difference between a happy working person and a miserable one," she says.

A 2014 survey in the *American Sociological Review* found many benefits to a flexible work schedule.

Researchers found that employees who were given greater control over when and where they worked, as well as more support from their workplace regarding their family lives, experienced a reduction in work-family conflict.

While there's no one-size-fits-all solution, offering and allowing a range of company-sanctioned options, and the flexibility to adjust once the realities of working motherhood set in, can have a major long-term impact on job satisfaction and retention rates.

PRIORITIZE WORK-LIFE BALANCE FOR EVERYONE

The women I spoke with who felt most supported in their workplaces were the ones who also felt like it was OK to be honest with their bosses and coworkers about the realities of being a working parent. Allison Benedikt, who is the executive editor of Slate and has three young children, feels she can be up front about the challenges of balancing her different responsibilities. (Disclosure: I worked at Slate from 2011–2014, before I was a parent.) She credits David Plotz, who had three young children when he was editor in chief at Slate, with creating an understanding culture.

In 2014, upon assuming the role of editor in chief, Julia Turner, mother of young twins, continued the culture promoting transparency about work-life challenges and conflicts. Now Slate has a Slack channel called "whereabouts" where people regularly post if they are working from home because of a childcare issue or will be in late because of a kid's dentist appointment. It's probably no coincidence that Slate has a strong track record of employing working mothers, and 31 percent of Slate's editorial staff are parents.

A study conducted by Deloitte University found that 61 percent of all employees felt they needed to downplay their personal differences from their coworkers, which is termed "covering" and can apply to everything from being a parent to being gay to being a member of a racial minority to dealing with a health issue. Management experts Dorie Clark and Christie Smith wrote in *Harvard Business Review* that "enabling employees to feel comfortable being themselves could unlock dramatic performance gains because they can focus their attention on work, rather than hiding parts of themselves." One of their recommendations for setting the tone in an organization is for leaders to share more about their personal challenges and strategies for dealing with work and life. "Everyone on our team knew that my boss's new baby was a bad sleeper. We'd all pitch in to help him out, too," says Elizabeth Bruenig of *The Washington Post*.

When a leader shows this kind of transparency, it can have clear benefits for parents, but it also creates a culture of inclusion, where anyone can feel supported in dealing with a wide range of challenges—whether that's a childcare crisis, caring for ailing parents, going through a divorce, or just owning up to needing to leave the office for regular therapy appointments.

Yet, the American workplace in general isn't all that great about encouraging work-life balance. A recent study found that the average American only uses 54 percent of their paid vacation time. Another study, with a small sample size, found that the realities of the profession may lead some journalists to self-medicate with alcohol and caffeine and not get enough sleep, resulting in lower than average abilities regarding creative thinking, problem solving, regulating emotions, and staying focused. How managers think about supporting employees should extend beyond just being understanding to parents about daycare pick-ups and school holidays. "If you create these systems that allow you to have a life outside of work but you're saying it's only related to

parenting, then you have just frozen everybody else in place," says Schulte.

"It's not fair in general, but it's also really bad for parents when you give parents a lot of choices that you don't give other people, because then everyone hates them," says Romper.com's Johnson. She believes flexibility and understanding should be applied to all employees equally. "I have a lot of young people without kids [on my team] who are so smart and work so many hours a day and are at such risk of burnout that I'm constantly encouraging people to take vacation."

In an era of cost-cutting and layoffs, ongoing technological disruption, lack of public trust in our work, and a hostile political climate, newsroom environments still matter. It's precisely because of these uncertainties that news organizations need to be smart about how to keep talented, diverse groups of journalists, including mothers with young children, in our ranks, doing the vital work that needs to be done. Paid family leave, inclusive, flexible work policies that benefit everyone, and improved office cultures are not tangential priorities; they are crucial to fostering a pipeline of young, innovative thinkers—the future leaders of our industry.

As the millennial baby boom begins, news organizations committed to their own longevity and success must act now to create mastheads that attract new readers and better reflect the communities we serve. Helping journalists with young families better manage work and parenthood is the place to start.

52. THE KIDS ARE OK

KEN W. KNIGHT, SARAH E. M. STEPHENSON, SUE WEST, MARTIN B. DELATYCKI, CHERYL A. JONES, MELISSA H. LITTLE, GEORGE C. PATTON, SUSAN M. SAWYER, S. RACHEL SKINNER, MICHELLE M. TELFER, MELISSA WAKE, KATHRYN N. NORTH, AND FRANK OBERKLAID (2017)

The current public debate about same-sex marriage raises a number of significant issues for medical professionals and researchers. . . . Misinformation is circulating in the public domain that children and adolescents with same-sex parents are at risk of poorer health and wellbeing than other children. An

increased public health risk exists as a result of homophobic campaign messages for the entire lesbian, gay, bisexual, transgender, intersex and queer (LGBTIQ+) community, including a mental health risk for same-sex couples, their children, and young people who identify as LGBTIQ+.

Here we provide an update on the evidence and outline implications for the . . . medical and research community.

WHAT THE RESEARCH TELLS US

The consensus of the peer-reviewed research is that children raised in same-sex parented families do as well emotionally, socially and educationally as children raised by heterosexual couple parents. These findings have been replicated across independent studies . . . internationally, some of which we discuss below.

REVIEWS AND META-ANALYSIS

In 2017, the Public Policy Research Portal at Columbia Law School reviewed 79 studies that investigated the wellbeing of children raised by gay or lesbian parents. The review concluded that there is "an overwhelming scholarly consensus, based on over three decades of peer-reviewed research, that having a gay or lesbian parent does not harm children."[1]

In 2014, an American Sociological Association review of over 40 studies also concluded that children raised by same-sex couples fare as well as other children across a number of wellbeing measures, including academic performance, cognitive development, social development, and psychological health.[2]

The Australian Institute of Family Studies' 2013 review of the Australian and international research on same-sex parented families found that being raised by same-sex parents does not harm children, with children in such families doing as well emotionally, socially and educationally as their peers.[3] In 2016, the Institute published a fact sheet on the same topic that reaffirmed the conclusions of the 2013 review.[4]

A 2010 meta-analysis of 33 studies similarly found that the gender or sexuality of parents did not adversely affect child health or wellbeing, with children raised by gay or lesbian parents faring as well as children raised by heterosexual parents across a range of measures including attachment security, behaviour problems and success at school.[5]

FAMILY PROCESSES MATTER MORE THAN FAMILY STRUCTURES

The findings of these reviews reflect a broader consensus within the fields of family studies and psychology. It is family processes (eg, parenting quality, parental wellbeing, the quality of and satisfaction with relationships within the family), rather than family structures (eg, the number, gender, sexuality or cohabitation arrangements of parents), that make a more meaningful difference to children's wellbeing and positive development.[6–10]

STUDIES CONCLUDING THAT CHILDREN WITH SAME-SEX PARENTS DO BETTER THAN OTHER CHILDREN

Some research has indicated that children with same-sex parents do better than other children. In addition to equivalent social and educational outcomes, these studies conclude that children raised by same-sex couples show better psychological adjustment, and greater open-mindedness towards sexual, gender and family diversity.[3,11,12] However, the authors note that these positive differences may reflect the high quality parenting, socio-economic status and family stability within the same-sex parented families studied.[11,12]

STUDIES CONCLUDING THAT CHILDREN WITH SAME-SEX PARENTS DO POORLY

A study using data from the New Family Structures Study—sometimes referred to as the Regnerus study[13]—is often cited as evidence that children do poorly when raised by gay or lesbian parents. The study analysed survey data from adults aged 18–39 years and concluded that those with a gay or lesbian parent fared worse on a range of social, emotional and relational outcomes when compared with adults raised by heterosexual, married, biological parents.[13] However, this and other studies reporting poor outcomes have been widely criticised for their methodological limitations.[3,14,15] The Regnerus study compared adults raised by a gay or lesbian parent in any family configuration with adults who were raised in stable, heterosexual, two-parent family environments. When re-analysed, taking family stability and having two active parents into account, the data showed that outcomes were similar for adults regardless of their parents' sexuality.[15]

THE IMPACT OF STIGMA AND DISCRIMINATION

SAME-SEX PARENTED FAMILIES

Children and adolescents with same-sex parents are emotionally affected when they and their families are exposed to homophobia, discrimination, prejudice and social stigma,[3,16,17] and do better when they live in communities that hold more accepting attitudes.[18] A 2008 study comparing the well-being of same-sex parented children raised in the United States and the Netherlands found that American children were significantly more likely than Dutch children to experience homophobic bullying, and less likely to disclose their family structure.[19] The authors concluded that these differences were likely due to the greater social acceptance of same-sex relationships in the Netherlands, which legalised same-sex marriage in 2001.[19]

Same-sex couples are at a higher risk of poorer mental health and suicide than heterosexual couples,[20] and living in a society that limits their legal and social rights results in negative psychological outcomes for same-sex parented families.[21] A 2009 study that compared the wellbeing of lesbian mothers in the US and Canada found that discriminatory policies in the US—including a prohibition on same-sex marriage—resulted in more symptoms of depression and caused unnecessary strain on the children of lesbian mothers.[21] Lesbian mothers in Canada, who had been able to marry since 2005, reported fewer symptoms of depression and concerns about discrimination even when they were not married.[21] Simply having access to the same social and legal resources as their heterosexual counterparts acted as a protective factor.[21]

Exposure to devaluing and discriminatory public messaging regarding LGBTIQ+ issues results in stark negative psychological and relational consequences for same-sex couples and their families.[22,23] This is particularly concerning as the current same-sex marriage debate has exposed same-sex parented families as well as young people who identify as LGBTIQ+ to homophobic and stigmatising material.

YOUNG PEOPLE WHO IDENTIFY AS LGBTIQ+

Young people who express diversity in their sexual orientation or gender identity experience some of the highest rates of psychological distress in Australia.[24] This cohort of young people is significantly more likely to experience depression, anxiety, post-traumatic stress disorder, self-harm and suicide than other young people.[24-26] These negative outcomes are largely attributed to the harassment, stigma and discrimination that they and other LGBTIQ+ individuals and communities regularly endure.[27]

Recent research indicates that legalising same-sex marriage has a positive impact on the mental health and wellbeing of LGBTIQ+ young people. Analysis of data from the Youth Risk Behavior Surveillance System, a nationally representative survey of school students in the US, revealed a 7% relative reduction in suicide attempts among sexual minority students living in states where same-sex marriage laws had been enacted.[28]

METHODOLOGICAL CHALLENGES

It should be acknowledged that there are methodological challenges in answering questions about children's wellbeing in same-sex parented families. Samples of children with same-sex parents tend to be small, and many population-based studies do not ask for information on parents' sexuality. This means that much of the research on same-sex parented families has used convenience or volunteer samples that can be biased. Despite this, the consensus of the available, high quality research is that children raised in same-sex parented families do as well as other children.

. . .

WHAT THE MEDICAL COMMUNITY CAN DO

We will of course continue to offer support and care to our patients and research participants, and conduct rigorous research that furthers our understanding of these issues. But when damaging misrepresentations of the evidence circulate unchecked, the potential for stigmatising rhetoric to generate greater harm to this community increases. This compels us to do more.

We have a duty of care to all groups in our society, particularly to those who are vulnerable. Our duty extends to calling for public statements based on accurate, objective interpretations of the best available evidence, the correction of inaccurate information, and efforts to reduce the destructiveness of public debate. This is exactly the course of action that we have taken on health issues such as immunisation and children in detention.

The research tells us that children and adolescents with same-sex parents are doing well, despite the discrimination that their families endure. This will not continue for long in the face of hostile debate.

The entire LGBTIQ+ community is at risk of harm in the current debate concerning same-sex marriage, and the most vulnerable are children and adolescents.

We need to speak up. Opportunities exist to add our voices to the public debate, through public statements as individuals and from our professional associations and workplaces.

Inaction is not an option when harm is the likely result.

NOTES

1. Columbia Law School. What does the scholarly research say about the wellbeing of children with gay or lesbian parents? http://whatweknow.law.columbia.edu/topics/lgbt-equality/what-does-the-scholarly-research-say-about-the-wellbeing-of-children-with-gay-or-lesbian-parents (accessed Sept 2017).
2. Manning WD, Fettro MN, Lamidi E. Child wellbeing in same-sex parent families: review of research prepared for American Sociological Association Amicus Brief. *Popul Res Policy Rev* 2014: 33: 485–502.
3. Dempsey D. Same-sex parented families in Australia. Melbourne: Australian Institute of Family Studies, 2013. https://aifs.gov.au/cfca/publications/same-sex-parented-families-australia (accessed Sept 2017).
4. Qu L, Knight K, Higgins D. Same-sex couple families in Australia 2016. Melbourne: Australian Institute of Family Studies, 2016. https://aifs.gov.au/publications/same-sex-couple-families-australia (accessed Sept 2017).
5. Biblarz TJ, Stacey J. How does the gender of parents matter? *J Marriage Fam* 2010; 72: 3–22.
6. Carlson MJ, Corcoran ME. Family structure and children's behavioral and cognitive outcomes. *J Marriage Fam* 2001; 63: 779–792.
7. Golombok S. *Parenting: what really matters.* London: Routledge, 2000.
8. Short E, Riggs DW, Perlesz A, et al. *Lesbian, gay, bisexual and transgender (LGBT) parented families.* Melbourne: The Australian Psychological Society, 2007.
9. Tasker F. Lesbian mothers, gay fathers, and their children: a review. *J Dev Behav Pediatr* 2005; 26: 224–240.
10. Wise S. *Family structure, child outcomes and environmental mediators: an overview of the Development in Diverse Families Study.* Melbourne: Australian Institute of Family Studies, 2003. https://aifs.gov.au/publications/family-structure-child-outcomes-and-environmental-mediators (accessed Sept 2017).
11. Crowl A, Ahn S, Baker J. A meta-analysis of developmental outcomes for children of same-sex and heterosexual parents. *J GLBT Fam Stud* 2008; 4: 385–407.
12. Miller BG, Kors S, Macfie J. No differences? Meta-analytic comparisons of psychological adjustment in children of gay fathers and heterosexual parents. *Psychol Sex Orientat Gend Divers* 2017; 4: 14–22.
13. Regnerus M. How different are the adult children of parents who have same-sex relationships? Findings from the New Family Structures Study. *Soc Sci Res* 2012; 41: 752–770.
14. Amato PR. The well-being of children with gay and lesbian parents. *Soc Sci Res* 2012; 41: 771–774.

15. Cheng S, Powell B. Measurement, methods, and divergent patterns: reassessing the effects of same-sex parents. *Soc Sci Res* 2015; 52: 615–626.

16. Crouch SR, McNair R, Waters E. Impact of family structure and socio-demographic characteristics on child health and wellbeing in same-sex parent families: a cross-sectional survey. *J Paediatr Child Health* 2016; 52: 499–505.

17. Crouch SR, Waters E, McNair R, et al. Parent-reported measures of child health and wellbeing in same-sex parent families: a cross-sectional survey. *BMC Public Health* 2014; 14: 635.

18. Crouch SR, Waters E, McNair R, et al. ACHESS—The Australian study of child health in same-sex families: background research, design and methodology. *BMC Public Health* 2012; 12: 646.

19. Bos HM, Gartrell NK, van Balen F, et al. Children in planned lesbian families: a cross-cultural comparison between the United States and the Netherlands. *Am J Orthopsychiatry* 2008; 78: 211–219.

20. Sanders EK, Chalk HM. Predictors of psychological outcomes in nonheterosexual individuals. *Psi Chi J Psychol Res* 2016; 21: 100–110.

21. Shapiro DN, Peterson C, Stewart AJ. Legal and social contexts and mental health among lesbian and heterosexual mothers. *J Fam Psychol* 2009; 23: 255–262.

22. Frost DM, Fingerhut AW. Daily exposure to negative campaign messages decreases same-sex couples' psychological and relational well-being. *Group Process Intergroup Relat* 2016; 19: 477–492.

23. Hatzenbuehler ML, McLaughlin KA, Keyes KM, Hasin DS. The impact of institutional discrimination on psychiatric disorders in lesbian, gay, and bisexual populations: a prospective study. *Am J Public Health* 2010; 100: 452–459.

24. Morris S. Snapshot of mental health and suicide prevention statistics for LGBTI people and communities. Sydney: National LGBTI Health Alliance, 2016. http://lgbtihealth.org.au/resources/snapshot-mental-health-suicide-prevention-statistics-lgbti-people (accessed Sept 2017).

25. Daraganova G. *Self-harm and suicidal behaviour of young people aged 14-15 years old. The Longitudinal Study of Australian Children annual statistical report 2016.* Melbourne: Australian Institute of Family Studies, 2017. https://aifs.gov.au/publications/self-harm-and-suicidal-behaviour-young-people-aged-14-15-years-old (accessed Sept 2017).

26. Strauss P, Cook A, Winter S, et al. *Trans Pathways: the mental health experiences and care pathways of trans young people. Summary of results.* Perth: Telethon Kids Institute, 2017. https://www.telethonkids.org.au/our-research/brain-and-behaviour/mental-health-and-youth/youth-mental-health/trans-pathways (accessed Sept 2017).

27. Almeida J, Johnson RM, Corliss HL, et al. Emotional distress among LGBT youth: the influence of perceived discrimination based on sexual orientation. *J Youth Adolesc* 2009; 38: 1001–1014.

28. Raifman J, Moscoe E, Austin SB, McConnell M. Difference-in-differences analysis of the association between state same-sex marriage policies and adolescent suicide attempts. *JAMA Pediatr* 2017; 171: 350–356.

53. IMMIGRATION POLICIES ARE HARMING AMERICAN CHILDREN

LEILA SCHOCHET (2017)

Daniel, a 6-year-old U.S. citizen, has been asking his parents more and more questions about Mexico since the 2016 election. "Mama says that we might move to Mexico," Daniel said to his father. "Am I gonna go also?"

Daniel's parents are unauthorized immigrants who came to the United States as young children. For the past several years, Daniel has been living in Texas with his mother, Carmen, while his father, Miguel, has been working in California.[1] Both Miguel and

Carmen are part of the Deferred Action for Childhood Arrivals (DACA) program instituted by the Obama administration in 2012, which allowed them each to get a work permit and a temporary reprieve from deportation.[2] Since the election, President Donald Trump has indicated that the future of DACA is unclear, fueling heightened concern and fear among DACA recipients.[3] That uncertainty has reached new heights in recent weeks, as attorneys general from several states have threatened to sue the administration to end DACA if the program is not terminated by September 5, 2017.[4] While Miguel had initially planned to join his family in Texas this past January, after the election, he put his plan on hold as he faces greater uncertainty about whether he will remain protected under his DACA status.

Miguel's biggest concern is how living under an administration that is openly targeting the unauthorized immigrant community could affect his son.

"We've taken steps to talk to him, let him know that Mom and Dad are a little bit worried or stressed out," Miguel said. "And we don't go too much into detail, being that he just turned 6, so we don't want to scare him too much."

President Trump's anti-immigrant agenda has forced millions of immigrants such as Miguel and Carmen to face the threat and consequences of deportation. During Trump's first 100 days in office, immigration arrests rose by more than 37 percent.[5] Despite his campaign promise to deport only those with criminal records, his administration has made all unauthorized immigrants a priority for deportation, with arrest rates more than doubling for hardworking immigrants without criminal records.[6] On top of an increased threat of deportation, immigrants and their children are also becoming targets of heightened racism and discrimination. Teachers have reported cases of children adopting Trump's rhetoric to bully their peers in school, telling Latino children that they will be deported and saying they should go back to where they came from.[7]

For the nearly 6 million U.S.-citizen children living with at least one unauthorized family member, life in Trump's America is frightening.[8] Since the election, adults across the country have reported spikes in fear and distress among young children from immigrant families.[9] Now more than ever, citizen children are worried that they could be separated from their parents or forced to leave their communities.[10]

Trump's harsh immigration policies create toxic stress for young children by breaking families apart, instilling fear in the immigrant community, and preventing families from accessing programs that meet children's most basic needs. Policies that cause children emotional distress and economic insecurity in early childhood interfere with their healthy development and derail their future success. Children such as Daniel will be the backbone of the nation's workforce in the coming years and could make critical contributions to the economy. But if the Trump administration continues to target immigrant families, it risks undermining the economic power of an entire generation.[11]

FEAR OF DEPORTATION CAN BE TOXIC

With the uptick in immigration arrests, immigrant parents must consider deportation as a serious possibility. Across the country, parents have been creating contingency plans that establish what will happen to their children if they are deported, granting power of attorney to a relative or trusted friend and telling children what may happen in the parent's absence.[12] Even DACA recipients such as Miguel—who are work-authorized—are fearful enough to create these contingency plans.

Miguel and Carmen decided that in the case of their deportation, Daniel would stay in the United States with his grandparents, who are now U.S. citizens, to maintain stability in his life.

"It's hard enough that [his] mom and dad would not be around to the degree that [Daniel's] used to, and so it just made more sense," Miguel said. "Daniel was born here, he's a U.S. citizen, he goes to school here, [so] let's keep him in a stable environment."

Not all children are fortunate enough to have a family member with whom they could stay in the case of parental deportation. Some parents must bring their citizen children back to their home country, which can force children to make a challenging transition to an unfamiliar culture and system. U.S.-citizen children have difficulties adapting to a new education system and often do not have adequate foreign language skills to reach their full potential in school; these children may also return to the United States at some point with limited English skills and interrupted schooling, leaving them perpetually behind.[13]

Being separated from a parent or caregiver—or even the idea of a separation—exposes young children to stress and trauma. In extreme cases, children may be present during immigration raids, where armed U.S. Immigration and Customs Enforcement agents may burst into a home and forcibly remove parents.[14] Children who have been separated from their parents frequently show signs of trauma, including anxiety, depression, frequent crying, disrupted eating and sleeping, and difficulties in school.[15] Many young children also have a misunderstanding of legal status in general, often equating being an immigrant with being unauthorized. These children may believe that they or their authorized relatives are also in danger of being deported, further escalating their fear.[16]

Regardless of whether they are separated from a parent or just facing the threat of parental deportation, young children are particularly vulnerable to the negative effects of heightened stress because they are in a critical developmental period.[17] Children in the broader Latino community can experience distress even if everyone in their family is authorized. In fact, there is evidence that immigrants—whether they are citizens, legal residents, or unauthorized— experience fear of deportation and feelings of vulnerability at similar rates.[18] Young children in the immigrant community can experience psychological distress after just seeing or hearing about their peers being separated from their families and friends.[19]

As children are exposed to increased stress within their households, schools, and communities, their own emotional well-being can be compromised. Enduring persistent levels of high stress can change a child's brain architecture and negatively influence their physical, cognitive, and emotional development.[20] As they grow up, many children who experience this toxic stress in early childhood are less equipped to cope with everyday instances of adversity, such as conflict with a friend or difficulties in the classroom.[21] This means that these children are more likely to have challenges with behavior, learning, emotional regulation, and physical health in the future.[22]

PARENTS' STRESS AFFECTS CHILDREN TOO

Like many parents, Miguel says that Daniel can sense when there is a shift in Miguel's mood and emotions.

"I've been pretty stressed since the election," Miguel said, "and [Daniel] does pick up on it. I'll read him a story and he'll interrupt and say, 'Hey Papa you look really sad or worried, what's wrong?' And I'll have to tell him, 'Oh well it was a long day at work,' but typically it's because I read something about some action that the [Trump] administration is taking."

As the threat of deportation for immigrant parents intensifies, they must cope with their own fear and stress while supporting their children. In addition to financial and emotional burdens, constant worry about being arrested or deported weighs on parents.

Just as Daniel quickly picked up on Miguel's stress, children are incredibly attentive to how their parents and caregivers feel. Young children look to their parents for emotional cues to help them learn how they should interpret a given situation, so when children notice that their parent is upset or scared, they may receive the message that they should feel the same way.[23] Research shows that an immigrant parent's legal vulnerability and fear trickle down to affect their children. As a parent's risk of deportation heightens, a child's emotional well-being and academic outcomes tend to worsen.[24]

The consequences of parental stress for young children can start even before birth. One well-documented instance of spillover from mother to child, and to the greater Latino community, was observed following one of the largest immigration raids in U.S. history. The 2008 immigration raid of a factory in Postville, Iowa, led to the detainment of 389 mostly Latino workers: Word of the raid spread quickly and triggered fear among Latino communities across the state.[25] In the nine months following the raid, babies born to Latina mothers in the state of Iowa—U.S. citizens and unauthorized immigrants alike—were 25 percent more likely to have low birth weight compared with the previous year, a result of maternal and fetal stress.[26] There was no change in birth outcomes for non-Latina white mothers.

Young children and adults alike are largely a product of their environment, and instilling a sense of fear and uncertainty into an entire community affects both citizens and immigrants.

DISTRUST OF PUBLIC SYSTEMS CAN AFFECT CHILDREN'S HEALTH, WELL-BEING, AND ACCESS TO EARLY EDUCATION

Early childhood is a critical stage in development when children need access to basic living standards— such as quality health care, nutritious food, and education—in order to thrive. Without these critical services, children can endure lifelong consequences. Specific programs target young children to help meet their needs, including Medicaid; the Special Supplemental Nutrition Program for Women, Infants, and Children (WIC); and Head Start. As a country, investing in these programs makes sense to help mitigate hardship in the short term and because they have been shown to pay off in the long run.

Children in unauthorized communities are historically underenrolled in important public programs to begin with, due to language barriers, lack of information, and their parents' or guardians' fear of interacting with public systems.[27] On top of these barriers, increased local immigration enforcement and a leaked draft executive order suggesting that immigrants could be deported for using public assistance has made immigrant parents even more afraid of getting their children the services they need.[28] While the services provided by these programs can help mitigate the detrimental effects of toxic stress on young children, not having healthy food or proper medical care can exacerbate the impact. Now more than ever, access to important programs is critical for keeping children's healthy development on track.

HARSH IMMIGRATION POLICIES UNDERMINE THE FUTURE U.S. WORKFORCE

President Trump's policies and rhetoric contribute to a toxic environment of fear that may alter the developmental outcomes of millions of children. While this generation has the potential to grow up and help the economy thrive, Trump's immigration policies could leave that economic power untapped.

Children of immigrants drive the economy, and promoting their success is one of the most important investments we can make as a nation. Research shows that children of immigrants grow up to be among the strongest contributors to the United States' economy, paying more in taxes than children with native-born parents.[29] In 2012, children of immigrants contributed 12 percent more per person, on average, in federal taxes than the rest of the native-born population— and contributed $30.5 billion at the state and local levels.[30] They are also slightly more likely to graduate from college and less likely to live in poverty than their native-born peers.[31]

Trump's anti-immigrant agenda compromises the economic security of immigrant families with children, which can negatively affect child outcomes. Separating families and deporting the primary breadwinner from a household can throw immigrant families into deep emotional and economic turmoil: Removing unauthorized residents from mixed-status households—those with both authorized and unauthorized members—could reduce the median annual household income by almost 75 percent, from $33,000 to $9,000.[32] For many children, this could mean going without nutritious food, consistent housing, or medical services that are critical for their healthy development.

While Trump argues that deporting unauthorized immigrants benefits the economy, research says otherwise. In states that ramped up their immigration enforcement efforts, low-income immigrant households with children experienced increased material hardship—such as difficulties paying for basic expenses, utilities, and medical care—while U.S.-citizen households saw no economic loss or gain.[33]

When taken to scale, this could imply that Trump's mass deportation agenda will drive citizen children of immigrants into poverty—and increase stress and psychological trauma—without accomplishing his goal of improving conditions for nonimmigrant citizens.

Together, the consequences of toxic stress and economic insecurity on young children could severely affect the nation's future workforce. Children who face adversity during early childhood—such as trauma, separation from a parent, or deep poverty—are more likely to have poor health, drop out of high school, be unemployed, and live in poverty in adulthood.[34] These outcomes can lower job prospects and inhibit people's ability to reach their full potential in the workforce, representing a lost opportunity for the economy.

CONCLUSION

The fear and anxiety that children are feeling because of President Trump's immigration policies will not fade when a new administration takes over; the experiences that this generation of children has now will continue to affect them for the rest of their lives. It is critical for the administration to consider carefully the true expense of a mass deportation agenda. In the meantime, it is everyone's duty to foster an environment of support for all children, regardless of their family's immigration status. Children such as Daniel—and our economy—depend on it.

NOTES

1. Miguel, phone interview with author, Washington, D.C., June 27, 2017. The author has changed the names of the family members profiled in this issue brief to protect their identities.

2. Philip E. Wolgin, "The Top 4 Things You Need to Know About DACA for Its 4th Anniversary," Center for American Progress, June 9, 2016, available at https://www.americanprogress.org/issues/immigration/news/2016/06/09/139044/the-top-4-things-you-need-to-know-about-daca-for-its-4th-anniversary/.

3. Michael D. Shear and Vivian Yee, "'Dreamers' to Stay in U.S. for Now, but Long-Term Fate Is Unclear," *The New York Times*, June 16, 2017, available

at https://www.nytimes.com/2017/06/16/us/politics/trump-will-allow-dreamers-to-stay-in-us-reversing-campaign-promise.html?_r=0.

4. Dara Lind, "The future of DACA suddenly looks very shaky," *Vox*, July 14, 2017, available at https://www.vox.com/policy-and-politics/2017/7/14/15966356/daca-dreamers-trump-amnesty.

5. Maria Sacchetti, "Immigration arrests soar under Trump; sharpest spike seen for noncriminals," *The Washington Post*, May 17, 2017, available at https://www.washingtonpost.com/local/immigration-arrests-up-during-trump/2017/05/17/74399a04-3b12-11e7-9e48-c4f199710b69_story.html?utm_term=.56ce15681cda.

6. Ibid.; U.S. Department of Homeland Security, "ICE ERO immigration arrests climb nearly 40%," available at https://www.ice.gov/features/100-days (last accessed July 2017).

7. Albert Samaha, Mike Hayes, and Talal Ansari, "The Kids Are Alt-Right," *BuzzFeed News*, June 6, 2017, available at https://www.buzzfeed.com/albertsamaha/kids-are-quoting-trump-to-bully-their-classmates?utm_term=.os7lym3ng#.xydpOmdJw.

8. Silva Mathema, "Keeping Families Together" (Washington: Center for American Progress, 2017), available at https://www.americanprogress.org/issues/immigration/reports/2017/03/16/428335/keeping-families-together/.

9. Anna Kamenetz, "'I Have Children Crying in the Classroom'," nprEd, March 9, 2017, available at http://www.npr.org/sections/ed/2017/03/09/518996780/i-have-children-crying-in-the-classroom; Roque Planas and Jessica Carro, "This Is What Trump's Immigration Crackdown Is Doing to School Kids," *The Huffington Post*, March 1, 2017, available at http://www.huffingtonpost.com/entry/elementary-school-kids-terrified-by-immigration-arrests_us_58a76321e4b07602ad548e14; Andrew Gumbel, "Doctors see a new condition among immigrant children: fear of Trump," *The Guardian*, November 25, 2016, available at https://www.theguardian.com/us-news/2016/nov/25/donald-trump-immigration-deportation-children-doctors.

10. Maureen B. Costello, "The Trump Effect" (Montgomery, AL: Southern Poverty Law Center, 2016),

available at https://www.splcenter.org/sites/default/files/splc_the_trump_effect.pdf.

11. National Academies of Sciences, Engineering, and Medicine, *The Economic and Fiscal Consequences of Immigration* (2016), available at https://www.nap.edu/catalog/23550/the-economic-and-fiscal-consequences-of-immigration.

12. Sarah Elizabeth Richards, "How Fear of Deportation Puts Stress on Families," *The Atlantic*, March 22, 2017, available at https://www.theatlantic.com/health/archive/2017/03/deportation-stress/520008/.

13. Randy Capps and others, "Implications of Immigration Enforcement Activities for the Well-Being of Children in Immigrant Families: A Review of the Literature" (Washington: Migration Policy Institute, 2015), available at http://www.migrationpolicy.org/research/implications-immigration-enforcement-activities-well-being-children-immigrant-families.

14. Albert Sabat, "An ICE Home Raid Explainer," ABC News, April 10, 2013, available at http://abcnews.go.com/ABC_Univision/News/ice-home-raid/story?id=18896252.

15. American Psychological Association Presidential Task Force on Immigration, "Crossroads: The psychology of immigration in the new century" (2012), available at http://www.apa.org/topics/immigration/immigration-report.pdf.

16. Joanna Dreby, "The Burden of Deportation on Children in Mexican Immigrant Families," *Journal of Marriage and Family* 74 (4) (2012): 829–845.

17. Wendy Cervantes and Christina Walker, "Five Reasons Trump's Immigration Orders Harm Children" (Washington: Center for Law and Social Policy, 2017), available at http://www.clasp.org/resources-and-publications/publication-1/Five-Reasons-Immigration-Enforcement-Orders-Harm-Children.pdf.

18. Capps and others, "Implications of Immigration Enforcement Activities for the Well-Being of Children in Immigrant Families"; Seline Szkupsinski Quiroga, Dulce M. Medina, and Jennifer Glick, "In the Belly of the Beast: Effects of Anti-Immigration Policy on Latino Community Members," *American Behavioral Scientist* 58 (13) (2014): 1723–1742.

19. Capps and others, "Implications of Immigration Enforcement Activities for the Well-Being of Children in Immigrant Families."

20. Barbara Milrod, "Why Children Bear the Brunt of Trump's America: The Stress Test," *Newsweek*, May 19, 2017, available at http://www.newsweek.com/why-child-anxiety-rise-trumps-america-612205; National Scientific Council on the Developing Child, "Persistent Fear and Anxiety Can Affect Young Children's Learning and Development," Working Paper 9 (Harvard University Center on the Developing Child, 2010), available at http://developingchild.harvard.edu/wp-content/uploads/2010/05/Persistent-Fear-and-Anxiety-Can-Affect-Young-Childrens-Learning-and-Development.pdf.

21. National Scientific Council on the Developing Child, "Persistent Fear and Anxiety Can Affect Young Children's Learning and Development."

22. Ibid.

23. Tedra A. Walden and Tamra A. Ogan, "The development of social referencing," *Journal of Child Development* 59 (5) (1988): 1230–1240.

24. Kalina Brabeck and Qingwen Xu, "The Impact of Detention and Deportation on Latino Immigrant Children and Families: A Quantitative Exploration," *Hispanic Journal of Behavioral Sciences* 32 (3) (2010): 341–361.

25. Arline T. Geronimus, "How Immigration Raids Affect Birth Outcomes," CRImmigration, March 14, 2017, available at http://crimmigration.com/2017/03/14/how-immigration-raids-affect-birth-outcomes/.

26. Nicole L Novak, Arline T Geronimus, and Aresha M Martinez-Cardoso, "Change in birth outcomes among infants born to Latina mothers after a major immigration raid," *International Journal of Epidemiology* (2017).

27. Edward Vargas, "Immigration enforcement and mixed-status families: the effects of risk of deportation on Medicaid use," *Children and Youth Services Review* 57 (2015): 83–89; Hirokazu Yoshikawa and Ariel Kalil, "The Effects of Parental Undocumented Status on the Developmental Contexts of Young Children in Immigrant Families," *Child Development Perspectives* 5 (4) (2011): 291–297; Cecilia Menjívar and Andrea Gómez Cervantes, "The effects

of parental undocumented status on families and children" (Washington: American Psychological Association, 2016), available at http://www.apa.org/pi/families/resources/newsletter/2016/11/undocumented-status.aspx; Katrina Fortuny and Juan Pedroza, "Barriers to Immigrants' Access to Health and Human Services" (Washington: Urban Institute, 2014), available at http://www.urban.org/research/publication/barriers-immigrants-access-health-and-human-services.

28. Greg Kaufman, "Why Immigrants in California Are Canceling Their Food Stamps," TalkPoverty, March 17, 2017, available at https://talkpoverty.org/2017/03/17/why-immigrants-california-canceling-food-stamps/; Annie Lowrey, "Trump's Anti-Immigrant Policies Are Scaring Eligible Families Away From the Safety Net," *The Atlantic*, March 24, 2017, available at https://www.theatlantic.com/business/archive/2017/03/trump-safety-net-latino-families/520779/?utm_source=twb.

29. National Academies of Sciences, Engineering, and Medicine, *The Economic and Fiscal Consequences of Immigration*.

30. Ibid.

31. Pew Research Center, "Second Generation Americans: A Portrait of the Adult Children of Immigrants" (2013), available at http://www.pewsocialtrends.org/files/2013/02/FINAL_immigrant_generations_report_2-7-13.pdf.

32. Randy Capps and others, "Deferred Action for Unauthorized Immigrant Parents: Analysis of DAPA's Potential Effects on Families and Children" (Washington: Migration Policy Institute, 2016), available at http://www.migrationpolicy.org/research/deferred-action-unauthorized-immigrant-parents-analysis-dapas-potential-effects-families.

33. Julia Gelatt and others, "State Immigration Enforcement Policies: How They Impact Low-Income Households" (Washington: Urban Institute, 2017), available at http://www.urban.org/research/publication/state-immigration-enforcement-policies#1.

34. Marilyn Metzler and others, "Adverse childhood experiences and life opportunities: Shifting the narrative" *Children and Youth Services Review* 72 (2017): 141–149, available at http://www.sciencedirect.com/science/article/pii/S0190740916303449.

54. THE RECIPROCAL RELATIONSHIP BETWEEN RELIGIOUS BELIEFS AND ACCEPTANCE OF ONE'S GAY OR LESBIAN FAMILY MEMBER

KATHERINE ZEININGER, MELLISA HOLTZMAN, AND RACHEL KRAUS (2017)

When discussing his coming out experience with news anchor Anderson Cooper, actor Ian McKellan said that disclosing created more benefits for his personal and professional life than challenges (*The Huffington Post* 2012). "I've never met a gay person who regrets coming out," McKellan told Cooper. "You're more at ease with your loved ones. . . . [H]onesty is the best policy" (*The Huffington Post* 2012). Coming out can be a personally liberating experience for gay and lesbian individuals in that it enables them to be honest about their sexual identity with those around them (Cant 2005), but it can also be incredibly stressful because they do not know if their disclosure will result in acceptance or rejection by the people closest to them. In fact, family members, particularly parents, are often the most difficult people to disclose to (Ben-Ari 1995), in part because their reactions frequently include disappointment, anger, shock, or guilt (Robinson, Walters, and Skeen 1989). While these reactions are influenced by a number of factors, studies show that religion plays a particularly important role in reactions to the coming out process (Lease and Shulman 2003).

For instance, families with highly traditional values react more negatively to disclosures of same-sex sexual attraction (Baiocco et al., 2015; Newman and Muzzonigro, 1993), and rates of disclosure are lower among gay men whose parents are highly religious (Schope, 2002). Likewise, Whitehead (2010) noted that individuals who belong to conservative denominations, attend church frequently, are biblical literalists, or embrace images of an angry God are highly likely to condemn same-sex behavior. These kinds of negative and ostracizing reactions are well documented within a number of religious traditions (McQueeney 2009).

Thus, there appears to be a link between religiosity and negative reactions to disclosures of same-sex sexuality, but this effect is not uniform. For instance, research conducted by Parents, Families, and Friends of Lesbians and Gays (PFLAG), a family-based organization that is committed to the civil rights of gay and lesbian individuals, notes that upon discovering that a family member identifies as gay or lesbian, individuals sometimes begin to question their faith and reevaluate their religious beliefs (PFLAG 1997). Rather than reject their family member, some people ultimately end up altering, if not entirely abandoning, their own religious beliefs. This is important because research consistently finds that acceptance by one's family member can significantly impact the mental health and well-being of gay and lesbian individuals (Ryan et al., 2009; Savin-Williams 1989). Understanding the processes that promote family acceptance, then, can have important and wide-reaching implications for lesbian and gay individuals.

Although research has begun to examine the relationship between family acceptance and religious beliefs (Lease and Shulman 2003), additional work is still needed. For instance, we know little about how the process of accepting one's gay or lesbian family member is both influenced by and influences one's religious beliefs. The stability of one's religious beliefs and the acceptance of one's family member are likely complex processes that interact with one another in distinct ways. Focusing on that interaction will contribute to scholarly understandings of the link between religion and acceptance of a gay or lesbian family member. To that end, we use interview data from family members of lesbian and gay individuals to examine the reciprocal effects of religion and acceptance of a sexual minority family member.

LITERATURE REVIEW

THE COMING OUT PROCESS

The term *coming out* refers to the process of accepting oneself as lesbian, gay, or bisexual and integrating this sexual orientation into different spheres of one's life (Cass 1996; D'Augelli and Patterson 1995; Savin-Williams 1990). The process usually begins in adolescence or young adulthood and consists of becoming aware of same-sex romantic feelings; initial same-sex sexual encounters; involvement in the lesbian, gay, and bisexual community; self-labeling as lesbian, gay, or bisexual; and disclosing this identity to others (Reynolds and Hanjorgiris 2000). Ultimately, the decision to disclose this information to friends, family members, and coworkers is motivated by the desire to validate one's own lifestyle and to establish authentic interpersonal relationships, while always balancing the potential costs of such disclosures (Bregman et al. 2013; Pelton-Sweet and Sherry 2008).

While personal experiences with coming out vary, studies in the United States have shown that the coming out process generally begins with one's awareness of same-sex attractions at about 9 to 11 years of age, followed by first same-sex sexual contact around 13 to 15 years, first self-labeling as gay, lesbian, or bisexual between 14 and 16 years, and the first disclosure of same-sex sexual orientation between 16 and 18 years (D'Augelli 2002; D'Augelli and Hershberger 1993; Herdt and Boxer 1993; Rosario et al. 1996; Savin-Williams and Diamond 2000). These transitions are not navigated without difficulty, however. Research suggests that levels of self-esteem, happiness, and life satisfaction initially decrease during these transitions, while levels of loneliness increase (Cole et al. 1996; Halpin and Allen 2004; Vincke and Bolton 1994). Self-esteem, happiness, and life satisfaction do eventually rebound for most individuals (Pelton-Sweet and Sherry 2008), but those effects are often contingent, to some degree, on the reactions of their family members to their coming out disclosures (Baiocco et al. 2015; Bregman et al. 2013).

FAMILIAL REACTIONS TO COMING OUT

One of the most difficult challenges that gay and lesbian individuals face during the coming out process is disclosing their sexual orientation to their family (Savin-Williams and Ream 2003). In fact, parents who have experienced a son or daughter coming out indicate that it resembles the grieving process after the death of a loved one, inducing shock, denial, anger, guilt, and sadness (Baptist and Allen 2008; D'Augelli 2006; Robinson et al. 1989; Savin-Williams 2001).

Familial reactions to the coming out of a family member are extremely important, as their acceptance or rejection can have adverse effects on gay and lesbian individuals (Bregman et al. 2013). For instance, family rejection has been associated with an increased likelihood of individuals experiencing depression, suicidal ideation, illicit substance abuse, and unprotected sex with casual partners (Ryan et al. 2009). Negative parental attitudes toward same-sex sexual orientation and a lack of family support for one's sexual identity have also been linked to more internalized oppression, such as having negative attitudes and feelings about one's sexual orientation, and less well-being among sexual minority individuals (Beals and Peplau 2005; Pedretti 2004; Sheets and Mohr 2009).

Familial reactions are not always negative, however. In some instances, families come to acknowledge and accept their gay or lesbian family member (Hilton and Szymanski 2011). Acceptance can be achieved through support groups, such as PFLAG; exposure to other gay or lesbian individuals; and learning more about same-sex sexual attraction through books, magazines, and other media outlets. Such efforts help family members overcome their anxieties and fears and develop healthy coping strategies (Heatherington and Lavner 2008; Phillips and Ancis 2008; Saltzburg 2004; Savin-Williams 2001). In turn, this acceptance can increase gay and lesbian individuals' personal comfort with their sexual orientation, increase their self-esteem, and lessen self-critical behaviors (Bregman et al. 2013; Savin-Williams 1989).

INFLUENCES BEHIND FAMILIAL REACTIONS

A number of factors are associated with familial reactions to the coming out process. Preexisting positive attitudes toward same-sex sexuality have been shown to predict positive reactions to disclosure (Heatherington and Lavner 2008), and family members who have had some positive exposure to gay culture are more likely to react positively to disclosure (Ben-Ari 1995). In addition, research suggests that parents who suspect that their child might be gay or lesbian are able to work through their feelings of guilt, fear for the child's welfare, and anticipated losses (e.g., grandchildren) early, thus enabling a more positive reaction when their child does come out (Goldfried and Goldfried 2001). Other factors, including the child's status in the home, age of disclosure, place of residence, involvement in a romantic relationship, and pride in same-sex attractions, have also been shown to influence parental reactions (Heatherington and Lavner 2008).

Important to note, regardless of whether familial reactions are positive or negative overall, parents of gay or lesbian children often report feeling concern for how their child will be treated by other people. In her study of PFLAG members across the United States, Conley (2011) showed that parents have three primary concerns when they learn about their child's gay or lesbian sexual orientation. Parents (although there are some notable differences between mothers and fathers) primarily focus on how their child's physical and emotional health will be impacted; whether their child will be accepted by other loved ones; and what society will think about them, as parents, and their child, as a gay or lesbian individual. In fact, stigma consciousness is the largest predictor of parental concern. Although Conley does not specifically account for the role of religion in these concerns about stigma, other research suggests that religion is one of the primary influences behind negative familial reactions to a gay or lesbian family member. For instance, gay men from families with highly traditional values perceived their family's feelings toward same-sex sexuality to be more negative than did those from less traditional families (Newman and Muzzonigro 1993). In addition, studies show that rates of disclosure are lower among gay men if their parents are very religious rather than nonreligious (Schope 2002). Religion often influences parents' preexisting attitudes toward same-sex sexuality, which in turn can influence how they respond to their child coming out. In a study asking parents to imagine that their son was gay, those who believed that same-sex sexuality was something that their child could control reported more negative reactions, less affection, and less willingness to help their hypothetical gay son (Armesto and Weisman 2001). The apparent link between parental religious beliefs and negative reactions to disclosure is, perhaps, not surprising given the highly negative attitudes toward same-sex sexuality reported by a number of religious denominations. Many of the world's most prominent religions condemn same-sex sexuality because people believe that it is a matter of choice; it violates and threatens important values; and it does not adhere to traditional, conservative ideals (Whitley 2009). Similar studies have also revealed that religions often condemn same-sex sexuality because it is seen as a sin and an abomination (Lease and Shulman 2003; McQueeney 2009; Sherkat 2002), or they categorize behaviors associated with it as unnatural, ungodly, and impure (Yip 2005).

Despite this rather extensive research on religion, same-sex sexuality, and negative parental reactions to disclosure, few studies have examined the relationship between family *acceptance* and religious beliefs. Lease and Shulman's (2003) study is one notable exception. They showed that many individuals eventually accept their gay or lesbian family members and, in turn, either seek out a religion that is accepting of same-sex sexuality or choose to discount their current religion's negative views on the subject. Two thirds of their research participants reported that, at the time of their family member's disclosure, their religion was unaccepting of same-sex sexuality, but fewer than half said their *current* religion promoted similarly negative attitudes. Of those who remained in their congregations despite their churches' unaccepting views on same-sex sexuality, most reported that they, as individuals, were nonetheless accepting of their family member's sexual orientation.

Although Lease and Shulman (2003) did not ground their findings in Hirschman's (1970) classic book *Exit, Voice, and Loyalty*, it can be used to provide context to their findings and thereby offer insight into how families, especially those rooted in traditionally conservative faiths, navigate their religion if they become disillusioned with their faith's teachings on same-sex sexuality (see also Dowding 2015). Specifically, Hirschman argued that when people are unsatisfied with something (a relationship, an organization, a product manufacturer, a company, etc.), they have three primary ways of responding. They can exit the situation, voice their concerns, or remain loyal to the relationship despite their dissatisfaction. An exit response involves leaving and/or finding a more attractive option or situation. A voice response involves making the source of their grievances aware of their discontent and asking for a resolution that will alleviate the dissatisfaction. A loyalty response involves continuing the relationship despite the discontent that has arisen. This typology, although not specifically designed to account for religious reactions to sexual orientation disclosures, may, by extension, offer important insights on that process.

We, therefore, argue that although Lease and Shulman's study expands scholarly understandings of the reciprocal relationship between religious beliefs and the acceptance of a sexual minority family member, further research is needed for two reasons. First, their study was based on survey responses to only two open-ended questions about the role of religion in promoting or hindering acceptance of a sexual minority family member and how individuals addressed conflict that arose because of nonaccommodating religions. Given the limited nature of their data, we do not yet understand the complex process that individuals likely engage in as they negotiate potentially negative religious ideologies and their own emotional reactions to their family members' disclosures. Second, and related, their study does not offer a strong theoretical explanation for the various ways that disclosure and religion impact one another. Thus, by relying on in-depth interviews and Hirschman's (1970) insights, this research provides a deeper analysis of the religious journeys family members go through in order to accept their loved ones. In so doing, it is able to extend, at least preliminarily, our understandings of how religion influences and is influenced by the disclosure of one's sexual orientation.

METHODS

SAMPLING PROCEDURES

For this study, we sought out individuals who had a background in a religious faith, who had a gay or lesbian family member, and who had already accepted their family member's sexual minority status. To maximize the number of participants, we recruited potential subjects through two primary methods. First, we used snowball sampling because we were examining a specific population that would otherwise be difficult to locate (Given 2008). We reached out to the first author's personal contacts with individuals involved in the gay and lesbian community, and we asked those people if they knew of others who might be interested in participating in our study. Along with snowball sampling, we also contacted members of the advocacy group PFLAG because, we reasoned, PFLAG members would likely have accepting attitudes toward their family member's sexual orientation. Given our focus on the relationship between family acceptance and religious beliefs, these focused sampling strategies were warranted. Our efforts resulted in 14 participants. This is a small sample, and thus we must treat our findings as preliminary, but given that we were targeting a very specific population of individuals and we were aiming for depth rather than breadth, we argue that these interviews provide a good starting point for further exploration of these issues.

PARTICIPANTS

Our research is based on interviews with 14 participants—12 parents of lesbian and gay individuals, 1 sibling, and 1 nephew. Among the participants, 10 were female and 4 were male; all were Caucasian except for one African American respondent; and they ranged in age from 27 to 80, with an average age of 59. Most participants had some college experience: One had an associate's degree, four had bachelor's degrees, and five had advanced graduate or professional degrees. The remaining four participants had high school diplomas (although two of those individuals had completed some college courses). Respondents represented two geographical areas of the United States—the Midwest and the South.

With respect to religious affiliations, at the time of the interviews four participants identified with a mainline Protestant denomination. According to Steensland et al. (2000:293–294),[1] mainline Protestant denominations have "typically emphasized an accommodating stance toward modernity, a proactive view on issues of social and economic justice, and pluralism in their tolerance of varied individual beliefs." Our participants in this classification identified as Episcopal, Presbyterian, Christian, or Quaker.

Three participants identified with an evangelical Protestant denomination. These denominations have been described as seeking "more separation from the broader culture, emphasiz[ing] missionary activity and individual conversion, and [teaching] strict adherence to particular religious doctrines" (Steensland et al. 2000:293–294). Our participants in this classification identified as Seventh Day Baptist or as Baptist.

In addition, one participant identified with Catholicism, one with Judaism, two with the liberal nontraditional denomination of Unitarian Universalism (UU), and three individuals no longer identified with an organized religion at all (two were agnostic and one was atheist). Notably, several participants had changed their religious affiliations following their gay or lesbian family member's disclosure.

Regarding the importance of their religion, six participants described their faith as being very important, four as important, one as somewhat important, and three as unimportant. When discussing their current religious attendance, seven participants reported attending worship services regularly (once a week or more), one occasionally (only on major holidays), and six not at all. With respect to current religious involvement, seven participants reported being involved (i.e., serving on committees or singing in the choir), while the remaining seven reported not being involved. Although we do not claim that our sample is representative or generalizable, we are satisfied with the religious diversity among our participants, and we believe that this diversity allows us to tap into a variety of religious experiences with coming out disclosures.

. . .

RESULTS

Emerging from these narratives is a pattern that suggests the process of accepting one's gay or lesbian family member involves a complex interaction between a general desire to accept them, the degree to which one's religion promotes or opposes the acceptance of same-sex relationships, and the level of investment an individual has in his or her church.

A TENDENCY TOWARD ACCEPTANCE

Our research set out to explore how the process of accepting one's gay or lesbian family member is both influenced by and influences one's own religious beliefs. Thus, although we started with an interest in acceptance, we did not anticipate that the general tendency of respondents would be the *immediate* acceptance of their family member. But, in fact, 10 of the 14 respondents reported accepting their family member's sexual orientation without hesitation. As one mother who belonged to a Quaker church noted, "It was not upsetting to me. . . . There was no question that I was still accepting of her." A Christian father reported merely asking his daughter if she was happy and when she said yes, he said, "'All right. Fine.' and went back to watching TV." And a mother who described herself as a "progressive Catholic" said she "talked to [her son] for a little while, just told him we love him no matter what, and [told him] it didn't surprise [her]."

In fact, a number of respondents reported that they were not surprised by the disclosure because they had already suspected their family member was gay or lesbian. According to a mother who belonged to the Episcopal Church,

> We had suspected for quite a while. We suspected since she was 13 and she came out at the Thanksgiving dinner table in 2010 when she was 16. And it's kind of a family joke because she's like, 10 minutes into the meal or so she said, "Okay, I might as well get this over with. I'm lesbian or bi and I have a girlfriend." And it was all just a non-event. . . . So kind of the family joke is, "Oh, that's nice! Can you pass the butter?"

Relatedly, because many respondents had suspected the sexual minority status of their family member, several expressed relief at the disclosure.

One mother said, "I was kind of relieved because [before disclosing] he'd been pretty unhappy," and others said they were glad that their family member "was at the point of being able to come out," "finally able to claim who [they were]," and no longer "living a lie." One mother even asked her son, "Why did it take you so long?"

Immediate acceptance was, therefore, very common among our participants. However, that did not mean that the process was entirely conflict free. Instead, two areas of concern arose that required some negotiation. The first was apprehension over the "harder life" that respondents perceived their family members would face. The second was difficulty reconciling their desire to accept their family member with religious doctrines that were not accommodating of a gay or lesbian lifestyle.

A HARDER LIFE

Similar to Conley's (2011) study that demonstrated various concerns parents felt when their children came out, 7 of the 10 participants in our study who reported immediately accepting their family member's disclosure also said that they felt some concern and anxiety over the difficulties their family member would likely face in society. For instance, a Christian participant whose sister is a lesbian said she felt some apprehension "knowing that it was going to make her life harder and not wanting that for her." A mother who left the Catholic church and joined a UU congregation said that although she "didn't have an issue with [her son's sexuality]," she did have "a long talk with him about AIDS and using condoms and all that kind of stuff because . . . that to [her] is the scariest part of being gay." She went on to say, "I certainly didn't want that for my son." Another parent echoed that sentiment when she said, "The thing that upset me most wasn't the fact that he was gay. It was how he would be treated by other people because he was gay. I worried about him in that respect."

This concern over treatment by others was often couched in recognition that U.S. society is not always kind to sexual minorities. As one formerly Methodist father noted,

> There were a lot of tears from all of us for the realization that she was going to have a more difficult life

than what we had envisioned . . . [because of] the way society would see her and the challenges that she would have to deal with.

Another formerly Presbyterian father said he was concerned not only for his daughter because he believed "people were discriminating against lesbians, gays, generally, and [he] was afraid she would be the victim of discrimination," but also for her son because his classmates and friends "could be very tough on him—make fun of him—because his mother is an out lesbian."

In response to a daughter's fear that her parents would "never be able to look [her] in the eyes again," a mother who currently belongs to a UU church said,

And I thought: What is wrong with this country and our society that our daughter, who we have always been supportive [of], loving, [and] close to, would have any suspicion that we might not want to look at her again? You know, when she said that I just grabbed her face and said, "You look at me. I love you!"

Thus, anticipated societal mistreatment of their family members often influenced initial reactions to disclosures, but these concerns did not inhibit acceptance of their family members. To the contrary, perceived negative societal attitudes spurred many participants to become advocates in the gay rights movement. According to one formerly Presbyterian mother, the realization that society may reject her daughter is "what really made us want to fight the fight." Participants reported forming support groups within their congregations, organizing documentary screenings at their churches, participating in community events, and even taking on leadership roles in PFLAG. This push toward advocacy, though, was also often a direct result of the second source of conflict that participants experienced: reconciling their immediate acceptance of their gay or lesbian family member with religious doctrines that did not support acceptance.

THE INFLUENCE OF RELIGIOUS DOCTRINE
Stability Within One's Faith

Among the 10 participants who immediately accepted their gay or lesbian family member, 5 were members of churches that they perceived to promote acceptance and 5 were members of churches that they perceived as not promoting acceptance. Considering first those individuals who were in accepting faiths, integrating their family member's sexual orientation into their own understandings of family life and their own religious beliefs was relatively easy given that the doctrines of their churches already promoted acceptance. A Christian participant whose sister is a lesbian said, "I feel like the type of Christianity that I was raised with was very much where it's about acceptance and forgiveness and welcoming and it's about those sorts of things more than anything else."

Another participant noted,

The Episcopal perspective is rooted in the Gospel of Jesus, of love not of condemnation. It doesn't come from the guilt perspective. It doesn't come from the "you have to believe this, that, and the other thing," so it's a much more inclusive, loving perspective. . . . The New Testament speaks so clearly of love and acceptance and I really honestly don't believe that message is, "Yeah, Jesus loves everyone unless you're gay."

Thus, some of our participants relied on religious passages that they believed promoted acceptance of their gay or lesbian family member, and these passages, in turn, influenced their acceptance of their relative's sexuality. When asked if their church's stance on same-sex sexuality influenced their reactions to their family member's disclosure, they routinely said yes and then followed up with statements such as "My religious beliefs made me the way I am," "My religious beliefs are a part of me," and "Yes, they obviously influenced our acceptance of our daughter." Of interest, the experience of accepting their family member also influenced their faith, not by shifting their beliefs—generally because "there was nothing about [their] beliefs that needed to change"—but by shifting their religious decision making. For instance, a woman whose sister is a lesbian reported that when she moved and was in search of a new church, the congregation's stance on gay rights was a "litmus test" for her and she routinely rejected otherwise "welcoming" and "great places" because of subtle "homophobic things" said during a sermon. She went on to say, "If it's clearly a place that wouldn't be welcoming to my sister, then I won't go."

. . .

Ultimately, though, these five respondents experienced only minor changes in their religious beliefs and at no time did they feel compelled to leave their churches or adjust their religious perspectives in any marked way. Most started in mainline denominations, such as Episcopal, Quaker, and Christian, that were open and affirming from the outset, and they remained in those denominations. The same, however, cannot be said of the other five respondents who immediately accepted their family members— nor of the four individuals who struggled with acceptance initially.

Changing One's Faith

Five of the individuals who immediately accepted their family members belonged to religious faiths that they perceived to promote relatively conservative stances toward same-sex relationships. Thus, these individuals struggled to reconcile their accepting attitudes with the doctrines of their Catholic, Presbyterian, or Methodist churches, and, as a result, they all eventually not only left their original churches but also altered many of the basic tenets of their faith. To use Hirschman's (1970) language, when these individuals became disillusioned with their faiths' teachings on same-sex sexuality, they exited their religious communities. For instance, one mother said that, following her son's disclosure, she worried that her Christian faith, as well as the "anti-gay" and "negative" sentiments that were promoted by President Bush during his bid for reelection, were "damaging [her] son." She went on to say that "during that time period the religious right became very loud . . . it became very personal. I thought they were attacking my kid . . . so I lumped all Christians together [and] became very anti-Christian." She and her family ultimately became atheists, arguing, "There's no heaven and hell. There's no sin. There are good choices and bad choices, and hell is created by your bad choices. Heaven is created when you make good choices. It's within yourself."

Similarly, a formerly Methodist father reported that "it was clear that our senior pastor was offended by our questions about [same-sex sexuality] and gave us the impression that we weren't really wanted in his community." Because the pastor routinely tried to "squelch" any discussion over the issue and because he, his wife, and his children did not want to continue "squirming in the pews" while listening to "offensive" sermons, they left the church and began to research religious positions on same-sex relationships. Once they did that, it "[opened] up a whole lot of other questions about how to interpret some of the other things that [they] had been taught traditionally." As a result, they "chose to redefine God . . . as being the spirit of goodness who resides within all of us. And our path in life, our journey, our choice, is to try and embrace that goodness that all of us share together." Thus, he and his family no longer embrace any organized religion. Instead, they refer to themselves as "optimistic agnostics." For this family, then, early attempts to "voice" (Hirschman 1970) concerns with church leadership were met with resistance and contempt. Consequently, they opted to exit not only their specific congregation but the larger Methodist community as well.

Important to note, both of these parents expressed concern over church doctrines that were "offensive" and "attacking." Others who changed their faith echoed those sentiments. One formerly Presbyterian mother said that she is now not only "prejudiced and biased against a lot of organized religions" but also "disgusted with [them] and their stand on homosexuality" because she has "[seen] the pain that organized religion has caused people." A mother said, "I really think that a lot of these Christian religions are really off track. They really are defeating their own purposes by not accepting people for who they are." She went on to say she is thankful that her son's disclosure "got [her] out of the Catholic church" because she now feels "free from all the guilt and stuff that gets put on [people] from religion." Both of these mothers "exited" (Hirschman 1970) their original churches and now attend UU churches because they feel UU philosophies are more congruent with their new perspective that "God is in each of us. . . . [W]e're all valuable and we all have God's spark."

Thus, because these participants immediately accepted their family member's sexual orientation but also belonged to churches that they viewed as not accepting of same-sex sexuality, they had to struggle to reconcile these divergent perspectives. This struggle ultimately resulted in their decision to shift their fundamental understandings of God and abandon their original churches entirely. . . .

As it turns out, individuals who left their churches were not heavily invested in them from the outset. They described religion as being less important to them, reported attending worship services with intermittent frequency, and noted that they were not actively involved in their churches (e.g., they did not serve on committees, sing in the choir, etc.). Their more tenuous connections to their churches, thus, may have made their exit easier. But their decision to alter their faith stands in sharp contrast to the compartmentalization in beliefs that were made by individuals who were heavily invested in their churches.

Compartmentalizing Aspects of One's Faith

Four respondents spoke of the difficulties associated with having strong ties to conservative churches yet having similarly strong desires to accept their family member's sexual orientation. They noted experiencing conflict between love for their child, which served as a strong motivator for acceptance, and deep ties to their church, which made blanket acceptance very difficult because it was in direct conflict with their long-held religious convictions. For instance, a woman who was a Seventh Day Baptist, whose husband was a church minister, and who described herself as heavily involved in a number of church functions said she was "heartbroken," "shocked," and "didn't know what to say, or think, or do" when her son disclosed his sexual orientation. She said her reaction was driven, in part, by her belief that "homosexuality . . . was a sin [based on her] religious upbringing," so she struggled with the news and initially was "hoping for change" in her son. However, because such change was not forthcoming, she started "searching for answers," getting "books from the library," attending "discussions in [her] community," and visiting with members of PFLAG. "As I studied more and began to think it through more, my previous religious inclination did not seem to be correct. . . . Now I believe that homosexuality is a natural condition. It is not a sin." She went on to note that "as far as my religious beliefs in this area are concerned, they have definitely changed," but she

also asserted that her connection to her church community remained "very important" to her and she had no intention of leaving her church or redefining her religious beliefs in any wholesale way. In short, a more segmented approach to changes in her faith made more sense to her. Thus, she chose to adjust her view on same-sex sexuality and simply ignore church teachings that suggested it was a sin.

Similarly, a father who is a Baptist minister said he was in "shock" and felt "numb" when both of his children told him they are gay. He believed same-sex sexuality was "a sickness and a sin," and he asserted that "there ought to be laws against it; we sure don't want them teaching it in our schools." But his love for his children sent him on a quest for information. He "started studying and [he] . . . realized that the Bible says very little about [same-sex sexuality]; really not enough to take a strong theological position about it." As a result, his beliefs about this issue are now "180 degrees different," he advocates for gay and lesbian rights, and he is no longer "in complete agreement with many other Christians in [his] denomination." Moreover, he is very comfortable with the fact that his beliefs diverge from others in his congregation: "[My] religious beliefs really only changed mainly just on this question [and] that's okay as far as I'm concerned. [We] don't have to agree."

In fact, comfort with the practice of disregarding aspects of doctrine that were incongruent with acceptance was critical for those who were heavily invested in their faith yet searching for a way to accept their gay or lesbian family member. Doing so allowed them to avoid the conflict associated with "having to choose" between their family member and their faith. As one Baptist mother noted, she "[didn't] like the . . . feeling that [she had] to choose," but if resolving the conflict had been impossible, she would have picked "[her] son over [her church] any day." Rather than make such a stark decision, however, she opted to compartmentalize and ignore teachings that were contrary to acceptance: "I'm not going to believe that my son is going to go to hell because of this like I was raised to believe my whole life." Although the conflict between her faith and accepting her son was "very difficult" and it "tested [her] beliefs," by disregarding select doctrine, she was able to proclaim,

"I'm not turning my back on the way I was raised. I just don't agree with that part of it at all." This resolution allowed her to maintain ties to two areas of her life that were critically important to her: her religion and her son.

These findings are consistent with Hirschman's (1970) argument that exiting can be easier when one is less invested in the source of discontent. When people are highly invested in something, they feel a stronger sense of "loyalty" to it and so are more inclined to continue the relationship despite some dissatisfaction. Because these respondents were all highly invested in their churches, their loyalty was likely quite high. Thus, exiting was a difficult proposition; instead, they had to find ways to remain connected to their religious communities even as they chose to accept their gay or lesbian family members. Ignoring anti-gay doctrine and agreeing to disagree with their church's teachings on same-sex sexuality was one way they could do this.

. . .

DISCUSSION

. . .

These findings offer important insights into how individuals respond to sexual orientation disclosures and suggest that the coming out process does not just impact those who are seeking acceptance; it also changes the way family members think about, talk about, and even advocate on behalf of gay and lesbian individuals. Moreover, these changes appear to not only be influenced by a person's religious beliefs, but to also reinforce, alter, or significantly limit those same beliefs. To that end, three prominent patterns regarding the reciprocal relationship between religious beliefs and acceptance emerged within our data.

First, the five respondents who were members of mainline congregations experienced relative stability within their faith because they believed that their churches already promoted acceptance. For these individuals, church doctrine encouraged positive reactions to their family member's disclosure. Important to note, this is similar to Dahl and Galliher's (2012) work on gay and lesbian adolescents whose religious and sexual identity was influenced by the degree to

which their church doctrine did or did not promote acceptance of same-sex sexuality. Thus, just as ideas of a loving God can positively influence self-acceptance among gay and lesbian youth, this study suggests the same may be true for family members who must confront the sexual orientation of their loved ones.

Just as important, not only did mainline denominations tend to promote acceptance of one's family member, but the sexual orientation of an individual's family member also appeared to influence that person's decisions about which churches to attend in the future, even if his or her gay or lesbian family member was not going to attend the chosen church. This is important for two reasons. First, it is consistent with the earlier finding that family members often experience personal and behavioral changes upon learning that their loved one is gay or lesbian. Second, and most critical, it also suggests that this tendency toward personal change extends to one's religious decision making. Thus, having a gay or lesbian family member may have implications for a person's religious decisions, irrespective of whether those decisions directly impact the gay or lesbian family member who served as their initial impetus.

The second and third patterns to emerge from our data are both associated with respondents who were members of more conservative churches. For these individuals, the relationship between their religion and their desire to accept their family member was more complicated because their church doctrines did not promote acceptance. This discrepancy between their lived experiences with a gay or lesbian family member and their religion's teachings resulted in interpersonal tensions with fellow congregants, tense feelings toward their houses of worship, and frustration with church doctrine—all of which had to be negotiated and ultimately resolved. Consistent with Lease and Shulman's (2003) findings and with Hirschman's (1970) work on "exiting," five individuals resolved this conflict by changing their religious beliefs, leaving their original churches, and in some instances dramatically redefining their beliefs about God and God's place within their lives.

In many ways this finding is similar to research that demonstrates that being a sexual minority often negatively affects that person's relationship with

God (Bradshaw et al. 2015). Family members of gay or lesbian individuals also sometimes have difficulty reconciling their desire for acceptance and their existing religious beliefs. Important to note, Zuckerman (2012:100) offered insight into why this might happen. Drawing on the insights of one of his respondents who said people must "make an effort to believe," Zuckerman suggested that religious beliefs are based on will, choice, and effort. In other words, unlike the experiences of children who typically just believe what their parents believe, for adults, religious belief does not just happen; it involves contemplation and effort. Thus, when faced with the challenge of reconciling large differences between their religious doctrines and the sexual orientation of their loved ones, it seems that for some people this reconciliation work is too burdensome—the gap between their faith and acceptance is too large and the work to bridge that gap is too onerous. As a result, they alter their beliefs, leave their original churches, and/or embrace new perspectives that are more congruent with their own desires.

Important to note, however, participants who left their churches were not heavily invested in them. They attended sporadically, did not serve on church committees, and did not participate in extra activities such as choir or bible study groups. When individuals with relatively tenuous connections to their churches leave religion, Zuckerman (2012) referred to this phenomenon as "mild apostasy," because the religious abandonment is not severe given that the person's religious connections are not strong in the first place. This stands in sharp contrast to individuals who do have strong ties to their houses of worship. In such cases, altering their religious beliefs will be much more challenging—a process Zuckerman referred to as "transformative apostasy" because the change is more intensely transformative given the existing strong investment.

However, our participants who were heavily invested in their religions prior to their family member's disclosure did not experience transformative apostasy—their level of investment kept them from abandoning their faith. They chose, instead, to compartmentalize and deprioritize those aspects of their religious doctrines that were not supportive of

same-sex relationships. Research shows that some gay and lesbian Mormons, Jews, and Christians ignore or reframe parts of their religious teachings that tend to condemn same-sex sexuality (Mahaffy 1996; Schnoor 2006; Walton 2006; Zuckerman 2012). Similarly, religiously invested individuals who want to accept their gay and lesbian family members appear to recognize that there are aspects of their religious doctrine with which they do not completely agree but which they can deprioritize and compartmentalize as only a small fraction of a greater set of religious beliefs. Because they value other aspects of their religion and identify strongly with their faith, some of these individuals choose to ignore those beliefs that do not promote acceptance. These findings are consistent with Hirschman's (1970) ideas regarding "exiting," and they provide nuanced examples of the strategies people may use to remain "loyal" to something with which they are not completely satisfied.

This is not to say, however, that all or even most members of conservative churches will be inclined toward this kind of compartmentalization. As Baker and Brauner-Otto (2015) demonstrated, evangelical Protestants are the least likely individuals to be accepting of sexual orientation disclosures by people close to them. But our research does suggest that among individuals who are highly motivated toward acceptance—such as the parents in our sample—compartmentalization might be a meaningful way to simultaneously preserve one's family relationships and religious ties, especially in situations where individuals are already highly invested in their churches.

The reciprocal relationships between religious beliefs and acceptance that our data reveal offer important preliminary insights into familial reactions to same-sex disclosures, but it is, nonetheless, important to note that our research focused primarily on parents of gay or lesbian individuals. It is possible that other types of family members utilize different strategies to manage their loved one coming out. It is also plausible that the closeness of a family member to the gay or lesbian individual may play some role in these various strategies. Arguably, if one is close to their gay or lesbian family member, their process may be more intense, complicated, or challenging compared to someone who does not feel close to their relative. Furthermore, it may be interesting to compare our research findings to the reactions of family members who do not affiliate with any particular religious group. Perhaps surprisingly, Barringer and Gay (2017) showed that gay and lesbian individuals who do not affiliate with any religion report lower levels of happiness compared to those who affiliate with at least some religious groups. It would be interesting to examine how nonreligious, atheist, and/or agnostic family members react to their loved one's sexual orientation disclosure.

Our research also focused on individuals who ultimately accepted their family member's sexual orientation. We did not interview individuals who rejected their gay or lesbian relative. As such, our results do not reflect the reactions of all religious individuals; instead they represent only those who have chosen to accept their loved one and must therefore wrestle with what that means for their religious beliefs. Future research should examine the reciprocal relationship between religious beliefs and the rejection of one's gay or lesbian family member. Ultimately, our qualitative interviews allowed us to expand upon previous but limited studies of individuals' religiosity and their acceptance of gay or lesbian family members (Lease and Shulman 2003). But our data are, nonetheless, limited in scope and restricted to only 14 participants. Our findings must, therefore, be considered preliminary. Future research should not only seek to replicate what we report here but also continue to explore the reciprocal relationship between acceptance and religious beliefs through additional in-depth, qualitative interviews.

NOTE

1. Steensland et al.'s (2000) classification system is not the only classification system used for religious groups. Sherkat's (2014) classification system is more nuanced, with 13 religious categories. Notable differences between the Steensland et al. and Sherkat classification systems include Sherkat placing Episcopalians in a separate category, separating Christian and Quaker as other Christian groups, and dividing Baptists into different categories. In addition to these differences

in categorizing religious groups, it is also important to note that Steensland et al. and Sherkat use somewhat different criteria for their classification systems. We decided to use the Steensland et al. classification scheme because the definitions of the various categories are a better fit for our data and allow us to make meaningful comparisons across categories. Using Sherkat's 13-category system would spread our data out across too many categories to make any meaningful comparisons.

REFERENCES

Armesto, Jorge and Amy Weisman. 2001. "Attributions and Emotional Reactions to the Identity Disclosure ('Coming-out') of a Homosexual Child." *Family Process* 40:145–162.

Baiocco, Roberto, Lilybeth Fontanesi, Federica Santamaria, Salvatore Ioverno, Barbara Marasco, Emma Baumgartner, Brian Willoughby, and Fiorenzo Laghi. 2015. "Negative Parental Responses to Coming Out and Family Functioning in a Sample of Lesbian and Gay Young Adults." *Journal of Child and Family Studies* 24:1490–1500.

Baker, Ashley and Sarah Brauner-Otto. 2015. "My Friend Is Gay, but . . . the Effects of Social Contact on Christian Evangelicals' Beliefs about Gays and Lesbians." *Review of Religious Research* 57:239–268.

Baptist, Joyce and Katherine Allen. 2008. "A Family's Coming Out Process: Systemic Change and Multiple Realities." *Contemporary Family Therapy* 30:92–110.

Barringer, M. N. and David Gay. 2017. "Happily Religious: The Surprising Sources of Happiness Among Lesbian, Gay, Bisexual, and Transgender Adults." *Sociological Inquiry* 87:75–96.

Beals, Kristin and Letitia Peplau. 2005. "Identity Support, Identity Devaluation, and Well-being among Lesbians." *Psychology of Women Quarterly* 29:140–148.

Ben-Ari, Adital. 1995. "The Discovery That an Offspring Is Gay: Parents', Gay Men's, and Lesbians' Perspectives." *Journal of Homosexuality* 30:89–112.

Bradshaw, William, Tim Heaton, Ellen Decoo, John Dehlen, Renee Galliher, and Katherine Crowell. 2015. "Religious Experiences of GBTQ Mormon

Males." *Journal for the Scientific Study of Religion* 54:311–329.

Bregman, Hallie, Neena Malik, Matthew Page, Emily Makynen, and Kristin Lindahl. 2013. "Identity Profiles in Lesbian, Gay, and Bisexual Youth: The Role of Family Influences." *Journal of Youth Adolescence* 42:417–430.

Cant, Bob. 2005. "Exploring the Implications for Health Professionals of Men Coming Out as Gay in Healthcare Settings." *Health and Social Care in the Community* 14:9–16.

Cass, Vivienne. 1996. "Sexual Orientation Identity Formation: A Western Phenomenon." Pp. 227–251 in *Textbook of Homosexuality and Mental Health*, edited by R. P. Cabaj and T. S. Sten. Washington, DC: American Psychiatric Press.

Cole, Steve, Margaret Kemeny, Shelley Taylor, and Barbara Visscher. 1996. "Elevated Physical Health Risk among Gay Men Who Conceal Their Homosexual Identity." *Health Psychology* 15:243–251.

Conley, Cynthia. 2011. "Learning about a Child's Gay or Lesbian Sexual Orientation: Parental Concerns about Societal Rejection, Loss of Loved Ones, and Child Well-being." *Journal of Homosexuality* 58:1022–1040.

Dahl, Angie and Renee Galliher. 2012. "The Interplay of Sexual and Religious Identity Development in LGBTQ Adolescents and Young Adults: A Qualitative Inquiry." *Identity: An International Journal of Theory and Research* 12:217–246.

D'Augelli, Anthony. 2002. "Mental Health Problems among Lesbian, Gay, and Bisexual Youths Ages 14 to 21." *Clinical Child Psychology and Psychiatry* 7:433–456.

D'Augelli, Anthony. 2006. "Stress and Adaption among Families of Lesbian, Gay, and Bisexual Youth: Research Challenges." Pp. 135–157 in *An Introduction to GLBT Family Studies*, edited by J. J. Bigner. New York, NY: Haworth Press.

D'Augelli, Anthony and Scott Hershberger. 1993. "Lesbian, Gay, and Bisexual Youth in Community Settings: Personal Challenges and Mental Health Problems." *American Journal of Community Psychology* 21:421–448.

D'Augelli, Anthony and Charlotte Patterson. (Eds.). 1995. *Lesbian, Gay, and Bisexual Identities Over the Lifespan: Psychological Perspectives.* New York, NY: Oxford University Press

Dowding, Keith 2015. "Albert O. Hirschman, Exit, Voice, and Loyalty: Responses to Decline in Firms, Organizations, and States." *Oxford Handbooks Online.* Oxford, UK: Oxford University Press.

Given, Lisa. 2008. *The SAGE Encyclopedia of Qualitative Research Methods.* New York, NY: Sage.

Goldfried, Marvin and Anita Goldfried. 2001. "The Importance of Parental Support in the Lives of Gay, Lesbian, and Bisexual Individuals." *Journal of Clinical Psychology* 57:681–693.

Halpin, Sean and Michael Allen. 2004. "Changes in Psychosocial Well-being during Stages of Gay Identity Development." *Journal of Homosexuality* 47:109–126.

Heatherington, Laurie and Justin Lavner. 2008. "Coming to Terms with Coming Out: Review and Recommendations for Family Systems-focused Research." *Journal of Family Psychology* 22:329–343.

Herdt, Gilbert and Andrew Boxer. 1993. *Children of Horizons: How Gay and Lesbian Teens Are Leading a New Way Out of the Closet.* Boston, MA: Beacon Press.

Hilton, Angela and Dawn Szymanski. 2011. "Family Dynamics and Change in Sibling of Origin Relationship after Lesbian and Gay Sexual Orientation Disclosure." *Contemporary Family Therapy* 33:291–309.

Hirschman, Albert. 1970. *Exit, Voice, and Loyalty: Responses to Decline in Firms, Organizations, and States.* Cambridge, MA: Harvard University Press.

Huffington Post, The. 2012. "Ian McKellen, 'Hobbit' Star, Talks Coming Out as Gay with Anderson Cooper." Retrieved September 3, 2015 (http://www.huffingtonpost.com/2012/12/14/ian-mckellen-coming-out-gay-anderson-cooper-_n_2303038.html)

Lease, Suzanne and Julie Shulman. 2003. "A Preliminary Investigation of the Role of Religion for Family Members of Lesbian, Gay Male, or Bisexual Male and Female Individuals." *Counseling and Values* 47:195–209.

Mahaffy, Kimberly. 1996. "Cognitive Dissonance and Its Resolution: A Study of Lesbian Christians." *Journal for the Scientific Study of Religion* 35:392–402.

McQueeney, Krista. 2009. "'We Are God's Children, Y'all': Race, Gender, and Sexuality in Lesbian- and Gay-affirming Congregations." *Social Problems* 56:151–173.

Newman, Bernie and Peter Muzzonigro. 1993. "The Effects of Traditional Family Values on the Coming Out Process of Gay Male Adolescents." *Adolescence* 28:213–227.

Parents, Families and Friends of Lesbians and Gays, Inc. (1997). *Faith in Our Families: Parents, Families and Friends Talk about Religion and Homosexuality.* Retrieved September 3, 2015 (http://www.pflag.org/fileadmin/user_upload/Publications/Faith_Families.pdf).

Pedretti, K. R. 2004. "After the Son Comes Out: Relationships with Parents and Levels of Homophobia of Disclosed Versus Undisclosed Gay Men" (Doctoral dissertation, California School of Professional Psychology, San Francisco, 2004). *Dissertation Abstracts International* 64–08:4056.

Pelton-Sweet, Laura and Alissa Sherry. 2008. "Coming Out through Art: A Review of Art Therapy with LGBT Clients." *Art Therapy: Journal of the American Art Therapy Association* 25:170–176.

Phillips, Mary Jane and Julie Ancis. 2008. "The Process of Identity Development as the Parent of a Lesbian or Gay Male." *Journal of LGBT Issues in Counseling* 2:126–158.

Reynolds, Amy and William Hanjorgiris. 2000. "Coming Out: Lesbian, Gay and Bisexual Identity Development." Pp. 35–55 in *Handbook of Counseling and Psychotherapy with Lesbian, Gay and Bisexual Clients,* edited by R. M. Perez, K. A. DeBord, and K. J. Bieschke. Washington, DC: American Psychological Association.

Robinson, Bryan, Lynda Walters, and Patsy Skeen. 1989. "Response of Parents to Learning that Their Child Is Homosexual and Concern Over AIDS: A National Study." *Journal of Homosexuality* 18:1–35.

Rosario, Margaret, Heino Meyer-Bahlburg, Joyce Hunter, Theresa Exner, Marya Gwadz, and Arden Keller. 1996. "The Psychosexual Development of Urban Lesbian, Gay, and Bisexual Youths." *Journal of Sex Research* 33:113–126.

Ryan, Caitlin, David Huebner, Rafael Diaz, and Jorge Sanchez. 2009. "Family Rejection as a Predictor of Negative Health Outcomes in White and Latino Lesbian, Gay, and Bisexual Young Adults." *Pediatrics* 123:346–350.

Saltzburg, Susan. 2004. "Learning that an Adolescent Child Is Gay or Lesbian: The Parent Experience." *Social Work* 49:109–118.

Savin-Williams, Ritch. 1989. "Coming Out to Parents and Self-esteem among Gay and Lesbian Youths." *Journal of Homosexuality* 18:1–35.

Savin-Williams, Ritch. 1990. *Gay and Lesbian Youth: Expression of Identity.* New York: Hempshire.

Savin-Williams, Ritch. 2001. *Mom, Dad. I'm Gay.* Washington, DC: American Psychological Association.

Savin-Williams, Ritch and Lisa Diamond. 2000. "Sexual Identity Trajectories among Sexual-minority Youths: Gender Comparisons." *Archives of Sexual Behavior* 29:607–627.

Savin-Williams, Ritch and Geoffrey Ream. 2003. "Sex Variations in the Disclosure to Parents of Same-sex Attractions." *Journal of Family Psychology* 17:429–438.

Schnoor, Randal. 2006. "Being Gay and Jewish: Negotiating Intersecting Identities." *Sociology of Religion* 67:43–60.

Schope, Robert. 2002. "The Decision to Tell: Factors Influencing the Disclosure of Sexual Orientation by Gay Men." *Journal of Gay and Lesbian Social Services: Issues in Practice, Policy, and Research* 14:1–22.

Sheets, Raymond and Jonathan Mohr. 2009. "Perceived Social Support from Friends and Family and Psychological Functioning in Bisexual Young Adult College Students." *Journal of Counseling Psychology* 56:152–163.

Sherkat, Darren. 2002. "Sexuality and Religious Commitment in the United States: An Empirical Examination." *Journal for the Scientific Study of Religion* 41:313–323.

Sherkat, Darren. 2014. *Changing Faith. The Dynamics and Consequences of Americans' Shifting Religious Identities.* New York: New York University Press.

Steensland, Brian, Lynn Robinson, Bradford Wilcox, Jerry Park, Mark Regnerus, and Robert Woodberry. 2000. "The Measure of American Religion: Toward Improving the State of the Art." *Social Forces* 79:291–318.

Vincke, John and Ralph Bolton. 1994. "Social Support, Depression, and Self-acceptance among Gay Men." *Human Relations* 47:1049–1062.

Walton, Gerald. 2006. "'Fag Church': Men Who Integrate Gay and Christian Identities." *Journal of Homosexuality* 51:1–17.

Whitehead, Andrew. 2010. "Sacred Rites and Civil Rights: Religion's Effect on Attitudes toward Same-sex Unions and the Perceived Cause of Homosexuality." *Social Science Quarterly* 91:63–79.

Whitley, Bernard. 2009. "Religiosity and Attitudes toward Lesbians and Gay Men: A Meta-analysis." *The International Journal for the Psychology of Religion* 19:21–38.

Yip, Andrew. 2005. "Queering Religious Texts: An Exploration of British Non-heterosexual Christians' and Muslims' Strategy of Constructing Sexuality Affirming Hermeneutics." *Sociology BSA Publications Ltd* 39:47–65.

Zuckerman, Phil. 2012. *Faith No More: Why People Reject Religion*. New York, NY: Oxford University Press.

55. BEYOND THE WALL

ASHLEY MCKINLESS (2017)

President Donald J. Trump's journey to the White House began with a simple promise. "I will build a great, great wall on our southern border," he announced in June 2015, when few took the hotel mogul's presidential ambitions, or chances, too seriously. "And I will have Mexico pay for that wall. Mark my words."

Mr. Trump himself would temper those words shortly after his election—"for certain areas . . . there could be some fencing," he said in an interview on "60 Minutes" on Nov. 13. But ultimately it does not matter whether it is a great wall or just a really long fence. If he builds it, they will still come.

They will come from Guatemala, Honduras and El Salvador, where a deadly mix of poverty, violence and corruption leaves families with no other option but to flee north. They will pay a *coyote* anywhere from $5,000 to $14,000 for three chances to roll the dice and make it across the border. They will risk extortion, kidnapping and rape on the 2,500-mile trek north, many riding atop *la bestia*, a train overflowing with other migrants, or fighting for air in the back of a crowded truck.

When the road ends, they will walk for miles in the punishing desert heat of northern Mexico, dodging Border Patrol agents, cartels and American vigilantes until the lucky ones cross undetected into the United States. Some will not make it out of the desert alive. The rest will be detained and flown back to their country of origin at an average cost to U.S. taxpayers of $12,500 each.

THE REVOLVING DOOR

I am standing in an empty deportation processing center in Guatemala City, where migrants returned from the U.S. border are welcomed, registered and sent on their way back into the country they had planned to leave behind. Cameras and recording devices are prohibited, and I am told not to initiate any conversations with the returnees, some of whom may be traumatized by their sudden reversal of fortune after traveling so far and coming so close to the finish line. The nondescript brick building is tucked into the corner of the national air force base at La Aurora International Airport. Inside, it feels like a high school cafeteria, complete with brown-bag lunches on white folding chairs. An elevated wooden counter and 12 aging computers at the front of the room suggest D.M.V.-level wait times ahead. Upbeat marimba music blares discordantly from above like a forced laugh.

A large sign behind the counter reads: "Ya estás en tu país y con tu gente"—"You are now in your country and with your people." It is a bittersweet welcome for many of the returning migrants, who say they love their country and would have stayed in Guatemala if they could have.

A football field away the returnees start leaving the plane. First 10 or so women and girls, walking in threesomes and pairs. Then a much longer line of men, young and old, make their procession across the tarmac. As they enter the building, some flash a wide, confident grin or wear a sheepish smile. Many look stoically ahead; others, exhausted and visibly upset, study the floor. More than a few are still wearing the white T-shirts they were given at detention centers in the United States. For security reasons, shoelaces and belts are not allowed. The chains and shackles that had bound them on the plane have been removed.

One hundred sixty-two Guatemalans fill the white folding chairs. Three or four times a day, four or five days a week, flights carrying as many as 260 returnees arrive at the base. Those numbers bear witness to the scale of the migrant crisis, though the scene is not entirely somber. Once everyone is seated, there is an animated call-and-response between the peppy representative from the Ministry of Foreign Affairs and the returning migrants.

"Thanks be to God because we are all alive when so many do not make it," she tells them. "Don't think of yourself as losers. You took a risk." Some roll their eyes, others cheer. It is clear that many of them have been through this routine before.

That includes Miguel, 30 years old with a sturdy build and quiet voice, who is eager to tell his story. He says he first left for the United States in 2000 at the age of 14 because there were no jobs in his small town in the north of Guatemala. He wound up in White Plains, N.Y., working as a landscaper for nine years. Six years ago, he returned to Guatemala to care for his ailing father. After his father died, he and his girlfriend, pregnant at the time, again made their way north. She made it across the border; he did not.

Two failed border crossings and a year and a half later, he still has not met his child. He says he will try his luck at the border again—maybe tomorrow, maybe in a few months.

Mr. Trump has not detailed how he plans to stem the flow of this desperate exodus. But the revolving door of Guatemala's deportation center makes one thing clear: A migration policy that begins and ends with fortifying the U.S. border is destined for expensive failure.

MIGRANT OR REFUGEE?

Few see the futility of a U.S. policy of wall-building more clearly than Mauro Verzeletti, C.S. The Scalabrini missionary, known to migrants and officials here as Padre Mauro, runs La Casa del Migrante, which provides returnees with a temporary place to stay, humanitarian assistance and psychological counseling. Every day he receives a schedule of the flight arrivals at Guatemala City's airport and dispatches a white van to pick up returning Guatemalans who have nowhere else to go. Padre Mauro spends much of his time tending to the immediate needs of these new arrivals, a ministry that he considers essential but merely a Band-Aid in the face of a migration crisis. What the country needs, he says, is for its leaders and the international community to address the conditions that push thousands of people like Miguel north every month.

The plight of Central American migrants and refugees briefly made front page news in 2014, when a surge in families and unaccompanied children overwhelmed the U.S. immigration system. While the alarm-raising headlines have dropped off, the number of unaccompanied children apprehended by the U.S. Border Patrol has not. In 2016, 18,914 Guatemalan youths were picked up—almost 2,000 more than the 17,057 apprehended two years prior.

North of the border, political debate has centered on whether these families and children should be considered economic migrants, who are subject to deportation, or refugees, who can claim a legitimate right to asylum. But such neat categories are not reflected in the lives of most Guatemalans, says Padre Mauro. Poverty and violence, past and present, are deeply intertwined in the country.

Like other countries in the region, Guatemala experienced a devastating, decades-long civil war between U.S.-backed military authoritarians and leftist rebels who drew their support from the indigenous Mayan community and the rural poor. The war ended in 1996, but patterns of exclusion and discrimination persist.

In 1993, Virginia Searing, S.C., came to Quiché, a region devastated by the government's scorched-earth policy, to establish a mental health program for victimized communities. She says parents and grand-parents in the area "saw their loved ones burned alive, macheted, tortured, raped. . . . They pass that on. How does a person live having experienced that?"

This unaddressed trauma, as well as impotent rage toward an economic system that still rewards the rich and the corrupt, Sister Searing says, is all too often expressed in the form of sexual violence, family abandonment and domestic and child abuse. Is a mother fleeing with children that she cannot feed, from a husband who abuses her, truly a migrant? Or is it more accurate to call her a refugee?

For decades, the United States has promoted neoliberal policies as the best economic response to this deadly mix of poverty and violence. Mean-while, they have directed foreign assistance to state security forces with shaky human rights records. The Central American Free Trade Agreement, signed in 2004, promised to bring jobs to the region and reduce migration to the United States. Instead, Padre Mauro says, CAFTA enriched the oligarchs and mul-tinational corporations and displaced small farmers. A decade later, Guatemala has a booming biofu-els export industry—and the fourth highest rate of chronic malnutrition in the world. Fifty percent of children under 5 are malnourished, and the rate is even higher for indigenous populations.

Padre Mauro believes the U.S. response to the 2014 border crisis will bring more of the same.

The Obama administration threw its sup-port behind the Alliance for Prosperity, a five-year, $22 billion plan drawn up by the governments of Guatemala, Honduras and El Salvador that aims to reduce incentives for migration by spurring private sector growth, strengthening the rule of law and com-bating gang- and cartel-driven violence. Roughly 60 percent of the funds are earmarked for policing and border security measures, and much of the develop-ment aid is focused on attracting foreign companies rather than investing in health, education and social security. These public services have been crippled by a culture of tax evasion among the country's busi-nesses and elite.

What the 60 percent of Guatemalans living in poverty need, Padre Mauro insists, is access to "las tres T's: trabajo, techo, tierra" ("the three L's: labor,

lodging, land"). It is the formulation used by Pope Francis in a forceful address to the Second World Meeting of Popular Movements, a gathering of grass-roots organizations of the poor and marginalized, in July 2015: "I wish to join my voice to yours in calling for land, lodging and labor for all our brothers and sisters. I said it and I repeat it: These are sacred rights."

A FUTURE WITH DIGNITY

The small farm holders of Nuevo Eden, a coffee coop-erative in San Marcos, a lush, mountainous district in Guatemala's western highlands, have been fighting for these rights for decades.

At the height of the civil war, families in the area fled to Mexico to escape atrocities perpetrated against indigenous Maya by military and paramili-tary groups. Whole villages were razed, women were raped, families were gathered into churches and burned in a brutal campaign considered by many here a genocide. The community was in exile for 16 years, and when the war ended, it took another two years of organizing and strikes to force the Gua-temalan government to hand over the money to buy back land promised in the peace accords.

That was not the end of their trials. Large deal-ers set the price for coffee beans. Turning a profit is difficult even in a good year. Then in 2012, *roya*—a fungus that because of climate change is reaching trees at altitudes once considered immune to the coffee leaf rust epidemic—wiped out 70 percent to 80 percent of their crop.

Production has bounced back. . . . But warming temperatures continue to push farmers in the area farther up the mountain. At some point, they will reach an altitude where even the most resilient seeds cannot take root.

What concerns these farmers most, however, is what the future will bring for young people in the region.

Young people like Angelita. At just 18 years of age, she is a volunteer firefighter, her community's de facto E.M.T. and a midwife—she has managed four deliveries so far. She is also a trained smoke-jumper, those fearless types who parachute into wildfires. She has studied literature and computers in high school, helps out her dad in the fields and her mom in the kitchen and plays soccer in her free time. She has a résumé and ambition that would make aspiring Ivy Leaguers look over their shoulders.

But, like most people under 30 here, she has no job and few prospects for further schooling. When her friends ask her why she does so much for no pay, she has a simple answer: "Es mi vocación"—to support her family, to strengthen her community, to build up her country is her vocation. And to listen to her talk is to know that if she had even the smallest opportunity, she would do all that and more.

Last summer, Angelita and some 20 other young people from surrounding communities were given the chance, with the support of C.R.S. and Caritas Internationalis, to travel to Guatemala City for a week-long training in cupping, a process to evaluate the aroma, flavor and body of coffee. These young people graduated from high school with degrees in teaching, business and computers, but they take pride in this new skill and want to share it with the cooperatives so that farmers can command a higher price for their harvest. But while a more competitive coffee product may benefit the community, it is not enough to provide the kind of formal employment young people desperately need if they are to stay in the region.

Angelita is one of 10 siblings; three of her four brothers are already living in the United States. Others in her community have also migrated or resorted to criminal activity to support themselves and their families. Susana, another participant in the coffee cupping program, graduated with a teaching degree three years ago and still cannot find work. The few coveted teaching posts are given to the family members of government officials, she says.

Susana has told her parents that she plans to leave for the United States to help support her younger sisters. She says she will take whatever work she can get up north: "Harvesting tomatoes, washing, cooking. I'm willing to do that."

Angelita has also been tempted to leave. But she cannot imagine leaving her family. She wants their strength and unity to be a model for their neighbors.

"I've had obstacles in my life," she says. But her father, a strong and loving influence, told her that whenever she encounters an obstacle, it means there is something good waiting beyond it.

THE WAY OUT

In his address in Bolivia, Pope Francis told the grass-roots organizers that there is no simple solution, no single social program that will tear down the many obstacles—corruption, inequality, environmental degradation, war—holding back bright, ambitious young people all over the developing world: "Don't expect a recipe from this pope."

Much less from the president of the United States. "The future of humanity does not lie solely in the hands of great leaders, the great powers and the elites," the pope said. "It is fundamentally in the hands of peoples and in their ability to organize."

Guatemalans know this. The two phrases one hears most from those contemplating a way out of the country's intractable cycle of corruption and poverty are "civil society" and "middle class"—neither of which can be built up with foreign aid alone.

But neither can the United States ignore the fate of the hundreds of thousands of people living with constant hunger, violence and economic despair beyond its border. Addressing another Meeting of Popular Movements, this time at the Vatican just days before the election of Mr. Trump, the pope offered a warning to those who would respond to the desperation of migrants and refugees by building walls: "There are so many cemeteries alongside the walls, walls drenched in innocent blood."

Mr. Trump can build his wall. But they will keep coming. Until deported mothers and fathers like Miguel are reunited with their children in the United States, they will keep coming. Until aspiring teachers like Susana are able to use and pass on their education, until someone like Angelita is able to support herself and her family, they will keep coming.

Eventually, as Pope Francis observes, "All walls collapse—all of them."

56. MY GRANDMOTHER WASHES HER FEET IN THE SINK OF THE BATHROOM AT SEARS

MOHJA KAHF (2003)

My grandmother puts her feet in the sink
of the bathroom at Sears
to wash them in the ritual washing for prayer,
wudu,
because she has to pray in the store or miss
the mandatory prayer time for Muslims
She does it with great poise, balancing
herself with one plump matronly arm
against the automated hot-air hand dryer,
after having removed her support knee-highs
and laid them aside, folded in thirds,
and given me her purse and her packages to hold
so she can accomplish this august ritual
and get back to the ritual of shopping for
    housewares

Respectable Sears matrons shake their heads and
    frown
as they notice what my grandmother is doing,
an affront to American porcelain,
a contamination of American Standards
by something foreign and unhygienic
requiring civic action and possible use of disinfec-
    tant spray
They fluster about and flutter their hands and I
    can see
a clash of civilizations brewing in the Sears bathroom

My grandmother, though she speaks no English,
catches their meaning and her look in the mirror
    says,
I have washed my feet over Iznik tile in Istanbul
with water from the world's ancient irrigation systems
I have washed my feet in the bathhouses of Damascus
over painted bowls imported from China
among the best families of Aleppo
And if you Americans knew anything
about civilization and cleanliness,
you'd make wider washbins, anyway
My grandmother knows one culture—the right one,
as do these matrons of the Middle West. For them,
my grandmother might as well have been squatting

in the mud over a rusty tin in vaguely tropical
    squalor,
Mexican or Middle Eastern, it doesn't matter which,
when she lifts her well-groomed foot and puts it
    over the edge.
"You can't do that," one of the women protests,
turning to me, "Tell her she can't do that."
"We wash our feet five times a day,"
my grandmother declares hotly in Arabic.
"My feet are cleaner than their sink.
Worried about their sink, are they?
I should worry about my feet!"
My grandmother nudges me, "Go on, tell them."

Standing between the door and the mirror, I can see
at multiple angles, my grandmother and the other
    shoppers,
all of them decent and goodhearted women, diligent
in cleanliness, grooming, and decorum
Even now my grandmother, not to be rushed,
is delicately drying her pumps with tissues from
    her purse
For my grandmother always wears well-turned pumps
that match her purse, I think in case someone
from one of the best families of Aleppo
should run into her—here, in front of the Ken-
    more display

I smile at the midwestern women
as if my grandmother has just said something
    lovely about them
and shrug at my grandmother as if they
had just apologized through me
No one is fooled, but I

hold the door open for everyone
and we all emerge on the sales floor
and lose ourselves in the great common ground
of housewares on markdown.

Source: *E-mails from Scheherazad* (University Press of Florida, 2003).

CHAPTER 9

WORK INSIDE AND OUTSIDE THE HOME

Worldwide, work— both paid and unpaid, and inside and outside the home—is a gendered phenomenon whereby certain activities are coded feminine and others masculine, and where the latter activities tend to be valued more. No matter who actually performs certain kinds of work like housework, it is devalued (even though when men perform household labor, especially child-rearing, it is often noted and celebrated). But the reality is that humans who identify as women are much more likely to do such devalued labor, and to be paid less than those who identify as men for the work they do. So while work is a gendered analytic construct, and there are social discourses and "regimes of truth" that construct meaning for work activities, there are important material realities for individuals performing the tasks of human subsistence.

Most people who identify as women work outside the home whether or not they are married or have children. Indeed, 40 percent of all families with children in the home have women as the primary breadwinner, and a major proportion of these are solo/single women. If you factor in the work that women also do in the home, then women are working very hard. In other words, in the United States and around the world, women work long hours because work for them tends to involve unpaid domestic labor and care of dependent family members as well as paid labor, often performed by "junior partners" as discussed in Chapter 8. In addition, when they do get paid for their work, women tend to earn lower wages compared with men and are less likely to have control over the things they produce and the wages they receive.

In this chapter we examine both domestic unpaid labor and women's employment in the labor force, with the latter discussion addressing the global economy and the changing nature and patterns of women's labor force participation, the dual economy, and the gender gap in wages. Again, although we recognize the problematics of this essentialized category of "women," we also know that society is organized around these gender binaries, research at all levels on this topic is conducted and data collected using these categories, and there are members of a distinct social group who identify as "women" who are involved in real, material practices based on those identities, and who are treated accordingly.

UNPAID LABOR IN THE HOME

Work done in the home is often not considered work at all: It is something done in the name of love, or because, somehow, one group of humans is better programmed to do this than others. The humorist Dave Barry, for example, declares that 85 percent of men in the United States are "cleaning impaired," satirizing men's supposed ineptitude or lack of participation in domestic activities as normalized or natural.

Women on average do about two-thirds of all domestic labor: work, as discussed later in the chapter, that tends to negatively affect their employment status and reduce their economic resources in terms of shorter and more horizontal career ladders and reduced social security benefits. Domestic work, often termed "reproductive labor," involves all the tasks associated with cleaning and household maintenance, purchasing and preparing food, taking care of children and/or aging or sick family members, and garden and yard work. Family work also involves "kin keeping," discussed shortly, which includes taking care of the emotional needs of family members.

Social discourses about gender that associate women, the home, and domesticity reinforce the assumption that housework and child care are feminine work. Such labor tends to be undervalued as women's formal "productive" paid labor in the workforce is prioritized. This is clearly the case in analyses of the effects of economic globalization, where statistics often tend to disregard reproductive labor. Economic globalization can be defined as processes that integrate economies toward a global marketplace or a single world market as illustrated by the rapid growth of transnational corporations and complex networks of production and consumption. Reproductive labor is rarely included in a country's national

---

GENDER AND HOUSEWORK

A simple Internet search on housework's impact on relationships reveals how a divide still exists when it comes to the division of labor within family structures. Hundreds of both popular and scholarly articles all agree that when it comes to housework, gender plays a significant role in who is actually doing the work.

Using the following resources, create a labor timeline that shows the division of housework progression since the 1950s. What is your assessment of the following trends?

1. How has the division of housework labor shifted with the increase of women in heterosexual relationships working outside of the home? What is the change when children are added to the home?
2. How does gender impact the division of housework in same-sex relationships?
3. What is the effect on the success of a relationship when labor is equitably divided? When it is not?
4. Does the household labor division that children experience affect how they will share housework in their adult relationships?

5. What are ways that traditional models of division of labor within the home can be challenged through the use of data and statistics?

Resources

Ausburg, Katrin, Iacovou, Maria, and Nicoletti, Cheti. (2017, August). "Housework Share Between Partners: Experimental Evidence on Gender-Specific Preferences." *Social Science Research*, 66, 118–139. https://www.sciencedirect.com/science/article/pii/S0049089X16302228

Burkeman, Oliver. (2018, February). "Dirty Secret: Why Is There Still a Housework Gender Gap?" *Guardian*. https://www.theguardian.com/inequality/2018/feb/17/dirty-secret-why-housework-gender-gap

National Science Foundation. (2008). "Chore Wars: Men, Women and Housework." https://www.nsf.gov/discoveries/disc_images.jsp?cntn_id=111458

Tejada, Chloe. (2017, September 9). "Women Still Do More Chores at Home Than Men, Study Finds." *Huffington Post*. https://www.huffingtonpost.ca/2017/09/27/women-chores-home_a_23224733/

LEARNING ACTIVITY

DOMESTIC WORKERS' BILL OF RIGHTS

In 2010 New York became the first state to pass a domestic workers' bill of rights, giving nannies, housekeepers, and household cooks the same protections as other workers. The campaign by Domestic Workers United leading up to it took six years of work, lobbying, and meetings. Along the way, the group made some eye-opening discoveries: Only 10 percent of domestic workers are provided with health insurance, 26 percent make less than minimum wage, and 33 percent had been verbally or physically abused by an employer. Ninety-three percent of New York's domestic workers are women, and 95 percent are people of color, and so those who are already marginalized and vulnerable are most affected by the lack of laws protecting domestic workers. To learn more, visit Domestic Workers United's website at www.domesticworkersunited.org.

To learn more about movements for domestic workers' rights worldwide, visit the website of the International Domestic Workers' Network Federation at http://www.idwfed.org/en and the National Domestic Workers Alliance at www.domesticworkers.org.

What does New York's bill provide for domestic workers? Why are these conditions important for domestic workers? Where are there other campaigns for a domestic workers' bill of rights? What is the status of domestic workers' rights in your state?

statistics of productivity such as the GNP (gross national product) and GDP (gross domestic product). See the sidebar "Domestic Workers' Bill of Rights" above for more information about the transference of reproductive labor to the paid labor force.

In the reading "Women Are Just Better at This Stuff," Rose Hackman focuses on the politics of housework in contemporary U.S. society. She emphasizes that housework is degrading, not because it involves manual labor but, instead, because it is embedded in degrading relationships that have the potential to reproduce domination from one generation to the next. When it comes to domestic work, it is also important to note that these hierarchies are not only gendered but classed and racialized. Although women generally are doing less housework today than in the past, the more privileged are more likely to outsource the work. In other words, a contemporary solution to the housework problem among those who can afford it is to hire someone else to do the work. That "someone" is most likely a working-class woman and very often a woman of color. Paid domestic work is one occupation traditionally held by women of color; it is also an occupation that is usually nonunionized and has low pay, little power, and few or no benefits. In addition, individual workers who used to contract services directly with employers are now being replaced by corporate cleaning services that control a good portion of the housecleaning business. Scholars emphasize that this new relationship between cleaners and those who can afford to employ them abolishes the traditional "mistress-maid" relationship and allows middle-class people who are sensitive to the political issues involved with hiring servants to avoid confronting these issues and feel less guilt.

Two major research findings emerge in the data on housework. The first concerns the amount of time certain individuals spend on household work, and the second the kinds of domestic labor they perform. Although these studies are revealing in helping us understand the gendered arrangement of our everyday lives and the implications for individuals, interpersonal relationships, families, and communities, it is important to recognize that traditional research on domestic labor is unfortunately fraught with assumptions about gender at the very same time that it uses gender as an interpretive lens. Note how this approach takes relatively fixed notions of woman and man and is centered on cisgender, heterosexual relationships.

With this in mind, let us now turn to the first research finding: time spent in domestic labor. According to the 2018 Bureau of Labor Statistics American Time Use Survey, individuals who identify as women perform about 14 hours a week and those who identify as men less than 5 hours. Most studies pin married men's contribution to housework at about 4 hours per week, up from 2 hours in 1965 but only slightly more than they were doing in

---

BRIDGING THE GENDER GAP IN AGRICULTURE

Phebean Adekunle

Agricultural produce are substances that sustain us as humans, irrespective of our location around the world. Women living in rural areas are identified as active contributors to the availability of food in local and global markets because they resort to farming as an option to sustain themselves and their families while the men in their households oftentimes migrate to cities in search of paid work. Women farmers perform tasks such as preparing and sowing seeds on farmlands, applying manures and fertilizers to plants, weeding, and harvesting crops with their hands. In some communities, farmwork also includes rearing animals and fishing. This means that the agricultural sector is the largest employer of women around the world.

Women typically make up 43 percent of the agricultural labor force in developing countries, and over 50 percent in Africa and Asia. In India, 80 to 100 million women (33 percent) are employed in the agricultural industry, while in Africa alone, 80 percent of the agricultural produce are delivered by rural women. Furthermore, 75 percent of women make up the agricultural labor force in Nigeria (Idowu, 2013).

Despite these great numbers, women lack control of and access to land resources that are significant to their income autonomy and growth in the informal economy to which agriculture belongs. Compared to men, women farmers are invisible in policies that affect change; this is due to existing inequity in gender roles across rural and urban communities that perpetuate the visible gender gap in the agricultural sector. Women farmers also have less access to machineries and fertilizers that can facilitate a reduction in the amount of time they spend on the farm and also increase the number of harvested crops for high income.

Moreover, if the population of the world is expected to increase to 9.1 billion people by 2050, ensuring zero hunger for this anticipated number would require a 70 percent increase in food production around the world. The question then is, How many humans would be needed

to achieve this goal? If women's contribution to the sustenance of the family, community, and the world remains undervalued, especially in the agricultural sector, that is an indicator that the marginalization and disempowerment of women will continue. To bridge the gap in the labor force, it is important to create an inclusive environment where women are recognized for their immense contribution to food security and are encouraged to participate in agricultural training and research, and given increased access to credit facilities that will support their empowerment.

LEARNING ACTIVITY

Visit the farmers market in your community and observe the number of women traders selling produce. Does your observation match any of the notable facts mentioned in this section? Talk to women farmers about their experiences. What do they suggest could be done to support women farmers in the United States and around the world? How can women farmers be made more visible and their work more valued?

You can read more about this topic by copying these sources in your browser.

http://www.wfo-oma.org/women-in-agriculture/
articles/the-role-of-rural-women-in-agriculture
.html
http://www.worldbank.org/en/news/
feature/2017/03/07/women-in-agriculture-the-
agents-of-change-for-the-food-system
http://indianexpress.com/article/opinion/columns/
the-invisible-women-farmers-agriculture-
labourer-4714072/
https://www.farmersweekly
.co.za/opinion/by-invitation/
the-crucial-role-of-women-in-african-agriculture/
http://www.fao.org/publications/sofa/2015/en/

Resources

Idowu, A. A. (2013). "Women's Rights, Violence, and Gender Discrimination: The Nigerian Circumstances." In Ronke Iyabowale Ako-Nai (ed.), *Gender and Power Relations in Nigeria* (pp. 31–45). Lanham, MD: Lexington Books.

1995. However, fathers have nearly tripled the amount of time they spend in direct care of children since 1965 to 8 hours a week, with more than half of these gains occurring since the 1990s. Also, twice as many men today are stay-at-home dads than 20 years ago, with four times as many saying they are doing it to care for their family. Still, although numbers have "tripled," they are still relatively low compared to women's child care hours, which is almost twice this figure at 14 hours a week. Nonheterosexual couples have more equitable divisions of domestic labor than heterosexual couples, but the partner who engages in more child care also tends to do more "feminine" household tasks.

A 2017 study of mostly white, educated, and middle-class heterosexual couples by Ohio State University researchers Drs. Claire Kamp Dush, Sarah Schoppe-Sullivan, and Jill Yavorsky followed families for three months after the birth of a first child. They found that although fathers' child care tended on the average to be lower than mothers' when both parents were working outside the home, the gender gap was smallest during the working week. On weekends, days off from work, and holidays, the researchers found that when mothers performed child care and housework, fathers relaxed or engaged in leisure activities 47 percent and 35 percent of the time, respectively. When fathers performed child care and housework, women relaxed or engaged in leisure activities 16 percent and 19 percent of the time, respectively. In hours spent in direct child care, mothers worked for an average of 99 minutes on work days and 92 minutes on non-employed-work days, while fathers worked an average of 38 minutes on work days and 34 minutes on non-employed work days. An interesting aspect of this research was that this held also for couples who considered themselves egalitarian and strove to provide gender equity in their relationship. This distinction between attitudes about sharing domestic labor and actually doing it is important here. As the 2018 U.S. General Social Survey (GSS) indicates, U.S. adults' positive attitudes toward gender egalitarianism have continued to increase since the mid-2000s. The amount of time men spend in reproductive labor, however, has not kept pace.

Sociologists suggest that once married, women do about twice the amount of work in the home as their spouses, increasing their stress and anxiety. When women marry, unfortunately most gain an average of 14 hours a week of domestic labor, compared with men, who gain an average of 90 minutes. Husbands tend to create more work for wives than they perform. A study from the University of Michigan estimated this husband-created labor at about 7 hours a week. This can cause stress-related problems and mental and physical exhaustion for women trying to juggle family responsibilities and paid employment. A 2018 study of 24 countries worldwide found that guilt over not being able to perform the domestic work that working-outside-the-home women still accept as their responsibility leads to stress that harms their health.

Drs. Daniel Carlson, Amanda Miller, and Sharon Sassler have noted the increase in contemporary couples sharing household tasks.[1] Although less than one-third of the respondents in their study actually shared housework equally, those couples who did reported the highest marital and sexual satisfaction. Shopping in particular was an activity

---

1 "Gendered Division of Housework and Couples' Sexual Relationships: A Reexamination," *Journal of Marriage and the Family* 78 (2016): 975–995.

that seemed to produce greater relationship satisfaction, especially for men. Those who shared the shopping reported not only greater sexual and relationship satisfaction than men who did the majority of this work, but also greater satisfaction than men whose partner did the majority of shopping. For women, the shared task that mattered most for their satisfaction with their relationship was dishwashing. Sharing responsibility for dishwashing was the single biggest source of satisfaction for women among all the household tasks, and lack of sharing of this task the single biggest source of discontent. Although this relationship between sharing of household tasks and interpersonal satisfaction holds true for LGBTQ couples, again it is important to recognize the more diverse gendered ways people behave in various kinds of household arrangements.

An Organization for Economic Cooperation and Development (OECD) report emphasized that domestic labor was one of the most important aspects of gender equality worldwide.[2] Indeed, cross-national comparisons of the gender gap in housework drawing on data from Japan, North America, Scandinavia, Russia, and Hungary by the Institute for Social Research (ISR) indicate that North American men are less egalitarian (meaning equally sharing power) than Scandinavians (Swedish men do an average of 24 hours of housework a week), but more egalitarian than Japanese men. Russian women do the least amount of housework, although they work the most total hours (employed plus domestic work), and Hungarian women do the most housework and have the least amount of leisure time.

All these comparative data must be interpreted with caution as questions are raised in terms of how household labor is defined, whether methods for reporting are standardized, and whether a discussion of "women doing less housework" means overall hours or as a proportion of total hours performed by women and men.

One of the most significant issues to consider in terms of the reliability of this housework data is that much family work is difficult to measure. This is especially true of the work involved in "kin keeping": remembering birthdays, sending cards, preparing for holidays, organizing vacations, keeping in touch with relatives, and providing "spousal career support" by entertaining, volunteering, and networking. These tasks are time-consuming and involve emotional work that is not easily quantified and is often invisible. Women tend to perform the bulk of this kin-keeping work. It is important to note that such work cannot easily be replaced with hired labor (which of course is usually the labor of another woman, often a woman of color or poor woman). Rose Hackman discusses this in her reading, focusing on emotional labor as a form of domestic labor that tends to be normalized in relationships as a particular gendered performance and does not reflect inherent and essentialized traits. Hackman makes the case for recognizing these repeated, taxing, and under-acknowledged acts as an important form of unpaid labor. Also implicit here is the reminder about the ways paid labor—and especially low-wage, service industry jobs, where "service-with-a-smile" is expected—mirrors gendered expectations in the home.

Finally, when it comes to household work, women seem to be better at multitasking and, as a result, often underestimate the work they do because they are performing

---

2   "Time spent in paid and unpaid work, by sex"; https://stats.oecd.org/index.aspx?queryid=54757

LEARNING ACTIVITY

WHO DOES THE WORK AT YOUR SCHOOL AND IN YOUR HOME?

Use the following charts to discover who does various kinds of work at your school and in your home. Discuss your findings with your classmates. What patterns do you notice? What do your findings suggest about how systems of inequality function in the institution of work, both inside and outside the home?

WHO DOES THE WORK AT YOUR SCHOOL?

Job Description	Gender	Race
Top administration		
Teaching		
Secretarial		
Groundskeeping		
Electrical/carpentry		
Janitorial		
Food preparation		
Security		
Intercollegiate coaching		

WHO DOES THE WORK IN YOUR HOME?

Job Description	Person in the Family Who Generally Does This Job	Gender of Person Who Generally Does This Job	Hours per Week Spent in Doing This Job
Laundry			
Mowing the lawn			
Maintaining the car			
Buying the groceries			
Cooking			
Vacuuming			
Washing dishes			
Making beds			
Cleaning bathroom			

multiple tasks at the same time. As a general trend, researchers find all survey respondents overreport the amount of housework and child care they perform, with men overreporting at almost twice the rate of women (about 150 percent compared to 68 percent).

If the first major finding is that irrespective of age, income, and own workload, individuals who identify as women perform the bulk of domestic labor, the second finding concerns the persistent gendered division of household labor: how domestic labor itself is gendered and performed accordingly. This means that individuals do different kinds of work in the home based on their own gender identities. According to U.S. Bureau of Labor Statistics data,[3] on an average day women spend twice as much time preparing food and drink, three times as much time doing interior cleaning, and almost four times as much time doing laundry as do men. Men spend twice as much time doing activities related to lawn, garden, and houseplants, and twice as much time doing interior and exterior maintenance, repairs, and decoration as do women. In other words, women tend to do the repetitive, ongoing, daily kinds of tasks, and men are more likely to perform the less repetitive or seasonal tasks, especially if these tasks involve the use of tools or machines. Studies show that heterosexual couples are more likely to share cooking and child care and less likely to share cleaning, the bulk of which is overwhelmingly performed by females (women and girls). Some tasks are seen as more masculine and some as more feminine. In this way, gender plays a significant role in the types of housework men and women perform.

It is important to note that the "feminine," frequently performed tasks are less optional for families and are also more likely to be thought of as boring by all respondents irrespective of gender. Among heterosexual couples who do share household work by each taking different tasks, there seems to be a focus on "equally shared" rather than "equally divided" tasks. "Equally shared" means that couples negotiate who does what to provide equity rather than divide up all tasks and each do an equal amount (equally divided). Although equal sharing takes into account personal preferences, efficiency, and vested interest and often is more "workable," it can run the risk of replicating gender-stereotyped behaviors that ultimately lead to inequities in the division of labor in the home. This is affirmed by a 2017 Canadian study by Rebecca Horne and colleagues who examined how household tasks were divided for couples across diverse life stages.[4] They found that irrespective of relative income, marital status, and responsibilities toward children, gender was the biggest predictor for who did what and for how long.

Many readers probably remember their father doing the housework or have a partner who identifies as a man who shares equally in domestic labor. According to several studies, men with a higher education are more likely to pick up and pitch in. Although there have been changes over the past decades, with more men taking on household responsibilities and "helping out," it is important to note how the term "helping" assumes that it is someone else's responsibility. Nonetheless, it is important to state that housework, although often dreary and repetitive, can also be creative and more interesting than some paid labor. And, although raising children is among the hardest work of all, it is also full of rewards. Those who do not participate in household work and child care miss the joys associated with this work even while they have the privilege of being free to do other things.

---

3 American Time Use Survey, https://www.bls.gov/tus/charts/household.htm
4 Horne, Rebecca, Johnson, Matthew, Galambos, Nancy, and Krahn, Harvey. "Time, Money, or Gender? Predictors of the Division of Household Labour Across Life Stages." *Sex Roles* 78, no. 11 (2018): 731–734.

HISTORICAL MOMENT

WAGES FOR HOUSEWORK

Women do two-thirds of the world's work but receive only 5 percent of the world's income. Worldwide, women's unpaid labor is estimated at $11 trillion. Early in the women's movement, feminists made the connection between women's unpaid labor and the profits accumulated by the businesses that relied on women's household and child-rearing work to support the waged laborers who produced goods and capital. They argued, then, that women should be compensated for the domestic labor that is taken for granted and yet depended on to maintain capitalist economies.

Several groups agitated for wages for housework, and in 1972 the International Wages for Housework (WFH) Campaign was organized by women in developing and industrialized countries to agitate for compensation for the unpaid work women do. They argued that this goal could best be reached by dismantling the military-industrial complex. In 1975 the International Black Women for Wages for Housework (IBWWFH) Campaign, an international network of women of color, formed to work for compensation for unwaged and low-waged work and to ensure that challenging racism was not separated from challenging sexism and other forms of discrimination.

Few American feminists advocated this position, although it constituted a significant position for feminists in Europe. Some feminists opposed the campaign, arguing that to pay women for housework would reinforce women's role in the home and strengthen the existing gendered division of labor.

Both the WFH and IBWWFH campaigns remained active into the early 2000s, advocating change in the ways women's work is valued and rewarded. They were involved in a campaign for pay equity and a global women's strike.

PAID LABOR

TRENDS AND LEGALITIES

The reading "A Brief History of Working Women" by sociologists Sharlene Hesse-Biber and Gregg Lee Carter reviews the changes in women's labor force participation over the past centuries for different groups of women. Briefly, as U.S. society became industrialized in the nineteenth century, the traditional subsistence economies of producing what families needed to survive from the home, taking in work (like spinning or washing), or working in others' homes or on their land were changed in favor of a more distinct separation between work and home. Factories were established, employees were congregated under one roof (and thus more easily controlled), and emerging technologies started mass-producing goods. Instead of making products in the home for family consumption, people were working outside the home and spending their earnings on these mass-produced goods. Urban centers grew up around these sites of production, and ordinary people tended to work long hours in often very poor conditions. These harsh conditions associated with women's wage labor coincided with continuing domestic servitude in the home. This double day of work was recognized by scholars over a hundred years ago and is still a central aspect of women's lives today.

At the same time that working-class women and children were working in factories, mines, and sweatshops, the middle-class home came to be seen as a haven from the cruel world, and middle-class women were increasingly associated with this sphere. From this developed the "cult of true womanhood": prescriptions for white, middle-class femininity that included piety, purity, and domesticity. Although these notions of femininity could be achieved only by privileged white women given structural arrangements in society, and they were resisted among certain groups, such norms came to influence gender performances. At the same time, some women were starting to enter higher education. With the founding of Oberlin Collegial Institute in 1833, other women's colleges such as Mount Holyoke, Bryn Mawr, and Wellesley were established as the century progressed. In addition, state universities (beginning with Utah in 1850) started admitting women. By the turn of the century, there were cohorts of (mostly privileged white) women who were educated to be full political persons and who helped shape the Progressive Era of the early twentieth century with a focus on reform and civic leadership. These women entered the labor force in relatively large numbers, and many chose a career over marriage and the family.

As the twentieth century progressed, more women entered the public sphere. The years of the Great Depression slowed women's advancement, and it was not until World War II that women were seen working in traditionally male roles in unprecedented numbers. The government encouraged this transition, and many women were, for the first time, enjoying decent wages. All this would end after the war as women were encouraged or forced to return to the home so that men could claim their jobs in the labor force. Child care centers were dismantled, and the conservative messages of the 1950s encouraged women to stay home and partake in the rapidly emerging consumer society. The social and cultural upheavals of the 1960s and the civil rights and women's movements fought for legislation to help women gain more power in the workplace.

The most important legislative gains of this civil rights era include, first, the Equal Pay Act of 1963, which protects men and women who perform substantially equal work in the same establishment from sex-based wage discrimination. This is the "equal pay for equal work" law. Second, Title VII of the Civil Rights Act of 1964 prohibits discrimination in employment based on race, color, religion, sex, and/or national origin in establishments with 15 or more employees. It makes it illegal for employers to discriminate against these protected classes in terms of the conditions and privileges of employment (hiring, firing, pay, promotion, etc.). Title VII says that gender cannot be used as a criterion in employment except where there is a "*bona fide* occupational qualification," meaning it is illegal unless an employer can prove that gender is crucial to job performance (for example, hiring male janitors for men's bathrooms). For the most part, the law had little influence until 1972 with the enforcement of the Equal Employment Opportunity Commission that had been established in 1965. The courts have fine-tuned Title VII over the years, and it remains the most important legislation that protects working women and people of color. For example, in 2009 the Lilly Ledbetter Fair Pay Act, the first bill signed into law by U.S. President Barack Obama, amended Title VII by stating that the 180-day statute of limitations for filing an equal-pay lawsuit regarding pay discrimination resets with each new paycheck affected by that discriminatory action. This legislation overturned previous time limits imposed on discrimination claims. Lilly Ledbetter was a production supervisor at a Goodyear tire plant in Alabama who filed an equal-pay lawsuit regarding pay discrimination under Title VII, 6 months before her early retirement in 1998. The courts gave opposite verdicts and eventually the case went to the U.S. Supreme Court in 2007, which ruled that Ledbetter's complaint was null because of time limits. The 2009 act amended this ruling.

In 1976 the Supreme Court expanded the interpretation of Title VII to include discrimination on the basis of pregnancy as sex discrimination, and in 1993 the Family and

LGBTQ EMPLOYMENT LAW

Lauren Grant

While the 2015 Supreme Court decision made marriage equality the law of the land, overturning marriage bans in 13 states and authorizing same-sex marriage in all 50 states, the ruling did not address the ongoing pressing problem of discrimination against LGBTQ people in employment. The UN Universal Declaration of Human Rights declares that everyone has the right "to work, to free choice of employment, to just and favourable conditions of work and to protection against unemployment . . . the right to just and favourable remuneration ensuring for [them]self and [their] family an existence worthy of human dignity, and supplemented, if necessary, by other means of social protection."[1]

In reality, enforcements of such protections often fail to meet the needs of the persons they are meant to protect as only 20 states prohibit discrimination on the basis of sexual and gender identity in the employment sector, and just 2 states prohibit discrimination on the basis of sexual identity only.[2] A Miami schoolteacher was fired from a Catholic school after she posted wedding photos online. In addition, in 2017 Trump administration lawyers argued that the Civil Rights Act of 1964 does not protect LGBT Americans from being fired.

In 2018, however, the U.S. Court of Appeals for the Sixth Circuit ruled that Title VII does include protection for transgender workers in the case of a funeral home worker who was fired when she announced she was transitioning and would begin to comply with the funeral home's dress code for women. Overall, however, many LGBTQ employees report discrimination at work but have little recourse in states that do not provide protections for LGBTQ workers.

Visit the Human Rights Campaign webpage here: https://www.hrc.org/state-maps/employment to find out your state laws on LGBTQ employment.

The American Bar Association claims that nearly 6.5 million employees in the United States belong to the LGBTQ community. Although the overwhelming majority of Americans believe that LGBTQ community members ought to be protected from employment discrimination, Congress has done very little to pass legislation that provides a legal backing for such protections.[3]

National Public Radio recently published a report that looked at the different kinds of discrimination most commonly experienced by those in the employment sector who identify as LGBTQ community members. The report claims that overall 57 percent of all LGBTQ people have experienced slurs at work, and 53 percent report being targeted with insensitive or offensive comments about their sexual or gender identity.[4] Additionally, LGBTQ people experience wage discrimination.[5] The Center for American Progress advises that given the potential for employment discrimination for LGBTQ people, "we need stronger laws and policies to [be put] in place to ensure all workers have equal workplace protections under the law no matter their sexual orientation or gender identity."[6]

What laws or policy changes do you think need to occur in order for LGBTQ people to feel a sense of protection under the law when it comes to employment?

1. Trevor G. Gates, "Why Employment Discrimination Matters: Well-Being and the Queer Employee," *Journal of Workplace Rights* 16, no. 1 (2012): 107–128.

2. Human Rights Campaign, "State Maps of Laws & Policies," www.hrc.org/state-maps/employment.

3. "Discrimination in Employment Issues for LGBT Individuals," ABA, October 13, 2017.

4. Harvard T. H. Chan School of Public Health, "Discrimination in America: Experiences and Views of LGBTQ Americans," November 2017, https://www.npr.org/documents/2017/nov/npr-discrimination-lgbtq-final.pdf.

5. https://www.americanprogress.org/issues/lgbt/news/2012/04/16/11494/the-gay-and-transgender-wage-gap/ and https://www.usatoday.com/story/money/2018/06/06/lgbtq-millennials-financial-survey/659754002/

6. Crosby Burns, "The Gay and Transgender Wage Gap," Center for American Progress, January 30, 2013, www.americanprogress.org/issues/lgbt/news/2012/04/16/11494/the-gay-and-transgender-wage-gap/ and https://www.usatoday.com/story/money/2018/06/06/lgbtq-millennials-financial-survey/659754002/.

Medical Leave Act was passed. It protected all workers by guaranteeing unpaid leave and protection of employment as a result of caring for a sick family member or the birth or adoption of a child. In 1986 the Supreme Court declared sexual harassment a form of sex discrimination and in 1993 broadened this ruling by stating that people suing on the basis of sexual harassment did not have to prove that they had suffered "concrete psychological harm." Sexual harassment legislation made a distinction between *quid pro quo* (sexual favors are required in return for various conditions of employment) and hostile work environment (no explicit demand for an exchange of sexual acts for work-related conditions but being subjected to a pattern of harassment as part of the work environment). In a poll conducted by the *Wall Street Journal* and NBC, 44 percent of working women said they had been discriminated against because of their gender and one-third said they had experienced sexual harassment. Scholars emphasize that such harassment denies employment opportunities and threatens physical safety and integrity. It is important to note that although some states have enforced state- and local-level legal protections against harassment targeted at LGBTQ individuals, currently 30 states have no such protections. Trans people are especially prone to job discrimination and harassment and may have little to no recourse.

The Age Discrimination in Employment Act, which was enacted in 1968 and amended in 1978 and 1986, outlaws mandatory retirement and prohibits employers with 20 or more employees from discriminating on the basis of age, protecting individuals who are 40 years of age and older. In 2005 courts restricted this law by interpreting it narrowly. Generally groups suing under Title VII of the Civil Rights Act of 1964 do not need to prove intentional discrimination and can declare "disparate impact" and claim they were disproportionately harmed by an employer's policy or behavior. Many courts now refuse to allow older workers to bring disparate-impact claims and require them to prove intentional harm. Fourth, the Americans with Disabilities Act (ADA) of 1990 prohibited employment discrimination against those with disabilities.

Finally, affirmative action policies that encouraged employers to take gender and race into account in terms of hiring were first initiated by President Kennedy in the 1960s. Since that time, affirmative action has helped diversify the workplace and encouraged the hiring of women and people of color. However, there is a lot of misunderstanding as well as serious hostility associated with affirmative action, as evidenced by the dismantling of affirmative action guidelines in many states. Basically, affirmative action creates positive steps to increase the representation of women and people of color in areas of employment, education, and government from which they may have been historically excluded. Affirmative action encourages the diversification of the job pool, but it does not encourage the hiring of unqualified women or people of color. It is a misunderstanding of these policies to think that white males now have a hard time getting jobs because they are being undercut by unqualified women or people of color. As of this writing, President Trump has limited the extent to which universities can use race in college admission protocol.

THE DUAL LABOR MARKET AND THE CHANGING ECONOMY

As the twenty-first century progresses it is important to understand the changing nature of the workplace in the United States and the connections between U.S. corporate capitalism and the global economy. Capitalism is an economic system based on the pursuit of profit and the principle of private ownership. Such a system creates inequality because this profit comes in part from surplus value created from the labor of workers. In other words, workers produce more value than they receive in wages, with this difference or surplus being reinvested into capital accumulation and corporate profit. The U.S. economy is able to maintain this profit accumulation through the perpetuation of a "dual labor market" that provides a "primary" market, with

IDEAS FOR ACTIVISM

- Advocate to your elected representatives for an increase in the minimum wage.
- Encourage your school to analyze pay equity and to make corrections where needed.
- Write your elected representatives to encourage legislation and funding for child care.

- Investigate exploitative employment practices of major national and multinational corporations and launch boycotts to demand improved conditions for workers.
- Encourage your elected representatives to support affirmative action.

relatively high wages and employee benefits and protections for workers, and a "secondary" market, where workers (disproportionately women and people of color) receive lower wages, fewer benefits, and less opportunity for advancement. For example, employees in the beauty industry tend to be working in the secondary market. Workers, such as those who work in nail salons, are often exposed to hazardous toxins that cause occupational health risks. These workers are often likely to be women of color earning very low pay and few if any benefits.

The dual labor market also maintains profits through globalization and U.S.-based strategies that include, first, the development of new technologies (especially electronic communications) that have revolutionized work and, in some cases, replaced workers and made some jobs obsolete. In cases where technology cannot replace workers, jobs have been exported overseas to take advantage of lower wages. Second, there has been a huge increase in the service sector and a shift from manufacturing to service-sector work. This has brought a change in the kinds of skills workers need in order to compete in this sector, reflecting the dual labor market and its distinctions between high-skilled service work (e.g., financial planning, public relations) and low-paid and low-skilled service work (food service, child and elderly care). Women and people of color are more likely to be found in the latter part of the service sector, illustrating the ways the economy is a conduit for the maintenance of systems of inequality and privilege. Consequences of the dual labor market are discussed in the following sections on women's labor force participation and issues of pay equity.

Third, economies around the world are increasingly connected to, and positioned differently within, a global economy. As explained in other chapters, globalization refers to the processes by which regional economies, societies, and cultures have become integrated through an interconnected global network of communication, transportation, and trade. As mentioned earlier, economic globalization is a component of these processes and involves the integration of national economies toward a global marketplace or a single world market as illustrated by the rapid growth of transnational corporations and complex networks of production and consumption. Wealthy nations in the global north have more influence in this global marketplace, in part because of their influence on and with such institutions as the World Trade Organization (WTO) and the World Bank. The WTO is an international financial institution that regulates trade and provides loans to developing countries for capital programs with certain social and economic strings attached, too complex to go into here. Basically the WTO supervises and regulates international trade deals by providing frameworks for negotiating and formalizing trade agreements. As of this writing, the WTO currently has 164 members and 23 observer governments. Liberia and Afghanistan joined in 2016. It is governed by a general council and holds a conference every two years. The World Bank is involved with loans and foreign investment and also has power over international trade and economic globalization generally. China became a member of the World Bank in 1980 and is increasingly becoming a powerful economic force in contributing a significant proportion of economic global growth each year.

Global multinational corporations have grown in size and influence, and mergers have resulted in a smaller number of corporations controlling a larger part of the global market. They have immense power and influence and often no longer correspond to national borders, functioning outside the jurisdiction of nation-states. Because many U.S.-based corporations rely on the cheaper, nonunionized labor force and looser environmental restrictions outside the United States, much manufacturing and increasingly service work is done overseas. Such processes of economic globalization involve vast numbers of women traveling across state borders and serving as cheap labor. In addition globalization encourages the immigration of women in both the formal economy (electronics and garment work, for example) and the informal economy (child care, sex work, street vendoring). As will be discussed in Chapter 11, the military has close ties to globalizing economies, creating what scholars call the military-industrial complex. Military operations and the presence of international military forces in developing countries serve in part to "stabilize" these nations and protect foreign business interests such as oil or other resources, often in the name of forging "peace" or "democracy."

The effects of the global economy include profound inequalities between rich and poor nations as well as between rich and poor citizens within individual countries. Often these inequalities are based on older inequities resulting from nineteenth- and early-twentieth-century colonization and imperialism. For individual women, although multinational corporations do give women a wage, they often upset subsistence economies and cause migration and cultural dislocation, which encourages increasing consumerism, sex trading, and the pollution of fragile environments. Women often work in poor and unhealthy conditions for little pay. In addition, many thousands of U.S. workers have lost their jobs as corporations have moved productive processes overseas. These events are not random but part of a broader pattern of global capitalist expansion.

WOMEN'S LABOR FORCE PARTICIPATION

When it comes to the labor force employment and status of those who identify as women, their notable progress is reflected in the relative increases among women in educational attainment, earnings, and occupational diversity, and an increased presence in leadership positions overall. However, women lag behind men and continue to face significant obstacles to economic stability and security such as occupational segregation and barriers to higher-level positions, lower wages and unequal pay, inadequate workplace flexibility given their tendency to perform a majority of domestic labor, and a greater likelihood that they will live in poverty. All of these barriers are exacerbated for women of color, who still lag behind white women on a majority of these dimensions.

Sexual harassment comprises a particular barrier for workers generally and women workers in particular. As we will discuss in the next chapter, sexual harassment ranges from misogynous and racist banter to sexual assault and abusive practices that demand sexual contact in return for job security and advancement. These practices are systematically incorporated into the structures of U.S. work life. The reading "The Age of Patriarchy: How an Unfashionable Idea Became a Rallying Cry for Feminism Today" by Charlotte Higgins addresses sexual harassment among celebrities and public officials and discusses the ways the #MeToo movement has helped shape the resurgence of patriarchy as a concept, capturing what she calls "the peculiar elusiveness of gendered power." She provides a history of the term and its usage, and encourages you to see the world through its multiple lenses.

A major change in terms of trends in workforce participation has been the increase in the number of women in paid employment or looking for work over the last century. According to a 2018 report from the Bureau of Labor Statistics, they made up 18 percent of the labor force in 1900, almost 30 percent in 1950, and almost 50 percent of all workers in 2018. About 57 percent of women in the United States are working in the labor force, and of these, about a third are women of color (approximately 62 percent are white, 17 percent Latina, 13 percent African American, and 6 percent Asian American). The projected numbers of women workers by 2025 anticipates a 30 percent increase for Latinas, an 11 percent increase for African Americans, a 24 percent increase for Asian Americans, and a 2 percent decrease for whites.

Approximately 71 percent of mothers with children younger than age 18 and 58 percent of those with infant children are in the labor force. In addition, about two-thirds of mothers generally are breadwinners or co-breadwinners. Only approximately one in five families involves a stay-at-home mother who does not also work outside the home, and, as already mentioned in Chapter 8, almost half of U.S. households with children younger than age 18 now include a mother who is either the sole or primary earner for her family. This means that women are more likely to be not only the primary caregivers in a family, but increasingly the primary breadwinners too. In terms of the latter, this reflects evolving family dynamics where it has become more acceptable and expected for married women to join the workforce, even those with young children, and especially for single women to raise children alone.

Scholars who address the contemporary situation of U.S. mothers working in both the labor force and at home emphasize the relative benefits for mothers in terms of physical and mental health—and especially lower rates of depression—of working outside the home. Wives' employment also lowers couples' risk of divorce in the United States, unless wives are compelled to work outside the home out of economic necessity and against their wishes, in which case they have the least happy marriages. An interesting finding is that although employed mothers today spend less time with their children than homemakers do, the former still spend more time with their children than stay-at-home mothers did in 1965. This reflects the increasingly child-focused aspect of contemporary families.

Effective labor force participation by parents requires affordable, accessible, and good-quality child care. The United States is unique among developed countries in leaving day care almost entirely to the private market and ranks last place among developed nations for support of working families. Many families spend a substantial portion of their monthly

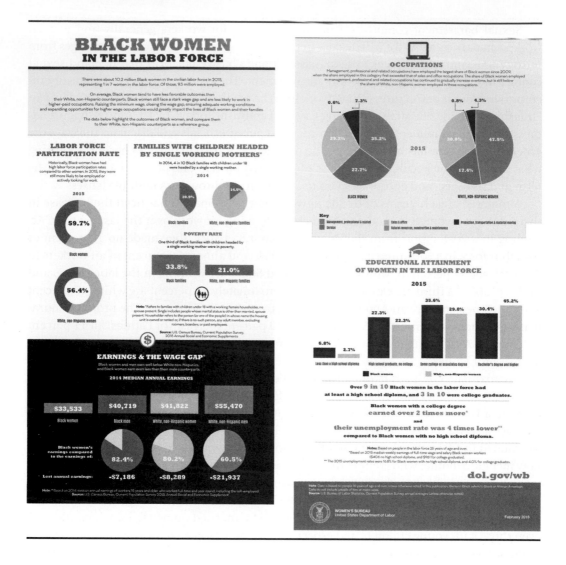

income on child care. In addition, women are more likely to work part time than men are (about 25 percent compared to 11 percent) because of their caretaking responsibilities. Because unemployment, retirement, and other benefits are contingent on full-time work, women, for example, receive lower Social Security checks than men. This is because worker benefits are calculated on their 35 highest-earning years and women lose an average of 12 years out of the paid labor force. Many scholars and activists emphasize that these caregiving years should be taken out of the equation or given a monetary value.

Given the large number of women in the labor force, what kinds of work are they doing? The answer is everything. Women are working in all segments of the labor force. At the same time, however, women are much more likely to be found in some sectors than others and are crowded into fewer fields, many of which are characterized as secondary sector jobs in the dual labor market. This aspect of segregating women and men into different jobs is called

$15 MINIMUM WAGE CAMPAIGN

Whitney Archer Jones

What is now a global movement in 300 cities across six continents, the Fight for $15, began in 2012 when 200 fast-food workers walked off the job in New York City demanding $15/hour and union rights (Fight for $15, n.d.). It has now become one of the most successful movements in the United States for an increased minimum wage in the last 40 years (Huizar & Gebreselassie 2016). This push for equitable pay works in tandem with the efforts of other groups focused on social justice. For example, the Fight for $15 is directly linked to goals of Black Lives Matter as well as the unfinished civil rights and women's rights movements that laid the foundation for today's fights for labor rights (Huizar & Gebreselassie, 2016; Leadership Conference Education Fund [LCEF] and Georgetown Center on Poverty and Inequality [GCPI], 2018).

In 1938, the Fair Labor Standards Act (FSLA), signed by President Franklin Delano Roosevelt, established the first federal minimum wage law. The FSLA set the minimum hourly wage at 25 cents, capped the workweek at 44 hours, and banned oppressive child labor (Grossman, 1978). The current federal minimum wage as of this writing, $7.25/hour, equates to an annual income of $15,080 for a full-time, year-round worker (RaisetheMinimumWage.com). Tipped workers may earn even less. Federal law allows tipped workers to be paid as little as $2.13/hour, a wage set in 1991, as long as earnings from tips bring up their hourly rate to the $7.25 minimum (LCEF and GCPI, 2018). Set in 2009, the current federal minimum wage has since lost 30 percent of its value (RaisetheMinimumWage.com) and is not a living wage. Forty-two percent of working people in the United States make less than $15 per hour (LCEF and GCPI, 2018), and women and people of color are overrepresented in this group: The majority of African American (54.1 percent), Latino (59.5 percent), and close to half of women (48.1 percent) workers in the United States earn less than $15/hour (Huizar & Gebreselassie 2016).

Movements for higher minimum wages are happening at the federal, state, and local levels. On January 1, 2018, minimum wages increased in 18 states and 19 cities, with additional increases in 3 more states and 18 cities/counties anticipated in the future (Lathrop 2017). It is important to interrogate current pay and wealth gaps as legacies of slavery and settler colonialism. When the FSLA was passed, it was crafted to maintain the racial order of Jim Crow laws and did not provide protections in occupations where African Americans were a majority of the labor force (LCEF and GCPI, 2018). On the federal level, the Raise the Wage Act, which proposes to raise the federal minimum wage to $15/hour by 2024, is stalled. Thirty percent of the workforce, nearly 41.5 million workers, would directly or indirectly benefit from raising the minimum wage to $15/hour by 2024 (Cooper 2017). Progress made through the Fight for $15 has been threatened under the Trump administration and its attack on unions; a crucial tool is fighting labor rights and fair pay (LCEF and GCPI, 2018). Raising the minimum wage is not just an issue of economic justice but one of racial justice and gender equity. A $15/hour minimum wage will not alone compensate for the legacies of exploited, uncompensated, and restricted participation in U.S. social and economic life, but it has the potential to assist in narrowing the pay and wealth gaps for people of color and women, and it could significantly impact future generations (Huizar & Gebreselassie, 2016).

Follow the progress of the Fight for $15 movement at https://fightfor15.org/, and visit https://raisetheminimumwage.com/ to view their interactive minimum wage map and to learn about active campaigns for raising minimum wages.

Works Cited

Cooper, D. (2017, April 26). "Raising the Minimum Wage to $15 by 2024 Would Lift Wages for 41 Million American Workers." Economic Policy Institute. Retrieved from https://www.epi.org/files/pdf/125047.pdf

Fight for $15. (n.d.). "About Us." Retrieved from https://fightfor15.org/about-us/

Grossman, J. (1978). "Fair Labor Standards Act of 1938: Maximum Struggle for a Minimum Wage." *Monthly Labor Review*, 101(6), 22–30. Retrieved from https://www.dol.gov/general/aboutdol/history/flsa1938

Huizar, L., and Gebreselassie, T. (2016). "What a $15 Minimum Wage Means for Women and Workers of Color" [Policy Brief]. National Employment Law Project. Retrieved from https://s27147.pcdn.co/wp-content/uploads/Policy-Brief-15-Minimum-Wage-Women-Workers-of-Color.pdf

Lathrop, Y. (2017, December 19). "Raises from Coast to Coast in 2018: Workers in 18 States and 19 Cities and Counties Seeing Minimum Wage Increases on January 1." National Employment Law Project. Retrieved from https://www.nelp.org/publication/raises-from-coast-to-coast-in-2018-minimum-wage-increases/

Leadership Conference Education Fund and Georgetown Center on Poverty and Inequality. (2018). "Bare Minimum: Why We Need to Raise Wages for America's Lowest-Paid Families." Retrieved from http://civilrightsdocs.info/pdf/reports/Bare-Minimum.pdf.

horizontal occupational segregation (meaning segregation of women and men across different kinds of jobs). Jobs held by women are often called "pink-collar" and tend to reflect extensions of reproductive labor or unpaid work in the home. Women are segregated into "feminine" occupations (especially working with people, the aged, and the young, replicating unpaid labor in the home) that are valued less than "masculine" occupations (such as working with technology or machines). This, which in part explains the gender gap in wages (discussed next).

Such horizontal occupational segregation is evident in office work: Ninety-five percent of administrative assistants and 82 percent of office clerks are women.[5] Nursing is also very heavily female-dominated: Ninety percent of registered and licensed practical nurses are women. They also predominate in education: 91 percent of teaching assistants, 97 percent of kindergarten and preschool teachers, 81 percent of elementary and middle-school teachers, and 60 percent of secondary schoolteachers are women. Not surprisingly, women congregate in other service-sector jobs: They comprise 89 percent of maids and housekeeping staff, 70 percent of waitstaff, and 85 percent of personal care aides. Finally, 84 percent of social workers are women.

In comparison, U.S. statistics show women's relative absence in STEM (science, technology, engineering, and mathematics) fields: Women comprise only 14 percent of the full-time workforce in engineering and architecture, 25 percent in computer science and mathematics, and 42 percent in life, physical, and social science. Among all women in STEM fields, white and Asian Americans predominate: Only 2 percent of African American women and 2 percent of Latinas work in engineering fields. The number of Native American women in this field is almost nonexistent. In addition, only 2–5 percent of working women are employed in occupations associated with precision production, craft, and repair, and less than 2 percent of electricians are women. These "masculine" occupations tend to be valued more than "feminine" occupations and pay more money independent of who actually performs the work.

Despite these traditional patterns, women's presence in certain once-male-dominated professions has increased somewhat. In 1970, 9 percent of practicing physicians were female, compared with about 35 percent in 2017. Not surprisingly, therefore, percentages are higher among newly licensed physicians and decrease as physician age climbs. Currently women make up approximately 51 percent of medical school applicants—although, as we discuss later, they are paid approximately 26 percent less, have difficulties accessing some medical specialties, are underrepresented in medical school faculty and administrative positions, report gender bias and sexual harassment, and report higher levels of conflict between domestic and professional responsibilities. Women are also increasingly entering dentistry. In 2018 over a quarter of all practicing dentists were women compared to only 3 percent in the 1960s. Currently they make up almost half of the dental school students. In addition, although women attorneys make up about a third of all practicing attorneys, 2016 was the first year the number of female enrollees surpassed male enrollees at U.S. law schools, and this trend is continuing currently. Similarly, female pharmacists also increased from 30 percent in 1985 to 58 percent in 2013.

---

5   Bureau of Labor Statistics, "Employment by Detailed Occupation," https://www.bls.gov/emp/tables/emp-by-detailed-occupation.htm

HISPANIC WOMEN
IN THE LABOR FORCE

There were about 11.1 million Hispanic women in the civilian labor force in 2015, representing 1 in 7 women in the labor force. Of those, 10.3 million were employed.

As a group, Hispanic women tend to have less favorable outcomes than Hispanic men and non-Hispanics, outcomes that could be improved by raising the minimum wage, closing the wage gap, ensuring adequate working conditions and expanding opportunities for higher wage occupations.

The data below highlight the outcomes of Hispanic women, and compares them to their White, non-Hispanic counterparts as a reference group.

SHARE OF THE LABOR FORCE

Hispanic women's share of the labor force has nearly doubled over the last 20 years.

FEMALE LABOR FORCE
- 8.0% — 1995
- 15.1% — 2015

TOTAL LABOR FORCE
- 3.7% — 1995
- 7.0% — 2015

By 2024, Hispanic women are projected to account for 18.1% of the female labor force and 8.5% of the total labor force.*

*Source: U.S. Bureau of Labor Statistics, Employment Projections program

LABOR FORCE PARTICIPATION RATE

Hispanic women are more likely to be in the labor force than 20 years ago, and their labor force participation rate is projected to surpass that of White non-Hispanic women, which has been declining over time.

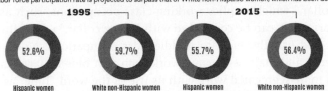

1995
- 52.6% — Hispanic women
- 59.7% — White non-Hispanic women

2015
- 55.7% — Hispanic women
- 56.4% — White non-Hispanic women

By 2024, the labor force participation rate of Hispanic women is projected to reach 57.4%, while White non-Hispanic women's participation rate will fall to 55.7%.*

*Source: U.S. Bureau of Labor Statistics, Employment Projections program

There are **4.5 million working Hispanic mothers** with **children under 18.**

16.9 % of Hispanic families with children under 18 with a single, female householder who works full-time and year-round **are in poverty.✝**

✝Source: U.S. Census Bureau, Current Population Survey 2016, Annual Social and Economic Supplement

EARNINGS**

Hispanic women and men earn well below White non-Hispanics, and Hispanic women earn even less than their male counterparts.

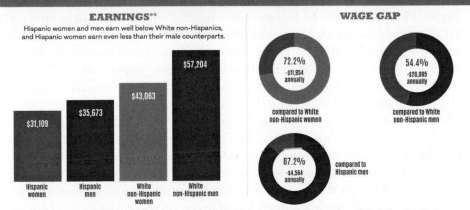

- $31,109 — Hispanic women
- $35,673 — Hispanic men
- $43,063 — White non-Hispanic women
- $57,204 — White non-Hispanic men

WAGE GAP

- 72.2% −$11,954 annually — compared to White non-Hispanic women
- 54.4% −$26,095 annually — compared to White non-Hispanic men
- 87.2% −$4,564 annually — compared to Hispanic men

**Note: Based on 2015 median annual earnings of workers 15 years and older who worked full-time and year round, including the self-employed.
Source: U.S. Census Bureau, Current Population Survey 2016, Annual Social and Economic Supplement

LEARNING ACTIVITY

SEX WORK

Lauren Grant

Feminists disagree about how society should respond to sex work. Some feminists argue for legalization—regulating sex work the same as any other business. Others argue for decriminalization. Decriminalization does not make sex work legal; it removes laws that criminalize it. Do some research on the web. What laws regulate sex work in the United States? In other countries? What has been the result of legalization? Of decriminalization? What are other options?

One of the most female-segregated jobs is sex work such as prostitution, where women workers have often struggled to control the conditions of their work against the demoralization and abuse by customers, pimps, and police. The reading "Aligned Across Difference: Structural Injustice, Sex Work, and Human Trafficking" by Corinne Schwarz, Emily J. Kennedy, and Hannah Britton brings together research on human trafficking with sex workers and research with members of the anti-trafficking community in an attempt to bridge differences. In particular, the reading explores the escalation of punitive carceral policies and growing sex workers' and human trafficking rights movements worldwide.

The term "blue collar," which implies working-class occupations, such as industrial, production, and factory work, can be contrasted with "white collar," which involves office or professional work and usually refers to middle-class occupations. Note the slippage between industrial work and male-segregated work such that blue collar means working class but also implies male-segregated work with its use of the word "blue" as opposed to "pink." The Bureau of Labor Statistics reports the following occupations as the most male segregated: engineers, mechanics and drivers, carpenters and construction trade workers, firefighters, airline pilots and navigators, and forestry and logging workers. You will note the obvious ways feminine jobs involve working with people, children, cleaning, and administrative support, whereas masculine employment tends to involve working with machines and inanimate objects. There are other differences too, such as wages for heavily male-segregated jobs tending to be higher than wages for female-segregated, pink-collar work. That is because, as already mentioned, these jobs are valued more. Finally, unionized women workers earn about 25 percent more than nonunion women workers and receive better health and pension benefits: Union membership helps narrow the gender wage gap. Currently only 1 in 10 employed women in the United States are union members, but they do make up 46 percent of unionized workers generally.

Another important aspect of occupational segregation by gender is that there is gender segregation even within the same job type. This is termed *vertical occupational segregation*, and, like horizontal occupational segregation (segregation across jobs), it functions as a result of, and as a conduit for, sexism and racism and other systems of inequality and privilege. For example, although the number of women physicians is increasing, as already mentioned, women are still overwhelmingly found in certain specialties such as pediatrics, family medicine, obstetrics and gynecology, and public health work, and are less likely to be found in surgical specialties, orthopedics, anesthesiology, and more entrepreneurial

ACTIVIST PROFILE
DOLORES HUERTA

Dolores Huerta is one of the most powerful and influential labor leaders in the United States. Born in Dawson, New Mexico, in 1930, Huerta grew up in Stockton, California, and eventually earned a teaching certificate from Stockton College. After one year of teaching, however, she quit to work with Community Service Organization (CSO). She thought she could do more to help the hungry children she saw at school by helping organize their farmworker parents.

While with CSO, she met Cesar Chavez, and in 1962 they founded the United Farm Workers of America (UFW). Although Chavez was more comfortable in the fields organizing workers, Huerta became the voice of the union, becoming the first woman and first Chicana negotiator in labor history. The UFW met with great success in the 1965 Delano Grape Strike, which won the first collective bargaining agreement for farmworkers, and Huerta was instrumental in the negotiations. She also became consciously involved with the feminist movement when she met Gloria Steinem in 1968, although she had always focused on issues specific to women farmworkers.

In 1972 she co-chaired the California delegation to the Democratic Convention, and she led the struggle for unemployment insurance, collective bargaining rights, and immigration rights for farmworkers under the 1985 amnesty legalization program. She was the first Latina inducted into the National Women's Hall of

Fame, and she received the National Organization for Women's Woman of Courage Award and the American Civil Liberties Union's Bill of Rights Award. She continues to struggle for farmworkers through the UFW and serve as a role model for Chicanas in their fight against discrimination.

positions where their numbers tend to hover between 7 and 38 percent. Observers note that the growing proportion of U.S. physicians and dentists in patient care who are female is improving the quality of medicine through more emotionally focused and patient-centered practice. The influx of women, however, is lowering physicians' average salaries overall. As already mentioned, female physicians on average earn about 26 percent less than male physicians, mostly because they enter the different specialties just discussed and fall prey to the consequences of vertical occupational segregation.

Similarly, female lawyers are less likely to practice criminal law and more likely to practice family law. They earn about 80 percent of male lawyers' salaries. Male teachers are more likely to teach sciences and to instruct older children; female professors teach more typically in the humanities and the social sciences and less often in the physical and applied sciences and technical fields. Usually specialties and fields that men occupy are more prestigious and the salaries are higher. In this way, women and men do not just tend to perform different jobs, but the jobs that they do are valued differently and have different levels of status and power and bring different problems associated with integration and

---

LEARNING ACTIVITY

WORKING WOMEN AND UNIONS

Visit the web page of the AFL-CIO at www.aflcio.org to learn more about women in the workforce. What are some of the key issues for working women identified by the AFL-CIO? What legislative issues does the AFL-CIO identify that would be beneficial to working women?

What is a union? What benefits do unions provide? Why are unions important for working women? What steps would people take to form a union at their workplace? Is your campus unionized? What are these unions doing to address gender inequality? Interview a union leader to learn more about the benefits of a union and the challenges faced by unions in the current political climate.

---

advancement. This differential is related to sexism in society generally as well as to other systems of inequality and privilege. Not surprisingly, when you look at women in professions such as law, pharmacy, human and animal medicine, and dentistry, overwhelmingly men are more likely to own their own practices and run their own businesses. Women of color are the most underrepresented among these more entrepreneurial professionals. The reasons for this are largely economic, as owning your own business takes wealth and capital.

Barriers to advancement in the labor force (what is often called the glass ceiling) have been challenged by individuals, the courts, and the organized women's movement. And, although these barriers are beginning to come down, they are still holding strong in many areas. Women tend not to be promoted at the same rate as men and they also continue to face obstacles when trying to enter the most prestigious and best-paid occupations. Normative gendered and racialized social discourses about women's place come into play in these public arenas, often in very unconscious ways as well as through institutionalized practices that systematically provide obstacles for certain individuals. There is a double standard of attitudes and expectations by gender at play in many occupational settings in the United States. For example, while 4 out of 10 employees have dated someone from work, women who do so are judged differently than men by both women and men. More negative judgments are directed against women, and it is often assumed that women are motivated by a desire to get ahead in their job.

Although U.S. women have made advancements in moving into middle-management business positions, they are relatively absent from top leadership positions.[6] Only 24 (or just under 5 percent) of Fortune 500 companies have women CEOs (chief executive officer) or presidents and only 8 of these CEOs are actually in the top Fortune 100. Of the 20 highest-earning executives (women still hold only 8 percent of the highest-earning slots), only 3 are women of color. Women make up about 17 percent of Fortune 500 boards of directors, and this drops to just over 3 percent for women of color. Indeed, two-thirds of all companies have no women of color on their board of directors at all. In addition, although women make up more than 60 percent of the nonprofit workforce (as opposed

---

6   Claire Cain Miller, "The Number of Female Chief Executives Is Falling," *New York Times* (May 23, 2018) nytimes.com/2018/05/23/upshot/why-the-number-of-female-chief-executives-is-falling.html

to the business for-profit workplace), they still lack access to top management positions, share of foundation dollars, and board positions. Women of color are relatively absent in the higher echelons of corporate power in all sectors.

Alongside consideration of the problems associated with the glass ceiling, it is important to recognize what researchers have called the "glass escalator" and the "glass precipice." The "glass escalator" refers to the practices whereby men who go into traditionally female-dominated professions such as teaching, nursing, and social work are disproportionately advanced into management and administrative positions where they receive more prestige, pay, and power than women. The "glass precipice" is the process whereby marginalized people are encouraged to go into leadership positions in failing organizations and companies and are disproportionately set up to fail professionally.

Finally, it is interesting to look at how the development of certain occupations as female segregated has affected the status and conditions of work. For example, clerical work, although low prestige, was definitely a man's job until the turn of the twentieth century, when women quickly became associated with this work. This was due to the following factors: There was a large pool of women with few other opportunities, clerical work's low status made it easier for women to be accepted, typewriter manufacturers began promoting the typewriter as something women used, and the personal service aspect of the work fit gender norms about the feminine aspect of secretarial work. As more women entered this profession, the gap between clerical wages and blue-collar wages generally increased, and the status of the clerical profession fell. A more recent example is the field of pharmacology. Two trends—the increasing number of pharmacies attached to chain drugstores and the increasing number of female pharmacists—have been seen as the reasons why the status of pharmacology has fallen as a profession, even while wages remain high. It remains to be seen whether the increase of women in human and animal medicine, and in the sciences generally, will decrease the status of these professions.

WAGES AND COMPARABLE WORTH

The most disparate wage gap in the United States is that between those who head corporations and those who work for corporations. In 2018 the average CEO pay was more than 300 times that of the average compensation of full-time, year-round workers in nonmanagerial jobs, not including the value of many perks that CEOs receive, nor their pension benefits. In 2018 a new federal regulation required publicly traded U.S. corporations to disclose the salaries of chief executives compared with workers in their organizations. A March 2018 *Guardian* newspaper article used this data to report that the CEO of Marathon Petroleum earned 935 times more than his typical employee, which means that the employee would have had to work for nine centuries to earn what the CEO made in a year. Some U.S. corporations would require their workers to work more than a millennium to equal the salaries of their CEOs—for example, the temp agency Manpower (2,483 years), Del Monte Produce (1,465 years), and amusement park owner Six Flags (1,920 years). A report from the Institute of Policy Studies emphasized that this gap between rich and poor increases to 364 times when the top 20 U.S. companies are used (average CEO salary rises to about $40 million/year) and the average salary for all workers is employed (average salary falls to about $35,000/year). Such CEO compensation far exceeds that of leaders in other fields and in other countries. Top managers in the United States made three times more than those in similar European companies, even though the Europeans tended to have higher sales numbers than their U.S. counterparts. It is important to keep in mind as already discussed, only about 4 percent, or 20, of the top 500 U.S. companies are led by women, and almost all of these women are white.

These data on wage inequities are one aspect of what scholars call the gender gap. Worldwide this is measured as the global gender gap of 144 countries measuring progress toward gender parity on four dimensions: economic participation and opportunity, educational attainment, health and survival, and political empowerment. In addition, the most recent gender gap data include analyses of the dynamics of gender gaps across industry talent pools and occupations. This is the topic of the reading by Vesselina Stefanova Ratcheva and Saadia Zahidi titled "Which Country Will Be the First to Close the Gender Gap—and How?" They discuss projections about which countries worldwide are making the fastest progress in closing gender gaps and offer strategies for gender parity.

As one aspect of the global gender gap, the gender wage gap—an index of the status of women's earnings relative to men's, expressed as a percentage—is calculated by dividing women's median earnings by men's median earnings. In the United States these data include only full-time, year-round workers and exclude all part-time or seasonal workers. This is relevant here because a large number of women work part-time jobs, and including these jobs would lower the numbers because part-time work tends to be lower paid and these workers receive fewer job-related benefits. They are also less likely to be unionized, which puts them in a vulnerable position in terms of wage negotiation.

According to 2018 data from the U.S. Bureau of Labor Statistics, the gender wage gap, or ratio of women's and men's median annual earnings, was 80.5 percent, meaning that women earn almost 81 cents for every dollar a man earns, and almost twice as many women as men earn minimum wage or less each year. This wage gap results in significant lost wages that continue to add up over a lifetime. Progress in closing this gender earnings gap based on median annual earnings has slowed since 2007. Economists report that if the pace of change in the annual earnings ratio continues at the current rate, it will take until 2059 for women and men to reach earnings parity. An alternative measure of the wage gap, the ratio of women's to men's median *weekly* earnings for full-time workers, was 81 percent in 2018. Women's median weekly earnings was $783, or 81 percent of the $965 median for men. The difference between these two measures is that the median annual earnings for full-time year-round workers includes self-employed workers and excludes seasonal workers. The weekly measure excludes self-employed and includes seasonal workers. The figures are based on the same Bureau of Labor Statistics data.

The U.S. Bureau of Labor Statistics data show that women of color, of course, earn less than this monolithic "woman," as do older women generally. African American women, for example, earn 92.5 percent of African American men's earnings and 68 percent of white men's annual median earnings. Similarly, Latinas earn 87 percent of Latinos' and 62 percent of white men's annual median income. Asian American women fare better, with 90 percent of Asian American men's and 87 percent of white men's annual median income. In other words, women of all major racial and ethnic groups earn less than men of the same group, and also earn less than white men. White women earn 82 percent of what white men earn. The latter percentage is close to the ratio for all women to all men because white workers represent the largest group in the labor force. No data are available for Native American women workers.

The educational attainment of women ages 25 to 64 in the labor force has risen substantially since the 1970s. In 2018, 42 percent of these women held a bachelor's degree and higher, compared with 11 percent in 1970. Six percent of women had less than a high school diploma—that is, did not graduate from high school or earn a GED—down from 34 percent in 1970. Women now earn the majority of college degrees. This education improves women's earnings: Female full-time wage and salary workers aged 25 and older with only a high school diploma earned about 81 percent of the median weekly earnings of women with an associate's degree and 56 percent of those of women with a bachelor's degree or higher, although all earned less than men with comparable degrees. The median annual earnings of female high school graduates are about 34 percent less than those of comparable men, those of women with bachelor's degrees and graduate degrees about 32 percent less, and those of women with doctoral degrees about 29 percent less than those of their male counterparts. One reason for this is that women and men choose different education and training that prepare them for different kinds of jobs that pay different wages (discussed in more detail shortly).

Since the Equal Pay Act was signed in 1963, the gender wage gap has been closing at a very slow rate. In 1963, women who worked full time, year round made 59 cents on average for every dollar earned by men. This means that the wage gap has narrowed by less than half a cent per year. If working women earned the same as men (those who work the same number of hours; have the same education, age, and union status; and live in the same region of the country), their annual family incomes would rise and reduce poverty rates by about half. The Institute for Policy Research reports that over a lifetime of work, the average 25-year-old woman who works full time, year round, until she retires at age 65 years will earn on the average almost a half-million dollars less than the average working man. Raising the minimum wage would help all people and support many families whose members are employed but still live in poverty.

So why do women earn less money than men on the average? The gender wage gap is explained by several factors. *First*, it is explained by the horizontal occupational segregation of the labor force: Women and men tend to work in different kinds of jobs, and the jobs women hold are valued and rewarded less. Such differences are not covered by the Equal Pay Act because women and men are engaged in different kinds of work. Indeed, when you compare similarly qualified and positioned men and women in the same occupation, the gender gap drops considerably, to about 4 percent, for example, in the case of computer engineers, and to 2 percent in the case of registered nurses, and only 1 percent in the case of elementary school teachers. In other words, whether you identify as a woman or a man, if you go into elementary teaching in the United States, your wages will be equally relatively low (although there are still differences: see the discussion of vertical occupational segregation that follows) compared to work in technology and engineering, where both women and men will have relatively higher wages. The reality, of course, as already discussed, is that many more women go into elementary education than men and more men go into computer engineering than women—hence a partial explanation for the difference in median weekly or annual salaries by gender. In addition, the jobs that men and women tend to take show differential wage growth over a life cycle (about 62 percent salary growth for computer engineers compared to 32 percent growth for registered nurses).

Second, the gap is explained by vertical occupational segregation, or the ways women and men are in different specialties within the same occupation. Currently it is estimated that women tend to earn less than men in 99 percent of all occupations. Indeed, comparable wages are a problem in every occupational category, even in occupations in which women considerably outnumber men. Women in professional and related occupations (sales and office occupations, for example) earn about a quarter less than their male counterparts. Female elementary and middle school teachers and registered nurses earn about 10 percent less than similarly employed men, despite comprising the majority of the field, and, as already noted, female physicians and attorneys earn less than male counterparts. This vertical segregation implies that women and other marginalized workers are in specialties or have work assignments within these professions that are less valued and rewarded than more "masculine" specialties and work assignments.

Finally, the total gender pay gap cannot only be explained by recognizing horizontal and vertical occupational segregation: It also involves overt and covert discrimination against women and other marginalized workers. After economists control for "human capital" variables (time spent in work, education, seniority, time since conferral of degree, prestige of institution awarding degree, etc.), there is still a proportion of unexplained variance between the wages of men and women in the same specialties or work assignments and within the same occupational category. Social discourses and disciplinary regimes about gender, race, age, sexuality, and social class work to create patterns of institutionalized inequalities that reinforce ideas concerning certain people's worth and the kinds of work those individuals should do. For example, as the reading "This Is the Hidden Financial Cost of Being an LQBTQ American Today" by Anna Swartz emphasizes, there are social discourses and disciplinary regimes about gender and sexual identities that produce significant workplace barriers for LGBTQ individuals that affect the wages they receive as well as their experiences in workplace communities. Twenty-eight states still lack protections for workplace discrimination based on sexual and gender identities.

Comparable worth, also known as pay equity, is one means to address the gender wage gap by providing a mechanism for paying women and men in different occupations comparably. Basically, comparable worth takes into account different jobs based on experience, skill, training, and job conditions and assigns relative points on these indices in order to determine their worth. There is no federal-level comparable worth legislation, although many states have enacted laws demanding comparable worth comparisons in determining pay for state workers. In addition, the courts have ruled both for and against workers who have brought comparable worth suits against various corporations. When the courts have ruled in favor of plaintiffs, it has often meant a considerable amount of money in back pay to compensate female workers for years of financial inequities.

Inequality in women's work lives thus has important consequences for inequality in other spheres of life. Because most women work both inside and outside the home and spend a considerable part of their lives working, it is of central importance to understand the conditions under which they work as well as to strive for equality in the workplace for all people.

THE BLOG

WE AIN'T AFRAID OF NO SEXISM: SCIENCE, POLITICS, ATHLETICS, AND *GHOSTBUSTERS*

Susan M. Shaw (2016)

Ask children to draw a picture of a scientist, and the vast majority of the time they'll draw a white man with messy hair. Think Bernie Sanders in a lab coat.

But it's not just children who think science is still a man's domain. Just ask the women scientists who endure the blatant and subtle forms of sexism that permeate science labs, classrooms, and fieldwork.

Or just watch the national news.

Already, in the past couple of years we've seen highly regarded male scientists who, despite being serial harassers, have been shielded by their universities. We watched one male astronomer give a press conference on his team's rather astonishing accomplishment of landing a probe on a comet—while he was wearing a shirt covered with drawings of scantily clad women in suggestive positions.

One woman scientist received a peer review that accompanied the rejection of a manuscript that suggested she find one or two male colleagues to co-author to prevent bias. When a postdoc asked an advice columnist at one of the premier science associations what to do about an adviser who kept looking down her shirt, she was told to put up with it because his attention to her science would be more important than his attention to her chest. A Nobel Prize-winning scientist told a group of women scientists that he didn't think women and men should be in the lab together because they fall in love and the women cry when the men criticize them. Or just read some of the uproar over the casting of four women as ghostbusters—and they're fictional scientists. The racism and sexism toward one of the stars was so vulgar and threatening that she left Twitter entirely. Apparently, women shouldn't even play scientists in the movies.

Hillary Clinton proclaimed she believes in science in contrast with the science denial of Donald Trump, and the Internet trolls attacked her—she only uses science when it helps her politically, she doesn't really understand science, she doesn't really mean it when she says she wants to transition to renewable energy or make other green policy changes because she's in the pocket of big oil, big ag, Wall Street, etc. Just read the comments section following any article about her statement.

So, in a nutshell, women can't be scientists, can't play scientists, and can't use science to support policy positions.

And yet women do. But when women do, they bring different experiences and different lenses to science that actually make science better—not because of some essential quality of womanhood but because their social location in a gendered world provides different insights and perspectives that are not available to the men whose privilege within the dominant culture of science (and higher education and politics and media) is largely invisible to them.

For example, seat belts and airbags in cars are designed for the average man. Having more women in engineering might mean such design assumptions are challenged. Research in medicine was almost always based on male bodies until more women entered the field.

Inclusion, however, is not enough. Women who start careers in science, technology, engineering, and mathematics (STEM) leave the field at high rates because of the culture of sexism that still pervades (as noted above). Women typically receive lower salaries, smaller labs, and less support than do their male colleagues. Policies do not take into account the added burdens of reproductive labor (childbearing, child-rearing, cooking, cleaning, buying birthday and sympathy cards—and doing departmental service at work) that still fall disproportionately to women.

Women want to do science, good science. And science needs women scientists. But the masculinist culture of science is threatened when women enter its domain. The presence of women challenges notions of hierarchy, power, privilege, objectivity, competition, and the sexualization, diminishment, and subordination of women that are essential elements of hegemonic masculinity.

(continued)

Just ask the women athletes in Rio about the presence of capable women in traditional male strongholds. Their accomplishments have been credited to the men in their lives; their appearance has been examined from every angle; they've been described as "giggling" and looking like they're at the mall; they've been named the "Michael Jordan of gymnastics" or "the female Michael Phelps"; they've been identified in the press by their husbands, not their own names. We've even been told that women fans, who watch the Olympics in greater proportion than men, are not really sports fans, less interested in the competitions and more in the backstories.

None of this is a new story. But perhaps the audacity of women who have so publicly challenged their exclusion from historically male spaces has made the issue so public that even the popular press can no longer ignore it. Will this audacity actually change the structures that perpetuate sexism? That remains to be seen, but women aren't going to stop making the challenge any time soon. After all, there's still another week left in the Olympics, and a woman is running for president on a major party ticket for the first time, and women, day after day, are doing good science.

Recently Gillian Anderson suggested she'd like to play Bond in the next 007 movie. The trolls went wild. "It's Bond," she tweeted, "Jane Bond."

Maybe in the not-too-distant future when asked to draw scientists or presidents or athletes or even 007, maybe, just maybe, children will be as likely to draw a woman as a man. But as Abby Yates says in *Ghostbusters*, "We need to reverse the portal. It's gonna take an insane amount of energy!"

57. A BRIEF HISTORY OF WORKING WOMEN

SHARLENE HESSE-BIBER AND GREGG LEE CARTER (1999)

WOMEN WORKERS IN PRE-INDUSTRIAL AMERICA

Seven hundred and fifty thousand Europeans came to America between 1600 and 1700. The bulk of them were from Britain, but the colonies also saw significant numbers from Holland, France, and Germany. Many came as indentured servants, exchanging their labor for the cost of passage to the American colonies. Indentured servants often worked from five to ten years to pay back their creditors. As early as the 1600s, prior to the slave trade, some Africans also came to the colonies as indentured servants; they often worked side by side with white indentured servants. Women's lives in this country differed drastically, depending on their race, class, and marital status.

WHITE WOMEN

European women usually arrived in the New World with their families, as daughters and wives, under the auspices of fathers or husbands. In the pre-industrial economy of the American colonial period (from the seventeenth century to the early eighteenth century), work was closely identified with home and family life. The family was the primary economic unit, and family members were dependent on one another for basic sustenance. Men performed the agricultural work, while women's work was done chiefly in the home, which was a center of production in colonial America. In addition to cooking, cleaning, and caring for children, women did spinning and weaving, and made lace, soap, candles, and shoes. Indeed, they manufactured nearly all articles used in daily life. This work was highly valued, and the colonies relied on the production of these "cottage industries."

Single women remained within the domestic sphere, living with relatives, often as "assistant homemakers." For married women, the nature of their work depended on the economic circumstances of their husbands:

> In cash-poor homes and among frontier families, women bore the burden of filling most of the family's basic needs. They worked to reduce cash expenditures by growing vegetables in the kitchen garden and making the family's clothes, candles, soap and household furnishings. If a husband were a craftsman or the proprietor of a shop or tavern, his wife and children might also work in the business, in addition to all the other tasks. In contrast, the wife of a successful farmer, plantation owner, or merchant did little actual work; instead, she supervised household servants and slaves who purchased or made the goods the family needed, cooked the meals, and maintained the house.

The social codes of colonial America did not exclude a woman from working outside the home, and many did so. Colonial women engaged in a great range of occupations, and as old documents are discovered and new histories of women's work are written, that range appears greater still. Women were innkeepers, shopkeepers, crafts workers, nurses, printers, teachers, and landholders. In the city of Boston during 1690, for example, women ran approximately 40 percent of all taverns. During that year, city officials also granted more than thirty women the right to saw lumber and manufacture potash. Women acted as physicians and midwives in all the early settlements, producing medicines, salves, and ointments. Many of the women who worked outside their homes were widows with dependent children, who took their husbands' places in family enterprises. It seems that at one time or another, colonial women engaged in many of the occupations practiced by men. Indeed, most models of the "patriarchal family economy" ill fit the historical evidence; for example, eighteenth-century diaries describe "a world in which wives as well as husbands traded with their neighbors" and "young women felt themselves responsible for their own support." Not surprisingly, however, women's wages in this period were significantly lower than those of men.

For poor women, there were special incentives to work outside the home. Local poor laws encouraged single poor women to work rather than become recipients of relief. The choice of jobs was much more limited, and many poor women became laundresses, house servants, or cooks. Again, however, female laborers were paid approximately 30 percent less than the lowest-paid unskilled, free, white male workers and 20 percent less than hired-out male slaves.

The fact that some women worked in so-called "masculine fields"—that they were merchants, tavern owners, shopkeepers, and so on—has sometimes been interpreted to mean that the colonial period was a "golden age of equality" for women. Contemporary historians argue instead, however, that these jobs were exceptions to the rule, and that in fact "colonial times were characterized by a strict and simple division of labor between men and women, which assigned them to fields and house, or to the public and private spheres, respectively." The dominant ideology was still that a woman's place was at home, raising children. . . .

WOMEN OF COLOR

Historically, the experiences of women of color have differed dramatically from those of white women. If we consider only the present time period, it may appear that women of color and white women have certain experiences in common—relatively low economic position, being the target of discriminatory practices in education and in work, and overall marginality in the power structure. But women of color and white women have reached their present circumstances through very different histories. Although white women's status was clearly inferior to that of white men, they were treated with deference, and they shared in the status privileges of their husbands. African American women almost never had the option of choosing between work and leisure, as did some white women. They were not included in the image of the "colonial housewife." African American women were not considered "weak" females, but were treated more like beasts of burden. Thus these women of color suffered a double oppression of sexism and racism.

Nowhere is this double oppression more clearly demonstrated than within the institution of slavery, which became established in late seventeenth- and early eighteenth-century colonial society—largely as a result of the demand for cheap agricultural labor, especially within the Southern plantation economy. Historians estimate the slave population in the United States, Caribbean, and Brazil consisted of 9.5 million blacks. More than double that number are estimated to have died in transit to the New World. Slave women in the Southern colonies were without doubt the most exploited of all women. They were exploited not only as workers but as breeders of slaves. The following advertisement was typical of the time:

> Negroes for Sale: A girl about twenty years of age (raised in Virginia) and her two female children, four and the other two years old—remarkably strong and healthy. Never having had a day's sickness with the exception of the smallpox in her life. She is prolific in her generating qualities and affords a rare opportunity to any person who wishes to raise a family of strong and healthy servants for their own use.

Slave women were also sometimes exploited as sex objects for white men. Like male slaves, they were considered intrinsically inferior. Slaves were property, not people. They faced severe cultural and legal restrictions: their family lives were controlled by their owners, their children were not their own, and their educational opportunities were almost nonexistent.

Sojourner Truth, formerly a slave and an activist in the abolitionist and women's rights movements, eloquently expressed the differences in treatment, under slavery, of black and white women: "That man over there says that women need to be helped into carriages and lifted over ditches, and to have the best place everywhere. Nobody ever helped me into carriages, or over mud puddles, or gives me any best place . . . and ain't I a woman?"

Before the Civil War, a black woman in one of the "cotton states," working on one of the larger plantations, would have been either a house servant or one of several million field hands who produced major cash crops. In the Southern plantation economy, we thus find a "bifurcated" concept of woman. The European woman became "the guardian of civilization," while the African American woman was "spared neither harsh labor nor harsh punishment," though the experience of slaves differed depending on the economic status and individual personality of the slave owner. Even pregnancy did not deter some slavemasters from cruel treatment: "One particular method of whipping pregnant slaves was used throughout the South; they were made to lie face down in a specially dug depression in the ground, a practice that provided simultaneously for the protection of the fetus and the abuse of its mother."

Some white women benefited from such slave labor and shared with their husbands the role of oppressor, although the slave-mistress relationship was psychologically complex: "In their role as labor managers, mistresses lashed out at slave women not only to punish them, but also to vent their anger on victims even more wronged than themselves. We may speculate that, in the female slave, the white woman saw the source of her own misery, but she also saw herself—a woman without rights or recourse, subject to the whims of an egotistical man." Conflict between white and African American women often resulted in

violence, in which "mistresses were likely to attack with any weapon available—knitting needles, tongs, a fork, butcher knife, ironing board, or pan of boiling water." Yet, while the relationship was often filled with strife, white and African American women "also shared a world of physical and emotional intimacy that is uncommon among women of antagonistic classes and different races."

Slavery was justified by notions of race involving the "biological superiority" of the colonists. It was assumed that Europeans in the colonies made up an easily identifiable and discrete biological and social entity—a "natural" community of class interests, racial attributes, political and social affinities, and superior culture. This was of course not exactly true, but given that the differences between white skin and black skin were more noticeable than many of the differences among Europeans themselves, and given that whites were in dominant positions politically and socially, it could easily *seem* to be true.

Slave families often resisted the oppressive workloads by banding together to help one another in the fields and to lessen the workloads of older, weaker, or sicker workers. The extended family was of vital importance under the slave system. African American mothers labored most of the day, some of them caring for white women's families, while their own children were left under the care of grandmothers and old or disabled slaves. While the two-parent, nuclear family may have been the most typical form of slave cohabitation, close relatives were often very much involved in family life. Stevenson's study suggests that in colonial and antebellum Virginia, the slave family was a "malleable extended family that, when possible, provided its members with nurture, education, socialization, material support, and recreation in the face of the potential social chaos that the slaveholder imposed."

Even though African American men were unable to own property, to provide protection and support for their children, or to work within the public sphere, there was a sexual division within the slave household. Men collected the firewood and made furniture—beds, tables, chairs—and other articles of wood, such as animal traps, butter paddles, and ax handles. They also wove baskets and made shoes.

African American women grew, prepared, and preserved foods; spun thread, wove and dyed cloth, and sewed clothes; and made soap and candles.

In the North, while slavery was an accepted practice, it was not nearly as widespread. Many African American women worked as free laborers as domestic servants; others worked as spinners, weavers, and printers.

NATIVE AMERICAN WOMEN

The work and family life experience of Native American women prior to European colonization differed depending on the region of the country and the type of tribal society. But in every Native American nation, women played very important roles in the economic life of their communities:

> They had to be resourceful in utilizing every aspect of the environment to sustain life and engaging in cultural exchanges to incorporate new productive techniques. They gathered wild plants for food, herbs for medicines and dyes, clay for pottery, bark and reeds for weaving cloth. In many nations, they also tilled the soil and sowed the seeds, cultivated and harvested, made cloth and clothing, dried vegetables, and ground grains for breads. In hunting societies, they cured the meats and dried the skins. They also assisted in the hunt in some cultures.

As a general rule, men hunted and women engaged in agricultural work. The more important hunting was to a community's survival, the more extensive the male power within the community; the greater the dependence on agriculture, the greater the power and independence of women. Women had the responsibility for raising children and maintaining hearth and home. Men engaged in hunting, fishing, and warfare.

In the East especially, many Indian communities were predominantly agricultural. Women constituted the agricultural labor force within these communities. An English woman who was held captive by a Seneca tribe observed that

> Household duties were simple and Seneca women, unlike English wives and daughters, were not slaves to the spinning wheel or the needle. In the summer, the women went out each morning to the fields,

accompanied by their children, to work cooperatively and in the company of friends and relatives, planting and tending the corn, beans, and squash at a pace to their individual rhythms and skills rather than to the demands of an overseer. They moved from field to field, completing the same tasks in each before returning to the first.

Women within agricultural communities would often maintain control over tools and land—as well as any surplus foods they gathered from the land. This often enabled them (especially elderly women who were heads of households) to garner some political clout within their tribal communities. For instance, if Iroquois women opposed war on certain occasions, they might refuse to let the men have the cornmeal they would have needed to feed their raiding parties or armies. These communities often had a matrilineal family structure (inheritance and family name were through the female line, with family connections through the mother) and matrilocal residence (upon marriage a man lived with his mother-in-law's relatives).

Through the lens of the white colonist, the work roles and family structure of Native American society appeared deviant and, in some cases, perverse. After all, English society was characterized by a patriarchal family structure with patrilocal residence:

> To Europeans, Indian family patterns raised the specter of promiscuous women, freed from accountability to their fathers and husbands for the offspring they produced. . . . Equally incomprehensible—and thus perverse—to many Europeans were the work roles accepted by Indian men and women. In the world the English knew, farming was labor and farmers were male. Masculinity was linked, inexorably, to agriculture: household production and family reproduction defined femininity. That Indian men hunted was not a sufficient counterpoise, for, in the England of the seventeenth century, hunting was a sport, not an occupation. Many concluded that Indian men were effeminate, lazy; Indian women were beasts of burden, slaves to unmanly men.

European colonization and conquest pushed Native Americans off their land, depriving them of food and livelihood, culture and traditions. Disease or warfare demolished whole societies. Others were radically transformed, especially with regard to the traditional gender and work roles. Having used military force to remove Native Americans from their lands onto reservations, the U.S. government "began a systematic effort to destroy their cultures and replace them with the values and practices of middle-class whites."

Confined to relatively small reservations, Native American men could no longer hunt as extensively as before (nor, defeated by U.S. forces, could they any longer carry on warfare). They therefore needed to redefine their social roles and to find new economic activities. In many a Native American tribe, the men took over agriculture, traditionally the women's work. Family structure also changed, at the prompting of missionaries and others including government officials, to become more like that of the Europeans, with less emphasis on the matrilineal extended family and more on the nuclear family and the husband-wife relationship.

THE ARRIVAL OF INDUSTRIALIZATION

The transformation from an agrarian rural economy to an urban industrial society ushered in a new era in women's work. With the advent of industrialization, many of the products women made at home—clothes, shoes, candles—gradually came to be made instead in factories. For a while, women still performed the work at home, using the new machines. Merchants would contract for work to be done, supplying women with the machines and the raw materials to be made into finished articles. The most common of these manufacturing trades for women was sewing for the newly emerging clothing industry. Since women had always sewn for their families, this work was considered an extension of women's traditional role, and therefore a respectable activity. As the demand for goods increased, however, home production declined and gave way to the factory system, which was more efficient in meeting emerging needs.

The rise of factory production truly separated the home from the workplace. With the decline of the household unit as the center of industrial and economy activity, the importance of women's economic role also declined. Male and female spheres of activity became more separated, as did the definitions of men's and women's roles. Man's role continued to be primarily that of worker and provider; woman's role became primarily supportive. She was to maintain a smooth and orderly household, to be cheerful and warm, and thus to provide the husband with the support and services he needed to continue his work life. The industrial revolution created a set of social and economic conditions in which the basic lifestyle of white middle-class women more nearly approached society's expectations concerning woman's role. More and more middle-class women could now aspire to the status formerly reserved for the upper classes—that of "lady." The nineteenth-century concept of a lady was that of a fragile, idle, pure creature, submissive and subservient to her husband and to domestic needs. Her worth was based on her decorative value, a quality that embraced her beauty, her virtuous character, and her temperament. She was certainly not a paid employee. This ideal was later referred to as the "cult of true womanhood" because of its rigid, almost religious standards.

Biological and social arguments were also often used to justify women's exclusion from the labor force. Women were seen as too weak and delicate to participate in the rough work world of men. It was believed they lacked strength and stamina, that their brains were small, that the feminine perspective and sensitivity were liabilities in the marketplace. Such arguments rationalized women's accepting the roles of homemaker and mother almost exclusively, as the industrial revolution spread across the country.

During the early years of industrialization, however, because many men were still primarily occupied with agricultural work and were unavailable or unwilling to enter the early factories, male laborers were in short supply. American industry depended, then, on a steady supply of women workers. Yet how could society tolerate women's working in the factories, given the dominant ideology of the times, which dictated that a woman's place was at home? Single white women provided one answer. Their employment was viewed as a fulfillment of their family responsibilities, during an interlude before marriage.

The employment of young, single women in the early Lowell (Massachusetts) mills is a prime example of the reconciliation of ideology with the needs of industry. Francis Cabot Lowell devised a respectable route into employment for such women. Recruiting the daughters of farm families to work in his mill, which opened in 1821 in Lowell, he provided supervised boardinghouses, salaries sufficient to allow the young women to offer financial aid to their families or to save for their own trousseaux, and assurances to their families that the hard work and discipline of the mill would help prepare them for marriage and motherhood.

In the early industrial era, working conditions were arduous and hours were long. By the late 1830s, immigration began to supply a strongly competitive, permanent workforce willing to be employed for low wages in the factories, under increasingly mechanized and hazardous conditions. By the late 1850s, most of the better-educated, single, native-born women had left the mills, leaving newly immigrated women (both single and married) and men to fill these positions.

While women thus played a crucial role in the development of the textile industry, the first important manufacturing industry in America, women also found employment in many other occupations during the process of industrialization. As railroads and other business enterprises expanded and consolidated, women went to work in these areas as well. In fact, the U.S. Labor Commissioner reported that by 1890 only 9 out of 360 general groups to which the country's industries had been assigned did not employ women.

By 1900, more than five million women or girls, or about one in every five of those 10 years old and over, had become a paid employee. The largest proportion (40%) remained close to home in domestic and personal service, but domestic service was on the decline for white working-class women at the turn of the century. About 25 percent (1.3 million) of employed women worked in the manufacturing industries: in cotton mills, in the manufacture of woolen and worsted goods, silk goods, hosiery, and knit wear. The third largest group of employed women (over 18%) were working on farms. Women in the trade and transportation industries (about 10%)

worked as saleswomen, telegraph and telephone operators, stenographers, clerks, copyists, accountants, and bookkeepers. Women in the professions (about 9 percent, and typically young, educated, and single, of native-born parentage) were employed primarily in elementary and secondary teaching or nursing. Other professions—law, medicine, business, college teaching—tended to exclude women. The fastest growing of these occupational groups were manufacturing, trade, and transportation. In the last thirty years of the nineteenth century, the number of women working in trade and transportation rose from 19,000 to over half a million. These women also tended to be young, single, native-born Americans; immigrants and minority women were excluded from these white-collar positions.

. . .

By the turn of the century, the labor market had become clearly divided according to gender, race, and class. Fewer manufacturing jobs were being defined as suitable for white women, especially with the rising dominance of heavy industry employment for which female workers were considered too delicate. Working-class women were increasingly devalued by their continued participation in activities men had primarily taken over (such as factory work), because these activities were regarded as lacking in the Victorian virtue and purity called for by the "cult of true womanhood." As the economy expanded and prosperity came to more and more white middle-class families, middle-class women could "become ladies." A "woman's place" was still defined as at home. If these women did work outside the home, the appropriate occupation was a white-collar job (sales, clerical, and professional occupations). White women's occupations shifted from primarily domestic service—which became increasingly identified as "black women's work"—and from light manufacturing to the rapidly growing opportunities in office and sales work. These jobs were also considered more appropriate for feminine roles as defined by the cult of true womanhood. Women of color did not share in this occupational transformation. In 1910, for example, 90.5 percent of African American women worked as agricultural laborers or domestics, compared with 29.3 percent of white women.

THE LEGACY OF SLAVERY

African American women were not part of the "cult of true womanhood." They were not sheltered or protected from the harsh realities, and "while many white daughters were raised in genteel refined circumstances, most black daughters were forced to deal with poverty, violence and a hostile outside world from childhood on." After emancipation, their employment and economic opportunities were limited, in part because the skills they had learned on the plantation transferred to relatively few jobs, and those only of low pay and status.

African American women's concentration in service work—especially domestic work—was largely a result of limited opportunities available to them following the Civil War. The only factory employment open to them was in the Southern tobacco and textile industries, and until World War I most African American working women were farm laborers, domestics, or laundresses. . . .

Despite the limited range of job opportunities, a relatively large proportion of African American women were employed. The legacy of slavery may partly account for the relatively high labor-force participation rate of African American women. Although women's labor-force participation rate is generally lower than men's, African American women's participation rate was historically much higher than that of white women. Thus, for example, white women's labor-force participation in 1890 was 16.3 percent, while African American women's rate was 39.7 percent.

WORLD WAR I AND THE DEPRESSION

World War I accelerated the entry of white women into new fields of industry. The pressure of war production and the shortage of male industrial workers necessitated the hiring of women for what had been male-dominated occupations. Women replaced men at jobs in factories and business offices, and, in general, they kept the nation going, fed, and clothed. The mechanization and routinization of industry during this period enabled women to quickly master the various new skills. For the most part, this wartime pattern involved a reshuffling of the existing female workforce, rather than an increase in the numbers of women employed. Although the popular myth is that homemakers abandoned their kitchens for machine shops or airplane hangars, only about 5 percent of women workers were new to the labor force during the war years. . . .

Thus the wartime labor shortage temporarily created new job opportunities for women workers, and at higher wages than they had previously earned. This was not necessarily the case for African American women, however. Although World War I opened up some factory jobs to them, these were typically limited to the most menial, least desirable, and often the most dangerous jobs—jobs already rejected by white women. These jobs included some of the most dangerous tasks in industry, such as carrying glass to hot ovens in glass factories and dyeing furs in the furrier industry.

World War I produced no substantial or lasting change in women's participation in the labor force. The employment rate of women in 1920 was actually a bit lower (20.4%) than in 1910 (20.9%). The labor unions, the government, and the society at large were not ready to accept a permanent shift in women's economic role. Instead, women filled an urgent need during the wartime years and were relegated to their former positions as soon as peace returned. As the reformer Mary Von Kleeck wrote, "When the immediate dangers . . . were passed, the prejudices came to life once more."

When the men returned from the war, they were given priority in hiring, and although a number of women left the labor force voluntarily, many were forced out by layoffs. Those remaining were employed in the low-paying, low-prestige positions women had always occupied and in those occupations that had become accepted as women's domain. . . .

The Great Depression of the 1930s threw millions out of work. The severe employment problems during this period intensified the general attitude that a woman with a job was taking that job away from a male breadwinner. Yet during the 1930s, an increasing number of women went to work for the first time. The increase was most marked among younger, married women, who worked at least until the first child, and among older, married women, who reentered the marketplace because of dire economic need or in response to changing patterns of consumer demand. Most jobs held by women were part-time, seasonal, and marginal. Women's labor-force participation increased slowly throughout this period and into the early 1940s . . . , except in the professions (including feminized professions such as elementary teaching, nursing, librarianship, and social work). The proportion of women in all professions declined from 14.2 percent to 12.3 percent during the Depression decade.

WORLD WAR II

The ordeal of World War II brought about tremendous change in the numbers and occupational distribution of working women. As during World War I, the shortage of male workers, who had gone off to fight, coupled with the mounting pressures of war production brought women into the workforce. A corresponding shift in attitudes about women's aptitudes and proper roles resulted. Women entered the munitions factories and other heavy industries to support the war effort. The War Manpower Commission instituted a massive advertising campaign to attract women to the war industries. Patriotic appeals were common.

. . .

Equal work did not mean equal pay for the women in these varied wartime occupations. Although the National War Labor Board issued a directive to industries that stipulated equal pay for equal work, most employers continued to pay women at a lower rate. Furthermore, women had little opportunity to advance in their new occupations.

World War II marked an important turning point in women's participation in the paid labor force. The social prohibition concerning married women working gave way under wartime pressure, and women wartime workers demonstrated that it was possible for women to maintain their households while also assuming the role of breadwinner with outside employment. More women than ever before learned to accommodate the simultaneous demands of family and work. The experience

"pointed the way to a greater degree of choice for American women."

However, at the war's end, with the return of men to civilian life, there was a tremendous pressure on women to return to their former positions in the home. During this time, a new social ideology began to emerge; Betty Friedan later called it "the feminine mystique." This ideology drew in social workers, educators, journalists, and psychologists, all of whom tried to convince women that their place was again in the home. As Friedan notes, in the fifteen years following World War II, the image of "women at home" rather than "at work" became a cherished and self-perpetuating core of contemporary American culture. A generation of young people were brought up to extol the values of home and family, and woman's role was defined as the domestic center around which all else revolved. Women were supposed to live like those in Norman Rockwell *Saturday Evening Post* illustrations. The idealized image was of smiling mothers baking cookies for their wholesome children, driving their station wagons loaded with freckled youngsters to an endless round of lessons and activities, returning with groceries and other consumer goods to the ranch houses they cared for with such pride. Women were supposed to revel in these roles and gladly leave the running of the world to men.

. . . .

Yet, unlike the post–World War I period, after World War II women did not go back to the kitchens. Instead, women's labor-force participation continued to increase throughout the post–World War II decades, so that by the late 1960s, 40 percent of American women were in the labor force, and by the late 1990s, 60 percent were. Who were the women most likely to be part of this "new majority" of women at work?

AFTER WORLD WAR II: THE RISE OF THE MARRIED WOMAN WORKER

Between 1890 and the beginning of World War II, single women comprised at least half the female labor force. The others were mostly married African American, immigrant, or working-class women.

The decade of the 1940s saw a change in the type of woman worker, as increasing numbers of married women left their homes to enter the world of paid work. . . . Although single women continued to have the highest labor-force participation rates among women, during the 1940s the percentage of married women in the workforce grew more rapidly than any other category. Between 1940 and 1950, single women workers were in short supply because of low birthrates in the 1930s. Furthermore, those single women available for work were marrying at younger ages and leaving the labor market to raise their families. On the other hand, ample numbers of older, married women were available, and these women (who had married younger, had had fewer children, and were living longer) were eager for paid employment. In 1940, about 15 percent of married women were employed; by 1950, 24 percent. This increase has continued: by 1960, 32 percent of married women; in 1970, over 41 percent; in 1980, 50 percent; and by 1995, 61 percent. Indeed, as the twentieth century comes to a close, we can see that labor-force participation rates of single and married women have become almost identical. . . .

During the 1940s, 1950s, and 1960s, it was mainly older, married women entering the workforce. In 1957, for example, the labor-force participation rate among women aged forty-five to forty-nine years exceeded the rate for twenty- to twenty-four-year-old women. During the 1960s, young married mothers with preschool- or school-age children began to enter the workforce. This trend continued for the next three decades; by 1995, more than three-quarters of married women with children between six and seventeen years of age were employed, and, most significantly, almost two-thirds of those women with children under the age of six were in the labor force. . . . In short, whereas before 1970 the overwhelming majority of married women stopped working after they had children, today the overwhelming majority of married women do not.

WOMEN OF COLOR

Denied entrance to the factories during the rise of industrialization and, for much of the twentieth century, facing discriminatory hiring practices that closed off opportunities in the newly expanded office and sales jobs, many women of color entered domestic service. From 1910 to 1940, the proportion of white women employed in clerical and sales positions almost doubled, and there was a decline in the numbers of white women in domestic work. Private household work then became the province of African American women: the percentage of African American household workers increased from 38.5 percent in 1910 to 59.9 percent in 1940. . . . For the next three decades, African American women remained the single largest group in domestic service.

African American women's economic status improved dramatically from 1940 through the 1960s, as a result of an increase in light manufacturing jobs, as well as changes in technology. African American women moved from private household work into manufacturing and clerical work, and made significant gains in the professions. Whereas in 1940, 60 percent of employed African American females worked in private households, by the late 1960s only 20 percent did. Their job prospects continued to improve, and by the 1980s, almost half of all working African American women were doing so in "white-collar" jobs—clerical and sales positions, as well as professional jobs in business, health care, and education. Through the 1990s, the historic, job-prestige gap between African American and white working women continued to close. Almost two-thirds of working African American women had jobs in the white-collar world by 1996, compared with nearly three-quarters of working white women. . . .

OTHER WOMEN OF COLOR AT WORK

Each minority group has had a different experience in American society and has faced different opportunities and obstacles. Women in each group share with African American women the concerns of all minority women; they share with the men of their ethnic groups the problems of discrimination against that particular ethnic minority.

NATIVE AMERICAN WOMEN

As we noted earlier, gender roles in Native American communities were disrupted during the conquest and oppression by whites. For example, Navajo society was traditionally matrilineal, with extended families the norm; Navajo women owned property and played an important role in family decisions. But beginning in the 1930s, government policy disrupted this system by giving land only to males. As they could no longer make a sufficient living off the land, more and more Navajo men had to seek employment off the reservations. Nuclear families became the norm. Navajo women became dependent on male providers. With the men away much of the time, these women are often isolated and powerless. They often face divorce or desertion and thus economic difficulties, because the community frowns on women seeking work off the reservation. Such disruption of the traditional Native American society left Native American women in very grim economic circumstances. But in recent decades, more and more of them have gotten jobs. Native American women's labor-force participation rate in 1970 was 35 percent (compared to 43% for all women). This rate rose sharply to 55 percent by the early 1990s and is now within a few percentage points of the rate for all women.

Like their African American counterparts over the past half century, Native American women have gradually moved out of low-skill farm and nonfarm work and domestic jobs into clerical, sales, professional, technical, and other "white-collar" jobs. In 1960, one in six working Native American women was employed as a domestic household worker; by the early 1990s only one in a hundred was. During the same period, the proportion of Native American women involved in agricultural work also went from [one in] ten to one in a hundred. Manufacturing work was increasingly replaced by white-collar work, reflecting the overall trends in the occupational structure; more specifically, while the percentage involved in factory work (much of it in textiles and traditional crafts) fell from 18.1 to 14.2, the percentage doing white-collar work soared from 28.9 to 61.3. Although many of these white-collar jobs are classified as "professional" (15.7% of all working Native American women) or "managerial" (9.4%), two-thirds of Native American women are still concentrated in the "secondary" sector of the labor market—which is characterized by low wages, few or no benefits, low

mobility, and high instability. They are kept there because of the "stagnation of the reservation economy," discrimination, and their relatively low level of educational attainment. A significant number do not have a high school diploma (in 1990, more than one-third of all those over the age of 25, compared to one-fifth of white women).

LATINA [CHICANA] WOMEN

. . . Large numbers of Chicanas migrated, usually with husband and children, from Mexico to the United States during the 1916–1920 labor shortage created by World War I. They found work in the sprawling "factory farms" of the Southwest, harvesting fruits, vegetables, and cotton in the Imperial and San Joaquin valleys of California, the Salt River valley of Arizona, and the Rio Grande valley of Texas. They also went to the Midwest, for instance to Michigan and Minnesota, to harvest sugar beets. Such migrant workers typically were exploited, spending long, tedious, and physically demanding hours in the fields for very low pay. Some became tenant farmers, which might seem a step up, except too often this system "created debt peonage; unable to pay the rent, tenants were unable to leave the land and remained virtually permanently indebted to their landlords."

During the 1920s, with a shortage of European immigration, new job opportunities opened up for Mexican Americans, and they began to migrate from rural, farm country to the urban, industrial centers, where they found work as domestics and factory workers. By 1930, one-third of working Chicanas were domestics and a quarter worked in manufacturing; at the time, the share employed in agriculture, forestry, and mining had fallen to 21 percent. Wage scales varied according to ethnicity, however. It was not uncommon to pay Chicana workers lower wages than "Anglo" (whites of European descent) women for doing the same job, whether as domestics, laundresses, or workers in the food-processing industries of the West and Southwest. Then the Depression years of the 1930s, with the general shortage of jobs, brought a backlash against Mexican American labor, and thousands of Mexicans were deported or pressured to leave.

World War II once again opened up the American labor market for Mexican migrants, as their labor was needed to offset wartime labor shortages. However, their treatment was deplorable by modern standards. In short, Mexican workers comprised a "reserve army" of exploited labor. Through the government-sponsored Bracero or "Manual Workers" program, Mexican workers were granted temporary work visas so that they could be employed on large corporate farms and elsewhere, but too often they were treated like slaves or prisoners.

World War II and the years following saw a massive shift in the occupational and geographical distribution of Chicana workers:

> Many left Texas for California, and the population became increasingly more urban. Women continued their move from the fields into garment factories throughout the Southwest. . . . [A] comparison of the 1930 and 1950 [census] data shows the magnitude of these shifts. For instance, the share of employed southwestern Chicanas working on farms dropped from 21 percent in 1930 to 6 percent in 1950, while the percentage in white-collar work doubled.

By the 1960s, the largest occupational category for Chicana workers was operatives, followed by clerical and service work. Chicanas became concentrated in particular industries—food processing, electronics (including telecommunications), and garments. Like their Native American counterparts, Chicana women have made some progress in entering professional and managerial occupations (primarily non-college teaching, nursing, librarianship, and social work). In 1960, 8.6 percent were in these occupations; by 1980, 12.6 percent, and by the early 1990s 17.5 percent. However, like the Native Americans, Chicana women are still overwhelmingly found in the secondary labor market (75%)—much more so than women (60%) and men (32%) of white European heritage.

The dominant reasons behind the low occupational prestige of all minority groups are the same: discrimination and low educational attainment. In the case of Chicana women, over 15 percent "are illiterate by the standard measure (completion of less than five years of schooling)," but studies of functional illiteracy during the 1970s and 1980s suggest "much higher rates—perhaps as high as 56 percent." At the other end of the educational attainment spectrum, only 8.4 percent of Latina women have completed four or more years of college—compared with 21.0 percent of white women and 12.9 percent of blacks. However, education is only part of the formula for success in the U.S. occupational system: for when education is held constant, Latina women make only between 84 and 90 percent of what white women do.

Beyond lack of education, Chicana women face other important obstacles in the labor market. They have high rates of unemployment and underemployment. Many of the jobs they hold are seasonal and often nonunionized. This lack of advancement translates into higher poverty rates (23 percent for Chicana/os in the early 1990s). The median income for full-time Chicana workers is lower than that of any other U.S. racial-ethnic group. For Latina women (in general) with children and no husband present, the poverty rate is even worse: 49.4 percent compared with 26.6 percent of white women in this situation.

Increasingly, Chicana women, like many female workers of color around the globe, are doing service or assembly work for multi-national corporations, especially in the apparel, food-processing, and electronics industries. These women have often displaced men in assembly work because they can be paid less and many do not receive job benefits. The work hours are long, and women are often assigned monotonous tasks that are dangerous to their health.

. . .

ASIAN AMERICAN WOMEN

. . . Asian Americans are considered to be the "model minority." . . . However, this is as much myth as fact. While many among both the native-born and the recent arrivals have high levels of education and professional skills and can readily fit into the labor market, others lack such advantages, often finding work only as undocumented laborers in low-paying jobs with long work days, little or no job mobility, and no benefits.

> We are told we have overcome our oppression, and that therefore we are the model minority. Model

refers to the cherished dictum of capitalism that "pulling hard on your bootstraps" brings due rewards. . . . Asian American success stories . . . do little to illuminate the actual conditions of the majority of Asian Americans. Such examples conceal the more typical Asian American experience of unemployment, underemployment and struggle to survive. The model minority myth thus classically scapegoats Asian Americans. It labels us in a way that dismisses the real problems that many do face, while at the same time pitting Asians against other oppressed people of color.

In 1996, 37.3 percent of Asian women who were 25 years and over had at least a bachelor's degree, compared with 23.2 percent of non-Latina whites. Filipina American women secured the highest college graduation rate of all women, a rate 50 percent greater than that of white males. Following closely behind are Chinese American and Japanese American women, who exceed both the white male and female college graduation rates. Yet, these educational achievements bring lower returns for Asian women than for whites. Census data reveal a gap between achievement and economic reward for Asian American women, who suffer from both race and sex discrimination within the labor market.

. . .

And it would be wrong to equate "Asian" with "well educated," because the majority of Asian women immigrating to the United States since 1980 have low levels of education. Though, as just noted, Asian women are much more likely to be college-educated than non-Latina white women, they are also much more likely—two and a half times more likely—to be grade-school dropouts: in 1996, 12.5 percent of Asian women had not gone beyond the eighth grade, compared to only 5.2 percent of their non-Latina white counterparts. This fact is linked to the other most obvious difference between Asian and white women . . . —the proportions working as "operators, fabricators, and laborers," where we find significantly more Asian women.

These women are most commonly employed as sewing machine operators at home or in small sweatshops in the Chinatowns of New York and San Francisco. Asian immigrant women are also heavily employed in the microelectronics industry. Women in general comprise 80 to 90 percent of assembly workers in this industry, and approximately "half of these assembly workers are recent immigrants from the Philippines, Vietnam, Korea, and South Asia." Within the microelectronics industry jobs are often "structured along racial and gender lines, with men and white workers earning higher wages and being much more likely to be promoted than women and workers of color." Karen Hossfeld's research on relationships between Third World immigrant women production workers and their white male managers in the high-tech Silicon Valley of California relates how immigrant women of color negotiate and often employ resistance to primarily white, middle-class management demands. One Filipina circuit board assembler in Silicon Valley puts it this way:

> The bosses here have this type of reasoning like a seesaw. One day it's "you're paid less because women are different than men," or "immigrants need less to get by." The next day it's "you're all just workers here—no special treatment just because you're female or foreigners."
>
> Well, they think they're pretty clever with their doubletalk, and that we're just a bunch of dumb aliens.
>
> But it takes two to use a seesaw. What we are gradually figuring out here is how to use their own logic against them.

As clerical or administrative support workers, Asian American women are disproportionately represented as cashiers, file clerks, office machine operators, and typists. They are less likely to obtain employment as secretaries or receptionists. Noting that there is an "overrepresentation of college-educated women in clerical work," Woo suggests that education functions less as a path toward mobility into higher occupational categories, and more as "a hedge against jobs as service workers and as machine operatives or assembly workers."

Asian American women with a college education who obtain professional employment are often restricted to the less prestigious jobs within this category. Asian American women "are more likely to remain marginalized in their work organization, to encounter a 'glass ceiling,' and to earn less than white men, Asian American men, and white women with comparable educational backgrounds." They are least represented in those male-dominated positions of physician, lawyer, and judge, and are heavily concentrated in the more female-dominated occupations of nursing and teaching.

Asian women have been subjected to a range of stereotypes. The "Lotus Blossom" stereotype depicts them as submissive and demure sex objects: "good, faithful, uncomplaining, totally compliant, self-effacing, gracious servants who will do anything and everything to please, entertain, and make them feel comfortable and carefree." At the opposite extreme, the Dragon Lady stereotype portrays Asian women

> as "promiscuous and untrustworthy," as the castrating Dragon Lady who, while puffing on her foot-long cigarette holder, could poison a man as easily as she could seduce him. "With her talon-like six-inch

fingernails, her skin-tight satin dress slit to the thigh," the Dragon Lady is desirable, deceitful and dangerous.

Asian American feminist Germaine Wong notes how stereotypes concerning Asian women operate in the workplace, serving to deter their advancement into leadership roles and to increase their vulnerability to sexual harassment. Additionally, these stereotypes have fostered a demand for "X-rated films and pornographic materials featuring Asian women in bondage, for 'Oriental' bathhouse workers in U.S. cities, and for Asian mail-order brides."

In sum, the notion of Asian Americans as the "model minority" deviates considerably from sociological reality. While Asian American women as a group have achieved some "success" in terms of high educational attainment, they receive lower returns on this investment compared to the white population. They have not "escaped the stigmatization of being minority and recent immigrants in a discriminatory job market."

58. STRUCTURAL INJUSTICE, SEX WORK, AND HUMAN TRAFFICKING

CORINNE SCHWARZ, EMILY J. KENNEDY, AND HANNAH BRITTON (2017)

INTRODUCTION

Feminist debates surrounding sex work and human trafficking are notoriously contentious, with a binary approach that sees pro-sex work and anti-human trafficking ideologies as incompatible. This article enters the debate among feminists working to end sexual violence, address human trafficking, and ensure the rights and agency of sex workers. These debates have pitted feminist against feminist as they try to create more livable lives for people globally. The stakes are high because the manifestations of this conflict have become entrenched in legislation, incarceration, and deportation—structures that affect real people's material conditions and lived experiences. The battle lines are drawn on these bodies attempting to survive deeply constrained environments, to imagine new forms of freedom and pleasure, and to escape coercion, violence, poverty, and abuse.

Consider those in the United States thought to be most vulnerable to exploitation and trafficking. The United States currently has 402,378 children in foster care, 14.5 million people in poverty under the age of 18, and an estimated 2.5 million homeless youth—20–40 percent of whom are LGBTQ youth (US Department of Health and Human Services 2014; US Census Current Population Survey 2016; National Center on Family Homelessness 2014). Homeless LGBTQ youth are at even greater risks for trafficking, sexual violence, abuse, and suicide (National Coalition for the Homeless 2009). Consider also the impact of the carceral state. In the United States, 56,575 persons were arrested for prostitution in 2012 (Bureau of Justice 2012), and 360,000–400,000 persons were deported from 2009 to 2014 (US Department of Homeland Security 2015).

This paper speaks across the contentious divide between sex work and human trafficking research. As members of the interdisciplinary Institute for Policy & Social Research (IPSR) at the University of Kansas, we were able to bring our projects into conversation to explore how structural injustices and carceral violence affect marginalized populations. These are not parallel projects; methodologically, we draw from two different samples of sex workers and anti-trafficking service providers, respectively. These interviews were conducted in different geographic regions at different times and had distinct research objectives. Even with these differences, both projects define sex work as commercial sexual activities exchanged for money and human trafficking as any commercial activity induced by fraud, force, or coercion. Even if it is a constrained choice, sex work is potentially agentive, while human trafficking involves having that agency compromised or even excised completely. Additionally, the themes and topics we encountered in our projects fit in a larger conversation about agency, vulnerability, and exploitation, and both directly address the growing divide between anti-trafficking activists and sex work advocates. This paper emerges from this normative conversation, indicating that these two camps share far more than either has acknowledged.

Neither of our projects sought out trafficked persons, as interviewing this population of survivors could be potentially retraumatizing, especially as trafficked persons are called upon to tell and retell their stories within the judicial system and research studies. Even with these goals, both research teams encountered trafficked persons in our participant pool, demonstrating the scope of trafficking across disparate populations: two sex workers interviewed in Kennedy's project experienced fraud; one service provider in Britton and Schwarz's study self-identified as a trafficking survivor.

We argue that, coerced or not, lives are harmed and made less livable—by structural injustice, anti-immigration rhetoric, deepening poverty, incarceration, and defunding the welfare state. Taking a cue from Butler (2004), we argue that these factors create the climate for lives to be made less livable: to be compromised, devalued, subject to violence, and removed from political legibility. We illuminate the statistics with rich qualitative data that begins to answer the call for accuracy about human trafficking and sex work. We assert the conflict between abolitionist and autonomy feminists distracts from substantive changes needed to decrease inequalities that disproportionately affect women, migrant populations, and racial and sexual minorities. While this paper focuses on human trafficking and sex work within the United States, the scope of this carceral framework clearly affects lives in similar ways outside our borders (Britton and Dean 2014; Chapkis 2003; Kempadoo 2001).

While others suggest that feminists could embrace a third way by uniting in opposition to sex trafficking while respecting women's agency (Cavalieri 2011), we argue instead that the debate itself is the problem. The oppositional framework shaping this debate is problematic, and the resultant proposals may further harm the "victims" they intend to protect. Current policies, and to a large degree the feminist debates surrounding them, do not make lives more livable or legible. They instead shift our gaze away from the real phenomena constraining choice, pleasure, and survival: systemic and structural inequalities that disproportionately affect LGBTQ persons, poor people, and trans people of color.

Our findings advocate for solutions that address the criminalization of economic migration, sex work, pleasure, poverty, and survival. We extend Sassen's (2002, 258) ideas of understanding how the "feminization of survival" operates, who benefits from it, and how we can alter the social institutions and practices that foster justice. We argue that activists and scholars need to develop new understandings of contentment that encompass context-specific agency, choice, and survival (Lewis and Marine 2015). Pleasure then becomes less important as a sense of enjoyment or satisfaction and more about the issues of livability and survival—how people survive under strict economic and carceral restraints while maintaining a sense of agency. We also re-envision the idea of danger as a series of threats located within the security state, criminality, and structural inequalities.

ANTI-TRAFFICKING MOVEMENT

Internationally, the anti-trafficking movement has polarized activists committed to ending the exploitation of women but with very different means to achieve that end. On one side are feminist abolitionists, who believe the root causes of women's exploitation are patriarchies of oppression that reduce women to commodities available for men's entitled purchase. Because gendered life outcomes remain unequal, these feminists understand most forms of sex work as prostitution and exploitation, much as the antipornography feminists see the porn industry as a site of commercialization and degradation. Abolitionist feminists often perceive sex workers as victims of patriarchy and male demand. Queer and transgender individuals are frequently left out of this framework, both as sex workers or clients of sex workers. The antiprostitution "End Demand" movement focuses its attention on prosecuting the *consumers* of sex work—the clients—and criminalizing the purchase of sex. While many do not advocate penalizing sex workers, this prosecution agenda leaves sex workers little room to navigate the carceral state. Because clients fear arrest, sex workers may be forced to make hasty negotiations in risky, less secure environments.

In the United States, the anti-trafficking movement has created a strange—but familiar—coalition of feminists, "progressive Democrats, and Republicans who closely identified with the evangelical Christian community" and decry prostitution and women's exploitation (Gulati 2011, 364). Radical feminists and Christian conservatives unite in ending trafficking (primarily sex trafficking) and are now oddly connected to growing anti-immigration sentiment (Shrage 2012; Sassen 2002). Indeed, as Chapkis argues, a slippage occurs when anti-trafficking advocates incorrectly demarcate between trafficked persons and migrants:

> The line drawn between the innocent victim and the willful illegal immigrant used to determine punishment and protection is not only a dangerous one, but it is also a distinction that does not hold. Most trafficking victims are also economic migrants. Their victimization most often involves high debts and abusive working conditions, not outright kidnapping and imprisonment. (2003, 931)

The anti-trafficking movement has been well funded, and, with its focus on policy and prosecution (Tilly and Wood 2012), it has been more successful than other movements in creating an international diffusion of anti-trafficking policies (Britton and Dean 2014). Governments know how to legislate and prosecute; they are less adept at changing attitudes and social structures—the root causes of trafficking and sex work stigma. For example, the Trafficking Victims' Protection Act (TVPA)—the first and prevailing federal-level policy on human trafficking—has provisions to prosecute traffickers and protect survivors, but not to prevent trafficking.

Policy goals of protecting survivors through access to safe living spaces, court orders of protection, and visas are imperative, as is prosecuting traffickers and market facilitators who perpetuate coerced labor. Problematically, these efforts only catch people after the crime of trafficking, while the structural factors promoting exploitation remain in place. The violence, abuse, and degradation experienced by trafficked persons are real and substantiated. The approaches taken by most states continue to be reactive, after the abuse has occurred, rather than proactive about the structural factors that lead to trafficking.

PRO-SEX WORK ACTIVISM

On the other side of the debate are autonomy feminists who also understand and appreciate the realities of patriarchy and women's oppression, but believe in the right to engage in sex work for reasons ranging from survival to freely chosen legitimate employment. These feminists and allies favor the decriminalization of sex work to ensure sex workers' safety and well-being (Beloso 2012; Cavalieri 2011). By treating sex work as similar to many other forms of service industry employment, they argue decriminalization will decrease abuse, harm, and illegal sex trafficking (Commission for Gender Equality 2014). This perspective, often considered harm reduction, takes a pragmatic approach to commercial sexual exchange.

Pro-sex work activists work to decouple commercial sexual exchange from trafficking and a hierarchy of sexual practices (Weitzer 2012; Hoang 2014).

These feminists believe that most sex workers actively choose this employment. When consent to engage in sex as an occupation is enacted—even in the many cases where sex work, because it is work, is not fun—it can still be understood as decision-making with agency (Rosen and Venkatesh 2008). Sex workers, much like other freelancers, can cultivate relationships with repeat clients (Ray 2007). This provides stability and increases the potential to refuse relationships with problem clients.

As pro-sex work feminists have demonstrated how sex work can be done with agency, critiques of the anti-trafficking movement have also emerged to reconsider the norms of human trafficking research and advocacy (Hoang and Parrenas 2014; Galusca 2012). Multiple scholars have argued that Europe's anti-trafficking movement is a thinly veiled attempt to surveil and maintain national borders (Davydova 2013; Agustin 2007; Bernstein 2007b). The anti-trafficking movement has been tied to the creation of women in the global South as a victim class by inciting fear of their transnational movement and sexualities (Desyllas 2007; Chapkis 2003; Kempadoo 2001; Doezema 2000). Scholarship has noted the similarities between the current anti-trafficking movement and the turn of the century US media panic over "white slavery," which led to a swift political response in the form of immigration restrictions, efforts to prosecute importers and traffickers, and provisions to deport immigrant prostitutes (D'Emilio and Freedman 2012; Spencer and Broad 2012; Donovan 2005; Doezema 2000; Stienstra 1996). A trend of US policy influenced by Protestant religious movements is considered the source of the abolitionist anti-trafficking movement from the 1990s to the present (Shrage 2012; Bernstein 2007a; Soderlund 2005).

Scholars have noted the anti-trafficking movement's creation of an "ideal victim" in need of—and, more importantly, worthy of—rescue (Chapkis 2003; Sassen 2002; Kempadoo 2001). Srikantiah (2007, 187–88) describes the iconic victim as gendered female, passive, compliant with traditional modes of justice, and legible as a citizen—"the iconic victim concept distances trafficking victims from the 'illegal alien' stereotype, thus avoiding any association

with economic migration." By portraying all sex workers as victims, some in the antipornography and anti-trafficking movements attempt to claim the moral high ground as they claim to be rescuing women from sex trafficking. The rhetorical distinction between deserving victims of trafficking and undeserving migrants solidifies a union between some anti-trafficking and anti-immigration proponents: "In this way, the Trafficking Victims' Protection Act helps to define 'compassionate conservatism': a willingness to provide assistance and protection for a few by positioning them as exceptions, proving the need for punitive measures against the many" (Chapkis 2003, 930).

THE PLEASURE/DANGER DICHOTOMY: CREATING UNLIVABLE LIVES

The current debates create opposition between human trafficking and sex work and encourage a dichotomy between pleasure and danger. This framework is ideologically restricted to what appears to be mutually exclusive worldviews: sex-positive feminists versus sex-suspicious feminists, constrained agency versus exploitation, labor versus slavery, rights-based policies versus rescue strategies, and so on.

Agentive Feminists	Abolitionist Feminists
Sex-positive feminist	Sex-suspicious feminist
Agency within constrained choice	Exploitation
Sensuality	Commodification of bodies
Labor	Slavery
Rights-based policies	Rescue strategies
Immigration reformers	Anti-immigration advocates
Decriminalization	End demand/criminalize purchasing sex
Global Alliance Against Traffic in Women	Coalition Against Trafficking in Women

Each side includes thoughtful, committed feminists working to ensure the full enfranchisement and expression of women, LGBTQ communities, and racial minorities—to use Butler's (2004) concept, to ensure the livability of all lives. However, this dichotomous framework does not reflect the lived experiences of our own research participants, who encounter pleasure and danger as interactive, intersecting forces. This narrow, binary approach to creating livable lives distracts from the very real threats that our participants face. We see our projects as offering a path outside of the gridlock of current debates that so frequently call upon these binary structures.

Specifically, we find the ideologies of carceral feminism—what Bernstein calls "a cultural and political formation in which previous generations' justice and liberation struggles are recast in carceral terms" (2012, 236)—undergird the pleasure/danger dichotomy, undermine the ways people create livable lives, and have material consequences for our participants. Carceral feminism operates within punitive avenues, a strategic tactic in the US carceral state. It advocates for policy change, which regulates and criminalizes, resulting in fines, arrests, and jail time. Not all policy is carceral; US law has at times been deployed to uphold sex workers' rights (Karalekas 2014). Policy may be used to promote autonomy and contentment, as in the case of antirape and prochoice legislation, or sex negativity, as was the case of antiporn legislation. Policy can also reinforce normative ideologies about pleasure and danger and how those forces expand or contract the options for a livable life. As Butler writes, "What is most important is to cease legislating for all lives what is livable only for some, and similarly, to refrain from proscribing for all lives what is only unlivable for some" (2004, 8). When policy upholds one half of the pleasure/danger binary—or conflates sex work with sex trafficking— some lives become unlivable, unrecognizable within its frames.

For all our participants, trafficking, exploitation, and abuse are egregious violations. But current anti-trafficking legislation applied within the carceral state fails to address the complex issues of sex work and human trafficking at great and unnecessary cost to our participants, operating with only one perception of how livable lives can flourish. Policy changes intended to produce humanitarian results— for example, the TVPA's protections for trafficking survivors—actually resulted in arrests or the denial of benefits under the basis of failing to prove one's victimization (Chapkis 2003). Using Butler's terms, we can reread the TVPA to show how those who could not prove their trafficking had "no norms of recognition" within the legislation and, thus, became "foreclosed from possibility" as a survivor, as a livable life (2004, 31). This is not to say that all anti-trafficking policies are inherently wrong. Rather, solutions to gender-based inequality and violence that perpetuate a prison industrial complex, which target certain populations—populations already oppressed by racism, sexism, and classism—for increased force and violence are the problem (Lawston and Meiners 2014).

The influence of the carceral state is evident in anti-trafficking policy. The numbers of human traffickers prosecuted within the framework of the TVPA reflect the disproportionate numbers of incarcerated young African American and Latino men nationally. Out of the 488 total trafficking suspects identified between 2008 and 2010, almost half were African American, and nearly one-fourth were Hispanic/Latino (US Department of Justice 2011). As police efforts to combat human trafficking increasingly focus on people of color as perpetrators, all persons engaged in street-level sex work—pimps, clients, and sex workers—and nonconsensual sex trafficking find themselves increasingly subject to the surveillance and punition of the carceral state (Bernstein 2012).

INTERDISCIPLINARY CONVERSATIONS

Our thinking on the current inadequacy of the pleasure/danger binary comes from an interdisciplinary conversation at the nexus of two ongoing but completely independent research projects: Kennedy's national research with sex workers and Schwarz and Britton's work studying the Midwest anti-trafficking movement. One would think based on the starting points of each of our projects (sex work versus trafficking) our findings would be mutually unintelligible, either fraught by inherent differences or reinscribing current sex war ideologies. Rather, our shared commitment to fostering conversations across departments, fostered by our membership in IPSR, gave us a platform to understand each other's work outside of this contentious divide. We began to think past our own narrowly focused research projects to larger normative understandings of criminality, risk, resilience, and agency that impact marginalized populations. It became clear that our findings—based in the actual experiences and voices of sex workers, trafficking survivors, and service providers—had more in common than any of us expected, though definitively not in the frequently circulated argument that all sex workers are trafficked. Participants were concerned with finding different paths toward livability and survival.

Kennedy's research began on the Internet, which has been identified as a key site of communication for nonnormative practice, to observe over one hundred self-identified sex work bloggers, then progressed to interviews with sex workers. She researches how the Internet affects the sex industry and sex work stigma. Kennedy is a sociologist and feminist. Her theoretical stance held that, while there is undoubtedly a hierarchical valuing of sex work in society—i.e., normatively stripping is somewhat acceptable, while street prostitution is intolerable—from the vantage point of many of the workers, this hierarchy is a useless social construction. A hierarchical valuing of sex work disadvantages sex workers who have worked in more than one sex work trade (a regular practice in this workforce), it justifies worse treatment of some sex workers relative to others, and it divides the workers, further discouraging their attempts at activism beyond the disadvantage currently resulting from arrests, incarceration, social isolation, and widespread sex work stigma. Observing sex workers on the Internet, she found many expressly criticize the sex work hierarchy, which some label the whoriarchy or the ho-iarchy. For this reason, she defines sex work as the commercial exchange of sex or sexual provocation for money, an umbrella definition that includes fourteen different kinds of work.

Kennedy began collecting interviews in 2013. She posted a Call for Participants (CFP) where she had been observing sex work bloggers, and she has to date conducted thirty-six in-depth interviews with people who answered the call or were referred to the project. The interviewees ranged in birth year from 1972 to 1994. Thirty-five of thirty-six were women including one trans woman. Twenty-eight interviewees self-identified their race/ethnicity status as white, one as Native American, two as Black, two as Asian American, and three as mixed (Asian Indian, Half-white/Half-Iranian, and Latina/white). Twelve identified their sexual orientation as bisexual, nine as queer, six as pansexual, two as heterosexual, one each as asexual, bicurious, heteroflexible, lesbian, omnisexual, straightish, and one said it depended on the day. The interviewees had worked or were currently working in the sex industry in thirty-three of the United States, plus Ontario, Canada, and Australia. Aggregating their responses, the following sex work trades are represented: cam play for pay, escorting, erotic writing, fetish modeling, nude dancing, nude modeling, phone sex service, pornographic acting, power play for pay, sensual massage, stripping, and sugaring.

Britton and Schwarz are gender studies scholars who approach human trafficking research from a human rights position of ending gender-based violence and finding upstream, structural solutions to vulnerability, exploitation, and trafficking. They have been lead researchers in an ongoing two-year project located across Kansas and Missouri to discern the sites of vulnerability to human trafficking, including both sex and labor exploitation. They have sought to map physical sites of vulnerability (truck stops along the major highways that bisect the country and the city; massage parlors; sporting and conference venues; military bases; agricultural and construction sectors populated by migrant labor), as well as locate moments within the life course that could create vulnerability (aging out of the foster care system, moments of child abuse and trauma, periods of homelessness, moments of income/healthcare insecurity).

To date, Britton's research team has conducted fifty-four intensive interviews with service providers in the Midwest. Utilizing a semistructured interview protocol, the researchers interviewed community stakeholders working for a variety of organizations that encounter vulnerable, exploited, or trafficked persons. These interviews range from thirty minutes to one hour, yielding rich narratives of vulnerability, agency, risk, and resilience. The research team has used both inductive and deductive analysis with ATLAS.ti software to understand how trafficking occurs as well as points of intervention to reduce vulnerability before exploitation occurs.

While we worked to understand and identify individual risk factors (such as homophobia, transphobia, cognitive and learning disabilities, undocumented status), we uncovered even more significant structural risk factors: poverty, homelessness, incarceration, and deportation. Similarly, these interview narratives demonstrate a nuanced picture of vulnerable populations' agency and resilience, including looking to their families and children as reasons to survive; having a belief in education as a pathway out of trafficking; and enduring violence and exploitation as a means to create a better future for their families and children. These become moments of agency that they use to survive and thrive.

While each project is shaped by our separate research agendas, all three researchers define themselves as feminist empiricists. We base our findings and our policy prescriptions on empirical work that is guided and framed by our participants' lived experiences.

FINDINGS

The interdisciplinary conversations occurring above and based on our very different research projects led us to some new normative understandings of risk, resilience, pleasure, survival, and danger. We argue the pleasure/danger binary distracts from the larger threats we are not tackling. Specifically, allowing the carceral, security state to define the argument, design the solutions and policies, and codify and criminalize pleasure perpetuates the gridlock that prevents structural changes that eliminate harm, which is the goal of both agentive and abolitionist feminists.

Our participants showed how the factors that compel someone into trafficking or coercive transactional sex are part of a *constrained choice*: many vulnerable or trafficked persons have some degree of agency that facilitated their engagement in certain forms of labor, even if that labor was coerced. Multiple push factors result from "situations of economic, political, religious, and military instability or tension" compounded by poverty (Srikantiah 2007, 163). These factors can be "atmospheric" or individual—for example, a person living in a stable environment might feel compelled to leave that environment because of "strained family circumstances," placing them in a similar position of vulnerability to someone leaving a war-torn country or living in poverty (Srikantiah 2007, 192). Acknowledging constrained choice-making reveals the complexity of agency within systems of trafficking (Weitzer 2014; Cavalieri 2011; Chapkis 2003; Sassen 2002).

The term "coercion" here is still problematic. Anti-trafficking scholars have shown how laborers were arguably coerced into certain exploitative practices through their relative poverty, family pressure, or the general lack of options. What might read as coercion to the anti-trafficking movement reads to the laborers as exercising their constrained agency; these people would be failed by a definition of trafficking specifically rooted in "coercion." Similarly, the line between an exploited trafficking victim and an exploited undocumented worker who chose to be smuggled into a country is narrow (Cavalieri 2011; Chapkis 2003; Sassen 2002). Denying exploited laborers state protection or threatening them with deportation because they were initially "culpable" in their migration contradicts the human rights goals of anti-trafficking efforts. Consent is no longer relevant in exploitation.

In place of a pleasure/danger binary, we envision pleasure and danger in new ways. Pleasure becomes a dynamic form encompassing both pleasure as autonomy and sensuality (such as joy in one's work) and pleasure as agency within a constrained environment (such as the ability to feed your family). Dynamic pleasure and contentment, as described in our data below, are worthy of feminist advocacy (Reger 2014). This has meaning especially in societies and systems that seek to deny livability through incarceration, deportation, violence, and so on. Danger, on the other hand, becomes the intertwined structural and individual-level risk factors that created material harm: the threat of incarceration or deportation, neoliberal economic policies that defund the welfare state, anti-LGBTQ policies that facilitate discrimination, and the privatization and defunding of key social services. A person's individual identities can also compound real danger of discrimination or vulnerability: race, citizenship status, poverty, LGBTQ identity, disability, homelessness, income insecurity, and health crises.

. . .

STRUCTURAL FACTORS CONTRIBUTING TO SEX WORK AND HUMAN TRAFFICKING

Our participants had various constraints, risk factors, or identities that affected their ability to make choices, experience pleasure, and have a livable life (Butler 2004). Britton and Schwarz found that the *vast majority* of the persons vulnerable to trafficking in their study faced poverty, unemployment, and income insecurity. Both domestic and foreign-born survivors faced an economic precarity that compelled them to take risks at work, to pursue work that was abusive, or to "consent" to work that eventually led to their trafficking. This economic insecurity often also translated into housing and health care insecurity. A lack of affordable healthcare and insurance were push factors for trafficking.

Each of these factors—poverty, housing insecurity, and a lack of affordable health care/insurance—was dramatically compounded for undocumented workers. Undocumented persons can have a fear of arrest and deportation that prevents them from seeking assistance. These vulnerabilities are exacerbated by limited English-language skills that prevent them from understanding their possible protection under trafficking laws.

Similarly, individuals—especially youth—who identified as LGBTQ faced familial rejection, social isolation, or harassment that drove many into homelessness and to engage in survival sex. These youth

may become targets of trafficking predators who offer protection. There is extensive documentation of the linkage of LGBTQ youth and homelessness (Ferguson-Colvin and Maccio 2012; Gordon and Hunter 2013), and trafficking scholars are beginning to document the vulnerability LGBTQ persons face to survival sex and trafficking (Dank et al. 2015). These vulnerabilities often continue into adulthood.

Schwarz and Britton found another pattern: individuals who had emotional, cognitive, or learning disabilities may be targeted by trafficking predators. Traffickers sought youth whose disability status isolated them, made them feel inferior or different, resulted in bullying, or enticed them into unhealthy relationships. While no one asserted that disabled persons need special protection, participants did indicate that there were "windows of missed opportunity" to identify these vulnerabilities, for example, interventions with case managers or social workers that failed to see exploitation or trafficking at play. Most of the sex-trafficking survivors in the study also had experienced some form of child abuse—sexual, emotional or physical. More resources in schools, foster care systems, and community social services would enable social workers to assist all these youth through such vulnerability.

Given the international economic downturn in the last two decades, our anti-trafficking participants indicated that the neoliberal economic policies constrained the choices of their clients. . . .

This precarity is also seen in the material realities of sex workers who are working to find other avenues of employment. . . .

Similarly, there are problems in trying to address vulnerability through legislation, which creates guidelines and scales and frameworks that do not match lived experiences. As Carol states, she sees that many sex workers are driven by economic constraints and material poverty:

> When they [the police] do their prostitution stings, they think they are really out there combating trafficking. They are getting a few tricks, they are getting their hands smacked, but they are not getting humiliated in court like the women. . . . You get these local girls who are just trying to survive, maybe they don't have a big pimp daddy, they just put themselves on Backpage or

Craigslist or whatever, she is just out there trying to get some money to pay for her kid's school shoes or whatever, she gets caught up in this mess. She doesn't have $1000 to pay for a fine. She doesn't have that. So how is she going to get it? If she is having to prostitute to buy her kid's school shoes, she is probably going to go out and prostitute to pay her fine.[1]

Here, Carol outlines how attempts to rescue trafficking victims led to the further impoverishment of sex workers, who were already vulnerable to structural poverty and now had to pay fines for their arrest. Rather than dealing with the factors causing poverty, punishing sex workers may drive them into more exploitative situations.

CONSTRAINED PLEASURE

Many of the participants in our two projects talked about pleasure in a range of forms—from experiencing sensuality, to having agency, to earning money on their terms, to surviving discrimination and alienation from families or communities. As we discussed the findings of our two studies, we began to conceive of pleasure not as a continuum, with opposed poles, but rather as a fluid, elastic form. Sex workers we spoke with described their occupations as often occurring in environments of their choice characterized by safety, control, and autonomy. They described worker/client exchanges of different but equal power. The exchanges were often mutually trusting, respectful, and communicative.

We argue one way to think about pleasure is the ability to express agency within a constrained environment. Service providers combating trafficking often worked to encourage their clients' agency, including the ability to state their own needs:

> Everybody is at a different space, so we do not have a set program. We determine in partnership with that person what they need. We let them tell us about their lives. We don't tell them, because they are the experts on their lives, even if they are crazy out of their minds. They are the experts on their lives, we are not, you know. They don't always know what is best for them . . . but they know what they want, they know what they need, and most of what we try to do, step one is building a trust relationship.[2]

In order to avoid retraumatizing trafficked persons coming from a position of constrained agency, Carol emphasized the collaboration between herself and her clients. There is no programmatic path from vulnerability to rehabilitation; rather, she uses a "survivor-first" model, allowing people to opt in and out of services and resources as needed while fostering their resilience during times of self-sufficiency (Schwarz and Britton 2015). These formerly trafficked persons experience pleasure by cultivating expertise and authority over their own rehabilitative processes, leading to an individually satisfying experience. Within Carol's organization, she does not require proof of fraud, force, or coercion (as would be required under the TVPA if she were a government agency), but instead grants her clients the ability to present their own experiences as worthy of whatever interventions each individual deems necessary, restorative, and critical to their own understandings of livability.

If your environment is heavily surveilled or very vulnerable, pleasure may be constricted, but it never fully disappears. Even the ability to survive has value and meaning. We are not in any way arguing that coercion, force, or fraud are pleasurable. We are saying that multiple effects can be experienced at one time: the achievement of survival *at the same time* as the crush of trafficking. For the sex worker, this was evident, for example, at a sensual massage facility where a sex worker spoke of enjoying camaraderie with coworkers, *at the same time* as the pain of stigma from doing a job that is judged as suspicious or immoral. The types and forms of agency and autonomy are obviously very different in situations of extreme exploitation. The very act of survival demonstrates agency. Alternatively, if someone exists in an environment with more social control, mobility, and autonomy, pleasure can be expansive, inviting exploration of new social norms and ideas.

. . .

Sex workers of all types of employment expressed a range of pleasure—from pleasure in the enjoyment of their work to pleasure in making a living. As Grace, a stripper, told Kennedy,

> I started when I was 21, and I started at a prominent club in Portland. From high school I always told all

my friends, if I ever have the body I'm gonna do it. I don't really know for what reason other than I can. I started up, and I've been doing it ever since, and now I work at another prominent club in Portland. I love it. I love my job. It was just part of my plan to take care of myself. I see it as a very independent type of job. I felt and I still feel that, while it is objectifying and I'm playing into social stereotypes and gender roles and all that, I still feel like I would be kinda silly not to take advantage of the type of money you can earn while basically doing nothing (laughter).[3]

While acknowledging that she works within a constrained environment—one she describes as objectifying and fulfilling particular gender roles—Grace has found that the independence and pleasure in her job is a driving force in her desire to stay in the industry. The ability to make money "while basically doing nothing" (though flirting and dancing for six hours in 5-inch heels is not nothing) is a source of real pleasure and power for her.

Britney, a transgender escort interviewed by Kennedy, spoke about having not only pleasure in her job as an escort but also autonomy:

And a lot of [the escorts who advised me] I confess were confused, the ones who were helpful to me were confused because they came from a background where they were turned out, they were turned out by a friend when they were in dire straits, and I was coming into it with a position of "if I really hate this, I don't have to do it, but I want to have the experience at least once. And see how I feel about it, because it could be a thing." And I loved it, I did. It was really intensely meaningful to me on a variety of different axes. And I still miss it. Even though obviously, you know, I ran into a lot of bullshit. But I do miss it.[4]

Britney was mentored by others in the industry who had been driven to escorting through isolation/vulnerability. Britney had much more agency and authority in her work. It was her choice to become an escort, and escorting was something she could choose to continue or stop. She describes the pleasure of fellowship with mentors as well as with the actual work. Sex work had not just agency, but great meaning for Britney.

. . .

CRITIQUE OF CARCERALITY AND STRUCTURAL VIOLENCE

Perhaps the most common thread between our projects was the danger our participants felt from the carceral state and from their own structural vulnerability. Whether someone was talking about a trafficking survivor who feared deportation or discussing the multitude of laws they broke to engage in commercial sex, there was a strong fear of incarceration and deportation. Even when crimes are committed during the course of being trafficked, many US states still limit—or do not have—vacatur statutes to expunge prior offenses. We were struck by how the danger of incarceration was linked in a vicious cycle with other structural risk factors, like poverty, homelessness, unemployment, and occupational criminalization. These risks intertwined with the danger of incarceration, such that being in poverty and identifying as a person of color is linked to a risk of criminalization. As Carol argued, prior arrests and prosecutions limit the ability for survivors to create new lives and new opportunities:

Most of our people have been arrested numerous times, a lot of them are carrying drug felonies, which is really too bad here . . ., because, if you are a drug felon here, you cannot get food stamps. So that leads to more crime, because when you cannot feed yourself and you're hungry, what are you going to do? You're going to go out to prostitute to get some money so you can eat or get a trick to feed you or find a pimp that will maybe feed you once a day or something. . . . So it's just this really poverty cycle that these folks get into, and because these are the really challenged people, they just kind of tend to stay stuck down in this poverty mire.[5]

While many argue that anti-trafficking and abolitionist feminists exclusively support carceral approaches, our empirical findings are more nuanced. As Carol indicates, some service providers hold more complex relationships toward the carceral state and acknowledge the violence it can perpetuate against their clients. Criminalized approaches to sex work *and* human trafficking run the risk of contributing to increased vulnerability. A precarity continuously reoccurs within poverty, risk, and exploitation when someone is operating in a carceral framework rather than a human rights framework. The carceral state "involves disciplinary mechanisms that operate to lock people's current and future life choices and possibilities into unequal and unfree capitalist social relations and to limit their social and physical mobility within these relations" (LeBaron and Roberts 2010, 20). Life is reduced to either imprisonment or possible future arrest.

Based on their prior involvement in the carceral state—involvement that is permanently marked a felony designation—these trafficking survivors remain locked into a system that denies them social benefits and limits their abilities to access basic goods. This restriction creates an environment where survivors of trafficking must return to those spaces of trauma and violence in order to escape the cycles of poverty, therein exchanging long-term exploitation for short-term survival.

. . .

CONCLUSION

Our research reveals that sex workers and human trafficking survivors in the United States operate within a space constrained by various types of restrictions, including economic and identity constraints. Sex workers and trafficked persons are negatively affected by carceral interpretations of state power: anti-immigration policies, the security state, the prison system, neoliberal economic policies, and the defunded welfare state. Individuals also had a deepening of these constraints based on their personal economic insecurity or identity factors such as a disability or LGBTQ status.

While it may seem that the dangers of the carceral state and structures like poverty are unrelated, we find they are interwoven so closely as to be mutually reinforcing. By approaching trafficking and sex work within a carceral framework, people's imperfect but working solutions to poverty, mental illness, and challenging parental responsibilities may become interpreted as crimes; the pursuit of criminals in turn creates and may drive poverty. The climate is such that almost all sex workers Kennedy interviewed harbored some fear they would get in trouble with the

police during the course of their work. Similarly, a key theme encountered by Britton and Schwarz in their interviews was the fear that labor and sex trafficking victims had of arrest or deportation. Rather than addressing poverty, the state increases funding of the security infrastructure at the cost of vital health care, housing subsidies, and poverty alleviation programs—programs that could by and large limit the number of people who are vulnerable to trafficking.

Compressed within these two sets of forces we find new ways to envision how to create livable lives: as the drive to establish autonomy, to identify one's own agency, to persist and live, and even to engage in rebellion against unjust policies. We interviewed people working within deeply constrained environments who were crafting ways to survive. We encountered people who were reacting against the hegemonic rhetoric of stigma and pushing back against the myth of an "ideal victim."

We argue there is no singular solution for the "danger" we have identified. Education funding, housing programs, employment programs, and health care access all represent upstream solutions that prevent exploitation and trafficking before they occur. Our policy recommendations include stronger rights-based education and English-language instruction for international migrants; reinvesting in education, housing, jobs training, and poverty alleviation programs; increasing the number of social workers and available funding for abused and neglected children, foster care programs, and disabled youth; the decriminalization of sex work; and strengthening state and local policies to support LGBTQ rights. Prosecutions, incarcerations, and the security infrastructure are reactive measures that have proven expensive and ineffective as deterrents—and they also are implemented after someone has been harmed, often resulting in causing further harm to those who are most vulnerable. Alleviating poverty gives individuals the agency to pursue education, work, and family on their own terms and without fear of exploitation or arrest.

Attempts to decriminalize migration and sex work are important policy debates to be examined apart from moralistic and sex-negative ideologies, and progress has been made in these types of discussions. For example, the human rights organization Amnesty International undertook a full-scale review of the research and has recommended decriminalization (amnesty.org 2015). While a full discussion of the decriminalization of sex work is outside the scope of this paper, there is a growing body of scholarship disputing the success of criminalizing the purchase of sex (the End Demand model) and arguing that decriminalization may make identification of exploitative sex work easier to identify (Weitzer 2012). Similarly, anti-immigration policies—even some anti-trafficking policies—may be driving more immigrants underground, exposing them to harsher exploitation and heftier transportation fees that make them vulnerable to violence and exploitation (Chapkis 2003; Sassen 2002). Approaching all of these problems with criminalization and prosecution misses the opportunity for economic reform that addresses these vulnerabilities before exploitation occurs. We also should examine new ways to understand pleasure as a means to craft a livable life—one of exercising autonomy, finding ways to survive, and creating lives free from violence and exploitation.

NOTES

1. Carol (anti-trafficking outreach organization), interviewed by Corinne Schwarz, October 15, 2013, transcript.
2. Carol (anti-trafficking outreach organization), interview by Corinne Schwarz, October 15, 2013, transcript.
3. Grace (stripper), interview by Emily J. Kennedy, March 6, 2014, transcript.
4. Britney (escort), interview by Emily J. Kennedy, February 28, 2014, transcript.
5. Carol (anti-trafficking outreach organization), interview by Corinne Schwarz, October 15, 2013, transcript.

REFERENCES

Agustin, Laura Maria. 2007. *Sex at the Margins: Migration, Labour Markets and the Rescue Industry.* London, UK: Zed Books.

amnesty.org. 2015. "Global Movement Votes to Adopt Policy to Protect Human Rights of Sex Workers." *Amnesty International*, last modified August 11, 2015. https://www.amnesty.org/en/latest/news/2015/08/global-movement-votes-to-adopt-policy-to-protect-human-rights-of-sex-workers/.

Beloso, Brooke M. 2012. "Sex, Work, and the Feminist Erasure of Class." *Signs* 38 (1): 47–70.

Bernstein, Elizabeth. 2007a. "The Sexual Politics of the 'New Abolitionism.'" *Differences: A Journal of Feminist Cultural Studies* 18 (3): 128–51.

———. 2007b. *Temporarily Yours: Intimacy, Authenticity, and the Commerce of Sex*. Chicago: University of Chicago Press.

———. 2012. "Carceral Politics as Gender Justice? The 'Traffic in Women' and Neoliberal Circuits of Crime, Sex, and Rights." *Theory and Society* 41 (3): 233–59.

Britton, Hannah, and Laura Dean. 2014. "Policy Responses to Human Trafficking in Southern Africa: Domesticating International Norms." *Human Rights Review* 15 (3): 305–28.

Bureau of Justice. 2012. *Arrests in the United States, 1980–2012*. Washington, DC.

Butler, Judith. 2004. *Undoing Gender*. New York: Routledge.

Cavalieri, Shelley. 2011. "Between Victim and Agent: A Third-Way Feminist Account of Trafficking for Sex Work." *Indiana Law Journal* 86: 1409–58.

Chapkis, Wendy. 2003. "Trafficking, Migration, and the Law: Protecting Innocents, Punishing Immigrants." *Gender and Society* 17 (6): 923–37.

Commission for Gender Equality (CGE). 2014. "Decriminalising Sex Work in South Africa." Braamfontein, South Africa. http://www.cge.org.za/wp-content/uploads/2014/05/CEG-Decr.pdf.

Dank, Meredith, Jennifer Yahner, Kuniko Madden, Isela Banuelos, Lilly Yu, Andrea Ritchie, Mitchylle Mora, and Brendan Conner. 2015. "Surviving the Streets of New York: Experiences of LGBTQ Youth, YMSM, and YWSW Engaged in Survival Sex." New York: Urban Institute. http://www.urban.org/sites/default/files/publication/42186/2000119-Surviving-the-Streets-of-New-York.pdf.

Davydova, Darja. 2013. "Criminal Networks, Unfortunate Circumstances, or Migratory Projects?

Researching Sex Trafficking from Eastern Europe." *Cultural Dynamics* 25 (2): 229–43.

D'Emilio, John, and Estelle Freedman. 2012. *Intimate Matters: A History of Sexuality in America.* 3rd ed. Chicago: University of Chicago Press.

Desyllas, Moshoula Capous. 2007. "A Critique of the Global Trafficking Discourse and US Policy." *Journal of Sociology & Social Welfare* 34 (4): 57–80.

Doezema, Jo. 2000. "Loose Women or Lost Women? The Re-Emergence of the Myth of White Slavery in Contemporary Discourses of Trafficking in Women." *Gender Issues* 18 (1): 23–50.

Donovan, Brian. 2005. *White Slave Crusades: Race, Gender, and Anti-Vice Activism, 1887–1917.* Champaign, IL: University of Illinois Press.

Ferguson-Colvin, Kristin M., and Elaine M. Maccio. 2012. "Toolkit for Practitioners/Researchers Working with Lesbian, Gay, Bisexual, Transgender, and Queer/Questioning (LGBTQ) Runaway and Homeless Youth." New York: National Resource Center for Permanency and Family Connections, Silberman School of Social Work. http://www.hunter.cuny.edu/socwork/nrcfcpp/info_services/download/LGBTQ%20HRY%20Toolkit%20September%202012.pdf.

Galusca, Roxana. 2012. "Slave Hunters, Brothel Busters, and Feminist Interventions: Investigative Journalists as Anti-Sex-Trafficking Humanitarians." *Feminist Formations* 24 (2): 1–24.

Gordon, Derrick M., and Bronwyn A. Hunter. 2013. "Invisible No More: Creating Opportunities for Youth Who are Homeless." New Haven, CT: The Consultation Center, Yale University School of Medicine. http://www.pschousing.org/files/InvisibleNoMoreReport.pdf.

Gulati, Giresh J. 2011. "News Frames and Story Triggers in the Media's Coverage of Human Trafficking." *Human Rights Review* 12: 363–79.

Hoang, Kimberly Kay. 2014. "Competing Technologies of Embodiment: Pan-Asian Modernity and Third World Dependency in Vietnam's Contemporary Sex Industry." *Gender & Society* 28 (4): 513–36.

Hoang, Kimberly Kay, and Rhacel Salazar Parrenas. 2014. *Human Trafficking Reconsidered: Rethinking the Problem, Envisioning New Solutions.* New York: IDebate Press.

Karalekas, Nikki. 2014. "Is Law Opposed to Politics for Feminists? The Case of the Lusty Lady." *Feminist Formations* 26 (1): 27–48.

Kempadoo, Kamala. 2001. "Women of Color and the Global Sex Trade: Transnational Feminist Perspectives." *Meridians* 1 (2): 28–51.

Lawston, Jodie M., and Erica R. Meiners. 2014. "Ending Our Expertise: Feminists, Scholarship, and Prison Abolition." *Feminist Formations* 26 (2): 1–25.

LeBaron, Genevieve, and Roberts, Adrienne. 2010. "Toward a Feminist Political Economy of Capitalism and Carcerality." *Signs* 36 (1): 19–44.

Lewis, Ruth, and Susan Marine. 2015. "Weaving a Tapestry, Compassionately: Toward an Understanding of Young Women's Feminisms." *Feminist Formations* 27 (1): 118–40.

National Center on Family Homelessness. 2014. *America's Youngest Outcasts Fact Sheet.* Waltham, MA: American Institutes for Research.

National Coalition for the Homeless. 2009. *LGBTQ Homelessness.* Washington, DC.

Ray, Audacia. 2007. *Naked on the Internet: Hookups, Downloads, and Cashing in on Internet Sexploration.* Berkeley, CA: Seal Press.

Reger, Jo. 2014. "Micro-Cohorts, Feminist Discourse, and the Emergence of the Toronto SlutWalk." *Feminist Formations* 26 (1): 49–69.

Rosen, Eva, and Sudhir Alladi Venkatesh. 2008. "A 'Perversion' of Choice: Sex Work Offers *Just Enough* in Chicago's Urban Ghetto." *Journal of Contemporary Ethnography* 37 (4): 417–41.

Sassen, Saskia. 2002. "Women's Burden: Counter-Geographies of Globalization and the Feminization of Survival." *Nordic Journal of International Law* 71: 255–74.

Schwarz, Corinne, and Hannah Britton. 2015. "Queering the Support for Trafficked Persons: LGBTQ Communities and Human Trafficking in the Heartland." *Social Inclusion* 3 (1): 63–75.

Shrage, Laurie. 2012. "Feminist Perspectives on Sex Markets." *The Stanford Encyclopedia of Philosophy Archive*, last modified July 11, 2012. http://plato.stanford.edu/archives/win2014/entries/feminist-sex-markets

Soderlund, Gretchen. 2005. "Running from the Rescuers: New U.S. Crusades Against Sex Trafficking and the Rhetoric of Abolition." *NWSA Journal* 17 (3): 64–87.

Spencer, Jon, and Rose Broad. 2012. "The 'Groundhog Day' of the Human Trafficking for Sexual Exploitation Debate: New Directions in Criminological Understanding." *European Journal on Criminal Policy and Research* 18 (3): 269–81.

Srikantiah, Jayashri. 2007. "Perfect Victims and Real Survivors: The Iconic Victim in Domestic Human Trafficking Law." *Boston University Law Review* 87: 157–211.

Stienstra, Deborah. 1996. "Madonna/Whore, Pimp/Protector: International Law and Organization Related to Prostitution." *Studies in Political Economy* 51: 183–217.

Tilly, Charles, and Lesley J. Wood. 2012. *Social Movements 1768–2012*. 3rd ed. Boulder, CO: Paradigm Publishers.

US Census Current Population Survey. 2016. "Income and Poverty in the United States: 2015."

https://www.census.gov/content/dam/Census/library/publications/2016/demo/p60-256.pdf.

US Department of Health and Human Services. 2014. *Adoption and Foster Care Analysis and Reporting System (AFCARS) Report, FY 2013*. http://www.acf.hhs.gov/sites /default/files/cb/afcarsreport21.pdf.

US Department of Homeland Security. 2015. *Immigration and Customs Enforcement Immigration Removals*. http://www.ice.gov/removal-statistics/.

US Department of Justice. 2011. "Characteristics of Suspected Human Trafficking Incidents, 2008–2010." http://bjs.ojp.usdoj.gov/content/pub/pdf/cshti0810.pdf.

Weitzer, Ronald. 2012. "Sex Trafficking and the Sex Industry: The Need for Evidence-Based Theory and Legislation." *The Journal of Criminal Law & Criminology* 101 (4): 1337–70.

———. 2014. "New Directions in Research on Human Trafficking." *The ANNALS of the American Academy of Political and Social Science* 653: 6–24.

59. WHICH COUNTRY WILL BE THE FIRST TO CLOSE THE GENDER GAP—AND HOW?

VESSELINA STEFANOVA RATCHEVA AND SAADIA ZAHIDI (2016)

Ten years ago the World Economic Forum started benchmarking gender gaps across the world. Each year, our annual report provides the global community —governments, companies and individuals—an opportunity to compare the relative position of women and men in economies across the globe.

As we reflect on a decade of data, we can make an educated guess on where gender gaps will close first, *ceteris paribus*. For 109 countries, sufficient historical data is available from the Global Gender Gap Index to calculate rates of change and estimate future trends. The projections are indicative of which countries are making the fastest progress on closing gender gaps, and where there may be a risk of stalling. While the rankings and the projections derived from them compare the position of women and men on education, economic, political and health indicators

within a country, parity within each country does not mean parity of outcomes between countries.

Iceland is set to be the first country in the world to close the gender gap in just 11 years. The United States and Germany are both set to close their gender gaps in more than 60 years, longer than countries which are currently ranked lower. Slovenia is likely to close its gender gap before Germany or Switzerland. Similarly, while Sweden ranks highly, akin to other Nordic states, change over the past 10 years has been slow. While in 2006, it was the best country for gender equality, its recent progress suggests it will be one of the slowest to close its gender gap in the future.

Still, past rates of change need not hold true in the future—they only provide a sense of the countries' trajectories to this point of time, relative to their starting point. Change can be accelerated using

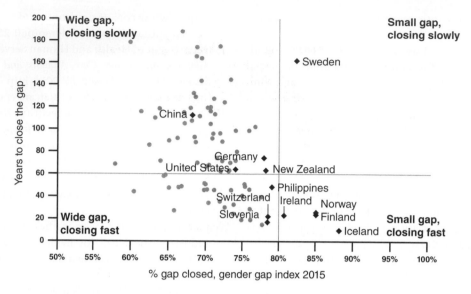

FIGURE 1 When will countries close their gender gaps at the current rate of progress?
Source: Global Gender Gap Report 2015, World Economic Forum

appropriate public policy measures, an improvement in the enabling environment provided by businesses, and more breadth in the roles and identities available to women in wider society.

The most striking changes have occurred in how and where women are integrated into the global talent value chain—from education through to labour market opportunities.

A hundred years ago, women were still unable to vote across most countries in the world. Today, they make up the majority of those in university in nearly 100 of the world's biggest economies. Many governments have sought to win the returns of this investment by introducing policies that help make female labour force participation feasible and an option which makes economic sense—for employers, individuals and families. Effective interventions have ranged from legislation promoting non-discrimination in hiring, appropriate paternity leave, child subsidies and tax credits, gender neutral taxation for families, as well as quotas in economic and political life. Mixed parental leave policies in particular, rather than pure maternity leave, have

begun to enable a more equitable division of labour between the sexes when it comes to child-rearing. Some governments have delivered a further disruptive jolt to the business community by legislating gender equality targets at different senior level positions, with a particular emphasis on boards.

And they have been informed by—indeed supported by—pioneering companies that have already gone a step beyond pure compliance. These companies have embraced new hiring and managerial practices which have enabled them to better promote and leverage female talent. Some businesses have further pursued the cause of promoting a more gender equal society by influencing the status of women along the value chain of their suppliers, distributors and partners. Recognizing the need to ensure women have the opportunity to work, businesses have also engaged with civil society to improve the position of women in society more broadly, promoted gender neutral images of women in their advertising, and actively campaigned with girls and young women in schools and universities to consider careers in their sectors.

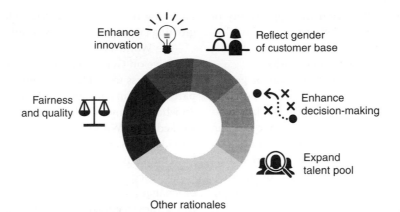

FIGURE 2 Industries' rationales for hiring and promoting women
Source: Future of Jobs Report, World Economic Forum

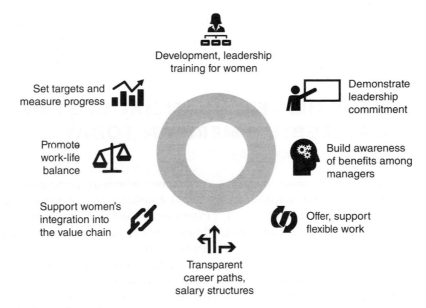

FIGURE 3 Strategies for gender parity

Successful companies have effectively introduced more transparency as part of internal measurement and monitoring—allowing them to understand their own gender gaps. They have built awareness and accountability among their senior staff, and provided training on understanding biases in management styles.

Businesses have also seized the opportunity of the overall disruptions in the structure of work—work 2.0—to empower female workers by offering flexible work and transparent career paths.

In addition, the social reproduction of gender stereotypes—nurture in the family environment, socialization in school and work, and media images—often means there is also a need for specific training and initiatives targeted at high-potential female leaders and a number of companies have supported their female workers by providing this form of training, mentoring and sponsoring. In parallel, pioneering voices have asked women to take on the personal work of leaning into the offer of career progression.

Although many employers have invested time and effort in these endeavours out of a strong belief in the value of fairness and equality for the social good, there is a significant part of the business community which has recognized the benefits of including women because of its effects on innovation, decision-making, diversity and their bottom line. This "business case" is compounded by the growing incomes of women—and the customer base they represent—as well as the rapid rise of women in tertiary education—and the growing talent pool they represent.

The World Economic Forum's Global Challenge Initiative on Gender Parity works with governments and business to accelerate progress on gender parity, particularly on education and economic gender gaps. So what—if any—of these numerous strategies have worked best? While no individual practice or policy provides a silver bullet, it is clear that countries that have successfully closed their gender gaps have deliberately used a combination of these systemic levers of change. The same holds true in companies—companies that have succeeded have not relied solely on CEO leadership or HR-driven change or corporate social responsibility initiatives, but rather sought to put in place a holistic combination of practices to create change.

On this International Women's Day, one critical message we can all carry forward is that accelerated change is entirely possible—but a search for deep collaboration between sectors and within organizations is likely to yield more results than any one practice or policy.

60. THIS IS THE HIDDEN FINANCIAL COST OF BEING AN LGBTQ AMERICAN TODAY

ANNA SWARTZ (2017)

It's true: Legal protections have increased measurably over the last decade for LGBTQ communities across the United States—most clearly with a 2015 Supreme Court decision that effectively legalized same-sex marriage. And yet, in many places it's still possible for LGBTQ people to be, as the oft-repeated phrase goes, married on Sunday, fired on Monday.

Indeed, whether or not you're married, navigating the already-tricky obstacle course of a career often comes with additional hurdles if you are gay, transgender or gender nonconforming: 28 states still lack protections against workplace discrimination based on sexual orientation, and research suggests nearly 1 in 10 workers have left jobs because of unwelcoming cultures.

"When it comes to employment, fundamentally, LGBTQ Americans are not on an even playing field,' Deena Fidas, director of the Workplace Equality Program at the Human Rights Campaign, said in a phone interview.

Crucially, new data suggest the barriers LGBTQ workers face—whether from bias, structural inequality, or other hurdles—have tangible consequences: There are quantifiable gaps in employment rates and pay based on sexuality. And for LGBTQ women or people of color, income and employment challenges may widen already large wage gaps driven by gender or race.

Here are three key ways LGBTQ workers face hidden financial and career costs—disproportionate to those borne by other Americans.

1. HIGHER RATES OF JOBLESSNESS

A newly published survey indicates that LGBTQ workers face higher rates of unemployment than the overall population.

While 9% of the general population of working-age Americans was unemployed between March and October of 2017, among LGBTQ Americans, that number was 13%—and among trans and nonbinary Americans it was 16%, the report found. Led by CivicScience, a consumer analytics company, the survey polled more than 153,000 Americans, including at least 10,000 who self-identify as LGBTQ.

Many of the numbers are in line with past data. For example, according to a 2011 report from the National Gay and Lesbian Task Force and the National Center for Transgender Equality, trans people faced an unemployment rate double the rate among the general population—and nearly half of trans people said they had been denied a job, fired or denied a promotion because of their gender identity.

What's driving these gaps? At least one factor, the CivicScience report suggests, is bias: Higher rates of unemployment may reflect "the many barriers and obstacles" LGBTQ workers face, "ranging from the interview process to in-office dynamics and policies."

2. WORKPLACE DISCRIMINATION

Even when LGBTQ people have jobs, they may still face bias and harassment at work. A 2011 report from the Williams Institute at UCLA School of Law found that 1 in 4 LGBT employees reported discrimination in the workplace in the past five years, and a Human Rights Campaign report found that 9% of LGBT employees had left a job because the environment was "not accepting."

Why do these problems persist in 2017? For one, in many states, workplace discrimination or harassment is perfectly legal.

According to Out and Equal, a nonprofit focused on LGBT workplace equality, in 28 states workers can still be fired for their sexual orientation, and in 30 states workers can be fired for being transgender.

"Federal law does not cover gender identity and sexual orientation," Fidas said, which leaves a "patchwork" of protections from state laws and municipal ordinances. Fidas said that more and more major employers have anti-discrimination policies on the books, but even when they're there in theory they may not exist in practice.

"A company may have a gender identity protection policy, but at the stage of a campus job fair or a local hiring manager, it's hard to account for whether that individual will approach the process and the candidate with full knowledge of that policy," Fidas said.

As it happens, employers who discriminate against LGBTQ employees may actually be hurting themselves: A 2013 report from the Williams Institute identified a host of benefits to companies that institute "LGBT-supportive employment policies"— those firms saw more job commitment from employees, better workplace relationships and better health outcomes for LGBT employees.

Fidas said there has been "significant progress" when it comes to employment and workplace discrimination—but that "for that individual who feels they have been frozen out of the application process," that progress just may not "feel fast enough."

3. THE LGBTQ WAGE GAP

There is also—much like that for women and people of color—a quantifiable income gap for certain LGBTQ communities.

According to Prudential's 2016–2017 LGBT financial experience report, lesbians made, on average, more than $5,000 less than straight women of a similar age. Bisexual women made, on average, about $15,000 less. And gay men earned $56,936 on average, compared to the $83,469 average income for straight male peers.

Notably, bisexual men, the report found, actually out-earned straight men of a similar age—by slightly less than $2,000 on average.

Generally, past data supports Prudential's finding that an income gap exists: A 2013 Pew survey found that 39% of LGBTQ respondents had annual family income of less than $30,000—compared to only 28% of all U.S. adults. And transgender respondents to the 2011 survey by the National Gay and Lesbian Task Force and the National Center for Transgender Equality were "nearly four times more likely to have a household income of less than $10,000 [per] year compared to the general population," according to [the] survey report.

On one hand, getting married may help mitigate financial challenges—for example, through preferential tax and health insurance treatment—and marriage is correlated with higher incomes, at least for some LGB people: According to data released by the U.S. Treasury in 2016, both same sex male couples and same-sex female couples had higher shared average adjusted gross income than married straight couples.

Still, same-sex partners of workers can't always get the same treatment as their straight peers: A study from the Kaiser Family Foundation released in 2016 and updated in 2017 found that just 43% of employers explicitly offer same-sex spouses health benefits.

While federal and state employees are guaranteed equal benefits to peers with opposite-sex partners, other private employers can choose to cover only opposite-sex spouses—unless the state or local government has explicitly instituted protection for same-sex couples.

In short, discrimination and barriers to employment—and equal pay—are a reality for many LGBTQ Americans. Without clearer federal protections for these workers, the hidden costs can only continue to pile up.

61. "WOMEN ARE JUST BETTER AT THIS STUFF"

ROSE HACKMAN (2015)

We remember children's allergies, we design the shopping list, we know where the spare set of keys is. We multi-task. We know when we're almost out of Q-tips, and plan on buying more. We are just better at remembering birthdays. We love catering to loved ones, and we make note of what they like to eat. We notice people's health, and force friends and family to go see the doctor.

We listen to our partner's woes, forgive them the absences, the forgetfulness, the one-track mindedness while we're busy organizing a playdate for the kids. We applaud success when it comes: the grant that was received, the promotion. It was their doing, and ours in the background. Besides, if we work hard enough, we can succeed too: all we need to do is learn to lean in.

But what if, much like childcare and house keeping, the sum of this ongoing emotional management is yet another form of unpaid labor?

If you think this is pushing it, you would be wrong.

The concept of emotional work and emotional labor—as repeated, taxing and under-acknowledged acts of gendered performance—has been a field of serious inquiry in the social sciences for decades.

It's just taken the rest of us a while to catch on.

Jennifer Lena, a sociologist and professor of arts administration at Columbia University, stares at me from across the rocky wooden café table we're sharing. Our two beers stand between us, ready for consumption.

Lena doesn't drink, though. She just stares, looking vaguely disappointed and plain unchallenged.

"Your next story is on emotional labor as the *next* feminist frontier?" she repeats back at me. "But that is so sociology 101! I have been teaching undergraduate students about that for years."

I take a sip of my beer and mumble, apologetic.

In all fairness, Lena's friendly dismissal makes a strong point. The concept has been around for over 30 years; it was first introduced by Arlie Hochschild, an academic who formally coined the concept in her 1983 book *The Managed Heart*.

But only recently has it slowly started to re-emerge in online debates and pop culture. Jess Zimmerman, who wrote about emotional labor for *The Toast*, says she was floored by the amount of feedback she received—hundreds and hundreds of women commented in fervent agreement, thanking her for finally giving them a vocabulary for what they experienced.

Zimmerman framed emotional labor as something especially occurring in private, while academics first focused on it as a formal workplace issue. It is perhaps because more and more women are entering formerly male dominated professions that they're noticing that extra emotional—say, "female type"—work is expected of them.

In a work context, emotional labor refers to the expectation that a worker should *manipulate* either her actual feelings or the appearance of her feelings in order to satisfy the perceived requirements of her job. Emotional labor also covers the requirement that a worker should *modulate* her feelings in order to influence the positive experience of a client or a colleague.

It also includes influencing office harmony, being pleasant, present but not too much, charming and tolerant and volunteering to do menial tasks (such as making coffee or printing documents).

Think of air hostesses, which was one of Hochschild's main examples in 1983, having to cater to clients' needs with an accommodating smile and a sympathetic ear, no matter how tired or disgusted they are by a vomiting child or a sleazy business class male customer.

Think too of the female politician, who is expected to be likable and fun, as well as intelligent and capable (if this rings a bell, it's because Hillary Clinton's aides are urging her to show more humor and heart).

Think of your morning Starbucks barista, who drew a smiley face on your cardboard cup of coffee this morning. Did she really want to go the extra mile today, or was it just part of the job expectation?

A few Stella sips in, Lena, the sociologist, throws me a bone.

"The way I think of emotional labor goes as follows: there are certain jobs where it's a requirement, where there is no training provided, and where there's a positive bias towards certain people—women—doing it. It's also the kind of work that is denigrated by society at large."

Research suggests that cumulatively, ongoing emotion work is exhausting but rarely acknowledged as a legitimate strain—and as such, is not reflected in wages.

The growth of low-wage, service industry jobs, where "service with a smile" is an expectation, has helped further entrench the phenomenon. Here, emotional work is not an added value; it is rather a requirement to get workers to the bare minimum.

In the US, where the federal tipped minimum wage is just $2.13 an hour, this is further accentuated. In those jobs, the employer is expecting emotional output, but is unwilling to pay for it. The duty to recognize emotion work is offloaded onto the client—who is then expectant of emotional fulfillment and satisfaction before providing the extra money.

This has nefarious consequences, especially for women. According to a study by ROC United, a worker center representing restaurant workers, women living off tips in states that have $2.13 minimum tipped wages are twice as likely to experience sexual harassment on the job compared to women in states with higher base wages.

Recent data suggests at least two-thirds of the low-wage industry is female, with half of these workers women of color.

Even in more prestigious industries, Jessica Collett, a professor of sociology at the University of Notre Dame, explains, men and women may both be engaged in the same degree of emotional labor formally, but women are expected to provide extra emotional labor on the side.

For example, boardroom members—male and female—may have to schmooze clients to the same extent (a formal expectation that goes with their jobs) but women may be expected, on top of this, to contribute to office harmony by remembering colleagues' birthdays, or making small chit-chat to staff. Male colleagues may do this too, but if they do it will be noticed as a plus ("isn't he sweet and generous with his time?").

This remark was echoed by a successful female human rights lawyer and friend of mine, who recently complained about the expectation that she should engage with office administrative staff every morning—something she was happy to do, but also felt she *had to do.* She needed to be seen as kind *and* competent in order to be respected, something her male colleague never bothered with.

Robin Simon, a sociology professor at Wake Forest University, turned the tables on herself and said that as a female professor, she was expected to be much more emotionally aware and available in and out of the classroom than her male colleagues.

"Students expect more emotion in women," she says, with female professors not just expected to be chirpy in the classroom (especially with the rise in student-evaluation-related employment), but also sometimes doubling up as therapists and faculty-politics peacekeepers. "I don't really get it. What is emotional labor?" one of my male friends asked me, busying around his kitchen, making us lunch as we took a break from working together out of his Manhattan home.

As I tried to break it down for my lunchtime cook, I saw his brows furrow in concentration and then slowly make way for confusion. My friend, a successful software engineer in his mid-30s who had shown himself an ally to feminist causes in many of our past conversations, clearly thought this one was a step too far.

"Why is the fact that women provide emotional support work, though? What if people actually enjoy it? What if women are just better at doing that? Why do we have to make that something negative?"

His questions may have betrayed some exasperation with me. He had, in all fairness, prepared all of the meals we had shared during our New York friendship without ever complaining.

"Why do you feminists always have to make normal things into issues to be debated?" he continued.

For him, framing emotional work as anything but natural was seen as needlessly picky; it was making something big out of something that was simply best left alone.

My friend would probably never dare say: "Oh, but women are better cooks," "Women are more talented cleaners" or "Women are better with children." And yet, that he was suggesting that maybe some women "are just like that"—better at emotions—seemed to be the argument I was bumping into most frequently when I brought up the argument.

But this essentialist view doesn't hold up academically.

In a 2005 seminal academic article on the subject using data on 355 employed and married parents, sociologist Rebecca Erickson found that not only was the brunt of emotion related work taken on by women at home, on top of child care and housework, it was also linked to gender construction, not sex.

"Part of what the research on this shows is that women's increased propensity to engage in emotion work is not related to their sex but really their gender and the position that they have served in the family and in friendship groups, in society," explains Collett.

This is a role we have simply become accustomed to: the woman as the emotion manager, throwing them into what Collett calls a "second shift."

In the bedroom too, women are expected to manage their male lovers' emotions and sensitivities.

In a recent article in the *Guardian*, Alana Massey talks of the ongoing sexual inequality that exists in a post-pseudo-sexual liberation world. We may have slowly come to terms with the idea of women having sex to the degree they want, but sex positivism has by no means been followed by widespread conversations on the *kind* of sex women want and need in order to be fulfilled.

You might therefore also think of women feeling the need to fake orgasms as not just a consequence of a society that still views sexual intercourse in a male-centric way, but as a way for women to cater first and foremost to the male ego.

A study published in 2011, collecting data from 71 sexually active heterosexual women, found that while all women reported experiencing orgasm generally (mostly during foreplay), 79% of them faked orgasms during penetrative vaginal sex over 50% of the time (25% of surveyed women faked 90% of the time).

The study found that 66% those women faking (or making "copulatory vocalizations," as the study put it) reported doing it in order to speed up their partner's ejaculation. Even more to the point, 92% of the women reported they very strongly felt the technique boosted their partner's self-esteem, which 87%

of them said was why they were doing it in the first place.

Sara Thompson, a teacher turned financial litigation lawyer in her early 30s, is by all means and purposes in a very egalitarian relationship.

Her husband and partner of 10 years is a successful researcher, administrator and professor at an Ivy League university. Together they share a life filled with formal and informal arrangements that keep their relationship sane and seemingly equal from the outside.

But get Thompson speaking about the emotion work and every day extra effort in household organization that goes on as part of her romantic relationship, and some clear disparities start to emerge.

Through an upbringing where she was reprimanded when she took up too much space, she has been shaped into being someone who is constantly, chronically paying attention to the environment around her.

"I am a person today who is very aware and conscious of the loudness of my voice, the presence of my body in a public space, the comfort level of the people around me," she explains.

Much of what she lists doing isn't simply cleaning and maintenance, but it is closely related. It involves thought, and planning:

"Hanging stuff on the walls, putting photographs in picture frames, thinking about whether we should buy new sheets because the old ones are getting old, thinking about the time that we are going to have dinner, thinking about what we are going to have for dinner."

It is not just that Thompson is cooking dinner, it is that she is planning dinner menus (what would he like to eat?), and thinking of what time to have it—all types of thoughtfulness that go unnoticed. "It really annoys me that I have to think about this. It's not fair, it's taxing on me," she says.

Birth control planning is another issue. "I am the one who has to do the entire research and break it down for him. 'How long does it take you to get pregnant after the IUD?' he asks me. Well, why wouldn't you make time to make that research if you are thinking we will have kids?"

The same is valid for smaller details of everyday life. "He is looking for stuff. Have you seen my nail filer? He goes to the closet and says he cannot see it. It's there. 'Where do we keep the kitchen towels?' He asks me time and time again. After the third or the fourth time, that shit needs to be learned."

She continues: "It suggests to me that there is a detachment to home that I do not have the luxury of having. Because if I did, then our everyday life would be a nightmare. So I take on that role. That's not my authentic self, but I have no choice," she says.

So Thompson picks her battles (don't we all?), and the question remains—if we are socialized from a young age to be this way, is it possible that we really are better at it, even if nature did not make us so? Should we just shut up and get on with it because the world would probably stop turning if we didn't?

Or is it time we started forgetting the birthdays too, time we stopped falsely screaming ecstasy, and demanded adequate, formal remuneration for emotion work provided in the workplace as a *skill*?

Now that, right there, would probably be a shake-patriarchy-to-its-core revolution.

62. THE AGE OF PATRIARCHY
CHARLOTTE HIGGINS (2018)

On 7 January this year, the alt-right insurgent Steve Bannon turned on his TV in Washington DC to watch the Golden Globes. The mood of the event was sombre. It was the immediate aftermath of multiple accusations of rape and sexual assault against film producer Harvey Weinstein, which he has denied. The women, whose outfits would normally have been elaborate and the subject of frantic scrutiny, wore plain and sober black. In the course of a passionate speech, Oprah Winfrey told the audience that "brutally powerful men" had "broken" something in the culture. These men had caused women to suffer: not only actors, but domestic workers, factory workers, agricultural workers, athletes, soldiers and academics. The fight against this broken culture, she said, transcended "geography, race, religion, politics and workplace."

Bannon, Donald Trump's former chief strategist, was one of 20 million Americans watching. In his view, the scene before him augured the beginning of a revolution "even more powerful than populism," according to his biographer Joshua Green. "It's deeper. It's primal. It's elemental. The long black dresses and all that—this is the Puritans. It's anti-patriarchy," Bannon declared. "If you rolled out a guillotine, they'd chop off every set of balls in the room . . . Women are gonna take charge of society. And they couldn't juxtapose a better villain than Trump. He is the patriarch." He concluded: "The anti-patriarchy movement is going to undo 10,000 years of recorded history."

Until very recently, "patriarchy" was not something rightwing men were even supposed to believe in, let alone dilate upon with such apocalyptic relish. It was the sort of word that, if uttered without irony, marked out the speaker as a very particular type of person—an iron-spined feminist of the old school, or the kind of ossified leftist who complained bitterly about the evils of capitalism. Even feminist theorists had left it behind.

Nevertheless, "patriarchy" has, in the past year or so, bloomed in common parlance and popular culture. Once you tune into it, you cannot escape it: it is emblazoned on banners and T-shirts; it is an unexpected recent addition to the vocabulary of the red-carpet interview; it is there in newspaper headlines, explaining everything from the Irish abortion vote to the recent murder of 10 people in Toronto in a van attack, allegedly by a violently misogynistic "incel"— a man who believes he has been denied a right to sex with women. Outside the anglophone world, the Spanish *patriarcado* has been getting a workout; so too the German *Patriarchat*, the Italian *patriarcato* and the French *patriarcat*. As the #MeToo campaign has grown, so has the use of "patriarchy." It has burst its way out of the attic of half-discarded concepts to greet a moment—one of fourth-wave feminist ferment—in

which there is a newly urgent need to name what women are still struggling against.

The resurgence of the term is all the more surprising when one considers the forces ranged against it. Many people would question the existence of something called "patriarchy" to begin with—pointing to the strides made in gender equality over the past century, and insisting that instances of sexism are individual and isolated, destined to fade further over time, rather than evidence of a persistent structure of inequality. There are others, meanwhile, who regard the term's very reappearance as another sign that #MeToo has "gone too far"—and see "patriarchy" as the hysterical war cry of McCarthyite feminists determined to hunt down men who are guilty of nothing more than past behaviours once considered perfectly acceptable.

For some sceptical liberals, there is a resistance to the ideological implications of grand concepts such as "patriarchy" (or "neoliberalism"), which are seen as oversimplifications of a more complex reality. Among gender studies academics, it is no longer in wide use. Once a term debated in endless articles, conferences and books, many theorists now regard it as too blunt and monolithic to capture the nuances of oppression. Paradoxically, some on the right have enthusiastically taken up the term— regarding it not as an evil to be stamped out, but as a "natural" difference between the genders, ordained by God or biology, to be protected against rampaging feminism.

But for those who have lost a basic trust in the forward motion of human progress—or who were born too recently to have known it—"patriarchy" seems exactly the word to explain the continued existence of pervasive, seemingly ineradicable inequality. The moment of #MeToo brought this into relief: it revealed to many feminists that despite all those years of working hard, of leaning in, of waiting till unfairness gradually ebbed away, of absorbing and internalising sexism, of building starry careers or else toiling away in menial jobs in the hope that their children would have it better, you could still be pinned to a bed or cornered at a party or groped, or leered at or catcalled by a man—simply because of your woman's body.

In this moment, the concept of "patriarchy" has offered itself as the invisible mechanism that connects a host of seemingly isolated and disparate events, intertwining the experience of women of vastly different backgrounds, race and culture, and ranging in force from the trivial and personal to the serious and geopolitical. For it allows us to ask, according to the philosopher Amia Srinivasan, "whether there is something in common between the Weinstein affair, the election of Trump, the plight of women garment workers in Asia and women farm workers in North America, and the Indian rape epidemic. It allows people to ask whether some machine is at work that connects all the experiences they're having with all the experiences others are having." The return of "patriarchy" raises the question: does the naming and understanding of this invisible mechanism offer the key to its destruction?

For much of human history, the persistence of male domination was so much part of the oxygen of life that patriarchy was not even identified as a concept—unlike democracy, autocracy or oligarchy, whose relative merits were vigorously debated by the Greeks. The notion that male supremacy was "natural" was self-fulfilling, since those who wrote the laws, the poems, the religious books, the philosophy, the history, the medical treatises and the scientific texts were, very largely, men writing for the benefit of men. As Jane Austen's character Anne Elliot says: "Men have had every advantage of us in telling their own story. Education has been theirs in so much higher a degree; the pen has been in their hands." You might even say that patriarchy's particular power is its capacity to make itself as invisible as possible; it tries very hard not to draw attention to the means of its endurance.

But if you look at the world with patriarchy in view, you might see how some intelligent, successful and apparently assertive women fail to leave men who humiliate them and monitor their every move (such are the hallmarks of "coercive control," now a criminal offence). You might see why even apparently liberal organisations, even those run by women, still have a gender pay gap. Or why about 80 women a year, in England, Wales and Northern Ireland, are murdered by a male partner or ex-partner. Why women do more childcare and housework than men, and why this domestic "second shift" has until recently been completely ignored by economists. Why the clothing of Angela Merkel and Theresa May is avidly critiqued, but that of Emmanuel Macron is not. Why there are so few meaningful female characters in films. Some concepts are like a pair of spectacles that allow otherwise invisible or inexplicable things to be seen with sudden sharpness: "patriarchy" is one of them.

The word literally means "rule of the father," from the ancient Greek. There are many different ideas about its extent and force. Some people have used it to describe patterns derived from the structure of the family; to others, it is an entire system of oppression built on misogyny and the exploitation and brutalisation of women. It is not simple, in fact, to produce a concise definition of patriarchy. But at its simplest, it conveys the existence of a societal structure of male supremacy that operates at the expense of women—rather in the way that "white supremacy" conveys the existence of a societal structure that operates at the expense of black people.

Part of the idea of "patriarchy" is that this oppression of women is multilayered. It operates through inequalities at the level of the law and the state, but also through the home and the workplace. It is upheld by powerful cultural norms and supported by tradition, education and religion. It reproduces itself endlessly through these norms and structures, which are themselves patriarchal in nature; and thus it has a way of seeming natural or inevitable, or else, in a liberal context, it is obscured by piecemeal advances in gender equality. Because it offers the idea of a structure of power relations, rather than a series of specific sexist acts, "patriarchy" accommodates the idea that not all men enthusiastically uphold it or benefit equally from it; and that some women may, on the other hand, do a great deal towards supporting it. It also allows for the fact that however much we might loathe it, we all, perforce, participate in it.

Only "patriarchy" seems to capture the peculiar elusiveness of gendered power—the idea that it does not reside in any one site or institution, but seems spread throughout the world. Only "patriarchy" seems to express that it is felt in the way individual examples of gender inequality interact, reinforcing each other to create entire edifices of oppression. Take the fact that only about 20% of rapes and sexual assaults in England and Wales are reported to the police, and that of those only a tiny proportion—7.5% in 2015—results in a conviction. Why should that be? The most immediate reason is that only a few are brought to trial—a fact that, in isolation, illuminates very little. But the concept of patriarchy helps to reveal that such a trial is merely the pinnacle of a structure supported on myriad props. These props might include all kinds of things without obvious connection: a legal system historically designed by men; the lingering misrecognition of rape as simply an excess of male desire; a police force carrying a legacy of sexism; the cultural and religious shaming of sexually active women; the objectification of women's bodies; pornography; the fact that women in general are discouraged from speaking out (and if they do, they may expect baleful consequences, as Mary Beard has shown in her book *Women and Power*). That is before you scrutinise the act of rape itself: for some feminists, sexual violence is so clearly a means of controlling women that it is not only an outrage often perpetrated under patriarchy, but its very underpinning.

Once you see the world through the lenses of "patriarchy," the thought naturally arises: what would the world be like if it weren't there? Some feminists have argued that if women gain equal rights in society, patriarchy will be at least sufficiently tempered. Others have argued that even if equality were achieved, patriarchy would still exist, because human institutions—political, legal, educational, cultural—are themselves, in their bones, patriarchal structures. But it says something about the nature of this inquiry that it has most vividly been answered by writers of speculative fiction. In the 19th-century novel *Herland*, Charlotte Perkins Gilman imagined a women-only society: one of calm justice, efficient agriculture and comfortable clothing with lots of pockets. In Naomi Alderman's novel *The Power*, published last year, women, through a kink of evolution, gain superior physical strength over men. A bloody revolution ensues, and there is no hint that the resulting reversal of patriarchy—matriarchy—will be any less

oppressive than what it has replaced. It seems to be a zero-sum game.

"Patriarchy" is not a stable concept. It has fallen in and out of fashion, flourishing at moments of feminist renewal. Nevertheless, feminism began without it. Mary Wollstonecraft was clear, in *A Vindication of the Rights of Woman* (1792) that there was such as thing as "the tyranny of men," but it was another 60 years before the term "patriarchy" was adopted as something like a theory of social relations.

By the mid-19th century, the world was coming to seem older, bigger and more unstable than it had done before. In 1859, Darwin's *On the Origin of Species* was published. Marx's *Das Kapital* would follow in 1867. At the same time, work by anthropologists and ancient historians was revealing that there were, and had been, family structures, legal systems and whole societies that looked radically different from those in modern Paris, Berlin or London. Industrialisation and urbanisation were underway in Europe, especially in Britain; women were rapidly entering the workforce.

Two years after *On the Origin of Species*, and six years before *Das Kapital*, a Swiss jurist and classicist called Johann Jakob Bachofen published a book whose influence remains nearly as pervasive—even though hardly anyone has heard of it now, its substantive claims have been repudiated, and it has never been fully translated into English from its original German. It was taken up strongly by Friedrich Engels; it deeply interested Sigmund Freud; and its theories were absorbed by early archaeologists and prehistorians. The book was called *Das Mutterrecht* ("Mother Right"), and its grand theory was that, in a distant prehistoric era, the father's role in begetting children had not been yet recognised, and women (and mother goddesses) held power in the world.

This highly speculative account of a matriarchy simultaneously birthed the idea of "patriarchy" as a historically contingent, manmade, societal structure that had, according to Bachofen, eventually superseded matriarchy. His method involved close readings of Greek literature and some contemporary anthropological studies. According to his interpretation of Aeschylus's *Oresteia*, for example, Orestes's acquittal for the murder of his mother, Clytemnestra, on the grounds that she was not a parent but only a "container" for his father's seed, echoed the moment when the patriarchy established itself—when "the Apollonian age [emerged] out of the ruins of mother right." Many academics would now argue that such myths are not really echoes of real matriarchal societies—but instead operated, as Mary Beard put it, "to justify the existence of the patriarchy, as charter myths for why men run things."

For Bachofen, matriarchy and patriarchy were opposites: dark versus light, "the bloody law of the earth" set against "the pure celestial power of the sun." His vision of the elementally opposed "female" and "male" has been hugely influential. The idea of an earthbound, essentially non-rational femininity has sometimes been claimed by feminists; in a very different way, you can hear the echoes of the rhetoric, roughly filtered through Nietzsche and Jung, in the statements of rightwing male supremacists of today, especially those who speak of the "chaos" of the feminine. Bachofen himself was no feminist. The idea of the Amazons—mythical female warriors—particularly disturbed him. They represented "an extreme and decadent form of gynecocracy . . . man-hating, man-killing, bellicose virgins," he wrote.

When the term "patriarchy" started to circulate in this new formulation, it opened up new avenues of thought on the left. Engels, in *The Origin of the Family, Private Property and the State*, drew deeply on Bachofen in order to argue that patriarchy was a crucial factor in the emergence of capitalism. For him, the arrival of patriarchy—which was associated with the recognition of fatherhood, the development of monogamous marriage and inheritable private property—represented "the world-historical defeat of the female sex. The man took command in the home also; the woman was degraded and reduced to servitude, she became the slave of his lust and a mere instrument for the production of children."

It took a female thinker, and a feminist, to pull "patriarchy" out of the realm of theory and into the zone of experience. Virginia Woolf's *Three Guineas* (1938) set "patriarchy" to work on the reality of her own circumstances. For her, it described the dynamics within families like hers—in which the father held economic power and authority, boys were trained for public life and girls were debarred from either a serious education or the opportunity to earn a living. The battle lines were drawn "between the victims of the patriarchal system and the patriarchs." In other words, it was "the daughters against the fathers."

Woolf did not here write of "patriarchy" as a social structure that went beyond the boundaries of the bourgeois household. Nor did she have time for feminine essentialism: she predicted that the opportunity for women to amass capital and property on equal terms as men would mean that women could change "from being the victims of the patriarchal system . . . to being the champions of the capitalist system." She expanded: "Behind us lies the patriarchal system: the private house, with its nullity, its immorality, its hypocrisy, its servility. Before us lies the public world, the professional system, with its possessiveness, its jealousy, its pugnacity, its greed." It is an ambiguous picture: she shows little admiration for the capitalist world she describes. And yet in her formulation—an idea that some later feminists would find themselves echoing—the "creative destruction" of capitalism had the capacity to leave patriarchy behind.

In the late 1960s and early 70s, amid the ferment of revolutionary thought on the campuses of western Europe and north America, a new generation of feminist activists emerged. It was clear to them that oppression continued to bear down on women despite their increased access to the rights that Woolf's generation fought for—access to education, the vote and the workplace. It was also obvious that existing theories of power were not equipped to explain this oppression: women had been of little interest as subjects for economics, history and sociology, with questions of gender inequality either ignored entirely or regarded as a natural byproduct of societal development. For the feminists of the second wave, part of the work was to bring women into the light. Oppression could be eradicated only if it could be identified, understood and effectively treated, quite possibly with radical or revolutionary medicine.

"Patriarchy" at first provided the most useful focus for this work. Kate Millett's *Sexual Politics* (1970) was an early text that attempted to flesh out "patriarchy" into society's "most fundamental concept of power." For her, patriarchy was everywhere; it was "the most pervasive ideology of our culture." Even ordinary, apparently harmless social norms were in fact tools of oppression, according to her analysis: romantic love, for example, was simply a means of emotionally manipulating the female by the male, tricking her into subservience. Female compliance was also ensured by force—by rape. Women were socialised into pleasing, flattering, entertaining and gratifying men. Millett called the assumed birthright of male dominance "a most ingenious form of 'interior colonisation,'" which was "sturdier than any form of segregation, and more rigorous than class stratification, more uniform, and certainly more enduring."

The feminist Rosalind Coward, author of *Patriarchal Precedents: Sexuality and Social Relations* (1983), one of the weightier academic tomes on the subject, recalls going to "endless conferences and meetings" in the 1970s and 80s where the idea of the patriarchy was discussed, analysed and thoroughly broken down. Her own book sets out some of the most pressing questions, not least the conundrum of where it actually came from. "Patriarchy offers itself as an account of the history of sexual relations, but at a certain point the same question has to be asked: why was it men who took control and what were the interests thus served? These questions lead back with an unerring certainty to the same divisions: are there natural sexual differences in which the sexes have distinct interests? Or are sexual dispositions produced by the patriarchal structure itself?" She had hit on a problem of circular thinking in relation to patriarchy—if it had emerged from some kind of a pre-patriarchal society, then surely the patriarchy would have been required in order to produce it in the first place.

"Patriarchy" sprouted dozens of reformulations and refinements as feminists attempted to theorise it into a coherent system of domination. The radical feminist Catharine MacKinnon took a hardline view: she saw patriarchy as inscribed into the very structures of the liberal state. "Men against women"

was precisely the fuel that kept society, as it is currently constituted, running. By contrast, the African American feminist bell hooks resisted the notion that the primary conflict in society was one of "men against women," which seemed inherent in radical definitions of "patriarchy." For her, it could be simply defined as "institutionalised sexism." In order to end it, everyone, male and female alike, must "let go of sexist thoughts and action."

Lived reality threw up problems with the concept. Experience tells us that some men are oppressed more than some women. Not all women are oppressed in the same way. Writers such as hooks pointed out that for African American women, the family was not necessarily the site of oppression it was for white people, representing a place of possible refuge from the traumas of white supremacy. The kind of workplaces available to many black women, too, were not of the liberating kind accessible to educated white women.

Queer theorist Judith Butler critiqued MacKinnon's universalising view of patriarchy on similar grounds, arguing that it involved "erasures" of other forms of subtle and layered oppression; it was a kind of "theoretical imperialism." Butler also sought to question the "naturalness" of gender. There were many possible categories of gendered and sexual practice, she argued, not simply the binary definitions that dominated the culture. And for psychoanalytically inclined feminist thinkers such as Jacqueline Rose, "the notion that all men are a category in opposition to all women breaks down because not all men are men," she told me. "That is, not all men embody the kind of masculinity that men are supposed to inhabit."

The eventual rejection by many feminists of the usefulness of "patriarchy" as a fine-grained analytic concept coincided with a general diminuendo in feminist debate in the 1990s and early 2000s—a period later identified by the feminist Beatrix Campbell as a time of "neoliberal neopatriarchy." Rapid globalisation and a culture of hyperindividualism, Campbell argued in *The End of Equality* (2013), had in fact led to yet more extreme forms of oppression, citing brutal conditions for labouring women in Mexico, the disproportionate number of female foetuses aborted in India and everywhere a working week "institutionalised in the interests of men un-encumbered by duties of care." While feminism had not died, during this period, it had certainly withered, she wrote.

A few years earlier, in her book *The Aftermath of Feminism* (2008), Angela McRobbie had questioned her own initial enthusiasm for the symbols of the "third-wave feminism" of that period: *Sex and the City*; "girl power"; pole-dancing classes. In those days, to throw around the word "patriarchy"—when many people assumed that moral and economic progress were destined to eradicate inequality—would have seemed eccentric, misguided or plain mad. Women, or so it seemed, had never had it so good.

Patriarchy is nimble and lithe. Its margins of operation always seem to be expanding. Feminists have naturally tended to arrange their battle lines in front of the aspect of oppression that they have regarded as the most pressing. If "patriarchy" has returned as an idea in public debate, it is because feminism has returned with renewed vigour; because inequality has not been eradicated.

In 1990, the feminist Sylvia Walby crisply laid out six areas of patriarchal oppression in her book *Theorizing Patriarchy*; they still seem to be ticking along nicely. In the home, women still do most of the domestic labour. In the workplace, a legal right to equal pay has not resulted in the eradication of the gender pay gap. At the level of the state, women are underrepresented nearly everywhere in the world in parliaments, legislatures, the military and other bodies. In terms of male violence, the charity Rape Crisis estimates that in Britain, 11 rapes are carried out or attempted every hour of every day. Women and men are still judged differently when it comes to sex. And the "patriarchal gaze" is still strong in education, religion, culture and the media. And so, for feminists right now, the uses of "patriarchy" are greater than its analytic flaws; it allows feminists to perceive the gap between the status quo and what they would like to achieve. "If patriarchy weren't effective, we wouldn't need feminism; if it were totally effective, we wouldn't have feminism," Jacqueline Rose told me.

Feminists of an older generation note that the popular revival of "patriarchy" has not (yet) been accompanied by the intense debate and academic theorising that flowered around it the 1970s. It is a slogan and a popular rallying cry rather than an analytic tool. "What I don't like about it," said Mary Beard, "is that it is convenient and simple. I don't really like 'misogyny' either, for the same reason. It's no more a tangible 'thing' than capitalism. Saying 'crush the patriarchy' has a nice ring, but it doesn't contain any political analysis."

While it is true that lots of intangible things are pressed into service as useful abstractions for helping us understand the world, some feminists still worry that "patriarchy" is in danger of being oversimplified in the course of being co-opted into public debate. "It is now seemingly used almost interchangeably with sexism," Rosalind Coward said, "and it certainly doesn't seem to be accompanied by a discussion about where it came from." Jacqueline Rose told me: "It's used as a call-out phrase, as if it explained everything. It's fine to use it as a tool, as long as you don't mistake it for a complete description of how the world is organised."

But then, perhaps the revival of "patriarchy" is a bellwether for today's feminism, which is presently more concerned with action than theory. The concept has survived its biggest theoretical challenge—that of intersectionality, which argues that "patriarchy" universalises and oversimplifies the subtle realities of oppression—because it offers a description of the world that many people recognise, and that unites the many people who want to fight against it. It is particularly suited to today's fast-moving, hyper-connected digital feminism, where immediate, personal connections can be made in an instant between feminists across the world and radicalising work done in a moment.

"Patriarchy" is also deeply energising to those who use it. There is a certain relief in giving a name to the affliction. It has a satisfying ring of old-fashioned radicalism about it, and it comes with a sharp flavouring of conflict. "Patriarchy" is a battle cry. That is not surprising: the internet has enabled the rapid expansion of feminist campaigning, but also the deep and sometimes violent radicalisation of those who fear and hate it. A reaction against the new feminism has arrived almost simultaneously, as the discontents of disgruntled and unsettled men are stirred and stoked online, in the so-called manosphere. Cynical politicians crusading against "political correctness," such as Trump, have fed off this baleful energy. In this clamorous world, "patriarchy" has become "the patriarchy," a further simplification that makes it seem even more crude and concrete—less of an invisible mechanism, more of a statue to be smashed.

One might reasonably ask whether the patriarchy is truly in any danger, as Steve Bannon fears. It is easier to topple patriarchs, as Susan Faludi pointed out in the wake of Weinstein, than patriarchy. Powerful men who have been called out by #MeToo have left the room, but the room itself still looks very much the same. (Some of the men, too, look very much as if they will be returning to the room quite soon.) If anything can unravel "the rule of the father," it is likely to be the gradual shift in the way gender and sexuality are being understood. New ways of bringing up children outside traditional family structures will chip away at it. So will the rising generation of bold young feminists who have not internalised oppression like their elders, and who are calling out sexism and misogyny where they see it.

But Bannon can relax. As Mary Beard said recently: "Patriarchy has had several thousand years of practice—of course it's good at it. It's very good at bolstering its own sexist values." If a horde of angry leading women did take a guillotine to the testicles of Harvey Weinstein, patriarchy would survive. The word "patriarchy" ought to be a reminder that Weinstein and his ilk are the symptom, not the disease—but it is easier to tackle individuals than structures, signs rather than causes.

At the moment—although the picture varies wildly across the globe—feminists are increasingly using the tool of "patriarchy" to recognise the subtle depth of the forces that keep oppression in place, from the expectations about the behaviour of women in the workplace to the way they are portrayed in fiction. It will be harder to unravel the effect of this cultural inheritance than it was to get the vote. As Max Weber observed, it is the very longevity of patriarchal traditions and norms that serve to prop it up—"the belief in the inviolability of that which has existed from time out of mind." The eradication of patriarchy looks like a task of enormous complexity; when it is smashed, it will take a lot down with it. And so the patriarchs—from the bully in the White House to the bully in your workplace—are still in charge. For now.

CHAPTER 10

RESISTING GENDER VIOLENCE

Gender violence in the United States and worldwide is an important public health and human rights issue. Violence, an assault on livelihood, safety, and the control of the body and life, can take many forms and has varying consequences depending on the type of assault, its context and interpretation, the chronicity of violence, and the availability of support. Gender violence implies that harm evolves from the imbalance in power associated with masculinity and femininity. In this chapter we introduce and define the issue of interpersonal gender violence and focus specifically on certain types of abusive behaviors that include stalking, bullying, and physical and sexual violence. Although our focus here is on interpersonal violence, we also make the point that gender violence concerns imbalances of power in society generally that facilitate violence perpetrated and condoned by the state in, for example, detention, incarceration, and police harassment, as well as in forms of violence associated with colonization, militarism, poverty, transphobia, and homophobia. These are examples of what scholars call structural violence. We make the point that these forms of violence stand alone as well as shape interpersonal experiences of violence in everyday lives.

And finally we want to emphasize again that even though we recognize the need to destabilize the normative categories of gender and resist binary aspects of opposing women to men as if these categories were "natural" ones, it is especially in this focus on violence that the material realities of identifying, and being identified, as a "woman" have real consequences. Living in certain bodies in the context of systemic and structured institutional power relationships means that women do exist as a knowable social group who are abused on the basis of misogynous attitudes and practices. This is true for both cisgender women and transwomen, although of course their experiences vary in terms of the consequences of gender conformity versus gender nonconformity as individuals are targeted specifically because of the latter. We emphasize these points because this chapter, like many others, incorporates statistics that assume and compare the categories "women" and "men."

In most societies, interpersonal gender violence (IPV) usually occurs when masculine entitlements produce power that manifests itself in harm and injury toward others. Overwhelmingly this gender power imbalance involves the violence of people who identify as men against others. Those who identify as women are especially vulnerable in intimate relationships. Most violence against them occurs in their own homes, where they are 10 times more likely to be victimized by an intimate partner. IPV is therefore among the most common forms of gender violence, is generally described as abuse within the context of an intimate partner relationship, and, while legal definitions vary by state, can include physical, sexual, and psychological abuse, as well as economic coercion. IPV affects millions of individuals, regardless of sexual and gender identity, race, ethnicity, national origin, age, religion, marital status, education, and social class. Because of the seriousness of this crime, the effects on victims and their families, and variations in the criminal justice system response, survivors of IPV tend to require a range of sustained resources, including access to emergency shelter, housing assistance, legal assistance, protection orders, safety planning, support groups, financial assistance, and other forms of support.

The range of IPV includes acts of intimidation and harassment (stalking; voyeurism; bullying and online/chat room, street, school, and workplace harassment; road rage; and obscene phone calls); forcing someone to watch or participate in pornography, prostitution, and other sex work; emotional/psychological, physical, and sexual abuse (including rape and attempted rape); and any other unwanted coercive act that harms and violates another person. The term "contact sexual violence" is often used to describe criminal acts that include rape, being made to penetrate a perpetrator, sexual coercion, sexual assault, and other unwanted sexual contact. Rates of IPV in the United States are quite alarming, although compared to figures from the early 1990s, rates of contact sexual violence have decreased somewhat, with the exception of stalking and online bullying. Overall, it is estimated that incidences of IPV cost the state and insurance companies, as well as communities, families, and individuals, billions of dollars every year, including lost wages and decreased productivity as well as trauma and distress. Survivors of abuse are disproportionately represented among the homeless and suicide victims.

Not surprisingly, physical and sexual violence, and especially IPV, are so very underreported that accurate statistics are difficult to collect, and the often tragic consequences are significant. The 1994 Violence Against Women Act (VAWA, passed as Title IV of the Violent Crime Control and Law Enforcement Act) provides some legal protection and rape shield laws, which prevent a victim's sexual history from being used by defense attorneys, and other various state reform laws have helped survivors. Mandatory arrest procedures and the creation of temporary restraining orders have also supported survivors, despite this carceral approach that relies on the police and courts and which is often shaped by racism, homophobia, and transphobia. As the reading by Homa Khaleeli, "#SayHerName," emphasizes, reliance on law enforcement is difficult in many communities because people of color, and especially African Americans, are subject to ethnic profiling by law enforcement

GENDERED VIOLENCE

Sam Shelton

On the surface, the term 'gendered violence' seems pretty straightforward, but it is actually a loaded concept. To fully grasp what this concept is pointing to, we have to break it down into its two parts: "gendered" and "violence." Let's start with violence. What comes to mind when you think about violence? Many people associate violence with the use of physical force against another person's body, but what makes something violent is more than just the means of inflicting harm. Violence is a method of social control that can take many different forms and exist in many different contexts. The threat of violence can prevent people from diverging too far from social norms, and the use of violence can force people back into boxes. Violence can be physical, but it can also be emotional, spiritual, economic, social, and/or anything else that takes autonomy away from the victim/survivor. The only defining characteristic of violence is that it is coercive—it places pressures on people to look and act in "normal" (or normative) ways.

To say violence is gendered is to recognize that the social construction of gender makes certain forms of social control possible. Gender constructs are grounded in systems of power, which means that the gender categories we are seen to occupy make us more or less vulnerable to different kinds of violence. Since violence is about containment and control, it tends to come from people in positions of privilege. Men, for example, are disproportionately the perpetrators of sexual and domestic violence. People on the opposite end of the spectrum, those who are disadvantaged by systems of power, more often have violence enacted against them by people who feel entitled to their bodies and lives. Transgender people experience astonishingly high

rates of interpersonal violence when in public, ranging from harassment and derision to assault and even murder. Perpetrators often attempt to justify violence by saying they were provoked by the appearance or behavior of the victim/survivor. This is victim-blaming.

The concept of gender violence helps us understand the relationships between constructions of gender and the workings of power, but it also poses the danger of essentialism. All too often, when people refer to gender violence, they fail to think about the ways that gender intersects with other sites of difference (e.g., race, class, and ability). When we consider only gender, we run the risk of erasing the experiences of people for whom gender violence is simultaneously racialized, or classed, or disabling. There is no "general" account of gender violence because we are never just gendered people. For example, women of color might experience gender violence in a very different way than white women. Racialized gender violence often depends on the stereotypes associated with particular racial groups. Asian women might be exoticized. Arab or Muslim women might experience gender violence that targets their cultural or religious beliefs. In any case, it is important to recognize the ways that gender violence looks different based on which gendered people we are talking about (Crenshaw 1991; Fuller 2004).

To learn more about gendered violence, visit INCITE! Women, Gender Non-Conforming, and Trans People of Color Against Violence at www.incite-national.org.

References

Crenshaw, K. (1991). "Mapping the Margins: Intersectionality, Identity Politics, and Violence Against Women of Color." *Stanford Law Review*, 43(6), 1241–1299.

Fuller, A. (2004). "What Difference Does Difference Make? Women, Race-Ethnicity, Social Class, and Social Change." *Race, Class, and Gender*, 11(4), 8–29.

and increased deaths as a result of police shootings. This reading focuses on the #SayHer-Name campaign that was created to raise awareness about the number of women and girls that are killed by law enforcement officers. Khaleeli's goal is to raise awareness of these issues and the ways state violence impacts women.

Violence against indigenous girls, women, and other marginalized people is a problem worldwide. The wars of the twentieth century and the new conflicts of the twenty-first, the increase in globalization, and the scope of global commerce and communications have all facilitated an increase in gender violence. It is broadly estimated that approximately one in three girls and women worldwide is beaten, coerced into sex, and otherwise abused. This violence involves economic exploitation and sexual abuse, as well as gender-based violence in situations of armed violence, insecurity, and communal conflicts. Such gendered violence must be understood in the context of ongoing discrimination against indigenous peoples as well as their marginalization in terms of violation of individual and collective rights, poverty, and displacement.

These problems occur despite United Nations Resolution 1325 on women and peace and security, adopted in 2000, which presents measures to protect women and girls from gender-based violence, particularly rape and other forms of sexual abuse, in situations of armed conflict. Still, some countries condone or legalize these crimes, and others accept such violence against women as necessary consequences of war and/or civil unrest and ethnic cleansing. Certainly increased militarism and military posturing among countries in the global north have important consequences for the safety of women and children in target societies, usually in the global south, facilitating prostitution and international sex trafficking in girls and women. The reading by Nadje Al-Ali, "Sexual Violence in Iraq: Challenges for Transnational Feminist Politics," addresses sexual violence by ISIS against women in Iraq, particularly Yezidi women, against the historical background of broader sexual and gender-based violence. It emphasizes the need to recognize imperialism and the forces of neoliberalism and globalization as well as local expressions of patriarchy and religious interpretations and practices. Al-Ali questions what a transnational feminist solidarity might look like in this context.

Gender violence is such a persistent problem worldwide that it is increasingly understood in many quarters as a human rights issue. In 2010 the International Violence Against Women Act (I-VAWA) was introduced into Congress and has still not yet passed, although as of this writing it has again been introduced into Congress. It would allocate more than a billion dollars over five years to make the prevention of gender-based violence a "strategic foreign-policy imperative." One key aspect of attempts to address gender violence worldwide includes a focus on international trafficking. In the reading "Gender Aspects of Human Trafficking," Emilie Linder discusses this "grave violation of human rights" and examines the role of poverty and gender inequality in understanding this phenomenon. Linder emphasizes the need to recognize changing patterns of migration as a result of global neoliberal economic policies, wars, and conflict in order to help understand why high numbers of women and girls become vulnerable to trafficking-related violence. It is important to emphasize that sex trafficking does not occur only in places like Southeast Asia, but also in communities within the United States. Indeed, according to the Department of Justice thousands of people are trafficked into the United States every year and

THE IMPACT OF WAR ON WOMEN AND CHILDREN IN SYRIA

Nancy Staton Barbour

The war in Syria began with what has become known as the "Arab Spring"—a wave of protests and anti-government uprisings in North Africa and the Middle East in 2010 and 2011. The overthrow of governments in Tunisia and Egypt, and the rise of similar movements in Oman, Algeria, Jordan, and Yemen, inspired Syrian protesters to demand the resignation of President Bashar al-Assad. The Assad regime responded violently, with security forces opening fire on pro-democracy demonstrators and subjecting protesters to arrest and torture. The government's forceful suppression of dissent only increased the numbers of protesters calling for the removal of Assad. Rebels took up arms to challenge the government's security forces, and a civil war ensued. In the midst of the Syrian conflict, and in the aftermath of the war and subsequent uprisings in neighboring Iraq, a group of jihadist fighters came together to form the Islamic State of Iraq and Syria (ISIS).

Since 2011, more than 5.6 million Syrians have fled the country to escape clashes between pro-government and opposition forces, bombings of cities and hospitals, chemical attacks, and ISIS kidnappings and killings. More than 6.6 million remain internally displaced within Syria. According to the United Nations High Commissioner for Refugees (UNHCR), the war in Syria has created "the biggest humanitarian and refugee crisis of our time" (2018).

The bombing and shelling of homes and buildings that provide social services is a key factor forcing displacement in Syria (Handicap International, 2017). For many displaced Syrian women and children, the lack of security is a constant issue. Women who have lost male family members and are unable to remain safely in their homes face increased economic hardship and vulnerability to crime. The destruction of medical facilities greatly reduces access to reproductive and other health services. In addition, the burden of caring for family members injured in attacks falls disproportionately on women.

Whether internally displaced or living as refugees outside of Syria, women and girls face a higher risk of sexual assault. A UNHCR survey of Syrian women refugees in Lebanon, Turkey, and Jordan found that 60 percent lived in fear of sexual violence. The refugees faced pervasive threats of assault and harassment from strangers in public places, including police officers, service providers, and cab drivers, as well as individuals known to them, like employers, landlords, and neighbors (Leitner Center, 2018). The desire to protect their daughters from the risk of sexual assault has led to higher rates of child marriages among Syrian refugees.

A 2018 report found that Syrian women refugees continued to face numerous threats, including "labor exploitation, discriminatory housing practices, lack of access to sexual and reproductive health services, sexual assault and harassment, child marriage, barriers to education, domestic violence, human trafficking, discrimination and violence based on their sexuality or gender identity, and lack of access to justice" (Leitner Center, 2018, p. 2). The report urged the inclusion of specific rights for female refugees in the Global Compact on Refugees, a document developed by the UNHCR in response to the global refugee crisis and presented to the UN General Assembly in November 2018.

References

Handicap International. (2017). "'Everywhere the Bombing Followed Us': Forced Displacement and the Use of Explosive Weapons in Populated Areas. Perspectives of Syrian Women Refugees in Lebanon." *UNHCR.* Retrieved from http://www.unhcr.org/en-us/events/conferences/5a86aa607/forced-displacement-use-explosive-weapons-populated-areas-perspectives.html?query=syrian%20women

Leitner Center for International Law and Justice. (2018). "Gendered-Approach Inputs to UNHCR for the Global Compact on Refugees (2018): Lessons from Abuses Faced by Syrian Female Refugees in Lebanon, Turkey, and Jordan." *UNHCR.* Retrieved from http://www.unhcr.org/5a3bb9b77.pdf

UNHCR. (2018). "Syria Emergency." Retrieved from http://www.unhcr.org/en-us/syria-emergency.html

approximately 70 percent end up working in the sex industry. These problems exist despite the fact that there are U.S. laws against human trafficking at the federal level such as the U.S. Trafficking Victims Protection Act (2000) and at state levels. It is important to recognize the need for law enforcement training and survivor services alongside legislation in addressing this national problem. It also is important to recognize the distinction between human trafficking and sex trafficking in terms of differences between coerced sex trafficking and women who freely cross national borders to engage in sex work. Feminists of the

SEX TRAFFICKING OF GIRLS IN NIGERIA

Folah Oludayo

In human trafficking people are forced, tricked, or threatened into situations in which they are exploited sexually or financially or through forced labor (Jorgen, 2006). Trafficking can be understood as a modern form of slavery. The trafficking of girls for the purpose of prostitution and other forms of exploitative labor is a widespread phenomenon in Nigeria, which has made this country a source, transit, and destination country for trafficked women and girls (Cullen-DuPont, 2009). Many hundreds of young Nigerian girls are sent to Europe and Asia every year, where they are put to work in brothels and strip clubs or sent out to prostitute themselves in the streets. Internal trafficking also occurs within Nigeria's borders (Ifedigbo, 2013).

In 2009 the United Nations Office for Drugs and Crimes estimated that between 3,000 and 6,000 girls are trafficked each year from West Africa. Women and children account for 80 percent of cases of human trafficking. The National Agency for the Prohibition of Trafficking in Persons (NAPTIP) and United Nations International Children's Emergency Fund (UNICEF) also report that 46 percent of repatriated victims of external trafficking in Nigeria are children, with a female-to-male ratio of seven to three (UNICEF, 2007). Children who are trafficked to other countries are engaged mainly in prostitution (46 percent), domestic labor (21 percent), forced labor (15 percent), and entertainment (8 percent). Among children who are trafficked within Nigeria, 32 percent are forced into labor, 31 percent into domestic labor, and 30 percent into prostitution.

According to a 2006 report issued by UNESCO, moving young girls from Nigeria to Europe for the purpose of sexual exploitation is one of the most persistent trafficking flows, as it is very well organized and difficult to detect. These victims often have to endure physical and psychological abuse and are under continuous threat of physical harm or deportation.

The *mama ke*, often the sponsor financing the journey, orders the girls and sometimes recruit them, leads the organizations, and monitors the process closely. The victims usually live and work under her control. Baby factories, often in the guise of orphanages, acquire and sell children. Boko Haram continues to kidnap girls for domestic servitude and sexual slavery. Trafficking not only affects girls' physical, emotional, and psychological well-being, but also adversely affects families, the economy, and wider national and transnational communities.

The Nigerian government is taking some, though still inadequate, steps to end trafficking. By creating and enforcing stronger laws, the government can slow trafficking in Nigeria (U.S. Department of State, 2017). More significantly, however, the social, political, and economic conditions that give rise to trafficking must be challenged and changed.

Learning Activity

1. Use online resources at www.unicef.org, unesco.org, and un.org/en to learn more about child trafficking around the world. What contributes to children's vulnerability to trafficking? How are various nations and organizations combating child trafficking?

2. Visit UNICEFUSA's resources for ending child trafficking at https://www.unicefusa.org/mission/protect/trafficking/end/resources. What concrete steps can you take to contribute to the movement to end child trafficking?

3. Plan an activity on your campus to raise awareness of child trafficking and advocate to end child trafficking.

References

"Child Trafficking in Nigeria Social Work Essay." (2015). UK Essays. https://www.ukessays.com/essays/social-work/child-trafficking-in-nigeria-social-work-essay.php?vref=1.

Deshpande N. A., & Nour, N. M. (2013). "Sex Trafficking of Women and Girls." *Reviews in Obstetrics and Gynecology*, 6(1), 22–27.

Cullen-DuPont, K. (2009). *Global Issues: Human Trafficking*. New York: Facts on File.

Ibirogba, L. (2014). "Tackling Menace of Human Trafficking." The Nation. http://thenationonlineng.net/tackling-menace-of-human-trafficking/.

Ifedigbo, S. N. (2013). "Child Trafficking in Nigeria." https://nzesylva.wordpress.com/tag/child-trafficking-in-nigeria/

Shelley, L. (2010). *Human Trafficking: A Global Perspective*. Cambridge: Cambridge University Press.

UNESCO (2006). Human Trafficking in Nigeria: Root Causes and Recommendations. *Policy Paper Poverty Series* 14.2 (E). http://nigerianlawguru.com/articles/human%20rights%20law/HUMAN%20TRAFFICKING%20IN%20NIGERIA%20-%20ROOT%20CAUSES%20&%20RECOMMENDATIONS.pdf

UNICEF Nigeria. (2007). Information Sheet: Child Trafficking. https://www.unicef.org/wcaro/WCARO_Nigeria_Factsheets_ChildTrafficking.pdf.

U.S. Department of State. (2017). "Trafficking in Persons Report." https://www.state.gov/j/tip/rls/tiprpt/countries/2017/271255.htm.

global north have been guilty of sensationalizing the issue in their desire to "save" women from such sex work, often in ways that ignore the complexity of women's decisions and experiences in this work, and especially the differences between migrating sex workers and those who are coerced into such practices. Of course it is problematic to automatically assume "free choice" in these decisions, because "choices" are often made from limited options and reflect structural realities such as poverty and violence.

Gendered violence is specifically linked to processes of globalization, as already discussed, because these processes often heighten problems associated with gender inequities in relationships, families, and communities at the same time that they often increase women's poverty and therefore their vulnerability. Violence against women in Juarez, Mexico, for example, where countless women have disappeared and been raped and killed, can be explained in part by forces of globalization cheapening women's labor power and therefore their bodies in the context of the forces of prostitution, organized crime, police corruption, and drug trafficking. In addition, globalizing forces have encouraged the status of women to be used as a marker of the level of "civilization" of a society, just as cultural interventions have been justified in part in the name of improving the status of women (as was most recently shown with the U.S. attacks on Afghanistan as "liberating" women from the Taliban, discussed in the reading by Andrea Smith, "Beyond the Politics of Inclusion"). These developments often create complexity for feminist activism as women and men in these countries seeking to address nationalist, patriarchal problems can be interpreted as "traitors"; similarly, they cause problems for feminists in the global north whose activism can be interpreted as ethnocentric meddling or support for the militarist strategies of their own societies.

It is important in all these discussions to understand the tendency to "exoticize" global gendered violence as something that happens elsewhere and to avoid reading such problems as dowry-related violence or acid throwing (when acid is thrown at the face or person to maim or kill) as examples of crimes caused by customs and culture. These crimes are no more exotic or culturally based than atrocities perpetuated against women in the global north on a daily basis. For example, "Nirbhaya," the 23-year-old who died after being gang raped with unspeakable brutality on a bus in New Delhi, India, in late 2012, became an icon of resistance and galvanized protests and calls for change in India. Although her tragic death highlighted the problem of chronic gender violence in India and its relationship to cultural misogyny, it is important for those in the global north to understand that cultural misogyny is present in all of our communities.

Violence is an inherent consequence of militarism in conflict zones; it is also present in the everyday lives of soldiers, who cope with a higher incidence of sexual assault than civilians. Prevalence figures gathered in 2016 show that rates of sexual assault decreased by half for active-duty women and by two-thirds for men over the past 10 years; however, a report released by the U.S. Defense Department in 2018 describes an increase of 10 percent in sexual assault cases compared to data from 2017 across all four military services. These numbers include soldiers who are sexually abused by fellow soldiers and community members affiliated with their service and reported cases of soldiers abusing nonservice troops. Men's rates of reporting IPV were relatively constant, and women's increased by about 13 percent. In part this reflects changes in reporting procedures: Currently about 1 in every 3 military members reports their sexual assault, up from about 1 in 14 in 2006.

It is important to emphasize that in all these situations where sexual, physical, and emotional abuse is recorded, violence is about the exercise of power and anyone can perpetrate it. But we do know that those who identify as men are most likely to suffer physical violence at the hands of other men, and boys are especially at risk during childhood and adolescence for suffering physical abuse by caretakers of all genders. They are especially at risk for sexual abuse by other boys and men. Given the norms about masculine invulnerability, it is often particularly difficult for these individuals to talk about their abuse and seek help. As a result, they are more likely to be in denial about such experiences, and some men who have been abused try to "master" the abuse by identifying with the source of their victimization and avoiding the weaknesses associated with being a "victim."

Trans individuals and those who are gender nonconforming are especially vulnerable to victimization by those with whom they have interpersonal relationships as well as by those who seek to harm them solely because of their identity. The latter is an example of a hate crime: a criminal offense motivated by prejudice, anger, and fear, and directed at someone (or a family, group, or whole community) because of their perceived identity. Hate crimes target victims because of their perceived membership in certain social groups and involve such criminal acts as damage to property or pets and offensive graffiti or letters (hate mail) as well as interpersonal violence such as physical and sexual assault, bullying, harassment, verbal abuse or insults, and murder. The U.S. Federal Bureau of Investigation (FBI) in its 2018 Uniform Crime Reporting (UCR) Program data reported approximately 7,000 hate crime cases in 2017 (59 percent motivated by race or ethnicity, with crimes against African Americans, Jews, and Muslims most predominant; 16 percent by disability; 18 percent by sexual identity; and 29 percent by gender). It is not clear how gender identity also plays a part in hate crimes not designated as only related to "gender," nor, of course, how statistics might skyrocket if crimes of misogyny directed against women (both cisgender and trans) that were not recorded as hate crimes were actually included. UCR data notoriously underestimates the extent of the problem, and some scholars suggest that about a quarter of a million such hate crimes based on disability, age, sexual identity, religion, race, or ethnicity as well as gender occur every year.

It is also important to understand the ways gender violence might be experienced differently based on different social identities. For example, although people with disabilities experience the same types of crime as people without disabilities, they may experience unique forms of these crimes because they often must rely on caregivers, limited transportation options, and limited access to sign language interpreters and assistive devices, and they may be vulnerable because of potential isolation, among other issues. In terms of IPV, therefore, these individuals often face diminished reporting opportunities, and they may experience denial of care or assistance; destruction of communication devices, medical equipment, and/or medications; and other controlling and abusive behaviors that harm them emotionally, physically, and/or sexually.

You may recall from Chapter 2 the importance of recognizing intersecting systems of discrimination and privilege and these systems' roles in shaping human experience. Sexual, psychological, and physical violence by the state can take a variety of forms that include, as Homa Khaleeli's reading "#SayHerName" emphasizes, the ways women and girls are treated by police and the criminal justice system. Women held in pretrial or prison facilities are at risk for physical and sexual assault. The mass incarceration of people of color is linked to structural forms of discrimination and oppression. Poor women, women of color, LGBTQ individuals, and those who are gender nonconforming are at great risk, as are those who work in the sex industry, migrants, and undocumented workers, to name just a few. In addition, gender-based violence is associated with lack of health and reproductive justice, including denials of care, provider-controlled contraceptive technologies, and forced sterilization. As already discussed in other chapters, women of color often receive inadequate health care, which puts them at risk for, among other things, higher mortality rates associated with childbirth and diseases such as cancer and diabetes. Structural violence is of course related to interpersonal violence because it shapes the conditions of the latter, the specifics of the experience, and the sources of potential support and healing. Andrea Smith makes this point in the reading "Beyond the Politics of Inclusion."

Knowledge about interpersonal gender violence in the United States relies on several sources of data. First is the National Crime Victimization Survey (NCVS) of the U.S. Bureau of Justice Statistics, which provides comprehensive information based on nationally representative samples of individuals and families interviewed in their homes about a broad range of crimes, including gender violence. As of this writing, the NCVS no longer asks 16- and 17-year-olds to voluntarily and confidentially disclose their sexual and gender identity, even though it provides crucial data on criminal victimization of LGBTQ people, who are subject to high rates of hate crimes that include gender-based violence. A National Research Council panel concluded that the NCVS was likely undercounting IPV as a result of the way the survey was designed and administered, and specifically the lack of privacy associated with interview protocol in respondents' homes.

Although the rate of intimate partner victimization declined over the last decade along with violent crime rates generally, currently an average of 24 people per minute are victims of physical and contact violence, including stalking, by an intimate partner in the United States. Over the course of a year this amounts to more than 12 million people. These findings emphasize that gender violence is an important and widespread public health problem. Eighty-one percent of women and 35 percent of men who experienced rape, physical violence, or stalking by an intimate partner reported at least one impact related to the experience, such as fear, concern for safety, injury, or absence of at least one day of work or school. Individuals who experienced rape or stalking by any perpetrator or physical violence by an intimate partner in their lifetime were more likely to report frequent headaches, chronic pain, difficulty sleeping, activity limitations, and poor physical and mental health than those who did not experience these forms of violence. In other words, nearly 3 in 10 women and 1 in 10 men in the United States has experienced contact sexual violence, physical violence, and/or stalking by an intimate partner and a related impact on everyday functioning.

VIOLENCE AGAINST WOMEN ACT OF 1994

For decades, feminist activists had worked to gain recognition of the extent and severity of violence against women in the United States. On the whole, violence against women had not been fully recognized as a serious crime within the criminal justice system. Often reports of sexual assault were greeted with skepticism or victim-blaming.

Prior to feminist activism in the 1970s, women had to present evidence of resistance to sexual assault, rules of evidence allowed consideration of a victim's entire sexual history, and husbands were exempt from charges of raping their wives. Following the opening of the first rape crisis centers in 1972, grassroots advocacy managed not only to provide care and services to victims, but also to change these laws.

Generally, domestic violence was considered by law enforcement to be a "family matter," and so police, prosecutors, and judges were often reluctant to "interfere." The first domestic violence shelters opened in the mid-1970s, but not until the 1980s did this problem receive widespread attention. Thanks to activists, laws did change in the 1980s to codify domestic violence as criminal conduct, to provide increased penalties, to create civil protection orders, and to mandate training about domestic violence for law enforcement.

Following a Washington, DC, meeting of representatives from various groups advocating for victims of sexual assault and domestic violence in the 1980s, activists turned their attention to ensuring the passage of federal legislation to protect women through interstate enforcement of protection orders, to provide funding for shelters and other programs for victims, and to provide prevention efforts. By demonstrating the need for these protections and programs, grassroots advocates and the National Organization for Women (NOW) Legal Defense Fund were able to develop bipartisan support in Congress and to pass the Violence Against Women Act (VAWA) in 1994.

The four subtitles of the act describe the target areas of concern: Safe Streets, Safe Homes for Women, Civil Rights for Women and Equal Justice for Women in the Courts, and Protections of Battered Immigrant Women and Children. VAWA changed rules of evidence, police procedures, penalties, and court procedures. It also authorized funding for prevention, education, and training.

Since 1994, VAWA has been reauthorized and modified several times. In 2013, the reauthorization for the first time included protections for lesbian, gay, bisexual, and transgender survivors and allowed tribal authorities to prosecute non-tribal members who commit crimes on tribal land. As of May 1, 2019, the bill reauthorizing the act has been passed in the House and awaits a vote in the Senate. To find out more about VAWA, visit the website of the U.S. Department of Justice's Violence Against Women Office at https://www.justice.gov/ovw.

Teen dating violence (TDV) is also an important problem in the United States, and one exacerbated by social media. Although it usually takes place in person, it can also include such behaviors as repeated texting or posting sexual pictures of a partner online without consent. When this dating violence occurs through text messaging, many teens often do not recognize controlling behaviors as abusive. This problem illustrates the ways communication technologies influence dating violence by redefining boundaries between dating partners. Teens are less likely than adults to report abusive behaviors out of fears of being ostracized by friends or of telling family members. Data from the Center for Disease Control's Youth Risk Behavior Survey and the National Intimate Partner and Sexual Violence Survey, however, show that TDV affects millions of teens in the United States each year. Almost 1 in 11 high school girls and 1 in 15 high school boys report having experienced physical dating violence in the last year. Sometimes physical abuse between adolescents involves mutual abuse, with both partners using violence against each other. However, it is clear that adolescents use force for different reasons and with different results. Researchers have found that girls suffer more from relationship violence, emotionally and physically. They are more likely than boys to have serious injuries and report being terrified. In contrast, male victims seldom fear violence by their girlfriends and often say the attacks did not hurt or that they found the violence amusing.

Data from the Center for Disease Control's Youth Risk Behavior Survey and the National Intimate Partner and Sexual Violence Survey also report that sexual dating violence occurs in relatively high numbers in teen relationships. These data suggest almost 1 in 9 high school girls and 1 in 36 high school boys report having experienced physical dating violence in the last year. Overall about 1 in 4 women and 1 in 12 who are survivors of contact sexual violence first experienced these or other forms of violence before age 18. It is important to note that that both girls and boys are more likely to be sexually abused by other boys. It is also important to note that over half to three-quarters of all teens surveyed report knowing others in violent relationships in their school or communities. The consequences of teen violence are immense, with rape victims in particular more likely to contemplate, and actually attempt, suicide.

An important aspect of teen violence is bullying, when someone verbally and/or physically harasses another person perceived as weaker. Bullies seek power through aggression and intimidation, and direct their attacks at vulnerable targets. Boys are more likely to bully than girls and to bully other boys, although girls are almost as likely to bully as boys through social media, but, as discussed below, in different ways than boys. Despite the most recent School Crime Supplement to the National Crime Victimization Survey, which reports that the rates of students reporting criminal victimization at school have decreased in the last decade (now about 4 percent of all K–12 students), bullying has increased, especially cyberbullying. The National Institute of Child Health reports that over 6 in 10 teenagers currently witness bullying in U.S. schools daily, and millions of children in grades 6 through 10 are bullied at least once a week. More than two-thirds of students report general bullying as an ongoing problem in their school, about 1 in 10 students drops out or changes schools because of repeated bullying, and more than 1 in 10 report school absences because of fear of bullying. Indeed, both the bully and the bullied are at greater risk of loneliness; lack of success in school; and involvement in drugs, alcohol, and tobacco. Almost half of all bullies have three or more police arrests by age 30. In addition, Asian American students are bullied in U.S. schools more than any other ethnic group, and particularly online in the form of cyberbullying. LGBTQ youth and those who are gender nonconforming are especially at high risk for bullying.

In terms of cyberbullying specifically, teenage boys and girls are equally likely to be targets, but there are differences in the specific types of harassment they encounter and girls appear to be more emotionally scarred as a result of the bullying. According to a Pew Research Center Internet and technology study, almost 60 percent of both girls and boys have experienced at least one of six abusive online behaviors, which include name-calling, spreading of false rumors, constant and repeated monitoring and policing, receiving explicit images they did not ask for, having explicit images of them shared without consent, and physical threats. While similar shares of boys and girls have encountered abuse such as name-calling or physical threats online, other forms of cyberbullying are more prevalent among girls. For example, 39 percent of girls say someone has spread false rumors about them online, compared with about 26 percent of boys who say this. Girls also are more likely than boys to report being the recipient of explicit images they did not ask for. When it comes to bullying online both girls and boys participate, but levels vary based upon the kind of bullying. Boys tend to use more overt aggression and intimidation and are likely to bully alone; girls are more secretive, use more indirect forms of emotional abuse intended to ostracize and humiliate, and bully as a group. Indeed, cyberbullying is currently a serious social problem that may lead to tragic consequences, such as youths committing suicide after experiencing bullying and harassment.

The prevalence of youths committing suicide due to long-term bullying has resulted in the term "bullycide." Again, this is especially pertinent for gender nonconforming and LGBTQ students who are at high risk of suicide after experiencing a variety of abusive behaviors. Alongside the high rates of ostracism and emotional humiliation, their isolation diminishes opportunities for seeking support. Lawmakers, school officials, and some companies that make and market online platforms are trying to address electronic harassment. For example, several states have enacted legislation prohibiting cyberbullying, schools have implemented policies and education, and social media companies are including anti-cyberbullying resources.In addition to these statistics on the bullying and victimization of children and youths is the tragic reality of school shootings, which have resulted in the killing and severe wounding of pupils and staff in schools across the United States.

GENDER AND SCHOOL SHOOTINGS

Nancy Staton Barbour

As Jill Filopovic points out in "It's Always Men," 98 percent of mass shootings in the United States have been perpetrated by males. School shootings are likewise overwhelmingly carried out by males, specifically young men under the age of 30. Research on school shooters has shown that these young men tend to commit violence against their peers out of frustration and anger stemming from their perceived failure to conform to socially constructed norms of masculinity (Farr, 2018; Langman, 2017). In a study of 31 school shooters—including the perpetrators of Jonesboro, Columbine, and Sandy Hook—Farr (2018) found that all of the shooters were troubled by challenges to their masculinity, for example, being bullied by male peers, having romantic difficulties with females, being called "homo" or "fag," or feeling otherwise emasculated by classmates and teachers. Langman (2017) observed that a combination of social, psychological, and biological factors contribute to feelings of inadequacy and "damaged masculinity" among school shooters.

While male identity is the main characteristic linking the vast majority of school shooters, it is also important to recognize that most shooters also identify as white and heterosexual—a demographic that typically enjoys the greatest social privilege in the United States. Thus, school shooters often feel that others have denied them the status to which they are entitled (Farr 2018). Early reports on the February 2018 shooting at Stoneman Douglas High School in Parkland, Florida, indicated that the perpetrator was motivated not only by damaged masculinity, but also by white supremacist ideology. Another common factor among men who commit mass shootings is misogyny. A growing group of male supremacists connecting on shadowy Internet sites and claiming to be "involuntarily celibate"—or "incel"—have celebrated mass shooters as avengers of marginalized men. The incel community, also predominantly white heterosexual males, blames women for denying them sex, and some members actively advocate violence against women and sexually active men.

The Stoneman Douglas shooting became a pivotal moment in the national debate on gun violence. One month after the incident, a million U.S. students coordinated school walkouts in response to the tragedy, and survivors of the shooting organized a massive protest to demand political action on gun control. Students from Stoneman Douglas High School went to Washington, DC, and spoke about their experiences at one of the largest youth-led demonstrations in American history. The March for Our Lives demonstration on March 24, 2018, saw more than two million people gather in cities across the United States and around the world to call for an end to mass shootings.

References

Farr, Kathryn. (2018). "Adolescent Rampage School Shootings: Responses to Failing Masculinity Performances by Already-Troubled Boys." *Gender Issues*, 35(2), 73–97.

Langman, Peter. (2017). "A Bio-Psycho-Social Model of School Shooters." *Journal of Campus Behavioral Intervention*, 5, 27–34.

That these shooters are overwhelmingly white boys is sometimes overlooked by media and academics alike. A more thorough analysis of contemporary white masculinities, as well as the role of firearms and violent media in the cultural landscape, needs to be performed in order to better understand this phenomenon.

Another disturbing trend is the increase in stalking behavior that causes fear and emotional and psychological trauma. Stalking can be defined as the act of a person who, on more than one occasion, follows, pursues, or harasses another person, and, by actively engaging in a pattern of conduct, causes the victim to believe the stalker will cause physical harm or mental distress to the victim. Behaviors include making unwanted phone calls; sending unsolicited or unwanted letters, texts, or emails; following or spying on the victim; showing up at places without a legitimate reason; waiting at places for the victim; leaving unwanted items, presents, or flowers; and posting information or spreading rumors about the victim on the Internet, in a public place, or by word of mouth. Stalking is generally defined as a pattern of behavior that would cause a reasonable person to feel fear. Although a crime throughout the United States, stalking varies widely across the states in terms of statutory classification and associated penalties because it is understood as a "course of conduct crime." This means that it consists of individual acts that could, in isolation, seem benign or non-criminal and be under-identified and underreported. Often linked to IPV, it can lead to significant trauma for those victimized.

Approximately 13 percent of women on college campuses report being stalked, and two-thirds of stalked women know their stalker. It is estimated that about 1 in 6 women and 1 in 20 men will experience stalking in their lifetimes. Eighty-five percent of women in the National Intimate Partner and Sexual Violence Survey reported that they were stalked by a man. Among men who are stalked, 46 percent report being stalked by a woman and 43 percent by a man. Native American women and those who indicate more than one racial identity report the highest rates of being stalked, at one-third and one-quarter, respectively.

All 50 states in the United States now have stalking laws, although as already mentioned states vary in how they handle the crime; some states require that victims prove they felt fear (and 4 states require proof that they feared for their life). Half of states require that there be two or more different instances of stalking, and the other half require evidence of an "established pattern" of stalking behavior. About one-third of those stalked report the problem to the police, with 20 percent of these indicating that law enforcement responded by taking no action.

As already mentioned, accounts of gender violence are generally underreported and sometimes difficult to interpret. Different studies ask about victimization in different ways and get different results. Some studies ask about current abuse, and some survey past histories; some ask only about physical abuse, while others include questions about emotional or psychological abuse and sexual abuse in the context of consent. It is always important to consider whether consent for sexual intimacy can occur in a relationship where physical violence and emotional intimidation are present.

However, any discussion attempting to address the issue of violence against women—either in the United States or worldwide—must involve several key points. *First*, violence must be understood in the context of socially constructed notions of gender. If one group of humans is raised to hide emotion, see sensitivity as a weakness, and view sexual potency as interwoven with interpersonal power, and others are raised to be passive, dependent, and support masculine entitlement, then interpersonal violence should be no

ANTI-LGBTQ VIOLENCE AROUND THE WORLD

Sayan Bhattacharya

A March 2017 article published in the *Guardian* asks the following question: "Where are the most difficult places in the world to be gay or transgender?" (Banning-Lover 2017). The article lists various countries—such as Iraq, Iran, Honduras, Uganda, Russia, and Egypt—that have had a long record of persecution and even murder of queer and transgender individuals. The fact sheet "Homophobic and Transphobic Violence" by United Nations Human Rights states that violence against LGBT people can range "from aggressive, sustained psychological bullying to physical assault, torture, kidnapping and targeted killings" (2017, 1). It notes that victims of homophobic and transphobic violence are sometimes not only murdered, but also brutalized through sexual torture, mutilation, and even burning.

Such violence can occur in public spaces, such as streets and parks; institutions, such as the workplace, hospitals, and schools; or the family home. Violence can also be carried out in prisons and by the police. It can be led by extremist groups too. For example, the *Guardian* article notes that the Islamic State has been concertedly attacking the LGBTQ population in the Middle East (Banning-Lover 2017). Amnesty International[1] (n.d.) reports that 76 countries in the world criminalize sexual activities between "same-sex" adults.

Still, we should not read these accounts of violence as representative of an entire culture. Different countries have specific histories and culture, and queer identities are mediated through these specificities. There are robust LGBTQ movements around the world that take into account these questions and accordingly design advocacy initiatives. However, often these local movements are rendered invisible in global analyses of anti-LGBTQ violence. For example, the *Guardian* article talks mostly about countries in the global south and how violent these countries are for LGBT people; while the incidents discussed are true, the analysis is incomplete because it does not take into account local movements of resistance in these countries. Moreover, it ends up giving the reader the impression that the global north has been able to create safe environments for LGBTQ people, which is far from the truth.

The Trump administration recently ordered the Bureau of Prisons to use "biological sex" to determine how transgender prisoners are assigned housing, thus rendering transgender folks more vulnerable to sexual abuse and other forms of discrimination. Yet the United States has often justified war with countries like Iraq and

Afghanistan and support for the Israeli occupation of Palestine by pointing out that LGBTQ people in these countries are unsafe under their respective governments (Puar 2007, 2017). Moreover, LGBTQ people of color and LGBTQ people with disabilities around the world are more at risk of hate violence compared to their white and able-bodied counterparts. Any analysis of hate crimes against LGBTQ people must also account for the ways race, class, and ability intersect with sexuality and gender.

Activity

Select two articles published in the United States that report anti-LGBTQ violence in a country outside of Europe and North America. Then compare that coverage with how the incidents were reported in the media of that country. Was there any difference in coverage? If yes, what were those differences? If no, why do you think there was no difference? Now imagine yourself in the journalist's shoes. How would you report the same incident? Is there anything that you would do differently?

Further Reading

Amnest International. (n.d.) "Gender, Sexuality, and Identity." https://www.amnestyusa.org/issues/gender-sexuality-identity/

Banning-Lover, R. (2017, March 1). "Where Are the Most Difficult Places in the World to Be Gay or Transgender?" *Guardian*. https://www.theguardian.com/global-development-professionals-network/2017/mar/01/where-are-the-most-difficult-places-in-the-world-to-be-gay-or-transgender-lgbt

Marzullo, M. A., & Libman, A. J. (2009, May). "Research Overview: Hate Crimes and Violence Against Lesbian, Gay, Bisexual and Transgender People." Human Rights Campaign Foundation. https://assets2.hrc.org/files/assets/resources/Hatecrimesandviolenceagainstlgbtpeople_2009.pdf?_ga=2.211618581.1200148078.1526426404-1353441099.1526234789

Puar, J. (2007). *Terrorist Assemblages: Homonationalism in Queer Times*. Durham, NC: Duke University Press.

———. (2017). *The Right to Maim: Debility, Capacity, Disability*. Durham, NC: Duke University Press.

United Nations Human Rights. (2017). "Fact Sheet: Homophobic and Transphobic Violence." https://www.unfe.org/wp-content/uploads/2017/05/Homophobic-and-Transphobic-Violence.pdf

---

[1] "Gender, Sexuality, and Identity," Amnesty International at https://www.amnestyusa.org/issues/gender-sexuality-identity/

surprise. As Debra Anne Davis explains in the reading "Betrayed by the Angel," women are raised in ways that may encourage victimization. *Second*, violence is a power issue and a consequence of masculine dominance in society. Such dominance also extends to control of political systems that address crime and create policy. Indeed, entitlements associated with masculinity produce a range that some scholars term the rape spectrum. This means that all sexist behaviors are arranged along a continuum—from unexamined feelings of superiority, for example, on one end to rape on the other. In this sense, all these behaviors, even though they vary tremendously in degree, are connected at some level.

In addition, scholars emphasize that these behaviors are often connected to "backlash" or resistance to gains made by women and other marginalized peoples. Though many support these gains and are working on ways to address interpersonal power and violence, hoping to enjoy more egalitarian relationships, some have not responded well to these gains. They have responded with anger and feelings of powerlessness and insecurity. Interpersonal violence occurs as people attempt to reestablish power they believe they have lost as a direct result of others' gains. As already discussed, hate crimes based on identity are significant problems in contemporary society as people marked as "different" or marginal are targeted as victims of violence. Finally, online gender-based harassment targeted at people who speak out in favor of social justice is also increasingly being understood as a form of backlash as well as a rampant social problem as the public virtual space gets constructed as a masculine sphere where misogyny is rife. In particular, those writing about feminism and misogynous violence are often silenced and controlled, sometimes through brutal online threats of violence.

Third, gendered sexual violence is also related to the ways violence is eroticized. Although pornography is the best example of this problem in its role in eroticizing power differences, women's magazines and advertising are often rife with these themes. Before turning our focus to specifically address issues associated with rape and sexual assault, physical abuse, and incest, we end this section with a discussion of pornography as an aspect of gender violence. Because many forms of pornography are legal, some people object to thinking about pornography in the context of gender violence and claim instead that it is a legitimate type of entertainment. Many people, scholars and laypeople, feminists and non-feminists alike, resist considering pornography in the context of gender-based violence. Indeed, there are sex-radical feminists who strongly endorse pornography and argue that it is empowering to women, especially when women are in control of certain aspects of the sex industry. Others respond that just because a person has consented (knowing also that "consent" does not always imply free choice), this does not alter the degrading character of the behavior. These debates are alive and well in feminist studies and sometimes bring about some interesting coalitions among those who normally do not work together, such as feminists and conservative religious groups.

Most feminist scholars and activists recognize the potentially positive aspects of some pornography that is created in more egalitarian contexts, but some emphasize it is still important to recognize that pornography eroticizes unequal power relations between people and often involves representations of coercive sex. Men as a social group are the major (although not only, of course) consumers of pornography, and women's bodies tend to be the ones on display for their pleasure. Critics suggest pornography thus represents a particular aspect of gender relations that reflects entitlements and power as well as sexual objectification, especially of marginalized people. They believe that people's rights to consume such materials are no longer rights when they violate the rights of others. In addition, some make the case that even if there is feminist disagreement over whether pornography entails objectification, and whether such objectification can ever serve social justice, pornography is still used as a tool of misogyny and domination in violent crime; otherwise some pornography would not be illegal.

Just as there are degrees of objectification and normalization of violence in pop culture forms, so too in pornography there is a continuum: from the soft porn of *Playboy* to *Hustler* and a host of hard-core Internet sites, along to illegal forms of representation such as child pornography and snuff films. Snuff films are illegal because women are actually murdered in the making of these films. Of course the Internet is one of the largest sites for pornography. In addition to online pornography, there is the problem of Internet prostitution, in which technology is utilized for live cam pornography as well as global trafficking and the sexual exploitation of women and children.

In conclusion, many people condone pornography because they believe it represents free speech, or because they feel that the women have chosen to be part of it. Some people make a distinction between hardcore and soft porn and feel that the former is harmful and the latter relatively harmless. Some see pornography as a mark of sexual freedom and characterize those who oppose it as prudish. Certainly sexual freedom requires sexual justice and pornography can be understood as a violation of this justice rather than an expression of it. In this way, pornography is opposed as a violation of rights even while others celebrate it.

SEXUAL ASSAULT AND RAPE

It is important to understand sexual abuse in terms of the normalization of violence in society. We live in societies where violence is used to solve problems every day, media are saturated with violence, militarism is a national policy, and rape is used as a weapon of war. Again, it is important to analyze the role of contemporary masculinity in these phenomena and consider the ways violent masculinity is normalized. What do you think would be the societal response if women and girls victimized men, boys, and other girls to the extent that men and boys routinely victimize girls, women, and each other?

Consider the following story told to us. A white, 30-something professional, whose pronouns are she/her/hers, had been having a drink with colleagues early one evening after work. A well-dressed man struck up a conversation with her, and they chatted a while. When she was leaving with her colleagues, the man asked if he could call her sometime, and she gave him her business card that provided only work information. He called her at work within the next week and asked her to have dinner with him, and, seeing no reason not to, she agreed to meet him at a popular restaurant after work. (She was careful to explain to us that on both occasions, she was dressed in her professional work clothes, and she met with him early in the evening in a public space. There was nothing provocative, she emphasized, about her clothes or her demeanor.) At some point during the meal, she started feeling uncomfortable. The man was flirtatious but also very pushy; he tried to choose and order her food and told her that if she wanted to date him, he had certain requirements about how his girlfriends dressed and acted. She panicked and felt a strong need to get away from him, so at some point she quietly excused herself, saying she needed to visit the rest room. She then exited quickly and did not return to the table. Unfortunately, this was not the end of the story. The man found out where her home was and started to stalk her, angry that she had humiliated him by rejecting his advances. One evening he forced his way into her apartment and beat her badly. Although she took out a restraining order on him, he managed to gain entrance into her apartment building again and beat her senseless one more time in the hallway outside her apartment.

This story is a tragic illustration of misogyny and masculine entitlement. The man felt he had the right to define the reality of women in his life and expected them to be subordinate. He believed it was his entitlement. He was so full of rage that when a woman snubbed him, he had to subdue her. In addition, the woman's telling of the story is illustrative of societal norms that blame women for their own victimization. When tearfully sharing her story, she had felt the shame and humiliation that comes with such an experience; she wanted it to be known that she had not been "asking for it." He had given no indication that he was anything but upstanding, she was dressed appropriately, she took no risks other than accepting a date, she gave him only her work numbers, and she agreed to meet him in a public place. What more could she have done except be wary of all men she might meet? This story sets the stage for our understanding of sexual assault.

Sexual assault can be defined as any sexual contact without consent that involves the use of force. Definitions of sexual contact violence also include forcing someone to engage in sexual contact, including the case where perpetrators make their victims penetrate them. Individuals may be sexually assaulted without being raped. Rape is a form of sexual contact violence, but sexual assault and abuse do not necessarily imply rape. More specifically, rape is the penetration of any bodily orifice by a penis or object without consent. Someone who is asleep, passed out, or incapacitated by alcohol or drugs cannot give consent. Silence, or lack of continued resistance, does not mean consent. You may recall the reading in Chapter 6 by Charlene Muehlenhard and colleagues, "The Complexities of Sexual Consent Among College Students," which makes these points. Although rape can be broadly defined as sex without consent, it is understood as a crime of aggression because the focus is on hurting and dominating. The sexual abuse of children is often termed molestation, which may or may not involve rape. When children are molested or raped by family members, it is termed incest. Although the rates of rape are very high, sexual assault rates generally (which include but are not limited to rape) are even higher.

Women are often victims of altruistic sex (where motivation for consent involves feeling sorry for the other person or feeling guilty about resisting sexual advances) and compliant sex (where the consequences of not doing it are worse than doing it). Neither of these forms of sexual intimacy involve complete consent. Consent is a freely made choice that is clearly communicated. Consensual sex is negotiated through communication in which individuals express their feelings and desires and are able to listen to and respect others' feelings and desires. Rape can happen to anyone—babies who are months old to women in their 90s, and people of all races, ethnicities, and socioeconomic statuses. Both women and men are raped, but, as already discussed, overwhelmingly it is a problem of men raping women and other men. Rape occurs relatively frequently in prisons; dominant men rape men they perceive as inferior. Often, dominant inmates refer to the victims as "women." In this way, rape is about power, domination, and humiliation and must be understood in this context.

As already mentioned, most reported sexual assaults are against girls and women, with the likelihood of one in three or four women experiencing sexual assault in their lifetime. In addition, approximately half of all women raped are under the age of 18 years, and about one-fifth are younger than 12 years old. Offenders were armed with a gun, knife, or other weapon in about 11 percent of rape or sexual assault victimizations, according to the National Crime Victimization Survey. The percentage of reported rape or sexual assault victimizations that resulted in an arrest either at the scene or during a follow-up investigation decreased from almost half in the late 1990s to less than a third in 2018. Overall, among both reported and unreported sexual assaults and rapes, approximately 1 in 10 results in an arrest. It is important to note again that NCVS surveys underreport IPV and include a higher relative proportion of stranger rapes, which are more likely to be reported and prosecuted.

Data from the Campus Sexual Assault (CSA) study suggests that almost a fifth of women are sexually assaulted during their enrollment in college, with the first few months of their college experience being the time of greatest vulnerability. When nonconsensual sexual contact rather than assault is considered, these estimates increase to about a quarter of all women undergraduates, with most incidents occurring on campus, and a majority associated with Greek life. The Association of American Universities (AAU) published a report on college sexual assault and misconduct that surveyed 150,000 students across the United States. Mirroring the takeaway message of the reading by Chelsea Spencer, Allen Mallory,

LEARNING ACTIVITY

HOW SAFE IS YOUR CAMPUS?

Investigate the safety and security of your campus by asking these questions:

- How many acts of violence were reported on your campus last year?
- Does your campus have a security escort service?
- What resources does your campus provide to ensure safety?
- What training and educational opportunities about safety does your college provide?
- What specialized training about violence is offered to fraternities and sports teams on your campus?

- How does your school encourage the reporting of violence?
- What support services does your school offer to victims of violence?
- What is your school administration's official protocol for dealing with complaints of violence?
- How does your school's code of conduct address violence?
- Are there dark areas of your campus that need additional lighting?
- Are emergency phones available around your campus?

Michelle Toews, Sandra Stith, and Leila Wood, "Why Sexual Assault Survivors Do Not Report to Universities," the report emphasized that the most common reason why survivors did not report sexual assault was because they worried that the victimization was not serious enough and they were embarrassed about its occurrence. In the AAU study, two-thirds of college rape survivors reported the incident to a friend, family member, or roommate, and less than 10 percent to school officials or police.

Over the last couple of decades the numbers of sexual offenses on college campuses have tripled, in part because of increased reporting procedures. Back in 1990 Congress passed the Campus Security Act ("Clery Act"), which mandated that colleges and universities participating in federal student aid programs complete and distribute security reports on campus practices and crime statistics. This was amended in 1992 to include the Campus Sexual Assault Victim's Bill of Rights to provide policies and statistics and to ensure basic rights to survivors of sexual assault. This act was amended again in 1998 to provide for more extensive security-related provisions, and, since then, the U.S. Department of Justice has given substantial grants to colleges and universities to address sexual and physical assault, harassment, and stalking on campus. It is estimated that women at a university with 10,000 women students could experience about 350 rapes a year with serious policy implications for college administrators. Still, however, a significant number of colleges and universities across the nation report zero known instances of rape on campus.

Rapes on college campuses (especially gang rapes) may be committed by fraternity members, and may be part of male bonding rituals. This does not mean, of course, that all fraternities are dangerous places for women, only that the conditions for the abuse of women can occur in these male-only living spaces, especially when alcohol is present. About 70 to 80 percent of campus rapes generally involve alcohol or other drugs (with alcohol most pervasive among all drugs). The most common "date rape" or predatory drugs are Rohypnol (commonly known as "roofies"), ketamine (commonly known as "special k"), and GHB (gamma hydroxybutyrate). These drugs are odorless when dissolved and are indiscernible when put in beverages. They metabolize quickly and make a person incapable of resisting sexual advances. Memory impairment is associated with these drugs, and a survivor may not be aware of such an attack until 8 to 12 hours after it has occurred. In addition, there may be little evidence to support the claim that drugs were used to facilitate the attack because of the speed at which these predatory drugs metabolize. It is imperative to be vigilant at social occasions where such attacks might happen; do not leave a drink unattended, get your own drinks from an unopened container, and watch out for your friends. A buddy system that includes a designated driver is essential!

One specific form of intimate partner violence is marital rape. In the United States the legal definition of marital rape varies across the states, but it is generally defined as any unwanted intercourse or penetration (vaginal, anal, or oral) obtained by force or threat of force, or when a spouse is unable to consent. Historically, rape was understood as a property crime against men because women were considered the property of husbands and fathers. As a result, it was considered impossible to violate something that was legally considered your property, and rape laws defined rape as forced intercourse with a woman who was not your wife. As of 1993, marital rape became illegal in all 50 U.S. states, but there are still a handful of states where marital rape continues to be handled in a substantially different way than rape outside of marriage, such as being charged under a different section of criminal code, restricted to a shorter reporting period, or held to a different standard of coercion and force. In addition, some states have lesser sentences for husbands than other rapists, and statutory rape laws often do not go into effect if a spouse is younger than the age of consent for that state.

Although marital rape is a form of violence both prevalent and illegal, it is often regarded as a much lesser crime than rape by a stranger, for example, or not really seen as a crime, as in "it's just having sex with your spouse when you don't want to." However, as research on marital rape suggests, it always involves emotional abuse and sometimes severe physical violence, threats of violence, and the use of weapons, usually by husbands against wives. Compared to batterers or those who only physically assault partners, individuals who batter and rape are particularly dangerous and more likely to severely injure and potentially murder a partner. Marital rape is also more likely to be ongoing and repeated because of physical access to victims, and is more likely to include anal and oral rape as well as vaginal.

A national study reported that 10 percent of all sexual assault cases involve a husband or ex-husband, and the National Resource Center on Domestic Violence suggests that taking into account the underreporting that occurs because women are less likely to label such actions as rape, 10 to 14 percent of married women in the United States have been raped by their husbands. Researchers generally categorize marital rape into three types: force-only rape, when a husband uses only enough force to enact the rape; battering rape, in which rape occurs in the context of an ongoing physically abusive relationship; and sadistic/obsessive rape, in which a husband uses torture or perverse acts to humiliate and harm his wife. Pornography is often involved in the latter case. Women are at particularly high risk for being raped when they are living with domineering partners who view them as "property"; when they are pregnant, ill physically or mentally, or recovering from surgery; and when they are separated or divorced.

As will be discussed in Chapter 11, political institutions in the United States have historically supported men's access to women as sexual property, and the history of racism and the lynching of black men for fabricated rapes of white women have influenced how our society and the courts deal with the interaction of race and sexual violence. Although most rapes are intraracial (they occur within racial groups), women of color are especially vulnerable as victims of sexual violence because of their marginalized status. They also have less credibility in the courtroom when rape cases go to trial. Men of color accused of rape are more likely to get media attention, be convicted, and receive longer sentences. While these differences result from the racism of a society that sees African American men in particular as more violent or dangerous, they also are related to class differences whereby men of color are generally less able to acquire superior legal counsel. As Andrea Smith explains in the reading "Beyond the Politics of Inclusion," gender violence functions as a tool of racism and colonialism for women of color. She emphasizes the need to make the needs of marginalized women central in the anti-violence movement and implores writers and activists to understand the intersectionality of racism and sexism in social movements for ending violence and supporting racial justice.

Very often, women realize that a past sexual encounter was actually a rape, and, as a result, they begin to think about the experience differently. They may have left the encounter hurt, confused, or angry but unable to articulate what happened. Survivors need to talk about what occurred and get support. It is never too late to get support from people who care. Feeling ashamed, dirty, or stupid is a typical reaction. It is not their/your/our fault.

Social myths about rape that encourage these feelings include the following:

- *Rape happens less frequently in our society than women believe. Feminists in particular blow this out of proportion by focusing on women's victimization, and women make up rape charges as a way to get attention.* This is false; rape happens at an alarming rate and is underreported. Rape is considered a crime against the state, and rape survivors are witnesses to the crime. As a result, the credibility of the "witness" is challenged in rape cases, and women are often retraumatized as a result of rape trials. This is among the many reasons why rape is underreported, and, as a proportion of total rapes committed, charges are rarely pressed and assailants rarely convicted. The FBI reports that the rate of false reporting for rape and sexual assault is the same as for other violent crimes: less than 3 percent. Although feminists care about the victimization of women, we focus on surviving, becoming empowered, and making changes to stop rapes from happening.
- *Women are at least partly responsible for their victimization in terms of their appearance and behavior (encouraging women to feel guilty when they are raped).* This is false; rape is the only violent crime in which the victim is not *de facto* perceived as innocent. Consider the suggestion that people who have been robbed were asking to have their wallets stolen.
- *Perpetrators are not totally responsible for their actions. Especially if a woman comes on to a man sexually, it is impossible for him to stop.* This is false; people are not driven by uncontrollable biological urges, and it is insulting to assume that this is how they behave. Likewise, it is wrong to assume that anyone has to "finish what they started." Everyone has the right to stop sexual behaviors at any time. Note how this myth is related to the previous one that blames the victim.

These myths not only support masculine privilege concerning sexuality and access and therefore support some men's tendency to sexually abuse women, but are also important

INTIMATE PARTNER VIOLENCE

Liddy Detar

Intimate partner violence hurts all who are involved and does so in forms that are physical, psychological, economic, emotional, and continuous. Violence is enforced in our legal, social, and institutional systems, as well as in our cultural constructions of gender, sex, and sexuality. These social identities intersect with race, ethnicity, class, ability, and nationality to shape our relationships to systems of power and to create certain bodies as vulnerable to violence. Traditional models for anti-violence work have drawn on a reductive "violence against women" framework and have turned to state forms of protection as solutions.

Queer feminist approaches have more recently centered the anti-violence movement around articulating conditions and identities that have historically been rendered invisible or relegated to the margins. Advocates and activists imagine anti-violence frameworks that recognize all bodies as vulnerable to violence, thus intervening in the criminalization of certain bodies and identities. This approach allows us to reimagine who is considered "worthy" of access to support and healing spaces. It also challenges ableist and other normative paradigms that define the terms of survivorship and who and which bodies are capable of healing. Drawing on queer and feminist lenses, the anti-violence movement can imagine new forms for resources, broader access, and different kinds of "safety" to address the needs of many historically isolated communities.

TRY THIS: Research your hometown; if you have moved around a lot, choose a place that has an important role in your life. Do an Internet search to explore the following:

1. Look up local newspapers or other media sources; check police logs and other emergency and call-response organizations. What sorts of crimes are reported? Pay attention to any crimes reporting sexual assault and/or involving the sex industry. How are they represented?

2. Look up resources in your town for victims of sexual and domestic violence. Perhaps you will find shelters or churches harboring children and their parents or guardians; perhaps you will find immigration advocacy groups or animal shelters that take in pets while their owners seek help. Look up churches, homeless shelters, and community centers for services they provide for survivors of intimate partner violence. If your town has limited resources, consider a search that asks how far someone must go to get help. Would they be able to walk or bike to a shelter? Would they need a car or public transportation?

3. Review the websites of resources and consider the following: What services are offered? Which bodies might feel welcome and find safety and access? Which bodies would not? What is the meaning of these findings?

IMAGINE: Drawing on a feminist intersectional perspective, create a list of needs for resources and access in your selected community and share it with a local shelter, town representative, or activist group involved in anti-violence work and in a position to implement change. Or volunteer at a shelter or anti-violence organization and participate in creating the change yourself.

Reference

Patterson, J. (2016). *Queering Sexual Violence: Radical Voices from Within the Anti-Violence Movement*. Riverdale, NY: Riverdale Avenue Books.

means for controlling women's lives. Recall again the discussion of sexual terrorism in Chapter 2. Such terrorism limits everyday activities and keeps people in line by the threat of potential sexual assault. Early research on rapists in the early 1980s revealed that although there are few psychological differences between men who have raped and those who have not, the former group were more likely to believe in the rape myths, were more misogynous and tolerant of the interpersonal domination of women generally, showed higher levels of sexual arousal around depictions of rape, and were more prone to use violence.

PHYSICAL ABUSE

Domestic violence hotlines receive over 20,000 calls in a typical day. A 2018 fact sheet from the National Coalition Against Domestic Violence (NCADV) reports an average of

20 people experiencing intimate partner physical violence every minute, with millions annually. The NCADV also reports 1 in 3 women and 1 in 4 men having experienced some form of physical violence by an intimate partner, with 1 in 7 women and 1 in 25 men reporting an injury. Not surprisingly, women have higher rates as perpetrators of physical violence compared to contact sexual violence, although the extent and severity of the violence tends to be less than that perpetrated by men. Of all survivors, women between the ages of 18 and 24 years incur the highest incidence of intimate partner physical violence. The National Coalition Against Domestic Violence (NCADV) reports that women who are pregnant are especially at risk, and physical violence especially. Consequences include miscarriages, stillbirths, and a two- to fourfold greater likelihood of bearing a low-birth-weight baby.

Individuals of all races and classes are abused, although rates are five times higher among families below poverty levels and among unemployed male partners. These differences reflect economic vulnerabilities and lack of resources, the ways certain families have extensive contact with authorities like social services that increase opportunities for reporting, and structural violence by the state as already discussed. Sadly, the impact of family violence on children is severe. More than half of all women who are victims of IPV live in households with children younger than 12 years, and studies indicate that between 3 and 10 million children witness some form of domestic violence every year. Violent juvenile offenders are four times more likely than non-offenders to have grown up in homes where they saw and experienced violence. Children who have witnessed violence at home are also about five times more likely to commit or suffer violence when they become adults. Approximately half of men who abuse women partners also abuse the children in those homes. Of course, women abuse children too, and these rates are quite high. Indeed, some estimates show mothers are more likely to neglect and abuse children than fathers. However, because mothers have greater ongoing contact with children through caretaking activities, when numbers are controlled for the relative proportion of such caretaking activities, mothers are less likely to abuse and neglect children than fathers or stepfathers.

Women who are physically abused are also always emotionally abused because they experience emotional abuse by virtue of being physically terrorized. Mariah Lockwood writes poignantly about the emotional abuse of battered women in the poem "She Said." This reading illustrates the ways women internalize messages about femininity, love, marriage, and romance that can make them vulnerable to being dominated in interpersonal relationships. The poem also speaks of the importance of friendship and emotional support for battered women. Emotional abuse, however, does not always involve physical abuse. Abusers, for example, who constantly tell partners that they are worthless, stupid, or ugly can emotionally abuse without being physically abusive. Sometimes the scars of emotional abuse take longer to heal than physical abuse and help explain why people might stay with abusive partners.

Why do people so often stay in abusive relationships? The research on this question suggests that when individuals leave abusive relationships they return about five to seven times before actually leaving for good. There are several complex and interconnected reasons why survivors stay. First, emotional abuse often involves feelings of shame, guilt, and low self-esteem. Like rape survivors generally, they often believe that the abuse is their fault. They may see themselves as worthless and have a difficult time believing that they deserve better. Low self-esteem encourages survivors to stay with or return to abusive partners. Second, some who are repeatedly abused become desensitized to the violence; they may see it as a relatively normal aspect of gender relationships and therefore something to tolerate.

A third reason people stay in abusive relationships is that abusers tend to physically isolate their partners from others. This often involves a pattern in which survivors may be prevented from visiting or talking to family and friends, left without transportation, and/ or have no access to a telephone. Notice how, when individuals are abused, the shame associated with this situation can encourage them to isolate themselves. An outcome of this isolation is that they do not get the reality check they need about their situation. Isolation thus helps keep self-esteem low, prevents support, and minimizes options in terms of leaving the abusive situation.

IDEAS FOR ACTIVISM

- Volunteer at a local domestic violence shelter.
- Organize a food, clothing, and toiletries drive to benefit your local domestic violence shelter.
- Interrupt jokes about violence against women.
- Organize Domestic Violence Awareness Month (October) activities on your campus.

- Create and distribute materials about violence against women on your campus. Write a blog about gender-based violence.
- Organize a poetry slam to feature poems about gender-based violence.

CHECK UP ON YOUR RELATIONSHIP

DOES YOUR PARTNER

- Constantly put you down?
- Call you several times a night or show up to make sure you are where you said you would be?
- Embarrass or make fun of you in front of your friends or family? Make you feel like you are nothing without him/her?
- Intimidate or threaten you? "If you do that again, I'll . . ." Always say that it's your fault?
- Pressure you to have sex when you don't want to?
- Glare at you, give you the silent treatment, or grab, shove, kick, or hit you?

DO YOU

- Always do what your partner wants instead of what you want? Fear how your partner will act in public?

- Constantly make excuses to other people for your partner's behavior? Feel like you walk on eggshells to avoid your partner's anger?
- Believe if you just tried harder or submitted more that everything would be okay?
- Stay with your partner because you fear what your partner would do if you broke up?

These indicators suggest potential abuse in your relationship. If you've answered yes to any of these questions, talk to a counselor about your relationship.

Remember, when one person scares, hurts, or continually puts down the other person, it's abuse.

Source: Created by the President's Commission on the Status of Women, Oregon State University.

A fourth reason survivors stay is that they worry about what people will think, and this keeps them in abusive situations as a consequence of the shame they feel. Most women in abusive relationships worry about this to some extent, although middle-class women probably feel it the most. The myth that this is a lower-class problem and that it does not happen to "nice" families who appear to have everything going for them is part of the problem. And, indeed, the question about what people will think is a relevant one: Some churches tell abused women to submit to their husbands and hide the abuse, neighbors often look the other way, mothers worry about their children being stigmatized at school, and certainly there is embarrassment associated with admitting your partner hits you, especially for men.

ACTIVIST PROFILE

INCITE! WOMEN OF COLOR AGAINST VIOLENCE

In 2000 a group of radical feminists of color organized a conference, "The Color of Violence: Violence Against Women of Color," at the University of California, Santa Cruz. Initially, the gathering was to be small, focused on analyzing violence against women of color and strategizing ways to address violence against women of color. The response was overwhelming, and more than 2,000 women of color attended. Another 2,000 had to be turned away. At this conference, the focus turned to women of color who had survived violence and challenged mainstream conceptualizations of the antiviolence against women movement.

One result of this conference was the founding of INCITE! Women of Color Against Violence, a national grassroots activist organization of radical feminists of color working to end violence against women of color and their communities. Using direct action, critical dialogue, and grassroots organizing, INCITE! Women of Color Against Violence works with women of color to create projects that address issues of violence against women of color and their communities. INCITE! identifies violence against women of color "as a combination of violence directed at communities, such as police violence, war, and colonialism, and violence within communities, such as rape and domestic violence." Projects include "producing a women of color radio show, challenging the non-profitization of antiviolence and other social justice movements, organizing rallies on street harassment, training women of color on self-defense, organizing mothers on welfare, building and running a grassroots clinic."

INCITE! utilizes a framework of intersectional analysis to understand and work against violence against women of color who are located in the intersection of racism and sexism, as well as other forms of oppression.

INCITE! also offers a challenge to the approach of many anti-violence organizations that are dominated by white women by placing women of color at the center of their analysis and work. Here are INCITE!'s principles of unity that guide the organization:

We at INCITE!:

- Maintain a space by and for women of color.
- Center our political analysis and community action in the struggle for liberation.
- Support sovereignty for indigenous people as central to the struggle for liberation.
- Oppose all forms of violence which oppress women of color and our communities.
- Recognize the state as the central organizer of violence which oppresses women of color and our communities.
- Recognize these expressions of violence against women of color as including colonialism, police brutality, immigration policies, reproductive control, etc.
- Link liberation struggles which oppose racism, sexism, classism, heterosexism, ableism, ageism, and all other forms of oppression.
- Support coalition building between women of color.
- Recognize and honor differences across cultures.
- Encourage creative models of community organizing and action.
- Promote shared leadership and decision-making.
- Recognize and resist the power of co-optation of our movements.
- Support these principles not only in our actions, but in the practices within our own organizations.
- Support the creation of organizational processes which encourage these principles and which effectively address oppressive individual and institutional practices within our own organizations.

A fifth reason survivors stay is that they cannot afford to leave. Women, who are more likely to be economically marginalized, fear for the financial welfare of themselves and their children should they leave an abusive situation. They often have less education and care of dependent children. They understand that the kind of paid work they could get would not be enough to support the family.

Reason six is that some survivors believe that children need a father and that even a bad father might be better than no father. Although this belief is erroneous in our view, it does keep women in abusive situations "for the sake of the children." Interestingly, the primary reason women do permanently leave an abusive relationship is also the children: When they see their children being hurt, this is the moment when they are most likely to leave for good.

Another reason survivors stay is that there is often nowhere to go. Although the increase in the numbers of crisis lines and emergency housing shelters is staggering given their absence only a few decades ago, some survivors still have a difficult time imagining an alternative to the abusive situation. This is especially true of those who live in rural areas and who are isolated from friends and family.

Reason eight is that survivors may fear what might happen to abusive partners in the criminal system, especially if they are men of color. They may also believe their partner will change. Part of the cycle of violence noted by scholars in this area is the "honeymoon phase" after the violent episode: First comes the buildup of tension when violence is brewing, second is the violent episode, and third is the honeymoon phase when abusers tend to be especially remorseful—even horrified that they could have done such a thing—and ask for forgiveness. Given that the profile of many batterers is charm and manipulation, such behavior during this phase can be especially persuasive. Survivors are not making it up when they think their partner will change.

Finally, people stay because they believe their partner might kill them—or hurt or kill the children—should they leave. Again, a batterer's past violence is often enough to establish this as no idle threat. Abusers do kill in these situations and often after partners have fled and brought restraining orders against them.

INCEST

This topic is especially poignant, as the reading by Grace Caroline Bridges, "Lisa's Ritual, Age 10," demonstrates. Incest is the sexual abuse (molestation, inappropriate touching, rape, being forced to watch or perform sexual acts on others) of children by a family member or someone with a kinship role in a child's life. There is now an evolving definition of incest that takes into account betrayals of trust and power imbalances, expanding the definition to include sexual abuse by anyone who has power or authority over the child. Perpetrators might include babysitters, schoolteachers, Boy Scout leaders, priests/ministers, and family friends, as well as immediate and extended family members. It is estimated that in about 90 percent of cases in which a child is raped, the perpetrator is someone they know. Studies suggest that 1 in every 3 to 5 girls has experienced some kind of childhood sexual abuse by the time she is 16 years old. For boys, this number is 1 in 6 to 10, although this may be underestimated because boys are less likely to admit that they have been victimized. Again, like other forms of abuse, incest crosses all ethnic, class, and religious lines. Power is always involved in incest, and, because

VIOLENCE AGAINST WOMEN: SELECTED HUMAN RIGHTS DOCUMENTS

International human rights documents encompass formal written documents, such as conventions, declarations, conference statements, guidelines, resolutions, and recommendations. Treaties are legally binding on states that have ratified or acceded to them, and their implementation is observed by monitoring bodies, such as the Committee on the Elimination of Discrimination Against Women (CEDAW).

GLOBAL DOCUMENTS

The Universal Declaration of Human Rights (1948) has formed the basis for the development of international human rights conventions. Article 3 states that everyone has the right of life, liberty, and security of the person. According to article 5, no one shall be subjected to torture or to cruel, inhuman, or degrading treatment or punishment. Therefore, any form of violence against a woman that is a threat to her life, liberty, or security of person or that can be interpreted as torture or cruel, inhuman, or degrading treatment violates the principles of this declaration.

The International Covenant on Economic, Social and Cultural Rights (1966), together with the International Covenant on Civil and Political Rights, prohibits discrimination on the basis of sex. Violence detrimentally affects women's health; therefore, it violates the right to the enjoyment of the highest attainable standard of physical and mental health (article 12). In addition, article 7 provides the right to the enjoyment of just and favorable conditions of work that ensure safe and healthy working conditions. This provision encompasses the prohibition of violence and harassment of women in the workplace.

The International Covenant on Civil and Political Rights (1966) prohibits all forms of violence. Article 6.1 protects the right to life. Article 7 prohibits torture and inhuman or degrading treatment or punishment. Article 9 guarantees the right to liberty and security of person.

The Convention Against Torture and Other Cruel, Inhuman or Degrading Treatment or Punishment (1984) provides protection for all persons, regardless of their sex, in a more detailed manner than the International Covenant on Civil and Political Rights. States should take effective measures to prevent acts of torture (article 2).

The Convention on the Elimination of All Forms of Discrimination Against Women (1979) is the most extensive international instrument dealing with the rights of women. Although violence against women is not specifically addressed in the Convention, except in relation to trafficking and prostitution (article 6), many of the antidiscrimination clauses protect women from violence. States parties have agreed to a policy of eliminating discrimination against women, and to adopt legislative and other measures prohibiting all discrimination against women (article 2). In 1992, CEDAW, which monitors the implementation of this convention, formally included gender-based violence under gender-based discrimination.

General Recommendation No. 19, adopted at the 11th session (June 1992), deals entirely with violence against women and the measures taken to eliminate such violence. As for health issues, it recommends that states should provide support services for all victims of gender-based violence, including refuges, specially trained health workers, and rehabilitation and counseling services.

The International Convention on the Elimination of All Forms of Racial Discrimination (1965) declares that states should undertake to prohibit and to eliminate racial discrimination in all its forms and to guarantee the enjoyment of the right to security of the person and protection by the state against violence or bodily harm, whether inflicted by government officials or by any individual group or institution (article 5).

The four 1949 Geneva Conventions and two Additional Protocols form the cornerstone of international humanitarian law. The Geneva Conventions require that all persons taking no active part in hostilities shall be treated humanely, without adverse distinction on any of the usual grounds, including sex (article 3). They offer protection to all civilians against sexual violence, forced prostitution, sexual abuse, and rape.

Regarding international armed conflict, Additional Protocol I to the 1949 Geneva Conventions creates obligations for parties to a conflict to treat humanely persons under their control. It requires that women shall be protected against rape, forced prostitution, and indecent assault. Additional Protocol II, applicable during internal conflicts, also prohibits rape, enforced prostitution, and indecent assault.

The Convention on the Rights of the Child (1989) declares that states should take appropriate legislative, administrative, social, and educational measures to protect the child from physical or mental violence, abuse, maltreatment, or exploitation (article 19). States shall act accordingly to prevent the exploitative use of children in prostitution or other unlawful sexual practices, and the exploitative use of children in pornographic performances and materials (article 34).

The International Convention on the Protection of the Rights of All Migrant Workers and Members of Their Families (adopted by the U.N. General Assembly in 1990 and put into force in 2003) asserts the right of migrant workers and their family members to liberty and security of person as proclaimed in other international instruments. They shall be entitled to effective protection by the state against violence, physical injury, threats, and intimidation, whether by public officials or by private individuals, groups, or institutions (article 16).

children are the least powerful group in society, the effects on them can be devastating. Approximately a third of all juvenile victims of sexual abuse are younger than six. Children who are abused often have low self-esteem and may find it difficult to trust.

Incest can be both direct and indirect. Direct forms include vaginal, oral, and rectal penetration; sexual rubbing; excessive, inappropriate hugging; body and mouth kissing; bouncing a child on a lap against an erection; and sexual bathing. Direct incest also includes forcing children to watch or perform these acts on others. Indirect incest includes sexualizing statements or joking, speaking to the child as a surrogate spouse, inappropriate references to a child's body, or staring at the child's body. Examples also include intentionally invading children's privacy in the bathroom or acting inappropriately jealous when adolescents start dating. These indirect forms of incest involve sexualizing children and violating their boundaries.

Often siblings indulge in relatively normal uncoerced sexual play with each other that disappears over time. When this involves a child who is several years older or one who uses threats or intimidation, the behavior can be characterized as incestuous. Indicators that a child has been sexually abused include excessive crying, anxiety, night fears and sleep disturbances, depression and withdrawal, clinging behaviors, and physical problems like urinary tract infections and trauma to the mouth and/or perineal area. Adolescent symptoms often include eating disorders, psychosomatic complaints, suicidal thoughts, and depression. Survivors of childhood sexual violence may get involved in self-destructive behaviors such as alcohol and drug abuse or cutting their bodies as they turn their anger inward, or they may express their anger through acting out or promiscuous behavior. In particular, girls internalize their worthlessness and their role as sexual objects used by others; boys often have more anger because they were dominated, an anger that is sometimes projected onto their future sexual partners as well as onto themselves. Although it takes time, we can heal from sexual violation.

In this way, acts of violence and the threat of violence have profound and lasting effects on all lives. We tend to refer to those who have survived violence as "survivors" rather than "victims" to emphasize that it is possible to go on with our lives after such experiences, difficult though that might be. Understanding and preventing gender violence has become a worldwide effort, bringing people together to make everyone safer.

THE BLOG

HARVEY WEINSTEIN'S NOT THE PROBLEM

Susan M. Shaw (2017)

Harvey Weinstein's not the problem. He's a symptom.

Of course, we act as if he's the problem, as if the problem is one of individual bad actors who do horrific things to women.

As if Harvey Weinstein and Bill Cosby and Roger Ailes and Bill O'Reilly and Donald Trump are simply individual men committing individual bad deeds toward individual women who happen to be at the wrong place at the wrong time.

As if they are aberrations. As if most men never do these things. As if there is no pattern, no discernable imprint of misogyny, no deep and pervasive system of sexism that means these things are not rare occasions but are ubiquitous parts of the intimate and daily fabric of women's lives.

Choosing to believe sexual harassment and sexual assault are individual problems rather than the systemic and violent enforcement of sexism and misogyny (with their interlocking companions of racism, heterosexism, classism, ableism, and ageism) is certainly easier. Men as a class don't have to be implicated, and so we can pretend that if we address the bad behavior of individual men—let's fire Roger Ailes or prosecute Bill Cosby—we've done our due diligence and taken care of the problem.

But we haven't even begun to address the real problem, which is the deep-seated misogyny and structural sexism embedded in our social institutions, ideologies, language, and relationships.

Take Harvey Weinstein. How many women had to come forward before most people believed any of them? A number of his Hollywood buddies jumped right to his defense when the first accusations were made public, but they quickly backed away from that support as the testimonies and accusations cascaded.

Woody Allen warned us not to get carried away in naming Hollywood's sexual harassment and sexual assault problem lest this become a witch hunt. How ironic given that historically witch hunts have often involved sexually repressed men murdering women who refused to fall under their control!

And why did women feel a need to participate in a #MeToo campaign to demonstrate how big the problem is? Why haven't men believed us so far when we've said sexual harassment and sexual assault are a problem? We've had the data. We've published the numbers.

But we know women are not believed. By custom and by law in this country, women have been afforded much less credibility than men. According to Lynn Hecht Schafran, director of the National Judicial Education Program to Promote Equality for Women and Men in the Court, "Sociological and legal research documents that women have less credibility in courts across the board than men."

The problem is not individual men like Harvey Weinstein. Men like him exist and get away with their barbarities because, despite the gains of feminist movements against sexism, we have not fundamentally transformed the interlocking systems of oppression that differentially disadvantage diverse women, transgender people, and gender nonbinary people and penalize them for not being cisgender men.

Think about how difficult the legal system makes prosecuting a rape, for example. Coincidence? Or evidence of a system created by men to maintain male dominance, particularly men's rights over women's bodies? Think of all the barriers to women's reproductive justice. The barriers to women's health care. The barriers to equal pay. Recent research has found that women of color face an astounding amount of harassment in space science. Not long ago, Boston University launched an investigation into a prominent Antarctic scientist accused of sexually harassing graduate students. *Mother Jones* published the story of an aspiring academic harassed by a star professor. *The Atlantic* ran a story of how women are harassed out of science.

These are not individual incidents of individual bad actors, any more than are the despicable actions of Harvey Weinstein or Bill Cosby.

These point to the larger systemic problem that will not be fixed by a few investigations, firings, or even prison sentences.

While women, transwomen, gender nonbinary people, and even a few men have taken to social media to tell their stories of sexual harassment and sexual assault, few men have spoken up beyond the cursory and expected condemnation of bad behavior. Some of Weinstein's former friends have called him out, but calling one man out for sexual harassment and sexual assault won't change the system that enables and preserves that behavior as a way to maintain male dominance.

What's needed is a gender revolution that tears apart the fabric of patriarchy itself. And that's not the responsibility of women, transgender folk, and gender nonbinary folk. That's the responsibility of men. The problem is systemic, and the response must be systemic. And it must come from men being accountable for the contours of patriarchal power and the violence that props it up.

Muriel Rukeyser wrote, "What would happen if one woman told the truth about her life? The world would split open."

Women have told the truth. Is it possible the world is now splitting?

63. BEYOND THE POLITICS OF INCLUSION
ANDREA SMITH (2004)

What was disturbing to so many U.S. citizens about the September 11, 2001, attacks on the World Trade Center is that these attacks disrupted their sense of safety at "home." Terrorism is something that happens in other countries; our "home," the U.S.A., is supposed to be a place of safety. Similarly, mainstream U.S. society believes that violence against women only occurs "out there" and is perpetrated by a few crazed men whom we simply need to lock up. However, the anti-violence movement has always contested this notion of safety at home. The notion that violence only happens "out there," inflicted by the stranger in the dark alley makes it difficult to recognize that the home is in fact the place of greatest danger for women. In response to this important piece of analysis, the anti-violence movement has, ironically, based its strategies on the premise that the criminal legal system is the primary tool with which to address violence against women. However, when one-half of women will be battered in their lifetimes and nearly one-half of women will be sexually assaulted in their lifetimes, it is clear that we live in a rape culture that prisons, themselves a site of violence and control, cannot change.

Similarly, the notion that terrorism happens in other countries makes it difficult to grasp that the United States is built on a history of genocide, slavery, and racism. Our "home" has never been a safe place for people of color. Because many mainstream feminist organizations are white-dominated, they often do not see themselves as potential victims in Bush's war in the U.S. and abroad. However, those considered "alien" in the United States and hence deserving of repressive policies and overt attack are not only people of color. Since 9/11, many organizations in LGBT communities have reported sharp increases in attacks, demonstrating the extent to which gays and lesbians are often seen as "alien" because their sexuality seems to threaten the white nuclear family thought to be the building block of U.S. society.

Furthermore, many mainstream feminist organizations, particularly anti-violence organizations, have applauded the U.S. attacks on Afghanistan for "liberating" Arab women from the repressive policies of the Taliban. Apparently, bombing women in Afghanistan somehow elevates their status. However, the Revolutionary Association of the Women from Afghanistan (RAWA), the organization comprised of members most affected by the policies of the Taliban, has condemned U.S. intervention and has argued that women cannot expect an improvement in their status under the regime of the Northern Alliance with which the United States has allied itself. This support rests entirely on the problematic assumption that state violence can secure safety and liberation for women

and other oppressed groups. Clearly, alternative approaches to provide true safety and security for women must be developed, both at "home" and abroad.

BEYOND INCLUSION: CENTERING WOMEN OF COLOR IN THE ANTI-VIOLENCE MOVEMENT

The central problem is that as the anti-violence movement has attempted to become more "inclusive" these attempts at multicultural interventions have unwittingly strengthened the white supremacy within the anti-violence movement. That is, inclusivity has come to mean taking on a domestic violence model that was developed largely with the interests of white, middle class women in mind, and simply adding to it a multicultural component. However, if we look at the histories of women of color in the United States, as I have done in other work, it is clear that gender violence functions as a tool for racism and colonialism for women of color in general (Smith 2002). The racial element of gender violence points to the necessity of an alternative approach that goes beyond mere inclusion to actually centering women of color in the organizing and analysis. That is, if we do not make any assumptions about what a domestic violence program should look like but, instead, ask what would it take to end violence against women of color, then what would this movement look like?

In fact, Beth Richie suggests we go beyond just centering women of color, to centering those most marginalized within the category of "women of color." She writes:

> We have to understand that the goal of our antiviolence work is not for diversity, and not inclusion. It is for liberation. If we're truly committed to ending violence against women, then we must start in the hardest places, the places like jails and prisons and other correctional facilities. The places where our work has not had an impact yet. . . . [W]e have to stop being the friendly colored girls as some of our anti-violence programs require us to be. We must not deny the part of ourselves and the part of our work that is least acceptable to the mainstream public. We must not let those who really object to all of us and our work co-opt some of us and the work we're trying to do. As if this antiviolence movement could ever really

be legitimate in a patriarchal, racist society. . . . Ultimately the movement needs to be accountable not to those in power, but to the powerless. (Richie 2000)

When we center women of color in the analysis, it becomes clear that we must develop approaches that address interpersonal and state violence simultaneously. In addition, we find that by centering women of color in the analysis, we may actually build a movement that more effectively ends violence not just for women of color, but for all peoples.

HUMAN RIGHTS FRAMEWORK FOR ADDRESSING VIOLENCE

Developing strategies to address state violence, then, suggests the importance of developing a human rights approach toward ending violence. By human rights I mean those rights seen under international law to be inalienable and not dependent on any particular government structure. When we limit our struggles around changes in domestic legislation within the United States, we forget that the United States government itself perpetrates more violence against women than any other actor in the world. While we may use a variety of rhetorical and organizing tools, our overall strategy should not be premised on the notion that the United States should or will always continue to exist—to do so is to fundamentally sanction the continuing genocide of indigenous peoples on which this government is based.

One organization that avoids this problem is the American Indian Boarding School Healing Project, which organizes against gender violence from a human rights perspective. During the nineteenth century and into the twentieth century, American Indian children were abducted from their homes to attend Christian boarding schools as a matter of state policy that again demonstrates the links between sexual violence and state violence. This system was later imported to Canada in the form of the residential school system. Because the worst of the abuses happened to an older generation, there is simply not sufficient documentation or vocal outcry against boarding school abuses.

Responding to this need, the International Human Rights Association of American Minorities issued a report documenting the involvement of mainline churches and the federal government in the murder of over 50,000 Native children through the Canadian residential school system (Annett 2001). The list of offenses committed by church officials includes murder by beating, poisoning, hanging, starvation, strangulation, and medical experimentation. In addition, the report found that church, police, business, and government officials maintained pedophile rings using children from residential schools. Several schools are also charged with concealing on their grounds the unmarked graves of children who were murdered, particularly children killed after being born as a result of rapes of Native girls by priests and other church officials. While some churches in Canada have taken some minimal steps towards addressing their involvement in this genocidal policy, churches in the United States have not.

As a result of boarding school policies, an epidemic of child sexual abuse now exists in Native communities. The shame attached to abuse has allowed no space in which to address this problem. Consequently, child abuse passes from one generation to the next. The American Indian Boarding School Healing Project provides an entryway to addressing this history of child sexual abuse by framing it not primarily as an example of individual and community dysfunction, but instead as the continuing effect of human rights abuses perpetrated by state policy. This project seeks to take the shame away from talking about abuse and provide the space for communities to address the problem and heal.

A human rights approach can even be of assistance to traditional service providers for survivors of violence. The human rights approach provides an organizing strategy to protest John Ashcroft's dramatic cuts in funding for anti-violence programs, particularly indigenous programs. Adequate funding for indigenous-controlled programs and services is not a privilege for states to curtail in times of economic crises. Rather, as international human rights law dictates, states are mandated to address the continuing effects of human rights violations. Hence, the United States violates international human rights law when it de-funds anti-violence programs. For indigenous women and women of color in general, sexual and domestic violence are clearly the continuing effects of human rights violations perpetrated by U.S. state policy.

CONCLUSION

For too long, women of color have been forced to choose between racial justice and gender justice. Yet, it is precisely through sexism and gender violence that colonialism and white supremacy have been successful. This failure to see the intersectionality of racism and sexism in racial justice movements was evident at the UN World Conference Against Racism, where the types of racism that women of color face in reproductive rights policies, for example, failed to even register on the UN radar screen. Women of color are often suspicious of human rights strategies because white-dominated human rights organizations often pursue the imperialist agenda of organizing around the human rights violations of women in other countries while ignoring the human rights violations of women of color in the United States. Nonetheless, an anti-colonial human rights strategy can be helpful in highlighting the violence perpetrated by U.S. state policy and combating U.S. exceptionalism on the global scale—as well as right here at home.

REFERENCES

Annett, Kevin. 2001. "The Truth Commission into the Genocide in Canada." Accessed August 31, 2003 (http://annett55.freewebsite s.com/genocide.pdf).

Richie, Beth. 2000. Plenary Address, "Color of Violence: Violence Against Women of Color" Conference, Santa Cruz, CA.

Smith, Andrea. 2002. "Better Dead than Pregnant: The Colonization of Native Women's Reproductive Health." In *Policing the National Body: Race, Gender, and Criminalization*, ed. Jael Silliman and Anannya Bhattacharjee. Cambridge: South End Press.

64. SHE SAID

MARIAH LOCKWOOD (2010)

I married because he asked me
she said, a matrimonial Miss Manners
   aching to please
    fearful to disappoint
He might not ask again.

I dreamed candlelight, roses, she said,
shameful now, love's blush a pallor
rolled thin like dough, thinner,
   edges curling, splitting wide.
It started with words, she said,

a drizzle brushed from summer clothes
then streaming, torrents, hail
   denting life itself.
Imagine, concealer was my first friend
she said, cream over plums ripened deep,
sugar over salt lips cracked, smiling,
   hiding contraband fruit.
But you were my sweetest friend, she said,
when sadness leached to hollow shell
brittle, bleached, but strong, stronger
   alive meeting the tide, she said.

65. GENDER ASPECTS OF HUMAN TRAFFICKING

EMILIE LINDER (2017)

DEFINITION

According to international law, trafficking in persons is a serious crime and a grave violation of human rights. It has dreadful effects on many aspects of the trafficked . . . victim's life such as exposition to physical, psychological, economic and sexual violence, amounting at times to torture.

Conforming to the UN Trafficking Protocol, a victim of human trafficking is considered as someone who has been coerced or brought into any kind of labour through force and fraudulent means. They may have been kidnapped, and/or brought in at an age or in a state where they had no capacity to give or withhold consent.

A GLOBAL PHENOMENON

Almost every country in the world is involved in human trafficking, whether as a country of origin, transit or destination for victims. The 2016 Global Report on Trafficking in Persons estimated that around 137 different nationalities were trafficked and identified in 106 different countries.

According to the International Labour Organization, in 2016, 24.9 million people were victims of forced labour, which includes 4.8 million trafficking victims used for sexual exploitation. Trafficking affects both men and women, however this phenomenon is not gender-neutral. Women and girls together account for about 71 percent of the victims.

But what can explain the high number of women and girls becoming more vulnerable to trafficking related violence?

MIGRATION

According to the Global Commission on International Migration, there are now around 258 million international migrants worldwide, of which nearly 50 percent are women. Traditionally, it was mainly men who sought jobs overseas; nowadays, migration is characterized by a growing number of women and girls. There are several reasons explaining this migration shift. For instance, migration is often cheaper and easier for women than for men, as education and skills requirements are lower for women. In addition, there has been an increased demand for female labour in areas such as household and care-giving work and other services of low-wage manufacturing.

It's key to understand that migration and human trafficking do not always go hand [in] hand. Every year, millions of women migrate freely and autonomously for diverse reasons. These women are not victims of trafficking. Trafficking starts out as recruitment or movement, and ends with exploitation. The connection between the increase of migration flow and human trafficking lay[s] in the fact that human traffickers are using migration flow and vulnerabilities of some migrants to force more people into modern slavery.

POVERTY

There is a strong link between gender, poverty and trafficking. Economic inequality is gendered as poverty impacts women more severely than men. This situation can be explained by several factors such as gender pay gaps, single mother households, as well as social and cultural exclusion women often face. A consequence of poverty is the fact that women living in precarious conditions are more likely to take extreme risks in order to access economic opportunities in others countries. This demand is attractive to individuals willing or looking to develop illegal businesses based on organized criminal networks and human trafficking.

According to Ms. Joy Ngozi Ezeilo, the Special Rapporteur on trafficking in Persons: "addressing the root causes that make people vulnerable to traffickers is necessary in order to fully suppress this practice. Awareness raising and empowerment through the realization of socio economic as well as civil and political rights could save many from falling in the traps of traffickers."

GENDER NORMS

Finally, the trafficking demand is often produced by discriminatory attitudes including cultural attitudes and beliefs which impact women politically, economically and socially. In 2000, Radhika Coomeraswamy, the former Rapporteur on Violence against Women declared that: "The lack of rights afforded to women serves as the primary causative factor at the root of both women's migration and trafficking." Indeed, unequal access to education, limited opportunities to access/own land and property and other forms of gender discrimination, increase the vulnerability of women and girls to trafficking. Moreover, in a society where gender ideology perceives women as weak and unpowered individuals, women are considered easier to manipulate and less likely to rebel, making them more susceptible to trafficking.

CONCLUSION

Thanks to numerous studies, we can now demonstrate with details how gender inequality and human trafficking are intrinsically linked. Therefore, there is an urgent need for a greater universal effort to eliminate gender inequality and to promote empowerment of women in order to eradicate human trafficking. Lastly, it's essential that any attempt to address the issue of gendered aspects of trafficking and the parallel anti-trafficking efforts must place the trafficked persons and their voices and agency at the centre of the discourse.

66. #SAYHERNAME

HOMA KHALEELI (2016)

When she speaks at public meetings, Professor Kimberlé Crenshaw has a trick. She asks everyone to stand up until they hear an unfamiliar name. She then reads the names of unarmed black men and boys whose deaths ignited the Black Lives Matter movement; names such as Eric Garner, Michael Brown, Tamir Rice, Freddie Gray, Trayvon Martin. Her audience are informed and interested in civil rights so "virtually no one will sit down," Crenshaw says approvingly. "Then I say the names of Natasha McKenna, Tanisha Anderson, Michelle Cusseaux, Aura Rosser, Maya Hall. By the time I get to the third name, almost everyone has sat down. By the fifth, the only people standing are those working on our campaign."

The campaign, #SayHerName, was created to raise awareness about the number of women and girls that are killed by law enforcement officers. For Crenshaw—who coined the term "intersectionality" in the 1980s to describe the way different forms of discrimination overlap and compound each other—it is a brutal illustration of how racism and sexism play out on black women's bodies.

In person, she is charming, warm and self-effacing. A passionate activist with a distinguished background in law, Crenshaw reels off cases of women killed by police officers in front of their families, friends or even cameras. Women such as Tanisha Anderson, who died 10 days before 12-year-old Tamir Rice was shot, in circumstances no less harrowing. Anderson's family had called the emergency services when she walked out in the street in her nightgown in the middle of winter. As her 16-year-old daughter watched from an upstairs window, officers tried to push Anderson, who was bipolar, into a police van.

When she refused and grew agitated, the family say officers performed a "take down," slamming her into the concrete pavement. By the time she arrived at hospital, she was dead. The coroner ruled her death as homicide.

Anderson is far from alone. Yvette Smith was killed in her own home after the police arrived to investigate a domestic disturbance complaint between two men. Smith, a single mother of two, was shot in the head when she opened the door for the officers. The police first alleged that Smith had a gun, then retracted the claim. The former Texas police deputy who killed Smith was cleared of her murder.

A year ago, Crenshaw, along with lawyer Andrea Ritchie, released a report looking at almost 70 such cases, many taking place in the past three years. But there could be many more. Until recently—when the *Guardian* launched its database, the Counted—the US had no comprehensive record of those killed by police officers. "More black people [in total] are killed—disproportionately to their rate in the population—and although the numbers are hard to assess, the reality is that black women are vulnerable to the same justifications used for killing black men," says Crenshaw.

One case that did catch the media and the public's attention was the death of Sandra Bland. Bland was pulled over for failing to use her indicator when she changed lanes. A video showed her being pinned to the ground and surrounded by officers after being charged with assault. She can be heard asking why her head is slammed on to the pavement. Three days later, she was found dead in a police cell.

However, unless the way women are killed is taken into account, says Crenshaw, we can't "broaden our understanding of vulnerability to state violence and what do we need to do about it." There are many cases, for instance, where women are killed by police who arrive as first responders to emergency calls for mental health crises. "Disability—emotional, physical and mental—is one of the biggest risk factors for being killed by the police, but it is relatively suppressed in the conversation about police violence," she points out.

Sometimes the victim is written off as collateral damage, as having been too close to an officer, such as in the case of Rekia Boyd. The 22-year-old was talking to her friends in an alley, she was told to quieten down, and then was shot by an off-duty police officer. In 2013, her family were given $4.5m (£3m) in a civil wrongful-death case, but the officer who shot her was cleared of involuntary manslaughter and the reckless discharge of a firearm. In other cases, the victims are caught up in other investigations; seven-year-old Aiyana Stanley-Jones was killed when her grandmother's house was raided.

Crenshaw points out that #SayHerName also serves to highlight other forms of state violence that impact women. Crenshaw cites the case of Daniel Holtzclaw, an Oklahoma police officer convicted of 18 of 36 charges of sexual assault against black women. Despite the number of women involved, the case was barely covered in the media. There is little public discussion of sexual abuse by police officers, Crenshaw says, although "according to some reports, they are the second most-common report of police abuse."

Crenshaw is a veteran activist and theorist, but it is young feminists who have enthusiastically turned intersectionality into a feminist cornerstone. When I ask her why, she laughs. "As a term, 'intersectionality' has been around since the late 80s," she says, "so there is something to be said about it being taken up in a robust way 30 years on. It's like a lazy Susan— you can subject race, sexuality, transgender identity or class to a feminist critique through intersectionality." But Crenshaw is aware of pitfalls. "Some people can use [intersectionality] as a way to deflect a critique of patriarchy—by saying: 'How can there be any full structural critique when we are so many different things at the same time?'"

Crenshaw is just as thoughtful about popular culture. On the day we meet, the feminist writer bell hooks publishes a scathing article on Beyoncé's new album, *Lemonade*, claiming it is more capitalism in action than the feminist masterpiece it has been lauded as. Crenshaw is diplomatic: "Formation and Lemonade speak to experiences that are too underrepresented in our culture. But there are costs to certain forms of visibility. I don't think it is a bad thing to discuss what these costs are.

"Having a monolithic view of feminism is suffocating," she continues. "What worries me is when it turns vitriolic and tracks on to other ways that women are marginalised. So, to call women old and out of touch is a traditional way to silence them. Nor do you want the trope of young and unaware to travel without interrogation. We don't want to undermine our collective voice."

So she isn't overwhelmed by feminist infighting? She laughs. "I think there is a more robust debate about feminism in the UK—what a great problem to have."

67. WHY SEXUAL ASSAULT SURVIVORS DO NOT REPORT TO UNIVERSITIES

CHELSEA SPENCER, ALLEN MALLORY, MICHELLE TOEWS, SANDRA STITH, AND LEILA WOOD (2017)

Over the past several years, increased attention from administrators, faculty, student advocates, survivors, and researchers has illuminated the epidemic of sexual assault on college campuses. The Campus Sexual Assault (CSA) Study found that approximately 19% of women were sexually assaulted during their enrollment in college (Krebs, Lindquist, Warner, Fisher, & Martin, 2007). Another study examining sexual assault and sexual misconduct on 27 college campuses found that 23.6% of female undergraduate students experienced nonconsensual sexual contact while enrolled at their university (Cantor et al., 2015). Further, given underreporting, these numbers may underestimate the incidence of sexual assault (Sinozich & Langton, 2014).

Sexual assault survivors experience an array of physical and mental health problems, including anxiety, depression, weight change, sleep problems, and a host of other traumatic reactions (Black et al., 2011), and these effects are often experienced over the long term (see Bordere, 2017). The impact of sexual assault can disrupt, or even end, college for survivors (White House Task Force to Protect Students from Sexual Assault, 2014). Cultural norms that hold victims accountable for sexual violence and allow for drinking to be used as an excuse for violence create a campus climate that negatively impacts the educational experience for many women (Buchwald, Fletcher, & Roth, 1993; Jordan, Combs, & Smith 2014). Rape culture is often embedded in university culture and leads to a tolerance and normalization of the occurrence of sexual assault through the use of tactics that shift the blame from the perpetrator to the victim (Buchwald et al., 1993; Sutton & Simons, 2015; Wade, Sweeney, Derr, Messner, & Burke, 2014). Men enact the majority of sexual violence, and a feminist analysis of sexual assault on campus must acknowledge the gendered nature of this violence (Johnson, 2005). Without an institutional commitment to fully support survivors when making a report about sexual assault, perpetrators have little to no accountability for their actions (Jordan et al., 2014), thus further perpetuating rape culture on college campuses.

There has been an increasing demand for universities to take action to protect students, provide meaningful and supportive interventions for survivors, and prevent future violence. Specifically, there has been increased government focus on university compliance with Title IX, the Violence Against Women Act, and the Clery Act, all of which mandate university response to survivors and consequences for perpetration (White House Task Force to Protect

Students from Sexual Assault, 2014). The majority of survivors (80%), however, do not report the assault to university authorities (Cantor et al., 2015; Sinozich & Langton, 2014). Therefore, universities may be underestimating the rate of sexual assault on campus (Cantor et al., 2015; Sinozich & Langton, 2014). Further, evidence suggests that universities may tend to underreport incidents to minimize the appearance of violence on campus. Specifically, Yung (2015) found that routine Clery audits would produce an increase in a university's report of sexual assault during the audit period, and that once the audit was completed, reports of sexual assault then reverted to preaudit numbers. Research has also found that universities "are failing to comply with the law and best practices in handling sexual violence on campus" (U.S. Senate, 2014, p. 4). As of June 2016, there were nearly 200 universities under investigation for mishandling sexual assault cases (*Chronicle of Higher Education*, 2016). Given underreporting by survivors, and the increasing attention on the performance of universities in addressing sexual assault, the goal of the present study was to understand, from female survivors' experiences, why they did not report their assault to university officials.

Most research examining reasons survivors give for not filing a report has focused on why the incident was not reported to the police rather than why it was not reported to university officials (e.g., faculty members, administrators, Title IX coordinators). Among the most common reasons provided for not reporting the incident to the police were because the survivors did not think the assault was serious enough to report, blamed themselves or felt guilty, were ashamed or felt embarrassed, feared retribution from the perpetrator or others, were afraid they would not be believed, lacked confidence in the criminal justice system, lacked evidence, or did not want family members or others to know what happened (Du Mont, Miller, & Myhr, 2003; Fisher, Daigle, Cullen, & Turner, 2003; Thompson, Sitterle, Clay, & Kingree, 2007). Although studies examining police reports provide important insight, sexual assault survivors might have different reasons for not reporting to university authorities than they have for not reporting to police. Furthermore, participants in these studies were provided a list of predetermined reasons for not reporting and asked to select the one(s) that applied to them, which may have limited respondents' ability to accurately report their rationales for not reporting. Thus, in the present study, we used an open-ended question asking survivors to describe, in their own words, why they did not report to university officials.

According to Title IX regulations, when a sexual assault is reported to university officials, they are obligated to connect the survivors with resources, such as counseling or legal services. Sinozich and Langton (2014) found that only 16% of female students who had been sexually assaulted received support from any public or private victim service agencies in their communities, although it was unclear whether the victims had reported to their universities or had been offered services and declined. Since July 2015, the Campus Sexual Violence Elimination (Campus SaVE) Act requires all universities to provide information about counseling, victim advocacy, legal assistance, and other services available to survivors who report to the university. By examining barriers to reporting sexual assaults to university officials, strategies may be developed that make reporting more accessible and desirable for survivors, which could result in more of them utilizing needed resources.

For decades, feminist scholars have helped illuminate the prevalence, predictors, and effects of sexual assault and other forms of gender-based violence (Armstrong, Hamilton, & Sweeney, 2006; Brownmiller, 1975; Fisher et al., 2003; Tutty & Rothery, 2002). The voices of feminist advocates and survivors of sexual assault have continued to fuel the movement to destigmatize reporting and to demand that the government and universities no longer ignore sexual assault occurring on college campuses (Hayes, 2012).

In the present study, we attempted to understand the perspectives of survivors on one college campus. Although survivors should not be mandated to report a sexual assault (Patterson, Greeson, & Campbell, 2009), understanding barriers to reporting will provide insight into what universities can do to help survivors feel safe and empowered to report sexual violence. We drew on feminist standpoint theory (Harding, 2009) to guide our framing and analysis of the data from survivors.

BASIC CONCEPTS: FEMINIST STANDPOINT THEORY

Feminist theories, similar to other critical approaches, focus on experiences of oppression and privilege and foreground the social construction of men and masculinity, and women and femininity (Payne, 2005; Samuels & Ross-Sheriff, 2008). One strand of feminism is standpoint feminism. Feminist standpoint theory places subordinate groups at the center of logical inquiry, exposing sexist, racist, and heterosexist biases in research methodology (Harding, 2012). The theory posits that disempowered individuals have a double consciousness—they see the world from their own perspective as well as that of their oppressor (Swigonski, 1994).

Several scholars have outlined characteristics that define the feminist standpoint (Harding, 2004, 2009; Hartstock, 2014; . . .). First, a standpoint is formed through scientific inquiry involving struggles of a subordinated group and highlighting a specific and socially situated knowledge that cannot come from the oppressor (Harding, 2009, 2012; Hartstock, 2014). The standpoint is formed through tension generated by social and political power, uncovering decentered knowledge (Harding, 2012). Localized knowledge exposes bias of the dominant viewpoint and challenges commonly accepted perceptions (Harding, 2012; Hartstock, 2014). Using a standpoint perspective that focuses on the everyday lives of people who have traditionally been marginalized, researchers strive for a more complete knowledge. In the college campus context, power is male identified, male centered, and male dominated (Johnson, 2005; see also Jozkowski & Wiersma-Mosley, 2017). Survivors may decide not to report their sexual assault to university officials because speaking out against a male (especially White, middle to upper class) perpetrator in a patriarchal society means risking blame, scrutiny, and disbelief (Grubb & Turner, 2012).

Critical examination of power and privilege are reflected in third-wave feminist theories wherein feminists have more closely attuned to intersecting forces of identity and experience. Intersectional feminism is a critique to the notion that all women share the same essential experience of womanhood

(Chamallas, 2010). Social identities vary by each woman's experience, social location (identity), and access to power (Shields, 2008). Intersectional models take into account identities based on race, gender, class, sexuality, citizenship, ability level, and other elements that form experience (Damant et al., 2008; Mehrota, 2010; Shields, 2008). Moreover, the more marginalized a survivor is relative to the imperialist White supremacist capitalistic patriarchy (hooks, 1994), the less incentive the marginalized individual has to believe that trusting the system will be beneficial. Thus, those who have the least power are the most likely to not report to university officials.

Feminist standpoint and intersectional feminist thought inspired the design of this study. We assumed that structural (e.g., race, sexuality), cultural, and institutional factors influence college women's decisions not to report to university officials. An anonymous survey was used to ensure that survivors of sexual assault would feel safe sharing their reasons for not reporting, which was particularly important because many survivors have experienced institutional betrayal (see Bordere, 2017).

METHOD

SAMPLE AND PROCEDURES

This study was part of a larger project examining the campus climate at a public university in the U.S. Southwest. The university consists of a relatively diverse student body (approximately 50% White, more than 30% Latina, and nearly 10% African American) of more than 30,000 undergraduate (87%) and graduate students. . . .

A total of 2,482 online surveys were completed. However, for the purpose of this study, the sample was drawn from female students who reported that they had "experienced any sort of nonconsensual or unwanted sexual contact" since enrolling at the university (n = 241). To be included in the final sample, participants had to indicate that they did not use formal reporting procedures to report the assault and offer an explanation for their decision not to report. As a result, 12 students were excluded because they did report their sexual assault to the university, and 9 were excluded because they did not provide a reason

for not reporting. This resulted in a final sample of 220 female survivors.

The majority of the sample were seniors (n = 82), followed by juniors (n = 43), sophomores (n = 41), freshmen (n = 33), graduate students (n = 20), and one survivor who did not indicate her year in school. Participants ranged from 18 to 51 years of age (M = 21.3). When identifying their race or ethnicity, participants were allowed to check all that applied to them. The majority selected White (n = 184), followed by African American (n = 21), other (n = 14), American Indian or Alaska Native (n = 12), Asian (n = 8), Middle Eastern or Arab (n = 2), and Native Hawaiian or other Pacific Islander (n = 1). Two participants did not report their race or ethnicity. In addition, the sample consisted of 57 individuals who identified as Hispanic or Latino. With regard to sexuality, 178 identified as heterosexual, 25 as bisexual, 8 as questioning, 5 as "other," and 4 as lesbian. The vast majority of survivors reported that the perpetrator was a man (n = 218); two indicated that the perpetrator was a female.

. . .

RESULTS AND DISCUSSION

If other campuses are similar to the one we studied—we have no reason to believe this campus is an anomaly—the overall finding that 220 of 232 female students who were survivors of sexual assault did not report their assault to university officials indicates that universities have a long way to go to enhance awareness, training, policies, and availability of services for survivors. The present study revealed eight themes that affected survivors' decision not to report their assault to university officials. Coming from the survivors themselves, these results, combined with the results from the logistic regression models, provide ways to reduce barriers for reporting sexual assaults to university officials. Although several themes were similar to those given by survivors in prior studies on police reports (e.g., Du Mont, Miller, & Myhr, 2003; Fisher et al., 2003; Thompson et al., 2007), we found a couple of important differences.

Our analysis revealed insights into why survivors did not report to university officials. Specifically, we discovered eight major themes: "It was not a big enough deal" (n = 64), "I didn't know who to report to or that I could report" (n = 42), "It wasn't related to the university" (n = 31), "I was afraid" (n = 23), "Because I was drunk" (n = 20), "Too ashamed to report" (n = 18), "I didn't want to get him in trouble" (n = 16), and "Felt as if I would be blamed for putting myself in the situation" (n = 11). For those themes reported by more than 20 participants, we ran a series of binary logistic regressions to determine which variables were associated with the likelihood of a survivor endorsing each of the themes. . . .

"IT WAS NOT A BIG ENOUGH DEAL"

The most frequent response was "It was not a big enough deal" (n = 64, 29.1%). To illustrate, one student said, "I did not feel the incident was serious enough to warrant any kind of investigation." Although this student did not elaborate on why she did not think the assault was serious enough to report, other students justified their decision by stating the type of assault did not warrant a report (e.g., "He just forcefully touched and kissed me. No fingering or penetrating"), or they did not feel threatened or frightened by the incident (e.g., "Wasn't a particularly traumatic or scary experience"). As one survivor stated, "The incident did not amount to something reportable in my eyes. I didn't think any crime was committed; just a slight violation of trust." Some survivors reported that they were able to handle the situation themselves and did not feel it was necessary to involve outside parties. For example, one survivor stated, "I just stopped talking to that person. I felt like I handled the situation responsibly on my own and did not need any assistance." These responses may indicate that the young women internalized messages from the dominant culture, encouraging them to dismiss and downplay the severity of the violence enacted on them. This is consistent with a rape culture in which the dominant discourse normalizes men's sexual violence against women (e.g., Hlavka, 2014) and heteronormative messages that view male sexuality as aggressive, powerful, and dominant are rampant (. . . Johnson, 2005). It is also possible that the women felt sufficiently capable to handle the experience in a way that suited them and did not see a need to report it to the university.

Results from the "It was not a big enough deal" logistic regression model . . . indicated that students who had ever received training in sexual assault prevention; experienced nonconsensual or unwanted oral sex, vaginal penetration, or anal penetration; or were fearful following their sexual assault were less than half as likely as their respective counterparts to provide a response coded as "It was not a big enough deal." In addition, for each year older they were, respondents were about 22% less likely to provide this type of response. These findings also support the notion of the rape culture minimizing or normalizing sexual assault; survivors often receive the message that a "real" sexual assault involves a stranger and fear (Phillips, 2000). It also underscores the importance of educational efforts on campus to inform students of consent, legal definitions of assault, and available resources. Students who had received training in sexual assault prevention were less than half as likely as those who had not to provide a response consistent with the theme that "it wasn't a big deal."

"I DIDN'T KNOW WHO TO REPORT TO OR THAT I COULD REPORT"

Another common reason for not reporting was "I didn't know who to report to or that I could report" (n = 42, 19.1%). One survivor indicated, "I was unaware that that [reporting] was even an option. I have never been informed by [the university] what to do if sexually assaulted." Other survivors reported that, although they might have known they could report the sexual assault, they were unaware of how to report the assault to the university. One survivor summarized this theme by stating, "I didn't know the procedures for reporting this type of thing." This finding has important implications for college administrators and Title IX coordinators; universities must figure out effective strategies to alert their students to the options. One way forward is to include this information in syllabi (see Sharp, Weiser, Lavigne, & Kelly, 2017).

One subtheme under "I didn't know who to report to or that I could report" was that the survivors felt it "would have been a lost cause" to report (n = 14, 6.4%). Specifically, they felt that there was a lack of evidence or that the university would not do anything. As one survivor stated, "No witnesses.

My word against his." Another survivor said, "I didn't think anyone would do anything about it." In a rape culture where women lack power, they often think that they will not be believed over the word of their assailant (see Weiser, 2017, for a brief review of this issue of not believing survivors).

Results from the logistic regression . . . indicated that students who had ever received training about policies and procedures regarding sexual assault were less than half as likely to provide a response consistent with this theme, which probably suggests that either training raises awareness about reporting or that those who attend trainings are more aware, or both. Students who reported that they believed the university would take the report seriously were substantially less likely to provide a response consistent with this theme, and those who reported higher levels of fear following their sexual assault were substantially more likely to indicate that they were unaware of their options for reporting.

"IT WASN'T RELATED TO THE UNIVERSITY"

In addition to not knowing how to report to university officials, many survivors (n = 31, 14.1%) reported that they did not report to the university because "it wasn't related to the university." In fact, many qualified this idea by stating that the sexual assault "did not happen on campus" or that "he [the perpetrator] was not a student." To illustrate, one survivor stated, "The incident didn't happen on campus so I didn't think it would apply or consider it important to report it." Another survivor stated, "It didn't involve a student nor occurred on campus." This speaks to the students' lack of knowledge regarding universities' Title IX obligations.

Results from the logistic regression analysis . . . indicated that students who had experienced a sexual assault before enrolling at the university were more than three times as likely to provide a response consistent with the theme "it wasn't related to the university," and those who were assaulted by a stranger were more than 10 times more likely to do so.

"I WAS AFRAID"

Many (n = 23, 10.4%) survivors reported they were afraid to report. Some survivors reported "I was afraid" without providing any further details

regarding why they were afraid (n = 12). Others reported that they were afraid of possible repercussions (n = 4), afraid of not being believed (n = 4), or afraid of the perpetrator (n = 3). As one survivor explained, "I was scared that he would harass me more and I didn't want to make him angry." Another survivor shared how a third party invoked fear in her: "The president of the club we were both in told me that no one would believe me and I would just get in trouble for slander." Fear of reporting the assault highlights the campus culture and lack of protection or support for survivors of sexual assault (Clark & Pino, 2016).

Results from the logistic regression . . . indicated that sexual minorities and students who reported that they were frightened during their sexual assault were roughly five and three times more likely to provide a rationale consistent with the "I was afraid" theme than were their respective counterparts. The finding on sexual minorities is consistent with previous research, which has found that LGBTQ individuals tend to not report discrimination because of safety concerns (Wickens & Sandlin, 2010).

"BECAUSE I WAS DRUNK"

Another common theme in the rationales provided was related to the role of alcohol or drugs in decision making regarding reporting sexual assaults (n = 20, 9.1%). Some respondents stated that being drunk made it difficult for them to decipher whether they had been sexually assaulted. One survivor stated, "Being drunk when it happened made it hard to tell if it was rape." Additionally, some survivors blamed themselves for being drunk:

> Personally, I felt somewhat responsible for the incident because of the amount of alcohol I had consumed. We were both very intoxicated, me to the point of blacking out and throwing up. This person may have been a predator and taken advantage of me, but I wasn't convinced that they too weren't at the same level of incomprehension as I was. How could I blame someone if we were guilty of the same things? We both drank a lot and I don't remember the incident vividly enough because of the blackout. I do remember waking up and being naked and seeing throw up all over my car and shower. It was a bad situation, but in some ways I put myself in it.

One particularly disturbing aspect of this theme was the way in which some students ($n = 6$) normalized these types of experiences. To illustrate, one student wrote that she did not report the incident because "it happens sometimes in college." Another survivor stated that she did not report "because it is socially acceptable on this campus to get as drunk as possible at fraternity parties and grind or hook up with anyone regardless if they are underage or too drunk to give consent." In a rape culture that seeks to shift the blame of sexual assault from the perpetrator to the victim, the normalization of excessive drinking and sexual assault serves as an excuse for the perpetrator (Wade et al., 2014).

"I DIDN'T WANT TO GET HIM IN TROUBLE"

Another theme is that the survivor "didn't want to get him [the perpetrator] in trouble" ($n = 18$, 8.2%). To illustrate, one survivor stated that she did not report the sexual assault to university officials because "an accusation of sexual assault ruins a person's life and options in their professional career." Similarly, another survivor stated: "He was a friend, [so] I didn't want to put a mark on his record for a stupid mistake." In a rape culture that values traditional gender roles (Grubb & Turner, 2012), women are socialized to be warm and caring, and to value relationships with others. Women are often expected to care for men, and in this culture, survivors of sexual assault still may feel that it is their role to protect their assailant, especially on college campuses, where survivors often know their assailants as fellow students, acquaintances, friends, or intimate partners.

"TOO ASHAMED TO REPORT"

In addition to feeling afraid or being drunk, some survivors stated that they did not report because they were "too ashamed to report" ($n = 16$, 7.3%). Various reasons were given as to why the survivor was too ashamed to report, such as "I was drugged and I feel incredibly embarrassed for allowing myself to be put in that situation" and "I didn't want to talk about it. I was embarrassed and thought it was my fault." Another student wrote, "I felt embarrassed that such a thing had happened to me." One survivor stated she did not report because "I didn't want anyone to know.

I was afraid and humiliated." The rhetoric of victim blaming is internalized in these examples, and they also speak to the shame that many women experience in the aftermath of sexual victimization, given a pervasive ideology that holds "women responsible for sexual victimization and differentiates 'good girls' from those who get raped" (Weiss, 2010, p. 303).

"I FELT AS THOUGH I WOULD BE BLAMED FOR PUTTING MYSELF IN THE SITUATION"

Similar to the theme of feeling too ashamed to report, several survivors indicated that they did not report their sexual assault because they "felt as though I would be blamed for putting myself in the situation" ($n = 11$, 5.0%). This theme included survivors who thought others would blame them, as well as survivors who stated that they blamed themselves for the incident. As one student reported, "I felt like it was my fault since I was drunk and kind of leading him on." Another survivor reported, "No one would believe me, I couldn't remember anything. I felt like a slut. I had a drink and I was blacked out; I'm sure I was drugged. I should have never gone dancing. I would have been blamed." This theme speaks directly to the campus environment that promotes rape culture, rape myth acceptance, and victim-blaming attitudes (Buchwald et al., 1993; Freyd & Birrell, 2013; Sutton & Simons, 2015). Survivors felt that they would be blamed for what happened to them, which suggests that the campus climate, as well as the greater social context, promotes the notion that survivors are at least partially to blame for the assault.

LACK OF INFORMATION

A salient theme that provides concrete and practical implications for universities is the finding that a considerable portion of students in our study were unaware of where to report, how to report, and to whom they could report a sexual assault. In a similar vein, Hayes-Smith and Levett (2010) found that students were knowledgeable of less than half of the sexual assault resources available to them at the university. Universities should make it clear to students how to report a sexual assault, as well as make information readily accessible to them. Perhaps, as Hayes-Smith and Levett (2010) suggest, disseminating information about sexual assault resources online would be the best way to provide students with this information. Some survivors in our study reported that they did not think that the university could help them, which suggests it is also important to share information with students about what the university can do to help sexual assault survivors, and for universities to be consistent in their approach. Faculty instructors could also aid in informing students, particularly in large introductory level and required general education courses where issues of assault and violence are likely discussed (e.g., introductory psychology, sociology, human development, family science classes).

In addition to not knowing who to report to or that they could report, some students believed that the sexual assault "wasn't related to the university." Some students believed that if the assault did not occur on campus, or if the perpetrator was not a student, they could not report it to the university. They did not understand that universities are required to offer victims remedies and resources whether or not the incident happened on or off campus and whether or not the assailant was a student. Such limited understanding may suggest that these survivors believe that the sole purpose of reporting is to punish perpetrators. According to the Campus SaVE Act, universities are required to provide resources to students who have been sexually assaulted, whether or not the assault occurred on campus. This suggests that universities should be clear in educating students that even if the assault happened off campus or the perpetrator was not affiliated with the university, they can still report the assault and get resources to assist them in healing and recovering from the assault.

Another form of misinformation was victims' limited definition of what constitutes sexual violence. Specifically, survivors whose sexual assault did not include oral sex, vaginal penetration, or anal penetration were more likely to indicate that "it was not a big enough deal" to report. These findings support previous research that found sexual assault survivors were less likely to label or acknowledge their assault if the experience did not match a narrow definition of "real" rape, characterized by penetration (Cleere & Lynn, 2013; Gavey, 2005). To reduce this barrier for reporting sexual assaults, universities

need to emphasize the wide spectrum of sexual violence in training, education, and policies concerning sexual violence.

NORMALIZATION OF SEXUAL VIOLENCE

The idea that "it's not a big enough deal" is also connected to a pattern of dismissing and discounting sexual violence against women. This theme arose more than any other in the rationales provided for not reporting. As with Hlavka's (2014) findings, the women in our study might have internalized notions that male violence against women is normal and not worth reporting. Hlavka found young women often respond to sexual aggression by ignoring the behavior, avoiding the perpetrator, or diverting attention, and some survivors in our study spoke about handling the situation themselves. This may suggest that survivors feel that the best option is to handle the assault privately. However, if universities are committed to providing support and resources for survivors of sexual assault, it is important that students be informed about the resources available, the mechanisms for reporting, and the value of reporting sexual assault to university support offices. Additionally, many women in our study blamed themselves and felt ashamed, which indicates that it is important for sexual assault training to address victim blaming myths and to stress that the university is mandated to assist survivors and hold offenders accountable.

BEING AFRAID TO REPORT

It is also important for universities to recognize that many young women are afraid to report the sexual assault. As our results indicated, this fear can be the fear of repercussions, harassment or revenge from the perpetrator, or fear that they would not be believed. In support of these findings, survivors who perceived that the university would not handle the sexual assault appropriately were more likely to report that they were afraid to report. Thus, universities should examine ways they have responded to survivors who filed a report to ensure they are not questioning the survivor's credibility. Those in positions responsible for implementing policies and procedures for reporting sexual assault (e.g., administrators, campus police, Title IX representatives) also need to make it known that all reports of sexual assault will be investigated and to take a clear stance that retaliation toward a sexual assault survivor will not be tolerated. Also, the fact that some sexual assault survivors report that they are ashamed or embarrassed to report their sexual assault to the university—a finding consistent with Vopni (2006)—suggests that there is still a stigmatization surrounding sexual assault. More education regarding sexual assault, combined with visible campus support for sexual assault survivors, may decrease the stigmatization that surrounds sexual assault.

Another important finding from the logistic regression models was that survivors who were sexual minorities were more likely to report fear as an explanation for not formally reporting the assault. Previous research has found that LGBTQ individuals tend to choose not to report any discrimination they face at universities because it would mean that they would have to report their sexual orientation in an unsafe environment (Wickens & Sandlin, 2010). In a rape culture that is based on heteronormativity, sexual minorities likely feel less safe or protected than their heterosexual counterparts. Universities need to take steps to make their campus safer for sexual minorities. For example, they may need to openly offer more support to LGBTQ students, especially to sexual minority students who have been sexually assaulted.

Finally, the finding that some survivors were afraid to report because they were drinking and "felt as though I would be blamed for putting myself in the situation" points to the importance of universities emphasizing the fact that consent cannot be legally given if an individual is drunk or has used drugs. It also highlights the need to focus on reducing the acceptance of rape myths—false beliefs that are often used to shift the blame of the sexual assault from the perpetrators onto the victims—on college campuses (see Weiser, 2017). Similarly, some students in this study reported that they did not report the assault because "it happens sometimes in college." This speaks to the college party culture in which excessive drinking and casual sexual relations are glamorized, normalized, and gendered (Armstrong, Hamilton, & Sweeney, 2006; Wade et al., 2014). Alcohol use by either the perpetrator or the victim is a risk marker for the occurrence of a sexual assault (Ullman, 2003). A culture that promotes excessive alcohol consumption and has little consequences for perpetrating sexual assault leads to a tolerance of sexual assault (Sutton & Simons, 2015; Wade et al., 2014). This tolerance could lead survivors to normalize their experience of being sexually assaulted while under the influence of alcohol, thus not reporting their sexual assault to university officials. This suggests that universities should examine the overall campus culture to create a culture that is safe for everyone. As the Centers for Disease Control and Prevention (2014) suggested, universities should

> identify opportunities to better understand the nature of sexual violence on campus; create a campus climate that supports safety, respect, and trust; create a comprehensive prevention plan to address sexual violence; select or develop strategies based on the best available research evidence; consider best practices for effective prevention when identifying strategies to implement; evaluate prevention strategies being implemented on campus. (pp. 12–13)

THE IMPORTANCE OF SEXUAL VIOLENCE TRAINING ON COLLEGE CAMPUSES

Our study offers some evidence of the value of sexual assault prevention training. The logistic regression models revealed that survivors who had ever received training about policies and procedures regarding incidents of sexual assault, or prevention of sexual assault, were less likely to provide rationales consistent with the themes "it wasn't a big enough deal" or "I didn't know who to report to or that I could report," indicating that educating students about what to report and how to report it might help students have more options available to label sexual assault experiences and to be more aware of what options are available. These findings support previous research that has found that sexual assault trainings increase rape knowledge among students who take the training (Anderson & Whiston, 2005). However, those who had ever received training were also more likely to provide rationales consistent with the theme "I was afraid." This, combined with the finding that those who provided responses consistent with the theme "I was afraid" were also more likely to think the university would not handle the sexual assault appropriately, points to the possibility that the training might need to be examined to ensure the message does not invoke fear in survivors. However, and just as important, it also suggests that universities may need to do more to support survivors (see Bordere, 2017), to reduce the fear of reporting the assault to the university, and to promote trust in the reporting process.

REFERENCES

Anderson, L. A., & Whiston, S. C. (2005). Sexual assault education programs: A meta-analytic examination of their effectiveness. *Psychology of Women Quarterly, 29,* 374–388. https://doi.org/10.1111/j.1471-6402.2005.00237.x

Armstrong, E. A., Hamilton, L., & Sweeney, B. (2006). Sexual assault on campus: A multilevel integrative approach to party rape. *Social Problems, 53,* 483–499. https://doi.org/10.1525/sp.2006.53.4.483

Black, M. C., Basile, K. C., Breiding, M. J., Smith, S. G., Walters, M. L., Merrick, M. T., . . . Stevens, M. R. (2011). *The National Intimate Partner and Sexual Violence Survey (NISVS): 2010 summary report.* Retrieved from http://www.cdc.gov/violenceprevention/pdf/nisvs_report2010-a.pdf

Bordere, T. (2017). Disenfranchisement and ambiguity in the face of loss: The suffocated grief of sexual assault survivors. *Family Relations, 66,* 29–45.

Brownmiller, S. (1975). *Against our will: Men, women, and rape.* New York, NY: Bantam Books.

Buchwald, E., Fletcher, P. R., & Roth, M. (Eds.). (1993). *Transforming a rape culture.* Minneapolis, MN: Milkweed Editions.

Cantor, D., Fisher, B., Chibnall, S., Townsend, R., Lee, H., Bruce, C., & Thomas, G. (2015). *Report on the AAU campus climate survey on sexual assault and sexual misconduct.* Retrieved from https://www.aau.edu/uploadedFiles/AAU_Publications/AAU_Reports/Sexual_Assault_Campus_Survey/AAU_Campus_Climate_Survey_12_14_15.pdf

Centers for Disease Control and Prevention. (2014). *Preventing sexual violence on college campuses: Lessons from research and practice.* Washington, DC: Office on Violence Against Women, U.S. Department of Justice. Retrieved from https://www.notalone.gov/assets/preventing-sexual-violence-on-college-campuses-lessons-from-research-and-practice.pdf

Chamallas, M. (2010). Past as prologue: Old and new feminisms. *Michigan Journal of Gender & Law, 17,* 157–174.

Chronicle of Higher Education. (2016, June 22). *Title IX: Tracking sexual assault investigations* [Data file]. Retrieved from http://projects.chronicle.com/titleix/investigations/?status=active

Clark, A. E., & Pino, A. L. (2016). *We believe you: Survivors of campus sexual assault speak out.* New York, NY: Holt.

Cleere, C., & Lynn, S. J. (2013). Acknowledged versus unacknowledged sexual assault among college women. *Journal of Interpersonal Violence, 28,* 2593–2611. https://doi.org/10.1177/0886260513479033

Damant, D., Lapierre, S., Kouraga, A., Fortin, A., Hamelin-Brabant, L., Lavergne, C., & Lessard, G. (2008). Taking child abuse and mothering into account: Intersectional feminism as an alternative for the study of domestic violence. *Affilia, 23*(2), 123–133.

Du Mont, J., Miller, K. L., & Myhr, T. L. (2003). The role of "real rape" and "real victim" stereotypes in the police reporting practices of sexually assaulted women. *Violence Against Women, 9,* 466–486. https://doi.org/10.1177/1077801202250960

Fisher, B. S., Daigle, L. E., Cullen, F. T., & Turner, M. G. (2003). Reporting sexual victimization to the police and others: Results from a national-level study of college women. *Criminal Justice and Behavior, 30,* 6–38. https://doi.org/10.1177/0093854802239161

Freyd, J., & Birrell, P. (2013). *Blind to betrayal: Why we fool ourselves—We aren't being fooled.* Hoboken, NJ: Wiley.

Gavey, N. (2005). *Just sex? The cultural scaffolding of rape.* New York, NY: Routledge.

Grubb, A., & Turner, E. (2012). Attribution of blame in rape cases: A review of the impact of rape myth acceptance, gender role conformity, and substance use on victim blaming. *Aggression and Violent Behavior, 17,* 443–452. https://doi.org/10.1016/j.avb.2012.06.002

Harding, S. (2009). Standpoint theories: Productively controversial. *Hypatia, 24*, 192–200. https://doi.org/10.1111/j.1527-2001.2009.01067.x

Harding, S. (2012) Feminist standpoints. In S. N. Hesse-Biber (Ed.), *Handbook of feminist research: Theory and praxis* (pp. 46–64). Thousand Oaks, CA: Sage. https://doi.org/10.4135/9781483384740.n3

Hartstock, N. C. (2014). The feminist standpoint: Developing the ground for a specifically feminist historical materialism. In C. McCann & S. K. Kim (Eds.), *Feminist theory reader: Local and global perspectives* (pp. 354–369). New York, NY: Routledge.

Hayes, D. (2012). Looking the other way? Calls for higher accountability intensify amid numerous recent sexual assault incidents on college campuses. *Diverse Issues in Higher Education, 29*(10), 8–9.

Hayes-Smith, R. M. & Levett, L. M. (2010). Student perceptions of sexual assault resources and prevalence of rape myth attitudes. *Feminist Criminology, 5*, 335–354. https://doi.org/10.1177/1557085110387581

Hlavka, H. R. (2014). Normalizing sexual violence: Young women account for harassment and abuse. *Gender and Society, 28*, 337–358. https://doi.org/10.1177/0891243214526468

hooks, b. (1994). *Outlaw culture: Resisting representations*. New York, NY: Routledge.

Johnson, A. G. (2005). *The gender knot: Unraveling our patriarchal legacy*. Philadelphia, PA: Temple University Press.

Jordan, C. E., Combs, J. L., & Smith, G. T. (2014). An exploration of sexual victimization and academic performance among college women. *Trauma, Violence, & Abuse, 15*(3), 191–200. https://doi.org/10.1177/1524838014520637

Jozkowski, K., & Wiersma-Mosley, J. (2017). The Greek system: How gender inequality and class privilege perpetuate rape culture. *Family Relations, 66*, 89–103.

Krebs, C. P., Lindquist, C. H., Warner, T. D., Fisher, B. S. & Martin, S. L. (2007). *The Campus Sexual Assault (CSA) Study*. Washington, DC: U.S. Department of Justice. Retrieved from https://www.ncjrs.gov/pdffiles1/nij/grants/221153.pdf

Mehrota, G. (2010). Toward a continuum of intersectionality theorizing for feminist social work scholarship. *Affilia, 25*, 417–430. https://doi.org/10.1177/0886109910384190

Patterson, D., Greeson, M., & Campbell, R. (2009). Understanding rape survivors' decisions not to seek help from formal social systems. *Health & Social Work, 34*, 127–136. https://doi.org/10.1093/hsw/34.2.127

Payne, M. (2005). *Modern social work theory* (3rd ed.). Chicago, IL: Lyceum Books.

Phillips, L. (2000). *Flirting with danger: Young women's reflections on sexuality and domination*. New York, NY: New York University Press.

Samuels, G. M., & Ross-Sheriff, F. (2008). Identity, oppression, and power: Feminisms and intersectionality theory. *Affilia, 23*, 5–9. https://doi.org/10.1177/0886109907310475

Sharp, E. A., Weiser, D., Lavigne, D., & Kelly, C. (2017). From furious to fearless: Faculty action and feminist praxis in response to rape culture on college campuses. *Family Relations, 66*, 75–88.

Shields, S. A. (2008). Gender: An intersectional perspective. *Sex Roles, 59*, 301–311. https://doi.org/10.1007/s11199-008-9501-8

Sinozich, S., & Langton, L. (2014). *Rape and sexual assault victimization among college females, 1995–2013*. Washington, DC: US Dept. of Justice. Retrieved from http://www.bjs.gov/content/pub/pdf/rsavcaf9513.pdf

Sutton, T. E., & Simons, L. G. (2015). Sexual assault among college students: Family of origin, hostility, attachment, and the hook-up culture as risk factors. *Journal of Child Family Studies, 24*, 2827–2840. https://doi.org/10.1007/s10826-014-0087-1

Thompson, M., Sitterle, D., Clay, G., & Kingree, J. (2007). Reasons for not reporting victimizations to the police: Do they vary for physical and sexual incidents? *Journal of American College Health, 55*, 277–282. https://doi.org/10.3200/JACH.55.5.277-282

Tutty, L. M., & Rothery, M. (2002). Beyond shelters: Support groups and community-based advocacy for abused women. In A. R. Roberts (Ed.), *Handbook of domestic violence intervention strategies* (pp. 396–418). New York, NY: Oxford University Press.

Ullman, S. E. (2003). A critical review of field studies on the link of alcohol and adult sexual assault in women. *Aggression and Violent Behavior, 8*, 471–486. https://doi.org/10.1016/S1359-1789(03)00032-6

U.S. Senate. (2014). *Sexual violence on campus: How too many institutions of higher education are failing to protect students*. Washington, DC: US Senate Subcommittee on Financial and Contracting Oversight. Retrieved from https://www.mccaskill .senate.gov/SurveyReportwithAppendix.pdf

Vopni, V. (2006). Young women's experiences with reporting sexual assault to police. *Canadian Woman Studies, 25*(1–2), 107–114.

Wade, L., Sweeney, B., Derr, A.S., Messner, M.A., & Burke, C. (2014). Ruling out rape. *Contexts, 13,* 16–25. https://doi.org/10.1177/1536504214533495

Weiser, D. (2017). Confronting myths about sexual assault: A feminist analysis of the false report literature. *Family Relations, 66,* 46–60.

White House Task Force to Protect Students from Sexual Assault. (2014). *Not alone: The first report of the White House Task Force to Protect Students from Sexual Assault*. Washington, DC: US Government Printing Office. Retrieved from https://www .notalone.gov/assets/report.pdf

Wickens, C. M., & Sandlin, J. A. (2010). Homophobia and heterosexism in a college of education: A culture of fear, a culture of silence. *International Journal of Qualitative Studies in Education, 23,* 651–670. https://doi. org/10.1080/09518390903551035

Yung, C. R. (2015). Concealing campus sexual assault: An empirical examination. *Psychology, Public Policy, and Law, 21,* 1–9. https://doi.org/10.1037/ law0000037

68. SEXUAL VIOLENCE IN IRAQ
Challenges for Transnational Feminist Politics
NADJE AL-ALI (2018)

INTRODUCTION

Recent developments in Iraq, in neighbouring Syria and elsewhere in the region where the so-called Islamic State (known as ISIS as well as Daesh)[1] has taken foothold, clearly raise the bar in terms of dehumanizing atrocities. The accounts of survivors of sexual violence at the hands of ISIS are beyond horrific. However, sexual violence, as we are witnessing now, did not emerge in a vacuum; Iraqi women and men were confronted with sexual and broader gender-based violence[2] [in] pre-invasion Iraq, as well as in the post-invasion period. Without wanting to belittle the carnage and cruelties committed by ISIS, I have felt uneasy about the limited interest displayed by the media, policy makers and the general public with respect to the broad continuum of sexual and gender-based violence in present-day Iraq, but also prior to the appearance of ISIS in Iraq. As feminist IR scholars like Cynthia Enloe (1987, 1990, 2000), Cynthia Cockburn (1999, 2004, 2007) and Annick TR Wibben (2004, 2011) among others, have argued, we need to recognize a continuum of violence before and after conflict and wars and from the personal/household to the international. More concretely, perpetrators of sexual and gendered violence exist on a broad spectrum in Iraq, including militia linked to the Iraqi government and other political parties, various insurgent groups who fought against the government and the former occupation, criminal gangs, family members and, until a few years ago, also the occupation forces.

. . .

INTERSECTIONAL POSITIONALITY

I am frequently faced with a conundrum when talking about sexual violence in Iraq. Sexual violence is rampant. There is no question about it. However, also widespread is the political instrumentalization of sexual violence, often sensationalized and exaggerated in terms of scope and threat. It is used as an othering and dehumanizing device, whether in relation to sectarian conflict, the fraud and complex relations between western and Middle Eastern political leaders, or the demonization of asylum seekers and migrants. For example, those of us living in Europe are familiar with the obsessive discussions of honour crimes in the European politics of immigration. Without doubt honour-based crimes and killings are a serious problem, particularly in relation to the Kurdish region and Kurdish diaspora communities in Europe (Alinia, 2013; Begikhani, 2005; Begikhani et al., 2010; Mojab, 2001, 2003). Yet, media and policy narratives around honour-based crimes are often incredibly essentializing, stigmatizing and glossing over complex situations and variations. The more recent debates about sexual harassment of women in Cologne by apparently largely Middle East/North African migrants and asylum seekers on New Year's Eve in Cologne have revealed the difficulty of addressing sexual violence and racism simultaneously.

Discourses on sexual violence are frequently deployed as part of wider racist and sectarian culturalist discourses: where their "barbaric" culture is essentially different from "our" civilized culture, and the way this difference is articulated most dramatically is over and with the bodies of women and the attitudes towards non-heteronormative sexualities. I agree with Lila Abu-Lughod's (2013) assessment in her book *Do Muslim Women Need Saving?* that blaming culture "means not just flattening cultures, stripping moral systems of their complexity, and hiding the most modern political and social interventions that no community escapes; it means erasing history" (Abu-Lughod, 2013: 136). I also concur with Abu-Lughod that what is often missing in discussions is the recognition of the dynamic historical transformations and specific political economies that are affecting women, men, families and everyday life in all communities (Abu-Lughod, 2013).

In my earlier joint work with Nicola Pratt (2009), published as *What Kind of Liberation? Women and the Occupation of Iraq*, we discussed how women in Iraq have fared since the fall of the Ba'th regime in 2003. Official rhetoric had put Iraqi women at centre stage, but we showed that in reality women's rights and women's lives have been exploited in the name of competing political agendas. We also tried to challenge the widespread view—even among some progressive anti-war and peace activists—that something inherent in Muslim, Middle Eastern or Iraqi culture is responsible for the escalating violence and systematic

erosion of women's rights. We argued that it was not Islam or "culture" that has pushed Iraqi women back into their homes. Instead, we blamed concrete and rapidly changing political, economic and social conditions as well as a wide range of national, regional and international actors (Al-Ali and Pratt, 2009).

Over the past years, I have spent lots of time and energy as an academic and as an activist to argue against the "culturalization" of gender-related issues—particularly with reference to gender-based violence in the Iraqi context. For years, I have felt compelled to say and write: It's not about "their culture," but it is about political economies. It is about authoritarian dictatorships and conservative patriarchal interpretations and practices. It is about foreign interventions and invasions and their gendered politics (Al-Ali, 2014). I have made a case for the significance of intersectionality, i.e. that the struggle for women's rights intersects with the struggle against other inequalities, which, in Iraq translates into the struggles against imperialism, neoliberal economics, authoritarianism, and, crucially as well, sectarianism.

Being based in London, my feminism certainly also intersects with the struggle against racism and Islamophobia. Throughout I have tried to not become an apologetic in terms of systematic human and women's rights abuses in Iraq and elsewhere. Yet I have to admit that I am personally frustrated by my own constant compulsion to fight Islamophobia and racism and, in that process, sometimes gloss over forms of gender-based and sexual violence, the political marginalization of women and men who do not fit heteronormative ideals, as well as extremely socially conservative attitudes towards gender norms and relations.

. . .

Obviously I cannot escape my positionality and audiences, being based in London, which comes with certain responsibilities and points of emphasis. Yet, rather than contributing to the taboo and silencing of sexual and wider gender-based violence within domestic Iraqi politics on the one hand, and the sensationalizing and essentialist culturalist discourses on the other, we need to find nuanced and truly intersectional ways to talk about it. Trying to avoid the straightjacket of location and positionality—however shifting that might be given people's multiple roles, transnational involvements and contextual identities—calls for historicizing to avoid essentialist notions of culture and identity. But it also requires attention to regional and local agencies, complicities, historically specific patriarchal articulations and practices, and, crucially, I would argue, a critical engagement with militarized and other newly emerging masculinities. In the Iraqi context today, this concretely translates into a recognition that US and UK actions and policies linked to the invasion and occupation have contributed to the deterioration of women's rights and the increase in gender-based and sexual violence, while simultaneously paying attention to and recognizing that local manifestations of militarized and neoliberal patriarchal gender norms and relations are also rooted in regional, (trans) national and local power dynamics and struggles as well as historically specific contestations over resources, cultures and identities. Crucially, gender-based and sexual violence did not simply emerge post-2003 but have a history linked to the Ba'th regime, which came into power in 1968 and lasted until 2003, and even further back to the formation of Iraq as a nation-state (Efrati, 2012). We also have to look carefully at the specific political and economic dynamics linked to the Kurdish Regional Government, particularly post-1991.

SEXUAL VIOLENCE DURING THE BA'TH REGIME

Despite its repressive nature, the first decade of the Ba'th regime has been largely characterized by its secularizing and modernizing policies. Women's education and labour force participation were integral to the regime's attempt at creating a productive population that could be governed through the centralized mechanisms of an increasingly authoritarian state. I have elsewhere discussed at length the state's active intervention in challenging prevailing gender norms and relations, largely to address the expanding economy and needs of the labour market (Al-Ali, 2007). Women's education and labour force participation was actively encouraged by the state which, throughout the 1970s and 1980s, provided free childcare and an infrastructure that facilitated women's entry into the expanding labour force (Al-Ali, 2007). An in-depth analysis of the 35 years of [the] Ba'th regime does point to contradictory and changing policies and attitude[s] towards women and gender, challenging any generalized and often simplistic assessments.

Clearly women living in urban areas not involved in opposition politics benefited much more from the modernizing state policies than either women in the countryside or those in opposition to the regime, in fear of their lives. Reports and personal accounts by Iraqi women and men who were in opposition to the regime reveal that sexual violence was integral to the horrific regime of torture in Iraqi prisons during the Ba'th era (Al-Ali, 2007; Amnesty International, 2005; Human Rights Watch, 2014). However, there appear to be more documented cases of women having experienced sexual violence in prisons than men, which might be a result of the greater social stigma attached for men experiencing sexual torture, abuse and rape.

From the 1980s onwards, in the context of the Iran–Iraq war and the atrocities against the Kurdish population, women were increasingly used to demarcate boundaries between communities and carry the heavy burden of honour in a society that became more and more militarized. Women's patriotic duties shifted to producers of loyal Iraqi citizens and future fighters. Their bodies became progressively the site of nationalist policies and battles (Rohde, 2010). During the Iraq–Iran war (1980–1988), a series of legal decrees were introduced to control women's marital and reproductive freedoms. In December 1982, the Revolutionary Command Council (RCC) issued a decree forbidding Iraqi women to marry non-Iraqis as well as another decree prohibiting Iraqi women married to non-Iraqis to transfer money or property to their husbands as inheritance (Omar, 1994: 63). At the same time, Iraqi men were encouraged to divorce their Iranian wives, while Iraqi Arab men were encouraged to marry Kurdish women as part of the regime's Arabization policies in the north. During this period, Islamist and Kurdish women were tortured and sexually abused, humiliating not only the female victims but "dishonouring" their male relatives as well (Al-Ali, 2007: 168–169).

The most known systematic killing but also sexual abuse took place during the 1987–1988 *Anfal* campaign, nominally a counterinsurgency operation against Kurdish resistance, but in reality a carefully planned and executed programme of ethnic cleansing in which 50,000–200,000 people are estimated to have been killed, most of them men and adolescent boys.[3] Thousands of Kurdish villages were systematically destroyed, and over a million and a half of their inhabitants deported to camps with no water, electricity or sewage. Others were executed on the way out of their villages. Under the leadership of Ali Hasan al-Majid, a cousin of Saddam Hussein, the *Anfal* campaign has been particularly associated with the use of chemical weapons, such as mustard and nerve gas. Long-term effects have included various forms of cancer, infertility and congenital diseases. It is beyond the scope of this article to discuss at any length the scale and depth of sexual violence carried out against Kurdish women at the time. Choman Hardi (2011) as well as Karen Mlodoch (2009) have written in great depth about women's experiences and memories of *Anfal*. Hardi's moving book, *Gendered Experiences of Genocide: Anfal Survivors in Kurdistan-Iraq* (2011), addresses systematic sexual abuse, including rape, of women in camps. She also stresses that despite the large body of documents, and evidence available, outside the immediate media coverage, *Anfal* "remained largely unrecognised by the international community" (2011: 33).

. . .

Nicola Pratt and I (2009) have argued previously that Iraqi women were instrumentalized in the run up to the invasion, and during the occupation. For example, high-ranking US officials, including then National Security Advisor Condoleezza Rice and Vice-President Dick Cheney, met with Women for a Free Iraq, a newly formed group of Iraqi opposition activists backed by the State Department post 9/11, to hear their personal stories and to discuss the future of the country (Al-Ali and Pratt, 2009: 56). The US State Department publicized the abuses experienced by women at the hands of the Iraqi regime—including beheadings, rape and torture (Office of International Women's Issues, 2003). In the UK, Tony Blair met a delegation of Iraqi women in November 2002 (Russell, 2002) and the Foreign and Commonwealth Office listed the regime's crimes against women as part of its dossier on human rights abuses in Iraq (Foreign and Commonwealth Office, 2002).

The timing of this sudden interest in the plight of Iraqi women cannot be overemphasized. For decades, many Iraqi women activists in the US and UK had tried to raise awareness about the systematic abuse of human and women's rights under Saddam Hussein, the atrocities linked to the *Anfal* campaign against the Kurds as well as the impact of economic sanctions on women and families (Al-Ali and Pratt, 2009: 56). Yet, throughout the 1980s and 1990s, their voices remained largely unheard among western politicians, who initially regarded Saddam Hussein as an ally in the fight against the Islamic regime in Iran. Later, after the invasion of Kuwait, when Saddam Hussein ceased to be regarded as an ally, the debate around economic sanctions and the broader humanitarian crisis subsumed more gender-specific forms of violence and human rights abuses. Yet, during the sanctions period (1990–2003), the combination of economic crisis, high levels of unemployment, changing state rhetoric and policies as well [as] a shift towards greater religiosity led to an increase in social conservatism and a growth in discriminatory practices and sexual forms of violence, such as domestic violence, polygamy and prostitution.

POST-INVASION AND OCCUPATION

The US partly justified its invasion of Iraq by calling attention to the abuse of women by the regime of Saddam Hussein (Al-Ali and Pratt, 2009). International agencies and NGOs received money (mostly from the US and the UK) to train women to enable their participation in peace-building, reconstruction and the transition to democracy (Al-Ali and Pratt, 2009). Delegations of self-selected Iraqi women visited Washington regularly after the invasion, holding press conferences hosted by the State Department and meeting President Bush at the White House in November 2003 (White House Office of the Press Secretary, 2003). When my colleague Nicola Pratt visited Washington, DC, in 2005, a number of officials were keen to stress the US administration's concern to support women in Iraq and to see them play a role in the country's future (Al-Ali and Pratt, 2009: 57).

However, despite the rhetoric of supporting and liberating women, women and gender issues quickly dropped off the agenda of both the occupation forces and Iraqi politicians. Since 2003, Iraqi women and men have faced high levels of insecurity, coupled with the lack of rule of law, both contributing to increasing and wide-ranging forms of gender-based and sexual violence. Other main challenges relate to an ongoing humanitarian crisis and lack of functioning and adequate infrastructure, widespread corruption and a non-functioning authoritarian and sectarian state that heavily relies on militia and repression. Rampant domestic violence, verbal and physical intimidation, sexual harassment, rape, forced marriage—as well as increases in *mut'ah* or so-called pleasure marriages[4]—trafficking, forced prostitution, female genital mutilation, and honour-based crimes, including killings, have been very much part of the post-invasion experience.

Several reports and interviews with Iraqi women's rights activists suggested already a few years after the invasion that in a context of widespread unemployment and poverty, women were particularly vulnerable to sexual exploitation. This view was also expressed by a leading women's rights activist from Baghdad, who told me: "The fragility of state institutions and the failure of the rule of law has created room for human trafficking gangs, especially for the trafficking of women and girls for sexual exploitation and prostitution." Women and girls from poor families in search of employment have been the most frequent victims of trafficking. It is not only Iraqi criminal gangs that have been involved in shipping women and girls to Syria, Jordan, Qatar and other Gulf countries but, according to Human Rights Watch (2011), some Iraqi police officers have also been involved.

According to a comprehensive report published in 2011 by the Heartland Alliance for Human Needs and Human Rights, gender-based violence has been institutionalized: violence against women is not sufficiently criminalized and victims face harsh laws and practices that treat victims as criminals. Any protective laws that might exist have been rarely implemented as the police and judges treat gender-based crimes and sexual violence leniently and allow perpetrators to act with impunity. No doubt, and as I stated earlier, sexual violence existed before 2003. Yet, the failure to protect women and establish proper awareness

mechanisms and procedures over the last years is one of the major failures and responsibilities of the international community, particularly the US and the UK, alongside the main Iraqi political actors, parties and governments. As early as 2005, an Iraqi women's rights activist stated in an interview with me:

> The Iraqi army and police are not just failing to prevent violence against women, but they are part of the problem. They treat women who have been victims of domestic violence or rape during kidnappings, for example, without any respect and some even consider them to be guilty. Also we know of cases where women have been harassed and even raped at police stations and inside prisons. We have tried to raise this with our politicians, but they are not listening. The Americans and British are also busy with other issues and do not pursue our complaints.

Almost a decade later, a Human Rights Watch report (2014) addresses the systematic corruption and flaws of the Iraqi criminal system. While both men and women are affected, women are particularly vulnerable as they are frequently detained as a punishment for male family members who have allegedly committed a crime or have been engaged in political activities. Due to the stigma attached to imprisonment, particularly given the risk of torture and sexual abuse, women face further harassment and ostracizing within their communities and families once freed. The report states that:

> . . . women are subjected to threats of, or actual sexual assault (sometimes in front of husbands, brothers, and children). Some detainees reported a lack of adequate protection for female prisoners from attacks by male prison guards, including those from adjoining male prisons. Two women reported that sexual assault by prison guards resulted in pregnancy. Women and officials reported that the likelihood of a woman being subject to sexual assault is far higher during arrest and interrogation, prior to a woman's confinement in prison. "[W]e expect that they've been raped by police on the way to the prison," Um Aqil, an employee at a women's prison facility told Human Rights Watch. (Human Rights Watch, 2014)

According to several reports, US forces knew that detainees were being tortured and ill-treated at places of detention under the control of the Interior Ministry, which they frequently visited (Amnesty International, 2006). Yet, British and American troops not only turned a blind eye to the violence committed by the Iraqi army, various militia and criminal gangs, but were also active perpetrators of sexual violence. Over the years, several of my respondents who are involved in human and women's rights activism have talked about various instances and cases of harassment at check points and during house searches, torture, sexual abuse and rape in prisons, mainly as part of counterinsurgency campaigns. In 2005, Amnesty International reported that female detainees had been tortured, threatened with rape, [and] subjected to sexual abuse, possibly including rape.

It is important to stress that gender-based and sexual violence does not only affect women and girls: men and boys are also targeted and impacted. Most visible have been the instances of sexual violence of male Iraqi prisoners at the hands of the US army in Abu Ghraib prison (Amnesty International, 2006; Human Rights Watch, 2004). The shocking images of naked hooded Iraqi men have become emblematic of larger human rights abuses and atrocities in the name of democracy and human rights at the hands of the occupation. However, men have also been attacked by militias linked to political parties as well as insurgent groups for not adhering to heterosexual gender norms. Men "suspected" of homosexual conduct or not being "manly" enough have become increasingly at risk and have been harassed and killed by Islamist militia (Human Rights Watch, 2009). In 2012, a wave of so-called emo killings targeted mainly teenage boys and young men whose hairstyles, clothes and music choice were perceived to be too effeminate by the attackers (Long, 2012). What emerges in central and southern Iraq is a toxic cocktail of Islamist sectarianism, authoritarianism and increased militarization of society, all exacerbating the glorification of militarized masculinities, often directly linked with ever more violent acts.

THE KURDISH REGION OF IRAQ (KRI)

In the Kurdish Region of Iraq (KRI), *de facto* autonomous since 1991, the situation is generally much better in terms of security, an improved infrastructure, a working parliament with active participation of female MPs and numerous women's organizations and rights activists who have managed to push through several relevant legal reforms. However, gender-based and sexual violence are also rampant, specifically in the form of honour-based crimes and killings, female suicides, self-burning and female genital mutilation (FGM). The Kurdish Regional Government (KRG) has used women's and gender-based issues to demarcate itself from the central government in Baghdad, stressing its democratic and more secular and progressive values. This has helped women's rights activists and female MPs to make some headway in relation to the legal protection of women and the criminalization of gender-based violence. Yet, as Begikhani (2005; Begikhani et al., 2010) and others have pointed out, in reality the KRG appears to be less invested in actually implementing new legislation and tends to pursue more traditional ways of addressing gender-based and sexual violence, using tribal and family dispute mechanisms, often to the detriment of women receiving justice. Despite the generally more secular and progressive context in comparison to central and southern Iraq, one cannot help but notice the way that Kurdish politicians instrumentalize gender issues.

Several authors have discussed and analysed gender-based and sexual violence in the KRI with reference to patriarchy, tribal culture, nationalism, militarism and Islamism (Begikhani, 2005; Begikhani et al., 2010; Mojab, 2001, 2003). More recently, Minoo Alinia (2013) has provided an in-depth analysis of honour-based crimes, paying attention to the way that various power structures intersect to produce a "hegemonic honour discourse." Looking at the intersections of ethnic and national oppression, economic marginalization, patriarchy, religion, tribal and kinship structures as well as displacement and militarization of society, Alinia also stresses the significance of prevailing notions of masculinity in controlling women's bodies, their sexuality and "honour."

While Alinia is moving away from the more generalized explanations pertaining to culture, religion, tribalism and nation, Mariwan Kanie (2015) provides further nuance and in-depth insight by pointing to shifts in social, political and economic norms and values as resulting in a "normative disorientation," and the emergence of new forms of masculinities alongside the older hegemonic *peshmerga* masculinities, all contributing to an increase in gender-based violence. In my view, "normative disorientation" is an excellent analytical lens to explore the impact of more recent political, social and economic changes in the KRI. But I would also argue that an intersectional approach is key, and that we need to be very specific in terms of the relevant intersecting oppressive structures as Alinia suggests. Patriarchy, nationalism, tribalism and Islamism, as well as hegemonic masculinities, shift in specific historical contexts and in line with changing political economies and require in-depth empirical research to adequately delineate them. This later insight is not only relevant for the KRI but more broadly applicable, and is certainly also poignant when analysing sexual violence in central and southern Iraq.

Throughout Iraq and the KRI, perpetrators of gender-based and sexual violence have cut across diverse ethnic, religious and class backgrounds and have ranged from the occupation forces, government officials and militants, resistance and insurgent groups, [and] criminal gangs to relatives and families. The various forms of violence are working to reconfigure masculinities and femininities in the post-invasion context. But they are also actively employed as tools for new forms of militarized, authoritarian as well as sectarian politics. Despite its rhetoric, the occupation forces, particularly the US, quickly dropped any initial commitment to gender-based equality and justice. Similar to the largely sectarian and corrupt Iraqi political elite, the US and UK politicians and the military not only compromised on gender issues as part of their overall shift from human to national security, but also contributed to the increase and intensity of sexual violence since the invasion.

ISIS: DOCTRINALLY JUSTIFIED SEXUAL VIOLENCE

Gruelling images and reports of sexually violated Yezidi women and girls have circulated widely within the media and policy circles since ISIS took over Mosul and key western cities in Iraq in 2014. Accounts of systematic and organized sexual slavery, forced marriages, sexual assault and rape have shocked and shaken many people around the world. In addition to the enormity and scale of the abuse, what has made these sexual atrocities and forms of dehumanization particularly appalling are the sexual enslavement and treatment of religious minorities by ISIS fighters.[5] Yezidis (Ezidis), an ancient religious minority with ethnically Kurdish background, have been most vulnerable, but other religious minorities such as Christian, Sabean, Shabak, Turkmen but also Shi'a and even Sunni women have been abused by ISIS fighters. There have been numerous accounts of widespread rape of religious minority women under the banner of *jihad al nikah* (sexual intercourse in pursuit of struggle) with fighters not waiting for unmarried girls to "volunteer" and offer themselves to the male fighters. The promise of sexual access to women and girls has been central to ISIS's recruitment strategy and propaganda materials (UN News Centre, 2015).

The unprecedented scale and level of brutality by ISIS fighters has been documented widely (Amnesty International, 2014; Human Rights Watch, 2015; UNAMI OHCHR, 2014; UN News Centre, 2015). The accounts of the survivors, mainly young female Yezidi survivors of captivity, sexual enslavement, beatings, forced marriage and rape are heart wrenching and impossible to summarize here. According to my interviews with Iraqi/Kurdish women's rights activists, many women seem to have been handed from one fighter to another, sometimes sold and sometimes given as presents. Rape and forced marriage appears to be part of a broader genocide of Yezidis and a systematic dehumanization of non-Muslim religious minorities. Regular occurrences of sexual violence are integral to ISIS's extreme form of asserting a militarized and dominant masculinity, embedded in a hyper-patriarchal system of rigid and polarized gender roles. Aside from the scale of the atrocities, what makes the violence so particularly gruesome is the way that ISIS engages in doctrinal justifications. In October 2014, for example, ISIS's English-language publication *Dabiq* stated that its fighters had given captured Yezidi women and girls to its members as "spoils of war." The publication justifies sexual violence claiming that Islam permits sex with non-Muslim "slaves," including girls, as well as beating and selling them

(Human Rights Watch, 2015). In a later issue of *Dabiq* (No. 9), in the section "From our sisters," a female ISIS member published a long essay on the role of female slaves within the so-called Islamic state, stressing the importance of conversion of infidels, including "slave girls" (Al-Muhajirah, 2015).

Yet, while the atrocities against Yezidi women and girls as well as other religious minorities are discussed widely within the media and policy circles, very little seems to be done to actually support those who escaped and survived. Several of my respondents stressed that general living conditions for Yezidi and Christian refugees are extremely difficult at a time when the KRG is already overstretched due to its hosting of hundreds of thousand of Syrian refugees and Iraqi internally displaced persons (IDPs) while being in an economic crisis due to a political stand off with the central government in Iraq. None of the European or North American countries outraged by ISIS violence has offered to take in a substantial number of Yezidi refugees or to seriously help the KRG to deal with the refugee crisis.

. . .

DILEMMAS FOR TRANSNATIONAL FEMINIST SOLIDARITY

Sexual and gendered violence is not merely employed as a racist and othering discourse by imperialist powers, and right-wing constituencies in the west, but discourses about sexual violence have emerged at every single moment of political and sectarian tension in modern Iraq as a central polarizing and political device among politicians and activists. Theoretically and politically, as I have argued previously (Al-Ali, 2014), we need to recognize that sexual and gender-based violence underwrites much of the broader structural and political violence we are witnessing. It is central to sectarianism and to extreme forms of authoritarianism. Too often thought about as an add-on, sexual violence is, in fact, central to all forms and processes of delineating, controlling, oppressing, marginalizing and governing communities.

Historicizing sexual violence allows us to challenge both the "presentism" so widespread within media and policy discourses as well as essentialist notions about "their culture" or "their religion." A historical approach reveals the complex interplay of inter- and transnational, regional, national and local factors in shaping the specific political economies and socio-historical contexts in which sexual violence might become more widespread. In my view, and as discussed in detail above, a positionality rooted in transnational feminist politics needs to go beyond dichotomous positions of macro power configurations linked to imperialism, neoliberalism and globalization on the one hand, and an attention to localized and regional inequalities and power configurations linked to patriarchy, cultural norms and religious interpretations and practices. Local practices of sexual and gendered violence are articulations not only of local patriarchies embedded in specific and often changing political economies but also transnational imperialism and neoliberalism. Crucially, however, I would argue that while macro processes clearly influence and shape local articulations and configurations of power, they cannot be collapsed into each other. Ironically, in my view, explaining away different forms of sexual violence solely by reference to the history of colonialism and imperialism, or in the Iraqi context, the history of the invasion and occupation, takes away agency of local actors, such as political leaders and militia, but also specific individual men, who historically have been complicit if not drivers of sexual violence, as my historical discussion has shown.

Talking about the ways in which sexual and gender-based violence is embedded within and productive of broader authoritarian, patriarchal and fascistic trends is a challenge. Mobilizing against sexual violence and engaging in advocacy work is even trickier and remains fraught with tensions (Al-Ali, 2014). As I tried to illustrate in this article, any political mobilization and demands are complicated by the continuum of sexual and gender-based violence evident at any given time, but rendered even more complex when taking a historical lens.

NOTES

1. The group was formerly called the Islamic State of Iraq and the Levant (ISIL) and is frequently referred to as Da'ish or Daesh, the Arabic equivalent

of ISIL. More recently, the group has renamed itself to the Islamic State (IS). In this article I use the ISIS, the term most commonly used in English media and academic circles.

2. Gendered or gender-based violence (GBV) refers to violence against a person based on the normative roles linked to each gender contributing to and reproducing unequal power relations in a given society. GBV could lead to psychological, economic, physical or sexual harm and is often used interchangeably with violence against women (VAW). Men can also be victims and survivors of gender-based violence, often linked to their non-normative masculinity and/or sexuality. Sexual violence is one specific continuum of GBV that refers to a wide range of threats, behaviours and acts that are sexual or sexualized, unwanted and committed without consent. Sexual violence might exist on an individual level but is often used more systematically to control, dominate and reinforce gender-based oppression and heteronormativity.

3. For more details, see Human Rights Watch (1993); and www.womenwarpeace.org/iraq/iraq.htm.

4. Within Shi'a Islam, *Nikāḥ al-mut'ah* (pleasure marriage) refers to an informal fixed-term marriage that can be contracted without any witnesses. In practice, *mut'ah* is often used to legalize prostitution, but might also be used to sanction mutually consensual sexual relations. Particularly for women, there is a stigma attached to engaging in *mut'ah* marriages.

5. In the fourth edition [of] *Dabiq*, ISIS's English-language digital magazine, states said, according to sharia and verses in the Qu'ran, female members of the Yezidi sect may legitimately be captured and forcibly made concubines or sexual slaves; media.clarionproject.org/files/islamic-state/islamic-state-isis-magazine-Issue-4-the-failed-crusade.pdf.

REFERENCES

Abu-Lughod L (2013) *Do Muslim Women Need Saving?* Cambridge, MA: Harvard University Press.

Al-Ali N (2007) *Iraqi Women: Untold Stories from 1948 to the Present*. London and New York: Zed Books.

Al-Ali N (2014) Reflections on (counter) revolutionary processes in Egypt. *Feminist Review* 106: 122–128.

Al-Ali N and Pratt N (2009) *What Kind of Liberation? Women and the Occupation in Iraq*. Berkeley: University of California Press.

Alinia M (2013) *Honor and Violence against Women in Iraqi Kurdistan*. New York and London: Palgrave Macmillan.

Al-Muhajirah US (2015) Slave girls or prostitutes? *Dabiq* No. 9: 44–49. Available at: media.clarionproject.org/files/islamic-state/isis-isil-islamic-state-magazine-issue%2B9-they-plot-and-allah-plots-sex-slavery.pdf.

Amnesty International (2005) Iraq—Decades of suffering: Now women deserve better. Available at: https://www.amnesty.org/en/documents/mde14/001/2005/en/.

Amnesty International (2006) Beyond Abu-Ghraib: Detention and torture in Iraq. March. Available at: www.amnestyinternational.be/doc/IMG/pdf/MDE140012006_IRAK.pdf.

Amnesty International (2014) Escape from hell: Torture and sexual slavery in Islamic State captivity in Iraq. December. Available at: https://www.amnesty.org/en/documents/mde14/021/2014/en/.

Begikhani N (2005) Honour-based violence among the Kurds: The case of Iraqi Kurdistan. In: Welchman L and Hussain S (eds) *Honour: Crimes, Paradigms and Violence against Women*. London and New York: Zed Books.

Begikhani N et al. (2010) Final report: Honour-based violence (HBV) and honour-based killings in Iraqi Kurdistan and in the Kurdish diaspora in the UK. Centre for Gender and Violence Research, University of Bristol/Roehampton University/Kurdish Women's Rights Watch.

Cockburn C (1999) *The Space Between Us: Negotiating Identities in Conflict*. London: Zed Books.

Cockburn C (2004) The continuum of violence: A gender perspective on war and peace. In: Giles W and Hyndman J (eds) *Sites of Violence: Gender and Conflict Zones*. Berkeley: University of California Press, pp. 24–44.

Cockburn C (2007) *From Where We Stand: War, Women's Activism and Feminist Analysis*. London: Zed Books.

Efrati N (2012) *Women in Iraq: Past Meets Present*. New York: Columbia University Press.

Enloe C (1987) Feminist thinking about war, militarism and peace. In: Hess BB and Feree MM (eds) *Analyzing Gender: A Handbook of Social Science Research*. Newbury Park, CA: Sage, pp. 526–547.

Enloe C (1990) *Bananas, Beaches and Bases: Making Feminist Sense of International Politics*. Berkeley: University of California Press.

Enloe C (2000) *Maneuvers: The International Politics of Militarizing Women's Lives*. Berkeley: University of California Press.

Foreign and Commonwealth Office (2002) Saddam Hussein: Crimes and human rights abuses. November. Available at: usiraq.procon.org/sourcefiles/FCOSaddamdossier.pdf.

Hardi C (2011) *Gendered Experiences of Genocide: Anfal Survivors in Kurdistan-Iraq*. Farnham: Ashgate.

Heartland Alliance for Human Needs and Human Rights (2011) Institutionalized violence against women and girls in Iraq. Available at: www.scribd.com/doc/49420024/Institutionalized-Violence-Against-Women-and-Girls-in-Iraq.

Human Rights Watch (1993) Genocide in Iraq, the Anfal campaign against the Kurds. Available at: www.hrw.org/reports/1993/iraqanfal/.

Human Rights Watch (2004) The road to Abu Ghraib. June. Available at: www.hrw.org/sites/default/files/reports/usa0604.pdf.

Human Rights Watch (2009) Iraq: Stop killings for homosexual conduct. 17 August. Available at: www.hrw.org/news/2009/08/17/iraq-stop-killings-homosexual-conduct.

Human Rights Watch (2011) At a crossroads: Human rights in Iraq eight years after the US-led invasion. February. Available at: www.hrw.org/sites/default/files/reports/iraq0211W.pdf.

Human Rights Watch (2014) "No one is safe": Abuses of women in Iraq's criminal justice system. Available at: www.hrw.org/reports/2014/02/06/no-one-safe.

Human Rights Watch (2015) ISIS escapees describe systematic rape: Yezidi survivors in need of urgent care. 14 April. Available at: www.hrw.org/news/2015/04/14/iraq-isis-escapees-describe-systematic-rape.

Kanie M (2015) Rethinking roots of rising violence against women in the Kurdistan Region of Iraq. *HIVOS, Knowledge Programme Civil Society in West Asia; Special Bulletin*, April.

Long S (2012) Massacre of emos in Iraq goes to the core of damaged society. *The Guardian*, 18 March. Available at: www.theguardian.com/commentisfree/2012/mar/18/iraq-massacre-emos-killing-gay.

Mlodoch K (2009) We want to be remembered as strong women and not as shepherds—Anfal surviving women in Kurdistan-Iraq struggling for agency and acknowledgement. *Journal of Middle East Women's Studies* 8(1): 63–91.

Mojab S (ed.) (2001) *Women of a Non-Nation State: The Kurds*. Mazda, CA: Costa Mesa.

Mojab S (2003) Kurdish women in the zone of genocide and gendercide. *Al-Raida* XXI(3): 20–25.

Office of International Women's Issues (2003) Iraqi women under Saddam's regime: A population silenced. 20 March. Available at: 2001-2009.state.gov/g/wi/rls/18877.htm.

Omar S (1994) Honour, shame and dictatorship. In: Hazelton F (ed.) *Iraq since the Gulf War: Prospects for Democracy*. London and New York: Zed Books.

Rohde A (2010) *State–Society Relations in Ba'thist Iraq*. London and New York: Routledge.

Russell B (2002) Blair hears Iraqi women's stories of abuse and suffering. *The Independent*, 3 December.

UNAMI OHCHR (2014) Report on the protection of civilians in armed conflict in Iraq. 6 July–10 September. Available at: www.ohchr.org/Documents/Countries/IQ/UNAMI_OHCHR_POC_Report_FINAL_6July_10September2014.pdf.

UN News Centre (2015) Sold for a packet of cigarettes: UN envoy fights to help women suffering sexual violence in the Middle East. 18 June. Available at: www.un.org/apps/news/story.asp?NewsID=51196#.VZ1NjO1VhHw.

White House Office of the Press Secretary (2003) President Bush meets with Iraqi women leaders. 17 November. Available at: georgewbush-whitehouse.archives.gov/news/releases/2003/11/20031117-4.html.

Wibben A (2004) Feminist international relations: Old debates and new directions. *Brown Journal of World Affairs* 10(2): 97–114.

Wibben A (2011) *Feminist Security Studies: A Narrative Approach*. London and New York: Routledge.

69. BETRAYED BY THE ANGEL
What Happens When Violence Knocks and Politeness Answers?
DEBRA ANNE DAVIS (2004)

Mrs. W. arranged us alphabetically, so I spent my entire third-grade year sitting next to a sadist named Hank C. Every day, several times a day, whenever the teacher wasn't looking, Hank would jab his pencil into my arm. He was shorter than me, and I'd look down on his straight brown hair and he'd glance up at me with a crooked smile and then he'd do it: jab jab jab.

He'd get up from his seat often to sharpen the point; I'd sit in my seat in dread, listening to the churn of the pencil sharpener in the back of the room, knowing the pencil tip would be dulled not by paper but by my skin. I'd go home with little gray circles, some with dots of red in the center, Hank's own bull's-eye, all up and down my left arm. I remember it was my left arm because I can see myself sitting next to him, wearing one of the outfits, not just a dress, but an *outfit*—matching socks, hair ribbon, even underwear—that my mother would put me in each morning. I look at him and hope *maybe not this time, please no more*, and he glances at me (or doesn't—he got so good at it that after a while he could find my arm without looking) and: jab jab jab. Each time I hope he won't and each time he does.

Mostly I'd just endure. *This is what is happening; there's nothing I can do about it.* One day after school I decided that I couldn't take it anymore. I decided that I would tell the teacher the very next time he did it. Of course I'd have to wait for him to do it again first. I felt relief.

When I went to school the next day, we had a substitute teacher instead of Mrs. W. I lost some of my resolve, but not all of it. Hank seemed in better spirits than usual. He started in soon after the bell rang while we were doing workbooks. Jab jab jab. I stood and walked to the front of the room, my lime green dress brushing against the gray metal of the teacher's desk. "Hank always pokes me with the pencil," I told the stranger. My voice was much smaller than I'd hoped. I'd said it like a whisper; I'd meant to sound mad.

"You go back to your seat and tell me if he does it again," she said. And that was it. I never could work up the nerve again to walk the 15 feet to the big desk and blurt out the nature of the boy's crime: Always, he pokes me. I continued going home each day with pencil wounds.

The problem, I think, was that I simply wasn't mad at him. When I went to tell the teacher, my voice wasn't loud in a burst of righteous anger; it was demure. I didn't want to bother her. Maybe I didn't want to see Hank punished. Maybe I didn't think I deserved not to be hurt. Maybe it just didn't seem that big an aberration. Even though no one else was being poked at every day, maybe this was just my lot in life.

I'm 25 years old. I'm alone in my apartment. I hear a knock. I open the door and see a face I don't know. The man scares me, I don't know why. My first impulse is to shut the door. But I stop myself: You can't do something like that. It's rude.

I don't invite him in, but suddenly he is pushing the door and stepping inside. I don't want him to come in; he hasn't waited to be invited. I push the door to close it, but I don't push very hard; I keep remembering that it's not polite to slam a door in someone's face.

He is inside. He slams the door shut himself and pushes me against the wall. My judgment: He is very rude. I make this conscious decision: Since he is being rude, it is okay for me to be rude back. I reach for the doorknob; I want to open the door and shove him outside and then slam the door in his face, rude or not, I don't care now. But frankly, I don't push him aside with much determination. I've made the mental choice to be rude, but I haven't been able to muster the physical bluntness the act requires.

Or maybe I realize the game is lost already. He is stronger than I am, I assume, as men have always been stronger. I have no real chance of pushing him aside. No real chance of it unless I am *very* angry. And I'm not very angry. I'm a little bit angry.

But, despite the fact that I didn't shove with much force, *he* is angry with *me*. I know why: It's because I've been rude to him. He is insulted. I am a bit ashamed.

We fall into our roles quite easily, two people who have never met each other, two people raised in the same culture, a man and a woman. As it turns out, a rapist and his victim.

I asked my students, college freshmen, these two questions once: What did your parents teach you that you will teach your own kids? What did they teach you that you won't teach your kids?

One young woman said, "My parents always told me to be kind to everyone. I won't teach my children that. It's not always good to be kind to everyone."

She was so young, but she knew this. Why did it take me so long to learn?

Working on this stuff makes me a little crazy. Sitting at my computer typing for hours about being raped and how it made me feel and makes me feel makes me distracted, jittery—both because I drink too much strong coffee and because writing goes beyond imagining into reliving.

I decided I needed to reread Virginia Woolf. I'd been making notes to myself for a while—"angel" or just "Woolf" scribbled on scraps of paper on my desk and in the front pocket of my backpack, to go buy the book, the book with the angel in it. (I could feel her hovering as I typed; I know the exact color and texture of her flowing gown.)

> *What could be easier than to write articles and to buy Persian cats with the profits? But wait a moment. Articles have to be about something. Mine, I seem to remember, was about a novel by a famous man. And while I was writing this review, I discovered that if I were going to review books I should need to do battle with a certain phantom. And the phantom was a woman, and when I came to know her better I called her after the heroine of a famous poem, "The Angel in the House." It was she who used to come between me and my paper when I was writing reviews. It was she who bothered me and wasted my time and so tormented me that at last I killed her*

> —"Professions of Women"
> *Virginia Woolf (1931)*

There was TV. Reruns of reruns of *I Love Lucy* and *The Flintstones. I Dream of Jeannie. Bewitched.* I can't even think of a show from my youth that had a single female character who was smart, self-confident, and respected by others. My sister and I would lie on our stomachs, heads propped on fuzzy cotton pillows with leopard-skin covers, watching, indiscriminate, mildly entertained, for hours.

Samantha was smarter than Darrin, it was obvious, but she hid her intelligence just as she hid her magical powers, powers Darrin didn't have, powers that made him angry. Samantha's mother, Endora, used her powers with confidence and even flair, but she cackled and wore flowing bright green dresses and too much makeup; she was a mother-in-law. I was supposed to learn how to be like Samantha, not like Endora, and I did.

None of this is news, of course; we can all see those sexist stereotypes quite easily now. But just because I can see, understand, and believe that something is false, that it's not right, now, doesn't mean it won't continue to be a part of me, always.

(Barbara Eden calling Larry Hagman "Master." How many times did I hear *that?*)

"It's big," I say. I turn my head up. I smile. Why do I say this? I ask myself, even then. Well it is big. . . . And I want to flatter him, so he won't hurt me any more than he already plans to. I, yes, I am trying to flirt with him. I've learned about flirting and how it works and what it can do. (It can get people to like you, to do things for you, to treat you well.) It's a skill I have honed. And I'm using it now. To save my life. (And, hey, it worked! Unless of course he hadn't planned to kill me in the first place.)

He smiles down at me (I'm on my knees, naked, leaning against my own bed, my hands tied behind me, my head in his crotch) proudly.

> *You who come of a younger and happier generation may not have heard of her—you may not know what I mean by the Angel in the House. I will describe her as shortly as I can. She was intensely sympathetic. She was immensely charming. She was utterly unselfish. She excelled in the difficult arts of family life. She sacrificed herself daily. If there was chicken, she took the leg; if there was a draught she sat in it—in short she was so constituted that she never had a mind or a wish of her own, but preferred to sympathize always with the minds and wishes of others.*

Back when he was pulling my jeans off, this is what happened: He kneeled behind me, reached around the waistband to the fly, and pulled until all the buttons popped open. Then he crawled back a few feet and began to pull the jeans off from the ankles—a stupid way to try to take someone else's pants off, but I didn't say anything.

He was having a little trouble because the pants weren't slipping off as, obviously, he'd envisioned they would. He tugged and then began yanking. "Stop fighting!" he growled at me. Ooh, *that* pissed me off! "I'm not *fighting!*" I sassed back at him. And I wasn't. How dare he! Accuse me, I mean. Of fighting.

> *Above all—I need not say it—she was pure. Her purity was supposed to be her chief beauty—her blushes, her great grace. In those days—the last of Queen Victoria— every house had its Angel. And when I came to write I encountered her with the very first words. The shadow of her wings fell on my page; I heard the rustling of her skirts in the room. Directly, that is to say, I took my pen in hand to review that novel by a famous man, she slipped behind me and whispered: "My dear, you are a young woman. You are writing about a book that has been written by a man. Be sympathetic; be tender; flatter; deceive; use all the arts and wiles of our sex. Never let anybody guess that you have a mind of your own. Above all, be pure."*

One thing being raped did to me: It caused me to be sometimes rude to strangers. Not out of anger, though, but out of fear.

I was 25 when I was raped. I'm 35 now. This happened last week.

I was in a coffee shop, reading a textbook for a class I'm teaching. After a while, I took a little break and brought my now-empty cup back to the counter. There was a guy at the counter waiting for his drink. "What are you reading?" he asked. He had a big smile on his face, a friendly smile. He wasn't creepy; he was being friendly. I sensed these things. "It's a textbook," I answered. I was looking at the floor now, not at his face any longer.

"Oh! What class are you studying for?" he asked.

"It's a class I'm teaching," I said. Oh no.

"Where do you teach? At _____ College?"

"No," I said flatly and tried to smile a little. I felt nervous, pinned. I knew the conversation wasn't over, but I simply turned and went back to my little

table. He stood there at the counter, probably watching me walk away and wondering why I wouldn't answer his question, why, against the unspoken code of our culture, I hadn't at least finished the exchange with a friendly word or a wave. But there was no way I would tell him (or you, notice) where I taught or what I taught or anything else about me. And there was no way I could explain this to him courteously; the whole exchange made me too nervous. I certainly wasn't angry at him, but I was a bit afraid. And right there in the coffee shop, I felt the presence of my angel, the rustling of her skirts: "Be sympathetic," I heard her reprimand me, sweetly. "Be tender. And pure." I couldn't be polite, but I did feel guilty.

Though I wasn't finished with my reading, when I got back to the table, I gathered up my things and left.

> *I turned upon her and caught her by the throat. I did my best to kill her. My excuse, if I were to be had up in a court of law, would be that I acted in self-defense. Had I not killed her she would have killed me.*

He bent down to gently arrange the towel over my bare and oozing body, after it was all over with. "You were so good-looking, I just couldn't resist," he told me.

And for the first time in my life, I didn't enjoy being complimented on my physical appearance. Why, I wondered at that moment, had I ever wanted to be considered pretty—or kind, or good? Compliments mean nothing. Or worse, compliments mean this. What good does such a compliment do *me*?

> *Thus, whenever I felt the shadow of her wing or the radiance of her halo upon my page, I took up the inkpot and flung it at her. She died hard. Her fictitious nature was of great assistance to her. It is far harder to kill a phantom than a reality.*

I haven't killed her. Yet. Maybe I need to go out and get an inkpot to fling at her. Hmm, I wonder how she'd hold up against a flying laptop. I can imagine hurling this 10-pound black plastic box at her (she's up in the corner, to my right). It easily tears through the soft blue, rough cotton of her ankle-length gown (she has a long, thin white lace apron tied around her waist). The computer crashes into the space where the walls and ceiling meet; she falls to the carpet. And then what? She's dead. And how do I feel about that? Guilty? Relieved? Well, I don't think I'd want to stuff my pockets with rocks and wade into a river. (Did Woolf ever really kill her angel? Or is it the angel that killed her?)

What I want to know is this: If I'm ever physically attacked again, will I fight to save myself? And will I be fighting out of righteous anger or out of unstrung fear?

What I need to know is this: Is the angel really the one who needs to die?

"I guess I'll get twenty years in the penitentiary for this," he says and waves his hand across the room at me.

Twenty years? Just for this? Just for doing this to me? Twenty years is a really long time.

In fact, he got 35 years. On a plea bargain. The police, the lawyers, the judge—the state, the legal system—even he, the criminal, the rapist, thought he deserved decades in jail for what he'd done to me. Why didn't I?

70. LISA'S RITUAL, AGE 10
GRACE CAROLINE BRIDGES (1994)

Afterwards when he has finished
lots of mouthwash helps
to get rid of her father's cigarette taste.
She runs a hot bath
   to soak away the pain
      like red dye leaking from her
         school dress in the washtub.

She doesn't cry
When the bathwater cools she adds more hot.
She brushes her teeth for a long time.

Then she finds the corner of her room,
curls against it. There the wall is
hard and smooth
as teacher's new chalk, white
as a clean bedsheet. Smells
fresh. Isn't sweaty, hairy, doesn't stick
to skin. Doesn't hurt much
when she presses her small backbone
into it. The wall is steady
while she falls away:
   first the hands lost

arms dissolving feet gone
   the legs dis- jointed
      body cracking down
         the center like a fault
          she falls inside
            slides down like
dust   like kitchen dirt
          slips off
the dustpan into
         noplace
a place where
nothing happens,
nothing ever happened.

When she feels the cool
wall against her cheek
she doesn't want to
come back. Doesn't want to
think about it.
The wall is quiet, waiting.
It is tall like a promise
only better.

CHAPTER 11

STATE, LAW, AND
SOCIAL POLICY

As we note in earlier chapters, societal institutions are established patterns of social behavior organized around particular needs and purposes. Institutions structure aspects of life in families and communities, and also produce social discourses or "regimes of truth" that create meaning and construct our notions of knowledge and truth. Gender, race, class, and other identities associated with systems of inequality and privilege structure social institutions, creating different effects on different people. The state, the focus of this chapter, is a major social institution organized to maintain systems of legitimized power and authority in society. The state plays an important role in both teaching and enforcing social values. It is a very powerful institution that has profound implications for people's everyday lives. A key focus of this chapter is the interaction between the state and gender relations in society. The state conceptualizes individuals as women and men and creates policies and practices that shape, privilege, and discriminate based on these gender categories. As a result, those who are gender nonconforming are not easily dealt with by the state and suffer the consequences of not fitting into these taken-for-granted models of citizenship.

The state is an abstract concept that refers to all forms of social organization representing official power in society: the government, law and social policy, the courts and the criminal justice system, the military, and the police. The state determines how people are selected to govern others and controls the systems of governance they must use. With considerable authority in maintaining social order, the state influences how power is exercised within society. The definition of state here differs from state as a geographic region, such as California or Ohio.

Because the state is a conduit for various patterns of social inequity, it does not always fairly regulate and control social order. Historically, white women and women and men of color—and especially those with little economic privilege—have been treated poorly by the state. There are still many problems and challenges at all levels of the political system. However, the state has also been a tool for addressing historical forms of social, political, and economic inequalities through laws and social policy (as evidenced by civil rights and affirmative action legislation). In this way, the state works both to maintain sources of inequality and as an avenue for social justice. As already discussed in other chapters, the legal gains of the mid- and late-twentieth century have been important in improving the lives of women and people of color. Title IX of the Education Amendments of 1972, which prohibits sex discrimination of all kinds (not just concerning athletics) at institutions that receive federal funds, is a case in point.

As already discussed in Chapter 2, the state works with other institutions, assigns roles, and distributes resources. In particular, it regulates other institutions, provides guidelines for expected behaviors, and channels resources and power. For example, it regulates the family (such as the Family Medical Leave Act, which recognizes the caregiving activities for only certain individuals recognized as "family"), education (such as Title IX), the economic system (such as antitrust laws that prevent monopolies and antidiscrimination policies), and religion (such as state rules for the separation of church and state). The state as nation-state also participates in international policymaking that has important implications for global economic development and military strategy. When the United States refuses to ratify international treaties such as CEDAW (the Convention on the Elimination of All Forms of Discrimination Against Women) or the Kyoto Treaty on environmental quality because it seeks to protect U.S. statutes and corporations and because the current president as of this writing resists scientific evidence that human activities cause global climate change, these actions have significant impact globally. The United States is often seen as a powerful symbol of urban secular decadence, with the emancipation of women a central feature. This highlights the importance of gender-sensitive conceptions of international aid and development.

Beyond national levels of state policy in the United States is the United Nations (UN), which has tremendous influence on global politics. Scholars emphasize that even though notions of women's "rescue" have been deployed to generate consent for military missions in Afghanistan and to some extent in Iraq, gender concerns remain peripheral to regional and international politics. Although the right to gender equality has been affirmed in international law, many nations still explicitly discriminate against women (including the United States). UN Resolution 1325 on women and peace and security was adopted by the UN Security Council in 2000 in response to this worldwide gender discrimination. As mentioned in Chapter 10, this resolution addresses gender-based violence against girls and women, especially in war zones. It also affirms the important role of women in the prevention and resolution of conflicts, peace negotiations, peace-building, peacekeeping, humanitarian response, and post-conflict reconstruction, and stresses the importance of women's equal participation and full involvement in all efforts for the maintenance and promotion of peace and security.

GOVERNMENT AND REPRESENTATION

Although the terms government and state tend to be used interchangeably, the government is actually one of the institutions that makes up the state. It creates laws and procedures that govern society and its citizens and is often referred to as the political system. It is important to note that the U.S. government is purported to be a democracy based on the

RESOURCE EXTRACTION IMPACTS

Luhui Whitebear

Natural resource extraction has devastating effects not only on the environment, but on Native/First Nation women in the United States and Canada as well. The exploitation of Indigenous lands and bodies have direct links to each other. In many places that extraction occurs, temporary camps are set up for the workers. These have been commonly referred to as "man camps" as they mostly house men. In the areas where these man camps are, rates of abduction, rape, sex trafficking, drug trafficking, and other related crimes increase (Nagle & Steinem). The camps may disappear, but the issues remain.

To further complicate matters, many loopholes exist in federal laws and policies that make it hard for non-tribal offenders to be prosecuted on tribal lands. The recent film *Windriver* highlights these loopholes as well as man camps and the disappearance of indigenous women. The hashtag #MMIW was created on social media by First Nation women in Canada to help raise awareness of the epidemic of murdered and missing indigenous women. The movement has gained momentum in the United States as well, but there is still much work to be done to fully grasp the extent of the impact in both countries. Natural resource extraction has resulted in pipelines traveling between Canada and the United States carrying not only oil and liquid natural gas, but a path of violence as well. The borders between the countries, states, and tribal territories do not act as barriers to this violence. Rather, violence becomes more difficult to address due to the jurisdictional issues that arise with borders.

Other natural resource extractions, such as strip mining, uranium mining, and water extraction, carry similar violence with them. Uranium and strip mining have polluted lands and bodies as shown by the high rates of chronic disease and illness on and near reservations on which these activities occur (Lewis, Hoover, & MacKenzie). The commodification of bottled water has left many communities with less access to clean water as well as the environmental impacts of the factories used to bottle the water.

Natural resource extraction changes the entire landscape in which it occurs. It takes generations to recover from the damage, and in some cases, areas are unrecoverable. Much like the land, Native/First Nation women have been changed dramatically. For the women not directly touched by these violences, they still feel the impact and are often wondering if they are next. However, Native/First Nation women are also the ones who are first to take a stand collectively against violence to both body and land. They find ways to survive and live through the realities that natural resource extraction brings to their communities.

Mapping Violence Activity Idea

1. Explore the U.S. Energy Information Administration energy mapping system at: https://www.eia.gov/maps/
2. Explore the map of U.S. reservations at: https://www.bia.gov/sites/bia.gov/files/assets/public/pdf/idc013422.pdf
3. Review the Violence Against Women Act Reauthorization of 2013 as related to tribes at: https://www.justice.gov/tribal/violence-against-women-act-vawa-reauthorization-2013-0
4. Reflect through a free write and/or small group discussion about how the maps relate as well as how you would address the violences mentioned earlier given the parameters of the law. How might this be different in Canada?

For More Information

> https://www.mmiwdatabase.com/
> http://www.cbc.ca/missingandmurdered/
> http://www.honorearth.org/sexual_violence
> http://www.niwrc.org/resource-topic/
> missing-and-murdered-native-women

References

Lewis, J., Hoover, J., & MacKenzie, D. (2017). "Mining and Environmental Health Disparities in Native American Communities." *Current Environmental Health Reports*, 4(2), 130–141. http://doi.org/10.1007/s40572-017-0140-5

Nagle, M. K., & Steinem, G. (2016, September 29). "Sexual Assault on the Pipeline." *Boston Globe*. https://www.bostonglobe.com/opinion/2016/09/29/sexual-assault-pipeline/3jQscLWRcmD12cfefQTNsL/story.html

principle of equal representation, but it is not representative of all people, and those who participate as elected officials do not necessarily represent all interests equitably. Recent attempts to restructure the electoral college to dilute numbers of low-income and/or people of color in any given constituency is a case in point. In addition, "citizen" is a constructed category that must be understood in historical context. Who is considered a U.S. citizen, for example, has changed over time along with the politics of immigration and the establishment of borders after the wars of the last centuries. President Trump is especially keen to revise and repeal immigration policy and set up strict notions of citizenship. He made immigration the centerpiece of his presidential campaign and since his election, as of this writing, he has banned nationals of eight mostly majority-Muslim countries from entering the United States; reduced refugee admissions to the lowest level; reversed the decline of unauthorized immigrants and for some time separated children from their parents; and cancelled the Deferred Action for Childhood Arrivals (DACA) program, which provides work authorization and temporary relief from deportation to unauthorized immigrants brought to the United States as children. He also has made disparaging remarks about immigrants and their families and threatened to build a wall separating the U.S. and Mexico and increase border patrol surveillance. This administration's support for legislation to dramatically cut legal immigration and reshape the selection of foreign-born workers has been met with public outrage and resistance. In response the courts and state and local jurisdictions have limited their cooperation with federal immigration enforcement, and Congress has slowed or stalled some of the administration's policies. The shifting face of the Supreme Court toward a more conservative ideological stance, however, will most likely continue to inform immigration policy and these important questions of citizenship.

The reading "Speech on Sweden's Feminist Foreign Policy," the text of the speech by Sweden's foreign minister Margot Wallström, discusses immigrant rights and Sweden's policy, which is guided by feminist ethics. It recognizes that gender inequalities often shape immigration laws and result in differential experiences for women compared to men when attempting to gain legal status. Wallström recognizes that immigration legislation must protect human rights for women.

Women have had a complicated relationship to the Constitution. The liberal doctrine of representation first included women as rights-bearing citizens and represented them as members of the body politic. They came to be excluded for a variety of political reasons, justified in part because the dominant culture assumed that politics and citizenship were purely masculine domains. The "founding fathers" believed that women's political identity should be restricted because their presence in politics was immoral, corruptive, and potentially disruptive, and that women should be represented by fathers, husbands, or brothers. It was understood that women should be confined to the private sphere of the home where they would be dependent on men, and, as a result, they had no separate legal identity and were legal beings only through their relationship to a man. They had no claims to citizenship rights as women until well into the nineteenth century. This is the notion of *femme couverte* discussed later.

As you know from Chapter 1, the Seneca Falls convention in 1848 produced the Declaration of Sentiments and Resolutions that aimed to ensure citizenship rights for women, even though they would have to wait until 1920 and the passage of the Nineteenth Amendment to the U.S. Constitution to receive the vote. In 1868, however, the Fourteenth Amendment was ratified, asserting that no state shall "make or enforce any law which will abridge the privileges or immunities of citizens of the United States, nor . . . deprive any person of life, liberty, or property without due process of law, nor deny to any person within its jurisdiction the equal protection of laws." This "person" was assumed to be male, and, as a result, women still could not vote, and the government did not (and, many people would argue, still does not) extend the same protection of the law to women as it did to men. Susan B. Anthony, one of the first feminists, who helped write the Declaration of Sentiments and Resolutions, wanted to test her belief that the Fourteenth Amendment should give women, as citizens, the right to vote. She voted in an election in Rochester, New York, and was fined. Hoping to push the case to the Supreme Court, Anthony refused to pay the fine. The case, however, was dropped in order to avoid this test of law. In the Anthony reading "Constitutional Argument," she argues her right to vote as a citizen under the terms guaranteed by the Fourteenth Amendment. This excerpt, published in 1898, is from a speech Anthony gave in 1873.

In 1923 the Equal Rights Amendment (ERA) was introduced into Congress to counter the inadequacies of the Fourteenth Amendment concerning women and citizenship. The ERA affirms that both women and men hold equally all of the rights guaranteed by the U.S. Constitution. It would provide a remedy for gender discrimination at the constitutional level and provide equal legal status to women for the first time in our country's history. It was rewritten in the 1940s to read: "Equality of rights under the law shall not be denied or abridged by the United States or by any state on account of sex"; and it eventually passed Congress (almost 50 years later) in 1972. Unfortunately, it failed to be ratified by the states and suffered a serious defeat in 1982. The most important effect of the ERA would have been to clarify the status of gender discrimination for the courts, whose decisions still show confusion about how to deal with such claims. "Sex" would become a suspect classification like race. It would require the same high level of "strict scrutiny" and have to meet the same high level of justification—a "necessary" relation to a "compelling" state interest—as the classification of race.

Although survey after survey showed overwhelming public support for the ERA among women and men, it was officially defeated on June 30, 1982, when it failed to be ratified by the states. It fell three states short of the 38 states needed for ratification. The ERA continues to be introduced into each session of Congress, but passage of the amendment has yet to regain the momentum it did during the 1970s (even though back in 1988 a Harris poll showed 78 percent approval). In order for the ERA to be fully amended, two-thirds of each house in Congress must pass it first, followed by its ratification by 38 states. As opposition to the ERA grew, some states retracted their prior ratification, and others, such as Illinois, changed laws in order to make ratification more difficult. Indiana became the 35th and last state to ratify the ERA in 1977, and the Republican Party removed ERA support from its platform. Many years later, ratification efforts continue, with women and men in many of the unratified states working under the "three-state strategy." This strategy argues that because there was no actual time limit for ratification in the original ERA, the amendment remains only three states short of official ratification. Currently 19 states have state ERAs or equal rights guarantees in their constitutions, and many groups are working together toward the legislation of the Equal Rights Amendment at all levels. These groups include the League of Women Voters U.S., American Association of University Women, Business & Professional Women/USA, National Organization for Women, National Women's Political Caucus, ERA Campaign, and the Equal Rights Amendment Organization.

Opponents of the ERA mistakenly claimed that the amendment was anti-family, reporting that it would deny a woman's right to be supported by her husband and encourage

LEARNING ACTIVITY

THE LEAGUE OF WOMEN VOTERS

The League of Women Voters was founded by Carrie Chapman Catt in 1920 during the convention of the National American Woman Suffrage Association, just six months before the Nineteenth Amendment was ratified. In its early years, the league advocated for collective bargaining, child labor laws, minimum wage, compulsory education, and equal opportunity for women in government and industry. Today the league is still involved in advocacy for justice, working on such issues as Medicare reform, campaign finance reform, and environmental preservation, as well as continuing the work begun more than 80 years ago to encourage women to use their political voices. To learn more about the League of Women Voters or to join the league, visit its website at www.lwv.org.

women to desert motherhood. There was also worry that it would legislate abortion and gay and lesbian rights as well as send women into combat. In addition, anti-ERA sentiments were voiced by business interests (such as members of the insurance industry) that profited from gender discrimination. The media sensationalized the issue and did not accurately report about what the ERA would and would not do, and conservative political organizations spent a lot of money and many hours organizing against it.

Most feminist leaders today agree that women would be better off if the ERA had been ratified in 1977. They would have received better opportunities for equality and would have been supported by stronger laws fighting gender discrimination in employment, education, and other areas of society. Some people feel that we no longer need a constitutional amendment because piecemeal federal and state laws have been enacted to protect against gender discrimination. However, as we have seen, federal laws are no longer as safe as they had been and can be repealed by a simple majority. Similarly, courts change policy as the makeup of the courts changes. A constitutional amendment requires three-quarters of the legislature to vote to repeal it. Although many people assume the continuity of women's rights, the U.S. Supreme Court is central in maintaining or potentially overturning several taken-for-granted rights. These rights include reproductive privacy, affirmative action, protection against gender-based discrimination, family and medical leave, and quality health care services.

An illustration of how the government has handled women and citizenship concerns the treatment of women who have married non-U.S. citizens. Prior to the mid-1920s, nonnative-born women who married male U.S. citizens automatically became American, and native-born women who married male non-U.S. citizens automatically lost their citizenship and were expected to reside in their husband's country. They also lost their right to vote, once women had been given the vote in 1920. When laws were passed to retain women's citizenship in the mid-1920s, still only men were able to pass on citizenship to their children. Laws equalizing citizenship on these issues were eventually passed in the mid-1930s. As already discussed, citizenship and who is classed as a citizen remains a highly volatile debate and often serves as a major conduit for inequality in many societies.

In addition to rights, citizenship entails such obligations as taxation, jury duty, and military service. Although women have shared taxation with men, in the past they had been prevented from service and/or exempted from jury duty because of their role as mothers and housewives. It was not until the 1970s that the Supreme Court declared that juries had to be representative of the community. Even then, juries were often racially biased

ACTIVIST PROFILE

WILMA MANKILLER

With her election as chief of the Cherokee Nation, Wilma Mankiller took both a step forward and a step backward. Although Mankiller was the first woman to serve as chief of a major Native American tribe in modern times, her election recalled the importance women had among the Cherokee before colonization by Europeans. Precontact Cherokee society was matrifocal and matrilineal. Women owned the property and maintained the home and were intimately involved in tribal governance.

Mankiller first became committed to involvement in Native American rights in 1969 when Native American activists, including some of her own siblings, occupied Alcatraz island in San Francisco Bay. The 19-month occupation became a turning point in Mankiller's life. She became director of the Native American Youth Center in Oakland, California, and in 1973 she watched as her brother joined other Native American activists as they held off FBI agents for 72 days at Wounded Knee, South Dakota.

Following a divorce, Mankiller returned to her family's land in Oklahoma and began to work for the Cherokee Nation; as an economic stimulus coordinator, she had the task of encouraging Cherokee people to train in environmental health and science and then return to their communities to put their knowledge to use. In 1981 she became director of the Cherokee Nation Community Development Department, and her work was so successful that she attracted the attention of Chief Ross Swimmer, who asked her to run as his deputy chief in 1983.

Despite sexist rhetoric and verbal threats from opponents, Swimmer and Mankiller won. In 1985 Swimmer was named head of the Bureau of Indian Affairs by President Ronald Reagan, and Mankiller became chief of the Cherokee Nation. In 1987 Mankiller ran on her own and was elected chief in her own right. That year, *Ms.* magazine named her Woman of the Year. She was re-elected in 1991, winning with 83 percent of the vote. During her tenure as chief, Mankiller focused on addressing high unemployment and low education rates among Cherokee people, improving community health care, implementing housing initiatives and child and youth projects, and developing the economy of northeastern Oklahoma. She created the Institute for Cherokee Literacy, emphasizing the need for Cherokee people to retain their traditions. She did not run for re-election in 1995. In 1998 President Bill Clinton awarded her the Presidential Medal of Freedom. She died at her Oklahoma home in 2010.

such that it was not unusual for an African American to face an all-white jury. A 1986 Supreme Court ruling stated that juries could not be constituted on the basis of race, and a 1994 ruling declared that gender too could not be used as a basis for jury competence. The obligation for military service, which many women have wanted to share with men, is outlined in more detail later in the chapter. Of course, women have served in auxiliary roles as nurses, transport drivers, and dispatchers for many years and are now able to participate in combat positions within most divisions of the armed services.

Although women tend to be as involved as men in electoral politics (and sometimes even more involved) in terms of voting, showing support, and volunteering for campaigns, there are markedly fewer women involved in official political positions associated with campaigns. Women still constitute a relatively smaller number of candidates for local, state, and national offices, and their presence is greater at the local than the national level. As political offices become more visible, higher level, better paid, and more authoritative or powerful, there are fewer women in these positions. There are several explanations for this

WOMEN IN POLITICAL LEADERSHIP IN LATIN AMERICA

Lisa Fernandez

For a moment in time, the countries of Latin America appeared to be leading the way for gender equality in politics: the president of Argentina was Cristina Fernandez de Kirchner, (2007–2015), Brazil had President Dilma Rousseff (2011–2016), President Laura Chinchilla in Costa Rica (2010–2014), and President Michelle Bachelet in Chile (2006–2010 and 2014–2018). All four women started their terms with high rates of popularity before public opinion plummeted due to accusations of unethical behavior. These progressive movements toward a feminist future led to the subjection of these women to misogynist, "macho" attitudes of critique by their peers, the media, the courts, and society. Although these politicians were initially seen as the hopeful alternative to male-dominated corrupted politics, each faced challenges due to the intersections of their gender and public leadership positions.

These cases turned into a challenge of values as these women moved away from traditional societal roles in the home to prominent, visible positions of power, politics, and economic decisions. This change in political status could be perceived as advancement for women in general, and that brings resistance from those who felt they were getting left behind: men. Patriarchy, a system in which men hold the power, has been the format for democracy since its implementation in the West. Even before these women began their terms, this societal norm of men in charge resulted in harsh media criticism and reinforced expectations of gendered disconnection of women to politics.

Each of the women was critiqued for her personality traits, family status, and appearance, all aspects that are often left out when covering male political candidates. Each was slandered publicly as an example of why men are the better choice in politics. President Kirchner called out this gender bias in a statement: "Implementing the misery and structural adjustment program once again requires the use of defamation and slander" (Gilbert 2016).

The slander took a particularly sexist turn in 2012 when a tabloid news magazine in Argentina, *Noticias*, published a scandalous cover drawing of President Kirchner appearing to be mid-orgasm; they further directed readers online to watch an animated video they created depicting her masturbating. This was an example of the gender equality paradox that existed in Latin America. Women were holding the highest positions of political office, yet the social attitudes—reducing women to sexual objects and hostility toward career women that is the basis of "machista" culture—have remained. Due to the extended media coverage of each of these women's court cases that led to the end of their terms, Latin America now faces uncertainty about the next wave of female presidents.

Learning Activity

Using an Internet search engine, find media coverage on current political scandals in your country. Are men and women discussed differently concerning appearance or personality? Does the coverage suggest different standards for women and men in political leadership in terms of how male and female politicians are regarded? Find examples of this from contemporary media. How are they described differently?

References

Gilbert, J. (2016, May 16). "Cristina Fernández de Kirchner, Ex-Argentine President, Indicted on Financial Charge." https://www.nytimes.com/2016/05/14/world/americas/cristina-fernandez-kirchner-indicted.html?smid=tw-nytimesworld&smtyp=cur

gap. Some suggest that women are just not interested and that they lack the credentials, but the main reasons are conflict between family and work roles, lack of political financing, and discrimination and sexist attitudes toward women in politics. Invariably social discourses about gender influence public opinion, and widespread sexism in media is one of the top problems facing women candidates and those from other marginalized identities.

The reading "I Knew America Was Not Ready for a Woman to Be President" by Angela N. Gist considers the 2016 presidential election through the lens of structural intersectionality: the notion that multiple identities come together to complicate and shape lived experiences. An important point here is that the workings of structural intersectionality do not necessary imply target group membership, but that people with combinations of various identities are all shaped by their confluence. In terms of the state and the political system in particular, Gist makes the case that "there is a social hierarchy embedded into the presidency [that] privileges masculinity and higher social class." She references Crenshaw's work about the ways social institutions—such as the state, the family, and the economic system—systematically work together to shape populations at the point of intersection between various identities. This influences the structure of the political systems as well as individuals' voting behaviors.

In 2016 Republican Donald Trump beat Democrat Hillary Rodham Clinton to take control of the Executive Office, the House of Representatives, and the Senate. However the midterm elections of 2018 that elected the 116th U.S. Congress shifted the balance of power in the House of Representatives from Republican to Democrat in the face of President Trump's low approval rating. As of this writing, 126 seats (23.5 percent) are held by women in the 116th U.S. Congress, a number that has more than quintupled since 1971 when women held only 3 percent of seats. Currently this includes 102 women (23 percent) in the House of Representatives; and 24 women (24 percent) in the Senate. In addition, two Democratic and two Republican women serve as Delegates to the House, representing Puerto Rico, American Samoa, the Virgin Islands, and Washington, D.C. Of the women serving in the 116th U.S. Congress, almost 40 percent are women of color, but the latter make up less than 10 percent of the total Congress. The 2018 election in particular saw the largest ever increase in elected women and people of color with half of all newly-elected Congressional representatives not identifying as white men. This is especially the case among Democrats. While 52 percent of newly-elected Democrats are women, only two or 4.5 percent of the incoming Republicans are women. Similarly, as with gender, the gain in representation for people of color is heavily concentrated in the Democratic Party with 34 percent of incoming House Democrats but only 2 percent of Republican colleagues identifying as people of color. The 116th Congress also saw some "firsts" with the election of the first Muslim and Native American women to Congress. This also marks the largest cohort of Black Congresswomen to ever serve: twenty two Black women in the House of Representatives. Vermont also narrowly missed the election of the first openly transgender governor.

Despite these historic gains in the 116th Congress with the largest numbers ever of women generally, and women of color in particular, these statistics still illustrate male and white domination in society and challenge the extent to which women and people of color are represented. The House of Representatives still consists of 60 percent white males, while the Senate is 71 percent white males. However, it is important to remember that women do not necessarily represent women's interests, just as people of color do not necessarily support issues that improve the status of non-white groups. Many feminists vote for men in political office over women candidates because they understand that a candidate's being female does not necessarily mean that her politics, or those of the party she represents, are pro-women.

The term *gender gap* in politics refers to differences between women and men in political attitudes and voting choices. Gender gaps are apparent in voting behavior, party identification, evaluations of presidential performances, and attitudes toward public policy issues.

WOMEN IN NATIONAL PARLIAMENTS, *Situation as of 1st June 2018*

WORLD CLASSIFICATION

Rank	Country	Lower or single House				Upper House or Senate			
		Elections	Seats*	Women	% W	Elections	Seats*	Women	% W
1	Rwanda	16.09.2013	80	49	61.3%	26.09.2011	26	10	38.5%
2	Cuba	11.03.2018	605	322	53.2%	—	—	—	—
3	Bolivia	12.10.2014	130	69	53.1%	12.10.2014	36	17	47.2%
4	Grenada	13.03.2018	15	7	46.7%	27.03.2013	13	2	15.4%
5	Namibia	29.11.2014	104	48	46.2%	08.12.2015	41	10	24.4%
6	Nicaragua	06.11.2016	92	42	45.7%	—	—	—	—
7	Costa Rica	04.02.2018	57	26	45.6%	—	—	—	—
8	Sweden	14.09.2014	349	152	43.6%	—	—	—	—
9	Mexico	07.06.2015	500	213	42.6%	01.07.2012	128	47	36.7%
10	South Africa[1]	07.05.2014	394	167	42.4%	21.05.2014	54	19	35.2%
11	Finland	19.04.2015	200	84	42.0%	—	—	—	—
12	Senegal	30.07.2017	165	69	41.8%	—	—	—	—
13	Norway	11.09.2017	169	70	41.4%	—	—	—	—
14	Mozambique	15.10.2014	250	99	39.6%	—	—	—	—
15	Spain	26.06.2016	350	137	39.1%	26.06.2016	266	101	38.0%
16	France	11.06.2017	577	225	39.0%	24.09.2017	348	102	29.3%
17	Argentina	22.10.2017	257	100	38.9%	22.10.2017	72	30	41.7%
18	Ethiopia	24.05.2015	547	212	38.8%	05.10.2015	153	49	32.0%
19	New Zealand	23.09.2017	120	46	38.3%	—	—	—	—
20	Iceland	28.10.2017	63	24	38.1%	—	—	—	—
21	Belgium	25.05.2014	150	57	38.0%	03.07.2014	60	30	50.0%
"	Ecuador	19.02.2017	137	52	38.0%	—	—	—	—
23	The F.Y.R. of Macedonia	11.12.2016	120	45	37.5%	—	—	—	—
24	Denmark	18.06.2015	179	67	37.4%	—	—	—	—
25	United Republic of Tanzania	25.10.2015	390	145	37.2%	—	—	—	—
102	United States of America	06.11.2018	431	102	23%	06.11.2018	100	24	24.0%

* Figures correspond to the number of seats currently filled in Parliament

1 - South Africa: The figures on the distribution of seats in the Upper House do not include the 36 special rotating delegates appointed on an ad hoc basis, and all percentages given are therefore calculated on the basis of the 54 permanent seats.

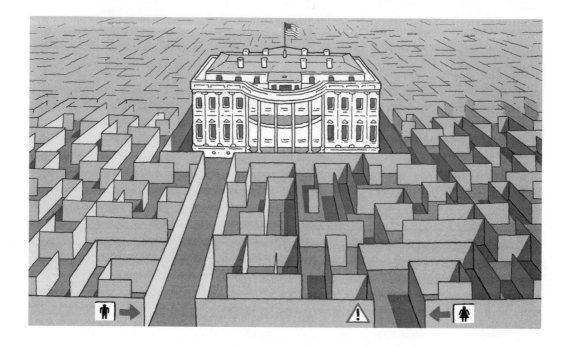

Polls find, for example, that compared with men, women are more likely to favor a more activist role for government; are more supportive of programs to guarantee health care and basic social services; more supportive of restrictions on firearms; more supportive of marriage equality; and more likely to favor legal abortion without restrictions.

In terms of the gender gap in voting behaviors, the measurable difference in the proportions of women and men who vote suggests that on the average women tend to lean toward the Democratic Party more than men because they are more concerned about such issues as education, welfare, health care, and the environment. In 2018, 60 percent of women compared to 47 percent of men who voted for one of the two major political parties voted Democrat. Though there are exceptions, men are more likely as a group to vote for strong defense, anti-welfare, and antiaffirmative action policies: the stance of the Republican Party. This does not, of course, imply that all men are Republican; only that as a group, they are more likely to favor the issues put forward by this political party. More women than men voted Democrat in the 2016 presidential election, but President Donald Trump still earned 42 percent of women's votes, overwhelmingly votes by white women. Fifty-four percent of women voted for Hillary Clinton with a higher relative proportion of women of color. This gender gap increased in the 2018 midterm elections with white college-educated women in particular increasing their support for Democratic candidates by eight percentage points compared to 2016. The reading "The Rise of the Valkyries: In the Alt-Right, Women are the Future, and the Problem" by Seyward Darby discusses the extreme fringe alternative-right or "alt-right," or white-nationalist faction, some of whom supported President Trump's campaign. Also popular in Europe, they represent an extreme populist nationalism fortified by fear and hatred of difference.

In 2016 forty-one percent of men voted for Clinton and 53 percent for Trump, again with many more white men voting for Trump. Specific differences by race include 58 percent of whites voting for Trump and 88 percent of African Americans voting for Clinton. Among Latinx and also Asian Americans, 65 percent voted for Clinton. There were also important differences in terms of age with younger people more likely to vote for Clinton (56 percent of those under 24 years and 52 percent of those 25-39 years). However this was a smaller bloc than the voters over 40 years who as a majority voted for Trump (50 percent of those 40-49 years and 53 percent of those over 50 years). These data on race and age also held true for the 2018 midterms. Although all age groups moved towards the Democratic party, 18 to 29 year old voters chose Democratic over Republican candidates by a 2-to-1 margin.

Not surprisingly, there were large differences by geographic region in 2016 with Trump securing the majority of rural as well as suburban votes (although the latter votes were significantly reduced for Republican candidates in 2018). Also differences by education revealed President Trump earning more votes among the less educated. Still, 45 percent of those with a college degree also voted for him (49 percent voted for Clinton). Finally in terms of income, President Trump did better among voters with lower incomes where he secured between 53 percent of the votes among those earning less than $30,000 a year, and just short of 51 percent of those earning between $30,000 and $99,900. Among those making over $100,000 the percentage slipped to about 48 percent voting for Trump.

Women (and what might be called women's issues) are also not equally represented in U.S. law, although now a third of the justices on the highest court, the U.S. Supreme Court, are female. Its membership currently consists of the chief justice of the United States and eight associate justices, all nominated by the president and appointed after confirmation by the U.S. Senate. As of this writing, there are three women on the court: Ruth Bader Ginsburg, appointed by President Bill Clinton, and Sonia Sotomayor and Elena Kagan, appointed by President Barack Obama. Only four women, including Associate Justice Sandra Day O'Connor, appointed by Ronald Reagan and now retired, have ever served, and Sotomayor is the first and only woman of color to serve.

The United States inherited British common law that utilized the doctrine of *femme couverte*, or covered woman: Husband and wife were one person under law, and she was his sexual property. As a result, married women could not seek employment without the husband's consent, keep their own wages, own property, sue, exercise control over their children, and control their reproductive lives. As already discussed in Chapter 10, rape within marriage was legally condoned. It was legally impossible to charge a husband with raping his wife because it would imply that the husband was raping himself. Although the Married Women's Property Act of 1848 allowed women to own and inherit property, the other constraints on their lives remained intact through the twentieth century. Even with the passage of these property acts, the law allowed the husband to control community property (jointly owned legally by husband and wife) until the 1970s.

Prior to the 1960s, most states decriminalized violence in the family (meaning violence within families was not legally understood as criminal acts), and operated marital rape exemption laws. It was not until the 1980s and 1990s that women had legal protections against violence; these protections include legislation such as the rape shield laws, mandatory arrest procedures in cases of domestic violence, public notification programs about convicted sex offenders in communities, the creation of protective or temporary restraining orders, state rape reform laws, and the 1994 Violence Against Women Act. Also prior to the 1960s, women's reproductive lives were a function of state control because the state had criminalized access to contraceptive information and procedures. As discussed in Chapter 7, before the passage of *Griswold v. Connecticut* in 1965, women had no legal right to contraceptives, and before the early 1970s with the passage of state abortion rulings and *Roe v. Wade*, they had no legal right to an abortion. The issue of reproductive justice is still controversial, of course, and the legal arena is the site for many of these battles today, especially in the area of parental notification and consent and the potential overturning of *Roe v. Wade*.

In terms of employment, *Muller v. Oregon* in 1908 reaffirmed the state's justification for limiting women's work. This legislation, supported by most feminists of the time, approved the right to prevent the often inhumane practice of women working in factories or similar facilities for more than 10 hours a day. It was based on the state's interest in protecting women's reproductive functions: considered important for the "well-being of the race." As discussed in Chapter 9, by the 1960s, various civil rights legislation was passed, including the Equal Pay Act and Title VII, preventing employers from discriminating against women and people of color. Affirmative action legislation of the 1970s and sexual harassment legislation of the 1980s further attempted to dismantle gender- and race-based inequities in the labor force. Challenges remain in this area, however, as systems of inequality still shape labor force experiences.

The state also affects individuals through the institution of marriage. Women had access to divorce in the nineteenth century, although it was often difficult to obtain. In addition, divorce carried a considerable stigma, especially for wives. Prior to the advent of no-fault divorce in the 1970s (divorce on demand by either or both parties), partners had to sue for divorce. Grounds to sue were based on a spouse's violation of the marriage contract such as by cruelty, abandonment, or adultery, and the courts needed to prove that someone had committed a crime. This procedure was difficult and expensive for women; it also tended to involve a double standard of behavior based on gender. Nonetheless, because this procedure allowed wives to show that husbands were "guilty," wives might receive relatively generous compensation. With the advent of no-fault divorce, this has changed because no one is charged with blame.

Likewise, alimony, the payment that women have traditionally received as compensation for their unpaid roles as wives and mothers, has been reduced or eliminated through various legislation since 1970. Although eliminating alimony indicates a more gender-neutral situation in which women are viewed not simply as dependent wives and mothers and may even have higher earnings than husbands, it has caused problems. This is because despite the gender-neutral language and intentions, society is stratified regarding gender, and women still tend to be financially subordinate to men. Although financial loss after divorce is significant for both men and women, women continue to bear the brunt of a breakup financially. This is because women tend to have lower salaries and therefore have less to live on, and also because women are more likely to have custody of children and endure more financial costs associated with single parenting. Financial hardship is often exacerbated by court-mandated

HISTORICAL MOMENT

SHIRLEY CHISHOLM FOR PRESIDENT

Shirley Chisholm was born to a mother from Barbados and a father from British Guiana. She grew up in Barbados and Brooklyn and graduated with honors from Brooklyn College with a degree in sociology. Following graduation, she worked at the Mt. Calvary Childcare Center in Harlem and became active in local politics. She completed a master's in education at Columbia University in 1952 and then managed day care centers.

Chisholm ran for a state assembly seat in 1964 and won, serving in the New York General Assembly until 1968. While in the New York legislature, she focused on issues of education and day care. In 1968 she ran for and won a seat in the U.S. Congress representing New York's Twelfth Congressional District, becoming the first black woman in the House of Representatives. Chisholm quickly distinguished herself as an outspoken advocate for the poor and for women's and civil rights and against the war in Vietnam.

During a speech on equal rights for women before the House of Representatives in 1969, Chisholm pointed out, "More than half of the population of the United States is female. But women occupy only 2 percent of the managerial positions. They have not even reached the level of tokenism yet. No women sit on the AFLCIO council or Supreme Court. There have been only two women who have held Cabinet rank, and at present there are none. Only two women now hold ambassadorial rank in the diplomatic corps. In Congress, we are down to 1 senator and 10 representatives. Considering that there are about 3½ million more women in the United States than men, this situation is outrageous."

In January 1972, Chisholm announced her candidacy for the Democratic nomination for the presidency: "I stand before you today as a candidate for the Democratic nomination for the Presidency of the United States. I am not the candidate of Black America, although I am Black and proud. I am not the candidate of the women's movement of this country, although I am a woman, and I am equally proud of that. I am not the candidate of any political bosses or special interests. I am the candidate of the people."

Chisholm became the first woman considered for the presidential nomination. Although she was defeated, she did garner more than 150 votes from the delegates to the Democratic National Convention in Miami. She continued to serve in Congress until 1982. She wrote two books: *Unbossed and Unbought* and *The Good Fight*. She died January 1, 2005, at the age of 80.

IDEAS FOR ACTIVISM

- Check out the National Organization for Women's "Take Action Campaign" at https://now.org/nap/ to find out what you can do to promote positive social change.
- Sign up to take action with Equality Now at http://www.equalitynow.org/actions.
- Work for a local candidate who supports human rights.

- Organize educational forums to examine political issues from perspectives of gender, race, class, and sexual identity.
- For more information about political issues of concern to women, visit the home page of the Feminist Majority Foundation at www.feminist.org. Follow the link to "Take Action" for ideas about what you can do to make a difference.

child support that does not get paid to women. Some states have enforced legislation to track errant child-support monies and enforce payment.

PUBLIC POLICY

State policies determine people's rights and privileges, and, as a result, the state has the power to exclude and discriminate against groups, and create policies in favor of certain other groups. By maintaining inequality, the state reflects the interests of the dominant groups in society and supports policies that work in their interests and reinforce their

AFFIRMATIVE ACTION: MYTHS AND MISCONCEPTIONS

MYTH: *Affirmative action is a form of reverse discrimination.*

REALITY: Affirmative action does not mean giving preference to any group. In fact, it stands for just the opposite. Included in the concept of affirmative action is the idea that all individuals must be treated equally and that a position should be given to the candidate most qualified. However, a hiring committee must make a good-faith effort to create a pool of candidates that reflects the number of women and minorities who possess proper training for the position. Once the qualified candidates are identified, a candidate's ability to provide cultural diversity to a department, to serve as a role model, and to offer a range of perspectives should be major elements in the evaluation and selection progress.

MYTH: *Affirmative action means establishing a "quota" system for women and minorities.*

REALITY: There is a difference between goals and quotas. Ideally, the percentage of women and minorities working in the position should be similar to the percentage of women and minorities qualified for such positions. Affirmative action does not mean showing partiality but rather reaching out to candidates and treating them with fairness and equity. Quotas, on the other hand, are court assigned to redress a pattern of discriminatory hiring.

MYTH: *Once you hire an affirmative action candidate, you can never fire him or her.*

REALITY: The terms of employment are the same for women and minorities as they are for men and non-minorities. In fact, in terms of affirmative action principles, standards of achievement, job requirements, and job expectations should be applied equally to all individuals.

MYTH: *To satisfy affirmative action responsibilities, all that needs to be done is to hire one or two women or minorities for dead-end jobs.*

REALITY: This is called tokenism. Hiring women and minorities for positions that are terminal in terms of advancement does not satisfy affirmative action goals. The same opportunities for employment and career advancement must exist for all individuals.

MYTH: *Affirmative action will result in lowering the standards and reputation of a department.*

REALITY: This will not happen if a qualified candidate is selected for a position. Diverse staff members providing varying talents and points of view increases effectiveness and vitality and can lead to an enhanced reputation.

MYTH: *Affirmative action and equal employment opportunity are the same things.*

REALITY: Equal employment opportunity means that all individuals must be treated equally in the hiring process and in advancement once on the job. Each person is to be evaluated as an individual on his or her merits and not based on a stereotypic conception of what members of specific groups are like. Affirmative action is a more proactive concept. It means that one will actively and aggressively seek to recruit women and minorities by making a positive and continuous effort in their recruitment, employment, retention, and promotion.

MYTH: *Affirmative action means applying a double standard, one for white males and a somewhat lower one for women and minorities.*

REALITY: Double standards are inconsistent with the principles and spirit of affirmative action. One standard should be applied to all candidates. This myth, of course, implies that women and minorities are inherently less qualified than white males.

MYTH: *Unqualified individuals are being hired and promoted for the sake of diversity/affirmative action.*

REALITY: Affirmative action plans that compromise valid job or educational qualifications are illegal. Plans must be flexible, realistic, reviewable, and fair. The U.S. Supreme Court has found that there are at least two permissible bases for voluntary affirmative action by employers under Title VII, the federal law that prohibits discrimination in employment on the basis of race, national origin, sex, or religion: (1) to remedy a clear and convincing history of past discrimination by the employer or union, and (2) to cure a manifest imbalance in the employer's workforce. Thus, affirmative action programs are intended to hire the most qualified individuals, while achieving equal opportunity for all.

Source: www.units.muohio.edu/oeeo/Myths.htm.

power. Native Americans, for example, have suffered because of state policies that required forced relocation, and African Americans have been harmed by Jim Crow laws that helped enforce segregation in the South and prevented African Americans from voting. As discussed in other chapters, there were miscegenation laws in the United States that prevented interracial marriage and aimed to maintain racial purity and superiority, and many states instigated laws that prevented African Americans from residing in certain communities, being in a town after sundown, and buying property in certain communities. Some of these laws were still on the books into the late twentieth century.

Welfare policy is especially illustrative of the ways the state is a conduit for the perpetuation of systems of inequality. Poverty in the United States is powerfully structured by racial and gender inequities, and patterns of income and wealth are strongly skewed along these lines. The federal poverty level is used by the U.S. government to define who is poor. It is based on a family's annual cash income rather than their total wealth, annual consumption, or their own assessment of well-being.

For 2018, the federal poverty level was an annual income of $12,140 for a solo person, $12,140 for a family of two, and $25,100 for a family of four. Add $4,320 for each additional person to compute the federal poverty level for larger families. These are the levels for the 48 contiguous states; Alaska and Hawaii are a little higher, since it is more expensive to live there. The federal poverty level is updated every year. It also includes the poverty threshold, used by the U.S. Census Bureau to report how many people in the United States live in poverty each year. In 2018 about 40.6 million people lived in poverty, 6 million fewer than in 2014. The official poverty rate was 12.7 percent, with approximately 22 percent of African Americans and just over 19 percent of Latinx with an income below the poverty level compared to about 9 percent of the white population.

Women generally had higher poverty rates, with about 1 in 8 or about 13 percent of women experiencing poverty. Not surprisingly, rates for women of color were higher. Twenty-three percent of African American and also Native American women, 21 percent of Latinas and almost 12 percent of Asian American women live in poverty. Although approximately one-fifth of all children live in poverty, African American children are three times more likely to be in poverty than white children. In addition, the poverty rate for women with disabilities was higher (32 percent) than women without disabilities (13 percent) or men with disabilities (25 percent).

In 2015 a national survey completed by the National Center on Transgender Equality reported widespread poverty facing the transgender community. People who are transgender were twice as likely to be living in poverty as the general U.S. population that year, compounded of course by other social identities that might also marginalize them. Transgender or gender nonconforming individuals, for example, had difficulties accessing the income supports and other resources to resist poverty, including facing negative treatment from government agencies. For example, over 1 in 10 transgender people reported negative treatment at a Social Security office, 14 percent at the Department of Motor Vehicles, and 13 percent at a courthouse.

Worldwide poverty is a major problem, with 2018 data from Oxfam International showing that 82 percent of the wealth generated in 2017 went to the richest 1 percent of the global population, while the 3.7 billion people—those who make up the poorest half of the world—saw no increase in their wealth. They also report that 42 people in the world now own the same wealth as the poorest half of humanity, and that billionaire wealth worldwide has risen on average 13 percent annually since 2010 (six times faster than the wages of ordinary workers, which have risen by a yearly average of just 2 percent). Further, the number of billionaires rose at an unprecedented rate of one every two days between

March 2016 and March 2017. Oxfam emphasizes that shareholders' and corporate profits are taken at the expense of workers' pay and conditions, which exacerbates world poverty. In the report, Oxfam challenged governments to use state policy to remedy poverty within nation-states. They made several suggestions for how to get this done: limiting returns to shareholders and top executives, and ensuring all workers receive a minimum "living" wage; eliminating the gender pay gap and protecting the rights of women workers (they estimate that it will take 217 years to close the gap in pay and employment opportunities between women and men worldwide); ensuring the wealthy pay their fair share through higher taxes and a crackdown on corruption and tax avoidance; and increasing spending on public services such as health care and education. Oxfam estimates that a global tax of 1.5 percent on billionaires' wealth could pay for every child to go to school.

"Regimes of truth" or social discourses (recall from other chapters that these are sets of beliefs and knowledge that support institutions in society) about who is deserving of wealth rely on the individualistic notion that success is a result of hard work and ambition; thus, those who work hard and push themselves should succeed economically. The corollary of this, of course, is that the fault associated with lack of economic success rests with the individual. This was referred to in Chapter 2 as the bootstrap myth. This myth avoids looking at structural aspects of the labor force and social systems that perpetuate classism and instead focuses on the individual.

The bootstrap myth helps explain the stigma associated with women on welfare in the United States and the many associated stereotypes—that they are lazy, cheat the system, and have babies to increase their welfare check. The reading by Brenda Della Casa discusses the actual realities of living on welfare. This personal testimony debunks these stereotypes and seeks respect for all people. In "What It Feels Like to Be on Welfare," Della Casa helps us understand that women on welfare often face a triple whammy: They are women facing lower-paid work, they are mothers with domestic responsibilities and child care expenses, and they are single with only one paycheck. Indeed, if women earned as much as comparable men, then solo women workers would see a rise in their incomes, poverty rates would be cut almost in half, and there would be a reduction in those seeking welfare. Having a job does not necessarily lift women out of poverty; it also does not guarantee sufficient retirement income, as the contemporary debate on Social Security reveals. Women will be disproportionately affected by Social Security reforms (and especially by any possible privatization of Social Security benefits).

Over 20 years ago, the passing of the 1996 Personal Responsibility and Work Opportunity Reconciliation Act (PRWORA) terminated the major source of welfare, Aid to Families with Dependent Children (AFDC), and replaced it with Temporary Assistance to Needy Families (TANF). No person could receive welfare for more than 5 years. In addition, welfare was transferred to the state through a block grant system, allowing some states to set their own agenda for distribution of funds. Critics of this and other policies of the 1990s have argued that not only have such policies failed to make low-income families self-sufficient, but they have kept wages low and undermined women's independence.

Since that time, welfare "reform" bills have, for example, cut safety net programs for the poor, reduced spending on Medicare and Medicaid, and raised the number of hours mothers receiving welfare have to work outside the home, study, or be involved in training, from

30 to 40 hours (at the same time that day care in most states is totally inadequate). Communities of color experience some of the most devastating consequences of poverty, and welfare "reform" has increased the vulnerability of individuals (especially solo mothers and children) in these communities. It is important to examine the argument that public assistance creates dependency: an argument generally made by people with a distorted picture of what it means to be poor. When survival is a constant struggle, people become ill-equipped to live in ways that facilitate steady employment. Imagine a mother who cannot afford to buy diapers for her child. No day care will take a child without a supply of diapers. How might the mother go on a job interview without clothes and transportation—or without an address beyond a homeless shelter to put on a resume? It is flawed thinking to believe that making poverty more unpleasant than it already is—coupled with lectures on ambition and self-reliance—might motivate people to improve their lot, because incentive tends usually not to be the problem. Meeting basic human needs would be a more productive solution.

A most obvious example of policies working to favor dominant groups is the practice often called "wealthfare," "welfare for the rich," or "aid to dependent corporations" (a play on AFDC) by some scholars. These policies reflect the ties political leaders have to the economic system and the ways the government subsidizes corporations and reduces taxes and other payments to the state for some corporations and businesses. Wealthfare involves five major types: direct grants; allowance of publicly funded research and development to be used free by private for-profit corporations; discounted fees for public resources (such as grazing fees on public land); tax breaks for the wealthy; and corporate tax reductions and loopholes. It has been estimated that more than $200 billion in corporate welfare could be saved over the next five years, as of this writing, if policies reining in these favors were instigated. Neither Republican nor Democratic lawmakers want to do this because they fear losing donations to their respective parties. The Occupy Wall Street (OWS) movement—an example of a leaderless resistance movement with people of many colors, genders, and political persuasions—originated in late 2011 to counter "wealthfare," among other issues. Their main concerns were social and economic inequality, greed, and corruption—especially the influence of corporate power on government and policy. The OWS slogan "We are the 99 percent" referred to income inequality and wealth distribution in the United States, between the wealthiest 1 percent and the rest of the population. The movement served as a source of collective resistance to U.S. national and international policy, and especially policies associated with the alliances among the government-military-industrial/economic complex. Spin-off from the movement continues in a variety of political endeavors aimed against corporate greed and institutionalized racism.

THE CRIMINAL JUSTICE SYSTEM

Laws can be defined as formal aspects of social control that determine what is permissible and what is forbidden in a society. The court system was created to maintain the law through adjudicating conflicts that may be unlawful and deciding punishments for people who have broken the law. The role of the police is to enforce these laws and keep public order. Prisons are responsible for punishing those who have broken the law and protecting society from people who have committed crimes. All these fit together to maintain the control of the state.

The U.S. prison system, the primary source of punishment and rehabilitation for criminal offenses, incarcerates more people than any other country in the world. In 2018 it was estimated that over two million people were in U.S. prisons, jails, and detention centers. Men of color, and especially young African American men, predominate in the criminal justice system. Among men, poor men and men of color are more likely to be considered a danger to society and tend to receive the longest sentences because of social stigma, racism and discrimination, poverty, lack of education, and the consequences of these structural variables on access to good legal counsel.

In 2018 the Federal Bureau of Prisons estimated that the almost 13,000 women who were convicted and incarcerated made up 7 percent of the inmate population in the United States. Currently, about 4 in 5 women in the correctional system are mothers. Although incarceration rates for women of color are significantly higher than those for white women, and their representation in the prison population higher than their representation in the total population, white women are currently being incarcerated at somewhat higher rates than women of color. As a group, women are more likely to have committed nonviolent property and drug crimes; these offenders account for about two-thirds of the population of women in prison. Along with drug offenses, women are more likely to commit crimes of shoplifting, bad-check writing, and embezzlement, and less likely to be involved in arson, armed theft, burglary, and acts of vandalism. The crimes that women commit are gendered in that they involve less potential for violent armed confrontation. These "safer" crimes reflect women's need for money to buy drugs or other personal wants, and/or survival and family needs. Women are also more likely to engage in the public order crime of prostitution, of course. Both men and women engage in the exchange of sex for money, but women are more likely to be arrested, and men's arrests are more likely to involve the purchase of sex as "johns" or are related to business management as "pimps."

Overall, about 80 percent of violent crime is committed by males. The disparity in rates is called the gender gap in crime commission. However, although women are much less likely to kill than men, among those who do, they are more likely to commit intimate partner murders. Men are more likely to commit stranger and acquaintance murder than women. This reflects the fact that women are more likely to kill in self-defense in domestic violence situations.

Most of the homicides enacted by women are first-time offenses, involve male victims, and most are likely to have taken place in the home, with kitchen knives and other

LEARNING ACTIVITY

WOMEN AND PRISON

To learn more about women in prison, visit www.womenandprison.org, a website created by incarcerated women. From this website, what do you learn about the gendered experiences of women in the criminal justice system? Why do these women argue that resistance to that system is necessary? What can you do to be an ally to incarcerated women around the world?

household implements rather than firearms. This evidence again suggests that much female homicide is done in self-defense. Although prior to the 1980s women who killed in self-defense almost always lost their plea, today juries are more understanding of the experiences of battered women. Even so, it is still sometimes very difficult for women to convince a jury that they were being abused, especially in terms of the question of "imminent danger" when an abused woman kills a partner while he is sleeping or not behaving violently at that moment. Defendants must meet two criteria for claiming justifiable homicide as self-defense: reasonable fear or perception of danger (such that killing was the only course of action to protect the defendant's life) and the confrontation of the defendant with deadly force by an assailant.

It is important to note that although women make up a small proportion of those "locked up," they are increasingly under correctional guidance of some kind. A 2017 Prison Policy Initiative report estimated that 16 percent of women in the system are "locked up," 9 percent are on parole, and 75 percent are on probation. This means that 3 out of 4 women under control of the correctional systems are on probation of some kind. Although it appears to be a positive alternative to incarceration, the Prison Policy Initiative report discusses fees associated with probation that are often unaffordable. A failure to pay these fees often violates probation. Domestic and child care responsibilities also complicate probation requirements that might require meetings with probation officers, with no extra money to spend on child care or transportation. These exacerbate women's vulnerability and increase their incarceration because they often cannot meet the burdensome obligations of probation supervision rather than because they commit crimes.

Compared to men's incarceration, where state prison systems hold many more men than local jails, the Prison Policy Initiative report states that incarcerated women are nearly evenly split between state prisons and such jails. In addition, about 60 percent of women in local jails have not been convicted of a crime and are awaiting trial. The report emphasized that avoiding pretrial incarceration is especially problematic for women because they are less likely to be able to meet the financial obligations of cash bail. Flight risk is a typical reason for pretrial incarceration, but the report suggests that women actually present a lower flight risk than men because they often have primary obligations for dependent children. And, once convicted, because state prisons tend to be set up for men, women are funneled into local jails: Approximately 25 percent of convicted incarcerated women are held in jails compared to 10 percent of all people incarcerated with a conviction.

Although jail stays are generally shorter than prison stays, local jails make it harder for inmates to communicate with family than do prisons because phone calls are more expensive and other communications restricted, such as those that limit mail contact to only postcards. This is problematic because, as already mentioned, most of the women are primary caretakers of their children. In addition, the report found that women in jails are more likely to suffer from mental health problems and experience serious emotional distress than either women in prisons or men in either correctional setting.

It is also important to recognize that approximately 57 percent of incarcerated women have suffered severe and prolonged physical and/or sexual abuse. The Bureau of Justice Statistics reports that just under half of all women (and one-tenth of all men) in correctional facilities indicated physical and/or sexual abuse before their current sentence.

LEARNING ACTIVITY
LGBTQ AND PRISON ABOLITION

Sam Shelton

Abolitionists see the prison industrial complex as a set of interconnected mechanisms of social control—such as surveillance, policing, criminalization, and incarceration—that benefit specific political interests and uphold multiple systems of power. They contend that the criminal (in)justice system and the police force are not apolitical entities serving the greater good, but rather tools that protect the existing social order through the containment of certain bodies/minds, such as those of people of color, people with disabilities, or people in poverty. The goal of abolitionists is to dismantle the prison industrial complex and to develop alternative solutions to social problems that do not rely on incarceration and violence (Spade 2011).

Unlike prison abolitionists, reformists seek to improve conditions within prisons so that they are more habitable for incarcerated people. Reformists also seek to make the criminal legal system and the police force more equitable by revising laws and policies that target people from specific social groups. They do not necessarily think about policing and incarceration as inherently oppressive; instead, reformists focus on addressing the conditions that make policing and incarceration inequitable or unjust, such as when incarcerated people are denied basic human rights. The goal of reformism is to create a criminal legal system that judges people impartially and a prison system that holds people accountable for their actions without being cruel or causing them excessive harm (UNODC 2018).

The following activity is meant to help you better understand the difference between abolitionists and reformists in relation to queer/trans politics. Either individually or in small groups, read the following scenario and figure out how you would respond to the prompts first as a reformist and then as an abolitionist. Next, compare your answers and reflect on how these two positions shaped your response to the scenario.

The scenario:

Two college students physically assaulted a queer person in your community. When this person sought assistance from a local shelter, they were denied access because of their assumed gender identity. When this person called the police for help, they were arrested on an unrelated charge, and were eventually sentenced to serve three months in jail. During this time, they experienced many other forms of violence, such as being sent to a men's prison and being placed in solitary confinement for long periods of time "for their own protection." Once their sentence was up, they were unable to get their old job back and had difficulty finding a new job that could cover their necessary expenses.

Discussion Questions

- What are the central issues going on in this scenario? What is causing them?
- What does social justice look like from your political stance?
- How can you prevent this situation from happening again in the future?
- What can you do to support queer and trans people in your community and those in prison?

For more information about prison abolition, visit criticalresistance.org. The activist group generation-FIVE also offers a transformative justice handbook that shows how an abolitionist approach can be applied to a specific social issue—child sexual abuse (http://www.generationfive.org/the-issue/transformative-justice/).

References

Spade, Dean. (2011). *Normal Life: Administrative Violence, Critical Trans Politics, and the Limits of Law.* Durham, NC: Duke University Press.

United Nations Office on Drugs and Crime [UNODC]. (2018). "Prison Reform and Alternatives to Imprisonment." https://www.unodc.org/unodc/en/justice-and-prison-reform/prison-reform-and-alternatives-to-imprisonment.html

A large number of these incidents occurred before the age of 18. These histories are then compounded by the high incidences of sexual abuse within correctional facilities. The Prison Policy Initiative report discusses women's subjection to sexual misconduct from both fellow prisoners and the correctional staff. Women inmates may suffer invasive procedures and violence, inflicted mostly by male prison guards, such as random and degrading searches and having guards observe their dressing and toiletry practices. The imbalance of power between inmates and guards means that the former are dependent on the latter for basic necessities. The full extent of this problem, however, is unknown because of underreporting and because female prisoners often fear retaliation. Angela Davis, a feminist activist and scholar, writes about the prison-industrial complex as a source of U.S. state-sanctioned human rights violations in which women prisoners represent a disenfranchised population. This reflects the power the state exercises over incarcerated women, who are more likely to be women of color, and illustrates the ways it perpetuates systemic gender and race domination. In response, the Dignity for Incarcerated Women bill was introduced to Congress in 2017 to address the inhumane and unjust conditions that incarcerated women often face.

THE MILITARY

The military, a branch of government constituted to defend against foreign and domestic conflict, is a central component of the state and political system. Militarism can be defined as the predominance of armed forces in state policies or the intent of a government or people for the maintenance of a strong military capability and its use to defend or promote (usually national) interests. Militarism is a central defining principle of many societies worldwide and is especially predominant in colonialist and imperialist societies intent on expansion and resource accumulation. It is important to understand the ways militarism functions as a mechanism of gendered power that perpetuates women's subordination within domestic, national, and international arenas. This includes women's experiences of war as combatants, victims, refugees, and survivors of violence, as well as workers (including sex workers) within the military-industrial complex. Contemporary wars of the late-twentieth and early-twenty-first centuries have utilized campaigns of fear and violence associated with nongovernmental agencies—or "terrorism"—that have changed the face of war and its responses.

As mentioned in Chapter 2, the military has strong ties to the economic system through a military-industrial complex that supports industries that manufacture weapons. Military presence overseas (as well as in civil wars) tends to be related to economic interests such as the need for oil or control of other resources, including the need for political "stability" in nations to maintain global corporate endeavors and strategic defense. The Pentagon has connections to other state entities, especially the government and its representatives. The military is a male-dominated arena, not only in terms of actual personnel who serve but in terms of the ways it is founded upon so-called masculine cultural traits such as violence, aggression, hierarchy, competition, and conflict. The military has a history of misogynistic and homophobic attitudes to enforce highly masculine codes of behavior. In the United States, military culture is integrated, often unknowingly, into our everyday lives, such as through camouflage fashions and ROTC on college campuses. Many scholars critique such normalization of militarism and call for a demilitarization of society.

Throughout most of history, women were not allowed to serve in the military except in such auxiliary forces as nursing. It was not until World War II that women who served in any military capacity were given formal status and not until 1976 that women were allowed into the military academies. As of 2016, all combat positions in the U.S. military—from infantry to special-operations forces—are open to women. Currently women make up 14.4 percent of active duty troops and 18 percent of reserve and guards. The Air Force and the Navy have the highest rates of enlisted women (19 percent for the Air Force and 18 percent for the Navy); women also comprise 21 percent of Air Force officers and 18 percent of Navy officers. Servicewomen make up 14 percent of the enlisted in the Army and 18 percent of its officers. The Marine Corps has the lowest proportion of women, with 8 percent of enlisted troops and 7.5 percent of officers.

In terms of race, the armed forces were officially segregated until 1948. According to the U.S. Council of Foreign Relations, currently people of color are overrepresented in the military, making up 30 percent of those on active duty and 24 percent of reserves and guards. Forty-three percent of servicemen and 56 percent of servicewomen are people of color, with African Americans overrepresented in the military compared to their proportion in the general population. In the Army in particular, there are almost as many African American women (about 40 percent) as white women (just over 40 percent of total servicewomen). Troops are younger than the civilian population, especially in the Marines, where 84 percent are aged 20 or younger. The Marine Corps is also the one branch of the military in which the proportion of African American men is less than their representation in the general population.

Resistance to the full integration of women in the military invokes several stereotypes. First is the "women are not strong enough to do this work" response. All soldiers must pass certain physical standards before landing in combat positions, so this will exclude certain individuals, both women and men. Outside of combat positions, some military standards, including the scores on mandatory physical fitness tests, may be scaled differently depending on gender and age. However, all military officials, including women and those supportive of full integration of the military, emphasize that standards for combat positions must not be altered and certainly not lowered in order that full respect and adequate safety is promoted and ensured.

A related response to women in combat positions is the notion that they will have problems experiencing the strain of combat duty and their presence will degrade control and morale, in part through inevitable sexual assault and harassment of women. President Trump, who called the issue of sexual assault "a massive problem" during the 2016 election, tweeted the following example of this: "26,000 unreported sexual assaults in the military—only 238 convictions. What did these geniuses expect when they put men and women together?" However, of course servicewomen have already proven themselves and served with distinction, and it is well known that women are easily able—and some suggest may be better—at tolerating pain and various hardships. Studies indicate that they tend to bring better communication skills, their presence often humanizes troops, and their integration helps promote more "natural" environments compared to men-only spaces. Still, the full integration of women into the military is complex, as the reading "New Military Femininities: Humanitarian Violence and the Gendered Work of War Among U.S. Servicewomen" by Jennifer Greenburg suggests. The author focuses on servicewomen and examines the ways women are integrated into combat violence through the promotion of certain gendered performances like domesticity alongside military violence. This reading shows how a new form of military femininity has emerged that tends to reject a rhetoric of humanitarianism and which instead emphasizes servicewomen's lethal capabilities.

Resistance to women in combat positions also centers on their reproductive lives, especially the way periods and potential premenstrual syndrome (PMS) might affect their ability to fight. Women tend to be insulted by these accusations of physiological frailty and emphasize their ability to manage their reproductive health. In a 2016 *Mother Jones* article, for example, one woman officer suggested that "if we are going to talk about women's PMS, we should talk about men's boners too," citing "reflex erections" that happen when men get scared or stressed, which she suggested is "a definite combat liability, particularly with younger male troops." The risk of pregnancy is also cited as a liability for servicewomen, even though time lost due to pregnancy is shorter than time lost due to men's disciplinary issues and addictions. It is emphasized that any sort of physical ailment might prevent someone from deployment; pregnancy is one, although not the most frequent "ailment" preventing service.

Sexualized violence and the harassment of women are recognized as widespread problems within the U.S. armed services. As discussed in Chapter 10, a 2018 Department of Defense report indicated that service members' reporting of sexual assault increased by about 10 percent during 2017. There were almost 7,000 reports of sexual assault involving service members as either victims or subjects of criminal investigation, which amounted to an almost 10 percent increase compared to the previous year. Recent reports of sexual misconduct by high-profile politicians and media personalities have reinvigorated public discussions about sexual harassment and assault that also extend to the U.S. military. In particular, the increase in reporting and the sheer number of allegations of sexual misconduct facilitated a demand for transparency and accountability within the armed forces.

Most recent data from the Department of Defense indicate that among the armed forces 1 in 4 women and 1 in 15 men faced severe and persistent sexual harassment or gender discrimination, usually by someone in their chain of command, although 4 out of

---

WOMEN IN BLACK: FOR JUSTICE, AGAINST WAR

Perhaps you've seen them—a small group of women dressed in black, standing silently on a street corner or in some other public place and perhaps on your campus. They are Women in Black, part of a global network of women advocating for peace and opposing injustice, war, militarism, and other forms of violence. They are especially committed to challenging militarism in the governments of their own countries. Women in Black began in Israel in 1988, as Israeli women stood in weekly vigils to protest the Israeli occupation of the West Bank. They did not chant or march. Rather, they stood at a busy intersection with simple signs that read "Stop the Occupation." Passers-by shouted at them, calling them "whores" and "traitors." They did not shout back but maintained a silent dignity.

Eventually, Women in Black vigils were organized around the world to support the women in Israel. As war came to Croatia and Bosnia in 1992, Women in Black groups began to oppose the violence there. And so the movement has continued to spread as women around the world have responded to war. In both the Gulf War and the wars in Afghanistan and Iraq, women across the globe and in the United States have stood in protest. Any group of women anywhere can hold a Women in Black vigil against any form of violence, militarism, or war. Women in Black also engage in nonviolent and non-aggressive action—blocking roads or entering military bases. In 2001 the United Nations Development Fund for Women (UNIFEM) and International Alert awarded Women in Black the Millennium Peace Prize for Women. To find out if there is already a vigil in your area or to learn how to start your own vigil, visit www.womeninblack.org.

5 survivors did not report the crime. Of those who did, 1 in 3 women and half of all men were dissatisfied with their treatment, only 8 percent of allegations ended in court martial, and only 3 percent resulted in offenders' convictions for nonconsensual sex offenses. Instead, retaliation was a norm, with 58 percent of women and 60 percent of men who reported a sexual assault facing some kind of retaliation and a third of all those reporting facing discharge from the military—typically within 7 months of filing a report. There is, therefore, low trust and satisfaction in the system. Of those who reported abuse, 1 in 10 eventually dropped out of the process. Of those who did not report, over 1 in 4 feared retaliation from their command or colleagues, and nearly 1 in 3 feared the process would be unfair or nothing would be done.

It is also important to recognize the specific plight of veterans who have experienced sexual abuse in the armed forces. The Department of Defense indicates that about 40 percent of homeless women veterans have experienced some kind of military sexual trauma and that veterans with this history are over twice as likely to experience homelessness. Healthcare for women veterans often tends not to take into account the physical, mental, and reproductive health needs of women. Female veterans are more likely to be solo parents and thus ineligible for transitional housing that exempts parents. In addition, only about a third of the Veteran Administration's medical centers have gynecologists on staff, for example. Families of service personnel are also at risk, as unique stresses—such as relocations, long work tours, frequent family separations, and dangerous work assignments—increase the risk for family violence and encourage alcohol and drug use and abuse. As already mentioned, abused female military personnel (and civilian spouses fearful of jeopardizing military husbands' prospects for continued service and promotion) often resist reporting incidents out of fear of lack of confidentiality, retaliation, and lack of available services.

Finally, the military has a long history of homophobia and transphobia that has included the execution, persecution, and dismissal of LGBTQ soldiers. Although polls consistently have continually shown support for the removal of antigay bans, arguments in favor of such prejudice mirror those already articulated about women and people of color in the military, including notions that the morale and fighting spirit of military personnel will drop if openly gay and lesbian personnel are present and that LGBTQ individuals pose a national security threat. Through the 1980s more than 15,000 military personnel were discharged because of homosexuality. By the mid-1990s President Clinton had created the "Don't Ask, Don't Tell" policy. In 2010 Congress voted to repeal the policy, and the law was signed by President Obama. In 2013 the Pentagon expanded benefits to same-sex partners of military personnel to include a range of services offered at various posts and bases, but did still withhold medical and dental coverage and housing allowances. Full benefits required the 2013 repeal of the Defense of Marriage Act (DOMA), the 1996 law that defined marriage as the union of a man and a woman. Because of the repeal of DOMA, military personnel now have full access to these services. Several years later, in 2016, the ban on military service by openly transgender persons was also repealed. As of this writing, President Trump has promised to reinstate the ban, but the Department of Defense has yet to change its policy.

TRANSGENDER AND THE MILITARY

Janet Lockhart

Serving Openly

Through history, people have concealed their true identities so they could serve in the military. Boys lied about their ages so they could enlist; women such as Deborah Samson disguised themselves as men to fight during the Revolutionary and Civil Wars. These soldiers had to hide their identities all day, every day—a strain in an already stressful situation.

Unfortunately, pressure to hide one's identity is not confined to history. Today, transgender people who wish to serve in the military may still have to do so in secrecy. Worldwide, fewer than 20 countries out of over 200 allow LGBTQ people to serve openly. The military of the Netherlands was the first, in 1974; and New Zealand's military was rated the most inclusive, in 2014 (O'Connor, 2017). Some militaries have support groups for LGBTQ individuals, and some participate in pride parades and other events. Unfortunately, these are the minority. Many countries forbid transgender people from serving at all.

In the United States, lesbian, gay, and bisexual people were barred from serving until the controversial Clinton-era "Don't Ask, Don't Tell" policy (1994), which gave legal protection—at least theoretically—to such people serving, provided their sexual orientations (and activities) remained secret. DADT was repealed, after much debate and resistance, in the Obama era (2011). In June 2016, transgender individuals finally gained the right to serve (Rosenberg 2016); but in July 2017, President Trump announced his intention to ban transgender individuals from serving "in any capacity," citing "tremendous medical costs and disruption that transgender in the military would entail" (*CBC News* 2017).

This "disruption" objection against inclusion of transgender people is also known as the "unit cohesion" argument (which has been used against inclusion of other groups, such as people of color and LGB people). The argument implies that because of their identity, transgender people will somehow interfere with the ability of the soldiers in their unit to bond, maintain morale, and function effectively as a fighting force. This viewpoint stigmatizes transgender individuals, assumes that cisgender (people whose gender identity coincides with the one assigned to them at birth) soldiers are intolerant, and ignores the responsibility of military commanders for setting an example and maintaining discipline.

Update the Issue

At the time of this writing (2018), transgender people's right to serve openly in the U.S. military is in flux. Update what has happened since this textbook was written.

What changes have occurred? How do the changes affect the lives and service of transgender people in the U.S. military?

Now do some more research and fill in the table for the following countries' policies on transgender people serving in the military. How are they similar and different from the current U.S. policy?

Country	Open service allowed? Year?	Notes
Australia	2010	Gay and lesbian service members allowed since 1992
Bolivia		
Botswana		
Canada		
Chad		
China		
Estonia		
Germany		
Israel		
Mexico		
North Korea		
Paraguay		
Philippines		
Russia		
Sweden		
Switzerland		

References

CBC News. (2017, July 26). "Trump Bans Transgender People from Military Service 'in Any Capacity.'" http://www.cbc.ca/news/world/trump-tweets-transgender-military-1.4222080

O'Connor, T. (2017, July 26). "Trump's Transgender Military Ban Leaves Only 18 Countries with Full LGBT Rights in Armed Forces." *Newsweek.* http://www.newsweek.com/trump-transgender-military-ban-leaves-few-countries-lgbt-rights-642342

Rosenberg, M. (2016, June 30). "Transgender People Will Be Allowed to Serve Openly in Military." *New York Times.* https://www.nytimes.com/2016/07/01/us/transgender-military.html

THE BLOG
MY STUDENTS MATTER

Susan M. Shaw (2015)

The president of a Christian university in Oklahoma just declared that his institution was a university, not a daycare, after he chided students for playing the victim over their hurt feelings when they hear something they don't like. I've seen a lot of chastising of college students over the past few weeks, especially students of color, because they've spoken out about their experiences of mistreatment on campuses.

The response from the dominant (well-off, white, straight, male) culture has primarily been to accuse students of being weak and self-absorbed opponents of free speech. Those are easy accusations for people to make who have never been interlopers in higher education. Our institutions of higher education, on the whole, were created by and for heterosexual white men. Changes resulting from the Civil Rights Movement, the Women's Movement, the LGBTQ Movement, Black Lives Matter, and other movements for social justice have challenged white male dominance in higher education, and many of the responses to recent challenges by students seem to me simply to be the good ol' boy system pushing back.

I'm a professor of Women, Gender, and Sexuality Studies at a large research university, and so I see a greater proportion of students of color, women students, and LGBTQ students than many professors in more traditional disciplines. I can't speak for students at Yale or Missouri, but my students are not asking to be coddled or protected from ideas they don't like. In fact, my students engage deeply with diverse ideas and care passionately about understanding the world around them.

What my students do want, as do I, is to be respected, to feel welcomed, and to feel valued by their institution. Many of the people criticizing students have never had the experience of being a minority of any kind on campus. They have not had to live with long histories of subordination and the psychological toll of oppression. So dismissing critiques of racist, sexist, classist, and heterosexist behaviors comes easily when one has never been targeted because of one's identity. One can simply believe that the playing field is level and everyone has an equal opportunity because that has been one's own experience. And, of course, acknowledging that others may not have had those same experiences would mean one would have to examine one's own privilege and systematic advantaging within social institutions.

What my students want is not to be called names. I get that. I don't want to be called b—h or c—t. I don't want to hear sexist jokes or have colleagues comment on my appearance. I don't want to see pictures of naked women on office walls in my workplace. All of those things create a hostile work environment.

Similarly, my students don't want to be asked to speak for their groups. They don't want to be singled out for their identities. They don't want to be stereotyped. They don't want to be reduced to a single identity. They don't want to see their cultures diminished by Halloween costumes or mascots that simply continue colonizing appropriations of their people and cultures. Those things also create a hostile environment, and learning in a hostile environment is not playing on a level field.

I know because I went to a Southern Baptist seminary in the early 1980s when Southern Baptists were fighting over the roles of women. I and other women at the seminary were told we didn't belong because of our gender. We listened to denominational leaders blame women—all women, including us—for the Fall of humankind. One of my fellow students once told me that he'd pray for me that I didn't get "messed up with this women in ministry thing." That was the day I became a feminist!

Asking for respect is not the same as asking to be coddled. Expecting professors to create inclusive, equitable, and just learning environments for each and every student in their classrooms is not asking for censorship.

My students want to be students. They want to learn. They want to see themselves represented in the curriculum alongside all the straight white men who still dominate course content. They want the range of ideas discussed broadened, not narrowed.

In my own classes, I welcome all ideas as long as they are argued responsibly and respectfully and are supported with evidence. I encourage students to examine conflicting ideas, including, and sometimes especially, ones with which they disagree. Sometimes, if all of the students seem to be agreeing, I argue an opposing viewpoint, just to expand the dialogue.

But I don't let students use slurs toward each other. If a student inadvertently says something offensive, I stop and address the comment—not targeting the student, but the student's words. I ask my students to read things they don't like, and sometimes I ask them to take the point of view of someone who liked what they read. I help them develop critical thinking skills. And they do.

Not surprisingly, the critics of diverse students use excesses as their evidence of the downward spiral of higher education. Of course, there are excesses. These are college students. They are young and idealistic and learning their way in the world. They are also making change. Have we forgotten how important a role college students played in stopping the war in Vietnam?

Our goal with students is to teach them. Rather than accusing them, we need to work with them, to hear them, to make change with them, because change is needed.

I am also the Principal Investigator on a large National Science Foundation funded project to transform institutional climate at my university. Why? Because despite the progress made over the last few decades, universities are still places where women, people of color, LGBTQ people, people from poor and working class backgrounds are disadvantaged in many ways that are often obscured by the veneer of equal opportunity.

My students are not wrong that we need to be better. What seems most overlooked in all the criticism of students, however, is the enduring optimism of students who have experienced discrimination and mistreatment and who still believe they can change the university and the world beyond it. I am heartened by their belief in a better university for all of us. After all, isn't that part of what a university should do? Send young people out in the world who have the skills, passion, and courage to make the world better.

71. CONSTITUTIONAL ARGUMENT

SUSAN B. ANTHONY (1898)

Friends and Fellow-Citizens:—I stand before you under indictment for the alleged crime of having voted at the last presidential election, without having a lawful right to vote. It shall be my work this evening to prove to you that in thus doing, I not only committed no crime, but instead simply exercised my citizen's right, guaranteed to me and all United States citizens by the National Constitution beyond the power of any State to deny.

Our democratic-republican government is based on the idea of the natural right of every individual member thereof to a voice and a vote in making and executing the laws. We assert the province of government to be to secure the people in the enjoyment of their inalienable rights. We throw to the winds the old dogma that government can give rights. No one denies that before governments were organized each individual possessed the right to protect his own life, liberty and property. When 100 or 1,000,000 people enter into a free government, they do not barter away their natural rights; they simply pledge themselves to protect each other in the enjoyment of them through prescribed judicial and legislative tribunals. They agree to abandon the methods of brute force in the adjustment of their differences and adopt those of civilization. Nor can you find a word in any of the grand documents left us by the fathers which assumes for government the power to create or to confer rights. The Declaration of Independence, the United States Constitution, the constitutions of the several States and the organic laws of the Territories, all alike propose to *protect* the people in the exercise of their God-given rights. Not one of them pretends to bestow rights.

> All men are created equal, and endowed by the Creator with certain inalienable rights. Among these are life, liberty and the pursuit of happiness. To secure these, governments are instituted among men, deriving their just powers from the consent of the governed.

Here is no shadow of government authority over rights, or exclusion of any class from their full and equal enjoyment. Here is pronounced the right of all men, and "consequently," as the Quaker preacher said, "of all women," to a voice in the government. And here, in this first paragraph of the Declaration, is the assertion of the natural right of all to the ballot; for how can "the consent of the governed" be given, if the right to vote be denied? Again:

> Whenever any form of government becomes destructive of these ends, it is the right of the people to alter or abolish it, and to institute a new government, laying its foundations on such principles, and organizing its powers in such form, as to them shall seem most likely to effect their safety and happiness.

Surely the right of the whole people to vote is here clearly implied; for however destructive to their happiness this government might become, a disfranchised class could neither alter nor abolish it, nor institute a new one, except by the old brute force method of insurrection and rebellion. One-half of the people of this nation today are utterly powerless to blot from the statute books an unjust law, or to write there a new and a just one. The women, dissatisfied as they are with this form of government, that enforces taxation without representation—that compels them to obey laws to which they never have given their consent—that imprisons and hangs them without a trial by a jury of their peers—that robs them, in marriage, of the custody of their own persons, wages and children—are this half of the people who are left wholly at the mercy of the other half, in direct violation of the spirit and letter of the declarations of the framers of this government, every one of which was based on the immutable principle of equal rights to all. By these declarations, kings, popes, priests, aristocrats, all were alike dethroned and placed on a common level, politically, with the lowliest born subject or serf. By them, too, men, as such, were deprived of their divine right to rule and placed on a political level with women. By the practice of these declarations all class and caste distinctions would be abolished, and slave, serf, plebeian, wife, woman, all alike rise from their subject position to the broader platform of equality.

The preamble of the Federal Constitution says:

We, the people of the United States, in order to form a more perfect union, establish justice, insure domestic tranquillity, provide for the common defence, promote the general welfare and secure the blessings of liberty to ourselves and our posterity, do ordain and establish this Constitution for the United States of America.

It was we, the people, not we, the white male citizens, not we, the male citizens; but we, the whole people, who formed this Union. We formed it not to give the blessings of liberty but to secure them; not to the half of ourselves and the half of our posterity, but to the whole people—women as well as men. It is downright mockery to talk to women of their enjoyment of the blessings of liberty while they are denied the only means of securing them provided by this democratic-republican government—the ballot. . . .

72 "I KNEW AMERICA WAS NOT READY FOR A WOMAN TO BE PRESIDENT"
ANGELA N. GIST (2017)

When people show you who they are, believe them the first time.

—*Maya Angelou*

As I reflect on the 2016 presidential election, I cannot stop thinking about social identity, structural intersectionality, and the history of U.S. voting rights. I keep trying to understand the mindset of the American people who support President Trump. Hillary Clinton and Donald Trump represented the intersection of myriad similar social identities that voters likely felt connected to, disconnected from, and/or ambivalent toward. The candidates' social identities overlap to some extent; they are both White, cisgender, heterosexual, middle/upper class, able-bodied, and of similar age, most of which are privileged social identity markers in the U.S. cultural context. Certainly, Clinton and Trump's social identities diverge on their gender, occupational background, political party affiliation, policy commitments, and public perceptions of past behaviors. Given the converging and diverging of Trump and Clinton's social identities, I ponder how (dis)identification could have driven voting behaviors.

If, as Ben-Bassat and Dahan argue, citizens link voting behaviors with their ability to identify socially with candidates, how might we think about voter patterns and social identity? According to Social Identity Theory (SIT) (Tajfel and Turner 13), people psychologically classify themselves and others into groups (i.e., organizational memberships, demographic groups, other affiliations) to metaphorically locate themselves in social geography; in essence, people construct their identities in relation to others (Ashforth and Mael 20). When we identify with others socially and express that connection, we can be said to express identification, which is defined as "the perception of oneness with or belongingness to some human aggregate" (Ashforth and Mael 21). Hence, voting could be an expression of identification and SIT could aid in the interpretation of voting trends.

Demographic analysis of voter turnout shows group-level phenomena in the 2016 election and many other elections. According to the Pew Research Center, "White non-Hispanic voters preferred Trump over Clinton by 21 percentage points (58% to 37%)," while "Clinton held an 80-point advantage among blacks (88% to 8%)" (Tyson and Maniam). Furthermore, women supported Clinton over Trump 54% to 42%. Almost the same percentages, 53% to 41%, of men voted for Trump. There are also disparities based on educational attainment, which is one indicator of social class. In what Tyson and Maniam describe as "by far the widest gap in support among college graduates and non-college graduates in exit polls dating back to 1980," college graduates voted for Clinton. Those without college degrees primarily supported Trump. These demographic statistics nod to potential identification between voters and candidates.

How do we make sense of these voting patterns in this election? SIT presents a plausible explanation (Tajfel and Turner 13). SIT explains the psychological categorization process, which constructs both identification according to salient in-groups or disidentification according to out-groups. Tajfel and Turner elaborate that individuals tend to favorably evaluate their own in-groups and negatively evaluate out-groups to construct a positive sense of self. In addition, Ben-Bassat and Dahan suggest that sources of (dis)identification or ambivalence inform political beliefs and behaviors. For example, more Black people voted for the first presidential candidate of color, just as more women voted for the first woman candidate (Tyson and Maniam). Given SIT, these demographic statistics point to some interesting points of divergence that manifest in voting behaviors. It is likely that people who vote, vote for someone they perceive to be part of their in-group (Ben-Bassat and

Dahan 205). Arguably, it all depends on one's source of identification. For example, women who voted for Trump might not have used gender as a source of identification, just as people of color who supported Trump may not have used race. It is plausible that men of color who voted for Trump may have identified via gender, not race, and so forth. These varied patterns signal the importance of intersectionality of identities. While group-level demographic statistics are telling, they miss the intersectionality and multiplicity of identity and identification, especially in relation to larger structures and systems of power.

Structural intersectionality, a concept originally introduced by Crenshaw, explains how the meeting of two or more social identities complicates and shapes lived experience both materially and discursively in qualitatively different ways that are constructed by societal structures (1245). Crenshaw argues that discursive, cultural, and social structures and systems, such as policy, legislation, capitalism, workforce barriers to entry, institutions of marriage, or notions of family, systematically work together to constrain/enable populations at the point of intersection between two or more social identities. For instance, the intersections of my personal social identities as a Black, cisgender, heterosexual, middle class, Christian, woman and scholar allowed me to view the election results from a simultaneously privileged and marginalized lens. My perspective reveals to me that there is a social identity hierarchy embedded into the presidency. That hierarchy explicitly privileges masculinity and higher social class status.

The structural intersectionality of the presidency, which implies a social identity hierarchy, defines the boundaries of a presidential "in-group" and legitimizes particular identities for candidacy. Arguably, Clinton's campaign pushed the boundaries of the presidential in-group not because of her race or social class status but because of her gender. Yet, Hillary Clinton was not "hired" for president. Her loss in this presidential campaign, despite the popular vote and Obama's previous success, nod to a social identity hierarchy structurally embedded into the presidency. While class status seems to be non-negotiable and race became negotiable as of Obama's 2008 election, gender is questionably nonnegotiable.

Karrin Anderson reminds us this is not Hillary Clinton's first defeat. In the 2008 and 2012 elections, I was able to connect to the racial identity of President Obama. In the 2016 election, I was able to connect with Secretary Clinton's gender identity. However, I suspect that shifting the embodiment of the presidency from White upper-class men to an upper-class man of color, and then to an upper-class White woman in consecutive elections was too much, too fast for some mainstream social identity groups in America. Societal change generally happens slowly, painfully, and chaotically. Unfortunately, there seemed to be some truth to what my 98-year-old African American grandmother told me after the 2016 election: "I knew America was not ready for a woman to be president."

The symbolism of change that President Obama represented was arguably overwhelming for some Americans and likely instilled fear because his race disrupted the norm. The possibility of Hillary Clinton's presidency could have aided in dismantling the gendered norm for presidency. The reaction to the Obama administration and to our new president seem to have strengthened the grip of "interlocking systems of oppression" (Combahee River Collective 1). From my perspective, this grip seems to more vehemently discriminate against members of the "out-group" and privilege members of the "in-group." Donald Trump represents the socially and structurally constructed in-group. He is White, hypermasculine, and upper class; he symbolizes and embodies a dominant structural intersectionality.

Thinking of structural intersectionality, I am reminded that history has foreshadowed this moment to some extent. This foreshadowing can be seen in the historical granting of voting rights to different demographic groups. In essence, our progress in diversifying the presidency parallels historical trends that follow the U.S. right to vote. White men who owned property have had the right to vote in the United States since the Declaration of Independence was signed in 1776 (MassVOTE 1). This law explicitly, structurally, and socially organizes the fundamental privilege of voting around privileged race, gender, and social class status; hence there are founding ideological assumptions legally embedded into U.S. history

and culture. These ideological assumptions construct and reify structural intersectionality and legitimate a particular combination of social identities over others. In 1776, it was not enough to be a member of one or two of those social categories (White, male, or upper class). Membership in all three was required to obtain the right to vote. Obviously, it is no coincidence that the first 43 presidents of our country were White men with middle- to upper-class status.

In 1869 and 1870, the Fifteenth Amendment was passed by Congress and ratified by states, granting the privilege to vote to men regardless of race (MassVOTE 1). This change took approximately 94 years and was the result of unrest, struggle, and resistance. This amendment is colloquially referred to as the amendment that granted Black men (note this amendment did *not* include Native Americans) the right to vote (MassVOTE 1). Because men of color were the second social identity group granted the right to vote, it is parallel then that the first successful presidential candidate who broke the racial barriers of the presidency was an upper-middle-class man of color. The forty-fourth president, Barack Obama symbolically represented progress for people of color; however, his presence as commander in chief still upheld a particular classed and gendered identity.

It was not until approximately 50 years later that women were granted the right to vote in 1919–1920 (MassVOTE 1). The quote by Maya Angelou used to open this essay conveys the parallel nature between the historical right to vote in the United States and the identities of our past U.S. presidents. The American population has to some extent foreshadowed who can be considered legitimately appropriate for president. Women's right to vote in the United States was deferred, just like the hope of our first woman president.

Native American populations were not granted to right to vote until 1924, and the last state laws denying Native Americans the right to vote were not overturned until 1948 (MassVOTE 1). American laws have historically disenfranchised certain populations and were vigorously enforced among the states. If we continue to follow the historical patterns that have been laid before us, then more resistance, struggle, and unrest is warranted.

While "the major systems of oppression are interlocking, [t]he synthesis of these oppressions creates the conditions of our lives" (Combahee River Collective 1). Structural intersectionality has marginalized identities in the United States and constrained the quality of life for many U.S. citizens in ways that strengthen the boundaries and walls between in-groups and out-groups. We must continue to resist such constraints and dichotomous oppositional thinking. Thus, it is important to remain "actively committed to struggling against racial, sexual, heterosexual, and class oppression" (Combahee River Collective 1). Gratefully the proverbial "underdogs" continue to protest the dominant narrative that being authentically American exclusively means the embodiment of White, upper-class masculinity. We have fought against interlocking systems of oppression for our *right* to vote and should also fight against structural intersectionality that constrains who is socially constructed as legitimate governmental leaders. Critical communication scholars, community activists, and feminists have a ripe opportunity to recognize structural intersectionality, communicate and educate for inclusion, and agitate for change.

I am increasingly concerned about the ways in which this new administration strengthens the grip of oppression on individual life. President Trump fuels the fire of festering fear, which will likely increase divisiveness, socially constructed hatred, and oppression. After all, divisiveness and opposition are exactly what SIT explains. What does the future hold for people with marginalized identities who reside in the United States and across the globe? America has shown the world who they believe they are and arguably who they want to remain: patriarchal, White, and wealthy.

As a woman, I was finally able to see a candidate on my ballot with whom I identified during this election. However, as a person of color, I was faced yet again with two White candidates who could not fully grasp my needs, desires, concerns, and hopes as an American citizen with an intersection of marginalized identities. How many others feel a loss of identification when they vote? As a scholar and citizen, I hope future generations will have more than two candidates from which to choose. I dream of a political system that can fully represent the multiplicity that makes up the beautiful, diverse tapestry of our multicultural population, not exclusively candidates that have been socially constructed as normative, legitimate, and acceptable by dominant structural intersections. Until then I will resist, struggle, and fight the good fight. I hope that you will be with me.

REFERENCES

Ashforth, Blake E., and Fred Mael. "Social Identity Theory and the Organization." *Academy of Management Review*, vol. 14, no. 1, 1989, pp. 20–39.

Ben-Bassat, Avi, and Momi Dahan. "Social Identity and Voting Behavior." *Public Choice*, vol. 151, no. 1–2, 2012, pp. 193–214.

Combahee River Collective. "The Combahee River Collective Statement." Apr. 1977, circuitous.org/scraps/combahee.html.

Crenshaw, Kimberlé. "Mapping the Margins: Intersectionality, Identity Politics, and Violence against Women of Color." *Stanford Law Review*, vol. 43, no. 6, 1991, pp. 1241–99.

MassVOTE. "History of Voting Rights." MassVOTE, 2013, massvote.org/voterinfo/history-of-voting-rights/. Accessed 15 Dec. 2016.

Tajfel, Henri, and John C. Turner. "The Social Identity Theory of Intergroup Behavior." *Psychology of Intergroup Relations*, edited by Stephen Worchel and William G. Austin, 2nd ed., Nelson-Hall, 1986, pp. 7–24.

Tyson, Alec, and Shiva Maniam. "Behind Trump's Victory: Divisions by Race, Gender, Education." *Fact Tank: News in the Numbers.* Pew Research Center, 9 Nov. 2016, www.pewresearch.org/fact-tank/2016/11/09/behind-trumps-victory-divisions-by-race-gender-education/. Accessed 4 Dec. 2016.

73. NEW MILITARY FEMININITIES
Humanitarian Violence and the Gendered
Work of War Among U.S. Servicewomen
JENNIFER GREENBURG (2017)

The U.S. military is currently in the process of opening ground combat positions to women. Until the combat exclusion policy was rescinded in 2013, women were technically banned from ground combat positions. The inclusion of women in combat raises a series of questions about what inclusion means, and how it has shifted military gender relations. To understand the stakes of inclusion, we need to examine how servicewomen were employed to search and question women in the post-September 11 (9/11) wars in Iraq and Afghanistan. Beginning in 2003, U.S. Marines assembled all-female 'Lioness' teams to search Iraqi women at checkpoints and during raids of homes. In early 2009, Marines began deploying 'female engagement teams' (FETs), which, like the Lioness teams, specifically employed servicewomen's labor to search Afghan women. The FETs became increasingly institutionalized and involved in health, education, and ostensibly humanitarian activities. By 2010, the army established all-female special operative teams called 'cultural support teams' (CSTs), which were attached to Ranger and Green Beret units. Recent, overtly gendered forms of military labor present a new military femininity that perpetuates violence through expressions of feminine domesticity. The centrality of combat to military femininity challenges long-standing feminist critiques of military institutions' marginalization of women, as well as more recent debates that have focused on female military teams' association with humanitarianism.

By tracking changes in military gender policy through the Lioness, FET, and CST programs, we see how each program was associated with transforming degrees of inclusion of different forms of servicewomen's military labor that variously combined humanitarian work, intelligence gathering and special operations, and direct participation in combat. These degrees of inclusion are associated with different formations of femininity and masculinity that dislodge certain long-standing gender essentialisms, while leaving others in place. For example, although the CSTs dislodged what some scholars argue has been the rendering of women's bodies 'foreign' within military combat roles (e.g. Dowler 2011), they have continued to define femininity through heterosexual marriage, domesticity, and biological reproduction (e.g. Lemmon 2015a). New forms of inclusion have left in place other violent subjugations of women, including the continued prevalence of military rape (Mesok 2016). The gender performances examined here are spatially dependent, with femininity often relying on the 'private' space of the home, and other spatial binaries of 'public' vs. 'private' that are fundamental to debates within feminist geography.

Much of the scholarship on gendered counterinsurgency in Iraq and Afghanistan has focused on how Lioness and FETs operated through the rhetoric of humanitarianism, and emphasized servicewomen's supposedly innate emotional capacity to relate to women and children (Fluri 2014; Khalili 2011; McBride and Wibben 2012; Mesok 2015; Terry 2009). However, military proponents of female counterinsurgent teams advocated for the teams' use in special operations and intelligence rather than humanitarianism. Proponents of female counterinsurgent teams advocated an equally lethal servicewoman to her male colleagues, while upholding gender essentialisms of heterosexual marriage, biological reproduction, and domestic caregiving. The all-female special operative CSTs provide an especially valuable example of the new military femininity because they emphasize women's value for military intelligence directly linked to targeted killing, eschewing many humanitarian aspects of the Lioness and FETs. At the same time, CSTs' military femininity enacted violence through feminine gender essentialisms. The CSTs represent a form of military femininity that does not fit neatly into either recent scholarship concerned with post-9/11 feminized counterinsurgency, or older feminist critiques of militarization that analyzed the military as a masculinist institution that both depends on and devalues women's labor (e.g. Enloe 1983). Feminist geopolitics offers to this conversation an attentiveness to the multiple, interconnected scales of geopolitical violence. Feminist geographical literature identifies the corporeal, the familial, and biological reproduction as key sites to examine geopolitical violence. Drawing on this geographical literature, as well as interventions from feminist international relations, critical military studies, and related fields, I trace how certain long-standing gender essentialisms have been replaced with women's integration into combat, while others remain deeply entrenched.

Between 2010 and 2012, I shadowed civilian contractors providing development expertise to military audiences as an element of counterinsurgency training (Greenburg 2017). Through a series of trips to five different military bases across the U.S., I spent between four days and eight weeks at each base, returning to some more than once. These trips opened into longer-term opportunities to observe other aspects of military training and more informal dimensions of military life. During this period there was intense debate within the military over the role of FETs and CSTs. My observations of military training gave me insight into the internal critiques of the FETs and CSTs, particularly from military women advocating for gender integration. In contrast to the humanitarian rhetoric analyzed in existing scholarship, the political forces I observed on military bases promoted the utility of women for intelligence and more overtly violent military operations—precisely the femininity that the CSTs embodied.

I discuss female counterinsurgent teams through debates within the military gleaned from my own ethnographic observations of military trainings, as well as policy documents, documentary footage, and the journalist Gayle Tzemach Lemmon's popular account of the first CST: *Ashley's War: The Untold Story of a Team of Women Soldiers on the Special Ops Battlefield* (2015a). As an important cultural artifact, *Ashley's War* helps us to understand a salient form of military femininity. The book's representations of white, middle-class domestic femininity mediate the combat military femininity valorized by the CSTs.

. . .

If gender is to be understood not as a synonym for 'women,' but rather a relational term that helps us to understand the production of masculinity and femininity, a gendered analysis of counterinsurgency questions how contemporary forms of war and violence reconfigure masculinities and femininities (Scott 1999). Laleh Khalili's work on the gendered coding of counterinsurgency as 'the civilianized option' is especially useful in this respect (Khalili 2013, 1473). Writing shortly after the U.S. military's adoption of counterinsurgency, she asserts that new forms of masculinity and femininity emerged in which white, literate, articulate, and educated forms of 'manliness' came to be valued over hypermasculine warrior grunts; as a result, this opened spaces for white, middle-class, educated women to enter the highest ranks of security institutions (1475). Khalili's attention to new gender formations of counterinsurgency provides a framework to consider what other masculinities and femininities produce female counterinsurgent teams. A certain echelon of upper- or middle-class, educated, white femininity is central to her argument. Without displacing this femininity—it is crucial to understanding the role of figures such as Hillary Clinton—I want to consider a military femininity that falls outside of the elite femininity Khalili describes. *Ashley's War* presents a femininity that is neither elite nor necessarily formally educated, though it does operate through middle-class domestic norms. The domestic norms at work here echo Fluri's argument regarding FETs that 'affirmative gender essentialism may help to increase women's combat roles in military units, but it risks "selling out" gender equality by presenting gender as a geopolitical tool that both relies on and strengthens "conservative gender regimes"' (Fluri 2014, 808).

Enloe has recently written about the integration of women into combat roles as the 'militarization of women's liberation'—the justification of women's rights in terms of military necessity, or as measured in terms of women's participation in waging war (Enloe 2013). Enloe's (1983) older work frames the military as a masculinist institution in which women's labor as camp followers, prostitutes, mothers, nurses, etc. is required yet simultaneously always cast out. Existing feminist critiques remain relevant to understanding ongoing military marginalizations of women. The continued relevance of a marginalization framework is perhaps most striking in the recent public outrage concerning military rape (Dick 2012; Human Rights Watch 2016; Mesok 2016). But at the same time, military femininity has been valorized, which raises the question of how and on what basis some women are included and even valorized alongside longer-standing exclusions and marginalizations. Military formations emphasizing servicewomen's value for intelligence collection directly linked to lethal targeting, such as the CSTs, are central to a concept of military femininity. It is necessary to look beyond feminized counterinsurgent teams that have operated through humanitarian claims, such as the FETs. By tracing how humanitarian rhetoric gave way to praise of servicewomen's violent utility, it is possible to identify a military femininity with a more complex relationship to marginalization than is available through foundational feminist literatures.

Enloe (1983) has previously written of a 'package of assumptions' about women and femininity within the military. In conversations occurring within the military that came to promote the CSTs over the FETs, I identified a new 'package of assumptions' about women and femininity in the context of liberal counterinsurgent warfare. Building on Belkin's notion of 'military masculinity' as 'a set of beliefs, practices, and attributes, that can enable individuals—men and women—to claim authority on the basis of affirmative relationships with the military or with military ideals,' I argue that an associated concept of 'military femininity' has become increasingly compelling in today's context (Belkin 2012, 3). Military advocates of servicewomen's utility for special operations devalorized military femininities operating through affect and humanitarianism, and introduced a distinct military femininity that promoted violence through gender essentialisms of what it is to be a woman.

SHIFTING MILITARY GENDER REGIMES: FROM 'FEMALE ENGAGEMENT' TO 'CULTURAL SUPPORT'

The army assembled the first all-female team to search Iraqi women at checkpoints in 2003. At the time, official military policy barred women from direct assignment to ground combat units. Officially, members of these teams—dubbed 'Lionesses'—were 'temporarily attached' to the combat units. The documentary, *Lioness* (2008), profiles five women who were members of the U.S. Army's First Engineering Battalion and were sent to Iraq to provide logistical support and supplies to combat battalions. As Lionessess, the women conducted house-to-house patrols and searches of women and children, receiving very little combat training prior to being sent into firefights. One of the most striking moments in the documentary combines footage of the April 2004 Battle of Ramadi with the Lionesses' memories of being deployed with a Marine Combat Brigade Team just after the four Blackwater contractors were killed in Fallujah. The Lioness team was deployed with the Second Battalion, Fourth Marine Regiment, or the '2–4,' nicknamed the 'Magnificent Bastards.' Several years ago on Memorial Day, a *New York Times* article described how Marines from the 2–4 gather at cemeteries in Nashville, Indianapolis, and the hill country of Texas, memorializing the 2004 Battle of Ramadi, in which 34 members of this battalion were killed, and over 250 wounded—more than any other American unit during a six-month tour of either Iraq or Afghanistan (*New York Times*, May 28, 2012; *Marine Corps Times*, March 7, 2014).

The Lioness team deployed with the 2–4 Marines is largely absent from any media coverage of the 2004 Battle of Ramadi. The Marines conducted a cordon-and-search operation to arrest two insurgent leaders, using the Lionesses to search Iraqi women at checkpoints, and to segregate and search women when the Marines entered homes. Shannon, a key figure in the documentary, recalls how it was her first time ever running with a fire team—the part of the battalion that goes first into battle. Shannon describes an insurgent attack that occurred during the search operation: 'They told me I was going to be on the back of the firing team. Especially because I had a SAW (Squad Automatic Weapon), they wanted me to cover their rear. And I was like, "oh god" . . . I was just, like, shaking. I was so scared.' Shannon made shooting sounds and her hands flew about: 'I was running with that Marine fire team . . . bullets everywhere.' She then described looking at Rainie, another member of the Lioness team, who was up on a roof, waving her hands frantically at Shannon to look behind her:

> All of a sudden I looked and everyone was gone. I was the only one in the street. There was insurgents all around me firing at me. I didn't know what to do . . . in the army, you tap back. You tap every man back. And you let 'em know you're moving. These bastards didn't say nothing to me. Just left me there. So I ran for my damn life and caught up with my firing team. And when I got there I kicked the squad leader right in the nuts. For leaving me. I sure did (McLagan and Sommers 2008).

One way to interpret Shannon's account, and the film *Lioness* more broadly, is in terms of early feminist historians' attempts to constitute women as historical subjects. This vein of 'her-story' literature aimed 'to give value to an experience that had been ignored (hence devalued) and to insist on female agency in the making of history' (Scott 1999, 18). Unproblematic incorporation of Shannon's participation into the historical record recalls the 'militarization of women's liberation' (Enloe 2013). At the same time, Shannon's account punctuates her lack of combat training, exposing her to greater harm than some of her male counterparts. Other members of Shannon's team also spoke about how their lack of training exposed them to harm, and the amplification of this exposure by their difficulty accessing health and disability services through the Department of Veterans Affairs (Glantz 2009; McLagan and Sommers 2008). Scott asserts that 'the radical potential of women's history comes in the writing of histories that focus on women's experiences *and* analyze the ways in which politics construct gender and gender constructs politics' (Scott 1999, 27). Shannon's account must then not only be inserted into gender-blind accounts of the Iraq war, but also call attention to the forms of masculinity and femininity being produced. When female counterinsurgent teams became more institutionalized, they were also seized upon by multiple forces advocating for gender integration of the armed forces. As all-female counterinsurgent teams came to represent the cause of gender integration, women's relationship not to humanitarianism, but to military violence, moved to the foreground of discourses and practices of military femininity.

In 2006, the Marines developed the 'Iraqi Women's Engagement Program' in Al Anbar Province, Iraq. Military publications describe sewing clinics and medical outreach undertaken as part of this program, and focus on the dialogues between uniformed and local women over cups of tea (Katt 2014). These programs prefigured the more widespread female engagement teams, or FETs. The first reported FET was assembled by pulling female service members from their regular jobs, with little additional training, to conduct a cordon-and-search operation in Western Afghanistan in February 2009 (ibid.). By late 2009, the program had become much more institutionalized when the International Security Assistance Force (ISAF) commander directed all military units to create FETs. The U.S. Army and Marine Corps recruited for these all-female teams who were trained in combat activities as well as Afghan culture, language, the use of interpreters, and activities like distributing school supplies, opening health clinics, conducting medical outreach, and even providing micro-credit.

In 2011, I observed Jones, a female Marine and FET trainer, while she was giving a shortened version of her regular training to a brigade combat team preparing to deploy to Afghanistan. Sharing her experience from previous deployments to Iraq and Afghanistan, Jones explained to the class, 'when we put on the uniform, we're a third gender: we're women, we're American, and we carry a gun.' She elaborated that what she called a 'third gender' category meant that she could talk about family with other Afghan civilian women, but she could also gain the respect of local men, which she attributed to carrying a gun. 'What I learned [in Afghanistan],' Jones continued, 'was that we [female Marines] were given the respect shown to men, but we were granted access to the household given to females. So we as women had the best of both worlds.' Jones's use of the term 'third gender' is striking. In gender studies literature, the term 'third gender' has often been applied to behaviors falling outside of dyadic male–female norms (Towle and Morgan 2002, 472). The term is also prominent in reference to societies providing clear examples of nonbinary gender practices (Herdt 2012; Roscoe 1998). Jones's use of the term is more in reference to 'Western' servicewomen's strategic positioning in Afghan society, which places them in a different social category than either Afghan women or American servicemen. Jones's use of the term has more in common with ethnographic writing on being treated like a 'third gender' person in the field (Schwedler 2006).

By using a nonbinary understanding of gender, however, Jones challenges the 'conservative gender regimes' some scholars argue could be strengthened by women's increasing role in military combat (Fluri 2014, 808). At the same time, how she uses a 'third gender' framework equates femininity with domesticity and access to other women and children, and masculinity with carrying a gun and access to other men. Jones argues that in adopting both these dyadic 'masculine' and 'feminine' traits, women serving on FETs became a 'third gender.' Gender studies critiques call into question the linking of one essential dualism of male–female with another, for instance, heterosexual–homosexual, and the limitations this places on any nuanced, nonbinary understanding of gender and sexuality (Herdt 2012, 48). Although Jones is not talking about sexuality here, it is possible to see how this particular iteration of 'third gender' servicewomen hardens gender essentialisms by linking a dualistic understanding of 'female' to 'masculine' traits of violence and male homosociality, while maintaining 'feminine' traits of domesticity, reproduction, and caregiving. Although military associations of femininity with domesticity remained in place as feminized counterinsurgency programs accelerated, the act Jones emphasized of 'carrying a gun' became even more pronounced as advocates of women in combat played up servicewomen's value in special operations.

On a different Marine Corps base, I observed another training focused on military interaction with civilians. FETs were a hot topic at the time, with many Marines, especially female Marines, indicting teams as untrained, unprofessional, immature, and, overall, too focused on humanitarian activities. One female major who had interacted with some FETs in Afghanistan described them as a 'bastard unit. They have no clear purpose and are used differently just depending on the whims of the

commander.' She explained that they had been 'set up for failure,' elaborating that the teams' institutional structure departed from the otherwise rigid military hierarchy:

> At the MEF [Marine Expeditionary Force] staff level, the most senior girl on the FETs was a first lieutenant, where everyone else on that staff was a full colonel. So of course nobody is going to listen to her. If they're going to take it seriously, they need to have a female colonel at the regimental level, a lieutenant colonel at the division, a major below that, and so on. The girls on them are also quite young—so you get 19-year-old corporals doing stupid stuff.

The major described servicewomen being plucked from other specializations to serve on FETs without much extra training, giving the teams a very different organizational structure than other military institutions. The major's use of the word *bastard* invokes not only the mixture of rank, training, and age making up the FETs, but also the mixing up of military gender roles the FETs represented, with women moving closer to the front lines through humanitarian work. In the major's description of the teams, it is also evident how military humanitarian labor evoked a limited degree of acceptance by male and female military personnel who interacted with the FETs. This limited acceptance was apparent in the discussion this Marine continued with a colleague in the room with us. In the training I was there to observe, they had been hearing 'rumblings from the top' that similar all-female teams were being assembled for intelligence gathering, and she had always thought the FETs would be better for 'intel,' but that this would violate the combat arms regulations for women. These 'rumblings' were precisely what grew into the CST program, and played an important role in the reversal of combat arms regulations banning women.

During a third army training on another base, I discussed the FETs with Marisa, a civilian contractor who had worked with FETs in Afghanistan, and referred to early FET deployments as 'window dressing,' or 'the fluffy bunny stuff,' which she and her colleagues explained as images of humanitarian relief that a commander could put into a PowerPoint slide to show his superiors. Her voice dripping with sarcasm, Marisa described the FETs like this: 'It's window dressing right now. You open up *Army Times* and there's some soldier with a headscarf looking really earnest and talking to women.' Marisa believed in the FET program. She had deployed as a civilian with Special Forces in Afghanistan early in the FET program. Here she conducted outreach to Afghan women, recalling to me how the meetings she organized with female Afghan villagers were specifically aimed to identify needs that could be filled by Quick Impact Projects: short-term, low-budget projects often used in a counterinsurgency to reward supporters of the counterinsurgents. Marisa was critical of the humanitarian aspects of the FETs, especially media representations of them. After returning from Afghanistan, she worked as a contractor for military trainings. Watching the FETs become more institutionalized and controversial within military circles, she explained:

> This was my big point for all the intel folks. For all the people who want to use FETs for DA, which stands for direct action. Like when they have to go on a night raid and they have to roll somebody up and they just want to use them for searching women in the home and seeing if they have anything on them. In the end, you get much more—even though I, personally, am not as interested in people having actionable intelligence for their target list—but if that's the goal, you're going to get much more authentic intelligence by someone calling you, on your cell phone, to tell you about something because they trust you. And you've established that you care more than about just that.

The 'trust' Marisa speaks of was related to the meetings she had with female villagers, during which emotional connection was certainly part of the work, but her point was that affect always had to be connected to its utility for intelligence—the prospect of 'rolling somebody up.' Marisa's account speaks to the importance of understanding how the affective and humanitarian representations of the FETs were always connected to the specter of violence. Her comments also clarify the space of the home as central to FETs' performances of gender. In both the FETs and CSTs, servicewomen's access to the private space of the Afghan family home

was considered a key asset, whether that was framed in terms of 'winning hearts and minds,' gathering intelligence, or some mixture of both.

Marisa commented that 'any time FETs are brought up in a large room, you can hear people snicker . . . For the male side, for them to consider it important, it has to get away from just sounding like development, wishy washy stuff, or women's issues. It has to be termed differently. And unfortunately it has to encompass this notion that that's how you get better intel.' This was the conclusion she had come to after her commanding officer in Afghanistan referred to her meetings with Afghan women as 'knitting circles.' I noticed these snickers in many of the military classrooms I observed. Marisa, and many of her civilian and military colleagues, arrived at the conclusion that the only way female teams would be taken seriously was through their connection to intelligence and combat.

FETs were mainly publicized through the language of humanitarianism and affect. However, the next iteration of all-female counterinsurgent teams moved away from what Marisa called 'development and wishy washy stuff,' and much more toward what the military calls 'kinetic' (violent) operations. At the same time as FETs were being praised in military public relations accounts for 'winning Afghan women's hearts and minds,' in 2010 the U.S. Army Special Forces Command was also beginning to assemble all-female teams to be attached to Army Rangers and Green Berets. Special Forces had realized that their operations would benefit from servicewomen capable of separating and questioning women and children during night raids of homes in Afghanistan. These all-female special operative teams were called cultural support teams, or CSTs. Precisely because they eschew some of the humanitarian aspects the FETs emphasized, CSTs present some of the most important clues about changes in gendered military structures occurring today. The form of military femininity valued by CSTs—which might be considered an amplification of the violent connection to intelligence in Marisa's narrative—is markedly different from the affect and humanitarianism other scholars emphasize.

ASHLEY'S WAR: GENDER ESSENTIALISM, VIOLENCE, AND THE NEW MILITARY FEMININITY

A recent exception to what is otherwise a dearth of literature on the CSTs is journalist Gayle Tzemach Lemmon's popular account of the first CST—*Ashley's War* (2015a). The book is named after First Lieutenant Ashley White, the first member of a CST to be killed in action when she died in an explosion during a night raid in Kandahar alongside two male Army Rangers. The book appeared on the *New York Times* best sellers list, was promoted by Sheryl Sandberg and Jon Stewart, and its rights have been sold to produce a Hollywood blockbuster. Lemmon describes the CSTs as 'the softer side of the hardest side of war' (Lemmon 2015a, 108). The book emphasizes the heteronormative femininity of the CST members, particularly the central character of Ashley White. Lemmon describes White as

> a petite blond dynamo who barely reached five foot three. And she was this wild mix of Martha Stewart and what we know as GI Jane. She was someone who loved to make dinner for her husband . . . She also loved to put 50 pounds of weight on her back and run for miles. And she loved to be a soldier. She was somebody who had a breadmaker in her office in Kandahar. And would make a batch of raisin bread and go to the gym and bust out 25 or 30 pull ups from a dead hang (Lemmon 2015b).

Throughout the book, Lemmon emphasizes White's feminine domesticity through recollections of the meals she would cook for her husband in their modest single-family home in North Carolina, and her continuation of this domestic caregiving via baking bread and cookies for Rangers in the field (Lemmon 2015a). Ashley's performance of domesticity is also spatially dependent on the place of her family home, aspects of which are transplanted to her deployment via the breadmaker she brings to the field and the proxy bodies of male Rangers she bakes for in her husband's absence. Such gendered forms of domestic labor are reminiscent of historical celebrations of women's contribution to war through hostessing, entertaining, or secretarial work (see Lutz 2001, 59–64). It is as if the author must remind the reader that Ashley is female even though she is doing military labor that was formerly restricted to men. The forms of domestic labor Ashley performs are uniquely articulated through military violence.

In the book, White is further celebrated for blending the role of a devoted domestic caretaker with that of a lethal soldier. Her connection to humanitarian endeavors is not emphasized, though tasks involving some level of emotional maturity, such as calming groups of women and children during a night raid, do figure prominently. Here the greater degree of servicewomen's acceptance by the dominant masculine military culture is apparent, in particular when servicewomen are not performing humanitarian work so much as participating in night raids of Afghan homes. The space of the home—here the Afghan family home that is to be infiltrated by a ground combat operation—is again significant in servicewomen's gendered labor. The gender formation associated with this degree of acceptance and amalgam of military labor blends hetero-normative femininity with military and physical skill. Khalili has written of the rise of a particular category of women and feminism that

> is indicative of a kind of femininity which is comfortable with, and in fact positively values, breaking through security spaces coded as masculine, and which appropriates many of the 'new masculine' qualities of the soldier-scholars, perhaps as a subspecies of what Judith Butler has provocatively called drag, or 'an uncritical appropriation of sex-role stereotyping' (Khalili 2011, 1473; Butler 1990).

. . . The gendered shift Khalili points to also identifies the civilian aspects of counterinsurgency with femininity, preserving the more mechanized, technologically advanced, higher-fire-power forms of war as masculine (ibid.). Yet Lemmon's representation of Ashley White does not adhere to the strict identification of femininity with civilians. Using Scott's notion of gender as a set of practices constituting femininity and masculinity, Khalili draws attention to femininity's association with civilians and masculinity's association with combatant. The advent of CSTs associated femininity with combat in a way that is different from femininity's association with the civilianization of war. This difference signals a change in the gendered politics that constitute knowledge about femininity and masculinity, and about military femininity in particular.

Within this broader framework of new gender dynamics of counterinsurgency, Khalili writes of 'a new hierarchy of power, in which white women were automatically placed in superior position to [Iraqi] men who in other circumstances would have been the expected superiors' (Khalili 2011, 1482). Female soldiers like White factor into this hierarchy well below elite civilian women, such as Emma Sky or Sarah Chayes, who advise male 'soldier-scholar' generals, but still above the racialized colonized man. . . .

There is a transgressive character to these elements of physical prowess and lethality but it is altogether different than the transgressive gender politics Khalili discusses in relation to Lynndie England and Sabrina Harman—two female soldiers at Abu Ghraib who became iconic figures of the torture inflicted on Iraqi men at the prison. Discussing how England and Harman uniquely became archetypes of U.S. torture, Khalili emphasizes how they were iconic representations of transgressive women, at the same time as they were subtly the embodiment of the new hierarchy of power that placed white women automatically in superior positions to Iraqi men (Khalili 2011, 1482). In Khalili's analysis of the racialized and gendered hierarchies produced in what she calls the 'seam of imperial encounter . . . the messy interstitial space in which the cross-hatching of race, gender, class, and empire all produce unexpected hierarchical positioning,' white working-class women play a particularly important role through their positioning in relation to Iraqi men (1481). Harman, for instance, was the daughter of a police detective, and England the daughter of a poultry factory worker.

If England and Harman became iconic by being demonized as transgressive military women, White embodies a military femininity that is decidedly untransgressive, involving middle-class domestic gender norms, and military norms governing acceptable vs. exceptional forms of violence. This is a femininity that 'plays by the rules' by embracing domestic caretaking and biological reproduction alongside military violence—in Lemmon's words, 'Martha Stewart meets GI Jane' (Lemmon 2015b). Mesok points to the Lioness teams' display of the military's racial diversity as 'a multicultural, multiracial site of freedom' offered to the women of Iraq (Mesok 2015, 67). In contrast, in her analysis of a White House promotional video of the FETs, Fluri notes that 'despite the racial diversity of the armed forces and FET program, all of the U.S. servicewomen in this video are phenotypically white, suggesting a dichotomized racialized aesthetic representation of female military personnel on the one hand and Afghan and Iraqi women and children on the other' (Fluri 2014, 806). In *Ashley's War* and other public representations, the participants in the CST program are also phenotypically white, suggesting the dichotomized racialized aesthetic representation to which Fluri refers, as well as the punctuation of whiteness in the broader configuration of military femininity. The white female soldier's body plays an especially significant role in public and media representations of all-female teams, in contrast to team members' direct experiences in Mesok's account.

CONCLUSION

Female counterinsurgent teams represent broader changes occurring today in military gender relations. I have presented the development of a new military femininity through the establishment of Lioness, female engagement, and cultural support teams, each of which was associated with transforming degrees of inclusion of servicewomen's military labor, at the same time as certain forms of repression and marginalization remained entrenched. Attention to the images, discourses, and practices associated with female counterinsurgent teams reveals how women's military labor has become increasingly accepted, even embraced, particularly as it has moved away from humanitarian work and emphasized women's utility to special operations. This acceptance has been achieved partly through a specific frame of femininity that emphasizes the servicewoman's equal combat capabilities to men, while maintaining a definition of femininity through heterosexual marriage, biological reproduction, and domestic caregiving.

The inclusion of women on the basis of a specific military femininity challenges the academic paradigm of women's marginalization within military institutions. At the same time, conceptual space for 'inclusion' can be made without completely abandoning an analysis of marginalization. There is a complex relationship between inclusion and marginalization that demands further research. Servicewomen's recent formal inclusion in ground combat through a very specific form of femininity is also occurring through various forms of violence and marginalization. The pervasiveness of military rape is one of the most disturbing examples of how the dominant military paradigm continues to exclude and marginalize many service members (male and female), including a disproportionate number of servicewomen. The absence of sexual assault in *Ashley's War* indicates how the new military femininity presents a very circumscribed notion of what it is to be a female soldier, a notion that disavows women who have been sexually assaulted by fellow military personnel. Further research is necessary on how the military's celebration of certain forms of femininity may be connected to other forms of exclusion, such as administratively discharging military sexual assault survivors and rendering them 'ineligible for compensation for service-related sexual trauma and for access to appropriate mental health services' (Tayyeb and Greenburg 2017, 6; also see Human Rights Watch 2016). The interplay between inclusion and violent repression is an important aspect of military femininity to follow in ongoing debates over military rape, inclusion of transgender service members, and the gendered work of war that informs so many aspects of military labor.

CSTs played an especially significant role in rescinding the combat exclusion policy. In contrast to their predecessors, CSTs display a form of military femininity that joins violence with white, middle-class feminine domesticity. This blend of 'Martha Stewart meets GI Jane' is situated in popular representations of servicewomen, such as *Ashley's War*, Congressional hearings, and debates internal to the military over the role of women in combat. The new military femininity provided a particularly compelling blend of hetero-normative domesticity to ongoing policy debates, alongside proof of women's value in combat. Following the formal inclusion of women in ground combat, understandings of femininity that circulate through the Lionesses, FETs, and CSTs inform the military's ongoing gender integration.

A *Military Times* poll taken just after the November 2016 election found that 55 percent of female troops contacted were concerned that their jobs would be 'adversely affected' under the Trump presidency (De Luce and McLeary 2016). One of these adverse effects is the possible return to the policy of excluding women from combat, as well as slowing or completely reversing the process of allowing transgender service members to openly serve. The emergent U.S. political landscape is a key terrain on which military femininities and masculinities will be performed and reformulated through the interplay between inclusion, exclusion, and ongoing forms of marginalization.

REFERENCES

Belkin, Aaron. 2012. *Bring Me Men: Military Masculinity and the Benign Facade of American Empire, 1898–2001.* New York: Columbia University Press.

Butler, Judith. 1990. *Gender Trouble: Feminism and the Subversion of Identity.* New York: Routledge.

De Luce, Dan, and Paul McLeary. 2016. "Female and Transgender Troops Fear Combat Exclusion in Trump's Pentagon." *Foreign Policy*, December 19.

Dick, Kirby, dir. 2012. *The Invisible War.* Documentary. New York: New Video Group.

Dowler, Lorraine, 2011. "The Hidden War: The "Risk" to Female Soldiers in the US Military." In *Reconstructing Conflict: Integrating War and Post-War Geographies*, edited by Scott Kirsch and Colin Flint, 295–314. Burlington, VT: Ashgate.

Enloe, Cynthia. 1983. *Does Khaki Become You?: The Militarisation of Women's Lives.* Boston, MA: South End Press.

Enloe, Cynthia. 2013. "Combat: The Zone of Women's Liberation?" *The Progressive*, January 24.

Fluri, Jennifer. 2014. "States of (In)Security: Corporeal Geographies and the Elsewhere War." *Environment and Planning D: Society and Space* 32: 795–814.

Glantz, Aaron. 2009. *The War Comes Home: Washington's Battle Against America's Veterans*. Berkeley, CA: UC Press.

Greenburg, Jennifer. 2017. "Selling Stabilization: Anxious Practices of Militarized Development Contracting." *Development and Change*. Advance online publication. doi:10.1111/dech.12348.

Herdt, Gilbert. 2012. "Introduction: Third Sexes and Third Genders." In *Third Sex, Third Gender—Beyond Sexual Dimorphism in Culture and History*, edited by Gilbert Herdt, 21–81. New York: Zone Books.

Human Rights Watch. 2016. *Booted: Lack of Recourse for Wrongfully Discharged US Military Rape Survivors*. New York: Human Rights Watch. https://www.hrw.org/node/288710/.

Katt, Megan. 2014. "Blurred Lines: Cultural Support Teams in Afghanistan." *Joint Forces Quarterly* 75: 106–113.

Khalili, Laleh. 2011. "Gendered Practices of Counterinsurgency." *Review of International Studies* 37 (4): 1471–1491.

Khalili, Laleh. 2013. *Time in the Shadows: Confinement in Counterinsurgencies*. Stanford, CA: Stanford University Press.

Lemmon, Gayle Tzemach. 2015a. *Ashley's War: The Untold Story of a Team of Women Soldiers on the Special Ops Battlefield*. New York: Harper.

Lemmon, Gayle Tzemach. 2015b. *Meet the Women Fighting on the Front Lines of an American War*. New York: TED Talk.

Lutz, Catherine. 2001. *Homefront: A Military City in the American 20th Century*. Boston, MA: Beacon Press.

McBride, Keally, and Annick Wibben. 2012. "The Gendering of Counterinsurgency in Afghanistan."

Humanity: An International Journal of Human Rights, Humanitarianism, and Development 3 (2): 199–215.

McLagan, Meg, and Daria Sommers, 2008. *Lioness*. Documentary. Room 11 Productions.

Mesok, Elizabeth. 2015. "Affective Technologies of War: US Female Counterinsurgents and the Performance of Gendered Labor." *Radical History Review* 2015 (123): 60–86.

Mesok, Elizabeth. 2016. "Sexual Violence and the US Military: Feminism, US Empire, and the Failure of Liberal Equality." *Feminist Studies* 42 (1): 41–69.

Roscoe, Will. 1998. *Changing Ones: Third and Fourth Genders in Native North America*. New York: St. Martin's Press.

Schwedler, Jillian, 2006. "The Third Gender: Western Female Researchers in the Middle East." *Political Science and Politics* 39 (3): 425–428.

Scott, Joan. 1999. *Gender and the Politics of History*. New York: Columbia University Press.

Tayyeb, Ali, and Jennifer Greenburg. 2017. "'Bad Papers': The Invisible and Increasing Costs of War for Excluded Veterans." Costs of War Project. Watson Institute for International and Public Affairs: Brown University. Accessed http://watson.brown.edu/costsofwar/papers.

Terry, Jennifer. 2009. "Significant Injury: War, Medicine, and Empire in Claudia's Case." *Women's Studies Quarterly* 37 (1–2): 200–225.

Towle, Evan B., and Lynn Marie Morgan. 2002. "Romancing the Transgender Native: Rethinking the Use of the 'Third Gender' Concept." *GLQ: A Journal of Lesbian and Gay Studies* 8 (4): 469–497.

74. SPEECH ON SWEDEN'S FEMINIST FOREIGN POLICY

MARGOT WALLSTRÖM (2016)

Minister Labidi, Mr. Dimiter Chalev, Ladies and Gentlemen, Students,

Four hundred and seventeen thousand. That is the number of internally displaced people in Libya. Many of them are women and children living under dire humanitarian conditions, without protection against gender-based and sexual violence, which is increasing according to recent reports.

Four percent. The number of signatories of 31 major peace processes between 1992 and 2011 that were women. In the same sample, only 2 percent of chief mediators and 9 percent negotiators are women.

I am here today to talk to you about why Sweden actively pursues a feminist foreign policy. With these two interlinked examples—Libya, a conflict with serious repercussions not least for Tunisia, and the lack of women involved in peace processes globally—I want to illustrate why it is so important that we include 100 percent of the population when we address war and conflict. But not only then: Tunisia is one of the best examples of how women's active political participation contributes to sustainable social change and democratic gains.

I am honoured to address you at this prestigious research institution and thank IHEC and the UN Office of Human Rights for hosting us.

Thank you, Mr. Chalev, for your introductory comments. I look forward to a discussion with you, Ms. Labidi. I am happy to see many familiar faces here today of women who have contributed to Tunisia's democratic consolidation, and the faces of many more whom I hope will do so in the future.

I have divided speech into three parts. First, I will describe the concept of a feminist foreign policy in more detail. Secondly, I will highlight some areas where the world can learn from Tunisia. I will conclude with some thoughts on how we can achieve real change.

***

WHAT A FEMINIST FOREIGN POLICY CAN DO

Sweden's feminist foreign policy aims at ensuring women's rights and participation in central decision-making processes. Gender equality is not just the right thing to do. As research is consistently telling us, it is the necessary and smart thing to do if we want to achieve our wider security and foreign policy objectives. We know for a fact that increasing gender equality has a positive impact on food security, extremism, health, education and various other key global concerns.

Feminist foreign policy is an integral part of the activities of the Swedish Foreign Service. Our methodology can be summarised in four words, all beginning with the letter "R."

Reality check is about getting the facts right from the outset. If we look to the needs and aspirations of 100 percent of the population, what is the situation on the ground? How should we then prioritize?

Rights. The fact is that human rights are also women's rights. Here, two fundamental tracks must be followed when pursuing a feminist foreign policy. Firstly, there are areas where we must aim for prohibition, such as gender-based discrimination, domestic violence and forced marriages. Secondly, there are areas where the aim is progress, for example equal rights to inheritance and access to education, employment and health, including sexual and reproductive health and rights. These areas are key to women's empowerment.

Representation, which includes influence over agenda-setting and starts by asking a simple question: who conducts policy? Whether it regards foreign or domestic policy, whether in Sweden or Tunisia, we see that women are still under-represented in influential positions in all areas of society. I am proud that the Swedish Ministry for Foreign Affairs might be an exception: five top positions—all three ministers and two out of three state secretaries—are held by women.

Resources refers to Sweden's ambitious international work, for example in development cooperation. The starting-point here is the need to apply a gender perspective when distributing aid and resources. To give an example: today, only one per cent of spending in security sector reform is allocated to initiatives which consider gender equality a significant objective. This is unacceptable. Global gender equality goals must have financial backing.

LEARNING FROM EACH OTHER: THE TUNISIAN EXAMPLE

It gives me particular pleasure to talk about gender issues here in Tunisia. Since Tunisia's independence 60 years ago, you have led the way in terms of advancing women's rights. Tunisian policies promoting women's education and participation in the labour market are unique in this part of the world. Women hold prominent positions in politics, social life and business, several of whom I see here today. I also see many bright and dedicated students, young men and women, the future leaders of Tunisia. To you I want to say: intellectual freedom is a cornerstone of democracy, cherish it, protect it. When you graduate, there is a world waiting for new leadership and strong values.

I also want to highlight the role that women played in the revolution five years ago and continue to play in consolidating your democracy. Tunisia's many democratic gains—new political parties, free democratic elections, freedom of speech and a vibrant civil society—are an illustration of how women's participation is crucial for sustainable development. The new Tunisian constitution that was adopted in 2014 guarantees equal human rights and citizenship for men and women and is a testament to the commitment, struggle and endurance of many passionate advocates in politics, civil society and media alike. I applaud you.

HOW CAN WE WORK TOGETHER TO ACHIEVE REAL CHANGE?

As you may know, Sweden yesterday inaugurated our embassy to Tunisia. I warmly welcome this strengthening of our bilateral ties and look forward to the work that we will do together in the future. Swedish aid to Tunisia includes support for human rights training in the justice sector and capacity building for female judges. Facilitated by the Swedish Institute, cooperation now also addresses the topic of gender equality through children's literature. Swedish companies employ over 5,000 Tunisians, a majority of them women. And I have learned that Beity, with Swedish support, has inaugurated a Centre d'Accueil for marginalized women here in Tunis. Sweden is proud to be a partner in all these ventures and more to come as we look forward to closer cooperation between our two countries.

* * *

Dear friends,

Gender equality is not a 'women's issue'. It is an issue of human rights, and of development. Our two countries have already pledged to work together towards the fulfilment of the Sustainable Development Goals by 2030. Gender equality is not just one of the 17 goals, but also precondition for the achievement of many of the others.

Sweden will join the UN Security Council as a non-permanent member for 2017–2018. We will prioritize the topic of women, peace and security in our work, pushing to operationalise the ground-breaking Security Council Resolution 1325 with regard to all phases including peacebuilding and conflict prevention. We will work to overcome the glaring underrepresentation of female mediators in UN peace processes.

Sweden's feminist foreign policy aims to respond to one of the greatest challenges of this century: the continued violations of women's and girls' human [rights]. Regardless of whether we struggle for gender equality at home—in Sweden or Tunisia, or in a context of conflict like neighbouring Libya—let's remember how the Swedish feminist and author Elin Wägner compared values and ideals to old-fashioned bicycle lights: they don't light up until you pedal forwards.

In our work for global gender equality, Sweden and Tunisia can do a great deal together. I am confident that many of you in this room will join in pedalling forward.

Thank you.

75. WHAT IT FEELS LIKE TO BE ON WELFARE
BRENDA DELLA CASA (2013)

Not too long ago, I woke up, grabbed my iPhone and popped onto Facebook to see what I had missed since falling asleep. What can I say other than I play on social media like it's my job. Normally my news feed is full of baby photos, food, and travel shots and the occasional questionable joke. On this particular morning, I was faced with a photo of a food stamp with a note to "those on welfare" who "don't work" and "milk the system." The post was calling for "accountability." I just shook my head in disappointment.

While most political comments don't hit me very hard (we all have a right to our opinion), I have a difficult time with those that group any set of people into a section and blame and berate them. It's especially disturbing when those I know make these kinds of statements and then look me in the eye and say it to me as though I am above some kind of fray. Quite frankly, it makes me sick to my stomach. Yes, there are people who abuse all kinds of systems, regardless of their tax bracket, but too often I hear people equate poverty with laziness or worse, criminal behavior, and it's heart-wrenching for me on a deeply personal level.

I have made no secret that I come from way down. I grew up in various cockroach-infested apartments with a violent, drug-addicted ex-felon father and a mother who did me both a favor and a great disservice by leaving. The only person I had to watch over me and make sure that I had food, water, and ice for my wounds was my beloved, hardworking and retired grandfather who supported me with a $500 monthly budget that was paid to him via pension and social security.

That included rent money.

When we lost our home (thanks to my father skipping bail) we moved into our fishing trailer and ate Pork and Beans nearly every weeknight for dinner. On weekends, we lived lakeside and ate the fish we caught. Finally, after we had to spend one third of our income on my eyeglasses, we went to sign up for food stamps, and stood in line for our boxed block of "government cheese." For a former foreman and a little girl who was already made fun of for a number of reasons and who was particularly sensitive to her grandfather's feelings, it was humiliating.

I hated seeing my proud and dignified hero standing in line for handouts. This was a man who prided himself on being self-sufficient and instilled a sense of duty and independence in me from day one. We were not drug addicts living the high life—we were just poor.

"You will be educated and life will be better for you when you get older, Brenda Lynn," he promised. He was going to fight like hell to see that it happened. "You just need to go to college and you'll never have to go through this again." But I was five years old.

We had a few years, hospital trips, pairs of shoes, and meals to worry about.

My grandfather had a moral fiber as thick as wool. He was a God-fearing man who treated everyone with dignity and respect, volunteered to help others, worked odd jobs to make money for us, and taught me to also treat everyone with dignity and respect, reminding me that "we are all equal, and we all put our pants on one leg at a time." He may not personally have agreed with your way of life, but he'd certainly vote for your right to live as you saw fit as long as it did not hurt anyone else.

He tipped his hat to women on the street. He firmly shook the hands of men. He opened doors. He gave what he had to help others, and he kept his word. He pressed and polished our cheap clothes and shoes to make us look as nice as possible. He didn't smoke, drink or do drugs. He paid his taxes—on time.

My grandfather wanted what all good, decent and loving fathers want for their daughters—the best, safest and most dignified life. While he'd have to save up for a few months to buy me a new dress at Sears in order to see the bright surprise flash across my face, I believe we were rich. Very few children enjoyed the conversation, love, companionship and connection we had. Having a hamburger and slice of pie once a week was our "big date" when we could afford it, and believe me when I tell you that there is still no better "date" for me today.

I was raised to believe in hard work, the value of education, human interaction, honoring your word, equality and making your own way in this world and helping others. When he passed away, everything beautiful in my world went with him.

I was bounced from home-to-home and turned to the system only once when I was cold and needed somewhere to sleep over Thanksgiving. I walked into Juvenile Hall and asked to stay there. Those two days were enough time for me to realize that I needed to stay under the radar.

God knows it would have been easier to have food stamps to offer someone to take me in or medical insurance, but I had to make due without both. On the occasion that I needed to go to the doctor, I went to Planned Parenthood. Not to exercise my right to choose, but for breast exams and free medical attention in a facility that treated me like a human being.

When I tried to work at 14, I was told I was not old enough to get a full time job. So, I worked under the table when I could and accepted food, clothes and shelter from those who felt sorry for me. Equally humiliating.

When it was time to go to college, I had the grades and essays to get in, but I was under 24 and that meant that I needed a parental signature. I was on my own and never a ward of the court, a painful purgatory for someone who ached to just get to the starting line like everyone else.

Thanks to President Clinton, an amendment was made, making it possible for kids who had been on their own and who had stayed out of the system (i.e., bounced from home-to-home or on the streets) to prove they were alone and apply for loans on their own and go to school. With that, a scholarship and loans, I attended American University, excelled where I could and Interned at The White House.

In the time since childhood and now, I have made an incredible family of friends who are on both sides of the political fence. Some of my friends feel very strongly about helping others whereas others feel we should all be responsible only for helping ourselves. Some of my friends are gay and have been humiliated, put down, abused, shut out and treated as second-class citizens by family members and strangers alike solely because they love the "wrong" gender.

I have friends who have started rehabilitation programs and others who have benefited from them. I have friends who go to church every week and others who have never stepped foot into one. I personally believe in God and God said that we should steer clear of judging others unless we want to be judged ourselves. I believe God judges deception, bigotry, cruelty and those who live their lives in ways that bring pain to others.

You may not believe this. We don't have to agree. But I will still show you respect, not only because that's how I was raised, but because it feels right on a deep and human level.

I am writing this because I want to say that I was one of those "welfare" people so many people callously group into the "lazy" section of the room. While I am now often told by these same people that I am one of the hardest working people they know, the reality is that there is no way I would be where I am today without the help I received in my past. Some tell me, "Yeah, but you are an exception."

No, I am not.

I am just one of the many people born under difficult circumstances who wanted to do better and needed a little help getting onto my feet. Now that I am on them, I do my best not to forget what it felt like when I was not. If anything, my past has benefited me in that it has served as a strong warning not to play the "we" VS "them" game as one day you might be the "them."

76. THE RISE OF THE VALKYRIES: IN THE ALT-RIGHT, WOMEN ARE THE FUTURE, AND THE PROBLEM

SEYWARD DARBY

A month after Donald Trump took office, an activist named Lana Lokteff delivered a speech calling on women to join the political resistance. "Be loud," Lokteff said in a crisp, assertive voice. "Our enemies have become so arrogant that they count on our silence."

Lokteff, who is in her late thirties, addressed an audience of a few hundred people seated in a room with beige walls, drab lighting, and dark-red curtains. The location, a building in the historic Södermalm neighborhood of Stockholm, Sweden, had been secured only the previous night, after several other venues had refused to host the event, billed as an "ideas" conference. Lokteff wore a white blouse and a crocheted black shawl over her trim figure, with a microphone headset fitted over her long blond hair. In addition to the attendees seated before her, she spoke to viewers watching a livestream. "When women get involved," she declared, "a movement becomes a serious threat."

Since Trump's election in November, that same idea had inspired more than 4,000 women to contact EMILY's List, an organization that backs female pro-choice candidates across the United States, about running for office. It had compelled women to organize a series of marches that brought millions of anti-Trump protesters into streets around the world.

To Lokteff, however, those women were the enemy. She is a member of the "alt-right," the insurgent white-nationalist faction that backed Trump's campaign. A motley coalition of online provocateurs, the alt-right opposes political correctness and multi-culturalism. Many of its supporters rhapsodize about the eventual creation of white ethnostates in Europe and North America. The group is the offspring of various extremist ideologies — the European New Right, identitarianism, paleoconservatism, and Nazism, to name a few.

The alt-right is widely considered a movement of young white men, and Lokteff was trying to rally women to the cause. "It was women that got Trump elected," she said. "And, I guess, to be really edgy, it was women that got Hitler elected."[1] The crowd applauded and cheered.

Lokteff said that "lionesses and shield maidens and Valkyries" would inspire men to fight political battles for the future of white civilization. "What really drives men is women," she explained, "and, let's be honest, sex with women." Lokteff, who has a penchant for diffuse historical references, asked her audience to imagine the *vesica piscis*, the shape created when two circles intersect, as in a Venn diagram. She pointed out that it adorns the doorways and windows of many old European churches. "It lured people in, making them feel warm," she said. "To get graphic, the vesica is reminiscent of the vagina."

Lokteff was the conference's only female speaker — perhaps because the alt-right has certain ideas about how women should behave. Another presenter, Matt Forney . . . once wrote a screed called "The Case Against Female Self-esteem." In his Stockholm speech, Forney bemoaned social norms telling white men that "your natural masculine instincts, your natural desires to bed and wed women, make you an oppressive misogynist." Paul Ramsey, who appeared at the event to decry a purported scourge of left-wing violence in America, is better known to his more than 38,000 Twitter followers as RAMZPAUL. Middle-aged with black, thick-rimmed glasses, he doesn't embrace the alt-right label, but his views align with those of many in the movement: He thinks women shouldn't vote, and has called gender equality "the mother of all delusions."

Other soldiers in the alt-right's fractious army regularly insult women on digital platforms such as Twitter, 4chan, and Reddit. The man who claims to have coined the term "alt-right," Richard Spencer, has said that women shouldn't make foreign policy because their "vindictiveness knows no bounds." Andrew Anglin, who runs a neo-Nazi website called the Daily Stormer, once criticized as a traitor any white woman who has mixed-race children. "It's OUR WOMB," he wrote. "It belongs to the males in her society."

Soon after the Stockholm conference, Lokteff's speech was posted on YouTube and several alt-right websites. One commenter called her an "Aryan goddess"; another joked, "I'm with her." Some, though, were less kind. "Those claims of . . . 'women being the force behind the men' etc., are just feminism infecting the so-called 'movement,' " a reader wrote on AltRight.com. "If women are busy giving speeches and making YouTube broadcasts, they are not going to have time to give birth."

Despite the vitriol she faces from ostensible ideological allies, Lokteff is a passionate warrior for the alt-right, the closest thing the movement has to a queen bee. And she isn't without her high-profile supporters. David Duke, the éminence grise of American white supremacy, has praised her as a "harder-hitting" Ann Coulter, with a "movie-star quality." Lokteff earned the endorsement with her prolific online broadcast work: She and her husband, Henrik Palmgren, run a media company called Red Ice. With studios full of high-end recording gear, blue lighting, and plush furniture, Red Ice is a slick propaganda platform for white nationalists.

Lately, Lokteff has been using Red Ice to amplify the voices of self-made female pundits. All of them are bitterly disappointed in the feminist agenda and believe that nationalism has their true interests at heart. They also embody a glaring contradiction: By supporting the alt-right, they stand shoulder to shoulder with men who think that female independence has undermined Western civilization. As the alt-right creeps out of the digital shadows and strives for civic legitimacy, however, these female commentators are trying to temper the movement's misogynist reputation. They describe the alt-right as a refuge where white women can embrace their femininity and their racial heritage without shame.

The question of why they've embarked on this crusade has a practical answer: No movement can survive on men alone. As one female pundit recently wrote, the prospect of the alt-right attracting women "terrifies the left, and it should, because they know that once a threshold of female involvement is reached, there's no going back." The philosophical answer is more complex — as are the intellectual contortions women must perform to justify participating in a movement so hostile to their freedom.

In an email exchange, Lokteff had extolled the alt-right as "incredibly diverse, just not racially," with "pagans, Christians, atheists, agnostics and even a few Satanists." . . . She spoke of ideological diversity: free-market capitalists and national socialists — Hitler references notwithstanding, she prefers not to use the term "Nazis" — who find common ground on matters of race. Alt-right men, she added, tend toward a certain comportment. "They're more alpha-male types," Lokteff told me. "Girls are kind of sick of the neutered-down, feminist, limp-wristed guy," she added, flopping one of her hands to demonstrate.

According to Keegan Hankes, a researcher at the Southern Poverty Law Center (S.P.L.C.), the alt-right is only superficially heterogeneous. "They have all these conflicting and complementary ideas entangled," he told me, "so that they can pivot" in arguments and interviews. However, Hankes noted, "Where there's smoke, there's fire."

The alt-right derives from the same impulses that have launched other white extremist groups, including a belief that "white civilization, the white race

in particular, is imperiled," said George Michael, a professor of criminal justice at Westfield State University, who studies right-wing extremism. This fear often emerges on the coattails of momentous change: the post-Civil War era of black emancipation, the transatlantic immigration waves of the early twentieth century, the Great Depression, the civil rights movement. Alt-right supporters point out that America was 80 percent white in 1980, but is barely 60 percent white today. They denounce rising rates of interracial marriage, liberal immigration policies, the Black Lives Matter movement, and the targeting of "white privilege" by academics and the media. The European contingent, meanwhile, bemoans the flow of refugees from Africa and the Middle East.

At the same time, social-science research sheds some light on the movement's appeal to individuals who profess to be seeking truth or purpose. The work of the political scientists Joseph E. Uscinski and Joseph M. Parent suggests that people who experience anxiety and loss of control over their personal circumstances are more likely to adopt fringe beliefs. This March, psychologists at Princeton published a study showing that ostracism also enhances belief in conspiracy theories.

The alt-right, Michael explained, benefits from the bullhorn the internet provides and from savvy branding engineered by its leaders. "They tend to frame their arguments less in the verbiage of supremacy and more in the verbiage of self-defense," he said. "It's more palatable." Nonetheless, the S.P.L.C. designates various entities in the alt-right as hate groups, including the Daily Stormer and Richard Spencer's "think tank," the National Policy Institute (N.P.I.).

On the internet, alt-right pundits can control their narratives and, if they want, hide behind handles and avatars. Acolytes say anonymity is necessary because they're part of a misunderstood counterculture; exposure could cost them jobs and friends, even invite violence. The digital netherworld, however, is also a haven for hate speech. Users kicked off Twitter for abusive language can easily start new accounts. Or they can move over to Gab, an alt-right-friendly messaging platform whose guidelines proclaim, "The only valid form of censorship is an individual's own choice to opt-out."

Lokteff explained how Red Ice entered this arena. Palmgren launched the company in 2002 in Gothenburg, Sweden. Its name refers to a Norse myth in which the world was created in a cosmic void between two realms — one frozen, one red-hot. Red Ice disseminated conspiracy theories about U.F.O.'s, Freemasons, the Illuminati, and 9/11. Then, around 2012, the outlet shifted its attention to conspiracies about race — the idea that liberals were perpetrating a white genocide, for instance. It also began to question the Holocaust. The company's tagline was "Dispelling the Mythmakers."[2]

Red Ice found a new audience in the nascent alt-right and now serves as a digital hub for the movement. It produces newscasts of events like the Stockholm conference and Spencer's protest in May against the removal of a Confederate monument in Virginia. Its bread and butter, though, is weekly talk-radio-style programs. The segments are available in audio and video formats, much like Rush Limbaugh's in-studio streams, and reach more than 120,000 subscribers on YouTube. Red Ice also has paying members, who can access additional content. Lokteff declined to reveal the number of members, but each one shells out seven dollars a month — "the cost of a hipster coffee," as she put it.

Lokteff hosts a program called Radio 3Fourteen — her birthday is March 14 — which frequently showcases women's perspectives on white nationalism. Her guests toe the alt-right's party line on gender, which mimics that of fascist and white-power movements of the twentieth century: By design, the sexes are not equal, physically or otherwise, but they are complementary and equally important. Men are strong and rational, women yielding and emotional; men are good at navigating politics, women at nurturing family units; men make decisions, women provide counsel. The survival of the white race depends on both sexes embracing their roles.

The group chat on Radio 3Fourteen seemed to speak to women who felt that an ever-liberalizing society was telling them how to be and what to believe, spurning them at any sign of parochial behavior. The bloggers noted how unhappy modern women are. To an extent, research bears out this idea: In 2009, the economists Betsey Stevenson and Justin Wolfers published a seminal study which found that as women's rights expanded, their happiness declined. They posited that "greater equality may have led more women to compare their outcomes to those of the men around them," resulting in disappointment when they found their relative positions lacking. But Lokteff and her klatch of commentators took a reductive view: If women are miserable, feminism must be to blame.

Two years ago, Lokteff, who identifies as pagan, discovered a YouTube personality who could speak to pro-white Christians: Ayla Stewart, a Utah woman whose handle is "Wife with a Purpose." She's in her thirties, with a round, dimpled face, wide blue eyes, and a warm voice. Stewart's homemade videos were often about her dramatic political transformation. She used to be a feminist, a supporter of gay rights, and an avowed pagan. She married at nineteen, studied women's spirituality in graduate school, and had a child. She wanted to be a stay-at-home mom. "I was really into home birth and extended breast-feeding," Stewart told me. Then her husband left, and she became a young single mother. She felt pressure to get a job and not worry about needing a man — or children, for that matter. But that wasn't what she wanted. "Children are so precious, we should do everything we can do to bring them into the best environment," she told me. "And a two-parent household with a mother and a father is that best environment." Stewart felt "shunned and ostracized and called down" for her beliefs by acquaintances and online critics.

After meeting her second husband, Stewart had more kids, joined the Mormon Church, and drifted even further from feminism. A friend recommended that she read *Fascinating Womanhood*, a conservative answer to The *Feminine Mystique*. Written in 1963 by Helen Andelin, a Mormon mother of eight, the book spawned a movement promoting traditional marriage. The text promises to teach women "how to cause a man to protect you," "how to bring out the best in your husband without pushing or persuasion," and "how to be attractive, even adorable, when you are angry." Stewart found comfort in Andelin's assertions that the sexes have different needs. "Men like to go out and earn a paycheck and feel respected and loved," she told me. "Women want to be cherished."

The book helped her see her first marriage in a new light: One reason it had failed, she decided, was that she hadn't provided her husband with the respect he required. *Fascinating Womanhood* also bolstered her belief that feminism demonized white men. "Being in liberal circles, the white man was the enemy — the guy who always had power and control, whom we had to get rid of and get women and people of color into power," Stewart said. "It dawned on me that I'd been incredibly sexist and racist."

In venting against feminism for betraying her, she began to draw connections with current events. In September 2015, she posted a tirade blaming feminism for the European refugee crisis. "Why, logically, would anyone allow hundreds of thousands of refugees to come over into your country, to live off of your social welfare programs, to increase horrible crimes like rape, and to, honestly, quite frankly, take over your culture?" she asked. Her answer was white guilt, which had seeped into politics because "women waste our votes" on liberal politicians. "Women see downtrodden people as their children," Stewart told me, "and want to be very motherly toward them and throw open their borders."

The video went viral — more than 122,000 views to date — and when Lokteff saw it, she invited Stewart onto Radio 3Fourteen. They quickly got onto the topic of Stewart's break from her political past. "Liberals think they're so enlightened, so much better than everyone else, but really they are just completely brainwashed, don't you think?" Lokteff asked. "Exactly," Stewart replied. Her relief was almost palpable.

The same month, Lokteff hosted Mary Grey (not her real name), another Christian white nationalist. Lokteff reached out after hearing "Good Morning White America," a weekly podcast that Grey hosts with her husband, who goes by Adam. Their appearance on Radio 3Fourteen was audio-only, and the discussion focused on the Greys' journey to the alt-right. Mary said she was skeptical when Adam began reading pro-white websites a few years ago and asked, "What would you do with all of the people that are non-white but are Christian?" His vague reply was, "They can have their own society, their own place to live — just over there." Mary laughed at her past skepticism. "After I heard that I was like, oh, okay, you're

not one of those evil racists that kill everyone," she said. (White nationalists almost never explain how they would create pure ethnostates.)

In January, Mary Grey self-published an illustrated children's book called *Walls and Fences*. "Why do we build walls? We have walls for protection," the text begins, set against a colorful image of the biblical city of Jericho as its walls tumble down at God's behest. Grey said she wrote the book "to help explain to my children why having a wall around our country" — like the one Trump has pledged to build along the U.S.-Mexico border — "is justified and a good and normal thing."

There is a long legacy of pro-white extremists trying to create illusions of normalcy. Kathleen Blee, a sociology professor at the University of Pittsburgh, wrote in her book Inside Organized Racism that "much about racist groups appears disturbingly ordinary, especially their evocation of community, family, and social ties." In a two-year study of thirty-four women across the United States, Blee found that her subjects, many of whom were educated and held good jobs, were "responsible for socializing their children into racial and religious bigotry."

Lokteff faces competing audiences: alt-right men who are skeptical or even disdainful of female strength, and confident women wary of a cause that might sideline them. Lokteff tries to reassure both groups, which requires twisting logic and concocting rationalizations as needed. She claims that many of the highest-rated Radio 3Fourteen episodes have female guests — to her eyes, a sure sign that male viewers like them. She doesn't argue that women shouldn't have the right to vote. Instead, she says that in an ethnostate, white households would vote as units. She doesn't apologize for being voluble but confesses to having overactive "guy brain" — the assertive and argumentative part of her. Stewart said something similar in our interview: "Intellectually, I tend to like to hang out with the boys."

In her speech, Lokteff said she didn't think women were cut out for national politics. But they could still help shape the public conversation. "Since we aren't physically intimidating," she said, "we can get away with saying big things."

"Big," in the context of the alt-right, can mean controversial, profane, or outright hateful. Eschewing political correctness is a virtue, a way to scandalize liberals. The movement's lingo is flippant, packed with vicious irony and inside jokes. It tends toward the extreme, even in the most mundane of formats.

With the exception of a few high-profile figures, all of them men, the alt-right is notoriously cagey with the mainstream media. Female pundits rarely grant interviews.

When we met, my first question to Lokteff was, why had she agreed to talk to me? "I wanted to give you a chance," she said. "You wrote me in a different way. You said you actually wanted to . . . hear what we're talking about." She added hastily, "It's not because you're a woman."

. . . Early in our conversation, Lokteff told me how similar we were. "You and I are a different kind of woman," she said, gesturing toward me with a freckled arm. In her left nostril, I spotted a piercing that I hadn't noticed online; I have one in the same spot. "We're more political, we ask questions, we're analytical," Lokteff continued. "Most women want to be beautiful, attract a guy, be taken care of, have their home, have their children."

If we were so alike, in her view, how would Lokteff pitch the alt-right to someone like me, who identifies as a feminist? She turned the question around. "What is feminism to you?" she asked.

My answer — that women should have equal opportunities and be able to choose, say, to stay at home or be the CEO of a company — left her exasperated. "In the West we already had that," she replied in a rush. "Our men have already propelled us like *crazy*." She ticked off examples: White women were the first women to fly a plane (France, 1908) and to go into space (Soviet Union, 1963). Societies like the Vikings (eighth century to eleventh) worshipped gods of both genders. Feminism, the genesis of which she pins roughly to the early twentieth century, did not make things better for women, Lokteff concluded. But it did make them worse for men. "It's easier for women to get a job because of affirmative action," she said. "The white male is on the shit list."

I asked how she would convince female Trump voters who, while conservative and maybe antifeminist, didn't share her pro-white views. Inspire fear, was the essence of her response. "There's a joke in the alt-right: How do you red-pill someone? Have them live in a diverse neighborhood for a while," she said. "Another thing that's attracting normies" — people not in the movement — "is rape. Women are scared of rape."

A few minutes later, Lokteff mocked liberals for being angry about Trump's "grab 'em by the pussy" statement. "All of a sudden, all these lefties are puritans when it comes to sex and vaginas," she scoffed. I suggested that the "grab 'em" part sounded like sexual assault. She shrugged it off, chalking up Trump's behavior to a Hollywood culture in which women throw themselves at rich and powerful men. "I think that he loves women," she said.

It was the same circular logic I'd heard her deploy when defending alt-right men from charges of sexism: How can they hate women if they love them?

. . . By the end of our conversation, it had started to rain, so Lokteff and I moved inside. I asked her about the alt-right's next steps. It was going to become a real political party, she replied, with platforms and candidates supporting white-nationalist policies, such as a ban on non-white immigration to the United States. She alluded to "a lot of people moving to D.C. right now"; Spencer recently set up an N.P.I. office in Alexandria, Virginia. "It's quite amazing when you look at just trolling and memes and people on the internet without any kind of organization . . . how much press and attention [we've gotten]," she said. "That's us not even organizing, not even pulling resources and funds and minds and skills together yet."

When I asked if she identified as a leader, she demurred. "Maybe on some level. I'm not sure I would take credit or put myself in that position," she said. Maybe not in the broad, hypermasculine constellation of the alt-right, but her position among the movement's women is a different matter. "There's always been the girl in the pack that's been more of the outspoken one," she continued. "I've never been the follower."

Her responses were as mystifying as the phenomenon of the alt-right itself. For months, America has tried to understand what the movement wants. Perhaps the better question is, who gets to decide? In grappling with how to set priorities, the alt-right is bumping up against ideological contradictions, divergent opinions, and other schisms in its ardent, loosely formed ranks. Assertive women are exposing some of these fissures, which seem likely to grow as the movement vies for a modicum of political acceptance.

Lokteff, though, is sanguine. "Ten years from now, a lot of these alt-right concepts are going to be very mainstream in white people's minds," she told me. Then, as though a light bulb had clicked on in her brain, she continued: "Look at feminism. It started as a fringe movement. Now it's mainstream, left and right."

NOTES

1. *Adolf Hitler lost a presidential race, but the Nazis earned enough votes in a parliamentary election in 1932 to become the dominant party in the Reichstag. Hitler was appointed Germany's chancellor the following year.*
2. *They changed it to "The Future Is the Past" earlier this year.*

HATE IN THE UNITED STATES

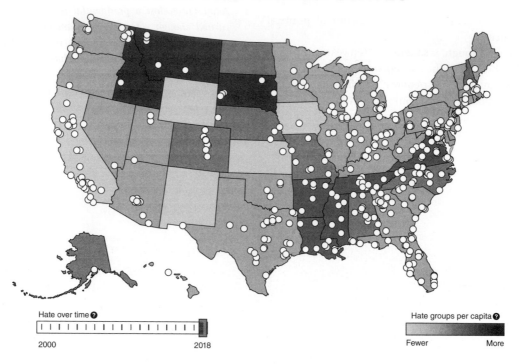

Hate over time ❓

2000   2018

Hate groups per capita ❓

Fewer   More

By the numbers

50	**40**	**1,234**
Percentage increase in total white nationalist groups in 2018	Estimated number of people killed in North America in radical right terrorist attacks in 2018	Number of hate group flyering incidents in 2018

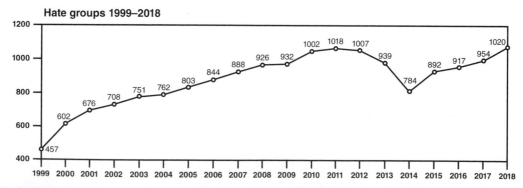

Hate groups 1999–2018

In 2018, the Southern Poverty Law Center tracked 1020 hate groups in the United States.
Source: splcenter.org

CHAPTER 12

RELIGION AND SPIRITUALITY

Religion is a complex and complicating feature of women's lives. Although many women feel empowered by religion because it offers them a place of belonging, comfort, acceptance, and encouragement, others feel oppressed by religion because it excludes and sometimes degrades women. In this way, as this chapter will explore, religion remains a significant personal and political force in women's lives. Many of the social and cultural battles raging in American society—abortion, marriage equality, sex education, racial violence, domestic violence, to name a few—are cast in religious terms, and many women organize their lives around their religious convictions.

The Southern Baptist controversy illustrates the experiences of many women in religious traditions. Throughout the 1980s and early 1990s, Southern Baptists, the nation's largest Protestant denomination with more than 14 million members, were embroiled in a controversy between fundamentalist and moderate leaders. The Baptist battles began over the issue of inerrancy (the notion that the Bible is without error in history, science, or doctrine) but quickly expanded to include, and then emphasize, social issues such as abortion, homosexuality, and the role of women in the home and church. As the fundamentalists grew in political power, they led the Southern Baptist Convention to pass resolutions excluding women from pastoral leadership in the churches and encouraging wives to submit to their husbands. Fundamentalist victory, however, did not come without a long, bitter conflict in which many women, particularly women in ministry, left the denomination. Other women decided to stay and focus their efforts on the autonomous local churches that carried on in the Baptist tradition of dissent, unbound by convention resolutions. Other women supported the denomination's stance and founded "women's studies" programs at the seminaries. These programs are anti-feminist and limit women's ministry to women and children.

Many moderate women became involved in alternative Baptist organizations that grew out of the controversy and promised women more visibility, opportunity, and support as seminary professors and denominational leaders. The women who found positions as

LEARNING ACTIVITY

PEOPLE OF FAITH

Interview three women and/or LGBTQ people who actively participate in a religious community. Ask about their experiences as women/LGBTQ people in their faith. Use the following questions or develop your own interview protocol.

- What is your religious community's stance on women's roles in home, society, and the religious community itself?
- What is your community's stance on LGBTQ issues?
- What roles do women fulfill in your religious community? What roles do LGBTQ people fulfill?
- In what activities do you participate in your religious community?

- In what ways has your religious community been empowering for you? Has your religious community ever been oppressive to you? Have issues of gender, race, or sexual identity played a role?
- What do you gain by your participation in your religious community?
- How might your religious community better serve women and LGBTQ people?

Gather the data obtained by several other students in your class and examine your findings. Do you see any common themes arising from your interviews? What do your data suggest about people's experiences in their faith communities? Can you make any generalizations from the data about how women and LGBTQ people experience religion as both empowering and oppressive?

---

seminary professors often faced resistance from students and misunderstanding from colleagues. Some became associate pastors in moderate Baptist churches, but very few were offered senior pastor positions. Women in the congregation heard the rhetoric of equality, but it came from the lips of the men who held the top positions in the churches and newly formed Baptist organizations. Women who were affirmed in their callings to pastoral ministry enrolled in new seminaries that offered little in the way of curricula focused on women.

In 2018, however, the #MeToo movement came at last to Southern Baptists with the firing of a seminary president who had been an architect of the fundamentalist takeover. Recordings from 2000 emerged of him telling wives to return to their abusers and making inappropriate comments about women's bodies. Encouraged by the #MeToo movement, women came forward to say he had discouraged them from reporting rape. Still, even as other fundamentalist leaders criticized him and the trustees of the seminary removed him from power, fundamentalist leaders continued to reiterate belief in women's submission and complementarianism (the belief that while women and men are equal before God, God assigns specific roles to women and men based on gender, including the requirement for wives to submit to husbands).

The willingness of so many moderate Southern Baptist women to stay in Baptist churches despite the anti-woman actions of the Southern Baptist Convention indicates the powerful pull of religion. Even women who strongly opposed the policy of the Southern Baptist Convention often became active participants in other Christian denominations; few left Christianity entirely. This simultaneous push and pull of religion, as exemplified by the experience of Southern Baptist women, merits careful feminist analysis. As a force that can both oppress and empower, religion has a dramatic potential to work politically either to continue women's oppression or to support women's liberation. Understanding this complex dynamic involves a close reading of the discourses of religion. The reading "Buddhist Nuns in Nepal" by Kathryn LaFever explores this push and pull of religion.

RELIGION AS OPPRESSIVE TO WOMEN

Southern Baptists are not alone in Christianity, nor is Christianity alone in world religions, in functioning as an oppressive force to women. This section discusses four ways that religion as belief and institutional practice has helped subordinate women. First, central to religion's oppressive function is the premise of a divinely ordained order of creation in which females are deemed inferior and men are seen not only as superior to women but also closer to God. As will be discussed in the next section, gendered language about the deity reinforces male domination of women. The notion of women's inferiority is often supported by creation myths that embed woman's inferior status in the religious community's narrative of identity; these are the stories a religious community tells about itself in order to make itself known to both members and the outside community. For example, a common interpretation of the second Hebrew myth of creation (although feminist biblical scholars take issue with this interpretation) is that Eve is created after Adam because she is to serve him and be his subordinate. Later in the Christian testament, writers argue that woman's secondary status is a result of Eve's role as temptress in the fall of humanity. As Elizabeth Cady Stanton pointed out in the reading "Introduction to *The Woman's Bible*" over a hundred years ago, the Bible has most often been used to maintain the oppression of women by excluding them from particular roles in church, family, and society. This deep-seated misogyny also plays a significant role in the religious oppression of sexual minorities. To a great extent, religious prohibitions on same-sex relationships are about maintaining gender distinctions and gender roles in support of male domination. Same-sex relationships challenge these distinctions and roles by denying that there is an essential "male role" or "female role" in the home or in sexuality. This is especially disturbing in gay relationships because of the shame that patriarchy associates with men being "used" like women or taking on stereotypically female roles in sexual relationships. In other words, the problem in the popular religious imagination is the association of gay male sex with the feminizing of men. To be a gay male is to be like a woman, and the worst thing for a man is to be like a woman.

Second, women's lower status is further maintained by excluding women from sacred rituals. Among the different world religions, women have not been allowed to celebrate the Eucharist, pray in public, participate in sacred dances, hear confession, baptize, enter the holy of holies, read sacred scriptures aloud in public, preach, lead prayers, or teach men.

LEARNING ACTIVITY

THAT OLD-TIME TV RELIGION

Watch several episodes of religious programming on television, such as the *700 Club* and two or three televised worship services. Who are the key personalities? What is their message? During the service, who is speaking? Who is singing? Who is leading? What messages about gender are conveyed, not only in the words themselves but also in the roles played by different people?

What messages about race, class, sexual identity, and/or ability are conveyed? Do you think these shows are helpful to people? Why or why not? Are they helpful to women? To LGBTQ people? Who do you think benefits from these shows? Are there ways in which these shows reinforce the subordination of women, LGBTQ people, and other non-dominant groups?

Keep a log of your observations to share with your classmates.

One argument for the exclusion of women from priesthood has been that the priest stands as a representative of God, and a woman cannot represent God because she is female. The underlying assumption is that men are more Godlike than women. When worshippers see only men as representatives of God, it reinforces the notion that men are more Godlike, and women's exclusion continues.

Third, religions maintain women's oppression very directly through church laws that require wives to submit to their husbands, regulate women's sexuality, and create highly defined gender performances for women and men. For example, these laws may keep women in abusive relationships or prevent them from having access to birth control and/ or abortion. Women may be told by church authorities that their role in the home is to be the support person for the husband and to submit to his divinely ordained authority. Then, when abuse occurs, a woman may be told that she is to continue to submit because that is her role and that God will change her husband because of her obedience to God's commandments. The husband's abusive behavior then becomes the wife's responsibility because his changing is contingent upon her submission. This situation is exacerbated by a prohibition on divorce in some denominations, preventing women from permanently leaving abusive or dysfunctional marriages.

Finally, historically and currently, religions also exercise power over women through church- and state-sanctioned control. During its early years, Christianity taught a spiritual unity that integrated the oppressiveness of Roman laws and gave women some status in the church (although women's place was still subordinate and Jesus's teachings about equality did not manifest in the teachings and practices of the church). Some women found solace in the devotional life of the convent where they could live a religious life as well as hold leadership positions and avoid the constraints of traditional femininity that included marriage and childbearing. In the "burning times" (between the eleventh and fourteenth centuries), tens of thousands of women in Europe were murdered as witches. For many of these women, "witchcraft" was simply the practice of traditional healing and spirituality and the refusal to profess Christianity. For other women, the charge of witchcraft had nothing to do with religious practices and everything to do with accusations rooted in jealousy, greed, and fear of female sexuality. But in the frenzy of the times, defending oneself against an accusation of witchcraft was practically impossible, and an accusation alone generally meant death. In 2012, the Vatican ordered a crackdown on the Leadership Conference of Women Religious, the umbrella organization for most nuns in the United States, for its "radical feminist" themes. Apparently, according to the Vatican, the nuns were putting too much emphasis on social justice issues such as poverty and hunger and not enough on moral issues such as abortion and homosexuality. The Vatican closed the investigation in 2015, praising the work done by the nuns but reminding them that in matters of contemporary religious issues they should have due regard for the Church's stances.

Other examples include the ways Christian imperialism has proved destructive for women and men of color and reinforced racism and ethnocentrism, despite the fact that in the Bible the Apostle Paul in his letter to the Galatians said that in Jesus Christ there is "neither Jew nor Greek, slave nor free, male nor female"—interpreted to mean that everyone is equal in the sight of God and should be treated so. The genocide of Native

Americans was conducted with the underlying belief that it was the God-given destiny of Europeans to conquer the native peoples of the Americas. Without understanding African cultures, Christian missionaries insisted that indigenous African peoples adopt Western ways. The legacy of Christian racism continued in the American South, where many Christians defended slavery based on their reading of scripture. Following Reconstruction, hate groups such as the Ku Klux Klan arose, calling for continued dominance by white, Anglo Christians. This continues today with the messages of such groups as the Christian Identity Movement and the Aryan Nation (as well as the Klan). In Germany, thousands of Christians joined in Hitler's plan to build a master race and contributed directly to the genocide of 6 million Jews. In the 1950s and 1960s, while many Christians worked tirelessly for the civil rights movement and African American churches in particular became sites of resistance to racism, many others defended segregation and participated in acts of racial hatred. Only in 2000 did Bob Jones University, a fundamentalist institution of higher education in South Carolina, repeal its rule against interracial dating. Despite the many advances in the twentieth century, the twenty-first century began with the continuing problems of racism and intolerance by many who profess Christianity. It continues with an association between the executive branch of government and policies providing a conduit for structured inequalities. In the reading "How Evangelicals became White," Kelly Brown Douglas develops the historical connection between "Christian Anglo-Saxon whiteness" and contemporary alignments between white supremacy and "white Christian America" as exemplified in the vote for Donald Trump.

In India, some Hindus believe self-immolation is the highest form of wifely devotion and leads to the spiritual salvation of a dead husband. The wife who commits *sati* by placing herself on the burning pyre with her husband's body is then revered as a goddess. While the practice was outlawed by British colonizers in the nineteenth century, around 40 cases of sati have been documented since Indian independence in 1947. While Indian feminists have argued against the practice, a number of women and men have argued that women should have the right to do it. Karen McCarthy Brown explains the story of Roop Kanwar, an 18-year-old woman who was burned alive on her husband's funeral pyre, as central in understanding religious fundamentalism in the reading "Fundamentalism and the Control of Women."

IDEAS FOR ACTIVISM

- Invite a group of women pastors, ministers, priests, and rabbis to participate in a panel discussion of women in ministry.
- Invite LGBTQ pastors, ministers, priests, and rabbis to participate in a discussion of LGBTQ people in religion.
- Organize a feminist spirituality group.
- Organize an educational event to explore women and LGBTQ people in the world's religions.

If possible, invite practitioners of various faiths to speak about their religious tradition.
- Investigate the official stance of your own religious tradition on women's roles and issues and LGBTQ roles and issues. Where there is room for improvement, write religious leaders to express your opinion.
- Organize an event to commemorate the women who died in the "burning times."

Currently the Religious Right, a political movement of religious conservatives in the United States that is intertwined with the conservative political establishment, is attempting to exert control over women, LGBTQ people, and people of color—especially immigrants—by influencing the U.S. legal system. In particular, during the campaign and presidency of Donald Trump, white evangelicals asserted themselves politically, with 80 percent voting for Trump—despite his history of adultery, disdain for women, and questionable business practices. For many white evangelicals, what matters most is whether or not a politician supports litmus test issues, such as opposition to abortion, marriage equality, trans inclusion, and most immigration. Faith-based initiatives that provide government funds to religious institutions tend to blur the line between church and state, and often serve to reduce women's choice and autonomy.

Religious influence on social policy, for example, has managed to chip away at abortion rights by convincing lawmakers to pass various restrictions. For many years, the Religious Right was also successful in preventing marriage equality for gay and lesbian couples. The Supreme Court's marriage equality decision has led leaders of the Religious Right to focus on legislation that restricts LGBTQ rights in the name of religious freedom. For example, they support laws that allow bakers and florists to refuse wedding service to gay and lesbian couples and exclude transgender people from using public restroom facilities that match their gender. In 2017, led by the Council on Biblical Manhood and Womanhood, a group of evangelical leaders issued "The Nashville Statement," a document that reiterates opposition to queer relationships and insists biological sex determines gender. The statement situates LGBTQ people as immoral and claims that even support for LGBTQ people is sinful. In 2019, the United Methodist Church's General Conference voted to reaffirm its 1972 statement that "the practice of homosexuality is incompatible with Christian teaching" and to strengthen enforcement of its ban on LGBTQ clergy and clergy participation in same sex marriage ceremonies.

Many young evangelicals' attitudes toward LGBTQ people, however, have changed in recent years in a more positive direction. In 2013 leaders of Exodus International, an organization that attempted to transform gay and lesbian Christians into heterosexuals through prayer and reparative therapy, formally apologized for the damage it had done and shut down the organization. Many young conservative leaders are also renouncing the culture wars of the past four decades and calling for a return to evangelical emphasis on conversion and compassion. Still, particular challenges exist in relation to transgender persons in the Christian church. Even as some parts of the church have become more welcoming to lesbian, gay, bisexual people, transphobia and trans exclusion are still quite common in the church.

Sharia is the sacred law of Islam that has been interpreted and integrated into some societies (such as Iran and Saudi Arabia) in ways that control women's lives. However, modernist, traditionalist, and fundamentalist Muslims (and those within different geographic regions) interpret it, and its scope, differently. Sharia deals with many public concerns addressed by secular law (such as economics) as well as personal and community issues that include family and sexuality.

The Muslim practice of wearing the veil (*hijab*) presents an especially complex example of the simultaneously oppressive and empowering role of religion in women's lives. From the perspective of the global north, the practice of veiling is often viewed as absolutely oppressing. Although many Muslim women are critical of coercive practices associated with veiling, they also see choosing to wear the headscarf as an empowering act of ethnic and cultural identity in the face of the influence of the global north. Muslim women often explain that they feel safer when veiled in public. The headscarf indicates that a woman is devout and virtuous, and therefore Muslim men will not objectify and sexualize her. In fact, very often these women express sympathy for North American women, who must constantly fear sexual assault in public places. The headscarf, they claim, protects them and therefore allows them the freedom to move about publicly without fear, and, in some cases, it allows them to claim their identity and take a stand against the hegemonic forces of the imperialism of the global north.

In this discussion it is important to recognize the differences between the teachings of the Qur'an and the interpretation of these teachings in some Muslim societies with the goal of keeping women subordinate to men. As the interview with Syafa Almirzanah demonstrates in the reading "The Prophet's Daughters," Islam is not a monolithic religion. Rather, more conservative and more progressive Muslims, respectively, interpret the Qur'an in their different ways—and indeed more progressive Muslims interpret the Qur'an to promote women's value and equality. In fact, Islamic feminism affirms equality as a divine mandate grounded in the Qur'an.

RELIGION AS EMPOWERING TO WOMEN

Despite religion's long history of oppression, women have also experienced profound support, encouragement, and satisfaction in religion. This section focuses on those aspects of empowerment. First, for many women, religion provides an environment in which they experience real community with other women. Women in traditional marriages who work in the home may find their only real social outlet in the church, mosque, or synagogue. Here, they build connections with other women and participate in personally meaningful experiences in a community context.

Second, religion may provide women with opportunities for building and exercising leadership skills within religious organizations. Particularly for women in traditional families, this allows them to develop skills they might not learn otherwise. For example, although Southern Baptists have generally excluded women from pastoral leadership in the churches, Woman's Missionary Union (WMU), auxiliary to the Southern Baptist Convention, has provided thousands of women with the opportunity to become lay leaders in their churches, as well as in associational, state, and national WMU organizations. WMU is a missions education organization for women, and in its local church organizations, women plan, budget, and implement programs for education and action. Its curriculum materials teach young girls that they can do anything God calls them to do. The subversive power of this message is clear in talking to Southern Baptist women in ministry. Many of them report first experiencing their call to ministry in a WMU organization. Similarly, Catholic women have been empowered through convent experiences, in which they exercise leadership and enjoy community with other women.

Third, leadership within the church or religious organization may facilitate women's power within their local or regional communities as well as encourage their participation in various forms of social activism. For example, in Santeria, a Caribbean religion, women who are healers, or *santeras*, have great personal power and hold immense social power in their communities. These women willingly enter into altered states of consciousness and allow the spirits to use them to bring about healing. Santeras see all the spirits with a person and are often able to reveal to the person what needs to be done. This ability puts the santera in an extremely powerful position, especially when the person consulting her is a politician or government official, as is often the case. Furthermore, as Caribbean women visit santeras, they see women who wield power in their culture and who can act as role models for them.

Another example of the role of religion in encouraging social activism is that of Jesse Daniel Ames, who helped organize the antilynching movement in the early part of the twentieth century. She worked through women's missions organizations in Methodist and Baptist Churches in the South. Black churches were at the heart of the 1950s and 1960s civil rights movement in which many early leaders of second-wave feminism had their first experiences of political organizing. A key component of Judaism is social justice, and Jewish women have long been actively involved in anti-defamationist, anti-racist, anti-sexist, and anti-heterosexist work. Ernestine Louise Rose, who fought for women's rights and against slavery during the 1840s and 1850s, challenged New York state lawmakers in 1854 to allow women to retain their own property and share equal guardianship of children with their husbands. When male politicians urged women to postpone their quest for suffrage and focus on the rights of former slaves, Rose declared, "Emancipation from

HISTORICAL MOMENT

BECOMING A BISHOP

Until 1984, no black woman had been elected bishop of a major religious denomination in the United States, but in that year, the Western Jurisdictional Conference of the United Methodist Church elected Leontine Kelly its first African American woman bishop and only the church's second female bishop.

Both Kelly's father and brother were Methodist ministers. Kelly married and had three children but divorced in the early 1950s. She remarried, this time to a Methodist minister, in 1956 and returned to college to earn a bachelor's degree and become a social studies teacher. Kelly was drawn to preaching and became a certified lay preacher. When her husband died in 1969, she accepted the church's invitation to become pastor. She earned a master of divinity (MDiv) from Wesley Theological Seminary in 1976 and became an ordained minister in the Methodist Church. From 1977 to 1983 she was pastor of Asbury-Church Hill United Methodist Church in Richmond, Virginia, and then became assistant general secretary of evangelism for the United Methodist General Board of Discipleship.

Kelly's nomination to the post of bishop by a group of California clergywomen was not without controversy. Some thought her unfit for the position because she was a black woman. Others opposed her nomination because she was divorced. Nonetheless, she was elected and then named bishop for the San Francisco Bay area, making her the chief administrator and spiritual leader for more than 100,000 United Methodists in Northern California and Nevada. She remained at that post for four years until her retirement in 1988.

In the fall of 2000, the United Methodist Church elected three African American women as bishops, the first since Leontine Kelly: Violet Fisher, Linda Lee, and Beverly Shamana. Kelly commented, "I will always be the first African American woman bishop of the United Methodist Church, but praise God I am no longer the only."

QUEER AND GENDER NONCONFORMING MUSLIM ACTIVISM

Sasha A. Khan

Queerness and gender nonconformity are often framed as mutually exclusive from Islam. Within North America and Western Europe, Islam is cast as an exceptionally *queermisic* (anti-queer) and *transmisic* (anti-trans) religion in order to justify racist and *xenomisic* (anti-foreigner) policies and rhetoric. For example, the first iteration of President Trump's executive order banning travel into the United States for citizens of six Muslim-majority nations was justified by claiming to uphold LGBTQ rights. The travel ban's underlying assumption was that Muslims are a threat to LGBTQ folks presumably because of the so-called inherent queermisia and transmisia of Islam. Further, within these logics the existence of queer and gender nonconforming Muslims is impossible. These narratives persistently obscure power relations and misrecognize queer and gender nonconforming Muslims. Can you think of any other examples?

Use this opportunity to research queer and gender nonconforming Muslims' activisms. Check out *Just Me and Allah: A Queer Muslim Photo Project* at http://queermuslimproject.tumblr.com/. Queer Muslim Southern artist Samra Habib published interviews and photographs of queer and gender nonconforming Muslims from around the globe. Additionally, queer and gender nonconforming folks have been developing spaces in which religion, gender, and sexuality are understood as inextricably linked. These include Islamic Healing Space of A2 and Ypsi in Michigan, El-Tawhid Juma Circle and Toronto Unity Mosque in Toronto, and Masjid Al-Rabia in Chicago. You may also want to check out *The Third Muslim: Queer and Trans* Muslim Narratives of Resistance and Resilience*, an exhibit co-curated by Zulfikar Ali Bhutto and Yas Ahmed that appeared at SOMArts Cultural Center.

When looking at these different queer and gender nonconforming Muslim activist projects, consider the following questions: What are the structural problems identified by each project? What are its goals? What are the convergences and divergences between them? How do these projects converge and diverge from dominant understandings of LGBTQ activism?

---

every kind of bondage is my principle." She also spoke out against anti-Semitism and set the tone for twentieth-century Jewish feminists' critique of Judaism's traditional attitudes toward women. The reading "Feminists in the Temple of Orthodoxy:" by Yitzhak Reiter explores these tensions in relation to Jewish women's struggle to pray at the Western Wall in Jerusalem, Judaism's most sacred site.

More recently, feminist Mormon women have taken to the Internet as activists calling for social change. Some of the move active websites include Feminist Mormon Housewives, Exponent, and Women Advocating for Voice and Equality (WAVE). Through their activism, these women seek to challenge the church's stances on feminist issues and reclaim the power they believe women held in earlier generations of Mormonism. The reading "I'm a Mormon Feminist" by Jessica Finnigan and Nancy Ross offers an overview of Mormon women coming together online. Within almost every religious tradition, women and LGBTQ people are resisting discrimination and injustice, using their religious faith to challenge the tenets of religion that marginalize, exclude, and dehumanize others.

Finally, for many women and LGBTQ people, religion provides a place in which they find a sense of worth as a valued person. The poem "God Says Yes to Me" by Kaylin Haught illustrates an accepting, loving God that has the potential to empower women. In the twenty-first century, many women are participating in revivals of ancient woman-centered religions and have become empowered through the revaluing of the feminine implicit in this spirituality. Wicca, or witchcraft (although not the witches we popularly think of at Halloween), is a Goddess- and nature-oriented religion whose origins predate both Judaism and Christianity. Current Wiccan practice involves the celebration of the feminine, connection with nature, and the practice of healing. As Wiccan practitioner Starhawk suggests, witchcraft encourages women to be strong, confident, and independent and to love the Goddess, the earth, and other human beings. This notion of witchcraft is very different from the cultural norms associated with witches that are propagated in society.

Indigenous cultures have also offered examples of valuing queer and gender diverse people. Before colonization, Two-Spirit people were accepted and often revered among many native peoples as counselors, storytellers, and healers. Two-Spirit identities are discussed in the reading "Native American Men-Women, Lesbians, Two-Spirit" by Sabine Lang that appeared in Chapter 3. Colonization brought homophobia and transphobia, and Two-Spirit people were often pushed to the margins as colonizers' heteronormative beliefs and practices influenced native cultures. Now, however, there are efforts to recover the place of Two-Spirit people in native communities.

GENDER AND GOD-LANGUAGE

Many theorists contend that one of the most powerful influences in molding gender and maintaining gender oppression is language. The words that religions use to talk about the divine are especially powerful in shaping the ways we think about men and women. Any language we use to talk about deities is of necessity metaphorical. We create images that can only partially represent the full reality of this concept. Unfortunately, those images sometimes become understood in literal, rather than metaphorical, ways. So, instead of thinking, for example, of God as Father, we may come to think God is Father. Throughout Jewish and Christian history, the preponderance of images for God have been masculine—Father, King, Lord, Judge, Master—and the effect has been that many people imagine God as male even though, intellectually, they might know this is not true. God is often imagined as white too.

In ancient times, the image of the Great Mother Goddess was primary in many cultures, but as war-centered patriarchal cultures developed, the life-giving Goddess had to be defeated by the warring God. In ancient Babylonian mythology, Tiamat was the Great Mother, but she was eventually slaughtered by her son Marduk, the god of war. Yahweh, the god of the ancient Israelites, was originally a consort of the Canaanite Mother Goddess, but, as the Israelites moved toward a patriarchal monotheism (belief in just one God), Yahweh became prominent as the Great Father God, and worship of the Goddess was harshly condemned by Yahweh's priests. The prominence of a single masculine image of deity then became reflected in the exclusion of women from the priesthood and eventually from the concept of Israel itself.

In response to the hegemony of masculine images of God, feminist theologians have constructed alternative feminine images of deity. Some theologians, such as Virginia Mollenkott, have returned to the Jewish and Christian testaments to point out the existence of feminine images within scripture. Other theologians, such as Sallie McFague, have challenged people to develop new models of God such as God as mother, God as lover, and

God as companion. And yet other women have returned to the ancient images of the Goddess herself. Others have reimagined God as transgender—the One who transcends, transgresses, transforms, crosses over.

The political nature of the decision to challenge normative God-language does not go unnoticed by traditionalists wishing to cling to male images. The Southern Baptist Convention issued a statement declaring that God is not like a father, but God is Father. And a group of mainline churchwomen created a furor within their denominations when at a conference they chose to call God "Sophia," a biblical, but feminine, name for deity.

LEARNING ACTIVITY

HOW WELL DO YOU KNOW THE GODDESS?

MATCH THE GODDESS TO HER NAME.

1. Odudua	a.	Egyptian mother Goddess and Goddess of the underworld, the queen of heaven and mother of light.
2. Coatlicue	b.	"Queen of Heaven." Assyrian creator of life, mother and guardian. Goddess of fertility, love, sexuality, and justice.
3. Izanami-no-kami	c.	Celtic creator of life. Mother Goddess of the earth and moon. The mother of all heroes or deities.
4. Demeter	d.	Scandinavian creator of life. Leader of the Valkyries.
5. Tho-og	e.	"Great, Invincible, and Magnificent Founder and Savior, Commander and Guide, Legislator and Queen." Creator and mother Goddess of Anatolia.
6. Kali	f.	The mother of Hawaii. Mother and guardian, mother of Pele and the Hawaiian people.
7. Astarte	g.	Creator of life who brings fertility and love. Goddess of the Yoruba people of Nigeria.
8. Kokyan Wuhti	h.	Tibetan primordial being. The eternal mother who is self-formed. She is the preexisting space.
9. Freyja	i.	"The Great Mother Goddess." Mesopotamian Goddess of justice, earth, nature, and goodness.
10. Haumea	j.	Hindu Goddess. She who gives life and also destroys it. The symbol of eternal time.
11. Po Ino Nogar	k.	"Spider Grandmother." Hopi creator of life. Beneficent deity who created humans, plants, and animals.
12. Hathor	l.	"Serpent Skirt." Mother Goddess of all Aztec deities of Mexico, the ruler of life and death.
13. Anu	m.	Greek mother and guardian. One of the 12 great Greek Olympian deities. She has power over the productivity of the earth and the social order of humans.
14. Asherah	n.	"Female-Who-Invites." Japanese creator of life, earth and nature, heaven and hell
15. Artemis Ephesus	o.	"Great One." Vietnamese creator of life. World fertility Goddess who brings rice to the people and protects the fields and harvests.

Answers: 1. g; 2. l; 3. n; 4. m; 5. h; 6. j; 7. b; 8. k; 9. d; 10. f; 11. o; 12. a; 13. c; 14. i; 15. e.

Source: Martha Ann and Dorothy Myers Imel, *Goddesses in World Mythology: A Biographical Dictionary* (New York: Oxford University Press, 1993).

LEARNING ACTIVITY

EXPLORING NEW METAPHORS FOR DEITY

Metaphors are images drawn from familiar human experiences, used in fresh ways to help explore realities that are not easily accessible in our everyday experience. All language about deity is metaphorical because no one image or analogy can capture the essence of deity. Throughout the history of Jewish and Christian faiths, in particular, deity has been variously imaged as Father, Shepherd, King, Lord, and Master. Originally, these metaphors helped many people explore and grapple with different aspects of the nature of deity. Many contemporary theologians, however, suggest the need for new metaphors for deity, shocking metaphors that will cause people to think about deity in new ways.

Theologian Sallie McFague contends, "The best metaphors give both a shock and a shock of recognition." In good metaphors, we see something about reality, and we see it in new ways.

What are some of the metaphors for deity with which you are familiar? In what ways have those metaphors

been helpful? In what ways are those metaphors limiting? What do you perceive as the consequences of taking these metaphors literally? Are there some metaphors you think have outlived their usefulness?

Following are a number of new metaphors for deity that are being utilized in current theological discussion. What do you think of these metaphors? In what new ways do they cause you to think about deity? What new ideas about deity do they suggest to you? In what ways do they call you to reappraise images of deity?

- God as mother
- God as lover
- God as companion
- God as gambler
- The earth as God's body

Can you think of any shocking new metaphors that help you think about deity in original ways?

REINTERPRETING, RECONSTRUCTING, AND DECOLONIZING TRADITIONS

For those feminists who have chosen to remain in religious traditions, the task of reworking oppressive elements has been great. Theology itself has been constructed with male experience as normative and has not taken into account the experiences of all genders. Since the 1960s, feminist theologians have undertaken the task of rethinking traditional theological notions from the perspective of women's experiences (across their intersecting differences of race, sexuality, social class, etc.). Elizabeth Cady Stanton started this work over a century ago, as the reading, "Introduction to *The Woman's Bible*" shows. For example, the traditional notion of sin expressed in the story of the Fall in Genesis is that of pride and the centrality of the self. Redemption in the Christian testament then involves the restoration of what humans lack—sacrificial love. Yet the normative experience for women is not pride and self-centeredness, given that women are generally socialized to be self-negating for the sake of their families—and, in fact, encouraging women to be self-sacrificing as a form of redemption simply exacerbates women's situation. Feminist theology brings women's experiences to the center and reconstructs theological concepts in keeping with those experiences.

Because of the predominance of Christianity in the United States, the Bible and its various interpretations play a large role in shaping women's lives. Given this importance, feminist re-examinations of religion fall on a continuum: from reinterpretation to reconstruction. Reinterpretation involves recognizing the passages that are particularly problematic for women and highlighting and reintegrating the passages that extol equality across genders. Proponents of such reinterpretation include Christian feminists who maintain a positive view of scripture as they continue to accept scripture as an authority in their lives. The goal of reconstruction, however, is to move beyond reinterpretation and recognize the patriarchal underpinnings of various interpretations and the ways they have been used to oppress women.

As an example of a reconstructionist account, Christian testament scholar Elisabeth Schussler Fiorenza encourages readers of scripture to look for the presence of women in the margins and around the edges of the text. She calls for biblical readers to re-create the narratives of women who were left out of (but hinted at) in the text. In a similar fashion, for example, Jewish feminist scholar Judith Plaskow calls for a reconceptualization of notions of God, Torah, and Israel that are inclusive of women. Other reconstructions of scripture include "womanist" biblical interpretations of women of color that analyze the Bible in light of the intersections of sexism and racism. In these accounts the Bible itself is subject

ACTIVIST PROFILE

NANNIE HELEN BURROUGHS

Nannie Helen Burroughs was only 21 years old when she delivered her stirring speech "How the Sisters Are Hindered from Helping" at the 1900 National Baptist Convention in Richmond, Virginia. This speech proved to be instrumental in the formation of the Women's Convention Auxiliary to the National Baptist Convention, the largest African American women's organization in the country at that time. The Women's Convention promptly elected Burroughs its corresponding secretary and continued to re-elect her every year from 1900 to 1948. In 1948 she became the convention's president and served in that role until her death in 1961.

Burroughs was also a tireless activist—challenging lynching and segregation, denouncing employment discrimination, opposing European colonization of Africa, and promoting women's suffrage. After the Nineteenth Amendment was passed, she founded the National League of Republican Colored Women and worked to encourage African American women to become politically involved. She also established the Women's Industrial Club, which offered short-term housing to African American women and taught them basic domestic skills. The club also offered moderately priced lunches for downtown office workers. During the Depression, Burroughs formed Cooperative Industrial, Inc., which provided free facilities for a medical clinic, hair salon, and variety store.

One of Burroughs's driving passions was the education of African American women. In 1909, with the support of the National Baptist Convention, she opened the National Trade and Professional School for Women and Girls in Washington, DC, and served as the institution's president. The school emphasized a close connection between education and religion. Its curriculum focused on the development of practical and professional skills and included a program in black history in which every student was required to take a course. Burroughs's motto for the school was "We specialize in the wholly impossible." In 1964 the school was renamed the Nannie Burroughs School. In 1975 Mayor Walter E. Washington proclaimed May 10 Nannie Helen Burroughs Day in the District of Columbia in recognition of Burroughs's courage in advocating for education for African American women despite societal norms.

to scrutiny in terms of its expressions of justice and injustice. Readers of the Bible with this perspective focus on the moral and ethical imperatives of justice contained therein and with an eye toward struggle for liberation for women of color. Similarly, LGBTQ readers of the Bible read to "queer" the text, looking for fissures in hegemonic gender and creating disruptions of heteronormative assumptions.

Women have begun to challenge and reconstruct religious traditions as well as scripture. For example, Jewish women have developed feminist Haggadot, texts containing the ritual for celebrating the Passover Seder. These feminist Haggadot commemorate the women of the Exodus, the liberation of the Israelites from slavery in Egypt. In one Haggadah, the four sons of the traditional ceremony become four daughters, and the lives of the women celebrating Passover are inserted in the ceremony to create a living history and a new story.

Perhaps one of the most contentious reconstructions of religious traditions is the ordination of women and LGBTQ people. Although feminist church historians have recovered a long tradition of women as rabbis, priests, pastors, bishops, and evangelists, most Christian denominations did not ordain women until the latter part of the twentieth century. Many still do not. One exception to this is the Quakers, who have a long and unique history of women's equality in the congregation. Although Quakers do not ordain anyone, some groups of Quakers do record ministers, and women have always been among the recorded. In silent Quaker meetings, women as well as men are assumed to be able to receive and speak a word from God.

Beginning in the 1960s, many mainline Protestant churches began to ordain women ministers, although men still make up the larger percentage of senior pastors in almost every denomination. The Episcopal Church elected the Most Rev. Dr. Katharine Jefferts Schori as its presiding bishop in 2006. Roman Catholics still prohibit women from becoming priests, although there is a growing movement within Catholicism, particularly American Catholicism, to change this policy. The Church of England first ordained women as priests in 1994, but the Church only consecrated its first woman bishop in 2015. Several churches—such as the United Church of Christ, the Unitarian Universalist Association, and the Episcopal Church—ordain openly LGBTQ clergy, although in the case of the Episcopal Church, this has caused tension between churches in the worldwide Anglican fellowship inside and outside the United States because many of the latter resist such ordination of LGBTQ clergy. In 2004, the church invested the Right Reverend V. Gene Robinson, an out gay man, bishop of the diocese of New Hampshire and in 2010 consecrated the Right Reverend Mary Douglas Glasspool as its first openly lesbian bishop. Although both the Presbyterian Church USA (PCUSA) and the United Methodist Church began ordaining women in the 1950s, full acceptance of LGBTQ people as ministers has come much more slowly. The PCUSA voted in 2011 to allow the ordination of people in same sex relationships, but the United Methodist Church still excludes people in same-sex relationships from ordination and prevents Methodists ministers from performing same-sex weddings.

Particularly for women in the global south and women of color in the United States, neither reinterpreting nor reconstructing go far enough in examining and challenging the colonial underpinnings of religious traditions. Postcolonial feminist theologians confront and call out the legacies of empire in religious texts and practices and the ways religions have been used as colonizing influences. For example, writers such as Musa Dube of Botswana point to colonial beliefs in "God, gold, and glory" as intersecting theological and economic supports for the conquest of Africa and its subsequent pillaging by colonizers. In response, women around the world have begun to develop their own spirituality, recapturing older religious traditions as a way to "decolonize" themselves from the influences of the religious traditions their people were forced to adopt during the colonial period.

Islamic feminists seek to recover the Qur'anic tradition of gender equality. They argue that patriarchy is not inherent in the religion but is a result of the ways patriarchal contexts and histories have taken precedence in Qur'anic interpretation. They also note that until recently Qur'anic interpretation had only been done by men. The goal of Qur'anic interpretation, they say, is to identify the unchanging principle in the text and implement it in the present. In so doing, they explain, Islamic feminists will recover Islam's foundational gender equality.

CREATING NEW SPIRITUAL TRADITIONS

Although some feminists believe in the reinterpretation and reconstruction of scriptures and choose to work within existing denominations, others prefer to create their own empowering religious texts and organizations. For some, traditional religious scriptures are so essentially androcentric, or male-centered, that they can reproduce only patriarchal social relations. They see no possibility of liberation in scripture because even reconstruction of biblical texts cannot change the patriarchal core of, for example, the Bible. Rather, these reconstructions simply perpetuate the patriarchal order. Feminist philosopher Mary Daly argued that patriarchal language is not accidental or incidental to the Bible but is an essential element of it, rendering the Bible useless in the liberation of women and other marginalized people. Women such as Daly look beyond traditional scripture for spiritual insight and understanding. Wiccan groups, discussed previously, fall into this category too.

In this way, although many women and LGBTQ people have expressed their spirituality within formal religious traditions, many others have created new forms of spiritual expression outside churches, synagogues, and mosques. These spiritualties are an empowering force that has taken such various forms as meditation, poetry, art, prayer, ritual, and social action. Spirituality enables marginalized people to experience connection with creation, with other human beings, and with the divine within themselves. The reading "Transgressing the Father Figure" by Allyson Dean and Whitney J. Archer describes the use of drag to subvert dominant theological norms and practices and suggests liberatory possibilities through queer transgressive performance.

For many feminists, spirituality is a central force in their politics. The awareness of the interconnectedness of all things motivates feminist action toward justice and peace and encourages women to work together across differences. Nature-based spiritualities affirm the connections among all living things and seek to protect the natural environment on which we all depend. Feminist spirituality values and affirms the diversity that makes up the unity of creation, and it challenges women to restructure the systems of power that create and maintain injustice. As feminist author Marge Piercy writes:

> Praise our choices, sisters, for each doorway
> open to us was taken by squads of fighting
> women who paid years of trouble and struggle,
> who paid their wombs, their sleep, their lives
> that we might walk through these gates upright.
> Doorways are sacred to women for we
> are the doorways of life and we must choose
> what comes in and what goes out. Freedom
> is our real abundance.*

---

*"The Sabbath of Mutual Respect," *The Moon Is Always Female* (New York: Knopf, 1980).

THE BLOG

CHRISTIAN FRAGILITY

Susan M. Shaw (2015)

Anyone in the U.S. with a social media account has undoubtedly seen the outcry from many members of the Christian Right over Friday's Supreme Court ruling on marriage equality. What many Americans celebrated as a triumph of love and social progress, many Christian conservatives decried as evidence of the country's moral decline and a precursor to the persecution of Christian pastors who preach against homosexuality or refuse to perform a same-sex wedding.

The force of this outcry is not simply about religious convictions. It's also about what I'm terming "Christian fragility."

In 2011 Robin DiAngelo published a pivotal article on "White Fragility" (International Journal of Critical Pedagogy, Vol 3 (3)(2011) pp 54-70). According to DiAngelo, white fragility is an emotional/psychological state for white people in which racial stress is intolerable. This racial stress arises when white folks are confronted by their own racial privilege or find themselves in situations that are not racially familiar. This state leads to a number of defensive maneuvers—including outward displays of emotion, argumentation, silence, and withdrawal—in order to restore racial equilibrium.

I see many parallels between DiAngelo's description of white fragility and the responses of certain conservative Christians to the marriage equality decision, as well as other social, political, and educational issues of the so-called "Culture Wars."

White dominance allows most whites to live in social environments that insulate them from challenging encounters with ideas or people who differ from themselves. Within this dominant social environment, whites come to expect social comfort and a sense of belonging and superiority. When this comfort is disrupted, whites are often at a loss because they have not had to build skills for constructive engagement with difference. They may become defensive, positioning themselves as victims of antiracist work and co-opting the rhetoric of violence to describe their experiences of being challenged on racial privilege.

Similarly, many conservative Christians segregate much of their lives into enclaves with people who share their values. Within the sharp subcultural boundaries of conservative Christianity, they insulate themselves from ideas and people who may issue direct and sustained challenges to their beliefs. They also often learn from their leaders that they know the Truth with certainty, that opposing beliefs are dangerous, and that they must hold fast against the onslaught of false ideas.

Since the 1980s, many conservative Christians have enjoyed political prominence and wide social acceptance of some of their ideals. As late as the early 2000s, most Americans opposed marriage equality. That framework provided an opportunity for conservative Christians to come to see some of their beliefs as normative, natural, and inherent, reinforced by broader support across the nation. Within this sphere of social comfort, many conservative Christians were not ready for the speed with which national norms around marriage equality changed and disrupted the assumptions of Christian entitlement and heteronormativity.

Unprepared to engage in constructive dialogue about marriage equality, many conservative Christians retreated into the defensive maneuvers of fragility—anger, fear, argumentation, resistance—as a way to try to reestablish an equilibrium. Presidential candidate Mike Huckabee called for conservative Christians to "resist and reject judicial tyranny, not retreat." Gov. Scott Walker of Wisconsin called for a constitutional amendment to allow states to define marriage. Louisiana's governor, Bobby Jindal, warned that the Court's decision "will pave the way for an all out assault against the religious freedom rights of Christians who disagree with this decision." Conservative Christian pastors railed against the decision in sermons that pitted God against the Supreme Court.

I'm guessing those who have never been insiders to conservative Christianity may wonder why the extreme and occasionally apocalyptic language about the marriage equality decision. As one who grew up a Southern Baptist fundamentalist, however, I do understand the fear and discomfort of Christian fragility. Rigid belief systems do not prepare people for encounters with difference. When one believes there is only one right way, one Truth, then the options for dialogue are limited. And the fear of turning away from The Truth is very real.

What is ignored in Christian fragility, however, is the social privilege accorded Christians of all stripes in this country—our holidays are embedded in the work calendar; we can easily find foods our religion allows us to eat; we can be elected President of the United States. By positioning conservative Christians as victims of religious oppression, many conservative Christians can then also ignore the privileges that come with the intersections of their Christian faith with heterosexuality and the very real consequences of heterosexism on the lives of LGBQ people—real violence, real economic disadvantage, real hate crimes—that are complicated and intensified as we include intersections with race, gender, gender identity, ability, age, and social class. The dominance of heterosexuality over other forms of sexual identity becomes obscured in arguments about the anticipated victimization of conservative Christians for their beliefs about homosexuality.

While the discomfort of disequilibrium seems intolerable for many conservative Christians, a new wave of conservative Christians has embraced the struggle to understand difference, and some have even come to support marriage equality. Many have offered alternative readings of the Bible that, while still holding the Bible in highest regard, also afford new understandings of LGBQ people and marriage equality. Christian fragility provides a framework for understanding the intense reactions of some conservative Christians to marriage equality, but Christian faith is only fragile when it is unwilling to engage difference with open hearts and open minds.

77. INTRODUCTION TO *THE WOMAN'S BIBLE*

ELIZABETH CADY STANTON (1895)

From the inauguration of the movement for woman's emancipation the Bible has been used to hold [woman] in the "divinely ordained sphere," prescribed in the Old and New Testaments.

The canon and civil law; church and state; priests and legislators; all political parties and religious denominations have alike taught that woman was made after man, of man, and for man, an inferior being, subject to man. Creeds, codes, Scriptures and statutes, are all based on this idea. The fashions, forms, ceremonies and customs of society, church ordinances and discipline all grow out of this idea.

...

The Bible teaches that woman brought sin and death into the world, that she precipitated the fall of the race, that she was arraigned before the judgment seat of Heaven, tried, condemned and sentenced. Marriage for her was to be a condition of bondage, maternity a period of suffering and anguish, and in silence and subjection, she was to play the role of a dependent on man's bounty for all her material wants, and for all the information she might desire on the vital questions of the hour, she was commanded to ask her husband at home. Here is the Bible position of woman briefly summed up.

...

These familiar texts are quoted by clergymen in their pulpits, by statesmen in the halls of legislation, by lawyers in the courts, and are echoed by the press of all civilized nations, and accepted by woman herself as "The Word of God." So perverted is the religious element in her nature, that with faith and works she is the chief support of the church and clergy; the very powers that make her emancipation impossible. When, in the early part of the Nineteenth Century, women began to protest against their civil and political degradation, they were referred to the Bible for an answer. When they protested against their unequal position in the church, they were referred to the Bible for an answer.

This led to a general and critical study of the Scriptures. Some, having made a fetish of these books and believing them to be the veritable "Word of God," with liberal translations, interpretations, allegories and symbols, glossed over the most objectionable features of the various books and clung to them as divinely inspired. Others, seeing the family resemblance between the Mosaic code, the canon law, and the old English common law, came to the conclusion that all alike emanated from the same source; wholly human in their origin and inspired by the natural love of domination in the historians. Others, bewildered with their doubts and fears, came to no conclusion. While their clergymen told them on the one hand that they owed all the blessings and freedom they enjoyed to the Bible, on the other, they said it clearly marked out their circumscribed sphere of action: that the demands for political and civil rights were irreligious, dangerous to the stability of the home, the state and the church. Clerical appeals were circulated from time to time conjuring members of their churches to take no part in the anti-slavery or woman suffrage movements, as they were infidel in their tendencies, undermining the very foundations of society. No wonder the majority of women stood still, and with bowed heads, accepted the situation.

78. GOD SAYS YES TO ME
KAYLIN HAUGHT (1995)

I asked God if it was okay to be melodramatic
and she said yes
I asked her if it was okay to be short
and she said it sure is
I asked her if I could wear nail polish
or not wear nail polish
and she said honey
she calls me that sometimes
she said you can do just exactly
what you want to
Thanks God I said
And is it even okay if I don't paragraph
my letters
Sweetcakes God said
who knows where she picked that up
what I'm telling you is
Yes Yes Yes

79. FUNDAMENTALISM AND THE CONTROL OF WOMEN
KAREN MCCARTHY BROWN (1994)

Religious fundamentalism is very difficult to define; yet many of us—scholars and journalists in particular—think we know it when we see it. For those attuned to gender as a category of analysis, a stab of recognition is often occasioned by the presence of high degrees of religiously sanctioned control of women. In conservative religious movements around the world, women are veiled or otherwise covered; confined to the home or in some other way strictly limited in their access to the public sphere; prohibited from testifying in a court of law, owning property, or initiating divorce; and they are very often denied the authority to make their own reproductive choices.

I propose to take up the thread of the control of women and follow it into the center of the maze of contemporary fundamentalism. Yet I will not argue, as might be expected, that the need to control women is the main motivation for the rise of fundamentalism, but rather that aggravation of this age-old, widespread need is an inevitable side effect of a type of stress peculiar to our age.

I will suggest that the varieties of fundamentalism found throughout the world today are extreme responses to the failed promise of Enlightenment rationalism. Fundamentalism, in my view, is the religion of the stressed and the disoriented, of those for whom the world is overwhelming. More to the point, it is the religion of those at once seduced and betrayed by the promise that we human beings can comprehend and control our world. Bitterly disappointed by the politics of rationalized bureaucracies, the limitations of science, and the perversions of industrialization, fundamentalists seek to reject the modem world, while nevertheless holding onto its habits of mind: clarity, certitude, and control. Given these habits, fundamentalists necessarily operate with a limited view of human activity (including religious activity), one confined largely to consciousness and choice. They deny the power of those parts of the human psyche that are inaccessible to consciousness yet play a central role in orienting us in the world. Most of all they seek to control the fearsome, mute power of the flesh. This characteristic ensures that fundamentalism will always involve the control of women, for women generally carry the greater burden of human fleshliness.

This essay is an exploratory one. Its topic is huge and it ranges widely, crossing over into several academic disciplines other than my own. Occasionally I am forced to paint with a broad stroke and a quick hand. Writing that is preliminary and suggestive can be risky, but the connections I see between religious fundamentalism and other, larger aspects of our contemporary world seem compelling enough to lead me to take that risk. My argument begins close to home, in the United States, with Christian anti-abortion activism.

THE ANTI-ABORTION MOVEMENT IN THE UNITED STATES

The "pro-life movement" emerged in the 1970s as a new type of religio-political organization. It was a bottom-up movement that used sophisticated, top-down technology. In the early stages of the movement, the organizing work was done around kitchen tables. But the envelopes stuffed at those tables were sent to addresses on computer-generated mailing lists, the product of advanced market-research techniques. This blend of grass-roots organization and advanced technology quickly brought a minority movement[1] to a position of significant political power. The combination of traditional and modern methods also reveals an ambivalence toward the ways of the modern world that I will later argue is characteristic of fundamentalist movements.

Many observers have noted an inconsistency in the pro-life position. The very groups who launch an emotional defense of the fetus's right to life are curiously indifferent to children outside the womb. As a rule, pro-lifers do not support social programs focused on issues such as child abuse, day care, foster care, or juvenile drug use. They oppose welfare programs in general and have taken no leadership in educational reform beyond concern with sex education, public school prayer, and the theory of evolution. Furthermore, their so-called pro-life argument is deeply compromised by staunch support for increased military spending and for the death penalty.

It seems clear that the pro-life position is not a consistent theological or philosophical stance. A quite different kind of consistency emerges from the full range of this group's social policy positions. Their overriding concern is that of maintaining strong and clear social boundaries—boundaries between nation-states, between law-abiding citizens and criminals, between the righteous and the sinful, between life and death, and not coincidentally, between men and women. This is a group centrally concerned with social order and social control.

Beyond the trigger of the 1973 Supreme Court decision in *Roe v. Wade*, stresses with a broader historical range have contributed to a focus on boundary maintenance in the anti-abortion movement. The upheavals of the 1960s created the immediate historical context of the anti-abortion movement of the 1970s. Student activists of the 1960s questioned the authority of parents, educators, and politicians. Black activists challenged the cherished American myths of equal opportunity and equal protection under the law. And the Vietnam War not only raised questions about U.S. military prowess but also planted doubts about the moral valence of the international presence and policy of the United States. These are very specific reasons why Americans in the 1970s might have felt that the social and moral orders were becoming dangerously befuddled.

. . .

A WORLD SUDDENLY TOO BIG

From the mid-nineteenth century into the early decades of the twentieth, the writings of travelers, missionaries, and, eventually, anthropologists were popular bedside reading materials in the United States. Americans were fascinated by exotic "others." They were concerned about their own place in this expanding, newly complex world. Most of these books did more than titillate. With their implicit or explicit social Darwinism, they also carried deeply comforting messages of progress and of Western superiority. Such messages, coming from many sources, infused an air of optimism into an otherwise disorienting age. During the same general time span, the seeds of American fundamentalism were sown and came to fruition.

Some of the social forces that shaped this period—expanding knowledge of and contact with the larger world, and increased communication—had emerged over a relatively long period of time. Others, such as the burgeoning of cities, the dramatic increase in immigrant populations, and a series of shifts in women's roles, had occurred more recently.[2] All of these forces came together in the second half of the nineteenth century to contribute to a general sense of vertigo; the world was becoming too big, too complicated, and too chaotic to comprehend. Most important, each individual's own place in it was uncertain. Religion, given its basic orientational role in human life, emerged as a natural arena for dealing with the resulting stress.

From that period until this in the United States, conservative Christians have come under a double attack. On one level, they have had to deal with the general stress of the times; and on the other, with the direct challenge of Enlightenment rationalism in the form of biblical higher criticism and evolutionary theory. The reaction of some groups of Christians has been ironic: they have responded to the threat by mimicking Enlightenment rationalism. The religion-versus-science debate pits against one another groups who share a common intellectual style: each claims to possess the truth. Believers, like rationalists, stress consciousness, clarity, and control.[3] Morality is codified; sacred narratives are taken literally and sometimes attempts are made to support them with "scientific evidence"; all sorts of truths are listed and enumerated; scripture becomes inerrant. Furthermore, conscious consent to membership in the community of belief, on the model of "making a decision for Christ," becomes increasingly important.

These are the religious groups we call fundamentalists. Their central aim is to make of their religion an Archimedean point in the midst of a changing world. But to do so, they must limit their religion's responsiveness to its social environment; and as a result they are left with little flexibility to respond to the complexity of their own feelings or to the challenge of a changing world. Sometimes they fall into aggressively defending brittle truths. This is what makes fundamentalism in the contemporary world problematic and, in some cases, dangerous.

. . .

FUNDAMENTALISM CROSS-CULTURALLY

Up to this point, I have been concerned with Christian fundamentalism in the United States, but in the process I have focused on dimensions of the story that serve, without denying the significance of local variations, to characterize fundamentalism around the globe. Religious fundamentalism is born in times and places where, for a variety of reasons, the world suddenly seems too complex to comprehend; and one's place in it, too precarious to provide genuine security.

One example is modern India, where the cult that developed around the recent immolation of a young woman on her husband's funeral pyre has been described as an instance of fundamentalism. John Hawley demonstrates that the background for the *sati* of Roop Kanwar was emerging Hindu nationalism in India augmented by a multitude of local destabilizing forces in Deorala, the site of the immolation. Furthermore, as Hawley and other authors have pointed out, Deorala is not a truly deprived area, and its residents are not traditionalists out of contact with the larger realities of modern India. I would therefore suggest, along with Hawley, that fundamentalism is not primarily a religion of the marginalized, as some have argued. Its more salient feature is that it develops among people caught off balance. Hence, fundamentalist groups often arise in situations where social, cultural, and economic power is up for grabs; many, like these groups now being referred to as Hindu fundamentalists, arise in postcolonial situations. Far from being essentially marginal to the societies in which they exist, fundamentalists are often directly involved in the political and economic issues of their time and place. And they often have a significant, if precarious, stake in them.

For the Rajputs in Deorala, traditional sources of pride and authority are being challenged by increasing contact with the cities of Jaipur and Delhi, and through them, all of India. These Rajputs are experiencing the disorientation of having to depend on economic and political systems beyond their control. Marwari merchants and industrialists, financial backers of the cult of the goddess Sati, are destabilized in another way. As their economic role expands throughout India, they risk their livelihood in a wider, less familiar, and less predictable world than the one in which earlier generations operated. The Marwari focus on the district around Jhunjhunu with its important Sati shrine gives them their emotionally saturated Archimedean point. The case of the Marwari businessmen suggests, even more directly than does that of the Rajputs, that fundamentalism is not a religion of the marginalized, but of the disoriented.

In the contemporary Indian context, rallying around the *sati* of Roop Kanwar (like anti-abortion activity in the United States) reasserts social control and demonstrates moral worth. It strengthens gender boundaries and provides an example of undiluted, innocent virtue that vicariously underwrites the virtue of Rajputs and Marwaris in general. Furthermore, as in the United States, insecurity about social control and moral rectitude is displaced onto the body of a woman. But in the sati ritual described by Hawley, the drive to kill the devouring, fleshly goddess and to enshrine the pure, spiritual one is much more painfully literal.

Both men and women attended the *sati* of Roop Kanwar, and both men and women subsequently revere her. At first glance this may seem difficult to understand, but the complicity of Indian women in the practice of *sati* has to be considered on more than one level. At the deepest level its explanation lies in the fear of women's will and women's flesh that men and women share, and in the relief that both feel when these forces are kept in check. But on another level there are explanations of a much more practical nature. Most Indian women's economic security heavily depends on marriage. A woman doing homage at a Sati shrine thus signals to her husband and to the world at large, as well as to herself, that she intends to be good and to do good, according to her society's standards. Thus she chooses to ignore any anger or fear she might feel about the practice, in the name of living a secure and ordered life. It is a herculean task for women to try to define the meaning and worth of their lives in terms different from those that prevail in their community. So some security can always be found in surrendering to, and even helping to strengthen, the accepted gender norms.

. . .

THE FAILED PROMISE OF ENLIGHTENMENT RATIONALISM

Modern communications, transnational economic pressures, and wars waged from the opposite side of the globe have brought many populations intimate knowledge of the vastness and complexity of their worlds. In the late twentieth century, the others in relation to whom we must define ourselves are more available to our experience and imagination than ever before; yet few if any of us have a satisfactory model for understanding ourselves within this complex, stressful world.

We all live in and are defined by a world too big and unstable for intellect or belief to comprehend, and we all react to intimations—as well as a few pieces of hard evidence[4]—of the failed promise of the Enlightenment. Academics, politicians, and ordinary folk the world over are immersed in this challenge and most commonly react to it (as fundamentalists do) by assuming that, with sufficient effort, the chaos can be first comprehended and then managed. In this way fundamentalists are simply extreme versions of the rest of us.

An emphasis on the control of women is characteristic of fundamentalism, but there is some of it everywhere in the world. The anti-abortion movement in the United States arises out of a much broader context in which, among other signals of misogyny, public power and authority have been denied to women for centuries. And the Sati cult could not have become an issue in Indian nationalism if in general Indian women were not seen as sources of pollution as well as of blessing—as a result of which they have been subject to a variety of social controls through the ages. When the mind and the spirit are cut off from the body, women become magnets for the fear raised by everything in life that seems out of control. The degree to which control is exercised over women is therefore a key to the profundity of stresses felt by most persons and groups. Fundamentalism is a product of extreme social stress.

Religion, whose primary function is to provide a comprehensible model of the world and to locate the individual safely and meaningfully within it, is an obvious place for this type of stress to express itself and seek redress. But as long as religions deal with this stress by positing a world that can be directly known, and in which it is possible to determine one's own fate, they only reinforce the controlling tendencies of Enlightenment rationalism and do nothing to move us beyond it to whatever comes next. We should be suspicious of any religion that claims too much certainty or draws the social boundaries too firmly. In this period marked by the gradual breakdown of Enlightenment rationalism and Euro-American hegemony in the world, something more is necessary. We need help in accepting ourselves as organic creatures enmeshed in our world rather than continuing to posture as cerebral masters granted dominion over it. This requires that we learn to trust the wisdom of our mute flesh and accept the limitations inherent in our humanity. If we could do this, it would radically diminish our scapegoating of women and all the other "others" who provide a convenient screen on which to project fears.

The resurgence of religion that we are experiencing at the turn of this millennium should not be viewed in an entirely negative light. If any system of orientation in the world can help us now, it seems likely to be a religious one. There is no small comfort in knowing that, as the grand ambitions spawned by the Enlightenment falter in the present age, what is likely to emerge is not what several generations of social scientists predicted. It is not civilization marching toward increasing secularization and rationalization. What is slowly being revealed is the hubris of reason's pretense in trying to take over religion's role.

NOTES

1. From the beginning of the anti-abortion movement to the present, opinion polls have consistently shown that the majority of people in the United States favor a woman's right to have an abortion.

2. Betty A. DeBerg, *Ungodly Women: Gender and the First Wave of American Fundamentalism* (Minneapolis: Fortress Press, 1990), has an excellent discussion of the general changes—and particularly the changes inn women's roles—attendant to the formation of fundamentalism in the United States. . . .

3. Often the only kind of control that fundamentalists can exercise over a chaotic and threatening world rests in their claim to have a privileged understanding of the deeper meaning of the chaos. Fundamentalists who engage in "end-time" thinking thus sometimes find themselves in the position of welcoming the signs of modern social decay because these signal the approach of the time when God will call home the chosen few.

4. The growing ecological crisis is one of the most tangible pieces of this evidence; it also reinforces the point that reason alone is an insufficient problem -solving tool, because we are incapable of holding in consciousness the full range of the interconnectedness of things.

80. "I'M A MORMON FEMINIST"
JESSICA FINNIGAN AND NANCY ROSS (2013)

In December 2012 the *Los Angeles Times* published an article entitled "For Mormon Feminists, Progress with an Asterisk" (Glionna 2012). The same day, *Jezebel* published a similar article, "Mormon Women Are 'Admired' but Still Not Equal" (Baker 2012). Baker asks, "So how can self-described feminists also be Mormon?" She concludes that Mormon feminism is an oxymoron and an unattainable identity, as Mormonism is a religion that is steeped in patriarchal authority. The same question has been reiterated in a number of publications over the last few decades (Basquiat 2001; Bell 1976; Dodwell 2003; Stack 1991). The same message is heard by Mormon feminists from their orthodox friends and family and from the leadership of the Church of Latter-day Saints (LDS). Such questions rely on a false binary between liberal feminism and a conservative religion, implying a lack of possible overlap or middle ground.

The situation for Mormon feminists today is different from that of previous generations. Mormon feminists use social media to connect previously isolated individuals and bring them into online communities that function as support networks. Mormon feminists started using blogs in the 2000s and recently expanded into closed Facebook groups. The use of Facebook groups coincides with the recent wave of Mormon feminist activism at the beginning of 2012.

There is some scholarship on how the Internet disrupts organized religion (Campbell 2010), but there is none on how social movements, such as Mormon feminism, use the Internet to advance and promote their cause within a larger religious community. In this study, we tracked the development of online Mormon feminist activism and identified how Mormon feminists use the Internet to raise awareness of issues and promote campaigns. We located Mormon feminist communities in different forms of social media and examined how they interact online. We concluded that social media make up an essential element in how Mormon feminists navigate the middle ground between conservative Mormonism and liberal feminism.

BACKGROUND

Activism within the LDS Church has a complicated history. Early female leaders mounted internal battles against polygamy in the 1840s, resulting in the disbanding of the Relief Society, the LDS Church's organization for women, from 1844 to 1868 (Derr, Cannon, and Beecher 2002; Newell and Avery 1994). Many scholars comment on the pro–women's suffrage position of LDS Church members and leaders in the United States, but they fail to recognize that this activism existed outside LDS Church policy and doctrine (Iversen 1984).

The ratification process and the defeat of the Equal Rights Amendment (ERA) in the 1970s and early 1980s, specifically the active anti-ERA position of the

LDS Church, brought forth a resurgence of Mormon feminist activism. This included civil disobedience, writing, and public speaking in favor of the ERA and in opposition to LDS Church leaders (Bradley 2005). In 1979, involvement in pro-ERA campaigns resulted in the excommunication—the most severe ecclesiastical punishment—of Sonia Johnson, an outspoken advocate for the group Mormons for ERA (Bradley 2005). Johnson's excommunication served as a warning to other feminists and pushed Mormon feminist conversations back into living rooms and small discussion groups (Bradley 2005).

After the failure to ratify the ERA, Mormon feminists continued to write, speak, and publish despite fear of church discipline (Bradley 2005). LDS Church leaders spoke openly about the dangers of church members reading non-church-approved texts and attending symposia that had not been officially endorsed by the LDS Church (Lindholm 2010). High-ranking LDS Church officials referred to feminists as one of the three greatest dangers to the Church (Packer 1993). Publications such as *Women and Authority* (Hanks 1992), which explored Mormon women's relationship to authority in the LDS Church and the decline of women's authority in the 20th century, resulted in a renewed round of church discipline. Six scholars were excommunicated in September 1993 (Lindholm 2010; *New York Times* 1993). The pattern of backlash and the accompanying high social cost to individuals who participated in Mormon feminism during those decades pushed visible collective movements underground and caused some commentators to ask whether Mormon feminism was dead (Stack 2003).

The Internet has reshaped Mormon feminism. In 2004, Lisa Patterson Butterworth founded the *Feminist Mormon Housewives* blog, providing 21st-century Mormon feminists with a discussion space (Cohen 2005). In subsequent years, Mormon feminists started other blogs, such as *The Exponent, Zelophehad's Daughters*, and countless others. Facebook added another dimension to the Mormon feminist community, allowing previously isolated individuals to meet and discuss issues in private groups.

LDS Church leaders were aware of Mormon feminist activism as a result of a series of campaigns in

2012 and 2013. In January 2013, Elaine Dalton, then General Young Women's President, stated:

> Young women, you will be the ones who will provide the example of virtuous womanhood and motherhood. You will continue to be virtuous, lovely, praiseworthy and of good report. You will also be the ones to provide an example of family life in a time when families are under attack, being redefined and disintegrating. You will understand your roles and your responsibilities and *thus will see no need to lobby for rights* (Dalton 2013; Stack 2013b).

In August 2013, Elder M. Russell Ballard, a member of the Quorum of the Twelve Apostles, said that Church members should be wary of the power of persuasion that is inherent in the Internet (Clegg 2013; Holman 2013). Ballard's talk also demonstrates the often contradictory statements about womanhood and female identity in the LDS Church, as he emphasizes the importance of women and at the same time limits their roles in the church.

. . .

In this sociocultural analysis, we combined quantitative and qualitative methods. We examined survey data as wells as blogs and social media sites. . . .

DISCUSSION

DEMOGRAPHICS: BREAKING DOWN THE MYTHS OF MORMON FEMINISTS

There are long-standing stereotypes that have been used to characterize people who participate in feminist activism (Israel-Cohen 2012). Conservative individuals within the LDS community identify Mormon feminists as a group of angry women who have no religious belief, are not active in their religious communities, are antifamily, do not attend church, and want simply to be ordained to the priesthood and steal power from men (Isackson 2013; Wilson 2013). Data from our study suggest that these stereotypes do not reflect the lives of the majority of Mormon feminists.

Mormon feminists are not exclusively female; 19 percent of those surveyed were male. Seventy-nine percent were aged 40 or younger. Ninety-five percent lived in the United States, and 91 percent identified as White/Caucasian. Eighty-one percent attended church at least two to three times per month, and 70 percent currently held a calling (a responsibility within the local congregation). Eighty-seven percent probably came from LDS families, as they reported having been baptized at the standard age of eight years. Seventy-seven percent reported levels of belief that are consistent with those of the mainstream population (Pew Research Center 2012). Ninety-one percent of married Mormon feminists were married in an LDS temple, a sign of faithfulness and orthopraxy. The majority of respondents (62 percent) were parents.

Of all the stereotypes, the only one that holds true is that most Mormon feminists want women to be ordained to the priesthood: 59 percent of survey respondents believe that women will be ordained to the priesthood in this life or the next. A further 26 percent believe that women already hold the priesthood. Only 16 percent believe that women will never hold the priesthood. These numbers are very different from a random sampling of Mormons by the Pew Trust, which found that just 13 percent of American Mormon men and 8 percent of Mormon women thought that women should be ordained to the priesthood (Pew Research Center 2012).

The most common emotion that was expressed in the open-ended response questions was fear. Mormon feminists fear that if they express their feminist views, they will be ostracized by family members, Church leaders, and friends. Only a minority of respondents (38 percent) had approached local leaders with feminist concerns, and of that group, only 37 percent reported that they felt heard and that their local leaders had made a positive change. Mormon feminists fear being denied or released from callings in consequence of their questions about gender. These fears are justified; 56 percent of Mormon feminists reported experiencing negative consequences as a result of expressing feminist views.

Despite their fears, a majority of Mormon feminists (74 percent) are hopeful that the LDS Church will in the future be more inclusive of women, and 58 percent of respondents feel that local leaders are including women in ward-level decisions. Respondents exhibited a high level of belief and participation, providing counterevidence to the stereotypes of Mormon feminists. Interview respondents also reported that their gender issues began organically and that finding online Mormon feminism sites allowed them to resolve their counteractive feelings and remain active in the LDS Church.

. . .

MORMON FEMINIST ACTIVISM CAMPAIGNS

Although the LDS Church has a long history of bottom-up innovation, this seems to have faded from memory (Christensen 2009). The current social and hierarchical framework of the LDS church clearly discourages grassroots activism, members are officially discouraged from engaging simple techniques, such as letter writing or personally attempting to contact church leaders at the highest levels (Church of Jesus Christ of Latter-day Saints 2010). Mormon feminist activism operates within these tensions. The following is an analysis of activist campaigns that demonstrate how Mormon feminists have used, mastered, and adapted to the limitations of activism in the LDS Church through the use of social media.

TEMPLE BAPTISMS AND MENSTRUATION

The first online Mormon feminist campaign took place in February 2012. Its goal was to get the LDS Church to clarify its policy on the participation of menstruating women in temple baptisms. Although many religious communities place restrictions on participation of women while they are menstruating, the LDS Church does not have any such policy. Nevertheless, many women reported having been excluded. Bloggers and commenters described in emotional terms their own experiences as teenagers, many of which included shame, humiliation, and feelings of being unworthy (Layne 2012). Survey respondents referred to their own shame at being excluded and were motivated by these negative feelings to participate in the campaign. Respondents did not want other teenage girls to have the same experience. One survey respondent said:

> Because as a teenager living in MO [Missouri], I worked all summer long to earn money to go on a temple trip to Dallas only to be told when I got

there that I couldn't do baptisms because I was on my period—it was humiliating and degrading—most of the other kids thought I didn't participate because of worthiness issues—I knew boys on that trip that weren't worthy to participate but they still got to do it—I was worthy but because I was a girl menstruating I was denied. I do think the campaign helped but my own girls have recently been told they couldn't participate—they were armed with the knowledge that they could and told the temple workers that it wasn't policy but there are sooo many girls that don't know, and the problem persists.

Mormon feminists created a Google spreadsheet listing 142 operating LDS temples that were contacted by telephone, with space to record the temple's policy, the name of the individual who called the temple, and additional comments on the phone call (Elisothel 2012). Twenty-eight individuals contacted sixty-eight temples on five continents. The data revealed inconsistent policies, some of which were exclusionary. Fifteen temples did not allow girls to participate in baptism during menstruation, sixteen temples allowed girls and women to participate if they used a tampon, five temples had other restrictions, and twenty-seven temples had no restrictions. The campaign resulted in a *Salt Lake Tribune* article that elicited a policy clarification from the LDS Church, stating, "The decision of whether or not to participate in baptisms during a menstrual cycle is personal and left up to the individual" (Stack 2012).

According to the traditional social movement literature, this movement was successful because it accomplished the goal that it set out to achieve. However, the real success of this campaign resides in the way in which Mormon feminists demonstrated their ability to come together online and coordinate activist campaigns.

. . .

WEAR PANTS TO CHURCH DAY

On December 5, 2012, responding to a *Jezebel* article (Baker 2012), a blogger for the *Mormon Child Bride* blog wrote, "Mormon feminists, I think it is time for some good old-fashioned Civil Disobedience" (Lauritzen 2012). Four days later, Mormon feminists created a new closed Facebook group called All Enlisted to discuss activism (Whitelocks 2012). They launched a campaign-specific Facebook page called Wear Pants to Church Day,[1] and an event was scheduled for a week later, on Sunday, December 16 (Gray 2012).

Women who wear pants to LDS Church services are not breaking any rules, but they are violating social norms. The LDS Church issued a statement in 1971 stating that women are free to wear pantsuits to church (Church of Jesus Christ of Latter-day Saints 1974). This statement was reiterated in December 2012 in response to the Wear Pants to Church event (Gray 2012).

Wear Pants to Church Day was reactionary and operated within a very small time frame. Although it was discussed in multiple Facebook groups, the initial idea lacked clear goals and was not well vetted over time by the Mormon feminist community. This makes it difficult to measure the movement's success by traditional metrics.

Negative comments played a significant role in the "Wear Pants to Church Day" campaign. Campaign organizers received numerous negative comments on the event's Facebook page, and one organizer received a death threat (Gray 2012). In our survey, many respondents reported that they were not intending to participate in Wear Pants to Church Day but changed their minds when they learned of the negative feedback. Two respondents wrote as follows:

> Originally, I wasn't planning on participating, but then I saw the backlash and realized that the people who were so upset were in people's wards. I felt I needed to show that Mormon feminists were everywhere.

* * * * *

> I saw women being treated terribly on Facebook by fellow church members for daring to have a voice in a church they are supposed to give equal consent to. I saw a microcosm of a larger problem play out. I wore pants because I wanted people to know which side of this ugliness I stood on, and I wanted any woman in my ward who had ever felt marginalized by the culture police to know that she had a friend in me.

THE "LET WOMEN PRAY" CAMPAIGN

The "Let Women Pray" campaign sought to address the fact that a woman had never, in its 183-year history, offered a prayer at an LDS General Conference,

the LDS Church's semiannual churchwide meeting (Stack 2013a). Previous policies preventing women from praying in church meetings were revoked in 1978 (Gardner 1978), and the LDS Church handbook specifically permits women to give opening and closing prayers in all church meetings (Church of Jesus Christ of Latter-day Saints 2010: Section 18.2).

Letter-writing campaigns as an act of protest are a distinct form of activism with a rich heritage in social movements (Earl and Kimport 2011; Staggenborg 1991). Many online activist campaigns have shifted from letter-writing to e-mail campaigns (Earl and Kimport 2011). The "Let Women Pray" campaign combined traditional letter-writing and e-mails, collecting both traditionally posted letters and printed e-mailed submissions. In an attempt to circumvent the restrictive letter-writing policy within the LDS Church, which specifically prevents members from writing letters directly to LDS Church leaders, coordinators mailed packets of letters rather than individual ones (Church of Jesus Christ of Latter-day Saints 2010).

Analyzing the success of this campaign is problematic. Statements in a January 2013 *Salt Lake Tribune* article indicated that prayers for the April meeting had been assigned months in advance (Stack 2013a). The LDS Church's statement did not indicate the gender of the individuals who were scheduled to pray. Just before the scheduled meeting, an LDS Church spokesman stated that women were indeed scheduled to pray (Stack 2013c). Two prayers at the April 2013 General Conference were offered by women (Berkes 2013), but the cause and effect of this cannot be determined from the available data. One respondent wrote: "I don't know if they would have allowed a woman to pray at general conference without the campaign or not, but I wanted my children to participate in a church where the question of why a woman has never prayed in conference before never even had to be asked."

. . .

THE "I'M A MORMON FEMINIST" PR CAMPAIGN

In 2011, the LDS Church launched a worldwide public relations campaign known as "I'm a Mormon"

(Coffman 2011). Mormon feminists created their own public relations campaign: "I'm a Mormon Feminist." This campaign builds not only on the LDS Church's campaign, but also on the "I Need Feminism" project (Porteous 2013). "I'm a Mormon Feminist" is a campaign that attempts to remove the negative stigma of feminism within the LDS Church. One respondent wrote:

> I think that Mormon Feminism sometimes gets lumped all together and that the mainstream body of the Church gets turned off to the more militant parts of the movement. I would like everyone in the Church to see that if they value women and the role of women in the Church, they are part of the feminist movement. If they think that women should be educated and valued, they are feminists. They can still be okay with women not holding the priesthood (which I am) and still be feminists. They can wear dresses to church (as I do) and be feminists. They can also like to bake and have kids. They just have to understand their own femininity as a daughter of God as separate from cultural expectations and express their role of women as it fulfills them and their role in eternal family and gospel structures.

The "I'm a Mormon Feminist" campaign involves a website, a Facebook page, a Twitter account, a Pinterest pinboard, and a YouTube channel. The website[2] provides a platform for individuals to submit a profile, stating why they identify as a Mormon feminism. In an attempt to further demystify Mormon feminism, the website also has a section entitled "MoFem 101," which includes a lengthy list of feminist and Mormon feminist terminology.

This campaign utilized new forms of media, including photographs and videos. It was also the first time that a website in a feminist campaign deactivated the comments section on a public page. Mormon feminists are still attempting to navigate public activism, exploring methods that help to mitigate the negative backlash and personal emotional toll associated with visible activism.

THE "ORDAIN WOMEN" MOVEMENT

The priesthood in the LDS Church has had a long evolution but has become inseparably linked to LDS male identity (Prince 1995). The "Ordain Women" campaign parallels similar movements in other religious traditions (Lee 2013). The issues that previous Mormon feminist campaigns addressed were restricted to policy and cultural norms. The "Ordain Women" campaign calls into question core LDS doctrines, challenging long-standing gender roles. Analysis of Mormon feminist blogs indicates that female ordination is a controversial topic that is still being debated in the online community (fMhAdmin 2013). Respondents to the survey expressed the same conflicted discussion as the blogs, as can be seen in the following three responses:

> I am undecided on this issue. I worried when I first heard of it that it was too much too fast and it might make it easy for those opposed to the feminist point of view to dismiss female ordination as too radical. But I believe with all my heart that the status quo is not what The Lord wants for women.

> * * * * *

> At first I didn't support it because I was unsure how to feel about the idea of women holding the priesthood. After reading a lot of Church History, I actually have come to support the Ordain Women campaign, but am still not participating in it because my bishop has made it very clear to me that he feels that the Ordain Women campaign is an apostate group and that my participation in it would make me ineligible for a temple recommend [TR]. I could simply participate in secret and hope he didn't find out—after all, there's no requirement to mention it in the TR interview . . . but that feels dishonest.

> * * * * *

> I'm not prepared to debate it without leaning heavily on online sources. I don't have an audience. Who can I talk to, to make a difference? No one. If I spoke about it, questioned it out loud to family or church leaders, I would become a pariah. And it's not the hill I want to die on in regards to my Feminism. I often talk about women having the priesthood in the temple, however, especially to young people (my kids, YW who babysit if I can sneak it in . . .). I don't know if the church in general is ready, because they certainly are sexist with a capital "S."

The center of the "Ordain Women" campaign is a professionally designed website that mirrors the look of official LDS Church websites ("Ordain Women" website 2013).[3] The site presents profiles of individuals giving their support to female ordination as well as a clearly worded mission statement, a FAQ section, a resource section, links to blogs, and links to media coverage. The website also provides resources beyond Mormonism, including a link to "198 Methods of Nonviolent Action" (Sharp 1973). In July 2013, the site displayed 108 profiles and had received over 250,000 views. This website is not interactive; comments cannot be left on posts or profiles. Despite the lack of conversation on the page itself, the website links to seventeen separate blog posts and one podcast that discuss the complexity and offer a platform for debate surrounding the "Ordain Women" movement.

The inherent complexity of a campaign that advocates female ordination in the LDS Church requires a movement that is moderated and vetted by many voices. Previous Mormon feminist campaigns and existing social networks refined the movement and provided a level of sophistication that was necessary for the successful formation and launch of the "Ordain Women" campaign.

The organizers of the "Ordain Women" campaign have a much broader age profile than did the organizers previous campaigns (Winslow 2013). Given the technological platforms on which online Mormon feminists congregate, it is not surprising that 79 percent of the survey respondents are under the age of 40. However, the 20 percent who are over 40 often bring broader life experiences. Together, these individuals provide a combination that has the potential to create a well-balanced set of campaigns within the movement.

CONCLUSION

. . .

Mormon feminists navigate a difficult space between conservative religion and liberal feminism. Previous generations of Mormon feminists had to navigate this territory alone or in small groups, but today's Mormon feminists can find significant support online. One of the biggest myths about Mormon feminists is that they leave the church. Our survey shows that the overwhelming majority of Mormon feminists are attending church and engaging in their local religious communities. Those who seek out blogs and groups online are looking for support. They find this support in conversations that validate their feelings and beliefs. These social media outlets serve as a support group that allows for sharing experiences and problem solving in addition to activism.

Mormon feminism is well archived in blogs, but the use of Facebook is not conducive to historical record keeping, especially in fast-moving, closed, or disbanded groups. In a vibrant and active Facebook group such as the FMH Society, only the most recent discussion threads are visible, and they are continually reordered according to popularity. The closed nature of the group also creates ethical boundaries for both reporting and access. This study of online Mormon feminism demonstrates that the only way to examine these conversations is to witness them as they are happening.

Every religious community will experience the impacts of the Internet (Campbell 2010) and the modernization of gender roles in a unique manner. The combination of liberal feminism and conservative religious communities provides a level of complexity and nuance that is essential to the larger theory. The further study of online religious feminist activism will add an essential dimension to the study of digitally enabled social media movements.

NOTES

1. www.facebook.com/WearPantsToChurchDay.
2. mormonfeminist.org.
3. ordainwomen.org.

REFERENCES

Baker, Katie J. M. 2012. "Mormon Women Are 'Admired' but Still Not Equal to Men." *Jezebel* December 3. Available at jezebel.com/5965164/mormon-women-are-admired-but-still-not-equal-to-men.

Basquiat, Jennifer Huss. 2001. "Reproducing Patriarchy and Erasing Feminism: The Selective Construction of History Within the Mormon Community." *Journal of Feminist Studies in Religion* 17: 5–37.

Bell, Elouise. 1976. "The Implications of Feminism for BYU." *BYU Studies* 16: 527–540. Available at byustudies.byu.edu/showtitle.aspx?title=5250.

Berkes, Howard. 2013. "A Woman's Prayer Makes Mormon History." *NPR.org*. Available at www.npr.org/blogs/thetwo-way/2013/04/08/176604202/a-womans-prayer-makes-mormon-history.

Bradley, Martha Sonntag. 2005. *Pedestals and Podiums: Utah Women, Religious Authority, and Equal Rights*. Salt Lake City, UT: Signature Books.

Campbell, Heidi. 2010. *When Religion Meets New Media*. New York, NY: Routledge.

Christensen, Clayton. 2009. "How to Be Successful at Missionary Work." Video recording of address given at 2009 Boston LDS Education Conference. Available at vimeo.com/7685569.

Church of Jesus Christ of Latter-day Saints. 1974. "Questions and Answers." *New Era* December. Available at https://www.lds.org/new-era/1974/12/qa-questions-and-answers.

Church of Jesus Christ of Latter-day Saints. 2010. *Church Handbook 2: Administering the Church*. Available at www.lds.org/handbook/handbook-2-administering-the-church.

Clegg, Christy. 2013. "Straight Thinking on the Role of Women." *Doves and Serpents* August 25. Available at www.dovesandserpents.org/wp/2013/08/straight-thinking-on-the-role-of-women.

Coffman, Keith. 2011. "Latter-day Saints Launch I'm a Mormon Ad Campaign." *Reuters* October 3. Available at www.reuters.com/article/2011/10/03/us-mormons-media-idUSTRE7911CM20111003.

Cohen, Debra Nussbaum. 2005. "Faithful Track: Questions, Answers and Minutiae on Blogs." *New York Times* March 5. Available at www.nytimes.com/2005/03/05/national/05religion.html.

Dalton, Elaine S. 2013. "Prophetic Priorities and Dedicated Disciples." *byutv.org*. Available at www.byutv.org/watch/de1638f4-c3d1-48ec-8999-cc8face48ab7/byu-devotional-address-elaine-s-dalton-11513.

Derr, Jill Mulvay, Janath Russell Cannon, and Maureen Ursenbach Beecher. 2002. *Women of Covenant: The Story of Relief Society*. Salt Lake City, Utah: Deseret Book Company.

Dodwell, Karen. 2003. "Marketing and Teaching a Women's Literature Course to Culturally Conservative Students." *Feminist Teacher* 14: 234–247.

Earl, Jennifer, and Katrina Kimport. 2011. *Digitally Enabled Social Change: Activism in the Internet Age*. Cambridge, MA: MIT Press.

Elisothel. 2012. "Drumroll Please: Temple 'Issue' Report." *Feminist Mormon Housewives*, 7 March. Available at www.feministmormonhousewives.org/2012/03/drumroll-please-temple-issue-report.

fMhAdmin. 2013. "Thoughts on the Ordination of Women?: Our Diversity of Views." *Feminist Mormon Housewives* March 21. Available at www.feministmormonhousewives.org/2013/03/thoughts-on-the-ordination-of-women-our-diversity-of-views.

Gardner, Marvin. 1978. News of the Church. *Ensign* November 1. Available at www.lds.org/ensign/1978/11/news-of-the-church.

Glionna, John M. 2012. "For Mormon Feminists, Progress 'with an Asterisk.'" *Los Angeles Times* December 3. Available at articles.latimes.com/2012/dec/03/nation/la-na-mormon-women-20121203.

Gray, Emma. 2012. "Mormon Women Wear Pants to Church, Get Threatened." *Huffington Post* December 21. Available at www.huffingtonpost.com/2012/12/21/mormon-women-wear-pants-to-church-threatened_n_2346737.html.

Hanks, Maxine. 1992. *Women and Authority: Re-emerging Mormon Feminism*. Salt Lake City, UT: Signature Books.

Holman, Marianne. 2013. "Women Are Essential to the Lord's Work, Elder Ballard Says." *DeseretNews.com* 21 August. Available at www.deseretnews.com/article/865585024/Women-are-essential-to-the-Lords-work-Elder-Ballard-says.html.

Isackson, Darla. 2013. "The Overwhelmed Woman and the Feminist Movement." *Meridian Magazine* July 26. Available at www.ldsmag.com/article/1/13033.

Israel-Cohen, Yael. 2012. *Between Feminism and Orthodox Judaism: Resistance, Identity, and Religious Change in Israel*. Boston, MA: Brill.

Iversen, Joan. 1984. "Feminist Implications of Mormon Polygyny." *Feminist Studies* 10: 504–524. doi:10.2307/3178041.

Lauritzen, Stephanie. 2012. "The Dignity of Your Womanhood." *Mormon Child Bride* December 5. Available at mormonchildbride.blogspot.co.uk/2012/12/the-dignity-of-your-womanhood.html.

Layne. 2012. "Blood in the Water." *Feminist Mormon Housewives* February 9. Available at www.feministmormonhousewives.org/2012/02/blood-in-the-water.

Lee, Frank. 2013. "Female Priests Risk Excommunication to Be Ordained." *USA Today* June 16. Available at www.usatoday.com/story/news/nation/2013/06/16/female-priests-risk-excommunication/2429187.

Lindholm, Philip. 2010. *Latter-day Dissent: At the Crossroads of Intellectual Inquiry and Ecclesiastical Authority.* Salt Lake City, UT: Greg Kofford Books.

New York Times. 1993. "Mormons Penalize Dissident Members." *New York Times* September 19. Available at www.nytimes.com/1993/09/19/us/mormons-penalize-dissident-members.html.

Newell, Linda King, and Valeen Tippetts Avery. 1994. *Mormon Enigma: Emma Hale Smith.* Champaign, IL: University of Illinois Press.

Packer, Boyd. K. 1993. *Talk to the All-Church Coordinating Council,* May 18. Available at www.lds-mormon.com/face.shtml.

Pew Research Center. 2012. *Mormons in America: Certain in Their Beliefs, Uncertain of Their Place in Society.* Available at www.pewforum.org/2012/01/12/mormons-in-america-methodology.

Porteous, Tom. 2013. "'I Need Feminism Because . . .': In Pictures." *The Tab Cambridge* April 23. Available at cambridge.tab.co.uk/2013/04/23/i-need-feminism-because-in-pictures.

Prince, Gregory A. 1995. *Power from on High: The Development of Mormon Priesthood.* Salt Lake City, UT: Signature Books.

Sharp, Gene. 1973. *The Politics of Nonviolent Action.* Boston, MA: P. Sargent, 1973.

Stack, Peggy Fletcher. 1991. "Mormonism and Feminism?" *Wilson Quarterly* 15: 30–32.

Stack, Peggy Fletcher. 2003. "Mormon Feminists?" *Beliefnet* November 12. Available at www.beliefnet.com/Faiths/Christianity/Latter-Day-Saints/2003/11/Mormon-Feminists.aspx.

Stack, Peggy Fletcher. 2012. "Menstruating Mormons Barred from Temple Proxy Baptisms?" *Salt Lake Tribune* March 5. Available at www.sltrib.com/sltrib/blogsfaithblog/53650972-180/temple-women-baptisms-mormon.html.csp.

Stack, Peggy Fletcher. 2013a. "'Wear Pants' Group to LDS Leaders: Let Women Pray at Conference." *Salt Lake Tribune* January 14. Available at www.sltrib.com/sltrib/blogsfaithblog/55627824-180/women-conference-general-church.html.csp.

Stack, Peggy Fletcher. 2013b. "LDS Women's Leader Stirs It Up with 'No Need to Lobby for Rights' Remark." *Salt Lake Tribune* January 22. Available at www.sltrib.com/sltrib/blogsfaithblog/55678907-180/women-dalton-rights-mormon.html.csp.

Stack, Peggy Fletcher. 2013c. "April Mormon Conference May Make History: Women Will Pray." *Salt Lake Tribune* March 22. Available at www.sltrib.com/sltrib/news/56026380-78/women-general-conference-lds.html.csp.

Staggenborg, Suzanne. 1991. *The Pro-Choice Movement: Organization and Activism in the Abortion Conflict.* Oxford, UK: Oxford University Press.

Whitelocks, Sadie. 2012. "Mormon Women Launch 'Wear Pants to Church Day' in Backlash over Strict Dress Code." *Daily Mail Online* December 13. Available at www.dailymail.co.uk/femail/article-2247550/Mormon-women-launch-wear-pants-church-day-backlash-strict-dress-code.html.

Wilson, J. Max. 2013. "Rules for Feminist Mormon Radicals: Moving the Overton Window." *Sixteen Small Stones* March 22. Available at www.sixteensmallstones.org/rules-for-feminist-mormon-radicals-moving-the-overton-window.

Winslow, Ben. 2013. "Feminists Call for LDS Church to Give Women the Priesthood." *FOX13Now.com* March 21. Available at fox13now.com/2013/03/21/feminists-call-for-lds-to-give-women-priesthood.

81. BUDDHIST NUNS IN NEPAL

KATHRYN LAFEVER (2017)

INTRODUCTION

For millennia Buddhist nuns have served as exemplars of cherished Buddhist values, models of diligence to end the suffering of sentient beings, and archetypes of devotion to the Buddha's promise of liberation or enlightenment that is possible for all sentient beings. In the words of the Buddhist feminist scholar Rita M. Gross (1993), "They have lived the eightfold path of Buddhist individual and social morality [which] involves non-harming and working for the benefit of all sentient beings on all levels" (p. 134). These nuns have "continued to take ordination and strive for liberation within a system which taught them that they were less likely to reach this goal than men . . . [in] religious systems created by men and intended to fulfil male needs . . . [demonstrating] . . . their spiritual needs and capacity are as great as men's, maybe even greater" (Allione, 2000, p. 83). Regardless of their marginalized social status, Buddhist nuns have clearly demonstrated they do not possess substandard spiritual capabilities (Adiele, 2004). They have endured, often propelled toward enlightenment by tragedy and adversity (Blackstone, 1998), spending at least one lifetime suffering implicit and explicit inequities as women. Despite their virtues and achievements, millions of Buddhist nuns have persevered, and continue to do so, in relative anonymity within a religious institution where precious few nuns have left any biographical mark. Karma Lekshe Tsomo, a fully-ordained bhikshuni nun and one of the most prominent Western leaders of Tibetan Buddhism (Gross, 1993; Haas, 2013), explains, "Buddhist women have actively worked for more than two millennia to implement Buddhist social ideals, yet rarely have their stories been told" (Tsomo, 2004a, p. 1). It is clear that, compared to monks, there exists few biographical accounts of the lives and work of Buddhist nuns. The omission of nuns' biographies from the corpus of Buddhist literature can be understood as one of myriad forms of gender exclusion and inequity to which nuns have quietly acquiesced for centuries, as a rich tradition of biographical writing developed around Buddhist monks, but not nuns. While Gutschow (2004) laments, ". . . why are humble nuns or elderly female renunciants so rarely honored?" (p. 234), there are any number of reasons for the absence of Buddhist nuns' biographies and life stories. A few factors include the "delicate tension" in Buddhist biography of expressing one's thoughts, feelings, and circumstances in the context of a religion that views the self or ego as an obstacle to enlightenment (Roesler, 2010, p. 4–5), or the endemic sexism fostered by "generations of monk editors" (Adiele, 2004, p. 90). Tsomo (2004a) asserts, "The contributions of Buddhist women . . . have largely gone unnoticed and unacknowledged, if not thwarted altogether . . . [So, it is] imperative to document the lives of Buddhist women, whether ordinary or exemplary, before these stories are lost forever" (Tsomo, 2004a, p. 17–19).

In that spirit, this study explores how contemporary nuns are utilizing and redefining their situated empowerment within their religious communities and beyond. It is predicated on the idea that nuns can be empowered by articulating and sharing their own narrative stories and experiences as well as by learning about Buddhist women who teach by their own example (Blackstone, 1998; Schaeffer, 2004; Schireson, 2009). Through in-depth interviews of Vajrayana Buddhist nuns living in an abbey in Kathmandu, Nepal, this study utilizes a biographical narrative methodological approach. This study examines ways in which these contemporary nuns exercise and contest power within a Buddhist institution, predicated on core religious teachings that profess egalitarianism, but situated within the highly-contextualized space of Kathmandu, where Tibetan culture converges with and diverges from Hindu culture in Nepal, a former Hindu kingdom notoriously oppressive to women and girls. This study explores women's empowerment, namely the empowerment opportunities and challenges they face as twenty-first century nuns in Nepal, and investigates what limits and enables them in achieving their aspirations. Are their roles and identities as Buddhist nuns evolving in empowering ways, and what do they indicate is possible to achieve in terms of fulfilling their monastic responsibilities in individual, local, and global contexts?

. . .

EMPOWERMENT & BIOGRAPHY

Empowerment, a central concept in this study, is also an integral and multifaceted principle of Vajrayana Buddhism. Buddhist empowerments, or *wang*, are initiations and rituals associated with tantric deities. "The word for empowerment is *wang* or *wang-kur*, literally translates to "dismantling," or removing ignorance in order to reveal the primordial power, the Buddha Nature, that all sentient beings possess (Phuntsok, n.d.). Among its interpretations, empowerment is synonymous with receiving wisdom as well as power through spiritual enlightenment and liberation (Yongey, 2003). It can correspond to wisdom based on sacred, not ordinary, perception, and is associated with physical and mental purification as well as liberation from illusions in the material world. It is considered a prerequisite to any ritual, initiation, or desired consequence associated with spiritual practice. While the Vajrayanas associate empowerment with attaining spiritual goals, this study equates empowerment with biography as well as a range of improvements linked to the material, secular, and socio-cultural conditions of the lives of Buddhist nuns.

. . .

HIMALAYAN WOMEN: A BRIEF HISTORICAL CONTEXT

Women in the Himalayan region are generally treated as second-class citizens and their inferior status commences at birth. Even the word *woman* in the Tibetan language literally translates to "born low" (Gross, 1993, p. 81; Tsomo, 1999, p. 177; Adiele, 2004). Historically, women in Himalayan cultures are regarded as without spiritual merit (Gross, 1993, p. 82, 100). They are considered spiritually unfit and physically unclean (particularly during menstruation, when they were banished from their houses or to special chambers; this practice was finally made illegal in

Nepal on August 10, 2017). The inextricable tie between suffering and the female body is found in early Buddhist literature, which includes references to five sufferings that are women's fate—Menstruation, leaving relatives to marry, domesticity, pregnancy, and childbirth (Schaeffer, 2004, p. 91). Schaeffer (2004) clarifies a salient point linking women to suffering in the material world, "the female body is not merely a symbol of samsara, nor receptacle for the seeds of samsara. It *is* samsara" (Schaeffer, 2004, Author's italics, p. 98). Further, women are among the evils—including desire, lust, beer, and sloth—from which good Buddhist male practitioners should abstain. During Buddha's lifetime in the fifth century B.C.E., most women were dependents controlled and protected by their male relatives. Defenseless women were generally ostracized, accused of adultery and prostitution, or of being the embodiment of a demon (Tsomo, 2004a, p. 48). It is evident that notions of innate suffering and evilness as determined by gender persist in Himalayan culture, where, for example, it manifests in many forms as violence against women, including the recent torture and murder of a woman accused of witchcraft in Nepal.

Male and female monastics look and dress essentially the same and were equally capable in the eyes of Buddha of attaining liberation, yet historically the status of nuns is much lower. Nuns vow to strictly adhere to the Eight Precepts, including a lifelong unremitting deference to all monks, which reflects but is not a defense of societal norms (Tsomo, 2004a, p. 22). Historically, full ordination has been widely available for monks but only for Buddhist nuns in a few countries, excluding Nepal and Tibet, where Vajrayana Buddhist nuns have been locked into the system as perpetual noviates (at present it is unclear if or when the full ordination of these nuns will be restored). Whereas Tibetan monks have been relatively well supported by the laity and had time to study and practice, the nuns have been fewer in number and generally less educated and materially sufficient (Gross, 1993, p. 80). Tibetan Buddhist nuns did not have the same access to resources—including the educational opportunities, financial support, and social prestige—enjoyed by monks. Moreover, "When people do show respect toward nuns, it is generally less deferential than the respect expressed to monks . . . these gender patterns of behavior toward nuns both reflect and perpetuate the lower status of nuns—and, by extension, all women—in Buddhist societies" (Tsomo, 2004a, p. 7).

. . .

The pervasive sexism and marginalization of women found among Himalayan cultures reflect the prevailing ideologies, not foundational Buddhist principles, through which Buddhism has evolved (Tsomo, 2004a). Similarly, Gross (1993) insists that gender privilege is incompatible with the Dharma (p. 154) and that core Buddhist teachings do not condone or justify "sexism, patriarchy, or androcentrism, let alone misogyny" (p. 116). Tsomo (2004a) argues that the most of the derogatory statements about women were not Buddha's words but interpretations provided by monks only in some parts of Asia long after the death of Buddha. Gross (1993) agrees, stating, "No major Buddhist teaching provides any basis for gender privilege or gender hierarchy and . . . [its] doctrines, in fact, mandate gender equality at the same time as they undercut the relevance of gender" (p. 153). Gross (1993) adds, "The view that one should not discriminate against women, and that gender is an irrelevant category in the spiritual life becomes stronger and more normative in later forms of Buddhism" (p. 115), a trend that finds resonance in the early twenty-first century among many Vajrayana nuns.

THE INTERVIEWS: INTRODUCTIONS

. . .

The six nuns who elected to participate in this study are referred to by the following pseudonyms: Jamma, Lumo, Ema, Nima, Zopa, and Tenzin. They range in age from 21 to 38 years-old and are proficient in speaking English. These nuns joined the abbey as novices when they were between the ages of eight and nineteen. These women have resided in the abbey, continually or off and on, from nine to twelve years. During their tenure, some had temporarily relocated, for a year or more, to work and study Buddhist and secular subjects at Buddhist facilities in northern and southern India. About 80% of the abbey's nuns, including Jamma, Lumo, Ema, and Zopa, have received the first or novice stage of ordination. Particularly in remote areas of the Himalayan region, illiteracy and school dropout rates are high among women and girls (Bangsbo, 2004). Yet, all of these nuns had achieved between six and twelve years of secular, or basic, education in reading, mathematics, and science as well as Nepali, English, and Tibetan language classes. Beyond basic education, four of the nuns had received between four and nine years of higher education in Buddhist philosophy.

There are two major points about how these nuns self-identify. First, even though some of the participants explained that they are fully ordained, each nun refers to herself and her monastic sisters as *anis*. Further, each nun reflexively writes her name beginning with the title of *Ani* followed by her first and last name. A Vajrayana nun in Kathmandu and Tibet is commonly referred to as an *ani*, pronounced "annie," meaning *aunt*. This common nomenclature, like their monastic robes, identifies these women as nuns and reinforces their solidarity as renunciants. Yet, it obscures their seniority, status, and ordination level to the general public and within the monastic order. In contrast, Tsomo (1999) points out that monks are not called "ahgoo" meaning *uncle* but, rather, a range of more referential designations that translate to *reverend, guru,* or *teacher*. Tsomo (1999) explains that Vajrayana nuns are increasingly addressed more respectfully as *chos.lags*, which translates to, "One who practices Dharma" (p. 178), but Salgado (2013) finds fully ordained or bhikshuni nuns referred to as *Tsunma* or *chola*, as the traditional and more respectful titles for female members of the Sangha (p. 104). Yet, this study finds *ani* a normative and inclusive but not particularly empowering or reverential title among these Vajrayana nuns in Kathmandu in 2014, where the traditional, humble designation of *ani* persists.

Second, while Nima indicates that most of the nuns at the abbey are ethnic Tibetans, all of the anis I interviewed self-identify as Vajrayana, not Tibetan, nuns. Historically the major religion of Tibet is Buddhism—more specifically, Vajrayana, Tantrayana, or Mantrayana—a form of Mahayana Buddhism. It can be confusing to distinguish Tibetan from Vajrayana Buddhism, since Vajrayana is "so integral a part of . . .

[Tibetan Buddhism] that it has become virtually identified with the religion of Tibet" (Lieberman & Lieberman, 2003) and ethnic Tibetans. As Havnevik (1994) states, "For centuries Tibetan Buddhism has been the core of Tibetan culture, and Buddhism has become integrated in the society to such a degree that it is impossible to talk of Tibetan Culture without reference to Tibetan Buddhism" (p. 263). *Tibetan nuns* is a term exclusively for nuns who self-identify or are recognized as Tibetan refugees. Ema kindly explains that it would be a misnomer for the nuns of the abbey to call themselves "Tibetan nuns" because enrollment in the abbey is open to all Vajrayana Buddhist women, not just those from Tibet. Further, even anis born in Tibet, or of Tibetan heritage, do not consider themselves Tibetan nuns. The majority of anis at the abbey are ethnic Tibetans. They reside in a Buddhist institution that prides itself on cultivating its Tibetan heritage, belong to a monastic order that flourished in Tibet between the eighth and twentieth centuries, and revere the Dalai Lama as their spiritual leader. A presumption is that their commitment to monastic life includes a commitment to the survival of the Tibetan cultural and people (Havnevik, 1994, p. 261). Despite these and myriad ethnic and cultural connections to Tibet, the nuns do not consider themselves *Tibetan nuns*. In other words, the participants include three of the nuns born in Tibet, and three born in Kathmandu to ethnic Tibetans living in exile in Nepal, all of whom are ethnic Tibetans yet refer to themselves as Vajrayana, not Tibetan, nuns. While this is a space by and for Tibet's hallmark form of Buddhism, it is not necessarily an empowering or appropriate setting in which to emphasize, for example, one's Tibetan nationalist sentiments or refugee status. Yet, identifying as Vajrayana rather than Tibetan nuns appears to represent a form of empowerment, in terms of the solidarity and inclusivity, among Buddhist renunciates and even members of the lay community, including those who may or may not self-identify as ethnically Tibetan.

FORMATIVE EMPOWERMENT EXPERIENCES

Each nun recalls the varied but ultimately empowering reactions from her parents when she first expressed the desire to become a Buddhist nun. While all of their parents were devout Buddhists, not all initially supported their daughter's desire to join the monastic order. The abbot explains, many parents have hard lives and did not have the opportunity to join the Sangha, so they often want their children to become ordained and attend to their "inner heart," or Buddhist values. A young woman requires the permission of her parents or guardian to enter the monastic order, but Jamma's father, a widower, resisted. He understood her aspiration but it took him years to support it, despite his own unrequited desire to be a monk. As a young adult, at his behest, Jamma stayed at home with him in Kathmandu but later attended a school of Chinese medicine in Beijing. After three years as a medical student, that experience affirmed that she wanted more than ever to become a nun. By the time Jamma was old enough to join without her father's permission, she finally received his blessing to do so. Zopa received consent from both parents, although they expressed concern that she needed more education to adequately prepare for monastic life. She explains that having more education helps to increase one's chances of being admitted to a nunnery and then as a member of the Sangha, keeping up with the rigors of requisite studies. Ema says that her father, so touched by the teachings of the Rinpoche Lama who founded this abbey, first suggested that his daughter join, although she maintains that she had secretly already decided to become a nun. All but Lumo insists it was her idea initially, not her parents', to become a nun. Historically to be a monastic is the most highly revered role in Tibet (Havnevik, 1994, p. 265); this and countless other reasons could have factored into why these young women became nuns. They felt empowered by choosing, usually at an early age and of their own volition, to become nuns and ultimately by their parents' robust support of their decision.

EMPOWERMENT AND EDUCATION

For many nuns, a major draw is to attend the abbey's renowned Shedra, a monastic college for upper-level Tibetan Buddhist studies. The Shedra provides a rarefied space where it is considered essential for female renunciants to study the Dharma as well as secular subjects, broadening access to spiritual and cultural training as well as preserving and improving monastic education (Lion's Roar Staff, 2016; Queen, 1996). Zopa had just graduated from the rigorous eight-year program, which currently enrolls about fifty-five nuns, including Ema and Nima. Three of the nuns, Jamma, Lumo, and Ema, teach at the Shedra. Jamma teaches Chinese and Tibetan, Lumo teaches Tibetan Buddhist logic and philosophy, and Ema teaches English and Tibetan. They are not among the abbey's six Shedra anis who have earned the prestigious Acharaya title and credential, the highest degree awarded at the Central Institute for Higher Buddhist Studies in Sarnath, Varnasi, India.

. . .

EMPOWERMENT THROUGH EXTRA-CURRICULAR PURSUITS

For these nuns, the ascetic lifestyle includes substantial work in the material world as students, teachers, translators, bookkeepers, and health care workers. While the nuns engage in individual and collective religious duties and spiritual pursuits, they shoulder responsibilities, such as caring for the lay community and procuring material resources from it, in order "to maximize both merit and material rewards" (Gutschow, 2004, p. 6). Although the nuns' responsibilities change depending upon the needs of the abbey and the interests and proclivities of each nun, they spend a significant amount of working, including studying and teaching as well as serving multiple and often vastly different roles to maintain the material organization of the abbey. All of the nuns participate in *Nyerpa* or *Ngodrup Tsokpa* duties, which involve the nuns' welfare. The nuns grow and harvest vegetables as well as cook and serve their own meals. Their self-sufficiencies include cleaning, laundry, sewing, bookkeeping, and gardening. Additionally, the nuns grow and harvest ingredients to make incense, which the abbey packages and sells in part to provide a source of revenue and be more self-supporting (Tsomo, 2004b, p. 357). The nuns aspire to be autonomous and self-supporting "so we don't have to rely on the monks," as Jamma states. Further,

the nuns now perform rituals and ceremonies, such as sand painting, for the monastic and lay communities, which in previous generations had been executed exclusively by monks.

Every interviewed nun, except Nima the youngest, had found it empowering to work in multiple capacities and hold several different jobs during her tenure at the nunnery. For example, Tenzin, who teaches early childhood education in the school, started work in the clinic, caring for elderly and infirm nuns. Jamma explains that normally the nuns have the freedom to change jobs once every two years. Yet, some nuns had held jobs for only one year, such as Zopa, who spent a year caring for the sick and serving as discipline master and chant master for one year each. Similarly, Tenzin had studied accounting and assisted with bookkeeping for only one and a half years. Some of the nuns liked changing jobs and responsibilities while others had found their niche early, notably in translation, education, and health care. But all voiced appreciation for the flexibility of trying different jobs and working in several capacities to become more well-rounded and thus empowered.

. . .

EMPOWERMENT AND WOMEN ATTAINING ENLIGHTENMENT

When asked what ideas or teachings had they been thinking about lately, three nuns, including the eldest and youngest, identified sexism in the world and the notion that only males can achieve enlightenment. These interlocutors understand, "the ultimately illusory nature of gender" (Gutschow, 2004, p. 234). They are well-versed in the fundamental Buddhist soteriological teachings that all living things possess an inherent Buddha nature and are therefore capable of achieving enlightenment or Buddhahood. They are aware that Buddha believed monks and nuns are equally capable of being monastics and achieving enlightenment (Gross, 1993; Adiele, 2004; Gutschow, 2004; Tsomo, 2004a, 2004b). Gender is irrelevant to the Dharma, the core teachings of Buddhism, which are neither female nor male (Gross, 1993). It disturbs them that while Buddhism teaches that all sentient beings, male and female, are equally capable of transcendence, the perception—perhaps more pronounced among rural populations—certainly has been that among the calculus of rebirths, a male human body, particularly that of a monk, ranks highest. Zopa recalls that many of the older women in the village where she grew up (as well as the majority of women in her parent's generation) aspire to reincarnate as men in the next life, which helps to explain something of "the Tibetan proverb that women are at least seven lifetimes behind men" (Gutschow, 2004, p. 212). Her memory substantiates the following observation by Gutschow (2004),

> When I asked several nuns if women gain enlightenment as easily as men, they gave me a variety of answers. Some said that women could, but only after making merit or overcoming bodily defilements. Others said that women can't gain liberation until they take rebirth as a male. (p. 234)

Further, Ema describes a point also found in Gross (1993): "Those who wish to serve the aims of being in a woman's body are few indeed" (p. 90). In other words, many Tibetan Buddhists concede that enlightenment is possible in a female body, yet few wish to endure such an arduous task, based on the perception that women must work harder than men to achieve enlightenment (Paul, 1979). Similarly, Gutschow (2004) recalls a senior Buddhist nun in Zangskar, India, admonishing, "Nobody in this region, male or female, had ever expressed a wish to be reborn as a female" (p. 3).

. . .

DEVELOPING EMPOWERING INTERPERSONAL QUALITIES

A goal of Buddhist education for women and girls is to overcome certain deeply-rooted cultural prejudices reinforced by Hindu and Buddhist society. Overcoming shyness and building self-confidence in this community of *anis* is a priority, the abbot explains. While it is not uncommon for novices to arrive painfully introverted with little or no self-confidence, young monks are often the opposite; too self-confident, self-centered, and domineering (Schireson, 2009). These young women, "have been

so invaded by the idea that they're not as worthy as male human beings" (Lion's Roar Staff, 2016), that it is a challenge for them to overcome the limitations of a range of "lady-like behaviors" (Schireson, 2009), including socially-conditioned docility, passiveness, obedience, and subservience. . . . .

Jamma explains that many Asian women are culturally conditioned to avert their eyes as a sign of respect and in general to be calm, quiet, and polite. Yet, through education and training, the nuns learn how to make eye contact and develop assertiveness and self-confidence. To build their self-confidence, nuns are often asked to do public speaking and to serve as representatives of the abbey. Jamma knows firsthand about the challenges of stepping out of her comfort zone to do public speaking and interact with monastics, laypersons, and non-monastics in communities in and around Kathmandu. She explains that these encounters help her not only to see how Buddhism applies to the world but also require her to be more social and outgoing than she is at the abbey, where nuns are expected to maintain a calm, quiet, and polite disposition. Both Jamma and Lumo explain that being required to represent the abbey in public has helped them to come out of their respective shells and develop a healthy self-confidence, as it has made it possible to apply their teachings in the physical world. Jamma admits that she was painfully shy, but eventually she discovered that she enjoys the daunting challenges posed by these public encounters. Because of her self-confidence and positive attitude, as well as her work in the community, her friends good-naturedly tease and call her a "Nun of the Twenty-First Century."

TWENTY-FIRST CENTURY NUNS

As Buddhism has evolved, so have the identities of Buddhist nuns. Compared to previous generations, this study finds twenty-first century nuns in a state of continuity—maintaining spiritual practices as they have for millennia—and flux—in that there are new and increasing empowerment opportunities for nuns to represent, explore, and apply their embodied spirituality in transformative ways. Throughout the Himalayan region, a significant number of nuns continue their time-honored spiritual practices and the traditional agriculturally-based physical labor required to sustain their nunneries, as they have for centuries. Yet, contemporary nuns increasingly combine traditional and innovative approaches in their daily lives and have educational opportunities and engage, "in translating, publishing, and a wide variety of other social welfare activities" (Tsomo, 2003, p. 607). Among the major factors credited with the development of the attitudes and convictions of twenty-first century nuns are the tandem influences of Western religion and feminism, "two independent streams of influence" (Gross, 1998, p. 219). Gross (1993) explains, "Buddhism is no longer developing in intellectual and spiritual isolation, but is undergoing mutual transformation through its encounter with the prophetic voices of Western religions and feminism" (p. 216).

Compared to previous generations, these nuns of the third millennium are increasingly self-sufficient. Jamma explains that nuns are less dependent on monks in two major ways. First, the nuns are increasingly self-reliant in all of the functions required to maintain their abbey. Second, with greater access to educational opportunities and Buddhist texts, contemporary nuns are less dependent upon monks to teach them, and can read and analyze Buddhist teachings for themselves. Gross (1993) finds nuns engaging in work that had been provided solely by the lay persons or non-monastics. Further, these nuns are officiating ceremonies and performing rituals that had previously been the exclusive domain of monks, including sand mandala painting and Tara dances. There are new creative and expressive potentialities for female members of the monastic community, as nuns are more actively engaged in perpetuating traditional arts but also in creative and even political self-expression (Norton, 2000; Havnevik, 1994). While many twenty-first century nuns still face serious and immediate concerns about having access to the bare necessities—such as adequate food, clean water, safe housing, as well as basic health care and religious instruction—indications are that compared to contemporary monks, and previous generations of nuns, are generally receiving more equitable support from the lay community as well as assistance from the international community.

. . .

CONCLUSIONS

This study explored the situated empowerment of a group of contemporary nuns within their religious community and beyond. Through in-depth interviews, this research examined ways that these contemporary nuns have exercised and contested power within a Buddhist institution, predicated on core religious teachings that profess egalitarianism yet situated within the highly-contextualized space of Kathmandu, Nepal.

Focusing on women's empowerment, namely the empowerment opportunities and challenges these women face as twenty-first century nuns, this study investigated some of what limits and enables them in achieving their aspirations. Predicated on the idea that nuns can be empowered by articulating and sharing their own narrative stories and experiences as well as by learning about Buddhist women who teach by their own example (Schireson, 2009), this study explored how their roles and identities as Buddhist nuns have evolved in increasingly empowering ways, and what they indicated was possible to achieve to fulfill their monastic responsibilities in individual, local, and global contexts.

. . .

More than earlier nuns, these women endeavor to gain agency and apply their spirituality through the work they do. They are improving societies and relieving the suffering of sentient beings in regional and global contexts. Among the values of biographical research is that it illustrates something of what these women have accomplished within Buddhist monasticism and the geographical and cultural spheres beyond. Evidence of how these Vajrayana nuns are empowered has the capacity to inspire contemporary and future nuns and others to achieve more ethical and empowering lives. Compared to men and women of privilege and even most monks, these Vajrayana nuns of Kathmandu are less empowered, but not unempowered, in their everyday social, material, and spiritual struggles.

With their shorn heads, androgynous robes, and lofty ambitions to renounce sexuality and maternity, these women have not completely avoided the burden of female gender roles, even within Buddhist institutions (Gutschows, 2004). There is a need for consciousness-raising about maintaining the status-quo and how men and women participate in re-creating the structures of oppression. There are indications that the social status of Vajrayana Buddhist nuns has been improving as they validate, legitimate, and exercise their own potentialities working inside and outside of the monastic community. These nuns have distinct voices that need to be heard, and they appear to be in the process of discovering them in tandem with defining their own identities and projects as twenty-first century nuns, devoted to easing the suffering of sentient beings in the material world. In the early decades of the third millennium, Buddhism offers scope and models for religious practitioners and provides solutions to many complex social issues. Yet, there is a need to go much further than Buddha did to end the gender-based subordination of women and help Buddhist nuns find their voices.

. . .

Examining the varied experiences and perspectives of nuns helps to enrich the Buddhist tradition, and the value of their biographies and teachings reverberate far beyond the female monastic community. It is hoped that this biographical study contributes to positively reshaping the evolving conceptualizations of these women, rare in their extreme commitment to their Buddhist religious avocation in the twenty-first century. The future is not only what is going to be but what also may be. As Vajrayana nuns continue to develop layers of identity, it is hoped that biographical writing on Buddhist nuns will flourish in ways that inspire and empower present and future generations to imagine and create a more equitable and just world for all.

REFERENCES

Adiele, F. (2004). *Meeting faith: The forest journals of a black Buddhist nun.* New York, NY: W. W. Norton & Company.

Allione, T. (2000). *Women of wisdom.* Ithaca, NY: Snow Lion Publications.

Bangsbo, E. (2004). *Teaching and learning in Tibet: A review of research and policy recommendations.* Copenhagen, Denmark: NIAS Press.

Blackstone, K. R. (1998). *Women in the footsteps of the Buddha: Struggle for liberation in the Therigatha.* Surrey, England: Curzon Press.

Gross, R. M. (1993). *Buddhism after patriarchy: A feminist history, analysis, and re-construction of Buddhism.* Albany, NY: State University of New York Press.

Gross, R. M. (1998). *Soaring and settling: Buddhist perspectives on contemporary social and religious issues.* New York, NY: The Continuum Publishing Company.

Gutschow, K. (2004). *Being a Buddhist nun: The struggle for enlightenment in the Himalayas.* Cambridge, MA: Harvard University Press.

Haas, M. (2013). *Dakini power: Twelve extraordinary women shaping the transmission of Tibetan Buddhism in the west.* Boston, MA: Snow Lion.

Havnevik, H. (1994). The role of nuns in contemporary Tibet. In R. Barnett (Ed.). *Resistance and reform in Tibet.* Bloomington, IN: Indiana University Press.

Lieberman, P., & Lieberman, M. R. (2003). Basic concepts of Tibetan Buddhism. *Brief introduction to basic concepts of "Tibetan" Buddhism* (p. 2). Retrieved from: https://library.brown.edu/cds/BuddhistTempleArt/buddhism2.html.

Lion's Roar Staff (2016, January 21). Waking up to patriarchy. *Lion's roar.* Retrieved from: http://www.lionsroar.com/waking-up-to-patriarchy/.

Norton, A. W. (2000). Women, art, and the Buddhist spirit. In E. B. Findly (Ed.). *Women's Buddhism, Buddhism's women: Tradition, revision, renewal* (pp. 357–372). Boston, MA: Wisdom Publications.

Paul, D. Y. (1979). *Women in Buddhism: images of the feminine in Mahayana tradition.* Berkeley, CA: Asian Humanities Press.

Phuntsok, N. (n.d.). On receiving wang (empowerment). "Empowerment." Retrieved from: http://www.khandro.net/TibBud_empowerment.htm.

Queen, C. S. (1996). Introduction: The shapes and sources of engaged Buddhism. In C. S. Queen, & S. B. King (Eds.), *Engaged Buddhism: Buddhist liberation movements in Asia* (pp. 1–44). Albany, NY: State University of New York Press.

Roesler, U. (2010). Introduction. In L. Covill, U. Roesler, & S. Shaw (Eds.). *Lives lived, lives imagined:*

Biography in the Buddhist traditions (pp. 1–14). Somerville, MA: Wisdom Publications.

Salgado, N. S. (2013). Buddhist nuns and gendered practice: In search of the female renunciant. *Oxford scholarship online* http://dx.doi.org/10.1093/acprof:oso/9780199760022.001.0001 http://www.oxfordscholarship.com.proxy.lib.miamioh.edu/view/10.1093/acprof:oso/9780199760022.001.0001/acprof-9780199760022-chapter-5.

Schaeffer, K. R. (2004). *Himalayan Hermitess: The life of a Tibetan Buddhist nun*. New York, NY: Oxford University Press.

Schireson, G. (2009). *Zen women: Beyond tea ladies, iron maidens, and macho masters*. Boston, MA: Wisdom Publications.

Tsomo, K. L. (1999). Mahaprajapati's Legacy: The Buddhist women's movement: An introduction. In K. L. Tsomo (Ed.). *Buddhist women across cultures [electronic resource]: Realizations* (pp. 1–48). Albany, NY: State University of New York Press.

Tsomo, K. L. (2003). Nuns. In R. E. Buswell Jr. (Vol. Ed.), *Encyclopedia of Buddhism. Vol. 2. Encyclopedia of Buddhism* (pp. 606–611). New York, NY: MacMillan Reference USA (M-Z).

Tsomo, K. L. (2004a). Family, monastery, and gender justice: Reenvisioning Buddhist institutions. In K. L. Tsomo (Ed.). *Buddhist women and social justice; ideals, challenges, and achievements* (pp. 1–22). Albany, NY: State University of New York Press.

Tsomo, K. L. (2004b). Tibetan nuns: New roles and possibilities. In H. von Welck (Ed.). *Exile as challenge: The Tibetan diaspora* (pp. 342–366). New Delhi, India: Orient Longman Private Limited.

Yongey, M. D. R. (2003). Vajrayana and the significance of the empowerment. Retrieved from: abuddhistlibrary.com. http://www.abuddhistlibrary.com/Buddhism/A%20-%20Tibetan%20Buddhism/Authors/Mingyur%20Rinpoche/Vajrayana%20and%20Empowerment/Vajrayana%20and%20Empowerment.htm.

82. THE PROPHET'S DAUGHTERS

AN INTERVIEW WITH SYAFA ALMIRZANAH (2009)

Syafa Almirzanah, a professor of comparative religion at Islamic University Sunan Kalijaga in Yogyakarta, Indonesia, could have continued her studies anywhere in the Muslim world, but she chose Catholic Theological Union in Chicago. . . .

"Dialogue is, for me, a must," she says. "In my tradition it is the obligation of Muslims to learn from others, to get knowledge from everywhere."

Almirzanah has been active in interreligious dialogue in both her home country of Indonesia and in the United States. She feels comfortable with Catholicism, she says, because of the many similarities between it and Islam.

One unfortunate similarity is the way scholars from both traditions have misused faith to repress women.

Almirzanah hopes that by learning about the history and theology of Islam—and by participating in interreligious dialogue—Muslims will embrace more female-friendly interpretations of the religion.

"I think one of the most important things in dialogue is having the courage to criticize our own tradition. We must learn from others, then come back and look at our tradition with a new horizon," Almirzanah says. "Learning from others enriches our traditions. We can be better Muslims and better Christians."

What does the Qur'an have to say about women?
The Qur'an is very positive about women. In the story of Creation, women and men are created from the same cells, so usually scholars say that means that men and women are the same before God.

The problem is that different Muslims understand the Qur'an in different ways. Islam is not the monolithic religion people think it is, just as Christianity is not monolithic.

If you read the Bible, you cannot ignore the context. When God revealed himself, it was not in a vacuum. People who receive the revelation of God have different backgrounds, experiences, and contexts, so they respond to it differently.

The same is true in Islamic tradition. Some more traditional Muslims only focus on what's written in the text and don't pay attention to the context of the verses; other more modern Muslims look at why God revealed a particular verse and how the community at that time understood it.

The verse on polygamy, for example, says that you can marry one or two or three or four women. More fundamentalist or traditional Muslims use this verse to justify having more than one wife, but actually the verse does not stop there. It continues: "If you cannot do justice, just marry one." They ignore that crucial part of the verse. This verse was revealed after a war, and there were a lot of widows and orphans, so men were allowed to marry multiple women in order to take care of them.

You also must look at verses in relation to other verses. The Qur'an says elsewhere that even if you wanted to, you could not do justice to more than one wife. So actually Islam and the Qur'an ban polygamy. It says if you cannot do justice, just marry one woman, but it also says you can never really do justice to more than one wife.

How were women treated during the seventh century in the Arabian Peninsula at the time of Muhammad?
This is also debatable. Scholars usually compare what it was like for women before Islam and after Islam.

Most scholars say that pre-Islamic times were worse for women. They say that before Islam men could marry more than four women. A Muslim scholar will argue that Muhammad limited polygamy and advocated the ideal marriage of one man and one woman. This is progress because some say that husbands could even sell women before Islam.

But there are also many scholars who write that before Islam women's conditions were not really bad because they were free and had rights. One author says that before Islam a lot of women were involved in war and managed businesses. There is evidence of cultures where husbands came into their wives' homes when they married, and the children would belong to the women's tribe. Our Prophet's first wife was a businesswoman, and she came from a very noble tribe, though she may be the exception.

I personally think it was almost like it is today. In certain communities where people are poor and have no access to education, of course women may not have the same opportunities as women who have rich families and live in an urban society. I can say that there were some good attitudes toward women before Islam, but Islam increased those good attitudes.

How did Muhammad treat his wives?
The first wife of the Prophet was a businesswoman. His youngest wife, Aisha, was a scholar and one of the interpreters of what the Prophet was saying. Because she was very close to the Prophet, a lot of people asked Aisha about what they should do in matters of love or matters of *Sharia*, or Muslim law. She also was involved in battle.

The Prophet didn't teach that women should just stay at home. These rules were introduced by the Prophet's companions after his death. The Qur'an gives women the right to pursue an education and be involved in worldly matters.

I think we need to get traditional Muslims to look at history, even at our Prophet's wives, and see that they were very active. Why should we now have to stay at home?

There is a verse that says men are above women, but *above* here does not mean women are naturally inferior. It means men are responsible for family welfare because they work outside the home and earn money-as they were in Muhammad's time.

Today, a woman can go outside of the home, work, and earn money, so she has the same status as a man. She also has responsibilities for her family, so for a more modern scholar, men are not above women.

How do more traditional Muslim scholars explain away the prominence of Muhammad's wives?
They say that his wives were exceptions. Most of the interpreters of the Qur'an have been men, so there is a lot of submission of women in Muslim teachings. When I was doing my graduate studies, my adviser told me that some of the interpreters were men who really hated women.

A lot of the misogynistic hadiths—the sayings of the Prophet—do not come from trusted sources, though.

Hadiths tell scholars about the life of the Prophet and the context of the revelations but aren't actually revelations themselves. They are passed on through generations of people from Muhammad's contemporaries, so scholars have to make sure there is a common link back to the time of the Prophet. In order to evaluate whether the Prophet said something, we have to study the transmission of the tradition and who it came from.

We have very strict requirements to accept that a saying really came from the Prophet. Most of the misogynistic hadiths come only from one source. These cannot be used as a resource for an edict. But some people choose the one that matches their thinking rather than the one that has the best source.

Who are other notable female figures in Islam beyond Muhammad's wives?

There are a lot. The ninth-century scholar Ibn Sa'd wrote biographies of important Islamic figures, and he had a whole book of women in Islamic history.

There are also women saints. Rabia al-Adawiyya is a very famous Sufi, or Muslim mystic. She was a pioneer for the idea of love for God in Islamic mysticism. She has a well-known prayer: "God, if I pray to you only so you do not put me in hell, just put me in hell, and if I pray to you only so I can go to paradise, don't put me in paradise, but if I pray to you only because I love you, don't hide your face from me."

Rabia is said to be in the rank of men because she was close to or one with God. A lot of Muslim women look at her as an example—the ideal mystic woman. She didn't marry, but there are a lot of women mystics who did marry. Some are the wives or daughters of male mystics. Sufi men had women teachers. A teacher of the famous Sufi Iban Arabi said, "I am his spiritual mother."

As in Christian spirituality, there are a lot of Muslim women mystics who are highly regarded. Mystics go beyond the text into the essence of the story. When you do that, every religion can meet. and men and women can meet. It is very conducive to dialogue.

Christian women sometimes struggle with male images of God. Is God thought of as male in Islam?

God is often described as having both a feminine and masculine aspect. One scholar compared it to yin and yang. In the Islamic tradition we call it *Jalal* and *Jamal*. *Jalal* is the might of God, and *Jamal* is the beauty of God. God has both of these aspects, feminine and masculine.

Yin and yang always are together, so women and men should be together. Man is not better than woman, and woman is not better than man. In Islam women and men should cooperate. Even in the Muslim Creation story, Eve is not the cause of the fall.

Still, the pronoun for God is a male pronoun, and that is a problem that feminists discuss. There are also certain verses in the Qur'an that only use a male pronoun, so Muslim feminists say that the male pronoun refers to both genders. For example, verses such as "you have to pray every day" use the male pronoun, but this doesn't mean that praying is only for males.

What does it mean to be a Muslim feminist?

Quite simply, I define it as someone who supports women's rights. There are a lot of male feminists who support the equal status of women, especially in Indonesia and Egypt. Some governments also promote equal rights.

Generally, what is the status of women in the Muslim world today?

As I said, Islam isn't a monolithic religion. The place of women depends a lot on the social, political, and cultural conditions of the community. Islam in Indonesia is very different from Islam in Saudi Arabia, for example.

In Indonesia it's common for women to study and be in politics, but still there is resistance. We had a female president before our current president. When she was to be appointed president, fundamentalist groups opposed it because they said that Islam prohibited women from leading them. She became our president anyway. There are no verses that prohibit a woman from being president.

Still, many believe that women's responsibilities are domestic tasks such as cooking and taking care of children. Even my in-laws still believe that. They wouldn't let my husband cook.

When a woman's husband comes home from his job, she is supposed to serve him. But both my husband and I work outside the home, so why should I serve him? I always say, "I am not his servant. I am his wife." If I serve him on an occasion, it's not because it's my responsibility; it's because I love him.

We also have to understand there are women themselves who really believe in the fundamentalist interpretation. They believe that they should be at home and that they might have to accept being a second wife because this is what Islam teaches.

How much of that is due to religion and how much is due to culture?
I think it has to do with both. Culture is there, but certain interpretations of religion are there, too. There is a certain interpretation of Islam that says women should stay at home, not go anywhere, and take care of the family.

This is why women have to study what Islam actually teaches about women and our position. Our Prophet cooked and even sewed his clothes himself. There is nothing to be ashamed of in that.

We have to improve Muslims' understanding of the Qur'an. A lot of laypeople are Muslim because their family is Muslim, and they have never really studied their own tradition. They depend on their religious leader: Whatever he says, they will follow it. We cannot just do that; we have to know the sources of Islam ourselves.

There are a number of schools of thought for Islamic law. I was taught that you don't have to follow one of them, but the most important thing is to know why they say what they do.

How can women's positions in the Muslim world improve?
There are a lot of ways to improve our status, but I think the key, again, is education. Unfortunately, there are still a lot of people who do not have access to it. A lot of families in my country still pay only for boys and not girls to study if they have limited resources.

I have a brother, and my father let me go to school even to the highest levels, but that's often not the case at the university level. As a professor in Indonesia, I do see a lot of female students studying theology, though.

. . .

What issues do Christian and Muslim women share?
I think Muslim and Christian women have the same struggle to gain equal positions to men within our traditions. Most of the interpreters in the Catholic tradition are male, just as in Islam. That's one of the reasons they underestimate women, and there are misinterpretations of both religions.

For example, Jesus had female followers, but the Catholic tradition doesn't really consider them to be apostles. From my perspective, the women of those days were Jesus' apostles. In Islam we also have women companions to the Prophet Muhammad. But for some reason, in both cases, these women have been forgotten.

Muslim and Christian women can work together. We need to interpret verses for ourselves and criticize the old male interpretations. We should study together and go deeper into the traditions to find out what our traditions are actually saying about the position of women.

83. FEMINISTS IN THE TEMPLE OF ORTHODOXY
YITZHAK REITER (2016)

INTRODUCTION

On April 24, 2013, something extraordinary happened at the Western Wall, the Jews' most central holy place. A group of religious, activist, and feminist women—the Women of the Wall (WoW)—succeeded in breaking the ritual status quo at the site. The

Jerusalem District Court Judge Moshe Sobel produced a ruling (interpreting a previous Supreme Court decision) that recognized the right of the WoW to conduct ritual worship at the Wall according to their custom, in a way that the majority of the worshippers at the place view as a disgraceful abomination.[1] The WoW's worship includes prayer and singing by women at Rosh Hodesh (the first day of each Jewish month), reading from the Torah while wrapped in colorful *tallitot* (prayer shawls) and wearing *tefillin* (phylacteries).

This ruling issued a dramatic change: it effectively opened the space for ritualistic pluralism at the Western Wall, a holy place that is open to everyone. It dealt a blow to the status of the hegemonic religious establishment that belongs to the Orthodox and Haredi/Ultra-Orthodox streams in Israel.[2] Indeed, for the religious Orthodox Jews currently dominating the Western Wall and Israel's religious institutions, the actions of the WoW are almost like bringing an "idol into the Temple"—a desecration of the holy place.

In April 2013, the same month in which Judge Sobel's ruling was published, the Chair of the Jewish Agency, Natan Sharansky, presented a new arrangement in an attempt to solve the controversy. It suggests erecting a third, egalitarian prayer plaza at the Wall, in what is known as the Robinson's Arch site (an area of the antiquities park south of the Mughrabi Ascent), identical in size and status to the current plaza dominated by the Orthodox Jews.

The Sharansky Plan promoted by the government may turn the achievements of the WoW upside down. Instead of bringing an end to the dispute, the court ruling has perhaps brought the beginning of a new conflict. Rather than granting women full egalitarian worship rights at the existing historic Western Wall (which was the WoW's main goal), this solution would create two different Western Walls: the historic Orthodox Western Wall plaza, and the new prayer platform at Robinson's Arch, which would have to fight for its recognition among the general public.

This case contributes to the existing research on holy places shared by more than one religious group, which mostly claims that holy places are indivisible and, by virtue of their status as "protected values," cannot be redivided without evoking a violent dispute. Ron Hassner and other scholars, for instance, have argued that at the religious level, the supreme spiritual force overpowers all else, and thus the congregation's commitment to protecting the sacredness of the place prevents the existence of any compromise or alternative on the custom of the place.[3] Hassner claims that the existence of division arrangements at

Samuel's Tomb and the Cave of the Patriarchs (Me'arat HaMachpela) is irrelevant because these are forced arrangements. I have studied the shared arrangements at the Cave of the Patriarchs/Al Haram Al-Ibrahimi and the Tomb of Samuel the Prophet/Nebi Samuel and conclude that the action of division arrangements creates, over time, a new reality, with which the parties come to terms. When a powerful governmental agent dictates and enforces amendments to the status quo, and when these are carried out over time, the nature of the change becomes a fact.[4]

. . .

The case of the WoW—a minority group that has challenged women's inferiority in Judaism—adds another dimension to the research on shared and divided holy spaces. The controversy over prayer exists not between two religions, but rather between different streams within Judaism, and by doing so also adds a case study to religious feminism. An analysis of this case allows us to explore a series of questions related to shared holy spaces and the breaking of the status quo: first, what has enabled legal and public recognition of a local custom of a minority group that challenges the hegemonic status quo at the Western Wall? Second, how has a small group of women succeeded over larger, more powerful forces in breaking the status quo in favor of a gender-oriented, pluralistic religious agenda, while other political movements and activists have failed? And third, what are the implications of these achievements for arrangements at the Western Wall and other contentious holy places?

. . .

Based on interviews with the major political actors of the dispute and content analysis of documents and publications, this article seeks to answer these questions and analyze the legal and public implications of the WoW's achievements. . . .

THE CONTROVERSY OVER THE STATUS OF THE WESTERN WALL AND LOCAL CUSTOM

The conflict over the right to pray at the Wall receives much attention because of the paradox that the Wall presents: on the one hand, the Wall is perceived by the public as a place that is sacred to the entire Jewish nation, but on the other, it is a place in which the custom patterns have been decided by the Orthodox stream alone. From the outset, the struggle of the WoW has evoked a public and legal question as to the meaning of local custom at the Western Wall. In particular, questions arose over whether or not local custom excludes the customs of other Jewish groups, what was the historical character of the Wall with regard to women's prayer, and whether the Wall has the status of a synagogue.

In 1967, when Israel gained control of the Western Wall, it determined a new status quo there, dictated by the Orthodox religious establishment in Israel, which over time became permanent as local custom. The religious establishment managing the Western Wall believes that local custom should reflect the historical continuity of the Jews praying at the Wall which, according to Orthodox opinion, included separation between men and women and did not include women's prayer except for personal pleas to God. However, this position is not supported by the historical sources.[5] In reality, mixed prayer and egalitarian prayer did historically exist at the Western Wall, when the practice there took the form of an individual prayer. It was only in the first years of Israel's rule at the Wall, when practices were determined by the Ministry of Religious Affairs (under Orthodox control), that separation between men and women at the lower prayer plaza was enforced, in line with the custom in Orthodox synagogues.

The Official in Charge of the Western Wall, Rabbi Shmuel Rabinowitz, claims that custom becomes permanent by the majority of those who worship at the Western Wall, who belong to the Orthodox stream.[6] In contrast, the position of the WoW and non-Orthodox movements is that the Western Wall is pan-Jewish, both a religious and national site, and it therefore belongs to all the Jews in the world. They believe the local custom should be pluralistic, reflecting the position of the majority of religious Jews in the world, who belong to the Reform, Conservative, and Modern Orthodox streams, as well as the position of the majority of Israel's residents, who are secular.

The WoW's main effort is to challenge the existing local custom at the Wall. Since 1988, they have been holding their prayer services with and without

interruptions according to their own custom—which includes praying every Rosh Hodesh, wrapped in colorful tallitot, some also wearing tefillin and reading aloud from the Torah. This raises the question: have the WoW, over time, created a new status quo and local custom at the Wall? The Supreme Court ruled that indeed, the WoW had earned their right to pray "according to their way."[7] However, as we will see, the WoW were not granted permission to read the Torah at the Wall, due to a possible offense to the (Orthodox and Ultra-Orthodox) worshippers' feelings. Instead, the WoW were requested to conduct this part of their service in the Archeological Park area.

THE REVOLUTIONARY CHALLENGE OF THE WOW

The WoW group was established following a definitive event. In November 1988, an international congress of Jewish feminist women was held at the Hyatt Hotel in Jerusalem. Towards the end of the conference, one participant, Rivka Haut, an Orthodox feminist from Brooklyn, suggested conducting a "gratitude prayer for the wellbeing of the State [of Israel]" at the Western Wall, with women reading from the Torah for the first time at this site, while still maintaining the Orthodox prayer approach.[8] Following this, the women from Jerusalem among them decided to make this a regular custom every Rosh Hodesh. Eight days later, on Rosh Hodesh Tevet, 5749 (December 9, 1988), the women brought a Torah scroll with them. When they began reading out loud from the Torah, wrapped in tallitot, a violent rampage broke out from the men's section, which included spitting, cursing, and snatching the Torah scroll from the women's hands.[9]

This event led to the formation of the Women of the Wall and the American parent organization named The International Committee for Women of the Wall. According to the WoW, it was the outburst of the Orthodox Jews towards them that revealed their power to challenge the Orthodox hegemony that discriminates against women, and the necessity of turning this act into a regular tradition.[10]

The Women of the Wall, then, arose out of the American feminist movement and served as a continuation of a women's network in North America that was tired of the marginal role of women in prayer. It unites Jewish women of all observances—Orthodox, Modern Orthodox, Conservative, and Reform—and currently has 160 listed female and male members. The International Committee for Women of the Wall provides substantial financial support for WoW, and a significant portion of this support comes from the Modern Orthodox community. Many American Modern Orthodox women who visit Israel have participated regularly in WoW from the beginning and have played a disproportionate role in WoW.[11] With their pluralistic composition, the WoW advocate for both genders to participate equally in Jewish practices, including prayer and reading from the Torah, while sitting together.[12] As Shakdiel writes, the WoW's great innovation was the inclusion of reading from the Torah and going up to the Torah, in particular on Jewish holidays like Purim, Rashey Hodesh (the first day of each Jewish month as a special religious festival for women) and Bat Mitzvah celebrations.[13]

In particular, the WoW seek to fight against the exclusion of women in the Orthodox space and bring about a change to Orthodox women's status by changing the perception of the religious woman and educating women about the political, religious, and social rights of women in Judaism.[14] The WoW demand prayer rights as an equal religious group at the Western Wall. As Dr. Bonna Haberman explained, "What occurs in a holy place has more ability to change . . . because it touches the Zionist world as well."[15] The WoW recognize the Wall as, according to WoW Chair Anat Hoffman, "an Archimedean point through which many sicknesses in the Israeli society can be rectified."[16] As Professor Frances Raday, who represented the WoW in their second appeal to the HCJ (1995), stated, any favorable change regarding women's status within the religious sector would in turn affect women's status in Israeli society at large, especially in the areas where Orthodoxy is dominant: marriage, divorce, and conversion to Judaism.[17]

Meanwhile, the heads of the conservative Orthodox stream in Israel, represented on this matter by the Official in Charge of the Western Wall, are unwilling to recognize women's prayer at the Wall. They view such worship as subversive because

it includes women's singing heard in the men's section, which Orthodox men (and some women) consider as erotic and forbidden (in Hebrew: "kol be isha erva"). They also deny women's right to lay tefillin, wrap themselves in tallitot, and read from the Torah, believing that these commandments are intended for men only. The WoW's alternative interpretation of the Halachic sources is thus subversive—and their egalitarian practice at the Wall is revolutionary—because it undermines the Orthodox hegemony that claims interpretational exclusivity. The Orthodox streams, meanwhile, consider the WoW as provocative agents that seek to deliberately harm the state-determined status quo and Orthodox hegemony.[18] Although the WoW have not been authorized to represent the Reform and Conservative movements, their struggle represents the effort of these streams—and particularly the interest in recognition and representation in the religious system in Israel. These non-Orthodox movements have long worked for recognition of their rabbis' conversion to Judaism and marriage ceremonies, and also to receive a section of the Western Wall for their worship. However, the Reform and Conservative movements do not view the WoW as representative of their cause, and until recently the movements even viewed the group as a nuisance and a disrupting agent.
. . .

ERECTING A NEW WESTERN WALL: THE SHARANSKY-MANDELBLIT PLAN

In the same month as Judge Sobel's ruling in April 2013, the Chair of the Jewish Agency, Natan Sharansky, publicized a plan for resolving the dispute that had broken out between the government and the North American Jewry, the non-Orthodox movements, and WoW. In the compromise that Sharansky suggested, known as the Sharansky Plan, the Western Wall Plaza would be enlarged southwards, almost reaching the southwestern corner of the Temple Mount, so that it would be equal in size to the Orthodox Wall plaza, and an elevated prayer podium would be erected, with the same height as the historic Wall plaza. The new prayer area, temporarily named

Ezrat Israel [Israel section], would be designed for anyone not wishing to pray at the Orthodox part of Wall. The entrance to the Western Wall from the south side would be shared by all, and from there each group would go to the part where it wished.[19]

The responses to the Sharansky Plan were mixed, and split the WoW into two camps. Some objected to the plan because it would move them away from their original objective of generating a change among Orthodox women.[20] However, others felt that in light of the HCJ rulings that offered the Robinson's Arch area as a prayer site for egalitarian prayer, the WoW could not reject the offer immediately. . . .

In considering the Sharanksy Plan, it is important to note that in places that are holy to more than one religious community, there are several ways of dividing official authority between the different communities. This is mainly done by dividing the access and prayer times of the different communities, or dividing the prayer space between them. These types of arrangements are in place, for example, at the Cave of the Patriarchs/Al Haram Al-Ibrahimi and the Tomb of Samuel the Prophet/ Nebi Samuel. Sharansky's Plan and the Mandelblit team's proposal are a third type of division: they suggest enlarging the sacred space—expanding the holy part of the Western Wall southwards and creating a second, pluralistic Western Wall. This proposal is one of the creative solutions for resolving disputes at holy places and providing recognition to excluded and discriminated-against groups. However, this solution has two disadvantages: first, the historic holy place would be considered more authentic—at least at the beginning—and as possessing a more elevated status than the holy space added to it. The second disadvantage is that an important part of the Archeological Park would be dramatically harmed. A related difficulty is a possible objection by Jordan and other political agents that will halt the construction. Not being able to fulfill the Sharansky-Mandelblit Plan will send the parties back to examining other alternatives, including giving the WoW an option of praying in the women's section at defined times, or on the upper plaza, or allocating a portion of the historic Wall in favor of the non-Orthodox streams.

THE ACTION STRATEGIES IN THE DISPUTE

The main actors in the intra-religious challenge posed by the WoW were the WoW themselves and the Official in Charge of the Western Wall. It was also influenced by the government and government officials' attitudes, the representatives of different movements in Judaism in Israel and the United States, and the attitudes of the non-religious public. Analyzing the action strategies used by these parties contributes to a comprehensive understanding of the WoW's achievements and consequently the achievements of the Reform and Conservative movements supported by many American Modern Orthodox members as well.

1. The WoW

The WoW's strategy included:

- Persistence and determination in arriving at the Wall to pray according to their custom for the duration of 26 years.
- Media coverage: The WoW succeeded in garnering public support, especially in the US, by reaching the public through extensive international media coverage and the use of social media. In turn, the North American posts put pressure on the Israeli Prime Minister.[21] However, the WoW were unable to extensively reach the public in Israel, even among the secular public, especially before the twenty-first century.[22] Their opposition in Israel portrayed the WoW a small group of strange and provocative women, most of them English speakers (foreign to the Israeli culture), who represent no one but themselves.
- Education and publicity: the WoW made various attempts to attract the public's sympathy through education and publicity actions, but with little success. Up until the 2000s, in which most of the secular public became fed up with the phenomenon of women's exclusion, the WoW did not succeed in

attracting this public to their struggle. They failed to clarify to the general public that their struggle also concerns the secular public, as part of the struggle against fanatical religious coercion.

- Activity among Orthodox women: the WoW worked to reach Orthodox women and change the norms of discrimination from within the Orthodox religious circles. In 2009, Orthodox women from the Kolech Organization joined the struggle, and two women from Kolech Organization even personally joined the Directorate of the WoW.[23]

- Holding Bat Mitzvah ceremonies: the aspiration of the WoW is to organize mass Bat Mitzvah ceremonies to educate and advocate for gender equality in observing Judaism's commandments. A limited number of Bat Mitzvah ceremonies have so far been held as part of the WoW's prayer at Robinson's Arch (and one at the women's section of the Wall), but they have not achieved their main goal. At the time of writing, this activity is only in its beginning stages.

- Obtaining support among American Jewry: the WoW acted in two spheres of action—in Israel and North America—in order to obtain public and financial support. In this realm, they have had great success, especially in the recent years.

- Turning to the HCJ (High Court of Justice): There are both benefits and risks in turning to a judicial body. The HCJ rulings granted the WoW recognition in principle, but withheld what they had wished to achieve: the right to pray according to their custom in the main women's section. Judge Sobel's ruling changed the public's awareness and attitudes in favor of the WoW's struggle.[24] Meanwhile, the government made two mistakes that led to the WoW's victory in the Jerusalem District Court ruling. The first mistake was the government's omission: it had not managed to construct and equip a proper prayer platform in the area of the antiquities site between the Mughrabi Ascent and Robinson's Arch, and one shared entrance to the Western Wall site. The second mistake was intensifying the enforcement of the Holy Places regulations at the Western Wall, which was accompanied by the arrest of the WoW.

2. The Reform and Conservative Movements

The WoW group came out of the Reform movement, the largest Jewish movement in the United States, and holding about 50 synagogues in Israel.[25] Importantly, the interests of the WoW differ from that of the Reform movement as well as the Conservative movement. While the WoW are struggling for recognition of their right to pray at the women's section, the latter two movements in Israel (supported by their American parent movements) are struggling for state recognition, including receiving a status at the Western Wall. Still, the WoW were forced to "align" with these movements in their mutual interests to receive recognition from the State of Israel and remain an active player in the negotiations over the status of the Western Wall.

The leaders of the Reform movement in Israel did not offer full support for the WoW's objectives. As Rabbi Kariv said, "I am not interested in poking a finger in the Haredim's eye." He continued, "If all you need is 11 hours a year, you are indicating that it is not an acute need, but only a symbol, so have the honor of praying at Robinson's Arch."[26] Nevertheless, Kariv began to support the WoW's struggle as a part of the Reform movement's struggle against the phenomenon of women's exclusion in Israeli religious society.

Kariv believes that in this process, and in the arrangement of the Sharansky-Mandelblit Plan, the non-Orthodox movements have made great achievements: clear, legislated recognition of the non-Orthodox streams; state recognition of the extension of the Western Wall area as a prayer zone; the establishment of public council for adminstering the Southern Western Wall, with representation equally divided between the state and the non-Orthodox streams; and the set-up of an egalitarian, pluralistic prayer administration, and establishing gender equality. He says that with a publicity campaign, the southern part of the Western Wall will become attractive and acceptable to the majority of the public within a decade, as a "separate but equal" alternative.

Despite these agreed-upon arrangements, the Reform movement and WoW feel that "the State is dragging its legs" on the issue of the physical planning due to Rabbi Rabinowitz's objection. Therefore, they set out on a Bat Mitzvah and Torah reading campaign in the women's section, as the WoW had done in October 2014, in order to put pressure on Rabbi Rabinowitz and the government to agree to the details of the requested construction drawings. Kariv calls this "maintaining public vigilance."[27]

The Conservative movement, meanwhile, supports the WoW but differs from them because it seeks to promote mixed prayer, not separate prayer. Nonetheless, the Conservative Movement is of the opinion that the WoW can compromise on a respectable prayer plot in the Robinson's Arch area.[28] In fact, the Conservatives' agreement to pray in the Robinson's Arch area has effectively destroyed the foundation of the WoW's demand to gain a status at the historic Wall.

3.   The Antiquities Authority

The Antiquities Authority was fundamentally against changes to the Archeological Park, including the erection of any prayer platforms at the expense of accessibility to and viewing of the archeological findings. Nonetheless, as the archeologist Dr. Yuval Baruch admits, the Authority belongs to the government, and the latter can put pressures on the Authority's chair. In this process, the Authority has cooperated with the government by agreeing both to the erection of a small prayer platform for the WoW, as well as to the allocation of the Herodian Road for prayer, as long as it does not disturb the visitors at the place. Since then, pressures to enlarge the prayer platform have increased in several steps, as has the current use of the prayer platform for celebrations. Yuval Baruch claims, "The Archeological Park is in danger."[29] However, as a branch of the government, the Antiquities Authority cannot do much against this trend.

4.   The Official in Charge of the Western Wall

The Official in Charge of the Western Wall, Rabbi Shmuel Rabinowitz, has, by his very personality and connections, great power in the government's corridors. In April 2013, he spoke before the Knesset committees and explained, "In the recent years I have been under two attacks . . . On the one hand, conservative fanatics—I am being attacked for my energetic activity,

for bringing thousands of student groups, for bringing thousands of soldiers to the Wall, groups, which in their opinion, do not follow the spirit of Grandfather Israel [the Jewish People along the generations] . . . on the other hand, liberal fanatics who wish to object to court decisions, or to the status quo at the Western Wall." Eventually, he continued, "we will light the fire of controversy at the Wall."[30] He believes that a hegmonic Orthodox status quo is good for everyone.

When dealing with the challenge of the WoW, Rabinowitz took a series of actions:

- Legislation and regulations: after the WoW turned to the HCJ in 1989, the Official in Charge sought to persuade the Minister of Religious Affairs to add a section to the regulations, forbidding religious ceremonies not in accordance with local custom. The government, however, did not accept his recommendation.

- Rabbi Rabinowitz also issued an instruction to prevent the WoW from bringing Torah scrolls and reading from the Torah in the women's section. The Torah scrolls that exist at the Western Wall are not available to the WoW, and that is why they bring a Torah scroll with them, which according to the regulations must remain in a closed bag in the main women's section.

- Tightening the procedures at the Wall Plaza: Rabbi Rabinowitz tightened the regulations at the Wall Plaza and frequently demanded separation between men and women even at state ceremonies in the upper plaza. For example, the singing of female soldiers at ceremonies for swearing-in IDF soldiers on the upper plaza was also stopped.

- Mobilizing Seminary and Yeshiva student protesters: In August 2013, 7,000 Seminary girls accepted the rabbis' calls and attended a prayer at the Wall, directed by Rabbi Rabinowitz at the same time of the WoW's Rosh Chodesh prayer. Consequently, the WoW's prayer was prevented, and they were forced to pray in a separate area from Wall.[31] Rabbi Rabinowitz claims that he was not the intiator, but rather, that he was subjected to pressure by the fanatic Ultra-Orthodox Haredim.

- Applying the police: the Official in Charge has direct authority to request the police's intervention to charge the WoW with violating public order and violating the regulations, and therefore to move them away from the Wall. Rabbi Rabinowitz used this authority as of 2009, leading to the arrest of women from WoW, as well as subsequent media attention and a change in public opinion.

- Development and improvement works: Rabinowitz acts tirelessly in the area of construction and development to expand the Wall Plaza, both in length and width. Andrew Sacks claims that Rabbi Rabinowitz has moved back (westward) the partition between the lower plaza and the upper plaza in order to enlarge the lower plaza where gender segregation exists, at the expense of the upper plaza.[32] In response to these complaints, Rabbi Rabinowitz states: "I have not made drastic changes, only not letting in musical instruments."[33]

- Orthodox hegemony: Levi Eshkol's government entrusted the management of the Western Wall with the Orthodox representatives, who possess political power in the Israeli Knesset and in most of the government's coalitions. The government has applied the judicial and law enforcement systems against the WoW, and has acted to move their prayer to the Robinson's Arch area, far away from the sight of the Orthodox and Ultra-Orthodox worshippers at the Western Wall. Even as the government has recently been lending a sympathetic ear to pluralism in Judaism and working to reach an acceptable arrangement to the WoW and the three main streams, Prime Minister Netanyahu is limited in his ability to generate radical changes due to the political power of the Ultra-Orthodox political parties.

IMPLICATIONS FOR STATUS QUO ARRANGEMENTS

Despite the definite names of the terms "status quo" and "local custom," these do not imply completely frozen situations. The main rationale for maintaining the status quo stems from the fear of the eruption of violence on the part of the hegemonic group at a holy place. Nevertheless, situations change, and even if they lead to acts of violence, a new status quo or custom becomes permanent. In June 1967, the government of Israel decided upon a new situation at the Western Wall, and it continues frequently to determine new situations in other holy places.

The change generated by the WoW can have implications for the status quo at the Temple Mount. In the ruling regarding the WoW's first petition, Supreme Court Justice Menachem Elon stated that in some cases, such as the Temple Mount, maintaining public order is prioritized over freedom of worship. MK Moshe Feiglin, who has been struggling for years to make free entrance and prayer of Jews at the Temple Mount possible, requested to stop carrying out arrests of the WoW while speaking "as one who has also been arrested for the transgression of trying to pray . . . at the Temple Mount." He added: "The Western Wall is a national site, a national heritage site, it belongs to the entire Jewish People, and obviously, one should allow Jews who want to pray in it to pray in it as they wish."[34]

Jewish prayer at the Temple Mount and the prayer of the WoW are not at the same level of risk to public safety. This is perhaps the reason that the WoW have received the court's recognition of their right to pray according to their special custom. Police protection of the WoW's prayer for the duration of one hour per month is not perceived as a burden that the police cannot handle. Nonetheless, changing the status quo in the matter of the WoW is a legal and political precedent whose importance, in my opinion, cannot be overstated. It is possible that in the future it will influence changes in the arrangement of rights and their fulfillment at the Temple Mount/Al-Haram al-Sharif compound and other places, such as the Room of the Last Supper above King David's Tomb.

CONCLUSION

The WoW's quarter-century struggle is the outcome of a successful political idea that crystallized out of the experience of violence that religious feminists experienced when they arrived on December 1988 at the Western Wall to pray with a Torah scroll. Anat Hoffman's political idea could be viewed as "bringing an idol into the Temple" of Orthodoxy. Under the auspices of the civil law, the WoW have succeeded in obtaining recognition from the courts for adding a new local custom to the hegemonic Orthodox status quo, thereby making an opening for a pluralistic approach within the historic Wall Plaza. Thus, the WoW, which began as a small group with tens of women, have succeeded where the Reform and Conservative movements in Israel have failed. This success has strengthened the national pan-Jewish character of the Western Wall space, and helped to restore the power of the civil system—the government and the courts.

Even beyond this important legal achievement, the WoW had two major political achievements: first, enlisting and consolidating American Jewry to support their demands in order to gain state recognition at the Western Wall; second, unifying the Reform, Conservative, and WoW movements within the framework of serious negotiations with the Israeli government to gain a recognized status at the Western Wall. Ironically, it is precisely these impressive political achievements that have contributed to the WoW's major resignation of power, as they had 'to align' with and compromise on the more modest interests of the Reform and Conservative Movements.

By doing so, the WoW sacrificed their revolutionary goal. They were forced to relinquish prayer at the stronghold of Orthodoxy and move southward "with all due respect" to a more inferior plot, Robinson's Arch, far away from the eyes of the Orthodox worshippers. They lost a central part of their identity as activists demanding change within the Orthodoxy, and they were forced to "reinvent themselves" as organizers of egalitarian Bat Mitzvah ceremonies at the Wall. The WoW have aspired to create a revolution in the perception of women's status within the religious system, and do this precisely in the "Temple of Orthodoxy" at the Western Wall. By contrast, the major interest of the Reform and Conservative movements was to gain state acknowledgement as recognized Jewish movements alongside the Orthodox at the Wall.

One can understand the WoW organization as the forerunner who paved the road to American-Jewish pressure on the Israeli government in favor of the non-Orthodox streams; however, once they had succeeded in their mission, they were forced to sacrifice the main justification for their existence.

It is still difficult to estimate the magnitude of the WoW's achievement. They have bequeathed the idea of "a woman wrapped in a tallit" and a woman reading from the Torah. However, it is unclear whether, and to what extent, the WoW have succeeded in spreading their idea among conservative Orthodox women watching them during their prayer in the women's section, and to what extent the media tumult has assisted this dissemination in Orthodox circles. Yet, certainly they influenced Modern Orthodox observants due to the fact that many of them supported their struggle. It is also unclear whether it will be possible to implement Sharansky's compromise, and if so, what its effect will be on the WoW's activity. If the WoW will be forced to pray at Robinson's Arch, will they succeed in bringing mass Bat Mitzvah ceremonies to the Wall? Or, once there is a solution, will the challenge disappear and with it, the supporters of the WoW?

The WoW's success in their struggle has created a precedent and a model to be imitated regarding the possibility of breaking a status quo at a holy place in favor of a discriminated-against minority group, in the name of the civil-legal norm of freedom of access and freedom of worship at holy places. Until recently it has been accepted that the existing situation named the "status quo" or "local custom" is "sacred" and must be strictly enforced. These arrangements perpetuate the old balance of power and the conservatism and hegemony of one religious group. They force the discrimination of minority groups at holy places that are open to all, which are worshipped by the members of different religious communities.

In June 1967, the government of Israel created a new status quo at the Western Wall, which transferred the Wall and the grand plaza to exclusive Jewish religious and national use. In the past quarter century, the WoW have broken this status quo at this site. The case in question is not a dispute between two religions, or two nationalities, but rather, an intra-Jewish, gender-oriented egalitarian dispute over the way of religious worship and women's rights in religion and society. It is probable that the important precedent of the recognition of the WoW's new local custom will have an influence on status quo arrangements at other controversial places, first and foremost, on the Temple Mount (Al-Haram Al-Sharif). The WoW's legal and political achievement challenges the general principle of a status quo at holy places, making it more flexible and challengeable in a multicultural society within the framework of a contemporary Western democracy.

NOTES

1. Appeal by the State of Israel 43832-42-33; HCJ 2512/87.
2. Barzilai, "The Political and Legal Culture in Israel."
3. Hassner, "To Halve and to Hold"; Atran et al., "Sacred Bounds"; Atran and Axelrod, "Reframing Sacred Values."
4. Reiter, "Contest and Co-habitation."
5. Ben Dov, Naor, and Aner, *HaKotel.*
6. Interview with Rabinowitz.
7. HCJ 257/89.
8. Shakdiel, "The Women of the Wall."
9. Lori, "It Interrupts the Wall."
10. Raday, "Demand for Equality," 405.
11. Judy Maltz, "The New Orthodox Face of Women of the Wall," *Haaretz*, April 1, 2013; on financial support: interview with Director of the WOW association, Leslie Sachs, Dec. 9, 2014.
12. Tavory, "Ha Yahadut HaReformit."
13. Shakdiel, "The Women of the Wall."
14. Raday, "Demand for Equality."
15. Interview with Haberman.
16. Interview with Hoffman.
17. Interview with Raday.
18. Raday, "Demand for Equality."
19. Sokol, Sharon, and Eisenbud, "Sharansky Proposes Egalitarian Section."
20. Ettinger, "The Women of the Wall's Compromise."
21. Interview with Sachs.
22. Lahav, "The Woes of WoW," 16.
23. Interview with Kehat.

24. Israel Democracy Institute, "With Court Ruling."
25. Interview with Kariv.
26. Interview with Kariv.
27. Interview with Kariv.
28. Interview with Sacks.
29. Interview with Baruch.
30. Knesset Committee, *Minutes*, 23.
31. Hasson, "Again."
32. Interview with Sacks.
33. Interview with Rabinowitz.
34. Knesset Committee, *Minutes.*

BIBLIOGRAPHY

Appeal by the State of Israel 43832-42-33, State of Israel v. Ras et al., interpreting HCJ 2512/87 Hoffman v. the Official in Charge of the Western Wall, IsrSC 48 (1774) 225 (2).

Atran, Scott, and Robert Axelrod. "Reframing Sacred Values." *Negotiation Journal* 24 (2008): 221-46.

Atran, Scott, Jeremy Ginges, Douglas Medin, and Khalil Shikaki. "Sacred Bounds on Rational Resolution of Violent Political Conflict." *Proceedings of the National Academy of Sciences of the USA* 104, no. 18 (2008): 7357-60.

Baruch, Yuval. Interview with author. November 4, 2014.

Barzilai, Gad. "The Political and Legal Culture in Israel." In *Megamot bachevra hayisraelit* [Trends in the Israeli Society] 2, edited by Efrayim Ya'ar and Ze'ev Shavit. Tel Aviv: Open University, 2003. [Hebrew]

Ben Dov, Meir, Mordechai Naor, and Zeev Aner. *Hakotel.* Ministry of Defense Press, 1981. [Hebrew]

Ettinger, Yair. "The Women of the Wall's Compromise: Erecting a Reform Compound." *Haaretz.* April 10, 2013. [Hebrew]

Haberman, Bonna. Interview with author. July 2, 2013.

Hassner, Ron. "To Halve and To Hold: Conflicts over Sacred Space and the Problem of Indivisibility." *Security Studies* 12, no. 4 (2013): 1–33.

Hasson, Nir. "Again: The Police Prevented the Women of the Wall from Praying at the Central Plaza." *Haaretz.* August 7, 2013. http://www.haaretz.co.il/news/education/1.209134 [Hebrew]

HCJ 2512/87. Anat Hoffman v. Official in Charge of the Western Wall, IsrSC 48 (1774) 225 (2).

HCJ 257/89. Anat Hoffman v. Official in Charge of the Western Wall, IsrSC 48(2) 265.

Hoffman, Anat. Interview with author. June 24, 2013.

Israel Democracy Institute. "With Court Ruling, Majority of Israeli Jews Back Women of the Wall." May 11, 2003. http://en-idi.org.il/about-idi/news-and-updates/with-court-ruling,-majority-of-israeli-jews-back-women-of-the-wall/

Kariv, Gilad. Interview with author. July 8, 2013.

Kehat, Hanna. Interview with author. November 24, 2014.

Knesset Committee for Internal Affairs and Environment Protection. Minutes. April 30, 2013.

Lahav, Pnina. "The Woes of WoW: The Women of the Wall as a Religious Social Movement and as Metaphor." Boston University School of Law Working Papers No. 13-2 (January 23, 2013).

Lori, Aviva. "It Interrupts the Wall." *Haaretz*. April 16, 2003. [Hebrew]

Rabinowitz, Shmuel. Interview with author. July 8, 2013.

Raday, Frances. "Demand for Equality in Defining Religious Identity: The Case of the WoW." *Hamishpat* 13 (2008): 401-25. http://hamishpat.colman.ac.il/Files.ashx?file=04_2011/J_FRhadi.pdf&objid=328&nsid=294&lcid=1037&boneid=12633 [Hebrew]

———. Interview with author. July 25, 2013.

Reiter, Yitzhak. "Contest and Co-habitation in Shared Holy Places: Samuel's Tomb and the Cave of the Patriarchs." In *Holy Places in the Israeli-Palestinian Conflict: Confrontation and Co-existence*, edited by Marshall J. Breger, Yitzhak Reiter, and Leonard Hammer, 158-77. London: Routledge, 2009.

Sachs, Lesley. Interview with author. December 9, 2014.

Sacks, Andrew. Interview with author. July 2, 2013.

Shakdiel, Leah. "The Women of the Wall: Radical Feminism as an Opportunity for a New Discourse in Israel." In *The Whirlpool of Identities: Critical Discussion of Religiosity and Secularism in Israel*, edited by Yossi Yona and Yehuda Gutman. Jerusalem: Van Leer Institute and Kibbutz Meuchad Publications, 2004. [Hebrew].

Sokol, Sam, Jeremy Sharon, and Daniel K. Eisenbud. "Sharansky Proposes Egalitarian Section at Kotel." *The Jerusalem Post*. April 10, 2013. http://www.jpost.com/Jewish-World/Jewish-News/Sharansky-proposes-egalitarian-section-at-Kotel-309285

Tavory, Efrayim. "Hayahadut Hareformit Be Israel: Hesegim ve Sikuyim" [Reform Judaism in Israel: Achievements and Chances.] 2002. http://www.ajc.org/atf/cf/%8B42D75369-D582-4380-8395-D25925B85EAF%7D/Hebrew3.pdf [Hebrew]

84. HOW EVANGELICALS BECAME WHITE

KELLY BROWN DOUGLAS (2018)

What values were really at stake for the 81 percent of white evangelicals who voted for a presidential candidate who uses crass language and admits to engaging in coarse behavior, and whose campaign was marked by vitriolic hatred of various people, particularly people of color?

I raised this question with a white male leader of a Christian foundation. In response, he told me to consider the "moral values"—such as pro-life concerns—that he said prompted, if not demanded, white evangelical support of Donald Trump's candidacy.

The Christian leader suggested that these particular concerns mitigated any misgivings that white evangelicals might have with Trump's dissolute behaviors and bigoted views. For many others, the moral imperatives *not* to support Trump were more overriding, especially for those who prioritize personal virtue as a core religious value.

The "value proposition" displayed by white evangelicals in the 2016 election, and the definition of what constitutes "moral values" and what doesn't, is inextricably related to the nation's upcoming demographic shift—the fact that, by the year 2044, the United States is expected to become majority nonwhite. This has significant implications for the wider faith community regarding issues of race. Much more may be at stake than the leader of the Christian foundation was able or willing to recognize.

'THE NEW ISRAELITES'

The value proposition of the Trump campaign was made clear in the campaign's "Make America Great Again" vision. This mantra tapped into America's defining Anglo-Saxon myth and revitalized the culture of white supremacy constructed to protect it.

The Anglo-Saxon myth was introduced to this country when America's Pilgrim and Puritan forebears fled England, intent on carrying forth an Anglo-Saxon legacy they believed was compromised in English church and society with the Norman Conquest in 1066. These early Americans believed themselves descendants of an ancient Anglo-Saxon people, "free from the taint of intermarriages," who uniquely possessed high moral values and an "instinctive love for freedom." Their beliefs reflected the thought of first-century Roman philosopher Tacitus (quoted above), who touted the unique superiority of an Anglo-Saxon people from the ancient woods of Germany. In his treatise *Germania*, Tacitus describes these Germanic tribes as a people for whom "good [moral] habits" were more effectual than "good laws" and argues that they possess a peculiar respect for individual rights and freedom.

Tacitus' writings not only played an influential role in determining systems of governance in America, but they also laid the foundation for the subjugation, if not elimination, of certain peoples: namely, those who were not members of the "unmixed race" that Tacitus described. Indeed, *Germania* has been called "one of the most dangerous books ever written," not so much for what Tacitus wrote but for how his words have been used to undergird horrific movements, such as the Nazis' monstrous program for "racial purity."

Considering themselves descendants of these mythic Anglo-Saxon people, the Puritans and Pilgrims crossed the Atlantic with a vision to build a nation that was politically and culturally—if not demographically—true to their "exceptional" Anglo-Saxon heritage.

They saw this as a divine vision. They traced their Anglo-Saxon heritage through the ancient woods of Germany back to the Bible. They considered themselves the "new Israelites," carrying forth a godly mission. Central to this mission was building not simply an Anglo-Saxon nation but a religious nation—one that reflected the morals and virtues of God, which in their minds were synonymous with the unsullied ways of their freedom-loving Anglo-Saxon ancestors. "The Lord will make [America] a city upon a hill," Puritan leader John Winthrop preached in 1630, "[with] the eyes of all people upon us."

From its beginning, America's social-identity, with a legitimating religious canopy, was Anglo-Saxon. Even Founding Fathers such as Thomas Jefferson and Benjamin Franklin envisioned America as a sacred witness to Anglo-Saxon character and values, if not people. (Jefferson wrote, "Tacitus I consider as the first writer in the world without a single exception.")

Jefferson's proposed language for a United States seal affirmed this belief. As John Adams described it, Jefferson's seal included "the children of Israel in the wilderness . . . and on the other side, Hengist and Horsa, the Saxon chiefs from whom we claim the honor of being descended, and whose political principles and form of government we have assumed." America's democracy was conceived of as an expression of a biblically ordained Anglo-Saxon mission.

A WHITEWASHED 'CITY ON THE HILL'

Anglo-Saxon America had a perpetually vexing problem. Anglo-Saxons were not native to American soil. Those native to American soil were decidedly not Anglo-Saxon. And not everybody who *looked* like Anglo-Saxons *were* Anglo-Saxon.

In 1751, Benjamin Franklin wrote that "the number of purely white people in the world is proportionally very small. . . . And in Europe, the Spaniards, Italians, French, Russians, and Swedes are generally of what we call a swarthy complexion; as are the Germans also, the Saxons only excepted, who with the English, make the [principal] body of white people on the face of the earth. I could wish their numbers were increased."

Yet, for most who came from Europe, there was a mitigating factor: They were "white"—and whiteness made all the difference. To safeguard the Anglo-Saxon vision, a pervasive culture of whiteness—with defined political, religious, and ethnic identities—was born. To be "white" eventually would be considered Anglo-Saxon enough. Whiteness became the passport into the exceptional space that was American identity.

During the First Great Awakening, when evangelical Protestantism spread across New England, revivalist Jonathan Edwards was convinced that the "glorious work of God" was destined to begin in America. Based on his interpretation of the prophecy of Isaiah, Edwards wrote, "It is signified that it shall begin in some very remote part of the world. . . . I cannot think that anything else can be here intended but America." Edwards further proclaimed that "in order to introduce a new and more excellent state of the church" where "the power of God might be more conspicuous," God had to start all over in a new world, America.

Such confidence in the divine nature of America's mission easily gave way to white evangelicals believing themselves to be God's uniquely "chosen" people. The white evangelical community assumed that spreading their brand of Christianity was essential to the nation remaining true to its divine mission—to build an Anglo-Saxon nation. Thus, the white evangelical community was alarmed when great numbers of non-Anglo-Saxon Europeans began to flood into the country. They offered what they believed to be an efficacious solution: Convert them to Anglo-Saxon Christianity and hence to "whiteness."

As evangelicals were spreading their brand of Christianity in the 18th and 19th centuries, they believed themselves to be also spreading Anglo-Saxonism. Their mission was as much an Anglo-Saxon mission as it was a Christian mission. Converting "foreigners" was for them a way to protect the Anglo-Saxon identity of America. "Conversion to [evangelical] Christianity was considered the only logical way to produce Anglo-Saxons out of the tired and huddled masses," explained sociologist Daniel B. Lee. By linking Anglo-Saxonism with godliness, evangelical Christianity has been historically complicit in promoting a "great" America that is equated with white supremacy.

"In a word, our national character is that of the Anglo-Saxon race," wrote 19th-century church historian Robert Baird. Baird argued that "essentially Germanic or Teutonic [are] the chief supports of the ideas and institutions of evangelical Christianity."

Christian Anglo-Saxon whiteness has subsequently served as the criterion, spoken or unspoken, for determining who is a "real" American, who is entitled to the rights of "life, liberty, and the pursuit of happiness," and who has the right to cross borders and occupy certain spaces. Essentially, whiteness provides the measure for what it means to be a legitimate citizen.

The "city on the hill" that the early Americans were building was to be nothing less than a sacred witness to Anglo-Saxon (white) supremacy.

WHEN CHARACTER NO LONGER MATTERS

Donald Trump's vision to Make America Great Again is a 21st-century effort to carry forth the legacy of the Anglo-Saxon myth and the culture of whiteness that protects that myth. Recovery of America's "greatness" was associated with the country ridding itself of nonwhite immigrants, whose very presence—according to Trump—has sent the nation spiraling into social disarray and moral decadence.

To bolster this prescription for America's greatness, Trump trafficked in disparaging misrepresentations of Mexican immigrants as rapists and of African-American communities as dangerous enclaves of criminality. His vision for "greatness" therefore resonates with those who have longed for an Anglo-Saxon/white America. In this way Trump's campaign served as a clarion call to "take back the country" from those detrimental to America's exceptionalist identity, namely nonwhite people.

The value proposition of Trump's Make America Great Again campaign is clear. It is the promise to make America *white* again—which is why so many people of color had a visceral reaction to this campaign mantra.

This brings us back to white evangelical support for Donald Trump. What does this unprecedented support say about their priority of values?

Given evangelical Protestantism's historical relationship to white supremacy, it is no wonder that

Trump's campaign appealed to a vast majority of white evangelical voters. Trump harkened back to this history by aligning America's greatness with evangelical Christian values, as he consistently linked a great America with a Christian America. He made it clear by suggesting that saying "Merry Christmas" was a sign of patriotism.

In this view, safeguarding the property of Anglo-Saxon white America takes priority over a commitment to individual morality. Ironically, that which was proclaimed as a mark of Anglo-Saxon exceptionalism—upright character—is dwarfed by a resolve to maintain a white supremacist nation.

THE 'DEATH RATTLE' OF WHITE CHRISTIAN AMERICA?

Most of white Christian America ignored Trump's intemperate behavior to support his vision of American greatness. In this regard, a majority of white Christian America found common cause with Trump's Anglo-Saxon exceptionalist values, eschewing any pretense of valuing personal morality. Such support reveals the corrupting nature of Anglo-Saxon exceptionalism.

To be fair, white evangelicals were not alone in their significant support of Trump's campaign. Fifty-eight percent of nonevangelical white Protestants and 60 percent of white Catholics did the same. Researcher Robert P. Jones argues that the 2016 presidential election represented the "death rattle" of white Christian America's attempt to protect the country from the consequences of a nonwhite America.

No one made this case more sharply than Michele Bachmann, who said to a gathering of "values-voter" evangelicals, "It's a math problem of demographics and a changing United States. . . . [T]his is the last election when we even have a chance to vote for somebody who will stand up for godly moral principles. This is it." The implication is clear: The more threatened the white demographic, the fiercer the defense of Anglo-Saxon white supremacy.

The bottom line is that in their support of Trump, much of white Christian America opted to support a white supremacist vision for the country. As for white evangelicals, far from abandoning their role as "values voters," they simply made clear what they value above all else.

Left to be determined is what those in the faith community who did *not* support the Make America Great Again campaign value most. Their real vote will be seen in their actions, because silence means consent.[1]

85. TRANSGRESSING THE FATHER FIGURE
ALLYSON S. DEAN AND WHITNEY J. ARCHER (2017)

INTRODUCTION

In the spring of 2012, we performed "Father Figure," a drag number at a university drag show. The university, one of the large institutions in a state typically associated with progressive ideals, hosts two shows a year and we both attended a few of them before coming to the conclusion that we should offer another drag narrative. Through our performance, we sought to re-center drag as a political act and to use the platform of performance to both critique systems of power in Catholicism and to engage the audience with questions about those powers.

We dressed like a Catholic priest and an altar boy donning clerical collar and red cassock respectively. In the process of the song, "Father Figure," a 1990 hit from then-closeted, later openly gay George Michael, we developed a romantic narrative imbued with transgressive power through transcending and playing with gender through drag. The performance incorporated commonly recognized Catholic rituals and symbols, including communion and the crucifixion. Both raised with influences of Christianity and Catholicism in our upbringings, this performance allowed us to unpack the legacy of those influences.

This article focuses on our use of drag performance as medium for engaging in theological discourse. The use of drag as a tool for "doing theology" has been personally liberating and thus we suggest that a possibility of liberation exists in bringing theology into queer spaces, extending theology beyond the realm of religious institutions or the academy. We examine the body and the performativity of gender as a starting point for theology, intending to present narratives of queer lives, those often erased or cast aside by Catholicism. We use the term queer to speak to queerness as it relates to gender and to sexuality.

. . .

PERFORMING DRAG

. . .

In our drag performance pieces, we seek to center queer experiences. Much of our performances grapple not only with sexuality, but also with gender. While drag often serves purposes of entertainment and campiness, our drag performances attempt to interact with the institutions and lived experiences often cast aside or easily compartmentalized as being anomalies or hot topic blips on a news cycle. In addition to taking on institutions and lived experiences of queer communities, we intentionally center the musical works of queer artists, a silence often prevalent in the drag performances in our local community.

We turned to drag as a way to confront and wrestle with some of the institutionalized challenges for LGBTQ+ folk and women in Catholicism, an institution that, up until the current papal leadership, often issued statements delegitimizing the existence of LGBTQ+ folk and devaluing the role of women, particularly the activism of nuns. The virtual non-existence of visible LGBTQ+ and women's involvement in the Church signaled an opportunity for us to re-write that narrative, centering queerness as pervasive, yet challenging within Catholicism.

Even under the conceivably liberal guidance of Pope Francis, LGBTQ+ lives remain unintelligible in Catholicism.[1] In this, we turn to Judith Butler's concept of performativity, one she illustrates through an examination of performing drag. Butler writes of drag's illustration of gender performativity, "The

point about drag is not simply to produce a pleasurable and subversive spectacle [of gender] but to allegorize the spectacular and consequential ways in which reality is both reproduced and contested."[2] With this consideration, we look to drag as the queer cousin of religious theater seen in Catholic ceremonies such as The Stations of the Cross, a re-enactment of the death and ascension of Christ.

Drag allowed us to disrupt the expected norms through our citation of gender. In performing as male bodies with access to the altar and power within the Church, our parodic gender performances produced a new understanding of the possibilities of women, of LGBTQ+ people, entering into the power space deemed previously inaccessible by our queer, female bodies. Though dressed in drag, neither of us took extra measures to further "masculinize" ourselves; to many, we would likely be deemed more androgynous than masculine in our drag. Our androgynous expressions sought to challenge and destabilize binary notions of gender perpetuated by the Church. This intentional effort to destabilize gender aligns with Althaus-Reid's *Indecent Theology*,[3] which introduces the concept of theology as destabilizing and grounded in subversion. Through our dragging, we disrupted the notion that the altar space, the conduit for conversation with God, was reserved for (presumed heterosexual or asexual) men only.

THE PERFORMANCE

The impetus for our drag performance stemmed from . . . observations we had about past University-sponsored drag shows; there were few, if any, performances that took up socio-cultural issues LGBTQ+ communities faced. In listening to George Michael's "Father Figure" for the first time in a number of years, we heard possibilities for attending to those observations that left us unsatisfied with the drag representations we saw re-occur frequently. We chose to take on an institution that simultaneously rejected queer identities while attempting to cover up the perverse actions of priests abusing youth, particularly young boys, in the Church.[4] In these cover-ups, the absence of a conversation about queerness and the Church pervaded. The erasure of queerness is a missed opportunity to establish a vital distinction between pedophilia and healthy consensual queer relations. The denouncement of homosexuality by the Church has strategically conflated it with the sexual abuse of minors to the extent that the Catholic League reported, "it makes no sense to pretend there is no relationship between homosexuality and the abuse of minors."[5] The explicit denouncement of homosexuality while not explicitly condemning pedophilia concurrently conflates the two and ironically demonizes the one that has the potential to exist in a consensual manner.

At the start of the performance, a large cross stood at the back of the stage while the spotlight shone on the priest, kneeling and praying. During the instrumental introduction to the song, the priest looked upwards, holding his hands toward the heavens, asking for forgiveness. When the altar boy entered the stage, the priest directed his gaze to the altar boy and moved closer. The priest watched the altar boy while preparing the altar for communion, singing to him as a sort of soliloquy, turning to look upwards in a sort of struggle to reconcile his desire for the boy with his responsibility to the divine. In the second verse, the priest moved toward the altar boy, catching his attention, and the two locked in a gaze, circling each other like two tigers about to pounce each other. The priest pulled away from the circle, turning his attention, once again, to the heavens, a continued demonstration of his torn desires. The teenage altar boy eventually pulled the priest away from his divine confession by singing to the priest, showing his lustful interest by beckoning the priest through directed song. This is one of several instances of a blurring of power between the two characters, as the priest followed the direction of the teen.

In this performance, we called on Althaus-Reid's and Isherwood's contention that queer theology is subversive,[6] we intended to subvert the traditional power structure of the religion at various points. The altar boy pushed the priest to his knees, administered the Eucharist to the priest, mouthing along to the song lyric, "I will be your preacher, teacher, anything you have in mind." In the administering of the Eucharist, the direct lineage of divinity from God to priest was disrupted and the altar boy offered the flesh of the savior to the priest, a metonymy for the flesh of his own body. The priest followed, stood up, pushed the altar boy to his knees, standing over him, and looked ready to receive oral sex. He held the wine goblet near his crotch, tipped it into the altar boy's mouth and wiped the altar boy's lip after he drank from it. The consumption of the Eucharist and the wine were both highly sensual, metaphoric for the consumption of Christ's body, a highly spiritual moment when one may feel closest to God.

Following the play with power in the administration of the Church's representation of Christ's body, the priest led the altar boy to a cross where he forced the altar boy's hands up to it and began to nail the boy to it. In designing our performance, we discussed the ending extensively. We considered the power of the Catholic Church and the considerable power structure that lies within it as an organization. We ended with a confirmation of that power as a commentary on the lengths to which the organization will go to uphold the sanctity of its clergy. We considered the messages we received within the Catholic and Episcopal traditions during our respective childhoods about sin, and the wrath God would have upon sinners should we commit sin. The nailing of the altar boy to the cross was an indication of the stronghold of power that will not be contested.

After the priest nailed the altar boy to the cross, he begged for forgiveness. In the final scene of the performance, the priest stood in front of the crucified altar boy, holding his hands up to God, confessing to the embodied spirituality about which Goss writes as often rejected or admonished in Catholicism.[7] As the priest realized a sensual, spiritual connection with the altar boy and engaged in power-shifting play, the priest's awakened sexuality ruptured the binary of flesh/spirit. Goss critiques this binary, writing that in Catholicism "[t]he body must be denied; it must be disciplined, bound, and restricted. The body must be abused in the name of self-conquest and spiritual transcendence."[8] In our performance, the priest wrestled with this ascetic need to be divorced of bodily pleasure in order to maintain spiritual piety. When the priest recognized he could not rectify the physical sexuality, could not control his own body, he turned instead to controlling the body who tempted him— the altar boy. He crucified the altar boy in a final attempt to discipline and restrict the body, turning from self-conquest to conquest over temptation.

The crucifying of the altar boy serves as the ultimate distraction of the Catholic conditions that serve to exert sexual control over priests and parishioners. The assemblage of Catholic sexual control tangles queerness with the blame for pedophilic interactions between priests and male altar servers.[9] Prior to the leadership of Pope Francis,[10] in response to calls for the Church to do something in the wake of multiple accusations, the Church excommunicated some accused priests. However, by singularly implicating a priest, and acting quickly to address it, or in some cases, cover it up, the priest became a scapegoat instead of the Church holding the mirror up to itself as institution.

In the crucifixion depicted during our performance, the priest serves as a representation of the Church and the altar server as an embodiment of the trail of destruction blazed by Catholicism. The priest was able to forget the teen, and his role in their romantic exchange through this erasure of the teen's life, much in the same vein as the Church has evaded responsibility for colonizing cultures away and distancing itself from any wrongdoings that allowed sexual abuse by those whom it granted authority and power.

We performed this piece as an act of commentary, transgression, and, ultimately, protest against an institution that has systematically denied the rights of both women and LGBTQ+ folks, indicating the second-class citizenship with which it views both populations. In complicating this assemblage of sexual control through our performance, our bodies appearing in Church vestments stood in stark contrast to key power structures of the Catholic Church: both of us identify as queer women. As women, we have been denied participation in the leadership of the Church because of the mere fact of being born, in "God's Kingdom," as women. Our role, according to the messages put forward by the Churches of our youth, is to be subservient to men, to provide the stability of the homestead while remaining non-participatory in the world outside of the home.

It was through our drag performance that we entered into the sphere of power from which we have been traditionally excluded. In playing out a sensual relationship wherein a mutual desire for each other and love for Christ was implied, we defied the discriminatory rhetoric of the Church that speaks so loudly about the abhorrent nature of homo- or "deviant" sexuality. By playing with the administration and consumption of the Eucharist as a sensual act where power shifted between the priest and altar boy, we hoped to destabilize the sacredness and hierarchy behind the Eucharistic service. Further, we wanted to open questions about what the consumption of the metaphoric body of Christ does to the consumer. Is it through consumption of the Eucharist that we become more like Christ? Is it only if certain rules are followed?

. . .

POWER, RITUAL AND THE SACRED

POWER

The structure of the Catholic Church upholds hierarchies of power that rest largely on individuals' ability to be recognizable as devoted and committed to the rituals of Catholicism. Buried in this is the subordination of women to peripheral roles and the near disenfranchisement of non-binary people. Positions of power are limited to men who are legible as devotedly Catholic. Historically, Catholicism exercised its power with centuries of Catholic missionaries colonizing "Others" into a theology deemed intelligible.[11]

The intelligibility, or lack thereof, of women in the Church has been recently contested. In his op-ed in *The New York Times* about Pope Francis's April 2015 address regarding the inequities in wages between men and women, Frank Bruni signals the hypocrisy of this address at the Vatican, where less than 20% of the wage-earning positions held are occupied by women.[12] Furthermore, Bruni points to the paradox of the Pope's comments in relation to the limited power women may hold in the Catholic Church. He writes,

> Men but not women get to preside at Mass. Men but never women wear the cassock of a cardinal, the vestments of a pope. Male clergy are typically called "father," which connotes authority. Women in religious orders are usually called "sister," which doesn't.[13]

Bruni states what Catholic women have known for centuries—there is a time and a limited place for our presence; and that presence is never at the altar for more than fulfilling a subservient role.

The patriarchal powers that lead the Catholic Church operate as if they are exempt from the values they profess. One needs to look no further than the rampant cover-up and lack of reporting of sex abuse within the Catholic Church to begin to understand the exempt status of clergy and the power of the Church. While the Catholic Church eschewed discussions about the motivations of priests who sexually abused children, particularly young boys, it held the stance that gay people were sinners because of their attractions. These two things, pedophilia and queerness, are not mutually constitutive, though this deflection of the Church's responsibility and intent focus on denouncing homosexuality create a false equation between the two. Instead of turning a critical eye inward to examine the psychological conditions of the priesthood and what changes the institution could make to prevent further abuses, the Church covered up some accusations and excommunicated priests after other accusations rose to international notoriety.

Further, the Catholic Church turned its attention to nuns like Sister Margaret McBride who was excommunicated for permitting an abortion at a Catholic hospital for a patient deemed likely to die if she did not terminate the pregnancy.[14] This diversion of attention away from the abuses of power by multiple priests to nuns aiming to assist or play greater leadership roles, such as Sr. Tish Rawles who sought ordination to lead a congregation,[15] reinforced patriarchal power imbued in the Church.

Our decision to don drag in the roles of priest and altar boy was in direct response to the power exuded by the Catholic Church. We wanted to interact with symbols and beliefs that are often held beyond reproach and throw them into question. Our performance subverted the power structure of the Catholic Church thus claiming our theological power as queer women. This piece served as an act of commentary, transgression and, ultimately, protest against Catholicism. In assuming positions of power never extended to women, as seen in the Catholic priesthood,

and eroticizing it by exposing a sexually perverse history of Catholicism, we felt we challenged the institution's sanctioned violence through destabilizing the sanctity of the priesthood.

Further, we saw our performance as a disruption to the power structures within drag spaces. At our local drag show and in drag communities in general, there tends to be a focus on queening. Would *Ru Paul's Drag Race*, now entering its tenth season, be as successful if it were a show about drag kings, instead of drag queens? We suggest, though perhaps contentiously, that it would not be and that the obsessions with drag queens and femininity, at the expense of marginalizing drag kings, are extensions of patriarchy. Male-bodied individuals performing as drag queens are conceptualizing ideas of femininity through a male perspective often playing to expressions of femininity held in high regard by the male-gaze.[16] Further, even while portraying women, it is the male performers given the spotlight. Female-bodied drag kings at our local drag show often did not play a leading role and when they did perform, they often embodied problematic misogynistic expressions of masculinity.

The structure of drag shows can be compared to the structure of mass. In each performance, the audience and performers know their role and there is an expected script. Our performance interrupted both scripts—it was an unexpected take on Catholicism and unexpected performance at a drag show.

ACTS AND RITUAL

. . .

We assert that ritual acts as a form of control, which serves to naturalize some actions, fuels the persistence as a norm only as long as it remains as a "daily social ritual of bodily life [in a context]."[17] The weekly repetition of Sunday Mass is a process through which ritual becomes naturalized and the values rituals profess become reified. Through taking on these rituals as performers, we sought to take control of and challenge those narratives.

In her work on the repetitive acts of gender, Judith Butler posits gender as a series of acts that produces "a hallucinatory effect of naturalized gestures."[18] This effect of naturalized gestures, which she constitutes as a ritual through its perpetual occurrence, produces a process by which one believes these gestures are a product of an internal essence; in turn, one "manufacture[s] [this essence] through a sustained set of acts, posited through the gendered stylization of the body."[19] This manufacturing of a supposed essence is the performativity, or the "doing" of gender.

The repetitive rituals situated within Catholicism present a performativity of Catholicism. As each of these ritualistic acts repeats in each service, it becomes a codified understanding of what constitutes the doing of Catholicism. The continuity of these physical and rhetorical acts across varied contexts of Catholic Churches establishes an expectation of Catholicism. We will kneel, we will stand, we will sit, we will eat the metaphoric body of Christ and drink the metaphoric blood, we will pray for forgiveness.

Jackson and Mazzei discuss Butler's performativity as a destabilization of gender:

> Butler's theory of gender performativity works to unsettle the stabilizing gender categories that attempt to normalize and regulate people, and accentuates a process of *repetition* that produces gendered subjectivity. This repetition is not a performance *by* a subject, but a performativity that *constitutes* a subject and thus produces the space of conflicting subjectivities.[20]

As scholars wishing to disrupt the controlling constitution of our subjectivities by rituals that do not allow us access into space or roles wherein power for LGBTQ+ women is possible, we embarked on a process of repeating these rituals. In this repetition of rituals, we did not follow the common script of control situated within the priest, as seen with the altar boy administering Eucharist, the body of Christ, to the priest. However, the administration was immediately recognizable to the audience. To some degree, we followed the communion script, as the altar boy lifted the wafer in the air, asking for God's blessing, before giving it to the priest, who then made the sign of the cross.

We used this ritual to make in-roads to our audiences, understanding our subjectivity and further realizing how our performing of these rituals looked different from the normative actions that serve to regulate certain actions by certain people

in the context of Catholic mass. Through our performance, we aimed to highlight the performativity of acts considered conduits to the divine, using those ritualistic acts as a means to queer the space and construct a new narrative wherein queer bodies, too, can (and often do) lead these rituals. The performance, however, brings the body politic into these rituals, wherein the mortal body plays out divine love in a destabilizing manner.

By applying a "doing" lens to our performance, we sought to challenge the subjectivities constructed for women and queer folk by using the tools of Catholicism to chip away at them. With our audiences experiencing us as recognizable figures doing recognizable acts, we flipped the script on these acts, destabilizing the audience's expectations of ritual performances of Catholicism. These rituals are commonly the most sacred ways parishioners experience the Church.

THE SACRED

From clergy vestments and baptismal fonts with holy water to marriage ceremonies and the understanding of the Bible as sacred scripture, concepts of the sacred exist across Catholicism. For the sake of our discussion we are focused on three constructions of the sacred: ritual, space and roles. We use our performance and the acts of communion and confession to demonstrate the manifestation of these three aspects of the sacred. We suggest that deeming something as sacred gives it power and thus the way in which our performance "plays" with the sacred is an ultimate act of subversion of the power imbued by Catholic notions of ritual, space and roles.

COMMUNION: CONSUMING CHRIST

In Catholicism, the Eucharist is often referred to as "communion," signaling the point in mass at which mortal Catholic congregation members become one with the divine through the consumption of that which is representative of the body and blood of Christ. Yet the ability to become one with the divine hinges on the singular role of the priest. The table for the Holy Eucharist is prepared and presided over by the priest who is understood to have the authority to bless the bread and wine in preparation for the consumption by the congregation. When parishioners are invited to partake of the Eucharist they are invited only to edge of the altar, often marked with a communion rail, thus restricting full and direct access to the altar. Additionally, the Catholic Church practices closed communion, inviting only those who are in a "full state of grace" to partake. According to the 1983 Code of Canon Law, which is still in effect today,

> A person who is conscious of a grave sin is not to . . . receive the body of the Lord without prior sacramental confession unless a grave reason is present and there is no opportunity of confessing; in this case the person is to be mindful of the obligation to make an act of perfect contrition, including the intention of confessing as soon as possible.[21]

Since homosexual acts are deemed a "grave depravity"[22] by the Catholic Church, queer folks are left uninvited to the altar and into full communion with the divine.

Stuart writes,

> The Eucharist is many things caught up in one action. At its heart is the great mystical transposition of bread and wine into the body and blood of Christ through which the mystery of redemption is once again enacted, stretched through time and space.[23]

Stuart contends that in this mystical transposition is the de-sexing of Christ's body, enabling it to become consumed by other bodies, synthesizing from two bodies into one, thus erasing sex from embodiment. Stuart claims that "the unity of the flesh becomes in the Eucharist a union of humanity and embodied divinity."[24]

In our performance, the consuming of Christ's body became an exchange that re-inscribed sex into Christ's embodiment in the Eucharist. It was an act of power subversion, as the priest dropped to his knees, begging for the Eucharist from the altar server who claimed to be his "preacher, teacher," willing to do "anything [the altar server had] in mind." The priest completed the communion ritual by offering and serving the altar boy the cup of wine, a symbolic offering of the blood they share, that which runs through both of their bodies, uniting them in their divine love.

After the altar server drank from the cup held to his lips by the priest, the priest slowly ran his thumb over the altar server's bottom lip, dripping with the liquid representative of Christ's blood, an exchange of the fluid between them in celebration of mutual love of Christ and of desire for each other. In the performance, this distribution and consumption of the Eucharist sexualizes and disturbs this sacred ritual in a way that gives new meaning to scriptural reference associated with the Last Supper, "And when He had taken some bread and given thanks, He broke it and gave it to them, saying, This is *My body which is given for you* [emp. ours]; do this in remembrance of Me."[25] In a way that made some uncomfortable, we used the Eucharist ritual to challenge the audience to think critically about bodies, gender, sexuality and spirituality. We sought to put on full display the assemblage of Catholic sexual control, wherein queerness and pedophilia become mutually constitutive for the sake of upholding the sanctity of both heteronormativity and celibacy.

CONFESSION

. . .

In our performance, we incorporated confession not as is traditionally expected—between parishioner and priest. Rather, we showed the confession as occurring between the priest and God. The priest, having wrestled with a sensual encounter through an exchange of Eucharist with the altar boy, crucifies the altar boy. In this, the audience witnesses the priest's confession of flaws as he is unable to maintain the piousness expected of his role.

Sara Ahmed writes that

> we can try and persuade ourselves that we do not want something by converting a happy object into an unhappy one, by removing that object from our field of preferences, by associating it with the unhappiness we anticipate it might cause.[26]

In the crucifixion of his desire-object, the priest satiated his desires through the eradication of his desire object, anticipating the consequences of allowing the desire to manifest further.

The priest, however, does not seem to confess directly to God, rather he turns to the crucified altar boy, falls on his knees, and prays for forgiveness, appearing as if he is confessing to the altar boy, the subject of his desire and of his apparent sin. Goss writes, "Body-deficit spiritualities manifest body loathing and provide a horizon for the hatred of bodies and the need to control bodies."[27] The altar boy becomes the embodiment of the priest's sin and lack of control; the priest crucifies the altar boy as a way of controlling bodies. His denial of his sexuality turns quickly to the need to eradicate the body that tempts him as a means of maintaining his ascetic celibacy and quashing the source of his confession. The priest's recognition and following attempt to deny the sexual and the erotic demonstrates Isherwood's point that the erotic is an ingredient of human condition and cannot be removed from any way of life including the celibate.[28]

...Confession produces a sort of knowledge-power by one being vulnerable with a priest, and receiving absolution from the priest acquiring that knowledge-power. The act of confession stands in stark contrast to the strategic silence much of the leadership, particularly that prior to the inauguration of Pope Francis, employed in the wake of multiple sexual abuse accusations by former altar servers; the Church, instead of seeking the confession of its abusive priests, resorted to conceal the truth to maintain its power.[29]

In the height of allegations of priests sexually abusing youth, the Catholic Church moved priests from parish to parish and when one was found guilty of the charge, the priest was dismissed without discussion. The Church maintained silence as a means of upholding the hegemonic discourses of celibacy and piousness. In our performance, we interrupt the desired silence, producing a narrative that shows this queer and manipulative interaction wherein power is not entirely located within the priest and the manifestation of that shifting power results in the drastic act of crucifying, something not far from the psychological damage done to those youth whose lives were altered by the abuse by their trusted priests in spaces deemed sacred conduits to God.

...

A THEOLOGY OF PERFORMANCE

Based on our experiences, we posit the potential of a theology of performance. Queer bodies in the Church operate within a framework of transgression. We move through the world, no matter how successfully the Church attempts to heteronorm us, peripherally, occupying and creating "the margins of imprecision and mismatches"[30] within the norms of a hetero- and gender-normative world. Whether or not we want to, we disrupt the "heterosexual matrix"[31] through our mere existence. Our experiences in this world require us to construct alternate meanings to those situated in a hetero- and gender-normative lens.

Simultaneously, queer bodies perform every day for survival. We read the cues of the hetero- and gender-normative worlds and determine to what extent we must perform those worlds' rituals in order to maintain physical, mental and emotional safety. We know performance well, as it often determines how we move through various spaces and contexts. Our performances determine to what extent we are able to "pass" in communities where our queerness is not wanted; we pay close attention to how hetero- and cisgender subjects are constituted[32] through the repeated acts and performances we, as queer bodies, must decide to either ignore or engage. Queer bodies consistently perform queerness in various ways, sometimes in accordance with mainstream norms and often in ways that destabilize the sanctity of those norms.

In suggesting a theology of performance, we look to what it offers as a theological compass for those of us for whom the performativity of hetero- and cis-normative Christianity, particularly Catholicism, does not compute. In the use of performance, variation is possible. Play is abundant. Performance generates possibility, in which both performer and audience member can suspend disbelief by imagining the narrative as a constructed reality, at least for the time the performance takes place. Performance, like other art forms, does not have a singular meaning; it allows for a theology that does not provide distinct answers.

In particular, performance spaces have historically served as sites of possibility and belonging for scores of LGBTQ+ individuals. From musicals to drag to performance art, performance spaces have, arguably, provided queer and trans* folks a home where play is valued, where narratives are able to be constructed and adapted instead of delivered dogmatically. In many of these performance spaces, LGBTQ+ performers jostle the normative constructions of gender, executing some seamlessly, while taking liberties to queer others. Performance spaces provide an outlet for expression, potentially providing emotional survival for LGBTQ+ folks. By pushing against and pulling on the rules of performativity, those which construct subjects, LGBTQ+ performers use performance as a way to break old molds of expected performance, opening up space to imagine new possibilities.

In thinking of a theology of performance, we focus on how performance operates in imagining the new. This is critical to queer theology, an arm of theology that seeks to "[see] things in a different light and [reclaim] voices and sources that previously ha[ve] been ignored, silenced, or discarded."[33] Through a theology of performance, LGBTQ+ folks are able to enter into the spaces and roles to which they have been denied access, transgressing the dogmatic principles dominating particular Christian denominations like Catholicism. This opens up space for queer bodies to re-engage in the theological discussions out of which they were once left. Performance theology brings art to theology. In the consumption of art, the consumer is left to draw conclusions on one's own, to make meaning of the piece for one's own understanding of a historical event, the intensity of a color, or the artist's intention. Like art, performance theology allows for multiple interpretations by both actor/performer and consumer/audience member. In this way, it aligns well with queer theology in that it acts transgressive, breaking down and obscuring boundaries and rules previously constructed through dogma.

Performance theology is distinctively different than the use of performance and evangelism. Performance theology is at its core a manifestation of transgression. Similar to other transgressive art forms, performance theology can cause discomfort in the ways it challenges and rewrites narratives that disrupt religious and social mores. In our performance we intentionally disrupted the dominant crucifixion narrative which almost always ends with celebrating the resurrection and subsequent ascension. By ending the performance with the crucifixion, we left the answers to theological questions about sin, forgiveness and the afterlife in the audience's minds. Our performance also posed the following questions: whose bodies are allowed to play a powerful role in Catholicism? How has ritual performance perpetuated the colonization of the mind/spirit and how can it be used to undo that same colonization? As well as, what constitutes a sacred space, and in what spaces is spirituality allowed to be explored? The emotions and critical inquiry that performance theology has the capacity to evoke allows theology to be a fully embodied experience which engages the body, mind and spirit.

In our previous section on acts/rituals, we emphasized how ritual becomes central to theology. Ritual, or the "doing of," serves as the residue of theology; those rituals become the tangible acts that become representative of their respective theological foundations. Where I (Allyson) may associate making the sign of the cross over my torso as how to begin prayer in Catholicism, this same act is a non-act in my mother's Lutheran Church. By thinking about ritual as the tangible performance of theology, we understand then how theology relies on ritual as reification.

Cheng writes about the use of drag in his discussion of queer theology. He writes,

> Drag is a parody in that it is a performance of a gendered role, but with the "critical difference" of disrupting societal norms about gender identities. These parodies dissolve categories because they attempt to replicate the thing to be parodied, but the copy is ultimately transformed into a new creation.[34]

It is in the use of parodic performance of theological traditions that new understandings can surface. The "new creation" of which Cheng speaks reveals how rituals may produce new meanings to rituals once deemed exclusionary of queer folks. In de-stabilizing those rituals through the performance of them *as performance*, those same rituals may be created as new possibilities for disruption, or for engagement.

A theology of performance provides a liberating framework with which to entertain and engage collaborative possibilities. In thinking of an audience, or perhaps a congregation, as the fourth wall, we can then think of the construction of the performance as a collaboration. Theology as performance is a theology of collaboration, of variation. Each performance produces new understandings, due in part to the perception and interactivity with the fourth wall. What happens when the wall breaks, when, in the middle of performance, a loud sigh reverberates and causes others in the audience to see or hear something not previously considered, simply because the sigh did not exist in previous iterations of the performance? The iterability of performance produces nuance. Nuance disrupts the dogmatic, emphasizing context as constantly shifting, calling for a fluidity of constructions and understanding. Dogma cannot hold a candle to nuance, as nuance will never stay still. A theology of performance satiates the unquenchable desire for theological progress. It brings theology out of the institutions and into the lived, embodied experiences of those seeking the divine outside the religious houses from which they were once evicted.

NOTES

1. Butler, *Undoing Gender*, 218.
2. Ibid.
3. Althaus-Reid, *Indecent Theology*.
4. Hurdle, "Philadelphia Priests Accused."
5. Donohue, "Homosexuality and Sexual Abuse."
6. Althaus-Reid and Isherwood, "Thinking Theology and Queer Theory," 308.
7. Ibid., 15.
8. Ibid., 11.
9. Donohue, "Catholic Church's Issue is Homosexuality, not Pedophilia."
10. San Martin, "Pope Calls Sexual Abuse Scandals a Grave Problem."
11. Butler, *Undoing Gender*, 30.
12. Bruni, "Catholicism Undervalues Women."
13. Ibid.
14. Hagerty, "Nun Excommunicated for Allowing Abortion."
15. Elliott, "Excommunicated Nun to Celebrate First Public Liturgy as a Woman Priest."
16. 17. Butler, *Undoing Gender*, 48.
18. Butler, *Gender Trouble*, xv.
19. Ibid.
20.-21. Code of Canon Law, cic. 916.

22. *Catechism of the Catholic Church*, 2357–9, accessed March 3, 2017, http://ccc.usccb.org/flipbooks/catechism/index.html.
23. Stuart, "The Priest at the Altar," 129.
24. Ibid.
25. Luke 29:19, New American Standard Bible.
26. Ahmed, *Willful Subjects*, 80.
27. Goss, *Queering Christ*, 13.
28. Isherwood, *The Power of Erotic Celibacy*.
29. Goldstein, "Sex Abuse and the Catholic Church."
30. Althaus-Reid, *Indecent Theology*, 64.
31. Althaus-Reid and Isherwood, "Thinking Theology and Queer Theory," 307.
32. Jackson and Mazzei, "Thinking Through Theory," 8.
33. Cheng, *Radical Love*, 6.
34. Ibid., 52.

BIBLIOGRAPHY

Ahmed, Sara. *Queer Phenomenology*. Durham, NC: Duke University Press, 2006.

Ahmed, Sara. *Willful Subjects*. Durham, NC: Duke University Press, 2014.

Althaus-Reid, Marcella. *Indecent Theology: Theological Perversions in Sex, Gender and Politics*. London: Routledge, 2000.

Althaus-Reid, Marcella, and Lisa Isherwood. "Thinking Theology and Queer Theory." *Feminist Theology* 15, no. 3 (2007): 302–314.

Bruni, Frank. "Catholicism Undervalues Women." *The New York Times*, May 6, 2015. http://www.nytimes.com/2015/05/06/opinion/frank-bruni-catholicism-undervalues-women.html?smprod=nytcore-iphone&smid=nytcore-iphone-share&_r=0.

Butler, Judith. *Gender Trouble: Feminism and the Subversion of Identity*. London: Routledge, 1990.

Butler, Judith. *Undoing Gender*. New York: Routledge, 2004.

Catechism of the Catholic Church. 2nd ed. Accessed March 3, 2017. http://ccc.usccb.org/flipbooks/catechism/index.html.

Cheng, Patrick. *Radical Love: An Introduction to Queer Theology*. New York: Seabury Books, 2011.

Code of Canon Law: Latin-English Edition. Washington, DC: Canon Law Society of America, 1983.

Donohue, Bill. "Catholic Church's Issue is Homosexuality, Not Pedophila." *On Faith*. Accessed March 9, 2017. https://www.onfaith.co/onfaith/2010/07/22/catholic-churchs-issue-is-homosexuality-not-pedophilia/6536.

Donohue, Bill. "Homsexuality and Sexual Abuse." *Catholic League*. Accessed March 3, 2017. http://www.catholicleague.org/homosexuality-and-sexual-abuse/.

Elliott, Elizabeth A. "Excommunicated Nun to Celebrate First Public Liturgy as a Woman Priest." *National Catholic Reporter*. Kansas City, MO, November 12, 2015.

Goldstein, Laurie. "Sex Abuse and the Catholic Church: Why Is It Still a Story?" *The New York Times*, April 20, 2016.

Goss, Robert E. *Queering Christ: Beyond Jesus ACTED UP*. Cleveland, OH: Pilgrim Press, 2002.

Hagerty, Barbara Bradley. "Nun Excommunicated for Allowing Abortion." *National Public Radio*, May 19, 2010. http://www.npr.org/templates/story/story.php?storyId=126985072.

Isherwood, Lisa. *The Power of Erotic Celibacy: Queering Hertopatriarchy*. New York: T&T Clark, 2006.

Jackson, Alecia Y. and Lisa A. Mazzei. *Thinking with Theory in Qualitative Research*. New York: Routledge, 2012.

San Martin, Ines. "Pope Calls Sexual Abuse Scandals a Grave Problem." *Crux: Talking Catholic Politics*, March 13, 2015. https://cruxnow.com/church/2015/03/13/pope-francis-calls-sexual-abuse-scandals-a-grave-problem/.

Stuart, Elizabeth. "The Priest at the Altar: The Eucharistic Erasure of Sex." In *Trans/Formations*, edited by Marcella Althaus-Reid and Lisa Isherwood, 127–138. London: SCM Press, 2008.

CHAPTER 13

ACTIVISM, CHANGE, AND FEMINIST FUTURES

THE PROMISE OF FEMINIST EDUCATION

In Chapter 1 we discussed the goals of women's and gender studies as a discipline. These objectives include, first, an understanding of the social construction of gender: the ways gendered personhood is mapped on to physical bodies; and second, the analysis of intersections of gender with other systems of inequality, including the effects of imperialism and globalization. These objectives encouraged you to question "woman" as an essentialized category and to think about the ways polarized and binary woman/man dichotomies imagine these categories as exclusively "natural" ones. But we also hope that you recognize woman as a social category organizing the practices and performances of gender and producing material and practical outcomes, such as work expected and performed, which inevitably results in certain outcomes within social hierarchies. In this sense "woman," a social category made up of both cisgender and trans individuals, exists at the same moment that the category is being destabilized by queer theory and trans perspectives. As a result, the third objective was to promote a familiarity with the status of marginalized social groups, including "women," and to consider individual and collective actions for change to improve the status and conditions of their/our lives.

A fourth and final objective of women's and gender studies is that you will start thinking about patterns of privilege and discrimination in your own life and understand your position vis-à-vis systems of inequality. We hope you will learn to think critically about how societal institutions affect individual lives—especially your own. We hope you will gain new insights and confidence and that new knowledge will empower you. Perhaps this knowledge will encourage you to get angry, as Laurie Penny, the author of the reading "Most Women You Know Are Angry," encourages you to do. Penny points out that women have a lot to be angry about and that recognizing it is empowering and using it as a political tool for change can be liberating. She also encourages us to think about anger as a product of larger social landscapes such as systemic racism and sexism rather than solely a personal response to injustice.

Feminist educators attempt to give students more inclusive and socially-just forms of knowledge and to support teachers using their power in non-exploitive ways. Women's and gender studies usually involves nonhierarchical, egalitarian classrooms where teachers respect students and hope to learn from them as well as teach them. The focus is on the importance of the student voice and experience and the encouragement for personal and social change. This is certainly the goal of Yvette Alex-Assensoh in the reading, "What's Love Got to Do With It?" Love here is imagined as transforming our college campuses into places where "I" does not rule at the expense of "We," and where love can promote inclusive environments and foster respectful and civil dialogue that mends the moral fabric of campus life, which Alex-Assensoh suggests is increasingly frayed. This kind of love guiding interactions between university administration, faculty, students, and staff might be especially useful for negotiating dialogue between parties divided and ideologically askance. For example, a good number of women's and gender studies classes occur within colleges and universities that do not necessarily share the same goals and objectives as the feminist classroom. Many feminist educators operate within the social and economic constraints of educational institutions that view "counter-hegemonic" education—that is, education that challenges the status quo—as problematic and/or subversive. Despite these constraints, feminist education, with its progressive and transformative possibilities, is an important feature on most campuses that can contribute to the dialogue to make this space more inclusive and diverse.

For many students, and perhaps for you too, the term feminism is still problematic. Many people object to the political biases associated with feminist education and believe knowledge should be objective and devoid of political values. It is important to emphasize that all knowledge is associated with power, as knowledge arises from communities with certain positions, resources, and understandings of the world. This means that all knowledge (and not just feminist knowledge) is ideological in that it is always associated with history and politics. To declare an unbiased objectivity or value neutrality is to ignore or mask the workings of power that are present in all forms of knowledge. Although feminist education is more explicit than other forms of knowledge in speaking of its relationship to power in society, this does not mean it is more biased or ideological than other forms of knowledge. It is important to note that some knowledge's claim to being objective, unbiased, and value neutral (these words essentially imply the same thing) is related to the claim to a scientific "truth." Feminist knowledge emphasizes that science is a human product and therefore hardly unbiased or value free either: All truth claims are relative and must be understood in the context of history, culture, and politics. This means that all knowledge, whether feminist or not, is "political."

ACTIVISM

We live in a complex time and some would say a very dangerous time with democracy under attack and the norms shaping civility and political discourse degrading rapidly. Many believe there is increasing prosperity in the United States, even though the gap between the rich and the poor is among the largest in industrialized nations and is increasing. In terms of our income inequality, as already discussed in other chapters, the top 10 percent average more than nine times as much income as the bottom 90 percent, and those in the

"Fighting supervillians is a cinch—fighting misogyny is the real challenge."

very top 1 percent average over 40 times more income than the bottom 90 percent. If we go even further and compare the nation's top 0.1 percent with everyone else, we find that their income is over 198 times the income of the bottom 90 percent. Indeed, U.S. Census data show more than 20 million people live in extreme poverty, and about one in five children goes to bed hungry. And despite the widespread belief that the United States remains a more mobile society than some others (meaning people can move out of poverty or move into more wealth), economists show that the typical child starting out in poverty here has less chance at prosperity than one in continental Europe or Canada. The United States and the United Kingdom stand out as the least mobile among postindustrial societies. Having a job also does not necessarily lift people out of poverty, and it is well known that U.S. workers tend to work eight or nine weeks more a year than their European counterparts.

Still, it is true that some groups in the United States have made significant progress over past decades and are integrated into most societal institutions. Others, however—and especially women of color and other marginalized social groups—lag behind the gains made by whites, although of course this latter group is stratified by social class and other intersecting identities. Whites may have race privilege, but they may not have class privilege or those associated with gender conformity, sexual identity, or ability, to name a few. In this way, an equitable sharing of power and resources in terms of gender, race, class, and other differences has not actualized. Indeed, in terms of bodies and behavior, those whose differences identify them as outside normative expectations are exposed to stigma and discrimination. They also endure both interpersonal violence (such as harassment and assault) and structural violence (such as poverty and homelessness) at increasing levels.

Wars and conflicts rage across the world, and many are suffering the displacements of militarism and economic globalization. Violence is rampant in all walks of life, and the balance of power in the world seems fragile. If this wasn't bad enough, global climate change is affecting all communities, human and nonhuman alike. Global capitalism, which has allowed the privileged to lead lives of relative security, has deleterious consequences on humanity in many regions of the world. These are the issues around which individual and collective feminist activism, both in the United States and worldwide, coalesce. The reading by Teresa Velásquez, "Mestiza Women's Anti-Mining Activism in Andean Ecuador," provides one template for intentional social action against injustice. These "defensora": women who defend lands and watersheds from state and multinational corporate mining projects use speech and "refusals" to portray the complexities of speaking and silence that they use to challenge gender, race, and class inequities.

As Audre Lorde, one of the most eloquent writers of the feminist second wave, once declared, "Silence will not protect you." Lorde wrote about the need to be part of social change efforts, and she encouraged us to speak out and address the problems in our lives and communities. Similarly, the reading by Byron Hurt, "Feminist Men," implores men to speak out and address inequities and learn how to be an ally to people who are different and who do not enjoy the privileges they enjoy. Hurt explains why black men should be embracing the "f" word (feminism) and emphasizes the necessity of men joining with women to make this world better for everyone. In this sense, coalitions are a central aspect of social change efforts.

And finally, the reading by Lucas Platero and Esther Ortega-Arjonilla, "Building Coalitions: The Interconnections Between Feminism and Trans* Activism in Spain," makes the case for just that, but within the discipline of women, gender, and feminist studies. They write about the shift in Spanish feminism toward integrating trans perspectives that pose important questions about feminism and prostitution, and transgender issues. They discuss the ways their research disrupts the oppositional nature of many of these debates and seeks instead negotiation and collaboration.

As these examples suggest, the strength of feminist justice-based movements involves their multi-issue and multi-strategic approaches. *Multi-issue* means organizing on many fronts over a variety of different issues that include political, legal, and judicial changes, educational reform, welfare rights, elimination of violence, workplace reform, and reproductive issues. Basically all of the issues in this text are components of a multi-issue approach to feminism. Key issues addressed by feminism that you might be dealing with include access to affordable higher education and preparation for work and professional careers. As you already know, currently women are earning more than half of all bachelor's degrees, and their presence is changing the face of many professions. Another key issue often mentioned as being at the forefront of students' minds is finding ways to balance work and family at a time when people increasingly want to combine a career and parenting. Access to affordable child care and equitable sharing of domestic responsibilities are also high priorities for families as are affordable health care and reproductive justice. We must speak out about injustice and help pave the way for a better world. Whether people consider themselves feminists or not is less important than personal and collective action

HOW TO LEARN THE MODERN ART OF PROTEST

INSTRUCTIONS

1. Focus on your target audience. Convincing people who already support you is a waste of time. Trying to change those diametrically opposed to you is pointless. Figure out who hasn't made up their mind yet but could be swayed to your side. Their support can help you get what you want.

2. Come up with an attention grabbing idea. PETA always gets on the news because they do outrageous things like having naked women go out in public to protest fur coats. The modern art of protest is all about media friendly events. Anything you decide to do should stop traffic. Otherwise the media won't care.

3. Organize your supporters. Gather together others who believe as you do. Enlist them to help you in your protest. Email, Facebook, Twitter, chat rooms, and phone trees can all help you recruit followers.

4. Schedule your protest for the greatest impact. If your protest takes place on a busy news day it is less likely to be covered by the media. Late mornings and early afternoons on weekends tend to be the slowest time for news. Consider scheduling your protest then. If your protest would make a great live shot on the TV news then do it during the local morning news from 5 a.m. to 7 a.m. or afternoon broadcasts from 4 p.m. to 7 p.m.

5. Advertise your intentions. Write out a media release and be sure every media outlet in town gets it. Send both email and regular mail copies to everyone. Follow up with phone calls the day before the protest. The media release should be straightforward and simple. State your intentions and details of who, what, where and when. Contact people and their phone numbers should be prominent in the media release.

6. Be media friendly. During your event have designated people looking for reporters. Approach them and ask if they need any elements for their story. Provide easy access to people to interview, video opportunities and information. Have a focused message. Do not try to tell them everything. Keep your argument simple and straightforward.

7. Follow up. Watch the news and read the newspaper to see how much buzz you created. Put pressure on those whom you are protesting and let them know you will do it again if your demands are not met. If you make progress approach the media with a story about your results. If little changed protest again. This time top yourself and come up with something even more memorable.

TIPS AND WARNINGS

- Be careful not to protest in the same way too often. The media will get bored quickly and ignore you. Be creative and choose your protests wisely.
- Understand the consequences of breaking the law during your protest. It is always best to obey the law, but historically some protesters have achieved change by being conscientious objectors. If you are planning to get arrested be sure you understand what will happen to you as a result of your arrest.

Source: Kent Ninomiya, eHow.com.

for change. "How to Learn the Modern Art of Protest," above, gives you some ideas about collective action that can be used to address these issues.

Sometimes feminist change requires collaborative multi-strategic activism. *Multi-strategic* means relying on working coalitions that mobilize around certain shared issues and involve different strategies toward a shared goal. Although human rights frameworks encourage coalitions to apply human rights standards associated with justice and human dignity to individual and community problems, they also promote a broad array of activist strategies from voting and policy changes—such as the inclusion of LGBTQ issues in nondiscrimination statements in higher education—to art and music. As reading by Li Maizi, "I Went to Jail for Handing Out Feminist Stickers in China," also emphasizes, women's rights are human rights. This author along with four colleagues was held for 37 days in a detention center in China after feminist activism that included handing out pamphlets on the Beijing subway about sexual harassment. A strong international response facilitated their release.

WHAT A DRAG! GENDER, PERFORMANCE, AND GENDERED PERFORMANCES

Gabrielle Boyle

When we think of performances, many of us may first think of performances on theater stages or big screens; but, in fact, we are *performing* all the time. We *perform* our gender and sexuality through our gender expression. How we dress and how we behave are all part of our gender expression and performance. Our understanding of how we *should* perform are influenced by dominant understandings of gender and sexuality.

How are you performing your gender today? What gendered objects do you have on you right now? How are these objects communicating your gender identity? Think about what section of the clothing store you shop in. Have you ever wanted to wear or use something that was made for a different gender? What would that mean if you wore or used that object? Would that change your gender identity?

What happens when performances of gender are produced on a theater stage or a big screen? Drag performances have traditionally taken tropes from the gender binary of normative white U.S. society and have amplified these tropes and trends for the stage (Taylor

and Rupp 2006). For example, the beauty norm for women in dominant U.S. society calls for small waists and big breasts. These beauty norms are established and enforced through the white, male-dominated beauty industries. So deeply ingrained in society, these norms and expectations often go unchallenged. Drag performances strive to bring attention to these norms by fashioning exaggerated representations of these norms for the stage.

While drag performances are specifically made for the stage, these constructed and performed critiques serve to challenge the ways we are expected to perform our genders and sexualities offstage. Drag shows are performances of activism that hold a mirror up to society.

Activity: Do a quick online search on drag performances. What messages about gender are the performers trying to make? What messages are these performances trying to send about race? About class? About beauty? Do these performances disrupt hegemonic gender or reinforce it?

Reference

Taylor, Verta, and Rupp, Leila J. (2006). "Learning from Drag Queens." *Contexts*, 5(3), 12–17.

LEARNING ACTIVITY

FEMINIST.COM

Visit the website www.feminist.com and follow the link to the activism page. There you'll find links to action alerts and legislative updates for a number of feminist organizations, including the National Organization for Women (NOW), Code Pink, Feminist Majority, the League of Women Voters, the White House Project, and Planned Parenthood. Follow these links to learn what actions you can take. Find links to articles, speeches, and other websites on feminist.com's resource page, and, for feminist spins on current events, check out the site's news page.

As discussed in Chapter 1, some liberal or reformist activists have worked within the system and advocated change from within. Their approach locates the source of inequality in barriers to inclusion and advancement, and they have worked to change women's working lives through comparable worth, sexual harassment policy, and parenting leaves. Legal attacks on abortion rights have been deflected by the work of liberal feminists working within the courts, and affirmative action and other civil rights legislation have similarly been the focus of scholars, activists, and politicians working in the public sphere. These organizations tend to be hierarchical with a centralized governing structure (president, advisory board, officers, and so forth) and local chapters around the country. Other strategies for change take a radical approach (for example, radical or cultural feminism) and attempt to transform the system rather than to adapt the existing system. Together these various

CONTEMPORARY SOCIAL JUSTICE PROTEST MOVEMENTS: BLACK LIVES MATTER

Rebecca Lambert

The Black Lives Matter movement started in 2013 in response to the acquittal of George Zimmerman, who shot and killed Trayvon Martin in Florida. Starting with the hashtag #BlackLivesMatter, Alicia Garza, Patrisse Cullors, and Opal Tometi built a political movement that centers black people and resists systemic oppression directed at black lives. The movement has grown and has chapters in cities across the country and across the world.

The BLM movement addresses a long history of violence against black bodies, especially state-sanctioned violence. This contemporary civil rights movement addresses the many police killings of unarmed black men, boys, and women. Natasha McKenna, Trayvon Martin, Eric Garner, Sandra Bland, Philando Castille, Michael Brown, Walter Scott, Yvette Smith, and Tamir Rice are all victims of police brutality. In highlighting this violence, Black Lives Matter shifts the focus from individuals to systemic oppression and highlights the violence and policing that the black community deals with on a daily basis (Taylor 2016).

Visit the movement's website, at https://blacklivesmatter.com. Hover over the "About" button, and follow the link to discover what they believe and how they structure their work. What strategies do they use for action? How does this movement use intersectionality to organize and why is this important?

References

Taylor, K. Y. (2016). *From# BlackLivesMatter to Black Liberation*. Chicago: Haymarket Books.

Funke, Daniel, and Susan, Tina. (2016, July 12). "From Ferguson to Baton Rouge: Deaths of Black Men and Women at the Hands of Police." *Los Angeles Times*. http://www.latimes.com/nation/la-na-police-deaths-20160707-snap-htmlstory.html

strategies work to advocate justice-based forms of equality. Contemporary feminism (both self-identified third-wave activism and others) uses both liberal and radical strategies to address problems and promote change.

Although differences in strategy are sometimes a source of divisiveness among activists and feminists, they are also a source of strength in being able to work on multiple issues from multiple approaches. Indeed, any given issue lends itself to both reformist and radical approaches. LGBTQ rights, for example, are something that can be tackled in the courts and in the voting booths as organizations work toward legislation to create domestic partner rights or community civil protections. At the same time, consciousness-raising activities and grassroots demonstrations, such as candlelight vigils for victims of hate crimes and Queer Pride parades, work on the local level. Together, different strategies improve the quality of life. This is what is meant by multi-strategic.

One important aspect to consider is that simply increasing the participation and leadership of marginalized people does not necessarily imply a more egalitarian or feminist future. As you know, there are individuals who are members of target groups in society who are still opposed to strategies for improving the general well-being of disenfranchised peoples. Changing the personnel—replacing people with those of other and different identities, for instance—does not necessarily secure a different kind of future. Although in practice liberal feminism is more sophisticated than, for example, simply considering female leaders merely because they are women, it has been criticized for promoting women into positions of power and authority irrespective of their stance on the social relations of gender, race, class, and other differences. Still, the encouragement of marginalized people into leadership positions is a central aspect of feminist change.

PIPELINES AND PROTESTS ON NATIVE LANDS

Luhui Whitebear

Pipelines have left many marks on native lands. In addition to the "man camps" and ensuing violence discussed in the resource extraction impacts section, pipelines—and the construction of them—disrupt native lands in very specific ways. First, it is important to know that treaties are described in the U.S. Constitution as the supreme law of the land. Therefore, the lands governed by sovereign tribal nations are supposed to be protected through treaties. However, due to historic Supreme Court cases ("the Marshall Trilogy"), the final say of what happens on native lands is up to the federal government rather than the tribal government. As a result, the needs and decisions of the tribes are not always upheld and protests ensue.

In recent years there has been much more media coverage on pipelines and protests on native lands, most notably with the Dakota Access Pipeline and the NoDAPL movement. One reason there was support for the NoDAPL movement was because of the ways in which it exposed environmental racism. The pipeline was deemed safe yet was diverted downstream from Bismarck, the largest city in North Dakota, to an area that threatened the drinking water of the Standing Rock Sioux Tribe (Worland 2016). The pipeline construction also crossed documented sacred sites and burial sites. Between the safety risk, the disregard for treaty rights, and the disregard for these sites, the NoDAPL movement quickly became the largest indigenous-led protest in recent history.

Similar to the NoDAPL movement, the Idle No More movement rose out of Canada in response to the construction of pipelines on native lands. Idle No More is credited to First Nations women who used the power of song and body to stand up against the oil companies destroying their ancestral homelands (Thomas-Muller 2014, 251). Among the biggest pipelines in Canada is the Keystone XL, which transports crude oil from the tar sands in Alberta, Canada. The environmental impact of the tar sands is monumental. During the Obama administration, an international protest of the Keystone XL occurred to prevent the pipeline from moving through native lands both in the United States and Canada. This resulted in the halting of the continued construction of the pipeline. However, one of the first moves of the Trump administration was to approve the construction of the Keystone XL pipeline and the Dakota Access Pipeline simultaneously. While the construction of the Dakota Access Pipeline was completed and the Keystone XL is under construction, the movements to stop them sparked further action with other pipelines on native lands. Oil and liquid natural gas pipelines continue to be protested across these lands many times with indigenous leadership at the forefront.

Activity Idea

Freewrite or engage in a small discussion on what you have heard about pipelines and oil spills. What types of impact on the environment and people have you heard about? What do you think can be done to help mitigate these types of conflicts in the future? What role, if any, do you see protests playing? Be sure to stay mindful of the rights of sovereign tribal nations.

For More Information

https://www.nodaplarchive.com/
http://www.idlenomore.ca/
https://www.theatlantic.com/photo/2014/09/the-alberta-tar-sands/100820/
https://academic.udayton.edu/race/02rights/native11.htm

References

Thomas-Muller, C. (2014). "The Rise of Native Rights–Based Strategic Framework: Our Last Best Hope to Save Our Water, Air, and Earth." In T. Black, S. D'Arcy, T. Weis, and J. K. Russell, *A Line in the Tar Sands: Struggles for Environmental Justice* (pp. 240–252). Toronto: Between the Lines.
Worland, J. (2016, October 28). "What to Know About the Dakota Access Pipeline Protests." *Time.* http://time.com/4548566/dakota-access-pipeline-standing-rock-sioux/

Contemporary U.S. feminism is concerned with issues that are increasingly global, inevitable in the context of a global economy and militarism worldwide. These concerns have resulted in the sponsorship of numerous international conferences and have promoted education about women's issues all over the world. And, as communication technologies have advanced, the difficulties of global organization have lessened. Transnational feminist groups have worked against militarism, global capitalism, and racism, as well as supported issues identified by immigrants and indigenous peoples around the world. This activism was demonstrated nearly 25 years ago in 1995 with the United Nations Fourth World Conference on Women held in Beijing, China. (The first conference was held in Mexico City in 1975, the second in Copenhagen in 1980, and the third in Nairobi in 1985.) More than 30,000 women attended the Beijing conference and helped create the internationally endorsed Platform for Action. This platform was a call for concrete action involving human rights of women and girls as part of universal human rights, the eradication of poverty of women, the removal of obstacles to women's full participation in public life and decision making, the elimination of all forms of violence against women, the assurance of women's access to educational and health services, and actions to promote women's economic autonomy. Since the Beijing conference, conventions under the leadership of the United Nations Commission on the Status of Women (CSW) continue to provide "progress reports" and re-formalize the platform in light of global changes since the conference. As of this writing, the most recent 62nd session of CSW took place March 2018 in New York, with a priority theme focusing on the challenges and opportunities in achieving gender equality and the empowerment of rural women and girls; participation in and access of women to media and communication technologies; and broadening the impact and use of communication technologies as an instrument for the advancement and empowerment of women and girls worldwide. Activism continues for U.S. ratification of the Convention on the Elimination of All Forms of Discrimination Against Women (CEDAW) and for other struggles to improve women's lives worldwide. There are currently 99 signatories and 188 state parties to CEDAW. The United States is the only signatory that has not yet ratified the Convention.

With these efforts in mind, certainly there is hope and much to celebrate, but the big picture is far from rosy and society has not transformed its core values in ways feminists throughout the world had hoped during the last century. The picture is thus one of simultaneous optimism and despair. Perhaps we can address the rage, cynicism, and often mean-spiritedness of this historical moment and come up with a transformational politics that encourages a consciousness shift and extends generosity and compassion toward others. Any movement for justice-based equity must have a strong moral foundation based on love, human dignity, and community.

IDEAS FOR ACTIVISM

- Organize an activism awareness educational event on your campus. Invite local activists to speak about their activism. Provide opportunities for students to volunteer for a wide variety of projects in your area.
- Find out about your school's recycling program. If there's not one in place, advocate with administrators to begin one. If there is one, try to find ways to help it function more effectively and to encourage more participation in recycling. If recycling services are not provided in your local community, advocate with city and county officials to begin providing these services.

- Find out what the major environmental issues are in your state and what legislative steps need to be taken to address these concerns. Then organize a letter-writing campaign to encourage legislators to enact laws protecting the environment.
- Identify a major polluter in your community and organize a nonviolent protest outside that business demanding environmental reforms.
- Sponsor a workshop on conflict management and nonviolence for campus and community members.

MATH CAMP FOR GIRLS

Emerald Stacy

To minimize the gender gap within science, technology, engineering, and mathematics (STEM) fields, concerned adults have founded dozens of after-school and summer programs dedicated to fostering a love of mathematics in girls. Here are a few examples of such programs.

> **After-school program:** Girls Excelling in Math and Science (GEMS) began in 1994 as an after-school program for fifth and sixth grade girls. Over the last 20 years, GEMS has expanded to hundreds of clubs around the United States, now reaching girls from preschool through middle school. All of the materials needed to begin your own club are provided by GEMS at no charge. http://www.gemsclub.org/
>
> **Math and dance:** In 2012, an MIT student launched SHINE, an after-school and summer intensive program for middle school girls that combines math and dance. In addition to helping girls build math skills through dance, SHINE trains high school and college women to be mentors in the program. There are currently programs established in seven states. All programs are free. http://www.shineforgirls.org/#home
>
> **Summer day camp:** Launched in the Seattle area in 2012, Girls Rock Math offers a series of summer camps to support going into STEAM[1]

[1] STEM +Art

fields. Although students must identify as a girl to participate, they need not be assigned female at birth. The curriculum used aligns with state and national standards, but goes further by focusing on problem solving skills, games, and art. Partial and full scholarships are available. http://www.girlsrockmathematics.com/

> **Summer residential camp:** The University of Nebraska–Lincoln offers a summer program, All Girls/All Math. This residential camp is for high school girls who have taken geometry, but not yet taken calculus. Throughout the week, students are exposed to various mathematical topics, with the freedom to develop their own mathematical style and preference. The cost varies from $175 to $500 per week, based on need and Nebraska residency. http://www.math.unl.edu/programs/agam/

Activity: Your Mathematics Autobiography

- Throughout your time in school, have there been times when you have felt good at math? What were those classrooms and teachers like?
- Have you seen, performed, or been on the receiving end of microaggressions in a math class?
- Which of your identities have helped you succeed in math classrooms? Which have not?
- How do you see yourself as a math student? How do others see you as a math student?
- Based on your experiences, how do you imagine we could close the gender gap in math?

FUTURE VISIONS

How might the future look? How will our knowledge of gender-, race-, and class-based in-equalities be used? Does our future hold the promise of prosperity and peace or economic unrest and increased militarization? Will technology save us or hasten our destruction? Will feminist values be a part of future social transformation? Future visions are meta-phors for the present; we anticipate the future in light of how we make sense of the present and have come to understand the past. This approach encourages us to look at the present mindfully, so that we are aware of its politics, and creatively, so that we can see the possi-bility for change. In her playful poem "Warning," Jenny Joseph looks to the future to offer some guidance in the present.

There are some social trends that have implications for the future. Given the higher fertility rates among the nonwhite population as well as immigration figures, whites in the United States will eventually become a relatively smaller percentage of the popula-tion until they are no longer a majority, and the proportion of mixed-race individuals will increase. Latinx are the largest growing group, estimated to increase from the current 18 percent of the U.S. population to more than 20 percent by 2025. In addition, the rise in births between 1946 and 1960 (the baby boomer cohort) and the decline through the 1970s means a large percentage of the population will be older than 65 years within the next couple of decades. Census reports suggest that by 2030 there will be about 70 million older persons (65 years and older): more than twice their number in 2000 and reaching approximately 20 percent of the population. Currently, persons 65 years and older repre-sent about 15 percent of the population. And, although some people have always lived to be 80, 90, and 100 years old, the number of aged will grow in response to better nutrition and health care among certain segments of the population. As the baby boomers age, they will create stress on medical and social systems. They might also influence family systems as several generations of aged family members could require care at the same time. This is complicated by the fact that families are becoming smaller, women are marrying later if at all, and many women are the primary breadwinners and raising children alone. Ties between stepfamilies and other non-familial or "chosen family" ties are most likely going to become more important in terms of care and support.

In our society, where the profit motive runs much of our everyday lives, where many citizens have lost respect for political and governmental institutions and are working longer hours and may feel disconnected from families and communities, the issue of integrity is something to consider. The definition of integrity has two parts: one, it is a moral position-ing about the distinction between right and wrong, and two, it is a consistent stance on this morality such that we act out what we believe and attempt to live our ideals. "Do as I say and not as I do" is an example of the very opposite of integrity. What might it mean to live with feminist-inspired integrity as well as envision a future where feminist integrity is central? We understand that this notion of feminist integrity is rather a nebulous concept and invite you to consider what it might mean for your life. We'll discuss seven implications here.

First, it is important to set feminist priorities and keep them. In a society where sound bites and multiple, fragmented pieces of information vie to be legitimate sources of

ACTIVIST PROFILE

MALALA YOUSAFZAI

At 17, Malala Yousafzai became the youngest person ever to win the Nobel Peace Prize. As a child, Malala defied the Taliban in Pakistan, demanding the right for girls to receive an education. A Taliban gunman shot her in the head in 2012, when she was only 15 years old. Malala survived and found herself with a global platform to advocate for girls' education.

Malala's father was an educator, and she attended a school he had founded. In 2007, the Taliban took control of the area of Pakistan where Malala lived and banned girls from attending school. Soon the Taliban began to attack girls' schools, and in 2008 Malala gave a speech titled "How Dare the Taliban Take Away My Basic Right to Education?" In 2009, she started blogging anonymously for the BBC about her struggles for an education, although her identity was soon revealed. For her work, she received Pakistan's National Youth Peace Prize in 2011 and was nominated for the International Children's Peace Prize.

The Taliban issued a death threat against her. Still she went to school and spoke out. She was shot on a bus on the way home from school. First she was taken to a military hospital in Peshawar and then to another hospital in the United Kingdom. Following multiple surgeries, she was able to finish her studies in Britain. And while the Taliban maintained its death threat, world support for Malala opened up greater opportunities for her to continue her advocacy. Malala writes, "It was then I knew I had a choice: I could live a quiet life or I could make the most of this new life I had been given. I determined to continue my fight until every girl could go to school. With my father, who has always been my ally and inspiration, I established Malala Fund, a charity dedicated to giving every girl an opportunity to achieve a future she chooses" (https://malala.org/malalas-story/).

On her 16th birthday, she gave a speech at the United Nations encouraging world leaders to support policies that ensured girls' education and women's

rights. She also advocated for urgently needed action against illiteracy, poverty, and terrorism.

In 2013, she was awarded the Sakharov Prize for Freedom of Thought by the European Parliament. In 2013, she was awarded the Nobel Peace Prize.

Malala has continued to work for girls and women around the world. In 2015, she opened a school for refugee girls from Syria supported by the Malala Fund. In 2018, she returned to Pakistan for the first time since being shot. She still travels the world speaking out on behalf of vulnerable girls and advocates with world leaders for change.

knowledge and facts get recast as "fake news," we must recognize that some things are more important than others. Priorities are essential. Postmodernism might have deconstructed notions of truth to the point where some argue that there is no such thing as the truth; yet some things are truer than others. Figure out your truths and priorities based on your own values and politics. Decide where to put your energy, and figure out which battles are worth fighting. This also means developing personal resilience to weather the

PRINCIPLES OF ENVIRONMENTAL JUSTICE

1. Environmental justice affirms the sacredness of Mother Earth, ecological unity and the interdependence of all species, and the right to be free from ecological destruction.
2. Environmental justice demands that public policy be based on mutual respect and justice for all peoples, free from any form of discrimination or bias.
3. Environmental justice mandates the right to ethical, balanced, and responsible uses of land and renewable resources in the interest of a sustainable planet for humans and other living things.
4. Environmental justice calls for universal protection from nuclear testing, extraction, production and disposal of toxic/hazardous wastes and poisons that threaten the fundamental right to clean air, land, water, and food.
5. Environmental justice affirms the fundamental right to political, economic, cultural, and environmental self-determination of all peoples.
6. Environmental justice demands the cessation of the production of all toxins, hazardous wastes, and radioactive materials, and that all past and current producers be held strictly accountable to the people for detoxification and containment at the point of production.
7. Environmental justice demands the right to participate as equal partners at every level of decision making, including needs assessment, planning, implementation, enforcement, and evaluation.
8. Environmental justice affirms the right of all workers to a safe and healthy work environment, without being forced to choose between an unsafe livelihood and unemployment. It also affirms the right of those who work at home to be free from environmental hazards.
9. Environmental justice protects the right of victims of environmental injustice to receive full compensation and reparations for damages as well as quality health care.
10. Environmental justice considers governmental acts of environmental injustice a violation of international law, the Universal Declaration on Human Rights, and the United Nations Convention on Genocide.
11. Environmental justice must recognize a special legal and natural relationship of Native Peoples to the U.S. government through treaties, agreements, compacts and covenants affirming sovereignty and self-determination.
12. Environmental justice affirms the need for urban and rural ecological policies to clean up and rebuild our cities and rural areas in balance with nature, honoring the cultural integrity of all our communities, and providing fair access for all to the full range of resources.
13. Environmental justice calls for the strict enforcement of principles of informed consent and a halt to the testing of experimental reproductive and medical procedures and vaccinations on people of color.
14. Environmental justice opposes the destructive operations of multinational corporations.
15. Environmental justice opposes military occupation; repression and exploitation of lands, peoples and cultures, and other life forms.
16. Environmental justice calls for the education of present and future generations that emphasizes social and environmental issues, based on experience and an appreciation of our diverse cultural perspectives.
17. Environmental justice requires that we, as individuals, make personal and consumer choices to consume as little of Mother Earth's resources and to produce as little waste as possible; and make the conscious decision to challenge and reprioritize our lifestyles to ensure the health of the natural world for present and future generations.

Source: People of Color Environmental Leadership Summit, 1991. www.umich.edurjrazerlnrelwhatis.html.

ups and downs (and, for some, the deeper trauma) of our lives. Survivors act not only from self-interest, but also in the interest of others. Having a relaxed awareness and the confidence that it brings allows us to prioritize and use our energy for things that really matter. Refusing to be controlled by improper laws or social standards, yet choosing to abide by them for the sake of others and with an eye to changing these structures, is what Bernie Siegel in *Love, Medicine and Miracles* calls "cooperative nonconformity."

WOMEN WORKING FOR PEACE

The International Peace Bureau (IPB) is the world's oldest and most comprehensive international peace federation. Founded in 1892, the organization won the Nobel Peace Prize in 1910. Its role is to support peace and disarmament initiatives. Current priorities include the abolition of nuclear weapons, conflict prevention and resolution, human rights, and women and peace. To learn more about the IPB, visit the website at www.ipb.org.

The Women's International League for Peace and Freedom (WILPF), founded in 1915 to protest the war in Europe, suggests ways to end war and to prevent war in the future; as well, it seeks to educate and mobilize women for action. The goals of the WILPF are political solutions to international conflicts, disarmament, promotion of women to full and equal participation in all society's activities, economic and social justice within and among states, elimination of racism and all forms of discrimination and exploitation, respect of fundamental human rights, and the right to development in a sustainable environment. For more information, including action alerts and readings, visit the WILPF homepage at www.wilpf org.

Second, it is important that we live in and envision a society that balances personal freedom and identity with public and collective responsibility. Transformational politics call for living with communal values that teach how to honor the needs of the individual as well as the group. The United States is a culture that values individualism very highly and often forgets that although the Constitution says you have the right to do something, we also have the right to criticize you for it. Similarly, we might question the limitations associated with certain rights. Is your right still a right if it violates our rights or hurts a community? And just because the Constitution says something is your right, that does not

FEMALE NOBEL PEACE LAUREATES

Sixteen women have been honored with the Nobel Peace Prize for their work for justice:

Baroness Bertha Von Suttner (1905): Austrian honored for her writing and work opposing war.

Jane Addams (1931): International president, Women's International League for Peace and Freedom.

Emily Greene Balch (1946): Honored for her pacifism and work for peace through a variety of organizations.

Betty Williams and Mairead Corrigan (1976): Founders of the Northern Ireland Peace Movement to build peace by bringing together Protestants and Catholics.

Mother Teresa (1979): Honored for her "work in bringing help to suffering humanity" and her respect for individual human dignity.

Alva Myrdal (1982): Honored with Alfonso Garcia Robles for their work with the United Nations on disarmament.

Aung San Suu Kyi (1991): Burmese human rights activist honored for nonviolent work for independence in Myanmar.

Rigoberta Menchu Tum (1992): Honored for her work for "ethno-cultural reconciliation based on respect for the rights of indigenous peoples."

Jody Williams (1997): Honored for her work with the International Campaign to Ban Landmines.

Shirin Ebadi (2003): Honored for her efforts to promote democracy and human rights.

Wangari Maathai (2004): Honored for her contribution to sustainable development, democracy, and peace.

Ellen Johnson Sirleaf, Leymah Gbowee, and Tawakkol Karman (2011): Honored for their nonviolent struggle for the safety of women and for women's rights to full participation in peace-building work.

Malala Yousafzai (2014): Honored for her struggle against the suppression of children and young people and for the right of all children to education.

Source: http://www.nobelprize.org/nobel_prizes/peace/laureates/.

necessarily make that act a moral choice. Just because we can do something doesn't mean we have to do it. Although the Constitution exists to protect choices and rights, it does not tell us which choices and rights are best.

Third, recognize that corporate capitalism does not function in everybody's interests. In this sense, economic freedom must not be confused with economic democracy. Because we can choose between 20 different kinds of breakfast cereal does not mean we have economic or political democracy where we actually all can afford to buy the cereal or live in neighborhoods where there actually are 20 different kinds of cereal available. Many of us have learned that capitalist societies are synonymous with democracies and that other economic systems are somehow undemocratic in principle. We live in a society that attempts a political democracy at the same time that economic democracy, or financial equity for all peoples, is limited. Unfortunately, capitalism has had negative effects on both physical and human environments, works hand in hand with imperialism and militarism, and has exacerbated global inequality. Poverty is probably the most serious social problem in the United States and worldwide. Starvation and hunger are often a result of inequity and politics, not a shortage of food. Consumerism has changed families and communities by encouraging people to accumulate material possessions beyond their immediate needs. Perhaps a motto for the future might be "pack lightly."

Fourth, to live in the present and the future with a core value of feminist integrity, we must understand the limitations of technology as well as its liberating aspects. The future vision must be one of sustainability: finding ways to live in the present so that we do not eliminate options for the future. It is important to balance economic, environmental, and community needs in ways that do not jeopardize sustainability. This means being in control of technology so that it is used ethically and productively, an issue that is related to the previous point about capitalist expansion. Corporations have invested heavily in new technologies that do not always work for the collective good. Certainly the recent oil spills—with their poignant consequences for human and nonhuman communities—is a case in point, as is the problem of global climate change and water shortages that are caused by industrialization and global capitalist expansion.

You might also wonder about the development of the Internet and virtual realities and the effects of these new ways of communication and entertainment on children and families. Do you think smart phones are actually making us smarter or not? How are these technologies affecting our relationships and everyday lives? How reliant are we on cell phones, and how is the way we live with our phones changing our brains as well as our social relationships? These are important questions that defy clear answers. Still, the questions are worth posing.

Closely related to understanding the limits of technology is our *fifth* notion of feminist integrity: the need to advocate a sustainable physical environment. There is only one world, and we share it; there is an interdependence of all species. Given this, it makes no sense to destroy our home through behaviors that bring about global climate change, environmental pollution, and species eradication. A source of clean and sustainable energy to replace reliance on oil and other fossil fuels is imperative at this moment. Sustainable environmental practices start with addressing issues associated with capitalist global expansion and technological development,

THE ENVIRONMENTAL JUSTICE MOVEMENT

Janet Lockhart

Seeing the (Really) Big Picture

> Every single part of the Earth reacts with every other part. It's one thing. . . . [Seeing the planet from above] makes you realize that, and makes you want to be a little more proactive in keeping it that way. If I could get every Earthling to do one circle of the Earth, I think things would run a little differently.
>
> —Karen Nyberg, International Space Station astronaut, on seeing Earth from orbit (Drake 2018, 74)

This astronaut's sentiment is one foundational principle of the environmental justice movement: the understanding that all of Earth's systems and species, including human beings, are interconnected and interdependent. Environmental activists highlight these connections, and hope that by doing so governments, militaries, corporations, and individuals change their behaviors to protect this complex but fragile web.

The other crucial principle of environmental justice is the *inclusion and empowerment of all people* in the process of deciding which natural resources will be developed and how, overseeing the implementation of these decisions, ensuring equal access to the use of resources, and protecting all people from the results of unhealthy development of resources in the past. It is vital to include the people most often living or working near environmental hazards such as garbage and toxic waste dumps, sources of air pollution, scarce or poisoned water, and depleted soil: these are mostly people of lower socioeconomic status (disproportionately people of color and females).

The environmental justice movement arose directly out people's experiences of responding to this "environmental racism." Government entities such as the Environmental Protection Agency were not always seen as allies in this movement. Even nonprofit advocacy groups such as the Natural Resources Defense Council acknowledge that they did not work directly with affected communities at first: They didn't see the "big picture" (Skelton and Miller 2016).

The environmental justice movement began in the United States, but is now global. Many events contributed to the movement. One important example (1982) involved the residents of Warren County, North Carolina, marching and taking legal action to challenge the proposed location of a toxic waste dump in their county (Skelton and Miller 2016). Even though the waste eventually was situated there, the actions taken by the people of the county shone a light on the nature of environmental racism and helped propel the environmental justice movement forward.

Activists start by *educating* people about the connections between environmental issues and factors such as race, gender, and socioeconomic status. What other actions are needed to bring about change? Environmental justice activism may include lobbying for state- and federal-level legislation, litigating, passing new environmental regulations, crafting international agreements, boycotting corporate offenders, taking grassroots actions, making individual conservation efforts, voting for change, and collaborating with affected groups.

Expand Your View

Check out the environmental justice groups on *The Green Spotlight* (http://www.thegreenspotlight.com/2017/07/environmental-justice-groups/). Scan the diverse list of groups and explore the website of one that appeals to you. Check that site's list of suggested activities and choose an individual or group action to take.

References

Drake, N. (2018, March). "They Saw Earth from Space. Here's How It Changed Them." *National Geographic.* https://www.nationalgeographic.com/magazine/2018/03/astronauts-space-earth-perspective/

Landman, Miriam. (2017, July 20). "Environmental Justice Groups & Multicultural Green Groups." *The Green Spotlight* [Blog]. http://www.thegreenspotlight.com/2017/07/environmental-justice-groups/

Skelton, R., and Miller, V. (2016, March 17). "The Environmental Justice Movement." National Resource Defense Council. https://www.nrdc.org/stories/environmental-justice-movement

as discussed previously. Is it possible to own the rivers and other natural resources of the land? What does it mean to turn precious resources into commodities, and what might be the consequences? Could we imagine such resources as sustainable communal property held in trust to be used in equitable ways by future generations? If this were possible, might we see air pollution, for example, as a violation of community property rights? Many young people are now making the case that environmental destruction is a violation of the Constitution and their right for future liberty and happiness. Central here is the need for environmental justice because the poor and communities of color have suffered disproportionately in terms of environmental pollution and degradation. As already discussed, environmental justice calls for protection from nuclear testing and extraction, production, and disposal of toxic and hazardous wastes and poisons that threaten the fundamental right to clean air, land, water, and food. It also demands that workers have the right to safe and healthy work environments without being forced to choose between unsafe livelihood and unemployment.

Sixth, a peaceful and sustainable future is one that respects human dignity, celebrates difference and diversity, and yet recognizes that diversity does not necessarily involve equality. It is not enough to be tolerant of the differences among us, although that would be a good start; it is necessary to recognize everyone's right to a piece of the pie and work toward equality of outcome and not just equality of access. Justice means that all individuals have the right to make their own way in the world. Celebrate the differences among us and recognize that thriving involves love, patience, and faith. We believe we must create social movements that derive from an ethic of caring, empathy, and compassion for all people.

Seventh and finally, we believe it is important to have a sense of humor and to take the time to play and celebrate. As socialist labor reformer Emma Goldman once said, "If I can't dance, it's not my revolution!" Often feminists are accused of having no sense of humor—but you know at this point that this is a false accusation!

A justice-based politics of integrity embraces equality for all peoples. It is an ethic with the potential to help create a peaceful and sustainable future, improving the quality of our lives and the future of our planet. An ethic that respects and values all forms of life and seeks ways to distribute resources equitably is one that moves away from dominance and uses peaceful solutions to environmental, societal, and global problems. As a blueprint for the future, a focus on justice and equality has much to offer. The struggle has begun and there is no end in sight!

THE BLOG

LOVE AS A RADICAL POLITICAL ACT

Susan M. Shaw (2017)

We progressives are facing difficult days as we watch the dismal failings of the Trump administration and the hateful machinations of Republicans on Capitol Hill. Authentic dialogue seems impossible when "alternative facts" and outright lies characterize most of the rhetoric we hear from Trump, Republican leaders, and the right-wing media, all of which is parroted by many Trump supporters.

The temptation to return insult for insult and injury for injury is enormous.

But if we are to offer an alternative vision to the insular nationalism and greed that characterize this administration, we cannot become what we abhor. Rather, we must engage in love as a political act that refuses the current moment's framing of us vs them and its attendant willingness to dehumanize and delegitimize those with whom we disagree.

Love is one of those words that is subject to a wide variety of interpretations—from the sentimentalized Hollywood version of romantic love to religion's highly abstract love of God that supposedly encompasses us all but rarely leads us to love one another in authentic ways.

I'm talking of love as a radical political tool, an act of resistance to the dividing and subordinating forces of bigotry, inequality, and oppression. In this instance, love is not simply a personal, individualistic act, but rather it is social force that calls for change through the creation of belonging, empowerment, and right relationships and institutional structures.

Feminist theorist bell hooks calls what I'm describing a "love ethic" (*All About Love: New Visions*. New York: William Morrow, 2000). She explains that a love ethic leads our choices to work with others, give all of ourselves to our relationships, and embrace "a global vision wherein we see our lives and our fate as intimately connected to those of everyone else on the planet." This means, she says, we consciously choose a different set of values to guide our living. In this way, she notes, love is not merely a feeling but is a practice—it is a way we choose to act. Awakening to this kind of love, she argues, "can happen only as we let go of our obsession with power and domination."

Love as a guiding ethic makes possible the transformation we seek—love is what motivates us to call for racial and gender justice; it is what drives our demands for inclusion, equity, accessibility, opportunity, and welcome. And our refusal to reject loving action, even in the face of insult, lies, and mistreatment must be what sets us apart from the current moment's tribalism, rage, and hatred.

Love must become our organizing principle on the Left. It must be our end and our means, lest we simply replicate the structures of power, hierarchy, divisiveness, exclusion, and dehumanization we see with such clarity in the current climate.

We must engage in unconditional, undeterred, radical love as a political act to challenge the forces of domination and exclusion that surround us. An ethic of love offers us alternative ways of being in the world and responding to the current political situation. It means we do not ignore current conflicts; nor does it mean we accept the status quo without challenge. It also means we do not respond in kind to those with whom we disagree. It means we choose a different way, a way that honors the humanity of all, even those whose views and actions we find repugnant, but it also means we choose to act, to resist the current administration's life-depleting rhetoric and policy and to offer alternative, life-affirming solutions to the pressing problems of our planet.

I cannot choose what the Trump administration does or what Trump supporters do. But I can choose what I do and who I want to be, and I do not have to allow those choices to be controlled by the chaos and anger emanating from this regime. I can choose not to become what I oppose. I can choose to love, politically, radically, in the face of opposition and even violence.

bell hooks says that fear keeps us from this kind of love. She says cultures of domination rely on fear to ensure our obedience and divide us from one another. She writes, "Fear is the primary force upholding structures of domination. It promotes the desire for separation, the desire not to be known . . . When we choose to love we choose to move against fear—against alienation and separation."

We progressives must choose to love. We must love one another, and we must love those against whom we struggle for justice. They are not the enemy. They are afraid. hooks quotes from the first epistle of John in the Christian Testament: "There is no fear in love; but perfect love casts out fear." Radical love overcomes fear, our own, and that of others.

We must have the courage to love radically and honestly, letting our love become the force that disrupts and subverts power and dominance and creates new possibilities for life, peace, and community.

---

86. FEMINIST MEN
BYRON HURT (2011)

Feminism: The word turns off a lot of men (insert snarky comment about man-hating feminazis here) and women. But here's why black men should be embracing the "f" word.

When I was a little boy, my mother and father used to argue a lot. Some mornings, I would wake up to the alarming sound of my parents arguing loudly. The disagreement would continue until my father would yell with finality, "That is it! I'm not talking about this anymore!" The dispute would end right there. My mother never got the last word.

My dad's yelling made me shrink in fear; I wanted to do something to make him stop raging against my mother. In those moments, I felt powerless because I was too small to confront my father. I learned early that he had an unfair advantage because of his gender. His size, strength and power intimidated my mother. I never saw my father hit her, but I did witness how injurious his verbal jabs could be when they landed on my mom's psyche.

My father didn't always mistreat my mother, but when he did, I identified with her pain, not his bullying. When he hurt her, he hurt me, too. My mother and I had a special bond. She was funny, smart, loving and beautiful. She was a great listener who made me feel special and important. And whenever the going got tough, she was my rock and my foundation. One morning, after my father yelled at my mom during an argument, she and I stood in the bathroom together, alone, getting ready for the day ahead of us. The tension in the house was as thick as a cloud of dark smoke. I could tell that my mother was upset. "I love you, Ma, but I just wish that you had a little more spunk when you argue with Daddy," I said, low enough so my father couldn't hear me. She looked at me, rubbed my back and forced a smile.

I so badly wanted my mother to stand up for herself. I didn't understand why she had to submit to him whenever they fought. Who was he to lay down the law in the household? What made him so special?

I grew to resent my father's dominance in the household, even though I loved him as dearly as I loved my mother. His anger and intimidation shut down my mother, sister and me from freely expressing our opinions whenever they didn't sit well with his own. Something about the inequity in their relationship felt unjust to me, but at that young age, I couldn't articulate why.

One day, as we sat at the kitchen table after another of their many spats, my mother told me, "Byron, don't ever treat a woman the way your father treats me." I wish I had listened to her advice. As I grew older and got into my own relationships with girls and women, I sometimes behaved as I saw my father behave. I, too, became defensive and verbally abusive whenever the girl or woman I was dating criticized or challenged me. I would belittle my girlfriends by scrutinizing their weight or their choices in clothes. In one particular college relationship, I often used my physical size to intimidate my petite girlfriend, standing over her and yelling to get my point across during arguments.

I had internalized what I had seen in my home and was slowly becoming what I had disdained as a young boy. Although my mother attempted to teach me better, I, like a lot of boys and men, felt entitled to mistreat the female gender when it benefited me to do so.

After graduating from college, I needed a job. I learned about a new outreach program that was set to launch. It was called the Mentors in Violence Prevention Project. As a student-athlete, I had done community outreach, and the MVP Project seemed like a good gig until I got a real job in my field: journalism.

Founded by Jackson Katz, the MVP Project was designed to use the status of athletes to make gender violence socially unacceptable. When I met with Katz, I didn't realize that the project was a domestic violence prevention program. Had I known that, I wouldn't have gone in for the job interview.

So when Katz explained that they were looking to hire a man to help institutionalize curricula about preventing gender violence at high schools and colleges around the country, I almost walked out the door. But during my interview, Katz asked me an interesting question. "Byron, how does African American men's violence against African-American women uplift the African-American community?"

No one had ever asked me that question before. As an African-American man who was deeply concerned about race issues, I had never given much thought about how emotional abuse, battering, sexual assault, street harassment and rape could affect an entire community, just as racism does.

The following day, I attended a workshop about preventing gender violence, facilitated by Katz. There, he posed a question to all of the men in the room: "Men, what things do you do to protect yourself from being raped or sexually assaulted?"

Not one man, including myself, could quickly answer the question. Finally, one man raised his hand and said, "Nothing." Then Katz asked the women, "What things do you do to protect yourself from being raped or sexually assaulted?" Nearly all of the women in the room raised their hand. One by one, each woman testified:

"I don't make eye contact with men when I walk down the street," said one.

"I don't put my drink down at parties," said another.

"I use the buddy system when I go to parties." "I cross the street when I see a group of guys walking in my direction."

"I use my keys as a potential weapon."

"I carry mace or pepper spray."

"I watch what I wear."

The women went on for several minutes, until their side of the blackboard was completely filled with responses. The men's side of the blackboard was blank. I was stunned. I had never heard a group of women say these things before. I thought about all of the women in my life-including my mother, sister and girlfriend-and realized that I had a lot to learn about gender.

Days after that workshop, Katz offered me the job as a mentor-training specialist, and I accepted his offer. Although I didn't know much about gender issues from an academic standpoint, I quickly learned on the j ob. I read books and essays by bell hooks, Patricia Hill Collins, Angela Davis and other feminist writers.

Like most guys, I had bought into the stereotype that all feminists were white, lesbian, unattractive male bashers who hated all men. But after reading the work of these black feminists, I realized that this was far from the truth. After digging into their work, I came to really respect the intelligence, courage and honesty of these women.

Feminists did not hate men. In fact, they loved men. But just as my father had silenced my mother during their arguments to avoid hearing her gripes, men silenced feminists by belittling them in order to dodge hearing the truth about who we are.

I learned that feminists offered an important critique about a male-dominated society that routinely, and globally, treated women like second-class citizens. They spoke the truth, and even though I was a man, their truth spoke to me. Through feminism, I developed a language that helped me better articulate things that I had experienced growing up as a male.

Feminist writings about patriarchy, racism, capitalism and structural sexism resonated with me because I had witnessed firsthand the kind of male dominance they challenged. I saw it as a child in my home and perpetuated it as an adult. Their analysis of male culture and male behavior helped me put my father's patriarchy into a much larger social context, and also helped me understand myself better.

I decided that I loved feminists and embraced feminism. Not only does feminism give woman a voice, but it also clears the way for men to free themselves from the stranglehold of traditional masculinity. When we hurt the women in our lives, we hurt ourselves, and we hurt our community, too.

As I became an adult, my father's behavior toward my mother changed. As he aged he mellowed, and stopped being so argumentative and verbally abusive. My mother grew to assert herself more whenever they disagreed.

It shocked me to hear her get in the last word as my father listened without getting angry. That was quite a reversal. Neither of them would consider themselves to be feminists, but I believe they both learned over time how to be fuller individuals who treated each other with mutual respect. By the time my father died from cancer in 2007, he was proudly sporting the baseball cap around town that I had given him that read, "End Violence Against Women." Who says men can't be feminists?

87. I WENT TO JAIL FOR HANDING OUT FEMINIST STICKERS IN CHINA
LI MAIZI (2017)

I often think of the day I was detained in Beijing. On the night of 6 March 2015, the police knocked on my door and took me to the station, where I was questioned nonstop for 24 hours. Later I was sent to a detention centre, where I was held for 37 days.

I was not alone. Four other female activists were also arrested. Though we had planned to hand out stickers on the Beijing subway to raise awareness about sexual harassment, we hadn't expected our actions to attract the attention of the Public Security Bureau.

Fellow Chinese feminists quickly responded to our detention: they bravely took to the streets with our pictures in the hope of showing the public that we were in danger. Thanks to their efforts, Free the Five became an international campaign. While communist China has officially always promoted gender equality, this incident reveals a different story.

Two years later, is there any hope for the Chinese feminist movement? Definitely, yes. Since my arrest, there has been both progress and a backlash against women's rights. On the one hand, the first legislation against domestic violence was passed in December 2015, an event of huge significance. Women who have been beaten by their husbands or partners now have the law on their side.

On the other hand, state surveillance of NGOs and feminist activists is increasing, and those who have tried to hold the government to account on human rights abuses have faced crackdowns.

An example of how progress and backlash can co-exist is what happened after a well-publicised allegation of sexual abuse. When a young girl called Xiao Zhu in Jiangxi province revealed on Xinlang Weibo—a social media platform often compared to Twitter—that she had been sexually assaulted by her father for four years there was an outpouring of sympathy and outrage. Two women's rights groups, Women Awakening Network and Yuanzhong Gender Development Centre, gave her legal support.

Local government officials found the attention from activists intolerable and, in less than a week, control of the case was taken over by the local branch of the Communist Youth League. The father faces up to three years in prison if found guilty, but the priority of the authorities is not justice for victims but social stability.

However, despite the pushback against grassroots organisations, and thanks to women's issues becoming more prominent on social media, women are becoming more active in the fight against gender discrimination. When I was released from detention, I faced a tough decision: should I continue my activism, or give up? I chose to continue. What I do is for the rights of women all over the world. But I can't help but be especially concerned about China. My own experiences, and the experiences of my friends in China, have had a profound effect on me.

Feminism is facing a backlash all over the world. In the US abortion rights are threatened. In Russia, some forms of domestic violence have been decriminalised. In Turkey, the murder of transgender activist Hande Kader shows that hate crime against marginalised communities is rife.

On International Women's Day, it is important to remember the struggles of all women. Women all over the world expressed solidarity with the Stanford University sexual assault survivor, posting photos and spreading the hashtag #Solidarity4StanfordSurvivor when she read her brave victim impact statement in court last year. When Irish activist and China scholar Séagh Kehoe told me about the campaign to repeal the Eighth Amendment to the Irish constitution—which equates the life of the "unborn child" with that of the mother, seriously restricting access to abortion across Ireland—I offered my support.

Because of China's two-child policy, abortions are readily available. If you get pregnant with a third child, abortion is compulsory. But I don't see our free access to abortion as a sign of progress, as reproductive rights only apply to married women. If you are unmarried, it is illegal to give birth and you will face heavy fines. Some NGOs are calling on the government to grant single women their reproductive rights.

In the era of the one-child policy, the reproductive rights of single women were denied as a means of controlling population growth. But now, even as propaganda encourages straight couples to reproduce, the state continues to discriminate against single women.

Until recently, single Chinese women over 27 were described as "leftover women". In 2007, the All-China Women's Federation (ACWF), the government body dealing with women's issues, called on women to marry as soon as possible. This year, however, the ACWF's newspaper China Women's News urged the media to stop referring to women as the leftover, a remarkable shift that I believe can be credited to feminist activism.

For activists such as me, it is difficult to work out where the boundaries are. Last month the Weibo account Feminist Voices was suspended for 30 days, because posts in support of the international women's strike and opposition to Donald Trump were said to have broken the law. Our first reaction was to make a big noise so the authorities would feel our rage about this censorship.

The Beijing government continues to push back the boundaries of acceptable resistance to the point where there is little room left, but at least women's issues are being discussed. That's why there is hope for feminism in China.

88. MESTIZA WOMEN'S ANTI-MINING ACTIVISM IN ANDEAN ECUADOR

TERESA A. VELÁSQUEZ (2017)

REPRESENTATIONAL SOVEREIGNTY 1: MAKING OF THE *DEFENSORA*

In 2001, the Ecuadorian Congress approved a neoliberal law to develop industrial mineral extraction that spurred conflicts across the country between (and at times, among) villagers, multinational mining companies, and the state. The rural parishes of Victoria del Portete and Tarqui, located in Ecuador's southern Andean region, began organizing around 2005, when lucrative gold and silver deposits were identified in the communal watershed that provide more than 1500 families with drinking and irrigation water. Farmers living downstream supply regional and local markets with thousands of liters of milk a day. Concerned that the proposed gold mine would adversely affect water supplies, they mobilized several community water boards against the Toronto-based IAMGOLD Corporation to stop the construction of the mine.

Mining conflicts reconfigured the fabric of community relations and kin networks in Victoria del Portete and Tarqui in various ways. First, mining became central in the reorganization of social alliances in the parish, pulling once friendly kin and neighbors into opposing camps while creating the possibilities for unprecedented cross-class and ethnic solidarities, similar to coalitions that emerged in Bolivia water and gas 'wars' (See Albro 2005; Postero 2007). IAMGOLD's offer for jobs and community development initiatives persuaded some rural residents, including the parish governing council, to align themselves with the company to receive moderate material benefits through their participation in corporate social responsibility programs. My collaborators described how disputes over community support for mining was played out in daily life with routine confrontations in the dairy pastures or on the street. Second, polarization of residents into two discernable camps was further complicated by divisions within the anti-mining movement. While it was initially men that filed state petitions against the proposed mine and organized direct action protests, sexism within the movement sparked a gendered critique, ultimately leading to the establishment of the anti-mining women's group Frente de Mujeres Defensoras de la Pachamama. Through this organization, *campesina* women took control over their political representation and developed their own gendered narratives and critiques of mineral extraction based on their unique position as agrarian women.

Over soft-boiled eggs and piping hot fava beans, then-president of the *defensoras*, Doña Rosita[1] told me about what motivated her to cofound the women's group. It was 2008, the start of my dissertation fieldwork, when we sat in her one-room adobe home. She recalled that before 'everyone was united'. However, this began to change following their blockade of the Pan-American Highway in June 2007, when the newly elected socialist government of Rafael Correa initially repressed the movement, jailing its most radical leaders, but then offered to include others into a high-level dialogue. Rosita recalled that a male leader, who was an influential advisor to the communal water board of Victoria del Portete and Tarqui, agreed to participate in the high-level dialogue with Minister of Energy and Mines, Alberto Acosta, breaking unity among the coalition.

Divisions among anti-mining organizations in Southern Ecuador may be interpreted as an effect of their differences in political ideology. A faction of radicalized Marxist leaders under the National Coordinating Committee for the Defense of Life and Sovereignty (Defensa de la Vida y la Soberanía, or CNDVS) rejected state dialogue, putting them at odds with other organizations willing to test the limits of a newly elected socialist government (see Moore and Velásquez 2013). Notwithstanding ideological differences, Doña Rosita offered an alternative explanation that underscores unequal gender power relations in community water boards. Rosita interpreted this leader's decision to participate in the dialogue without full support of the community as an example of his own self-interest. She accused him of *protagonismo*—when someone asserts their own agenda over community wills and norms (see Speed 2008). Rosita commented that in deciding unilaterally to engage in state dialogues, this leader wanted to 'be big. Like Herod'. Rosita was also a catechist and viewed his transgressions through the moral prism of Catholicism: He violated a moral principal by placing his own individual desires for political authority and power over the desires of the community.

In February 2008, less than a year after the rupture over state dialogue and with the help of CNDVS, Doña Rosita and her neighbors established the Frente de Mujeres Defensoras de la Pachamama, bringing together *campesina* women from different anti-mining struggles across the country. Although most of the women self-identify as *campesinas*, they do not comprise a socially homogeneous group. The women vary in ethnic ancestry, access to markets and migrant remittances, age, and place of origin. Julia Salazar, an urban mestiza from Cuenca and co-director of CNDVS, spearheaded the formation of the organization in response to increasing threats and harassment against women involved in the anti-mining movement. Some of the women reported being insulted by neighbors who call them stupid for not being in favor of the mine, and one *defensora* reported she was hit by a male relative and received death threats from him. Moreover, Julia and Soledad (another urban mestiza feminist) were among 32 activists who faced penal charges for their participation

in anti-mining protests in the previous year when the Correa administration clamped down on region-wide road closures, heightening tensions between the state and social movement activists. In response to the growing atmosphere of repression, one *defensora* joked that the organization should be called the 'Frente Mujeres Teroristas', (Women Terrorist Front).[2] The joke drew attention to the ways in which their activism placed them as 'public' women, or women out of place and hence vulnerable to state and gendered violence (see Wright 2006).

Through the organization of workshops and conference activities, the *defensoras* were able to develop a critique of mining based on their unique position as agrarian women. For instance, only 2 months after the group was formed, Julia organized an international conference that brought together mestiza and indigenous women activist from anti-mining struggles in Ecuador, Peru, Bolivia, Venezuela, and Guatemala, among other countries. Referencing a conversation with a woman from Peru that she met during the conference, Doña Rosita told me, 'They say . . . their land isn't good for anything . . . the dirt doesn't produce anymore. In turn, here we have milk, we have meat, cheese . . . corn, beans . . . everything that we sow grows. But, later [with mining] we won't be able to sow anything . . . this is why we are worried'. Doña Beatriz shared similar concerns: 'I was reading the pamphlets from Bolivia [brought by the women at the conference], and it says that at the beginning they [mining company] paid them . . . when the earth didn't produce anymore the mining company had to pay them more and more . . . and they told them, "here take this liquidation so that you leave this." This is not what we want. Here it will be the same thing'. In contrast to men who have the opportunity to migrate to the coast for work or become intermediaries (who buy/sell and transport raw milk locally), women are charged with the task of tending the dairy cows and subsistence garden plots. These activities provide important sources of income and sustenance to maintain the household because they supplement, if not supplant, the erratic remittances sent by their husbands or adult children living in the United States. The exchanges with other agrarian women generated a greater understanding of how mining would impact their livelihoods and subsistence activities.

Through the process of collective organizing, the group established an identity among the *campesina* women as *defensoras*; however, as an organization, the Frente de Mujeres Defensoras de la Pachamama group remained an affiliate of the CNDVS. The *defensoras* brought the language of gender to anti-mining protests. Shortly after the international conference, the CNDVS staged a road blockade along the Pan-American Highway as a way to pressure the government to emit the Mining Mandate—a legal document that would extinguish mineral concessions in wetlands or in communities that were never consulted regarding proposed mineral projects. Because gold mining requires large volumes of water to extract and process gold, water was a central concern for the women who need access to water to irrigate their fields and sustain their animals.

On 2 April 2008, the *defensoras* joined other CNDVS members in a road blockade and confronted the riot police demanding them to leave. I caught up with *defensora* Lourdes during a break. She sat on the rounded curb of a traffic circle with two other women and declared into my digital recorder, 'This [mining] is going to seriously affect us. Like many, we are starting to understand this. Firstly, the *guagua's* [Quechua for children]. [Mining] will bring leukemia, cancer. We don't want this. We want clean water, sweet water, pure water, that is what we want'. Lourdes was neither married nor a mother, but she did help raise her siblings' children while they lived and worked in New York. Evelyn, the single and recently crowned *Reina* of the parish, similarly deployed the language of motherhood: 'we are here for reasons that affect all of us. Mining affects water . . . [and] also destroys the environment. [With mining development], it will dry out the earth, the children will be born with genetic mutations, we will all get illnesses that we have never seen before. That's why we are here at the road blockade'.

Across Latin America, women collectively organized in defense of their livelihoods also make political use of motherhood. Neoliberal policies have uniquely affected the subsistence base of peasant women, motivating them to join social movements

(Nash 1990). Safa (1990) and Stephen (1997) document how poor women draw upon their socially legitimate roles as mothers and wives to reconfigure their relationships to the state and expand the meaning and practices of democracy. While the *defensoras* do not necessarily seek participation or recognition by the state, they use the language of motherhood to make an ethical–moral argument against an extractivist economy. By articulating a concern about mining's effects on the future generations, the *defensoras* position themselves as fulfilling their traditional gender roles. Despite the shifts in gender roles that may result from sustained international migration in the area, women do not question their social roles as a mother. However, by politicizing traditional gender roles, they transformed motherhood from a biological fact into a social and political construction (Taylor 1997).

Furthermore, the *defensoras* play upon on the language of motherhood when they invoke the Pachamama in their protests. Lourdes continued, 'We are here with the *compañeras* defending the Pachamama, *nuestra madre tierra* (our mother earth), we will be here until victory, *compañera*'. Later, Rosita, who also made multiple references to protect the Pachamama, explained what the term meant to her: 'Quimsacocha *is* Pachamama, she nourishes, she sustains us . . . if the miners take out the gold, its like taking out a liver or a kidney'. The *defensoras* used the term 'Pachamama' to contest state and corporate representations of the Quimsacocha watershed as a gold-mining project. By reframing Quimsacocha as Pachamama, the women draw attention to the interconnection between human and 'other-than-human beings' that sustain the lives of current, past, and future generations in the rural Andes (de la Cadena 2010, 341).

The language of 'motherhood' cast in social and environmental terms enabled the women to 'present a more cohesive identity and narrative' that creates space for their activism and generates legitimacy for their actions (Jenkins 2015, 453). By drawing parallels between their role as mothers in social reproduction and that of Pachamama, the *campesinas* are able to iron out the complexities of organizing a heterogeneous group of women. As an organization, the Frente de Mujeres Defensoras de la Pachamama gave them a space to create and control their own narrative framework for anti-mining activism that reflected their position as agrarian women rather than adhere to an indigenous narrative frame employed by the communal water board constituted by their growing links with the national and regional indigenous movement. In contrast, the *defensoras* simultaneously embrace Andean culture as part of their collective politics but strategically distance themselves from indigenous identity, emphasizing that they are instead 'mestizas'. They view themselves as upwardly mobile peasants who are 'more evolved' than their indigenous parents and grandparents.[3] Similar to processes of mestizaje identified by Marisol de la Cadena in Peru, '"indigenous culture" is not the same as "being Indian"—a label that carries a historical stigma of colonized inferiority' (2000, 6). While their emphasis on gender, space, and class over racial/ethnic identifications maintains the ongoing invisibility of racial systems that *campesino* mestizos are embedded within, it nonetheless provides them with an alternative way to validate and legitimate their unique struggles as women.

CHALLENGING SEXISM

Exerting a greater control over their own political narratives, the *defensoras* established a veritable challenge to sexism within the anti-mining movement and, by extension, local water politics. Because the communal water boards spearheaded local activism against mining, it meant that gender inequalities present in Andean water board systems were also reproduced within anti-mining activism. Although *campesina* women participate in the 'family farming system' (Deere and León 1982), they are seldom involved in the formal decision-making processes related to the community-run irrigation and drinking water systems of which they are members (Zwarteveen and Bennett 2005). In the Andes, although women are not explicitly barred from attending meetings, 'prevailing class, gender, and ethnic relations and contradictions in both intracommunity and wider sociopolitical arenas' (Boelens 2008, 49) can affect women's ability to actively participate in water management systems. In the northern Ecuadorian Andes, Bastidas writes

that attending water board meetings is perceived as a male activity. One of her rural mestiza collaborators notes that even if she were to attend the meeting, 'men are the ones who talk and discuss. They know what to say and how to say it' (cited in Bastidas 2005, 160). Similarly, Doña Beatriz confirmed that women are not visible leaders in the local anti-mining movement because they would never be elected as a water board director: 'they are men, they are educated . . . were are just *sencillas*, [with little schooling]'. Lack of formal education and the perception that women do not know how to 'talk' is a powerful force in the Andes that reinforces sexism within social movement organizing (Cervone 2002).

The transformation from a silenced woman to a collective speaking subject, albeit uneven, was shaped by the political practices of CNDVS, the umbrella organization. CNDVS organized forums called the *Diálogo por La Vida*, or Dialogue for Life, in rural parishes and towns embroiled in mining conflicts. One by one people gave their *testimonios* in front of an assembly (usually at a community band shell or at a church). These narratives were not always spontaneous and unscripted, rather they often followed the narrative format set out by more experienced leaders in which mining was rejected as an environmental threat. The *defensoras* were encouraged to travel to other parishes and towns and give their *testimonio* to the community facing similar struggles, which often was inseparable from the public *denuncia* (denouncement) of multinational companies and the Correa administration. This particular genre of public *testimonio/denuncia* is a strategy to give voice to subaltern subjects with little political power, and also worked to expand CNDVS' membership base and create collective subjectivities. These dialogues were an important place where women gained experience speaking in front of crowds and employed narrative frameworks from their position as agrarian women.

Opportunity for public speaking became transformative for women such as Doña Laura, the first president of the *defensoras*. In 2008, as part of the CNDVS delegation, she traveled to a public forum to discuss the government's water policy. Upon her return, we spoke after a *defensora* meeting. Doña Laura said that there were *campesinos* there but that the event was *'frio'* (literally 'cold' or without much contestation) because people feared speaking up. She recounted that *campesinos* were there, but the presence of urban mestizo state functionaries and intellectuals dominated the space. In reference to *campesinos*, Doña Laura commented, 'They don't know how to talk, afraid that they will talk bad'. She proudly added that even if she spoke 'good or bad', she did speak. In interviews and private conversations, other *defensoras* also shared how they became more emboldened by grabbing the microphone at rallies and community meetings, and by speaking out without caring, even if it came out 'bad'.

'Speaking' connotes both a racial and gendered form of privilege that is expressed in speech that is eloquent or articulate. In other words, 'good' speech presumes the embodiment of a certain social position as well as access to education. For Doña Laura, her act of speaking, regardless if it came out 'good or bad', was a radical refusal of the exclusionary nature of 'speech' that implies membership in a dominant or hegemonic social group. The act of coming to voice or of speaking was a powerful medium through which *defensoras* took control over their own political representation. However, it also generated considerable opposition among other anti-mining farmers in the parish, who perceived the women as *'bravas'*, or angry women for forming a break-off group and involving themselves in a bitter battle against male water board leaders.

REPRESENTATIONAL SOVEREIGNTY 2: PERFORMING REFUSALS

The *defensora's* defied dominant representations of *campesina* women in the regional imaginary as folkloric women who are spoken about, but who never speak. In early 2009, they staged a protest that symbolically contested the racial, gendered, and class constructions of urban space. The protest took place shortly after the Correa administration unveiled a draft mining law that would allow the government to push through contentious gold and copper projects. Rejected by some, the proposed law declared mining activity a public utility and did not provide affected communities with a binding consultation process (Dosh and Kligerman 2009). Activists argued that declaring mining a 'public utility' could lead to the expropriation of community resources when such lands and watersheds were needed to develop the mining project (Moore 2009). Moreover, opposition lawyer Wilton Guaranda observed that the mining law that was ultimately approved (based largely on the draft circulated) violated territorial rights conferred to indigenous people in the 2008 National Constitution and key aspects of the United Nation's Declaration on the Rights of Indigenous Peoples. Yet, the proposed law gained some traction and support because it addressed the popular critique of neoliberal extractivism as a squandering of national patrimony. Derlis Palacios, then Minister of Mines and Energy, defended the proposed law as a benefit to the nation because 60% of mining royalties would be reinvested into surrounding communities and stringent regulations would ensure that the environmental impact would be minimal.[4]

Heated debates over the proposed law were illustrative of the challenges to neo-extractivism, a development strategy adopted by progressive governments in Latin America in which the state 'plays an active role and gains a greater legitimacy through the redistribution of some of the profits generated by such extractivism' (Gudynas 2010, 188). People most affected by the proposed law and their allies organized marches and road blockades to pressure the interim legislative commission to shelve the law. The protests grew and by early 2009, a new round of street blockades was staged resulting in the arrests of some leaders. In the province of Azuay, community water system leader Carlos Pérez Guartambel organized a hunger strike in collaboration with Salvador Quishpe, a key figure of the indigenous movement. Meanwhile, the *defensoras* organized their own action that demonstrated the 'politics of refusal' (Simpson 2014), a critical dimension to their collective subjectivities that is predicated upon 'knowing how to speak'.

On 12 January 2009, a small group of *defensoras* staged a protest in Cuenca's central plaza called the Parque Calderón. Some of the women wore *polleras* while others donned baseball hats and pants in the heat of the day. The women sat on the outside of the rotunda, with a chain around their hands to appear as if they had locked themselves to the wrought iron bars. A piece of simple, rectangular white tape covered their mouths. They were silent and let the lively hand-written protest signs around them shout their demands: 'Down with the fascist and repressive government in service of imperialist miners [mining companies]'; 'Stop the criminalization of protest'; 'Liberty for the Imprisoned, Enough of Illegal Detentions'; and 'Stop the Persecution of Campesinos of Molleturo'. In January, at least 12 anti-mining activists were arrested and jailed, and least one male leader charged with sabotage and terrorism.[5] It was rumored that the police were looking for additional community leaders from the parish of Molleturo, where the defensoras had a strong base.

The tensions between speech and silence were shaped by the worsening political conditions of state repression. At the April 2008 protest, where women deployed motherhood as a framework for their opposition to mining, 17 members of the CNDVS were arrested. Doña Rosita was violently detained. She and at least two other defensoras were temporarily jailed and faced penal charges. A few days after the April protest, President Correa denounced the CNDVS as a 'handful of nobodies' and used gendered insults against Julia claiming 'we have to send her to a psychiatrist', referencing the sexist stereotype of outspoken women as mad or crazy.[6] In addition, he encouraged the public to defend mining by going out to the street to confront activists in the following round of planned mobilizations slated for late April. Although the government eventually emitted the Mining Mandate the same month to curb illegal mining concessions, much of 2008 was marked by increased hostility between the Correa administration and activists because his government was unwilling to fully implement legislation that would jeopardize the viability of the five most important mineral projects at the time.[7] These tensions further seeped into community relations as the defensoras regularly received threatening phone calls. In December 2008, defensora Lucrecia and her husband were stopped on their way back to their home in the campo and badly assaulted by unknown people. Many speculated that they were thugs paid for by the company or even the state.

The 12 January 2009 protest in Parque Calderón spoke directly against the use of violence and intimidation tactics against activists but failed to generate full public support. For instance, while they tethered themselves to the glorieta, the defensoras' bodies were subjected to insults and aggression from passersby. Some of the comments were ideological and spoke directly to the mining issue. Commentary such as, 'do what you will but you won't take out the miners, mining is going to happen, get out of here', or simply, '¡vive La minería!', was common. Other commentary took on racialized insults. As one of the defensoras held a sign that read, 'Down with Fascism . . .', a well-dressed woman walked by and yelled, 'you shouldn't use words you don't know'. Her tone smacked of urban racism that positioned rural women as 'illiterate Indians'. In another instance, an elderly man walked by and commented with disgust, 'ociosas viejas!', which translates to 'lazy old hags'. A campesina peeled back the tape covering her mouth and shouted in response, 'callase viejo sin huevos' or 'shut up old man without balls'. Each one hurled gendered insults to the other. His comment suggested that the women should be doing some sort of 'real' work—perhaps in the home or in the market. Playing with traditional gender roles, the women insulted his masculinity by suggesting that he lacked 'balls', or the bravery that it takes to stand up against the government. They positioned themselves as having such 'balls', and thus as more masculine than the man. After the woman's indignant riposte, the other women burst into laughter and peeled off part of the tape to take delight in making jokes about the old man's huevos.

One could explain the lack of support by the public as an effect of the intimidation campaign that Correa waged against anti-mining activists. A study authored by the Ecuadorian ombudsman office, the Defensoría del Pueblo, concluded that the Correa administration created a system of criminalization in which discursive intimidation worked as a way to 'consolidate social support to delegitimize the actions of protesters that defend the constitution' (Reyes, Mora, and Loachamín 2010, 23). This largely rested on the identification of an 'internal enemy', rooted in Cold War security strategies. Indeed, the media campaign to identify anti-mining activists as internal enemies largely seemed to work. While Correa repeatedly insulted anti-mining activists on his Saturday radio program, several *Cuencanos* I spoke with supported mineral extraction and echoed the words of Correa that Ecuadorians should not be 'beggars sitting on sacks of gold'. These sentiments were particularly strong during the time of the women's protest in Parque Calderón as evident in several newspaper editorials. Published in Cuenca's most important newspaper *El Mercurio* on 10 January—a mere 2 days before the *defensoras* protest—one editorial titled, 'Absurd Savagery' called for authorities to 'use an iron fist against the abuse and prepotency of the [protestors] who should be more concerned with producing more for the economic benefit of the country'.[8]

. . .

The crisis in political representation is exacerbated by the Correa administration, which has chosen Cuenca's political elite to spearhead pro-mining policies. Throughout his 2-term presidency, Correa selected *cuencanos* to serve in key cabinet posts, including Derlis Palacios, the former Minister of Mines and Petroleum, and José Serrano, the former Subsecretariat of Mines (http://www.eltiempo.com.ec/noticias-cuenca/156019-cuencanos-una-presencia-constante-en-el-gobierno/). President Correa replaced the president of the National Constituent Assembly Alberto Acosta with Corcho Cordero to fast track the writing of the constitution and advance a legal framework in favor of progressive neo-extractivism. On 12 January 2009, the same day of the *defensoras* protest, Cordero convened the interim National Assembly for the second and definitive debate over the controversial mining law, ignoring months of mobilizations and calls for the respect of human and environmental rights. The mining law passed with an overwhelming 50–6 majority vote.[9] Political support for mineral extraction was inextricably linked to regional political processes dominated by bureaucratic elite that had made strategic alliances with Correa's administration. As such, the *defensoras'* protest against state policing simultaneously called into question the political authority and legitimacy of regional politicians as well as the constructions of race, class, and gender that have created and empowered a new elite political class.

In their theorization of political refusals, Tuck and Yang (2014, 241) write that 'refusals shift the gaze from the violated body to the violating instruments'. By tethering themselves with chains to the rotunda and taping their mouths shut during the 2009 protest, the women performed the experiences of incarceration. If bodies are critical sites for disciplinary power aimed at order and control, they may also be the means to channel and fuel the affective experiences of such forms of state power (see Fabricant and Postero 2013; Taylor 1997). Their intention was to demonstrate and contest the embodied experiences of state violence and repression that marked public debates over the Correa's support for large-scale industrial mining in environmentally and socially sensitive areas. Read against Cuenca's official cultural narratives, I would argue that their bodies did more than just speak back to national politics, rather they also transformed the prevailing scripts for rural women as mere folkloric Others whose place is largely in the countryside. By bringing their protest to the city, *campesina* women simultaneously embodied the *chola cuencana* while at the same time unwittingly challenging it at every turn, talking back to the symbolic associations of *cuencano* men with political authority. Choosing to be silent accompanied with moments of critical back talk to passersby was a reversal of the forms of every day silence. Mary Weismantel notes that popular markets are the only space in Cuenca where *chola* vendors do have a voice that can temporarily invert social hierarchies; however, when a *chola* leaves the market, 'the loud, vulgar voice she had as a vender is muted, if not silenced completely' (Weismantel 2001, 118).

The women's effort to influence state policing and the mineral law did not generate a widespread support for the cause because urbanites may well have interpreted them as *cholas* that exceeded the boundaries of their externally imposed social scripts. Similar to the rural migrants who return from the United States to build lavish homes in Cuenca, the *defensoras'* protesting bodies could have easily been viewed as being out of place. Rural families migrate as a way to side step a weak economy and the limits of a rigid caste social structure that impedes social mobility (Miles 2004). *Cuencano* elites deride the *malgusto* or bad taste of rural families who use remittances to build garish multistory, glass mirrored homes that clash with 'traditional' or 'European' aesthetics of the city. Acosta writes that counterposing the *'mal gusto'* of the *cholos* with the *'buen gusto'* of the nobles of Cuenca 'constitutes expressions of racialized and classist imaginaries, that although unintentional are incorporated into the habitus that still circulates in Cuencano society' (Mancera Acosta 2012, 131).

. . .

CONCLUSION

. . .

In Ecuador, the *defensoras'* refusal to be represented by community water board leaders implicated a turn toward gender-based organizing. By appropriating gender-specific discourses, the women embarked on a politics that deployed traditional narratives of motherhood and indigenous environmentalism to create their own political spaces and underscore the ways in which agrarian women would be uniquely affected by mining in upland páramos. Women were empowered to become 'speaking subjects' in which their discursive practices challenged both the sexism within the rural anti-mining movement and regional narratives of folkloric women—women who were spoken about but who never spoke. Their simultaneous use of the *pollera* and embrace of mestizaje accompanied by a refusal to embody the *chola cuencana* means that similar to the Mohawk who have been written and spoken about, the *defensoras'* own representation differs from the official ones defined by artists, poets, politicians, and even academics. Furthermore, the enactments of refusals in an otherwise collaborative research relationship provides an interesting example of how collective political practices shape and affect the relationship between activists and politically engaged researchers.

The *defensoras'* political practices are not without their own contradictions. Although their 2009 protest challenged the prevailing racial symbolic order of urban space, their embrace of mestizaje means that they may be unable to challenge their racialization as indigenous women in the rural contexts. Similar to the urban nobility, rural families in the parish of Victoria del Portete use a combination of last names, color, and dress to assert their racial and economic hegemony in the parish. Small and subsistence farmers of indigenous descent have long battled with their wealthy neighbors over water and land (see Arevalo 2006). In recounting a past dispute over pasture lands, one *defensora* described the people with a term that I was not familiar with. When I asked, she clarified, 'oh you know those rich people from Victoria [del Portete], the whites, who think they are better [than us] . . .'. Tensions among *'indios'* and *'blancos'* within the parish were often discussed during the course of my fieldwork by both groups. One *'blanco'* in particular would flippantly refer to people living in downstream communities as *'indios'*. In turn, a few *defensoras* not only told tales of long lines and mistreatment in city offices but also had numerous stories of abusive white neighbors in the rural areas. An awareness of racism often understood as 'discrimination' does not translate into a greater ethnic/racial solidarity, because women embrace the promise of social advancement of mestizaje and use a narrow definition of *indígena*. Rosita, for instance, asserts that she is more evolved than her great-grandparents who were true *indígena*, who went 'bare foot and had woolen hats and spoke more Quechua and didn't understand . . . we understand everything through our education (*estudios*) because before the elders didn't have much education'.

In contrast, community water board leaders forged a political alliance that effectively placed a defense of water from mineral activity within the agenda of the indigenous movement and set the conditions under which Guartambel was twice elected as the president of Ecuarunari (a historically powerful highland Andean indigenous organization).[10] Guartambel's hybridization of Catholic and indigenous spiritual practices and savvy use of indigenous imagery in protests have motivated *campesinos* (including a couple of 'white' families) in the parishes of Victoria del Portete and Tarqui to affiliate themselves with the indigenous movement and its political arm, the Pachakutik Party. While some participate in the indigenous movement as mestizos, others from Victoria del Portete and Tarqui are reevaluating their mestizo identities and are starting to claim an indigenous

Kichwa or Cañari identity. Because Andean indigenous identity is a product of ongoing struggles for resources. and political rights rather than a social category of naturalized cultural differences (Jimeno 2014; Pallares 2002), the debates over mining are shifting the ways in which some (though not all) think about their individual and collective identities. In a conversation about Carlos Pérez Guartambel's involvement in Pachakutik, Ceci mentioned, 'I don't understand how he can say we are indigenous. I don't deny my indigenous roots, but we are not indigenous. We don't speak Quechua anymore'.[11]

An embrace of the main tenets of mestizaje as well as a gender critique of the anti-mining movement has limited the possibilities for a broad-based alliance among the *defensoras* and the national indigenous movement. Nonetheless, the *defensoras* have been instrumental in revealing the kind of gendered political violence that makes mineral extraction possible in new areas. Opting for radical refusals over dialogues with the state, the *defensoras* have continued street protests and demonstrations as their primary political strategy. Since 2009, *defensoras* faced charges of organized terrorism, obstruction of public roads, and harassment.[12] In addition, an organized protest against the Chinese-owned Rio Blanco mine project resulted in the assault and arbitrary detention of eight women.[13] Physical harassment is not unique to the *defensoras*. Amazonian indigenous and nonindigenous women, including urban environmental activists against oil extraction have also experienced similar abuses. The widely publicized murder of Honduran activist Berta Cáceres is yet another testament to the region-wide phenomenon experienced by women defenders of the environment. Threats and physical harassment against women defenders of the environment have prompted multiple complaints against the Ecuadorian government in the Inter-American Human Rights Court. *Defensoras* have travelled to Washington, DC to provide testimonies of such incidents. Given the critiques of international court systems as disciplinary mechanisms of neoliberal governance, their struggle to carve out sovereign spaces are partial at best. Although the *defensoras* do not struggle in alignment with the indigenous movement, their continued coordination

of political rallies, events, radio programs, and workshops contribute to the plurality of voices critical to gold-mining projects.

NOTES

1. I use pseudonyms except in the case of national public figures. Although many women from the Frente de Mujeres Defensoras de la Pachamama participate in public protests, I have chosen to use a pseudonym to protect their identities given their ongoing criminalization and harassment.

2. I learned about threats against the women through my participation in workshops and meetings of the women's group in 2008.

3. Personal communication, 22 April 2008.

4. *El Tiempo*, 'Nuevas condiciones para la minería', 11 January 2009.

5. *El Tiempo*, 'Antimineros cierran tres vías', 6 January 2009.

6. Dialogo con el presidente, Radio Program, #63, 5 April 2008.

7. If applied, the mining mandate would have affected the following projects on the basis of a lack of community consultation: IAMGOLD's Quimsacocha project (INV's Loma Larga project); International Mineral Corporation's Rio Blanco project (now owned by Junefield); Kinross' Fruta del Norte project (now owned by Lundin Mining); and Corriente Resources' Mirador project. All of the projects were in the exploratory phase.

8. Armando Albornoz Ventimilla, *El Mercurio*, 'Salvajismo Absurdo', 10 January 2009.

9. The 50 vote majority came largely from Alianza País, Correa's political party who dominated the interim legislative committee; see http://ecuadorinmediato.com/index.php?module=Noticias&func=news_user_view&id=95439&umt=asamblea_nacional_aprobu_-ley_minera_ecuador

10. His election to Ecuarunari provoked public debate as to whether Pérez Guartambel is indigenous or mestizo. Public debate over his identity was provoked by an article from *El Telégrafo*, a newspaper closely aligned with the government, see http://www.eltelegrafo.com.ec/noticias/pagina-dos/1/un-lider-mestizo-dirigira-al-movimiento-indigena-ecuarunari

for the original article; for a subsequent discussion by Pachakutik Assemblywoman Lourdes Tiban, see http://www.asambleanacional.gob.ec/es/contenido/quien_define_lo_indigena_el_nuevo_presidente_de_la_ecuarunari

11. Field notes, 26 July 2016.

12. See the report titled 'Modalidades de Criminalización y limitaciones a la efectiva participación de mujeres Defensoras de derechos ambientales, los territorios y la naturaleza en las Américas', prepared for the Inter-American Commission on Human Rights on the 'Situation of Defenders of Women's Rights and the Environment in America', October 2015; see http://issuu.com/fondodeaccionurgente-al/docs/informe_cidh_esp_2015

13. For Frontline defenders report, see https://www.frontlinedefenders.org/en/case/case-history-frente-de-mujeres-Defensoras-de-la-pachamama

REFERENCES

Acosta, Mónica Mancero. 2012. Nobles y cholos : raza, género y clase en Cuenca, 1995-2005. FLACSO. Sede Ecuador.

Albro, R. 2005. "The Water Is Ours Carajo! Deep Citizenship in Bolivia's Water War." In *Social Movements: An Anthropological Reader*, edited by J. Nash, 249–271. Oxford: Blackwell.

Arevalo, B. 2006. "Las comunidades locales y la microcuenca del río Irquis En La Provincia Del Azuay." MA Thesis, Facultad Latinoamericana de Ciencias Sociales, Quito, Ecuador.

Bastidas, E. P. 2005. "Women and Water in the Northern Ecuadorean Andes." In *Opposing Currents: The Politics of Water and Gender in Latin America*, edited by V. Bennett, S. Dávila-Poblete, and M. N. Rico, 154–169. Pittsburgh: University of Pennsylvania Press.

Boelens, R. 2008. "Water Rights Arenas in the Andes: Upscaling the Defence Networks to Localize Water Control." *Water Alternatives* 1 (1): 48–65.

Cervone, E. 2002. "Engendering Leadership: Indigenous Women Leaders in the Ecuadorian Andes." In *Gender's Place: Feminist Anthropologies of Latin America*, edited by R. Montoya, J. Frazier, and J. Hurtig, 179–196. New York: Palgrave MacMillan.

De La Cadena, M. 2000. *Indigenous Mestizos: The Politics of Race and Culture in Cuzco, Peru, 1919-1991.* Durham, NC: Duke University Press.

de la Cadena, M. 2010. "Indigenous Cosmopolitics in the Andes: Conceptual Reflections beyond 'Politics'." *Cultural Anthropology* 25 (2): 334–370. doi:10.1111/cuan.2010.25.issue-2.

Deere, C. D., and M. León. 1982. *Women in Agriculture: Peasant Production and Rural Wage Employment in Colombia and Peru.* Geneva: International Labour Organization.

Dosh, P., and Kligerman. 2009. "Correa Vs. Social Movements: Showdown in Ecuador." *NACLA Report on the Americas* 42 (5): 21–24. doi:10.1080/10714839.2009.11725465.

Fabricant, N., and N. Postero. 2013. "Contested Bodies, Contested States: Performance, Emotions, and New Forms of Regional Governance in Santa Cruz, Bolivia." *The Journal of Latin American and Caribbean Anthropology* 18 (2): 187–211. doi:10.1111/jlca.2013.18.issue-2.

Gudynas, E. 2010. "El Nuevo Extractivismo Del Siglo 21: Diez Tesis Urgentes Sobre El Extractivismo Bajo El Progresismo Sudamericano Actual." *Americas Program, Center for International Policy (CIP).*

Jenkins, K. 2015. "Unearthing Women's Anti-Mining Activism in the Andes: Pachamama and the 'Mad Old Women'." *Antipode* 47 (2): 442–460. doi:10.1111/anti.12126.

Jimeno, M. 2014. The Story of My Life: Juan Gregorio Palechor. Translated by Andy Klatt. Durham, NC: Duke University Press.

Miles, A. 2004. *From Cuenca to Queens: An Anthropological Story of Transnational Migration.* Austin: University of Texas Press.

Moore, J. 2009. "Ecuador: Mining Protests Marginalized, But Growing." *Upside Down World*, January 21.

Moore, J., and V. Teresa[Velasquez, T.]. 2013. "Water for Gold: Confronting State and Corporate Mining Discourses in Azuay, Ecuador." In *Subterranean Struggles: New Dynamics of Mining, Oil, and Gas in Latin America*, edited by A. Bebbington and J. Bury, 119–148. Austin: University of Texas Press.

Nash, J. 1990. "Latin American Women in the World Capitalist Crisis." *Gender & Society* 4 (3): 338–353. doi:10.1177/089124390004003005.

Pallares, A. 2002. *From Peasant Struggles to Indian Resistance: The Ecuadorian Andes in the Late Twentieth Century.* Norman: University of Oklahoma Press.

Postero, N. 2007. *Now We are Citizens: Indigenous Politics in Postmulticultural Bolivia.* Stanford: Stanford University Press.

Reyes, A. C., L. J. Mora, and R. N. Loachamín. 2010. *Los Escenarios de la Criminalización a Defensores de Derechos Humanos y de la Naturaleza en Ecuador: Desafíos para un Estado Constitucional de Derechos.* Quito: Defensoría del Pueblo del Ecuador.

Safa, H. 1990. "Women's Social Movements in Latin America." *Gender and Society* 4 (3): 354–369. doi:10.1177/089124390004003006.

Simpson, A. 2014. *Mohawk Interruptus: Political Life across the Borders of Settler States.* Durham, NC: Duke University Press.

Speed, S. 2008. "Forged in Dialogue: Towards a Critically Engaged Activist Research." In *Engaging Contradictions: Theory, Politics, and Methods of Activist Scholarship*, edited by C. R. Hale, 213–226. Berkeley: University of California Press.

Stephen, L. 1997. *Women and Social Movements in Latin America: Power from Below.* Austin: University of Texas Press.

Taylor, D. 1997. *Disappearing Acts: Spectacles of Gender and Nationalism in Argentina's "Dirty War.".* Durham, NC: Duke University Press.

Tuck, E., and K. Wayne Yang. 2014. "R-Words: Refusing Research." In *Humanizing Research: Decolonizing Qualitative Inquiry with Youth and Communities*, edited by D. Paris and M. Winn, 223–247. Thousand Oaks, CA: SAGE Publications.

Weismantel, M. 2001. *Cholas and Pishtacos: Stories of Race and Sex in the Andes.* Chicago: University of Chicago Press.

Wright, M. W. 2006. "Public Women, Profit, and Femicide in Northern Mexico." *South Atlantic Quarterly* 105 (4): 681–698. doi:10.1215/00382876-2006-003.

Zwarteveen, M., and V. Bennett. 2005. "The Connection between Gender and Q Water Management." In *Opposing Currents: The Politics of Water and Gender in Latin America*, edited by V. Bennett, S. Dávila-Poblete, and M. N. Rico, 13–29. Pittsburgh: University of Pennsylvania Press.

89. BUILDING COALITIONS
The Interconnections Between Feminism and Trans* Activism in Spain
R. LUCAS PLATERO AND ESTHER ORTEGA-ARJONILLA (2016)

INTRODUCTION

Nunca tuve una reacción negativa desde el feminismo. Si hubo alguna, debió ser cosa de silencio. . . . Pero en aquellos años [1993] después incluso, me sentí arropadísima por la gente. Más que arropada, es que había surgido una especie de vínculo de simpatía mutua. Tengo que usar la palabra catártica, porque se puede decir que yo nunca he tenido una experiencia tan fuerte de ser aceptada por un colectivo, como aquella [las jornadas feministas de 1993]. Y realmente, no podíamos medir la importancia que tenía . . . hasta ese momento no estábamos cerca del movimiento feminista.

—*Entrevista con Kim Pérez, activista trans* sobre las Jornadas Feministas de 1993*

I never had a negative reaction within feminism. If there ever was one, it must have been in terms of silence. . . . But in those years [1993] and even later, I felt very supported by people. More than supported, it is that a type of link based on mutual sympathy had grown. I have to use the word cathartic, because you could say that I had never had such a strong experience of acceptance from a collective as I had there [the 1993 Feminist Conference]. And, really, we could not then measure the import it had . . . up to that point, we were not close to the feminist movement.

—*Interviewee Kim Pérez, trans* activist, on the 1993 Feminist Conference*

This article intends to answer one key question: what makes it possible for trans* women in Spain today to be part of the feminist movement with little resistance? Based on in-depth interviews with relevant activists, and using literature reviews, we explore the relevant factors that facilitated the active participation of trans* women in Spanish feminism since, at least, the early 1990s. This question emerges from our own experiences as activists and academics involved in the recent history of feminism and trans* rights in Spain. This question has also informed our research, leading us to design a participatory action research study in which knowledge is collectively produced, and where the question and the results are relevant for the community (Reason & Bradbury, 2008). Not only is there an active presence of trans* women and trans* issues in Spanish feminism, but there is also a widespread presence of "transfeminism," which needs to be explained in terms of its vernacular nuances, processes, and alliances. As one of the interviewees, Juana Ramos, stated:

> En el Estado español, a diferencia de otros sitios, ha habido una alianza importante porque se han dado unas circunstancias concretas, que incluyen el liderazgo y receptividad, tanto por parte de determinadas personas pertenecientes al movimiento feminista como por parte de activistas trans*.

> In Spain, quite differently from other countries, there has been a strong alliance [between feminist and trans* activists] because of certain specific circumstances that were present, including the leadership and receptiveness, on the side of certain feminist activists, as well as the trans* activists.

Our starting hypothesis was that the particular political context of Spain and the formation of the feminist movement—in which lesbian feminists have played a relevant role since its emergence and not only as part of independent groups—were key in connecting feminism with trans* women and vice versa. In particular, we wanted to explore to what extent lesbian feminist collectives had facilitated the inclusion of trans* women, first in feminist events, such as the National Conferences, and later as part of feminist ideology. Lastly, we also wanted to explore how they

promoted a shift in feminist paradigms. With regards to our hypothesis, we were aware that there were a multiplicity of factors that we would find through the research process, along with the knowledge that a discussion on the resistance to trans* activists' participation was missing from the feminist movement, as well as from the research conducted to date. These were questions that we tackled in our interviews.

METHODOLOGY: MAPPING THE NARRATIVES

As activists and researchers, we are part of the communities we are studying and aware of the situated knowledge we produce (Haraway, 1991), which is rooted in conversations and shared experiences with other activists. We are aware of the political importance of these phenomena, along with the lack of discussion in sociological and historical terms. By revealing the multiple circumstances that make this coalition possible, we defy a linear understanding of the struggle for trans* rights, in which Anglo-Saxon and European-centered narratives are often presented as universal. Missing from many historical analyses, both in the context of Spanish discourses and in many hegemonic debates, is the possibility of trans* and feminist movements co-existing without conflict.

Our research is based on two sources: literature reviews and oral history. We started by reviewing the Spanish feminist literature that covered the debates on trans* and feminist alliances from the mid 1970s to the present, which had not previously been the subject of a comprehensive analysis. At the same time, we employed snowball sampling (Goodman, 1961) to locate and conduct interviews with eight activists: Aitzole Araneta, Laura Bugalho, Cristina Garaizabal, Nancy Losada, Justa Montero, Kim Pérez, Empar Pineda, and Juana Ramos. The in-depth interviews were recorded and transcribed. For our analysis, we took the approach of Carol Bacchi, who states that "discourses are not the direct product of intentional manipulation by a few key political actors but neither are they transhistorical structures operating outside of human intervention" (Bacchi, 1999: 43). This approach allows for an unveiling of power relationships in a Foucauldian sense and for an examination of processes of agency.

Given the young history of Spanish feminism, we chose significant events in which the presence of trans* women and trans* issues could be traced, such as the *Jornadas Feministas Estatales* (National Feminist Conferences), the March 8th demonstrations, and, to a lesser extent, the impact of feminism on the *Octubre Trans* (Trans October) events. The activists interviewed saw the *Jornadas Feministas Estatales* as particularly essential in setting the stage for the debates and evolution of feminist thought. According to the interviewee Justa Montero, the role of these conferences was:

> Una apuesta determinada por situar debates novedosos o debates vinculados a la práctica política. . . . La Coordinadora, que, mucho más en aquella época quizás que ahora, era una red donde todos los grupos discutíamos las cosas que iban planteando. Todas estábamos muy permeadas por los temas novedosos que se iban tratando a partir de colectivos concretos.

> A determined proposal to hold new debates or debates linked to political practice. . . . The Feminist Coordination Group, probably more so then than now, was a network in which all groups discussed the topics that were proposed. Everyone was really sensitive to new issues that were dealt with within specific collectives.

We are fully aware that these conferences are only one part of feminist debates, and we do not intend to magnify their impact, but at the same time they have been chosen strategically as a clear signpost in feminist memory and a fruitful locus for the discussion of trans* rights.

SPANISH FEMINISM AND TRANS* ACTIVISM (1975–2015)

In order to show the relationship between the feminist and trans* movements in Spain, we will structure our narrative around the National Feminist Conferences. After the inclusion of trans* identity issues in the 1993 National Feminist Conference, trans* experiences took root within the feminist movement at the 2000 Conference in Córdoba, and blossomed at the 2009 Conference in Granada, where feminist analyses were directly challenged by trans* issues and theories.

To provide some context, present-day Spain is a parliamentary monarchy that underwent a democratic transition that started in the mid 1970s. This was possible only after the death of dictator Francisco Franco in 1975 and the convergence of the different political actors who introduced the Constitution of 1978. This young democracy set the minimum conditions for social participation, which included allowing the discussion of critical, progressive ideas in public realms and facilitating the emergence of social movements, such as feminism and the "homosexual liberation movement" (Platero, 2011). In record time, laws were passed granting most basic democratic rights (such as freedom of speech and assembly, the ability to vote and elect a Parliament, equality for women and for children born out of marriage, etc.). Before joining the European Union in 1986, Spain had established the foundations needed to achieve many of the liberties already present in other democratic countries. During the transition to democracy, social movements had to fight hard, often in coalition with left-wing organizations, to gain rights for women, sexual minorities, and other disenfranchised citizens, in defiance of discriminatory legislation like the so-called "Social Danger Act" (*Ley 16/1970, de 4 de agosto, sobre peligrosidad y rehabilitación social*, 1970). Under that law, homosexuality (including lesbianism and transvestism) and prostitution were banned and persecuted in Spain. The construction of new political identities took place in the context of a new democracy in which basic rights had just been granted.

The feminist movement in Spain had been organized prior to the transition, during the Francoist dictatorship, but the struggle for women's rights did not gain a large following until the Spanish state became a democracy. The creation of large, organized women's groups in all of the major cities took place as an indirect consequence of those struggles. The groups were coordinated through a federation, which began to organize large feminist conferences.

In January 1977, quite soon after Franco's death, some Spanish feminist groups established the

Federación de Organizaciones Feministas del Estado Español (Federation of Spanish Feminist Organizations; FOFEE). Major issues related to women's rights, such as legal equality, abortion, sexual and reproductive rights, and divorce, were included in the manifesto of the Federation, as was the repeal of the "Social Danger Act" (Moreno Sardá, 1977; Uría Ríos, 2009).

Although the first national Feminist Conference was organized in 1975, clandestinely, and before the formation of the FOFEE, the creation of the Federation made possible the strategic coordination and the organization of the subsequent national feminist conferences. These conferences discussed the most relevant issues at each moment, including women's liberation, violence against women, pornography, pleasure, divorce, and motherhood. The topics were strategically chosen by the Feminist Coordination network to start discussions that may not have been taking place in all Spanish cities. In the words of the interviewee Justa Montero:

> Todas las Jornadas Estatales son jornadas que se organizan con un, digamos, con un planteamiento de qué es lo que se quiere que esté presente en el debate, o sea que son jornadas muy abiertas, pero sí que hay un enfoque determinado y una apuesta determinada por situar algunos debates y, siempre, con una voluntad de situar debates novedosos o debates vinculados a la práctica política.

> All National Conferences are organized with a plan regarding what we want to have present in the debate. That is, the conferences are very open but, indeed, there is a certain approach and a certain commitment to give rise to some debates, and always there is a willingness to raise novel debates or discussions related to political practice.

These conferences are highly relevant for Spanish feminism. It is worth noting that they were convened infrequently and the participants paid for their own expenses. They were organized by grassroots groups, although some academics were also invited. The number of attendees ranged from two to five thousand people, mostly women. As shown in Table 1, the 1980s and early 1990s were a time of consolidation of feminism in Spain. Four of the seven Feminist Conferences took place between 1979 and 1993.

ORIGIN OF THE TRANS* MOVEMENT IN SPAIN

The trans* movement in Spain was initially framed within the demands of the "homosexual liberation movement," which arose in the midst of the Spanish Transition in the late 1970s. The primary demand of the time was the derogation of the aforementioned Social Danger Act (1970). We should mention that trans* activists—then called and seen as "travestis" (cross-dressers)—were an active and visible part of the first protests carried out at the end of the 1970s, such as the first protest in Barcelona in 1977 that demanded the elimination of the Social Danger Act (Pineda, 2008; Platero, 2009; Ramos Cantó, 2003). The strategic alliance between an incipient trans* movement and the homosexual rights movement fell apart during the 1980s, due to the effects of the AIDS pandemic and the various political responses to it. At the time, gay groups tried to disassociate homosexuality from AIDS by normalizing gayness. In this context, the gay movement left trans* people by the wayside, because society's facile association of trans* people with prostitution resulted in them being considered counterproductive to the movement's political strategy (Ramos Cantó, 2003; Vázquez, 2001).

There has not yet been a detailed study of when the term *travesti* stopped being used in Spain to signify the rupture with gender norms and someone's disidentification with their sex assigned at birth, and when the term *transexual* became preponderant. The shift became visible at the start of the 1990s, and may have begun in the mid 1980s. In this regard, it is important to state that at least until the mid 2000s, *transexual* was used predominantly as an inclusive, umbrella term, while *transgénero*, in the Spanish context, had a more restrictive meaning, reserved for those who do not identify with the medical diagnosis of *transexual*. This usage is quite different in the English-speaking world, where "transgender" is the umbrella term and "transsexual" refers to someone who identifies as a gender completely different from the gender assigned to them at birth and often changes their body to match how they identify. In this article, we use "trans*" and "transgender" as encompassing terms for all possible identifications and

TABLE 1. FEMINIST CONFERENCES IN SPAIN WITH A NATIONAL SCOPE (1975–2015).

Date	Slogan and city	Main topics	Discussion of trans rights
1975	"Liberación de la mujer," Madrid, clandestine	Women's liberation	No
1979	II Jornadas Estatales sobre la Mujer, Granada. 3,000 participants	Equality and difference feminism debates, class and sexuality	No
1985	10 años de lucha feminista, Barcelona.	Independent feminism, no—violence, mental health, violence, sexuality, political lesbianism, pornography	No
1988	Jornadas feministas sobre violencia machista, Santiago de Compostela.	Violence, pornography vs. antipornography	No
1993	"Juntas y a por todas," Madrid.	Women's diversity (youth, prostitution, domestic workers, Roma, rural, disability, maternity), equality institutions, philosophy, and so on	Yes. Round Table discussing transgenderism and the challenges faced by women who are trans prostitutes.
2000	"Feminismo es y será!," Córdoba.	Globalization, multiculturalism, gender violence, can aggressors be rehabilitated?, sexuality.	Yes. Two papers by trans women. Relationship between feminism and transgender movements, trans women approaches to sexuality.
2009	"Treinta años después, ¡aquí y ahora!," Granada.	Transfeminism, intersectionality, identities, bodies, sexualities, neoliberalism, feminist culture.	Yes. Two round tables and six papers. Shift in feminist paradigm toward transfeminism.

corporealities, using the asterisk to open up a greater range of meanings (Tompkins, 2014: 26).

The 1980s were an important decade for trans* rights in Spain. In 1983, the ban against sex reassignment surgeries (castration) was removed from the Spanish Penal Code. Shortly thereafter, in 1987, the first trans* association with a national scope, *Transexualia*, was created by transgender women, many of whom were sex workers in Madrid and other cities in Spain. The police systematically harassed trans* women in sex work, and *Transexualia* was mainly created to fight against this abuse. The group also struggled against the fears generated by the emergence of AIDS (Vázquez, 2001).

As shown in Table 1, trans* women and trans* issues were formally discussed at the last three feminist conferences (1993, 2000, and 2009). At this point, it is important to note how a young feminist movement that had focused on issues relating to

cis and heterosexual women shifted in order to include trans* issues in the 1993 feminist conference, which was entitled *"Juntas y a por todas"* ("Together and All the Way"). This approach was carried out in conjunction with trans* people and required a significant amount of idea sharing and developing a level of trust. Some feminist groups, especially women from the *Colectivo de Feministas Lesbianas de Madrid* (CFLM), had been working on a special commission created against sexist violence (*Comisión Antiagresiones*), and had also participated in a previous feminist conference against sexist violence, in Santiago de Compostela (1988). These women, most of whom were lesbian feminists, were more open-minded than previous feminist organizers and promoted the discussion of women's sexuality at the conference, supporting explicitly the issue of pornography and considering prostitution in terms of sex work. . . .

At the same time, trans* sex workers in *Transexualia* were interested in building coalitions with other collectives that could support their demands for recognition and their struggle against discrimination and harassment. . . .

We want to emphasize the gap between the Santiago Conference, in December 1988, and the Madrid Feminist Conference, "*Juntas y a por todas*" in 1993. During those four years, feminists formed *Hetaira*, an association in defense of women sex workers, which also included some trans* women. As a result, the entry of trans* people and trans* issues into Spanish feminism was directly related to activism around sexuality and sex work.

The effect of trans* issues on the 1993 Feminist Conference was great, in keeping with the trend in Anglo-Saxon countries at that time of including trans* issues in women's and gender studies (Enke, 2012: 1). Some participants in the 1993 Conference explained the already-mentioned influence of these debates on sexuality in terms of their own personal experience. Kim Pérez, a trans* activist not involved in sex work, gave a talk about the many years she struggled with a mental illness diagnosis and her feeling of freedom when she found the medical category "transsexual." Cristina Garaizabal recalls the impact of Kim Pérez's talk:

> Creo que a partir del 93 empieza ya la discusión, en todo el movimiento (sobre lo trans) . . . Kim explicó toda la parte suya, que yo creo que fue lo que impactó más. La parte personal de que llevaba desde lo veintitantos años de psiquiatra en psiquiatra, que la habían diagnosticado delirios, paranoia, psicosis, todo tipo de elementos psiquiátricos. La liberación que le supuso el asignarse la categoría *transexual*, por mucho que fuera una categoría medicalizada.

> I think that from '93 onwards is when the discussion starts in the entire movement [regarding trans issues] . . . Kim explained her experiences, which I think is what had the biggest impact. The personal question, that she had been, since her twenties, bouncing from one psychiatrist to the next, that she had been diagnosed with delirium, paranoia, psychosis, all manners of psychiatric issues. The freedom that meant

assigning herself the category *transsexual*, no matter how much it was a medicalized category.

Trans* issues became even more central to the feminist movement in the first decade of the twenty-first century. The 2000 Conference in Córdoba, "Feminism is . . . and will be," included talks on transgenderism by trans* activists Laura Bugalho of the *Colectivo Trans Galicia* and Kim Pérez, who had given a talk at the 1993 Conference (Asamblea de mujeres de Córdoba Yerbabuena, 2001). Since the previous conference, Pérez had become a highly respected voice within the Spanish feminist movement.

From the 1990s to the early 2000s, the link between transgenderism and sex work gradually dissipated, as more trans* people with non-sex work backgrounds became involved, and the trans* movement became more organized. This increased activism led to the start of a concerted struggle for the legal, social, and health-care rights of trans* people. In 1996, the *Federación de Asociaciones de Transexuales* (Federation of Transsexual Associations; FAT) was created to coordinate the work of the different trans* rights organizations.

In the 2000s, the coordination of the various trans* associations was carried out through the transgender section of the Spanish Federation of lesbian, gay, transgender, and bisexual (LGTB) organizations (FELGTB). Beginning in 2004, FELGTB had taken on the role of lobbying national political authorities to recognize the legal and health-care rights of trans* people (Platero, 2011). With the legalization of same-sex marriage in 2005, a new window of opportunity opened for sexual rights, and some trans* organizations entered into negotiations with the Socialist government. But because of resistance, the "Gender Identity Law," which permitted trans* people to change their name and sex in the Civil Registry, was not approved until 2007.

Held after the law was passed, the 2009 Granada Feminist Conference reflected a qualitative difference from previous feminist conferences in the relationship between its trans* and feminist participants. There was a clear commitment to place gender identity at the center of the Spanish feminist agenda, leading to the development of Spanish "transfeminism."

The first time that the term "transfeminism" was used at the Conference was in Córdoba in 2000. Kim Pérez used the word in her talk, "Woman or Trans? The Insertion of Transgender Women within the Feminist Movement." However, in 2009, transfeminism became not so much a translation of an Anglo concept, but rather a local concept with its own definitions, and its use signaled that Spanish feminist movements (and not just trans* women with a feminist conscience) were willing to question binaries like man/woman, homosexual/heterosexual, and cis/trans. Transfeminism led to Spanish feminism in general becoming more queer, more decolonial, and intersectional. The organizers of the Conference put together two transfeminist round tables, but there were also many sessions led by young grassroots feminists, which included six papers and numerous informal actions and gatherings. The result was the consolidation of a new generation of *cis* and *trans* activists who had internalized the criticism of the gender binary system. This "transfeminist turn" involved people from different subject positions and placed discussions about identities, bodies, and sexualities at the core of feminism (Coordinadora Estatal de Organizaciones Feministas, 2010). . . .

What happened in Granada was likely what Justa Montero mentioned, the birth of a new feminist perspective that was already being formed through the debates that were occurring in various spaces. Discussions about feminism and trans* rights were taking place not only in the respective organizations and by political actors who claimed to represent these rights, but also in such disparate spaces as social movements, squatter houses, political parties, universities, museums, and trade unions. These various spaces were helping to generate a "critical mass" that was influenced by Third Wave feminism, which addresses intersectionality and plurality and that encourages a complex understanding of issues that challenge binarisms.

The Conferences have left a significant wake, in terms of the incorporation of transfeminist points of view and practices. These repercussions include participation in the annual march and events that take place under the umbrella of "Trans October" in various Spanish cities, the publication of books such as Miriam Solá and Elena Urko's (2014) *Transfeminismos. Epistemes, fricciones y flujos* (*Transfeminisms: Epistemologies, Frictions and Fluids*), and the growing demand to depathologize trans* identities.

BUILDING COALITIONS

En el Estado Español, a diferencia de otros sitios ha habido una alianza importante, tanto desde mujeres pertenecientes al movimiento feminista, como por parte de activistas *trans*.—Juana Ramos

In Spain, contrary to other places, there has been an important alliance between women belonging to the feminist movement, as well as by trans activists.—Juana Ramos

Our initial hypothesis regarding the influence of lesbian feminism in facilitating the participation of trans* women within feminism has been supported by all the participants in our research. However, we think it necessary to add nuance to this initial hypothesis, in order to avoid falling into a kind of unidirectional triumphalism that overstates the role of lesbian feminism. In fact, we must acknowledge the active role and agency of trans* women, who struggled to establish links with feminism, as Juana Ramos states in the above quote. This alliance did not only have a political objective, but also was based on personal relationships, where the knowledge of each person's biography helped to better understand the impact of transgenderism and prostitution— issues that had been extremely controversial within feminism itself. Cristina Garaizabal remembers in her interview:

Recuerdo que el impacto fue grandioso, porque no las conocíamos, teníamos la duda de cómo tratarlas, si en masculino o en femenino. Duda que, ya digo, nada más tratarlas se te pasaba porque era evidente que lo raro hubiera sido tratarlas en masculino, eso nos hubiera costado, pero por cómo se movían y eso. A partir de ahí, empezamos una relación . . . digamos, más personal. No fue tanto desde el colectivo (CFLM) a *Transexualia* sino un grupo de ellas y un grupo de nosotras, que era más a nivel de relación personal, y de hablar de nuestras cosas . . . Y sobre todo, ellas hablar de sus vidas, que para nosotras eran un fenómeno completamente desconocido.

I recall that the impact was enormous, because we did not know them [trans women], we had doubts about how to address them, whether in the masculine or the feminine. Doubts that, I tell you, became moot the moment we interacted, because it was evident that it would have been weird to address them in the masculine. That would have been hard. Because of how they moved and so on. From there on, we began a more, shall we say, personal relationship. It wasn't so much a work that came from the collective (CFLM) toward *Transexualia*, but rather that a group of them and a group of us came together, that it was more a matter of personal relationship, of talking about our things. . . . And, especially, having them talk about their lives, which for us were a completely unknown subject.

Empar Pineda says simply:

Nos hicimos muy amigas [las chicas del CLFM y de Transexualia] y hasta el día de hoy.

We [cis women from the lesbian feminist collective and trans* women from *Transexualia*] became very good friends, and we still are.

This was about a relationship between women, which took place fundamentally from the 1990s onward. A kind of "unexpected sorority," if you will, which was based on a shared political interest in sexual freedoms, but that was also rooted in interpersonal links for mutual care. In those early years, the trans* movement was basically led by women, as Juana Ramos mentions in her interview:

Hubo una apertura del movimiento feminista hacia la realidad transexual y en el caso concreto de las mujeres transexuales. Porque en aquella época, la transexualidad masculina todavía no era muy conocida aquí, en el Estado Español. Básicamente, quienes estaban representando el movimiento *trans* eran mujeres. Luego ya, a partir del año 95, 96, empezaron a aparecer en los colectivos hombres transexuales, pero antes no. Simplemente no éramos conscientes de que podía haber hombres transexuales, pensábamos que era una cuestión de mujeres.

There was an opening of the feminist movement toward transgender realities, especially in the specific case of transgender women. Because, at that time, male transgenderism was still not well-known here in Spain. Basically, here in Spain, those who were representing the trans movement were women. Later, after '95, '96, we start to see the birth of associations representing trans men, but not before. We were simply not aware that there could be transgender men, we thought this was a women's issue.

. . .

At the same time, the participation of trans* women in the feminist movement, which the more veteran members see as very positive, is not free of conflicts. These conflicts speak directly to the political subject of feminism, as well as to intergenerational differences regarding how to conceive of feminism itself. . . .

Another conflict is evident in the recollection of the Conference by the interviewee Aitzole Araneta:

Las mayores resistencias que nos encontrabamos en el transfeminismo . . . es cuando el protagonismo lo tiene alguien *trans* (énfasis) y no es una chica, es un chico trans.

The biggest resistance that transfeminism faced . . . is when the protagonist is someone *trans* (with emphasis), and it is not a woman, but a trans man.

In this regard, it is more than a question of trans* men's participation. It involves a broader discussion of the participation of men and the political subject of feminism, which locates this debate within a contemporary global feminist context. In retrospect, feminism has experienced an evolution, which has led to the use of the plural "feminisms," whereby discrimination and how to confront it are considered intersectionally, instead of women being the sole political subject of analysis. Cristina Garaizabal points out:

Supone un reto, más que un cambio. Supone un reto, lo que yo no sé si eso se va a trasladar en un cambio de paradigma. En todo caso es evidente que es un reto ya abierto . . . al feminismo. El tema en el 93 era: "¿Quién decide quién es mujer y por qué?". El problema es que en el 2009 no es ese el debate. Porque en el 93 el sujeto del feminismo siguen siendo las mujeres. Cada cual que lo entienda como le dé la gana y ese es el debate: "¿Qué es ser mujer?". Pero en el 2009 el problema que se plantea ya no es ese porque, como entran los *trans* masculinos, el asunto es "¿por qué los hombres no?", "¿todos los hombres son opresores?",

"¿el sujeto del feminismo son solo las mujeres?" El sujeto del feminismo son los . . . discriminados por el sistema de géneros.

This is more of a challenge than a change. It is a challenge, what I don't know is if this will translate into a paradigm shift. In any case, it is evident that it is an open challenge . . . to feminism. The issue in '93 was "Who decides who is a woman, and why?" The problem is that in 2009 that was not the debate. Because in '93, the subject of feminism is still women. Each person can define that however they damn well please and that is the debate: "What does it mean to be a woman?" But in 2009 the issue that is raised is not that one anymore, because trans men are present, and now the question is "Why not men?", "Are all men oppressors?", "Is the subject of feminism only women?" The subject of feminism is . . . anyone who is discriminated against by the gender systems.

To state that there were conflicts does not mean that these issues necessarily blocked the debates or the evolution of transfeminism itself. . . .

Laura Erickson-Schroth describes transfeminism as "an approach to feminism that is informed by trans politics" (2014:620). In contrast, Spanish transfeminism is not simply about feminism learning more about transgenderism. Nor is it only a matter of concern for trans* women, so that they incorporate feminism in their personal and political practices. It has more to do with a paradigm shift, so that feminism can go beyond "attending the demands of those affected by the gender system [which would be a direct allusion to women and sexual and gender minorities] to address itself to combating the binary gender system itself," as Cristina Garaizabal stated in her interview.

CONCLUSION

Our qualitative research was carried out in conjunction with its protagonists, and is based on an open dialogue that informs, helps rethink, and raises new questions. Our intent was to escape from a homogeneous and globalized narrative about how the relationship between feminisms and the trans* movement has been crafted. With this aim in mind, we have tried to explain, in a situated fashion, the Spanish case, which, in our opinion, breaks with this homogeneity, presenting its own definition of transfeminism.

We do not claim that relationships between cis and trans* feminists have been unproblematic, but that they do break with the traditional Anglo narrative (and also the Latin American one) of being two different and opposing movements. Their leaders recognize that they are interdependent movements, wherein sexual and gender rights are intertwined. Therefore, women's rights have to include trans* women's rights.

The Spanish case can help rethink the narratives that habitually frame trans* and feminist rights, as it challenges a linear historical narrative of the achievement of rights for each separately. We argue that Spanish trans* and feminist movements are part of a geopolitically localized history, with its own nuances and where the importance of the vernacular is paramount. In this regard, we want to point out the lack of studies about the leadership of the Spanish trans* movement in this political moment.

The resistances from within Spanish feminism to trans* issues serve to forefront the importance of the feminist debates regarding the nature of feminism, the participation of men (specifically trans* men), and the need to present the plurality of intersectional experiences that cross-cut these topics.

Finally, we would like to make clear that our work is limited because the narrative we describe is still unfolding. Thus there is a need to continue studying the evolution of this tide of transfeminism, as well as the role played by transfeminism in today's environment, with the current economic crisis and the austerity policies that have resulted. Today, we are moving into a new situation, with a shifting political climate after the May 2015 regional and municipal elections, in which leftist coalitions consisting of grassroots activists made significant gains. Some trans* activists have being appointed to public positions, which opens up new possibilities for transfeminist leadership and initiatives.

REFERENCES

Asamblea de mujeres de Córdoba Yerbabuena (Ed.). (2001). *Jornadas feministas Córdoba 2000: Feminismo.es y será*. Córdoba, Spain: Servicio de Publicaciones de la Universidad de Córdoba.

Bacchi, C. (1999). *Women Policy and Politics: The Construction of Policy Problems*. London, UK: Sage Publications.

Coordinadora estatal de organizaciones feministas. (Ed.). (2010). *Granada, treinta años después: aquí y ahora*. Madrid, Spain.

Enke, A. F. (Ed.). (2012). *Transfeminist Perspectives in and beyond Transgender and Gender Studies*. Philadelphia, PA: Temple University Press.

Erickson-Schroth, L. (Ed.). (2014). *Trans Bodies, Trans Selves: A Resource for the Transgender Community*. Oxford and London, UK: Oxford University Press.

Goodman, L. A. (1961). Snowball sampling. *Annals of Mathematical Statistics*, 32(1), 148–170. doi: 10.1214/aoms/1177705148.

Haraway, Donna J. (1991). *Simians, Cyborgs, and Women. The Reinvention of Nature*. London and New York: Routledge.

Ley 16/1970, de 4 de agosto, sobre peligrosidad y rehabilitación social. 1970. http://www.boe.es/diario_boe/txt.php?id=BOE-A-1970-854

Moreno Sardá, A. (1977). *Mujeres en lucha: el movimiento feminista en España*. Barcelona, Spain: Anagrama.

Pineda, E. (2008). Mi pequeña historia del lesbianismo organizado en el movimiento feminista de nuestro país. In R. Platero (Coord.), *Lesbianas. Discursos y Representaciones* (pp. 31–60). Barcelona, Spain: Melusina.

Platero, R. (L.). (2009). Transexualidad y agenda política: una historia de (dis)continuidades y patologización. *Política y Sociedad* 46 (1–2), 107–128.

———. (2011). The narratives of transgender rights mobilization in Spain. *Sexualities* 14 (5), 597–614. doi:10.1177/1363460711415336

Ramos Cantó, J. (2003). Las asociaciones de transexuales en España. In A. Becerra-Fernández (Ed.), *Transexualidad: La búsqueda de una identidad* (pp. 125–142). Madrid, Spain: Díaz de Santos.

Reason, P. & Bradbury, H. (Eds.). (2008). *The Sage Handbook of Action Research: Participative Inquiry and Practice*. London, UK: Sage.

Solá, M. & Urko, E. (2014). *Transfeminismos. Epistemes, fricciones y flujos*. Tafalla, Spain: Txalaparta.

Tompkins, I. (2014). Asterisk. *Transgender Studies Quarterly* 1(1–2), 26–27. doi:10.1215/23289252-2399497

Uría Ríos, P. (2009). *El feminismo que nunca llegó al poder*. Madrid, Spain: Talasa.

Vázquez, J. (2001). *Los inicios del movimiento transexual en el Estado español*. Conference presented November 8 at the LGTB Collective of Madrid (COGAM).

90. MOST WOMEN YOU KNOW ARE ANGRY

LAURIE PENNY (2017)

Many women you know are angrier than you can possibly imagine. Most are pretty good at hiding it, having been taught to do so since childhood.

One of the questions I am asked most often, when I give talks about my books on gender and politics, is about anger. Young women ask me how I get away with expressing anger with such apparent ease, and they worry about men's reactions if they do the same. These questions are usually a veiled request for permission. Female anger is taboo, and with good reason—if we ever spoke about it directly, in numbers too big to dismiss, one or two things might have to change.

Young women who come to my events often tell me that they want to be more forthright, but they're extremely worried about "coming across as too angry." I usually reply that there are worse things to be. If you stand up for yourself, if you assert your right to self-respect and bodily autonomy, if you raise your voice above a whisper, if you leave the house without a sweet smile slathered across your face, some people will inevitably call you shrill, a scold, a nag, bitter, a bitch. And that's all right. Bitches, in the fragrant words of Tina Fey, get stuff done.

You'll never guess quite how furious the women around you are, until you ask them. Some of the angriest women I know are also the sweetest, the kindest, the most personable and generous. Inside, they might be seething with rage they have been taught never to express, anger they can barely acknowledge even to themselves. They'd probably be surprised to find out how common that feeling is. They have learned that showing their anger is an invitation to mockery, shame, or shunning, so they displace their anger, try to smother it into silence, because they've learned that nice girls don't get cross. Nice girls don't speak out or stand up for themselves. It's unladylike. It's unbecoming. Worst of all, it's threatening to men. Case in point: period jokes. How many times have you heard people dismiss and belittle a woman who dares to express emotion by telling her she's probably menstruating? How many times have men in power—including Donald Trump—tried to push back and put down women who criticize them by implying that our opinions are nothing more than a mess of dirty, bloody hormones, none of it rational, none of it real? These jokes are never just jokes. They're a control strategy.

The patriarchy is so scared of women's anger that eventually we learn to fear it, too. We walk around as if we were bombs about to go off, worried about admitting how livid we really are, even to ourselves. There are real social consequences for coming across as an "angry woman"—especially if you're not also white, straight, and cisgender. In my work as a political writer and speaker, I've learned that the privileges I was born with mean I can "get away with" being angrier in public than other women I know. As a tiny white lady who passes as cis, I come across as "fiery" or "feisty," but someone else saying the same things might face more damaging stereotyping. "Race," writes Roxane Gay in *The New York Times*, "complicates anger."

If angry women manage to successfully hide their inconvenient feelings, they are praised for being "strong." So often, "strong woman" is used to mean "a woman who doesn't complain." At most, we are allowed to speak about fear, about upset. Society can cope with girls who are "broken"—but girls who burn with fury are a problem, and they need to be controlled. Whenever my friends and I have to deal with harassment, abuse, and threats from people who would rather we not talk about women's rights, we can expect some sympathy as long as we talk only about how frightened we are. But we're not just

frightened. We're furious. We're livid, because what is happening to us is unfair and unjust.

Boys learn to disguise their hurt and vulnerability as anger—girls, all too often, learn the opposite. Unfortunately, denying your anger does not make it disappear. It grows in the dark, away from daylight, into something twisted and unhealthy, eating away at you from inside. When I was a teenager and going through a difficult time, I didn't know what to do with my rage, so I treated it like a stained shirt and turned it inside out, keeping the rancor close to my skin where nobody could see. I directed my frustration inward and took it out on my own body, hurting and starving myself. In the slow, painful years of recovery, I learned that there were better ways of dealing with my anger, and I didn't have to be afraid of it. Part of me was always afraid that if I stopped hurting myself, I would start hurting other people—but anger does not have to lead to violence.

Anger is not the same as hatred, although it's easy to confuse the two, especially in a political climate where hatred of others comes easy and rational rage is met with mockery. Anger is a feeling. Hatred is an action. Hatred is anger applied indiscriminately, anger attached to cruel—rage reworked into an excuse to lash out at another person because of who or what they are. Anger itself is no more or less than the human heart rebelling against injustice, real or imagined, and often it has damn good reason.

It's all right to feel angry. It's all right to feel anything, in fact—as a society, we still fail to distinguish between emotions and actions, but it's what we do, not what we feel, that delineates the difference between right and wrong. What matters is not how angry you feel, but what you do with it. Choosing to control your rage, to use it for good, is better by far than squashing it down or letting it eat you away from inside. Anger can be useful. It can keep you moving and working when you want to give up. It can give you courage when you need it. It can focus your attention on what has to change, in your life, in your community. Anger can be a tool as well as a weapon, and it's a tool we shouldn't let rust away and never learn to use.

We worry too much about how men and boys will respond to our anger. One of the things I hear most often when I speak about female anger is that angry women are unattractive. This is supposed to end the discussion, because more than anything else, women and girls are supposed to want to be attractive. If we let on that we're cross, boys won't want to date us, especially not if it's them we're cross with. If we show our teeth, nobody will love us. I'm here to tell you that that's not true. Being honest about my anger has made me surer of myself, and my life is now gloriously full of friends and partners who don't require me to take up less space. The responsibility of making men feel safe and unthreatened was interfering with my plan of taking down the patriarchy and helping to build a world where the common human experience of being a woman doesn't have to hurt so much. As far as I'm concerned, boys who want to be with only "cool, chill girls" should try dating in the morgue.

As I've grown up, I've stayed angry—but my anger has grown up, too. It has boiled down and condensed into something strong and subtle, something that I can control. Writing out my rage is cathartic—and useful, too. I'm lucky that my coping mechanism is also my career. Plenty of women are angry, and why wouldn't they be? It's bad enough that women and girls are still being attacked and undermined, as individuals and as a group—when our basic rights to health care are stripped away, when we are blamed for the violence that is done to us and shamed for our sexuality, when we have to get up every day and deal with racism and homophobia and class prejudice. It's bad enough that we still have to fight to be treated as full, equal human beings without also being shamed and silenced if the whole situation makes us furious. Yes, we're angry. Why shouldn't we be? Why aren't you?

91. WHAT'S LOVE GOT TO DO WITH IT?

YVETTE ALEX-ASSENSOH

Our institutions of higher education are among the most intellectually, technologically and administratively well-endowed in history. Despite the successes of this "innovate or die" era, however, the moral fabric of our campuses is becoming increasingly frayed. Public support for colleges and universities is at an all-time low, while conflict, violence and vitriol are invariably seen as synonymous with campus life. Recent conflicts on our college campuses over the last year demonstrate that business as usual is no longer an option.

How did this happen?

In our pursuit of academic rankings and financial endowments, we forgot about love—not the second-hand emotion that Tina Turner sang about, but the "sacrificial love" that puts the needs of others before our own, with the goal of ensuring that everyone's needs are met. Innovation does not exist in a vacuum. It is born in inclusive environments where people are free to study, research, engage and give back, unfettered by disrespect, hatred and violence. These environments cannot exist without sacrificial love. As humanity becomes increasingly pragmatic

and self-centered, higher education must play a key role in bringing love back to the forefront.

Our present academic climate emphasizes evidence and objectivity. For many, the idea of sacrificial love seems too esoteric, too risky. Some even dismiss it as a cheap way to accommodate the academically unqualified, opting instead to search for viable answers in policies, legal counsel, strategic planning, unions, endowments and technology. These elements are not in short supply, yet the issues plaguing campus life continue to persist, seemingly unhindered.

Campus violence, sexual assault, suicide, dishonest and unethical research practices; disharmony and ideological warfare; binge drinking; financial mismanagement; and academic misconduct are among the problems dominating headlines and creating inhospitable campus climates. What binds many of these crises is a focus on the "I" at the expense of the "we," which is the antithesis of sacrificial love. Whereas this type of love calls on us to be more patient, kind, respectful and truthful as well as look for the best in other people and situations, focusing on the "I" prioritizes individual gain and self-aggrandizement at the expense of fair play and broader institutional interests.

Yet, the purpose of higher education is not merely to produce new knowledge and prepare our students to lead in a diverse world, it is to steward them and society toward boundless excellence and full humanity, which includes not just a love for learning but love for others. A good dose of this kind of love is just what colleges and universities need to reclaim their leadership role.

But what does this love look like, and how do we incorporate it into our 21st-century colleges and universities?

Leaders serve with love by listening respectfully and thoughtfully to diverse viewpoints and including perspectives different from their own, especially when they are beneficial to the commonwealth.

While valuing the importance of free speech, love embraces the highest forms of truth telling, in ways that involve empathy and inclusivity.

Love welcomes individuality and tradition but values the need to question and disrupt the status quo to create new forms of knowledge and new ways of thinking across disciplinary boundaries, methodologies or cultural norms.

Love encourages faculty, staff and students to take care of themselves and their families in ways that allow them to be their best selves when they work, learn and live.

Love perpetuates forward thinking leadership that addresses the here and now, while also investing in future generations through partnerships with K-12 institutions, nonprofits, businesses and civic organizations.

To take root, sacrificial love must be activated, practiced and incentivized at all levels of college and university life. Here are some ways we can make that happen:

Incorporate the practice of love as a guiding principle of engagement in course syllabi, faculty meetings, university governing bodies, policymaking and budgeting. Students can encourage our colleges and universities to embrace our full humanity by modeling sacrificial love in the classroom and in co-curricular activities. Governing Boards can make sacrificial love a guiding principle in resource allocation and agenda setting.

What's love got to do with college and university life? Not enough, but with time and commitment, we can ensure that it guides everything we do!

92. WARNING

JENNY JOSEPH

When I am an old woman I shall wear purple
With a red hat which doesn't go, and doesn't
   suit me.
And I shall spend my pension on brandy and
   summer gloves
And satin sandals, and say we've no money for
   butter.
I shall sit down on the pavement when I'm tired
And gobble up samples in shops and press
   alarm bells
And run my stick along the public railings
And make up for the sobriety of my youth.
I shall go out in my slippers in the rain
And pick the flowers in other people's gardens
And learn to spit.

You can wear terrible shirts and grow more fat
And eat three pounds of sausages at a go
Or only bread and pickle for a week
And hoard pens and pencils and beermats and
   things in boxes.

But now we must have clothes that keep us dry
And pay our rent and not swear in the street
And set a good example for the children.
We must have friends to dinner and read the papers.

But maybe I ought to practise a little now?
So people who know me are not too shocked
   and surprised
When suddenly I am old, and start to wear purple.

CREDITS

READINGS

Reading 1: "Claiming an Education", from On Lies, Secrets, and Silence: Selected Prose 1966–1978 by Adrienne Rich. Copyright © 1979 by W.W. Norton & Company, Inc. Used by permission of W.W. Norton & Company, Inc.

Reading 2: "Feminism Is Sensational," in Living a Feminist Life, Sara Ahmed , pp. 21–42. Copyright, 2017, Duke University Press. All rights reserved. Republished by permission of the copyright holder. www.dukeupress.edu"

Reading 3: Dear Sisters: Dispatches from the Women's Liberations Movement. Basic Books.

Reading 4: Manifesta: Young Women, Feminism and the Future. Farrar, Straus & Giroux, LLC.

Reading 5: Meridians 15/1, 2016, 86–104.

Reading 6: Composition Studies 45.2 (2017): 210–211.

Reading 7: "My heroines" by Marge Piercy. Copyright © 2010 by Marge Piercy. Used by permission of The Wallace Literary Agency.

Reading 8: Race, Sex, & Class journal Vol. 1 #1, Fall 1993. Jean Belkir, Editor.

Reading 9: Rethinking Women's and Gender Studies, Catherine Orr, Ann Braithwaite, Diane Lichtenstein, p. 158–170

Reading 10: There is No Hierarchy of Oppressions: From I AM YOUR SISTER (Oxford University Press) Copyright © 1983, 2009 by Audre Lorde. Used herewith by permission of the Charlotte Sheedy Literary Agency

Reading 11: Gina Crosley-Corcoran," Explaining White Privilege to a Broke White Person" (Huffington Post blog, 5/8/14)

Reading 12: Robert Bird and Frank Newport, "What Determines How Americans Perceive Their Social Class?" (Gallup, 2/27/17)

Reading 13: Evan Taylor, "Cisgender Privilege", Seal Press, member of the Perseus Books Group.

Reading 14: The Poet's Job: To Go Too Far. Edited by Margaret Honton.

Reading 15: © 2016 The Author(s). Published by Informa UK Limited, trading as Taylor & Francis Group. This is an Open Access article distributed under the terms of the Creative Commons Attribution License (http://creativecommons.org/licenses/by/4.0/), which permits unrestricted use, distribution, and reproduction in any medium, provided the original work is properly cited.

Reading 16: Jim Ferris "Poems with Disabilities"

Chapter 3 opener: Qwo-Li Driskill, "FOR MARSHA P. (PAY IT NO MIND!) JOHNSON"

Reading 17: The Sciences (July/August 2000).

Reading 18: Paradoxes of Gender. Yale University Press.

Reading 19: Journal of Lesbian Studies, 20/3–4, 2016, 299–323. Reprinted by permission of the publisher Taylor & Francis Ltd, http://www.tandfonline.com

Reading 20: Arvind Dilawar, "The Connection between White Men, Aggrievement, and Mass Shootings," Pacific Standard, March 28, 2018

Reading 21: This Bridge Called My Back. Persephone Press.

Reading 22: International Journal of Qualitative Studies in Education" 30/3, 2017, 245–265.

Reading 65: Emilie Linder/makeeverywomancount.org

Reading 66: Copyright Guardian News & Media Ltd 2018

Reading 67: Family Relations, 66, 2017, 166–179.

Reading 68: Al-Ali, N. Sexual violence in Iraq: Challenges for transnational feminist politics. European Journal of Women's Studies 25(1), pp. 10–27. Copyright © 2016 by the Author. Reprinted by permission of SAGE Publications, Ltd.

Reading 69: "Betrayed by the Angel: What Happens When Violence Knocks and Politeness Answers?" from Harvard Review (Spring 2004): 40–45. Debra Anne Davis.

Reading 70: Looking for Home: Women Writing About Exile. Minneapolis: Milkweed Editions 1990.

Reading 71: Public Domain

Reading 72: Women's Studies in Communication, 40/2, 2017, 150–154. Copyright © The Organization for Research on Women and Communication (ORWAC), www.orwac.org, reprinted by permission of Taylor & Francis Ltd, http://www.tandfonline.com on behalf of The Organization for Research on Women and Communication (ORWAC).

Reading 73: Gender, Place, & Culture, 24/8, 2017, 1107–1126.

Reading 74: Margot Wallstrom, "Speech on Sweden's Feminist Foreign Policy"

Reading 75: https://www.huffingtonpost.com/brenda-della-casa/welfare-what-its-like_b_4255553.html

Reading 76: Copyright © 2017 Harper's Magazine. All Rights reserved. Reproduced from the September issue by special permission.

Chapter 12 opener: "TINNE: The sabbath of mutual respect" from MOON IS ALWAYS FEMALE by Marge Piercy, copyright © 1980 by Middlemarsh, Inc.. Used by permission of Alfred A. Knopf, an imprint of the Knopf Doubleday Publishing Group, a division of Penguin Random House LLC. All rights reserved."

Reading 77: Public Domain

Reading 78: Kaylin Haught, "God Says Yes to Me"

Reading 79: Fundamentalism and Gender, OUP, p. 175–201

Reading 80: Interdisciplinary Journal of Research on Religion, 9, 2013.

Reading 81: Women's Studies International Forum, 64, 2017, 41–50.

Reading 82: The Editor's of U.S. Catholic, "The Prophet's Daughters: The editors interview Syafa Almirzanah." U.S. Catholic, http://www.uscatholic.org/church/2009/01/the-prophet%E2%80%99s-daughters

Reading 83: Shofar, 34/2, 2016, 79–107.

Reading 84: Reprinted with permission from Sojourners, www.sojo.net

Reading 85: Theology & Sexuality, 23/1–2, 2017, 67–92.

Reading 86: "Feminist Men." 3/16/2011.

Reading 87: Copyright Guardian News & Media Ltd 2018

Reading 88: 2017, Latin American and Caribbean Ethnic Studies 12 (3) 250–272.

Reading 89: Journal of Lesbian Studies, 20/1, 2016, 46–64. Reprinted by permission of the publisher Taylor & Francis Ltd, http://www.tandfonline.com

Reading 90: Laurie Penny, "Most Women You Know are Angry" (Teen Vogue, 8/2/17)

Reading 91: Reprinted with permission from Diverse: Issues In Higher Education, Vol. 34 No.16, www.Diverse Education.com

Reading 92: Copyright © Jenny Joseph, SELECTED POEMS, Bloodaxe 1992. Reproduced with permission of Johnson & Alcock Ltd.

IMAGES

INDEX